Does your blood flow hot and redder
because I have stripped petals from hearts of roses
according to some code of grammar?
As you say, Vincent, we represent echoes—
yours more intense than mine.
After our pains over white squares,
the voice of sunflower and rosebud remain.

SECOND PLACE
Steven M. Thomas

Haiku In A Hurricane

I'm pulled between two types of poetry.
Sometimes I get so sick of being eclipsed
By gangster flicks and semi-lewd T.V.,
So tired of poetry's diminishment,
I want to smash the mental windows screaming,
To lay the language open with a blade
And make it bleed disturbing visions, streaming
Strange sex, half seen, and gore too deep to wade.
At other times I think the art can best
Be served more quietly, by choosing plain
Words carefully—the right word from the rest;
By honesty, economy and aim.
It's great to screech and rave like crazy larks;
Effective, too, the whisper in the dark.

D0122858

For information about how the 1997 contest was judged—
and tips on submitting to competitions—read Contest
Judging: No Quick Walk in the Park on page 4.

For complete details about the *1998 Poet's Market* Poetry
Contest, turn to page 5.

1997
POET'S
MARKET

1 9 9 7
POET'S
MARKET

WHERE & HOW TO PUBLISH

YOUR POETRY

EDITED BY

CHRISTINE MARTIN

ASSISTED BY

CHANTELLE BENTLEY

WRITER'S DIGEST BOOKS
CINCINNATI, OHIO

If you are a poetry publisher and would like to be considered for a listing in the next edition of *Poet's Market*, send a SASE (or SAE and IRC) with your request for a questionnaire to *Poet's Market*—QR, 1507 Dana Ave., Cincinnati OH 45207. Questionnaires received after March 14, 1997, will be held for the 1999 edition.

Managing Editor, Annuals Department: Constance J. Achabal.
Supervising Editor: Michael Willins.

This 1997 hardcover edition of *Poet's Market* features a "self-jacket" that eliminates the need for a separate dust jacket. It provides sturdy protection for your book while it saves paper, trees and energy.

International Standard Serial Number
0883-5470
International Standard Book Number
0-89879-746-2

Cover Illustration: Celia Johnson

Attention Booksellers: This is an annual directory of F&W Publications. Return deadline for this edition is December 31, 1997.

Contents

The Markets

Resources

Indexes

From the Editor

In preparing this, the 12th edition of *Poet's Market*, it was impossible to overlook the increasing presence of poetry in today's world. Not only is poetry in all sorts of publications (including some telephone books), but it's also on radio and television. It's literally in the air. And we're delighted to be part of its "renaissance."

After all, if you're interested in writing and publishing poetry, you're interested in *Poet's Market*. In this volume we provide information about hundreds of publications and presses seeking poetry—in all, more than 1,700 possible markets for your work. And the good news is that approximately 300 of them are new to this edition.

In addition, you'll find information about contests and awards, conferences and workshops, writing colonies, and organizations and publications useful to poets. Each of these sections also has new listings—which means our book has grown. In fact, at 592 pages, this edition of *Poet's Market* is the largest ever.

But we don't expect you to rely on our word—or our page count—as proof poetry is enjoying a renaissance. We asked the editors and publishers listed in this directory if *they* believe interest in poetry is increasing, and what it means for poets. Read Trends in the Field: Interest and Opportunities Up, on page 8, for details.

We are also delighted to announce the winners of our *1997 Poet's Market* Poetry Contest, for poetry about writing or submitting poetry. On the endleaves, you can read the three winning poems and learn about the winners. On page 6, you'll learn how we judged our contest. And, on page 7, you can read the rules for our 1998 contest, for poetry about the "role" of the poet.

To learn more about the roles of poets today, read our interviews with poets **Max Garland**, **J. Patrick Lewis**, **Susan Ludvigson**, **Gerald Stern**, and poet and editor **Gary Whitehead**. For different views, don't miss the interviews with **Sapphire**, who sees her role as "town crier," and **William Bronk**, who simply views himself as a "vessel" through which poems flow. And to illustrate that poetry is not just of interest in the United States, we have interviews with Australian poet and editor **Sally Clarke**, Canadian poet **Barbara Klar**, and "American-Irish" poet **Julie O'Callaghan**.

In essence, this volume helps you learn about the field *and* get your work published. If you've never submitted work before, read Charting Your Path to Poetry Publication, on page 10, which offers a step-by-step approach to every aspect of the process. If you're wondering where to submit first, read How to Use Your *Poet's Market*, on page 4. It explains our various indexes, which now include double daggers to highlight new listings. And, if you just need time to write, read our interview with **Elizabeth Guheen**, who provides an in-depth look at a writing colony.

With our book in your hands, you can bet your work will makes its presence known in today's world. Tell us about it. Besides strains of poetry in the air, we love to hear word that a new poet has been published!

Christine Martin

wdigest@aol.com

How to Use Your *Poet's Market*

To reap the benefits of *Poet's Market*, you need to know how to use it. After all, this directory not only provides listings of poetry publishers, but it is also designed to help you determine which ones are the best markets for your work.

The first step, however, is to examine your poetry. Do you write poetry that makes a political statement? poetry about wildlife? religious symbols? other poets? Do you write sonnets? prose poems? about a certain area? in a language other than English?

Maybe you don't write any specific type of poetry. Maybe the answer depends on which one of your works we're talking about. No matter. If you've put craft into your poems, you'll find places for them.

START WITH THE INDEXES

All Publishers of Poetry listings are coded as to the category of poetry they are seeking. Publishers that desire poetry within certain realms—on certain subjects, in certain forms, or by certain folks—can be quickly identified by a **IV** and terms denoting the specialization(s). For example, *The Leading Edge* is coded **IV-Science fiction/fantasy** because it seeks material related to those genres.

Once you've defined your own poetry, you don't need to comb each page for compatible listings. Turn to the Subject Index (where you will find all publishers with **IV** codes divided according to their specializations) and scan the boldface headings to locate the specialization that matches your work. If you write haiku, for instance, check under **Form/Style**. If you're an older adult who writes about the woods near your home, check under both **Senior Citizen** and **Nature/Rural/Ecology** and write down the names of those publishers that sound interesting.

Publishers may classify themselves as **Regional** in the Subject Index, but checking the Geographical Index is also helpful. There you'll discover the publishers located in your state or country. While some don't consider themselves "regional" in terms of the poetry they accept, they are often more open to writers from their own areas.

Also useful, particularly if you're trying to publish a small collection of poems, is the Chapbook Publishers Index, which lists publishers who consider chapbook manuscripts (typically 20-25 pages of poetry connected by a theme). You'll find more information about both chapbook and book publishing in Charting Your Path to Poetry Publication, on page 10.

Finally, if you've heard about a particular publisher, but can't seem to find its listing, check the General Index. All imprints and publications located at the same address are grouped together. The General Index lists *all* titles in the book, however, and includes cross-references where necessary.

CHECK MARKET CODES

Once you have a list of possible markets for your work—because of specialization or location or an interest in chapbooks—look up each listing and check the market category code(s) following the title to discover how open it is to submissions.

Besides a **IV** code, a publisher can also have **I, II, III** or **V**. Those with **I** are open to beginners' submissions, so if you're just starting out, try sending to them. Publishers with **II** codes are general markets which expect you to be familiar with literary journals and magazines. Those coded **III** are limited as to the number of submissions they accept, so your chances of publishing with these folks are limited too. Finally, those with **V** are not accepting unsolicited manuscripts. Although you may have picked such a publisher out of the Geographical Index, you can't submit your poetry to it at this time. That's okay. Cross it off your list and move on to the next one.

When you discover publishers with more than one code, read their listings to determine if they're still possible markets for your work. For instance, a publisher may be **I, IV-Religious**, which means it either wants religious material as well as poetry from beginners or religious material only, including poetry from beginners. To learn more about market category codes, see the Publishers of Poetry introduction.

Also, as you read the listings based on the indexes, others will attract your eye. Don't feel limited by those on your list. Many publications don't want to be noted for a specialization and are open to ALL types of work.

READ CAREFULLY

When you've refined your list of possible markets by checking market categories, study each listing *carefully*. Look for the general purpose of the publisher and statements about its interests in poetry. For example, *Hellas* accepts any kind of poetry but especially welcomes poems in meter. In their listing, they say, "We prize elegance and formality in verse, but specifically encourage poetry of the utmost boldness and innovation, so long as it is not willfully obscurantist."

Also, the names of recently published poets and sample lines of poetry will indicate what level of writing an editor is seeking and provide insight into editorial tastes.

Consider the date a publisher was founded as well. Older publishers have more stability, and sometimes more prestige. However, newer publishers, especially those new to this edition (designated by a ‡), are often more receptive to submissions.

Carefully reading the description of a publication's format will help you visualize how your poetry will appear in its pages. Better yet, review sample copies. This is the best way to determine whether your poetry is right for a publication. Sample copies can be ordered from publishers or often found in your library or local bookstore.

However, don't just locate a sample copy, decide your work is appropriate, and submit to that market without knowing submission procedures. Inappropriate submissions will not only leave a bad impression of your work, but they can also affect a publisher's willingness to accept unsolicited manuscripts from others as well.

If you haven't already done so, read Charting Your Path to Poetry Publication. It offers a step-by-step approach to every aspect of the submission process. Most publishers also include specific submission procedures in their listings. And many offer guidelines for a self-addressed, stamped envelope (SASE). Send for them. The goal, after all, is to increase—not decrease—your chances of acceptance.

OTHER RESOURCES

As you develop your craft, take advantage of the various resources for poets. For support services and feedback from others, for example, join one of the groups listed in Organizations Useful to Poets. If you're searching for a place to get away and write, check Writing Colonies. Or, if you're seeking instruction and marketing tips, attend one of the events in Conferences and Workshops or consult one of the magazines listed in Publications Useful to Poets.

Finally, if you don't recognize a symbol or an abbreviation being used, refer to the Key to Symbols on page 18 or the Glossary on page 546. And, for easy reference, you will find a list of U.S. and Canadian Postal Codes on page 545.

Contest Judging:
No Quick Walk in the Park

The mathematical chances for winning the *1997 Poet's Market* Poetry Contest were 1 in 628. And choosing only three winning entries from the more than 600 poems was no quick walk in the park. But regardless of how daunting the task, we enjoyed reading every entry and delighted in knowing *Poet's Market* touched folks in locations as far away as England and Egypt, as well as those across the United States and Canada.

As the Call for Entries in the 1996 edition of *Poet's Market* stated, our first contest was on the topic of "writing and submitting poetry." This theme led to some very creative work. We received poems comparing writing to childbirth, tapestry weaving and being lost at sea; poems where poets searched for the muse in vain; and even poems where poets found the muse but lost their pen. To judge this huge variety of work as fairly as possible, we rated each poem, from zero to five, on the basis of relevance to the topic, accessibility, craft and imagery.

REASONS FOR ELIMINATION

Unfortunately, some poems were rejected for failing to adhere to contest rules. In fact, almost 90 entries were eliminated because they did not relate to our interest in poetry about writing or submitting poetry. Also, we discovered a number of poems containing typos or spelling errors and some exceeding the 32-line limit. But, overall, the entries were mechanically sound.

Those poems that passed the first elimination round were compared on their craft, creativity and originality. Then three more comparison rounds followed. Finally, weeks of carefully reading and reciting poems, and discussing their various points, brought us to our winners. The three winning poems all view the topic of writing and submitting poetry from very unusual perspectives, and do so with craft. (To read the winning poems, see the front and back endleaves of this edition.)

GOOD NEWS!

With the successful completion of our first poetry contest, we are happy to announce the *1998 Poet's Market* Poetry Contest. This year the contest theme is the "role" of the poet—either today or in years past. (See A Call for Entries for details.) We are also happy to announce that the prize money has been increased to $150, $100 and $75. However, if we may offer one piece of advice for entering any contest, it would be: Follow the rules to the letter. As editors of a directory that constantly reminds poets to follow submission guidelines, nothing could be more disheartening than to have your own guidelines go unheeded.

Finally, as we leave you to your pen, paper, and search for that elusive muse, we want to wish you the best of luck with your poetry whether you submit it to our contest or to one of the many contests, journals or publishers listed in this book.

A CALL FOR ENTRIES

To see *your* work in the next edition of *Poet's Market*, simply write a great poem(s) about the "role" of the poet—either today or in years past—and enter your work in our poetry contest. The best three poems will be published in the *1998 Poet's Market*. And the three winners will receive a free copy of our annual directory and a cash prize of $150, $100 or $75, respectively. Read the following rules for details.

1. All poems must be original, unpublished, and not under consideration by any other publisher or in any other contest.

2. *Poet's Market* retains first publication rights to the three winning poems, which will be published in the 1998 edition (to be released in September 1997). All other rights will be returned. Note: *Poet's Market* does not claim *any* rights to any other work.

3. Each poem must relate to the topic: the "role" of the poet. Poems may be in any form, rhymed or unrhymed, but no poem can exceed 32 lines in length.

4. You may enter as many poems as you like, but each poem counts as one entry and must be accompanied by a $3 handling fee. (Make checks or money orders payable to Writer's Digest Books.)

5. Poems must be clearly typed (single-spaced with double-spacing between stanzas) on one side of $8\frac{1}{2} \times 11$ or $8\frac{1}{4} \times 11\frac{3}{4}$ (A4) white paper.

6. You must submit two copies of each entry. On one copy, include your name, address and telephone number in the upper left corner. The second copy must only contain the poem. Entries will be separated on arrival to allow for blind judging.

7. All entries must be postmarked by midnight, January 31, 1997. **Note that manuscripts cannot be acknowledged or returned**.

8. Every entry will be read and judged by the staff of *Poet's Market*. In the event of a tie, an outside judge will be consulted.

9. Winning poets will be notified by phone on or before March 14, 1997. To receive the names of the winning poets (after March 28, 1997), you must enclose a self-addressed, stamped envelope (or self-addressed envelope and International Reply Coupon) with your entry.

10. The three winning poets will receive $150, $100 or $75, respectively, and a copy of the *1998 Poet's Market*.

11. Employees of F&W Publications, Inc. and their immediate family members are not eligible.

12. *Poet's Market* reserves the right to forego publication of any winning entry. In such cases, first rights will be returned.

Note: Failure to comply with these guidelines will result in disqualification.

Send entries to: *1998 Poet's Market* Poetry Contest
1507 Dana Ave.
Cincinnati, OH 45207

Deadline: January 31, 1997

Trends in the Field: Interest and Opportunities Up

BY CHRISTINE MARTIN

Poetry. It's everywhere. Turn on the radio and you can hear a commercial delivered as if the announcer is participating in a poetry slam. Log on to your favorite online service and you're sure to find a forum for poets. Stop by your local bookstore and—if you don't catch a reading in progress—you can discover details about upcoming events, including readings, workshops, and new publications.

Indeed, poetry has gone mainstream. Or has it? To find out we asked the editors and publishers listed in this directory whether *they* believe interest in poetry is increasing and on what factors they base their responses. We also asked whether an increased interest in poetry translates into increased sales of poetry publications—and, perhaps most important, increased opportunities for poets, particularly those who have yet to publish their work.

WHAT EDITORS SAID

Overwhelmingly, editors do believe interest in poetry is increasing—though some see it as a rapid increase, while others view it as a gradual one. Many, however, say increasing interest is coming from aspiring poets—more than from the general public. They are receiving more submissions but not necessarily selling more of their releases.

Of course, most editors are glad to receive work from new writers, and many say submissions are coming from folks in all walks of life, all around the world. As Ruth Daigon, editor of ***Poets On:***, says, "We've received poems from migrant workers, nurses, lawyers, factory workers, the unemployed and dispossessed, prisoners and computer troubleshooters as well as younger and younger students. It's very refreshing."

At the same time, editors are dismayed that many new writers do not appear to be readers of their publications or any others. For instance, Richard Mathews, editor of Florida's ***Tampa Review***, says, "Unfortunately, most new writers seem more interested in getting published than in reading and supporting poetry through the purchase of books and subscriptions. This means our publication budget remains the same. We can't afford to increase the number of pages we're printing, and the competition to appear on those pages is greater because of the increased number of submissions."

FURTHER EVIDENCE

Editors add that the mounting interest in poetry can be seen not only in the swell of submissions, but also in the wide range of poetry readings, including events at bars, cafés and coffeehouses, in addition to more traditional readings at bookstores, colleges and universities. As Jordan O'Neill, editor of ***The Unforgettable Fire***, says, "Living in New York City, I am amazed at the increase in poetry readings and the number of poets appearing. Any given night I can go out and listen to someone read, and that is simply wonderful." Editors make similar comments about Baltimore, Chicago, Los Angeles and San Francisco.

Yet it would be a mistake to think only large cities (or only U.S. cities) are hotbeds for poetry readings. For example, Georgette Perry, editor of Catamount Press, says that in Huntsville, Alabama, open-mike readings are now regular occurrences at churches as well as bookstores.

Editors also see growth in the number of poetry workshops and creative writing programs; the number of poetry groups (including online poetry clubs) and members; and the number of poetry magazines and journals. A few editors whose publications are not solely devoted to poetry, such as Alice Ansfield, publisher and editor of *Radiance: The Magazine for Large Women*, and Carol S. Lawson, editor of *The Chrysalis Reader*, add that readers' interest has prompted them to increase their space for verse.

PRIMARY FACTORS

If the above serves as evidence that interest in poetry is increasing, then what caused this increase in the first place? A number of editors say it's simply a result of poetry having more media exposure. Whether it actually stems from widely-viewed events like Maya Angelou reciting her work at Bill Clinton's inauguration or the release of *Il Postino*, the film which featured the work of Pablo Neruda, is hard to determine. But it's true that poetry is presented more on television and radio, and many daily and weekly newspapers now include coverage of poets and poetry events.

However, the main factor, according to most editors, is the development of new technologies. Steven Zytveld, coordinating editor of Canada's *Carleton Arts Review*, says it best: "Photocopiers, desktop-publishing programs, and e-mail have made publishing easier, submitting quicker, and writers more in touch with each other."

Yet while the development of technology has encouraged aspiring editors to create publications to feature the work of aspiring writers—and thus more outlets for poetry—it may also be, as a few editors suggest, that folks are using poetry to combat the effects of an increasingly technological society. As Ken Butler, editor of *Liberty Hill Poetry Review*, says, "The more people become involved and engaged in a technologically sophisticated society, the greater the need for simple human basics . . . in today's environment that translates to poetry."

WHAT THIS MEANS FOR YOU

Whatever the reasons for the increased interest, it is important to note that more outlets for poetry do exist—which is generally good news for aspiring poets. However, with more people interested in writing and submitting poetry, competition for space on an editor's pages remains keen. So it should come as little surprise that, more than ever before, editors are encouraging poets to submit only their best work.

Most editors are also quick to add that, without the support of the burgeoning number of new writers, their publications can neither increase the space they devote to poetry nor can they continue to exist for long. Though new publications will always spring up, the demise of older publications will ultimately mean opportunities for poets could stagnate or, ultimately, decrease.

As it stands now, the nature of the market is already changing. The prevalence of poetry readings, combined with little or no increase in the sale of poetry publications, has some editors wondering whether the increased interest in poetry is really an increased interest in the spoken word rather than the written word. Also, new technologies, including increased accessibility to the Internet, have lessened the need for poets to purchase printed publications when so much is available free online. And desktop publishing has prompted poets to self-publish, only supporting their own endeavors.

In essence, interest and opportunities are up, but editors and publishers agree that for poets to continue to see their work on the printed page, they need to support the written word, and each other.

Charting Your Path to Poetry Publication

BY CHRISTINE MARTIN

Say, you've just spent the last few months writing (and polishing) your first poems and are anxious to start sending them to editors and publishers. Or, perhaps, you've been writing poetry for years and have just been convinced by your spouse, sibling or best friend that your poetry deserves a wider audience. In either case, if you're like most of the folks we've met at workshops this past year, you probably have a number of questions about how to properly submit your work.

Let's even say your first question is quite basic: "Where do I begin?" Well, you don't need to wonder any longer. Here we'll answer—with up-to-date, detailed information—the most often asked questions about submitting poetry.

WHERE TO BEGIN

So, where *do* you begin to look for editors and publishers who might be interested in your work? The easiest answer of course is in this directory. Included along with listings for contests and awards and resources such as organizations and publications, you'll find about 1,700 publishers of poetry from around the world. And most of these magazine and book publishers specifically indicate what they do and do not want to see in the way of poetry for their pages. The biggest challenge you'll have here is narrowing down our list of markets. (For help on this matter, read How to Use Your *Poet's Market* on page 4.)

Yet, if you're just beginning, don't overlook the publications you have right on your living room coffee table. Those small (and often specialized) publications, such as your local church bulletin, the weekly neighborhood newspaper, your inhouse company magazine and the regional garden club gazette, are probably not listed within these pages. That's okay. Unless you're strictly out for literary fame, they're considered viable options. After all, the best way to determine whether your poetry is appropriate for a publication is to read several sample issues, and you've been reading these magazines for months, perhaps even years. You're already familiar with their contents and you probably have much in common with their other readers. So even if your weekly newspaper does not have a poetry page, the editor might publish an occasional poem—particularly if it relates to life in your neighborhood.

We should also add that new magazines are established all the time—even as you're reading these pages. To keep up with new literary journals and small presses, read publications such as *Poets & Writers Magazine* or *Writer's Digest*, both which regularly contain information about new markets. On a more local level, check the notices posted on the bulletin board at your library or nearest bookstore. There you may discover a new publication particularly interested in the work of regional writers.

APPEARANCE IS EVERYTHING

When preparing to submit your work to any publication, however, remember that neatness counts. Use a typewriter or personal computer with a letter-quality (or at least near letter-quality) printer to type or print your poems on good, white, standard-size (generally 8½ × 11) bond paper. Do not handwrite your poems and do not use onion skin or erasable bond. Proofread your work carefully, and make sure the type is dark and clear. Sloppy manuscripts with spelling or typographical errors are likely to be returned without comment.

Except for haiku, no matter how short your work, editors prefer that you submit each poem on a separate page with the title centered above it and your name, address and telephone number (typically) in the upper right or left corner. Some editors want poems double-spaced. Others prefer single spacing (with double spacing between stanzas) to give them an idea of how your poem will appear on their pages. If your poem carries over to a second sheet, note whether the lines at the top are a continuation of the same stanza or the start of a new one. Don't leave an editor wondering about such details. In all aspects, submit your work exactly as you would like it printed.

WHAT TO SEND

How many poems should you submit? In general, send only three to five poems to any editor at any given time. A few editors, particularly those who like to "feature" poets, prefer to receive seven or eight poems in a submission. But this is rare. Many of the listings in this directory note exactly how many poems an editor will consider. You can also avoid irritating an editor with too many (or too few) poems by requesting a copy of the publication's submission guidelines (which may indicate how many poems you should send *and* exactly how they should be typed).

As many editors and publishers have very specific submission policies, it is always a good idea to send a self-addressed, stamped envelope (SASE) to receive a copy of a publisher's guidelines before submitting any work. If you're interested in a magazine or book publisher outside of your own country, send a self-addressed envelope (SAE) and International Reply Coupons (IRCs), which can be purchased from many post offices. If a publisher does not have guidelines or if the guidelines do not indicate the number of poems you should submit, don't worry. Sending three to five poems is considered standard.

Choosing which poems to send—and their arrangement—is up to you. More than anything else, an editor wants to see your best work. Of course, you also want to send work that is appropriate for the publication in question. And in arranging your poetry, your goal is simply to entice an editor to continue reading.

TO COPYRIGHT OR NOT TO COPYRIGHT

Before you send off the poems you have spent months perfecting, however, you may be wondering about copyright protection. The good news is that you own the copyright to your work from the moment of creation. And, you can, if you wish, put the copyright symbol (©) on your poetry, followed by the year of creation and your name. Yet, copyright notices are typically considered unnecessary as most editors know you own the copyright to your work and few, if any, will steal your ideas. For some, in fact, copyright notices signal the work of amateurs who are distrustful of editors and publishers.

While the decision is certainly yours, it is important to note that most magazines are copyrighted and book publishers will usually register copyrights in your name. In addition, those who are inclined to "borrow" your ideas will do so whether or not the copyright notice is attached. If you wish to register your copyright, however, or if you would like more information, write to the Copyright Office, Library of Congress, Washington DC 20559. For answers to specific questions (but not legal advice), call the Copyright Public Information Office at (202)707-3000 weekdays between 8:30 a.m. and 5 p.m. (EST).

RIGHTS IN GENERAL

Related to the question of copyright protection are questions about rights in general. The most common is: "What rights do I have to my work once I let someone publish it?" Well, the answer all depends on what rights the publisher acquires from submitting poets.

It's safe to say that most magazine editors and publishers seek first rights—that is, they want to be the first to publish the work in question. It's important to note, however, that first North American serial rights means the editor will be the first to publish your work in a U.S. or Canadian periodical. Your work can still be submitted to editors outside North America, or those open to reprint rights.

Editors and publishers who seek reprint rights are open to submissions of previously published work—provided you tell them when and where the work was previously published so they can properly credit the periodical in which your work first appeared. You'll notice that many poetry collections list such "credits," often on the copyright page. In essence, they've acquired reprint rights.

Still other publishers, however, require poets to relinquish all rights, which means you cannot submit that particular work for publication anywhere else—not even as part of your own poetry collection—unless you negotiate to get reprint rights returned to you. A few publications, including *Highlights for Children*, request all rights but are noteworthy publications that typically pay poets in cash as well as copies. Other publishers seeking all rights may not be as generous, or as reputable. If you're asked to relinquish all rights, you can request that the publisher consider first rights instead, or you can simply refuse payment and withdraw your work.

Since the issue of rights can be so important, almost all editors and publishers will specifically state (in their directory listings or guidelines) what rights they typically acquire. And once your work is accepted for publication, a number of editors and publishers will ask you to sign an agreement which not only tells you what rights are being requested, but also asks you to certify that the poetry is your own.

Unless you and the publisher agree otherwise (in writing), the Copyright Law states that you are primarily offering one-time rights to your work—that is, the editor or publisher may only publish your work once. If an editor requests something different, such as the right to also later publish the work in a retrospective anthology, and you are open to such an arrangement, make sure the agreement is documented.

For more information on rights, including electronic rights, refer to the second edition of *The Writer's Essential Desk Reference*, published by Writer's Digest Books in 1996.

COVER LETTERS

Another issue poets have had to grapple with—though one of a far less serious nature—is whether to include cover letters with their submissions. In the past, most editors and publishers did not state their preferences, so poets had to decide for themselves. Recently, however, many editors are specifically indicating a desire for cover letters in their market listings and submission guidelines.

Overall, a cover letter allows you to personally present yourself—and your work—to specific editors. To do so graciously, you'll not only want to list the titles of the poems you are submitting, but you'll also want to demonstrate some familiarity with the publication in question. Editors, of course, like to know their contributors are among their readers. Include a few of your most recent publishing credits as well. And what

SAMPLE COVER LETTER

Samantha Brown
10 Yellow Creek Dr.
Kennekenec PA 24680
(987)654-3210

August 15, 1996

Crystal Evans, Poetry Editor
Keep the World Green
36 Pleasant Ave.
Quiet Springs VT 13579

Dear Crystal Evans,

Enclosed are three of my poems for your consideration: "Cool Streams," "The Mating of Monarchs" and "Silence of the Woods."

As a fulltime naturalist and manager of an 80-acre city park, I am very concerned about the natural world and have found your magazine enjoyable and enlightening. The photographs are beautiful and the articles are tremendously helpful on both a personal and professional level. For instance, after reading your June issue, I redesigned our park compost system, as well as the compost heap at home. Now we are reviewing the safety of the water within our creek.

In addition to overseeing activities in the park, I give school presentations on nature and the environment and write a monthly nature column for a regional parents magazine. I have also recently published poetry in *Beauty in Nature*, *Parks for the People* and *Untouched Treasures*.

Needless to say, it would be an honor to see my poetry within a publication whose philosophy is so close to my own. Thank you for your time and consideration.

Sincerely,

Samantha Brown

Samantha Brown

if you haven't published a poem yet? Then note that. Some editors are particularly interested in new writers and have special sections for beginners' work.

Before you compose your cover letter, though, check to see if the editor has requested biographical information for the magazine's contributors' page. If so, add a few lines about your job or hobbies, particularly if either relates to the enclosed poems. Above all, refrain from praising your work. Let your poems speak for themselves. And, no matter how much information is requested, keep your cover letter to one page.

Finally, address your letter to the person listed as the poetry editor (or the editor if the publication is small). Most of the publications in this directory have a particular individual to whom you should direct your submissions. If no one is listed, however, check the publication's guidelines or the masthead of a recent copy. If you are still unable to locate a specific name, simply address your letter to "Poetry Editor." Of course, use an acceptable business-style format and make sure your letter is free of misspellings and grammatical errors. (For an example, refer to the Sample Cover Letter on page 13.)

SIGN, SEAL AND DELIVER

Once you have decided which poems you are going to submit, place them together and fold them into thirds. Do not fold your poems individually as the hassle of having to unfold and read each poem is apt to annoy editors, many of whom are already overworked. If you have elected (or are required) to also enclose a cover letter, fold the letter into thirds and place it on top of your batch of poems. Then put all of this material into a business-size (#10, 4⅛ × 9½) envelope.

To ensure a response from the editor or publisher in question, you must also include a SASE. You can use either a #9 (4 × 9) envelope or a #10 envelope folded into thirds. If you're submitting poetry to a publication outside of your own country, include a SAE and IRCs. One IRC, by the way, is usually enough for one ounce by surface mail. For airmail return, you need one IRC for each half-ounce. In either case, make sure your reply envelope contains enough postage to cover the cost of returning your submission. And make sure your outside envelope has enough postage attached to get your poetry to the editor in the first place. (In general, three pages of poetry, a cover letter and a SASE can be mailed for one first-class stamp.)

KEEPING RECORDS

But don't just send the only copy of your poems winging its way through the wild blue yonder. Always keep extra copies for yourself. In fact, you may want to keep the original typewritten or computer-printed version of your work and submit good, clean photocopies to editors and publishers. After all, you never know when your poetry will end up lost in the mail or somewhere in the heap of other submissions at a publisher's office. If you submit the one-and-only copy of your work and it gets lost in the process, you're simply out of luck.

It's also important to keep a record of which poems you have submitted, where and when. You can record such information on 3 × 5 cards arranged alphabetically (by poem title) in a metal storage container. Or you can use sheets of paper arranged in file folders (in which you can also keep the original copy of each poem). Or you can create a database on your personal computer. In any case, list the title of each poem, the name of the magazine to which it was submitted, and the date your work was mailed. Also note the date of each editor's reply, the outcome of your efforts, and any comments that may prove useful when you're next submitting to that market (such as changes in editors, reading periods or frequency of publication).

TRACKING RESPONSES

By keeping detailed records of when and where you are submitting your work—and the date of the editor's reply—you are also tracking response times. Most editors and publishers indicate (in their market listings and submission guidelines) approximately how long you must wait before you can expect to receive a reply. If an editor does not specify when you will receive a report, it is generally expected to be within three months. Many times, however, the approximate date (or three-month benchmark) will come and go without a word from the editor or publisher.

What should you do when you haven't heard from an editor within the specified time period? Wait another month, then send a note inquiring about the status of your submission. Note the titles of your poems and the date sent. Ask when the editor anticipates making a decision. And enclose a SASE or self-addressed, stamped postcard for the editor's response. If you still do not hear from the market, send a postcard withdrawing your poems from consideration. Then submit your work elsewhere.

By all means, do *not* call editors with questions about submissions. Phone calls are only likely to irritate those who must divide their time between publishing a small press magazine and maintaining a fulltime job and family obligations. And you stand little chance of accomplishing your goal anyway as many editors simply cannot supply such answers over the phone. Why risk having your poems completely dropped from consideration?

PREVIOUSLY PUBLISHED POEMS

When you submit your poetry to magazine editors and publishers, by the way, they not only assume the work is original (that it is yours and nobody else's), but they also assume the work has not been previously published and is not being simultaneously submitted. Nothing is wrong with sending an editor a poem that has already been published. Some editors, however, are simply not open to such submissions. As stated earlier, these folks want to be the first to publish new work—not the second. They are looking to acquire first rights to your poetry—not reprint rights. So before you send any previously published material, check market listings or submission guidelines to see if the editor or publisher in question is willing to consider such work. If so, note (in your cover letter) where the particular poem(s) first appeared.

. . . AND SIMULTANEOUS SUBMISSIONS

As many editors and publishers take months to reply to submitted work, poets in recent years have responded by sending the same package of poems to several editors at the same time. This is considered simultaneously submitting. And most who engage in this practice believe that a batch of three to five poems submitted to two or more editors has a better chance of resulting in an acceptance. However, if you submit your work simultaneously and an editor accepts one of your poems, you must contact the other editor(s) immediately and withdraw your work from consideration. This is likely to annoy (or even anger) the other editor(s) still in the process of making a decision. And future submissions to these markets may no longer be welcome.

To lessen the risks involved with this practice, you need to tell editors up front (in your cover letter) that you are simultaneously submitting your work. This is not only a way of forewarning them, but it may also prompt an editor to make a more timely decision. However, if you're going to tell editors that you're simultaneously submitting your material, make sure they are actually open to such submissions. If not, it is unlikely they will even consider your work. In addition, simultaneously submitting your work only to those publications open to the practice greatly decreases your chances of irritating any editors in the process. Again, check market listings or submission guidelines for specific information.

Yet the question still remains whether you should simultaneously submit your work in the first place. Why rush the process? You certainly don't try to take shortcuts in writing your poems. Why take shortcuts in submitting? After all, if you're just beginning or are still perfecting your craft, you're likely to quickly collect rejections. That can be discouraging. And if you're already regularly publishing, you're more likely to garner two acceptances at once—which puts you back at the point of having to contact editors and withdraw your work. The final decision, of course, is yours.

CHAPBOOKS AND OTHERS

Book publishers, by the way, expect some of the poems in your manuscript to be previously published. And, knowing the difficulty poets face in placing a collection, they are more accepting of the practice of simultaneous submissions. Yet you should only begin to think about book publication once you have gathered a fair number of publication credits in literary or small press magazines. Often, publishing a chapbook is a good middle step.

A chapbook is a small volume of 20-25 pages (or less). As such a volume is less expensive to produce than a full-length book collection (which may range from 48 to 80 pages), a chapbook is a safe way for a publisher to take a chance on a lesser-known poet. Most chapbooks are saddle-stapled with card covers. Some are photocopied publications. Others contain professionally printed pages. While chapbooks are seldom noted by reviewers or carried by bookstores, they are good items to sell after readings or through the mail. You'll discover that, in addition to some book publishers, a number of magazine publishers also publish chapbooks (for a complete list, refer to the Chapbook Publishers Index on page 547).

Whether you're planning to submit your work to either chapbook or book publishers, however, you should always examine sample copies of their previously published collections. This is not only the best way to familiarize yourself with the press' offerings, but it is also a good way to determine the quality of the product. To solicit a publisher's interest in your work, the standard procedure is to first query. Send a sampling of your poems (three to five, unless a publisher has noted otherwise), with a cover letter including brief biographical information and a few of your more noteworthy publication credits. Also let the publisher know that you are familiar with their other collections. And don't forget to include a SASE (or SAE and IRCs) for the publisher's reply.

BOOK PUBLISHING OPTIONS

Once you develop an interest in having a collection of your work published, you'll soon discover that publishing arrangements vary. Some, in fact, are more beneficial to poets than others. Consider the following options carefully.

• **Standard publishing.** In a standard publishing contract, the publisher usually agrees to assume all production and promotion costs for your book. You receive a 10% royalty on the retail (or sometimes wholesale) price, though with some small presses you are paid with a percentage of the press run instead. Such publishers only release a small number of poetry volumes each year.

• **Cooperative publishing.** This arrangement is exactly that: cooperative. Although the details of such contracts vary, they require some type of investment of either time or money on your part. Some require involvement in marketing. Others specify money for production costs. In any case, know what you're signing. While cooperative publishing is respected in the literary and small press world (and many such publishers can bring your work the attention it deserves), some vanity/subsidy presses try to label themselves as "cooperative." True cooperative publishing, however, shares both the risks and the profits.

• **Self-publishing.** This option may be most appealing if your primary goal is to publish a small collection of your work to give to family and friends. It is also a good choice for those who prefer complete control over the creative process. In this scenario, you work hand-in-hand with a local printer and invent a name for your "press." Most important is that you pay all the costs but own all the books and net all the proceeds from any sales (which you must generate). For details, read *The Complete Guide To Self-Publishing* by Tom and Marilyn Ross (Writer's Digest Books, 1994).

• **Vanity/subsidy presses.** This is probably the least desirable option. Companies in this category usually advertise for manuscripts, lavishly praise your work, and ask for fees far in excess of costs (compare their figures to those of your local printer for a book of similar size, format and binding). These companies also make a habit of collectively advertising their books, that is, your work will simply receive a line along with 20 or so other books in an ad placed in the general media rather than a specific market. Worse yet, sometimes you own all copies of your book; sometimes you don't.

It's important to note that some anthology publications also fall under "vanity/ subsidy" publishing as you must pay a tidy sum to purchase the volume containing your work. If you have concerns about a particular publisher call the Poets & Writers Information Center at (212)226-3586. Calls are welcome weekdays from 11 a.m. to 3 p.m. (EST).

KEY TO SYMBOLS AND ABBREVIATIONS

‡—new listing
ms—manuscript; **mss**—manuscripts
b&w—black & white (photo or illustration)
p&h—postage & handling
SASE—self-addressed, stamped envelope
SAE—self-addressed envelope
IRC—International Reply Coupon (IRCs should be sent with SAEs for replies from countries outside your own)

IMPORTANT MARKET LISTING INFORMATION

• Listings are based on questionnaires and verified copy. They are not advertisements *nor* are markets necessarily endorsed by the editors of this book.

• Information in the listings comes directly from the publishers and is as accurate as possible, but publications and editors come and go, and poetry needs fluctuate between the publication date of this directory and the time you use it.

• If you are a poetry publisher and would like to be considered for a listing in the next edition, send a SASE (or SAE and IRC) with your request for a questionnaire to *Poet's Market*—QR, 1507 Dana Ave., Cincinnati OH 45207. Questionnaires received after March 14, 1997, will be held for the 1999 edition.

• *Poet's Market reserves the right to exclude any listing that does not meet its requirements.*

The Markets
Publishers of Poetry

If you're seeking outlets for your poetry, you've undoubtedly come to the right place! In this section you'll find listings for all types of poetry markets—everything from small, stapled newsletters published by one or two dedicated individuals to larger, perfect-bound journals produced by volunteers at colleges and universities to slick magazines with paid staffs. You'll also discover listings for chapbook publishers and publishing houses that release perfect-bound, paperback collections.

Even more encouraging, perhaps, is that approximately 300 of the markets included here are new to this edition—and new listings are often more receptive to submissions.

To locate this year's new listings, look for the double daggers (‡) preceding the listing titles. As in years past, some new listings are publications that were in earlier editions of *Poet's Market* but not the previous one. We're happy to welcome back, for example, *The American Voice*, *Arc: Canada's National Poetry Magazine*, *Mobius* and *Whetstone*, a journal published in the Canadian province of Alberta.

Other listings new to this edition are actually "new," that is, they are magazines or presses that began publishing in the last few years. These include *The Brownstone Review*, *Faultline*, *Hootenanny*, *Many Mountains Moving* and *The Yalobusha Review*. Dead Metaphor Press and Pavement Saw Press, by the way, are both new presses which sponsor annual chapbook contests.

All told, this section contains about 1,700 poetry publishing markets, includes ten in-depth interviews with folks in the field, and showcases the covers of 11 different publications. And if we had to describe it in one word, that word would be "diverse!"

LOCATING SPECIFIC MARKETS

Yet, given the number of listings (and the number of pages), how do you find information about a particular publisher, say one you've heard about at a writer's conference? Simple. Check the General Index for the page number. Although we list all publishers of poetry in this section alphabetically, information about related markets is grouped together in one listing to provide an overview of a publisher's entire operation. Yet *all* titles are included in the General Index.

The listing for *Amelia* is a classic example. If you look up our entry for *Amelia*, you'll also find information about *Cicada* and *SPSM&H*, as well as the numerous awards offered by the same publisher. When all of these activities are noted in one listing, it's easy to understand why the publisher's response to your submission may take a bit longer than expected. Nevertheless, if you were specifically looking for *Cicada*, you would find it listed in the General Index with a cross-reference to *Amelia* and the appropriate page number.

This also applies to publications that have changed names. Though you will find a publication listed in this section under its new name, you will find the previous name with the appropriate cross-reference in the General Index. The General Index also lists those publishers from the 1996 edition who are not included in this edition. And, if known, it provides reasons for their absence.

As you make your way through the listings—and we encourage you to review them all—you will discover publications and presses as diverse as the names themselves. Some editors, for instance, publish magazines solely devoted to certain types of poetry. Others produce publications open to both poetry and fiction. And still others, particu-. larly editors of very specialized publications, welcome poetry on specific topics but have space for only a few poems each issue. Discovering each publisher's focus will help you determine if your work is appropriate for his or her pages.

WATCH SUBMISSION DETAILS

Besides uncovering a publisher's objective, however, you must pay attention to submission details if you want your work to be given serious consideration. While a number of practices are considered standard, more and more editors are opting for variations. Thus, each year we ask editors and publishers to not only update the general information within their listings (such as their reporting times and payment policies) but also to clarify specific submission details.

For example, it is important to know if, and when, editors publish theme issues. While some editors develop all of their issues around themes, others only publish one or two theme issues a year (or even every few years). Of course, whenever an editor is reading for a theme issue, that's the type of work he or she wants to receive. If you send unrelated work, even if the editor does not normally publish theme-based material, your work will probably not be considered.

Once again we specifically asked editors to supply details about their upcoming themes and related deadlines. Though a number of editors were able to provide this information for 1997, many had not yet finalized their plans when we contacted them. To be sure that your submission will be welcome, it is always best to send a self-addressed, stamped envelope (SASE) to receive up-to-date information about themes, deadlines, and other submission guidelines.

By the way, as you read the listings in this section, you will also notice an increasing number of fax numbers and e-mail addresses. Be careful when contacting editors by these means. While some actually encourage submissions via fax or computer, most simply supply fax numbers and e-mail addresses to facilitate requests for guidelines or other additional information. If you submit material in an undesired manner, you may not receive any response.

INCLUDE REPLY ENVELOPES!

Speaking of responses, although we didn't specifically ask editors and publishers if they had complaints about submissions, many of them said they still receive submissions without SASEs (or without sufficient return postage on SASEs). This is discouraging. Throughout this book, readers are repeatedly instructed to include a SASE or a SAE (self-addressed envelope) and IRCs (International Reply Coupons—for replies from countries outside your own) with all submissions, queries or requests for information.

It's simple: If you want to know if an editor accepts or rejects your material, you must include a vehicle for a reply. And it only makes sense that if it takes you two stamps to mail material, it will take two stamps for the material to be returned—unless you are sending a disposable manuscript. But if you do not want your poems returned to you (that is, the manuscript can be discarded), the editor needs to be told that the SASE is only for his or her response.

It's not surprising that frustrated editors are creating policies about submissions lacking SASEs. As one editor wrote a few years ago (and it bears repeating): "In the past two years, I have been receiving more and more submissions without SASEs. This gets to be a terrible drain on a budget that runs in the red as it is. As it stands now, the problem has gotten so bad that I feel I have to include a disclaimer regarding SASEs with my notice: 'Submissions without a SASE cannot be acknowledged.' "

Some editors are not so kind; they are discarding submissions without SASEs before the material is even read. Although we have started noting these policies within listings, your safest bet is to make a habit of sending a SASE (or SAE and IRCs) with all correspondence. Also, to make sure you're following other expected submission procedures, read (or reread) Charting Your Path to Poetry Publication, on page 10.

EVALUATING PUBLISHERS

Still other types of information within listings are editorial comments designed to help you evaluate the quality of various publications and the interests of various publishers. Such comments include a detailed description of a publication's physical appearance and notes about its content.

Of course, the best way to evaluate any publication is to actually review a sample copy. However, our descriptions provide you with general ideas about what publications look like and how much space they have for poetry. Although it's tempting to aim only for very high-profile, attractive magazines, some of the smaller, more simply produced publications are the most receptive to as-yet-unpublished poets. (Note: A number of printing and production terms, such as saddle-stapled and perfect-bound, are defined in the Glossary on page 546.)

As another way of helping you evaluate publishers, we have also included information about awards and honors that have been bestowed on editors and publishers or their magazines and books. For instance, we continue to note which publications have had poetry selected for inclusion in recent volumes of *The Best American Poetry*, an annual anthology highlighting the best poetry published in periodicals during the previous year.

Once again, thanks to David Lehman, who edits *The Best American Poetry* series, and his assistant, Maggie Nelson, we were able to obtain an advance list of those publications that have work included in the 1996 volume, guest edited by Adrienne Rich. As a different guest editor compiles the anthology every year, knowing which publications have work included, especially in a number of the most recent volumes, can provide insight into the type and quality of material used.

In addition, *The Best American Poetry* (published by Scribner, 1230 Avenue of the Americas, New York NY 10020) can help you develop a sense for trends in the field. The 1996 volume, by the way, is published at the same time as this edition of *Poet's Market*. So, when you're ready to read the poetry that has been selected from the publications listed here, check your nearest library or bookstore.

UNDERSTANDING MARKET CATEGORIES

Finally, all listings in this section include one or more Roman numerals in their headings. These "codes," selected by editors and publishers, can help you determine the most appropriate markets for your poetry. (For details see How to Use Your *Poet's Market* on page 4.) The market category codes and their explanations are as follows:

I. Publishers very open to beginners' submissions. For consideration, some may require fees, purchase of the publication or membership in an organization, but they are not, so far as we can determine, exploitative of poets. They publish much of the material received and frequently respond with criticism and suggestions.

II. The general market to which most poets familiar with literary journals and magazines should submit. Typically they accept 10% or less of poems received and usually reject others without comment. They pay at least one copy. A poet developing a list of publication credits will find many of these to be respected names in the literary world.

III. Limited markets, typically overstocked. This code is often used by many prestigious magazines and publishers to discourage widespread submissions from poets who have not published elsewhere—although many do on occasion publish relatively new or little-known poets.

IV. Specialized publications encourage contributors from a specific geographical area, age-group, gender, sexual orientation or ethnic background or accept poems in specific forms or on specific themes. In most **IV** listings we also state the specialty (e.g., **IV-Religious**). Often a listing emphasizes more than one subject area; these listings are marked with two codes. To quickly locate such markets, refer to the Subject Index which lists publishers according to their specialties.

V. Listings which do not accept unsolicited manuscripts. You cannot submit to these without specific permission to do so. If, for some reason, the press or magazine seems especially appropriate for you, query with a SASE. But, in general, these folks prefer to locate poets themselves. Sometimes they are temporarily overstocked; other times they have projects lined up for years.

We have included these listings because it is important to know not only where to send your poetry but also where NOT to send it. In addition, many are interesting publishers, and this book is widely used as a reference by librarians, researchers, publishers, suppliers and others who need to have as complete a listing of poetry publishers as possible.

‡**A.L.I. (THE AVON LITERARY INTELLIGENCER) (II)**, 20 Byron Place, Clifton, Bristol BS8 1JT England, e-mail dsr@maths.bath.ac.uk, founded 1991, editor Daniel Richardson. *A.L.I.* is a quarterly literary newsletter which publishes poetry, fables, fiction, reviews, true stories and news of meetings, courses and performances in the Bristol, Bath and Somerset area. **They want "idealistic, eclectic work; writing in which it is possible to hear the voice of the writer. Nothing unsurprising."** They have recently published poetry by Philip Gross and Pamela Gillilan. As a sample the editor selected these lines from "Aubade" by Len Jenkinson:

> We were going to Barlow's for nails,
> bright morning comes down to me over the years.
> Blue sky, orange chimney pots and birds,
> a seagull from the dump crying round
> across to the blue pearl town woken to its haze of sound.

A.L.I. is 12 pgs. (actually six 11⅝×16½ sheets of white paper folded in half), photocopied and unbound. They receive about 200 poems a year, accept approximately 20%. Press run is 150 for 100 subscribers, 20 shelf sales. Single copy: $1.50; subscription: £3 UK or $10 US. **Sample postpaid: $5. Make checks payable to** *Avon Literary Intelligencer.* **"Payment is also accepted in the equivalent value of unused postage stamps." Submit 4 poems at a time. No previously published poems or simultaneous submissions. Cover letter preferred. E-mail submissions OK. Seldom comments on rejections. Reports in about 3 months. Sometimes sends prepublication galleys. Pays 1 copy.** Reviews books of poetry when time allows. Open to unsolicited reviews. Poets may also send books for review consideration. They also offer an annual poetry competition with £3/poem entry fee and £100 first prize. Send SASE (or SAE and IRC) for details.

ABBEY; ABBEY CHEAPOCHAPBOOKS (II), 5360 Fallriver Row Court, Columbia MD 21044, e-mail greisman@aol.com, founded 1970, editor David Greisman. **They want "poetry that does for the mind what that first sip of Molson Ale does for the palate. No pornography or politics."** They have published poetry and artwork by Richard Peabody, Vera Bergstrom, D.E. Steward, Carol Hamilton, Harry Calhoun, Wayne Hogan and Cheryl Townsend. *Abbey*, a quarterly, aims "to be a journal but to do it so informally that one wonders about my intent." It is 20-26 pgs., magazine-sized, photocopied. They publish about 150 of 1,000 poems received/year. Press run is 200. Subscription: $2. **Sample postpaid: 50¢. Send SASE for guidelines. Reports in 1 month. Pays 1-2 copies.** *Abbey Cheapochapbooks* come out 1-2 times a year averaging 10-15 pgs. **For chapbook consideration query with 4-6 samples, bio and list of publications. Reports in 2 months. Pays 25-50 copies.** The editor says he is "definitely seeing poetry from two schools—the nit'n'grit school and the textured/reflective school. I much prefer the latter."

ABIKO QUARTERLY WITH JAMES JOYCE STUDIES (II, IV-Translations), 8-1-8 Namiki, Abiko-Shi, Chiba-Ren 270-11 Japan, phone 011-81-471-84-7904, founded 1988, founding editor Laurel Sicks, poetry editor Jesse Glass, is a literary-style quarterly journal **"heavily influenced by James Joyce's *Finnegan's Wake*. We publish all kinds, with an emphasis on the innovative and eclectic. We sometimes include originals and translations. However, we no longer consider unsolicited poetry and fiction. All of our new work comes from our annual international poetry and fiction contest. See *Writer's Digest*, *Poets & Writers* and *AWP Chronicle* for details." Contest runs from September 1 to December 31 and is judged by a well-known poet.** They have recently published poetry by Alice Friman, Carrie Ivenson, Kenji Miyazawa, Jon Silkin, Cid Corman, Lew Turco, William Bronk and Edith Shiffert. It is about 600 pgs., 7 × 10, desktop-published with Macintosh laser printer and perfect-bound with coated paper cover. Press run is 500 for 150 subscribers of which 10 are libraries, 100 shelf sales. **Sample postpaid: $30.** Open to unsolicited reviews. Poets may also send books for review consideration. The editor says, "Poets are in a hurry to publish. Poets, educate yourselves! Read contemporary poetry. In fact, read all poetry! Work at your craft before you attempt to publish. Please remember U.S. postage does not work in Japan with SAEs!"

ABORIGINAL SF (IV-Science fiction), Box 2449, Woburn MA 01888-0849, founded 1986, editor Charles C. Ryan, appears quarterly. **"Poetry should be 1-2 pgs., double-spaced. Subject matter must be science fiction, science or space-related. No long poems, no fantasy."** The magazine is 100 pgs., with 10 illustrations. Press run is 12,000, mostly subscriptions. Subscriptions for "special" writer's rate: $17/4 issues. **Sample postpaid: $5.95. No simultaneous submissions. Send SASE for guidelines. Reports in 2-3 months, no backlog. Always sends prepublication galleys. Pays $20/ poem and 2 copies. Buys first North American serial rights.** Reviews related books of poetry in 100-300 words.

‡ABOVE THE BRIDGE MAGAZINE; THIRD STONE PUBLISHING (I, IV-Regional), P.O. Box 416, Marquette MI 49855, phone (906)228-2964, founded 1985, poetry editor Sean MacManus. *Above the Bridge* is a quarterly magazine designed to reflect life and living in Michigan's Upper Peninsula. **"All poetry must relate to life in the Upper Peninsula of Michigan. There is rugged, magnificent country here. Material should reflect that."** The editor says the magazine is 60 pgs., 8½ × 11, and includes line art and graphics. They receive about 200 poems a year, accept approximately 10%. Press run is 2,500 for 1,000 subscribers of which 50 are libraries. Single copy: $3.50; subscription: $13. **Sample postpaid: $4. Submit 2-3 poems at a time. Previously published poems and simultaneous submissions OK. Cover letter preferred. Often comments on rejections. Send SASE for guidelines. Reports in 4 months. Pays $5 and 1 copy. Acquires one-time rights.** Staff reviews books of poetry only if author or topic is related to Michigan's Upper Peninsula. Send related books for review consideration.

ABRAXAS MAGAZINE (V); GHOST PONY PRESS (III), 2518 Gregory St., Madison WI 53711, *Abraxas* founded 1968, Ghost Pony Press in 1980, by editor/publisher Ingrid Swanberg, who says "Ghost Pony Press is a small press publisher of poetry books; *Abraxas* is a literary journal publishing contemporary poetry, criticism, translations and reviews of small press books. *Do not confuse these separate presses!*" *Abraxas* **no longer considers unsolicited material, except as announced as projects arise.** The editor is interested in poetry that is **"contemporary lyric, concrete, experimental, narrative." Does not want to see "political posing; academic regurgitations."** They have published poetry by William Stafford, Ivan Argüelles, Denise Levertov, César Vallejo and Andrea Moorhead. As a sample the editor selected the final lines of an untitled poem by próspero saíz:

> the beautiful grief of the moon is my beam of silence
> Dawn
> the splendor of the moon dies
> my lips open to a gentle breeze
> she rides a silken yellow scarf into the vanishing clouds
> i am still here.

The magazine is up to 80 pgs. (160 pgs., double issues), 6 × 9, flat-spined (saddle-stitched with smaller issues), litho offset, with original art on its matte card cover, using "unusual graphics in text, original art and collages, concrete poetry, exchange ads only, letters from contributors, essays." It appears "irregularly, 4- to 9-month intervals or longer." Press run is 600 for 300 subscribers of which 150 are libraries. Subscription: $16/4 issues, $20/4 issues Canada, Mexico and overseas. **Sample postpaid: $4 ($6 double issues). Submit 5 poems at a time.** *Abraxas* **will announce submission guidelines as projects arise. Publishes theme issues. Send SASE for details. Pays 1 copy plus 40% discount on additional copies.** To submit to Ghost Pony Press, inquire with SASE plus 5-10 poems and cover letter. **Previously published material OK for book publication by Ghost Pony Press.** Editor sometimes comments briefly on rejections. **Reports on queries in 1-3 months, mss in 3 months. Payment varies per project. Send SASE for catalog to buy samples.** They have published *zen concrete & etc.*, a "definitive collection" of poetry by d.a. levy. That book is a 245-page, 8½ × 11, perfect-bound paperback available for $27.50. They have also published *the bird of nothing & other poems* by próspero saíz. It is a 168-page, 7 × 10, perfect-bound paperback available for $20 (signed and numbered edition is $35). For either book, add $2 p&h.

ACM (ANOTHER CHICAGO MAGAZINE) (II); LEFT FIELD PRESS (V), 3709 N. Kenmore, Chicago IL 60613, founded 1977, poetry editor Barry Silesky. *ACM* is a literary biannual, with **emphasis on quality, experimental, politically aware** prose, fiction, poetry, reviews, cross-genre work and essays. **No religious verse.** They have published prose and poetry by Albert Goldbarth, Michael McClure, Jack Anderson, Jerome Sala, Nance VanWinkel, Nadja Tesich, Wanda Coleman, Charles Simic and Diane Wakoski. As a sample the editor selected these lines by Dean Shavit:

> Just the facts. Forgotten on purpose.
> This is our land. *Yes, you said, "ours."*
> A gang of teenagers, too young for the army, too stupid for respect.

Silesky says *ACM* is 220 pgs., digest-sized, offset with b&w art and ads. Editors appreciate traditional to experimental verse with an emphasis on message, especially poems with strong voices articulating social or political concerns. Circulation is 2,000 for 500 subscribers of which 100 are libraries. **Sample postpaid: $7. Submit 3-4 typed poems at a time. No previously published poems; simultaneous submissions OK. Reports in 2-3 months, has 3- to 6-month backlog. Sometimes sends prepublication galleys. Pays $5/page and 1 copy. Buys first serial rights.** Reviews books of poetry in 250-500 words. Open to unsolicited reviews. Poets may also send books for review consideration. **They do not accept unsolicited submissions for chapbook publication.** Work published in *ACM* has been included in *The Best American Poetry* (1992, 1994, 1995 and 1996) and *Pushcart Prize* anthologies. The editor says, "Buy a copy—subscribe and support your own work."

THE ACORN; EL DORADO WRITERS' GUILD (II, IV-Regional), P.O. Box 1266, El Dorado CA 95623, phone/fax (916)621-1833, founded 1993, poetry consultant Hatch Graham, is a quarterly journal of the Western Sierra, published by the El Dorado Writers' Guild, a nonprofit literary organization. It includes "history and reminiscence, story and legend, and poetry." **They want poetry "up to 30 lines long, though we prefer shorter. Focus must be on western slope Sierra Nevada. No erotica, pornography or religious poetry."** They have recently published poetry by Nell Hutchison, Rebecca Conrad Lawton and Joyce Odam. As a sample the poetry consultant selected these lines from "Camouflage Cat" by Taylor Graham:

> All night she hunts,
> black by the light of her two
> green moons. Come dawn
> it's stubblefield silver, gossamer
> of grasses drying.

The poetry consultant says *the Acorn* is 44 pgs., 5⅜ × 8½, desktop-published on quality paper and saddle-stapled. They receive about 250 poems a year, use approximately 15% (10-12/issue). Press run is 200 for 90 subscribers, 100 shelf sales. Subscription: $12. **Sample postpaid: $4.75. Submit 3-7 poems, neatly typed or printed, at a time. Previously published poems OK; simultaneous submissions discouraged. Cover letter with short (75-word) bio required.** "Our issues favor topical items suitable for the season." **Deadlines are February 1, May 1, August 1 and November 1.** Time between acceptance and publication is 1 month. **"Five editors each score poems for content, form and suitability. Poetry consultant selects top group. Graphics editor selects to fit space available." Often comments on rejections. Reports within 3 weeks after deadline. Pays 1 copy. All rights revert to author on publication.** The editor says, "If your poetry is about nature, be accurate with the species' names, colors, etc. If you describe a landscape, be sure it fits our region. Metered rhyming verse had better be precise. (We have an editor with an internal metronome!) Slant rhyme and free verse are welcome. Avoid trite phrases."

ACORN WHISTLE (II), 907 Brewster Ave., Beloit WI 53511, founded 1994, first issue published in spring 1995, editor Fred Burwell, appears twice yearly. "We seek writing that moves both heart and mind. **We seek accessible poetry: narrative, lyrical, prose poem. No length requirements. We are not interested in experimental, religious, erotic or New Age work.** We also publish fiction, memoir and personal essay." They have recently published poetry by Ruth Daigon, Joanne Mollosk Riley and Allison Joseph. As a sample the editor selected the first stanza of "Out on the Water" by Denise Pendleton:

> Lights blaze and I can feel
> how lit up it is inside. Either hand I reach
> will touch them from any spot I stand in. My mother
> stirs soup simmering at my elbow while my father's

> *bushy arms crowd the table I set. All day*
> *we have sailed with the wind behind, lifting*
> *us toward sky and at last we are held*
> *where we are, drinking iceless drinks*
> *while breathing in the small cabin's air.*

The editor says *AW* is 90 pgs., 8½×11, staple-bound, using b&w photos and art, no ads. Press run is 500. Subscription: $10. **Sample postpaid: $5. No previously published poems; simultaneous submissions OK. Often comments on rejections. Send SASE for guidelines. Reports in 1-8 weeks. Pays 2 copies. Acquires first North American serial rights.** The editor says, "We publish no reviews, although we plan to mention publications by our past authors. We wish that more writers would focus on material that matters to them, rather than trying to impress an audience of editors and teachers. We seek accessible writing for an audience that reads for pleasure and edification. We encourage a friendly, working relationship between editors and writers."

ACUMEN MAGAZINE; EMBER PRESS (I, II), 6 The Mount, Higher Furzeham, Brixham, South Devon TQ5 8QY England, phone (01803)851098, press founded 1971, *Acumen* founded 1984, poetry editor Patricia Oxley, is a "small press publisher of a general literary magazine with emphasis on good poetry." **They want "well-crafted, high quality, imaginative poems showing a sense of form. No experimental verse of an obscene type."** They have published poetry by Elizabeth Jennings, William Oxley, Gavin Ewart, D.J. Enright, Peter Porter, Kathleen Raine and R.S. Thomas. As a sample the editor selected this poem, "Northbound Train," by Ken Smith:

> *Birds rising. These flecks*
> *white on the brown ploughland*
> *flakes of fine snow, they are birds,*
> *they are gulls suddenly flying.*

Acumen appears 3 times a year (in January, May and September) and is 100 pgs., A5, perfect-bound. "We aim to publish 120 poems out of 12,000 received." Press run is 650 for 400 subscribers of which 20 are libraries. **Sample copy: $15. Submit 5-6 poems at a time. No previously published poems; simultaneous submissions OK, if not to UK magazines. Reports in 1 month. Pays "by negotiation" and 1 copy.** Staff reviews books of poetry in up to 300 words, single format or 600 words, multi-book. Send books for review consideration to Glyn Pursglove, 25 St. Albans Rd., Brynmill, Swansea, West Glamorgan SA2 0BD Wales. Patricia Oxley advises, "Read *Acumen* carefully to see what kind of poetry we publish. Also read widely in many poetry magazines, and don't forget the poets of the past—they can still teach us a great deal."

ADASTRA PRESS (II), 101 Strong St., Easthampton MA 01027-2536, founded 1980 by Gary Metras, who says, "I publish poetry because I love poetry. I produce the books on antique equipment using antique methods because I own the equipment and because it's cheaper—I don't pay myself a salary—it's a hobby—it's **a love affair with poetry and printing of fine editions**. I literally sweat making these books and I want the manuscript to show me the author also sweated." All his books and chapbooks are **limited editions, handset, letterpress**, printed with handsewn signatures. "Chances of acceptance are slim. About 1 in 200 submissions is accepted, which means I only take 1 or 2 unsolicited mss a year." The chapbooks are in flat-spine paper wrappers, cloth editions also hand-crafted. He wants **"no rhyme, no religious. Poetry is communication first, although it is art. Long poems and thematic groups are nice for chapbooks. No subjects are tabu, but topics should be drawn from real life experiences. I include accurate dreams as real life."** Poets recently published include W.D. Ehrhart, Jim Daniels, Cortney Davis and Miriam Sagan. As a sample the editor selected these lines from "How To Burn" by Christopher Locke:

> *Beyond the breath*
> *Fogged windows, city blocks*
> *Lurch head first towards*
> *The tar papered walls of evening.*

1-4 chapbooks are brought out each year. **Author is paid in copies, usually 10% of the print run. "I only read chapbook manuscripts in the month of February, picking one or two for the following year. Queries, with a sample of 3-5 poems from a chapbook manuscript, are read throughout the year and if I like what I see in the sample, I'll ask you to submit the ms in February. I prefer a cover letter and a) samples from a completed chapbook ms or b) a completed chapbook ms. Do not submit or query about full-length collections. I will only be accepting chapbook manuscripts of 12-18 double-spaced pages. Any longer collections would be a special invitation to a poet. If you want to see a typical handcrafted Adastra chapbook, send $5 and I'll mail a current title.** If you'd like a fuller look at what, how and why I do what I do, send a check for $12 ($10 plus $2 p&h) and I'll mail a copy of *The Adastra Reader: Being the Collected Chapbooks in Facsimile with Author Notes, Bibliography and Comments on Hand Bookmaking*, published in 1987. This is a 247-page anthology covering Adastra publishing from 1979-1986."

ADRIFT (II, IV-Ethnic), 46 E. First St., #3D, New York NY 10003, founded 1980, editor Thomas McGonigle, who says, "The orientation of the magazine is Irish, Irish-American. I expect the reader-writer knows and goes beyond Yeats, Kavanagh, Joyce, O'Brien." The literary magazine is open to all kinds of submissions, but does not want to see "junk." They have published poetry by James Liddy, Thomas McCarthy, Francis Stuart and Gilbert Sorrentino. *Adrift* appears twice a year and is 32 pgs., magazine-sized, offset on heavy stock, saddle-stapled, with matte card cover. Circulation is 1,000 with 200 subscriptions, 50 of which go to libraries. Single copy: $4; subscription: $8. **Sample postpaid: $5. Make checks payable to T. McGonigle. Simultaneous submissions OK. Magazine pays, rate varies; contributors receive 1 copy.** Reviews books of poetry. Open to unsolicited reviews. Poets may also send books for review consideration.

ADVOCACY PRESS (V, IV-Children), P.O. Box 236, Santa Barbara CA 93102, founded 1983, contact William Sheehan, publishes children's books. "**Must have rhythm and rhyme.**" They have published 3 books of rhymes for children: *Father Gander Nursery Rhymes* (nonsexist, nonviolent, nonracist version of *Mother Goose*), *Mother Nature Nursery Rhymes* and *Nature's Wonderful World in Rhyme*. Their books are 32-48 pgs., illustrated in full color. "**Publish no other poetry at this time.**" **Query with description of concept and sample. SASE required for reply.** "All Advocacy Press books have gender equity, self-esteem themes."

ADVOCATE, PKA's PUBLICATION (I), 301A Rolling Hills Park, Prattsville NY 12468, phone (518)299-3103, founded 1987, editor Remington Wright, is a bimonthly advertiser-supported tabloid, 12,000 copies distributed free, using "**original, previously unpublished works,**" such as feature stories, essays, 'think' pieces, letters to the editor, profiles, humor, fiction, poetry, puzzles, cartoons or line drawings." **They want "nearly any kind of poetry, any length, but not religious or pornographic. Poetry ought to speak to people and not be so oblique as to have meaning only to the poet. If I had to be there to understand the poem, don't send it."** As a sample the editor selected the opening lines from "You Brought Me Lilacs" by Tilitha Waicekauskas:

> *I was young and slender, and in your eyes*
> *I was more beautiful than morning skies.*
> *My hair was as black as a raven's wing*
> *And the love in your eyes made my spirit sing.*
> *For I adored you and on my hand*
> *Was your diamond of promise—a platinum band*
> *—And you brought me lilacs.*

They accept approximately 25% of poems received. **Sample postpaid: $4. No previously published poems or simultaneous submissions.** Time between acceptance and publication is an average of 4-6 months. **Editor "occasionally" comments on rejections. Reports in 6-8 weeks. Pays 2 copies. Acquires first rights only.** Reviews books of poetry. Open to unsolicited reviews. Poets may also send books to the attention of J.B. Samuels for review consideration. Offers occasional contests. The editor says, "All submissions and correspondence must be accompanied by a self-addressed, stamped envelope with sufficient postage."

AEGINA PRESS, INC.; UNIVERSITY EDITIONS (I, II), 59 Oak Lane, Spring Valley, Huntington WV 25704-9590, founded 1983, publisher Ira Herman, is **primarily subsidy,** strongly committed to publishing new or established poets. Publishes subsidy titles under the University Editions imprint. They have also published non-subsidized poetry as well. **Authors of books accepted on a non-subsidized basis receive a 15% royalty**. "We try to provide a way for talented poets to have their collections published, which otherwise might go unpublished because of commercial, bottom-line considerations. We will publish quality poetry that the large publishers will not handle because it is not commercially viable. We believe it is unfair that a poet has to have a 'name' or a following in order to have a book of poems accepted by a publisher. Poetry is the purest form of literary art, and it should be made available to those who appreciate it." They have recently published *Manortown* by Barry D. Kukovich, *Glad Tidings* by Florence Berg and *Poetry by Gladys* by Gladys Nichols. As a sample the editor selected these lines from "replicated" in *Her Space-Time Continuum* by Yuria Julia Kumagai:

> *water and powder were my beginning;*
> *into the mold;*
> *i became milky, dry and then fragile*
> *out of the mold;*
> *i was knifed, sponged and then fired*

"**Most poetry books we accept are subsidized by the author.** In return, the author receives all sales proceeds from the book, and any unsold copies left from the print run belong to the author. Minimum print run is 500 copies. We can do larger runs as well. Our marketing program includes submission to distributors, agents and other publishers." **Mss should be typed and no shorter than 40 pages. There is no upper length limit. For a query, submit 3 or more poems. Simultaneous submissions OK.**

Reports in 1 month for full mss, 7-10 days for queries. Always sends prepublication galleys. They publish perfect-bound (flat-spined) paperbacks with glossy covers. **Sample books are available for $6 each plus $1.50 p&h.**

AERIAL (V), P.O. Box 25642, Washington DC 20007, phone (202)244-6258, founded 1984, editor Rod Smith, is an occasional publication. Issue #8 (published in May 1995) was the Barrett Watten issue (available for $15). They have published work by Jackson MacLow, Melanie Neilson, Steve Benson, Phyllis Rosenzweig and Charles Bernstein. A special issue is in the works, on Bruce Andrews, therefore **they're not looking for new work at this time.** As a sample the editor selected these lines from "subtracted words" by P. Inman:

> still dollar in its pale
> mice sight. Parts of knock
> in a river of propellor blade.
> Wage sand gist. Keyhole
> college, its brink on. An
> ash stelm of mind ball

The magazine is 200-300 pgs., 6×9, offset. Circulation is 1,000. **Sample postpaid: $7.50.** Also publishes critical/political/philosophical writing.

AETHLON: THE JOURNAL OF SPORT LITERATURE (IV-Sports), Dept. PM, English Dept., East Tennessee State University, Box 70270, Johnson City TN 37614-0270, phone (615)929-4339, founded 1983, general editor Don Johnson, Dean, Arts & Sciences, ETSU. **Submit poems to poetry editor Robert W. Hamblin, Professor of English, Southeast Missouri State University, Cape Girardeau MO 63701.** *Aethlon* publishes a variety of sport-related literature, including scholarly articles, fiction, poetry and reviews; 6-10 poems/issue; two issues annually, fall and spring. **Subject matter must be sports-related; no restrictions regarding form, length, style or purpose. They do not want to see "doggerel, cliché-ridden or oversentimental" poems.** Poets published include Neal Bowers, Joseph Duemer, Robert Fink, Jan Mordenski, H.R. Stonebeck, Jim Thomas, Stephen Tudor and Don Welch. The magazine is 200 pgs., digest-sized, offset printed, flat-spined, with illustrations and some ads. Circulation is 1,000 for 750 subscribers of which 250 are libraries. Subscription is included with membership ($30) in the Sport Literature Association. **Sample postpaid: $12.50. "Only typed mss with SASE considered."** No simultaneous submissions. Submissions are reported on in 6-8 weeks and the backlog time is 6-12 months. Contributors receive 5 offprints and a copy of the issue in which their poem appears.

AFRICA WORLD PRESS (V, IV-Ethnic), P.O. Box 1892, Trenton NJ 08607, phone (609)844-9583, fax (609)844-0198, founded 1983, president/publisher Kassahun Checole, publishes **poetry books by Africans, African-Americans, Caribbean and Latin Americans**. They have published *Under A Soprano Sky* by Sonia Sanchez, *From the Pyramid to the Projects* by Askia Muhammad Toure and *The Time: Poems and Photographs* by Esther Iverem. However, they are currently not accepting poetry submissions. Send SASE for catalog.

AFRICAN AMERICAN REVIEW (IV-Ethnic), Dept. of English, Indiana State University, Terre Haute IN 47809, phone (812)237-2968, founded 1967, poetry editors Sterling Plumpp, Thadious M. Davis, Pinkie Gordon Lane and E. Ethelbert Miller, is a "magazine primarily devoted to the analysis of African American literature, **although one issue per year focuses on poetry by African Americans."** No specifications as to form, length, style, subject matter or purpose. They have published poems by Amiri Baraka, Gwendolyn Brooks, Dudley Randall and Owen Dodson. *AAR* is 6×9, 200 pgs. with photo on the cover. They receive about 500 submissions/year, use 50. Individual subscriptions: $24 US, $31 foreign. **Sample postpaid: $10. Submit maximum of 6 poems to editor Joe Weixlmann. The editors sometimes comment on rejections. Publishes theme issues. Send SASE for guidelines. Reports in 3-4 months. Always sends prepublication galleys. Pays in copies.** The *African American Review* received a Special Merit Award for Editorial Content from the 1995 American Literary Magazine Awards.

AFRICAN VOICES (I, II, IV-Ethnic), 270 W. 96th St., New York NY 10025, phone/fax (212)865-2982, founded 1992, contact poetry editor, is a bimonthly "art and literary publication that **highlights the work of people of color. We publish ethnic literature and poetry on any subject. We do not wish to limit the reader or author."** They have published poetry by Reg E. Gaines, Maya Angelou, Tony Medina and Louis Reyes Rivera. As a sample we selected these lines from "Which patent leather shoe belong to which found leg" by Letta Simone-Nefertari Neely (which also appears in *Gawd and alluh huh sistahs*, published by the Collective Effort Coalition Press):

> 30 years later and ahm bout to start a funeral dirge cuz they
> wuz
> sittin at the 16th street baptist church swingin too short legs

> *back and forth in pews and giglin like kids do if they ain't*
> *thinkin bout death*
> *they wuz*
> *thinkin bout what they wuz gonna do after sunday school/how*
> *they wuz gonna sang in the choir/bout who they thought wuz*
> *cute*
> *thinkin bout everything but being bombed outta they skins*

They receive about 100 submissions a year, accept approximately 30%. Press run is 20,000 for 5,000 subscribers of which 30 are libraries, 40% shelf sales. Single copy: $1; subscription: $15. **Sample postpaid: $3. Previously published poems and simultaneous submissions OK. Cover letter and SASE required. Three poetry editors make final selections. Seldom comments on rejections. Send SASE for guidelines. Reports in 6-8 weeks. Pays 5 copies. Acquires first or one-time rights.** Reviews books of poetry in 500-1,000 words. Open to unsolicited reviews. Poets may also send books for review consideration, attn. Layding Kaliba. Sponsors periodic poetry contests. Send SASE for details. The editor says, "We strongly encourage new writers/poets to send in their work and not give up if their work is not accepted the first time. Accepted contributors are encouraged to subscribe."

AFRO-HISPANIC REVIEW (IV-Ethnic), Romance Languages, #143 Arts & Sciences, University of Missouri, Columbia MO 65211, founded 1982, editors Marvin A. Lewis and Edward J. Mullen, appears twice a year, in the fall and spring, using some **poetry related to Afro-Hispanic life and issues.** They have recently published poetry by Cristina Rodriguez Cabral, Luz Argentina Chiriboga and Lemuel Johnson. **Sample copy: $7.50. Submit 2 poems at a time. "Prefer clean copy with accents." Reports in 6 weeks. Pays 5 copies.** Reviews books of poetry in "about 500 words."

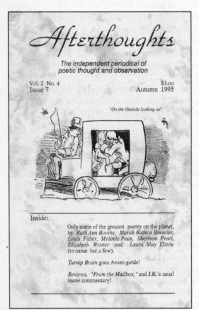

Afterthoughts

The independent periodical of
poetic thought and observation

Vol. 2 No. 4 $3.00
Issue 7   Autumn 1995

"On the Outside looking in"

Inside:

Only some of the greatest poetry on the planet,
by *Ruth Ann Boothe, Marah Bianca Rhoades,
Louis Faber, Melinda Paas, Sherman Pearl,
Elizabeth Rosner* and *Laura May Elston*
(to name but a few).

Turnip Bruin goes Avant-garde!

Reviews, *"From the Mailbox,"* and J.K.'s usual
inane commentary!

"I wanted to capture the periodical's lighthearted side, especially amid the sea of very serious, socially-conscious poems," says J.K. Andromeda, editor and publisher of the Canadian quarterly *Afterthoughts.* "I also felt the illustration conveys the passion I want our contributors to put into their work." Published in London, Ontario, *Afterthoughts* contains about 80 percent poetry, but also publishes short essays on social issues and personal growth as a complement to the poems. "The poems are selected to express, in an artistic and creative way, the thoughts, emotions, and experiences of our readership and people from all walks of life," says Andromeda. The cover illustration is by Wilhelm Busch, a 19th century German artist and writer, and the journal's "Resident Artist from Beyond the Corporeal Realm."

AFTERTHOUGHTS (II, IV-Social issues), Pacific Centre North, 701 Granville St., P.O. Box 54039, Vancouver, British Columbia V7Y 1K6 Canada, founded 1994, editor J.K. Andromeda, is an "independent periodical of poetic thought and observation," published 3 or 4 times a year (or as funds permit). **The editor is looking for "poems dealing with life experience, episodes of irony, emotional conflict, animal rights, veganism, environmental protection, racial harmony, inspiration, and anything else that will touch the very core of the reader's heart. All forms of poetry welcome— quality and originality are the only criteria."** They have recently published poetry by Nancy Berg, John Grey, Katherine Gordon, Marah Bianca Rhoades, Monika Lee, Laura Mae Elston and Paul Karan. As a sample the editor selected these lines from "Addendum to My Will" by Sylvia Parusel:

> *Spare me the dogma and piety:*
> *I want my eulogy written in limerick*
> *—the bawdier the better—*
> *and afterwards*
> *usher in all of the homeless*

>*and friendless people in town,*
>*serve them beer and cookies*
>*and seat then next to*
>*Aunt Louise*

Afterthoughts is 72 pgs., digest-sized, professionally printed and perfect-bound with quality cover stock and b&w illustrations and photos throughout. Press run is 300-500 for 60 subscribers including 15 libraries. Subscription: $12 US, $15 CAN for 4 issues. **Sample postpaid: $5. Cheques or money orders payable to *Afterthoughts*. Previously published poems and simultaneous submissions OK. "Please include an International Reply Coupon with your SAE if you are submitting from the U.S. or overseas. U.S. stamps can't be used in return mail from Canada, and due to high postage costs, we are unable to reply to submissions lacking IRC. SASE required for *Canadian* writers." Cover letter with brief bio required. Reports in 4-6 weeks. Pays 1 copy. "We reserve the right to reprint accepted poetry in future issues. Other than that, all rights revert back to the poet after publication."** They also publish 1- to 3-page essays dealing with veganism and social concerns similar to the periodical's poetic themes. The editor says, "Please make your work accessible and sincere. Write for your own joy and enlightenment and that of your readers—not for poetry editors and workshop coordinators."

AGENDA EDITIONS; AGENDA (II), 5 Cranbourne Ct., Albert Bridge Rd., London SW11 4PE England, founded 1959, poetry editors William Cookson and Peter Dale. *Agenda* is a quarterly magazine (1 double, 2 single issues/year). **"We seek poetry of 'more than usual emotion, more than usual order' (Coleridge).** We publish special issues on particular authors such as T.S. Eliot, Ezra Pound, David Jones, Stanley Burnshaw, Thomas Hardy, etc." Some of the poets who have appeared in *Agenda* are Geoffrey Hill, Seamus Heaney, C.H. Sisson, Patricia McCarthy and W.S. Milne. As a sample the editors selected these lines (poet unidentified):

>*How will you want the snowy impermanence of ash,*
>*your dust, like grass-seed, flighted over heathland,*
>*drifting in spinneys where the boughs clash,*
>*with matted needles laying waste beneath them.*

Agenda is 80 pgs. (of which half are devoted to poetry), 5×7. They receive some 2,000 submissions/year, use 40, have a 5-month backlog. Circulation is 1,500-3,000, 1,500 subscriptions of which 450 are libraries. Subscription: $44 individuals US, $54 libraries and institutions US. **Sample: £4 ($8 surface mail). Submit around 6 poems at a time. Reports in 1 month. Sometimes offers a small payment for poetry.** Reviews books of poetry. Open to unsolicited reviews. Poets may also send books for review consideration. **To submit book ms, no query necessary, "as little as possible" in cover letter. SAE and IRCs for return. Reports within a month. Pays copies.** The editors say poets "should write only if there is an intense desire to express something. They should not worry about fashion."

AGNI (II), Boston University, 236 Bay State Rd., Boston MA 02215, phone (617)353-5389, founded 1972, editors Askold Melnyczuk and Erin Belieu. *AGNI* is a biannual journal of poetry, fiction and essays "by both emerging and established writers. **We publish quite a bit of poetry in forms as well as 'language' poetry, but we don't begin to try and place parameters on the 'kind of work' that *AGNI* selects."** Editors seem to select readable, intelligent poetry—mostly lyric free verse (with some narrative and dramatic, too)—that somehow communicates tension or risk. They have published poetry by Derek Walcott, Patricia Traxler, Thom Gunn, Maxine Scates, Mark Halliday and Ha Jin. As a sample the editors selected these lines from "The Owl" by Joe Osterhaus:

>*So Hegel's Owl of Minerva spreads*
>*its wings at dusk, beginning its long flight*
>*when depth and outline are the most obscure—*
>*how true the image is, yet how unclear,*
>*as if the thinker wanted both the night*
>*and the raptor's shadow gliding over the dry beds.*

AGNI is typeset, offset-printed and perfect-bound with about 40 poems featured in each issue. Circulation is 1,500 by subscription, mail order and bookstore sales. Subscription: $18. **Sample: $7. Submit 3 poems at a time. "No fancy fonts, gimmicks or preformatted reply cards. Brief, sincere cover letters." They will consider simultaneous submissions but not previously published poems. Reads submissions October 1 through April 30 only. Mss received at other times will be returned unread. Reports in 2-5 months. Pays $10/page, $150 maximum, plus 2 copies and one-year subscription. Buys first serial rights.** Work published in *AGNI* has been included in *The Best American Poetry* (1992, 1993, 1994 and 1995) and *Pushcart Prize* anthologies.

AG-PILOT INTERNATIONAL MAGAZINE (IV-Specialized), P.O. Box 1607, Mt. Vernon WA 98273, phone (206)336-9737, publisher Tom Wood, "is intended to be a fun-to-read, technical, as well as humorous and serious publication for the ag pilot and operator. Interested in **agricultural aviation**

(crop dusting) and aerial fire suppression (air tanker pilots) related poetry ONLY—something that rhymes and has a cadence." As a sample we selected these lines from "Freedom" by Jack B. Harvey:

> So now I dress in faded jeans
> And beat up cowboy boots.
> My flying's done on veg'tables,
> The row crops, and the fruits.
>
> My wife now drives the flaggin' truck
> And marks off all my fields.
> She tells me all about the crops
> And talks about the yields.

It appears monthly, 48-64 pgs., circulation 8,400. **Buys 1 poem/issue. Pays $20-50**.

THE AGUILAR EXPRESSION (I, II, IV-Social issues), P.O. Box 304, Webster PA 15087, phone (412)379-8019, founded 1986, editor/publisher Xavier F. Aguilar, appears 2 times/year, and is **"open to all types of poetry, including erotica that is well written. We insist that all writers send a SASE for writer's guidelines before submitting."** They have published poetry by Kimberly Harwell and Dann Ward. As a sample the editor selected the poem "Unnoticed" by Kathleen Lee Mendel:

> I am blank paper
> kept in the back
> of your black leather
> address book.

The editor describes it as 6-12 pgs., magazine-sized. Circulation is 200. **Sample postpaid: $6. Submit 3 poems at a time. "Send copies; mss will not be returned." Cover letter, including writing background, and SASE for contact purposes, required with submissions. Reports in 2 months. Pays 1 copy.** Open to unsolicited reviews. **"We are also seeking poetry manuscripts as we wish to publish 1 or 2 chapbooks in 1996-1997. Send SASE for details."** The editor says, "In publishing poetry, I try to exhibit the unique reality that we too often take for granted and acquaint as mediocre. We encourage poetics that deal with *now*, which our readers can relate to. We are particularly interested in poetry dealing with social issues."

AHSAHTA PRESS; COLD-DRILL; COLD-DRILL BOOKS; POETRY IN PUBLIC PLACES (IV-Regional), English Dept., Boise State University, Boise ID 83725, phone (208)385-1999. Ahsahta Press is a project to publish **contemporary poetry of the American West**. But, say editors Tom Trusky, Orv Burmaster and Dale Boyer, **"Spare us paens to the pommel, Jesus in the sagebrush, haiku about the Eiffel Tower, 'nice' or 'sweet' poems."** The work should **"draw on the cultures, history, ecologies of the American West."** They publish collections (45 pgs.) of individual poets in handsome flat-spined paperbacks with plain matte covers, with an appreciative introduction, at most 3/year. Occasionally they bring out an anthology of their authors on cassette. And they have published *Women Poets of the West*, an anthology (94 pgs.) with an introduction by Ann Stanford. "We are currently producing our MONSTER Twentieth-Year Anniversary anthology." Some of their poets are Susan Deal, Leo Romero, David Baker, Linda Bierds, Philip St. Clair and Gretel Ehrlich. As a sample here are lines from Gerrye Payne's "Machines," in the collection *The Year-God*:

> Machines sit to hand, vortices of possibility.
> Under their blank gaze biological life
> Flares and dies, is ashamed.
> The neighbor's tractor hums, clearing brush,
> inventing geometry in random chaparral.

They are not reading manuscript samplers until 1998. At that time, you may submit only during their January 1 through March 31 reading period—a sample of 15 of your poems with SASE. Multiple and simultaneous submissions OK. They will report in about 2 months. If they like the sample, they'll ask for a book ms. If it is accepted, **you get 25 copies of the 1st and 2nd printings and a 25% royalty commencing with the 3rd. They seldom comment on the samples, frequently on the mss.** Send SASE for their catalog and order a few books, if you don't find them in your library. "Old advice but true: Read what we publish before submitting. **75% of the submissions we receive should never have been sent to us. Save stamps, spirit and sweat."** *cold-drill* publishes **"primarily Boise State University students, faculty and staff, but will consider writings by Idahoans—or writing about Idaho by 'furriners.' "** They do some of the most creative publishing in this country today, and it is worth buying a **sample of *cold-drill* for $9** just to see what they're up to. This annual "has been selected as top undergraduate literary magazine in the U.S. by such important acronyms as CSPA, CCLM and UCDA." It comes in a box stuffed with various pamphlets, postcards, posters, a newspaper, even 3-D comics with glasses to read them by. **No restrictions on types of poetry**. As yet they have published no poets of national note, but Tom Trusky offers these lines as a sample, from Patrick Flanagan, "Postcard From a Freshman":

> *The girls here are gorgeous, studying hard,*
> *many new friends, roommate*
> *never showers, tried to*
> *kill myself, doctor says*
> *i'm getting better*

Circulation is 400, including 100 subscribers, of which 20 are libraries. **"We read material throughout the year, notifying only those whose work we've accepted December 15 through January 1. Manuscripts should be photocopies with author's name and address on separate sheet. Simultaneous submissions OK. Payment: 1 copy."** They also publish two 24-page chapbooks and one 75-page flat-spined paperback/year. **Query about book publication**. "We want to publish a literary magazine that is exciting to read. We want more readers than just our contributors and their mothers. Our format and our content have allowed us to achieve those goals, so far." Poetry in Public Places is a series of 8 monthly posters/year "presenting the poets in Boise State University's creative students series and poets in BSU's Ahsahta Press poetry series." The posters are on coated stock. These, like all publications emanating from BSU, are elegantly done, with striking art.

AILERON PRESS; AILERON: A LITERARY JOURNAL; VOWEL MOVEMENT (II), P.O. Box 891, Austin TX 78767-0891, founded 1980, editor Lyman Grant. *Aileron* is a biannual periodical consisting of poetry and occasional short fiction, with some art. **They want "poetry that moves us, that makes us want to read it again and again. We are especially keen on innovative uses of language—the unexpected word and the unusual cadence. We would like to see more poetic craft displayed, and, though not inimical to rhymed work, feel that few contemporary poets handle rhyme well."** They have published poetry by Anselm Hollo, Simon Perchik, Hal J. Daniel III and Tomaz Salamun. As a sample the editor selected these lines by Elkion Tumbalé:

> *Blue cup modal gorges*
> *Lurk frondly on*
> *Orchid Zontal*
> *Obsidian felines*

Aileron is digest-sized, saddle-stapled, typeset (in small type), with b&w original line art and stiff cover with art. Each issue contains 40-60 pages of poetry garnered from 600-800 submissions each year of which 80-100 are used, 6-month backlog. Circulation is 350, with 25 subscribers. Subscription: $20 for 4 issues. **Sample postpaid: $6. All formats acceptable; must have name and address on each page; no limitations on form, length or subject matter. Send SASE for guidelines. Reports in 6 weeks. Pays 1 copy.** *Vowel Movement*, "a 'pataphysical journal,' is published occasionally as a special issue of *Aileron*. It contains **avant-garde humor, satire, and work that is outrageous or experimental in nature."**

AIM MAGAZINE (IV-Social issues, ethnic), 7308 S. Eberhart Ave., Chicago IL 60619, phone (312)874-6184, founded 1974, poetry editor Henry Blakely, is a quarterly, **"dedicated to racial harmony and peace." They use 3-4 poems ("poetry with social significance mainly"—average 32 lines) in each issue.** They have published poetry by J. Douglas Studer, Wayne Dowdy and Maria DeGuzman. *Aim* is magazine-sized with glossy cover, circulation 10,000. They receive about 30 submissions a year, use half. They have 3,000 subscribers of which 15 are libraries. Subscription: $10. **Sample postpaid: $4. Simultaneous submissions OK. Reports in 3-6 weeks. Pays $3/poem. You will not receive an acceptance slip: "We simply send payment and magazine copy."** The editor's advice: "Read the work of published poets."

AIREINGS (II, IV-Women), Brudenell Rd., #24, Leeds, West Yorkshire LS6 1BD United Kingdom, phone 01132-785893, founded 1980, editor Jean Barker, appears twice a year. "Poems acceptable from all over the world. **Primarily like women's work** as we are a Women's Co-op running the mag and like to redress the balance a bit, but we are **happy to receive work by men also. Poetry on all subjects. We do draw a line on sexist/racist stuff, but we like a broad spectrum of work as long as it is not too long, as we only run to 40 pgs."** They have published poetry by Geoffrey Holloway, Pauline Kirk, Jane Legge, Mary Sheepshanks, C.A. de Lomallini and Linda Marshall. As a sample the editor selected these lines (poet unidentified):

> *For what's so indestructible as names,*
> *Though so haphazard, like those seeds, en masse,*
> *blown out across the graves; and some are lost.*
> *Yet, see the golden harvest in the grass,*
> *each seed a planting and each plant a word.*

Aireings is 40 pgs., digest-sized, saddle-stapled, photocopied from typescript with matte b&w card cover, "illustrated by our own artist. No ads yet, but we may have to later, if we are under extreme financial pressure." They publish about 5% of the poetry received. Their press run is 300-350 for 100 subscribers (10 libraries) and shelf sales. It costs £2/copy, which includes UK postage (overseas: Payment in sterling £6. Other currencies: check equivalent of £11 or in notes equivalent of £6.50.).

Submit 4 poems at a time. "Work should be typed if possible—just legible if not." Simultaneous submissions and previously published poems (if not in the North of England) OK, "if declared." Reports "after our editorial deadlines, which are the 1st of January and July." Pays 2 copies. Staff reviews books of poetry in 500 words.

ALABAMA LITERARY REVIEW (II), English Dept., Troy State University, Troy AL 36082, phone (334)670-3286, fax (334)670-3519, poetry editor Ed Hicks, a biannual, **wants contemporary poetry that is "imagistic—***but*** in motion." Will look at anything, but does not want to see "lyrics sent as poetry. We want serious craft."** They have recently published poetry by David Musgrove, R.T. Smith, Ed Peaco, Joanne M. Riley, Martha Payne, Edward Byrne and Katherine McCanless. As a sample the editor selected these lines from "Late Fall" by Diane Swan:

> It's hard to tell birds
> from wind-rushed leaves
> as they skirl up in the funnels
> of blinking October light

The beautifully printed 100-page, 7×10 magazine, matte cover with art, b&w art and some colored pages inside, receives 300 submissions/year, uses 30, has a 2-month backlog. **Sample postpaid: $5. Submit 2-5 poems at a time. "SASE with appropriate postage is paramount." Will consider simultaneous submissions. Reads submissions September 1 through July 31 only.** Sometimes comments on rejections. **Reports in 2-3 months. Sometimes sends prepublication galleys. Pays copies, sometimes honorarium. Acquires first rights.** Open to unsolicited reviews. Poets may also send books for review consideration.

ALASKA QUARTERLY REVIEW (II), College of Arts and Sciences, University of Alaska Anchorage, 3211 Providence Dr., Anchorage AK 99508, phone/fax (907)786-4775, founded 1981, executive editor Ronald Spatz. "A journal devoted to contemporary literary art. **We publish both traditional and experimental fiction, poetry, literary nonfiction and short plays.**" They have recently published poetry by Nancy Eimers, Hayden Carruth, Lisel Mueller, John Balaban and Dorianne Laux. Editors seem to welcome all styles and forms of poetry with the most emphasis perhaps on voice and content that displays "risk," or intriguing ideas or situations. They publish two double-issues a year, **each using between 25-50 pgs. of poetry.** They receive up to 3,000 submissions a year, accept 40-60. They have a circulation of 1,500 for 450 subscribers of which 32 are libraries. Subscription: $8. **Sample postpaid: $5. Manuscripts are *not* read from May 15 through August 15. They take up to 4 months to report, sometimes longer during peak periods in late winter. Pay depends on funding. Acquires first North American serial rights.** Work published in *AQR* has been selected for inclusion in *The Best American Poetry 1996* and a *Pushcart Prize* anthology.

ALBATROSS; THE ANABIOSIS PRESS (II, IV-Nature), P.O. Box 7787, North Port FL 34287-0787, phone (941)426-7019, founded 1985, editors Richard Smyth and Richard Brobst. *Albatross* appears: "as soon as we have accepted enough quality poems to publish an issue. **We consider the albatross to be a metaphor for an environment that must survive. This is not to say that we publish only environmental or nature poetry, but that we are biased toward such subject matters. We publish mostly free verse, 200 lines/poem maximum, and we prefer a narrative style, but again, this is not necessary. We do not want trite rhyming poetry which doesn't convey a deeply felt experience in a mature expression with words.**" They have recently published poetry by Simon Perchik, Lyn Lifshin, Ann Newell, William Virgil Davis and Errol Miller. As a sample the editors selected these lines by Michael McMahon:

> a one bulb noon in the manger
> of childhood
> birth blood steaming
> on the straw as the black mare
> exhaled pain and angels

The magazine is 28-36 pgs., $5\frac{1}{2} \times 8\frac{1}{2}$, laser typeset with linen cover, some b&w drawings, and sometimes, in addition to the poetry, has an interview with a poet in each issue. Circulation is 200 for 75 subscribers of which 10 are libraries. Many complimentary copies are sent out to bookstores, poets and libraries. Subscription: $5/2 issues. **Sample postpaid: $3. Submit 3-5 poems at a time. "Poems should be typed single-spaced, with name and address in left corner and length in lines in right corner." No simultaneous submissions. Cover letter not required; "We do, however, need bio notes if published." Send SASE for guidelines. Reports in 4-6 months, has 6- to 12-month backlog. Pays 1 copy. Acquires all rights. Returns rights provided that "previous publication in *Albatross* is mentioned in all subsequent reprintings."** Also holds a chapbook contest. **Submit 20-24 pgs. of poetry, any theme, any style. Deadline is May 31 of each year. Include name, address and phone number on the title page. Charges $7 reading fee (check payable to *Albatross*). Winner receives $100 and 25 copies of his/her published chapbook. All entering receive a free copy of the winning chapbook.** "The Anabiosis Press is a nonprofit, tax-exempt organization. Membership fee is $20/

year." Comments? "We expect a poet to read as much contemporary poetry as possible."

ALICEJAMESBOOKS; BEATRICE HAWLEY AWARD (IV-Regional, women, ethnic), University of Maine at Farmington, 98 Main St., Farmington ME 04938, phone/fax (207)778-7071, founded 1973, is "an author's collective which only publishes **poetry. Authors are primarily from the New England Area**. We strongly encourage submissions by poets of color." They publish flat-spined paperbacks of high quality, both in production and contents, no children's poetry. Their books have won numerous awards and been very respectably reviewed. "Each poet becomes a working member of the co-op with a two-year work commitment." That is, you have to live close enough to **attend meetings and participate in the editorial and publishing process**. They publish about 4 books, 72 pgs., each year in editions of 1,000, paperbacks—no hardbacks. **Query first, but no need for samples: simply ask for dates of reading period, which is in early fall and winter. May contact by phone or fax for submission guidelines only. Send 2 copies of the ms. Simultaneous submissions OK, but "we would like to know when a manuscript is being submitted elsewhere." Reports in 2-3 months. Pays authors 100 paperback copies.** Offers Beatrice Hawley Award for poets who cannot meet the work requirement due to geographical restraints. Their book *The Moon Reflected Fire*, by Doug Anderson, won the Kate Tufts Discovery Award for 1995.

ALIVE NOW (IV-Spirituality, themes); POCKETS (IV-Religious, children, themes); DE-VO'ZINE (IV-Religious, youth, themes); WEAVINGS; THE UPPER ROOM (V), 1908 Grand Ave., P.O. Box 189, Nashville TN 37202, phone (615)340-7200. This publishing company brings out about 20 books a year and five magazines: *The Upper Room, Alive Now, Pockets, Devo'Zine* and *Weavings*. Of these, three use unsolicited poetry. *Pockets, Devotional Magazine for Children*, which comes out 11 times a year, circulation 68,000-70,000, is for children 6-12, "offers stories, activities, prayers, poems—all **geared to giving children a better understanding of themselves as children of God. Some of the material is not overtly religious but deals with situations, special seasons and holidays, and ecological concerns from a Christian perspective**." It uses 3-4 pgs. of poetry/ issue. **Sample free with 7½ × 10½ SAE and 4 first-class stamps. Ordinarily 24-line limit on poetry. Send SASE for themes and guidelines. Pays $25-50.** The second magazine which uses poetry is *Alive Now*, a bimonthly, circulation 75,000, for a general Christian audience interested in reflection and meditation. **They buy 30 poems a year, avant-garde and free verse. Submit 5 poems, 10-45 lines. Send SASE for themes and guidelines. Pays $10-25.** The third magazine that uses poetry is *Devo'Zine: Just for Teens*, a bimonthly devotional magazine for youth ages 12-18, offers meditations, scripture, prayers, poems, stories, songs and feature articles to **"aid youth in their prayer life, introduce them to spiritual disciplines, help them shape their concept of God, and encourage them in the life of discipleship." Ordinarily 20-line limit on poetry. Send SASE for theme and guidelines. Pays $20.** *The Upper Room* magazine does not accept poetry.

ALLARDYCE, BARNETT, PUBLISHERS (V), 14 Mount St., Lewes, East Sussex BN7 1HL England, founded 1982, editorial director Anthony Barnett. Allardyce, Barnett publishes "literature, music, art. **We cannot consider unsolicited manuscripts**." They have published books of poetry by J.H. Prynne, Douglas Oliver, Veronica Forrest-Thomson, Anne-Marie Albiach and César Vallejo. In the US, their books can be obtained through Small Press Distribution in Berkeley, CA.

ALLEGHENY REVIEW (I, IV-Undergraduate students), Dept. PM, Box 32, Allegheny College, Meadville PA 16335, founded 1983. "Each year *Allegheny Review* compiles and publishes a review of the nation's best **undergraduate literature**. It is entirely composed of and by college undergraduates and is nationally distributed both as a review and as a classroom text, particularly suited to creative writing courses." In the Fall of 1995, they added a section of essays on poetry and literature. (Submit 10-15 typed pgs., double-spaced.) "We will print **poetry of appreciable literary merit on any topic, submitted by college undergraduates. No limitations except excessive length (2-3 pgs.)** as we wish to represent as many authors as possible, although exceptions are made in areas of great quality and interest." They have published poetry by Eric Sanborn, Cheryl Connor, Rick Alley and Kristi Coulter. The *Review* appears in a 6×9, flat-spined, professionally-printed format, b&w photo on glossy card cover. Single copy: $5. **Sample: $3.50 and 11×18 SAE (back issue: $3). Submit 3-5 poems, typed. Submissions should be accompanied by a letter "telling the college poet is attending, year of graduation, any background, goals and philosophies that the author feels are pertinent to the work submitted." Reports 1-2 months following deadline. Poem judged best in the collection earns $50-75 honorarium.** "Ezra Pound gave the best advice: 'Make it new.' We're seeing far too much imitation; there's already been a Sylvia Plath, a Galway Kinnell. Don't be afraid to try new things. Be innovative. Also, traditional forms are coming 'back in style,' or so we hear. Experiment with them; write a villanelle, a sestina or a sonnet. And when you submit, please take enough pride in your work to do so professionally. Handwritten or poorly typed and proofed submissions definitely convey an impression—a negative one."

ALLY PRESS CENTER (V), Dept. PM, 524 Orleans St., St. Paul MN 55107, founded 1973, owner Paul Feroe, **publishes and distributes work by Robert Bly, Michael Meade, James Hillman and Robert Moore, including books, cassette tapes and videotapes.** Four times a year a newsletter is mailed out along with information about Bly's reading and workshop schedule. **The press is not accepting unsolicited mss at this time.** Newsletter is free on request.

ALMS HOUSE PRESS; THE ALMS HOUSE JOURNAL (I), P.O. Box 217, Pearl River NY 10965-0217, founded 1985, poetry editors Lorraine De Gennaro and Alana Sherman, publishes the biannual *Alms House Journal* and 3-4 chapbooks/perfect-bound books per year. **"We have no preferences with regard to style as long as the poetry is high caliber. We like to see previous publication in the small press, but we are open to new writers. We look for variety and excellence and are open to experimental forms as well as traditional forms. Any topics as long as the poems are not whiny or too depressing, pornographic or religious."** They have recently published chapbooks by Lenore Balliro and Robert Hudzik. As a sample the editors selected these lines of poetry:

> Later, the hay moon will rise white & bellied out
> like some great thumbprint over the pond,
> and in the lingering warmth
> the moon drifts in and out of the clouds
> the scent of new mown grass rises up
> in and out of your dreams like summer.

For *AHJ*, submit 3-5 poems at a time with $5 reading fee. For chapbooks, submit 16- to 24-page ms with $15 reading fee; for longer collections, submit up to 50 pages with $25 reading fee. All mss must be typed with 1 poem/page. No previously published poems or simultaneous submissions. Reads submissions September 1 through December 31 only. Send SASE for guidelines. Reports in 2-3 months. Press pays $25 plus 10 copies and 7% of all sales over first 100 books. They sponsor a poetry reading series and offer a critical and editorial service for $50. The editors say, "We treat every poem, every manuscript and every author with respect. We believe poetry should be well presented."

ALOHA, THE MAGAZINE OF HAWAII AND THE PACIFIC (IV-Regional), 1240 Ala Moana Blvd., Suite 320, Honolulu HI 96814, phone (808)593-1191, fax (808)593-1327, editorial director Cheryl Chee Tsutsumi, is a bimonthly (every 2 months) "consumer magazine with Hawaii and Pacific focus. **Not interested in lengthy poetry. Poems should be limited to 100 words or less. Subject should be focused on Hawaii."** As a sample the editorial director selected these lines by Sheri Rice:

> Sea touching sand
> Licks the silent shore
> Footsteps melting into smoothness
> Erasing ridges, indentations
> As each slap and pull of the ocean
> Planned by tides and moonlit nights
> Delivers one more day.

Aloha is 64 pgs., magazine-sized, flat-spined, elegantly printed on glossy stock with many full-color pages, glossy card cover in color. They publish 6 of more than 50 poems received/year. Circulation is 75,000. **Sample: $2.95 plus $2.62 p&h. Ms should be typed, double-spaced, with name, address and phone number included.** Poems are matched to color photos, so it is "difficult to say" how long it will be between acceptance and publication. **Send SASE for guidelines. Reports within 2 months. Pays $30 plus 1 copy (and up to 10 at discount).**

ALPHA BEAT SOUP; ALPHA BEAT PRESS (I, IV-Form/style), 31 Waterloo St., New Hope PA 18938-1210, phone (215)862-0299, founded 1987, poetry editor David Christy, appears irregularly **emulating the Beat literary tradition.** *Alpha Beat Soup* is "an international poetry and arts journal featuring Beat, 'post-Beat independent' and modern writing." Christy says that **25% of each issue is devoted to little known or previously unpublished poets.** They have recently published works by Pradip Choudhuri, George Dowden, Jack Micheline, Steve Richmond and A.D. Winans. As a sample the editor selected these lines by Ana Christy:

> the alley in its
> complacency surrenders
> to
> morning scavenger birds
> squawking an Ornette
> Coleman sax.

ABS is 50-75 pgs., 7 × 8½, photocopied from IBM laser printer, card cover offset, graphics included. They use 50% of the poetry received. Press run is 600 for 400 subscribers of which 11 are libraries. Single copy: $8; subscription: $15. **Sample postpaid: $10. Submit 3-6 poems at a time. Simultaneous** submissions and previously published poems OK. Cover letter, including "an introduction to the poet's work," required. Editor comments on rejections "only on request." Sometimes sends prepublication galleys. Pays 1 copy. Reviews books of poetry in approximately 700 words, multi-book format. Open to unsolicited reviews. Poets may also send books for review consideration. **Alpha Beat Press publishes chapbooks and supplements as well as a monthly broadside series featuring unknown poets. They offer cooperative publishing of chapbooks, "as a way to fund our press and also showcase the unknown poet." Write for details.** Also see the listings for *Bouillabaisse* and *Cokefish*.

‡**AMARANTH (II)**, P.O. Box 184, Trumbull CT 06611, phone (203)452-9652, founded 1995, editors Becky Rodia and Christopher Sanzeni, is a biannual poetry journal. **The editors would like to see "formal and free verse with clear, concrete imagery; a good sense of sound and rhythm; and attention to line and stanza breaks. Though any subject matter or form is welcome, we especially enjoy prose poems, humor and 'personal' poems. However, we don't have the space to print anything over 70 lines. Please refrain from sending us poems without punctuation and poems which employ the lowercase 'i.' We also do not appreciate abstract meditations/screamfests on 'topics' such as bliss, freedom, alienation, ecstasy, etc."** They have recently published poetry by Mordecai Marcus, Joe Benevento and Sally Jo Sorensen. As a sample the editors selected these lines from "Mormon Barbie" by Denise Duhamel:

> *Sometimes one of Barbie's earthly days seems forever,*
> *her personalized pink planet swirling high above the world as she knows it.*
> *She dreams of her Maker, the Lord Jesus Christ,*
> *and Ken who will, in the afterlife, call out her secret marriage name*
> *so she will fly to him, no longer Barbie,*
> *no longer misunderstood at every turn.*

Amaranth is 36-40 pgs., 5½×8½, professionally printed and saddle-stapled with glossy card cover with full-color artwork. They receive about 500 poems a year, accept approximately 10%. Press run is 1,000. Subscription: $10. **Sample (including guidelines) postpaid: $6. Submit 3-5 poems at a time, name and address on each. No previously published poems; simultaneous submissions OK, "but please notify us immediately if the work is accepted elsewhere." Cover letter preferred. Often comments on rejections. Send SASE for guidelines alone. Reports in 3 months, longer if under serious consideration. Sometimes sends prepublication galleys. Pays 2 copies, additional copies available at a discount. Rights revert to authors upon publication.** The editors plan to start reviewing chapbooks and books in under 1,000 words, single format. Poets may send books for review consideration. They also plan to run occasional contests. Watch the trade publications for announcements. They add, " 'Amaranth' means 'flower which never fades' and we look for poems that are beautiful, but timeless, hardy, universal and human."

AMBER; MARSH & MAPLE (I, II), 40 Rose St., #404, Dartmouth, Nova Scotia B3A 2T6 Canada, phone (902)461-4934, founded 1967, editor Hazel F. Goddard, appears 4 times/year (in January, April, July and October). "*Amber* and its one-page supplement, *Marsh & Maple*, promote and distribute current work. *Amber* is nonprofit, entirely subscription-supported." **They want "free verse, half page, regular line lengths (not over 56 characters preferred), also haiku and occasional sonnet. Any subject, but must be in good taste, *not vulgar.* Original, bright content. No religious verse. Prefer poems to be seasonal, if on nature."** They have published poetry by John D. Engle, Jr., Diana K. Rubin and Tony Cosier. As a sample the editor selected these lines (poet unidentified):

> *i am a symphony*
> *blazing syllables of light*
> *across each phrase*
> *lengthening like eighth notes*
> *from a phantom violin*
> *to touch the inner ear*

Amber is 28 pgs., digest-sized, photocopied on colored paper and saddle-stapled with paper cover. They receive about 500 poems a year, use roughly 70%. Press run is 100 for 90 subscribers of which 3 are libraries. Single copy: $2.50; subscription: $10. **Sample postpaid: $1. Submit 2 poems at a time. Every sheet should bear the poet's name. Previously published poems OK; no simultaneous submissions.** Time between acceptance and publication is 1-6 months. **Seldom comments on rejections. Publishes theme issues. Send SASE for upcoming themes.** "First acceptance paid for with

---

‡ **THE DOUBLE DAGGER** before a listing indicates that the listing is new in this edition. New markets are often the most receptive to submissions.

1 free copy; continuing submissions expected to be covered by a subscription." The editor says, "I receive many books of poets' poems. If up to an average standard I select from them for publication in my magazine. Most poems are from well-crafted poets, a few new writers. Need not be professional but *must* be good work. When space allows, I list contests poets may like to enter, comment on books poets send and devote centrefold to personal chatting, poets' successes, etc."

AMBIT (III), 17 Priory Gardens, Highgate, London N6 5QY England, phone 0181-340-3566, editor Martin Bax; poetry editors Edwin Brock, Carol Ann Duffy and Henry Graham; prose editor J.G. Ballard; and art editor Mike Foreman. *Ambit* is a 96-page quarterly of **avant-garde, contemporary and experimental work.** As a sample the editor selected these excerpts from "Two Poems For Two Suicides" by Henry Graham:

> *1*
>
> *All right then*
> *who would fardels bare?*
> *Or the world away out of earshot*
> *careless of your one foot in too many graves*
> *every waking hour.*
>
>
> *2*
> *It got to seem like a war,*
> *casualties*
> *I used to say,*
> *though no one was shooting at us.*
> *Or were they?*

Subscription: £22 individuals, £33 institutions (UK); £24 ($48) individuals, £35 ($70) institutions (overseas). **Sample: £6. Submit 6 poems at a time, typed double-spaced. No previously published poems or simultaneous submissions. Pay is "variable plus 2 free copies."** Staff reviews books of poetry. Send books for review consideration, attn. Review Editor.

AMELIA; CICADA; SPSM&H; THE AMELIA AWARDS (II, IV-Form), 329 "E" St., Bakersfield CA 93304 or P.O. Box 2385, Bakersfield CA 93303, phone (805)323-4064. *Amelia*, founded 1983, poetry editor Frederick A. Raborg, Jr., is a quarterly magazine that publishes chapbooks as well. Central to its operations is a series of contests, most with entry fees, spaced evenly throughout the year, awarding more than $3,500 annually, but they publish many poets who have not entered the contests as well. Among poets published are Pattiann Rogers, Stuart Friebert, John Millett, David Ray, Larry Rubin, Charles Bukowski, Maxine Kumin, Charles Edward Eaton and Shuntaro Tanikawa. As a sample the editor selected these lines by Robert Gibb:

> *Yours is not the whole handprint*
> *Left palmed on the walls of a cave*
> *Or the bright sides of a pony.*
> *This darkness is yours which rolls*
> *From beneath the nails, prints*
> *Gleaming like the back of fist,*
> *Freshly gutted and spread flat.*
> *They are boxy as Mayan glyphs, ten*
> *Small likenesses, ten little mirrors*
> *which flash as black as obsidian. . . .*

They are **"receptive to all forms to 100 lines. We do not want to see the patently-religious or overtly-political. Erotica is fine; pornography, no."** The digest-sized, flat-spined magazine is offset on high-quality paper and sometimes features an original four-color cover; its circulation is about 1,556, with 612 subscribers, of which 28 are libraries. Subscription: $25/year. **Sample postpaid: $8.95. Submit 3-5 poems at a time. No simultaneous submissions except for entries to the annual Amelia Chapbook Award. Reports in 2-12 weeks, the latter if under serious consideration. Pays $2-25/ poem plus 2 copies. "Almost always I try to comment."** The editor says, "*Amelia* is not afraid of strong themes, but we do look for professional, polished work even in handwritten submissions. Poets should have something to say about matters other than the moon. We like to see strong **traditional pieces as well as the contemporary and experimental. And neatness *does* count**." Fred Raborg has done more than most other editors to ensure a wide range of styles and forms, from traditional European to Asian, from lyric to narrative. Typically he is swamped with submissions and so response times can exceed stated parameters. *Amelia* continues to place in outside surveys as a top market, because of editorial openness. Brief reviews are also featured. As for Raborg's other publications, *Cicada* is a quarterly magazine that publishes **haiku, senryu and other Japanese forms**, plus essays on the form—techniques and history—as well as fiction which in some way incorporates haiku or Japanese poetry in its plot, and reviews of books pertaining to Japan and its poetry or collections of haiku. Among poets published are Roger Ishii, H.F. Noyes, Knute Skinner, Katherine Machan Aal, Ryah

Tumarkin Goodman and Ryokufu Ishizaki. These sample lines are by Elizabeth St. Jacques:

> *shrinking*
> *the small garden plot*
> *a silver-striped melon*

> *the quiet search over rocks*
> *of a thin green vine*

They are **receptive to experimental forms as well as the traditional. "Try to avoid still-life as haiku; strive for the *whole* of an emotion, whether minuscule or panoramic. Erotica is fine; the Japanese are great lovers of the erotic."** The magazine is offset on high-quality paper. Circulation is 600, with 432 subscribers of which 26 are libraries. Subscription: $14/year. **Sample postpaid: $4.95. Submit 3-10 haiku or poems. No simultaneous submissions. Reports in 2 weeks. No payment, except three "best of issue" poets each receive $10 on publication plus copy. "I try to make some comment on returned poems always."** SPSM&H is a quarterly magazine that publishes **only sonnets, sonnet sequences**, essays on the form—both technique and history—as well as romantic or Gothic fiction which, in some way, incorporates the form, and reviews of sonnet collections or collections containing a substantial number of sonnets. They are **"receptive to experimental forms as well as the traditional, and appreciate wit when very good."** Among poets published are Margaret Ryan, Harold Witt, Sharon E. Martin, Rhina P. Espaillat and Robert Wolfkill. These sample lines are by Michael J. Bugeja:

> *She knew the steps, the key. The cadence*
> *When she came to him with another minuet,*
> *Sheeted music in her satchel like a poem:*
> *Heavy, black. But even she could dance*
> *Later as he taught her, timing the duet*
> *With the indifference of a metronome.*

Perhaps it may help to know the editor's favorite Shakespearean sonnet is #29, and he feels John Updike clarified the limits of experimentation with the form in his "Love Sonnet" from *Midpoint*. The magazine is offset on high-quality paper. Circulation is 600, for 432 subscribers and 26 libraries. Subscription: $14/year. **Sample postpaid: $4.95. Submit 3-5 poems at a time. No simultaneous submissions. Reports in 2 weeks. No payment, except two "best of issue" poets each receive $14 on publication plus copy. "I always try to comment on returns."** The following annual contests have various entry fees: The Amelia Awards (six prizes of $200, $100, $50 plus three honorable mentions of $10 each); The Anna B. Janzen Prize for Romantic Poetry ($100, annual deadline January 2); The Bernice Jennings Traditional Poetry Award ($100, annual deadline January 2); The Georgie Starbuck Galbraith Light/Humorous Verse Prizes (six awards of $100, $50, $25 plus three honorable mentions of $5 each, annual deadline March 1); The Charles William Duke Longpoem Award ($100, annual deadline April 1); The Lucille Sandberg Haiku Awards (six awards of $100, $50, $25 plus three honorable mentions of $5 each, annual deadline April 1); The Grace Hines Narrative Poetry Award ($100, annual deadline May 1); The Amelia Chapbook Award ($250, book publication and 50 copies, annual deadline July 1); The Johanna B. Bourgoyne Poetry Prizes (six awards of $100, $50, $25, plus three honorable mentions of $5 each); The Douglas Manning Smith Epic/Heroic Poetry Prize ($100, annual deadline August 1); The Hildegarde Janzen Prize for Oriental Forms of Poetry (six awards of $50, $30, $20 and three honorable mentions of $5 each, annual deadline September 1); The Eugene Smith Prize for Sonnets (six awards of $140, $50, $25 and three honorable mentions of $5 each); The A&C Limerick Prizes (six awards of $50, $30, $20 and three honorable mentions of $5 each); The Montegue Wade Lyric Poetry Prize ($100, annual deadline November 1).

AMERICA; FOLEY POETRY CONTEST (II), 106 W. 56th St., New York NY 10019, phone (212)581-4640, founded 1909, poetry editor Patrick Samway, S.J., is a weekly journal of opinion published by the Jesuits of North America. They primarily publish articles on religious, social, political and cultural themes. **They are "looking for imaginative poetry of all kinds. We have no restrictions on form or subject matter, though we prefer to receive poems of 35 lines or less."** They have published poetry by Howard Nemerov, Fred Chappell, William Heyen and Eve Shelnutt. *America* is 24 pgs., magazine-sized, professionally printed on thin stock with thin paper cover. Circulation is 35,000. Subscription: $33. **Sample postpaid: $1.75. Send SASE for excellent guidelines. Reports in 2 weeks. Pays $1.40/line plus 2 copies.** The annual Foley Poetry Contest offers a prize of $500, usually in late winter. Send SASE for rules. "Poems for the Foley Contest should be submitted between January and April. Poems submitted for the Foley Contest between July and December will normally be returned unread." The editor says, *"America* is committed to publishing quality poetry as it has done for the past 87 years. We encourage beginning and established poets to submit their poems to us."

AMERICAN ATHEIST PRESS; GUSTAV BROUKAL PRESS; AMERICAN ATHEIST (IV-Specialized), P.O. Box 140195, Austin TX 78714-0195, phone (512)458-1244, founded 1958, editor

Frank Zindler, publishes the biannual magazine with 40,000 circulation, *American Atheist*, and under various imprints some dozen books a year reflecting "concerns of atheists, such as separation of state and church, civil liberties and atheist news." **Poetry is used primarily in the poetry section of the magazine. It must have "a particular slant to atheism, dealing with subjects such as the atheist lifestyle. Anticlerical poems and puns are more than liable to be rejected. Any form or style is acceptable. Preferred length is under 40 lines."** They have published poetry by Julia Rhodes Pozonzycki, Allan Case and Thomas A. Easton. The magazine-sized format is professionally printed, with art and photos, glossy, color cover. They receive over 20-30 poetry submissions/week, use about 12/year. Of their 17,000 subscriptions, 1,000 are libraries. Single copy: $2.95; subscription: $25. **Sample free. Submit 6-8 poems at a time, typed and double-spaced. Simultaneous submissions OK. Time-dependent poems (such as winter) should be submitted 4 months in advance. Guidelines and upcoming themes available for SASE, but a label is preferred to an envelope. Reports within 3-4 months. Pays "first-timers" 10 copies or 6-month subscription or $12 credit voucher for AAP products. Thereafter, $15/poem plus 10 copies. Buys one-time rights. Sometimes comments on rejected mss.** Reviews related books of poetry in 500-1,000 words. They do not normally publish poetry in book form but will consider it.

THE AMERICAN COWBOY POET MAGAZINE (I, IV-Cowboy), Dept. PM, P.O. Box 326, Eagle ID 83616, phone (208)888-9838, fax (208)887-0082, e-mail acpm@cyberhighway.net, founded 1988 as *The American Cowboy Poet Newspaper*, magazine format in January 1991, publisher Rudy Gonzales, editor Rose Fitzgerald. *ACPM* is a quarterly "about real cowboys" using **"authentic cowboy poetry. Must be clean—entertaining. Submissions should avoid 'like topics.' We will not publish any more poems about Old Blackie dying, this old hat, if this pair of boots could talk, etc. We do not publish free verse poetry. Only traditional cowboy poetry with rhyme and meter."** They also publish articles, including a "Featured Poet," stories of cowboy poetry gatherings, and news of coming events. Subscription: $12/year US, $15 Canada, $20 Overseas. **Sample postpaid: $3.50. Cover letter required with submissions. Send SASE for guidelines or request via e-mail. Editor always comments on rejections.** Staff reviews related books and tapes of poetry. Send books and cowboy music tapes for review consideration.

‡**AMERICAN INDIAN STUDIES CENTER; AMERICAN INDIAN CULTURE AND RE-SEARCH JOURNAL (IV-Ethnic/nationality)**, 3220 Campbell Hall, Box 951548, UCLA, Los Angeles CA 90095-1548, phone (310)825-7315, fax (310)206-7060, e-mail aisc@UCLA.edu, website http://www.sscnet.UCLA.edu/Indian/, founded 1975. The *American Indian Culture and Research Journal* is a quarterly which publishes new research and literature about American Indians. **All work must have Native American content.** The editor says the journal is 300 pgs., 5×9, perfect-bound. They receive 20-50 poems a year, publish 10-15. Press run is 1,200 for 1,000 subscribers of which 400 are libraries, 10 shelf sales. Subscription: $25 individual, $35 institution. **Sample: $7.50. Make checks payable to Regents of the University of California. Submit 5-6 poems at a time. No previously published poems or simultaneous submissions. Cover letter preferred.** Time between acceptance and publication is 6 months. **Poems are circulated to members of an editorial board. Often comments on rejections. Publishes theme issues. Reports in 2 months. Always sends pre-publication galleys. Pays 1 copy.** The American Indian Studies Center also publishes 1-2 paperback books of poetry in their Native American Literature Series. They have published *The Light on the Tent Wall: A Bridging* by Mary TallMountain and *Old Shirts & New Skins* by Sherman Alexie. **Pays author's copies and offers 40% discount on additional copies.** Send SASE for a complete list of the center's publications.

AMERICAN LITERARY REVIEW (II), University of North Texas, P.O. Box 13827, Denton TX 76203, phone (817)565-4670, editor Barbara Rodman, poetry editor Bruce Bond, is a biannual publishing **all forms and modes of poetry, but "less interested in poetry in the personal mode."** They have published poetry by Penelope Austin, Wendy Barker, Bruce Bond, Kevin Cantwell, David Citino, Wyn Cooper, Elizabeth Dodd, Joseph Duemer, Pattiann Rogers, William Stafford, Lee Upton and Ralph Wilson. As a sample the editor selected these lines from "Double or Nothing" by Jack Myers:

> And, now, like an amnesiac trying to feel special on his birthday,
> I've decided that death must be what it's like before we're born.
> Have I finally broken through? Unafraid of the nothing that's eternal
> in favor of the nothing that will pass?

Sample postpaid: $8. Submit up to 5 poems at a time. Reports in 2 months. Sometimes sends prepublication galleys. Pays copies.

AMERICAN POETRY REVIEW (III), Dept. PM, 1721 Walnut St., Philadelphia PA 19103, phone (215)496-0439, founded 1972, is probably the **most widely circulated (18,000 copies bimonthly) and best-known periodical devoted to poetry in the world**. Poetry editors are Stephen Berg, David Bonanno and Arthur Vogelsang, and they have **published most of the leading poets writing in**

English and many translations. The poets include Gerald Stern, Brenda Hillman, John Ashbery, Norman Dubie, Marvin Bell, Galway Kinnell, James Dickey, Lucille Clifton and Tess Gallagher. *APR* is a newsprint tabloid with 13,000 subscriptions, of which 1,000 are libraries. The editors receive about 8,000 submissions/year, use 200. This popular publication contains mostly free verse (some leaning to the avant-garde) with flashes of brilliance in every issue. Editors seem to put an emphasis on language and voice. Because *APR* is a tabloid, it can feature long poems (or ones with long line lengths) in an attractive format. Translations are also welcome. In all, this is a difficult market to crack because of the volume of submissions. **Sample and price per issue: $3.50. No simultaneous submissions. Reports in 3 months, has 1- to 3-year backlog. Always sends prepublication galleys. Pays $2/line.** The magazine is also a major resource for opinion, reviews, theory, news and ads pertaining to poetry. Each year the editors award the Jerome J. Shestack Prizes of $1,000, $500 and $250 for the best poems, in their judgment, published in *APR*. Poetry published here has also been included in the 1992, 1993, 1994 and 1995 volumes of *The Best American Poetry*.

THE AMERICAN SCHOLAR (III), 1811 Q St. NW, Washington DC 20009, phone (202)265-3808, founded 1932, associate editor Sandra Costich, is an academic quarterly which **uses about 5 poems/ issue. "We would like to see poetry that develops an image, a thought or event, without the use of a single cliché or contrived archaism. The most hackneyed subject matter is self-conscious love; the most tired verse is iambic pentameter with rhyming endings. The usual length of our poems is 30 lines. Up to 4 poems may be submitted at one time; *no more* for a careful reading."** They have published poetry by Robert Pack, Alan Shapiro and Gregory Djanikian. What little poetry is used in this high-prestige magazine is accomplished, intelligent and open (in terms of style and form). Study before submitting (**sample: $6.95, guidelines available for SASE). Reports in 2 months. Always sends prepublication galleys. Pays $50/poem. Buys first rights only.**

AMERICAN TOLKIEN SOCIETY; MINAS TIRITH EVENING-STAR; W.W. PUBLICA-TIONS (IV-Specialized, themes), P.O. Box 373, Highland MI 48357-0373, phone/fax (813)585-0985, founded 1967, editor Philip W. Helms. There are special poetry issues. Membership in the ATS is open to all, regardless of country of residence, and entitles one to receive the quarterly journal. Dues are $10 per annum to addresses in US, $12.50 in Canada and $15 elsewhere. Their journal and chapbooks use **poetry of fantasy about Middle-Earth and Tolkien.** They have published poetry by Thomas M. Egan, Anne Etkin, Nancy Pope and Martha Benedict. *Minas Tirith Evening-Star* is magazine-sized, offset from typescript with cartoon-like b&w graphics. Press run is 400 for 350 subscribers of which 10% are libraries. Single copy: $3.50; subscription: $7.50. **Sample postpaid: $1.50. "Please make checks payable to American Tolkien Society." No simultaneous submissions; previously published poems "maybe." Cover letter preferred. "We do not return phone calls unless collect." Editor sometimes comments on rejections. Publishes theme issues occasionally. Send SASE for guidelines. Reports in 2 weeks. Sometimes sends prepublication galleys. Pays contributor's copies.** Reviews related books of poetry; length depends on the volume, "a sentence to several pages." Open to unsolicited reviews. Poets may also send books to Paul Ritz, Reviews, P.O. Box 901, Clearwater FL 34617 for review consideration. Under imprint of W.W. Publications they publish collections of poetry 50-100 pgs. **For book or chapbook consideration, submit sample poems. Publishes 2 chapbooks/year.** They sometimes sponsor contests.

‡THE AMERICAN VOICE (II), 332 W. Broadway, Louisville KY 40202, phone (502)562-0045, founded 1985, editor Frederick Smock, is a literary quarterly publishing North and South American writers. They prefer **free verse, avant-garde, in areas such as ethnic/nationality, gay/lesbian, trans-lation, women/feminism and literary.** They have published poetry by Olga Broumas, Odysseus Elytis, Cheryl Clarke, Marge Piercy and Ernesto Cardenal. *TAV* is 140 pgs. of high-quality stock, elegantly printed and flat-spined with matte card cover. Editors seem to prefer lyric free verse, much of it accessible, by well-known and new writers. Circulation is 2,000 with 1,000 subscriptions of which 100 are libraries. Subscription: $15/year. **Sample postpaid: $7. No simultaneous submissions. Cover letter requested. Occasionally comments on rejections. Reports in 6 weeks, has a 3-month back-log. Pays $100/poem and 2 copies. (They pay $50 to translator of a poem.)** Open to unsolicited reviews. Poets may also send books for review consideration. *The American Voice* has received an *Utne Reader* Alternative Press Award and has had work included in *The Best American Poetry* (1995 and 1996 volumes) and *Pushcart Prize* anthologies.

AMERICAN WRITING: A MAGAZINE; NIERIKA EDITIONS (IV-Form/style), 4343 Ma-nayunk Ave., Philadelphia PA 19128, founded 1990, editor Alexandra Grilikhes, appears twice a year using **poetry that is "experimental and the voice of the loner, writing that takes risks with form, interested in the powers of intuition and states of being. No cerebral, academic poetry. Poets often try to make an experience 'literary' through language, instead of going back to the original experience and finding the original images. That is what we are interested in: the voice that speaks those images."** They have published poetry by Ivan Argüelles, Antler, Eleanor Wilner, Diane

Glancy and Margaret Holley. As a sample the editor selected these lines from "Coyote" by Shelley M. Miller:

> There is pain, Coyote, that you have not known yet.
> It is good your legs still carry you
>   tirelessly away from peace;
> that your grin still frightens away false caretakers,
> that you long ago ate your own heart to survive.
>
> There is pain ahead, Coyote.
> Muscle, cunning, speed? These will never set you free.

AW is 80 pgs., digest-sized, professionally printed and flat-spined with matte card cover. Press run is 2,000 for 350 subscribers. Subscription: $10. **Sample postpaid: $6. Submit 8 poems at a time. No previously published poems; simultaneous submissions OK. Guidelines on subscription form. Reports anywhere from 6 weeks to 6 months. Pays 2 copies/accepted submission group.** Since *American Writing* began in 1990, 15 of the authors they have published won national awards after publication in the magazine. The editor says, "Many magazines print the work of the same authors (the big names) who often publish 'lesser' works that way. *AW* is interested in the work itself, its particular strength, energy and voice, not necessarily in the 'status' of the authors. We like to know *something* about the authors, however."

‡THE AMETHYST REVIEW (I, II), 23 Riverside Ave., Truro, Nova Scotia B2N 4G2 Canada, phone (902)895-1345, founded 1992, editors Penny Ferguson and Lenora Steele, is a biannual publication of poetry, prose and black ink art. **They want "quality, contemporary poetry to 200 lines. No bad rhyme and meter."** They have recently published poetry by Joe Blades and Liliane Welch. As a sample the editors selected "Prayer" by Carol Rose:

> in Jerusalem
> mothers press
> their bodies
> against stone
> go wild
> like moss

TAR is 84 pgs., about 7×8½, perfect-bound with colored recycled paper cover and b&w art on the cover and inside. They receive 500-600 poems a year, accept approximately 10%. Press run is 150 for 100 subscribers of which 5 are libraries, 25 shelf sales. Single copy: $6 Canadian; subscription: $12 Canadian, $14 US. **Sample (including guidelines) postpaid: $4 US or Canadian. Submit 5 poems at a time. No previously published poems or simultaneous submissions. Cover letter preferred. Always comments on rejections. Send SASE (or SAE and IRC) for guidelines alone. Reports in 6 months maximum, "usually in 1-2 months." Pays 1 copy. Acquires first North American serial rights.** Occasionally reviews books of poetry published by contributors only. They also sponsor an annual contest with a theme which changes each year. The contest fee is the cost of (and includes) a subscription. First prize is $50 Canadian. Send SASE (or SAE and IRC) for details. The editors add, "Therapy is not always good poetry. The craft must be the important focus."

THE AMHERST REVIEW (II), Box 1811, Amherst College, P.O. Box 5000, Amherst MA 01002-5000, is an annual literary magazine seeking quality submissions in fiction, poetry, nonfiction and photography/artwork. **"All kinds of poetry welcome."** The editor says the review is 50 pgs., 5×8, soft cover with photography, art and graphics. They receive 300-500 poems a year, accept around 10. Most copies are distributed free to Amherst students. **Sample postpaid: $6. No previously published poems; simultaneous submissions OK. Reads submissions from September to February only. Magazine staff makes democratic decision. Seldom comments on rejections. Send SASE for guidelines. Reports in late March. Pays 1 copy.**

THE AMICUS JOURNAL (IV-Nature/rural/ecology), 40 W. 20th St., New York NY 10011, phone (212)727-4412, fax (212)727-1773, e-mail amicus@nrdc.org, website http://www.nrdc.org/nrdc, poetry editor Brian Swann, is the quarterly journal of the Natural Resources Defense Council. *Amicus* **publishes about 15 poems a year and asks that submitted poetry be "rooted in nature."** They have published poetry by some of the best known poets in the country, including Mary Oliver, Gary Snyder, Denise Levertov, Reg Saner, John Haines and Wendell Berry. As a sample the editors selected these lines from "To Give" by Mark Irwin:

> Floating along the tops of the Sangre de Christos
> the slow popcorn of clouds.
> All day the summer wears us like an invisible gown
> and the wind whispers It is the outside
> you can never have, whispers this through the trees,
> their great breathing lungs. Rivers flood . . .

The Amicus Journal is finely-printed, saddle-stapled, on high quality paper with glossy cover, using art, photography and cartoons. Circulation is 175,000. **Sample postpaid: $4. "All submissions must be accompanied by a cover note (with notable prior publications) and self-addressed, stamped envelope." Pays $50/poem plus a year's subscription.**

ANACONDA PRESS; FUEL (II), P.O. Box 146640, Chicago IL 60614, e-mail alowry@mcs.com, editor-in-chief Andy Lowry. Currently publishes *fuel*, "a wiry, highly energized mini-magazine using lots of cool poetry, art and fiction." Also publishes **3-4 poetry chapbooks/year. "We're looking for daring, eccentric works. No academia allowed!" Sample postpaid: $3. Submit up to 6 poems at a time. "Previously published poems are OK if not too terribly recent. Simultaneous submissions are frowned upon. We appreciate cover letters." Send SASE for most recent guidelines. Sometimes sends prepublication galleys. Pays 1-2 copies if published in 'zine. Chapbook payment is negotiable. Rights revert to authors.**

ANALECTA (IV-Students), Dept. PM, Liberal Arts Council, FAC 17, University of Texas, Austin TX 78712, phone (512)471-6563, founded 1974, contact Marc Faletti and Jason Hayter, is an annual of literary works and art by **college/university students and graduate students chosen in an annual contest. No restrictions on type; limited to 5 poems/submission. Submissions cannot be returned.** "Our purpose is to provide a forum for excellent student writing. **Works must be previously unpublished.**" As a sample, the editor selected this excerpt from "Jitterbug Puppet" by Alex Travgott:

> She dances in the garden
> with tiger lilies in her white arm
> like a swarm of clouds before a storm.
>
> Her legs pound down the dirt in time. . .

It is a 150-page magazine, glossy plates for interior artwork in b&w, 7×10, flat-spined, soft cover. Of about 800 submissions received, they publish about 40. Press run is 800 for 700 subscribers, 100 shelf sales. **Sample postpaid: $7.50. Entries must be typed; name should appear on cover sheet only. Send SASE for guidelines. Deadline is in mid-October. Prizes in each category. Pays 2 copies and $100 for each prize.**

‡**ANAMNESIS PRESS; ANAMNESIS CHAPBOOK CONTEST (II)**, P.O. Box 7212, Redwood CA 94063, phone/fax (415)255-3190, e-mail kdaniels@ix.netcom.com, website http://www.iquest.net/ap/, founded 1990, publisher Keith Allen Daniels, primarily publishes chapbooks selected through its annual contest, though occasionally publishes a larger volume "to preserve poetry that might otherwise be forgotten. **We wish to see poems of intellectual and emotional depth that give full rein to the imagination, whether free verse or formalist. Please don't send us trite, sappy, maudlin or 'inspirational' poetry.**" They have recently published poetry by Joe Haldeman, James Blish, David R. Bunch and Steven Utley. Chapbooks are 25-40 pgs., photo offset and saddle-stapled with 2-color covers. **For the Anamnesis Chapbook Contest, submit 20-30 pgs. of poetry with a cover letter and $10 entry fee between January 1 and June 15 only. Previously published poems (if author provides acknowledgments) and simultaneous submissions OK. Winners are selected in September. First prize: $500, publication and 20 copies. Second prize: $200, publication and 20 copies.** The publisher adds, "We encourage poets to purchase a sample chapbook for $3 before submitting, to get a feel for what we're looking for. We use free verse and well done formal poetry."

ANATHEMA REVIEW (II), P.O. Box 891, Bowling Green OH 43402, founded 1993, editors Edward Atlee Gore and Matthew David Gengler, appears approximately 1-2 times a year depending on quality of submissions. "**We seek thoroughly crafted, intelligent poetry and fiction that bears meaning and significance. Writing that is void of thought or purpose is rarely considered. Traditional forms receive a fair reading. We refuse seasonal, overly sentimental or trite writing.**" They have published poetry by Simon Perchik, Gary Whitehead and Barbara Van Noord. As a sample we selected these lines from "Lambis Reads My Palm" by David Hassler:

> When I return to Greece, I'll say to my friends
> I drove a cadillac in America.
> *Already he has a contract to record,*
>
> *His life running a course, sure*
> *as the music he played this evening.*
> Truth of silence! *he warns his students*
>
> *before they touch the keys.*
> In my country, we sing our poetry.
> That's how we know it's good.

AR is 30-40 pgs., $5\frac{1}{2} \times 8\frac{1}{2}$, professionally printed and saddle-stapled with card cover, b&w art and photos. They accept less than 5% of poetry and fiction received. Press run is 150-200 for 50% shelf sales. Subscription: $10 for 5 issues. **Submit up to 5 poems at a time. No previously published poems; simultaneous submissions OK. Cover letter required.** Time between acceptance and publication is 9-12 months. **Send SASE for guidelines. Reports in 1-3 months. Pays 1 copy.** The editors say, "We accept submissions of reviews and submissions of books for us to review."

‡**ANGELFLESH; ANGELFLESH PRESS (I)**, P.O. Box 141123, Grand Rapids MI 49514, founded 1994, editor Jim Buchanan. *Angelflesh* appears 3 times/year ("plus extras") and publishes "today's best cutting-edge fiction, poetry and art." **They want poetry that is "strong, real and gutsy, with vivid images, emotional and spiritual train wrecks. No taboos, no 'Hallmark' verse."** They have recently published poetry by Antler, Catfish McDaris and Ana Christy. As a sample the editor selected these lines from an untitled poem by élliott:

> *I came here to live*
> *a poet crawling over the*
> *bones of Byron and Kerouac*
> *with chipped words from the*
> *street I came*
> *here like the wolf*
> *like a man stumbling under the*
> *weight of his own cross.*

The editor says *Angelflesh* is 40-50 pgs., various sizes, photocopied and saddle-stitched. They receive about 500 poems a year, accept 40-50%. Press run is 100. Subscription: $10. **Sample postpaid: $4. Submit 3-5 poems at a time. Previously published poems and simultaneous submissions OK. Cover letter preferred.** Time between acceptance and publication is 1-3 months. **Seldom comments on rejections. Send SASE for guidelines. Reports in around 1 month. Pays 1 copy.** Under Angelflesh Press the editor also publishes about 1 perfect-bound paperback and 2-4 chapbooks/year. Chapbooks are usually 30-40 pgs., 5½ × 8, photocopied and saddle-stitched with some artwork. **Query first with sample poems and cover letter with brief bio. Replies to queries in 1 month, mss (if invited) in 2-4 weeks. Pay negotiable. For a sample chapbook, send $4 or send a SASE for further details about their chapbook series.**

ANHINGA PRESS; ANHINGA PRIZE (II), P.O. Box 10595, Tallahassee FL 32302-0595, phone (904)575-5592, fax (904)442-6323, founded 1972, poetry editors Rick Campbell and Van Brock, publishes **"books and anthologies of poetry. We also offer the Anhinga Prize for poetry—$2,000 and publication—for a book-length manuscript each year. We want to see contemporary poetry which respects language. We're inclined toward poetry that is not obscure, that can be understood by any literate audience."** They have recently published *Unspeakable Strangers* by Van K. Brock and *Isle of Flowers: Poems by Florida Individual Artists Fellows* edited by Donna J. Long. As a sample the editors selected these lines from *The Secret Life of Moles* by P.V. LeForge:

> *The sun migrates across whatever scenes*
> *death can spare:*
> *and we have many of these small reprieves*
> *living within us.*
> *When we die, will life stop again?*
> *And for whom?*

Considers simultaneous submissions. Send SASE for rules (submissions accepted January 1 to March 15) of the Anhinga Prize for poetry, which requires a $20 entry fee. The contest has been judged by such distinguished poets as William Stafford, Louis Simpson, Henry Taylor, Hayden Carruth, Marvin Bell, Donald Hall and Joy Harjo.

ANJOU (V), P.O. Box 322 Station P., Toronto, Ontario M5S 2S8 Canada, founded 1980, edited by Richard Lush and Roger Greenwald, publishes broadsides of poetry. **"We do not wish to receive submissions because we publish only by solicitation."**

ANTERIOR POETRY MONTHLY; ANTERIOR BITEWING LTD. (I), 993 Allspice Ave., Fenton MO 63026-4901, e-mail 72247.1405@compuserve.com, founded 1988, editor Tom Bergeron, appears 12 times a year using **"poems of excellence. We prefer articulate, logical writing that follows traditional poetic practices. Submissions welcome from everyone; however, there is a $1 reading fee per poem submitted unless you are a subscriber. The top four poems in each issue receive awards of $25, $15, $10 and $5 respectively. Other poems may be published with no payment to the author. Entries received after the 15th, extra submissions and poems more suited to later seasons are automatically entered in future month's contest."** They have published poetry by J. Alvin Speers, Pearl Bloch Segall, Katherine Brooks and Marian Ford Park. As a sample the editor selected these lines from "The Light" by Barbara N. Paul-Best:

> *Cold are the winds that blow,*

> Cold as December ice and January snow;
> Soothing as a blanket of snow-starred down;
> Peaceful as the absence of every sound.

APM is 20 pgs., digest-sized, desktop-published and saddle-stapled with colored paper cover. Press run is 200-300 for 110 subscribers. Subscription: $20. **Sample postpaid: $1. Make checks payable to Anterior Bitewing Ltd. Submit 5 poems at a time. Name and address on each page. "We like cover letters." Include sufficient first-class postage to cover returns. Send SASE for guidelines. Acquires one-time rights.** The editor says, "Always resubmit. There's some editor out there somewhere who will love your work. Take advice, make changes accordingly and keep on resubmitting."

ANTHOLOGY OF MAGAZINE VERSE & YEARBOOK OF AMERICAN POETRY (III, IV-Anthology), % Monitor Book Company, P.O. Box 9078, Palm Springs CA 92263, phone (619)323-2270, founded 1950, editor Alan F. Pater. The annual *Anthology* is a selection of the **best poems published in American and Canadian magazines during the year and is also a basic reference work for poets.** Alan F. Pater says, "We want poetry that is 'readable' and in any poetic form; we also want translations. **All material must first have appeared in magazines.** Any subject matter will be considered; we also would like to see some rhyme and meter, preferably sonnets." They have published poetry by Margaret Atwood, Stanley Kunitz, Robert Penn Warren, Richard Wilbur, Maxine Kumin and John Updike. Indeed, the anthology is a good annual guide to the best poets actively publishing in any given year. 90% of selections are made by the editor from magazines, but some poets are solicited for their work which has been in magazines in a given year. **Cover letters should include name and date or issue number of magazine in which the poem was originally published.**

ANTIETAM REVIEW (IV-Regional), Washington County Arts Council, 7 W. Franklin St., Hagerstown MD 21740-4804, phone/fax (301)791-3132, founded 1982, poetry editor Crystal Brown, appears annually and looks for **"well-crafted literary quality poems. We discourage inspirational verse, haiku, doggerel."** Uses poets (natives or residents) from the states of Maryland, Pennsylvania, Virginia, West Virginia, Delaware and District of Columbia. Needs 20 poems/issue, up to 30 lines each.** Poets they have recently published include Eleanor Ross Taylor, William Aiken and Barbara F. Lefcowitz. As a sample the editor selected these lines from "3 A.M." by Angie Estes:

> Sucked tight to the mattress
> like a rock climber nursing
> at the blank chest of a cliff, she lifts
> one knee to her elbow and crawls
> the way the iris, espaliered
> in bas relief, inch each Egyptian
> hip another notch toward what they think
> is heaven.

AR is 54 pgs., 8½ × 11, saddle-stapled, glossy paper with glossy card cover and b&w photos throughout. Press run is 1,000. **Sample postpaid: $3.15 back issue, $5.25 current. Submit 5 typed poems at a time. "We prefer a cover letter stating other publications, although we encourage new and emerging writers. We do not accept previously published poems and reluctantly take simultaneous submissions."** Do not submit mss from February through August. "We read from September 1 through February 1 annually." Send SASE for guidelines. Sends prepublication galleys, if requested. Pays $20/poem, depending on funding, plus 2 copies. Buys first North American serial rights.** The editors seem open to all styles of poetry, free and formal, as long as the author is from the designated region. Overall, a good read; but poems have to compete with prose. Ones used, however, are featured in attractive boxes on the page. Sponsors a contest for natives or residents of DC, DE, MD, PA, VA and WV. Send SASE for details. Work published in *Antietam Review* has been included in a *Pushcart Prize* anthology.

THE ANTIGONISH REVIEW (II), St. Francis Xavier University, P.O. Box 5000, Antigonish, Nova Scotia B2G 2W5 Canada, phone (902)867-3962, fax (902)867-2448, e-mail tar@stfx.ca, founded 1970, editor George Sanderson, poetry editor Peter Sanger. This high-quality quarterly "tries to produce the kind of literary and visual mosaic that the modern sensibility requires or would respond to." They want poetry **not over "80 lines, i.e., 2 pgs.; subject matter can be anything, the style is traditional, modern or post-modern limited by typographic resources. Purpose is not an issue."** No "erotica, scatalogical verse, excessive propaganda toward a certain subject." They have recently published poetry by Andy Wainwright, W.J. Keith, Michael Hulse, Jean McNeil, M. Travis Lane and Douglas Lochhead. *TAR* is flat-spined, 6 × 9, 150 pgs. with glossy card cover, offset printing, using "in-house graphics and cover art, no ads." They accept about 10% of some 2,500 submissions/year. Press run is 850 for 700 subscribers. Subscription: $20. **Sample postpaid: $3. Submit 5-10 poems at a time. No simultaneous submissions or previously published poems. Include SASE or SAE and IRCs if outside Canada. Editor "sometimes" comments on rejections. Pays 2 copies.**

THE ANTIOCH REVIEW (III), P.O. Box 148, Yellow Springs OH 45387, phone (513)767-6389, founded 1941, poetry editor Judith Hall, "is an independent quarterly of critical and creative thought . . . **For well over 50 years, creative authors, poets and thinkers have found a friendly reception . . . regardless of formal reputation**. We get far more poetry than we can possibly accept, and the competition is keen. Here, where form and content are so inseparable and reaction is so personal, it is difficult to state requirements or limitations. Studying recent issues of *The Review* should be helpful. No 'light' or inspirational verse." They have published poetry by Ralph Angel, Jorie Graham, Mark Strand, Gillian Conoley and Adrian C. Louis. They receive about 3,000 submissions/year, publish 20 pages of poetry in each issue, and have about a 6-month backlog. Circulation is 5,000, of which 70% is through bookstores and newsstands. Large percentage of subscribers are libraries. Subscription: $35. **Sample: $6. Submit up to 10 poems at a time. No previously published poems. Reads submissions September 1 through May 15 only. Send SASE for guidelines. Reports in 6-8 weeks. Pays $10/ published page plus 2 copies.** Reviews books of poetry in 300 words, single format. This is a beautiful journal featuring some of the best poems being written by new and well-known writers. *AR* received a First Place Award for Editorial Content from the 1995 American Literary Magazine Awards. Work published in this review has also been included in *The Best American Poetry 1995* and *Pushcart Prize* anthologies.

ANTIPODES (IV-Regional), 8 Big Island, Warwick NY 10990, e-mail pakane@vassar.edu, founded 1987, poetry editor Paul Kane, is a biannual of Australian poetry and fiction and criticism and reviews of Australian writing. They want **work from Australian poets only. No restrictions as to form, length, subject matter or style.** They have published poetry by A.D. Hope, Judith Wright and John Tranter. As a sample the editor selected these lines from "Poetry and Religion" by Les Murray:

> *Religions are poems. They concert*
> *our daylight and dreaming mind, our*
> *emotions, instinct, breath and native gesture*
> *into the only whole thinking: poetry*

The editor says *Antipodes* is 180 pgs., 8½×11, perfect-bound, with graphics, ads and photos. They receive about 500 submissions a year, accept approximately 10%. Press run is 500 for 200 subscribers. Subscription: $20. **Sample postpaid: $17. Submit 3-5 poems at a time. No previously published poems or simultaneous submissions. Cover letter with bio note required. The editor says they "prefer submission of photocopies which do not have to be returned." Seldom comments on rejections. Reports in 2 months. Pays $20/poem plus 1 copy. Acquires first North American serial rights.** Staff reviews books of poetry in 500-1,500 words. Send books for review consideration.

APALACHEE QUARTERLY; APALACHEE PRESS (II, IV-Themes), P.O. Box 10469, Tallahassee FL 32302, founded 1971, editors Barbara Hamby, Bruce Boehrer, Beth Meekins, Pat McEnulty, Rikki Clark and Kim MacQueen. They have published poetry by David Kirby, Peter Meinke, Alfred Corn and Virgil Suarez. *Apalachee Quarterly* is 160 pgs., 6×9, professionally printed and perfect-bound with card cover. There are 55-95 pgs. of poetry in each issue. "Every year we do an issue on a special topic. Past issues include Dental, Revenge, Cocktail Party and Noir issues." Circulation is 700 for 350 subscribers of which 75 are libraries. Subscription: $15. **Sample postpaid: $5. Submit clear copies of up to 5 poems, name and address on each. Simultaneous submissions OK. "We don't read during the summer (June 1 through August 31)." Sometimes comments on rejections. Send SASE for guidelines. Pays 2 copies.** Staff reviews books of poetry. Send books for review consideration.

APHRODITE GONE BERSERK: A JOURNAL OF EROTIC ART (IV-Erotica), 233 Guyon Ave., Staten Island NY 10306, founded 1995 (first issue published early 1996), editor C. Esposito, is a semiannual journal of erotic art, including poetry, fiction, memoirs and photography. **They want "poetry that deals with the erotic or sexuality in any form and from any orientation or perspective."** The editor says *AGB* is 50 pgs., 8½×11. They expect to receive about 200 submissions a year and accept approximately 10%. Press run is 1,000. Single copy: $6; subscription: $10. **Previously published poems and simultaneous submissions OK. Time between acceptance and publication is 6-12 months. Send SASE for guidelines. Reports in 1 month. Pays 1 copy. Acquires one-time rights.** "We accept books, chapbooks, magazines and videos that deal with the erotic and sexuality for possible review in *AGB*." Also open to unsolicited reviews. The editor says, "Especially when writing erotic poetry, stay away from the cliché and write honestly."

THE APOSTOLIC CRUSADE (I, IV-Religious), (formerly *The Dreambuilding Crusade*), P.O. Box 995, La Mirada CA 90637-0995, founded fall 1992, editor and publisher Art Garcia. *The Apostolic Crusade* is a bimonthly newsletter promoting spiritual growth through divine inspiration. **They want "short, simple poems relating to spirituality and divine inspiration."** They have recently published poetry by K. Brittany Fedorev Vanderkleed, Betty J. Silconas, Jan Lattimer, Anna Rose Whitlock and Kathryn Smeets. As a sample the editor selected this poem, "What Is Truth?" by Marilyn Kay Giuliana:

Truth is following the footsteps of Christ.
Forever focused on His guiding light.
Listen carefully to the voice within.
Speaking in whispers what's wrong & right.
Truth followed, sets one free.
No chains of sin enslaving us in.

The newsletter is 4 double-sided, 8½ × 11 pages, corner-stapled. It includes announcements, birthdays, poetry and information on pen pal networking and networking newsletters. "We accept 80% of submitted poetry." Press run is 100 for 50 subscribers. Single copy: $2; subscription: $12. **Sample postpaid: $3. Submit up to 5 poems at a time. Include name and address on all submissions. Previously published poems and simultaneous submissions OK. "We like to receive cover letters explaining a little bit about the poet and the reasons for publication."** Time between acceptance and publication is 2-6 months. **Publishes theme issues. Upcoming themes include: "The Birth of Jesus" (deadline: October 15, 1996), "Passion of Jesus" (deadline: February 15, 1997) and "Virgin Mary" (deadline: April 15, 1997). No reply or return of rejections. Rather, the authors of the accepted poems simply receive the issues in which their poems are included. Pays 1 copy, "more only on request."** The editor adds, "We would appreciate any donation of monies or stamps to help defer cost. Make checks payable to *The Apostolic Crusade*."

APPALACHIA; THE APPALACHIA POETRY PRIZE (II, IV-Nature), 5 Joy St., Boston MA 02108, phone (617)523-0636, founded 1876, poetry editor Parkman Howe, editor-in-chief Sandy Stott, is a "semiannual journal of mountaineering and conservation which describes activities outdoors and asks questions of an ecological nature." **They want poetry relating to the outdoors and nature—specifically weather, mountains, rivers, lakes, woods and animals. "No conquerors' odes."** They have published poetry by Reg Saner, Warren Woessner, Susan Lier, Mary Oliver and Thomas Reiter. The editor says *Appalachia* is 160 pgs., 6×9, professionally printed with color cover, using photos, graphics and a few ads. They receive about 200 poems a year, use 10-15. Press run is 10,000. Subscription: $10/year. **Sample postpaid: $5. Submit maximum of 6 poems. "We favor shorter poems—maximum of 36 lines usually." No previously published poems or simultaneous submissions. Cover letter required.** Time between acceptance and publication is 1 year. **Seldom comments on rejections. Send SASE for guidelines. Reports in 4-6 weeks. Pays 1 copy. Acquires first rights.** Staff reviews "some" books of poetry in 200-400 words, usually single format. Offers an annual award, The Appalachia Poetry Prize, given since 1972. The editor says, "Our readership is very well versed in the outdoors—mountains, rivers, lakes, animals. We look for poetry that helps readers see the natural world in fresh ways. No generalized accounts of the great outdoors."

APPALACHIAN HERITAGE (IV-Regional), Hutchins Library, Berea College, Berea KY 40404, phone (606)986-9341 ext. 5260, fax (606)986-9494, founded 1973, editor Sidney Saylor Farr, a literary quarterly with Southern Appalachian emphasis. The journal publishes several poems in each issue, and the editor wants to see **"poems about people, places, the human condition, etc., with Southern Appalachian settings. No style restrictions but poems should have a maximum of 14 lines, prefer 8-10 lines."** She does not want "blood and gore, hell-fire and damnation, or biased poetry about race or religion." She has published poetry by Jim Wayne Miller, James Still, George Ella Lyon and Robert Morgan. The flat-spined magazine is 6×9, professionally printed on white stock with b&w line drawings and photos, glossy white card cover with 4-color illustration. Issues we have scanned tended toward lyric free verse, emphasizing nature or situations set in nature, but the editor says they will use good poems of any subject and form. **Sample copy: $6. Submit 2-4 poems at a time, typed one to a page. No previously published poems; simultaneous submissions OK. Requires cover letter giving information about previous publications where poets have appeared. Publishes theme issues occasionally. Send SASE for upcoming themes. Reports in 2-4 weeks. Sometimes sends prepublication galleys. Pays 3 copies. Acquires first rights.** Reviews books of poetry. Open to unsolicited reviews. Poets may also send books for review consideration. The Denny C. Plattner Awards go to the authors of the best poetry, article or essay, or short fiction published in the four issues released within the preceding year. The award amount in each category is $200.

ALWAYS include a self-addressed, stamped envelope (SASE) when sending a ms or query to a publisher within your own country. When sending material to other countries, include a self-addressed envelope and International Reply Coupons (IRCs), available for purchase at many post offices.

APROPOS (I, IV-Subscribers), Ashley Manor, 450 Buttermilk Rd., Easton PA 18042, founded 1989, editor Ashley C. Anders, **publishes all poetry submitted by subscribers except that judged by the editor to be pornographic or in poor taste. Maximum length 40 lines—50 characters/line.** $25 for 6-issue subscription plus free entry to 2 special contests. As a sample the editor selected her own "Simple Poem":

> *If I can write a simple poem*
> *that makes somebody smile,*
> *or wipes away a teardrop,*
> *then my poem will be worthwhile.*
>
> *It need not win a trophy,*
> *for that would not mean as much,*
> *as knowing that my simple poem*
> *and someone's heart will touch.*

It is 90 pgs., digest-sized, plastic ring bound, with heavy stock cover, desktop-published. **Sample postpaid: $3. Submit 1 poem at a time. Simultaneous submissions and previously published poems OK. Send SASE for guidelines. All poems are judged by subscribers.** Prizes for regular issues are $50, $25, $10 and $5. Prizes for special contests are $25, $10 and $5.

AQUARIUS (II), Flat 10, Room A, 116 Sutherland Ave., Maida-Vale, London W9 England, poetry editor Eddie Linden, is a literary biannual publishing quality poetry. Issue 19/20, guest edited by Hilary Davies, contains poetry, fictional prose, essays, interviews and reviews. The latest issue is on the English poet Roy Fuller and contains prose and poetry. **"Please note the magazine will not accept work unless writers have bought the magazine and studied the style/form of the work published."** Single copy: $10. Subscription in US: $50. **Payment is by arrangement.**

ARARAT (IV-Ethnic), Dept. PM, A.G.B.U., 31 W. 52nd St., New York NY 10019, phone (212)765-8260, editor-in-chief Leo Hamalian, is a quarterly magazine **emphasizing Armenian life and culture for Americans of Armenian descent and Armenian immigrants. They use about 6 poems/issue and want any verse that is Armenian in theme. They do not want to see traditional, sentimental love poetry.** Their circulation is 2,400. Subscription: $24 ($32 foreign). **Sample copy: $7 plus 4 first-class stamps. Previously published submissions OK. Submit seasonal/holiday material at least 3 months in advance.** Publishes ms an average of 1 year after acceptance. **Reports in 6 weeks. Pays $10.** Buys first North American serial rights and second (reprint) rights to material originally published elsewhere.

‡ARC: CANADA'S NATIONAL POETRY MAGAZINE (II), P.O. Box 7368, Ottawa, Ontario K1L 8E4 Canada, founded 1978, co-editors Rita Donovan and John Barton, is a biannual of poetry, poetry-related articles, interviews and book reviews. **"Our tastes are eclectic. Our focus is Canadian, but we also publish writers from elsewhere."** They have published poetry by Anne Szumigalski, Heather Spears, Robert Priest and Erin Mouré. *Arc* is 80-88 pgs., perfect-bound, with laminated 2-color cover, artwork and ads. They receive about 500 submissions a year, accept 40-50 poems. Press run is 580 for 200 subscribers of which 30 are libraries, 100 shelf sales. Single copy: $7.50 Canadian/Canada, $8.50 Canadian/US, $10 Canadian/Overseas; subscription (4 issues): $20 Canadian/Canada, $25 Canadian/US, $28 Canadian/Overseas. **Cost of sample varies. No previously published poems or simultaneous submissions. Cover letter required. Submit 5-8 poems, single spaced, with name and address on each page. Send SASE for guidelines and upcoming themes. Reports in 3-6 months. Pays $25 Canadian/page plus 2 copies. Buys first North American serial rights.** "We do not accept unsolicited book reviews." The Confederation Poets Prize is an annual award of $100 for the best poem published in *Arc* that year.

‡ARC PUBLICATIONS (III), Nanholme Mill, Shaw Wood Rd., Todmorden, Lancashire OL14 6DA United Kingdom, phone (01706)812338, fax (01706)818948, founded 1969, partners Tony Ward, Angela Jarman and Rosemary Jones, publishes 8 paperback books of poetry a year. **They want "literary, literate, contemporary poetry. No religious or children's verse. We specialize not only in contemporary poetry of the U.K. but also in poetry written in English from across the world."** They have recently published books of poetry by Don Coles (Canada), Dinah Hawken (New Zealand), John Kinsella (Australia) and Ivor Cutler (UK). Their books are 64-100 pgs., 5½ × 8½, offset litho and perfect-bound with card covers in 2-3 colors. **Query first with 10 sample poems and a cover letter with brief bio and publication credits. Previously published poems and simultaneous submissions OK. Mss are read by at least 2 editors before possible acceptance.** Seldom comments on rejections. **Replies to queries in up to 4 months. Pays 7-10% royalties and 6 author's copies (out of a press run of 600). Send SASE (or SAE and IRCs) for current list to order samples.** They say, "Poets should have a body of work already published in magazines and journals, and should be acquainted with our list of books, before submitting."

ARGONAUT (V, IV-Science fiction/fantasy), P.O. Box 4201, Austin TX 78765, founded 1972, editor/publisher Michael Ambrose, is a **"semiannual magazine anthology of science fiction and weird fantasy, illustrated."** They publish **"speculative, weird, fantastic poetry with vivid imagery or theme, up to 30 lines. Prefer traditional forms. Nothing ultramodernistic, non-fantastic."** They have published poetry by John Grey, David Lunde, William John Watkins and Joey Froehlich. The editor describes it as 64 pgs., digest-sized, typeset. They accept 5-8 of 100-200 poems received. Press run is 800 for 50 subscribers of which 3 are libraries. Subscription: $8. **Sample postpaid: $4.95.** *Argonaut* **was closed to submissions in 1996. Query for 1997. If open, submit no more than 5 poems at a time. No previously published poems or simultaneous submissions. Editor comments on submissions "occasionally." Send SASE for guidelines. Reports in 1-2 months. Sometimes sends prepublication galleys. Pays 1 copy.** The editor says, "Too much of what I see is limited in scope or language, and inappropriate for the themes of *Argonaut*. Poets should know what the particular market to which they submit is looking for and not simply shotgun their submissions."

ARIEL, A REVIEW OF INTERNATIONAL ENGLISH LITERATURE (III), English Dept., University of Calgary, Calgary, Alberta T2N 1N4 Canada, founded 1970, is a "critical, scholarly quarterly with about 5-8 pgs. of poetry in each issue." Though subject matter is open, editors seem to prefer mostly lyric free verse with attention to form—line, stanza and voice. As a sample here are lines from "Ecstasy!" by Fritz Hamilton:

> being the
> Jackson Pollock of
> poetry I
>
> dance over the paper in
> the street with
> my pen poised to
>
> pour my words of
> poetry onto
> the world . . .

Ariel is 114-144 pgs., digest-sized, professionally printed and flat-spined with glossy card cover. They receive about 300 submissions of poetry/year, use 20-30. Circulation is 850, almost all subscriptions of which 650 are libraries. Subscription: $29.50 institutions; $19.50 individuals. **Sample postpaid: $8. Submit 4-8 poems at a time. No long poems. No simultaneous submissions. Cover letter required. Editor comments on rejections, "only occasionally and not by request." Canadian postage (or IRCs) required with SAE for return of submissions. Pays 10 offprints plus 1 copy.**

ARJUNA LIBRARY PRESS; JOURNAL OF REGIONAL CRITICISM (V), 1025 Garner St. D, Space 18, Colorado Springs CO 80905-1774, library founded 1963, press founded 1979, editor Dr. Baron Joseph A. Uphoff, Jr. "The Arjuna Library Press is avant-garde, designed to endure the transient quarters and marginal funding of the literary phenomenon (as a tradition) while presenting a context for the development of current mathematical ideas in regard to theories of art, literature and performance; photocopy printing allows for very limited editions and irregular format. Quality is maintained as an artistic materialist practice." He publishes **"surrealist prose poetry, visual poetry, dreamlike, short and long works; not obscene, profane (will criticize but not publish), unpolished work."** He has recently published work by R.D. Pileggi and Susanne Lutz, and translations by K.A. Kopple of the work of Marosa Di Giorgio. As a sample the editor selected these lines from "The March Hare" by Marosa Di Giorgio:

> . . . I wandered through the forest and saw the sun set,
> all at once, in various places; four or five suns,
> round, white as snow, with long threads.
> Or square and red, with long threads.
> My father was the prince of the fields. . .

JRC is published on loose photocopied pages of collage, writing and criticism, appearing frequently in a varied format. Press run: 1 copy each. Reviews books of poetry "occasionally." Open to unsolicited reviews. Poets may also send books for review consideration. "Upon request will treat material as submitted for reprint, one-time rights." Arjuna Library Press publishes 6-12 chapbooks/year, averaging 50 pgs. **However, he is currently overstocked and is not accepting submissions for the journal or the press.** The editor says, "Poets should be aware that literature has become a vast labyrinth in which the vision of the creative mind may be solitary. One can no longer depend upon an audience to entertain the storyteller. The writer may be left lonely in the presence of the creation which should, therefore, be entertainment in its own right if not for an audience then at least for the holder of the copyright."

THE ARK (V), 115 Montebello Rd., Jamaica Plain MA 02130-2907, phone (617)522-1929, founded 1970 (as BLEB), poetry editor Geoffrey Gardner, publishes books of poetry. **"We are unable to take**

on new projects at this time." They have published poetry by David Budbill, John Haines, Joseph Bruchac, Elsa Gidlow, W.S. Merwin, Eliot Weinberger, Kathy Acker, George Woodcock, Kathleen Raine, Marge Piercy and Linda Hogan. The editor selected these lines by Kenneth Rexroth (a translation from the Sanskrit) as a sample:

> You think this is a time of Shiva's waking
> You are wrong
> You are Shiva
> But you dream

THE UNIVERSITY OF ARKANSAS PRESS (V); ARKANSAS POETRY AWARD (I, II), 201 Ozark, Fayetteville AR 72701-1201, founded 1980, acquisitions editor Kevin Brock, publishes flat-spined paperbacks and hardback collections of individual poets. Miller Williams, director of the press, says, **"We are not interested in poetry that is obscure or private or self-consciously erudite."** They have published poetry by Frank Stanford, Henri Coulette, Enid Shomer and John Ciardi. As a sample, here is a stanza from "Joy" by William Dickey:

> Now I am driving in my small car up the Coast Highway.
> The motor is regular, the headlights are dipped and raised
> to accommodate other travellers. I am warm and alone
> between the dark vigorous sea and the dark mountains.
> This is contentment, surely, but it is not joy.

That's from his book *In The Dreaming*, 106 pgs., digest-sized, flat-spined, elegantly printed on egg-shell stock with matte 2-color card cover. **Query with 5-10 sample poems. Replies to queries in 2 weeks, to mss (if invited) in 2-4 weeks. No replies without SASE. Always sends prepublication galleys. Offers 10% royalty contract plus 10 author's copies. Send SASE for catalog to buy samples.** First-book mss are not considered except as submissions for the Arkansas Poetry Award. The Arkansas Poetry Award competition is open to any original ms by a living American poet whose work has not been previously published or accepted for publication in book form. Chapbooks, self-published books, and books produced with the author's subsidy are not considered previously published books. No translations. Submit 50-80 pgs., not more than one poem/page, counting title page in page count. An acknowledgments page listing poems previously published should accompany ms. Author's name should appear on the title page only. $15 reading fee. Postmark deadline: May 1. Publication the following spring. A $500 cash advance is part of the award.

ARNAZELLA (II), Bellevue Community College, 3000 Landerholm Circle SE, Bellevue WA 98007-6484, phone (206)649-3084, established 1979, advisor Jeffrey White, is a literary annual, published in spring, using **well-crafted poetry, no "jingles or greeting card" poetry**. They have published poetry by William Stafford, Judith Skillman and Colleen McElroy. The editor describes this student publication (which uses work from off campus) as 75 pgs., 6×8, offset, using photos and drawings. **They are currently accepting submissions only from poets in Washington, Oregon, Idaho, Alaska and British Columbia.** Of 150-200 poems received/year they use about 30. Press run is 500 for 3 subscriptions, one of which is a library. **Sample postpaid: $5. Submit up to 3 poems. Deadline is usually at the end of December. Send SASE for guidelines. Reports in 1-4 months. Pays 1 copy.**

ARROWSMITH (I, II), P.O. Box 2148, Bellaire TX 77402, founded 1993, editor Keddy Ann Outlaw, is a biannual publication of poetry, short short fiction, b&w photos and collages. **"All styles of poetry considered, as long as well crafted. Length no more than 2 pages per poem. No greeting card doggerel, clichéd statements of self pity or Sunday school verse."** They have recently published poetry by Sharron Crowson, Larry Fontenot, Mary Winters, André de Korvin and Pat Little Dog. As a sample the editor selected these lines from "The Astronaut's Ex-Wife" by Sandra Reiff:

> The wife began to sharpen her scissors
> her brushes   her wits   and cut
> off her organdy shadow   leave it on the bed
> with her obedient iron shoes and other
> empty rockets

Arrowsmith is 36-44 pgs., digest-sized, laser printed and saddle-stapled. They currently accept about 1 out of 100 poems received. Press run is 350 for 60 subscribers of which 10 are libraries. Subscription: $8. **Sample postpaid: $4. Submit up to 5 poems at a time. Previously published poems OK by invitation only. Simultaneous submissions OK, if indicated. Cover letter with brief bio preferred.** "Indicate if a yes-or-no reply is sufficient in lieu of poems being returned. **May comment on strong points of poems that almost made it, if time allows." Send SASE for guidelines. Reports in 2-8 weeks. Pays 1 copy. Acquires first-time rights only.** The editor says, "When a poem is finished, sharp and true, it is ready to fly, to pierce its readers with all its singleness, authenticity and intensity.

Arrowsmith is the place such ammunition is gathered, a literary quiver let loose on the world."

ARSENAL PULP PRESS (V), 103-1014 Homer St., Vancouver, British Columbia V6B 2W9 Canada, founded 1980, publishes 1 paperback book of poetry/year. They only publish the work of Canadian poets and are **currently not accepting any unsolicited mss.**

ARSHILE (III), P.O. Box 3749, Los Angeles CA 90078-3749, founded 1993, editor Mark Salerno. *Arshile* is a biannual "Magazine of the Arts," including poetry, fiction, drama, essays on art and interviews. **They want poetry "that shows evidence of formal innovation."** They have recently published poetry by Notley, Myles, Moriarty, Ashbery, Koch, Guest, Baraka, Malanga and Towle. The editor says *Arshile* is 5½ × 8½, professionally printed and perfect-bound with 4-color cover and b&w art and ads inside. Press run is 1,000 for 100 subscribers of which 25% are libraries, 30% shelf sales. Subscription: $18 for 2 issues. **Sample postpaid: $10. No previously published poems or simultaneous submissions. Reports in 3 months. Pays 2 copies. Rights revert to authors/artists.**

ART TIMES: A LITERARY JOURNAL AND RESOURCE FOR ALL THE ARTS (II), P.O. Box 730, Mount Marion NY 12456-0730, phone (914)246-6944, poetry editor Cheryl A. Rice, is a monthly tabloid newspaper devoted to the arts. *Art Times* focuses on cultural and creative articles and essays, but also publishes some poetry and fiction. The editor wants to see **"poetry that strives to express genuine observation in unique language; poems no longer than 20 lines each."** As a sample she selected these lines from "Quietest Plastics" by Donald Zirilli:

> *Touch your face, touch mine*
> *with your face. I said to kiss me*
> *but this noise in the night,*
> *this mystery, prevented you*
> *from hearing me. Cotton breathes,*
> *but we are the quietest plastics.*

Art Times is 16-24 pgs., newsprint, with reproductions of artwork, some photos, advertisement-supported. They receive 300-500 poems/month, use only 40-50/year. Circulation is 16,000, of which 5,000 are by request and subscriptions; most distribution is free through galleries, theatres, etc. Subscription: $15/year. **Sample: $1 postage cost. Submit 4-5 typed poems at a time. "Simultaneous submissions discouraged." Criticism of mss is provided "at times but rarely." They have an 18-month backlog. Send SASE for guidelines. Reports in 6 months. Pays 6 copies plus 1-year subscription.**

ARTFUL DODGE (II, IV-Translations), Dept. of English, College of Wooster, Wooster OH 44691, founded 1979, poetry editor Daniel Bourne, is an annual literary magazine that "takes a strong interest in poets who are continually testing what they can get away with successfully in regard to subject, perspective, language, etc., but who also show mastery of current American poetic techniques—its varied textures and its achievement in the illumination of the particular. What all this boils down to is that we require high craftsmanship as well as a vision that goes beyond *one's own* storm windows, grandmothers or sexual fantasies—to paraphrase Hayden Carruth. **Poems can be on any subject, of any length, from any perspective, in any voice, but we don't want anything that does not connect with both the human and the aesthetic. Thus, we don't want cute, rococo surrealism, someone's warmed-up, left-over notion of an avant-garde that existed 10-100 years ago, or any last bastions of rhymed verse in the civilized world.** On the other hand, we are interested in poems that utilize stylistic persuasions both old and new to good effect. We are not afraid of poems which try to deal with large social, political, historical, and even philosophical questions—especially if the poem emerges from one's own life experience and is not the result of armchair pontificating. We often offer encouragement to writers whose work we find promising, but *Artful Dodge* **is more a journal for the already emerging writer than for the beginner looking for an easy place to publish. We also have a sustained commitment to translation, especially from Polish and other East European literatures,** and we feel the interchange between the American and foreign works on our pages is of great interest to our readers. We also feature interviews with such outstanding literary figures as Jorge Luis Borges, W.S. Merwin, Nathalie Sarraute, Stanislaw Baranczak, Omar Pound, Gwendolyn Brooks, John Giorno, William Least Heat-Moon, Cynthia Macdonald, Tim O'Brien, Lee Smith and William Matthews. Recent and forthcoming poets include Naomi Shihab Nye, Julia Kasdorf, Charles Simic, Denise Duhamel, Lola Haskins, Ron Wallace, Alberta Turner, Tim Seibles, Roger Mitchell, Khaled Mattawa, David Ignatow, Peter Wild, Karl Krolow (German), Tomasz Jastrun (Polish), Jorge Luis Borges (Spanish), U Sam Oeur (Khmer), Laureano Alban (Spanish), Mahmud Darwish (Palestinian) and Tibor Zalan (Hungarian)." As a sample the editor selected these lines from "Houdini" by Joel Brouwer:

> *. . . Look at these arms,*
> *the exhausted rubber muscle. This*
> *is God's work: to trick you*
> *into magic not through illusion nor divinity,*

CLOSE-UP

Craft must accompany enthusiasm

J. Patrick Lewis

Photo by Judy Lewis

"Enthusiasm is a necessary but not a sufficient condition for writing poetry," says J. Patrick Lewis. "There must be first and always a sense of craft."

Lewis, an economics professor at Otterbein College in Westerville, Ohio, who has written both fiction and poetry (including work for both adults and children), is perhaps best known for his wide range of children's verse. Of his 13 published children's books, eight are poetry, and the collections range from rhyming, nonsense verse and narrative poems in a variety of strict forms to a children's book of haiku.

Yet, before Lewis ever saw his name on a book jacket, the instructor admits he had to learn a lesson himself: He had to spend time studying the craft. "I first began writing poetry around 1980—terrible stuff—treacly, didactic, forced rhyme doggerel. Of course I thought it was pretty good . . . until I came to my senses," he says.

Part of what helped him come "to his senses," were the reactions of his three children, whom Lewis fondly refers to as his "first fans." They were also "stern critics," who never let him get away with anything, and it was only after sharing his work with them that he decided to go back to learn the poet's trade.

So, Lewis stopped writing for three years and immersed himself in the study of metrics and the masters—both adult's and children's poets. "Only when I felt pretty solidly grounded there did I presume to try again," he says. "Less so than adult poetry, children's poetry and verse, I believe, depend as much for their effect upon *sound* as *sense*. Oftentimes, though not exclusively, form and rhyme facilitate that appeal to children."

Of course, Lewis is speaking of "clever, eccentric, well-honed rhyme—not doggerel." And while most of his poetry for children does follow strict metrics, whereas his work for adults relies somewhat less on strict forms, he says the particular form matters little. "Quality ought to be the sole criterion, which means that poems should be wonderfully eccentric and unexpected."

However, even after Lewis became a quality student of the craft, publication of his first collection of children's poetry did not come easily. In fact, when he began submitting his poetry manuscripts, he was told that a half dozen children's poets—Dr. Seuss and Shel Silverstein among them—had the market pretty much to themselves.

But Lewis persevered and, in 1990, after the manuscript had been rejected 20 times, his first collection of animal poems, *A Hippopotamusn't*, was published by Dial. Since then, he has published numerous works, including two other collec-

CLOSE-UP, *Lewis*

tions of animal poems as well as a book of nature poems, a collection of poems about the months of the year, and, most recently, a delightful book of riddle poems.

This year should see the appearance of *The Boat of Many Rooms*, the story of Noah's ark in verse, and *The La-di-da Hare*, a nonsensical tale in narrative verse, published by Atheneum; *Long Was the Winter Road They Traveled*, a nativity ballad published by Dial; and *Boshblobberbosh: Runcible Poems for Edward Lear*, published by Creative Editions. The latter is Lewis's tribute to the Victorian nonsense writer and children's poet, who has been his inspiration.

"The Gentleman Bookworm"

There once was a Gentleman Bookworm
Ate his words with a fork and a spoon.
When friends crawled down
From Book End Town
He offered them **Goodnight Moon**.

He fed them **The Wind In The Willows**
And a page out of **Charlotte's Web**.
They were eating bizarre
Where The Wild Things Are.
When one of the guestworms said,

"How sinfully rich and delicious!
Why should anyone bother to cook?
You've done it, dear boy!
Now sit down and enjoy
A bite of this poetry book!"

(from *The Bookworm's Feast*, to be published by Dial in 1998, reprinted by permission of the author)

Given the wide range of his subject matter, it seems only natural to wonder where Lewis gets his ideas. The answer is simple. In any form of writing, he says, ideas come from ideas, that is, from reading. "The first lesson of the classroom ought to be that you can't even hope to become a good writer without being a good reader. Second, ideas come from observation—from looking at things, for a long time . . . then looking some more . . . then taking pictures, but only with your words. And the final source of ideas is remembering."

A poet for children, for instance, ought to spend as much time as possible in "remembered childhood." The "back alleys of memory," particularly times in the schoolyards, are great places for ideas, he says. "I think the single most important difference [between writing for children and adults] is that a child's experiences are limited, and so the poetry he or she reads must fall within that experience."

CLOSE-UP, *continued*

Actually, with barely a handful of quality magazines for children, and the tightening market for children's books, the most difficult task for aspiring children's poets is overcoming the desire for instant gratification, Lewis says. "If a half dozen rejections are enough to make you want to bury your head in the sand, then perhaps there are other, less stressful pursuits that would interest you. If, on the other hand, you are in for the long haul, it's just possible that patience and hard work will find their reward."

The same could be said to those seeking to publish a book of adult poetry. Though Lewis has published work in about 70 literary journals and small magazines, including *Artful Dodge*, *The Gettysburg Review*, *New Letters*, *Southern Humanities Review*, *West Branch* and *Yankee*, he has yet to secure a publisher for his first adult poetry collection.

Nevertheless, Lewis continues to write, and to experiment with different forms and different mediums. He is not only working on his own nursery rhyme collection, but he is also collaborating with folksinger Sally Rogers on a collection of children's songs for a book and, hopefully, a compact disc.

As for publication of his adult work, Lewis remains optimistic. A writer must expect to run the gauntlet of rejection, he says. "If that's too painful, time-consuming or inconvenient, then get out of the game early. But if you believe in what you've done—and you've put craft into your work—send out the manuscript, even if the cows *don't* come home very soon."
—*Christine Martin*

> but by beating my scant and bleeding hands
> against the darkness—and worse
> and more important: to never be fooled myself.

The digest-sized, perfect-bound format is professionally printed, glossy cover, with art, ads. There are about 60-80 pgs. of poetry in each issue. They receive at least 2,000 poems/year, use 60. Press run is 1,000 for 100 subscribers of which 30 are libraries. **Sample: $5 for recent issues, $3 for others. "No simultaneous submissions. Please limit submissions to 6 poems. Long poems may be of any length, but send only one at a time. We encourage translations, but we ask as well for original text and statement from translator that he/she has copyright clearance and permission of author." Reports in up to 6 months. Pays 2 copies, plus, currently, $5/page honorarium because of grants from Ohio Arts Council.** Open to unsolicited reviews; "query first." Poets may also send books for review consideration; however, "there is no guarantee we can review them!"

‡ARTISAN, A JOURNAL OF CRAFT (I), P.O. Box 157, Wilmette IL 60091, e-mail artisanjnl@ao l.com, founded 1995, editor Joan Daugherty, is a bimonthly publication based on the idea that "anyone who strives to express themselves with skill is an artist and artists of all kinds can learn from each other. **We want poetry that is vital, fresh and true to life; evocative. Nothing trite, vague or pornographic.**" As a sample the editor selected these lines from "Miami Beach" by Karen Mittelman:

> an island breathes huge
> against the arms of ocean,
> and every fish in the
> dark waters,
> swollen with moonlight,
> breathes back.

artisan is 20 pgs. (including cover), 8½ × 11, offset-printed and saddle-stitched with card stock cover, minimal graphics and classified ads. They receive about 140 poems a year, use approximately 25%. Press run is 200 for 50 subscribers, 100 distributed free to coffeehouses and local libraries. Subscription: $12. **Sample postpaid: $2.50. Make checks payable to artisan, ink. Submit 2-5 poems at a time. No previously published poems; simultaneous submissions OK. Cover letter preferred, however** "**if you send a cover letter, make it personal. We don't need to see any writing credentials; poems should stand on their own merit.**" Time between acceptance and publication is 2-6 months. **Often comments on rejections. Publishes theme issues. Send SASE for guidelines and upcoming themes. Reports in 1-2 months. Pays 3 copies. Acquires first rights.** *artisan* sponsors an annual contest that rotates between poetry, fiction and nonfiction. First prize is $100, second is $50. Prize winners and works meriting honorable mention are published in an expanded issue. Entry fee varies. Send SASE for guidelines. The editor says, "One of our founding goals was to provide an outlet for beginning writers *but* they should always remember to be honest when writing, to be themselves and not their favorite writer."

ARTS END BOOKS; NOSTOC MAGAZINE (II), P.O. Box 162, Newton MA 02168, founded 1978, poetry editor Marshall Brooks. "**We publish good contemporary writing. Our interests are broad and so are our tastes.**" People considering sending work to us should examine a copy of our magazine and/or our catalog; check your library for the former, send us a SASE for the latter." Their publications are distinguished by excellent presswork and art in a variety of formats: postcard series, posters, pamphlets, flat-spined paperbacks and hardbacks. As a sample the editor selected the poem "Mr. Green Again" by Bill Costley:

> after I got out of jail   —   cold   —   grey   —   steel
> by way of the courthouse   —   hot   —   red   —   brick
> & picked up my pay   —   check   —   double   —   check

> *I went down to the Public Gardens*
> *& rode on the Swanboats*

> *to feel how it was to be back*
> > *in the green again.*

The magazine appears irregularly in print runs of 300-500, about 30 pgs. of poetry in each, 100 subscriptions of which half are libraries. They receive a few hundred submissions/year, use 25-30. **Sample postpaid: $4. Query before sending submissions. Submit 5-6 poems at a time with name and address on each page. "SASE essential."** They offer "**modest payment plus contributor's copies.** A cover letter is a very good idea for any kind of submission; we receive *very* few good, intelligent cover letters. What to include? That's up to the writer, whatever he/she feels important in terms of the work, in terms of establishing a meeting." **Discourages simultaneous submissions. Frequently comments on rejected mss. Tries to report within a few weeks. Always sends prepublication galleys.** Reviews books of poetry "on occasion, length varies." Brooks says, "We try to respond warmly to writers interested in making genuine contact with us and our audience."

ARUNDEL PRESS; MERCER & AITCHISON (V), 8380 Beverly Blvd., Los Angeles CA 90048, phone (213)852-9852, founded 1984, managing editor Phillip Bevis. Arundel Press "publishes only major texts (as we see them) in limited editions printed letterpress. **We no longer consider unsolicited manuscripts.** Most work is illustrated with original graphics. Mercer & Aitchison publishes definitive editions of major (as we see them) works of poetry, literature and literary criticism."

ASCENT (II), Dept. of English, Concordia College, Moorhead MN 56562, e-mail olsen@gloria.cord. edu, founded 1975, editor W. Scott Olsen, appears 3 times/year, using **poetry that is "eclectic, shorter rather than longer."** They have published poetry by Thomas Reiter, Michael Bugeja and Kathleen Lynch. As a sample the editor selected these lines from "The Poems Escape" by Dan Campion:

> *Suppose all sense drained from their stricken hands,*
> *All light chased from their eyes, their tongues a gag.*
> *That's how it was inside, and where they're bound.*
> *Once mad to climb the wall and leap the fence,*
> *Though, they skin out. Then hounds can't match their stride.*

The editor describes *Ascent* as 64 pgs., 6×9, perfect-bound, professionally printed with matte card cover. They receive about 750 poems a year, accept approximately 5%. Press run is 900 for 250 subscribers of which 90 are libraries. Subscription: $9/year. **Sample postpaid: $3.50. Submit 3-6 poems at a time. Always sends prepublication galleys. Pays 3 copies.** This continues as one of the "best buys" in the literary world for its low price, openness to all forms and styles, and relatively quick and encouraging response times. The editor says, "Poems are rejected or accepted from 2-8 weeks, usually closer to 2 weeks. Acceptances are usually published within the year." Poetry published here has also been included in *The Best American Poetry 1994*.

THE ASHLAND POETRY PRESS (V, IV-Anthologies, themes), Ashland University, Ashland OH 44805-3799, founded 1969, editor Robert McGovern, publishes anthologies on specific themes and occasional collections. He has published the collection *American Lit* (a sonnet sequence) by

Harold Witt and the anthology *Scarecrow Poetry: The Muse in Post-Middle Age*. As a sample he selected these lines from "Jacqueline Du Pré" by Leonard Trawick:

> *Jacqueline du Pré, when your muscles came untuned,*
> *wasn't the music still there, all those silent years——*
> *just as, after the last note, when players poise their bows*
> *triumphant for one still moment before the applause,*
> *the whole quartet hangs perfect in the air?*

That poem appears in *80 on the 80's: A Decade's History in Verse* edited by Robert McGovern and Joan Baranow. **"Watch publications such as *Poets & Writers* for calls for mss, but don't submit otherwise. We do not read unsolicited mss; anthology readings take quite a bit of time." Considers simultaneous submissions. On collections, poet gets 10% royalty; anthologies, poets are paid stipulated price when sufficient copies are sold. Write for catalog.**

ASIAN PACIFIC AMERICAN JOURNAL; ASIAN AMERICAN WRITERS' WORKSHOP (I, II, IV-Ethnic/nationality, anthology), 37 St. Mark's Place, #B, New York NY 10003, phone (212)228-6718, fax (212)228-7718, e-mail aaww@panix.com, website http://www.panix.com/~aaww, founded 1992. The *APA Journal* is a biannual published by the AAWW, a not-for-profit organization. It is **"dedicated to the best of contemporary Asian-American writing."** They have recently published poetry by Arthur Sze, Cathy Song and Eric Gamalinda. As a sample the editor selected these lines from "Sound among Sounds" by Koon Woon:

> *And so because the leaves flutter, we know wind from their gaps.*
> *While the thought of wind is tame, yet by it,*
> *One room inflates, another deflates; one world inflates, another deflates.*

APA Journal is 140-190 pgs., digest-sized, typeset and perfect-bound with 2-color cover and ads. They receive submissions from about 80 poets/year, accept about 30%. Press run is 1,500 for 400 subscribers of which 50 are libraries, 800 shelf sales. Single copy: $10; subscription: $20. **Sample postpaid: $12. Submit 4-6 poems at a time. Previously published poems and simultaneous submissions OK. Cover letter with phone and fax numbers and 1- to 4-sentence biographical statement required. Submissions on 3.5 Macintosh disk (or IBM, if necessary) welcome. Deadlines are usually May 15 and December 15 for October 1 and April 1 issues, respectively.** "We will work with authors who are promising." **Send SASE for guidelines or request via e-mail. Reports in 3 months. Pays 2 copies. Acquires one-time rights.** In 1996 they also published *Contours of the Heart*, a South Asian American anthology and *Flippin,* a Filipino American anthology. The AAWW offers creative writing workshops, a newsletter, a bookselling service, readings and fellowships to young Asian-American writers. Write for details.

ATHENA INCOGNITO MAGAZINE (I), 1442 Judah St., San Francisco CA 94122, founded 1980, editor Ronn Rosen, is an annual of experimental writing and other arts. **They want poetry that is "experimental, surrealist, Dada, etc. 3 pgs. max. No greeting card verse, overly religious poetry or epics."** They have recently published poetry by Collette Robbins and Jamie Erfurdt. As a sample the editor selected these lines (poet unidentified):

> *Arrow strikes*
> *Swims out*
> *Narrow gap lapped up that vulture*
> *Heron heron heron*
> *Of summer brambled.*

The editor says the magazine is usually 20-30 photocopied pgs. They receive about 50 poems a year, use approximately 15%. Press run is 200 for 50 subscribers of which 2 are libraries, 50 shelf sales. **"All people submitting poetry *must* buy a sample copy—$5.50 postpaid." Previously published poems and simultaneous submissions OK. "Name and address required on all pages. SASE also required." Often comments on rejections. Reports in 1-2 months. Pays 1 copy.** The editor says, "Be well read in world poetry, surrealism and Dada, and get inspired."

ATLANTA REVIEW; POETRY 1997; POETRY ATLANTA, INC. (II), P.O. Box 8248, Atlanta GA 30306, founded 1994, contact poetry editor, is a semiannual primarily devoted to poetry, but also featuring fiction, interviews, essays and fine art. **They want "quality poetry of genuine human appeal."** They have published poetry by Seamus Heaney, Charles Simic, Linda Pastan, Maxine Kumin, Josephine Jacobsen and Mark Jarman. As a sample the editor selected these lines from "The sin of giving short measure" by Irish poet Biddy Jenkinson:

> *May my eyes have vision in them tonight*
> *and may my hand have sensitivity.*
> *May my lines lie close to the truth. . . .*
>
> *May one consecrated inspiration*
> *last three hours tonight.*

May I put a contour,
to the best of my ability,
around humanity.

AR is 112 pgs., 6×9, professionally printed on acid-free paper and flat-spined with glossy cover and b&w artwork. They receive about 10,000 poems a year, use about 1%. Press run is 4,000 for 300 subscribers of which 15 are libraries, 2,500 shelf sales. Single copy: $6; subscription: $10. **Sample postpaid: $5. No previously published poems. Issue deadlines are June 1 and December 1.** Time between acceptance and publication is 2 months. **Editors alternate as final issue editor. Seldom comments on rejections. Each spring issue has an International Feature Section: the Caribbean 1997. Send SASE for guidelines. Reports in 2 months. Pays 2 copies plus subscription. Acquires first North American serial rights.** *AR* also sponsors POETRY 1997, an annual international poetry competition. Prizes are $1,000, $500 and $250, plus numerous International Merit Awards. Winners are announced in leading international literary publications. All entries will be considered for publication in *Atlanta Review*'s Fall 1997 issue. Entry fee is $5 for the first poem, $2 for each additional. No entry form or guidelines necessary. Send to POETRY 1997 at the above address. Postmark deadline: May 1, 1997. They say, "We are making a serious effort to give today's poets the wider audience they truly deserve."

THE ATLANTIC (II), Dept. PM, 745 Boylston St., Boston MA 02116, phone (617)536-9500, founded 1857, poetry editor Peter Davison, assistant poetry editor David Barber, publishes 1-5 poems monthly. **Some of the most distinguished poetry in American literature** has been published by this magazine, including work by William Matthews, Mary Oliver, Stanley Kunitz, Rodney Jones, May Swenson, Galway Kinnell, Philip Levine, Red Hawk, Tess Gallagher, Donald Hall and W.S. Merwin. The magazine has a circulation of 500,000, of which 5,800 are libraries. They receive some 75,000 poems/year, of which they use 35-40 and have a backlog of 6-12 months. **Sample postpaid: $3. Submit 3-5 poems with SASE. No simultaneous submissions. Publishes theme issues. Always sends prepublication galleys. Pays about $3/line. Buys first North American serial rights only.** Wants "to see poetry of the highest order; we do *not* want to see workshop rejects. **Watch out for workshop uniformity. Beware of the present indicative. Be yourself."** Poetry published here has been included in the 1992, 1993, 1995 and 1996 volumes of *The Best American Poetry*.

ATLANTIS: A WOMEN'S STUDIES JOURNAL (IV-Feminist), Dept. PM, Institute for the Study of Women, Mount Saint Vincent University, Halifax, Nova Scotia B3M 2J6 Canada, phone (902)457-6319, fax (902)443-1352, founded 1975, appears twice a year using "a little" **poetry "certainly no longer than 5 ms pgs.; should have a feminist perspective, preferably academic."** They have published poetry by Liliane Welch. The editor describes it as 150 pgs., magazine-sized, flat-spined with card cover. They accept about 5-10% of submissions. Press run is 1,000 for 600 subscribers of which 55% are libraries. Subscription: Canada: individual $20, institution $40; US: individual $30, institution, $50; international: individual $35, institution $55 (all in Canadian dollars). **Sample postpaid: $7.50 Canadian. Submit no more than 3 poems at a time, one poem/page. Reports in 3-4 months. Pays 1 copy.**

ATOM MIND (II); MOTHER ROAD PUBLICATIONS (V), P.O. Box 22068, Albuquerque NM 87154-2068, first founded 1968-70, reestablished 1992, editor Gregory Smith. *Atom Mind* is a quarterly journal of "alternative literature, mostly influenced by the Beats, Steinbeck, John Fante and Bukowski. **Narrative, free verse, 20-80 lines preferred, although length restrictions are not set in stone. No light verse, inspirational poetry, doggerel, 'moon-spoon-June' rhyming verse."** They have published poetry by Lawrence Ferlinghetti, Charles Plymell and Wilma Elizabeth McDaniel. As a sample we selected these lines from "good stuff" by Charles Bukowski:

beer from China.
think of it.
this is some a.m.
Caesar and Plato hulk in the
shadows and I love you all
for just a
moment.

The editor says *AM* is 120 pgs., 8½×11, offset, with illustrations and photographs. They receive approximately 2,000 submissions annually, publish perhaps 5%. Press run is 1,000 for 750 subscribers of which 25 are libraries. Subscription: $20. **Sample postpaid: $6. Prefers to consider submissions of 5-8 poems at a time, rather than 1 or 2 poems. Previously published poems OK; no simultaneous submissions.** Time between acceptance and publication is 8-12 months. **"*Atom Mind* is very much a one-man operation; therefore, submissions are subject to the whims and personal biases of the editor only." Often comments on rejections. Send SASE for guidelines. Reports in 1-2 months. Pays copies, number varies. Acquires first or one-time rights.** Mother Road Publications also publishes 2 paperback and 2 hardback collections of poetry/year. **"Book-length poetry manuscripts considered by invitation only." Send SASE for catalog.**

AURA LITERARY/ARTS REVIEW (II), Dept. PM, Box 76, Hill University Center, University of Alabama at Birmingham, Birmingham AL 35294-1150, phone (205)934-3216, founded 1974, editor Steve Mullen, is a semiannual magazine that publishes "fiction and art though majority of acceptances are poetry—90-100 per year. **Length open, style open, subject matter open. We are looking for quality poetry. Both first-time and often published poets are published here."** *Aura* has published work by Lyn Lifshin, Adrian C. Louis and William Miller. The 6×9 magazine is 100-140 pgs., perfect-bound, printed on white matte with b&w photos, lithography and line art. Circulation is 500, of which 40-50 are subscriptions; other sales are to students and Birmingham residents. Subscription: $6. **Sample postpaid: $2.50. Writers should submit "3-5 poems, with SASE, no simultaneous submissions, will take even neatly handwritten." Send SASE for guidelines. Reports in 2-3 months. Pays 2 copies.**

‡THE AUROREAN: A POETIC QUARTERLY; ENCIRCLE PUBLICATIONS (II), P.O. Box 219, Sagamore Beach MA 02562, phone (508)833-0805, press founded 1992, magazine founded 1995, editor Cynthia Brackett-Vincent. *The Aurorean*, which appears in March, June, September and December, seeks to publish **"poetry that is inspirational, meditational or reflective of the Northeast. Strongly encouraged topics: positivity, recovery and nature. Maximum length: 36 lines. Typographical oddities are OK as long as we can reproduce them on our page. No hateful, overly religious or vulgar poetry."** They have recently published poetry by P. Carey Reid, Beverly Tricco and Linda Renaud. As a sample the editor selected the opening lines from "Twentieth (century) Maine" by Mark Walsh:

> "Stand firm you boys from Maine."

> *These words run through my mind and I can almost hear*
> *the voice of that stoic rhetorician, on sabbatical to fight a war.*
> *He stands stone-jawed, stone eye gazing over the stone wall*
> *the smoke from a western battle rolling through the trees*
> *hiding the grey men as they move in for the last time.*

The Aurorean is 24-40 pgs., 5½×8½, desktop-published and saddle-stapled with light card cover. Press run is 250. Subscription: $14. **Sample postpaid: $4. Make checks payable to Encircle Publications. Submit 3-5 poems at a time. No previously published poems or simultaneous submissions. Cover letter preferred. Often comments on rejections. Send SASE for guidelines. "We notify authors of receipt of manuscripts immediately. We report on decisions in one week to two months." Always sends prepublication galleys. Pays 3 copies/poem. Also features a "Poet-of-the-Quarter" each issue with publication of up to 3 poems and an extended bio. Featured poets receive 10 copies and a 1-year subscription.** The editor says, "Study *Poet's Market*. Read samples before you submit. Always have a ms out there. Stop saying you want to be a writer. You are a writer if you write. Remember, editors are people too. What one editor rejects one day, another may jump at the next. Invest in the small press with samples. Invest in yourself with postage. Always include enough postage for the return/reply process!!! Read more poetry than you write, and read your poetry out loud."

‡AUTHORS (I, IV-Membership), 501 Cambridge St. SE, Medicine Hat, Alberta T1A 0T3 Canada, phone/fax (403)526-2524, e-mail authmag@aol.com, website http://members.gnn.com/wwwmedia/aui ndex.htm, founded 1992, editor/publisher Philip Murphy, is a membership-driven, monthly contest publication for writers in all genres. **They want poetry in all forms and styles, and on all subjects. No poetry in "poor taste or that is insincere."** As a sample the editor selected these lines from "Sunrise of Your Love" by Leonardo Osorio (Buenos Aires, Argentina):

> *Because my soul*
> *is confused with your soul,*
> *because my dream*
> *about your name in every star*
> *lives inside me palpitating*
> *from the skin to the heart*

Authors is 80-100 pgs., 8½×11, saddle-stitched and printed on colored paper with b&w artwork. They receive 40-50 poems a year, publish most of them. Press run is 350 for 300 subscribers, 50 distributed free to the media. Subscription: $29/6 months, $49/year. **Sample (including guidelines) postpaid: $6. Membership/subscription is not required. However, "space for nonmembers is currently limited—up to six-month waiting period. This space is tied to membership base. Ratio 75/25." Submit up to 3 poems at a time. Previously published poems and simultaneous submissions OK. Cover letter preferred. "DOS disks in any major word processing format appreciated with accompanying hard copy."** Time between acceptance and publication is 1-5 months. **Reports**

in about 3 weeks. Pays 1 copy. Sponsors monthly contest with three levels of achievement. "Each level is rewarded with a certificate. The top level (Gold) awards cash prizes ($75 plus 1-year membership—$49 value) for the best story or poem of the month." Winners are chosen by fellow members. The editor says, "Our philosophy is to publish as many works as our membership base will allow (both novice and professional), to provide feedback to published works, and to offer ever increasing cash incentives for quality submissions. All serious inquiries in any genre in good taste are given due consideration. We are reluctant to send out rejection slips."

BABY SUE (I), P.O. Box 8989, Atlanta GA 30306-8989, founded 1985, editor/publisher Don W. Seven, appears twice a year publishing harsh, rude humor for the extremely open-minded. **"We are open to all styles, but prefer short poems." No restrictions.** They have published poetry by Edward Mycue, Susan Andrews, Stephen Fievet and Barry Bishop. The editor says *baby sue* is 32 pgs., offset. "We print prose, poems and cartoons. We usually accept about 5% of what we receive." Single copy: $3; subscription: $12 for 4 issues. **Sample postpaid: $2. Previously published poems and simultaneous submissions OK. Deadlines are March 30 and September 30 of each year. Seldom comments on rejections. Reports "immediately, if we are interested." Pays 1 copy.** "We do occasionally review other magazines." The editor adds, "We have received no awards, but we are very popular on the underground press circuit and sell our magazine all over the world."

‡BACKSPACE (IV-Gay/lesbian/bisexual), 33 Maplewood Ave., Suite 201, Gloucester MA 01930-6201, e-mail charkim@tiac.net, website http://www.tiac.net/users/charkim, founded 1991, managing editor Kim Smith. *Backspace*, published 3 times a year, is a collection of queer poetry and fiction, provides a forum for gay/lesbian writers to share their work with their peers." **They want any kind of poetry, prefer gay and lesbian themes, but nothing more than 50 lines. "No explicitly sexual or violent works."** The editor says *Backspace* is about 36 pgs., digest-sized, laser-printed and saddle-stitched with glossy cover stock. They receive 15-30 poems a year, accept approximately 35%. Press run is 400. Single copy: $4; subscription: $7/year. **Sample postpaid: $2. Make checks payable to Charlotte Stratton. Submit 6 poems at a time. No previously published poems; simultaneous submissions OK. Cover letter with brief bio (no more than 30 words) required. Material on diskette or via e-mail also accepted. Send SASE for guidelines. Reports immediately. Pays 1 copy.** Reviews books of poetry. Open to unsolicited reviews. Poets may also send books for review consideration to Charlotte Stratton, assistant managing editor. The editor says, "Don't hold yourself back—share your work."

BAGMAN PRESS (I), P.O. Box 81166, Chicago IL 60681-0166, founded 1989, publisher Bill Falloon, publishes 1 paperback/year—**"emphasis is on 'new' writers who can create powerful first impressions."** They have published *Joe the Dream*, poetry by J.J. Tindall, and *Playing Soldiers in the Dark*, fiction by Stephen Dueweke. **Submit complete ms with SASE. Previously published poems OK; no simultaneous submissions. Cover letter required. Seldom comments on rejections. Replies to queries in 2 weeks, to mss in 6 months or less. Pays 5-10% royalties and 30 author's copies.** "Small Press Distribution is our primary distributor." The publisher says, "Our aim is to publish writers whose voices have not yet had the opportunity to be heard. We want to publish writing that is consistently strong from beginning to end, writing that will challenge readers to respond to the nuance of a writer's imagination."

BAKUNIN (II), P.O. Box 14245, Irvine CA 92713-4245, founded 1990, editor Jordan Jones, is an annual publication. **"We are looking for poems that challenge accepted pieties and norms. We are also interested in powerful personal poems."** They want **"avant-garde, surrealist, Beat, visceral and mainstream poetry of humor, pathos and social comment. No trite or hackneyed verse; no poem that uses but does not earn the word love."** They have published poetry by Sandra McPherson, Dennis Schmitz, Benjamin Saltman and William Stafford. As a sample the editor selected the opening lines of "The Aqueduct" by Dorianne Laux:

> We played there on hot L.A. summers, kids poking through
> the slick algae and bloated tires, the delicate rafts
> of mosquito eggs. Open boxcars pulled gray squares
> of sky overhead as we took apples and crackers
> from our pockets and ate, watched the cursing workers
> from the can factory gathering at the silver lunch truck

MARKET CATEGORIES: (I) Beginning; **(II)** General; **(III)** Limited; **(IV)** Specialized; **(V)** Closed.

Bakunin is 200 pgs., 6×9, offset on acid-free recycled paper and perfect-bound with laminated cover, b&w artwork and some ads. They receive about 750 submissions a year, publish approximately 5%. The free verse is mostly lyric, and the poems tend to be one-page. Press run is 1,000 for 100 subscribers, 450 shelf sales. Subscription: $10, $12 foreign, $20 institutional. **Sample postpaid: $10; back issue: $5. Submit up to 5 poems at a time. No previously published poems; simultaneous submissions OK, "if the author indicates they are such." Cover letter required.** Time between acceptance and publication is 1-2 years. **Seldom comments on rejections. Send SASE for guidelines. Reports in 3-6 months. Pays 2 copies. Acquires first North American serial rights.** "We publish 250- to 750-word reviews of single books, magazines or whole presses." The editor says, "*Bakunin* is a magazine for the dead Russian anarchist in all of us."

BANTAM DOUBLEDAY DELL PUBLISHING GROUP (V), 1540 Broadway, New York NY 10036, phone (212)354-6500, **only accepts mss from agents**.

BAPTIST SUNDAY SCHOOL BOARD; CHRISTIAN SINGLE (IV-Religious, themes); HOME LIFE (IV-Religious); MATURE LIVING (IV-Religious, senior citizen), 127 Ninth Ave. N., Nashville TN 37234, the publishing agency for Southern Baptists. "We publish magazines, monthlies, quarterlies, books, filmstrips, films, church supplies, etc., for Southern Baptist churches. **We want poetry with a message to inspire, uplift, motivate, amuse.**" *Christian Single*, founded in 1979, managing editor Ivey Harrington, is a monthly magazine for single adults, ages 25-45. **"We need inspirational poetry targeted to single adults. Poetry that is happy, positive and shows people living single successfully. This will be thought-provoking, spiritual poetry to tie in with monthly themes."** *Christian Single* is 50 pgs., magazine-sized, with a circulation of 70,000. Uses 12-20 poems/ year. **Previously published poems OK; prefers not to receive simultaneous submissions. For sample, send 9×12 SAE with 4 first-class stamps.** Publishes 6-12 months after acceptance. **Reports in 2 months. Pays upon acceptance; payment varies.** The biggest of the monthlies is *Home Life*, which began in 1947. Circulation 600,000; 20,000 subscribers. It is a magazine-sized, saddle-stapled, slick magazine, 60 pgs., illustrated (no ads). Its Editor-in-Chief, Charlie Warren, says he wants **"religious poetry; poetry treating marriage, family life and life in general from a Christian perspective. We rarely publish anything of more than 25 lines." Sample: $1 to authors with 9×12 SASE. Submit 5 poems at a time. Query unnecessary. Send SASE for guidelines. Reports in 6-8 weeks. Pays $25-50.** *Mature Living: A Christian Magazine for Senior Adults*, founded in 1977, is a monthly mass circulation (360,000) magazine providing **"leisure reading for senior adults. All material used is compatible with a Christian life-style."** The poetry they use is of Christian content, inspirational, about "nature/God," rhymed, 8-24 lines. **You do not have to be a senior citizen to submit.** *Mature Living* is 52 pgs., magazine-sized, saddle-stapled, using large print with color art. They "receive hundreds" of poems/year, use 50-100. Most of their distribution is through churches who buy the magazine in bulk for their senior adult members. **For sample, send 9×12 SAE and 4 first-class stamps. Reports in 6-8 weeks, but possibly a 3-year delay before publication. Pays $13-25.**

WILLIAM L. BAUHAN, PUBLISHER (V, IV-Regional), P.O. Box 443, Old County Rd., Dublin NH 03444, phone (603)563-8020, founded 1959, editor William L. Bauhan, publishes poetry and art, especially New England regional books. **Currently accepts no unsolicited poetry.** They have published books of poetry by Sarah Singer, Anne Marx, Phoebe Barnes Driver and May Sarton.

BAY AREA POETS COALITION (BAPC); POETALK (I), P.O. Box 11435, Berkeley CA 94712-2435, founded 1974, direct submissions to Editorial Committee. Coalition sends bimonthly poetry letter, *Poetalk*, to over 300 people. They also publish an annual anthology (17th—180 pgs., out in February 1996), giving one page to each member of BAPC (minimum 6 months) who has had work published in *Poetalk* during the previous year. *Poetalk* publishes approximately 75 poets each issue. BAPC has 160 members, 70 subscribers, but *Poetalk* is open to all. **No particular genre. Short poems (under 30 lines). "Rhyme must be well done."** Membership: $15 for 12 months of *Poetalk*, copy of anthology and other privileges; extra outside US. Also offers a $50 patronage, which includes a subscription and anthology for another individual of your choice, and a $25 beneficiary/memorial, which includes membership plus subscription for friend. Subscriptions: $6/year. As a sample the editors selected this complete poem, "Pretense," by LaDonna Fehlberg:

> The brown, dry leaf scurries
> across the driveway
> into the garage,
> sneaks inside the house-
> pretending it's a mouse.

Poetalk is 6 legal-sized pgs., photocopied and folded in half to make 24 pgs. total. **Send SASE with 64¢ postage for a free complimentary copy. Each poem should be 3×4 maximum, 4 to a page. Typewritten, single-spaced OK. Simultaneous and previously published work OK, but must be noted.** "All subject matter should be in good taste." **Send 4 poems (on 1 page) with SASE every**

6 months. Response time is 2 weeks to 4 months. You'll get copy of *Poetalk* **in which your work appears.** BAPC holds monthly readings, yearly contest, etc.; has mailing list open to local members. People from many states and countries have contributed to *Poetalk* or entered their annual contests. Send SASE in early September for contest guidelines. The editors say, "We differ from many publishers in that we are very actively involved in working with the poets to make their poems publishable. We try to help people get to the point where we can publish their work, i.e., we make editorial comments on almost everything we reject. If you don't want suggested revisions you need to say so clearly in your cover letter."

BAY WINDOWS (IV-Gay/lesbian), 1523 Washington St., Boston MA 02118, e-mail rudyk@aol.c om, founded 1983, poetry editor Rudy Kikel. *Bay Windows* is a weekly gay and lesbian newspaper published for the New England community, regularly using **"short poems of interest to lesbians and gay men. Poetry that is 'experiential' seems to have a good chance with us, but we don't want poetry that just 'tells it like it is.' Our readership doesn't read poetry all the time. A primary consideration is giving** *pleasure.* **We'll overlook the poem's (and the poet's) tendency not to be informed by the latest poetic theory, if it** *does* **this: pleases. Pleases, in particular, by articulating common gay or lesbian experience, and by doing that with some attention to form. I've found that a lot of our choices were made because of a strong image strand. Humor is** *always* **welcome— and hard to provide with craft. Obliquity, obscurity? Probably not for us. We won't presume on our audience."** They have recently published poetry by Judith Saunders, David L. Skeens, Nasira Alma, Charles Bridgeman, Lawrence Schimel and Leslea Newman. As a sample Rudy Kikel selected these lines from "Trust" by Scott Hightower:

> *These are not the hands you want. But*
> *they are the hands you want tonight.*
>
> *These are not the lips you want. But*
> *they are the ones you want tonight*
>
> *pressing down on your mouth, your eye lids,*
> *your shaft, your neck, and throat.*

"We try to run four poems each month." They receive about 300 submissions/year, use 1 in 6, have a 3-month backlog. Press run is 13,000 for 700 subscribers of which 15 are libraries. Single copy: 50¢; subscription: $40. **Sample postpaid: $2. Submit 3-5 poems at a time, "5-25 lines are ideal; include short biographical blurb and SASE. No submissions via e-mail, but poets may request info via e-mail." Reports in 2-3 months. Pays 1-2 copies. Acquires first rights. Editor "often" comments on rejections.** They review books of poetry in about 750 words—"Both single and omnibus reviews (the latter are longer)."

BEACH HOLME PUBLISHERS; PORCÉPIC BOOKS (II, IV-Regional), 4252 Commerce Circle, Victoria, British Columbia V8Z 4M2 Canada, phone (604)727-6514, fax (604)727-6418, e-mail bhp@softwords.bc.ca, website http://www.swifty.com/sw/cover.html, founded 1971, editor Joy Gugeler, publishes 3-4 paperback books of poetry each year under the imprint Porcépic Books. They want **"excellent quality writing—all subjects, cultures, etc.—by Canadian authors."** They have published *The Self-Completing Tree* by Dorothy Livesay, *Oedipal Dreams* by Evelyn Lau, *Cocktails at the Mausoleum* by Susan Musgrave and *Love As It Is* by Marilyn Bowering. **Query first, with sample poems and cover letter with brief bio and publication credits. Previously published poems and simultaneous submissions OK, if indicated. No fax or e-mail submissions.** Time between acceptance and publication is 12-18 months. **Seldom comments on rejections. Replies to mss (if invited) in 3-4 months, sometimes longer. Pays 10% royalties and 5-10 author's copies. Samples may be ordered directly from Beach Holme Publishers or through a bookstore.** The editor says, "We are open to new authors, although we are most interested in poets who have had individual poems published in magazines, etc., or who have some familiarity with the literary scene. We appreciate authors who are familiar with our recent or backlist titles and our company."

BEACON (IV-Regional), Southwestern Oregon Community College, 1988 Newmark Ave., Coos Bay OR 97420-2956, phone (503)888-7335, editor changes yearly. *Beacon* is a small, college literary magazine that appears twice a year and publishes the work of local writers and artists. **They want poetry only from those who have had their beginnings or currently reside in Southwestern Oregon. No specifications as to form, length, subject matter or style. "Submissions limited to five poems per term, prefer non-saga poems; one story per term, maximum 3,000 words."** The editor says *Beacon* is 75-100 pgs., 5½×8, professionally printed with color cover and b&w art within; no ads. They receive about 400 poems a year, accept approximately 25%. Press run is 300, all shelf sales. **Sample postpaid: $3.50. No previously published poems or simultaneous submissions. Cover letter required. Reads submissions December 1 to January 15 and March 1 to April 15.** Time between acceptance and publication is 2 months. **Seldom comments on rejections. Reports "on**

publication." **Pays 1 copy. Acquires first rights.** The editor says, "We encourage poets to visit for readings and bring works to offer for sale. We do not compensate in any way for these readings. The purpose of our magazine is to heighten the value of literature in our community."

‡**THE BEAR ESSENTIAL (IV-Nature/rural/ecology)**, P.O. Box 10342, Portland OR 97210-0342, phone (503)242-2330, fax (503)243-2645, e-mail orlo@teleport.com, website http://www.teleport.com/~orlo/, founded 1993, editor Tom Webb, is a semiannual that "maintains a street-level and hands-on perspective regarding the world around us. Urban and rural in focus, the magazine discusses both new and traditional environmental subject matter." **They want poetry with "innovative environmental perspectives, not much longer than 50 lines. No rants."** They have recently published poetry by Brian Christopher Hamilton, Heather Joyner and Derek Sheffield. As a sample the editor selected these lines from "The Tick" by Craig Thompson:

> my companions had no mercy either
> ridiculing my shock with endless reference
> to those hungry suckers sapping out life
> from deer, rodent, coyote, bear,
> whatever passing mammal chances by

The Bear Essential is 76 pgs., 11 × 14, newsprint with brown Kraft paper cover, saddle-stitched, with lots of original graphics and b&w photos. They receive about 200 poems a year, publish 15-20. Press run is 15,000 for 750 subscribers of which 10 are libraries, 14,000 distributed free on the streets of the Western US and beyond. Subscription: $10. **Sample postpaid: $2. Make checks payable to Orlo. Submit 3-5 poems at a time. Previously published poems and simultaneous submissions OK. Cover letter required. Poems are reviewed by a committee of 7-9 people. Publishes theme issues. Send SASE for guidelines and upcoming themes. Reports in 6-8 weeks. Pays 5-20 copies, subscription and "invitation to great events." Acquires first or one-time rights.** Note: *The Bear Essential* is published by Orlo, a nonprofit organization exploring environmental issues through the creative arts.

BEDLAM PRESS (V), Church Green House, Old Church Lane, Pateley Bridge, N. Yorkshire HG3 5LZ England, phone 01423 711508, founded 1982, is a "small press publisher of poetry books, specializing in **long poems or sequences, mainly concerned with public affairs.**" They are **currently not accepting unsolicited mss.**

‡**BEGGAR'S PRESS; THE LAMPLIGHT; RASKOLNIKOV'S CELLAR; BEGGAR'S REVIEW (I)**, 8110 N. 38th St., Omaha NE 68112-2018, phone (402)455-2615, founded 1977, editor Richard R. Carey. *The Lamplight* is a semiannual (more frequent at times) publication of short stories, poetry, humor and unusual literary writings. **"We are eclectic, but we like serious poetry, historically orientated. Positively no religious or sentimental poetry. No incomprehensible poetry."** They have published poetry by Fredrick Zydek and John J. McKernan. As a sample the editor selected these lines (poet unidentified):

> Lord, why did you curse me with doubt!
> I'm a shot discharged in a wood without trees,
> like a scream that began as a shout.
> Never too far from famine or mire;
> hunger and cold, and all creatures turn bold—
> But, Lord, why did you give me desire!

The Lamplight is 40-60 pgs., 8½ × 11, offset printed and perfect-bound with 65 lb. cover stock. They receive about 600 poems a year, use only 10-15%. Press run is 500 for 300 subscribers of which 25 are libraries. Single copy: $9.50. **Sample: $7 plus 9 × 12 SASE. No previously published poems; simultaneous submissions OK. Cover letter required—"must provide insight into the poet's characteristics. What makes this poet different from the mass of humanity?"** Time between acceptance and publication is 4-12 months. **Often comments on rejections. Also offers "complete appraisals and evaluations" for $4/standard sheet, double-spaced. Brochure available for SASE. Reports in 2 to 2½ months. Pays 2 copies plus discount on up to 5. Acquires first North American serial rights.** *Raskolnikov's Cellar* is an irregular magazine of the same format, dimensions and terms as *The Lamplight*. However, it deals in **"deeper psychologically orientated stories and poetry. It is** more selective and discriminating in what it publishes. Guidelines and brochures are an essential to consider this market." **Send SASE and $1 for guidelines. Brochures require only SASE.** *Beggar's Review* is 20-40 pgs., 8½ × 11, offset printed and saddle-stitched. It lists and reviews books, chapbooks and other magazines. "It also lists and reviews unpublished manuscripts: poetry, short stories, book-length, etc. Our purpose is to offer a vehicle for unpublished work of merit, as well as published material. We like to work with poets and authors who have potential but have not yet been recognized." Lengths of reviews range from a listing or mere caption to 1,000 words, "according to merit." Single copy: $6. Beggar's Press also plans to publish 4-6 paperbacks/year—**some on a subsidy basis. "In most cases, we select books which we publish on a royalty basis and promote ourselves. Borderline** books only are author-subsidized." **Query first with a few sample poems and a cover letter with brief bio and publication credits.** "We also like to know how many books the author himself will be able to market to friends, associates, etc." **Replies to queries in 1 month, to mss in 2½ months. Pays 10-15% royalties and 3 author's copies. Terms vary for subsidy publishing. "Depending on projected sales, the author pays from 20% to 60%."** The editor says, "Our purpose is to form a common bond with distinguished poets whose poetry is marketable and worthy. Poetry is difficult to market, thus we sometimes collaborate with the poet in publishing costs. But essentially, we look for poets with unique qualities of expression and who meet our uncustomary requirements. We prefer a royalty arrangement. Beggar's Press is different from most publishers. We are impressed with concrete poetry, which is without outlandish metaphors. Keep it simple but don't be afraid to use our language to the fullest. Read Poe, Burns and Byron. Then submit to us. There is still a place for lyrical poetry."

BEGINNER'S MIND PRESS (V), 1059 27th St., Apt. 2, Des Moines IA 50311, founded 1992, editor Christien Gholson, publishes both chapbooks (2/year) and broadsides. However, **during 1997 BEgiNNer's MIND Press will not be accepting unsolicited mss.** When accepting submissions, the editor looks for **"poetry that has depth, ideas, music; that can be read out loud. No rhyme (unless blues oriented); no vague introspection; no poetry from the world of TV, suburbia; no academic verse (poetry with the poetry edited out of it)."** They have published poetry by Kevin Bezner, Christopher Conlon, Andrew Gettler and Louis McKee. As a sample the editor selected these lines from "Candelabra, for Pablo Nervoa" by Maia:

> between us, oceanic
> murmur of the sheets
>
> where we lie together
> under the long bells
>
> the green gaze
> of time

The chapbooks are generally 16 pgs., digest-sized, printed on plain white paper and saddle-stapled with b&w graphic on paper cover. The editor says, "All chaps and broadsides are given away free-for-postage (55¢ for a chap, 32¢ for a couple B'sides). Price can never define the worth of Art. Art has very little to do with being published—it's a way of life."

BELHUE PRESS (III, IV-Gay), 2501 Palisade Ave., Suite A1, Riverdale, Bronx NY 10463, founded 1990, editor Tom Laine, is a small press **specializing in gay male poetry**, publishing 3 paperbacks/year—no chapbooks. **"We are especially interested in anthologies, in thematic books, in books that get out of the stock poetry market."** They want **"hard-edged, well-crafted, fun and often sexy poetry. No mushy, self pitying, confessional, boring, indulgent, teary or unrequited love poems—yuck!"** As a sample the editor selected these lines from "Thoth" in the book *Sex-charge* by Perry Brass:

> How I lie
> in your winding sheet, sleeping
> > past the wake
> of our small end,
> a whiter corner in your light,
> curled toe to toe
> against your parts.

"Poets must be willing to promote book through readings, mailers, etc." Query first with 6 pgs. of poetry and cover letter. Previously published poems and simultaneous submissions OK. Time between acceptance and publication is 1 year. **Often comments on rejections. Will request criticism fees "if necessary." Replies to queries and submitted mss "fast." No payment information provided. Sample: $7.95.** "The only things we find offensive are stupid, dashed off, 'fortune cookie' poems that show no depth or awareness of poetry. We like poetry that, like good journalism, tells a story."

THE BELLINGHAM REVIEW; THE SIGNPOST PRESS; 49TH PARALLEL POETRY AWARD (II), M.S. 9053, Western Washington University, Bellingham WA 98225, founded 1975, editor Robin Hemley, publishes *The Bellingham Review* twice a year, runs an annual poetry competition and publishes other books and chapbooks of poetry occasionally. **"We want well-crafted poetry but are open to all styles,"** no specifications as to form. Poets they have published recently include David Shields, Tess Gallagher, Gary Soto, Jane Hirshfield, Albert Goldbarth, R.T. Smith and Rebecca McClanahan. As a sample the editor selected these lines from "Sitting at Dusk in the Back Yard After the Mondrian Retrospective" by Charles Wright:

> Form imposes, structure allows—
> > the slow destruction of form

> *So as to bring it back resheveled, reorganized,*
> *Is the hard heart of the enterprise.*
> *Under its camouflage,*
> *The light, relentless shill and cross-dresser, pools and deals.*
> *Inside its short skin, the darkness burns.*

The *Review* is 6×9, perfect-bound, with art and glossy cover. Each issue has about 60 pgs. of poetry. They have a circulation of 1,000 with 500 subscriptions. Subscription: $10/year, $19/2 years. **Sample postpaid: $5. Submit up to 10 poems at a time. Simultaneous submissions OK. Reads submissions September 1 through May 1 only. Reports in 1-4 months. Pays 1 copy, a year's subscription plus monetary payment (if funding allows). Acquires first North American serial rights.** Reviews books of poetry. Send books for review consideration also between September 1 and May 1. Send SASE for guidelines for the next 49th Parallel Poetry Award and query regarding book publication before sending a ms.

BELLOWING ARK PRESS; BELLOWING ARK (II), P.O. Box 45637, Seattle WA 98145, phone (206)545-8302, founded 1984, editor Robert R. Ward. *Bellowing Ark* is a bimonthly literary tabloid that **"publishes only poetry which demonstrates in some way the proposition that existence has meaning or, to put it another way, that life is worth living. We have no strictures as to length, form or style; only that the work we publish is to our judgment life-affirming." They do not want "academic poetry, in any of its manifold forms."** They have recently published poetry by Benjamin Green, Jay Udall, Crysta Casey, Peter Russell, Hannah B. Adams, Muriel Karr and Teresa Noelle Roberts. As a sample the editor selected these lines from "Air with Air—for the Marriage of Paula and Robert" by Margaret Hodge:

> *Those who weave nature sounds with music*
> *say air can relieve the mind, played*
>
> *through soothing flute, spirited penny whistle,*
> *the slow jig of an ocean storm,*
>
> *skirling wind lifting a tent flap.*
> *Air signs who marry bring this to mind.*
>
> *Here on water and land, friends learn*
> *of the distant wedding by surprise.*
>
> *We leave part of the wishes we could give them*
> *up in the air, think of hugs to keep them grounded.*

The paper is 32 pgs., tabloid-sized, printed on electrobright stock with b&w photos and line drawings. It is a lively publication. Almost every poem is accessible, enjoyable and stimulating. All styles seem to be welcome—even long, sequence poems and formal verse. Circulation is 1,000, of which 200 are subscriptions and 600 are sold on newsstands. Subscription: $15/year. **Sample postpaid: $3. Submit 3-6 poems at a time. "Absolutely *no* simultaneous submissions." They reply to submissions in 2-6 weeks and publish within the next 1 or 2 issues. Occasionally they will criticize a ms if it seems to "display potential to become the kind of work we want." Sometimes sends prepublication galleys. Pays 2 copies.** Reviews books of poetry. Send books for review consideration. Bellowing Ark Press publishes collections of poetry by invitation only.

BELL'S LETTERS POET (I, IV-Subscribers), P.O. Box 2187, Gulfport MS 39505-2187, founded 1956, publisher and editor Jim Bell, is a quarterly which **you must buy ($5/issue, $20 subscription) to be included.** The editor says "many say they stop everything the day it arrives," and judging by the many letters from readers, that seems to be the case. **Though there is no payment for poetry accepted, many patrons send awards of $5-20 to the poets whose work they especially like. Poems are "4 to 20 lines in good taste."** They have recently published poetry by Paul Pross, A.L. Dotson, James Wilson and Winnie Fitzpatrick. As a sample of the spirit of *BL* poetry the editor selected these lines from "The Stalker" by Deborah Vandereyk:

> *Hurriedly moving on*
> *I hear a voice say, "where will you*
> *go?" as it darts up and down.*
> *Various shades of gray*
> *slip through my mind, only*
> *to develop into a dim configuration.*
>
> *Past opportunities and future possibilities*
> *begin to take shape.*
> *Once again I turn to notice my*

shadow, as I swiftly move on . . .
BL is 64 pgs., digest-sized, offset from typescript on plain bond paper (including cover). **Sample (including guidelines) postpaid: $5. Submit 4 poems a year. Ms may be typed or even handwritten. No simultaneous submissions. Previously published poems OK "if cleared by author with prior publisher." Accepted poems by subscribers go immediately into the next issue. Deadline for poetry submissions is 3 months prior to publication.** Reviews books of poetry by subscribers in "one abbreviated paragraph." "The Ratings" is a competition in each issue. Readers are asked to vote on their favorite poems, and the ratings are announced in the next issue, along with awards sent to the poets by patrons. *BL* also features a telephone exchange among poets and a birth-date listing. *BL* celebrated its 40th anniversary in 1996. The editor asks, "Tired of seeing no bylines this year? Subscription guarantees a byline in each issue."

THE BELOIT POETRY JOURNAL; CHAD WALSH POETRY PRIZE (II)

THE BELOIT POETRY JOURNAL; CHAD WALSH POETRY PRIZE (II), RFD 2, Box 154, Ellsworth ME 04605-9616, phone (207)667-5598, founded 1950, editor Marion K. Stocking, is a well-known, long-standing quarterly of quality poetry and reviews. **"We publish the best poems we receive, without bias as to length, school, subject or form**. It is our hope to discover the growing tip of poetry and to introduce new poets alongside established writers. **We publish occasional chapbooks on special themes to diversify our offerings."** They want **"fresh, imaginative poetry, with a distinctive voice. We tend to prefer poems that make the reader share an experience rather than just read about it, and these we keep for up to 3 months,** circulating them among our readers, and continuing to winnow out the best. At the quarterly meetings of the Editorial Board we read aloud all the surviving poems and put together an issue of the best we have." They have recently published poetry by Hillel Schwartz, Molly Tenenbaum, Albert Goldbarth and Sharon Olds. As a sample the editor selected these lines from "Defending Walt Whitman" by Sherman Alexie:

God, there is beauty in every body. Walt Whitman stands
at center court while the Indian boys run from basket to basket.
Walt Whitman cannot tell the difference between
offense and defense. He does not care if he touches the ball.
Half of the Indian boys wear t-shirts damp with sweat
and the other half are bareback, skin slick and shiny.
There is no place like this. Walt Whitman smiles.
Walt Whitman shakes. This game belongs to him.

The journal is 48 pgs., digest-sized, saddle-stapled, and attractively printed with tasteful art on the card cover. All styles of verse—providing they articulate ideas or emotions intelligently and concisely—are featured. The editor is also keen on providing as much space as possible for poems and so does not include contributors' notes. They have a circulation of 1,400 for 575 subscribers of which 325 are libraries. **Sample copy with guidelines: $4. SASE for guidelines alone. Submit any time, without query, any legible form.** *"No previously published poems or simultaneous submissions.* **Any length of ms, but most poets send what will go in a business envelope for one stamp. Don't send your life's work."** No backlog: **"We clear the desk at each issue." Pays 3 copies. Acquires first serial rights.** Staff reviews books of poetry in an average of 500 words, usually single format. Send books for review consideration. The journal awards the Chad Walsh Poetry Prize ($3,500 in 1995) to a poem or group of poems published in the calendar year. "Every poem published in 1997 will be considered for the 1997 prize." Poetry published in *The Beloit Poetry Journal* has also been included in *The Best American Poetry* (1994 and 1996) and *Pushcart Prize* anthologies. The editor says, "We'd like to see more strong, imaginative, experimental poetry; more poetry with a global vision; and more poetry with fresh, vigorous language."

BENEATH THE SURFACE (II)

BENEATH THE SURFACE (II), % The Dept. of English, Chester New Hall, McMaster University, Hamilton, Ontario L8S 4L9 Canada, e-mail u9316827@muss.CIS.mcmaster.ca, founded 1911, editor changes yearly, is a biannual using **"top quality poetry/prose that achieves universality through individual expression."** They want **"quality poetry; any form; no restrictions." Also interested in short stories.** They have published poetry by Dorothy Livesky and John Barlow. As a sample the editor selected these lines from "Johnny Kneels On" by Sean Brendan-Brown:

Johnny kneels on
red plastic prayer pad
and thinks how weird it is
Major is a priest
when Moses said thoushaltnotkill
and Jesus said dountoothers
but Johnny kneels on.

BTS is 30-50 pgs., professionally printed, saddle-stapled, with cover art, drawings and b&w photographs. They receive about 250 submissions/year, use approximately 10%. Press run is 150 for 8 subscribers of which 3 are libraries, 92 shelf sales. Subscription: $8/year. **Sample postpaid: $4. No previously published poems or simultaneous submissions. Submit poems with cover letter, includ-**

ing short bio and summary of previous publications, if any. E-mail submissions welcome until April 1997. Reads submissions September through April only. Pays 1 copy. Acquires first North American serial rights. Rarely reviews books of poetry, "though we do include literary essays when submitted."

BENNETT & KITCHEL (IV-Form), P.O. Box 4422, East Lansing MI 48826, phone (517)355-1707, founded 1989, editor William Whallon, publishes 1-3 hardbacks/year of **"poetry of form and meaning. No free verse or blank verse, no sestinas or haiku."** As an example of what he admires, the editor selected these lines by Rhina P. Espaillat:

> Aloof from self, the apple tree
> regretless shall unbloom to death;
> my epitaph's in every breath:
> "Remember me, remember me."

Bennett & Kitchel has recently published *Severe* by Anthony Lombardy. **Sample postpaid: $8. Simultaneous submissions and previously published poems OK if copyright is clear. Minimum volume for a book "might be 750 lines."** If a book is accepted, publication is within 9 months. Editor seldom comments on submissions. Reports in 2 weeks. Terms are "variable, negotiable." He remarks, "To make a bad rhyme not from incompetence but willfully is like stubbing your toe on purpose."

BERKELEY POETRY REVIEW (II), 201 Heller Lounge, University of California, Berkeley CA 94720-4500, founded 1973, is an annual review "which publishes poems and translations of local as well as national and international interest. **We are open to a broad range of poetry but are always looking for innovation."** They have recently published poetry by Bob Hass, Lyn Hejinian, Albert Goldbarth, Ishmael Reed and Thom Gunn. The editors describe it as a flat-spined paperback, averaging 150 pgs. Circulation 500. Subscription: $10/year. **Submit 4 poems at a time *with SASE*. No previously published poems or simultaneous submissions. Reads submissions September through March only. Reports in 1-3 months. Pays 1 copy.**

‡BIG HEAD PRESS; BIG HEAD PRESS BROADSIDE SERIES (V), P.O. Box 17657, Beverly Hills CA 90209-3657, founded 1991, editor Scott C. Holstad, associate editor Lisa Lundgren. **"Note: We will not be reading any submissions until July, 1997. Social commentary preferred. 40 lines max. No love poetry."** They have published poetry by Antler, Rod Farmer, Arthur Winfield Knight, Lyn Lifshin and Robert Howington. As a sample the editor selected these lines from "Do You Mind" by Sal Salasin:

> Some are born to greatness
> and some have greatness thrust
> upon them for blowing off the
> hands and feet of Nicaraguan
> coffee harvesters.
> The rest of us are
> forced to work.

Broadsides are printed on 4½ × 8 card stock, with author's photo and bio. Of hundreds of submissions, they say they accept 10-15 poems/year. Press run is 250-500, most distributed free. **Sample broadside: $1. Beginning in July 1997, submit 4-10 poems with b&w photo. Previously published poems and simultaneous submissions OK, if noted. Cover letter with brief bio and phone number required.** Time between acceptance and publication is 6-15 months. **Often comments on rejections. Send SASE for guidelines. Reports in 2 weeks to 3 months. Pays 10-15 copies. Acquires one-time rights. "Due to financial constraints, we currently require full subsidation for chapbooks."** Authors then receive 50% of press run. Sample chapbook: $3. The editor says they would like to see "more politically didactic material."

BILINGUAL REVIEW PRESS; BILINGUAL REVIEW/REVISTA BILINGÜE (IV-Ethnic/Hispanic, bilingual/Spanish), Hispanic Research Center, Arizona State University, Box 872702, Tempe AZ 85287-2702, phone (602)965-3867, journal founded 1974, press in 1976. Managing editor Karen Van Hooft says they are "a small press publisher of U.S. Hispanic creative literature and of a journal containing poetry and short fiction in addition to scholarship." The journal contains some poetry in each issue; they also publish flat-spined paperback collections of poetry. **"We publish poetry by and/or about U.S. Hispanics and U.S. Hispanic themes. We do not publish translations in our journal or literature about the experiences of Anglo Americans in Latin America. We have published a couple of poetry volumes in bilingual format (Spanish/English) of important Mexican poets."** They have published poetry by Alberto Ríos, Martín Espada, Judith Ortiz Cofer and Marjorie Agosín. The editor says the journal, which appears 3 times a year, is 96 pgs., 7 × 10, offset and flat-spined with 2-color cover. They use less than 10% of hundreds of submissions received each year. Press run is 2,000 for 1,200 subscriptions. Subscriptions are $18 for individuals, $32 for institutions. **Sample postpaid: $6 individuals/$11 institutions. Submit "2 copies, including ribbon original if possible, with loose stamps for return postage." Cover letter required. Pays 2 copies. Acquires all rights.** Reviews books of US Hispanic literature only. Send books, Attn: Editor, for review consideration. **For book submissions, inquire first with 4-5 sample poems, bio and publication credits. Pays $200 advance, 10% royalties and 10 copies.** Over the years, books by this press have won five American Book Awards and two Western States Book Awards.

BIRMINGHAM POETRY REVIEW (II, IV-Translations), English Dept., University of Alabama at Birmingham, Birmingham AL 35294, phone (205)934-8573, founded 1988, co-editors Robert Collins and Randy Blythe. The review appears twice a year using poetry of **"any style, form, length or subject. We are biased toward exploring the cutting edge of contemporary poetry. Style is secondary to the energy, the *fire* the poem possesses. We don't want poetry with cliché-bound, worn-out language."** They have published poetry by Hague, Hopes, McDonald, Richards, Call and Miltner. As a sample the editors selected these lines from "Charisma Revisited" by Brendan Galvin:

> *Still, there was something to be said*
> *for their peasant reticence, though*
> *it leaves us confounded as to why*
> *the country has been empty*
> *these hundred years.*

They describe their magazine as 50 pgs., 6×9, offset, with b&w cover. Press run is 700 for 300 subscribers. Subscription: $4/year; $7/2 years. **Sample postpaid: $2. Submit 3-5 poems, "no more. No cover letters. We are impressed by good writing; we are unimpressed by publication credits." SASE required. No simultaneous or multiple submissions, and previously published poems only if they are translations. Editor sometimes comments on rejections. Send SASE for guidelines. Reports in 1-4 months. Pays 2 copies and one-year subscription.** They say, "Advice to beginners: Read as much good contemporary poetry, national and international, as you can get your hands on. Then be persistent in finding your own voice."

BISHOP PUBLISHING CO. (IV-Specialized), 2131 Trimble Way, Sacramento CA 95825, phone (916)971-4987, professor Roland Dickison, is a "small press publisher of **folklore in paperbacks, including contemporary** and out-of-print."

BITS PRESS (V), English Dept., Case Western Reserve University, Cleveland OH 44106, phone (216)795-2810, founded 1974, poetry editor Robert Wallace. **"Bits Press is devoted to poetry. We publish chapbooks (and sometimes limited editions) by young as well as well-known poets."** However, they are currently inactive.

‡**BKMK PRESS (II)**, University House, University of Missouri-Kansas City, 5101 Rockhill Rd., Kansas City MO 64110-2499, phone (816)235-2558, fax (816)235-2611, founded 1971, associate editor Michelle Boisseau, managing editor Kelly Freeman, generally publishes 4-5 paperbacks and 1-3 chapbooks a year. BkMk Press seeks to publish "well-known and beginning poets fairly and equally." **They have no specifications regarding form, length or subject matter but do not want to see "pretentious, unserious poetry."** They have published books of poetry by Howard Schwartz and Neal Bowers. Their books are generally 64 pgs., 5½×8½, professionally printed and perfect-bound with laminated covers with art and photographs. **Query first with sample poems and a cover letter with brief bio and publication credits. Previously published poems and simultaneous submissions OK.** Seldom comments on rejections. **Replies to queries in 1 month, to mss in 1-3 months. Pays 10% royalties and 20 author's copies (out of a press run of 600).** Call or write for catalog to order samples.

BLACK BEAR PUBLICATIONS; BLACK BEAR REVIEW (II, IV-Social issues), 1916 Lincoln St., Croydon PA 19021-8026, founded 1984, poetry and art editor Ave Jeanne, review editor Ron Zettlemoyer. *Black Bear Review* is a semiannual international literary and fine arts magazine that also publishes chapbooks and holds an annual poetry competition. **"We like well-crafted poetry that mirrors real life—void of camouflage, energetic poetry, avant-garde, free verse and haiku which relate to the world today. We seldom publish the beginner, but will assist when time allows. No traditional poetry is used. The underlying theme of *BBR* is social and political, but the review is interested also in environmental, war/peace, ecological and minorities themes. We would like to receive more ideas on AIDS awareness, life styles and current political topics."** Poets recently published in *BBR* include Richard Peabody, John Grey, R.M. Host, John Sullivan, Sean Brendan-Brown and Marc Swan. As a sample from *BBR*, the editor selected these lines from "Windshield Washer" by Ben Passikoff:

> *My face is sidewalk*
> *printed with the cities*
> *that left me in weather.*

> *My pants stay up with stolen rope.*
> *If I own soul*
> *it radiates tatters*
> *that stitch my skin*
> *together by inference. . . .*

BBR is 64 pgs., digest-sized, perfect-bound, offset from typed copy on white stock, with line drawings, collages and woodcuts. Circulation is 500 for 300 subscribers of which 15 are libraries. Subscription: $10, $15 overseas. **Sample postpaid: $5; back copies when available are $4. Submit 5 poems at a time, one to a page. "Please have name and address on each page of your submissions." Simultaneous submissions are not considered. "Submissions without SASE will be discarded."** Time between acceptance and publication is 6 months. **Send SASE for guidelines. Reports in 2 weeks. Pays contributor's copy. Acquires first North American serial rights.** Considers reviews of books of poetry and recent issues of literary magazines, maximum 250 words. Send books for review consideration. **They also publish 2 chapbooks/year.** Published: *Rubato Jitter* by John Sullivan. **Chapbook series requires a reading fee of $5, complete ms and cover letter. Send SASE for guidelines.** For book publication, they require that *"BBR* has published the poet and is familiar with his/her work." **Author receives one-half print run.** They say, "We appreciate a friendly, brief cover letter. Tell us about the poet; omit degrees or any other pretentious dribble. All submissions are handled with objectivity and quite often rejected material is directed to another market. If you've not been published before—mention it. We are always interested in aiding those who support small press. We frequently suggest poets keep up with the current edition of *Poet's Market* and read the listings and reviews in issues of *Black Bear*. Most recent issues of *BBR* include reviews on small press markets—current releases of chapbooks and the latest literary magazines. We make an effort to keep our readers informed and on top of the small press scene. Camera-ready ads are printed free of charge as a support to small press publishers. We do suggest poets and artists read issues before submitting to absorb the flavor and save on wasted postage. Send your best! Our yearly poetry competition offers cash awards to poets." Deadline: November 1. Send SASE for guidelines. The editors add, "We receive too many submissions with the right topic but the wrong style. We do not have time for poems with 'dirty' words where no poetry surrounds them. We also do not want to see 'Hallmark' poetry."

BLACK BOOKS BULLETIN: WORDSWORK; THIRD WORLD PRESS (IV-Ethnic), 7822 S. Dobson, P.O. Box 19730, Chicago IL 60619, phone (312)651-0700, fax (312)651-7286. *BBB* is a periodic journal of Black culture, including **"Black literature and current issues facing the African-American community."** They have published poetry by Gil Scott Heron, Brian Gilmore, Sonia Sanchez, Keorapetse Kgositsile and Amiri Baraka. They also publish book reviews, essays, interviews, short stories and literary criticism. **Write, fax or call for further information.**

BLACK BOUGH (II, IV-Form), 7 Park Ave., Flemington NJ 08822, founded 1991, editor Charles Easter, is a triannual that publishes "haiku and related poetry that uses the Eastern form in the Western milieu." **They want "haiku, senryu, tanka, haibun (in particular) and sequences. No academic essays or extremely long poems."** They have recently published work by Nasira Alma, Jim Kacian and Yvonne Hardenbrook. As a sample the editor selected this haiku by Edward J. Rielly:

> *newborn boy*
> *wailing at the world,*
> *window fan on high*

bb is 30 pgs., digest-sized, professionally printed, saddle-stitched, with photos, no ads. They receive about 5,200 poems a year, use 5-10%. Press run is 200 for 100 subscribers. Subscription: $13.50. **Sample postpaid: $5. "Submit no more than 20 haiku; prefer several haiku/page."** No previously published poems or simultaneous submissions. Time between acceptance and publication is 3-6 months. **Comments on rejections "if requested." Reports in 1-2 months. Pays $1/verse, up to $4 for a long poem or haiku sequence. Acquires first rights.**

BLACK BUZZARD PRESS; BLACK BUZZARD REVIEW; VISIONS—INTERNA-TIONAL, THE WORLD JOURNAL OF ILLUSTRATED POETRY; THE BLACK BUZ-ZARD ILLUSTRATED POETRY CHAPBOOK SERIES; INTERNATIONAL—VISIONS POETRY SERIES (II), 1110 Seaton Lane, Falls Church VA 22046, founded 1979, poetry editor Bradley R. Strahan, associate editor Shirley G. Sullivan. "We are an independent nonsubsidized press

---

USE THE GENERAL INDEX to find the page number of a specific publisher. Also, if a publisher from last year's edition is not included in this edition, the General Index will tell you why.

dedicated to publishing fine accessible poetry and translation (particularly from lesser-known languages such as Armenian, Gaelic, Urdu, Vietnamese, etc.) accompanied by original illustrations of high quality in an attractive format. **We want to see work that is carefully crafted and exciting, that transfigures everyday experience or gives us a taste of something totally new; all styles except concrete and typographical 'poems.' Nothing purely sentimental. No self-indulgent breast beating. No sadism, sexism or bigotry. No unemotional pap. No copies of Robert Service or the like. Usually under 80 lines but will consider longer."** They have published poetry by Ted Hughes, Michael Mott, Louis Simpson, Marilyn Hacker, James Dickey, Naomi Shihab Nye and Lawrence Ferlinghetti. Bradley Strahan says that "no 4 lines can possibly do even minimal justice to our taste or interest!" *Visions*, a digest-sized, saddle-stapled magazine finely printed on high-quality paper, appears 3 times a year, uses 56 pages of poetry in each issue. Circulation 800 with 400 subscribers of which 50 are libraries. **Sample postpaid: $3.75. Current issue: $4.75.** They receive *well* over a thousand submissions each year, use 150, have a 3- to 18-month backlog. "*Visions* is international in both scope and content, publishing poets from all over the world and having readers in 48 U.S. states, Canada and 24 other countries." *Black Buzzard Review* is a "more or less annual informal journal, dedicated mostly to North American poets and entirely to original English-language poems. In *BBR*, we are taking a more wide-open stance on what we accept (including the slightly outrageous)." **Sample postpaid: $3.50. Current issue: $4.50.** It is 36 pgs., magazine-sized, side-stapled, with matte card cover. **Submit 3-6 poems at a time. "Poems must be readable (not faded or smudged) and *not* handwritten. We resent having to pay postage due, so use adequate postage! No more than 6 pages, please." No previously published poems or simultaneous submissions. Publishes theme issues. Send SASE for upcoming themes. Theme for Spring 1997 issue is Translations from Celtic tongues. Deadline: December 1, 1996. Reports in 3 days to 3 weeks. Pays 1 copy or $5-10 "if we get a grant." Buys first North American serial rights.** Staff reviews books of poetry in "up to 2 paragraphs." Send books for review consideration. **To submit for the chapbook series, send samples (5-10 poems) and a *brief* cover letter "pertinent to artistic accomplishments." Reports in 3 days to 3 weeks. Pays in copies. Usually provides criticism. Send $4 for sample chapbook.** They also publish the International-Visions Poetry Series. Send SASE for flyer describing titles and order information. Bradley Strahan adds that in *Visions* "We sometimes publish helpful advice about 'getting published' and the art and craft of poetry, and often discuss poets and the world of poetry on our editorial page."

‡**BLACK CROSS (I)**, 3121 Corto Place #2, Long Beach CA 90803, e-mail wstien@csulb.edu, website http://www.csulb.edu/~wstien, founded December 1995, editors Jim Guess and Erik Jensen, is a quarterly that features poetry and art "with a heavy-metal edge and mild touches of psychosis and perversion. **We want image heavy work, any length, subject, style or form. No greeting card rhymes. Don't be boring or lame."** They have recently published poetry by Rev. Randy Tin-Ear, Richard Craig, Kristine Sanders, Charles Ellik and Andrew Demcak. As a sample the editors selected "Divorce" by Erik D. Feten:

> "I've been divorced many times."
> *He stated this matter-of-factly as if he meant to say . . .*
> "I've changed my underwear many times."
> *The commonplace mutates with every new gray hair.*

Black Cross is 50 pgs., about 5½×8½, photocopied and saddle-stapled, with heavy card stock cover with b&w art and b&w cartoon-like art and collages inside. They receive about 350 poems a year, accept approximately 30%. Press run is 150 for 50 shelf sales. Subscription: $7.50/year. **Sample postpaid: $2. Make checks payable to James Guess. Submit 2-5 poems at a time. No previously published poems or simultaneous submissions. "Cover letters are appreciated, but not required. Electronic submissions are welcome. Postal submissions should be typed or at least legible." Comments on rejections if requested. Publishes theme issues. Send SASE for guidelines and upcoming themes. Brief guidelines are also included inside the magazine or can be obtained via e-mail or website. Reports in 1-4 weeks. Pays 1 copy. Acquires first rights.** Jim Guess says, "Particularly good submissions are featured on the *Black Cross* website. Online, poets can discover other internet resources relating to poetry, view art and poetry samples from various issues of the magazine, and find submission guidelines and updates." He adds, "The end result of any poem should be heavy images and killer lines that dismay your loved ones. Remember, fear your government, not your genitals."

BLACK MOUNTAIN REVIEW; LORIEN HOUSE (IV-Themes), P.O. Box 1112, Black Mountain NC 28711-1112, phone (704)669-6211, founded 1969, editor David A. Wilson. Lorien House is a small press publishing many books (poetry on a subsidy basis) and the literary periodical, *Black Mountain Review*. The review focuses on **work about American authors.** "Poetry is an important part of each issue, but **must be on the theme. If not, please do not send it.**" Recent themes have included William Faulkner, Margaret Mitchell and Sidney Lanier. As a sample the editor selected these lines from "Death Doesn't Like Crowds. It Comes To You When You're Alone." by Laurel Speer, published in *BMR* issue #9 on Tennessee Williams:

> *Tennessee Williams said that, but often it's not true.*
> *Death doesn't have to be discriminate. Sometimes you're*
> *caught in a crowd, hitting a beach, climbing a fence*
> *at a soccer match or biting into a fish sandwich*
> *at a fast food restaurant. Who knows?*

Send SASE for guidelines and upcoming themes. Pays small monetary amount plus 2 copies. Query regarding subsidized book publication. Editor comments on submissions "occasionally," and offers "full analysis and marketing help" for $1/typed page of poetry. "Only material with full return postage will be returned."

‡BLACK RIVER REVIEW (II, IV-Translations), Dept. PM, 855 Mildred Ave., Lorain OH 44052-1213, phone (216)244-9654, e-mail brr@freenet.lorain.oberlin.edu, founded 1985, poetry editor Sherlene Roush, editorial contact Kaye Coller or Deb Gilbert, is a literary annual using **"contemporary poetry, any style, form and subject matter, 50 line maximum (usually), poetry with insight, energy and a distinctive voice. Do** *not* **want Helen Steiner Rice, greeting card verse, poetry that mistakes stilted, false or formulaic diction for intense expression of feeling. We receive too many well-written, polished poems that have nothing to distinguish them from the thousands of other well-written, polished poems we've read over the years."** They have recently published poetry by Adrian Louis, Diane Glancy, Timothy Russell, B.Z. Niditch, Nathaniel Smith and Lyn Lifshin. As a sample the editor selected these lines from "The River's Wife" by Sandra Reiff:

> *The River's Wife*
> *was dry as a hymn*
> *he was deep   cunning*
> *able to shed his skin*
> *   they were fated for each other*
> *She'd sit and watch the traffic*
> *in lost souls*
> *recede across his muscles*
> *   an enigma*
> *she couldn't hold him   he was slippery*
> *fleeting   fascinating how*
> *he got into her mind*
> *and out came gates   fences   walls*
> *   whole cities*

BRR is about 60 pgs., magazine-sized, offset printed on quality stock, saddle-stapled with glossy cover with art. Circulation is 400 (sold in college and area bookstores and by mail). **Sample: $3.50 (back copy); $4 (current issue); plus $1.50 p&h. Prefers no simultaneous submissions but will consider with the understanding that no submission may be withdrawn after May 1. Will consider previously published poems if acknowledged. Submit between January and May 1. Send SASE for guidelines or request via e-mail. Pays 1 copy.** Reviews books of poetry. Kaye Coller comments, "We want strong poems that show a depth of vision beyond the commonplace. We don't care if a poet is well-known or not, but we don't publish amateurs. An amateur is not necessarily a new poet, but one who doesn't believe in revision, tends to be preachy, writes sentimental slush, tells the reader what to think and/or concludes the poem with an explanation in case the reader didn't get the point. If we think we can use one or more of a poet's poems, we keep them until the final choices are made in June; otherwise, we send them back as soon as possible. Follow the ms mechanics in *Poet's Market*. **We are also looking for poems written in Spanish. If selected, they will be published with English translation by either the poet or one of our staff."**

THE BLACK SCHOLAR; THE BLACK SCHOLAR PRESS (IV-Ethnic), P.O. Box 2869, Oakland CA 94618, founded 1969, publisher Robert Chrisman, uses **poetry "relating to/from/of the black American and other 'Third World' experience."** The quarterly magazine is basically scholarly and research-oriented. They have published poetry by Ntozake Shange, Jayne Cortez, Andrew Salkey and D.L. Smith. The editor says it is 64 pgs., 7×10, with 10,000 subscribers of which 60% are libraries, 15% shelf sales. "We only publish one issue every year containing poetry." Subscription: $30, institutions $60; foreign $45, foreign institutions $75. **Sample issue: $6, institutions $10. Enclose "letter and bio or curriculum vita, SASE, phone number, no originals." Send SASE for guidelines. Pays 10 copies and subscription.** Reviews books of poetry. They also publish 1-2 books a year, average 100 pgs., flat-spined. **Send query letter. For sample books, send $8\frac{1}{2} \times 11$ SASE for catalog, average cost $10.95 including p&h.** The publisher says, "Please be advised—it is against our policy to discuss submissions via telephone. Also, we get a lot of mss, but read *every single one,* thus patience is appreciated."

BLACK SHEETS (III, IV-Erotica, themes, gay/lesbian/bisexual), P.O. Box 31155, San Francisco CA 94131-0155, fax (415)431-0172, e-mail blackb@ios.com, website http://www.queernet.org/

BlackBooks, founded 1993, editor Bill Brent, appears 3-4 times a year. *Black Sheets* is "a kinky, queer, intelligent, and irreverent zine of sex and popular culture." **They want "sexual outlaw poetry that is sexy, thought-provoking and funny. We are a sex zine, so don't send any non-erotic poetry. Any sexual orientation or gender is fine. Don't submit unless you have bought a sample issue first. Also, each issue has a specific theme and poets have a better chance if their themes conform to ours. A schedule is sent with the purchase of a sample issue."** They have recently published poetry by Simon Sheppard, Trebor Healey, Dossie Easton and Keith Hennessy. As a sample the editor selected these lines from "this really happened on 8/25/93," a poem of his own:

> *"hi i'm bill what's your name"*
> *"ramon"*
> *he smiles*
> *my dick is a rock i want to throw at him*

Black Sheets is 52 pgs., 8½×11, offset and saddle-stitched with a 2- to 3-color glossy cover and cartoons and illustrations. Much of the content—from graphics to writing to ads—is sexually explicit. They accept about 5% of the poetry received and publish up to 6 poems each issue. Press run is 3,000 for 200 subscribers, 1,000 shelf sales and 300 additional single copy sales. Subscription: $20 for 4 issues. **Sample postpaid: $7, age statement required. Previously published poems and simultaneous submissions OK. IBM-compatible disk submissions OK.** Time between acceptance and publication is 6 months to 1 year. **Occasionally comments on rejections. Reports anywhere from 1-6 months. Pays $5/poem and 1 copy. Requires signed agreement before publication. Prefers to retain anthology rights for possible "best of" collections.** Open to unsolicited reviews. The editor says, "Truth is brief. We prefer graphic to romantic, terse to verbose."

BLACK TIE PRESS (III), P.O. Box 440004, Houston TX 77244-0004, fax (713)789-5119, founded 1986, publisher and editor Peter Gravis. "Black Tie Press is committed to publishing innovative, distinctive and engaging writing. We publish books; we are not a magazine or literary journal. We are not like the major Eastern presses, university presses or other small presses in poetic disposition. To get a feel for our publishing attitude, we urge you to buy one or more of our publications before submitting." He is **"only interested in imaginative, provocative, at risk writing. No rhyme."** They have published poetry by Steve Wilson, Guy Beining, Sekou Karanja, Craig Cotter, Harry Burrus, Dieter Weslowski, Laura Ryder, Toni Ortner and Jenny Kelly. As a sample the editor selected these lines from "Prediction" in *Duende* by Donald Rawley:

> *I am the child of black crows,*
> *iguanas and all monsters of balana.*
> *I am cagey limbed,*
> *fetal lipped and mute.*
>
> *I am cut at the stalk and bled.*

Sample postpaid: $8. "We have work we want to publish, hence, unsolicited material is not encouraged. However, we will read and consider material from committed, serious writers as time permits. Query with 4 sample poems. Write, do not call about material. *No reply without SASE.*" Cover letter with bio preferred. Reports in 2-6 weeks. Always sends prepublication galleys. Author receives percent of press run. Peter Gravis says, "Too many writers are only interested in getting published and not interested in reading or supporting good writing. Black Tie hesitates to endorse a writer who does not, in turn, promote and patronize (by actual purchases) small press publications. Once Black Tie publishes a writer, we intend to remain with that artist."

THE BLACK WARRIOR REVIEW (II), P.O. Box 2936, Tuscaloosa AL 35486-2936, founded 1974, is a semiannual review. They have recently published poetry by David Wojahn, Lisel Mueller, Brendan Galvin and Dara Wier. As a sample the editor selected these lines from "Coleman Valley Road" by Gerald Stern:

> *The strings are stretched across the sky; one note*
> *is almost endless—pitiless I'd say*
> *except for the slight sagging; one note is*
> *like a voice, it almost has words, it sings*
> *and sighs, it cracks with desire, it sobs with fatigue.*
> *It is the loudest sound of all. A shrieking.*

BWR is 200 pgs., 6×9. Circulation is 2,000. **Sample postpaid: $6. Address submissions to Poetry Editor. Submit 3-6 poems at a time. Simultaneous submissions OK if noted. Send SASE for guidelines. Reports in 1-3 months. Pays $30-45/poem plus 2 copies. Buys first rights.** Awards one $500 prize annually to a poet whose work appeared in either the fall or spring issue. Reviews books of poetry in single or multi-book format. Open to unsolicited reviews. Poets may also send books for review consideration to Mindy Wilson, editor. Poetry published in *BWR* has been included in *The Best American Poetry 1993*. The editor says, "We solicit a nationally-known poet for a chapbook section. The remainder of the issue is chosen from unsolicited submissions. Many of our poets have substantial publication credits, but our decision is based simply on the quality of the work submitted."

BLANK GUN SILENCER; BGS PRESS (II), 1240 William St., Racine WI 53402, phone (414)639-2406, founded 1991, editor Dan Nielsen, is "an independent art/lit mag" which appears twice a year "publishing Buk-heads, post Dada freaks and everything in between." **They want poetry that is "tight, concise, startling, funny, honest, causing leaps of recognition—a good solid kick in the head. Nothing flowery, overly 'poetic,' too academic, rhyming or blatantly pointless."** They have published poetry by Charles Bukowski, Gerald Locklin, Fred Voss and Ron Androla. As a sample the editor selected these lines from "Edge" by Mark Weber:

> *where are my John Coltrane records?*
> *o, i sold them when*
> *i was a junkie*
> *they sold good*
> *but now i want to hear them*
> *need to hear the cycle of 5ths played backwards*
> *on "Giant Steps"*
> *one of the purest musicians ever*

The editor says *BGS* is 60-80 pgs., digest-sized, photocopied and saddle-stapled with card stock cover and b&w art. They accept approximately 200 poems a year. Press run is 300 for 50 subscribers of which 7 are libraries. Single copy: $4; subscription: $8. **Sample postpaid: $3. Submit 6 poems at a time. Fresh copies preferred. Previously published poems OK, if notified. No simultaneous submissions. Cover letter required.** Time between acceptance and publication is up to 1 year. **Often comments on rejections. Send SASE for guidelines. Reports within 3 months. Pays up to 3 copies. Acquires first or one-time rights.** Reviews books of poetry in up to 3 pages. Open to unsolicited reviews. Poets may also send books for review consideration. BGS Press **publishes 4 chapbooks/ year. Query first with sample poems and cover letter with bio and publication credits. Replies to queries in 1 week, to mss within 1 month. Sometimes sends prepublication galleys. Pays 30 copies. For sample chapbook, send $2.**

BLIND BEGGAR PRESS; LAMPLIGHT EDITIONS; NEW RAIN (IV-Ethnic, anthology, children), P.O. Box 437, Williamsbridge Station, Bronx NY 10467, phone/fax (914)683-6792, founded 1976, literary editor Gary Johnston, business manager C.D. Grant, publishes **work "relevant to Black and Third World people, especially women."** *New Rain* is an annual anthology of such work. Lamplight Editions is a subsidiary which publishes "educational materials such as children's books, manuals, greeting cards with educational material in them, etc." They want to see **"quality work that shows a concern for the human condition and the condition of the world—art for people sake."** They have published work by Judy D. Simmons, A.H. Reynolds, Mariah Britton, Kurt Lampkin, Rashidah Ismaili, Jose L. Garza and Carletta Wilson. As a sample the editor selected the opening lines of Brenda Connor-Bey's "Crossroad of the Serpent":

> *Like a serpent*
> *splitting open fields*
> *this road always brings me back*
> *to this magical place of healing*
> *to this place of hidden waters*

New Rain is a 60- to 200-page chapbook, digest-sized, finely printed, saddle-stapled or perfect-bound, with simple art, card covers. **Sample postpaid: $5.** They also publish about 3 collections of poetry by individuals each year, 60-100 pgs., flat-spined paperback, glossy, color cover, good printing on good paper. **Sample: $5.95. For either the anthology or book publication, first send sample of 5-10 poems with cover letter including biographical background, philosophy and poetic principles. Considers simultaneous submissions. Reads submissions January 15 through September 1 only. Replies to queries in 3-4 weeks, to submissions in 2-3 months. Pays copies (the number depending on the print run). Acquires all rights. Returns them "unconditionally."** Willing to work out individual terms for subsidy publication. Catalog available for SASE.

‡**THE BLIND HORSE REVIEW (II)**, P.O. Box 81305, Lincoln NE 68501-1305, founded 1992, editor Todd Kalinski, assistant editor Brett Kunde, is a poetry and prose publication that appears about twice a year. **They do not want poetry that is "overtly sentimental in nature. No particular qualms as to length, and subject matter or language may be what it may [and they mean that]. No academic writing for the sake of strictly writing it, and no globs of despair for no sensible reason."** They have recently published poetry by Kurt Nimmo, Steve Richmond, Cheryl Townsend and Gerald Locklin. As a sample the editor selected these lines from "Locked Out" by Chris Mortenson:

> *It would be preferable to contemplate*
> *and to discuss important things*
> *but most people don't.*

Humanity more easily accepts the insubstantial,
though some have a bit more depth,
it is not much.

The Blind Horse Review is 36-48 pgs., digest-sized and saddle-stapled with heavy, colored, matte paper cover. They accept about 5% of the poetry received and feature 11-14 writers in each issue. Press run is 300 for 50 subscribers. Subscription: $13 for 3 issues. **Sample postpaid: $5. Make checks payable to Todd Kalinski. Submit 10 poems at a time. No previously published poems or simultaneous submissions. Include SASE "and, if you may, a cover letter without awards and publications, but a letter of interest, something maybe of insight." Often comments on rejections. Send SASE for guidelines. Reports in up to 1 month. Pays 1 copy. Rights revert to authors.** The editor says, "Type yourself into a certain sensibility that one can actually persevere in this vocation; because it doesn't seem to come easily to most of the writers writing today."

BLOCK'S POETRY COLLECTION; BLOCK PUBLICATIONS (II), 1419 Chapin St., Beloit WI 53511-5601, founded 1993, editor Alan J. Block, is a quarterly. **"Poems of shorter length (two pages or less), high quality and unique perspective have a home here. We also publish poetry-related reviews and b&w artwork." They do not want erotica or religious verse.** They have recently published poetry by Robert K. Johnson, Pearl Mary Wilshaw and John Grey. As a sample the editor selected these lines from "Intervention" by Corrine DeWinter:

Clio lingers over Ambrosia,
Licking the tips of her fingers
As she contemplates
The casualty of time.
The sand convenes
Around her toes.

The editor says *BPC* is 60 pgs., 5½ × 8½, offset, saddle-stapled, with cover art and ads. Press run is 500 for 50 subscribers. Subscription: $20. **Sample postpaid: $6. Submit 5 poems at a time. No previously published poems or simultaneous submissions.** Time between acceptance and publication is 6-8 months. **Always comments on rejections. Reports in 1-3 months. Pays copies.** Awards 4-issue subscription to best poet in each issue; $100 award to poet of the year. The editor says, "I am open to most kinds of poetry. I see too much trite verse and not enough skillful rhyme. If you submit, be prepared to receive critical comments with returned poems."

BLOODREAMS: A MAGAZINE OF VAMPIRES & WEREWOLVES (I, IV-Specialized), 1312 W. 43rd St., North Little Rock AR 72118, phone (501)771-2047, founded 1991, editor Kelly Gunter Atlas, is an annual appearing in October. They primarily publish short fiction, with poetry and artwork used as fillers. **"All styles of poetry (including traditional) are considered, but all poetry *must* relate to vampires or werewolves. We prefer poetry that is 25 lines or less, but will consider longer works if especially well-written. However, we do not accept poems which are longer than one typewritten page, single-spaced, unless solicited by the editor."** They have published poetry by Dirk Roaché and Lisa S. Laurencot. As a sample the editor selected these lines from Laurencot's "Mender of the Wounded Spring":

Wolf and Red Man, their mother, Dawn,
shared earth with seasons' wonders.
Ever round spring's pristine coils,
mirrored esteem thrust symbolic nexus.

Bloodreams is 40-50 pgs., 8½ × 11, computer typeset and photocopied on 20 lb. paper, bound by plastic spiral, with 60 lb. colored paper cover, b&w drawings and 3-5 pgs. of ads. They receive about 60 poems/year, use 4-5/issue. Press run is 100 for 75 subscribers. **Sample postpaid: $4. Make check or money order payable to Kelly Atlas. Submit up to 4 poems at a time. Previously published poems OK, if author includes name and date of publication. Cover letter required. Reads submissions February through July. "Poems are accepted or rejected depending on availability of space in the issue and on the impact the poem has on the editor." Seldom comments on rejections. Reports in 1-2 weeks. Pays 1 copy. Acquires one-time rights.** "We have a review column, 'Fang and Claw,' where books, comics and vampire/werewolf-related poetry chapbooks are reviewed. It varies from issue to issue." The editor says, "We look for poetry that has mood, atmosphere and description. Make us feel that we are not merely reading it, but experiencing it."

THE BLOWFISH CATALOG (IV-Erotica), 2261 Market St., #284, San Francisco CA 94114-1600, fax (415)864-1858, e-mail blowfish@blowfish.com, founded 1994, appears 2-3 times/year. "*The Blowfish Catalog* is a catalog of mail-order erotic products. **We include fiction and poetry as well and are interested in short, erotic pieces of any format. All material must be on the general subject of sex, sexuality, gender or related matters."** As a sample we selected these lines from "Hit and Run" by James E. Myers:

I ran over a myth last night

> *I think it might have been true love*
> *It wasn't really my fault*
> *It's always so dark out*
> *And the headlights don't help much*
> *Not really . . .*

The Blowfish Catalog is 64 pgs. (plus cover), 8½×11, web offset and saddle-stapled with a few b&w photos and graphics. The issue we received contained 2 poems. Press run is 10,000. **Sample postpaid: $3. Previously published poems and simultaneous submissions OK.** Time between acceptance and publication is 2 months. **Send SASE for guidelines. Reports in approximately 1 month. Pays $25-75. "We will also pay 25% additional in merchandise credit, if desired." Buys one-time rights.**

BLUE LIGHT PRESS (V), P.O. Box 642, Fairfield IA 52556, phone (515)472-7882, founded 1988, partner Diane Frank, publishes 3 paperbacks, 3 chapbooks/year. **"We like poems that are imagistic, emotionally honest and uplifting. Women, Visionary Poets, Iowa Poets, San Francisco Poets. No rhymed poetry or dark poetry." They are currently accepting work by invitation only. Interested poets should query.** They have published poetry by Rustin Larson, Nancy Berg, Viktor Tichy, Tom Centolella and Meg Fitz-Randolph. As a sample the editor selected these lines from *The Houses Are Covered in Sound* by Louise Nayer:

> *There was something*
> *moving in a garbage can,*
> *a white light glowing in a spiral.*
> *I thought it was a child,*
> *no the wind, no the part*
> *of myself that glowed.*

That book is 60 pgs., digest-sized, professionally printed and flat-spined with elegant matte card cover: $10. They have also published two anthologies of Iowa poets. They have an editorial board, and "work in person with local poets, have an ongoing poetry workshop, give classes, and will edit/critique poems by mail—$30 for 4-5 poems."

BLUE MESA REVIEW (II, IV-Themes), Dept. of English, Humanities Bldg. #217, University of New Mexico, Albuquerque NM 87131-1106, phone (505)277-6347, fax (505)277-5573, e-mail psprott@unm.edu, website http://www.unm.edu/~english/bluemesa/, founded 1989 by Rudolfo Anaya, managing editor Patricia Lynn Sprott, faculty editor Dr. David Johnson, is an annual review of poetry, short fiction, creative essays and book reviews. **They want "all kinds of free, organic verse; poems of place encouraged. No length limits; no greeting card verse."** They have recently published poetry by Virgil Suarez, David Axelrod and Brian Swann. As a sample they selected these lines from "Modern Love" by Robert Burlingame:

> *A lifetime, says Buddha,*
> *is like a flash of lightning, or*
> *a torrent rushing down a steep*
> *canyon. On this rainy afternoon,*
> *this close to the mountain, we*
> *confront these analogies.*

BMR is about 250 pgs., 6×9, professionally printed and flat-spined with glossy cover, photos and graphics. This hefty publication includes a number of long poems—several spanning three pages. They receive about 1,000 poems a year, accept 10% or less. Press run is 1,600 for 600 shelf sales. Single copy: $10. **Sample postpaid: $12. No previously published poems or simultaneous submissions. Cover letter required. Accepts mss from May 15 through October 31 only. Poems are then passed among readers and voted on. Seldom comments on rejections. Publishes special theme sections. Theme for the special section in the Spring 1997 issue is "Borderlands: Bilingual Literature from La Frontera." Send SASE for upcoming themes. Reports on mss by mid-December. Pays 2 copies.** Reviews books of poetry. Open to unsolicited reviews. Poets may also send books to Patricia Sprott for review consideration.

BLUE MOUNTAIN ARTS, INC. (IV-Specialized: greeting cards), Dept. PM, P.O. Box 1007, Boulder CO 80306-1007, e-mail bma@rmii.com, founded 1971, contact editorial staff. Blue Mountain Arts is a publisher of greeting cards, calendars, prints and mugs. They are looking for poems, prose and lyrics (**"usually nonrhyming"**) appropriate for publication on greeting cards and in poetry anthologies. "Poems should reflect a message, feeling or sentiment that one person would want to share with another. We'd like to receive **sensitive, original submissions about love relationships, family members, friendships, philosophies and any other aspect of life. Poems and writings for specific holidays (Christmas, Valentine's Day, etc.) and special occasions, such as graduation, anniversary and get well, are also considered.** Only a small portion of the material we receive is selected each year and the review process can be lengthy, but be assured every manuscript is given serious consideration." **Submissions must be typewritten, one poem/page or sent via e-mail. Prefers original material.**

Simultaneous submissions OK, "if notified of acceptance elsewhere." Submit seasonal material at least 4 months in advance. Send SASE for guidelines or request via e-mail. Reports in 3-6 months. Pays $200/poem for the worldwide, exclusive right to publish on a greeting card; $25/ poem for one-time use in an anthology. They advise, "We strongly suggest that you familiarize yourself with our products before submitting material, although we caution you not to study them too hard. We do not need more poems that sound like something we've already published. Overall, we're looking for poetry that expresses real emotions and feelings."

BLUE PENNY QUARTERLY (II), Metronetics Publications, 7 Elliewood Ave., 3rd Floor, Charlottesville VA 22903, e-mail imlac@aol.com (best way to contact), website http://ebbs.english.ut.edu/ olp/bpq/front-page.html, founded 1994, editor Doug Lawson, poetry editor Leigh Palmer (address submissions to "Poetry Editor"), is a quarterly designed to promote fine literature in the electronic communities. **"We welcome a variety of forms and themes—except inspirational verse, randomness jury-rigged to back up literary theory, and therapeutic journalism. We value the wild and the well-made."** They have recently published poetry by Ioana Ieronim (in translation), Wendy Battin, Eva Shaderowfsky and Robert Klein Engler. *BPQ* is an electronic publication, more than 100 pgs., using full-color artwork. It is printable by the reader's home computer and readers are encouraged to pass the software along to others. They accept 10% of the poetry received. **No previously published poems; simultaneous submissions OK. Cover letter required. Submissions via e-mail recommended as regular mail address may change.** Time between acceptance and publication is 1 month to 1 year. **Guidelines available via website. Reports in up to 3 months. Acquires first North American or one-time rights and electronic rights. Electronic rights returned upon request.** Reviews books of poetry in about 1,000 words. Open to unsolicited reviews. Poets may also send books for review consideration, attn: Doug Lawson. They also offer Readers' Choice Awards of $50 for the best poem of the issue and an Editor's Choice Award of $100 for the best poem published during the year.

BLUE UNICORN, A TRIQUARTERLY OF POETRY; BLUE UNICORN POETRY CONTEST (II, IV-Translations), 22 Avon Rd., Kensington CA 94707, phone (510)526-8439, founded 1977, poetry editors Ruth G. Iodice, Martha E. Bosworth and Fred Ostrander, wants **"well-crafted poetry of all kinds, in form or free verse, as well as expert translations on any subject matter. We shun the trite or inane, the soft-centered, the contrived poem. Shorter poems have more chance with us because of limited space."** They have published poetry by James Applewhite, Kim Cushman, Charles Edward Eaton, Patrick Worth Gray, Joan LaBombard, James Schevill, John Tagliabue and Gail White. As a sample the editors selected these lines from "Memory" by Harold Witt:

> At Jackie's funeral Caroline read a poem,
> "Memory of Cape Cod" by Edna Millay—
> the genteel first lady had heard the ash leaves blowing
> that sounded like the sea with its rustling spray;
> "we'll find you another beach like the beach at Truro—"
> a poem of memory that caught in her mind somehow
> and echoes still now she has no tomorrow,
> which is the thing memorable poems do.

Blue Unicorn is **"distinguished by its fastidious editing, both with regard to contents and format."** It is 56 pgs., narrow digest-sized, finely printed, saddle-stapled, with some art. It features 40-50 poems in each issue, all styles, with the focus on excellence and accessibility. They receive over 35,000 submissions a year, use about 200, have a year's backlog. **Sample postpaid: $5. Submit 3-5 typed poems on 8½×11 paper. No simultaneous submissions or previously published poems. "Cover letter OK, but will not affect our selection." Send SASE for guidelines. Reports in 1-3 months (generally within 6 weeks), sometimes with personal comment. Pays 1 copy.** They sponsor an annual contest with small entry fee, with prizes of $100, $75, $50 and sometimes special awards, distinguished poets as judges, publication of 3 top poems and 6 honorable mentions in the magazine. Entry fee: $4 for first poem, $3 for others to a maximum of 5. Write for current guidelines. **Criticism occasionally offered.** The editors add, "We would advise beginning poets to read and study poetry— both poets of the past and of the present; concentrate on technique; and **discipline yourself by learning forms before trying to do without them.** When your poem is crafted and ready for publication, study your markets and then send whatever of your work seems to be compatible with the magazine you are submitting to."

‡BLUE VIOLIN (II, IV-Form/style), P.O. Box 1175, Humble TX 77347-1175, founded 1995, editor Mary Agnes Dalrymple, is a biannual publication of free verse poetry. **The editor wants "free verse poetry *only*, no longer than 60 lines. Shorter poems have a better chance of being accepted."** *Blue Violin* is 40 pgs. (including cover), digest-sized, neatly printed and saddle-stapled with colored card cover and graphics done by the editor. She receives about 10,000 poems a year, accepts less than 1%. Press run is 200-300. Subscription: $10. **Sample postpaid: $5. Submit 3-7 poems at a time,**

Book I   January, 1996

As editor, publisher and cover artist of *Blue Violin*, Mary Agnes Dalrymple bases the illustrations she draws on the "feel" she gets from the poems selected for each issue. "Even though I do not have a theme in mind when I select poems, I am drawn to poems about people, and the difficulties we all face in our everyday lives. This drawing, entitled 'Consolation,' is about one of those difficult moments," says Dalrymple. Based in Humble, Texas, the biannual publication is solely devoted to free verse poetry. While Dalrymple says poetry is the reason for the publication's existence, she is quick to add that poems under 60 lines have a greater chance of being accepted.

typed one to a page, name and address on each. **"Please include SASE with proper postage."** Previously published poems and simultaneous submissions OK. **Cover letter and letter-sized envelope preferred.** Time between acceptance and publication is 6-12 months. **Often comments on rejections. Reports in 2-4 weeks. "Poets who are accepted receive a free copy of the issue in which their poem appears.** Patron donations are accepted (and greatly appreciated). Patrons receive a free copy and are named in subsequent issues. These funds help pay printing and postage costs."

BLUELINE (IV-Regional), Dept. PM, English Dept., Potsdam College, Potsdam NY 13676, fax (315)267-3256, e-mail tylerao@potsdam.edu, founded 1979, editor-in-chief Anthony Tyler, and an editorial board, "is an annual literary magazine dedicated to prose and **poetry about the Adirondacks and other regions similar in geography and spirit."** They want **"clear, concrete poetry pertinent to the countryside and its people. It must go beyond mere description, however. We prefer a realistic to a romantic view. We do not want to see sentimental or extremely experimental poetry."** They usually use poems of 75 lines or fewer, though "occasionally we publish longer poems" on "nature in general, Adirondack Mountains in particular. Form may vary, can be traditional or contemporary." They have published poetry by Phillip Booth, George Drew, Eric Ormsby, L.M. Rosenberg, John Unterecker, Lloyd Van Brunt, Laurence Josephs, Maurice Kenny and Nancy L. Nielsen. It's a handsomely printed, 112-page, 6×9 magazine with 40-45 pgs. of poetry in each issue. Circulation is 400. **Sample copies: $4 for back issues. Submit 5 poems at a time. Include short bio. No simultaneous submissions. Submit September 1 through November 30.** They have a 3- to 11-month backlog. **Occasionally comments on rejections. Send SASE for guidelines. Reports in 2-10 weeks. Pays copies. Acquires first North American serial rights.** Reviews books of poetry in 500-750 words, single and multi-book format. "We are interested in both beginning and established poets whose poems evoke universal themes in nature and show human interaction with the natural world. We look for **thoughtful craftsmanship rather than stylistic trickery."**

BOA EDITIONS, LTD. (IV), 92 Park Ave., Brockport NY 14420, phone (716)637-3844 or (716)546-3410, founded 1976, poetry editor A. Poulin, Jr., **"We regret that we cannot consider unsolicited manuscripts for publication. Due to restricted funds, our annual publishing schedule is very limited."** They have published some of the major American poets, such as W.D. Snodgrass, John Logan, Isabella Gardner, Richard Wilbur and Lucille Clifton, and they publish introductions by major poets of those less well-known. For example, Gerald Stern wrote the foreword for Li-Young Lee's *Rose*.

BOGG PUBLICATIONS; BOGG (II), 422 N. Cleveland St., Arlington VA 22201-1424, founded 1968, poetry editors John Elsberg (USA), George Cairncross (UK: 31 Belle Vue St., Filey, N. Yorkshire YO 14 9HU England), Sheila Martindale (Canada: P.O. Box 23148, 380 Wellington St., London, Ontario NGA 5N9 Canada) and Robert Boyce (Australia/New Zealand: 48 Academy Ave., Mulgrave,

Victoria 3170 Australia). "We publish *Bogg* magazine and occasional free-for-postage pamphlets."
The magazine uses a great deal of poetry in each issue (with several featured poets)—"**poetry in all
styles, with a healthy leavening of shorts (under 10 lines). Prefer original voices. Our emphasis
is on good work per se and Anglo-American cross-fertilization. We are always looking for American work with British/Commonwealth themes/references.**" This is one of the liveliest small press
magazines published today. It started in England and in 1975 began including a supplement of American
work; it now is published in the US and mixes US, Canadian, Australian and UK work with reviews
of small press publications from all of those areas. It's thick (68 pgs.), typeset, saddle-stitched, in a
6×9 format that leaves enough white space to let each poem stand and breathe alone. They have
recently published work by Jon Silkin, John Millett, Richard Peabody, Peter Bakowski, Elliot Richman,
Janine Pommy Vega and Laurel Speer. As a sample the editors selected these lines from "Wallace
Stevens and I try 'Oh Susannah'" by New Zealand poet Bernard Gadd:

> we image only too lucidly,
> wallace and i, ourselves among
> israel's elders spying spying
> from the branchy screens
> bright nipples loosing
> lucent drops upon the brown flesh

**They accept all styles, all subject matter. "Some have even found the magazine's sense of play
offensive. Overt religious and political poems have to have strong poetical merits—statement
alone is not sufficient. Submit 6 poems at a time. Prefer typewritten manuscripts, with author's
name and address on each sheet. We will reprint previously published material, but with a credit
line to a previous publisher." No simultaneous submissions. Cover letters preferred. "They can
help us get a 'feel' for the writer's intentions/slant." SASE required for return of ms.** There are
about 50 pgs. of poetry/issue. Press run is 850 for 400 subscribers of which 20 are libraries. Subscription: $12 for 3 issues. **Sample postpaid: $3.50.** They receive over 10,000 American poems/year, use
100-150. "We try to accept only for next 2 issues. SASE required or material discarded (no exceptions)." **Send SASE for guidelines. Reports in 1 week. Pays 2 copies. Acquires one-time rights.**
Reviews books and chapbooks of poetry in 250 words, single format. Open to unsolicited reviews.
Poets may also send books to relevant editor (by region) for review consideration. Their occasional
pamphlets and chapbooks are by invitation only, the author receiving 25% of the print run, and you
can get **chapbook samples free for 6×9 SASE.** Better make it at least 2 ounces worth of postage.
John Elsberg advises, "Become familiar with a magazine before submitting to it. Long lists of previous
credits irritate me. Short notes about how the writer has heard about *Bogg* or what he or she finds
interesting or annoying in the magazine I read with some interest."

‡**BOHEMIAN BRIDGE (II, IV-Regional)**, P.O. Box 1780, Shepherdstown WV 25443, founded
1993, is a bimonthly publication devoted to promoting the work of writers of the Appalachian region.
It contains poetry, short stories, quotes and a calendar of events. **They want poetry from Appalachian
writers. "Unlimited as to style or perspective; prefer less than 100 lines; new styles and innovation
welcome. No sentimental love poetry or religious poetry."** *Bohemian Bridge* is 44 pgs., approximately 7×8½, photocopied and saddle-stapled with heavy card stock cover and b&w graphics and
ads. They receive about 500 poems a year, accept approximately 10%. Press run is 300-500 for about
100 subscribers, 20-40 shelf sales. Subscription: $7.95 for 6 months, $14.95 yearly. **Sample postpaid:
$2.95. Submit up to 3 poems at a time, typed with name and address on each page. Previously
published poems and simultaneous submissions OK. Cover letter preferred. Often comments on
rejections. Send SASE for guidelines. Reports in approximately 2 months. Pays 1 copy. Acquires
one-time rights.**

BOHEMIAN CHRONICLE (I), P.O. Box 387, Largo FL 34649-0387, founded 1991, editor/pub-
lisher Emily Skinner, is a monthly publication "promoting sensitivity in the arts." **They want experimental poetry no longer than one page. No rhyming poetry.** They have recently published poetry
by Eileen Malone. The editor simply describes it as 12 pgs., stapled. They receive about 200 poems
a year, use 40. Press run is 500 for 100 subscribers, 400 sent abroad free. Subscription: $12. **Sample:
$1 and #10 SASE. Submit 4 poems maximum. No previously published poems; simultaneous
submissions OK. Reads submissions January through September only.** Time between acceptance
and publication is 9-12 months. **Always comments on rejections. Send SASE for guidelines. Reports
in 1-3 months. Pays $2 and 2 copies. Buys all rights or first rights. If all rights, does not return
them.** "We select the year's best for our anniversary issue and award Bohos to the best in each
category." The editor says, "We are not formula-oriented. We only buy what we like, good or bad."

BOMB MAGAZINE (III), 594 Broadway, Suite 905, New York NY 10012, founded 1981, managing
editor Lawrence Chua, is a quarterly magazine that "encourages a dialogue among artists of various
media. **Experiments with form and language are encouraged. No limericks, inspirational verse,
clever or greeting card styles.**" They have published poetry by David Mamet, Harold Pinter and

A.C. Purcell. As a sample the editors selected these lines by Agha Shahid Ali:

> *Cries Majnoon:*
> *Those in tatters*
> *May now demand love:*
> *I've declared a fashion*
> *of ripped collars.*
> *The breezes are lost*
> *travellers today,*
> *knocking, asking*
> *for a place to stay.*
> *I tell them*
> *to go away.*

Bomb is 96 pgs., saddle-stitched with 4-color cover. "We receive about 100 manuscripts a month; we accept 2 or 3 every 4 months." Press run is 12,000 for 2,000 subscribers of which 600 are libraries. Single copy: $4.50; subscription: $18/year. **Sample postpaid: $5. No previously published poems; simultaneous submissions OK. Cover letter including name, address, telephone number and previous publications required. "Poetry should be legibly typed."** Time between acceptance and publication is 4-6 months. **Reports in 4 months. Pays $50. Buys first North American serial rights.**

BONE & FLESH PUBLICATIONS (III), P.O. Box 728, Concord NH 03302-0728, founded 1988, editors Susan Bartlett, Lester Hirsh, Frederick Moe and Amy Shea, managing editor Monica A. Cruickshank-Nagle. In 1997, there will be two issues of *Bone & Flesh* literary journal, one of which will feature New Hampshire writers. "We are looking for **quality work from *seasoned* writers/artists: prose, poems, fiction, essays, reviews and art. Themes vary and tend to focus on the substance of our lives and the links with other lives and times.**" They have published works by Lyn Lifshin, Mara Attina, Tim Hoppey, Mary Winters and Arthur Kagle. As a sample the editors selected these lines from "Raking Leaves" by Bruce MacMahon:

> *All day the gathering*
> *these cupped hands full*
> *of sky to a ground*
> *rasped into piles*
>
> *taking a select few*
> *I burn them in silence*
> *to an aged night wind. . .*

Bone & Flesh is 50-75 pgs and the format is changing to include 6-12 in-depth features per issue, with a blend of prose, verse and art. Subscription: $14. **Sample postpaid: $7. Submissions are accepted February through May only. "Submissions received outside of this time will not be read or returned." Editors will comment on work "when appropriate." Reports in 3-6 months. Pays copies. Acquires first North American serial rights.** They recently published "Symposium on Song," an issue related to folk music and verse.

BOOG LITERATURE; BOOGLIT (I, II), P.O. Box 221, Oceanside NY 11572-0221, founded 1991, editor/publisher David Kirschenbaum. BOOG Literature publishes *BOOGLIT* (formerly *MA!*), a quarterly zine of poetry, prose and arts reviews, as well as 5-10 chapbooks/year and occasional broadsides. The editor says he **would like to see more "true poetry written from personal experience."** They have published poetry by Eileen Myles, Bernadette Mayer, Todd Colby and Anne Waldman. As a sample the editor selected these lines from "Rosebud Memorium" by Geoffrey Cook:

> *Let a thousand rosebuds bloom*
> *like shepherdesses & nymphs*
> *in a war scattered city park*

BOOGLIT is 40 pgs., 8½ × 11 offset printed on newsprint with art, graphics and small press ads. "We accept 10-15 poems per issue, sometimes more, never less." Press run is 1,500—distributed free throughout New York City. **Sample postpaid: $3. Make all checks payable to David Kirschenbaum. Submit up to 5 poems; 6 short poems can count as 1 poem or page of poetry. Previously published poems and simultaneous submissions OK. "A friendly cover letter is always appreciated. Most small presses have low circulations, so if your piece was (or may be) published elsewhere, but you think it deserves/needs to be read by more people, send it along (but please tell us when and where it was or will be published)."** Time between acceptance and publication is "usually no more than 3 months." **Often comments on rejections. Send SASE for guidelines. Reports in 6-12 weeks. Pays 1 copy. Acquires first North American serial or reprint rights.** "We welcome and will write reviews of either chaps or mags in 250-1,000 words, single or multi-book format." **For chapbook or broadside publication, query with sample poems and cover letter including brief bio and publication credits. Replies to queries within 2 months, to mss within 3 months. Pays 10% of press run; first printing is 100-200 copies.** Recent chapbooks include *Art Against Art Not* by Amiri Baraka,

Conditional by Mark DuCharme and *Versions Neveu* by Barry Gifford. For sample chapbook, "send check or money order for $4, and we will select a chap to send in return." The press also publishes occasional spoken word cassette compilations. Query before sending tapes. The editor says, "The job of the small press is to get the word out. If it's solid, we will publish it. It's quality, not résumé."

‡**THE BOOKPRESS: THE NEWSPAPER OF THE LITERARY ARTS (III)**, The DeWitt Bldg., 215 N. Cayuga St., Ithaca NY 14850, phone (607)277-2254, founded 1990, editor/publisher Jack Goldman, associate editor Isaac Bowers, appears 8 times/year, each month except January and June, July and August. As for poetry, the editor says, **"The only criterion is a commitment to the aesthetic power of language. Avoid the hackneyed and formulaic."** They have recently published poetry by Phyllis Janowitz, Ruth Stone and Debra P. Patnaik. As a sample the editor selected these lines from "Nordau Beach in August" by Amy Zalman:

> *Our bodies draw toward what we can hold, and so I*
> *swim out from the mouth of the sea, to take*
> *handfuls of the pale seeds foaming, of water*
> *from water, to string a necklace*
> *of violet light.*

The editor says *The Bookpress* is a 12-page tabloid. They receive about 50 poems a year, accept approximately 10%. Press run is 7,500 for 300 subscribers of which 15 are libraries. Subscription: $12/year. **Sample copies free. No previously published poems or simultaneous submissions. Cover letter preferred. Reads submissions August 1 through April 1 only. SASE required.** Time between acceptance and publication is 1 month. **Often comments on rejections. Send SASE for guidelines. Reports in 3 months. Pays 2 copies. Acquires first North American serial rights.** Reviews books of poetry. Length of reviews varies, typically between 1,500-2,000 words, sometimes longer. Poets may also send books for review consideration.

BORDERLANDS: TEXAS POETRY REVIEW (II), P.O. Box 49818, Austin TX 78765, founded 1992, appears twice a year publishing "high-quality, outward-looking poetry by new and established poets, as well as brief reviews of poetry books and critical essays. Cosmopolitan in content, but particularly welcomes Texas and Southwest writers." **They want "outward-looking poems that exhibit social, political, geographical, historical or spiritual awareness coupled with concise artistry. We also want poems in two languages (one of which must be English), where the poet has written both versions. Please, no introspective work about the speaker's psyche, childhood or intimate relationships."** They have recently published poetry by Naomi Shihab Nye, John Knoepfle, Laurel Speer, James Ulmer and Ronald Wallace. As a sample the editors selected these lines from "Gold in the Black Hills" by Robert James Tillett:

> *You could hear their women's children crying*
> *within the circled-wagon barricades.*
> *But still those copper voices clicked and thrummed*
> *that metal language—and later, explosions*
> *in the hills, a new war sounding in the canyons*
> *and men raging underground.*

Borderlands is 80-120 pgs., 5½ × 8½, offset, perfect-bound, with 4-color cover, art by local artists. They receive about 2,000 poems a year, use approximately 120. Press run is 800. Subscription: $17/year; $33/2 years. **Sample postpaid: $8.50. Submit 3-6 typed poems at a time. No previously published poems; simultaneous submissions OK. Include SASE (or SAE and IRCs) with sufficient postage to return poems and a response. Seldom comments on rejections. Reports in 4-6 months. Pays 1 copy. Acquires first rights.** Reviews books of poetry in one page. Also uses 3- to 6-page essays on single poets and longer essays (3,500-word maximum) on contemporary poetry in some larger context (query first). Sponsors a poetry and essay contest awarding one $500 prize in poetry and five $100 prizes for essays. Entry fee: $10 for poems, $5 for essays. Postmark deadline: March 1 through April 30, 1997. Send SASE for details. They say, "We believe it's possible—though not easy—for poetry to be both involved with the world and high-quality."

BOREALIS PRESS; TECUMSEH PRESS LTD.; JOURNAL OF CANADIAN POETRY (V), Dept. PM, 9 Ashburn Dr., Nepean, Ontario K2E 6N4 Canada, founded 1972. Borealis and Tecumseh are imprints for books, including **collections of poetry, by Canadian writers only, and they are presently not considering unsolicited submissions.** Send SASE (or SAE with IRCs) for catalog to

---

THE SUBJECT INDEX, located before the General Index, can help you select markets for your work. It lists those publishers whose poetry interests are specialized.

buy samples. Poets recently published include Carol Shields and Diane Dawber. As a sample the editor selected this poem, "Uncle," by Shields:

> *When he speaks*
> *it is with the privileged*
> *angular paragraphs*
> *of old essays,*
> *his phrases antique*
> *and shapely as jewelry.*
>
> *But when he laughs*
> *he touches new territory*
> *somewhere sad between*
> *language and breath*
> *just missing the edge*
> *of what he really*
> *means.*

The *Journal* is an annual that publishes articles, reviews and criticism, not poetry. **Sample postpaid: $15.95.**

THE BOSTON PHOENIX: PHOENIX LITERARY SECTION (PLS) (III), 126 Brookline Ave., Boston MA 02215, phone (617)536-5390, founded 1966, poetry editor Lloyd Schwartz, is a monthly book review with one poem in almost every issue. Press run is 150,000. Single copy: $1.50. **Submit 1-3 poems at a time, under 50 lines each. "Please include cover letter and SASE." Reports in 1 month. Pays $50.** Open to unsolicited reviews. Poets may also send books for review consideration to Tom deKay, book editor. Poems published in this review appear in the 1992 and 1995 volumes of *The Best American Poetry*.

BOSTON REVIEW (II), E53-407, MIT, 30 Wadsworth St., Cambridge MA 02139-4307, phone (617)253-3642, fax (617)252-1549, website http://Polisci~mac~2.mit.edu/BostonReview/BostonRevie w.html, founded 1975, poetry editors Mary Jo Bang and Timothy Donnelly, is a bimonthly magazine of arts, culture and politics which uses about **three pages of poetry/issue, or 25 poems a year**, for which they receive about 700 submissions. Poems in select issues seem to echo or somehow comple-ment the prose, which concerns social or literary affairs. The poetry features lyric and narrative verse with an emphasis on voice, often plaintive-sounding or dream-like in tone. They have a 4- to 6-month backlog. Circulation is 20,000 nationally including subscriptions and newsstand sales. **Sample postpaid: $4.50. Submit no more than 6 poems at a time. Simultaneous submissions discouraged. Cover letter listing recent publications encouraged. Submissions and inquiries are accepted via regular mail only. Reports in 2-4 months "if you include SASE." Always sends prepublication galleys. Pay varies. Buys first serial rights.** Reviews books of poetry. Only using *solicited* reviews. Poets may send books for review consideration. Poetry published by this review has been included in *The Best American Poetry 1993*. The editor advises, "To save the time of all those involved, poets should be sure to send only *appropriate* poems to particular magazines. This means that a poet should not submit to a magazine that he/she has not read. Poets should also avoid lengthy cover letters and allow the poems to speak for themselves."

BOTTOMFISH (II), De Anza College, 21250 Stevens Creek Blvd., Cupertino CA 95014, founded 1976, editor David Denny. This college-produced magazine appears annually. They have recently published poetry by Chitra Divakaruni, Walter Griffin and Edward Kleinschmidt. As a sample the editor selected the closing lines from "Bread and Salt" by Ioanna-Veronika Warwick:

> *A bride and groom*
> *are greeted at the door*
> *with bread and salt.*
> *The streets are layered*
> *with steep shadows,*
> *lost in the lucky light.*

Bottomfish is 80 pgs., 7×8¼, well-printed on heavy stock with b&w graphics, perfect-bound. Circula-tion is 500, free to libraries, but **$5/copy to individual requests. "Before submitting, writers are strongly urged to purchase a sample copy." Best submission times: September through February. Deadline: February 15 each year. Reports in 1-6 months, depending on backlog. Pays 2 copies.**

BOUILLABAISSE (I, IV-Form/style), % Alpha Beat Press, 31 Waterloo St., New Hope PA 18938-1210, phone (215)862-0299, founded 1991, editors Dave Christy and Ana Christy, is a biannual using **"poetry that reflects life and its ups and downs."** They want **"modern, Beat poetry; poetry from the streets of life—no limit. No rhythm, Christian or sweet poetry."** They have recently published poetry by Jan Kerouac, Allen Ginsberg, t.k. splake and Joseph Verrilli. As a sample the editors selected these lines by Janine Pommy Vega:

> Archangel Mary falls into the water
> killing the bridges, the Tappanzee and
> railroad tresks. Her backside against the pier, they promenade
> across her, River Edge to Harlem
> and time runs out

The editors say *Bouillabaisse* is 160 pgs., 8½ × 11, offset, saddle-stitched, with graphics. They receive 200 submissions a year, accept 40%. Press run is 500 for 350 subscribers of which 9 are libraries. Subscription: $17. **Sample postpaid: $10. Submit 5 poems at a time. Previously published poems and simultaneous submissions OK. Cover letter required. Always comments on rejections. Send SASE for guidelines. Reports "immediately." Pays 1 copy.** Reviews books of poetry in 250-500 words. Open to unsolicited reviews. Poets may also send books for review consideration. They publish 2 paperbacks and 10 chapbooks/year. "We work with each individual on their project." **Replies to queries "immediately," to mss within 3 weeks. Always sends prepublication galleys for chapbooks. Pays author's copies.** Also see the listings for *Alpha Beat Soup* and *Cokefish*.

BOULEVARD (II), % editor Richard Burgin, P.O. Box 30386, Philadelphia PA 19103, phone (215)568-7062, founded 1985, appears 3 times a year. **"We've published everything from John Ashbery to Howard Moss to a wide variety of styles from new or lesser known poets. We're eclectic. Do not want to see poetry that is uninspired, formulaic, self-conscious, unoriginal, insipid."** They have published poetry by Amy Clampitt, Molly Peacock, Jorie Graham and Mark Strand. As a sample the editor selected these lines from "Three Soundings of January Snow" by Stuart Lishan:

> Snow arias the ground tonight. It quilts
>   the house; it sounds like a samba of whispers,
> Muffled, like a mitten slipped over love, like guilt.

Boulevard is 200 pgs., digest-sized, professionally printed, flat-spined, with glossy card cover. Poetry herein—mostly free verse but wide-ranging in content, length and tone—is accessible and exciting. Poems have one thing in common: careful attention to craft (particularly line, stanza and voice). Their press run is 3,000 with 700 subscribers of which 200 are libraries. Subscription: $12. **Sample postpaid: $7. "Prefer name and number on each page with SASE. Encourage cover letters but don't require them. Will consider simultaneous submissions but not previously published poems." Reads submissions October 1 through May 1 only. Editor sometimes comments on rejections. Pays $25-250/poem, depending on length, plus 1 copy. Buys first-time publication and anthology rights.** Open to unsolicited reviews. Poetry published in *Boulevard* has also been included in the 1992, 1993, 1994 and 1995 volumes of *The Best American Poetry*. Richard Burgin says, "We believe the grants we have won from the National Endowment for the Arts, etc., as well as the anthologies that continue to recognize us, have rewarded our commitment. My advice to poets: 'Write from your heart as well as your head.' "

‡BRASS CITY; BRASS CITY PRESS (I, II), 77 Williamson Dr., Waterbury CT 06710-1131, founded 1995, editor Scott Keeney. *Brass City* is a bimonthly poetry zine designed to present "high-caliber poetry that finds itself outside of the mainstream." **They want "poetry influenced by surrealism, Dada, Beat, NY School, Black Mountain, deep image and language poetry—poetry with close attention to language as well as imagery. No traditional or confessional poetry or poetry by people who aren't familiar with postmodern forms."** They have recently published poetry by Errol Miller, David Fedo, John Bradley and Phebe Davidson. As a sample the editor selected these lines from "Sea" by Nava Fader:

> My lover is not my muse. He
> tells me what distance is. He is
> captain of some sea I can not understand.
> Under the blankets he
> charts some vast stretch and
> shuts his eyes—he might be
> navigating by stars I don't see.

Brass City is 16-24 pgs., digest-sized, photocopied from laser-printed script and saddle-stapled with colored paper cover. They accept about 5% of the submissions received. Press run is 150 for 50 subscribers. Subscription: $10/1 year, $18/2 years. **Sample postpaid: $2. Make checks payable to Brass City Press. Submit 3-5 poems at a time. Previously published poems OK "depending on where and when"; no simultaneous submissions. Cover letter with bio for contributor's note required.** Time between acceptance and publication is 2-6 months. **Often comments on rejections. Send SASE for guidelines. Reports in 1-8 weeks. Pays 1 copy. Acquires all rights but returns them upon publication.** The editor says, "It would behoove a poet to support the magazines which support (i.e. publish) him/her. We are especially interested in publishing work by 'younger' poets."

‡(the) **BRAVE NEW TICK (I, IV-Gay/lesbian/bisexual)**, P.O. Box 24, S. Grafton MA 01560, phone/fax (508)799-3769, e-mail tick@ultranet.com, website http://www.ultranet.com/~tick/index.ht ml, founded 1985, editor Paul N. Dion-Deitch, is a gay bimonthly, art and literary publication designed for networking. **They want gay and lesbian work. No Christian "religious right" material.** They have recently published poetry by Brian Duley, Kevin Hibshman and John Mark Ivey. The editor says it is 10-12 pgs., 8½×11, photocopied. They receive 200-300 poems a year, "try to publish most." Press run is 100. Subscription: $10/year. **Sample postpaid: $1. Make checks payable to Paul N. Dion-Deitch. Cash also OK. Previously published poems and simultaneous submissions OK. Cover letter with bio preferred. "Submissions on disk (PC) are much appreciated!" Often comments on rejections, if asked. Publishes theme issues. Send SASE for guidelines. Guidelines are also included inside the publication or may be obtained via e-mail or website. Reports in about a month. Pays 1 copy.**

GEORGE BRAZILLER, INC. (II), 171 Madison Ave., New York NY 10016, phone (212)889-0909, founded 1955, editor Adrienne Baxter, is a major literary publisher. In 1980 they published *Classic Ballroom Dances* by Charles Simic, from which this sample poem, "Bedtime Story," was selected:

> When a tree falls in a forest
> And there's no one around
> To hear the sound, the poor owls
> Have to do all the thinking.
>
> They think so hard they fall off
> Their perch and are eaten by ants,
> Who, as you already know, all look like
> Little Black Riding Hoods.

It is 64 pgs., digest-sized, professionally printed, flat-spined, with glossy card cover, $3.95. **"We consider reprints of books of poetry as well as new poems. If submitting a book for reprint, *all* reviews of the book should be submitted as well. Submit sample of work, never *entire* original pgs." Reports in 1 month or less. Payment varies in each case. Buys all rights.** The editor says, "We are a small publishing house that publishes few books (in general) each year. Still, we have published many well-known authors and are always receptive to new writers of every kind—and from all parts of the world."

THE BRIAR CLIFF REVIEW (II, IV-Regional), Briar Cliff College, 3303 Rebecca St., Sioux City IA 51104-2340, website http://www.briar-cliff.edu/www/bcchomep/publicat/bccrevie/bcreview.htm, founded 1989, poetry editor Jeanne Emmons, is an attractive annual "eclectic literary and cultural magazine focusing on (but not limited to) Siouxland writers and subjects." **They want "quality poetry with strong imagery; especially interested in regional, Midwestern content with tight, direct, well-wrought language. No suicide notes, anguished teen-aged reflections or allegorical emotional landscapes."** They have published poetry by Karen Jobst, James Autry, Ken McCullough and Ann Struthers. As a sample the editor selected these lines from "Custer Nat'l Park" by Diane Glancy:

> There are times I think
> how the wilderness is a wool sweater dried on high
> when cleaners are called for in the label
> at the back of the neck.
> Even the sky comes around with a sack.

BCR is 64 pgs., 8½×11, professionally printed on 70 lb. matte paper, saddle-stapled, four-color cover on 10 pt. coated stock, b&w photos inside. They receive about 100 poems a year, accept 12. Press run is 500, all shelf sales. Single copy: $4. **Sample postpaid: $5. No previously published poems; simultaneous submissions OK. "We will assume that submissions are not simultaneous unless notified." Cover letter with short bio required. "No manuscripts returned without SASE." Reads submissions August 1 through November 1.** Time between acceptance and publication is 5-6 months. **Seldom comments on rejections. Reports in 6 months. Pays 2 copies. Acquires first serial rights.** *Briar Cliff Review* has been awarded the Gold Medalist Award from the Columbia Scholastic Press Association and the All American (with five marks of Distinction) from the National Scholastic Press Association at the University of Minnesota, for both its 1994 and 1995 issues.

‡**BRILLIANT STAR (IV-Children, religious)**, % Baha'i Subscriber Service, Baha'i National Center, Wilmette IL 60091, is a Baha'i bimonthly for children, appearing in a magazine-sized format. **"Poems are always illustrated, so think about how your poem will look. Our readers are ages 5-14. Write for *them* not for yourself. We do not want to see Christmas themes in any form. If you are not familliar with the Baha'i Faith, research is encouraged."** As a sample the editor selected these lines from "Hooray for Skin" by Susan Engle:

> Suppose, when God created skin,
> He turned the skinside outside in

So when you talk to Mrs. Jones,
Your eyes meet over fat and bones
And tissues, blue and white and red,
That stretch from toe to hand to head.
It makes me glad to have a skin
To keep the outside boneside in.

Sample free with 9 × 12 SASE (sufficient postage for 5 oz.); objectives are printed in the masthead. Considers simultaneous submissions. "Contributors receive two copies." The editor urges children who wish to write poetry to avoid "writing about tired subjects like 'dogs as friends' and being 'afraid of the dark.' Write about today's world in fun, exciting language. Write about a realistic fear—guns, drugs, the school dance, my ugly feet, will my parents divorce. Make your poem an engaging short story." This is also good advice for adults who wish to write children's poetry for this publication.

BROKEN STREETS (I, IV-Religious), 57 Morningside Dr. E., Bristol CT 06010, founded 1979, editor Ron Grossman, is a **"Christian-centered outreach ministry to poets."** The editor wants **"Christian-centered poetry, feelings, etc., usually 5-15 lines, but also haiku. No more than 3 poems at a time. Not necessary to query, but helpful."** He has published Bettye K. Wray and Naomi Rhoads. The magazine, which appears twice a year, is 40-80 pgs., digest-sized, photocopied typescript with card cover. Uses about 300 of the 500 poems submitted/year—by folks of all ages, including children and senior citizens. Press run is 1,000. Subscription: $10 (includes "all mailings and current chapbook"). **Sample postpaid: $4. No previously published poems. Cover letter required. Reports in 1 week. Pays copies.** Reviews books of poetry. Open to unsolicited reviews. Poets may also send books for review consideration.

‡BROODING HERON PRESS (V), Bookmonger Rd., Waldron Island WA 98297, founded 1984, co-publishers Sam and Sally Green, **publishes 3 chapbooks/year.** They have **"no restriction other than excellence."** They do not want **"prose masquerading as poetry or poems written for form's sake."** However, **"we're too backlogged to look at anything new until 1998."** They have published poetry by Denise Levertov, James Laughlin and Gary Snyder. **Query in late 1997 to determine when the press will be reading again. If open to submissions, submit complete ms of 16-20 poems; no query. Previously published poems OK; no simultaneous submissions. Cover letter required.** Time between acceptance and publication varies. **Always comments on rejections. Reports within 6 weeks. "We print 300 books per title, bound in paper and cloth. Payment is 10% of the press run. Author retains copyright."** This press has received many awards for fine printing. **Write for catalog to order samples.**

BROOKLYN REVIEW (II), 2900 Bedford Ave., Brooklyn College, Brooklyn NY 11210, founded 1974, editors change each year, address correspondence to poetry editor. They have published such poets as Allen Ginsberg, Elaine Equi, Amy Gerstler, Eileen Myles, Alice Notley, Honor Moore, Ron Padgett and David Trinidad. *BR* is an annual, 128 pgs., digest-sized, flat-spined, professionally printed with glossy color cover and art. Circulation is 750. **Sample postpaid: $6. "Please send no more than four poems." Cover letter with brief history required. Reads submissions September 1 through December 1 only. Reports in 6 weeks to 6 months. Pays copies.** Poetry published in *BR* has also been selected for inclusion in *The Best American Poetry 1992*.

‡THE BROWNSTONE REVIEW (II), 331 16th St. #2, Brooklyn NY 11215, founded 1995, poetry editor Aaron Scharf, appears twice a year. **"We will consider poems of any form, length and style as long as the language is fresh and vivid."** They do not want to see "anything trite or pretentious—nor generic workshop poems." The editor says the review is 60 pgs., 7 × 8½, side-stapled, and receives 300-400 poems a year. Press run is 100. Single copy: $6; subscription: $10. **Make checks payable to Keith Dawson. Submit 3-5 poems at a time. No previously published poems; simultaneous submissions OK. Cover letter preferred. Seldom comments on rejections. Send SASE for guidelines. Reports within 3 months. Pays 2 copies.**

BRUNSWICK PUBLISHING CORPORATION (I), 1386 Lawrenceville Plank Rd., Lawrenceville VA 23868, phone (804)848-3865, founded 1978, poetry editor Dr. Walter J. Raymond, is a **partial subsidy publisher. Query with 3-5 samples. Response in 2 weeks with SASE. If invited, submit double-spaced, typed ms. Reports in 3-4 weeks, reading fee only if you request written evaluation. Always sends prepublication galleys. Poet pays 50-80% of cost, gets same percentage of profits for market-tester edition of 500-1,000, advertised by leaflets mailed to reviewers, libraries, book buyers and bookstores.** As a sample we selected these lines from "'Round And 'Round We'd Twirl" by Dee Brown:

I remember when I was just a little girl
You would pick me up and 'round and 'round we'd twirl

> *You'd stop to catch your breath*
> *All the while, I begged for more*
> *Now, as I reminisce of those days so long ago*
> *I close my eyes, to watch us twirl across the floor*

That's from her book *Beyond What You See*, 54 pgs., digest-sized, flat-spined, neatly printed, glossy cover with photo. Cost: $9.95. **Send SASE for catalog to order samples and "Statement of Philosophy and Purpose," which explains terms**. That Statement says: "We publish books because that is what we like to do. Every new book published is like a new baby, an object of joy! We do not attempt to unduly influence the reading public as to the value of our publications, but we simply let the readers decide that themselves. We refrain from the artificial beefing up of values that are not there. . . . We are not competitors in the publishing world, but offer what we believe is a needed service. We strongly believe that in an open society every person who has something of value to say and wants to say it should have the chance and opportunity to do so."

‡BUFFALO BONES (II), Evergreen Poets & Writers, P.O. Box 714, Evergreen CO 80437, founded 1994, contact editors (editorial staff rotates), appears 2 times/year, is a nonprofit publication containing "nothing elitist. Poems by known and unknown poets stand side by side. We look for high quality." **They want "any form of poetry, 40-line limit, strong imagery, narratives with a new twist, and a bit of fun once in awhile. No profanity, graphic/sexual, or woe-is-me poems."** They have recently published poetry by Robert Cooperman, Judith Herschemeyer, Donna Park, Carolyn Campbell and Lyn Lifshin. *Buffalo Bones* is 40 pgs., digest-sized, nicely printed on quality paper. They receive about 4,000 poems a year, accept approximately 150. Press run is 1,000 for 80 subscribers, 75% distributed free to libraries and bookstores. Subscription: $12. **Sample postpaid: $4. Make checks payable to Evergreen Poets & Writers. Submit 3-5 poems at a time. "Poems are not returned." Previously published poems and simultaneous submissions OK. Reads submissions September 1 through May 1. Poems are circulated to an editorial board. "We have a rotating editorship in order to insure variety and a fresh look in every issue." Send SASE for guidelines. Reports in 3 months. Pays 2 copies. Acquires first or one-time rights.** Sponsors contest. Deadline: November 1. "All contest entries are also considered for publication." Send SASE for guidelines. The editors say, "The response to *Buffalo Bones* has been overwhelming. The first year we received 1,000 submissions, the second year 4,000. Every poem gets attention from several readers. There are many fine poems—so little space. Our editorial staff rotates for each issue, therefore, try us again."

BUFFALO SPREE MAGAZINE (II), 4511 Harlem Rd., Buffalo NY 14226, founded 1967, poetry editor Janet Goldenberg, is the quarterly regional magazine of western New York. It has a controlled circulation (21,000) in the Buffalo area, mostly distributed free (with 3,000 subscriptions, of which 25 are libraries). Its glossy pages feature general-interest articles about local culture, plus book reviews, fiction and poetry contributed nationally. It receives about 300 poetry submissions/year and uses about 25, which have ranged from work by Robert Hass and Carl Dennis to first publications by younger poets. As a sample the editor selected these lines from "Alien in Spring" by Martha Bosworth:

> *I am a tall pale animal in boots*
> *trampling forget-me-nots and scaring birds*
> *from the lemon tree: with my long-handled claw*
> *I pull down lemons—tear-shaped, dimpled, round,*
> *bouncing they vanish into vines and weeds.*

They use 5-7 poems/issue, **these are selected 3-6 months prior to publication. Sample postpaid: $3.75. Submit up to 6 poems at a time. Considers simultaneous submissions, "but we must be advised that poems have been or are being submitted elsewhere." Pays $25/poem on publication.**

BUTTON MAGAZINE; THIMBLE PRESS (I, II), P.O. Box 26, Lunenburg MA 01462, founded 1993, poetry editor Mark P. Timms, "is New England's tiniest magazine of fiction, poetry and gracious living." **They want poetry about the quiet surprises in life, not sentimental, and true moments carefully preserved. Brevity counts.** They have recently published poetry by William Corbett, David Barber, Amanda Powell and Norah Dooley. As a sample the editor selected this haiku, "for an author," by Chris Mulholland:

> *Ernest Hemingway*
> *Put your shiny gun away*
> *Ernest Hemingway*

Button appears twice a year and is 30 pgs., 4¼ × 5½, saddle-stitched, card stock cover with illustrations that incorporate one or more buttons (our favorite shows the Statue of Liberty holding needle and thread). *The Boston Globe* called it charmingly homemade in feel and liked "its lack of pretension and its quirky humor." Press run is 1,200 for more than 450 subscribers; 750 shelf sales. Subscription: $5/year. **Sample postpaid: $1. Submit up to 4 poems at a time. No previously published poems. Cover letter required.** Time between acceptance and publication is 6-12 months. **Poems are circulated to an editorial board. Often comments on rejections. Send SASE for guidelines. Reports in**

7-8 weeks. Pays 2-year subscription and author's copies. Acquires first North American serial rights. Thimble Press **publishes 1 chapbook/year. Query first, with sample poems and cover letter with brief bio and publication credits. Replies to queries in 2 months. Pays half net profit and 30 author's copies. For sample, send $1.** The editor says, "*Button* was started so that a century from now when people read it they'll say, 'Gee, what a wonderful time to have lived. I wish I lived back then.' Our likes include wit and humanity, intelligence and eccentricity. We dislike whining, cheap sentimentality and 'writing as therapy,' and strongly recommend you spring the buck to see what's in the magazine. All correspondence handled with graciousness and consideration."

BYLINE MAGAZINE (IV-Writing), P.O. Box 130596, Edmond OK 73013-0001, phone (405)348-5591, founded 1981, editor Marcia Preston, poetry editor Betty Shipley, is a **magazine for the encouragement of writers and poets, using 8-10 poems/issue about writers or writing.** As a sample the editor selected these lines from "Cone" by Darrell Fike:

> The crimson-tipped calligraphy
> of the morning glory vine
> scrawled across the top of the fence rail
> spells out a message perhaps
> the lost instruction manual for this world

ByLine is magazine-sized, professionally printed, with illustrations, cartoons and ads. They have about 3,000 subscriptions and receive about 2,500 poetry submissions/year, of which they use 144. Subscription: $20. **Sample postpaid: $4. Submit up to 4 poems at a time, no reprints. Send SASE for guidelines. Reports within 6 weeks. Pays $5-10/poem. Buys first North American serial rights.** Sponsors monthly poetry contests. Send #10 SASE for details. Marcia Preston advises, "We are happy to work with new writers, but please read a few samples to get an idea of our style. We would like to see more serious poetry about the creative experience (as it concerns writing)."

THE CAFÉ REVIEW (III), c/o Yes Books, 20 Danforth St., Portland ME 04101, e-mail writer@main elink.net, website http://www.mainelink.net/~writer/cafehtml/index.html, founded 1989, editors Steve Luttrell and Wayne Atherton, is a quarterly which has grown out of open poetry readings held at a Portland cafe. The editors say they aim "to print the best work we can!" **They want "free verse, 'beat' inspired and fresh. Nothing clichéd."** They have recently published poetry by Charles Bukowski, Robert Creeley, Janet Hamill and Diane Wakoski. As a sample the editor selected these lines from "Cream Hidden" by Michael McClure, beginning with lines by Rumi:

> "*LIKE CREAM HIDDEN IN THE SOUL OF MILK*
> *no-place keeps coming into place.*"
> *No-place is where I am at.*
> *My soil is where no toil*
> *will upearth it.*

The Review is 70-80 pgs., 5½ × 8½, professionally printed and perfect-bound with card cover, b&w art, no ads. They receive over 1,000 submissions a year, accept approximately 15%. Press run is 300 for 70 subscribers of which 10 are libraries, 75-100 shelf sales. Subscription: $20. **Sample postpaid: $6. No previously published poems or simultaneous submissions. Cover letter with brief bio required. "Poems only may be sent via e-mail. All other requests should be sent via U.S. mail. We usually respond with a form letter indicating acceptance or rejection of work, seldom with additional comments." Reports in 2-4 months. Pays 1 copy.** They also publish 1-2 chapbooks/year.

CALAPOOYA COLLAGE; $1,000 CAROLYN KIZER POETRY AWARDS (V), P.O. Box 309, Monmouth OR 97361, phone (503)838-6292, founded 1981, editor Thomas L. Ferte. *CC* is a literary annual using **"all kinds" of poetry. However, the annual will not be published again until August 1997. Submissions welcome beginning January 1997.** They have published poetry by Robert Bly, Joseph Bruchac, Octavio Paz, Marge Piercy, Etheridge Knight, Vassar Miller, William Stafford, Ursula K. LeGuin, Patricia Goedicke, David Wagoner and David Ray. It is 48 pgs., tabloid-sized. Press run is 1,500 for 250 subscribers of which 16 are libraries. They accept about 6% of 6,000 poems received annually. **Sample postpaid: $5. Reads submissions September 1 through June 1 only. Best times for submissions are January and February. Reports in 1-2 months. Pays 2 copies.** Reviews books of poetry in 600-1,000 words. Open to unsolicited reviews. Poets may also send books for review consideration. All poems accepted for publication are eligible for annual $1,000 Carolyn Kizer Poetry Awards.

CALDER PUBLICATIONS LTD.; RIVERRUN PRESS INC.; ASSOCIATION CALDER (V), 179 Kings Cross Rd., London WC1X 9BZ England, phone 0171-833-1300, publisher John Calder, is a literary book publisher. On their list are Samuel Beckett, Breyten Breytenbach, Erich Fried, Paul Eluard, Pier Paolo Passolini and Howard Barker. **"We do not read for the public,"** says John Calder, and he wants **no unsolicited mss.** "Any communication which requires a response should be sent with a SAE."

CALLALOO (IV-Ethnic), Dept. PM, Dept. of English, 322 Bryan Hall, University of Virginia, Charlottesville VA 22903, phone (804)924-6616, founded 1976, editor Charles H. Rowell. Devoted to **poetry dealing with North America, Europe, Africa, Latin and Central America, South America and the Caribbean**. They have published poetry by Rita Dove, Jay Wright, Alice Walker, Yusef Komunyakaa, Aimé Césaire, Nicolás Guillén and Jimmy Santiago Baca. Visually beautiful and well-edited with thematic, powerful poems in all forms and styles, this thick quarterly journal features about 15-20 poems in each issue (along with concise and scholarly book reviews). Circulation is 1,400, with 1,400 subscriptions of which half are libraries. Subscription: $27, $54 for institutions. **"We have no specifications for submitting poetry except authors should include SASE." Reports in 6 months. Pays copies.** Poetry published in *Callaloo* has been included in the 1992, 1994, 1995 and 1996 volumes of *The Best American Poetry.*

CALYX, A JOURNAL OF ART & LITERATURE BY WOMEN (IV-Women, lesbian); CA-LYX BOOKS (V), P.O. Box B, Corvallis OR 97339-0539, phone (541)753-9384, fax (541)753-0515, founded 1976, managing editor M. Donnelly, is a journal edited by a collective editorial board, **publishes poetry, prose, art, book reviews and interviews by and about women.** They want **"excellently crafted poetry that also has excellent content."** They have published poetry by Diane Glancy, Robin Morgan, Carole Boston Weatherford and Eleanor Wilner. As a sample the editor selected these lines from "Surviving" by Gail Tremblay:

> *I dream of dancing naked under stars,*
> *the dew on grass dampening my ankles,*
> *the moon, sensuous ancestor, calling*
> *to my blood. I dream the impossible*
> *moment when tongues touch, try to forget*
> *how much I've lost.*

Calyx appears 3 times every 18 months and is 7×8, handsomely printed on heavy paper, flat-spined, glossy color cover, 125-200 pgs., of which 50-60 are poetry. Poems tend to be lyric free verse that makes strong use of image and symbol melding unobtrusively with voice and theme. **Sample for the single copy price: $8 plus $1.50 postage. In 1996 and 1997, *Calyx* is open to submissions October 1 through November 15 only. Mss received when not open to reading will be returned unread. Send up to 6 poems with SASE and short bio. "We accept copies in good condition and clearly readable. We focus on new writing, but occasionally publish a previously published piece." Simultaneous submissions OK, "if kept up-to-date on publication." Send SASE for guidelines. Reports in 2-6 months. Pays copies and subscription.** Open to unsolicited reviews. Poets may also send books for review consideration. *Calyx* received a Special Merit Award for Editorial Content from the 1995 American Literary Magazine Awards and a 1996 Oregon Governor's Award for the Arts. Calyx Books publishes 1 book of poetry a year. All work published is by women. Recently published: *The Country of Women* by Sandra Kohler. **However, they are not accepting book submissions at this time.** They say, "Read the publication and be familiar with what we have published."

CAMELLIA; CAMELLIA PRESS INC. (II), P.O. Box 417, Village Station, New York NY 10014-0417, editor Tomer Inbar, associate editor Beth Stevens. *Camellia* is published biannually as a fold-out magazine/poster "available for free in New York City, the San Francisco/Oakland Bay area, Seattle, Ithaca, D.C., Northern Virginia and Baltimore, or by sending 55¢ postage. **We publish poetry in the W.C. Williams tradition. The poetry of things, moment and sharpness. We encourage young writers and like to work with the writers who publish with us. Our main goal is to get the poetry out. We do not want to see poetry where the poem is subordinate to the poet or poetry where the noise of the poetic overshadows the voice. We look for poetry that is honest and sharp and unburdened."** As a sample the editor selected this poem, "Dear Bill," by Jeff Vetock:

> *These bees matter*
> *for a day, from the door*
> *in summer he moves*
> *willingly often enough*
> *outside to tree*
> *no longer weather*
> *like a page turns*
> *to notice in time*
> *some sunlit sparrow*
> *for now, this*

Camellia's exact dimensions, the theme for a given issue and the mix of poetry and other art will be determined on an issue by issue basis. "We will keep the basic graphic design consistent with the style we have used for the past seven years, however we will be inviting guest designers to work with that design, bringing something new to each issue. We will continue to publish special project issues from time to time using various formats and mediums. We receive approximately 300-350 poems/issue and publish about 20." Press run is 1,000-2,000. Subscription: $5/year, $7 overseas. **Sample: 55¢ postage.**

Submit 8 poems at a time. Simultaneous submissions and previously published poems OK. "Cover letters are helpful, but shouldn't go overboard. Sometimes the cover letters are more interesting than the poetry received." Reports "ASAP." Pays 2 copies. Editor comments on submissions "if asked for or if I want to see more but am not satisfied with the poems sent." A chapbook of poems by Jerry Mirskin, entitled *Picture A Gate Hanging Open And Let That Gate Be The Sun*, is available for $5 from Camellia Press Inc. Also available is a poster of poetry, photographs and design using poems from the first 6 years of *Camellia*. They send prepublication galleys only for chapbooks.

CANADIAN AUTHOR; CANADIAN AUTHORS ASSOCIATION (III), Box 419, Campbellford, Ontario K0L 1L0 Canada, phone (705)653-0323, fax (705)653-0593, e-mail canauth@redden.on.ca, poetry editor Sheila Martindale. *Canadian Author*, a quarterly, is 28 pgs., magazine-sized, professionally printed, with paper cover in 2 colors. It contains articles useful to writers at all levels of experience. **Sample postpaid: $4.75. Buys 40 poems a year. "The trend is toward thematic issues and profiles of featured poets, so query letters are recommended." Pays $15 plus one copy.** (See also Canadian Authors Association Literary Awards in the Contests and Awards section.)

CANADIAN DIMENSION: THE MAGAZINE FOR PEOPLE WHO WANT TO CHANGE THE WORLD (III, IV-Political), 401-228 Notre Dame Ave., Winnipeg, Manitoba R3B 1N7 Canada, phone (204)957-1519, fax (204)943-4617, e-mail info@canadiandimension.mb.ca, founded 1964, editorial contact Brenda Austin-Smith, appears 6 times/year, using **"short poems on labour, women, native, gay/lesbian and other issues. Nothing more than one page."** They have published poetry by Tom Wayman and Milton Acorn. It is 48-56 pgs., magazine-sized, slick, professionally printed, with glossy paper cover. Press run is 3,500 for 2,500 subscribers of which 800 are libraries, 1,000 shelf sales. Subscription: $30.50 US ($24.50 Canadian). **Sample postpaid: $2. Submit up to 5 poems at a time. Previously published poems are unlikely to be accepted. Simultaneous submissions OK, if notified. Editor comments on submissions "rarely." Publishes theme issues. Send SASE (or SAE and IRC) for upcoming themes.** Reviews books of poetry in 750-1,200 words, single or multi-book format. They say, "We are broadly political—that is, not narrowly sloganeering, but profoundly sensitive to the connections between words and the state of the world. Topics can be personal as well as political. Also, American writers are reminded to include Canadian return postage or its equivalent in reply coupons, etc."

CANADIAN LITERATURE (IV-Regional), 167-1855 West Mall, University of British Columbia, Vancouver, British Columbia V6T 1Z2 Canada, phone (604)822-2780, website http://www.swifty.com/cdn_lit, founded 1959, editor E.M. Kröller, is a quarterly review which publishes **poetry by Canadian poets. "No limits on form. Less room for long poems."** They have published poetry by Atwood, Ondaatje, Layton and Bringhurst. As a sample the editor selected these lines from "A Reader's Deductions" by M. Travis Lane:

> *Disruption, too, is a convention.*

> *Today is new to the old; yesterday is new to the young.*
> *What is wholly familiar no longer is true.*

> *I am the story I tell. You are my different story.*

Each issue is professionally printed, digest-sized, flat-spined, with 175-200 pgs., of which about 10 are poetry. They receive 100-300 submissions/year, use 10-12. Circulation is 1,500, two-thirds of which are libraries. **Sample for the cover price: $15 Canadian plus postage and GST. No simultaneous submissions or reprints. Cover letter and SASE required. Reports within the month. "Accepted poems must be available on diskette." Pays $10/poem plus 1 copy. Buys first rights.** Reviews books of poetry in 500 words.

CANADIAN WRITER'S JOURNAL (IV-Writing); WIND SONGS (IV-Form/style), Gordon M. Smart Publications, P.O. Box 6618, Depot 1, Victoria, British Columbia V8P 5N7 Canada, is a small quarterly, publishing mainly short "how-to" articles of interest to writers at all levels. They use a few **"short poems or portions thereof as part of 'how-to' articles relating to the writing of poetry and occasional short poems with tie-in to the writing theme."** The Wind Songs column of *CWJ* accepts **unpublished poems including haiku, senryu, tanka, sijo, one-liner renga and sequences. Maximum 15 lines.** Subscription: $15 for 1 year, $25 for 2 years. **Sample: $4. Submit up to 5 poems (identify each form)** to Elizabeth St. Jacques, Poetry Editor, 406 Elizabeth St., Sault Ste. Marie, Ontario P6B 3H4 Canada. **Include SASE ("U.S. postage accepted; do not affix to envelope"). Token payment.** The magazine runs an annual poetry competition with closing date June 30. Send SASE for current rules.

‡CANDLELIGHT POETRY JOURNAL; ARMADILLO POETRY PRESS (I), P.O. Box 3184, St. Augustine FL 32085-3184, phone (904)794-0294, founded 1995, editors Carl Heffley and Robin

Sherwood. *Candlelight Poetry Journal* is a quarterly **"seeking an eclectic mix of form, free verse and avant-garde work from the poets of today. Limit 30 lines, though this may be relaxed for exceptional work. Form poetry is preferred, but please no cliché, hearts-and-flowers, moon-June poetry."** They have recently published poetry by Yvonne Sapia, William Middleton, Chris Hensler, Walter Stormont and Teri Van Dyken. As a sample the editors selected these lines from "Bodice Ripper" by Patricia A. Smith:

> *Exotic place,*
> *Rich bazaar.*
> *Kiwis, mangos, persimmons, papayas,*
> *But, I don't speak these languages.*

> *If I meet a pirate, a gypsy, a king,*
> *How will we communicate?*

CPJ is 52-58 pgs., 8½×11, offset and saddle-stapled with a coated card cover with art. They accept about 50% of the poetry received. Press run is 800 for 400 subscribers of which 12 are libraries. Subscription: $25. **Sample postpaid: $6.50. Make checks payable to Armadillo Poetry Press. Submit 5 poems at a time. Previously published poems OK ("after a period of years"); no simultaneous submissions. Cover letter with brief bio preferred. "Poems are selected on a basis of form, imagery, creativity and originality." Always comments on rejections. Send SASE for guidelines. Reports in 2-4 weeks. Pays "publication," which means you must purchase a copy if you want to see your work in print. However, they also offer 4 Editors' Choice Awards of $10 and give $10 to "the poet receiving the most votes from readers in each issue." Acquires first (or occasionally reprint) rights.** Always includes market listings and articles on writing poetry. Also reviews books of poetry. Open to unsolicited reviews. Poets may also send books for review consideration. Armadillo Poetry Press also offers a series of contests (with reading fees of $2 for the first poem and $1 for each additional poem and prizes of $75, $100 and $125) and publishes perfect-bound anthologies, 120-180 pgs., which entrants may purchase if they want to see their work in print. Cost for an anthology, including p&h, is $14.

‡**CANNEDPHLEGM (I)**, 37 Lafayette, San Francisco CA 94103, phone/fax (415)252-8768, founded 1995, editor Jeff Fleming. *Cannedphlegm*, which appears every 1-3 months, is a literary magazine containing poetry, short fiction, columns, sketches and a few b&w photos. **The editor says he is open to any type of poetry—no specifications.** He has recently published poetry by Jim Dewitt, John Grey and Michael H. Brownstein. As a sample the editor selected these lines from "Wish I Were," a poem of his own:

> *The lip prints you left as a joke*
> *on the window of my car make me wish*
> *I were glass. That you might casually*
> *place your soft lips against me*
> *lives on as my one hopeful image, encouraging me*
> *to rise from my deathbed each morning.*

Cannedphlegm is 24-36 pgs., 7×8½, photocopied and saddle-stapled with paper cover. They receive 200-300 poems a year, accept approximately 75%. Press run is 125 for 100 subscribers. Subscription: $10 for 6 issues. **Sample postpaid: $2. Make checks payable to Jeff Fleming. Submit up to 5 poems at a time. Previously published poems and simultaneous submissions OK. Cover letter preferred. Often comments on rejections. Send SASE for guidelines. Reports within 2 weeks. Pays 1 copy.** The editor says, "One rejection to one poem could just as easily indicate a poor editor as a poor poem."

THE CAPE ROCK (II), Dept. of English, Southeast Missouri State University, Cape Girardeau MO 63701, phone (314)651-2500, founded 1964, editor Dr. Harvey Hecht, appears twice yearly and consists of **64 pgs. of poetry and photography, with a $200 prize for the best poem in each issue and $100 for featured photography. "No restrictions on subjects or forms. Our criterion for selection is the quality of the work. We prefer poems under 70 lines; no long poems or books; no sentimental, didactic or cute poems."** They have published poetry by Stephen Dunning, Joyce Odam, Judith Phillips Neeld, Lyn Lifshin, Virginia Brady Young, Gary Pacernick and Laurel Speer. As a sample the editor selected these lines from "At The Rodin Museum, Stanford" by Fred D. White:

> *The lovers unleash their passion on the hot*
> *summer grass of the sculpture garden,*
> *surrounded by metal longing.*

> *They drop wild desires into each other's mouths*
> *like mother birds.*

It's a handsomely printed, flat-spined, digest-sized magazine. Their circulation is about 500 for 200 subscribers of which half are libraries. Single copy: $5; subscription: $7/year. **Sample: $4. Submit**

3-7 poems at a time. **Do not submit mss in May, June or July. Send SASE for guidelines.** They have a 2- to 8-month backlog and **report in 1-3 months. Pays 2 copies.** This is a solid publication that features a wide selection of forms and styles, leaning in recent years toward free verse that establishes a mood or milieu.

CAPERS AWEIGH MAGAZINE (I, IV-Regional), P.O. Box 96, Sydney, Nova Scotia B1P 6G9 Canada, founded 1992, publisher John MacNeil, is a quarterly of **poetry and short fiction "of, by and for Cape Bretoners at home and away." They want work by Cape Bretoners only. Nothing profane.** The publisher says it is 50-60 pgs., 5×8, desktop-published, stapled, including computer graphics and trade ads. Press run is 500. Subscription: $20. **Sample postpaid: $5. No simultaneous submissions. Cover letter required. Seldom comments on rejections. Pays 1 copy.**

THE CAPILANO REVIEW (III), 2055 Purcell Way, North Vancouver, British Columbia V7J 3H5 Canada, phone (604)984-1712, fax (604)983-7520, website http://www.capcollege.bc.ca, founded 1972, editor Robert Sherrin, is a literary and visual media review appearing 3 times/year. **They want avant-garde, experimental, previously unpublished work, "poetry of sustained intelligence and imagination."** They have recently published poetry by Robin Blaser, Daphne Marlatt and Betsy Warland. *TCR* comes in a handsome digest-sized format, 150 pgs., flat-spined, finely printed, semi-glossy stock with a glossy full-color card cover. Circulation is 1,000. **Sample: $9 prepaid. Do not submit mss during June and July. No simultaneous submissions. Reports in up to 6 months. Pays an honorarium plus 2 copies.**

CAPPER'S (I, IV-Nature, inspirational, religious, humor), 1503 SW 42nd St., Topeka KS 66609-1265, fax (913)274-4305, founded 1879, editor Nancy Peavler, is a biweekly tabloid (newsprint) going to **370,000 mail subscribers, mostly small-town and farm people. Uses 6-8 poems in each issue. They want short poems (4-10 lines preferred, lines of one-column width) "relating to everyday situations, nature, inspirational, humorous."** They have recently published poetry by Elizabeth Searle Lamb, Robert Brimm, Margaret Wiedyke, Helena K. Stefanski and Claire Puneky. As a sample the editor selected this poem, "Sugar maple matinee," by Linda Roth:

> Forty thousand sun-
> burned hands,
> Applaud them-
> selves
> Then drop down
> into autumn's
> lap.

Send $1.50 for sample. Not available on newsstand. "Most poems used in *Capper's* are upbeat in tone and offer the reader a bit of humor, joy, enthusiasm or encouragement. Short poems of this type fit our format best." Submit 4-6 poems at a time. No simultaneous submissions. Now returns mss with SASE. Publishes theme issues. Send SASE for upcoming themes. Reports within 2-3 months. Pays $10-15/poem. Buys one-time rights. The editor says "Poems chosen are upbeat, sometimes humorous, always easily understood."

THE CARIBBEAN WRITER; THE DAILY NEWS PRIZE; THE PAIEWONSKY PRIZE (IV-Regional), University of the Virgin Islands, RR 02, P.O. Box 10,000, Kingshill, St. Croix, USVI 00850, phone (809)692-4152, founded 1987, editor Dr. Erika Waters, is an annual literary magazine **with a Caribbean focus. The Caribbean must be central to the literary work or the work must reflect a Caribbean heritage, experience or perspective.** They have recently published poetry by Derek Walcott, Kamaw Brathwaite and Opal Palmer Odisa. As a sample the editor selected the opening lines of "Nineteen Ninety-Two" by Howard Fergus:

> Dawns 1992 a magic landfall
> on a brand new world of gold
> in Europe. Columbus makes a second
> coming after five hundred years
> not to violate virgin peoples
> but to carnival God for earlier conquests

The magazine is 190 pgs., 6×9, handsomely printed on heavy pebbled stock, flat-spined, with glossy

---

THE GEOGRAPHICAL INDEX, located before the Subject Index, can help you discover the publishers in your region. Publishers often favor poets (and work) from their own areas.

card cover, using advertising and b&w art by Caribbean artists. Press run is 1,000. Single copy: $9 plus $1.50 postage; subscription: $18 for 2 years. **Sample: $5 plus $1.50 postage. Send SASE for guidelines. (Note: Postage to and from the Virgin Islands is the same as within the US.) Simultaneous submissions OK. Blind submissions only: name, address, phone number and title of ms should appear in cover letter along with brief bio. Title only on ms. Deadline is September 30 of each year.** The annual appears in the spring. **Pays 2 copies. Acquires first North American serial rights.** Reviews books of poetry and fiction in 500 words. Open to unsolicited reviews. Poets may also send books for review consideration. The magazine annually awards The Daily News Prize of $300 for the best poem or poems and The Paiewonsky Prize of $100 for first-time publication.

‡**CARLETON ARTS REVIEW (II)**, Box 78, 18th Floor, Davidson Dunton Tower, Carleton University, Ottawa, Ontario K1S 5B6 Canada, phone (613)520-2310, founded 1982, is a 60-page biannual publishing poetry, prose, visual art (b&w) and reviews. **"All kinds of poetry accepted and encouraged."** They have published poetry by Stan Rogal, Brian Burke, Calvin White and Alan Packwood. They receive 200-300 poems a year, publish about 10%. Press run is 400 for 50 subscribers most of which are libraries, 150 shelf sales. Subscription: $8. **Sample postpaid: $4. No previously published poems or simultaneous submissions. "Please include a short biography and list of publications plus a SASE or SAE and international reply coupon." Submit in September or December. Always comments on rejections. Reports in 1-2 months. Pays 2 copies.**

CARN; THE CELTIC LEAGUE (IV-Ethnic), 11 Hilltop View, Braddan, Isle of Man, phone/fax (UK)(0)1624-627128, founded 1973, general secretary Bernard Moffatt, is a magazine-sized quarterly, circulation 2,000. "The aim of our quarterly is to contribute to a **fostering of cooperation between the Celtic peoples**, developing the consciousness of the special relationship which exists between them and making their achievements and their struggle for cultural and political freedom better known abroad. Contributions to *Carn* come **through invitation to people whom we know as qualified to write more or less in accordance with that aim. We would welcome poems *in the Celtic languages* if they are relating to that aim.** If I had to put it briefly, we have a political commitment, or, in other words, *Carn* **is not a literary magazine.**" Reviews books of poetry only if in the Celtic languages.

CARNEGIE MELLON MAGAZINE (II, IV-Specialized: university affiliation), Carnegie Mellon University, Pittsburgh PA 15213, phone (412)268-2132, editor Ann Curran, is the **alumni magazine** for the university and **limits selections to writers connected with the university.** As a sample the editor selected these lines from "Raw October" by Jim Daniels, associate professor of English:

> We toss eggs
> at cars, houses,
> Crazy Eddie chases
> us down the street
> Larry rips
> his shirt on a fence . . .

Submit 3 poems at a time (typed, double-spaced, with SASE) to Gerald Costanzo, poetry editor. No payment. Only uses staff-written reviews.

THE CAROLINA QUARTERLY; THE CHARLES B. WOOD AWARD (II), 510 Greenlaw Hall, CB #3520, University of North Carolina, Chapel Hill NC 27599-3520, founded 1948, poetry editor Carrie Blackstock, appears 3 times a year primarily publishing fiction and poetry. **They have no specifications regarding form, length, subject matter or style of poetry.** They have published poetry by Stephen Dunn, Mark Doty, Denise Levertov and X.J. Kennedy. As a sample the editor selected these lines from "Jacob" by George Garrett:

> Came then in the dark
> Out of the dark a dark
> Man without name or number
>   a brute fact
>   a sweet dream
>   labor of love and death

TCQ is about 90 pgs., 6×9, professionally printed and perfect-bound with one-color matte card cover, a few graphics and ads. They receive about 6,000 poems a year, accept less than 1%. Press run is 1,500 for 200 library subscriptions and various shelf sales. Single copy: $4; subscription: $10. **Sample postpaid: $5. No previously published poems or simultaneous submissions. "Every manuscript is read by at least two people. Manuscripts that make it to the meeting of the full poetry staff are discussed by all. Any poem with strong support of one or more people is accepted." Seldom comments on rejections. Send SASE for guidelines. Reports in 2 months. Pays 4 copies. Acquires first rights.** Reviews books of poetry. Open to unsolicited reviews. Poets may also send books for review consideration (attn: Editor). The Charles B. Wood Award for Distinguished Writing is given to the author of the best poem or short story published in each volume of *The Carolina Quarterly*.

Only those writers *without* major publications are considered and the winner receives $500.

CAROLINA WREN PRESS (II, IV-Women, ethnic, gay/lesbian, social issues), 120 Morris St., Durham NC 27701, phone (919)560-2738, founded 1976, publishes 1 book/year, **"primarily women and minorities, though men and majorities also welcome."** They have published poetry by Jaki Shelton Green, Mary Kratt and Steven Blaski. **Send book-length mss only. Reports in 2-4 months. Pays 10% of print run in copies. Send 9½ × 12 SASE for catalog and guidelines (include postage for 3 ounces).**

‡**CAROUSEL MAGAZINE (III)**, Room 274, University Centre, University of Guelph, Guelph, Ontario N1G 2W1 Canada, founded 1983, editors Dan Evans and Amber Wilson, is an annual which features "the best in North American fiction, poetry, essays and visual art by both established and emerging talent." They have recently published poetry by Timothy Findley, Leon Rooke, Lorna Crozier, Terry Griggs and Steven Heighton. It is 200 pgs., flat-spined. Their press run is 500. **Sample postpaid: $12. Type name and address on each page. Cover letter with short bio and info on past publications required. Send SASE (or SAE and IRCs) for more information. Pays 1 copy.**

‡**CASCANDO: THE NATIONAL STUDENT LITERARY MAGAZINE (IV-Students)**, P.O. Box 1499, London SW10 9TZ United Kingdom, phone (0171) 267-5899, fax (0171) 209-2428, founded 1992, co-editors Lisa Boardman and Emily Ormond, appears 3 times/year. *Cascando* is designed to publish new poetry, fiction, drama, essays, reviews and articles by students in part-time or full-time education in the UK and abroad. **"We prefer poetry 40-50 lines maximum, but will accept longer. We are very open in terms of form, subject matter and style. Work must be by students."** As a sample the editors selected these lines from "Portrait" by Charles Bennett:

> *I have a small black and white television*
> *for which I am grateful, actually.*
> *Absurd and sassy, Carmen Miranda*
> *restored me fully*
> *when order and reason*
> *began to meander.*

The editors say *Cascando* is 130 pgs., large, square and perfect-bound with full-color glossy cover, photos throughout and some ads. They receive 1,000 submissions a year, accept approximately 5%. Press run is 3,000 for 2,000 subscribers of which 600 are libraries, 500 shelf sales. Single copy: $9; subscription: $30. **Sample postpaid: $13. Make checks payable to Cascando Press Ltd. Submit 6 poems at a time. No previously published poems; simultaneous submissions OK. Cover letter with brief bio preferred. Often comments on rejections. Publishes theme issues. Send SASE (or SAE and IRCs) for guidelines and upcoming themes. Reports in 4-5 months. Sometimes sends prepublication galleys. Pays 1 copy.** Reviews books of poetry in 500-1,500 words. Open to unsolicited reviews. Poets may also send books for review consideration.

CAT FANCY (IV-Animals), P.O. Box 6050, Mission Viejo CA 92690, phone (714)855-8822, founded 1965, editor Debbie Phillips-Donaldson. *Cat Fancy* is a magazine-sized monthly that uses poems on the subject of cats. **"No more than 30 short lines; open on style and form, but a conservative approach is recommended. In our children's department we occasionally use longer, rhyming verse that tells a story about cats. No eulogies for pets that have passed away."** Circulation is 300,000. Subscription: $25.97. **Sample postpaid: $5.50. Submit ms with SASE; editors do not respond to submissions without SASE. Reports in 10-12 weeks. Pays $20/poem plus 2 copies.**

CATAMOUNT PRESS (II, IV-Anthology), 2519 Roland Rd. SW, Huntsville AL 35805, founded 1992, editor Georgette Perry, publishes 1-2 chapbooks and 1 anthology/year. **During 1997, Catamount will continue to use short to mid-length poems on nature and conservation. Single-author chapbooks will be 4 × 5½ micro-size. "Before submitting a chapbook ms, send 3 unattached 32¢ stamps for guidelines and sample, so that your submission will fit the format."** Poets recently published include Vincent Peloso, Amanda Kay and Jill Carpenter. As a sample the editor selected these lines from "winter, spring, summer, falling" by Kaye Bache-Snyder from the chapbook-anthology *Fingerlings*:

> *swallows*
> *sleep now on wing,*
> *sailing the sea of stars*
> *on an ancestral route of lights*
> *to spring*

The editor says, **"The best chance for publication is to submit 5-6 pgs. of poems, including some short ones, with SASE and cover note."** Previously published poems OK if author holds copyright. **Reports in 1 month. Pays copies.**

THE CATHARTIC (II), P.O. Box 1391, Ft. Lauderdale FL 33302, phone (305)967-9378, founded 1974, edited by Patrick M. Ellingham, "is a **small biannual poetry magazine devoted to the unknown poet** with the understanding that most poets are unknown in America." He says, "While there is no specific type of poem I look for, **rhyme for the sake of rhyme is discouraged. Any subject matter except where material is racist or sexist in nature. Long poems, over 60 lines, are not right for this magazine normally. I would like to see some poems that take chances with both form and language.** I would like to see poems that get out of and forget about self ['I'] and look at the larger world and the people in it with an intensity that causes a reader to react or want to react to it. I am gravitating toward work that looks at the darker side of life, is intense and uses words sparingly." **Considers sexually explicit material.** Recently published poets include Joy Walsh, John Grey, Rod Farmer and Errol Miller. It's a modest, 28-page pamphlet, offset printed from computer-generated text, MSWord and Pagemaker, consisting mostly of poems and b&w drawings and photos. He receives over 1,000 submissions/year, uses about 60. No backlog. **Sample postpaid: $3. Make checks payable to Patrick M. Ellingham. Submit 5-10 typed poems at a time. No previously published poems; simultaneous submissions OK. "Submissions without SASE are not considered or returned." Send SASE for guidelines. Reports in 1 month. Pays 1 copy.** The editor advises, "The only way for poets to know whether their work will get published or not is to submit. It is also essential to read as much poetry as possible—both old and new. Spend time with the classics as well as the new poets. Support the presses that support you—the survival of both is essential to the life of poetry."

CATS MAGAZINE (IV-Animals), P.O. Box 290037, Port Orange FL 32129, phone (904)788-2770, fax (904)788-2710, e-mail cats@pwr.com, website http://www.catsmag.com, editor Tracey Copeland, is a monthly magazine **about cats, including light verse about cats in a column called "Few Lines 'Bout Felines,"** for cat enthusiasts of all types. They have recently published poetry by Neva Davis, Frank Lloyd Kramer, Nancy Norton and Marcy Stewart Froemke. As a sample the editor selected this complete poem, "It's a Furrin Tongue" by Glenn Lybbert:

> When I meow, he dignifies
> My feeble sounds with long replies.
> On each attempt, I then opine
> I'll never learn the tongue Feline;
> For when I try, his eyes say that
> I make a most inferior cat.

Sample copy and writer's guidelines for $5 (including p&h). All submissions must have SASE. Publishes theme issues. Send SASE for upcoming themes. Reports in 3-4 months. Pays $5-30/ poem on publication.

CAVEAT LECTOR (III), 400 Hyde St., Apt. 606, San Francisco CA 94109, founded 1989, editors Christopher Bernard, James Bybee and Andrew Towne, appears 2 times/year. "*Caveat Lector* is devoted to the arts and to cultural and philosophical commentary. We publish visual art and music as well as literary and theoretical texts." **They want poetry that is "technically polished and deeply felt—if humorous, actually funny. Classical to experimental. 300-line limit."** They have recently published poetry by Marianne Milton, Christy Soto, Taylor Graham and Alfred Robinson. As a sample the editors selected these lines from "Matthew, do you ride?" by Zoon:

> How can you rule a god
> who doesn't speak your language?
> Why? When the shadow of god's passage touches you
> you don't deny the awful unanticipated call —
> you rise.

The editors say *CL* is 32-36 pgs., 4¼×11, offset and saddle-stitched. They receive about 500-600 poems a year, accept less than 5%. Press run is 300 for 50 subscribers of which 12 are libraries, 200 shelf sales. Single copy: $2.50; subscription: $10 for 4 issues. **Sample postpaid: $3. Simultaneous submissions OK.** Time between acceptance and publication is 6 months. **Often comments on rejections. Reports in 1 month. Pays 5 copies. Acquires first publication rights.** Christopher Bernard says, "The two rules of writing are: 1. Rewrite it again. 2. Rewrite it again. The writing level of most of our submissions is pleasingly high. A rejection by us is not always a criticism of the work, and we try to provide comments to our more promising submitters."

WM CAXTON LTD. (I, IV-Regional), 12037 Hwy. 42, Ellison Bay WI 54210, phone (414)854-2955, founded 1986, publisher K. Luchterhand. **"About 50% of our books involve an author's subvention of production costs with enhanced royalties and/or free copies in return,"** and the publisher acquires all rights. They want **"any serious poetry, not children's or doggerel." Poetry must have Northern Midwest author or subject.** They have published books of poetry by David Koenig (**Green Whistle**), Marilyn Taylor (**Shadows Like These**), William Olson (**North of Death's Door**) and Caroline Sibr (**Moon Gold**). Write or call to purchase sample copies.

THE CENTENNIAL REVIEW (II), 312 Linton Hall, Michigan State University, East Lansing MI 48824-1044, phone (517)355-1905, e-mail cenrev@pilot.msu.edu, founded 1957, editor R.K. Meiners, appears 3 times/year. **They want "that sort of poem which, however personal, bears implications for communal experience."** They have published poetry by David Citino and Dimitris Tsaloumas. As a sample the editor selected these lines from "Those Who Claimed We Hated Them" by Sherri Szeman:

> . . . *We clicked tongues in sympathy*
> *at the blue-black scratchings on their forearms.*
>
> *But we had all suffered during the war.*
> *We suffered, as they did. We had only*
>
> *feigned gaiety at their misfortunes, to*
> *convince our oppressors to spare our homes.*

It is 240 pgs., 6×9, desktop-published, perfect-bound, with 3-color cover, art, graphics and ads. They receive about 500 poems a year, accept about 2%. Press run is 1,000 for 800 subscribers. Subscription: $12/year. **Sample postpaid: $6. Submit 5 poems at a time. No previously published poems or simultaneous submissions. Seldom comments on rejections. Publishes theme issues. Send SASE for guidelines and upcoming themes. Reports in about 2 months. Pays 2 copies plus 1-year subscription. Acquires all rights. Returns rights "when asked by authors for reprinting."**

CENTER PRESS; MASTERS AWARD (III), Box 16452, Encino CA 91416-6452, founded 1980, editor Gabriella Stone. Center Press is "a small press presently publishing 6-7 works per year including poetry, photojournals, calendars, novels, etc. We look for quality, freshness and that touch of genius." In poetry, **"we want to see verve, natural rhythms, discipline, impact**, etc. We are flexible but **verbosity, triteness and saccharine make us cringe. We now read and publish only mss accepted from the Masters Award."** They have published books by Bebe Oberon, Walter Calder, Exene Vida, Carlos Castenada and Claire Bloome. As a sample the editor selected these lines from "Mostly the Moon" by Scott Alejandro Sonder (the 1996 Masters Award Winner):

> *It is mostly the moon*
> *she said, so let's not talk*
> *of love as the crescent*
> *rolls slowly to silver*
> *and luminous shadows*
> *wove jasmine over*
> *coats of night.*

Their tastes are for poets such as Charles Bukowski, Sylvia Plath, Erica Jong and Bob Dylan. **"We have strong liaisons with the entertainment industry and like to see material that is media-oriented and au courant.** We sponsor the Masters Awards, established in 1981, including a poetry award with a $1,000 grand prize annually plus each winner (and the five runners up in poetry) will be published in a clothbound edition and distributed to selected university and public libraries, news mediums, etc. There is a one-time only $10 administration and reading fee per entrant. Further application and details available with a #10 SASE." The editor says, "Please study what we publish before you consider submitting."

UNIVERSITY OF CENTRAL FLORIDA CONTEMPORARY POETRY SERIES (II), % English Dept., University of Central Florida, Orlando FL 32816-1346, phone (407)823-2212, founded 1968, poetry editor Judith Hemschemeyer, publishes **two 50- to 80-page hardback or paperback collections each year. "Strong poetry on any theme in the lyric-narrative tradition."** They have published poetry by Robert Cooperman, Katherine Soniat and John Woods. As a sample the editor selected these lines from "The Everly Brothers" in *Music Appreciation* by Floyd Skloot:

> *My brother thought they were freaks*
> *of nature, voices fitting together*
> *through some fluke of chemistry.*
> *He said they might just as well*
> *have been Siamese twins sharing*
> *a heart, or the Everly humpbacks.*

Submit complete paginated ms with table of contents and acknowledgement of previously published poems. Simultaneous submissions OK. "Please send a reading fee of $7, a SASE for return of ms, and a self-addressed postcard for acknowledgment of receipt of ms." Reads submissions September through April. Reports in 3 months. Time between acceptance and publication is 1 year.

‡CHAFF (I), 1061 NW 84th Ave., Plantation FL 33322, founded 1996, first issue expected April 1997, editor Jordan Taylor Young, is a semiannual publication "for the express purpose of uniting Christian poets through the publication of their work." **They want "free verse poetry—rhyme and**

meter only if exceptional quality—romantic, Christian, or concerning nature, growing older or friendship. Nothing satanic, obscene, violent, sensual, erotic or homosexual." As a sample of the type of works they are seeking, the editor selected an excerpt from "Lost Friend" by Carrie Lyons:

> And you my dear
> are one long streak
> of moonbeam and star
> Not of this world,
> not really mine.
> Where have you gone—
> When can I follow?

The editor says *Chaff* will be 20-24 pgs., 5½×8, laser-printed and stapled. Estimated press run is 50-100. **Submit 5 poems at a time with $1/poem reading fee. Previously published poems and simultaneous submissions OK. Cover letter required. Seldom comments on rejections. Publishes theme issues. Send SASE for upcoming themes. Reports in 3-4 weeks. Pays 2 copies.** The editor says, "Often poets are not recognized for their artistry, separated like chaff from wheat. We intend to provide a stronger link to self, helping new and aspiring poets to find their own voices through the publication of their work."

CHAMINADE LITERARY REVIEW (II, IV-Regional), 3140 Waialae Ave., Honolulu HI 96816, founded 1986, editor Loretta Petrie, appears annually giving **special consideration to Hawaii's writers or Hawaii subject matter. "No jingles or pop poetry."** They have recently published poetry by Eleanor Wilner, William Heyen and Rob Wilson. As a sample the editor selected these lines from "The Waking Stone" by Michael McPherson:

> The sharks here cannot be trusted.
> Poisons in their meat make them crazy,
> they feel no bond of loyalty or kinship
> nor any longer honor the ancient ways.
> Living seas near shore are stained
> with runoff from the burning fields,
> effluents open like brown dark flowers
> and coax the grey swimmers to frenzy.
> Spirit warriors are returning to land,
> they stand and cast a spectral gaze
> over plains now littered with debris.

CLR features the work of many well-known creative writers and thus, at first blush, seems like a mainstream literary magazine. But poems, prose and artwork play off each other for added effect and unify such themes as ecology, love, nature, etc. The handsomely printed magazine averages over 200 pgs., 6×9, flat-spined with glossy card cover. They accept about 25% of 500 poems received/year. Press run is 500 for 350 subscribers of which 6 are libraries. Subscription: $10/year, $18/2 years. **Sample postpaid: $4. Previously published poems OK. Pays year's subscription**. Open to unsolicited reviews.

CHAMPION BOOKS, INC.; NEW SHOES SERIES (II), P.O. Box 636, Lemont IL 60439, phone (800)230-1135 or (708)257-9655, fax (800)827-7415, founded 1993, president Rebecca Rush, publishes 3-12 flat-spined paperback books of poetry/year through their New Shoes Series. They say, "In their prime, Kerouac and Ginsberg were never literary stars; they were the unknown and the unheard, speaking their minds and breaking new literary ground. But, now, decades after their heyday, they have become the pantheon for the mainstream of today's youth. Combined with the crossover between music and literature by such artists as Henry Rollins, William Burroughs and Jim Morrison, this has created a new era of readers with an appreciation for the great authors of the past as well as an interest in the direction of writing in the future. **Champion Books seeks obscure and unrenowned authors interested not in following in the footsteps of others, but in creating their own new shoes to walk in.**" As a sample the editor selected "Untitled" from *My Gradual Demise & honeysuckle* by Douglas A. Martin:

> licking wounds like a deranged dog,
> I fall to the altar of a desk,
> drink communion from a fountain pen,
> and bleed onto an empty page of redemption.
> I will come again.

Query first, with 5-10 sample poems, cover letter with brief bio. Previously published poems and simultaneous submissions OK. Replies to queries in 1-3 months. Pays 7-10% royalties and about 4 author's copies. Write for catalog to order samples. Rebecca Rush says, "As an editor I am more interested in the content and tone of the poetry rather than the number of periodicals in which the poems have previously appeared. I am also impressed with authors who take initiative to promote their own works through self-published chapbooks and readings; it's always helpful if an author is willing to extend their own time and effort in order to get their works out to the public."

‡CHANGING MEN: ISSUES IN GENDER, SEX AND POLITICS (IV-Feminist), P.O. Box 3121, Kansas City KS 66103, phone (816)374-5969, founded 1979, poetry editor Bob Vance, is described as **"a pro-feminist journal for men—politics, poetry, graphics, news."** He wants work by men and women that "expresses the emotional, intellectual and sensual complexity of living in America in an age enlightened by but not yet freed by feminism, gay liberation, socialism and ethnic beauty. A concern for form and invention is appreciated." They have published poetry by Sidney Miller, Diane Kendig, T. Obatala, Sesshu Foster, Assotto Saint and Denis O'Donovan. Though the poetry is "so varied" the editor felt he could not select 4 representative lines, here are the opening lines of Sholom Aram's "Two Poems on the Theme of Incest" to illustrate the quality, if not variety, of poetry in the magazine:

> Shameful secrets bind us and hold us apart
> like the plastic rings on a six pack of beer.
> Who do I protect not to say what they are?

They use about 6 pgs. of poetry in each magazine-sized issue. Circulation is 6,000 for 2,000 subscribers of which 10% are libraries. **Sample postpaid: $6. Submit up to 5 poems. Simultaneous submissions OK.** Cover letter not required but appreciated: **"short, personal, fun, no credit lists, no descriptions of enclosed poems. Let the poems speak for themselves, but I don't mind short discussion of why one chooses to write (of all things) poetry."** Editor sometimes comments on rejections. **Send SASE for guidelines. Reports in 2-8 months. Pays copies.** The editor says, "I am not limited to publishing poems directly related to pro-feminist men's issues, and would prefer to see work that relates to these issues by chance or in an original unexpected way. I am inundated with poems about fathers!"

CHANTRY PRESS (III), 32 Oak Place, Hawthorne NJ 07506, founded 1981, poetry editor D. Patrick, publishes **perfect-bound paperbacks of "high quality" poetry. No other specifications.** They have published work by Laura Boss, Anne Bailie, Ruth Lisa Schechter, Susan Clements and Joanne Riley. These sample lines are from *Winter Light* by Maria Gillan:

> Remember me, Ladies,
> the silent one?
> I have found my voice
> and my rage will blow
> your house down.

That's from an 80-page book (usually books from this press are 72 pgs.), flat-spined, glossy cover, good printing on heavy paper, author's photo on back, $5.95. **Don't send complete ms. Query first, with sample poems and SASE, no cover letter necessary. Simultaneous submissions OK. Submission period October through April. Replies in 4 months. Always sends prepublication galleys. Pays 15% royalties after costs are met and 10 author's copies. Very short comment "sometimes" on rejected mss.** The editor advises: "Do not be rude in inquiring about the status of your manuscript."

CHANTS (II, IV-Translations), Dept. of English, Kennesaw State College, 1000 Chastain Rd., Kennesaw GA 30144-5591, founded 1988, editors Austin Hummell and Michael Fournier, appears twice a year. The editors "publish the **best translations and the most ambitious lyric poetry we can find. We encourage all poets, particularly younger ones, for whom poetry is a ruling passion.**" They have published poetry by Jorie Graham, Ron Rash and Ricardo Pau-Llosa. As a sample the editors selected the following lines from "Rerun" by Pamela McClure:

> Rivervalley, unusual eddy
> And cerulean's the seizure above
> So in the daylight noise the road ahead
> Drops us back to the house and its cover
> Of shadow, hollyhock limbs limbering
> Up the rerun of vine-braid and ivy.

Chants is 64 pgs., digest-sized, professionally printed, flat-spined, with photo or graphic on cover but no inside art. They accept about 5% of poems received. Single copy: $4. **Sample: $4 plus $1 postage. No previously published poems or simultaneous submissions.** Time between acceptance and publication is up to 6 months—occasionally longer. **Sometimes comments on rejections. Reports in 1-3 months. Pays 2 copies.** The editors say, "We favor the lyric above other modes, but will publish any poem, formal or informal, that has heart and imagination. We discourage timid and anecdotal verse, and bloodless experiment. We publish poetry exclusively, and are fond of translation. We feature one poet per issue, and try to include a brief essay to accompany each feature."

CHAPMAN (IV-Ethnic); CHAPMAN PRESS (V), 4 Broughton Place, Edinburgh EH1 3RX Scotland, phone (0131)557-2207, fax (0131)556-9565, founded 1970, editor Joy Hendry, "provides an outlet for new work by **established Scottish writers and for new, up-and-coming writers also,**

for the discussion and criticism of this work and for reflection on current trends in Scottish life and literature. But *Chapman* is not content to follow old, well-worn paths; it throws open its pages to new writers, new ideas and new approaches. In the international tradition revived by MacDiarmid, *Chapman* **also features the work of foreign writers and broadens the range of Scottish cultural life."** They have published poetry and fiction by Alasdair Gray, Liz Lochhead, Sorley MacLean, T.S. Law, Edwin Morgan, Willa Muir, Tom Scott and Una Flett. As a sample the editor selected these lines from Judy Steel's poem "For Nicole Boulanger" who, Steel says, "was born in the same year as my daughter and died in the Lockerbie air disaster of 1988":

> *You died amongst these rolling Border hills:*
> *The same our daughters played and rode and walked in -*
> *They make a nursery fit to shape and mould*
> *A spirit swift as water, free as air.*
>
> *But you, west-winging through the Christmas dark*
> *Found them no playground but a mortuary -*
> *Your young life poised for flight to woman's years*
> *Destroyed as wantonly as moorland game.*

Chapman appears 4 times a year in a 6×9, perfect-bound format, 104 pgs., professionally printed in small type on matte stock with glossy card cover, art in 2 colors. Press run is 2,000 for 900 subscribers of which 200 are libraries. They receive "thousands" of poetry submissions/year, use about 200, **have a 4- to 6-month backlog. Sample: £3.50 (overseas). Cover letter required. No simultaneous submissions. Reports "as soon as possible." Always sends prepublication galleys. Pays £8/page plus 1 copy.** Staff reviews books of poetry. Send books for review consideration. **Chapman Press is not interested in unsolicited mss.** The editor says poets should not "try to court approval by writing poems especially to suit what they perceive as the nature of the magazine. They usually get it wrong and write badly." Also, they are interested in receiving poetry dealing with women's issues and feminism.

THE CHARITON REVIEW PRESS; THE CHARITON REVIEW (II), Northeast Missouri State University, Kirksville MO 63501, phone (816)785-4499, founded 1975, editor Jim Barnes. *The Chariton Review* began in 1975 as a twice yearly literary magazine and in 1978 added the activities of the press, producing "limited editions (not chapbooks!) of **full-length collections . . . for the purpose of introducing solid, contemporary poetry to readers**. The books go free to the regular subscribers of *The Chariton Review*; others are sold to help meet printing costs." The poetry published in both the books and the magazine is, according to the editor, **"open and closed forms—traditional, experimental, mainstream. We do not consider verse, only poetry in its highest sense, whatever that may be. The sentimental and the inspirational are not poetry for us. Also, no more 'relativism': short stories and poetry centered around relatives."** They have published poets such as Michael Spence, Neil Myers, Sam Maio, Andrea Budy, Charles Edward Eaton, Wayne Dodd and J'laine Robnolt. There are 40-50 pages of poetry in each issue of the *Review*, a 6×9, flat-spined magazine of over 100 pages, professionally printed, glossy cover with photographs. Circulation is about 600 with 400 subscribers of which 100 are libraries. They receive 7,000-8,000 submissions/year, of which they use 35-50, with never more than a 6-month backlog. Subscription: $9 for 1 year, $15 for 2 years. **Sample postpaid: $5. Submit 5-7 poems at a time, typescript single-spaced. No simultaneous submissions. Do *not* write for guidelines. Always sends prepublication galleys. Pays $5/printed page. Buys first North American serial rights. Contributors are expected to subscribe or buy copies.** Open to unsolicited reviews. Poets may also send books for review consideration. *The Chariton Review* continues to be a lively magazine open to all styles and forms with only one criterion: excellence. Moreover, response times here are quick, and accepted poems often appear within a few issues of notification. **To be considered for book publication, query first. Samples of books: $3 and $5. Payment for book publication: $500 with 20 or more copies. Usually no criticism is supplied.**

THE CHATTAHOOCHEE REVIEW (II), DeKalb College, 2101 Womack Rd., Dunwoody GA 30338, phone (404)551-3166, founded 1980, editor-in-chief Lamar York, poetry editor (Mr.) Collie Owens, is a quarterly of poetry, short fiction, essays, reviews and interviews, published by DeKalb College. **"We publish a number of Southern writers, but *CR* is not by design a regional magazine. In poetry we look for vivid imagery, unique point of view and voice, freshness of figurative language, and attention to craft. All themes, forms and styles are considered as long as they impact the whole person: heart, mind, intuition and imagination."** They have published poetry by Peter Meinke, David Kirby, Allan Peterson, Bin Ramke, Peter Wild and Cory Brown. As a sample the editors selected these lines from "A Good Date" by David Staudt:

> *We walked onto the ice dams after supper,*
> *cool floors powdered for a two-step.*
> *Snowfall we couldn't see hissed like sparks*

> *doused on our wet faces. Under the cliffs,*
> *reliefers from Packerton drank and howled,*
> *and domes of visible flakes, thick as glitter*
> *in souvenirs from the Poconos,*
> *flickered over cans of sterno or sticks*
> *where fishermen hunkered in lawnchairs*
> *over blue slots routed in the ice.*

The Review is 90 pgs., 6×9, professionally printed on white stock with b&w reproductions of artwork, flat-spined, with one-color card cover. Its reputation as a premiere literary magazine continues to grow. Recent issues feature a wide range of forms and styles augmenting prose selections. Circulation is 1,250, of which 300 are complimentary copies sent to editors and "miscellaneous VIP's." Subscription: $15/year. **Sample postpaid: $5. Writers should send 1 copy of each poem and a cover letter with bio material. No simultaneous submissions.** Time between acceptance and publication is 3-4 months. **Publishes theme issues. Send SASE for guidelines. Queries will be answered in 1-2 weeks. Reports in 3 months. Pays 2 copies. Acquires first rights.** Staff reviews books of poetry and short fiction in 1,500 words, single or multi-book format. Send books for review consideration.

A biannual nonprofit publication, **Chelsea** encourages its cover designers to be creative. "It's in keeping with our eclectic outlook," says Editor Richard Foerster. "For the last 38 years, each cover of **Chelsea** has been different." The New York-based journal primarily publishes poetry, fiction and essays by new and established writers. However, poetry is **Chelsea**'s primary focus. In fact, until recently, all the editors have been poets, Foerster says. The cover for issue number 58 was designed by New York City freelance designer Donald Martiny.

CHELSEA; CHELSEA AWARD COMPETITION (III, IV-Translations), P.O. Box 773, Cooper Station, New York NY 10276-0773, founded 1958, editor Richard Foerster, associate editors Alfredo de Palchi and Andrea Lockett, is a long-established, high-quality literary biannual aiming to promote intercultural communication. **"We look for intelligence and sophisticated technique in both experimental and traditional forms. We are also interested in translations of contemporary poets. Although our tastes are eclectic, we lean toward the cosmopolitan avant-garde. We would like to see more poetry by writers of color. Do not want to see 'inspirational' verse, pornography or poems that rhyme merely for the sake of rhyme."** They have recently published poetry by Renée Ashley, Ellen Bass, Roald Hoffmann, Ben Howard, James Laughlin and Michael Waters. As an example of "the kind of attention to language and imagery" wanted for *Chelsea*, the editor selected these lines from "The Eye-mote" by Sylvia Plath:

> *What I want back is what I was*
> *Before the bed, before the knife,*
> *Before the brooch-pin and the salve*
> *Fixed me in this parenthesis;*
> *Horses fluent in the wind,*
> *A place, a time gone out of mind.*

Chelsea is 192-240 pgs., 6×9, flat-spined, offset, cover art varies, occasional photos, ads. Circulation is 1,400 for 800 subscriptions of which 200 are libraries. Subscription: $13 domestic, $17 foreign. **Sample: $7. Submissions of 5-7 pgs. of poetry are ideal; long poems should not exceed 10 pgs.; must be typed; include brief bio. No previously published poems or simultaneous submissions.**

"We try to comment favorably on above-average mss; otherwise, we do not have time to provide critiques." Reports within 3 months. Always sends prepublication galleys. Pays $15/page and 2 copies. Buys first North American serial rights and one-time nonexclusive reprint rights. Guidelines for their annual Chelsea Award Competition (deadline December 15), $750 for poetry, available for SASE to P.O. Box 1040, York Beach ME 03910. Work published in *Chelsea* has been included in the 1993, 1994 and 1995 volumes of *The Best American Poetry*. Richard Foerster, editor, comments: "Beginners should realize that editors of little magazines are always overworked and that it is necessary haste and not a lack of concern or compassion that makes rejections seem coldly impersonal."

‡**CHERRY STREET GRILL (I, II)**, P.O. Box 278, Alamo CA 94507-0278, phone (510)930-6762, e-mail cherrystrt@aol.com, founded 1995, editor Mark Hoehner, is a quarterly "eclectic collection of lively, unpredictable poetry that makes the reader think, feel, and want to read the magazine cover to cover, and then go back to the beginning and do it again." **They want "well-crafted, down-to-earth, accessible poetry on any subject. Put away your rhyming dictionary and avoid clichés. Don't send in a poem you wrote today—good poetry takes time to mature. Prefer poems under 50 lines in length. No love sonnets, overly sentimental verse or 'inspirational' poetry. Only about 5% of accepted poems rhyme."** They have recently published poetry by Romola Robb Allrud, Caron Andregg and Raphael Seth. As a sample the editor selected this poem, "To Be in the Same Room with Beauty," by Robert Klein Engler:

> *The overhead fans mill their portions of smoky air.*
> *Paintings hang like ash on the edge of glaciers.*
>
> *You are reading in the corner—asleep and awake.*
>
> *Once, when you turn to look at a noise in the street,*
> *I feel the lance of your eyes wind by.*

Cherry Street Grill is 24-32 pgs., digest-sized, photocopied from laser-printed originals and saddle-stapled, with colored card stock cover. They receive approximately 350 poems a year, accept about 20%. Press run is 150 for 45 subscribers. Single copy: $3; subscription: $10. **Sample postpaid: $2. Make checks payable to Mark Hoehner. Submit 5 poems at a time, typed with name and address on each page. Previously published poems and simultaneous submissions OK. Cover letter preferred. If submitting via e-mail, save work as "text" prior to sending. Poems are read by the editor and two assistant editors. Seldom comments on rejections. Send SASE for guidelines or obtain via e-mail. Guidelines are also included in each issue of the magazine. Reports in 6-8 weeks. Pays 3 copies.**

CHICAGO REVIEW (III, IV-Translations), 5801 S. Kenwood, Chicago IL 60637-1794, website http://www.uchicago.edu/humanities/review/crhomepage.html, founded 1946, poetry editor Devin Johnston. **"We publish high quality poetry. About 20% of the work we select is unsolicited; the remainder is solicited from poets whose work we admire. Translations are welcome, but please include a statement of permission from the original publisher if work is not in the public domain."** They have recently published poets as diverse as Alice Fulton, Yusef Komunyakaa, Turner Cassity, Nathaniel Mackey, August Kleinzahler, Meena Alexander and Adrian C. Louis. Editors seem to prefer lyric free verse—some of it leaning toward avant-garde and some quite accessible. Circulation is 2,800. **Sample postpaid: $5. New submissions read year-round. Reports in 3 months, longer in some cases. Sometimes sends prepublication galleys. Pays 3 copies and one-volume subscription.** Occasionally reviews books of poetry. Open to unsolicited reviews.

CHICKADEE MAGAZINE; THE YOUNG NATURALIST FOUNDATION (IV-Children, nature), 179 John St., Suite 500, Toronto, Ontario M5T 3G5 Canada, founded 1979, managing editor Catherine Jane Wren, is a magazine **for children 3-9 about science and nature** appearing 10 times/year. **They want "evocative poetry; poems that play with words; humorous poetry; no longer than 50 lines. Nothing religious, anthropomorphic; no formal language; no poetry that is difficult to understand."** As a sample the editor selected this complete poem, "Snow Stars," by Goldie Olszynko Gryn:

> *I'm stepping on snow stars,*
> *small glittery glow stars.*
> *I'm stepping on snow stars*
> *that fall from the sky.*
>
> *I'm stepping on snow stars,*
> *cold crystally pole stars,*
> *but now there are no stars*
> *where I have walked by.*

Chickadee is 32 pgs., magazine-sized, professionally printed in full-color, with paper cover. They accept 1-2% of every 500 poems received. Circulation: 25,800 within US and 100,000 within Canada. Subscription: $14.95 US. **Sample postpaid: $3.75. Submit up to 10 poems at a time. Simultaneous submissions considered. Send SASE (or SAE and IRC) for writers' guidelines. Pays $10-75/poem plus 2 copies. Buys all rights.** "*Chickadee* is a 'hands-on' science and nature publication designed to entertain and educate 3- to 9-year-olds. Each issue contains photos, illustrations, an easy-to-read animal story, a craft project, puzzles, a science experiment and a pullout poster."

CHICORY BLUE PRESS (IV-Women, senior citizens), 795 East St. N., Goshen CT 06756, phone (860)491-2271, founded 1988, publisher Sondra Zeidenstein, publishes **2-3 chapbooks/year. She is currently open to receiving queries for chapbooks by women poets over age 60. Submit 5-7 poems and cover letter with only "a brief introduction of self and work." Replies to queries and mss (if invited) in 3 months. Seldom comments on rejections. Pays royalties, honorarium or 10 author's copies.** She has published poetry by Honor Moore and Pattiann Rogers. **Samples can be ordered from the press.**

CHILDREN'S BETTER HEALTH INSTITUTE; BENJAMIN FRANKLIN LITERARY AND MEDICAL SOCIETY, INC.; HUMPTY DUMPTY'S MAGAZINE; TURTLE MAGAZINE FOR PRESCHOOL KIDS; CHILDREN'S DIGEST; CHILDREN'S PLAYMATE; JACK AND JILL; CHILD LIFE (IV-Children), 1100 Waterway Blvd., P.O. Box 567, Indianapolis IN 46206-0567. This publisher of magazines stressing health for children has a **variety of needs for mostly short, simple poems.** For example, *Humpty Dumpty* is **for ages 4-6;** *Turtle* is for preschoolers, similar emphasis, uses many stories in rhyme—and action rhymes, etc.; *Children's Digest* is **for preteens (10-13);** *Jack and Jill* is **for ages 7-10.** *Child Life* is **for ages 9-11.** *Children's Playmate* is **for ages 6-8.** All appear 8 times a year with cartoon art, very colorful. **Sample postpaid: $1.25. Send SASE for guidelines. Reports in 8-10 weeks. Pays $15 minimum.** Staff reviews books of poetry. Send books for review consideration. The editors suggest that writers who wish to appear in their publications **study current issues carefully.** "We receive too many poetry submissions that are about kids, not for kids. Or, the subject matter is one that adults think children would or should like. We'd like to see more humorous verse."

‡**CHINOOK PRESS (IV-Regional); THE CHINOOK QUARTERLY (I, II)**, 1432 Yellowstone Ave., Billings MT 59102, phone (406)245-7704, founded 1996, editor/publisher Mary Ellen Westwood. *The Chinook Quarterly* is a literary magazine containing prose, poetry, art and nonfiction "combining the traditional values and the contemporary spirit of the West. **I am open to work of any kind, but want real human themes with some purpose and message about life. As a Westerner, I favor themes of change and redemption, nature and harmony. I will also take some poems on seasonal themes. I do not want poems that shock, just for the sake of shocking. But I am willing to take on difficult themes of human importance."** In their first issue, they published poetry by Josephine Jones, Mela Mlekush and Dan Burke. As a sample the editor selected these lines from "Luck of the Draw" by Paul Zarzyski:

> high above the Missouri River's silent swirls,
> the flicking together of leaves
> is the applause of small green hands, children
> thrilled by a winning ride, by their wildest wish
> beginning, as everything begins, with luck
> of the draw, with a breeze in the heat . . .

The editor says *TCQ* is 60-80 pgs., $7 \times 8\frac{1}{2}$, flat-spined with glossy cover, some color. They accept 48-60 poems a year. Subscription: $20. **Sample postpaid: $7. Submit 4-6 poems at a time, name and address on each page. No previously published poems; simultaneous submissions OK, if identified as such. Cover letter required; include brief bio and brief statement about why you wrote the work.** Time between acceptance and publication is 2-12 months. **Always comments on rejections. Send SASE for guidelines. Reports within 2 months. Always sends prepublication galleys. Pays $5/poem plus 4 copies.** Reviews books and chapbooks and includes general literary criticism. Open to unsolicited reviews. Poets may also send books for review consideration. Chinook Press, **which has a Northwest regional bias,** also plans to publish 2 paperback books of poetry/year. **Prefers to see complete ms. Replies to mss in 2-6 months.** As for payment, "individual arrangements will be made with each poet based on the book and the market. All poet will contribute is promotion

THE CHAPBOOK INDEX, located before the Geographical Index, lists those publishers who consider chapbook manuscripts. A chapbook, a small volume of work, is often a good middle step between magazine and book publication.

time." **Call or write to purchase sample.** The editor says, "I want real, true-to-life poetry commenting on and challenging change in the human condition. I do not want a lot of 'ivory tower' musings. I admire risk-takers because I am one, and I will publish both new and established writers who take a risk with their work."

CHIRON REVIEW; CHIRON BOOKS; CHIRON REVIEW POETRY CONTEST (I, II), 522 E. South Ave., St. John KS 67576-2212, phone (316)549-3933, founded 1982 as the *Kindred Spirit*, editor Michael Hathaway, assistant editor Jane Hathaway, contributing editor (poetry) Gerald Locklin, is a quarterly tabloid using photographs of featured writers. **No taboos.** They have published poetry by Charles Bukowski, Marge Piercy, Antler, Wilma Elizabeth McDaniel and Ron Androla. As a sample the editor selected these lines from "The Wild Turkey" by Lynn Trombetta:

> There was not one worthy thing about her, unless it was
> her willingness to be attentive, to be true.
> And see then, how the sun lifted, hurried forward
> towards her, gilding her with gladness
> touching her all over with star bright hands.

Each issue is 24-32 pgs. and "contains dozens of poems." Their press run is about 1,000. **Sample postpaid: $4 ($8 overseas or institutions). Submit 3-6 poems at a time, "typed or printed legibly." No simultaneous submissions or previously published poems. Very seldom publishes theme issues. Send SASE for guidelines and any upcoming themes. Reports in 2-4 weeks. Pays 1 copy. Acquires first-time rights.** Reviews books of poetry in 500-900 words. Open to unsolicited reviews. Poets may also send books for review consideration. **For book publication submit complete ms.** They publish 1-3 books/year, flat-spined, professionally printed, **paying 25% of press run of 100-200 copies.** Their annual poetry contest offers awards of $100 plus 1-page feature in Winter issue, $50, and 5 free subscriptions and a Chiron Press book. Entry fee: $5/poet.

THE CHRISTIAN CENTURY (II, IV-Religious, social issues), Dept. PM, 407 S. Dearborn St., Chicago IL 60605, phone (312)427-5380, founded 1884, named *The Christian Century* 1900, founded again 1908, joined by *New Christian* 1970, poetry editor Dean Peerman. This "ecumenical weekly" is a liberal, sophisticated journal of news, articles of opinion and reviews from a generally Christian point-of-view, **using approximately one poem/issue, not necessarily on religious themes but in keeping with the literate tone of the magazine. "No pietistic or sentimental doggerel, please."** They have published poetry by Robert Beum, Joan Rohr Myers, Ida Fasel, Jill Baumgaertner, David Abrams, Catherine Shaw, J. Barrie Shepherd and Wendell Berry. As a sample the editor selected this poem, "Grain Silos," by James Worley:

> Cathedrals of the oldest preached religion,
> towers erected to the oldest useful god
> (the one now worshiped three times every day
> by those who can, invoked by those who can't)
> these cylinders of homage (oblong praise)
> project a plenty that is its own reward,
> a yearning that has grown its own response:
> the deity whom these raised prayers rise to laud
> resides (when crops are good) in grateful guts.

The journal is magazine-sized, printed on quality newsprint, using b&w art, cartoons and ads, about 30 pgs., saddle-stapled. **Sample postpaid: $2. No simultaneous submissions. Submissions without SASE or SAE and IRCs will not be returned. Pays usually $20/poem plus 1 copy and discount on additional copies. Acquires all rights. Inquire about reprint permission.** Reviews books of poetry in 300-400 words, single format; 400-500 words, multi-book.

CHRISTIAN POET; REDWOOD FAMILY CHAPEL PUBLICATIONS (I, IV-Religious), 2745 Monterey Hwy. #76, San Jose CA 95111-3129, e-mail soos@soos.com, website http://www.soos. com/poetpark, founded as Realities Library in 1975, as CCR Publications in 1987, now Redwood Family Chapel Publications, editor and publisher Ric Soos. He has published books of poetry by Ruth Daigon and Ella Blanche Salmi. "Because of economic conditions, we have discontinued our book series. To replace the book series we have started *Christian Poet*. It will be published as often as we have time, poetry and finances." As a sample the editor selected this poem, "The Test," by Pete Green:

> Lugging wood from yard to stove
> I come to the kitchen step and door;
> The Test, with arms loaded numb,
> groping, groping, never grasping that
> Christ is a door nailed open.

Christian Poet is published free at the website mentioned above. **Poets may submit one poem via e-mail. Include short bio with submission. Previously published poems OK. Seldom comments on**

rejections. The editor says, "Please keep in mind when you contact me that I believe in Jesus Christ, and that anything I publish will be to help further the Gospel if it is for that purpose. **In poetry, I look for items that will not hinder the spread of the Gospel. In other words, the poet need not be Christian, does not need to mention Christ by name, but I will no longer be publishing for shock value."** He publishes those "who support me in some respect . . . Support is not always financial."

THE CHRISTIAN SCIENCE MONITOR (II), The Home Forum Page, 1 Norway St., Boston MA 02115, phone (617)450-2474, founded 1908, is an international daily newspaper. **Poetry used regularly in The Home Forum, poetry editor Elizabeth Lund. They want "finely crafted poems that celebrate the extraordinary in the ordinary. Seasonal material always needed. Especially interested in poems about life in the city. No violence, sensuality or racism. Short poems preferred."** They have published work by William Stafford, Diana der-Hovanessian, Steven Ratiner and Lyn Lifshin. As a sample the editor selected these lines from "Working in the Rain" by Robert Morgan:

> *My father loved more than anything to*
> *work outside in wet weather. Beginning*
> *at daylight he'd go out in dripping brush*
> *to mow or pull weeds for hog and chickens.*

Submit no more than 5 poems at a time, single-spaced. SASE must be included. No previously published poems or simultaneous submissions. Usually reports within 1-2 months. Pays varying rates, upon publication.

‡CHRISTIANITY AND THE ARTS (I, II, IV-Religious), P.O. Box 118088, Chicago IL 60611, phone (312)642-8606, fax (312)266-7719, e-mail chrnarts@aol.com, founded 1994, editor/publisher Marci Whitney-Schenck, poetry editor Robert Klein Engler **(and submissions should go directly to him at Richard J. Daley College, 7500 S. Pulaski, Chicago IL 60652)**. *Christianity and the Arts* is a quarterly magazine designed "to celebrate the revelation of God through the arts and to encourage Christian artistic expression." **They want poetry of "excellence—open to all styles—with a Christian viewpoint."** They have recently published poetry by Nick Patricca and N. Kenneth Heffley. It is 48 pgs., 8½ × 11, professionally printed on coated stock and saddle-stapled, with b&w and color photos. They accept 20% of the poetry received. Press run is 4,000 for 2,700 subscribers, 700 shelf sales. Single copy: $4.50; subscription: $15. **Sample postpaid: $6. Previously published poems and simultaneous submissions OK.** Time between acceptance and publication is 6 months. **Publishes theme issues. Send SASE for upcoming themes. Reports within 2 weeks. Always sends prepublication galleys. Pays 2 copies. Acquires first or one-time rights.** The editor says they prefer poets subscribe.

THE CHRISTOPHER PUBLISHING HOUSE (II), 24 Rockland St., Commerce Green, Hanover MA 02339, phone (617)826-7474, fax (617)826-5556, founded 1910, managing editor Nancy Lucas, who says **"We will review all forms of poetry."** They have recently published *Heartbeats: A Book of Wisdom* by Ron J. Flemming, *My Love, My Friend, and My Dreams* by Gabriela Freitas and *Poems 1942-1992* by I. Lesley Briggs. **Submit complete ms of at least 65 poems. Enclose SASE for return of ms. Always sends prepublication galleys.**

THE CHRONICLE OF THE HORSE (IV-Specialized), P.O. Box 46, Middleburg VA 22117, phone (703)687-6341, founded 1937, assistant editor Tricia Booker, is a weekly magazine using **short poetry related to horses "the shorter the better. No free verse."** The magazine is devoted to English horse sports, such as horse shows and steeplechasing. It averages 68 pgs., magazine-sized. Subscription: $47. **Sample postpaid: $2. No simultaneous submissions. Summer "is not a good time" to submit. 1-3 editors read poems. Reports in 4-6 weeks. Pays $20/poem. Buys first North American rights.** "We review books submitted to us but do not accept reviews for publication."

THE CHRYSALIS READER (II, IV-Spirituality, themes), Rt. 1 Box 184, Dillwyn VA 23936-9616, fax (804)983-1074, founded 1985, editor Carol S. Lawson, poetry editor Robert F. Lawson. *The Chrysalis Reader* is published by the Swedenborg Foundation as a "contribution to the search for spiritual wisdom." It appears intermittently and is now a "book series that draws upon diverse traditions to engage thought on questions that challenge inquiring minds. Each issue addresses a topic from varied perspectives using literate and scholarly fiction, essays and poetry dealing with spiritual aspects of a particular theme." **They want poetry that is "spiritually related and focused on the particular issue's theme. Nothing overly religious or sophomoric."** They have recently published poetry by Jan Frazier and Robert Bly. As a sample the editor selected these lines from "Burning the Long Boat" by Robert F. Lawson:

> *We stand on the flagstones.*
> *Such a small opening for a big man to disappear into.*
> *Alone in the dark, he broke down the coffee table,*
> *in his haste to save his heart;*

> the vial of pills showed its teeth
> just out of reach at the top of the chest.

TCR is 150 pgs., 7 × 10, professionally printed on archival paper and perfect-bound with coated cover stock, illustrations, photos and ads for other literary publications. They receive about 150 poems a year, use 8-10%. Press run is 3,500. **Sample postpaid: $10. Submit no more than 6 poems at one time. No previously published poems or simultaneous submissions. Submissions via fax OK.** Time between acceptance and publication is 18 months maximum. **Seldom comments on rejections. Send SASE for themes and guidelines or request via fax. Themes for Summer 1997 and Winter 1997 are symbols and choices, respectively. Reports in 2 months. Always sends prepublication galleys. Pays $25 and 3 copies. Buys first-time rights. "We like to be credited for reprints."** The editor says *The Chrysalis Reader* is devoting more attention and space to poetry.

THE CHURCHMAN'S HUMAN QUEST (IV-Political), (formerly just *The Human Quest*), 1074 23rd Ave. N., St. Petersburg FL 33704-3228, editor Edna Ruth Johnson, is a "humanistic bimonthly dealing with society's problems, especially peace. We use practically no poetry." It is magazine-sized and appears 6 times a year. Circulation is 10,000, of which 1,000 go for library subscriptions. **Send for free sample. Pays copies.**

THE CHURCH-WELLESLEY REVIEW; XTRA! (IV-Gay/lesbian), 491 Church St., Suite 200, Toronto, Ontario M4Y 2C6 Canada. *The Church-Wellesley Review* is the annual supplement for *Xtra!* (Canada's largest gay/lesbian newspaper.) **"We want wild humour, fast-paced drama, new takes on old themes, gays and lesbians in other contexts. Our aim is always quality, not style. Although we prefer non-traditional poetry,** we have in the past published a contemporary 30-line 'up-dating' of Chaucer called 'Provincetown Tales.' **Amaze us or amuse us, but just don't bore us."** They have published Patrick Roscoe, Jane Rule, Timothy Findley, Chocolate Waters and David Watmough. The magazine receives over 1,000 submissions/year. Press run is 37,000 in Toronto plus 22,000 in Vancouver and is distributed free. **Poetry can be any length ("no epics, please"), but no more than 10 poems per writer per year. Mss should include 8 poems with name on every page, daytime phone number and 50-word bio. Submissions are accepted March 1 through July 1. "We do not respond at other times. We report as soon as possible, definitely by publication in early fall." Payment is made in Canadian funds within one month of publication.** Staff reviews books of poetry. Send books for review consideration to the attention of Fiction Editor. *Xtra!*, the review's parent magazine, has received several community awards as well as a journalism award for a column on Living with AIDS.

CIMARRON REVIEW (II), 205 Morrill Hall, Oklahoma State University, Stillwater OK 74078-0135, founded 1967, poetry editors Sharon Gerald, Doug Martin, Mark Cox, Lisa Lewis, James Cooper and Sally Shigley, is a quarterly literary journal. **"We emphasize quality and style. We like clear, evocative poetry (lyric or narrative) controlled by a strong voice. No obscure poetry. No sing-song verse. No quaint prairie verse. No restrictions as to subject matter, although we tend to publish more structured poetry (attention to line and stanza).** Also, we are conscious of our academic readership (mostly other writers) and attempt to accept poems that everyone will admire." Among poets they have published are Robert Cooperman, James McKean, David Citino, Tess Gallagher and Albert Goldbarth. This magazine, 100-150 pgs., 6 × 9, perfect-bound, boasts a handsome design, including a color cover and attractive printing. Poems lean toward free verse, lyric and narrative, although all forms and styles seem welcome. There are 15-25 pages of poetry in each issue. Circulation is 500 of which most are libraries. Single copy: $3; subscription: $12/year ($15 Canada), $30 for 3 years ($40 Canada), plus $2.50 for all international subscriptions. **Submit to Poetry Editor, anytime, 3-5 poems, name and address on each, typed single- or double-spaced. No simultaneous submissions. Send SASE for upcoming themes. Reports within 3 months. Pays $15 for each poem published. Buys all rights. "Permission for a reprinting is granted upon request."** Reviews books of poetry in 500-900 words, single-book format, occasionally multi-book. All reviews are assigned.

CINCINNATI POETRY REVIEW; CINCINNATI WRITERS' PROJECT (II, IV-Regional), Humanities Dept., College of Mount St. Joseph, 5701 Delhi Rd., Cincinnati OH 45233, founded 1975, editor Jeffrey Hillard, "attempts to set local poets in a national context. Each issue includes **a quarter to a third of work by local poets (within about 100 miles of Cincinnati)**, but most are from all over." They use **"all kinds" of poetry** and have published such poets as Enid Shomer, Lynne Hugo deCourcy, Pat Mora, Marilyn Krysl, David Citino, Jeff Worley, Harry Humes, Walter Pavlich and Ray Gonzalez. They publish one issue/year, usually a fall/winter issue. *CPR* is 80 pgs., digest-sized, handsomely printed and flat-spined, all poems with art on the glossy card cover. They receive about 2,000 submissions a year, use 40-60. Circulation is about 1,000 for 130 subscribers of which 30 are libraries. Subscription: $9 for 4 issues. **Sample: $2. Submit typed mss with address on each poem.** "Occasionally" publishes theme issues. Theme for a special section of *CPR* #25 was Cuban poetry and it included an interview with Cuban poet Julia Calzadilla. **Note, however, that the editor solicits**

material for special sections. **Reports in 1-3 months. Pays 2 copies.** *CPR* is published by the Cincinnati Writers' Project. Other publications include *The Shadow Family* by Jeffrey Hillard, *The Kansas Poems* by Dallas Wiebe, *Dismal Man* by Jon Christopher Hughes, *River Dwellers—Poems on the Settling of the Ohio River* by Jeffrey Hillard, *Living in Cincinnati* by Kevin Walzer and *Down the River—A Collection of Fiction & Poetry on the Ohio River Valley*, edited by Dallas Wiebe.

THE CINCINNATI POETS' COLLECTIVE (II), 716 Maple Ave., Newport KY 41071, founded 1988, editor Rebecca M. Weigold, is an annual poetry magazine **accepting only well crafted poems. No rhyme or greeting card verse; no cartoons or artwork.** *TCPC* is digest-sized, saddle-stapled. Circulation is approximately 150 through bookstore sales and subscriptions. **Submit up to 5 poems at a time. SASE required for consideration. No previously published poems. Simultaneous submissions OK, if noted. Reports in 4-6 months. Pays 1 copy.** The editor says, "Work your poetry, rework and revise it again and again before submitting. You know you are done when every word is paramount to the poem's survival and you are completely exhausted."

CITY LIGHTS BOOKS (III), 261 Columbus Ave., San Francisco CA 94133, phone (415)362-1901, founded 1955, edited by Lawrence Ferlinghetti and Nancy J. Peters, is a paperback house that achieved prominence with the publication of Allen Ginsberg's *Howl* and other **poetry of the "Beat" school.** They publish **"poetry, fiction, philosophy, political and social history." Simultaneous submissions OK. "All submissions must include SASE." Reports in 6-8 weeks. Payment varies.**

THE CLAREMONT REVIEW (I, IV-Teens/young adults), 4980 Wesley Rd., Victoria, British Columbia V8Y 1Y9 Canada, phone (604)658-5221, fax (604)658-5387, e-mail aurora@island.net.com, founded 1991, is a biannual review which publishes poetry and fiction **written by those ages 13 to 19.** Each fall issue also includes an interview with a prominent Canadian writer. **They want "vital, modern poetry with a strong voice and living language. We prefer works that reveal something of the human condition. No clichéd language nor copies of 18th and 19th century work."** They have recently published poetry by Charlotte Stewart, Nicola Chalke and Gabrielle Gray. As a sample the editors selected these lines from "After the Rain" by Meaghan Strimas:

> No angels with white wings, fluttering above,
> dusty silver feathers falling on your lap
> just you and me.

The Claremont Review is 110 pgs., 6×9, professionally printed and perfect-bound with an attractive color cover. They receive 600-800 poems a year, publish 120. Press run is 700 for 200 subscribers of which 50 are libraries, 250 shelf sales. Subscription: $12/year, $20/2 years. **Sample postpaid: $6. Submit poems typed one to a page with author's name at the top of each. No previously published poems; simultaneous submissions OK. Cover letter with brief bio required. Reads submissions September through June. Always comments on rejections. Send SASE (or SAE and IRC) for guidelines. Reports in 2-6 weeks (excluding July and August). Pays 1 copy and funds when grants allow it. Acquires first North American serial rights.** Sponsors contest. Submit up to 3 poems. Entry fee: $12. Deadline: November 15. Send SASE (or SAE and IRC) for details. The editors add "We strongly urge potential contributors to read back issues of *The Claremont Review*. That is the best way for you to learn what we are looking for."

THE CLASSICAL OUTLOOK (IV-Specialized, translations), Classics Dept., Park Hall, University of Georgia, Athens GA 30602-6203, founded 1924, poetry editors Prof. David Middleton (original English verse) and Prof. Jane Phillips (translations and original Latin verse), "is an internationally circulated quarterly journal (4,000 subscriptions, of which 250 are libraries) for high school and college Latin and Classics teachers, published by the American Classical League." **They invite submissions of "original poems in English on classical themes, verse translations from Greek and Roman authors, and original Latin poems. Submissions should, as a rule, be written in traditional poetic forms and should demonstrate skill in the use of meter, diction and rhyme if rhyme is employed. Original poems should be more than mere exercise pieces or the poetry of nostalgia. Translations should be accompanied by a photocopy of the original Greek or Latin text. Latin originals should be accompanied by a literal English rendering of the text. Submissions should not exceed 50 lines."** They have recently published work by James Fowler and Peter Huggins. As a sample we selected these lines from "Pan's Lament" by Patricia Snyder:

> Pan piped at dawn,
> trembling, tumbling trills
> that called the rising winds their own,
> enchantments sent to woo
> and win the virgin day.

There are 2-3 magazine-sized pgs. of poetry in each issue, and they use 20% of the approximately 350 submissions they receive each year. They have a 12- to 18-month backlog, 4-month lead time. **Submit 2 anonymous copies, double-spaced, no more than 5 poems at a time. Receipt is acknowledged** by letter. Poetry is refereed by poetry editors. Send SASE for guidelines. Reports in 6-9 months. Pays 2 complimentary copies. Sample copies are available from the American Classical League, Miami University, Oxford OH 45056 for $7.50. Reviews books of poetry "if the poetry is sufficiently classical in nature." The editors add, "Since our policy is to have poetry evaluated anonymously, cover letters, names and addresses on poems, etc., just make work at this end. Also, we never knowingly publish any works which have been or will be published elsewhere."

CLEANING BUSINESS MAGAZINE; CLEANING CONSULTANT SERVICES, INC. (IV-Specialized), P.O. Box 1273, Seattle WA 98111, phone (206)622-4241, fax (206)622-6876, founded 1976, poetry editor William R. Griffin. *CBM* is "a quarterly magazine **for cleaning and maintenance professionals**" and uses some poetry relating to their interests. **"To be considered for publication in *Cleaning Business*, submit poetry that relates to our specific audience—cleaning and self-employment."** He has published poetry by Don Wilson, Phoebe Bosche, Trudie Mercer and Joe Keppler. The editor says it is 100 pgs., 8½×11, offset litho, using ads, art and graphics. Of 50 poems received, he uses about 10. Press run is 5,000 for 3,000 subscribers of which 100 are libraries, 500 shelf sales. Single copy: $5; subscription: $20. **Sample postpaid: $3. Send SASE and $3 for guidelines. Simultaneous submissions OK; no previously published poems. Pays $5-10 plus 1 copy.** William Griffin suggests "poets identify a specific market and work to build a readership that can be tapped again and again over a period of years with new books. Also write to a specific audience that has a mutual interest. We buy poetry about cleaning, but seldom receive anything our subscribers would want to read."

CLEVELAND STATE UNIVERSITY POETRY CENTER; CSU POETRY SERIES (II); CLEVELAND POETS SERIES (IV-Regional), Cleveland State University, Cleveland OH 44115, fax (216)687-6943, coordinator Rita Grabowski, editors Leonard Trawick, David Evett and Ted Lardner. The Poetry Center was founded in 1962, first publications in 1971. **The Poetry Center publishes the CSU Poetry Series for poets in general and the Cleveland Poets Series for Ohio poets. "Open to many kinds of form, length, subject matter, style and purpose. Should be well-crafted, clearly of professional quality, ultimately serious (even when humorous). No light verse, devotional verse or verse in which rhyme and meter seem to be of major importance."** They have recently published poetry by Jared Carter, Richard Jackson, Jan Freeman and Susan Firer. As a sample Leonard Trawick selected these lines from *Hurdy-Gurdy* by Tim Seibles:

> When a man is killed
> the wind doesn't cool his face
> and the sky is like an urn, like
> a painted bowl turned over on him.
> He's so weak lying there—his hand
> is like a starfish too far from the sea.

Books are chosen for publication from the entries to the CSU Poetry Center Prize contest. (Write for free catalog and sampler of some 75 Poetry Center books.) Deadline: March 1. Entry fee: $15. The winner receives $1,000 and publication. They publish some other entrants in the Poetry Series, providing 50 copies (out of a press run of 1,000) and 10% royalty contract. The Cleveland Poets Series (for Ohio poets) offers 100 copies of a press run of 600. To submit for all series, send ms between December 1 and March 1. Reports on all submissions for the year by the end of July. Mss should be for books of 50-100 pgs., pages numbered, poet's name, address and phone number on cover sheet, clearly typed. Poems may have been previously published (listed on an acknowledgment page). Simultaneous submissions OK, if notified and "poet keeps us informed of change in status." Send SASE for guidelines. The Center also publishes other volumes of poetry, including chapbooks (20-30 pgs.), with a **$10 reading fee for each submission (except for Ohio residents).**

THE CLIMBING ART (IV-Specialized: mountaineering), Fairfield Communications, P.O. Box 1378, Laporte CO 80535, phone (303)221-9210, founded 1986, editor Scott Titterington, fiction and poetry editor C. Langenberg, is a biannual journal **"read mainly by mountain enthusiasts who appreciate good writing about mountains and mountaineering. We are open to all forms and lengths. The only requirement is that the work be fresh, well-written and in some way of interest to those who love the mountains."** They have published poetry by Terry Gifford, Allison Hunter, Paul Willis, Denise K. Simon and Barry Govenor. As a sample we selected "Our Mission" by John Grey:

> The mountain has size on its side,
> the sense that things that big
> need not have opinions
> or make peace with the world.
> We, on the other hand,
> are at the bottom,

suburbs, impossible affairs,
promotions missed.

TCA is 160 pgs., digest-sized, professionally printed on heavy stock with glossy card cover. They use 8-10 poems/issue, receive 50 submissions/month. Press run is 1,500 for 700 subscribers of which 10 are libraries, 500 shelf sales. Subscription: $18. **Sample postpaid: $4. Simultaneous submissions and previously published poems OK. Reports in 2 months. Sometimes sends prepublication galleys. Pays 2 copies and subscription. Acquires one-time rights.** Reviews books of poetry only if they concern mountains. Open to unsolicited reviews. They also sponsor an annual poetry contest; first prize: $100.

‡**CLÓ IAR-CHONNACHTA (IV-Bilingual/foreign language)**, Indreabhán, Co. Galway Ireland, phone (091)593307, fax (091)593362, founded 1985, contact Nóirin Ni Ghrádaigh, publishes paperback books of **Irish language poetry**, one of which is selected through a competition. They have published collections of poetry by Cathal Ó Searcaigh and Gabriel Rosenstock. **Query with 20 sample poems and a cover letter with brief bio and publication credits. No previously published poems; simultaneous submissions OK. Mss are read by an editorial panel. Often comments on rejections. No payment information provided.** The poetry competition offers a £5,000 first prize in addition to publication. Deadline: December 1. Send SASE (or SAE and IRC) for details.

CLOCKWATCH REVIEW (I, II), Dept. of English, Illinois Wesleyan University, Bloomington IL 61702, phone (309)556-3352, founded 1983, editor James Plath, associate editors Lynn Devore, James McGowan, Robert Bray, Brian Burt and Pamela Muirhead. "We publish a variety of styles, leaning toward poetry which goes beyond the experience of self in an attempt to SAY something, without sounding pedantic or strained. **We like a strong, natural voice, and lively, unusual combinations in language.** *Something fresh, and that includes subject matter as well.* It has been our experience that extremely short/long poems are hard to pull off. Though we'll publish exceptions, we prefer to see poems that can fit on one published page (digest-sized) which runs **about 32 lines or less.**" They have published Peter Wild, Martha Vertreace, John Knoepfle, Rita Dove and Peter Meinke. Asked for a sample, the editors say "trying to pick only four lines seems like telling people what detail we'd like to see in a brick, when what we're more interested in is the design of the *house.*" The 80-page, semiannual *CR* is printed on glossy paper with colored, glossy cover. They receive 2,080 submissions/year, use 20-30. They use 7-10 unsolicited poems in each issue, with 1 featured poet. Circulation is 1,400, with 150 subscribers, of which 25 are libraries. They send out 300 complimentary copies and "the balance is wholesale distribution and single-copy sales." **Sample postpaid: $4. Submit 5-6 poems at a time.** "We are not bowled over by large lists of previous publications, but brief letters of introduction or sparse bios are read out of curiosity. One poem per page, typed, single-spacing OK." No backlog. **Comments on rejections "if asked, and if time permits." Reports in 4 months. Pays 3 copies, and, when possible, small cash awards—currently $5/poem.** Only uses staff-written or solicited reviews. Send books for review consideration if not self-published.

CLOUD RIDGE PRESS (V), 815 13th St., Boulder CO 80302, founded 1985, editor Elaine Kohler, is a "literary small press for unique works in poetry and prose." They publish letterpress and offset books in both paperback and hardcover editions. In poetry, they publish **"strong images of the numinous qualities in authentic experience grounded in a landscape and its people."** The first book, published in 1985, was *Ondina: A Narrative Poem* by John Roberts. The book is 6 × 9¼, handsomely printed on buff stock, cloth bound in black with silver decoration and spine lettering, 131 pgs. 800 copies were bound in Curtis Flannel and 200 copies bound in cloth over boards, numbered and signed by the poet and artist. This letterpress edition, priced at $18/cloth and $12/paper, is not available in bookstores but only by mail from the press. The trade edition was photo-offset from the original, in both cloth and paper bindings, and is sold in bookstores. The press plans to publish 1-2 books/year. **Since they are not accepting unsolicited mss, writers should query first. Queries will be answered in 2 weeks and mss reported on in 1 month. Simultaneous submissions are acceptable. Royalties are 10% plus a negotiable number of author's copies. A brochure is free on request; send #10 SASE.**

CLUBHOUSE; YOUR STORY HOUR (I, IV-Children, teens), Dept. PM, P.O. Box 15, Berrien Springs MI 49103, poetry editor Krista Phillips. The publication is printed in conjunction with the **Your Story Hour** radio program, founded 1949, which is designed to teach the Bible and moral life to children. The magazine, *Clubhouse*, started with that title in 1982, but as *Good Deeder*, its original name, it has been published since 1951. The editor says, **"We do like humor or mood pieces. Don't like mushy-sweet 'Christian' poetry. We don't have space for long poems. Best—16 lines or under."** They have published poetry by Lillian M. Fisher, Audrey Osofsky, Sharon K. Motzko, Bruce Bash and Craig Peters. As a sample the editor selected these lines from "Nurses Office" by Eileen Spinelli:

And it hurts behind my ear,

And I've got a cut right here,
And a rash between my toes,
And a pimple on my nose.
Ouch, my knee feels sore and tender-
Bumped it on my bike's back fender.
I can't tell you all I've got.
Where's the aspirin?
Bring the cot!
I need T.L.C. and rest.

Too bad I'll miss that spelling test!
"*Clubhouse* has been downscaled to 8 pages from 32—to make it possible to print on inhouse equipment. However, the number of issues per year has increased to 12." The magazine has a circulation of 6,000, with 6,000 subscriptions of which maybe 5 are libraries. Subscription: $5 for 12 issues/year. **Sample cost: 3 oz. postage. Submit mss in March and April. Simultaneous submissions OK. The** "evaluation sheet" for returned mss gives reasons for acceptance or rejection. *Writer's guidelines* **available for SASE. Pays about $12 for poems under 24 lines plus 2 contributor's copies. Negotiates rights.** The editor advises, "Give us poetry with freshness and imagination. We most often use mood pieces and humorous poems that appeal to children."

CLUTCH (II), 554 Natoma St., San Francisco CA 94103, founded 1991, editors Dan Hodge and Lawrence Oberc, is an irregular (1 or 2 issues/year) "alternative/underground literary review." **They want "poetry which explores or reveals an edge, societal edges especially. *Take chances*. Academic, overly studied poems are not considered."** They have published poetry by Charles Bukowski, Lorri Jackson, Todd Moore and Robert Peters. As a sample the editors selected these lines from "1492" by Mitchel Cohen:

and the syringe is the size of a lover, O yes!
and the kisses, and the bodies,
and the fleshy zipless hallucinations
that pass for lovers
are no cure, no cure at all . . .

The editors describe *Clutch* as 60-70 pgs., approximately 5½ × 8½. "Printing, binding and graphics vary with each issue. We receive approximately 300 unsolicited submissions a year, but we accept less than 10% of unsolicited material. The majority of material is solicited." Press run is 200-500 for 40 subscribers of which 6 are libraries, approximately 70 shelf sales. Subscription: $5/issue for as many future issues as specified. **Sample postpaid: $5. Make checks payable to Dan Hodge. Previously published poems and simultaneous submissions OK. Cover letter required. Seldom comments on rejections. Reports in 1-4 months. Pays 1 copy. Rights revert to authors.** "Open to publishing reviews of books/magazines from underground press." Poets may also send books for review consideration. The editors say, "We advise obtaining a sample copy or otherwise becoming familiar with the kind of poetry we've previously published before considering a submission."

‡**COAL CITY REVIEW (II)**, English Dept., University of Kansas, Lawrence KS 66045, founded 1989, editor Brian Daldorph, is an annual publication of poetry, short stories, reviews and interviews— "the best material I can find." **As for poetry, the editor quotes Pound: " 'Make it new.' " They do not want to see " 'experimental' poetry, doggerel, five-finger exercises or beginner's verse."** They have recently published poetry by Taylor Graham and Elliot Richman. As a sample the editor selected these lines from "photograph" by Steve Dolgin:

i ate donuts with coke and vodka
and was not privileged

except for one smile
that i won't give back

CCR is 60 pgs., 5 × 8, professionally printed on recycled paper and saddle-stapled with light card cover. They accept approximately 5% of the material received. Press run is 200 for 50 subscribers of which 5 are libraries. Subscription: $6. **Sample postpaid: $4. Submit 6 poems at a time. Accepts previously published poems occasionally; prefers not to receive simultaneous submissions. Seldom comments on rejections. Send SASE for guidelines. Reports in 1-3 months. Pays 1 copy.** Reviews books of poetry in 300-1,000 words, mostly single format. Open to unsolicited reviews. Poets may also send books for review consideration. *CCR* also publishes occasional chapbooks as issues of the magazine but does not accept unsolicited chapbook submissions. Their most recent chapbook is *Casualties* by Taylor Graham. The editor says, "Care more (much more) about writing than publication. If you're good enough, you'll publish."

COCHRAN'S CORNER (I, IV-Subscribers), 1003 Tyler Court, Waldorf MD 20602-2964, phone (301)870-1664, founded 1985, poetry editor Billye Keene, is a **"family type" quarterly open to beginners, preferring poems of 20 lines or less. You have to be a subscriber to submit. "Any subject or style (except porn)."** She has published poetry by J. Alvin Speers, Becky Knight and Francesco BiVone. *CC* is 58 pgs., desktop-published, saddle-stapled, with matte card cover. Press run is 500. Subscription: $20. **Sample: $5 plus SASE. Submit 5 poems at a time. Simultaneous submissions and previously published poems OK. Cover letter welcome. Send SASE for guidelines. Reports in average of 3 months. Pays 2 copies. Acquires first or one-time rights.** Reviews books of poetry. Send books for review consideration. Contests in March and July; $3 entry fee for 2 poems. "We provide criticism if requested at the rate of $1 per page." The editor says, "Write from the heart, but don't forget your readers. You must work to find the exact words that mirror your feelings, so the reader can share your feelings."

THE COE REVIEW (II), Coe College, 1220 First Ave. NE, Cedar Rapids IA 52402, phone (319)399-8760, founded 1972, editor Amanda Moore, is "an annual little literary magazine with **emphasis on innovative and unselfconscious** poetry and fiction. We are **open to virtually any and all subject matter."** They have published poetry by James Galvin and Jan Weissmiller. The annual is 100-150 pgs., flat-spined, digest-sized with matte card cover. "Each issue includes 4-8 reproductions of works of art, usually photographs, lithography and etched prints." Circulation is about 500. **Sample postpaid: $4. Submit 3-5 poems at a time. No simultaneous submissions. Accepted work appears in the next issue, published in Spring. Include "brief cover letter with biographical information. One of the fun things about *The Coe Review* is the Contributor's Notes at the end. We only accept submissions from August 31 through March 15 due to the academic school year." Send SASE for guidelines. Pays 1 copy.** The editor says, "We are supportive in the endeavors of poets whose material is original and tasteful. We are eclectic in our publication choices in that variety of subject matter and style make *The Coe Review* exciting."

COFFEE HOUSE PRESS (III), 27 N. Fourth St., Suite 400, Minneapolis MN 55401, phone (612)338-0125, founded 1984, editorial assistant Chris Fischbach, publishes 15 books/year, 6 of which are poetry. **They want poetry that is "challenging and lively; influenced by the Beats, the NY School or Black Mountain."** They have published poetry collections by Victor Hernandez Cruz, Anne Waldman, Andrei Codrescu and Linda Hogan. As a sample the editor selected these lines from "Heading North" by Steve Levine:

> *The family that eats together*
> *eats together and eats together, rides a*
> *tiny Honda together, two of them, huge*
> *matching bellies heading north*

Submit 8-12 poems at a time. Previously published poems OK. Cover letter required. "Please include a SASE for our reply and/or the return of your ms." Seldom comments on rejections. Replies to queries in 1 month, to mss in 6 months. Always sends prepublication galleys. Pays 8% royalties, $750 advance and 15 author's copies. Send SASE for catalog to order sample. Coffee House Press books have won numerous honors and awards. As an example, *The Book of Medicines* by Linda Hogan won the Colorado Book Award for Poetry and the Lannan Foundation Literary Fellowship. The editor says, "We'd like to see more books by writers of color."

COFFEEHOUSE (I, II), P.O. Box 77, Berthoud CO 80513, founded 1990, editor Ray Foreman, is a quarterly that focuses exclusively on **"free verse narrative poetry, prose poems and short shorts that are imaginative and clear with opening lines that hook the reader."** They have recently published poetry by Hugh Fox, Will Inman, Errol Miller and T.N. Turner. As a sample the editor selected these lines from "My Aunt Louella (December Song)" by Josephine George:

> *Aunt Louella hasn't cut her hair since her*
> *wedding when she had it bobbed and finger*
> *waved at the 2nd floor Inez Salon of Beauty*
> *in Sioux City. Now she keeps it "Rita Hayworth" red*
> *wears it long falling down her back to her waist.*
> *Aunt Louella was a virgin when she married*
> *Charlie Waldschmidt 45 years ago, stayed a virgin for*
> *a few years when Charlie got hurt on the John Deere.*
> *Charlie died last year; Louella took some of the*
> *insurance money, got a hundred dollar make-over in*
> *Omaha, some new clothes, lost weight and "cut loose."*

Coffeehouse is 20 pgs. They accept about 5% of 3,000 poems submitted/year. Press run is 500 for 200 subscribers. Subscription: $4 for 1 year (4 issues). **Sample postpaid: $1. Submit up to 5 poems at a time. Previously published poems and simultaneous submissions OK. "However, please send SASE for guidelines *before* submitting." Reports in about 2 weeks.** The editor has changed his "payment" policy as follows: **"Poets whose work is accepted are required to purchase a contributor's pack of 14 copies for $5 (postpaid) and expected to give, send or distribute these copies to people they know,** thus insuring their work will be read by someone other than other poets in the same magazine." He adds, "All I want to do is select prime material, publish it, and send it out to the poets. Frankly, my criteria of good work is that people other than poets enjoy it. We look for work with three qualities: It must be interesting, must be entertaining and must be well-written. Why would anyone want to read it if it doesn't have these qualities?"

COKEFISH; COKEFISH PRESS (I), 31 Waterloo St., New Hope PA 18938-1210, phone (215)862-0299, founded 1990, editor Ana Christy, is an irregular journal **with an entry fee of $1/3 poems. "I want to see work that has passion behind it. From the traditional to the avant-garde, provocative to discreet, trivial to the significant. Am interested in social issues, alternative, avant-garde, erotica and humor for people with nothing to hide."** They have recently published poetry by Yusukekeida, Paul Weinman, Dale Russell, Joan Reid and Dan Crocker. As a sample the editor selected these lines from "Contortionist" by Albert Huffstickler:

> The hardest parts the recovery
> Unkinking limbs locked into place
> Till distortions become the truer way
> There's pain and exposure in realignment . . .
> And a blood-deep sorrow you can't account for

The format is 60 pgs., side-stapled on heavy paper with a cover printed on both sides on colored photocopy paper. They accept 30% of mss received. Press run is 300 for 150 subscribers. Subscription: $15. **Sample postpaid: $4. Submit 5-7 poems at a time. Note entry fee: $1/3 poems, additional $1 for additional poems. Simultaneous submissions and previously published poems OK. Cover letter "explaining why the poet chose *Cokefish*" required. Send SASE for guidelines. Reports in 1 week. Sometimes sends prepublication galleys. Pays 1 copy.** "We publish a mostly poetry broadside and will work with poets on publishing their chapbooks and audiotapes through Cokefish Press. Manuscript length up to 40 pages—$5 reading fee." Cokefish Press also publishes cooperative chapbooks. Write for details. The editor advises, "Spread the word; don't let your poems sit and vegetate in a drawer. Send me stuff that will make my hair stand up on end." Also see the listings for *Alpha Beat Soup* and *Bouillabaisse*.

COLD MOUNTAIN REVIEW (II), English Dept., Appalachian State University, Boone NC 28608, phone (704)262-2154, editors Maria Tabor and Alexa Maddox. *CMR* is published twice a year by students in the English Department at Appalachian State University and features poetry, short fiction, b&w line drawings and photographs. **They have no specifications regarding form, length, subject matter or style of poetry.** They have recently published poetry by Jeff Nelson, Stephen Beauchamp and Beth Ann Fennelly. As a sample the editors selected these lines from "Heyday" by Mary Rudbeck Stanko:

> When I was a boyandgirl
> the night flipped a full penny moon
> into my hand
> and fate smiled from the side of a mouth
> which, when slightly angled,
> seemed not to be harmful at all.

CMR is about 60 pgs., 6×9, neatly printed with 1 poem/page (or 2-page spread), saddle-stitched, with light card stock cover. They publish about 10% of the submissions received. **For sample, send SASE or make donation to ASU Visiting Artist Series. Previously published poems and simultaneous submissions OK. "Please include short biographical description." Reads submissions September 1 through November 20 and January 10 through March 15. Send SASE for guidelines. Reports within 6 weeks. Pays 3 copies.**

COLLAGES & BRICOLAGES, THE JOURNAL OF INTERNATIONAL WRITING (II, IV-Translations, feminist, political, social issues, themes), P.O. Box 86, Clarion PA 16214, founded in 1986, editor Marie-José Fortis. *C&B* is a "small literary magazine with **a strong penchant for literary, feminist, avant-garde work.** Strongly encourages poets and fiction writers, as well as essayists, whether English-speaking or foreign. **(Note: Writers sending their work in a foreign language must have their mss accompanied by an English translation.)** We are presently looking for **poetry that is socially aware—politically engaged. No sexism, racism or glorification of war. We are going towards focus-oriented issues."** As a sample the editor selected these lines by Anne Blonstein:

> on Sunday   even the devil
> must rest   let us
> plant provisionally   paradise in our heads

The annual is 100-150 pgs., magazine-sized, flat-spined, with card cover. They accept 7% of 900 poetry submissions/year. Press run is 800. **Sample postpaid: $7.50, $3 for back issue. Submit up to**

5 poems at a time, no more. Reads submissions August 15 through November 30 only. Publishes theme issues. Send SASE for upcoming themes. Reports in 1-3 months. Always sends prepublication galleys. Pays 2 copies. Acquires first rights. "It is recommended that potential contributors order a copy, so as to know what kind of work is desirable. We understand that nobody's budget is unlimited, but remember that most lit mags' back issues are half price. *C&B*'s are only $3. Be considerate to editors, as many of them work on a voluntary basis and sacrifice much time and energy to encourage writers. And please, do not send a tiny SASE in which we will have to fold material a zillion times—use at least a 9½×4 envelope." Marie-José Fortis says, "Show me that you write as if nothing else mattered."

COLLEGE & CAREER PUBLISHING; CALIFORNIA WORK WORLD (I, II, IV-Children/ teen/young adult, students), P.O. Box 900, Ontario CA 91762-8900, founded 1989. *California Work World* is a "monthly newsletter/workbook to help junior high and high school students learn about college and jobs as well as how to be a good citizen in our world and cope with problems encountered along the way." **They want "rhyming poems with messages for teenagers; 5-40 lines. Particularly interested in humorous poems, social issues and poems about life on the job. No non-rhyming, free-form verse. No poems about love and personal relationships, please."** As a sample the editor selected these lines by Beverly Bassler:

> *Success with life's struggles begins with one's self,*
> *Jump in, get your feet wet, get off the shelf!*
> *We're all in this world on a stage, in a play;*
> *Each person's unique in his style and his way.*

CWW is 16 pgs., glue bound, with puzzles and illustrations. Press run is 10,000. **Sample postpaid: $1. Submit 3 poems at a time. Previously published poems and simultaneous submissions OK.** Time between acceptance and publication is 3-4 months. "Poems are tested with groups of teenagers, and they choose favorites." **Often comments on rejections. "If comments are desired, poet must include SASE." Send SASE for guidelines. Reports in 3-4 months. Pays $35 and 20 copies.**

COLLEGE ENGLISH; NATIONAL COUNCIL OF TEACHERS OF ENGLISH (II), Dept. of English, University of Massachusetts-Boston, 100 Morrissey Blvd., Boston MA 02125-3393, e-mail collengl@umbsky.cc.umb.edu (for queries only), editor Louise Z. Smith, poetry editor Thomas O'Grady. This journal, which is sent 8 times/year to members of the National Council of Teachers of English (membership: $40, includes subscription to *CE*), is a scholarly journal for the English discipline, but includes poems in each issue. Poets recently published include Sherman Alexie, W.D. Ehrhart and Catherine Phil MacCarthy. As a sample the editor selected these lines from "In Praise of Ravens" by Charles Hood:

> *They praise the horizon by using it,*
> *going from cloud to noon like hawks*
> *or peregrine angels, and when the light*
> *is right they can row white with each*
> *wing beat, flashing silver as they cut*
> *tinsel from the sun, beating home.*

CE is 100 pgs., perfect-bound, with matte card cover, 7½×9½, circulation 18,000. Poems tend to be wide-ranging in style, form and content. **Sample postpaid: $6.25, from NCTE, 1111 W. Kenyon Rd., Urbana IL 61801-1096. Submit a "letter-quality copy" of each poem with cover letter including titles of poems submitted. Reports in 2 months maximum, except for summer submissions. Pays 2 copies.**

COLOR WHEEL; MINK HILLS JOURNAL; SUGAR MOUNTAIN PRESS (II, IV-Nature/ ecology, spiritual), 36 W. Main St., Warner NH 03278-9202, phone (603)456-3036, founded 1990, editor Frederick Moe, associate editor Carol Edson, appears approximately 2 times/year. "*Color Wheel* uses high quality prose and **poetry related to spiritual, ecological and mythological themes. We want poetry that explores more deeply and intensely our relationships with the earth and one another. All forms of poetry are welcome, including longer poems (2-4 pages). No rhymed verse."** They have published poetry by R.D. Savage, Lynn Kozma, David Sparenberg, Jeanne Shannon and Walt Franklin. The editor says it is 32-40 pgs., 8×11, flat-spined, with heavy cover stock, cover art, graphics and line drawings. They receive about 300 submissions a year, use an average of 5%. Press

MARKET CONDITIONS are constantly changing! If you're still using this book and it is 1998 or later, buy the newest edition of *Poet's Market* at your favorite bookstore or order directly from Writer's Digest Books.

run is 300 for 30 subscribers of which 4 are libraries, more than 100 shelf sales. Single copy: $6; subscription: $14 (2 issues). **Sample back issue postpaid: $5. Make checks payable to Frederick Moe. Submit 5 poems at a time. No simultaneous submissions. Cover letter required—include "something that does not keep the writer 'anonymous'!" Reads submissions September through May only. Comments on "close" rejections. Publishes theme issues. Send SASE for guidelines, publication list and upcoming themes. Reports in up to 1 month. Pays copies. Retains one-time reprint rights for special editions.** Sugar Mountain Press (formerly 700 Elves Press) also publishes an annual titled *Mink Hills Journal* which publishes poetry and creative nonfiction **"with a focus on the Northeast region. Submissions to** *Color Wheel* **may also be considered for** *Mink Hills Journal."* The premier issue was published autumn 1995. Subscription: $12 (2 issues). Frederick Moe says, "*Color Wheel* is esoteric yet focused in content. Poets should be familiar with the evolution of the magazine and type of material we publish before sending work. I encourage 'new' voices and appreciate creative approaches to the material. I am annoyed by poets who enclose postcards for response rather than a SASE and expect me to recycle their manuscript. I do not respond to such submissions. Inclusion of a SASE allows me to return press information with response and demonstrates concern on the part of the writer for their work. It is worth the extra expense! I would also like to note that we would appreciate audio submissions of poetry/music/performance/creative work for a potential audiotape issue or anthology. Sugar Mountain Press is known for publishing deeply ecological poetry, with intricate in-depth exploration of self in relation to nature. We have published several challenging long poems and are not afraid to take risks."

COLORADO REVIEW (II, IV-Translations, themes), Dept. of English, 359 Eddy Bldg., Colorado State University, Ft. Collins CO 80523, phone (970)491-5449, fax (970)491-5601, founded 1955 as *Colorado State Review*, resurrected 1977 under "New Series" rubric, renamed *Colorado Review* 1985, editor David Milofsky, poetry editor Jorie Graham. *Colorado Review* is a journal of contemporary literature which appears twice annually; it combines short fiction, poetry, interviews with or articles about significant contemporary poets and writers, articles on literature, culture and the arts, translations of poetry from around the world and reviews of recent works of the literary imagination. **"We're interested in poetry that explores experience in deeply felt new ways; merely descriptive or observational language doesn't move us. Poetry that enters into and focuses on the full range of experience, weaving sharp imagery, original figures and surprising though apt insight together in compressed precise language and compelling rhythm is what triggers an acceptance here."** They have published poetry by Tess Gallagher, James Galvin and Brendan Galvin. They have a circulation of 1,500, 300 subscriptions of which 100 are libraries. They use about 10% of the 500-1,000 submissions they receive/year. Subscription: $15/year. **Sample postpaid: $8. Submit about 5 poems at a time. Reads submissions September 1 through May 1 only. "When work is a near-miss, we will provide brief comment and encouragement." Publishes theme issues. Send SASE for upcoming themes. Reports in 3-6 months. Always sends prepublication galleys. Pays $10/printed page for poetry. Buys first North American serial rights.** Reviews books of poetry, both single and multibook format. Open to unsolicited reviews. Poets may also send books for review consideration. Poetry published in *Colorado Review* has been included in the 1993, 1994, 1995 and 1996 volumes of *The Best American Poetry*. They say, "Our attitude is that we will publish the best work that comes across the editorial desk. We see poetry as a vehicle for exploring states of feeling, but we aren't interested in sentimentality (especially metaphysical)."

COMMON LIVES/LESBIAN LIVES (I, IV-Lesbian), P.O. Box 1553, Iowa City IA 52244, founded 1980, contact poetry editor, is a quarterly publication that "seeks to document the experiences and thoughts of lesbians as we claim our past, name our present conditions, and envision our evolving futures. *CL/LL* will reflect the complexity and richness of those experiences and thoughts by describing the lives of ordinary lesbians—women who have always struggled to survive and create a culture for ourselves. **The magazine is a forum for developing and clarifying our lesbian-defined social and political relationships."** It features stories, journals, graphics, essays, humor and **poetry by lesbians.** They have published poetry by Libré Cory, Pamela Gray, Ellen Grove and Cassidy Sims. As a sample we selected this poem, "Trust," by Patricia Victour:

> Before love must come trust,
> and I begin, slowly,
> to trust her with raw pieces of myself
> no one ever touched before—
> stretch marks on my belly,
> old nightmares,
> echos in my heart
> that whisper, "Not so fast. . .
> pain goes there."

CL/LL is 127 pgs., digest-sized, attractively printed, flat-spined, glossy cover with b&w photo, containing b&w photos, some illustrations and ads. "We receive a lot of poetry and publish 10 or so poems each issue." Press run is 2,000 for 1,000 subscribers, 700 shelf sales. "Free back issues to lesbians in prisons, mental institutions and old-age homes." Single copy: $5; subscription: $15/year. **Sample postpaid: $4.50. Submit 3 poems or 5 pages ("whichever is shorter") at a time. No previously published poems or simultaneous submissions. Cover letter with brief description of work and 2 copies of a short personal bio required. Mail submissions flat, not folded. Poems are circulated to an editorial board. Often comments on rejections. Send SASE for guidelines. Pays 2 copies.** "Unless an author requests otherwise, **all copyable manuscripts submitted to** *CL/LL* **become a part of the** *Common Lives/Lesbian Lives* **Special Collection at the Lesbian Herstory Archives.** In this way the voices of all the lesbians we hear are preserved and accessible." They say, "*CL/LL* feels a strong responsibility to insure access to women whose lives have traditionally been denied visibility and to encourage lesbians who have never before thought of publishing to do so."

COMMONWEAL (III, IV-Religious), 15 Dutch St., New York NY 10038, phone (212)732-0800, poetry editor Rosemary Deen, appears every 2 weeks, circulation 20,000, is a general-interest magazine for college-educated readers **by Catholics. Prefers serious, witty, well-written poems of up to 75 lines. Does not publish inspirational poems.** As a sample the editor selected these lines from "One is One," a sonnet by Marie Ponsot:

> *Heart, you bully, you punk, I'm wrecked, I'm shocked*
> *stiff. You? you still try to rule the world—though*
> *I've got you: identified, starving, locked*
> *in a cage you will not leave alive . . .*

In the issues we reviewed, editors seemed to favor free verse, much of it open with regard to style and content, appealing as much to the intellect as to the emotions. **Sample: $3. Considers simultaneous submissions. Reads submissions September 1 through June 30 only. Pays 50¢ a line. Buys all rights. Returns rights when requested by the author.** Reviews books of poetry in 750-1,000 words, single or multi-book format.

COMMUNICATIONS PUBLISHING GROUP; CAREER FOCUS, FOR TODAY'S RISING PROFESSIONAL; COLLEGE PREVIEW, A GUIDE FOR COLLEGE-BOUND STUDENTS; DIRECT AIM, A GUIDE TO CAREER ALTERNATIVES; JOURNEY, A SUCCESS GUIDE FOR COLLEGE AND CAREER-BOUND STUDENTS; VISIONS, A SUCCESS GUIDE FOR NATIVE AMERICAN STUDENTS; FIRST OPPORTUNITY, A GUIDE FOR VOCATIONAL TECHNICAL STUDENTS (IV-Youth, themes, ethnic), Dept. PM, 106 W. 11th St., #250, Kansas City MO 64105-1806, phone (816)221-4404, editor Georgia Clark. These six publications are 40% freelance written. All are designed to inform and motivate their readers in regard to college preparation, career planning and life survival skills. All except *First Opportunity*, which is quarterly, appear in spring and fall. *Career Focus* **is for Blacks and Hispanics, ages 21-50.** Circ. 250,000. *College Preview* **is for Black and Hispanic young adults, ages 16-21.** Circ. 600,000. *Direct Aim* **is for Black and Hispanic young adults, ages 18-25.** Circ. 500,000. *Journey* **is for Asian-American high school and college students, ages 16-25.** Circ. 200,000. *Visions* **is for Native American students and young adults, ages 16-25.** Circ. 100,000. *First Opportunity* **is for Black and Hispanic young adults, ages 16-21.** Circ. 500,000. **Sample copy of any for 9 × 12 SAE with 4 first-class stamps. Simultaneous and previously published submissions OK. Submit seasonal/holiday material 6 months in advance. "Include on manuscript your name, address, phone and Social Security numbers." They use free verse. Each magazine buys 5 poems/year. Submit up to 5 poems at one time. Length: 10-25 lines. Writer's guidelines for #10 SASE. Reports in 2 months. Pays $10-25/poem on acceptance.**

COMMUNITIES: JOURNAL OF COOPERATIVE LIVING (IV-Specialized), P.O. Box 169, Masonville CO 80541-0169, founded 1972, editor Diana Christian, is a "quarterly publication on **intentional communities and cooperative living," occasionally using poetry relevant to those topics.** It is 76 pgs., magazine-sized, professionally printed on recycled white stock with 2-color glossy paper cover, saddle-stapled. **Submit any number of poems at a time. SASE required. Previously published poems and simultaneous submissions OK. No comment on rejections. Publishes theme issues. Send SASE for upcoming themes. Pays 1 copy.** They also publish the *Communities Directory*.

A COMPANION IN ZEOR (IV-Science fiction/fantasy), 307 Ashland Ave., McKee City, Egg Harbor Township NJ 08234-5568, phone (609)645-6938, founded 1978, editor Karen Litman, is a **science fiction, fantasy fanzine appearing** *very* **irregularly (last published issue November 1994; hopes to publish again this year). "Material used is now limited to creations based solely on works (universes) of Jacqueline Lichtenberg. No other submission types considered. Prefer nothing obscene. Homosexuality not acceptable unless very relevant to the piece. Prefer a 'clean' publication image."** As a sample we selected these lines from "Song of the Captive" by Gail Ray Barton:

> *Nerves burning, blood drying,*

> *Can't you hear me or care?*
> *You're deafened by legend,*
> *The bars are made of air.*
> *I am caged inside your fear,*
> *With attrition torment here;*
> *And the sun says, it's too late;*
> *And the bars are made of hate.*

It is magazine-sized, photocopied from typescript. Press run is 100. **Send SASE for guidelines. Cover letter preferred with submissions; note whether to return or dispose of rejected mss. Sometimes sends prepublication galleys. Pays 1 copy, "but can negotiate." Acquires first rights. "Always willing to work with authors or poets to help in improving their work."** Reviews books of poetry. Open to unsolicited reviews. Poets may also send books for review consideration.

COMPENIONS; STRATFORD WRITER'S WORKSHOP (I), P.O. Box 2511, St. Marys, Ontario N4X 1A3 Canada, founded 1983, contact Marco Balestrin, is a quarterly publication of the Stratford Writer's Workshop. "We print works by the members of the S.W.W. and have expanded our mandate to include poetry and short fiction by other writers." **They want "original, sincerely-written poetry of any form, 30 lines maximum. No clichéd or trite poetry. No pornography."** They have recently published poetry by Peter Stavropolous, Leslie Dolin and Edward Garcia. As a sample Marco Balestrin selected these lines from "Winter Sun" by Alice McMullin:

> *Huge winter sun*
> *red with fusion fire*
> *moves low before our car.*
> *We travel through the leafless chill*
> *withdrawn.*

Compenions is 14-20 pgs., 8½×11, photocopied and side-stapled, with computer graphics. They receive about 80 poems a year, use approximately 60%. Press run is 30 ("will increase after further submissions are received"). **Sample postpaid: $4. Submit up to 6 poems at a time *with $3.50 reading fee*. Include name and address on each poem. (Make cheques or money orders payable to Stratford Writer's Workshop). Previously published poems and simultaneous submissions OK. Cover letter required. "Please include a SASE (if within Canada) or SAE and 2 IRCs (if outside Canada)." Members read over submissions and choose suitable poems. Often comments on rejections. Publishes theme issues. Themes for September 1996, December 1996, March 1997, June 1997 and September 1997 are north, south, work, play and rest, respectively. Reports in 2-3 months. Pays 2 copies.** Balestrin says, "We would like to be a forum providing writers (especially beginners) the opportunity to get published, thereby also exposing ourselves to what is going on 'out there,' in other words, to have a literary relationship beneficial to both parties!"

THE COMSTOCK REVIEW; COMSTOCK WRITERS' GROUP INC. (II), 907 Comstock Ave., Syracuse NY 13210, phone (315)475-0339, founded 1987 as *Poetpourri*, published by the Comstock Writers' Group, Inc., co-editors Jennifer B. MacPherson and Kathleen Bryce Niles, appears biannually. **They use "work that is clear and understandable to a general readership, that deals with issues, ideas, feelings and beliefs common to us all—well-written free and traditional verse. No obscene, obscure, patently religious or greeting card verse."** They have published poetry by Gayle Elen Harvey, Katharyn Howd Machan, Robert Cooperman, Michael Scofield and Susan A. Manchester. As a sample they selected these lines from "When Women Went Downtown" by Patricia Fargnoli:

> *Evenings, far over the tiny houses*
> *the wind swept the black pines like a broom,*
> *stars swirled in their boiling cauldron of indigo*
> *and the children floated to sleep to the women's song*
> *zipping the night together, to the story*
> *of the snow goose who went farther and farther*
> *and never returned.*

The Comstock Review is 100 pgs., digest-sized, professionally printed, perfect-bound, raised cover. Circulation 550. Subscription: $10. **Sample postpaid: $5. Poems may be submitted anytime for possible publication, 3-6 at a time, name and address on each page, unpublished poems only. Cover letter with short bio of poet preferred. Return time is about 6 weeks. Editors usually comment on returned submissions. Pays copies. Acquires first North American serial rights.** They offer a yearly contest with over $400 in prizes, $2/poem fee, 30-line limit.

CONCHO RIVER REVIEW; FORT CONCHO MUSEUM PRESS (IV-Regional), 213 E. Ave. D, San Angelo TX 76903, phone (915)942-2281, fax (915)942-2155, founded 1984, poetry editor Gerald M. Lacy. "The Fort Concho Museum Press is entering another year of publishing *Concho River Review*, a literary journal published twice a year. **Work by Texas writers, writers with a Texas**

connection and writers living in the Southwest preferred. **Prefer shorter poems, few long poems accepted; particularly looking for poems with distinctive imagery and imaginative forms and rhythms. The first test of a poem will be its imagery.**" Short reviews of new volumes of poetry are also published. *CRR* is 120-138 pgs., digest-sized, flat-spined, with matte card cover, professionally printed. They use 35-40 of 600-800 poems received/year. Press run is 300 for about 200 subscribers of which 10 are libraries. Subscription: $12. **Sample postpaid: $4. "Please submit 3-5 poems at a time. Use regular legal-sized envelopes—no big brown envelopes; no replies without SASE. Type must be letter-perfect, sharp enough to be computer scanned." Publishes theme issues. Send SASE for upcoming themes. Reports in 1-2 months. Pays 1 copy. Acquires first rights.** The editor says, "We're always looking for good, strong work—from both well-known poets and those who have never been published before."

‡**CONDUIT (II)**, 3142 Lyndale Ave. S. #6, Minneapolis MN 55408, e-mail conduit@bitstream.net, founded 1993, editors William D. Waltz and Brett Astor, is a quarterly designed "to explore language, art, life without ulterior motives; to publish work that is 'essential.' " **They want "lively, honest poetry that is attuned to language."** They have recently published poetry by Richard Jones, Daniil Kharms and Dara Wier. *Conduit* is 52 pgs., 4¼×11, neatly printed on recycled paper and saddle-stapled with matte card cover and art. They receive about 2,000 poems a year, publish about 50. Press run is 600-1,000 for 100 subscribers, 100-200 shelf sales. Single copy: $2.75; subscription: $11. **Sample postpaid: $3.75. Submit 3-5 poems at a time. No previously published work.** Time between acceptance and publication is 6-12 months. **Seldom comments on rejections. Send SASE for guidelines. Reports in 6-10 weeks. Pays 3 copies. Rights revert to authors upon publication.** Reviews books of poetry in 500 words. Open to unsolicited reviews. Poets may also send books for review consideration. The editors say, "*Conduit* is dedicated to the work of poets and artists who wear the stains of a life lived and whose edges are neither affected nor accidental. *Conduit* will grow and evolve, but one thing will remain constant: quality writing that risks annihilation."

CONFLUENCE; OHIO VALLEY LITERARY GROUP (II), P.O. Box 336, Belpre OH 45714, phone (304)422-3112, founded 1983 as *Gambit*, 1989 as *Confluence*, editor J. Scott Bond, assistant editor David Prather. *Confluence* is an annual "credible platform for outstanding student work complemented by established/emerging authors. This literary magazine is published at Marietta College, Marietta, Ohio, and was named to represent the merging of the Ohio and Muskingum Rivers as well as the collaboration of the Ohio Valley Literary Group with Marietta College." **As for poetry, they want "truths retold in vital, economical language. Nothing cliché, sentimental, same old ax to grind."** They have recently published poetry by Lyn Lifshin, Denise Duhamel, Margaret Gibson and Louis Phillips. As a sample the editor selected these lines from "The breathtaking indigo of their clothes" by Brigitte Oleschinski, translated by Gary Sea:

> *Fissures, footprint, shingles.*
> *On the stones spreads a topography of weather*
> *of time, Thirst*
> *and questions. You*
> *wonder over torrent-scarred rock onto*
> *rivers of sand, sun-blanched clefts, stumbling—hear*
> *the barometer's dispatch like*
> *a saxophone and all things blue*
> *are oceans in your head.*

Confluence is 96-112 pgs., digest-sized, professionally printed and perfect-bound with 2-color matte card cover and b&w graphics. They receive 800-1,000 submissions a year, accept approximately 2%. Press run is 500 for 300 subscribers of which 10 are libraries, about 150 shelf sales. Single copy: $5. **Sample: $3 plus $1.25 postage. No previously published poems or simultaneous submissions. Cover letter with brief bio required. Reads submissions January 1 to March 1 only.** Time between acceptance and publication is 6 months. **Always comments on rejections. Send SASE for guidelines. Reports in 3 months. Pays 1-3 copies. Returns rights upon publication.**

CONFRONTATION MAGAZINE (II), English Dept., C.W. Post Campus of Long Island University, Brookville NY 11548-0570, phone (516)299-2391, fax (516)299-2735, founded 1968, editor-in-chief Martin Tucker, is "a semiannual literary journal with **interest in all forms. Our only criterion is high literary merit.**" We think of our audience as an educated, lay group of intelligent readers. **We prefer lyric poems. Length generally should be kept to 2 pages. No sentimental verse.**" They have published poetry by Karl Shapiro, T. Alan Broughton, David Ignatow, Philip Appleman, Jane Mayhall and Joseph Brodsky. As a sample the editor selected these lines from "Imagination" by Scott Thomas:

> *He builds things in my cellar. He fashions things*
> *From wood and glass, flesh and bone, green eyes*
> *And dirt. One day while I was down there washing*
> *Bedclothes, he was at his workbench tinkering*

With a small electric motor. "Rewiring
A soul," he said.

Confrontation is 190 pgs., digest-sized, professionally printed, flat-spined, with a circulation of about 2,000. A well-edited, visually beautiful journal, each issue features about 30-40 poems of varying lengths. The magazine is recommended not only for its "showcase" appeal, but also for the wide range of formal and free styles, displaying craft and insight. They receive about 1,200 submissions/ year, publish 150, have a 6- to 12-month backlog. **Sample postpaid: $3. Submit no more than 10 pgs., clear copy. No previously published poems. Do not submit mss June through August. "Prefer single submissions." Publishes theme issues. Send SASE for upcoming themes. Reports in 6-8 weeks. Sometimes sends prepublication galleys. Pays $5-50 and copy of magazine.** Staff reviews books of poetry. Send books for review consideration. Basically a magazine, they do on occasion publish "book" issues or "anthologies." Their most recent "occasional book" is *Phantom Pain*, story and drawings by Alfred Van Loen.

CONJUNCTIONS (III), Dept. PM, Bard College, Annandale-on-Hudson NY 12504, founded 1981, managing editor Michael Bergstein, editor Bradford Morrow, is an elegant journal appearing twice a year, using work that is **"stylistically innovative. Potential contributors should be familiar with the poetry published in the journal."** They have published poetry by John Ashbery, Robert Kelly, Charles Stein, Michael Palmer, Ann Lauterbach and Fanny Howe. As a sample here are lines from "Paulownia" by Barbara Guest:

ravenous the still dark a fishnet—
robber walk near formidable plaits
a glaze—the domino overcast—
violet. shoulder.

This publication is distributed by Consortium. It is 350 pgs., 6×9, flat-spined, professionally printed. Issues reviewed feature mostly lyric free verse with occasional sequences and stanza patterns (some leaning toward the avant-garde). Poems compete with prose, with more pages devoted to the latter. Press run is 5,500 for 1,000 subscribers of which 250 are libraries. Subscription: $18. **Sample postpaid: $12. Pays $100-175.**

THE CONNECTICUT POETRY REVIEW (II), P.O. Box 818, Stonington CT 06378, founded 1981, poetry editors J. Claire White and Harley More, is a "small press that puts out an annual magazine. **We look for poetry of quality which is both genuine and original in content. No specifications except length: 10-40 lines."** The magazine has won high praise from the literary world; they have published such poets as John Updike, Robert Peters, Diane Wakoski and Marge Piercy. Each issue seems to feature a poet. As a sample the editors selected these lines by Odysseus Elytis (translated by Jeffrey Carson):

Maybe I'm still in the state of a medicinal
herb or of a cold Friday's snake
Or perhaps of one of those sacred beasts
with its big ear full of heavy sounds
and metallic noise from censers.

The flat-spined, large digest-sized journal is "printed letterpress by hand on a Hacker Hand Press from Monotype Bembo." Most of the 45-60 pgs. are poetry, but they also have reviews. Editors seem to favor free verse with strong emphasis on voice (and judicious use of image and symbol). They receive over 1,200 submissions a year, use about 20, have a 3-month backlog. Press run is 400 for 80 subscribers of which 35 are libraries. **Sample postpaid: $3.50. Reports in 3 months. Pays $5/poem plus 1 copy.** The editors advise, "Study traditional and modern styles. Study poets of the past. Attend poetry readings. And write. Practice on your own."

CONNECTICUT RIVER REVIEW; BRODINE CONTEST; CONNECTICUT POETRY SOCIETY (II), 35 Lindsley Place, Stratford CT 06497, founded 1978, appears twice yearly, editor Norah Christianson. They are looking for **"original, honest, diverse, vital, well-crafted poetry. Translations and long-poems accepted."** They have recently published poetry by Rennie McQuilkin, Paul Petrie, Cortney Davis, Dick Allen, Thom Ward and Roberta Marggraff. As a sample the editor selected these lines from "After my son" by Andrew Dillon:

. . . for fathers are waiting for sons
to take up the strides of Orion,
and let daddy out
like a great foolish wolf
to lope the horizons of death.

Each of the attractively printed, digest-sized issues contains about 40 pgs. of poetry, has a circulation of about 500 with 175 subscriptions of which 5% are libraries. They receive about 2,000 submissions/ year, use about 80. Subscription: $12. **Sample postpaid: $6. Submit no more than 3 poems. No previously published poems or simultaneous submissions. Guidelines available with SASE. Pays**

1 copy. The Brodine Contest has a $2 entry fee/poem and three cash awards plus publication in the *Connecticut River Review*. Entries must be postmarked between May 1 and July 31.

CONSCIENCE (II), CFFC, 1436 U St. NW, Suite 301, Washington DC 20009-3997, founded 1980, poetry editor Andrew Merton, is a quarterly newsjournal of prochoice Catholic opinion, published by Catholics for a Free Choice. **They want poetry up to 45 lines maximum. "We're topically broad and broadminded. However, no polemics (about abortion/choice/religion) nor poems in conflict with a prochoice—albeit not stiflingly politically correct—organization."** They have published poetry by Mekeel McBride and Romana Huk. As a sample the editor selected these lines from "Autobiography" by Lysa James:

> Sometimes they tell me I lie.
> I am only trying to find
> which story is mine.
> This pattern of moving
> away from all memory
> did not stop

Conscience is 48 pgs., $8 \times 10\frac{1}{2}$, web press newsprint, saddle-stitched with some b&w art, photos and ads. They accept less than 10% of poetry received. Press run is 15,000. Single copy: $3.50; subscription: $10/year. **Sample free for 9×12 SAE with $1.01 postage. Submit 3-5 poems at a time. No previously published poems; simultaneous submissions OK, if noted.** Time between acceptance and publication is 1-8 months. **Seldom comments on rejections. Reports in 2 months. Pays $10 and 5 copies. Buys first serial rights.** Interested poets are strongly urged to read a few issues of this publication before submitting. The editor says, "*Conscience* explores ethical and social policy dimensions of sexuality and reproductive health and decision-making, church-state dynamics and related topics. CFFC is a nonprofit educational organization that shapes and advances sexual and reproductive ethics that are based on justice, reflect a commitment to women's well-being, and respect and affirm the moral capacity of women and men to make sound and responsible decisions about their lives."

CONSERVATIVE REVIEW (II), 1307 Dolley Madison Blvd., Room #203, McLean VA 22101, phone (703)893-7302, fax (703)893-7273, founded January 1990, poetry editor Mattie F. Quesenberry, is a bimonthly magazine that includes "political articles, political statistics, political cartoons and especially strong articles on foreign affairs. **We want to see poetry of any form exploring our relationship to religion and the natural world, especially poems exploring the impact of 20th century science and technology on traditional values. We do not want to see any political poetry. Poetry transcends political divisions because it captures universal experiences."** They have recently published poetry by Barbara N. Ewell, Linda Jenkins, Filemann Waitts, Barry Butson and Jay Liveson. As a sample the editor selected these lines from "When I Finally Turn off the Lamp" by Hans J. Stahlschmidt:

> All sounds are swallowed up by a dampness
> so thick that I have to walk into my daughter's
> room and bend over her dreaming face
> to hear her breath and see her fingers moving
> across her blue dotted blanket like fingers
> following the strings of a nocturnal instrument.

CR is 40 pgs., $8\frac{1}{2} \times 11$, offset printed and saddle-stitched with glossy card cover. They use one page of poetry in each issue. Press run is 900 for 700 subscribers of which 150 are libraries. Subscription: $29/year. **Sample postpaid: $5. Submit 3 poems at a time. Simultaneous submissions OK. "Unsolicited manuscripts must be accompanied by a letter certifying the material is the original work of the author and involves no contravention of copyright or unauthorized use of another author's material."** Time between acceptance and publication is up to a year. **Often comments on rejections. Reports in 1-2 months. Pays 3 copies. Acquires all rights. Returns rights upon request.** "We will review books and chapbooks, and print short critical essays." Open to unsolicited reviews. Poets may also send books for review consideration. The editor says, "There is no real division between poetry and our 20th century science and technology. Even the most specialized specialists live their lives with consciences housed in flesh and blood. Even our most unscientific writers and poets must live and react in the modern world."

CONTEXT SOUTH (III), 2100 Memorial Blvd., #4504, Kerrville TX 78028, founded 1988, editor/publisher David Breeden, appears once a year using **"any form, length, subject matter. Looking for strong rhythms, clear vision. Nothing sentimental."** They have published poetry by Andrea Hollander Budy, Simon Perchik and Peter Drizhal. As a sample the editor selected these lines from "Curiosity" by Kirpal Gordon:

> If he could only open his fist banging
> a hollow sound against his chest
> sorrows could never invade him

> *for his hand would always be opening*
> *like a rose in contradiction.*

CS is 65 pgs., digest-sized, saddle-stapled, using fiction, criticism and book reviews as well as poetry. They accept less than 1% of poems received. Press run is 500 for 60 subscribers of which 6 are libraries. **Sample: $5. Simultaneous submissions OK. Reads submissions January 1 through March 31 only. Publishes theme issues. Pays 1 copy. Acquires first serial rights.** Reviews books of poetry in 500 words maximum. Open to unsolicited reviews. Poets may also send books for review consideration. The editor advises, "Read every poem you can find from the beginning of time. Every poem encapsulates the tradition."

COPPER BEECH PRESS (III), Box 1852, English Dept., Brown University, Providence RI 02912, phone (401)863-3744, founded 1973, poetry editor Randy Blasing, publishes **books of all kinds of poetry**, about three 64-page, flat-spined paperbacks a year. They have recently published Phillis Levin, Jeffrey Harrison, Robert B. Shaw and Kay Ryan. **Query with 5 poems, biographical information and publications. Considers simultaneous submissions. Do not submit queries from Memorial Day to Labor Day. Replies to queries in 1 month, to mss in 3 months. Always sends prepublication galleys. Pays 5% royalties. For sample books, call or write for free catalog.**

COPPER CANYON PRESS (III), P.O. Box 271, Port Townsend WA 98368, phone (360)385-4925, fax (360)385-4985, founded 1972, editor Sam Hamill, publishes 10 paperback books of poetry/year, one of which is through the National Poetry Series Annual Open Competition (for details, see the listing in the Contests and Awards section). They have published books of poetry by Lucille Clifton, Hayden Carruth, Carolyn Kizer and Olga Broumas. **Query first with sample poems and cover letter with brief bio and publication credits. No queries via fax. Replies to queries and mss (if invited) in 1 month.** Time between acceptance and publication is 2 years. **Write for catalog to order samples.**

CORNERSTONE (IV-Religious), Jesus People USA, 939 W. Wilson, Chicago IL 60640-5706, phone (312)561-2450 ext. 2088, poetry editor Tammy Boyd, is a mass-circulation (50,000), low-cost ($2.50/copy) publication appearing 2-4 times/year, **directed at young adults (20-35), covering "contemporary issues in the light of Evangelical Christianity." They use avant-garde, free verse, haiku, light verse, rarely traditional—"no limits except for epic poetry. (We've not got the room.)"** As a sample the editor selected these lines from "Learning to Walk" by Larry Woiwode:

> *I lay my life down and it looks like a blade of grass,*
> *That narrow and rigidly green. Our daughter, five last*
> *Month, has lived in seven houses, if I'm counting right,*
> *But seems intact; my spurious child, the unending, undone*
> *Book that undoes me unendingly lies in a gutted jukebox*
> *Left by the renter before us.* No songs in it! *she cries.*

They buy 10-25 poems/year, use 1-2 pgs./issue, and have a 6- to 9-month backlog. **Sample: $2.50. Submit maximum of 5 poems at a time. Cover letter required. Send SASE for guidelines. Pays $10 for poems having 1-15 lines, $25 for poems having 16 lines or more. Buys first or one-time rights.** Open to unsolicited reviews. Poets may also send books for review consideration. In past years, *Cornerstone* has received numerous awards from the Evangelical Press Association (including second place for poetry) as well as a Medal of Distinctive Merit from the Society of Publication Designers and a Certificate of Design Excellence from *Print* magazine.

CORONA (II), Dept. of History and Philosophy, Montana State University, Bozeman MT 59717, phone (406)994-5200, founded 1979, poetry editors Lynda and Michael Sexson, "is an interdisciplinary occasional journal bringing together reflections from those who stand on the edges of their disciplines; those who sense that insight is located not in things but in relationships; those who have deep sense of playfulness; and those who believe that the imagination is involved in what we know." In regard to poetry they want **"no sentimental greeting cards; no slap-dash."** They have published poems by Wendy Battin, William Irwin Thompson, Frederick Turner and James Dickey. The journal is 125-140 pgs., perfect-bound, professionally printed. They use about 20-25 pgs. of poetry/issue. Press run is 2,000. **Sample postpaid: $7. Submit any number of pages. No simultaneous submissions. Reports in 1 week to 9 months. Payment is "nominal" plus 2 contributor's copies.** The editors advise, "Today's poet survives only by the generous spirits of small press publishers. Read and support the publishers of contemporary artists by subscribing to the journals and magazines you admire."

COSMIC TREND; PARA*phrase (I, IV-Themes, love/romance/erotica), Sheridan Mall Box 47014, Mississauga, Ontario L5K 2R2 Canada, founded 1984, Cosmic Trend poetry editor George Le Grand, *PARA*phrase* editor Tedy Asponsen. Cosmic Trend annually publishes 1 chapbook anthology and 1 special project with narrated music cassettes of **"New Age, and Post-New-Age, sensual and mind-expanding short material of any style, but preferably unrhymed; also: humorous, unusual or zany entries (incl. graphics) with deeper meaning. We ignore epics, run-of-a-mill romantic**

and political material. Would like to publish more free verse." They have recently published poetry by Iris Litt, Charles David Rice and Shula Robin. As a sample the editor selected these lines by Jiri Jirasek:

> The power of stone
> is encased light
> of waiting—
> in the mating season
> of all galaxies . . .

PARA*phrase*—Newsletter of Cosmic Trend (irregular: 2-3 times a year)—publishes "poetry related to our major anthologies advertised there." **Submit up to 10 poems at a time with name and address on each sheet. Submission fee: $1 for each two poems submitted, plus $1 for postage. Minimum fee is $2 plus postage. ("No US postal stamps, please.") They will consider simultaneous submissions and previously published poems "with accompanied disclosure and references." Publishes theme issues. Themes for Spring 1997 and Winter 1997 are "Gardens from Beyond" (deadline: October 30, 1996) and "Forgotten Alien Skies" (deadline: May 15, 1997), respectively. Send $1 for guidelines and upcoming themes or $6 for sample publication, guidelines and upcoming themes. Response time is usually less than 3 weeks. Editor "often" comments on submissions. Poets purchase a copy of the publication in which their work appears for the "discounted price" of $6. Rights revert to authors upon publication.** Reviews books of poetry. Open to unsolicited reviews. Poets may also send books for review consideration, attn. Tedy Asponsen. Cosmic Trend publishes electronic music cassette tapes in addition to their poetry/music anthology accompaniments. They say, "Share your adventure of poetry beyond the usual presentation! Cosmic Trend can choose your poems for narration with music and inclusion into our cassette accompaniments to our illustrated anthologies."

COSMOPOLITAN (IV-Women), 224 W. 57th St., New York NY 10019, founded 1886, is a monthly magazine "aimed at a female audience 18-34," part of the Hearst conglomerate, though it functions independently editorially. They want **"freshly-written free verse, not more than 25 lines, either light or serious, which addresses the concerns of young women. Prefer shorter poems, use 1-4 poems each issue. Poems shouldn't be too abstract. The poem should convey an image, feeling or emotion that our reader could perhaps identify with. We do publish mostly free verse, although we're also open to well-crafted rhyme poems. We cannot return submissions without SASE."** They have a circulation of 2,987,970. **Buy sample at newsstand. Mail submissions to "Poetry Editor" at above address. Reports in 3-5 weeks. Pays $25.** "Please do not phone; query by letter if at all, though queries are unnecessary before submitting."

COTEAU BOOKS; THUNDER CREEK PUBLISHING CO-OP; WOOD MOUNTAIN SE-RIES (II, IV-Regional, children), 401-2206 Dewdney Ave., Regina, Saskatchewan S4R 1H3 Canada, phone (306)777-0170, fax (306)522-5152, founded 1975, publisher Geoffrey Ursell, is a "small literary press that publishes poetry, fiction, drama, anthologies, criticism, young adult novels—**only by Canadian writers."** They have recently published poetry by Louise Halfe, Paul Wilson, Judith Krause, Barbara Klar, Dennis Cooley, Bruce Rice and Tonja Gunvaldsen Klaassen as well as 2 anthologies of Saskatchewan poetry. As a sample they selected these lines from "Exiles Among You" by Kristjana Gunnars:

> how we know a season is over
> and we must be older, the daylight
> deeper, more experience
> to draw on, further disappointments
> and wisdom in the aftermath: a bundle
> we pack on our backs as we go

"We publish theme anthologies occasionally." However, writers should submit 30-50 poems "and indication of whole ms," typed; simultaneous and American submissions not accepted. Cover letter required; include publishing credits and bio and SASE or SAE with IRC if necessary. Queries will be answered in 2-3 weeks and mss reported on in 3-4 months. Always sends prepublication galleys. Authors receive 12.5% royalty; 10 copies. Their attractive catalog is free for 9 × 12 SASE, or SAE with IRC, and sample copies can be ordered from it. The editor says: "Membership has changed through the years in the Thunder Creek Publishing Co-op, but now stands at eight. Each member has a strong interest in Canadian writing and culture. Generally, poets would have published a number of poems and series of poems in literary magazines and anthologies before submitting a manuscript." However, the imprint Wood Mountain Series is for first collections, reflecting their commitment to publishing new writers. Coteau Books published *Voice*, by Anne Szumigalski, winner of the 1995 Governor General's Award for Poetry and *Beyond My Keeping*, by Elizabeth Philips, winner of the 1995 Saskatchewan Poetry Award.

CLOSE-UP

Writing powerful poetry takes both tenacity and time

Barbara Klar

With striking images that burn the page with their lust and honesty, Barbara Klar's poetry explores topics ranging from abortion to nature, from sex to writing. These poems, which sometimes border on erotica, take center stage in Klar's life and are a culmination of persistence, patience and perfectionism, and the desire to write poetry that "tells it like it is" even at the risk of offending readers.

"I think a lot of readers *are* offended by my work," says Klar. "The ones who aren't are less afraid of reality, which I try to present in my poetry. Reality *is* the metaphorical penis left inside a woman after a breakup. Reality *is* menstruation, abortion, drunkenness. Most reality isn't pretty, but poetry that tries to be pretty is often weak."

A resident of Ruddell, Saskatchewan, but born of parents who immigrated to Canada from Germany, Klar was raised with a stoic work ethic that manifests itself in her writing. "This work ethic gives me the persistence to write, but also makes me put very high and sometimes unrealistic expectations on myself."

She has revised some of her poems 50 to 100 times over a period of several years. Others are never completed to her satisfaction and are simply abandoned. The writing of her imagistically powerful poems, however, isn't quite as laborious as their revision. "I don't really have a writing process," Klar says. "Each poem develops differently, at its own speed. I go with whatever seems to work."

Another factor Klar sees as important in developing good, strong poetry is time. "Often leaving a poem alone for several months is the best thing for it—something happens to your idea of the poem in that time. Distance and time write the poem more than involvement." Her need to step back from the work seems to stem from Klar's younger years when she first used writing as a way to understand herself and her surroundings. "I was a tomboy who spent lots of time alone, thinking about what struck me as important in the world. As a lonely kid with a poor self-image, poetry made me feel as if I had something to give and say."

To be able to give as much of herself to her writing as possible, Klar, who graduated from the University of Saskatchewan with a B.A. in English, works summers as a tree planter in various areas of Saskatchewan. "I had loved the forest and the outdoors since I was a kid, and I'd heard good money could be made tree planting." And even though only working summers means being relatively poor most of the time, it allows Klar to focus her winters on her main

CLOSE-UP, *Klar*

priority—writing. But having time to write isn't the only reason she returns every summer to the physically and mentally exhausting work, Klar says. "I enjoy working hard. I enjoy the people I meet. Tree planting is rather addicting—I experience an adrenalin withdrawal when the season ends."

A love of the natural world shows in much of Klar's work. In fact, regardless of the topic she is exploring, many of the metaphors and images she uses are taken from nature and its creatures. Klar began submitting her sensual, earthy poetry in the mid-1980s to journals in western Canada. "In the beginning I sent my work to small, fairly low profile journals. I thought I'd have a better chance with them than with some of the journals which published, it seemed, only established writers. But as my work improved, I got braver and began sending it to really good journals."

"I Wanted Them Not To Be Lovers"

From the next room of this hotel
in the middle of nowhere comes the sound
of the evening's centre, the silence
after she comes, after her breath
quick and animal, his delicate laughter,
after the music downstairs, people dancing,
the two of them talking, nervous hands
around their beers.

We have been strangers
stranded in a snowstorm. Two women
and one man. From the edge of the evening's circle
I watched them move around the table
toward each other and wanted them to move
no closer. If they became only friends
I would sleep. If they became lovers I would be
the only other person staying the night
upstairs, hearing them turn
without me toward this point.

(from **The Night You Called Me A Shadow**, 1993, reprinted by permission of Coteau Books, Regina, Saskatchewan, Canada)

Then, in 1989, Klar received an acceptance from **Grain** magazine, the well-known Canadian literary quarterly. However, this first publication didn't make getting other poems into print any easier. She says, "The quality of my work was still the same, and that is what editors go by, that and their own taste. . . . There was a long gap until the next acceptance."

But Klar continued submitting her work and was eventually published in numerous journals, including **Border Crossings**, **Dandelion**, **Fort Sanity** and the

CLOSE-UP, *continued*

NeWest Review. She also submitted her work to contests she read about in *Freelance*, the Saskatchewan Writers Guild's newsletter. In 1990, her poem "Smoking" (about a young girl's first experience with cigarettes) received an honorable mention from *Grain*'s Short Grain Contest. And, in 1992, she won Third Prize in the prose poem category of that contest with her poem "The Parting Gift," a brutally honest telling of what "baggage" is left behind after a breakup.

About the same time, Klar completed a collection of poetry and entered it into the long manuscript category of the Saskatchewan Writers Guild Awards. The manuscript, entitled *The Night You Called Me A Shadow*, won its category and went on to be published by Coteau Books in 1993 as part of their Wood Mountain Series, which publishes first collections of poetry. "It felt good to have the manuscript in the hands of a publisher who treats their writers well and produces beautiful books," she says. Klar was particularly impressed with Coteau's willingness to allow her to make some of the decisions concerning the book's design. "I was quite picky about the layout, but they did everything I asked them to."

Even though Klar's experience with Coteau was very positive, she offers this advice: "When it comes to suggestions after acceptance, stand your ground. It's your book. Don't let them make it into something you don't want it to be. Trust your editor, but don't make all the changes he or she suggests. Know why you are making the decisions you are making. Do what's best for your poems. They are your children."

Since Klar's poetry can be construed by some as pornographic, standing up for her work is a task with which Klar is familiar. "The difference between my work and pornography is that I deal with the subject of sex with some respect and intelligence," she says. "I also try to leave more up to the reader's imagination, rather than 'tell it all.' To me that's the nature of good erotica, allowing the reader to take most of the clothes off the poem."

Klar's final advice to others seeking success in publication is reminiscent of her advice for writing successful poetry: "Be ready. Don't rush publication. Put your soul into your poems. Make them as good as they can be before they go into print."

—*Chantelle Bentley*

"Often leaving a poem alone for several months is the best thing for it . . . Distance and time write the poem more than involvement."

—*Barbara Klar*

COTTONWOOD; COTTONWOOD PRESS (II, IV-Regional), Box J, 400 Kansas Union, University of Kansas, Lawrence KS 66045, phone (913)748-0853, founded 1965, poetry editor Philip Wedge. The press "is auxiliary to *Cottonwood Magazine* and publishes material by authors in the region. Material is usually solicited." The press recently published *Violence and Grace* by Michael L. Johnson. For the magazine they are looking for "strong narrative or sensory impact, non-derivative, not 'literary,' not 'academic.' Emphasis on Midwest, but publishes the best poetry received regardless of region. Poems should be 60 lines or less, on daily experience, *perception*." They have published poetry by Rita Dove, Allen Ginsberg, Walter McDonald, Patricia Traxler and Ron Schreiber. The magazine, published 3 times/year, is 112 pgs., 6×9, flat-spined, printed from computer offset, with photos, using 15-20 pages of poetry in each issue. They receive about 2,000 submissions/year, use about 30, have a maximum of 1-year backlog. They have a circulation of 500-600, with 150 subscribers of which 75 are libraries. Single copy: $6.50. **Sample postpaid: $4. Submit up to 5 pgs. of poetry at a time. No simultaneous submissions. Sometimes provides criticism on rejected mss. Reports in 2-5 months. Pays 1 copy.** The editors advise, "Read the little magazines and send to ones you like."

COUNTRY WOMAN; REIMAN PUBLICATIONS (IV-Women, humor), P.O. Box 643, Milwaukee WI 53201, founded 1970, managing editor Kathy Pohl. *Country Woman* "is a bimonthly magazine dedicated to the lives and interests of country women. Those who are both involved in farming and ranching and those who love country life. In some ways, it is very similar to many women's general interest magazines, and yet its subject matter is closely tied in with rural living and the very unique lives of country women. We like short (4-5 stanzas, 16-20 lines) traditional rhyming poems that reflect on a season or comment humorously or seriously on a particular rural experience. Also limericks and humorous 4- to 8-line filler rhymes. No experimental poetry or free verse. Poetry will not be considered unless it rhymes. Always looking for poems that focus on the seasons. We don't want rural putdowns, poems that stereotype country women, etc. All poetry must be positive and upbeat. Our poems are fairly simple, yet elegant. They often accompany a high-quality photograph."** They have published poetry by Hilda Sanderson, Edith E. Cutting and Ericka Northrop. *CW* is 68 pgs., magazine-sized, glossy paper with much color photography. They receive about 1,200 submissions of poetry/year, use 40-50 (unless they publish an anthology). Their backlog is 1 month to 3 years. Subscription: $16.98/year. **Sample postpaid: $2. Submit maximum of 6 poems. Photocopy OK if stated not a simultaneous submission. Reports in 2-3 months. Pays $10-25/poem plus 1 copy. Buys first rights (generally) or reprint rights (sometimes).** They hold various contests for subscribers only. One of their anthologies, *Cattails and Meadowlarks: Poems from the Country*, is 90 pgs., saddle-stapled with high-quality color photography on the glossy card cover, poems in large, professional type with many b&w photo illustrations. The editor says, "We're always welcoming submissions, but any poem that does not have traditional rhythm and rhyme is automatically passed over."

THE COVENANT COMPANION; COVENANT PUBLICATIONS (II, IV-Religious), 5101 N. Francisco Ave., Chicago IL 60625, phone (312)784-3000, founded 1923, executive secretary of publications John E. Phelan Jr., is a monthly designed to "gather, stimulate and enlighten the church it serves—The Evangelical Covenant Church—on the way to promoting Christ's mission in the world." **They want brief poems with Christian viewpoint. Nothing sing-songy.** The editor says it is 40 pgs., 8×10, some 4-color, some 2-color, some b&w, with self cover, pictures, graphics and ads. They receive about 200 poems a year, use 5-10. Press run is 21,000 for about that many subscribers. Subscription: $26. **Sample postpaid: $2.25. Submit 3-6 poems at a time. Previously published poems and simultaneous submissions OK.** Time between acceptance and publication is 3 months. **Seldom comments on rejections. Reports on submissions "as we get around to them." Pays $10-15 and 3 author's copies. Buys first or one-time rights.**

COVER MAGAZINE (II), P.O. Box 1215, Cooper Station, New York NY 10276, phone (212)673-1152, founded 1986, editor/publisher Jeffrey C. Wright, poetry editor Lita Hornick, is a "broad-based arts monthly covering all the arts in every issue, a 40-page tabloid sold on newsstands and in select bookstores nationwide." **They want "shorter poems—2-24 lines generally, modern, favoring new romantic work. Nothing stodgy or simplistic."** They have published poetry by John Ashbery, Lawrence Ferlinghetti, Allen Ginsberg, Robert Creeley and Molly Peacock. As a sample we selected these lines from "Notes From My Pockets" by Ira Cohen:

> *"I Left three days ago*
> *but no one seems to know*
> *   I'm gone."*
>   popular song
>
> *Having left yet still here*
> *perhaps the poem can sustain me*

> *still yearning for your touch*
> *I'm afraid it will burn me. . .*

Cover tries "to reach a cutting-edge/front-line audience in touch with the creative fields." They receive about 1,000 poems a year, accept approximately 50. Entirely supported by subscriptions, sales and ads. Press run is 20,000 for 3,400 subscribers (20 of them libraries), 4,000 shelf sales. Two-year subscription: $18. **Sample postpaid: $5. Submit 4 poems with cover letter.** Time between acceptance and publication is 4-6 months. **Editor often comments on submissions. Send SASE for upcoming themes. Reports in 4 months. Pays nothing, not even a copy.** Open to unsolicited reviews. Poets may also send books for review consideration. Offers annual poetry contest, for subscribers only.

COYOTE CHRONICLES: NOTES FROM THE SOUTHWEST (I, II, IV-Political, regional), 222 W. Brown Rd., Suite #9, Mesa AZ 85201, founded 1993, editor Jody Namio, is a "small press publisher of fiction, poetry, nonfiction and scholarly publications, publishing a biannual literary journal. Limited subsidy publishing services offered to selected authors." She wants **"poetry with emphasis on progressive political themes and ideas, ecology etc. No religious, fantasy or 'scenery' poetry."** They have published poetry by Norman German, John Grey, Mark Maire and Richard Davignon. As a sample she selected these lines (poet unidentified):

> *Last night I went to bed intoxicated again. You watched*
> *"Ghandi," repressing violence.*
> *Today, I am drinking too much coffee,*
> *smoking too many cigarettes.*
> *You say you'll be late . . .*

CC is 80 pgs., 8½ × 11, professionally printed on recycled paper, saddle-stitched. They accept 10-15% of 1,000 poems received a year. Subscription: $12. **Sample postpaid: $4. Guidelines available for SASE. They consider simultaneous submissions and previously published poems. Submit with cover letter and bio.** "Backlog of submissions at this time." **Editor sometimes comments on rejections, "more substantial critiques on request." Reports in 6-8 weeks. Pays 5 copies. "Contributors encouraged to buy additional copies."** Publishes several chapbooks a year averaging 64 pgs. **For chapbook consideration either query or send ms with cover letter and bio. Reports in 12-14 weeks. "Large backlog at this time, but we welcome all submissions."** Payment "varies with author." Send SASE for catalog to buy samples.

CQ (CALIFORNIA STATE POETRY QUARTERLY); CALIFORNIA STATE POETRY SOCIETY (II), P.O. Box 7126, Orange CA 92613, phone (714)854-8024, founded 1972, editorial board chair Julian Palley. *CQ* is the official publication of the California State Poetry Society (an affiliate of the National Federation of State Poetry Societies) and is designed "to encourage the writing and dissemination of poetry." **They want poetry on any subject, 60 lines maximum. "No geographical limitations. Quality is all that matters."** They have published poetry by Michael L. Johnson, Lyn Lifshin and Robert Cooperman. As a sample they selected "The Fading" by Anne Marple:

> *I dream you back again*
> *but after waking*
> *I must strain to remember*
> *as though peering at a faded snapshot*
> *where the knitted hat and muffler*
> *are still distinct*
> *but the face has disappeared.*

CQ is 50-60 pgs., 5½ × 8½, offset and perfect-bound, heavy paper cover with art. They receive 3,000-4,000 poems a year, accept approximately 5%. Press run is 500 for 300 subscribers of which 24 are libraries, 20-30 shelf sales. Membership in CSPS is $12/year and includes a subscription to *CQ*. **Sample (including guidelines) postpaid: $4. Send SASE for guidelines alone. Submit up to 6 "relatively brief" poems at a time; name and address on each sheet. Generally no previously published poems or simultaneous submissions. Seldom comments on rejections. Reports in 1-4 months. Pays one copy. Acquires first rights.** CSPS also sponsors an annual poetry contest. Awards vary. All entries considered for *CQ*. They say, "Since our editor changes with each issue, we encourage poets to resubmit. Also, we are not opposed to rhyme, but it should be used with great discretion."

ALWAYS include a self-addressed, stamped envelope (SASE) when sending a ms or query to a publisher within your own country. When sending material to other countries, include a self-addressed envelope and International Reply Coupons (IRCs), available for purchase at many post offices.

CRAB CREEK REVIEW (V, IV-Anthology, themes), 4462 Whitman Ave. N., Seattle WA 98103-7347, phone (206)633-1090, founded 1983, editor Linda J. Clifton. Previously a biannual publication, *CCR* now appears approximately once every 2 years as a theme-based anthology. They publish **poetry which is "free or formal, expresses complex notions through clear imagery, has wit and a voice that is interesting, energetic and gives a strong sense of the individual; accessible to the general reader rather than full of very private imagery and obscure literary allusion."** They have published poetry by Laurel Speer, Olga Popova, Diane Glancy, Michael Lassell, David Romtvedt and Eastern European, Japanese, Chinese and Latin American writers. As a sample the editor selected these lines from "Listening at Little Lake Elkhart" by William Stafford:

> What signal brought us, following the faintest of trails?
> Is there bread for this hunger, this long exile from earth?
> Listening as well as we can, we hear the loon cry—
> from a dark shore it echoes; it tells how far
> the northland goes, one gray lake then another
> all the way to the edge of the wind.

The editor says *CCR* is a 160-page, perfect-bound paperback. **Sample copy of Spring 1996 Anthology postpaid: $8. They are currently not accepting unsolicited submissions. Poets can check *Poets & Writers* or send SASE for upcoming themes and reading periods.** Back issues of the biannual publication are available for $3. They also sponsor an annual contest with prizes of $100, $50 and $25. Entry fee: $12 for up to 5 poems. Send SASE for details.

CRAZYHORSE (II), Dept. PM, Dept. of English, University of Arkansas at Little Rock, Little Rock AR 72204, phone (501)569-3161, founded 1960, poetry editor Ralph Burns, fiction editor Judy Troy, is a highly respected literary magazine appearing twice a year. They have published poetry by Alberto Rios, Mark Jarman, Bill Matthews, Yusef Komunyakaa and Lynda Hull. As a sample we selected these lines from "Freshman English Poetry Anthology (University of Minnesota, 1964)" by Maura Stanton:

> I looked at the two lyres
> Printed across the cover
> Of my thick green anthology,
> I knew the lyre was the symbol
> For Poetry, but I wondered
> Why there were two, not one.
> I opened the brand new book
> And wrote my name in pencil
> Across the white front page.

Crazyhorse is 145-180 pgs., 6×9, offset, color cover. Press run is 1,000. Subscription: $10. **Sample postpaid: $5. Prefers submissions of 3-5 poems at a time. No previously published poems. Always enclose SASE. No submissions May through August. Reports usually within 3 months. Pays $10/ printed page plus 2 copies. Offers two $500 awards for best poem and best story.** Reviews books of poetry. *Crazyhorse* received a Special Merit Award for Editorial Content from the 1995 American Literary Magazine Awards. To get a sense of the quality of the magazine, the editors suggest poets purchase a sample copy.

CRAZYQUILT QUARTERLY (II), P.O. Box 632729, San Diego CA 92163-2729, phone (619)688-1023, fax (619)688-1753, founded 1986, editor Jackie Ball, is a literary quarterly which has recently published poetry by Robert Edwards, Robert Frank and Ruth Good. As a sample the editor selected these lines from "Sweet Alyssum" by Jennifer Lagier:

> On the day of vernal equinox
> erotic crocus press their blunt blooms
> beyond rigid earth.
> Hen's eggs mysteriously balance erect
> upon their wide ends
> Spring spatters wedding rice petals
> over rough granular sand.

CQ is 90 pgs., digest-sized, saddle-stapled, professionally printed on good stock with matte card cover. Circulation 200. Subscription: $19 (2 years for $32). **Sample: $5 plus $1 postage; back issue: $3. Submit up to 5 poems at a time, one poem to a page. Previously published poems and simultaneous submissions OK. Reports in 10-12 weeks, time to publication is 12-18 months. Pays 2 copies. Acquires first or one-time rights.**

CREAM CITY REVIEW (II), P.O. Box 413, Dept. of English, University of Wisconsin at Milwaukee, Milwaukee WI 53201, editor Andrew Rivera, poetry editor Kristin Terwelp, is a nationally distributed literary magazine published twice a year by the Creative Writing Program. The editors will consider **any poem that is well-crafted and especially those poems that "have a voice, have place or play with the conventions of what poetry is. We get very little humor or parody, and would enjoy**

getting more." They have published poetry by Albert Goldbarth, Audre Lorde, Marge Piercy, May Sarton, Philip Dacey, Amiri Baraka, Tess Gallagher, Cathy Song, Mary Oliver and Philip Levine. They do not include sample lines of poetry; "We prefer not to bias our contributors. We strive for variety—vitality!" *CCR* is averaging 300 pgs., 5½×8½, perfect-bound, with full-color cover on 70 lb. paper. This journal is fast becoming a leader in the literary world. It's lovely to look at—one of the most attractive designs around—with generous space devoted to poems, all styles (but favoring free verse). Press run is 2,000 for 450 subscribers of which 40 are libraries. **Sample postpaid: $5. "Include SASE when submitting and please submit no more than 5 poems at a time." Simultaneous submissions OK when notified. "We have had a strange string of problems with simultaneous submissions. We will continue to look at them, but authors need to be more responsible in notifying us that work has been accepted elsewhere." Editors sometimes comment on rejections. Send SASE for guidelines. Reports in 2-4 months, longer in summer. Payment includes choice of 2 copies or 1-year subscription. Buys first rights.** Reviews books of poetry in 1-2 pgs. Open to unsolicited reviews. Poets may also send books to the poetry editors for review consideration. Sponsors an annual contest for poems under 100 lines. Submit 3-5 poems/entry. Entry fee is $5. Awards $100 plus publication and one-year subscription for first place; publication and one-year subscription for second through fifth place. Poetry published in this review has been included in *The Best American Poetry 1996*.

CREATIVE WITH WORDS PUBLICATIONS (C.W.W.); SPOOFING (IV-Themes); WE ARE WRITERS, TOO (I, IV-Children, seniors), P.O. Box 223226, Carmel CA 93922, founded 1975, poetry editor Brigitta Geltrich, **offers criticism for a fee**. It focuses "on furthering **folkloristic tall tales** and such; creative writing abilities in **children** (poetry, prose, language art); creative writing in **senior citizens** (poetry and prose)." The editors publish on a wide range of themes relating to human studies and the environment that influence human behaviors. **$5 reading fee/poem, includes a critical analysis.** The publications are anthologies of children's poetry, prose and language art; anthologies of special-interest groups such as senior citizen poetry and prose; *Spoofing: An Anthology of Folkloristic Yarns and Such*; and anthologies with announced themes (nature, pets, love, sports, etc.). **"Want to see: folkloristic themes; poetry for and by children; poetry by senior citizens; special topic (inquire). Do not want to see: too mushy; too religious; too didactic; expressing dislike for fellowmen; political; pornographic; death and murder poetry." Send SASE for guidelines and upcoming themes.** They have recently published poetry by Randi A. Shedlosky, Monica Taylor, Deborah Stoeckel and Nicola Fleming. As a sample the editor selected these lines by Katie Lande:

> . . . *Too hot to concentrate*
> *Too hot to move*
> *Weakened by humidity*
> *I gaze beyond wavy curtains of heat*
> *and dream . . .*

Spoofing! and *We are Writers, Too!* are low-budget publications, photocopied from typescript, saddle-stapled, card covers with cartoon-like art. **Submit 20-line, 40 spaces wide maximum, poems geared to specific audience and subject matter. "Query with sample poems (one poem/page, name and address on each), short personal biography, other publications, poetic goals, where you read about us, for what publication and/or event you are submitting. Also include SASE for response."** They have "no conditions for publication, but C.W.W. is dependent on author/poet support by purchase of a copy or copies of publication." They offer a 20% reduction on any copy purchased. The editor advises, "Trend is proficiency. Poets should research topic; know audience for whom they write; check topic for appeal to specific audience; should not write for the sake of rhyme, rather for the sake of imagery and being creative with the language. Feeling should be expressed (but no mushiness). Topic and words should be chosen carefully; brevity should be employed; and author should proofread for spelling and grammar. We would like to receive more positive and clean, family-type poetry."

THE CREATIVE WOMAN (IV-Women, feminist, themes), 126 E. Wing, Suite 288, Arlington Hts. IL 60004, phone (847)255-1232, founded 1977, editor Margaret Choudhury, is a quarterly publishing nonfiction articles, fiction, poetry and book reviews. **"We focus on a special topic in each issue, presented from a feminist perspective."** They want poetry **"recognizing, validating, celebrating women's experience, especially fresh and original style."** They have published poetry by Marge Piercy and Larissa Vasilyeva. As a sample the editor selected these lines from "Custom as a Veil" by Carol Ciavonne:

> *Women do not cry at weddings,*
> *they grieve with open ears.*
> *Let there be compensation they say,*
> *let it be beautifully phrased.*

The Creative Woman is 52 pgs., magazine-sized, saddle-stapled, professionally printed with b&w photos, graphics and ads. They use about 5% of several hundred poems received each year. Press run is 1,000 for 600 subscriptions (65 libraries). Subscription: $16, $26 outside US. **Sample postpaid: $5.**

Mss should be double-spaced, name and address on each page. No simultaneous submissions or previously published poetry. Cover letter required. Send SASE for upcoming themes. Theme for Winter 1996 issue: "Rock and Rap Music," for Spring 1997: "Women & the Law," for Summer 1997: "Women in Hard Hats" and for Autumn 1997: "Women's Fashions & Society." Reports in up to 1 year. Pays 3 copies and opportunity to purchase more at half price. Staff reviews related books of poetry. Send books for review consideration.

CRESCENT MOON PUBLISHING; PASSION (II, IV-Anthology, gay/lesbian, love/romance/erotica, occult, religious, spirituality, women/feminism), 18 Chaddesley Rd., Kidderminster, Worcestershire DY10 3AD England, founded 1988, editor Jeremy Robinson, publishes about 25 books and chapbooks/year **on arrangements subsidized by the poet.** He wants **"poetry that is passionate and authentic. Any form or length."** Not **"the trivial, insincere or derivative.** We are publishing a new quarterly magazine, *Passion* ($4 each, $17 subscription). It features poetry, fiction, reviews and essays on feminism, art, philosophy and the media. Many American poets are featured, as well as British poets such as Jeremy Reed, Penelope Shuttle, Alan Bold, D.J. Enright and Peter Redgrove. **Contributions welcome. We are also publishing two anthologies of new American poetry each year entitled** *Pagan America*." They have also published studies of Rimbaud, Rilke, Cavafy, Shakespeare, Beckett, German Romantic poetry and D.H. Lawrence. As a sample the editor selected these lines from Peter Redgrove's poem "Starlight":

> Her menstruation has a most beautiful
> Smell of warm ripe apples that are red,
> And an odour of chocolate, a touch of poppy,
> And bed-opiums roll from her limbs
> Like the smokes of innumerable addicts between the sheets . . .

The above is from the book *Sex-Magic-Poetry-Cornwall: A Flood of Poems*, by Peter Redgrove, 76 pgs., flat-spined, digest-sized. Anthologies now available ($8.99 or $17 for 2 issues of *Pagan America*) include: *Pagan America: An Anthology of New American Poetry, Love in America: An Anthology of Women's Love Poetry, Mythic America: An Anthology of New American Poetry* and *Religious America: An Anthology of New American Poetry.* **Submit 5-10 poems at a time. Cover letter with brief bio and publishing credits required ("and please print your address in capitals"). Send SASE (or SAE and IRCs) for upcoming anthology themes. Replies to queries in 1 month, to mss in 2 months. Sometimes sends prepublication galleys.** The editor says, "Generally, we prefer free verse to rhymed poetry."

CRICKET; SPIDER, THE MAGAZINE FOR CHILDREN; LADYBUG, THE MAGAZINE FOR YOUNG CHILDREN; BABYBUG, THE LISTENING AND LOOKING MAGAZINE FOR INFANTS AND TODDLERS (IV-Children), P.O. Box 300, Peru IL 61354-0300, *Cricket* founded 1973, *Ladybug* founded 1990, *Spider* founded 1994, *Babybug* founded 1994, editor-in-chief Marianne Carus. *Cricket* (for ages 9-14) is a monthly, circulation 100,000, **using "serious, humorous, nonsense rhymes" for children and young adults. They do not want "forced or trite rhyming or imagery that doesn't hang together to create a unified whole." They sometimes use previously published work.** The attractive 8×10 magazine is 64 pgs., saddle-stapled, with color cover and full-color illustrations inside. *Ladybug*, also monthly, circulation 143,000, is similar in format and requirements but is aimed at younger children (ages 2-6). *Spider*, also monthly, circulation 80,000, is for children ages 6-9. Format and requirements similar to *Cricket* and *Ladybug*. *Babybug*, published at 6-week intervals, circulation 28,000, is a read-aloud magazine for ages 6 months to 2 years; premier issue published November 1994. It is 24 pgs., 6¼×7, printed on cardstock with nontoxic glued spine and full-color illustrations. The magazines receive over 1,200 submissions/month, use 25-30, and have up to a 2-year backlog. **Do not query. Submit no more than 5 poems—up to 50 lines (2 pgs. max.) for** *Cricket*; **up to 20 lines for** *Spider* **and** *Ladybug*, **up to 8 lines for** *Babybug*, **no restrictions on form. Sample of** *Cricket, Ladybug* **or** *Spider*: $4; **sample of** *Babybug*: $5. **Guidelines available for SASE. Reports in 3-4 months. Payment for all is up to $3/line and 2 copies. "All submissions are automatically considered for all four magazines."** *Cricket* and *Spider* hold poetry contests every third month. *Cricket* accepts entries from readers of all ages; *Spider* from readers ages 10 and under. Current contest themes and rules appear in each issue. *Cricket* has received Parents' Choice Awards every year since 1986 and the Golden Lamp Award in 1995. *Ladybug*, launched in 1990, has received Parents' Choice Awards every year since 1991 and the EdPress Golden Lamp Award in 1994.

CRIPES! (II), 514½ E. University Ave., Lafayette LA 70503, fax (318)482-2506, e-mail jet9006@usl.edu (for queries and requests for information only), founded 1994, co-editors Jim Tolan and Kelly Stern, is a biannual publication of poetry, prose and artwork. **They want "the well made, the eccentric, the imaginatively precise, the evocative and provocative." They do not want to see "formal exercises, sensationalism, the shoddily crafted or the soulless."** They have recently published poetry by Sean Brendan-Brown, Allen Johnson, Tom Whalen and Adrienne Goering. As a sample the editor selected these lines from "Preservation" by A.D. Fallon:

> With thin wooden tongs
> we slowly pull our brains out
> our noses, placing each chunk in
> a hand-thrown jar. They surround
> our skulls in clay mosaic halos—
> We are the angels of dust.

Cripes! is 36-48 pgs., digest-sized, offset and saddle-stitched with 2-color card cover, artwork and graphics; no ads. They accept 3-5% of submissions. Press run is 300 for 50 subscribers, 10% shelf sales. Subscription: $10 for 3 issues. **Sample postpaid: $4. Make checks payable to Jim Tolan. No previously published poems; simultaneous submissions OK. "Though we don't require a cover letter, we do like to know how a person has come to know about *Cripes!*" Often comments on rejections. Reports within a month. Pays with a 3-issue subscription.** "We publish reviews of books, chaps and other zines in no more than one to two pages." Poets may send books for review consideration. Jim Tolan says, "We see *Cripes!* as a carefully gnawed niche between the formally competent but soulless verse of academic and avant-garde journals and the emotionally charged but poorly crafted poeming of the zines. And we encourage others who acknowledge the possibility of such a place to submit to our magazine."

CROSS ROADS: A JOURNAL OF SOUTHERN CULTURE (IV-Regional, themes), P.O. Box 726, University MS 38677, e-mail crossrds@um.cc.olemiss.edu, founded 1992, editor William Bland Whitley, is semiannual. "*Cross Roads* serves as a forum for a wide range of responses to the South from creative, academic, popular and folk perspectives; one fourth to one half of each issue is creative writing (poetry, fiction, drama and nonfiction essays)." **They want "poetry by Southerners and poetry (by anyone) about the South. We would like to see high-quality poetry about any aspect of Southern culture (Southern history, Southern folkways, Southern identity, Southern art/music, etc.—in short, any aspect of the Southern experience). Nothing overly sentimental, stereotyping or awkwardly rhyming."** They have recently published poetry by Sheryl St. Germain, Ron Smith, Walter McDonald and Don Hoyt. As a sample the editor selected these lines from "The Crater, Vicksburg" by Franz K. Baskett:

> Standing on the lip of The Crater
> I think about what it feels like
> To hold a gun and shoot.
> The heft of two and a half pounds
> Of blue steel. To shoot. To feel
> The kick. To aim and squeeze off.
> But not like it was done here.
> No Sir.

Cross Roads is 112 pgs., digest-sized, perfect-bound, with artwork, b&w photographs, music notation, and several ads. They receive 200 poems a year, use 20. Press run is 800 for 70 subscribers of which 25 are libraries. Subscription: $9 for individuals, $12 for institutions. **Sample postpaid: $4.50. No previously published poems or simultaneous submissions. Cover letter required. Include "a short biographical statement explaining background and connection with the South or interest in the study of Southern culture. One paragraph is enough." Seldom comments on rejections. Publishes theme issues. Send SASE for upcoming themes or request via e-mail. Reports within 3 months. Pays 1 copy. Acquires first North American serial rights.**

CROSS-CULTURAL COMMUNICATIONS; CROSS-CULTURAL REVIEW OF WORLD LITERATURE AND ART IN SOUND, PRINT, AND MOTION; CROSS-CULTURAL MONTHLY; CROSS-CULTURAL REVIEW CHAPBOOK ANTHOLOGY; INTERNATIONAL WRITERS SERIES (II, IV-Translations, bilingual), 239 Wynsum Ave., Merrick NY 11566-4725, phone (516)868-5635, fax (516)379-1901, founded 1971, Stanley H. and Bebe Barkan. Stanley Barkan began CCC as an educational venture, a program in 27 languages at Long Island University, but soon began publishing collections of poetry translated into English from various languages—some of them (such as Estonian) quite "neglected"—in bilingual editions. During the 70s he became aware of Antigruppo (a group against groups), a movement with similar international focus in Sicily, and the two joined forces. **CCR** began as a series of chapbooks (6-12 a year) of collections of poetry translated from various languages and continues as the **Holocaust, Women Writers, Latin American Writers, African Heritage, Asian Heritage, Italian Heritage, International Artists, Art & Poetry, Jewish, Israeli, Yiddish, Cajun, Dutch, Finnish, Swedish, Scandinavian, Turkish,** and **Long Island** and **Brooklyn Writers Chapbook Series** (with a number of other permutations in the offing)—issued simultaneously in palm-sized and regular paperback and cloth-binding editions and boxed and canned editions, as well as audiocassette and videocassette. **Cross-Cultural International Writers Series,** focusing on leading poets from various countries, includes titles by Leo Voman (Holland) and Pablo Neruda (Chile). **All submissions should be preceded by a query letter with SASE. The Holocaust series is for survivors. Send SASE for guidelines. Pays 10% of print run. In**

addition to publications in these series, CCC has published anthologies, translations and collections by dozens of poets from many countries. As a sample the editor selected the beginning of a poem by Rainer Maria Rilke, as translated by Stephen Mitchell:

> She was no longer that woman with blue eyes
> who once had echoed through the poet's songs,
> no longer the wide couch's scent and island,
> and that man's property no longer.
>
> She was already loosened like long hair,
> poured out like fallen rain,
> shared like a limitless supply.

That's from the bilingual limited poetry and art edition, *Orpheus. Eurydice. Hermes: Notations on a Landscape*, published in 1996. It is 35 pgs., 10½×13½, smythe-sewn cloth. **Sample chapbook postpaid: $10.** *Cross-Cultural Monthly* focuses on bilingual poetry and prose. Subscription: (12 issues/editions): $50. **Sample postpaid: $7.50. Pays 1 copy.** CCC continues to produce the International Festival of Poetry, Writing and Translation with the International Poets and Writers Literary Arts Week in New York.

CRUCIBLE; SAM RAGAN PRIZE (I, II), Barton College, College Station, Wilson NC 27893, phone (919)399-6456, founded 1964, editor Terrence L. Grimes, is an annual using **"poetry that demonstrates originality and integrity of craftsmanship as well as thought. Traditional metrical and rhyming poems are difficult to bring off in modern poetry. The best poetry is written out of deeply felt experience which has been crafted into pleasing form. No very long narratives."** They have published poetry by Robert Grey, R.T. Smith and Anthony S. Abbott. As a sample the editor selected these lines from "Toward Short Off Mountain" by Mary C. Snotherly:

> So dense the fog, each man trudged alone,
> accompanied only by a stumble of boots,
> slap of laurel, by his own separate breathing,
> and like thunder roll, the barks resounding.

It is 100 pgs., 6×9, professionally printed on high-quality paper with matte card cover. Good type selection and point sizes highlight bylines and titles of poems. Press run is 500 for 300 subscribers of which 100 are libraries, 200 shelf sales. **Sample postpaid: $6. Send SASE for guidelines for contests (prizes of $150 and $100), and the Sam Ragan Prize ($150) in honor of the Poet Laureate of North Carolina. Submit 5 poems at a time between Christmas and mid-April. No previously published poems or simultaneous submissions. Reports in 3 months or less. "We require 3 unsigned copies of the manuscript and a short biography including a list of publications, in case we decide to publish the work."** Editor leans toward free verse with attention paid particularly to image, line, stanza and voice. However, he does not want to see poetry that is "forced."

CUMBERLAND POETRY REVIEW; THE ROBERT PENN WARREN POETRY PRIZE (II, IV-Translations), Dept. PM, P.O. Box 120128, Acklen Station, Nashville TN 37212, founded 1981, is a biannual journal presenting poets of diverse origins to a widespread audience. "Our aim is to support the poet's effort to keep up the language. We accept special responsibility for reminding American readers that not all excellent poems in English are being written by U.S. citizens. We have published such poets as Debra Marquart, Richard Tillinghast and Rachel Hadas." As a sample the editorial board selected these lines from "Gesualdo" by Arthur Gregor:

> Although the father of two boys, he talked
> as the child in him still might,
> of the happiness he felt in the music,
>
> the happiness of being one with all that is
> outside yourself, vast as the clear autumn sky,
> tall as the poplars already turned yellow.

CPR is 75-100 pgs., 6×9, flat-spined. Circulation 500. **Sample postpaid: $9. Send poetry, translations or poetry criticism with SASE or SAE with IRC. Submit up to 6 poems at a time. No previously published poems. "We accept, but do not like to receive simultaneous submissions."** Cover letter with brief bio required. Reports in 6 months. Pays 2 copies. Acquires first rights. Returns rights "on request of author providing he acknowledges original publication in our magazine."** They award The Robert Penn Warren Poetry Prize annually. Winners receive $500, $300 and $200 and publication in the review. For contest guidelines, send SASE.

CURMUDGEON; BUT(T) UGLY PRESS (I, II), 2921 Alpine Rd., #112, Columbia SC 29223, phone (803)736-1449, founded 1991, editor Erik C. McKelvey, assistant editor Lori Ann Larkin, is a biannual of "reality." **As for poetry, they want "reality. Stuff that can be seen. All forms. No surrealism. I'm not a big fan of reading for the way the words are on the page. I like a meaning**

to grab me." They have recently published poetry by James Michael Ward, Kevin Keck, Bruce Williams and Diane Robertson. As a sample the editor selected these lines from "Karma dances a Zen movement" by elliott:

> at the foot of my brass bed
> My past lives devour my false guilt
> I pin the spider beneath my weight
> Her taut web drawing me to her
> My juices, her venom, sing
> We recreate Eden.

The editor says *Curmudgeon* is 40-60 pgs., 8½×11, folded, photocopied with color cover, art and ads. They receive about 200 poems a year, accept approximately 25%. Press run is 100 for 20 subscribers. Subscription: $6. **Sample postpaid: $3. Submit 5 poems at a time. Previously published poems and simultaneous submissions OK. Cover letter, "telling us where the poet found our name," required.** Time between acceptance and publication is 6 months. **Seldom comments on rejections. Offers criticism for a fee. "A short, critical spiel is free; but if there needs to be more, terms can be worked out between the individual and the editors." Send SASE for guidelines. Reports in 2-3 weeks. Pays 1 copy.** Reviews books and chapbooks of poetry in 500 words. Open to unsolicited reviews. Poets may also send books for review consideration. The editor adds, "I want reality. I frown on surrealism. We like new poets for every issue of the magazine."

‡CURRICULUM VITAE LITERARY SUPPLEMENT; SIMPSON PUBLICATIONS (I), Grove City Factory Stores, P.O. Box 1309, Grove City PA 16127, e-mail proof114@aol.com, website http://www.well.com/user/ruz/cv/cv3toc.html, founded 1995, editor Michael Dittman. *Curriculum Vitae Literary Supplement* appears 3 times a year. **"We'd like to see more metrical work, especially more translations, and well-crafted narrative free verse is always welcome. However, we do not want to see rambling Bukowski-esque free verse or poetry that overly relies on sentimentality.** We are a relatively new publication and focus on unknown poets." As a sample the editor selected these lines from "Flicker, Fade, Die" by Jason Shaffer:

> Flicker, fade, die.
> Flicker, fade, die.
> Most nights the signals none too clear
> 'round here. You roll your eyes at
> old men's stories . . .

The editor says *CVLS* is 26 pgs., digest-sized, photocopied and saddle-stitched with a 2-color card stock cover. They receive about 50 poems a year, accept about 10. Press run is 1,000 for 300 subscribers of which 7 are libraries, 200 shelf sales. Subscription: $6 for 6 issues. **Sample postpaid: $1.50. Submit 3 poems at a time. Previously published poems and simultaneous submissions OK. Cover letter preferred.** Time between acceptance and publication is 8 months. **Poetry is circulated between 3 board members. Often comments on rejections. Publishes theme issues. Send SASE for guidelines and upcoming themes. Reports within a month. Pays 3 copies.** Reviews books of poetry; length and type of reviews vary. Open to unsolicited reviews. Poets may also send books for review consideration. Simpson Publications also publishes about 5 chapbooks a year. Interested poets should query.

CUTBANK; THE RICHARD HUGO MEMORIAL POETRY AWARD (II), English Dept., University of Montana, Missoula MT 59812, phone (406)243-5231, founded 1973, has revolving editors. *Cutbank* is a biannual literary magazine which publishes regional, national and international poetry, fiction, reviews, interviews and artwork. It also offers 2 annual awards for best poem and piece of fiction, The Richard Hugo Memorial Poetry Award and The A.B. Guthrie, Jr. Short Fiction Award. Winners are announced in the spring issue. They have published poetry by Seamus Heaney, Norman Dubie, James Tate, Amiri Baraka and Gerald Stern. As a sample the editors selected these lines from "Faces" by Mark Levine:

> We can't make the faces go away
> The bodies are not such a problem
> We pull them apart with chemicals and stretch them out
> Along the cracked surface of the old freeway.

There are about 100 pgs. in each issue, 50 pgs. of poetry. Circulation is 400 for 250 subscribers of which 30% are libraries. Single copy: $6.95; subscription: $12/two issues. **Sample postpaid: $4. Submit 3-5 poems at a time, single-spaced. Simultaneous submissions discouraged but accepted with notification. "We accept submissions from August 15 through March 15. Deadlines: Fall issue, November 15; Spring issue, March 15." Send SASE for guidelines. Reports in 2 months. Pays copies. All rights return to author upon publication.** Staff reviews books of poetry in 500 words, single or multi-book format.

DAGGER OF THE MIND; K'YI-LIH PRODUCTIONS; BREACH ENTERPRISES (IV-Science fiction/fantasy, horror), 1317 Hookridge Dr., El Paso TX 79925-7808, phone (915)591-0541, founded 1989, executive editor Arthur William Lloyd Breach, wants **"poetry that stirs the senses and emotions. Make the words dance and sing, bring out the fire in the human soul. Show flair and fashion. No four-letter words, nothing pornographic, vulgar, blasphemous, obscene and nothing generally in bad taste."** They have published poetry by Jessica Amanda Salmonson. The quarterly *DOTM* is magazine-sized, saddle-stapled, with high glossy covers. They receive 300-450 poems a year, use about 75. Press run is 4,000-5,000 with 400 subscribers. Subscription: $8/half year, $16/year. **Sample postpaid: $3.50. "Send in batches of 10. I will consider simultaneous submissions only if told in advance that they are such. Include cover letter with published credits, a very brief bio and kinds of styles written. Length is open as is style. Be creative and try to reflect something about the human condition. Show me something that reflects what is going on in the world. Be sensitive but not mushy. Be intelligent not sophomoric. Don't try to carbon copy any famous poet. You lead the way—don't follow. I don't like the trend toward blood and gore and obscenity. Report back in 3 months tops."** Pays $1-5/poem plus 1 copy. Buys first North American serial rights and reprint rights. *"DOTM* is devoted to *quality* horror. The key word is quality. *DOTM* is a publication under the division of K'yi-Lih Productions." The editor will evaluate work and review books of poetry for a fee, depending on length and quantity. Send books for review consideration. He says, "I'm planning an anthology of Lovecraftian related material. The paperback will be predominantly Cthulhu Mythos fiction, but I do intend to publish some poetry."

THE DALHOUSIE REVIEW (II), Sir James Dunn Bldg., Suite 314, Halifax, Nova Scotia B3H 3J5 Canada, phone (902)494-2541, fax (902)494-1665, e-mail dalrev@ac.dal.ca, founded 1921, is **a prestige literary journal preferring poems of 40 lines or less**. They have recently published poetry by Rose Marie Hunold, Gary Margolis, Heather Gardam, E. Russell Smith and Jeanne Shannon. As a sample the editor selected these lines from "Personations: 7" by Stan Rogal:

> *The reason one mask is as good as another.*
> *Masks. For this (or looking deeper),* bent,
> *Each object puts on its ugly face.*

> *Whether I appear or not depends upon the means.*
> *An arriving (of sorts), of form. Like,* here, *in this light,*
> *I star. I flicker.*

> Insist (always), on the verb.

The Dalhousie Review is 144 pgs., 6 × 9, professionally printed on heavy stock with matte card cover. Relatively few poems are featured in each issue, but ones that are tend to be free verse with emphasis on image and voice. Individual copies range in cost from $8.50-25. Subscription: $30/year within Canada and US, $40/year outside (both in Canadian dollars). **Submit 6-10 poems at a time. No previously published poems; simultaneous submissions OK. Cover letter welcome. OK to submit work or request information via e-mail. Contributors receive $3 for a first poem, and for each poem after (in the same issue) he or she will receive $2/poem; 2 complimentary copies of issue and 15 offprints.**

DAMAGED WINE (II, IV-Form), P.O. Box 722, Palos Park IL 60464-0722, founded 1993 (first issue fall/winter 1994), editor-in-chief Daniel A. Scurek, appears irregularly. *"Damaged Wine*'s purpose is to publish the finest free verse poetry received and to help give greater definition and respect to the much (and often deservedly) maligned form. **We seek only high-quality free verse. We like poetry that takes a more traditional approach; poetry with meaning, attention to detail and clarity, a sense of structure. Length, subject matter, style and content are open, though we encourage poets to stay clear of self-indulgent writing, a problem typical in free verse. No metered poetry, overtly experimental poetry, poems that extend obviously into prose."** They have published poetry by Richard Calisch, Effie Mihopoulos and John Dickson. *DW* is approximately 50 pgs., 4¼ × 11, laser typeset, saddle-stapled with card cover and artwork (mostly line drawings). They receive about 1,500 poems a year, accept approximately 10%. Press run is about 300. Single copy: $4; subscription: $12 for 3 issues. **Sample postpaid: $5. "All submissions must be typed; only one poem per page; name and address on each. Send no fewer than 2 poems and no more than 6. Please include a short bio note listing previous credits."** Previously published poems and simultaneous submissions OK, **if notified upon submission. Cover letter welcome but not required.** Time between acceptance and publication is 2 years. **Seldom comments on rejections ("unless requested"). Send SASE for guidelines or order a sample copy as guidelines are printed in each issue. Reports in 4 months. Pays 2 copies. Acquires one-time rights.** "We do accept books and chapbooks for review, provided they are books of free verse poetry. Reviews run from 5-10 pages and are typically but not exclusively in single-book format. We are not open to unsolicited reviews, but poets may send books for review consideration." The editor adds, "Free verse has defined modern poetry, not always in the most flattering way. We look to give free verse a stronger distinction and more defined quality. We feel that strongly experimental and prose poetry, for example, are fine stylistically, and may even define the

CLOSE-UP

Making the effort worthwhile

"The best advice I've ever been given," says Gary Whitehead, "is 'Let the writing be the most important part of being a writer.' For me, the joy of discovery, the joy of creating, is more rewarding than seeing a poem published. Sometimes, after writing a poem I'm particularly proud of, I can hardly contain my happiness. And that makes all the effort worthwhile."

Effort indeed. For almost ten years, Whitehead has been earnestly writing—and studying—poetry. His interest in the genre began in an introductory creative writing course with a very "inspirational" teacher—one who instantly recognized him as a writer and not only encouraged him to change his college major to English from sociology, but also encouraged him to submit his work to the school's poetry contest.

Gary Whitehead

Photo by Sharen Barboza

Since that class (and his second place contest finish), Whitehead has earned not just one, but three degrees in English—the most recent of which is a Master's in English from Iowa State University, where he was awarded a fellowship in poetry. He has also published hundreds of poems in publications such as *The Christian Science Monitor*, *Green Mountains Review*, *Southern Humanities Review*, *Southern Poetry Review* and *Yankee*.

Perhaps Whitehead has studied the craft so diligently because reviewing his early work causes him to grimace. Yet, those imitative poems, which "reek of obvious rhyme," were an important part of the process. "I think every beginning poet must write poorly," he says. "Doesn't a juggler drop the balls a few times before keeping them aloft? Most poets begin by imitation. For me it was Frost, Yeats, or whatever poet I was reading at the time.

"Even now, after reading Seamus Heaney, my lines suddenly shorten, my word choices ripen, my vowels jump from line to line like juncos on live wires. But imitation isn't satisfying for long. I think poets ultimately find they only want to be themselves. And if they've got any talent, and they write often, sooner or later they'll write a good poem."

For Whitehead, publication only increases the desire to write a "good" poem. Publication not only furthers one's career as a writer, but it also improves one's writing, he says. It reinforces the desire to write. Another valuable aspect of publication is that when you're published in a magazine, you usually receive a copy and can read everything else in the issue, which keeps you aware of what others are writing. Publication also increases your network with other writers. "I've received letters from people I don't know commending me on poems of mine they've read in magazines. Knowing someone else might read what I've

CLOSE-UP, *Whitehead*

"The Velocity of Dust"

We're here three days and everything
but us is set in its ordered place,
so we refinish our kitchen table.

We remove the old layer of dark varnish
like seven years of getting sober,
like one year of being married.

The sanding nearly wears me out.
Somehow it's like we've done this before,
taken something old and made it young again.

Through the universe of floating dust
spinning in the open door of the garage
I watch you work the sandpaper in the nooks,

and I realize that we've always done this.
I imagine your hands moving over me
in the way you have of removing blemishes,

and I think of the scars you don't know about.
The dust, predictable in its velocity,
settles around us like November snow.

Wiping with tack cloth, I tell you about
another garage and the thought of running
the car with the door closed,

drunk and hiding, first snow of that year.
You dust me off with your baseball cap
and take me outside for some air.

(originally published in *Poetry Digest*, Fall 1994; reprinted by permission of the author)

---

written, I think I'm more apt to write a better poem."

Yet Whitehead does more than just advocate publication. As founder, editor and publisher of the poetry magazine **Defined Providence**, he annually provides the benefits of publication to other poets. Whitehead decided to start a literary magazine when he discovered his work in a publication he had sent poems to months before, but which never sent a reply. Right then he vowed to be the editor that always replied to submissions, and in a timely manner.

He also strives to make his publication unique by organizing poems in relation to one another—"around certain themes as they might develop"—and by

CLOSE-UP, *continued*

including the work of unknown poets alongside the work of more established ones. "My reason for the latter is that I remembered the first time I had a poem in a magazine alongside [a poem by] James Merrill. I was thrilled," Whitehead says.

"As short-lived as the thrill was, it gave me a long-lasting sense of optimism. And this is what I've always hoped to do with my magazine, and that's why I'll put a poem by Richard Cambridge—a wonderful, but little-known poet—alongside poems by Mark Doty and Fred Chappell. A little bit of hope goes a long way."

During his time at Iowa State, Whitehead taught writing and offered hope to poets through the pages of his own magazine while also serving as poetry editor for another unique publication, *Flyway*, formerly the well-known literary magazine *Poet & Critic*. "What makes *Flyway* different from all other literary magazines is that it includes, alongside each creative piece, an author's commentary on the origins, inspirations and processes of the art's creation. In essence, the magazine has *Poet & Critic*'s original goal of being 'a workshop in print.' "

Working on *Flyway* was also a learning experience for Whitehead. Whereas *Defined Providence* is a one-man operation, with the responsibility for selecting poetry falling solely on Whitehead's shoulders, *Flyway* is a team effort, where every poem accepted must be approved by the poetry editor and the editor. "Springing as it did from the long-running *Poet & Critic*, and having a university affiliation, *Flyway* is of a different class than *Defined Providence*," he says.

Whitehead also admits that *Defined Providence* is a bit more conservative than *Flyway*, which takes more risks in the kinds of poems it chooses. That's why, no matter what type of publication you are submitting to, it's important to read the magazine before sending work. You'll obviously save time and postage if you don't send sonnets to a magazine of L-A-N-G-U-A-G-E poetry, he says. "I like a poem to make sense, to take me somewhere emotionally, and to make me feel somehow changed. All too often I see poems that don't accomplish this.

"The kinds of poems that are hardest to place are poems that are either really long or really short, probably because either type of poem is difficult to write well. A long poem risks being verbose, a small poem [risks] being underdeveloped."

Though Whitehead now serves as a contributing editor to *Flyway*, and continues to edit and publish *Defined Providence*, he remains more poet than editor and says the most difficult task for a poet trying to publish today is to get a book published. "With individual poems, it's not so hard. It all depends on where you want to publish them. What I found is that when I took all those well-published individual, miscellaneous poems and attempted to put them into a collection, many of them sounded too much alike.

"Poets fall back on what they're best at, and in my case, I realized I was writing strong balanced lyrics that focused inward rather than projected outward. And when I saw all those poems together, I realized the speaker was contextualized in the same way in many of them. Now, when I sit down to write, I'm thinking less about lyricism, more about narrative. I'm looking out instead of looking in."

—*Christine Martin*

poetry of the future, but are, in form, different from free verse. Free verse doesn't necessarily mean absence of meter, absence of logic or absence of internal flow. Poets should concentrate on the strengths of quality free verse: strong visual imagery and a sense of rhythm. Remember, good free verse is actually more difficult to write than metered poetry. We'd even suggest that poets analyze some of the masters of meter (be it Pope or Frost) as well as the masters of free verse (from Williams to Plath)."

DANCE CONNECTION (IV-Specialized), 815 First St. SW, #603, Calgary, Alberta T2P 1N3 Canada, phone (403)228-5780, fax (403)228-5773, e-mail eltonh@cuug.ab.ca, website http://www.can uck.com/Esalon/index.html, founded 1983, editor Heather Elton, appears 5 times a year and uses **poems about dance—"contemporary poetry dealing with 'issues' rather than lyrical poetry about young ballerinas. Something tough/challenging that deals with the body in a postmodern context."** It is 60 pgs., magazine-sized, desktop-published and saddle-stapled. Press run is 5,000 for 3,000 subscribers of which 35 are libraries, 1,500 newsstand sales. Subscription: $21 individuals, $33 institutions. **Sample postpaid: $5. Reports in 3 months. Sometimes sends prepublication galleys. Pays 3 copies and "occasional honorarium." Acquires all rights. Returns rights.** The editor says they "very occasionally publish poetry. When we get larger we will publish more, but now space is a precious commodity for review/calendars/news/columns and feature departments."

‡DANCING JESTER PRESS; CASSANDRA BOOKS OF VERSE (II); ONE NIGHT IN PARIS SHOULD BE ENOUGH (I, II), 3411 Garth #208, Baytown TX 77521, phone (713)427-9560, e-mail djpress@aol.com, founded 1994, acquisitions editor Shiloh Daniel. Dancing Jester Press publishes "work of intellectual distinction and literary excellence in a series called the Cassandra Books of Verse." They publish 5 paperbacks a year. **"We welcome all forms and styles of poetry. We are looking for a certain seriality and synchronicity. However, we eschew poetry we feel is no more than a copy of a copy of reality. To spark our interest you must capture the moment."** They recently published a three-volume Odyssean Trilogy by Gabriel Thomson. As a sample the editor selected these lines from "How Can Such Ignorance Have Its Own Way?" which appears in *Dwelling Amongst Fruit: Odysseus at Ithaca, An Odyssean Trilogy, Volume 3*:

> "How can such ignorance
> \have its own way?"
> \Muse, when they speak of me
> this is what they say.

The editor says books are usually 60 pgs., soft flat-spined, with fine art graphic covers. They also publish audio-books. **Query with 3 sample poems, a cover letter with short bio and publication credits. "Please include all illustrations connected with the writing." Previously published poems and simultaneous submissions OK.** Time between acceptance and publication is 18 months. **Poems are circulated to an editorial board.** "We read sympathetically, critique fairly and so edit evenly." **Replies to queries in 3 months. Pays 14% royalties and 5 author's copies (out of a press run of 500).** For a catalog, mail a request along with SASE plus $2.50 p&h. They also sponsor the One Night In Paris Should Be Enough contest, for poems of any style or form, no more than 300 lines total. First prize is one night in Paris, France (airfare and accommodations included). Entry fee: $15; 3 poems/ entry. Send SASE for entry form and guidelines. Deadline: December 22. The editor says, "There are but 24 hours in each day. If you have poetic aspirations, spend your time wisely reading and writing poetry rather than spending your time foolishly talking about reading and writing poetry. Poets are those who write, rather than those who talk about writing poetry."

DANCING SHADOW PRESS; DANCING SHADOW REVIEW (I, II), P.O. Box 9778, Baldwin MD 21013, phone (410)557-0110, founded 1992, editors Alan C. Reese, Sam Schmidt and Virginia Crawford. *Dancing Shadow Review* is a biannual "dedicated to publishing outstanding poetry and fiction without regard for political, ideological, social or stylistic constraints." **They want "poetry in which the form and language hammer home the poet's vision. We want to see it all, but tend to shy away from preachy or sentimental claptrap."** They have recently published poetry by Harvey Lillywhite and Richard Peabody. As a sample the editors selected these lines from Lillywhite's poem "Finding the Mother-Country":

> No myth illuminates the all-night driving
> That is our poverty, except how memory is
> A country of myth—the road curves over
> The planet, seems to start at the beginning

✝ **THE DOUBLE DAGGER** before a listing indicates that the listing is new in this edition. New markets are often the most receptive to submissions.

And to end in kingdom come—

DSR is 80-100 pgs., digest-sized and perfect-bound with glossy card cover and b&w artwork. Press run is 500 for 100 subscribers, 50 shelf sales. Single copy: $6.95; subscription: $14. **Sample postpaid: $8. Submit 3-5 poems at a time with a biographical sketch. Previously published poems OK; no simultaneous submissions. Reads submissions September 1 through June 30 only. Often comments on rejections. Pays 1 copy.** Dancing Shadow Press also publishes 2-4 chapbooks/year. **Query first with sample poems and cover letter with brief bio and publication credits. Replies to queries in 4-6 weeks, to mss in 2-4 months. Pays author's copies, 10% of the press run.** They have recently published *The Algebra of Hooves*, stories and poems by Nora Myers. It is 32 pgs., digest-sized and saddle-stapled with light card stock cover. Sample postpaid: $6.

DANDELION (II); BLUE BUFFALO (IV-Regional), The Alexandra Centre, 922 Ninth Ave. SE, Calgary, Alberta T2G 0S4 Canada, phone (403)265-0524, founded 1975, poetry editor Jenine Werner-King, managing editor Bonnie Benoit, appears twice a year. **They want "quality—We are open to any form, style, length. No greeting card verse."** They have published poetry by Claire Harris, Susan Ioannou and Robert Hilles. As a sample the editor selected these lines by Roger Nash:

> *On Sabbath evenings, a slow hand*
> *tuned the guitar. A fast hand*
> *moved the shifting stars. And, somewhere,*
> *while we were growing up, there was a street still*
> *made of gold of tin of slush*

Dandelion is 102 pgs., 6×9, professionally printed and bound with full-color cover. They accept about 10% of 600 mss received. Press run is 750. **Sample postpaid: $7. Submit 4-7 poems at a time. No previously published poems or simultaneous submissions. Cover letter with brief bio "appreciated. All submission requests require SASE (or SAE and IRCs). Only collect long distance calls will be returned." Reads submissions January through March and July through September for issues in June and December. Send SASE (or SAE and IRC) for a short statement of their needs and upcoming themes. Reports in 4-6 weeks. Pays honorarium plus 1 copy. Acquires first rights.** Reviews books of poetry in 500-1,200 words; preference is for books by Alberta writers. Open to unsolicited reviews. Poets may also send books for review consideration to Reviews Editor. *blue buffalo* is a magazine which falls under the Dandelion Magazine Society umbrella. *blue buffalo* is also published twice yearly, but **submissions are accepted** *only* **from Alberta writers.**

JOHN DANIEL AND COMPANY, PUBLISHER; FITHIAN PRESS (II), a division of Daniel & Daniel, Publishers, Inc., P.O. Box 21922, Santa Barbara CA 93121-1922, phone (805)962-1780, founded 1980, reestablished 1985. John Daniel, a general small press publisher, specializes in literature, both prose and poetry. Fithian Press is a subsidy imprint open to all subjects. **"Book-length mss of any form or subject matter will be considered, but we do not want to see pornographic, libelous, illegal or sloppily written poetry."** He has recently published *Amaranth-Sage Epiphanies: The Collected Poems of Hugo Walker*; *Sex Scells*, light verse by Kenneth Leonhardt; and *Shared Sightings: An Anthology of Bird Poems*, edited by Sheila Goldburgh Johnson. As a sample John Daniel selected "Housewife" from the book *The Shape of a Pear*, by Estelle Gershgoren Novak:

> *All week folding clothes*
> *Even when she rests,*
> *looking at the clouds*
> *she sees the soiled sheets*
> *of her laundry.*

He publishes 10 flat-spined paperbacks, averaging 64 pgs., each year. **For free catalog of either imprint, send #10 SASE. To submit material send 12 sample poems and bio. Reports on queries in 2 weeks, on mss in 2 months. Simultaneous submissions OK. Always sends prepublication galleys. Pays 10-75% royalties of net receipts. Buys English-language book rights. Returns rights upon termination of contract.** Fithian Press books (50% of his publishing) are subsidized, the author paying production costs and receiving royalties of 50-75% of net receipts. Books and rights are the property of the author, but publisher agrees to warehouse and distribute for one year if desired. John Daniel advises, "Poetry does not make money, alas. It is a labor of love for both publisher and writer. But if the love is there, the rewards are great."

DAUGHTERS OF SARAH (IV-Feminist, religious, social issues, themes), 2121 Sheridan Rd., Evanston IL 60201, phone (708)866-3882, e-mail cfa944@lulu.acns.nwu.edu, founded 1974, editor Elizabeth Anderson, is a quarterly magazine "integrating feminist philosophy with biblical/Christian theology and making connections with social issues." The magazine includes 1-3 pieces of poetry. The editor says, **"Please no rhymed couplets; must be short enough for one (or two) 5½×8½ page, but prefer less than 20 lines. Topics must relate to Christian feminist issues, but prefer specific to abstract terminology."** She does not want "greeting card type verse or modern

poetry so obscure one can't figure out what it means." As a sample the editor selected these lines by Geri Lynn Bawnblatt from an issue on AIDS:

> *Gazes, like lichens, attach to the floor,*
> *solidify encrusted.*
> *April released left the labyrinth*
> *where tied tissue laced scrambled veins.*
> *Cindered wings dropped in delay—*
> *amassed malignant hours.*

The magazine is 64 pgs., digest-sized, web offset, with photos and graphics. Circulation is 4,500 for 4,400 subscribers of which 250 are libraries; bookstore sales are 50. Single copy: $6; subscription: $22/year. Back issues available for $4. **Prefers shorter poems. Submit no more than two at once to Cathi Falsani, associate editor. "If submitting via e-mail, please type 'D of S' in the subject line."** Time to publication is 3-18 months. **Publishes theme issues. Send #10 SASE for guidelines and upcoming themes. Reports in 2-3 months.** *Daughters of Sarah* **pays $15-30/poem plus 2-3 copies. Buys one-time rights.** *Daughters of Sarah* received the Associated Church Press Honorable Mention for Poetry and Chicago Women in Publishing's 2nd Place Award for Literature. The editor says, **"Write first for list of upcoming themes, since we usually choose poetry to fit with a particular theme."**

DBQP; ALABAMA DOGSHOE MOUSTACHE; A VOICE WITHOUT SIDES; &; HIT BROADSIDES; THE SUBTLE JOURNAL OF RAW COINAGE; DBQPRESCARDS (IV-Form), 875 Central Pkwy., Schenectady NY 12309-6005, founded 1987, poetry editor Ge(of Huth).

"dbqp is the name of the overall press. *Alabama Dogshoe Moustache* publishes **language poetry (usually very short) & visual poetry.** *A Voice Without Sides* is an occasional magazine in very small runs (about 24 copies) and in strange formats (in jars, as earrings, etc.); it uses the same type of poem as *ADM. &* is a series of leaflets each featuring a single poem. *Hit Broadsides* is a broadside series. *The Subtle Journal of Raw Coinage* is a monthly that publishes coined words but occasionally will publish an issue of *pwoermds* (one-word poems such as Aram Saroyan's 'eyeye') or poems written *completely* with neologisms. *dbqprescards* is a postcard series publishing mostly poetry. These publications are generally handmade magazines, leaflets, broadsides and objects of very small size. **I am interested only in short language poetry and visual poetry. No traditional verse or mainstream poetry."** They have published poetry by John M. Bennett, Bob Grumman and Jonathan Brannen. As a sample the editor selected this complete poem by damian lopes:

> *the small boy walks*
> *like turning pages*
> *& runs like an alphabet*
> *without vowels*

Their major poetry magazine is *Alabama Dogshoe Moustache*, which appears in various formats up to 15 pgs., magazine-sized, held together with thread, staples, fasteners, or packaged inside containers. Its press run is 100-125 with 10 subscriptions. Single copy: 40¢-$2.50. **Sample postpaid: $1-2. Make checks payable to Geof Huth. Catalog available for SASE. Reports within 2 weeks. Pays "at least 2 copies."** Staff occasionally reviews books of poetry. Send books for review consideration. The editor says, "Most of the poetry I reject is from people who know little about the kind of poetry I publish. I don't mind reading these submissions, but it's usually a waste of time for the submitters. If you are familiar with the work of the poets I publish, you'll have a much better idea about whether or not I'll be interested in your work."

‡**DEAD METAPHOR PRESS (II),** P.O. Box 2076, Boulder CO 80306-2076, phone (303)939-0268, e-mail wilmartr@colorado.edu, founded 1985, contact Richard Wilmarth, publishes 1-3 chapbooks of poetry and prose a year, primarily through an annual chapbook contest. **"No restrictions in regard to subject matter and style."** They have recently published poetry by Anselm Hollo, Jack Collom and Aimée Grunberger and prose by Tracy Davis. As a sample we selected these lines from "The Bed" by Tree Bernstein from her chapbook, *Journal of the Lingering Fall*:

> *We lay down together mother, father, and I*
> *between them, on the crack between the beds,*
> *our hands folded across our chests*
> *dress rehearsal for a mausoleum dance*
>
> *Small now, like a deflated balloon,*
> *her body nearly spent of air*
> *her thin cold hand reaches for mine as she dreams*
> *of the stranger who offers his bed and rest at last*

Chapbooks are usually 24-60 pgs., 6×9, printed or photocopied, saddle-stitched, some with illustrations. **Submit 24 pgs. of poetry with a bio, acknowledgments and SASE. "Entries must be typed or clearly reproduced and bound only by a clip. Do not send only copy of manuscript."** Previously published poems and simultaneous submissions OK. **Reading fee: $8. Deadline: October 31. Winner will be announced in** *Poets & Writers* **and** *The Small Press Review.* **Winner receives 10% of press run plus discounted copies.** For sample chapbooks, send $6.

DEAD OF NIGHT PUBLICATIONS; DEAD OF NIGHT MAGAZINE (IV-Horror, science fiction/fantasy, mystery), 916 Shaker Rd., Suite 228, Longmeadow MA 01106-2416, founded 1989, editor Lin Stein. *Dead of Night* is an annual magazine that primarily publishes horror, fantasy, mystery, suspense and science fiction stories as well as reviews, interviews and an average of 2-3 poems per issue. **They want "genre poetry only: horror/fantasy/mystery/science fiction/suspense. All forms acceptable, including haiku. Works 32 lines or under preferred. No poetry which is outside these genres or of a 'general' theme."** They have recently published poetry by Michael J. Bielawa, Ann K. Schwader, S.G. Johnson and Jacie Ragan. As a sample the editor selected these lines from "The Bleeding" by John Grey:

> . . . *upon you,*
> *I am not the dagger*
> *you imagine*
> *but the vessel*
> *flying your dark spaces,*
> *parachuting my horror*
> *down into places*
> *deeper inside you*
> *than you are*

Dead of Night is 100 pgs., magazine-sized, newsprint, saddle-stapled with slick four-color cover; b&w art and ads inside. Press run is 3,000 for 700 subscribers, various shelf sales. Single copy: $5; subscription: $9 for 2 issues. **Sample postpaid: $2.50 (back issue). "No multiple submissions, please, unless the poems are VERY short (6-8 lines). In that case, 2-3 poems at one time are OK."** No previously published poems or simultaneous submissions. Cover letter required. Reads submissions January 1 through May 31 only. Time between acceptance and publication is 6-18 months. Occasionally comments on rejections. Send SASE for guidelines. Reports in 4-6 weeks. Pays $7/poem plus 1 copy. Buys first North American serial rights.** The editor says, "We advise poets to study our guidelines and/or a sample issue or back issue before submitting."

DEATHREALM (IV-Horror, fantasy), 2210 Wilcox Dr., Greensboro NC 27405-2845, e-mail s.rain ey@geis.com, founded 1987, editor Mark Rainey, is a quarterly using **"mostly tales of horror/dark fantasy. Small amount of poetry in each issue. No poetry reviews. Poems may be any style or length, though epic-scale pieces are** *not* **recommended. Rhyme or freestyle OK."** They have published poetry by Ardath Mayhar, Jessica Amanda Salmonson, Michael Arnzen and Chad Hensley. It is 64-72 pgs., magazine-sized, saddle-stapled with color cover. They receive 200-300 poems a year, accept 10-12. Press run is 3,000 for 500 subscribers, 2,500 shelf sales. Subscription: $15.95. **Sample postpaid: $4.95. Submit no more than 4 poems at a time. No simultaneous submissions. "Cover letters welcome, but limit to brief bio information, how writer found out about** *Deathrealm***, et. al. Do not open cover letter with poetry excerpts." Closed to submissions annually January 1 through May 1. Send SASE for guidelines. Reports in 6-9 weeks. Pays $4-8 plus 1 copy. Buys first North American serial rights.**

DEFINED PROVIDENCE; DEFINED PROVIDENCE PRESS (II), P.O. Box 16143, Rumford RI 02916, founded 1992, editor Gary J. Whitehead. *Defined Providence* is an annual which aims to publish "unknown poets alongside some of those poets considered to be the best in America." They **want "well-crafted lyrical or narrative poems grounded in experience. No overly religious, pornographic; singsong or conspicuous rhyme. Nothing too long. Shorter poems have a better chance."** They have recently published poetry by Fred Chappell, Mark Doty, Neal Bowers, X.J. Kennedy, Jack Myers and Vivian Shipley. As a sample the editor selected these lines from "Evening Walk" by Eric Trethewey:

> *The stars, haphazard in their swarming,*
> *blink on—remote, precise in themselves,*
> *as though to pinpoint anew the aim*
> *of each impossible longing.*

DP is an average of 72 pgs., digest-sized, offset from laserprint, perfect-bound with color card cover and exchange ads. "I receive about 1,500 poems per year and accept about 60 of them." Press run is 300 for 60 subscribers, 40 shelf sales. Subscription: $4, $7 for 2 years. **Sample postpaid: $3. Submit no more than 4 poems at a time, single-spaced. No previously published poems or simultaneous submissions. Cover letter preferred. Comments on rejections that show promise. Send SASE for guidelines. Reports in 1-3 weeks. Pays 1 copy.** The magazine also includes book reviews (in both single and multi-book format), and considers essays and interviews. Defined Providence Press publishes chapbooks through a contest. Winner receives stipend and 25 copies of a perfect-bound book,

24-56 pgs. $10 reading fee required. The 1994 selection was *Road Against Wind*, by Ronald J. Goba, 54 pgs., available for $5. They also hold an individual poem contest ($3/poem fee, any number of poems, 3 prizes, judged by a well-known poet). The editor says, "I see too much poetry that is hurried and uninteresting. I like poems surprising in their use of language, unpredictable, that have closure. I encourage poets to read a copy prior to submitting, and I remind poets that small mags stay alive through subscriptions."

DELAWARE VALLEY POETS, INC. (IV-Membership, anthology), P.O. Box 6203, Lawrenceville NJ 08648, publications director Coleen Schlaffer. "We publish contemporary anthologies and broadsides of **poetry by invitation to submit and books or chapbooks by members who are ready to publish."** They have published poetry by Maxine Kumin, Theodore Weiss and Geraldine C. Little. As a sample they selected these lines from "Mr. Kurtz, I Presume" by John Falk:

> *and a blue mantle of water unclasps,*
> *Slides down from the clouds and reclothes*
> *The worn and broken armature of stones.*

Members submit 6 samples, bio, publications. Reports in 6 months. "For anthologies, poets must have some connection with the basic organization. Anthologies are paid for by DPV, Inc., and all sales go to the organization. Individual authors pay printing costs; individual editorial services and distribution are provided by DVP. All sales go to the author." They add, "Poets serious about their work need to read all the poetry they can find, write poetry, attend poetry readings and find someone to trade poetry and criticism with. If there is no workshop available, start one."

DENVER QUARTERLY; LYNDA HULL POETRY AWARD (II), Dept. of English, University of Denver, Denver CO 80208, phone (303)871-2892, founded 1965, editor Bin Ramke, is a quarterly literary journal that publishes fiction, poems, book reviews and essays. **There are no restrictions on the type of poetry wanted.** Poems here focus on language and lean toward the avant-garde. Length is open, with some long poems and sequences also featured. They have published poetry by John Ashbery, Ann Lauterbach and Marjorie Welish. *Denver Quarterly* is about 130 pgs., 6×9, handsomely printed on buff stock and flat-spined with two-color matte card cover. Press run is 1,400 for 700 subscribers of which 300 are libraries, approximately 300 shelf sales. Subscription: $15/year to individuals and $18 to institutions. **Samples of all issues after Spring 1985 are available for $5 postpaid. Submit 3-5 poems at a time. Simultaneous submissions discouraged. No submissions read between May 15 and September 15 each year. Publishes theme issues. Send SASE for guidelines and upcoming themes. Reports in 2-3 months. "Will request diskette upon acceptance." Pays 2 copies and $5/page.** Reviews books of poetry. The Lynda Hull Poetry Award is awarded annually for the best poem published in a volume year. All poems published in the *Denver Quarterly* are automatically entered. Poetry published here has also been included in *The Best American Poetry 1992*.

DEPTH CHARGE; JOURNAL OF EXPERIMENTAL FICTION (II), P.O. Box 7037, Evanston IL 60201, phone (708)733-9554, founded 1986, editor Eckhard Gerdes. The *Journal of Experimental Fiction*, which appears irregularly (approximately twice a year), is a "literary and scholarly journal focusing on the limits of fiction, especially areas where it interfaces other art forms, including poetry, visual art and music." **They want "poetry from the interface zone, where it meets experimental fiction and the avant-garde."** They have published poetry by Richard Kostelanetz, Arthur W. Knight and Tim W. Brown. The editor says it is 100 pgs., $5\frac{1}{2} \times 8\frac{1}{2}$, perfect-bound with a 2-color cover (occasionally 4-color), some b&w artwork and ads. They receive 100-200 submissions a year, accept 5-10. Press run is 500 for 250 subscribers of which 100 are libraries, 100 shelf sales. **Sample postpaid: $9. No previously published poems or simultaneous submissions. Cover letter required.** Time between acceptance and publication is 2 months to 1 year. **Always comments on rejections. Send SASE for guidelines. Reports in 2 weeks to 2 months. Pays 3-5 copies. Acquires first North American serial rights.** Reviews books of poetry in 100-200 words. Open to unsolicited reviews. Poets may also send books for review consideration. Depth Charge also publishes 2-4 paperback books of poetry a year. **Query first, with sample poems and cover letter with brief bio and publication credits. Replies to queries and mss (if invited) in 2 weeks to 2 months. Pays 10% royalties and 20 author's copies.** The editor says, "Please familiarize yourself with our publications before submitting."

DESCANT (III, IV-Regional), Box 314, Station P, Toronto, Ontario M5S 2S8 Canada, phone (416)593-2557, founded 1970, editor-in-chief Karen Mulhallen, is "a quarterly journal of the arts committed to being the finest in Canada. **While our focus is primarily on Canadian writing we have published writers from around the world."** Some of the poets they have published are Lorna Crozier, Stephen Pender and Libby Scheier. As a sample the editor selected these lines from "Isla Grande" by Lake Sagaris:

> *I had caught children in my womb like clams*
> *watched them pried open and consumed and tossed away*

and still I was young.

Descant is 140 pgs., over-sized digest format, elegantly printed and illustrated on heavy paper, flat-spined with colored, glossy cover. They receive 1,200 unsolicited submissions/year, of which they use less than 10, with a 2-year backlog. Circulation is 1,200 for 800 subscribers of which 20% are libraries. **Sample postpaid: $8. Submit typed ms of no more than 6 poems at a time, name and address on first page and last name on each subsequent page. Include SASE with Canadian stamps or SAE and IRCs. No previously published poems or simultaneous submissions. Send SASE (or SAE and IRC) for guidelines and themes. Reports within 4 months. Pays "approximately $100." Buys first rights.** Karen Mulhallen says, "Best advice is to know the magazine you are submitting to. Choose your markets carefully."

DESCANT: TEXAS CHRISTIAN UNIVERSITY LITERARY JOURNAL (II), English Dept., Box 297270, Texas Christian University, Fort Worth TX 76129, phone (817)921-7240, founded 1956, editors Neil Easterbrook, Stan Trachtenberg and Steve Sherwood, appears twice a year. **They want "well-crafted poems of interest. No restrictions as to subject matter or forms. We usually accept poems 40 lines or fewer but sometimes longer poems."** It is 80 pgs., 6×9, professionally printed and saddle-stapled with matte card cover. Poems in issues we read tended to be lyric free verse under 50 lines with short line lengths (for added tension). "We publish 30-40 pgs. of poetry per year. We receive probably 4,000-5,000 poems annually." Their press run is 500 for 350 subscribers. Single copy: $6; volume: $12, $18 outside US. **Sample postpaid: $4. No simultaneous submissions. Pays 2 copies.**

THE DEVIL'S MILLHOPPER PRESS; THE DEVIL'S MILLHOPPER; KUDZU POETRY CONTEST; SAND RIVER POETRY CONTEST (II), English Dept., Box 26, University of South Carolina at Aiken, 171 University Parkway, Aiken SC 29801-6309, phone/fax (803)641-3239, e-mail gardner@univscum.csd.scarolina.edu, founded 1976, editor Stephen Gardner, publishes one magazine issue of *The Devil's Millhopper* each year and one chapbook, winner of an annual competition. **They want to see any kind of poetry, except pornography or political propaganda, up to 100 lines.** Some of the poets they have published are Susan Ludvigson, Ann Darr, Lynne H. deCourcy, Ricardo Pau-Llosa, Katherine Soniat, Walt McDonald, R.T. Smith, Dorothy Barresi and Richard Frost. The magazine is 32-40 pgs., digest-sized, printed on good stock and saddle-stapled with card cover and uses beautiful b&w original drawings inside and on the cover. The print run of *Devil's Millhopper* is 500. The annual chapbook has a print run of 600, going to 375 subscribers of which 20 are libraries. **Sample postpaid: $4. Submit 5-6 poems at a time. Send regular, non-contest submissions September and October only. They want name and address on every page of submissions; simultaneous submissions acceptable. Sometimes the editor comments on rejected mss. Reports usually in 2 months. Sometimes sends prepublication galleys. Pays copies. Acquires first North American serial and reprint rights. Rights automatically revert to author upon publication.** Send SASE for their annual Kudzu Poetry Contest rules (prizes of $150, $100 and $50, $3/poem entry fee), annual Sand River Contest for poetry in traditional fixed forms (prizes of $250, $150 and $50, $3/poem entry fee), chapbook competition rules, and guidelines for magazine submissions. Send Kudzu Contest submissions September 1 to October 31; Sand River Contest submissions June 1 to July 31; chapbook contest submissions January 1 to February 28. Chapbook competition requires $10 reading fee (which includes a one-year subscription). Pays $50 plus 50 copies. The editor advises, "There is no substitute for reading a lot and writing a lot or for seeking out tough criticism from others who are doing the same."

‡DIAL BOOKS FOR YOUNG READERS (V, IV-Children), 375 Hudson St., New York NY 10014, publishes some illustrated **books of poetry for children. "Poetry should be fairly straight forward."** Do not submit unsolicited mss. Query first with sample poems and cover letter with brief bio and publication credits. SASE required with all correspondence. No previously published poems; simultaneous submissions OK. Send queries to Attn: Submissions. Replies to queries in 1-2 months, to mss (if invited) in 1 month. Payment varies.

JAMES DICKEY NEWSLETTER (III), DeKalb College, 2101 Womack Rd., Dunwoody GA 30338, founded 1984, editor Joyce M. Pair, is a biannual newsletter devoted to critical articles/studies of James Dickey's works/biography and bibliography. They **publish a few poems of *high* quality. No poems lacking form or meter or grammatical correctness.** As a sample here are the opening lines from "Haft Blossom" by R.T. Smith:

> *Long-sleeping, I rose in the morning*
> *and opened the door to sunlight.*
> *Trough water woke me with sunlight,*
> *dark and the other stars having*
> *yielded their power . . .*

It is 30 pgs. of ordinary paper, neatly offset (back and front), with a card back-cover, stapled top left corner. The newsletter is published in the fall and spring. Subscription to individuals: $12/year (includes membership in the James Dickey Society), $14 to institutions. **Sample available for $3.50 postage. Contributors should follow MLA style and standard ms form, sending 1 copy, double-spaced. Cover letter required. Pays 5 copies. Acquires first rights.** Reviews "only works on Dickey or that include Dickey." Open to unsolicited reviews. The editor's advice is: "Acquire more knowledge of literary history, metaphor, symbolism and grammar, and, to be safe, the poet should read a couple of our issues."

THE DISABILITY RAG & RESOURCE (IV-Specialized), P.O. Box 145, Louisville KY 40201-0145, founded 1980, fiction/poetry editor Anne Finger, appears 6 times a year and "is the nation's leading disability rights magazine." **The editors have no restrictions as to form, length or style of poetry. "We are interested in vivid material by disabled writers or about the disability experience. Nothing sappy, sentimental, stereotyped or clichéd."** They have published poetry by Kenny Fries, Margaret Robison, Bill Abrams and Barbara Seaman. As a sample we selected the opening lines of "A Quiet Heard" by Nancy Bigelow Clark:

> In the silence of an old growth forest
> She speaks in layers, a fluency
> of flesh and air where even swear words
> Are a litany of fern, wild grape
> Growing undisturbed because few take
> The time to learn her language.

The editor says *The Rag* is approximately 48 pgs., 8 × 10⅝, b&w graphics on newsprint, some advertising. They receive about 100 poems a year, accept approximately 15%. Press run is 5,000 for 4,500 subscribers of which approximately 10% are libraries, 350 shelf sales. Single copy: $3.95; subscription: $17.50 individuals, $35 institutions, $42 international. **Sample postpaid: $4.50. Previously published poems OK, "provided they have not appeared in a publication that circulates to the disabled community." No simultaneous submissions. Cover letter required.** Time between acceptance and publication is 6-12 months. **Often comments on rejections. Send SASE for guidelines and upcoming themes. Reports within 1 month. Pays $25/poem plus 2 copies. Buys first North American serial rights.** "We publish reviews of disability-related poetry collections; our reviews run approximately 250-500 words." They have also published *The Ragged Edge*, an anthology of essays and poems from *The Rag*'s first 15 years.

‡**DJINNI (II)**, 29 Front St., #2, Marblehead MA 01945, fax (617)631-8595, e-mail kaloclarke@aol.com, founded 1990, editors Kalo Clarke and Kim Alan Pederson, is an annual international magazine publishing contemporary poetry, short fiction, short drama, essays and drawings by well-knowns and new talent. **The editors are especially interested in work that explores new directions.** *Djinni* is published "when sufficient quality material has been selected—usually late fall or early winter." The handsome magazine is 60-100 pgs., digest-sized, professionally printed and perfect-bound with matte card cover. Subscription or **sample: $5. Reads submissions May through November only. Reports in 1-3 months. Pays 1 copy.**

DOC(K)S; EDITIONS NEPE; ZERROSCOPIZ; ANTHOLOGIES DE L 'AN 2.000; LES ANARTISTES (II, IV-Bilingual/foreign language), Le Moulin de Ventabren, 13122 Ventabren, France 13122, uses **"concrete, visual, sound poetry; performance; mail-art; metaphysical poetry,"** not **"poesie à la queue-leu-leu"** . . . whatever that means. They have published work by J.F. Bory, Nani Balestrini, Bernard Heidsieck, James Koller, Julien Blaine and Franco Beltrametti. The magazine *Doc(k)s* is published 4 times a year and has a circulation of 1,100, of which 150 are subscriptions. It is an elegantly produced volume of over 300 pgs., 7 × 10, flat-spined, using heavy paper and glossy full-color card covers. Most of it is in French. "We cannot quote a sample, because concrete poetry, a cross between poetry and graphic art, requires the visual image to be reproduced." **There are no specifications for submissions. Pay for poetry is 5 copies.** Nepe Editions publishes collections of poetry, mostly in French.

DOLPHIN LOG (IV-Children, themes), 777 United Nations Plaza, New York NY 10017-3585, phone (212)949-6290, fax (212)949-6296, founded 1981, editor Lisa Rao, assistant editor Anna Prokos, is a bimonthly educational publication for children offered by The Cousteau Society. "Encompasses all areas of science, ecology and the environment as they relate to our global water system. Philosophy of magazine is to delight, instruct and instill an environmental ethic and understanding of the interconnectedness of living organisms, including people." They want to see **"poetry related to the marine environment, marine ecology or any water-related subject matter to suit the readership of 7- to 13-year-olds and which will fit the concept of our magazine. Short, witty poems, thought-provoking poems encouraged. No dark or lengthy ones (more than 20 lines). No talking animals."** The editor excerpted these sample lines from "Garbage Pirates" by Marianne Dyson:

> Their treasure bags ready

The garbage pirates three,
Set sail in a wagon boat
Upon the Sidewalk Sea.

They steer around bottle fish
With broken, jagged teeth,
And pinch their noses at the smell
Of trash on Driveway Beach.

It is 20 pgs., magazine-sized, saddle-stapled, offset, using full-color photographs widely throughout, sometimes art, no advertising. It circulates to 80,000 members, approximately 860 library subscriptions. Membership: $35/year for a Cousteau Society family membership, $15/year for *Dolphin Log* only. **Sample: $2.50 plus 9×12 SAE with 3 first-class stamps. Prefers double-spaced submissions. Publishes theme issues. Reports within 2 months. Always sends prepublication galleys. Pays $25-100 on publication and 3 copies. Rights include one-time use in *Dolphin Log*, the right to grant reprints for use in other publications, and worldwide translation rights for use in other Cousteau Society publications.** The editor advises, "Become familiar with our magazine by requesting a sample copy and our guidelines. We are committed to a particular style and concept to which we strictly adhere and review submissions consistently. We publish only a very limited amount of poetry each year. We are looking for longer poetry about entire ecosystems rather than one specific animal. For example, a poem about the wetlands or tidepools would be great."

DOLPHIN-MOON PRESS; SIGNATURES (II, IV-Regional), P.O. Box 22262, Baltimore MD 21203, founded 1973, president James Taylor, is **"a limited edition (500-1,000 copies) press which emphasizes quality work (regardless of style), often published in unusual/'radical' format."** The writer is usually allowed a strong voice in the look/feel of the final piece. "We've published magazines, anthologies, chapbooks, pamphlets, perfect-bound paperbacks, records, audio cassettes and comic books. **All styles are read and considered, but the work should show a strong spirit and voice. Although we like the feel of 'well-crafted' work, craft for its own sake won't meet our standards either."** They have published work by Michael Weaver, John Strausbaugh, Josephine Jacobsen and William Burroughs. They have also previously published a collection by the late Judson Jerome, *The Village: New and Selected Poems*, $10.95 paperback, $15.95 hardcover. **Send SASE for catalog and purchase samples or send $15 for their 'sampler' (which they guarantee to be up to $25 worth of their publications). To submit, first send sample of 6-10 pgs. of poetry and a brief cover letter. Replies to query or to submission of whole work (if invited) in 2-4 weeks. Always sends prepublication galleys. Pays in author's copies, negotiable, though usually 10% of the run. Acquires first edition rights.** Three of the books published by this press have been nominated for the Pulitzer Prize and another for a National Book Award. "Our future plans are to continue as we have since 1973, publishing the best work we can by local, up-and-coming and nationally recognized writers—in a quality package."

THE DOMINION REVIEW (II), Bal 220, English Dept., Old Dominion University, Norfolk VA 23529-0446, phone (804)683-3991, founded 1982, faculty advisor Janet Peery, Creative Writing, says, **"There are no specifications as to subject matter or style, but we are dedicated to the free verse tradition and will continue to support it."** They have published poetry by Donald Morrill, Ioanna-Veronika Warwick, Peter Spiro and Brighde Mullins. *TDR* is 150 pgs., digest-sized, professionally printed, flat-spined, and appears each spring. They have 500 subscriptions. **Sample: $5. They will not consider previously published poems. Cover letter and brief bio requested. Submissions read from September 1 through January 31; allow to March 15 for replies. Sometimes sends prepublication galleys. Pays 1 copy plus "nominal cash prizes are awarded for best work within each genre." Acquires first North American serial rights.**

DOUBLE-ENTENDRE (II), 3941 Legacy Dr., #204-206A, Plano TX 75023, founded 1993, editor Joshua Friend, is a biannual which contains poetry, short fiction and b&w line art. In regard to poetry, **they are open to all forms, lengths, subjects, etc. However, they do not want "that which is melodramatic, overly abstract or propagandizing."** They have recently published poetry by Philip Miller, Nancy Berg, John Grey, Robert Cooperman and Mary Winters. As a sample the editor selected these lines from "Vietnamese Supper" by Mary Hale Jackson:

Stay with me pickled radishes,
my love. Comfort me

With vegetable wedges dipped
in Thai fish-sauce

Express your trust with chicken
tender as smoke

The editor says it is 50-60 pgs., 5½×8½, desktop-published and staple bound, no ads. Press run is 100. Single copy: $4; subscription: $8. **Submit 4-7 poems at a time. Previously published poems and simultaneous submissions OK. "Work that is submitted without SASE cannot be returned."** Time between acceptance and publication is up to 8 months. **Seldom comments on rejections. Reports in 2-3 months. Pays 2 copies. Rights remain with authors.** The editor says, "Believe in your work. Sometimes great works get rejected many times, and the only things that will keep the possibility of publication alive are your continued faith in yourself and your persistence in submitting."

DRAGON'S TEETH PRESS; LIVING POETS SERIES (III), El Dorado National Forest, 7700 Wentworth Springs Rd., Georgetown CA 95634, founded 1970, poetry editor Cornel Lengyel. Published poets include Francis Weaver, Marcia Lee Masters and Stanley Mason. As a sample, the editor selected the beginning lines of "Not Just By Word of Mouth Alone" from *The Thirteenth Labor* by Ronald Belluomini:

> My sole being elliptic
> I have now and anciently dreamt in
> the treasuries of hope about
> a scheme to elude delusion's wrath,
> but I have broken
> my egg-shaped dream with collusion's fact.

Dragon's Teeth Press **"subsidy publishes 25% of books** if book has high literary merit, but very limited market"—which no doubt applies to books of poetry. They publish other books on 10% royalty contract. **Simultaneous submissions OK. Reports in 2 weeks on queries, 1 month on mss.**

DREAM INTERNATIONAL QUARTERLY (I, IV-Specialized), % Tim Scott, 2104 W. Foster Ave., Chicago IL 60625, founded 1981, senior poetry editor Tim Scott. **"Poetry must be dream-inspired and/or dream-related. This can be interpreted loosely, even to the extent of dealing with the transitory as a theme. Nothing written expressly or primarily to advance a political or religious ideology. We have published everything from neo-Romantic sonnets to stream-of-consciousness, ala 'the Beat Generation.'"** They have recently published poetry by Gary Jurechka, Maria Silvagnia and Linda Calendrillo. As a sample the editor selected these lines from "Two Simple Words" by Myrtle Archer:

> She was.
> No other line could tell her days
> No public praises came her way
> She scaled no Alps. She plumbed no depths.

DIQ is 120-150 pgs., 8½×11, with vellum cover and drawings. They receive about 150 poems a year, accept about 20. Press run is 300 for 200 subscribers of which 4 are libraries. Subscription: $30 for 1 year. **Sample postpaid: $8. Submit up to 5 typed poems at a time. Previously published poems and simultaneous submissions OK. Disk submissions welcome** (details available in guidelines). **Cover letter including publication history, if any, and philosophy of creation required. "As poetry submissions go through the hands of two readers, poets should enclose one additional first-class stamp, along with the standard SASE."** Do not submit mss October through December. Time between acceptance and publication is 1 year. **Comments on rejections if requested. Send SASE for guidelines. Reports in 1-4 weeks. Sometimes sends prepublication galleys. Pays 1 copy, "less postage." Also, from time to time, "exceptionally fine work has been deemed to merit a complimentary subscription." Acquires first North American serial or reprint rights.** Staff considers reviewing books of poetry "if the poet is a former contributor to *DIQ*. Such reviews usually run to about 500 words." Tim Scott says, "Don't get discouraged. Discouragement is the beginning writer's biggest enemy. If you are good at your craft, you will eventually find an outlet for it. Know your literary predecessors and the tradition in which you are working. Read everything from Shakespeare and Donne to Baudelaire and Rimbaud, from Crane and Hopkins to Plath and Sexton."

THE DREAM SHOP; VERSE WRITERS' GUILD OF OHIO; OHIO HIGH SCHOOL POETRY CONTESTS (IV-Membership, students), 233 E. North St., Medina OH 44256-1947, founded 1928, editor J.A. Totts. The Verse Writers' Guild of Ohio (Amy Jo Zook, treasurer, 3520 St. Rte. 56, Mechanicsburg OH 43044) is a state poetry society open to members from outside the state, an affiliate of the National Federation of State Poetry Societies. *The Dream Shop* is their poetry magazine, appearing twice a year. **Only members of VWG may submit poems. They do not want to see poetry which is highly sentimental, overly morbid or porn—and nothing over 40 lines. "We use beginners' poetry, but would like it to be good, tight, revised. In short, not first drafts. Too much is sentimental or prosy when it could be passionate or lyric. We'd like poems to make us think as well as feel something."** They have recently published poetry by Yvonne Hardenbrook, Betsy Kennedy, Rose Ann Spaith and Dalene Workman Stull. As a sample the editor selected these lines from "In Dubiis" by Timothy Russell:

> . . . as the boy practices the limited part

> *for tenor sax of a popular theme*
> *for the twentieth time tonight.*
> *He's had it perfect for two days.*
> *Warped images dance in the bell*
> *of the boy's polished instrument:*
> *his father sitting like a gargoyle*
> *on the wooden steps, wiping his eye.*

The magazine is 52 pgs., digest-sized, computer typeset, with matte card cover. "Ours is a forum for our members, and we do use reprints, so new members can get a look at what is going well in more general magazines." Annual dues including *The Dream Shop*: $15. Senior (over 65): $12. Single copies: $2. **Previously published poems OK, if "author is upfront about them. All rights revert to poet after publication."** The Verse Writers' Guild sponsors an annual contest for unpublished poems written by high school students in Ohio with categories of traditional, modern, and several other categories. March deadline, with 3 money awards in each category. For contest information write Verse Writers' Guild of Ohio, 1798 Sawgrass Dr., Reynoldsburg OH 43068.

DREAMS AND NIGHTMARES (IV-Science fiction/fantasy), 1300 Kicker Rd., Tuscaloosa AL 35404, phone (205)553-2284, e-mail d.kopasks-me@genie.com, founded 1986, editor David C. Kopaska-Merkel, is published twice a year. The editor says, **"I want to see intriguing poems in any form or style under about 60 lines (but will consider longer poems). All submissions must be either science fiction, fantasy or horror (I prefer supernatural horror to gory horror). Nothing trite or sappy, no very long poems, no poems without fantastic content, no excessive violence or pointless erotica. Sex and/or violence is OK if there is a good reason."** He has recently published poetry by Charlee Jacob, Herb Kauderer, D.F. Lewis, Wendy Rathbone, Greg Stewart and John Grey. As a sample the editor selected these lines from "The Names of the Moon" by John Gesang:

> *. . . One imagines*
> *H.G. Wells living there now*
> *in a somewhat picturesque little*
> *cottage of late Victorian design,*
> *tucked away near one end of his own*
> *Small crater on the far or "dark" side*

Dreams and Nightmares is 24 pgs., digest-sized, photocopied from typescript and saddle-stapled with a colored card stock cover and b&w illustrations. They accept about 80 of 1,000-1,500 poems received. Press run is 250 for 90 subscribers. Subscription: $10/6 issues. Lifetime subscription: $100 (includes available back issues). **Samples: $2. Submit up to 5 poems at a time. "Rarely" uses previously published poems. No simultaneous submissions. Send SASE for guidelines. Information requests and comments via e-mail are welcome; e-mail submissions are accepted but not encouraged. Reports in 2-10 weeks. Pays $3/poem plus 2 copies. Buys first North American serial rights.** The editor reviews books of poetry. Send books for review consideration. *Dreams and Nightmares* received an award from the Professional Book Center for "advancing the field of speculative poetry." The editor says, "There are more magazines publishing fantastic poetry than ever before, and more good fantastic poetry is being written, sold for good money and published. The field is doing very well."

THE DRY CREEK REVIEW (II), Aims Community College, Loveland Center, 104 E. Fourth, Loveland CO 80537, founded 1990, faculty advisor Tony Park, is an annual. "We accept creative nonfiction, fiction, translations, and quality poetry." **They are open to all forms/styles. "We want poems built around vivid imagery, rich language and risk. We do not want to see the abstract based on the insignificant."** They have recently published poetry by Joy Harjo, Evan Oakley, Greg Grummer, Linda Aldrich and Deanna Kern Ludwin. As a sample the editor selected these lines from "When I was Blond" by Veronica Patterson:

> *When I was blond*
> *I played with the amber monkeys in pines*
> *and none could tell us*
> *from the night. I grew*
> *morning glories from an apple. All said*
> *the blossoms were the color of my eyes.*

The attractive *Review* is 95-150 pgs., 6×9, professionally printed and perfect-bound with 4-color light card cover with art and occasional b&w art and photos inside. They receive 300-400 poems a year,

---

MARKET CATEGORIES: (I) Beginning; **(II)** General; **(III)** Limited;
(IV) Specialized; **(V)** Closed.

accept 10-15%. Press run is 750, all distributed free. **No previously published poems; simultaneous submissions OK. Reads submissions September 15 through April 30 only. Poems are circulated to an editorial board. Seldom comments on rejections. Reports in 3-6 months. Rights revert to author on publication.** Open to unsolicited reviews. Poets may also send books for review consideration.

DUST (FROM THE EGO TRIP); CAMEL PRESS (IV-Specialized), General Delivery, Big Cove Tannery PA 17212, phone (717)573-4526, founded 1981, poetry consultant Katharyn Howd Machan, publisher James Hedges, who describes himself as "editor/printer of scholarly and scientific journals, does occasional poetry postcards and chapbooks for fun." *Dust (From the Ego Trip)* is "an intermittent journal of personal reminiscences." For it he wants **autobiographical material (can address any subject, but written from the viewpoint of an active participant in the events described). Mss should be between 1,000 and 2,500 words and can be one long poem or a collection of related shorter poems. Any style OK, including haiku, and any language using the roman alphabet. No religious (evangelizing) material or other material written primarily to advance a point of view. Any topic is OK, and coarse language is OK, but only if used artistically."** As a sample James Hedges selected these lines from "The Deaf Child" by Duane Locke:

> Once, the child rubbed a thumb
> over a series of green scales,
> found that a joy grew within.
>
> The lips of the other odd figure
> are speaking what the child has never heard,
> speaking to a curtain cord swayed by wind.

He publishes 1-2 chapbooks a year under the Camel Press imprint, average 20 pgs. **Query with "a few sample poems." Cover letter not required, "but I like the personal contact and the show of sincere interest." No bio or publications necessary because, "we judge on material only, status of poet is irrelevant." Simultaneous submissions and previously published material OK. Reports in 10 days. Always sends prepublication galleys. Pays 50 copies plus half of net after production costs are recovered.** He is open to subsidy publishing poetry of "artistic merit." To buy samples, request catalog. He says, "I always write a cover letter, but I'm not a poetry critic, just a considerate publisher. I do a bit of poetry because I want to encourage the art and broaden my catalog. Everything I publish is handset in metal type and letterpress printed on fine paper. The authors are expected to do most of the promotion. Press run is normally 500, and I give away about 400 copies to friends, plus 50 for the author. The author can order more copies in advance if he expects to sell a large number. Financial arrangements are negotiable."

DWAN (I, IV-Gay/lesbian, translations), Box 411, Bellefonte PA 16823, founded 1993, editor Donny Smith, appears every 2 to 3 months. *Dwan* is a "queer poetry zine; some prose; some issues devoted to a single poet or a single theme ('Jesus' or 'Mom and Dad,' for instance)." The editor wants **"poetry exploring gender, sexuality, sex roles, identity, queer politics, etc. If you think Charles Manson is cool—or even Charles Bukowski—you might not feel welcome at *Dwan*."** They have recently published poetry by Charly Earley, Roman Adu and Michael Gregg Michaud. As a sample the editor selected these lines from "Girl Kiss Girl" by Maria Goodman:

> she does, but with a smile as
> generous as the way she
> shared her pillow. A kiss on the
> cheek, you are numb, then pleased,
> then scared. She backs away.

Dwan is 16 pgs., 5½ × 8½, photocopied on plain white paper, and stapled. They receive 400-500 pgs. of poetry/year ("that's no exaggeration!"), accept less than 10%. Press run is 75. **Sample available for 2 first-class stamps. Submit 5-15 poems typed "in black on white please, no colored paper, no blue ink." Previously published poems and simultaneous submissions OK. Cover letter required.** Time between acceptance and publication is 6-18 months. **Often comments on rejections. Send SASE for upcoming themes. Reports in 1-3 months. Pays copies.** The editor reviews books, chapbooks and magazines usually in 25-150 words. Send books for review consideration. "Heterosexuals always welcome."

EAGLE'S FLIGHT; EAGLE'S FLIGHT BOOKS (I, IV-Translations), P.O. Box 465, Granite OK 73547, phone (405)535-2452, founded 1989, editor/publisher Shyamkant Kulkarni, is a quarterly "platform for poets and short story writers—new and struggling to come forward." **They want "well-crafted literary quality poetry, any subject, any form, including translations." Translations should have permission of original poets.**" They have recently published poetry by Han Shan, Leeda Warren and Mike Cluff. As a sample the editor selected these lines from "Life" by Susan K. Behm:

> Universe so grand, reaches

beyond man. Planet so fragile
Containing life so delicate,
Nature so cycling, brings
Everything back to its origin,
Animals so bonding, working for
Survival, man so selfish, ignores
All until its destruction.

Eagle's Flight is 8-12 pgs., 7 × 8½, printed on colored paper and saddle-stapled, including simple art, few ads. They receive about 50 poems/year, accept 10%. Press run is 200 for 100 subscribers. Subscription: $5. **Sample postpaid: $1.25. Submit up to 5 poems at a time, no more than 21 lines each. No previously published poems or simultaneous submissions. Cover letter required; include short bio, up to 4 lines. Reads submissions January 1 to June 30.** Time between acceptance and publication is 1-3 years. **Seldom comments on rejections. Send SASE for guidelines. Reports in 2-3 months. Pays 2 copies. Acquires first publication rights.** Reviews books of poetry in 250-750 words, single format. Sponsors the "Poem of the Year" award for the best poem published in *Eagle's Flight* in the previous year. Under Eagle's Flight Books, they publish 1 paperback/year. "Up to now we have been publishing our own books, but **if somebody wants to share publishing cost, we can help or undertake publishing a book/anthology. We don't have selling organizations. Anybody interested in this may enquire." Replies to queries in 1 month.** The editor says, "We expect poets to be familiar with our publication and our expectations and our limitations. To be a subscriber is one way of doing this. Everybody wants to write poems and, in his heart, is a poet. Success lies in getting ahead of commonplace poetry. To do this one has to read, to be honest, unashamed and cherish decent values of life in his heart. Then success is just on the corner of the next block."

EARTH'S DAUGHTERS: A FEMINIST ARTS PERIODICAL (IV-Women/feminism, themes), P.O. Box 41, Central Park Station, Buffalo NY 14215, founded 1971. The "literary periodical **with strong feminist emphasis**" appears 3 times a year, irregularly spaced. Its "format varies. Most issues are flat-spined, digest-sized issues of approximately 60 pgs. We also publish chapbooks, magazine-sized and tabloid-sized issues. Past issues have included broadsheets, calendars, scrolls and one which could be assembled into a box." **Poetry can be "up to 40 lines (rare exceptions for exceptional work), free form, experimental—we like unusual work. All must be strong, supportive of women in all their diversity. We like work by new writers, but expect it to be well-crafted. We want to see work of technical skill and artistic intensity. We rarely publish work in classical form, and we never publish rhyme or greeting card verse."** They have published poetry by Christine Cassidy, Rose Romano, Lyn Lifshin, Helen Ruggieri, Joan Murray, Susan Fantl Spivack, "and many fine 'unknown' poets, writers and artists." They publish poetry by men if it is supportive of women. As a sample the editor selected "On Saving Letters From Friends" by Jean LeBlanc from *#43/44 The Girlfriends Issue*:

. . . Time, folded deliberately into thirds—
past, present, future—
can, for an instant, be held fast between our fingers,
replayed, reviewed, remembered,

understood, accepted, forgiven,
then refolded and neatly ordered in a drawer. . . .

"Our purpose is to publish primarily work that otherwise might never be printed, either because it is unusual, or because the writer is not well known." Subscription: $14/3 issues for individuals; $22 for institutions. **Sample postpaid: $5. Simultaneous submissions OK. "Per each issue, authors are limited to a total of 150 lines of poetry, prose or a combination of the two. Submissions in excess of these limits will be returned unread. Business-size envelope is preferred, and use sufficient postage—we do not accept mail with postage due." Send SASE for guidelines.** Some issues have themes, which are available for SASE after April of each year. **Length of reporting time is atrociously long if ms is being seriously considered for publication, otherwise within 3 weeks. Pays 2 copies and reduced prices on further copies. Editor comments "whenever we have time to do so—we want to encourage new writers."** The collective says: "Once you have submitted work, please be patient. We only hold work we are seriously considering for publications, and it can be up to a year between acceptance and publication. If you must contact us (change of address, notification that a simultaneous submission has been accepted elsewhere), be sure to state the issue theme, the title(s) of your work and enclose SASE."

EASTERN CARIBBEAN INSTITUTE (I, IV-Regional), P.O. Box 1338, Frederiksted, U.S. Virgin Islands 00841, phone (809)772-1011, fax (809)772-3463, founded 1982, editor S.B. Jones-Hendrickson, editorial contact Cora Christian, is a "small press publisher with plans to expand," **especially interested in poetry of the Caribbean and Eastern Caribbean.** As a sample the editor selected these lines from "The AIDS Watch" in *Of Mask and Mysteries* by Lillian Sutherland:

> Today I watched a mother
> > just sitting there and crying
> Today I watched a mother
> > just sitting there and dying
> Today I watched a mother
> > put her husband in his grave

Their books are softcover, averaging 60 pgs. Sample copies available for purchase. **Submit 5 sample poems and cover letter with bio and previous publications. Simultaneous submissions and previously published poems OK. Reads submissions January to May only. Reports in 1 month. Pays 50 copies.** The editor says, "In our part of the world, poetry is moving on a new level. People who are interested in regional poetry should keep an eye on the Caribbean region. There is a new focus in the Virgin Islands."

ECHOES MAGAZINE (I, II), P.O. Box 3622, Allentown PA 18106-0622, fax (610)776-1634, e-mail echoesmag@aol.com or 73200.1446@compuserve.com, website http://users.aol.com/echoes mag/, founded 1993, is a bimonthly designed to "provide a forum for people in all walks of life to share their experiences and perspectives in creative ways—poetry, stories, plays, drawings. **We want poems that speak to the reader, sharing the writer's unique perspective and inspiring new insights or understanding. We look for imaginative use of imagery, metaphor, and language that is meaningful to the average reader.**" They have published poetry by both well-known poets and talented newcomers. As a sample we selected these lines from "After the Battle" by John Grey:

> The bruising of an August morning.
> Hoping the sun will peel away the
> bad tissue. He stands to lonely attention
> at the French windows, too ashamed for warming.
> Her pain makes her feel out of place
> in a slight, see-through nightdress.

Echoes is 64 pgs., 6 × 9, offset printed and perfect-bound with card stock cover and original drawings and artwork. They receive about 1,500 poems a year, accept less than 10%. Press run is 1,200. Subscription: $24 for 6 issues. **Sample postpaid: $5. Submit 4-5 poems at a time, name and address on each page. Previously published poems OK, "if publication was to a limited audience." No simultaneous submissions. Cover letter required;** include brief description of background and writing experience. **"We also accept ASCII text files via e-mail or on 3.5 computer disks, Mac or DOS."** Time between acceptance and publication is 2-5 months. **Poems are circulated to 2-3 members of an editorial review panel and to each editor. Often comments on rejections. Send SASE for guidelines, also available via website. Reports in 6-8 weeks. Pays 6 copies. "We ask all writers of accepted work to authorize the Library of Congress to include their work in its programs of Braille and sound recordings for the handicapped. We also request exclusive magazine, reprint, and anthology rights for one year, including the right to publish audio or electronic issues, and nonexclusive rights thereafter. All negotiable to fit author's situation."** They are also planning to hold a contest and a conference in 1997. Interested poets should send SASE for information. The editor says, "We see too much poetry that is full of abstractions, or deals with familiar subjects in an all-too-familiar way, or delights in its own obscurity. The result is not interesting or meaningful to the average reader."

EDICIONES UNIVERSAL (IV-Ethnic, foreign language, regional), 3090 SW Eighth St., Miami FL 33135, phone (305)642-3234, founded 1964, general manager Marta Salvat-Golik, is a small press subsidy publisher of **Spanish language books. "We specialize in Cuban authors and themes."** They have published books of poetry by Olga Rosalo and Amelia del Castillo. **Poets "must be able to purchase in advance 75% of the copies, due to the fact that poetry does not sell well." Poets receive the copies they paid for. Submit sample, bio, publications. Reports in 1 month.**

EIDOS MAGAZINE: SEXUAL FREEDOM & EROTIC ENTERTAINMENT FOR WOMEN, MEN & COUPLES (IV-Erotica, women), P.O. Box 96, Boston MA 02137-0096, phone (617)262-0096, fax (617)364-0096, e-mail eidos4sex@aol.com, website http://www.io.org/~do mina/org/EIDOS.HTML, founded 1982, poetry editor Brenda Loew Tatelbaum. "Our press publishes erotic literature, photography and artwork. Our purpose is to provide an alternative to women's images and male images and sexuality depicted in mainstream publications like *Playboy, Penthouse, Playgirl*, etc. We provide a forum for the discussion and examination of two highly personalized dimensions of **human sexuality: desire and satisfaction. We do not want to see angry poetry or poetry that is demeaning to either men or women. We like experimental, avant-garde material that makes a personal, political, cultural statement about sensu-sexuality."** They have recently published poetry by Sheree Anne Slaughter, Lorraine A. Williams, Corrine DeWinter and Frank Moore. As a sample we selected this poem, "Source Mythology," by John Hulse:

> When I was young someone told me

Winter 1995-1996

ECHOES
the magazine for creative communication

$5.00

Most cover illustrations for the bimonthly magazine *Echoes* are based on a poem or story in that particular issue. "This drawing [drawn to complement the short story 'I Am a Rock' by Susan Dugan] is attractive, eye-catching, and conveys a feeling of the personality and artistic quality a reader will find inside," says Editor Peter Crownfield. Published in Allentown, Pennsylvania, *Echoes* contains poems and stories by beginning and professional writers from "all walks of life, experiences and perspectives." The magazine also publishes plays and drawings, and focuses on giving writers and artists a way to communicate their emotions and ideas. "We look for good, clear writing that is personal and 'alive,'" says Crownfield. "Unfortunately, we can publish only about five percent of the poetry and stories we receive." The cover artist is Victoria Perry, a lifelong resident of upstate New York.

> that to really please a woman
> I had to learn how to balance a nickel
> on the tip of my tongue.

Eidos is a newsprint tabloid, professionally printed with photography and art, **number of poems/issue varies.** They receive hundreds of poems/year, use about 100. No backlog right now. Press run is 10,000 for over 7,000 subscribers. Subscription: $55 for 4 issues. **Sample postpaid: $15. Only accepts sexually explicit material. 1 page limit on length, format flexible. Camera-ready, "scannable" poems preferred, but not required. No previously published poems; simultaneous submissions OK. "Poets must submit their work via regular 'snail' mail. No faxes or e-mail submissions accepted." Do not send computer disks. Publishes bio information as space permits. Comment or criticism provided as often as possible. Send SASE for guidelines. Reports in 1 month. Pays 1 copy. Acquires first North American serial rights.** Open to unsolicited reviews. Poets may also send books for review consideration. The editor advises, "There is so much poetry submitted for consideration that a rejection can sometimes mean a poet's timing was poor. We let poets know if the submission was appropriate for our publication and suggest they resubmit at a later date. Keep writing, keep submitting, keep a positive attitude."

1812 (III), Box 1812, Amherst NY 14226, phone (716)834-1067, e-mail doctrbook2@aol.com, founded 1993, editors Dan Schwartz and Richard Lynch, is an annual literary arts publication **"looking for material with a *bang*."** The editor says *1812* is 100 pgs., 6×9, with glossy cover and b&w art. They receive about 1,000 poems a year, accept 1-3%. **Previously published poems OK; no simultaneous submissions. Cover letter required. "Submission may be arranged by e-mail with permission."** Time between acceptance and publication is 6-12 months. **Sometimes comments on rejections. Send SASE for guidelines. Payment is "arranged." Buys one-time rights.** Open to unsolicited reviews. Sponsors the Overture Award for poetry. Reading fee is $5 for first poem, $2 for each additional entry. Award is $100 and publication. Send SASE for guidelines.

THE EIGHTH MOUNTAIN PRESS; EIGHTH MOUNTAIN POETRY PRIZE (IV-Women, feminist), 624 SE 29th Ave., Portland OR 97214, founded 1985, editor Ruth Gundle, is a "small press publisher of **feminist literary works by women.**" They have recently published poetry by Karen Mitchell, Maureen Seaton, Lori Anderson and Elizabeth Woody. They publish 1 book of poetry averaging 128 pgs., every other year. **"We now publish poetry *only* through the Eighth Mountain Poetry Prize." Pays 8-10% royalties. Buys all rights. Returns rights if book goes out of print.** The Eighth Mountain Poetry Prize is a biennial award of a $1,000 advance and publication for a ms of 50-120 pgs. written by a woman; no restrictions as to subject matter. Send SASE for rules. **Submit during January in even-numbered years. Postmark deadline: February 1.** Entry fee: $20. "The selection will be made anonymously. Therefore, the ms must have a cover sheet giving all pertinent information (title, name, address, phone number). No identifying information except the title should appear on any other ms page. The contest will be judged by a different feminist poet each year, whose name will be announced after the winning ms has been chosen." Previous judges have included Audre Lorde, Linda Hogan, Marilyn Hacker, Judy Grahn, Lucille Clifton and Naomi Shihab Nye.

EKSTASIS EDITIONS (II), Box 8474, Main Postal Outlet, Victoria, British Columbia V8W 3S1 Canada, phone/fax (604)385-3378, founded 1982, publisher Richard Olafson, annually publishes 12 paperbacks, 2 hardbacks and 10 chapbooks of "well crafted" poetry. **They have no specifications regarding form, length, subject matter or style of work.** They have recently published collections of poetry by Robin Skelton, Michael Bullock, Pierre Reverdy and Richard Stevenson. **Query first, with sample poems and cover letter with brief bio and publication credits. Previously published poems and simultaneous submissions OK. Replies to queries and mss (if invited) in 4 months. Pays 5-10% royalties and author's copies.**

ELECTRIC CONSUMER (III), P.O. Box 24517, Indianapolis IN 46214, founded 1951, editor Emily Born Schilling, is a monthly publication for rural electric consumers in Indiana including electrical/ energy information and general interest features. **"We very rarely publish poetry and prefer contributors to be rural electric members from Indiana."** The editor says *EC* is a 16-page, stitched and trimmed tabloid. They receive 30-50 poems a year, "may run 6." Press run is 280,000 for 279,000 subscribers. Subscription: $7/year. **No previously published poems or simultaneous submissions. On *rare* occasions poems are published as needed to fill space. However, they have a 3-year backlog, do not generally report on submissions, and do not pay.**

11TH ST. RUSE; BIG FISH (I), 322 E. 11th St., #23, New York NY 10003, phone/fax (212)475-5312, founded 1987, editor Lucid. *11th St. Ruse* appears every 5 months, 4 pgs. mimeo, wants **poems "short, without glut, preferably written very quickly. Especially interested in angry, obscure, humorous, religious, primitive or mysterious poetry and minority poets."** They have recently published poetry by Tinkerbelle, John Alan Douglas, Mike Topp, J thi Wilson and Jay Link. As a sample the editor selected these lines from "Scissors" by Adam Woo:

> living
>> alone
>>> I scratch
>> my back
>>> with a
>> pair of
>>> scissors

Press run is 250. Single copy: 33¢. **Sample postpaid: 50¢. Make checks payable to Ellen Carter. Submit 5 poems at a time. "We prefer pseudonyms." Simultaneous submissions OK. Reports in 1 day to 3 months. Pays 1 copy.** Open to unsolicited reviews. Poets may also send books for review consideration. The editor says, "I have another magazine, *Big Fish*, and I am currently seeking poems in foreign languages without translations."

ELF: ECLECTIC LITERARY FORUM (ELF Magazine) (II), P.O. Box 392, Tonawanda NY 14150, phone/fax (716)693-7006, e-mail neubauer@buffnet.net, website http://www.cais.com/aesir/ fiction/elforum, founded 1990, editor C.K. Erbes, is a quarterly. **"Subject matter and form are open, but we are looking for well-crafted poetry. We prefer poems of 30 lines or less, but will consider longer poems. No trite, hackneyed, ill-crafted effluvia."** They have published poetry by Gail White, R.S. Gwynn, John Dickson, Dana Gioia, X.J. Kennedy, Nikki Giovanni and John Haines. As a sample the editor selected these lines from "Third Planet from the Sun" by Martha Vertreace:

> Around the roofless theatre, a six-foot fence.
>> Plywood men in hard hats
> carry plywood ads; announce what comes,
>> trompe l'oeil,
> the gift eyes have for naming what they know.

ELF is 52-56 pgs., magazine-sized, professionally printed and saddle-stapled with semi-gloss cover. They use approximately 140 poems/year. Circulation 6,000. Subscription: $16. **Sample postpaid: $5.50. Submit 3 poems at a time. Hard copy with SASE required for submission. Send SASE for guidelines or view on website. "Accepted writers are asked to submit a bio of 25 words or less." Poems are circulated to an editorial board of professional poets and writers. Editor comments when possible. Reports in 4-6 weeks. Sometimes sends prepublication galleys. Pays 1 copy. Acquires first North American serial rights.** Staff reviews books of poetry. Publishers only may send books for review consideration. They also sponsor the Ruth Cable Memorial Prize for Poetry (annual deadline March 31). Send SASE for guidelines.

ELK RIVER REVIEW (V), 606 Coleman Ave., Athens AL 35611-3216, founded 1991, editor John Chambers, is an annual "devoted only to poetry and associated reviews, articles, essays and interviews.

Open to all types of poetry, no line limit. We want poems that are well-crafted, musical, provocative. However, we are currently overstocked through 1997 and are not accepting submissions at this time." They have published poetry by Vivian Shipley, Dan Leidig, Charles Clifton, Carolyn Moore, Kennette Wilkes, Joanne Lowery and Greg Ling. As a sample we selected these lines from "Snowflakes and Satellites" by Bettye Cannizzo:

> One delights the eye like a baby's smile,
> tickles the tongue like a Margarita.
> The other jolts the imagination like poetry,
> stimulates the mind like philosophy.

The editor says **ERR** is approximately 128 pgs., 6×9, professionally printed, perfect-bound with glossy cover and b&w drawings inside. Press run is 600 of which 25 go to libraries. Subscription: $12. **Sample postpaid: $6.50. Submit 3-5 poems at a time; name, address and phone number on each page. No previously published poems. Cover letter required. Include "succinct biographical facts and publishing credits (if any)." Often comments on rejections. Send SASE for guidelines. Reports in 2-4 months. Always sends prepublication galleys. Pays 1 copy. Acquires first rights.** Reviews poetry collections (including chapbooks) of regional interest. Open to unsolicited reviews; query first. Poets may also send books for review consideration. Sponsors Marjorie Lees Linn Poetry Award, an annual contest that awards a $750 grand prize and a $250 prize split by second and third places. "All winners will be published in an issue of **ERR**, receive 3 copies of the issue and receive a free book of poetry by Marjorie Lees Linn." Submit 2 copies each of as many poems as desired; open length, poem and subject matter. Entry fee: $10 for 1-3 poems; $2 each additional. "Those submitting 5 or more poems will receive a free subscription." Judge changes every year. Send SASE for details.

ELLIPSE (V, IV-Translations, bilingual), C.P. 10, FLSH Université de Sherbrooke, Sherbrooke, Quebec J1K 2R1 Canada, phone (819)821-7000 ext. 3268, fax (819)821-7285, founded 1969, editors M. Grandmangin and C. Bouchara, **publishes Canadian poetry in translation.** That is, on facing pages appear either poems in English and a French translation or poems in French and an English translation. **Currently they are not accepting unsolicited mss.** They have published poetry by Patrick Lone, Gwen McEwen and Anne Hébert. As a sample, the editors selected these lines from "La Malemer" by Rina Lasnier:

> Malemer, mer stable et fermée à la foudre comme à l'aile—
> mer prégnante et aveugle à ce que tu enfantes,
>
> emporte-moi loin du courant de la mémoire—et de la longue flottaison des souvenirs;

translated by D.G. Jones:

> Malemer, firm sea impervious to the lightning as to the
> whispering wing—pregnant and oblivious to your generation,
>
> bear me far away from the currents of memory—and the long
> hulls cargoed with recollection;

The magazine appears twice yearly in an elegant, flat-spined, 6×9 format, professionally printed, 120 pgs. Subscription: $12. **Sample postpaid: $5.**

ELLIPSIS MAGAZINE (II), Westminster College of Salt Lake City, 1840 S. 1300 East, Salt Lake City UT 84105, phone (801)488-4158, founded 1967, appears twice a year using **"good literary poetry and fiction. Limited on space."** They have published work by William Stafford, William Kloefkorn, David Lee, Dixie Partridge and Ron Carlson. The editor describes it as 90 pgs., digest-sized, perfect-bound. Subscription: $18/year. **Sample postpaid: $10. Send ms with SASE and contributor notes. Does not read submissions from April 15 through August 31. Responds within 4 months. Pays $10/poem, $20/story, plus 1 copy.**

EMERALD COAST REVIEW; WEST FLORIDA LITERARY FEDERATION; FRANCIS P. CASSIDY LITERARY CENTER; THE LEGEND; BACK DOOR POETS; WISE (WRITERS IN SERVICE TO EDUCATION) (IV-Regional), 400 S. Jefferson St., Pensacola Cultural Center, Pensacola FL 32501. The WFLF was founded in 1987 and began the Cassidy Literary Center, a regional writers' resource and special collection library. One of their programs is WISE, which provides over 50 area writers who volunteer their time to share their writing and writing experiences with local students. They sponsor a Student Writers Network for students in grades 9-12 and scholarships for area college student writers. WFLF also sponsors a PEN-WISE poetry contest for grades 1-12. The contest awards publication in a chapbook. They publish *The Legend*, a newsletter bringing literary arts news to 800-1,000 area writers and their supporters. Back Door Poets, one of their subgroups, conducts open microphone poetry readings the third Saturday of each month. Also, WFLF hosts a writing workshop the first Saturday of every month. Membership in WFLF ranges from $10/year for students to $500 and up for life-time memberships. The *Emerald Coast Review* is an **annual limited**

to Gulf Coast regional writers. **Sample postpaid: $12. Send SASE for guidelines. Submit with required form (included in guidelines) May 1 to July 31. Pays copies.**

EMRYS JOURNAL (II), P.O. Box 8813, Greenville SC 29604, founded 1982, editor Jeanine Halva-Neubauer, an annual, wants **"all kinds of poetry, though we don't publish poems of more than 2-3 pgs."** They have published poetry by Jan Bailey, Gil Allen and Cecile Goding. As a sample the editor selected the first stanza from "Motor without a Boat" by Mary Matthews:

> An enormously wealthy oil company
> had thousands of things to sell and so
> they took their things to an enormously
> barren lot where no wildflowers or
> weeds would grow and where the prints
> of a working man's shoes left no impression.

EJ is up to 120 pgs., 6×9, handsomely printed, flat-spined. "For a past issue we received about 1,200 poems from 300 people. We printed 15." Press run is 400 for 250 subscribers of which 10 are libraries. **Sample postpaid: $10. Submit 5 poems maximum. Editor sometimes comments on rejections. Send SASE for guidelines. Pays 5 copies.** They say, "We try to report within 6 weeks of receipt. We read from August 15 through December 1."

THE EMSHOCK LETTER (IV-Subscribers), Randall Flat Rd., P.O. Box 411, Troy ID 83871-0411, phone (208)835-4902, founded 1977, editor Steve Erickson, appears 3-12 times a year, occasionally with **poetry and other writings by subscribers**. It is **"a philosophical, metaphysical, sometimes poetic expression of ideas and events. It covers a wide range of subjects and represents a free-style form of expressive relation. It is a newsletter quite unlike any other."** The editor describes it as 5-7 pgs., magazine-sized, photocopied from typescript on colored paper. Subscription: $25. **"Poets (who are subscribers) should submit poetry which contains some meaning, preferably centering on a philosophic theme and preferably 50 lines or less. Any good poetry (submitted by a subscriber) will be considered for inclusion and will receive a personal reply by the editor, whether or not submitted material is published in *The Emshock Letter*. Editor will promptly discard any and all material submitted by nonsubscribers. Poets must become subscribers prior to submitting any material!"** Reviews books of poetry only if written by subscribers.

ENCODINGS: A FEMINIST LITERARY JOURNAL (IV-Women/feminism), P.O. Box 6793, Houston TX 77265, founded 1989, co-editors Jacsun Shah and Lazette Jackson, with occasional guest editors. *Encodings* appears "randomly, twice a year," using **"high quality poetry with a feminist perspective; especially interested in women's ways of knowing, women's invention and use of language."** As a sample the editors selected these lines from "Dressing Down" by Allison Joseph:

> How free it is to be homely,
> to walk streets unfettered
> by the lavish complications
> of ornate jangles of jewelry,
> taut skirts, strict belts
> and high heels . . .

Encodings is 40-60 pgs., 7×8½, photocopied from typescript and saddle-stapled with glossy card cover. Subscription: $10. **Sample postpaid: $5. Submit up to 5 poems at a time. Cover letter with brief bio preferred. Send SASE for guidelines. Reports in 2-3 months. Pays 2 copies.**

ENITHARMON PRESS (V), 36 St. George's Ave., London N7 0HD England, phone (0171)607-7194, fax (0171)607-8694, founded 1969, poetry editor Stephen Stuart-Smith, is a publisher of fine editions of poetry and literary criticism in paperback and some hardback editions, about 15 volumes/year averaging 100 pages. They have published books of poetry by John Heath-Stubbs, Phoebe Hesketh, David Gascoyne, Jeremy Hooker, Frances Horovitz, Ruth Pitter, Ted Hughes, Thom Gunn, Edwin Brock and Jeremy Reed. **"Substantial backlog of titles to produce, so no submissions possible before 1999."**

ENVOI (II), 44 Rudyard Rd., Biddulph Moor, Stoke-on-Trent, Staffs ST8 7JN United Kingdom, founded 1957, editor Roger Elkin, appears 3 times/year using poetry, articles about poetry and poets, and reviews. "1) *Envoi* does not subscribe to any one particular stable, school or style of contemporary poetry writing and has catholic tastes; 2) To be selected, **poetry must be sincere in its emotional and intellectual content, strongly integrated in form and contemporary in its subject matter—while a poem may be set in classical times or depend heavily on mythic archetypes, its overall 'texture' must have contemporary relevance; 3) *Envoi* requires writing that is daring in its subject matter and challenging in its expressive techniques— in short, work that takes risks with the form, the language and the reader; 4) *Envoi* is, however, still interested in traditional verse structures (the villanelle, pantoum, sonnet) but these must subscribe to the points listed in 2); and 5) *Envoi* is**

looking for writing that sustains its creative strengths over a body of poems, or sequence. These criteria are prescriptive, rather than proscriptive; gates rather than hurdles. The over-riding concern is the creation of access for writers and readers to as wide a variety of contemporary poetry as space will allow." *Envoi* is 176 pgs., digest-sized, professionally printed and perfect-bound with matte card cover. "The emphasis is on giving space to writers so that the reader can begin to assess the cumulative strengths of any one author over a body of work. This means that competition for space is very keen. I handle between 300 and 500 poems per week and can only feature the equivalent of 100 poems three times a year!" Press run is 1,000 including 20 library subscriptions. Single copy: £4 ($10); subscription: £15 ($30—"US funds preferably in bills rather than checks because of the high cost of conversion rates"). **Sample: £3 ($8). Submit no more than 6 poems, or a long poem of up to 6 sides; each poem on a separate page, bearing name and address; an accompanying SAE with 3 IRCs for return. Reports in 1-2 months. Pays 2 copies.** Roger Elkin says "*Envoi* presents the work of any one poet by a group of poems, up to six. Space is given to long(er) poems and short sequences, or extracts from longer sequences. We have a First Publication Feature for writers who have not appeared in national publications previously, and each issue contains a 'reading' of a modern poem or an article on poetic style. The Review section has been expanded in length to feature more comprehensive articles. Each issue also features a competition with prizes totalling £200; prize-winning poems are published along with a full adjudicator's report. We also feature poems in collaboration, as well as translations."

EPICENTER (II), P.O. Box 367, Riverside CA 92502, founded 1994, is a quarterly poetry and short story forum **open to all styles.** They have published poetry by Mike Cluff, Max Berkovitz, Stan Nemeth and Vicki Solheid. As a sample the editors selected this poem by Todd Raboy:

> talking
> i accidentally
> sipped your coffee
>   4 years later
> someone asked me
> if i had ever kissed
>   you
> i answered
>   yes
> honestly believing
> i had

Epicenter is 24 pgs., digest-sized and saddle-stapled with semi-glossy paper cover and b&w graphics. They receive about 300 submissions a year, use approximately 15%. Press run is 400 for 250 shelf sales. Single copy: $3. **Sample postpaid: $3.50. Make checks payable to Rowena Silver. Previously published poems and simultaneous submissions OK. Seldom comments on rejections. Send SASE for guidelines. Pays 1 copy. Acquires one-time rights.** The editors add, "*Epicenter* is looking for ground-breaking poetry and short stories from new and established writers. No angst-ridden, sentimental or earthquake poetry."

EPOCH; BAXTER HATHAWAY PRIZE (III), 251 Goldwin Smith, Cornell University, Ithaca NY 14853, phone (607)255-3385, founded 1947, has a distinguished and long record of publishing **exceptionally fine poetry** and fiction. They have published work by such poets as Ashbery, Ammons, Eshleman, Wanda Coleman, Molly Peacock, Robert Vander Molen and Alvin Aubert. The magazine appears 3 times a year in a 6×9, professionally printed, flat-spined format with glossy color cover, 100 pgs., which goes to 1,000 subscribers. They use less than 1% of the many submissions they receive each year, have a 2- to 12-month backlog. Mostly lyric free verse, with emphasis on voice and varying content and length, appears here (and, occasionally, avant-garde or "open" styles)—some of it quite powerful. **Sample postpaid: $5. "We *don't read* unsolicited mss between April 15 and September 15." Reports in 2 months. Occasionally provides criticism on mss. Pays $5-10/page. Buys first serial rights.** The annual Baxter Hathaway prize of $1,000 is awarded for a long poem or, in alternate years, a novella. At this time, however, the Baxter Hathaway Prize has been temporarily suspended. Poetry published in *Epoch* has also been included in the 1992 and 1993 volumes of *The Best American Poetry*. The editor advises, "I think it's extremely important for poets to read other poets. I think it's

---

USE THE GENERAL INDEX to find the page number of a specific publisher. Also, if a publisher from last year's edition is not included in this edition, the General Index will tell you why.

also very important for poets to read the magazines that they want to publish in. Directories are not enough."

EQUINOX PRESS (V); BRITISH HAIKU SOCIETY; BLITHE SPIRIT (IV-Form/style, translations), Sinodun, Shalford, Braintree Essex CM7 5HN England, phone 01371-851097, founded 1990, c/o Mr. David Cobb. Equinox publishes poetry (mainly haiku and senryu), 1-2 volumes/year. **They have a waiting list at present and are unable to consider submissions.** BHS publishes a quarterly journal, *Blithe Spirit*, a quarterly newsletter and other occasional publications (pamphlets, folios). *Blithe Spirit* **publishes mainly haiku, senryu and tanka sent in by society members,** but one section, "The Pathway," accepts **originals in any language plus a translation in one of English, French or German, and is open to non-members.** As a sample the Equinox editor selected this haiku (poet unidentified):

> a cloudless sky
> painters stretch ladders
> to their farthest rungs

Staff reviews books of poetry. Send books for review consideration. The Museum of Haiku Literature, Tokyo, gives a quarterly best-of-issue award (£50). In addition, BHS administers the annual James W. Hackett Haiku Award (currently £100). Rules of entry are available annually in the spring. Send SASE (or SAE and IRC from outside England) to J.W. Hackett Award, % R. Goring, 27 Park St., Westcliff-on-Sea, Essex SS0 7PA England.

ESSENCE (V, IV-Women, ethnic), 1500 Broadway, New York NY 10036, phone (212)642-0647, founded 1970, poetry editor Angela Kinamore. "*Essence* caters to the **needs of today's Black women.**" **They publish poetry with humor or poetry dealing with love/romance, politics, religion, social issues or spirituality.** They have published poetry by Margaret Walker Alexander and Pinkie Gordon Lane. As a sample the editor selected these lines from "Ode to My Sons" by Mari Evans:

> I am the vessel from whence you came
> the lode filled with imaginings
> aside from dreams my longing cannot
> touch your reaching nor can I direct
> your quest . . .

Essence is a mass-circulation consumer magazine with an upscale tone. It is 140 pgs., slick stock with full-color art, photos and ads. **They are currently not accepting poetry submissions.**

EUROPEAN JUDAISM (IV-Religious, ethnic), Kent House, Rutland Gardens, London SW7 1BX England, founded 1966, poetry editor Ruth Fainlight, is a "twice-yearly magazine with emphasis on European Jewish theology/philosophy/literature/history, with **some poetry in every issue. It should preferably be short and have some relevance to matters of Jewish interest.**" They have published poetry by Linda Pastan, Elaine Feinstein, George Szirtes and Dannie Abse. As a sample the editor selected these lines from a poem by Micheline Wandor:

> we scions of the wooden spoon
> must spit the coal dust
> and the tailor's chalk
> and wipe
> the black and the white
> from the corners
> of our mouths.

It is a glossy, elegant, 6×9, flat-spined magazine, rarely art or graphics, 110 pgs. They have a press run of 950, about 50% of which goes to subscribers (few libraries). Subscription: $27. **Submit 3-4 poems at a time. SASE (or SAE with IRCs) required. "We cannot use American stamps. Also, I prefer unpublished poems, but poems from published books are acceptable." Cover letter required. Pays 1 copy.**

EVENT (II, IV-Themes), Douglas College, P.O. Box 2503, New Westminster, British Columbia V3L 5B2 Canada, founded 1971, editor David Zieroth, appears 3 times/year and is "a literary magazine publishing **high-quality contemporary poetry**, short stories and reviews. **In poetry, we tend to appreciate the narrative and sometimes the confessional modes. In any case, we are eclectic and always open to content that invites involvement. We publish mostly Canadian writers.**" They have recently published poetry by Tom Wayman, Elisabeth Harvor and Lorna Crozier. These sample lines are from "Poetry" by Don Domanski:

> is it a side street or a cat's jaw?
> cerecloth or the body's flesh?
> I've named it the heart's pillow
> wind in a mirror   cloud-rope
> lighthouse on the edge of a wound

> beadwork   the mote's halo   wolf-ladder

Event is 140 pgs., 6×9, finely printed and flat-spined with glossy cover. Circulation is 1,000 for 700 subscribers of which 50 are libraries. **Sample postpaid: $6. Submit 5 poems at a time. No previously published poems. Brief cover letter with publication credits required. Include SASE or SAE and IRCs. "Tell us if you'd prefer your manuscript to be recycled rather than returned."** Time between acceptance and publication is within 1 year. **Comments on some rejections. Reports in 3-4 months. Pays honorarium. Buys first North American serial rights. Sometimes they have special thematic issues, such as: work, feminism, peace and war, coming of age.**

THE EVER DANCING MUSE; WHO WHO WHO PUBLISHING (II), P.O. Box 7751, East Rutherford NJ 07073-1624, founded 1993, editor John Chorazy, is a "semiannual collection of poetry and short prose, publishing fine work in a small press format." **The editor wants "thinking, feeling poetry; poems no longer than two typed pages, prose no longer than four typed pages. Does not use rhyming poetry. I like short, tight poems, from 1-20 lines, but will consider everything sent. Submit 3-5 poems that you care deeply about, and want me to care about as well as the readers."** They have recently published poetry by Lyn Lifshin, Mary Winters and Errol Miller. As a sample the editor selected these lines from "no man likes a whore" by Rita D. Costello:

> I've been raped for money
> a cup of coffee   a bottle of wine
> shoved up against the wall
> and bleeding   for the clothes I wear
> sometimes   the screams are mine
> and harder than their curses

The Ever Dancing Muse is 20 pgs., 5½×8½, saddle-stapled with light card cover. Press run is 150 for 50 subscribers. Subscription: $8 for 3 issues, 1 back issue free. **Sample postpaid: $3. Previously published poems and simultaneous submissions OK, "if stated as such, and author holds the rights to the work. Cover letters are interesting and appreciated but not required."** Seldom comments on rejections. **Reports in 1 day to 1 month. Pays 2 copies. Acquires one-time rights.** The editor reminds poets, "This magazine, and all small press publications, need the support of poets and poetry readers to continue. Read a sample issue!"

THE EVERGREEN CHRONICLES (IV-Gay/lesbian), P.O. Box 8939, Minneapolis MN 55408, phone (612)649-4982, is "a triquarterly journal of arts and cultures dedicated to presenting the best of lesbian and gay literary and visual artists. **The artistry presented is not limited to 'gay' or 'lesbian' themes, but extends to life, in all its dimensions."** Subscription: $20. **Sample postpaid: $8.95. "Send 4 copies of your work, up to 10 pgs. of poetry. Please include cover letter with short biographical paragraph describing yourself and your work. Deadlines: July 1 and January 1." Their third issue is a contest issue. Send SASE for guidelines and upcoming themes. Pays 1 copy and honorarium. Acquires first rights.** Staff reviews books of poetry in 500 words, single format. Send books for review consideration.

EXCURSUS LITERARY ARTS JOURNAL (II), P.O. Box 1056, Knickerbocker Station, New York NY 10002, founded 1994, publisher Giancarlo Malchiodi, is an annual "eclectic collection of quality work from both new and established poets. **All literary excursions are welcome . . . from the idyllic to the rebellious, formal and traditional to free form and avant-garde, imagistic to concrete to narrative to 'language' to Beat, to everything in between and beyond." However, they do not want "religious poetry nor any romantic pablum."** As a sample the publisher selected these lines from "Watching Willy Wonka Alone on a Saturday Night" by Meredith Schuman:

> And fantasy floats through my 12-inch set
> up a broken antenna as I spoon gummy pink
> Amoxil into my flushed cheeks like Violet
> chewing an illicit blueberry Gobstopper.
> Solitude sticks like static to the screen, its dusty knobs
> decaying like a tootsie roll in my fevered mouth.

Excursus is about 120 pgs., 8½×11, offset printed and perfect-bound, with glossy card stock cover and b&w art and photos. They receive upwards of 2,500 submissions a year, accept 5-10%. Press run is 1,000. **Sample postpaid: $5. Submit up to 3 poems at a time, "not to exceed 170 lines total," addressed "Attn: Poetry." Simultaneous submissions and previously published poems OK, "if notified of previous placement." Personalized cover letter required. Reads submissions September 1 through June 30 only. "Publisher initially screens all submissions and forwards quality work to Editorial Collective. Seldom comments on rejections. Send SASE for guidelines. Reports within 5 months. Pays 1 copy. Acquires one-time rights.** They sponsor an annual contest. Entry fee: $5 for 5 poems, addressed "Attn: Contest." Deadline: June 30. The winner receives $200, 4 pages of dedicated space in the magazine, 5 copies, and an invitation to join the Editorial Collective. The publisher says "Don't be concerned with 'fads' in poetry, whether 'formal,' 'performance,' or whatever . . . write from your instincts. Assimilate what you read and enjoy, but don't copy."

EXIT 13 (IV-Specialized: geography/travel), % Tom Plante, 22 Oakwood Ct., Fanwood NJ 07023-1162, phone (908)889-5298, founded 1987, editor Tom Plante, is a "contemporary poetry annual" using **poetry that is "short, to the point, with a sense of geography."** They have recently published poetry by Mina Kumar, Gerard Coulombe, Robert Cooperman, Ray Mizer and Madeline Hoffer. As a sample the editor selected these lines by Jennifer A. Zogott:

> *in this land dominated by*
> *memory, ghosts, skeletons*
>
> *presiding, ex-officio,*
> *the Parachute Jump*
> *silently observes the sturdy inaugural turn*
> *of the Wonder Wheel*

Exit 13, #7, was 60 pgs. Press run is 300. **Sample postpaid: $6.** *Make checks payable to Tom Plante.* **They accept simultaneous submissions and previously published poems. Send SASE for guidelines. Reports in 3 months. Pays 1 copy. Acquires one-time and possible anthology rights.** Staff reviews books of poetry and magazines in a "Publications Received" column, using 25-30 words/ listing. Send books for review consideration. The editor advises, "Write about what you know. Study geography. *Exit 13* looks for adventure. Every state and region is welcome. Send a snapshot of an 'Exit 13' road sign and receive a free copy of the issue in which it appears."

EXPEDITION PRESS (III, IV-Love, religious), 105 E. Walnut St., #2306, Kalamazoo MI 49007-5253, publisher Bruce W. White, publishes chapbooks of **love poems and religious poems. "I dislike violence."** He likes to see **"experimental, fresh new approaches, interesting spatial relationships, as well as quality artwork. I dislike political diatribes."** He has recently published poetry by J. Kline Hobbs, Jim DeWitt, Todd Zimmerman, Margaret Tyler, Martin Cohen and C. VanAllsburg. As a sample the publisher selected this haiku of his own:

> *a tree by a lake.*
> *the same tree in winter.*
> *a harvest moon over the lake.*

Submit typed ms of 20-30 pgs. and cover letter with brief bio. No previously published poems or simultaneous submissions. Ms on cassette OK. Reports in 1 month. Sometimes sends prepublication galleys. Pays 100 copies. Bruce White provides "much" criticism on rejected mss.

EXPLORATIONS (II), UAS, 11120 Glacier Highway, Juneau AK 99801-8761, phone (907)465-6418, fax (907)465-6406, e-mail jnamp@acadl.alaska.edu, founded 1980, editor Professor Art Petersen, is the annual literary magazine of the University of Alaska, Southeast. **"The editors respond favorably to 'language really spoken by men and women.' Standard form and innovation are encouraged as well as appropriate and fresh aspects of imagery (allusion, metaphor, simile, symbol . . .)."** As a sample the editor selected these lines from "Seven come eleven" by Charles Bukowski:

> *I've never ever quite met*
> *anybody*
> *like myself—*
> *living with deadly calm*
> *inside this hurricane of hell.*

Explorations is digest-sized, nicely printed and saddle-stapled, with front and back cover illustration in one color. The editors tend to go for smaller-length poems (with small line breaks for tension) and often print two on a page—mostly lyric free verse with a focus on voice. **Sample postpaid: $4.** In 1996, they again offered first prizes of $500 for poetry and prose and published the best of the submissions received. Each year a prominent poet or writer serves as judge (1996: Peggy Shumaker). **An entry/reading fee is required: $4 for 1 poem (60 lines/poem maximum), $2/poem for 2-5 poems (5 maximum, no more than 60 lines each), $4/story (up to 2, each 3,000 words maximum); those paying reader/contest entry fees receive a copy of the publication. Checks should be made payable to "UAS Explorations." Mss must be typed with name, address, and 3- or 4-line biography on the back of each first page. Simultaneous submissions OK. Submit January through March. Mss are not returned. Send SASE for guidelines. Submissions are reported on in May or June, publication is annual, out in May or June. Pays 2 contributor copies. Acquires one-time rights.**

EXPLORER MAGAZINE; FLORY LITERARY FOUNDATION (I, IV-Inspirational, nature, love), P.O. Box 210, Notre Dame IN 46556-0210, phone (219)277-3465, founded 1960, editor/publisher Raymond Flory, is a semiannual magazine that contains **short inspirational, nature and love poetry** as well as prose. The editor wants **"poetry of all styles and types; should have an inspira-**

tional slant but not necessary. Short poems preferred—up to 20 lines—the shorter the better. Good 'family' type poetry always needed. Seasonal material also welcome. No real long poetry or long lines; no sexually explicit poetry or porno." He has recently published poetry by Joan Olivieri, Terry Peterson, L.J. Cardin, Rita Collura and Philip Huss. As a sample the editor selected "Christmas Eve" by Rosemary Lauturner:

> Christmas eve
> Snowflakes falling,
> Late night
> Cosmic peacefulness,
> As the moon rises.

Explorer is 32-48 pgs., digest-sized, photocopied from typed copy in a variety of fonts (some of it dot-matrix) and saddle-stapled with card cover. Their 35th Anniversary issue contained the work of 74 authors. Circulation is 250-400. Subscription: $6/year. **Sample available for $3, guidelines for SASE. Subscribers vote for the poems or stories they like best and prizes are awarded; four prizes each issue: $25, $20, $15 and $10; first-prize winner in each issue receives a plaque along with the cash prize. In addition to the regular cash prizes, there is also an editor's choice award, the Joseph Flory Memorial Award, named after the editor's late father. Award is $10 and a plaque. Latest winner: Ann Lewandowski. The editor also awards the Angel Light Award, given to the author whose prose or poetry most emphasizes the "spiritual." Award is $10 and a plaque. The most recent award winner is Elizabeth Miller for "Robin." Writers should submit 3-4 poems, typed, camera-ready. Material must be previously unpublished; simultaneous submissions OK. Submit seasonal material 8 months to 1 year in advance. Reporting time is 1-2 weeks and time to publication 1-2 years. Pays 1 copy only to those appearing in the magazine for the first time.** The editor says, "Over 90% of the poets submitting poetry to *Explorer* have not seen a copy of the magazine. Order a copy first—then submit. This will save poets stamps, frustration, etc. This should hold true for whatever market a writer is aiming for!"

EXPRESSIONS (I, IV-Specialized: people with disabilities/ongoing health problems), P.O. Box 16294, St. Paul MN 55116-0294, founded 1993, editor Sefra Kobrin Pitzele, is a nonprofit semiannual, subtitled "Literature and Art by People with Disabilities and Ongoing Health Problems," designed "to provide a place for talented people to be published." **They are open to any topic provided entry is written by people with disabilities and/or ongoing health problems.** They have recently published poetry by Mark Franz, Stephanie R. Bird and Susan Dion. As a sample the editor selected these lines from "La Loba" by Hayley R. Mitchell, winner of their 1995 Poetry Contest:

> She walks the wilds, collects
> bones, bit by bit, in a woven
> basket strapped to her hunching
> back. She preserves that which
> is in danger of being lost.

Expressions is 80 pgs., 5½×8½, perfect-bound with 60 lb. glossy card cover. They publish about 25% of the poetry received. Press run is 700 for 120 subscribers. Subscription: $12 US, $17 foreign and institutions. **Sample postpaid: $6. Submit no more than 5 poems at a time with $5 reading fee. Previously published poems and simultaneous submissions OK. Cover letter with 4- to 5-line bio and statement of ownership required. Do not submit mss from December 15 to January 15.** "Six others read each submission and grade it—independently—from 1 to 5. Most 5's are published." **Often comments on rejections. Send SASE for guidelines and upcoming themes. Reports in 3-5 months. Pays 2 copies. Acquires one-time rights.** They sponsor an annual poetry, art and prose contest. Deadline: December 15. Write for details. "At the end of each issue, we print book reviews appropriate to our audience. We only review informational books on disability or illness." However, they are open to unsolicited reviews of such materials.

EXPRESSIONS FORUM REVIEW (I), 2837 Blue Spruce Lane, Wheaton MD 20906-3167, founded 1991, is a semiannual of poetry, **"any kind, any form, 20 lines maximum. No sex-related matters, no obscenity."** They are currently looking to receive more traditional forms of poetry. Single copy: $3; subscription: $12. **Submit up to 4 poems with $3 reading fee. Previously published poems and simultaneous submissions OK. Typewritten poems preferred; do not send original copies. Seldom comments on rejections. Send SASE for guidelines. Reports in 4 months. Pays 1 copy.** Open to unsolicited reviews. Poets may also send books for review consideration. Reading fee includes entry into spring and fall poetry contests. 1st prize: $100; 2nd: $50; 3rd: $25 (and 25 honorable mentions). The editor says, "Speak from the heart and soul."

EXQUISITE CORPSE (II), P.O. Box 25051, Baton Rouge LA 70894, founded 1983, editor Andrei Codrescu (whom you can often hear in commentary segments of "All Things Considered," The National Public Radio news program). This curious and delightful monthly ($20/year), when you unfold it, is 6″ wide and 16″ long, 20 pgs., saddle-stapled, professionally printed in 2 columns on quality stock. The flavor of Codrescu's comments (and some clues about your prospects in submitting here) may be judged by this note: "A while ago, alarmed by the number of poems aimed at the office—a number only the currency inflation and Big Macs can hold candles to—we issued an edict against them. Still they came, and some even came live. They came in the mail and under the door. We have no poetry insurance. If we are found one day smothered under photocopy paper, who will pay for the burial? The *Corpse* wants a jazz funeral. Rejections make poets happy. Having, in many cases, made their poems out of original, primal, momentary rejections, the rejection of these rejections affirms the beings forced to such deviousness." He has published poetry by Carol Bergé, Charles Plymell, Lawrence Ferlinghetti, Alice Notley and many others. You'll find all styles and forms here, even short light verse. Most examples are freestyle, leaning toward expressionism (effective use of symbol), and accessible, too. Translations also seem welcome. **Payment: "Zilch/Nada." You take your chances inserting work into this wit machine. As of 1990 this is their policy: ". . . we are abolishing the SASE-based privacy system . . . Your submissions will be answered directly in the pages of our publication. Look for your name and for our response to your work in the next *Corpse*. We will continue returning your submissions by SASE if you wish, but as to what we think of your *écriture*, please check 'Body Bag,' our new editorial column. Please rest assured that your work will receive the same malevolently passionate attention as before. Only now we are going to do it in public."** Here's an example: "We were excited by 'The Wind Got Excited' until the puppy-hero got too excited and leapt off the 13th floor. That was cruel . . . " Comments you want, comments you get! Poetry published in this magazine has been included in *The Best American Poetry 1992*.

FABER AND FABER, INC. (V), 53 Shon Rd., Winchester MA 01890, phone (617)721-1427, editor-in-chief Dan Weaver, senior editor Valerie Cimino, has a distinguished list of poetry publications but is **not accepting mss.**

FAR GONE (II), P.O. Box 43745, Lafayette LA 70504-3745, founded 1995, editor/publisher Todd Brendan Fahey, is an annual journal "stalking the giants of tomorrow." It includes fiction, poetry and interviews. **They want "a sure voice in any style of poetry. Nothing not accomplished."** They have recently published poetry by Skip Fox, Minal Hajratwala and Juliet Rodeman. *Far Gone* is 42-48 pgs., $11 \times 8\frac{1}{2}$ (landscape format), offset and handsewn. The cover is professionally printed on 64 lb. fine-laid paper with halftone reproduction of classic art. It's a striking package. They accept 3-8 poems/issue. Press run is 100 for 20 subscribers of which 10 are libraries, 20 shelf sales. **Sample postpaid: $7. No previously published poems; simultaneous submissions OK ("though they may cause one heartache"). Cover letter required. Seldom comments on rejections. Pays 1 copy. Rights returned to contributors upon written request.** Staff reviews small press books of poetry (no chapbooks) in 250 words. Send books for review consideration. They offer $50 and publication to the Best Interview-of-Year ("of literary persons of note"). Entry fee: $5. (The inaugural issue features interviews with Ken Kesey and Timothy Leary.) The editor says, "Each issue of *Far Gone* will be a piece of art (check out #1). Poetry selected will meet such a standard."

When the editors of the Elgin, Illinois-based *Farmer's Market* selected the cow clip art to go on the cover of this issue, they were not only thinking of their Midwestern origin, but also of simplifying their cover images. "We wanted a clean, sharp graphic image, and felt this illustration worked on that level," says Patrick Parks, editor of the biannual journal. "And, to be honest, the three of us who edit the magazine are partial to our bovine neighbors." *Farmer's Market* devotes about half of its pages to poetry and looks for quality, structured work. And although Midwestern themes are not necessary, "a good eggplant poem is always welcome."

Farmer's Market
A journal of contemporary writing
Fall/Winter 1995

FARMER'S MARKET; MIDWEST FARMER'S MARKET, INC. (II), Elgin Community College, 1700 Spartan Dr., Elgin IL 60123-7193, founded 1981, editors Patrick Parks, Rachael Tecza and Joanne

Lowery, is a biannual seeking **poems that are "tightly structured, with concrete imagery, reflective of the clarity, depth and strength of Midwestern life. Not interested in highly abstract work or light verse."** They have published poetry by Larry Starzec, Melanie Richards, Philip Dacey, Edward C. Lynskey and Marjorie Maddox. As a sample, they offer these lines from "Everything Changes to Beauty" by Kathryn Burt Winogrod:

> The clear skimming line of my father's fishing pole
> rides its twinned self off the brightening pond,
> a lifting rain of light returning to light,
> and beneath, where fish round their mouths
> like moons to swallow it, the lure
> tiny and shimmering, make-believe.

FM is 100-200 pgs., digest-sized, perfect-bound with card cover, handsomely printed with graphics and photos. The poems are almost always accessible . . . clear, crafted lyric free verse. All in all, this is an enjoyable read. They receive about 1,500 submissions/year, of which they use 50-60, have a 6-month backlog. Circulation 700 for 200 subscribers, of which 25 are libraries. **Sample: $4.50 plus $1 p&h. Submit 4-6 poems at a time, typed. Would rather not have simultaneous submissions. Comments on rejections, "only if we think the work is good." Send SASE for upcoming themes. Reports in 6-8 weeks (summer replies take longer). Pays 2 copies. Acquires one-time rights.** This publication has received numerous Illinois Arts Council Literary Awards and poetry published here has also been included in *The Best American Poetry 1996*.

FARRAR, STRAUS & GIROUX/BOOKS FOR YOUNG READERS (II, IV-Children), 19 Union Square W., New York NY 10003, phone (212)741-6900, founded 1946, contact Editorial Dept./ Books for Young Readers. They publish one book of children's poetry "every once in awhile," in both hardcover and paperback editions. **They are open to book-length submissions of children's poetry only.** They have published collections of poetry by Valerie Worth and Deborah Chandra. As a sample the editor selected "Suspense" from Chandra's book *Balloons*:

> Wide-eyed
> the sunflowers
> stare and catch their summer
> breath, while I pause, holding basket
> and shears.

Query first with sample poems and cover letter with brief bio and publication credits. Poems previously published in magazines and simultaneous submissions OK. Seldom comments on rejections. Send SASE for reply. Replies to queries in 1-2 months, to mss in 1-4 months. "We pay an advance against royalties; the amount depends on whether or not the poems are illustrated, etc." Also pays 10 author's copies.

FAT TUESDAY (II), 560 Manada Gap Rd., Grantville PA 17028, phone (717)469-7159, founded 1981, editor-in-chief F.M. Cotolo, other editors Kristen von Oehrke, B. Lyle Tabor, Thom Savion and Lionel Stevroid, is an annual which calls itself **"a Mardi Gras of literary and visual treats featuring many voices, singing, shouting, sighing and shining, expressing the relevant to irreverent.** On Fat Tuesday (the Tuesday before Ash Wednesday, when Lent begins) the editors hold The Fat Tuesday Symposium. In over ten years no one has shown up." **They want "prose poems, poems of irreverence, gems from the gut. Usually shorter, hit-the-mark, personal stuff inseparable from the voice of the artist. Form doesn't matter, but no rhyming greeting-card stuff. Also particularly interested in hard-hitting 'autofiction.' "** They have published poetry by Mark Cramer, Mary Lee Gowland, Chuck Taylor, Patrick Kelly, Charles Bukowski, Gerald Locklin and Kilgore Rimpau. As a sample they offer these lines by John Quinnett:

> It is enough to be alive,
> To be here drinking this cheap red wine
> While the chili simmers on the stove
> & the refrigerator hums deep into the night.

The digest-sized magazine is typeset (large type, heavy paper), 36-60 pgs., saddle-stapled, card covers, (sometimes magazine-sized, unbound) with cartoons, art and ads. Circulation 200 with 20-25 pgs. of poetry in each issue. They receive hundreds of submissions each year, use 3-5%, have a 3- to 5-month backlog. **Sample postpaid: $5. Submit 4 poems at a time. "Handwritten OK; we'll read anything." No previously published poems or simultaneous submissions. "Cover letters are fine, the more amusing the better." Reads submissions June through December. Reports in 1-2 weeks. Pays 1 copy. Rights revert to author after publication.** The editors say, "Our tip for authors is simply to be themselves. Poets should use their own voice to be heard. Publishing poetry is as lonely as writing it. We have no idea about current trends, and care less. We encourage all to buy a sample issue to see what they have which best fits our style and format, and also to help support the continuation of our publication. We rely on no other means but sales to subsidize our magazine, and writers should be sensitive to this hard fact which burdens many small presses."

‡**FAULTLINE (II)**, P.O. Box 599-4960, Irvine CA 92716-4960, fax (714)824-2916, e-mail faultline@ uci.edu, founded 1991, is an annual journal of art and literature occasionally edited by guest editors and published at the University of California, Irvine. **"We are looking for top, top quality poetry from poets who are obviously acquainted with contemporary poetry."** They have recently published poetry by Thomas Lux, Heather McHugh and Sabina Grogan. As a sample we selected the opening lines of "Gravediggers" by Linda Thomas:

> *At first I am sure*
> *the sea once covered our backyard.*
> *With each spadeful of dirt*
> *come cones and sea slippers,*
> *the dry dishes of scallops and jackknives,*
> *and I am sure*
> *this neglected plot of hard clay*
> *once served as the ocean floor.*

Faultline is approximately 120 pgs., $7 \times 8\frac{1}{4}$, professionally printed on 60 lb. paper, perfect-bound with 80 lb. cover stock and featuring b&w art and photos. They receive about 1,500 poems a year, accept approximately 5%. Press run is 500 for 50 subscribers, 175 shelf sales. Single copy: $10. **Sample postpaid: $5. Submit up to 5 poems at a time. Simultaneous submissions OK. Cover letter preferred. Do not include name and address on ms to assist anonymous judging. Reads submissions October 1 to April 30 only. Poems are selected by a board of up to 6 readers. Seldom comments on rejections. Publishes theme issues. Send SASE for guidelines and upcoming themes. Reports in 3 months. Always sends prepublication galleys. Pays $20/poem (when possible) and 1 copy. Buys first or one-time rights.** Poetry published by this journal has also been selected for inclusion in a *Pushcart Prize* anthology.

FAUQUIER POETRY JOURNAL (I), P.O. Box 68, Bealeton VA 22712-0068, founded 1994, managing editor D. Clement, is a quarterly that contains poetry and poetry comment; "purpose is to encourage new and developing poets with talent." **They want "fresh, creative, well-crafted poetry, any style. Due to format, longer poems over 40 lines are not often used. Do not want overly sentimental or religious themes, overdone subjects, or overly obscure work."** They have recently published poetry by Marylin Faith Rumph, R.G. Ribble, Nancy Ryan, T.E. Harper and Michael Musante. As a sample the editor selected these lines from "Dinner at the Parthenon" by Robert Hentz:

> *Dinner to the vibrant beat*
> *and seductive strains of music*
> *that animate the deadest feet*
> *not in Athens but on Halsted Street—*
> > *saganaki and gyros,*
> > *salad graced with feta cheese, . . .*

FPJ is 40-50 pgs., digest-sized, laser-printed on plain white paper and saddle-stapled with bright colored paper cover. Press run is more than 100 for 50 subscribers. Subscription: $20. **Sample postpaid: $5. The editor encourages subscriptions by requiring a reading fee for nonsubscribers ($5 for 1-5 poems); no reading fee for subscribers. Submit poetry with name and address in the upper left corner of each page and include SASE. Simultaneous submissions OK. Rarely accepts previously published poems. Often comments on rejections. Send SASE for guidelines. Reports in 2-6 weeks. Offers Editor's Choice Awards of $5-25 for the best entries in each issue. Pays 1 copy to remainder of published poets. Acquires one-time rights.** They sponsor quarterly poetry contests, explained in the journal. Entry fee: $5. Prizes range from $5-50, and winners are published in the following issue. In addition to poetry, *FPJ* occasionally prints articles by guest columnists. Articles should deal with some aspect of poetry, the writing experience, reactions to particular poems or poets, the mechanics (how to), etc. No reading fee, no guidelines other than word limit (around 1,000 words). "Pretty much anything goes as long as it's interesting and well-written." Pays 2¢/word. The editor says, "Let us see a variety in your submission; what one editor likes, another won't. Send a range of work that illustrates the breadth and depth of your talent; this helps us decide if there's something we like. We encourage submissions from anyone who is writing mature, well-crafted poetry."

FEELINGS: AMERICA'S BEAUTIFUL POETRY MAGAZINE; ANDERIE POETRY PRESS; QUARTERLY EDITOR'S CHOICE AWARDS (I, II), P.O. Box 85, Easton PA 18044-0085, phone (610)559-9287, founded 1989, editor Carole J. Heffley, a quarterly magazine, uses **"high-quality poetry in both free verse and form, rhyme and non-rhyme, no more than 30 lines."** Any theme that is well written, no pornography. They have recently published poetry by Michael Steffen, Mary Gribble and Ronald Ribble, Ph.D. As a sample here are the opening lines from "Rhode Island" by Terry Lerdall Fitterer:

> *How picturesque, the sand beneath my feet*
> *and rushing waves—above where seagulls soar,*

> the fishing rigs that hold a lobster fleet,
> and nightly calm except the ocean's roar.

Feelings is magazine-sized, professionally printed on lightweight paper, saddle-stapled with heavy paper cover, using "photography appropriate to the season or subject." Subscription: $24. **Sample postpaid: $6.50. Cover letter with background, credits ("something about the writer") required with submissions. "SASE must accompany all correspondence." Send SASE for guidelines. Reports in 6 weeks. Pays $10 for 3 Editor's Choice Awards in each issue. Acquires first rights.** Also runs several contests throughout the year with prizes ranging from $25-100. **"We publish chapbooks; info/price list upon request with SASE."** Mss on "how-to" write/publish poetry welcome. Payment for articles varies.

FEH! (IV-Humor), 196 Alps Rd., Suite 2-316, Athens GA 30606-4068, founded 1986, editor Tony Arnold, appears 3 times a year, using **"silliness and nonsense, but *good* silliness and nonsense; humor, satire, irreverence, eccentricity, fanaticism, etc.; rhyming and non."** They have recently published poetry by Richard Ball and Mary Bradford. As a sample the editor selected these lines by Ferdinand "Skeet" Giaclepousse:

> I believe in God and Bigfoot
> and the right to worship as I please.
> I've seen angels, demons and the Virgin Mama
> in the midst of my D.T.'s

feh! is 50 pgs., 5½ × 8½, with photocopied card cover. Their press run is 200 with about 50 subscriptions, and sales through bookstores. **Sample postpaid: $3. Submit up to 6 poems at a time. Considers simultaneous submissions and previously published poems. Editor sometimes comments on rejections, if asked. Send SASE for guidelines. Reports within 2 months. Pays 1 copy. Acquires one-time rights.**

FELLOWSHIP IN PRAYER (IV-Religious), 291 Witherspoon St., Princeton NJ 08542, phone (609)924-6863, fax (609)924-6910, founded 1950, contact Editor, is an interfaith bimonthly **"concerned with prayer, meditation and spiritual life"** using short poetry **"with deep religious (or spiritual) feeling."** It is 48 pgs., digest-sized, professionally printed, saddle-stapled with glossy card cover. They accept about 2% of submissions received. Press run is 10,000. Subscription: $16. **Sample free. Submit 5 poems at a time, double-spaced. Simultaneous submissions and "sometimes" previously published poems OK. Cover letter preferred. Reports in 1 month. Pays 5 copies.** Staff reviews books of poetry in 75 words, single format.

FEMINIST STUDIES (IV-Women/feminism), %Dept. of Women's Studies, University of Maryland, College Park MD 20742, phone (301)405-7415, fax (301)314-9190, founded 1969, poetry editor Alicia Ostriker, **"welcomes a variety of work that focuses on women's experience, on gender as a category of analysis, and that furthers feminist theory and consciousness."** They have published poetry by Janice Mirikitani, Paula Gunn Allen, Cherrie Moraga, Audre Lorde, Judith Small, Milana Marsenich, Lynda Schraufnagel, Valerie Fox and Diane Glancy. The elegantly printed, flat-spined, 250-page paperback appears 3 times a year in an edition of 8,000, goes to 7,000 subscribers, of which 1,500 are libraries. There are 4-10 pgs. of poetry in each issue. **Sample postpaid: $12. No simultaneous submissions; will only consider previously published poems under special circumstances. Manuscripts are reviewed twice a year, in May and December. Deadlines are May 1 and December 1. Authors will receive notice of the board's decision by June 30 and January 30. Always sends prepublication galleys. No pay.** Commissions reviews of books of poetry. Poets may send books to Claire G. Moses for review consideration.

THE FIDDLEHEAD (I, II, IV-Regional, students), Campus House, University of New Brunswick, P.O. Box 4400, Fredericton, New Brunswick E3B 5A3 Canada, founded 1945, poetry editors Robert Gibbs, Robert Hawkes and Don MacKay. From its beginning in 1945 as a local little magazine devoted mainly to student writers, **the magazine retains an interest in poets of the Atlantic region and in young poets** but prints poetry from everywhere. It is **open to excellent work of every kind, looking always for vitality, freshness and surprise.** Among the poets whose work they have recently published are Brett Hursey and Ruth Warat. As a sample, we selected these lines from "A Little Poem About Commitment" by Kim Roberts:

> Truth to the spirit of the event in this narrative takes precedence
>   over a strict adherence to history.
> Due to the earth's curvature, the map plates in this book cannot
>   conform to borders.
> If you are not fully satisfied, a refund will be provided.
> We cannot be responsible for loss or damage of personal property.
> I have not hesitated to invent wherever it seemed fictionally right
>   to do so.

If swallowed, drink a glass of water to dilute.
The Fiddlehead is a handsomely printed, 6×9, flat-spined paperback (120 pgs.) with b&w graphics, colored cover, paintings by New Brunswick artists. They use less than 10% of submissions. Circulation is 1,000. Subscription: $20/year plus $6 postage (US). **Sample: $7 (US). Submit 3-10 poems at a time. No simultaneous submissions. For reply or return of ms, send SAE with Canadian stamps, IRCs or cash. Reporting time is 2-6 months, backlog 6-18 months. Pay is $10-12/printed page.** Reviews books by Canadian authors only.

FIELD; FIELD TRANSLATION SERIES; CONTEMPORARY AMERICAN POETRY SE-RIES; O.C. PRESS (II, IV-Translations), Rice Hall, Oberlin College, Oberlin OH 44074, phone (216)775-8408, fax (216)775-8124, founded 1969, editors Stuart Friebert, David Young, Alberta Turner and David Walker, is a literary journal appearing twice a year with "emphasis on poetry, translations and essays by poets." **They want the "best possible" poetry.** They have published poetry by Thylias Moss, Yusef Komunyakaa, Charles Simic and Sharon Olds. The handsomely printed, digest-sized journal is flat-spined, has 100 pgs., rag stock with glossy card color cover. Although most poems fall under the lyrical free verse category, you'll find narratives and formal work here on occasion, much of it sensual, visually appealing and resonant. Circulation 2,500, with 800 library subscriptions. Subscription: $14/year, $24/2 years. **Sample postpaid: $7. Reports in 2 weeks, has a 3- to 6-month backlog. Always sends prepublication galleys. Pays $20-30/page plus 2 copies.** They publish books of translations in the Field Translation Series, averaging 150 pgs., flat-spined and hardcover editions. **Query regarding translations. Pays 7½-10% royalties with some advance and 10 author's copies.** They have also inaugurated a Contemporary American Poetry Series with the publication of a collection of new and selected poems by Dennis Schmitz. This series is by invitation only. Write for catalog to buy samples. Work published in *Field* has also been included in the 1992, 1993, 1994 and 1995 volumes of *The Best American Poetry*. Stuart Friebert says they would like to see more poetry from "minority" poets "of any and all cultures."

5TH GEAR (I, II), 724 Humphries Lane, Chesapeake VA 23322-4444, phone (804)482-5796, founded 1994, first issue September 1995, editor Andy Fogle, who says, "*5th Gear* comes out at least once a month in a 4×5 leaflet format, distributed free at record stores, bookstores, libraries and the like, and once a year in a large, magazine-sized issue, collecting the work of everyone I've published during the year. Think of it as a band releasing 12 or more free singles every year and then releasing a monster collective album around December or January and charging you five bucks." **As for poetry, "I'll consider absolutely anything; I have pretty wide tastes, but I also have my biases. Put simply, I publish what I want, what I like best."** They have recently published poetry by M. Jayanti Van Hoose, Larry Grady, Graham Foust, Meara Day, Andy Fenwick, Dennis Saleh, Alicia Bayer, Harding Stedler and Tricia Mueller. The editor says *5th Gear*'s annual issue is 8½×11, professionally printed, saddle-stapled. They receive about 1,500 poems a year, accept 100. Monthly press run is 300, annual press run 100 for 40 subscribers. Subscription (at least 12 leaflets, large annual issue and several supplements): $10. Make checks payable to Paul A. Fogle. **Several sample monthlies are available for free with SASE. No previously published poems; simultaneous submissions OK.** Time between acceptance and publication can run up to a year. **Reports in 2 months. Pays "as many monthlies within season and one annual." Acquires first rights and requests mention "if poem later appears somewhere else."** The editor says, "Guidelines are available with a SASE, but I'd rather you just send the poetry. I'd like submissions to be typed, but will consider handwritten poems. I'd rather not see any staples, paper clips or separately folded poems but those are just tics. I comment on rejections pretty often and like to think I can be helpful at times, but I can also be blunt, so be prepared either way. The best advice I can give is Jack Kerouac's: 'Be in love with your life.'"

THE FIGURES (V), 5 Castle Hill Ave., Great Barrington MA 01230-1552, phone (413)528-2552, founded 1975, publisher/editor Geoffrey Young, is a small press publishing poetry and fiction. They have published poetry by Lyn Hejinian, Clark Coolidge, Ron Padgett and Christopher Dewdney. **They pay 10% of press run. However, they currently do not accept unsolicited poetry.**

FILLING STATION (II), P.O. Box 22135, Bankers Hall, Calgary, Alberta T2P 4J5 Canada, founded 1993, appears 3 times/year (February, June and October). *Filling Station* is a magazine of contemporary writing featuring poetry, fiction, interviews, reviews and other literary news. **"We are looking for all forms of contemporary writing. No specific objections to any style."** They have recently published poetry by Robert Hilles, Adeena Karasick, Suzette Mayr and Erin Mouré and say, "as an editorial collective, to pick one specific example goes against our objective of representing many different voices." *FS* is 48 pgs., 8½×11, saddle-stapled with card cover and includes photos, artwork and ads. They receive about 100 submissions for each issue, accept approximately 10%. Press run is 500 for 100 subscribers, 250 shelf sales. Subscription: $15/1 year, $25/2 years. **Sample postpaid: $6. Submit typed poems with name and address on each page. No previously published poems; simultaneous submissions OK. Cover letter required. Deadlines are November 15, March 15 and July 15.**

Seldom comments on rejections. **Send SASE (or SAE with IRC) for guidelines. Reports in 3 months. Pays 1 year subscription. Acquires first North American and second reprint rights.** Reviews books of poetry in both single and multi-book format. Open to unsolicited reviews. Poets may also send books for review consideration. Here's what the collective has to say about *Filling Station* and the philosophy behind this publication: "You stop between these 'fixed' points on the map to get an injection of something new, something fresh that's going to get you from point to point. . . . We want to be a kind of connection between polarities: a link. We'll publish any poem or story that offers a challenge: to the mind, to the page, to writers and readers."

FINE MADNESS (II), P.O. Box 31138, Seattle WA 98103-1138, founded 1982, editors Sean Bentley, C. Deavel, John Malek and J.W. Marshall. *Fine Madness* publishes 3 issues every 2 years (a new issue roughly every 8 months). **They want "contemporary poetry of any form and subject. We look for highest quality of thought, language and imagery. We look for the mark of the individual: unique ideas and presentation; careful, humorous, sympathetic. No careless poetry, greeting card poetry, poetry that 10,000 other people could have written."** They have recently published poetry by Pattiann Rogers, Albert Goldbarth and Caroline Knox. As a sample the editor selected these lines from "Natural History of an Idea" by Melinda Mueller:

> Ice is over with quickly, while a knife, say, keeps happening,
> long after skin has healed. And the mind that thinks this—
> this is strangely consoling—is another event among the rest.

> Not that that's the end of it. There's the phone
> that rings, the avalanche of lights on that suburban hill
> across the lake, the incessant evening . . .

Fine Madness is 64 pgs., digest-sized, perfect-bound, offset with color card cover. They accept about 40 of 1,500 poems received. Their press run is 1,000 for 100 subscribers of which 10 are libraries. Subscription: $9. **Sample postpaid: $4. Guidelines available for SASE. Submit 2-5 poems, preferably originals, not photocopy, 1 poem/page. No previously published poems or simultaneous submissions. Reports in 1-4 months. Pays 1 copy plus subscription.** Poets may send books for review consideration to John Malek. *Fine Madness* has had poetry selected for inclusion in the 1990, 1991, 1992, 1993 and 1994 volumes of *The Best American Poetry* and a *Pushcart Prize* anthology. Editor Sean Bentley says, "If you don't read poetry, don't send us any."

FIREBRAND BOOKS (IV-Feminist, lesbian, ethnic), 141 The Commons, Ithaca NY 14850, phone (607)272-0000, founded 1984, editor and publisher Nancy K. Bereano, "is a **feminist and lesbian** publishing company committed to producing quality work in multiple genres by ethnically diverse women." They publish both quality trade paperbacks and hardbacks. As a sample, here is a stanza of a sestina, "great expectations," from the book *Living As A Lesbian* by Cheryl Clarke:

> dreaming the encounter intense as engines
> first me then you oh what a night
> of rapture and risk and dolphin
> acrobatics after years of intend-
> ing to find my lesbian sources in the window
> of longing wide open in me

The book is 94 pgs., flat-spined, elegantly printed on heavy stock with a glossy color card cover, a photo of the author on the back, $7.95. **Simultaneous submissions acceptable with notification. Replies to queries within 2 weeks, to mss within 1 month. Pays royalties.** Send for catalog to buy samples.

FIREWEED: A FEMINIST QUARTERLY (IV-Women), P.O. Box 279, Station B, Toronto, Ontario M5T 2W2 Canada, phone (416)504-1339, founded 1978, edited by the Fireweed Collective, is a feminist journal of writing, politics, art and culture that **"especially welcomes contributions by women of color, working-class women, native women, lesbians and women with disabilities."** As a sample we selected the opening lines of "These Military Men" by Joy Hewitt Mann:

> My husband was
> a military man.
> Dinner
> 5:30
> sharp.
> No give.   No take.

Fireweed is 88 pgs., 6¾×9¾, flat-spined, with 3- or 4-color cover. Poems tend to be freestyle lyrics leaning toward avant-garde, with some room for rhymed verse and stanza patterns. Press run is 2,000. Subscription: $20 individuals, $30 institutions in Canada; $28 individuals, $42 institutions in US. **Sample: $6.50 in Canada, $7 in US. Simultaneous submissions OK. Reports in 6-12 months.**

"Please include SAE and IRC for reply." Pays $20 for first printed page, $10 for remaining full or partial printed page and 2 copies.

FIREWEED: POETRY OF WESTERN OREGON (IV-Regional), 1330 E. 25th Ave., Eugene OR 97403, founded 1989, is a quarterly publishing the work of **poets living in Western Oregon or having close connections to the region. However, poems need not be regional in subject; any theme, subject, length or form is acceptable.** They have recently published poetry by Jane Glazer, Charles Goodrich, Wes Vollmer and Stephanie Van Horn. As a sample they selected these lines from "Sunday Voices" by Jenny Fowler:

> *I envy their high notes.*
> *So I sit like a choirgirl,*
> *a golden rod moving up my spine,*
> *and the music streaks full of yellow whistle*
> *from my lips.*
> *GlorIa, glorIa, glorIa.*

Fireweed is 44 pgs., digest-sized, laser printed and saddle-stapled with card cover. "We receive several hundred poems and publish about ¼ or ⅓ of them." Press run is 250 for 180 subscribers of which 20 are libraries, 25 shelf sales. Subscription: $10. **Sample postpaid: $2.50. Submit 3-5 poems at a time, name and address on each page. No previously published poems; simultaneous submissions OK. Cover letter with brief bio required. Often comments on rejections. They do not publish guidelines for poets but will answer inquiries with SASE. Reports in 2-4 months. Pays 2 copies. Acquires first North American serial rights.** Reviews books of poetry by Oregon poets in 500-750 words, single format. Open to unsolicited reviews. Oregon poets may also send books for review consideration. They add, "We occasionally have special issues organized by theme, compiled by a guest editor or focused on newcomers to *Fireweed*. Support your local magazines by sending work and buying subscriptions! Submit to the smaller publications *first!*"

‡FIRM NONCOMMITTAL: AN INTERNATIONAL JOURNAL OF WHIMSY (II, IV-Humor), 5 Vonda Ave., North York, Ontario M2N 5E6 Canada, founded 1995, editors Brian Pastoor and Jeff Bersche, is an annual forum for international light verse and humorous, short fiction and nonfiction. **"Short poems under 40 lines are preferred, in all forms and styles from visual to villanelle. There is a morass of morose writing out there. We seek writers who find the sunshine in the saturnine, who 'take the utmost trouble to find the right thing to say and then say it with the utmost levity'—G.B. Shaw."** They have recently published "levity" by bill bissett (Canada), K.V. Skene (England), Deborah Shapiro (Israel) and Craig Griffiths (Wales). As a sample the editors selected these lines from "Pre-Dawn Aphorisms" by Libby Scheier (Canada):

> *I accidentally planted the garden twice this year,*
> *there will be a war of the seeds*
> *and the fittest will survive.*

Firm Noncommittal is 40-48 pgs., 6¼ × 8¼, professionally printed and perfect-bound with matte card cover, using mirthful, b&w art. They accept "nearly 10%" of the submissions received. Circulation is 100 and growing, "thanks to support from *Krax* and other light-minded magazines." **Sample postpaid: $5 (Canadian funds). Make checks payable to Brian Pastoor. Submit up to 6 poems in May or June only. Previously published poems OK; no simultaneous submissions. Cover letter required; include a brief bio, "preferably under 50 words, preferably factual. Unless of edificial genius, mss without SASE or SAE and IRCs will be binned (sorry)." Often comments on rejections. Send SASE (or SAE and IRCs) for guidelines. Reports in 2 months. Sometimes sends prepublication galleys. Pays 2 copies.** Brian Pastoor says, "While we do admit a bias to the ironist here, we shy away from satire that is too heavy. We're after light, perspicuous writing that reveals a quickness of mind about the spiritual or mundane (all themes universal), writing that is characterized by imagination, ingenuity and/or self-conscious verbal artifice. Tom Robbins, as always, put it best: 'Those who fail to see the whimsy of things will experience rigor mortis before death.' "

FIRST HAND (IV-Gay, subscribers), Box 1314, Teaneck NJ 07666, phone (201)836-9177, founded 1980, poetry editor Bob Harris, is a **"gay erotic publication written mostly by its readers."** The digest-sized monthly has a circulation of 70,000 with 3,000 subscribers of which 3 are libraries and uses 1-2 pgs. of poetry in each issue. They have published poetry by Michael Swift and Robert Patrick. As a sample the editor selected these lines from "Hustler" by Christopher Thomas:

THE SUBJECT INDEX, located before the General Index, can help you select markets for your work. It lists those publishers whose poetry interests are specialized.

> *We celebrate the skin—*
> *I, for the joy of unzipping,*
> *he, for the thirty-five dollars cash—*
> *our mouths wet and wonderful around it all.*

Submit poems no longer than 1 typed page. No queries. Editor Bob Harris sometimes comments on rejected mss. Reports in 6 weeks. Pays $25/poem. Reviews books of poetry. The editor advises, "Make sure what you're writing about is obvious to future readers. **Poems need not be explicitly sexual, but must deal overtly with gay situations and subject matter."**

‡FIRST TIME; NATIONAL HASTINGS POETRY COMPETITION (I, II), Burdett Cottage, 4 Burdett Place, George St., Hastings, East Sussex TN34 3ED England, phone/fax 01424 428855, founded 1981, editor Josephine Austin, who says the biannual magazine is **open to "all kinds of poetry—our magazine goes right across the board—which is why it is one of the most popular in Great Britain."** The following lines are from "Why a Poet?" by R.M. Griffiths:

> *Of all types of people*
> *and all their differences in depth,*
> *the poet is the deepest,*
> *Or is it just the most vacuous?*

The digest-sized magazine, 24 pgs., saddle-stapled, contains several poems on each page, in a variety of small type styles, on lightweight stock, b&w photographs of editor and 1 author, glossy one-color card cover. Subscription: $13. **Sample: $2 plus postage. "Please send dollars." Poets should send 10 poems. Poems submitted must not exceed 30 lines, must not have been published elsewhere, and must have name and address of poet on each. Cover letter required. Maximum time to publication is 2 months. "Although we can no longer offer a free copy as payment, we can offer one at a discounted price of $3."** The annual National Hastings Poetry Competition for poets 18 and older offers awards of £100, £50 and £25, £1/poem entry fee. Editor Josephine Austin has received The Dorothy Tutin Award "for services to poetry." She advises, "Keep on 'pushing your poetry.' If one editor rejects you then study the market and decide which is the correct one for you. Try to type your own manuscripts as longhand is difficult to read and doesn't give a professional impression. Always date your poetry — ©1996 and sign it. Follow your way of writing, don't be a pale imitation of someone else—sooner or later styles change and you will either catch up or be ahead."

‡FISHDRUM (II), P.O. Box 966, Murray Hill Station, New York NY 10156, founded in 1988 by Robert Winson (1959-1995), now edited by Suzi Winson, is a literary magazine appearing once a year. They want **"West Coast poetry, the exuberant, talky, often elliptical and abstract 'continuous nerve movie' that follows the working of the mind and has a relationship to the world and the reader. Philip Whalen's work, for example, and much of** *Calafia, The California Poetry*, **edited by Ishmael Reed. Also magical-tribal-incantatory poems, exemplified by the future/primitive** *Technicians of the Sacred*, **ed. Rothenberg.** *FishDrum* **has a soft spot for schmoozy, emotional, imagistic stuff. Literate, personal material that sings and surprises, OK?"** They have published poetry by Philip Whalen, Joy Harjo, Arthur Sze, Nathaniel Tarn, Alice Notley, John Brandi, Steve Richmond, Jessica Hagedorn, Leo Romero and Leslie Scalapino. As a sample the editor selected these lines from "Glossolalia" by Kate Bremer:

> *Everywhere I look I see amino acids on the ground.*
> *When I close my eyes, I see molecules and pieces of Sanskrit:*
> *I hear syllables and alphabets.*

FD is approximately 80 pgs., perfect-bound, professionally printed. "Of 300 or so unsolicited submissions, accepted fewer than twenty." Press run is 500 for 100 subscribers of which 10 are libraries, 400 shelf sales. Subscription: $20 for 4 issues. **Publishes theme issues. Sometimes sends prepublication galleys. Pays 2 copies. Contributors may purchase advance copies at $3 each. Acquires first serial rights.** Reviews books or chapbooks of poetry in long essays and/or capsule reviews. Open to unsolicited reviews. Poets may also send books for review consideration. The editor says, **"We're looking for prose, fiction, essays, what-have-you, and artwork, scores, cartoons, etc.—just send it along. We are also interested in poetry, prose and translations concerning the practice of Zen. We publish chapbooks, but solicit these from our authors."** She also adds, "It is my intention to complete Robert's work and to honor his memory by continuing to publish *FishDrum*."

‡FIVE LINES DOWN; FIVE LINES DOWN PRESS (I, IV-Form/style), 10 Wayne Court, Redwood City CA 94063, phone (415)368-8472, founded 1994, editor Kenneth Tanemura. *Five Lines Down* is a biannual journal devoted to publishing English language tanka, articles on tanka, and reviews of tanka books. **They want tanka only—no other poetry.** They have recently published tanka by Sanford Goldstein, David Rice and Tom Clausen. As a sample the editor selected this tanka by Pat Shelley:

> *The year after your death*

> *all the pelargoniums you loved*
> *froze one winter night*
> *Ten years later*
> *I am not yet consoled.*

Five Lines Down is 28 pgs., digest-sized, attractively printed and saddle-stapled with card stock cover with b&w art. They receive about 500 poems a year, publish less than one fifth. Press run is 100 for 70 subscribers. Subscription: $10. **Sample postpaid: $5. Make checks payable to Kenneth Tanemura. No previously published tanka or simultaneous submissions. Cover letter preferred. Seldom comments on rejections. Reports within a few weeks. Pays nothing—not even a copy.** Reviews books of tanka. Open to unsolicited reviews. Poets may also send books for review consideration. Under Five Lines Down Press, they also publish books of tanka, typically in chapbook format. **Poets must first be published in** *Five Lines Down.* **Replies to queries in 3 weeks, to mss (if invited) in 1 month. Pays 20 author's copies (out of a press run of 100).** The editor says, "Poets should be familiar with both translations of Japanese tanka and English language tanka, and be aware of the position of tanka in the short-poem community."

FLEETING MONOLITH ENTERPRISES (II); VERTICAL IMAGES (IV-Regional), 62 Langdon Park Rd., London N6 5QG England, phone (0181)340-5807, founded 1986, editor Mike Diss. Fleeting Monolith publishes about 3 chapbooks/year. *Vertical Images* is an annual using primarily poets connected with the Vertical Images poetry group: "All those submitting work are given equal representation in the magazine, which grows largely out of consistent workshop practice every two weeks. We suggest moving to London, joining the group and taking it from there." For their chapbooks, Fleeting Monolith wants **"inspired/delirious/challenging/manic/radical/subversive work—who cares about form! Nothing dead/academic/po-faced/sensitive stuff."** They have published poetry by Slaughter District, A.W. Kindness, D. Nasty and the editor, who selected the following complete poem (by Mark E. Jackson) as a sample:

> *The wind favours those who offer no resistance. Bingo*
> *vikings come down from the clouds with their wrestling*
> *equipment, perky-nosed & smelling of catfish. You know,*
> *almost all of the brain's capacity is unused. As it must*
> *seem to a trouserpress. It's my party & I can buy a goat.*
> *Any way you go, you upset the average.*

Their chapbooks are in a variety of formats and **payment depends "entirely on the format and scope of each work." Sample postpaid: £2.** "Series of free poetry broadsheets available on request—IRC preferred." The editor says, *"L'art, c'est un connerie-.* Artaud said that, but we wish we had. Poetry can be a garden shed: Michaux said that (who cares about form! count this, count that!) and he wasn't English either—in fact, not many poets are, now that Keats and Lewis Carroll are dead. Buster Keaton was a poet and Jean Tinguely is a poet. At Fleeting Monolith, only a small part of the living process of poetry gets crystallized into books. Write us a letter, send us something, join the network of creative discontent."

FLIPSIDE (II), 109 Dixon Hall, California University of Pennsylvania, California PA 15419, founded 1987, poetry editors Cindy Speer and Derek C.F. Pegritz, is a literary tabloid appearing twice a year. **"We publish highly imageable poetry about concrete people, places and things. We tend to publish poems that deal with a darker, more unusual side of life. We don't publish melodramatic love poems or mushy ballads, nor do we publish bitter poetry."** They have published poetry by Charles Bukowski and Arthur Winfield Knight. As a sample the editors selected the poem "Mother Lover" by Michael Bagamery:

> *Make-up on that face*
> *Like rubble.*
> *Ivy won't run up a building*
> *Unless it stands.*

The tabloid is 48 pgs., professionally printed on newsprint with b&w photos and line drawings inside, some ads. They accept less than 5% of hundreds of poems submitted. Press run is 5,000, distributed free to the public, libraries, writing schools, colleges, advertisers, poets, etc. **Sample postpaid: $2. Send SASE for guidelines. Reports in 2 months. Pays as many copies as you want.**

‡FLOATING BRIDGE PRESS (IV-Regional), P.O. Box 18814, Seattle WA 98118, founded 1994, publishes **limited edition chapbooks by Washington state poets, selected through an annual contest.** They have recently published chapbooks by Nance Van Winckel and Joannie Kervran. As a sample the editors selected these lines from "Love Apples" in Kervran's chapbook, *A Steady Longing for Flight*:

> *Each cut and push of the shovel sings inside her*
> *and she imagines the summer garden*
> *awash in lavender and meadow rue.*

> *In the darkest corner she'll plant a bleeding heart,*
> *fleshy pendants dripping ruby in the shade.*

That chapbook is 32 pgs., digest-sized and offset printed on acid-free recycled paper with a letterpress linocut matte cover. **Sample postpaid: $6. For consideration in the contest, Washington poets (only) should submit a chapbook ms of 20-24 pgs. of poetry with $10 reading fee and SASE (for results only) between September and January. Previously published individual poems and simultaneous submissions OK. Author's name must not appear on the ms; include a separate page with title, name, address, telephone number and acknowledgments of any previous publication. Deadline: January 15.** Mss are judged anonymously and will not be returned. **In addition to publication, the winner receives $100 (minimum), 50 copies and a reading in the Seattle area. All entrants receive a copy of the winning chapbook. Send SASE for guidelines.**

THE FLORIDA REVIEW (II), Dept. of English, University of Central Florida, Box 25000, Orlando FL 32816, phone (407)823-2212, founded 1972, editor Russ Kesler, is a "literary biannual with emphasis on short fiction and poetry." **They want "poems filled with real things, real people and emotions, poems that might conceivably advance our knowledge of the human heart."** They have published poetry by Knute Skinner, Elton Glaser, Silvia Curbelo and Walter McDonald. It is 128 pgs., professionally printed, flat-spined, with glossy card cover. Press run is 1,500 for 500 subscribers of which 50 are libraries, 300 shelf sales. **Sample postpaid: $4.50. Submit no more than 6 poems at a time. Simultaneous submissions OK. Editor comments on submissions "occasionally." Send SASE for guidelines. Reports in 1-3 months. Always sends prepublication galleys. Pays 3 copies, small honorarium occasionally available. Acquires all rights. Returns rights "upon publication, when requested."** Reviews books of poetry in 1,500 words, single format; 2,500-3,000 words, multi-book. Send books for review consideration. The editor says they would like more formal verse.

FLUME PRESS (II), 773 Sierra View, Chico CA 95926, phone (916)342-1583, founded 1984, poetry editors Casey Huff and Elizabeth Renfro, publishes poetry chapbooks. **"We have few biases about form, although we appreciate control and crafting, and we tend to favor a concise, understated style, with emphasis on metaphor rather than editorial commentary."** They have published chapbooks by Tina Barr, Randall Freisinger, Leonard Kress, Carol Gordon, Gayle Kaune, Luis Omar Salinas, Judy Lindberg, Ava Leavell Haymon, Martha M. Vertreace, Joanne Allred and Mary Matthews. As a sample the editors selected these lines from "Touch Pool" by Pamela Uschuk:

> *Around and around*
> *the holding pool, rays soar*
> *like squadrons of angels, now and then lifting*
> *a wing to test the edge*
> *as if they would swim through the glass to the sea*

Chapbooks are chosen from an annual competition, March 1 through May 30. $7 entry fee. Submit 20-24 pgs., including title, contents and acknowledgments. Considers simultaneous submissions. Brief cover letter preferred. "Flume Press editors read and respond to every entry." Sometimes sends prepublication galleys. Winner receives $100 and 25 copies. Sample: $7.

FLYWAY (II), 203 Ross Hall, Iowa State University, Ames IA 50011-1201, fax (515)294-6814, e-mail flyway@iastate.edu, founded 1961, editor Stephen Pett, appears 3 times a year. *Flyway* "is one of the best literary magazines for the money; it is packed with some of the most readable poems being published today—all styles and forms, lengths and subjects." The editor shuns elite-sounding free verse with obscure meanings and pretty-sounding formal verse with obvious meanings. It is 6×9, 76 pgs., professionally printed and perfect-bound with matte card cover with color. Circulation is 600 for 400 subscribers of which 100 are libraries. Subscription: $18. **Sample postpaid: $8. Submit 4-6 poems at a time. Cover letter preferred. "We do not read mss between the end of May and mid-August." May be contacted by fax or e-mail, but "work should come by mail." Reports in 4-6 weeks (often sooner). Pays 1 copy. Acquires first rights.**

FOLIO: A LITERARY JOURNAL (II), Dept. of Literature, Gray Hall, The American University, Washington DC 20016, founded 1984, is a biannual. Editors change annually. They have published poetry by Jean Valentine, Henry Taylor and William Stafford. There are 12-20 poems published in each issue. *Folio* is 64-72 pgs., 6×9, perfect-bound, neatly printed from typeset. **Sample postpaid: $5. Submit up to 6 pgs. with brief bio/contributor's note from August to March 1. Considers simultaneous submissions. Reads submissions September 1 through March 1 only. Pays 2 copies. Acquires first rights.** They also sponsor a contest open to all contributors with a $75 prize for the best poem of the fall and spring issue.

FOOTWORK: THE PATERSON LITERARY REVIEW; HORIZONTES; ALLEN GINSBERG POETRY AWARDS; THE PATERSON POETRY PRIZE; PASSAIC COUNTY COMMUNITY COLLEGE POETRY CENTER LIBRARY (II, IV-Regional, bilingual/foreign

language), Poetry Center, Passaic County Community College, Cultural Affairs Dept., 1 College Blvd., Paterson NJ 07505-1179, phone (201)684-6555. A wide range of activities pertaining to poetry are conducted by the Passaic County Community College Poetry Center, including the annual literary magazine *Footwork*, founded 1979, editor and director Maria Mazziotti Gillan, using **poetry of "high quality" under 100 lines; "clear, direct, powerful work."** They have published poetry by David Ray, Diane Wakoski, William Stafford, Sonia Sanchez, Laura Boss and Marge Piercy. *Footwork: The Paterson Literary Review* is 160 pgs., magazine-sized, saddle-stapled, professionally printed with glossy card 2-color cover, using b&w art and photos. Circulation 1,000 with 100 subscribers of which 50 are libraries. **Sample postpaid: $10. Send no more than 5 poems/submission. Simultaneous submissions OK. Reads submissions September through January only. Reports in 1 year. Pays 1 copy. Acquires first rights.** *Horizontes*, founded in 1983, editor José Villalongo, is an annual Spanish language literary magazine using **poetry of high quality no longer than 20 lines. Will accept English translations, but Spanish version must be included**. They have published poetry by Nelson Calderon, Jose Kozer and Julio Cesar Mosches. *Horizontes* is 120 pgs., magazine-sized, saddle-stapled, professionally printed with full color matte cover, using b&w graphics and photos. Circulation 800 with 100 subscribers of which 20 are libraries. **Sample postpaid: $4. Accepts simultaneous submissions. "On occasion we do consider published works but prefer unpublished works." Reads submissions September through January only. Reports in 3-4 months. Pays 2 copies. Acquires first rights.** Staff reviews books of poetry. Send books for review consideration. The Poetry Center of the college conducts The Allen Ginsberg Poetry Awards Competition each year. Entry fee: $12. Prizes of $300, $150 and $100. Deadline: April 1. Send SASE for rules. They also publish a *New Jersey Poetry Resources* book, the *PCC Poetry Contest Anthology* and the *New Jersey Poetry Calendar*. The Paterson Poetry Prize of $1,000 is awarded each year (split between poet and publisher) to a book of poems published in the previous year. Publishers should write with SASE for application form to be submitted by February 1. Passaic County Community College Poetry Center Library has an extensive collection of contemporary poetry and seeks small press contributions to help keep it abreast. The Distinguished Poetry Series offers readings by poets of international, national and regional reputation. Poetryworks/USA is a series of programs produced for UA Columbia-Cablevision.

FOREVER ALIVE (IV-Specialized: physical immortality), P.O. Box 12305, Scottsdale AZ 85267-2305, phone (602)922-0300, fax (602)922-0800, e-mail herbbowie@aol.com, founded 1989, editor Herb Bowie, is a quarterly, published by People Forever International, which includes news, articles, essays, fiction and poetry on the subjects of health, aliveness and physical immortality. **They want "poems expressing a positive attitude toward living forever."** As a sample the editor selected the opening lines of "A Prayer Spontaneous" by Joe Bardin:

> There is a poetry of us,
> a prayer spontaneous:
> driving the car,
> or in the sudden stillness of parking
> sunshine warming the steering wheel,
> or in the shower
> hot water washing the muscle, the flesh.

FA is 52 pgs., 8½ × 11, web press printed and saddle-stapled with glossy 4-color paper cover and b&w inside. They publish one poem each issue. Press run is 2,000 for 400 subscribers, 300 shelf sales. Single copy: $6; subscription: $24. **Sample postpaid: $3. No previously published poems or simultaneous submissions. Cover letter required. Seldom comments on rejections. Reports in 3 months. Pays 10 copies. "All published submissions become the property of People Forever International, unless specific rights are reserved by the author."**

‡FORKROADS: A JOURNAL OF ETHNIC-AMERICAN LITERATURE (IV-Ethnic), P.O. Box 150, Spencertown NY 12165, founded 1995, editor David Kherdian. *Forkroads* is designed to promote "understanding and tolerance of our differences, around which we need to unite as one nation of rich and varied parts." **They want poetry from ethnic writers—poetry about the ethnic-American experience or sensibility only."** They have recently published poetry by Sherman Alexie, Luis J. Rodriguez, Michael Lally and Diane di Prima. The editor says *Forkroads* is 96 pgs., 8×10, offset, glossy, with full-color cover art and graphics, photos, drawings and ads inside. They receive several hundred poems a year, publish 30-35. Press run is 5,000. Single copy: $6; subscription: $25. **Sample postpaid: $8. Make checks payable to Forkroads Press. Submit 6 poems at a time. No previously published poems; simultaneous submissions OK. Cover letter preferred.** Time between acceptance and publication can be up to 1 year. **Often comments on rejections. Reports in 6 weeks. Always sends prepublication galleys. Pays $25. Buys first serial rights.** Reviews books of poetry in both single and multi-book format. Open to unsolicited reviews. Poets may also send books for review consideration.

THE FORMALIST; HOWARD NEMEROV SONNET AWARD (II, IV-Form, translations), 320 Hunter Dr., Evansville IN 47711, founded 1990, editor William Baer, appears twice a year, **"dedicated to contemporary *metrical* poetry written in the great tradition of English-language verse."** This is one of a handful of magazines that publish formal (metered, rhymed) poetry *exclusively*. The poems here are among the best in the genre—a joy to read—tastefully edited so that each verse plays off the other. They have published poetry by Richard Wilbur, Donald Justice, Mona Van Duyn, Derek Walcott, John Updike, Maxine Kumin, James Merrill, Karl Shapiro, X.J. Kennedy, May Swenson, W.S. Merwin, W.D. Snodgrass and Louis Simpson. As a sample the editor chose the opening stanza from "The Amateurs of Heaven" by Howard Nemerov:

> Two lovers to a midnight meadow came
> High in the hills, to lie there hand in hand
> Like effigies and look up at the stars,
> The never-setting ones set in the North
> To circle the Pole in idiot majesty,
> And wonder what was given them to wonder.

"We're looking for well-crafted poetry in a contemporary idiom which uses meter and the full range of traditional poetic conventions in vigorous and interesting ways. We're especially interested in sonnets, couplets, tercets, ballads, the French forms, etc. We're also interested in metrical translations of the poetry of major, formalist, non-English poets—from the ancient Greeks to the present. We're not, however, interested in haiku (or syllabic verse of any kind) or sestinas. Only rarely do we accept a poem over 2 pages, and we have no interest in any type of erotica, blasphemy, vulgarity or racism. Finally, like all editors, we suggest that those wishing to submit to *The Formalist* become thoroughly familiar with the journal beforehand." Subscription: $12/year; $22/2 years. **Sample postpaid: $6.50. *The Formalist* considers submissions throughout the year, 3-5 poems at one time. No simultaneous submissions, previously published work, or disk submissions. A brief cover letter is recommended** and a SASE is necessary for a reply and return of ms. **Reports within 2 months. Pays 2 copies. Acquires first North American serial rights.** The Howard Nemerov Sonnet Award offers $1,000 and publication in *The Formalist* for the best unpublished *sonnet*. The final judge for 1996 was Anthony Hecht. Entry fee: $3/sonnet. Postmark deadline: June 15. Send SASE for guidelines. See also the contest listing for the World Order of Narrative and Formalist Poets. Contestants must subscribe to *The Formalist* to enter. Work published in *The Formalist* also appears in *The Best American Poetry 1992*.

‡FOUND STREET PRESS; FOUND STREET (II, IV-Form/style), 2260 S. Ferdinand Ave., Monterey Park CA 91754, founded 1991, editor Larry Tomoyasu. *Found Street* is a "*visual* exploration of language and meaning" appearing 1-2 times a year. The editor says, **"I would like to see truly 'creative' writing; writing that expands the boundaries of what writing *is*; poems that are almost drawings and drawings that are almost words. Nothing seen; nothing taught; nothing approved."** He has recently published experimental and verbal/visual poetry by John M. Bennett, Jack Skelley, James Haining and Spencer Selby. The format of the publication changes from issue to issue. One issue we received was 3×4¼ with foldout pages; another issue was 5½×8½. The editor receives about 200 poems a year, accepts approximately 20%. Press run is 40. **Sample postpaid: $2. Make checks payable to Larry Tomoyasu. Submit 3-5 poems at a time. "All verbal/visual work should be camera-ready (b&w only)." No previously published poems or simultaneous submissions. Cover letter preferred.** Time between acceptance and publication is 3 months to 1 year. **Seldom comments on rejections. Send SASE for guidelines. Reports usually within 1 month. Pays 1-2 copies. Acquires first rights.** The editor says, "Found Street Press specializes in small publications and gets its name from where most people find our publications: on the street." He adds, "My advice to beginners: If you can't get your work published, start your own zine. Give it away free to all your friends and anyone who will take it, and send it to other poets and publishers, because if people aren't interested when it's free, they sure as hell aren't gonna pay for it. Read poetry, write poetry and *buy* poetry—we are our own market."

THE FOUR DIRECTIONS; SNOWBIRD PUBLISHING COMPANY (IV-Ethnic), P.O. Box 729, Tellico Plains TN 37385, phone (423)253-3680, founded 1991, publisher William Meyer. *The Four Directions* is an American Indian literary journal designed to further American Indian literature. **All authors must be of American Indian heritage, and they want poetry that reflects or touches commom/uncommon American Indian concerns.** They have published poetry by Susan Clements and Shirley Hill Witt. The editor says it is 60-68 pgs. with approximately 54 pgs. of poetry, short stories, articles and reviews. They receive about 200 poems a year, use approximately 48. Press run is 2,000 for 180 subscribers of which 90 are libraries, 1,800 shelf sales. Subscription: $21, $25 institutions. **Sample postpaid: $7. Previously published poems and simultaneous submissions OK. Cover letter required. Often comments on rejections. Publishes theme issues. Send SASE for upcoming themes. Reports in 6-9 weeks. Sometimes sends prepublication galleys. Pays $10 for full-page of poetry. Buys one-time rights.** Accepts reviews of all media, including books of poetry. Reviews range from 200 to 2,000 words. Snowbird Publishing Company publishes books but "so far we have not published any books of poetry." **Query first with sample poems and cover letter with brief bio and publication credits. "Poetry may be previously published or not, but must be of professional quality." Replies to queries and mss in 6-9 weeks. Pays 10-18% royalties and 10 author's copies.** The editor says, "The field of American Indian literature is the fastest growing literary effort in North America. We tend to seek writing that furthers the growth of the Indian spirit. We would like to see more traditional American Indian poetry and poetry in bilingual (American Indian and English or Spanish and English) forms."

FOX CRY (II), University of Wisconsin Fox Valley, 1478 Midway Rd., P.O. Box 8002, Menasha WI 54952-8002, phone (414)832-2662, founded 1973, editor Professor Don Hrubesky, is a literary annual using **poems up to 50 lines long, deadline February 15.** They have published poetry by Shirley Anders, Ellen Kort, David Graham, Curtis Brown, Robert Cooperman and Laurel Mills. As a sample the editor selected these lines from "Valentine's Day 1994," a poem of his own:

> *And, therefore, I come on this St. Valentine's Day,*
> *To write what words of comfort I can*
> *To leave this card*
> *And one small white, fragile rose,*
> *Inadequate emblem of a bitter father's love*
> *that nourished with sadness relentlessly grows.*

Their press run is 400. **Sample postpaid: $5. Submit maximum of 3 poems from September 1 through February 15 only. Simultaneous submissions considered. Send SASE for guidelines. Pays 1 copy.**

FRANK: AN INTERNATIONAL JOURNAL OF CONTEMPORARY WRITING AND ART (II, IV-Form, translations), 32 rue Edouard Vaillant, 93100 Montreuil France, phone (33)(1)48596658, fax (33)(1)48596668, e-mail david@paris-anglo.com, website http://www.paris-angl o.com, founded 1983, editor David Applefield. *Frank* is a literary semiannual that **"encourages work of seriousness and high quality which falls often between existing genres. Looks favorably at true internationalism and stands firm against ethnocentric values. Likes translations. Publishes foreign dossier in each issue. Very eclectic." There are no subject specifications, but the magazine "discourages sentimentalism and easy, false surrealism. Although we're in Paris, most Paris-poems are too thin for us. Length is open."** They have published poetry by Rita Dove, Derek Walcott, Duo Duo, Raymond Carver, Tomas Tranströmer, James Laughlin, Breytenbach, Michaux, Gennadi Aigi, W.S. Merwin, Edmond Jabes, John Berger, and many lesser known poets. The journal is 224 pgs., digest-sized, flat-spined and offset in b&w with color cover and photos, drawings and ads. Circulation is 4,000 of which 2,000 are bookstore sales and subscriptions. Subscription: $38 (individuals), $60 (institutions) for 4 issues. **Sample postpaid: $10 airmail from Paris. Queries via e-mail OK. Guidelines and upcoming themes available for SAE and IRCs. Poems must be previously unpublished. The editor often provides some criticism on rejected mss. Submissions are reported on in 3 months, publication is in 3-6 months. Pay is $5/printed page and 2 copies.** Editor organizes readings in US and Europe for *Frank* contributors. He says, "Send only what you feel is fresh, original, and provocative in either theme or form. Work of craft that also has political and social impact is encouraged."

FREE FOCUS (I, IV-Women/feminist); OSTENTATIOUS MIND (I, IV-Form/style), P.O. Box 7415, JAF Station, New York NY 10116, *Free Focus* founded 1985, *Ostentatious Mind* founded 1987, poetry editor Patricia D. Coscia. *Free Focus* "is a literary magazine **only for creative women, who reflect their ideas of love, nature, beauty and men and also express the pain, sorrow, joy and enchantment that their lives generate.** *Free Focus* **needs poems of all types on the subject matters above. Nothing x-rated, please. The poems can be as short as 2 lines or as long as 2 pages.** The objective of this magazine is to give women poets a chance to be fullfilled in the art of poetry, for freedom of expression for women is seldom described in society." They have published poetry by Helen Tzagoloff, Elizabeth Hahn Ph.D., Patricia A. Pierkowski, D.R. Middleton, Crystal Beckner, Elaine F. Powell, Kris Anderson, Carol L. Clark and Mary Anderson. As a sample the editor selected these lines from "A Woman I Once Knew" by Maura Schroeder:

> *She sleeps in the desert alone,*
> *Carving ancestral bone,*
> *from waking mountains.*
> *She sleeps in the desert alone,*
> *Wading in salt-soaked rivers,*
> *with wounds unfolded.*

Ostentatious Mind "is a co-ed literary magazine **for material of stream of consciousness and experimental poems. The poets deal with the political, social and psychological."** They have published poetry by Paul Weinman, Rod Farmer, L. Mason, Dr. John J. Soldo, Carl A. Winderl, James W. Penha and Joe Lackey. As a sample the editor selected this poem, "Poetic Wax," by Sheryl L. Nelms:

> comes in 1.5 liter
>
> bottles
>
> at Majestic
> Liquors

Both magazines are printed on 8×14 paper, folded in the middle and stapled to make a 10-page (including cover) format, with simple b&w drawings on the cover and inside. The two magazines appear every 6-8 months. **Sample of either is $3.50 postpaid. Submit only 3 poems at a time. Poems should be typed neatly and clearly on white typing paper. Simultaneous submissions and previously published poems OK. Publishes theme issues. Send SASE for guidelines and upcoming themes. Reports "as soon as possible." Sometimes sends prepublication galleys. Pays 1-2 copies.** The editor says, "I think that anyone can write a poem who can freely express intense feelings about their experiences. A dominant thought should be ruled and expressed in writing, not by the spoken word, but the written word."

FREE LUNCH (II), P.O. Box 7647, Laguna Niguel CA 92607-7647, founded 1988, editor Ron Offen, is a **"poetry journal interested in publishing the whole spectrum of what is currently being produced by American poets. Occasionally offers a 'Reprise Series' in which an overlooked American poet is reexamined and presented. Among those who have been featured are Kenneth Patchen, Maxwell Bodenheim, Stephen Vincent Benet and Kenneth Fearing.** Also features a 'Mentor Series,' in which an established poet introduces a new, unestablished poet. Mentors have included Maxine Kumin, James Dickey, Lucille Clifton, Kenneth Koch, Stephen Dunn and Diane Wakoski. **Especially interested in experimental work and work by unestablished poets. Hope to provide all serious poets living in the US with a free subscription. For details on free subscription send SASE. No restriction on form, length, subject matter, style, purpose. Don't want cutsie, syrupy, sentimental, preachy religious or aggressively 'uplifting' verse. No aversion to form, rhyme."** Poets recently published include Sherman Alexie, James Broughton, Billy Collins, Judson Crews, Dave Etter, Paul Genega, Mekeel McBride and Todd Moore. As a sample the editor selected these lines from "Training Camp" by Neal Bowers:

> I am coaching my heart to quit,
> calling it "fat boy," "loser,"
> feeding it greasy fries
> and the lonely fast food of 3 a.m.,
> saying, "Stay down! Stay down!"
> like a manager who has money
> on the other fighter, . . .

FL, published 2-3 times a year, is 32-40 pgs., digest-sized, attractively printed and designed, saddle-stapled, featuring free verse that shows attention to craft with well-knowns and newcomers alongside each other. Press run is 1,200 with 200 subscribers of which 15 are libraries. Subscription: $12 ($15 foreign). **Sample postpaid: $5 ($6 foreign). "Submissions must be limited to 3 poems and are considered only between September 1 and May 31. Submissions sent at other times will be returned unread. Although a cover letter is not mandatory, we like them. We especially want to know if a poet is previously unpublished, as we like to work with new poets."** They will consider simultaneous submissions. Editor usually comments on rejections and tries to return submissions in 2 months. Send SASE for guidelines. Pays 1 copy plus subscription. Work published in *Free Lunch* has been included in *The Best American Poetry 1993*. The editor quotes Archibald MacLeish, " 'A poem should not mean/ But be.' I have become increasingly leery of the ego-centered lyric that revels in some past wrong, good-old-boy nostalgia, or unfocused ecstatic experience. Poetry is concerned primarily with language, rhythm and sound; fashions and trends are transitory and to be eschewed; perfecting one's work is often more important than publishing it."

‡FREEZER BURN MAGAZINE (I, IV-Science fiction/fantasy, horror), 10 Becket St. #3, Salem MA 01970, phone (508)745-7379, founded 1994, editors David G. Rogers and Teresa C. Cerrato, is a quarterly of science fiction, horror and fantasy short stories, poetry and artwork. **They want science fiction, horror and fantasy poetry. "Avoid epic length poems. Poems under 30 lines stand the best chance. Nothing pornographic."** They have recently published poetry by Nancy Bennett, James S. Dorr and Deidra Cox. As a sample we selected these lines from "New Arrivals on Antaur IV to Their Little Boy" by John Grey:

> Don't worry about playmates.
> I'm sure these green scaly things
> will come around eventually.
> When it comes
> to picking sides

you'll be the first one chosen.
Two eyes can focus on a fly ball
so much easier than five.

Freezer Burn is 36-48 pgs., 7 × 8½, photocopied and saddle-stapled with 70 lb. color cover, b&w art and ads from other publications. They receive "hundreds" of poems a year, accept approximately 65%. Press run is 100 for 10 subscribers, 60 shelf sales. Subscription: $12. **Sample postpaid: $3. Make checks payable to David G. Rogers. Submit 5 poems at a time. Previously published poems and simultaneous submissions OK. Cover letter strongly preferred. "Give us a sense of who you are."** Time between acceptance and publication is 3-9 months. **Always comments on rejections. Send SASE for guidelines. Reports in 3 weeks. Pays $20 (flat fee) and 1 copy. Acquires first or one-time rights.**

FRENCH BROAD PRESS (V), Dept. PM, The Asheville School, Asheville NC 28806, phone (704)255-7909, founded 1989, publishers Jessica Bayer and J.W. Bonner, publishes 20- to 40-page chapbooks. French Broad Press **does not accept unsolicited material**.

FRIENDS JOURNAL (II, IV-Specialized: Quakerism), 1501 Cherry St., Philadelphia PA 19102-1497, phone (215)241-7277, founded 1827 as *The Friend*, 1844 as *Friends Intelligencer*, 1955 as *Friends Journal*, appears monthly, magazine-sized, circulation 9,500. Subscription: $25/year. **"We seek poetry that resonates with Quakerism and Quaker concerns, such as peace, nonviolence and spiritual seeking." No multiple or simultaneous submissions. Pays 2 copies/poem.**

FROGMORE PAPERS; FROGMORE POETRY PRIZE (III), 42 Morehall Ave., Folkestone, Kent CT19 4EF England, founded 1983, poetry editor Jeremy Page, is a biannual literary magazine with emphasis on new poetry and short stories. **"Quality is generally the only criterion, although pressure of space means very long work (over 100 lines) is unlikely to be published."** They have published poetry by Geoffrey Holloway, Myra Schneider, Frances Wilson, Linda France, Pauline Stainer, R. Nikolas Macioci and John Latham. As a sample the editor selected these lines by Elizabeth Garrett:

I rock on my heels and test
My breath's spillage on the air.
I shall fold it with the weather
For safe keeping, in a camphor chest.

The magazine is 38 pgs., saddle-stapled with matte card cover, photocopied in photoreduced typescript. They accept 3% of the poetry received. Their press run is 300 with 120 subscriptions. Subscription: £6 ($12). **Sample postpaid: £1 ($3). (US payments should be made in cash, not check.) Submit 5-6 poems at a time. Considers simultaneous submissions. Editor rarely comments on rejections. Reports in 3-6 months. Pays 1 copy.** Staff reviews books of poetry in 2-3 sentences, single format. Send books for review consideration to Sophie Hannah, reviews editor, 127 Horton Rd., Manchester M14 7QD England. They also publish *Crabflower* pamphlets and have published collections by Geoffrey Holloway, Robert Etty, David Lightfoot and Sophie Hannah as well as several anthologies. Write for information about the annual Frogmore Poetry Prize. The editor says, "My advice to people starting to write poetry would be: Read as many recognized modern poets as you can and don't be afraid to experiment."

FROGPOND: QUARTERLY HAIKU JOURNAL; HAIKU SOCIETY OF AMERICA; HAIKU SOCIETY OF AMERICA AWARDS/CONTESTS (IV-Form, translation), % Japan Society, 333 E. 47th St., New York NY 10017, has been publishing *Frogpond* since 1978, now edited by Kenneth C. Leibman, PhD., and **submissions should go directly to him** at P.O. Box 767, Archer FL 32618-0767. *Frogpond* is a saddle-stapled quarterly of 48 pgs., 5½ × 8½, of haiku, senryu, sequences, linked poems (renga/renku), haibun, tanka and haiku translations. It also contains essays and articles, book reviews, some news of the Society, contests, awards, publications and other editorial matter—a dignified, handsome little magazine. Poets should be familiar with modern developments in English-language haiku as well as the tradition. **Haiku should be brief, fresh, using clear images and non-poetic language. Focus should be on a moment keenly perceived. Dr. Leibman hopes contributors will be familiar with contemporary haiku and senryu as presented in** *The Haiku Handbook* **(William J. Higginson) and** *The Haiku Anthology* **(Cor van den Heuvel, editor).** Recent contributors include Kenneth Tanemura, Lenard D. Moore, Michael Dylan Welch, Bruce Ross, Ion Codrescu and Patricia Neubauer. Considerable variety is possible, as these two examples from the magazine illustrate:

I climb the mountain with my eyes never ending snow
—Pamela A. Babuski

Sardine clouds—
the salty breath

> *of the fisherman*
> —Margaret Chula

Each issue has between 25 and 30 pages of poetry. They receive about 8,000 submissions/year and use about 400-450. The magazine goes to about 600 subscribers, of which 15 are libraries, as well as to over a dozen foreign countries. **Sample back issues postpaid: $10 (biannual issues of 1992, 1993); $5 (quarterly issues). Make checks payable to Haiku Society of America. They are flexible on submission format, but Dr. Leibman prefers 5-20 poems on 1 or 2, 8½×11 sheets. No single poems. No simultaneous submissions. Seasonal material should be submitted 3-4 months before seasonal issue is due; non-seasonal material read anytime. Reports within 6 weeks. They hope contributors will become HSA members, but it is not necessary, and all contributors receive a copy of the magazine in payment. Send SASE for Information Sheet on the HSA and submission guidelines.** Poetry reviews usually 1,000 words or less. Open to unsolicited reviews. Poets may also send books for review consideration. Four "best-of-issue" prizes are given "through a gift from the Museum of Haiku Literature, Tokyo." The Society also sponsors The Harold G. Henderson Haiku Award Contest, The Gerald Brady Senryu Award Contest, The Haiku Society of America Renku Contest, The Nicholas A. Virgilio Memorial Haiku Competition for High School Students and gives Merit Book Awards for books in the haiku field.

FRONTIERS: A JOURNAL OF WOMEN STUDIES (IV-Feminist), %Susan Armitage, Wilson 12, Washington State University, Pullman WA 99164-4007, founded 1975, is published 3 times a year and **uses poetry on feminist themes.** They have published work by Audré Lorde, Janice Mirikitani, Carol Wolfe Konek and Opal Palmer Adisa. The journal is 200-208 pgs., 6×9, flat-spined. Circulation 1,000. **Sample: $8. No simultaneous submissions. Reports in 3-5 months. Pays 2 copies.** "We are not currently publishing reviews of books, poetry, essays or otherwise."

THE FUDGE CAKE (I, IV-Children/teens), P.O. Box 197, Citrus Heights CA 95611-0197, founded 1994, editor/publisher Jancarl Campi, is a bimonthly children's newsletter designed to showcase the work of young writers. **They want poetry and short stories written by children ages 6-17. "Any form is fine. Open to any style or subject matter. Poetry: 30 lines or less. Short stories: 300-400 words."** As a sample we selected these lines from "The Sentry of the Highway" by Alice Martin:

> *The sentry of the highway*
> *Stands guard over the desert*
> *Mankind glides by*
> *Not pausing to fight.*

The Fudge Cake is 20 pgs., 5½×8½, desktop-published and saddle-stapled with colored paper cover and computer-generated graphics. Press run is 300 for 50 subscribers; 150 distributed free to libraries and bookstores. Subscription: $10 US, $12 Canada. **Sample postpaid: $3. Submit 1-4 poems at a time. "Submissions should be typed or neatly printed on 8½×11 white paper." Previously published poems OK. Cover letter required with SASE for notification. "Copies of poems and stories are not returned." Often comments on rejections or suggests revisions. Send SASE for guidelines. Reports in 2 months. Pays 1 copy. Authors retain all rights.** Holds bimonthly contests. Winners are published in the winners' section of the next edition. The editor adds, "We value the work of today's children and feel they need an outlet to express themselves."

FUGUE (I), Room 200, Brink Hall, University of Idaho, Moscow ID 83844-1102, website http://www.uidaho.edu/Letters_and_Science/Eng/Fugue, founded 1991, is a biannual literary digest of the University of Idaho. **They have "no limits" on type of poetry. "We're not interested in trite or quaint verse. Nothing self-indulgent or overly metaphoric to the point of being obscure."** They have published poetry by Ricardo Sanchez and Maria Theresa Maggi. As a sample the editor selected these lines from Maggi's "The Appointment":

> *. . . the conceptual warble of arms and legs*
> *caught me in cold waves*
> *at the isinglass window, slicing*
> *its heavy and not quite*
> *willing prisoners, my parents*
> *and all parents, in a tide*
> *of dulled longing and shadows.*

The editor says *Fugue* is 42 pgs., digest-sized, saddle-stapled. They receive approximately 400 poems/semester, use 5-10 poems/issue. Press run is 200 plus an electronic version on the World Wide Web. **Sample postpaid: $3. No previously published poems or simultaneous submissions. Reads submissions September 15 through April 15 only. Send SASE for guidelines. Reports in 1-3 months. Pays at least 1 copy. Buys first North American serial rights.** The editor says, "Proper manuscript format and submission etiquette is expected; submissions without proper SASE will not be read or held on file."

FULL-TIME DADS (IV-Specialized), P.O. Box 577, Cumberland ME 04021, phone (207)829-5260, e-mail fulltdad@aol.com, website http://www.parentsplace.com/fulltdad/index.html, founded 1991, editor/publisher Stephen Harris, is a bimonthly journal that seeks "to encourage and support men in their work as fathers." **They want material about fathers, fatherhood, and parenting from a father's perspective. As for poetry, "short is better. Not overly sentimental, but must come from the heart. Humor a plus. Absolutely no violence or anti-child, anti-male attitudes."** As a sample we selected these lines from "Becoming A Father" by Gary H. Stern:

> *You are crying at night.*
> *Soon you will stay up later than I do,*
> *and you will turn off the TV for me.*
> *While I read the morning paper you will ask questions,*
> *And I am supposed to know all the answers. . . .*

Full-Time Dads is 24 pgs., 8½ × 11, attractively designed, printed on white paper and saddle-stapled, including occasional graphics. They accept about 10 poetry submissions a year. Press run is 400 for 325 subscribers. Subscription: $26. **Sample postpaid: $5. Previously published poems and electronic submissions OK; no simultaneous submissions. Always comments on rejections. Send SASE for general writer's guidelines. Reports in 2 weeks. Pays 1 copy. Acquires one-time rights.** Reviews books, etc., that deal with fatherhood. Open to unsolicited reviews. Poets may also send related books for review consideration.

FURRY CHICLETS: A LAWPOETS CREATION (I, IV-Themes), 269 Nepal Rd., Ashland OR 97520, e-mail lawpoet@mind.net, founded 1990, editor Charles Carreon, an annual, wants **"poetry that cares enough about meaning to be brief, cares enough about being read to be interesting, and yet is utterly unconcerned with how it is classified. Poems: 1 page."** As a sample the editors selected these lines from "those who abide (cybernetic foreskin)" by Robert O'Neal Schultz:

> *he drives himself hard.*
> *those who abide drive him*
> *   to the breaking point.*
> *before he can hold the truth,*
> *know it is good,*
> *clocks ring midnight down.*
> *he is crushed under the hour.*
> *neurons misfire.*
> *his typewriter grunts.*

FC consists of approximately 75 photocopied pages stapled at the top to a blue matte backing. **Back issues available for $5. Make checks payable to Charles Carreon.** "*FC* tends to pick up the odd poems that other publications overlook. Too much angst, chaos or exuberance? We can help." **Editors often comment on submissions. They try to respond in 3 months.**

G.W. REVIEW (II), Marvin Center Box 20B, 800 21st St. NW, Washington DC 20052, phone (202)994-7288, founded 1980, editor Merrell K. Maschino, appears twice a year publishing **unconventional, solid work and some translations.** The magazine is published for distribution to the George Washington University community, the Washington, D.C. metropolitan area and an increasing number of national subscribers. They have recently published poetry by Maxine Claire, E. Ethelbert Miller and Linda Pastan. As a sample the editor selected these lines from "On Muranowska Street" by Myra Sklarew:

> *I have always loved particulars: the angels*
> *bearing a martyr's palm, the way the hair*
> *of the worshippers forms waves or*
> *filaments, the flowers embroidered*
> *on your sleeve.*

It is 64 pgs., perfect-bound with b&w illustration or photo on the cover. They receive about 3,300 poems a year and accept 20-30. Their annual press run averages 4,000 copies. Subscription: $5/year, $8/2 years. **Sample postpaid: $3. Submit 1-5 poems at a time. They consider simultaneous**

THE GEOGRAPHICAL INDEX, located before the Subject Index, can help you discover the publishers in your region. Publishers often favor poets (and work) from their own areas.

submissions but not previously published poems. Cover letter, including list of enclosures, recent publications and phone number, required. The staff does not read manuscripts from May 15 through August 15. Editor sometimes comments on rejections when the staff likes the work but thinks it needs to be revised. Reports in 1-3 months. Pays 5 copies.

GAIRM; GAIRM PUBLICATIONS (IV-Ethnic, foreign language), 29 Waterloo St., Glasgow G2 6BZ Scotland, phone/fax (0141)221-1971, editor Derick Thomson, founded 1952. *Gairm* is a quarterly which uses **modern/cosmopolitan and traditional/folk verse in Scottish Gaelic only.** It has published the work of all significant Scottish Gaelic poets, and much poetry translated from European languages. An anthology of such translations, ***European Poetry in Gaelic***, is available for £7.50 or $15. *Gairm* is 96 pgs., digest-sized, flat-spined with coated card cover. Circulation is 2,000. **Sample: $3.50. Submit 3-4 poems at a time. Reads submissions October 1 through July 31 only.** Staff reviews books of poetry in 500-700 words, single format; 100 words, multi-book format. Occasionally invites reviews. Send books for review consideration. **All of the publications of the press are in Scottish Gaelic.** 1995 publications include *A' Gabhail Ris* by Maoilios Caimbeul, *Meall Garbh/ Rugged Mountain* by Derick Thomson and *Fon T-Slige/Under the Shell* by Anne Frater. Catalog available.

‡GASLIGHT: TALES OF THE UNSANE (IV-Horror, science fiction/fantasy), P.O. Box 21, Cleveland MN 56017, founded 1992, editor Melissa Gish, appears 3 times/year. **All poetry must be related to the genres of horror, dark fantasy, or sci-fi and must be under 50 lines. No high fantasy, sword and sorcery, or gaming themes."** They have recently published poetry by Ruth Berman and Herb Kauderer. The editor says *Gaslight* is 60 pgs., digest-sized and saddle-stitched with colored paper cover and b&w art. They receive about 100 poems a year, accept approximately 30%. Press run is 300 for 275 subscribers. Single copy: $4; subscription: $10/year. **Sample postpaid: $2. Submit 3 poems at a time. No previously published poems or simultaneous submissions. Cover letter preferred. Reads submissions May 1 through September 1 only.** Time between acceptance and publication is 3-12 months. **Always comments on rejections. Send SASE for guidelines before submitting. Reports in 1 month. Pays up to 10¢/line and 1 copy. Buys first North American serial rights.** Includes brief reviews of genre material. Open to unsolicited reviews. Poets may also send related books for review consideration. The editors are organizing a new contest for female poets who have published less than 5 poems. Query (with SASE) for guidelines and dates.

GAZELLE PUBLICATIONS (V), 1906 Niles-Buchanan Rd., Niles MI 49120, phone (616)465-4004, e-mail wadeted@aol.com, website http://www.goshen.net/Gazelle/, founded 1976, editor Ted Wade, is a publisher for home schools and compatible markets including **books of verse for children but is not currently considering unsolicited manuscripts.**

GENERATOR; GENERATOR PRESS (V), 8139 Midland Rd., Mentor OH 44060, founded 1987, poetry editor John Byrum, is an annual magazine "devoted to the presentation of **all types of experimental poetry, focusing on language poetry and 'concrete' or visual poetic modes."** They have published poetry by Susan Smith Nash, Jessica Grim, Jane Reavill Ransom, Deborah Meadows, Liz Waldner and Carla Bertola. As a sample the editor selected these lines by W.B. Keckler:

> or char ds of
> st one or cha
> r ds of st one
> who looks through sad pylons
> roasted in belief. ripe river lotus. lotioned.
>   flax seed asphalt in a constant mash
> bee technology, ham radio, cream pink feet
>   crocodile colors in eyes in silky glass

Generator is magazine-sized, photocopied, side-stapled, using b&w graphics, with matte card cover. Press run is 200 copies for 25 subscribers of which 20 are libraries. **Sample postpaid: $8.** Generator Press also publishes the **Generator Press chapbook series. Approximately 2-4 new titles/year. They are currently not accepting unsolicited manuscripts for either the magazine or chapbook publication.** Together with Score (see listing in this section), Generator Press has published *CORE: A Symposium on Contemporary Visual Poetry*, described as "an international survey of the methods, opinions and work of over 75 contemporary visual poets" (photocopy version available for $25). The editor adds, "Worthwhile writers do not need advice and should not heed any but their own."

THE GENTLE SURVIVALIST (I, IV-Ethnic, nature, inspirational), Box 4004, St. George UT 84770, website http:/www.infowest.com/gentle/, founded 1991, editor/publisher Laura Martin-Bühler, publishes "11 issues over a 13-month period" (not published in February and August). *The Gentle Survivalist* is a newsletter of "harmony—timeless truths and wisdom balanced with scientific developments. For Native Americans and all those who believe in the Great Creator." **They want poetry that**

is "positive, inspirational, on survival of body and spirit, also man's interconnectedness with God and all His creations. Nothing sexually oriented, occult, negative or depressing." They have published poetry by Keith Moore and C.S. Churchman. As a sample the editor selected these lines from Moore's poem, "A Line in Motion":

> Little else pleases like
> Seven-o'clock downing sun
> On the faces and flanks of beasts,
> An hour of crisp clarity and
> The highest flattery in nature

TGS is 8 pgs. (two 11 × 17 sheets folded in half). The issues we have received warn readers about the dangers of aluminum and formaldehyde, discuss herbal medicine, and offer spice and food alternatives for those "stuck in a rut." They also offer money-saving tips and ideas on writing a personal history. "We print four poems average per issue." Press run is 200. Subscription: $20. **Sample postpaid: $2. Submit 4 poems at a time. Previously published poems and simultaneous submissions OK. Cover letter required; "just a note would be fine. I find noteless submissions too impersonal."** Time between acceptance and publication is 3-4 months. **Send SASE for guidelines. Reports within 2 months. Does not return poetry. Pays 1 copy.** Sponsors annual contest. Awards a 1-year subscription to the winner. Winner announced in December issue. Send SASE for details. The editor says, "To succeed, one must not seek supporters, but seek to know whom to support. *TGS* receives a great deal of poetry that is general in nature. We seeks poems of inspiration about God, Man and our interconnectedness with all living."

‡GEORGE & MERTIE'S PLACE: ROOMS WITH A VIEW (I, II), P.O. Box 10335, Spokane WA 99209-1335, founded 1995, editors George Thomas and Mertie Duncan, appears monthly except for January. *GMP* is "a Spokane home for wayward literature, a monthly journal of opinion and imagination or any realm between. **We are open to any form but our limited format prohibits long poetry. Social realism is just one interest."** They have recently published poetry by Tom Gribble, Iris Neal and Geoff Peterson. As a sample the editors selected these lines from "The Last Time I Heard from Sean" by Tom Hunley:

> I felt harried that morning & hurried,
> because I'd set my alarm for p.m.
> instead of a.m. & had to catch
> the 24 at 8:58.
> I reached College Street
> at 8:56, shook
> my wallet & heard a lack
> of jingling coins. . . .

GMP is a 4- to 8-page, 8½ × 11, "micromagazine", printed (unbound) on colored paper with b&w graphics. In addition to poetry it may contain essays, short short stories, letters, opinions and "tidbits with a twist." Press run is 50 for 20 subscribers, 20 shelf sales. Single copy: $1.50; subscription: $12/year. **Sample postpaid: $2. Submit 3 poems at a time. No previously published poems or simultaneous submissions. Cover letter preferred, "but not a long list of credits; we're looking for personal historical comments to personalize our content."** Time between acceptance and publication is 3 months. **Seldom comments on rejections. Reports in 1-2 months. Pays 1¢/word ($2 minimum) and 1 copy.** They say, "We think most poetry is sterile and not attached to the world where men and women struggle to survive in an ever more alienating environment. We have more than enough data—we need value now."

GEORGETOWN REVIEW (II), P.O. Box 6309, Southern Station, Hattiesburg MS 39406-6309, founded 1992 (first issue Spring 1993), is a biannual literary journal publishing fiction and poetry—no criticism or reviews. **They want "honest, quality work; not interested in tricks."** They have published poetry by Fred Chappell, John Tagliabue, William Greenway, Elton Glaser, X.J. Kennedy, Peter Wild, Michael Cadnum and Alan Feldman. *GR* is 100-120 pgs., 5½ × 8½, perfect-bound, with heavy stock cover with art. They receive about 1,000 submissions a year, "take maybe 10%." Press run is 1,000. Subscription: $10/year. **Sample postpaid: $5. Submit no more than 5 poems at a time, name and address on each page. No previously published poems; simultaneous submissions OK. Reads submissions September 1 through May 1 only. Poems are read by at least 3 readers. Sometimes comments on rejections. Reports in 2-4 months. Always sends prepublication galleys. Pays 2 copies. Acquires all rights. Returns rights provided "our name is mentioned in any reprint."** Sponsors annual poetry contest. $500 first prize; runners-up receive publication and subscription. Entry fee: $5 for the first poem, $2 each additional poem. Deadline: September 1. Winner and runners-up announced in fall issue each year.

GEORGIA JOURNAL (IV-Regional), P.O. Box 1604, Decatur GA 30031-1604, phone (404)377-4275, poetry editor Janice Moore. *Georgia Journal* is a bimonthly magazine covering the state of

Georgia. **They use poetry "from Georgia writers or poetry about Georgia. It should be suitable for the general reader."** They have published poems by former President Jimmy Carter, Stephen Corey, Blanche Farley and Adrienne Bond. As a sample Janice Moore selected these lines from "Next Door" by John Stone:

> *of a sudden*
> *with no fanfare*
> *but much finesse*
>
> *the gingko that*
> *has blazed all month*
> *has acquiesced*

Georgia Journal is 80 pgs., 8½ × 11, saddle-stapled and professionally printed on glossy paper with color cover. Circulation is 15,000. Recent issues feature accessible narrative and lyric free verse. Content is genuinely open and varied, from nature and personal poems to war and meditative verse. About 4 poems appear in each issue. **Sample: $3. Submit maximum of 3-4 poems, maximum length 30 lines. "A brief cover letter with previous publications is fine, but keep it brief." Send SASE for guidelines. Reports in 2-3 months. Pays copies. Acquires first rights.** Staff selects books by Georgia authors to review.

UNIVERSITY OF GEORGIA PRESS; CONTEMPORARY POETRY SERIES (II), 330 Research Dr., Suite B100, University of Georgia, Athens GA 30602-4901, phone (706)369-6140, press founded 1938, series founded 1980, series editor Bin Ramke, publishes four collections of poetry/year, **two of which are by poets who have not had a book published,** in paperback editions. They have published poetry by Martha Collins, Marjorie Welish, Arthur Vogelsang and C.D. Wright. As a sample the editor selected these lines from "The Sciences Sing a Lullabye" by Albert Goldbarth:

> *Physics says: go to sleep. Of course*
> *you're tired. Every atom in you*
> *has been dancing the shimmy in silver shoes*
> *nonstop from mitosis to now.*
> *Quit tapping your feet. They'll dance*
> *inside themselves without you. Go to sleep.*

That is from the book *Heaven and Earth: A Cosmology* for which Goldbarth won a National Book Critics Circle Award. **"Writers should query first for guidelines and submission periods. Please enclose SASE." There are no restrictions on the type of poetry submitted,** but "familiarity with our previously published books in the series may be helpful." **$10 submission fee required.** Manuscripts are *not* returned after the judging is completed. **Always sends prepublication galleys.**

THE GEORGIA REVIEW (II), The University of Georgia, Athens GA 30602-9009, phone (706)542-3481, founded 1947, editor Stanley W. Lindberg, associate editor Stephen Corey, assistant editor Janet Wondra. They have published poetry by Galway Kinnell, Yusef Komunyakaa, Pattiann Rogers, Gerald Stern, Lisel Mueller, Seamus Heaney, Linda Pastan, Albert Goldbarth, Rita Dove and Charles Simic. "Also have featured first-ever publications by many new voices over the years, but encourage all potential contributors to become familiar with past offerings before submitting." As a sample Stephen Corey selected these lines from "Still Life with Tropical Flowers" by Carolyn Miller:

> *But it is not still:*
> *. . . The shiny red plastic heart*
> *of the anthurium flaunts an erect, barbed*
> *organ; the protea's shattered edges are*
> *orange crystals growing toward the sun. Even the air*
> *around these hard, hostile flowers seems startled*
> *by the strangeness of the world.*

This distinguished quarterly is 200 pgs., 7 × 10, professionally printed, flat-spined with glossy card cover. They use 60-70 poems a year, less than one-half of one percent of those received. Circulation is 7,000. Subscription: $18/year. **Sample postpaid: $6. Submit 3-5 poems at a time. No simultaneous submissions. Rarely uses translations. No submissions accepted during June, July and August. Publishes theme issues occasionally. Reports in 1-3 months. Always sends prepublication galleys. Pays $3/line. Buys first North American serial rights.** Reviews books of poetry. "Our poetry reviews range from 500-word 'Book Briefs' on single volumes to 5,000-word essay reviews on multiple volumes." *The Georgia Review* is one of the best literary journals around. It respects its audience, edits intelligently and has won or been nominated for awards in competition with such slicks as *The Atlantic*, *The New Yorker* and *Esquire*. Work appearing here has also been included in the 1992 and 1995 volumes of *The Best American Poetry*. Needless to say, competition is extremely tough. All styles and forms are welcome, but response times can be slow during peak periods in the fall and late spring. Yet the editor says they would like to receive "the very best work from an even wider slate of poets."

GEPPO HAIKU WORKSHEET; YUKI TEIKEI HAIKU SOCIETY ANNUAL MEMBERS' ANTHOLOGY; KIYOSHI TOKUTOMI MEMORIAL HAIKU CONTEST (I, IV-Form, membership), 20711 Garden Place Court, Cupertino CA 95014, *Geppo* founded 1977, published by the Yuki Teikei Haiku Society, editor Jean Hale. *Geppo* is a bimonthly offset newsletter for members only. **Traditionally structured haiku are encouraged: "a poem illuminating the perception of nature (humans included) focused at a moment in time, of 17 syllables in 3 lines of 5, 7, and 5 syllables, and having one season word or *kigo.*"** *Geppo* also publishes poems from the society's workshops, retreats, readings, and contest, as well as short invited articles on haiku form and practice by established haiku poets. As a sample we selected the following haiku by Alice Benedict:

> cry of a night bird—
> paleness of the hazy moon
> sifts into the dunes

Membership in the Yuki Teikei Haiku Society is $15/year and includes 6 issues of *Geppo*. **Sample of *Geppo* available for SASE.** Press run is 200. The New *Annual Member's Anthology* contains haiku in traditional form submitted by members and selected by an editorial board. It is about 40 pgs., 5½×8½, and printed on heavy paper with card stock cover. Press run is about 300. Members who submit poems receive a copy for a mailing fee of $2; nonmembers can order it from the society for $5/copy. The Kiyoshi Tokutomi Memorial Haiku Contest is open to anyone. First prize is $100. Deadline: April 15. For guidelines, send SASE to Haiku Contest Coordinator, 782 Del Mar, Livermore CA 94550.

‡GERBIL: A QUEER CULTURE ZINE; GERBIL PRESS (II, IV-Gay/lesbian/bisexual), P.O. Box 10692, Rochester NY 14610, phone (716)262-3966, e-mail GerbilZine@aol.com, website http://www.multicom.org/gerbil/gerbil.htm, founded 1994, editors Tony Leuzzi and Brad Pease. *Gerbil* is a quarterly designed to provide "an open forum for lesbian/gay-identified writers and artists to express themselves and their work." **They seek poetry with gay/lesbian content but are not limited to that. They are "open to all forms as long as the poetic voice is honest and clear. We look for lively, personal material of literary merit. No angst, pointless experimentation or abstraction."** They have recently published poetry by Rane Arroyo, David Trinidad, Beth Bailey and Ken Pobo. As a sample the editors selected these lines from "Randy Poem" by Glenn Sheldon:

> At first six hands busy themselves
> unwinding time's new tonight; you say
> you've thrown caution to the wind,
> let it rain cats and dogs, let me be judged or
> not, *but then you flip on yourself, toss us
> out of the bed you borrowed.*

Gerbil is 28 pgs., about 7½×9½, offset and saddle-stitched with coated paper cover and b&w photos and graphics and lots of spot color inside. They receive about 500 poems a year, accept about 20. Press run is 1,500 for 100 subscribers, 700 shelf sales. Subscription: $10. **Sample postpaid: $3. Submit 3-5 poems at a time. No previously published poems. "Friendly" cover letter required. Disk submissions (for Mac) welcome.** Time between acceptance and publication is up to 1 year. **Always comments on rejections. Publishes theme issues occasionally. Reports in 1-3 months. Pays 2-3 copies. Acquires first rights.** Reviews books of poetry and other magazines. Open to unsolicited reviews. Poets may also send books for review consideration. Occasionally sponsors poetry contests; watch website or zine for details. **Gerbil Press also occasionally publishes chapbooks on a cooperative basis. They usually work with poets who first published in the magazine, and their publishing arrangements vary based on the writer and project.** As for the zine, they say, "If you're a beginning writer, don't be afraid to submit work! We publish a wide range of work of literary merit."

THE GETTYSBURG REVIEW (II), Gettysburg College, Gettysburg PA 17325, phone (717)337-6770, founded 1988, editor Peter Stitt, is a multidisciplinary literary quarterly considering **"well-written poems of all kinds."** They have recently published poetry by Rita Dove, Donald Hall, Susan Ludvigson, Pattiann Rogers, Charles Wright and Paul Zimmer. As a sample the editor selected these lines by Frankie Paino:

> If each bone of the body is holy
> it is because it gives shape to
> mortal love—bowl of the pelvis
> like a cradle, sickles of the
> hips like two moons, every angle
> open as the mouth to a kiss—

They accept 1-2% of submissions received. Press run is 4,500 for 2,700 subscriptions. **Sample postpaid: $7. Submit 3 poems at a time, with SASE. No previously published poems or simultaneous submissions. Cover letter preferred. Reads submissions September through May only. Publishes theme issues occasionally. Pays $2/line.** Essay-reviews are featured in each issue. Open to unsolicited essay-reviews. Poets may also send books for review consideration. Editor Peter Stitt, a leading literary critic and reviewer, has created a well-edited and -respected journal that features a tantalizing lineup of poems in all styles and forms. Competition is keen, and response times can be slow during heavy submission periods, especially in the late fall. Work appearing in *The Gettysburg Review* has been included in *The Best American Poetry* (1993, 1994 and 1995) and *Pushcart Prize* anthologies. As for the editor, Peter Stitt won the first PEN/Nora Magid Award for Editorial Excellence.

GINGER HILL (II), c/o English Dept., Room 314, Spotts World Cultures Building, Slippery Rock University, Slippery Rock PA 16057, founded 1963, is an annual literary magazine using **"academic poetry, with preference for excellent free verse, but all forms considered. 27-line limit. No greeting card verse, no sentimentality, no self-serving or didactic verse."** They have recently published poetry by Elizabeth R. Curry, B.Z. Niditch, Lyn Lifshin and Robert Cooperman. It is digest-sized, "varies in format and layout every year," perfect-bound, with 2,000 distributed free. **Submit 3 poems at a time in duplicate. No previously published poems. Submissions must be postmarked on or before December 1 of each year. Send SASE for guidelines. Pays 2 copies.** They say, "We choose about 5-10% of all submissions. Excellence is stressed."

THE GLASS CHERRY PRESS; THE GLASS CHERRY (II), 901 Europe Bay Rd., Ellison Bay WI 54210-9643, phone (414)854-9042, founded 1994, editor Judith Hirschmiller. *The Glass Cherry* is a quarterly literary magazine composed primarily of contemporary poetry. **They want "original poetry that is stunning; poetry that clings, leaves a scar. Any form, length, style or subject matter, except pornographic."** They have published poetry by Simon Perchik and James Liddy. As a sample the editor selected these lines from "Cold Wind" by Duane Locke:

> The child wrapped the wind
> Around his throat,
> As if the cold wind were a wool scarf.

The Glass Cherry is 40-60 pgs., 5½×8½, saddle-stapled with card stock cover. Each issue has a featured poet whose work comprises approximately 40% of the issue, and a photo of the featured poet appears on the back cover. They receive about 2,000 poems a year, accept less than 10%. Press run is 500 for 25 subscribers ("and growing"), 5% shelf sales. Single copy: $5; subscription: $15. **Sample postpaid: $6. Make checks payable to Judith Hirschmiller. Submit up to 5 poems at a time, name and address on each page. Previously published poems OK, "only if requested." No simultaneous submissions. Cover letter with brief bio required. "Please limit phone calls to situations which cannot be resolved by the written word." Seldom comments on rejections. Send SASE for guidelines and upcoming themes. Reports in 1 month. Pays 1 copy. Acquires first or one-time rights. Requests acknowledgment and notification from author when work is reprinted elsewhere. Re**views books of poetry. Open to unsolicited reviews. Poets may also send books for review consideration. They also sponsor contests related to specific themes or occasions. Rules vary, but reading fees are required. Winning poems are published on the back covers of special issues. The Glass Cherry Press also plans to publish 3 books of poetry a year. Recently published: *My Mother's Fire* by Lyn Lifshin. **Poems included in book-length mss need not be previously published. The editor reads book-length submissions (20-60 pgs.) from January through April only. Send SASE for guidelines. Reports in 1-4 months. Samples are available from the press for $10 and a SASE.** The editor says, "Writers are encouraged to read back issues of *The Glass Cherry* prior to submitting."

GLB PUBLISHERS (III, IV-Gay/lesbian/bisexual), P.O. Box 78212, San Francisco CA 94107-8212, phone (415)621-8307, founded 1990, associate editor John Hanley. "We are **cooperative publishers. Founded for gay, lesbian and bisexual writers. Authors share cost of printing and promotion but have much control over cover design, typefaces, general appearance."** They publish 2-4 paperbacks and 1-2 hardbacks/year. **They want "book-length collections from gay, lesbian or bisexual writers. Nothing antagonistic to gay, lesbian or bisexual life-styles."** They have published poetry by Robert Peters, Paul Genega and Thomas Cashet. **Previously published poems OK; no simultaneous submissions. Cover letter required.** "Author should explain intention for poems and expectations for sales of books." Often comments on rejections. **Replies to queries in 10 days, to mss in 1 month. Always sends prepublication galleys. Pays 15-25% royalties and 20 author's copies.** Check bookstores for samples.

GLOBAL TAPESTRY JOURNAL; BB BOOKS (II), Spring Bank, Longsight Rd., Copster Green, Blackburn, Lancs, BB1 9EU United Kingdom, founded 1963, poetry editor Dave Cunliffe. **"Experimental, avant-garde—specializing in exciting high-energy new writing. Mainly for a bohemian and counter-culture audience. Poetry in the Beat tradition. Don't want contrived, traditional, pompous and academic or pretentious mainstream."** Also considers sexually explicit material. In addition to the magazine, *Global Tapestry Journal*, BB Books publishes chapbooks. "We want honest, uncontrived writing, strong in form and content. We don't want 'weekend hobby verse' and poetry without energy." They have recently published poetry by David Tipton, Kenneth Patchen, Jeff Cloves and Joy Walsh. As a sample the editor selected these lines by Liza Kucharski:

> *the system doesn't fit where our*
> *body's going to*
> *we make square corners*
> *and walk around them in curves*

GTJ is 72 pgs., 9 × 6, saddle-stapled, typeset in a variety of mostly small sizes of type, rather crowded format, casual pasteup, with b&w drawings, photos, collages, display and classified ads, with a 2-color matte card cover. Circulation 1,150 with 450 subscribers of which 50 are libraries. Subscription: £8 sterling for 4 issues mailed seamail to USA. **Sample postpaid: $3. Considers previously published poems. Cover letter, with clear address, telephone number and short publishing history, required. Send SASE (or SAE and IRC) for guidelines. Responds "soon," has an 18-month backlog. Pays 1 copy.** Open to unsolicited reviews. Poets may also send books for review consideration. **BB Books publishes about 4 chapbooks of poetry/year. To submit for chapbook publication send 6 samples and cover letter giving publication credits. Pays 10% of press run in copies. Send SASE (SAE with IRCs if foreign) for catalog to buy samples.** David Cunliffe comments, "The United Kingdom has a limited number of magazines and small press ventures publishing poetry from unknowns. Many little mags are self-publishing cliques or small-time vanity operations. Simultaneous submissions and simultaneous publication are often resented. There is much readership crossover among the non-poet subscribers and they resent seeing the same work in many magazines over a short period. We typeset for a few United Kingdom mags and publishers and we see this in the setting jobs we do every week. Many of the editors circulate poet blacklists to help prevent this tendency from spreading."

DAVID R. GODINE, PUBLISHER (V), P.O. Box 9103, Lincoln MA 01773. They have recently published *New and Selected Poems* by Ron Padgett and *The Stonecutter's Hand* by Richard Tillinghast. They say, **"Our poetry program is completely filled through 1997, so we are not accepting any unsolicited materials at this time."**

GOLDEN ISIS MAGAZINE; AGE OF AQUARIUS; GOLDEN ISIS PRESS; POEM OF THE YEAR CONTEST (I, IV-Mystical/Occult), P.O. Box 525, Fort Covington NY 12937, founded 1980, editor Gerina Dunwich. "*Golden Isis* is a mystical literary magazine of poetry, magick, pagan/Egyptian artwork, Wiccan news, occult fiction, letters, book reviews and classified ads. **Occult, Egyptian, cosmic, euphonic and Goddess-inspired poems, mystical haiku and magickal chants are published. We are also interested in New Age spiritual poetry, astrological verses and poems dealing with peace, love and ecology. All styles considered; under 60 lines preferred. We do not want to see pornographic, Satanic, sexist or racist material.**" They have recently published poetry by Elisa Rowen, Blackheart, and Michael DeWitt. As a sample the editor selected these lines from "The Sabbat Circle" by Crystal Miller:

> *Listen, the song of the night calls*
> *A midnight ritual of magick*
> *Back to the womb of our Mother*
> *Reborn in the light of the Moon*

The magazine is 15-20 pgs., digest-sized, desktop-published, saddle-stapled with paper cover. International circulation is 5,000. Single copy: $3; subscription: $10/year. "No postal money orders, please." **Submit 1 poem/page, typed single-spaced, name and address on upper left corner and the number of lines on upper right corner. No limit on number of poems submitted. Previously published poems and simultaneous submissions OK. Occasionally comments on rejected material. Reports within 2-3 weeks. No payment or free copies. "We can no longer afford it." All rights revert to author upon publication.** Reviews books of poetry, "length varies." Open to unsolicited reviews. Poets may also send books for review consideration. *Age of Aquarius* is a digest-sized "psychedelic journal of 60s counter-culture in the 90s." Sample: $3. Circulation: 3,600. **Golden Isis Press currently accepts mss for chapbook publication. Send complete ms and $5 reading fee. "Please make checks payable to Golden Isis. We offer a small advance, 10 free copies of the published work, and 10% royalty on every copy sold for as long as the book remains in print." Sample chapbook** (*Circle of Shadows* by Gerina Dunwich): **$3.95.** The magazine sponsors an annual "Poem of the Year" contest that offers cash prizes. Entry fee: $1/poem. Deadline: December 1. No limit on number of poems entered. Poems should be up to 60 lines, any form, with author's name and address on upper left corner of each page. Free guidelines and contest rules for SASE. *Golden Isis* is a member of W.P.P.A. (Wiccan/Pagan Press Alliance).

GOOSE LANE EDITIONS (V, IV-Regional), 469 King St., Fredericton, New Brunswick E3B 1E5 Canada, phone (506)450-4251, fax (506)459-4991, acquisitions editor L. Boone, founded 1956, is a small press publishing Canadian fiction, poetry and literary history. **Writers should be advised that Goose Lane considers mss by Canadian poets only.** They receive approximately 400 mss/year, publish 10-15 books yearly, 2 of these being poetry collections. Writers recently published include John Thompson and Kwame Dawes. As a sample the editor selected these lines from "What Are You Thinking, My Sisters," published in *Dipped in Shadow* (1996) by Claire Harris:

> *O what are we dreaming my sisters my sisters*
> *what are we dreaming deep*
> *in our skins the bones of our*
> *thought have been curved by our cultures*
> *our flesh hung like curtains my sisters*
> *dear friends and we change like the continents*
> *what ever our saying*
> > *slow*
> > > *inexorable*
> *scattered*
> > *and hiding*
> > *deep   O our skins*

They are not currently reading submissions. "Call to inquire whether we are reading submissions after January 1997. Always sends prepublication galleys. Authors may receive royalty of up to 10% of retail sale price on all copies sold. Copies available to author at 40% discount.

GOSPEL PUBLISHING HOUSE (IV-Religious); PENTECOSTAL EVANGEL (V); LIVE (IV-Religious); TEEN LIFE (V); WOMAN'S TOUCH (V); TAKE FIVE; JUNIOR TRAILS (IV-Religious, children/teens), The General Council of the Assemblies of God, 1445 Boonville Ave., Springfield MO 65802-1894, phone (417)831-8000 ext. 4276, fax (417)862-7566. **Gospel Publishing House produces the Spirit of Praise Bulletin Series. Poems accepted for back cover of bulletins. For more information, call or write to Promotions.** *Pentecostal Evangel* is a weekly magazine containing **inspirational articles and news of the Assemblies of God for members of the Assemblies and other Pentecostal and charismatic Christians**, circulation 250,000. **"Presently, the** *Pentecostal Evangel* **is not accepting poetry."** *Live* is a weekly **for adults in Assemblies of God Sunday schools**, circulation 200,000. **Traditional free and blank verse, 12-20 lines. "Please do not send large numbers of poems at one time." Submit seasonal material 1 year in advance; do not mention Santa Claus, Halloween or Easter bunnies. Sample copy and writer's guidelines for 7×10 SAE and 2 first-class stamps. Letters without SASE will not be answered. Pays 25¢/line on acceptance. Buys first and/or second rights.** *Teen Life* is a weekly magazine of **Christian fiction and articles for teenagers, 12-17,** circulation 78,000. *Woman's Touch* is a bimonthly **inspirational magazine for women**, circulation 21,000. **However,** *Woman's Touch* **is currently not accepting poetry.** *Take Five* is a **youth devotional accepting poetry written by teens. Poetry should be typed, double-spaced, and must include the teen's name, complete address, church and age. Pays $15 upon acceptance.** *Junior Trails* is a weekly tabloid covering **religious fiction and biographical, historical and scientific articles with a spiritual emphasis for boys and girls ages 10-11,** circulation 65,000. **Buys 10-15 poems/year. Free verse and light verse. Submit seasonal/holiday material 15 months in advance. Simultaneous and previously published submissions OK. Sample copy and writer's guidelines for 9×12 SAE and 2 first-class stamps. Reports in 2-4 weeks. Pays 20¢/line on acceptance. Buys first and/or second rights.** "We like poems showing contemporary children positively facing today's world. **For all our publications, submit 1-2 poems at a time."**

GOTTA WRITE NETWORK LITMAG; MAREN PUBLICATIONS (I, IV), 612 Cobblestone Circle, Glenview IL 60025, phone/fax (847)296-7631, e-mail netera@aol.com, founded 1988, editor/publisher Denise Fleischer, features "contemporary poetry, articles, short stories and market listings. *GWN* now spans 40 states, Canada and England. Half of the magazine is devoted to science fiction and fantasy in a section called 'Sci-Fi Galleria.' **A short checklist of what I look for in all poems and stories would be: drawing the reader into the protagonist's life from the beginning; presenting a poem's message through powerful imagery and sensory details; and language that is fresh and dynamic. I prefer free verse. Would also like to receive experimental, multicultural, feminist, humor, contemporary and translations. The poetry we publish expresses today's society openly and honestly. Our contributors dive into the subjects where others turn away. They speak of moments before the bomb hit the Japanese, life in prison, anorexia, suicide attempts, and life in a nursing home."** She has recently published poetry by Mary Gallagher, Lyn Lifshin, Robin Bayne, Roxanne Sadovsky and Debbie McIntyre. As a sample the editor has selected the poem "Street Gaines" by Sharon Anderson:

> *Children tossing stones on bloodstained chalk*
> *drawings. . . . a new kind of hopscotch*
> *played in alleys of bullet-ridden tenements.*

The semiannual is 76 pgs., magazine-sized, desktop-published, saddle-stapled. "*Gotta Write Network* subscribers receive more than a magazine. In subscribing, they become part of a support group of both beginners and established poets. Readers are from all walks of life. I'm striving to give beginners a positive starting point (as well as promote the work of established writers and editors) and to encourage them to venture beyond rejection slips and writer's block. Publication can be a reality if you have determination and talent. There are over a thousand U.S. litmags waiting for submissions. So take your manuscripts out of your desk and submit them today!" Subscription: $12.75. **Sample postpaid: $5. Submit up to 5 poems at a time. Name and address on each page. No previously published poems or simultaneous submissions. Include a cover letter and SASE. Accepts poetry submissions via e-mail. "GWN's folder is posted in AOL's Writer's Club bulletin board." Reports in 2-4 months. Sometimes sends prepublication galleys. Pays 1 copy. Acquires first North American serial rights. Pays $5 for assigned by-mail interviews with established paperback authors and small press editors.** Maren Publications now offers a small press magazine distribution service." She adds, "Write the way you feel the words. Don't let others mold you into another poet's style. Poetry is about personal imagery that needs to be shared with others."

GRAFFITI OFF THE ASYLUM WALLS (IV-Humor, erotica, fetishes), P.O. Box 1653, Hot Springs AR 71902-1653, founded 1991, "curator" BrYan Westbrook, is an "illiterary journal published whenever I receive enough suitable material." He wants **"stuff you would be afraid to show your mother, priest and/or shrink; also anything that can make me laugh. No formal poetry; no pro-religious or animal rights poetry; nothing boring; no submissions by minors. We live in a time of crusading censors and I will not have my publication jeopardized by an offended parent."** They have published poetry by Cheryl Townsend, Belinda Subraman, harland ristau and Scott C. Holstad. As a sample the editor selected these lines from "Cheap Date" by Richard Cody:

> His hands played over her fine young body,
> seeking to unleash forbidden pleasures.
> "You better enjoy this . . ." he whispered.
> "You're going back to the graveyard tomorrow."

Press run and format vary. Subscription: $10 for 4 issues. **Sample postpaid: "$3 (checks made out to BrYan Westbrook) or will trade copies with other editors." Submit no more than 5 poems at a time. Previously published poems and simultaneous submissions OK. Cover letter and SASE required. "I do not want to just see a list of previous publications. I want to know who you are more than where you've been." Often comments on rejections. Reports "usually next day, rarely more than 3 months." No payment, but offers contributors unlimited copies at discount price of $2. Acquires one-time rights.** Staff will review "*anything* someone wants to send me. Length varies with how much I think needs to be said." BrYan Westbrook says, "Throughout history the preserved literature of any period has mainly been what the people of that time actually enjoyed. Scholars have placed these works upon lofty pedestals and declared them the only true art. It's time we stop trying to imitate what others have considered entertainment and get on with creating the art we really want for ourselves. *GOTAW* is my contribution to this endeavor."

GRAIN; SHORT GRAIN CONTEST (II), Box 1154, Regina, Saskatchewan S4P 3B4 Canada, phone (306)244-2828, fax (306)665-7707, e-mail grain@bailey 2.unibase.com, website http://www.sasknet.com/corporate/skwriter, founded 1971, is a literary quarterly. "*Grain* strives for artistic excellence and seeks material that is accessible as well as challenging to our readers. Ideally, a *Grain* poem **should be well-crafted, imaginatively stimulating, distinctly original." They want poetry with substance.** They have published poetry by Evelyn Lau and Jay Meek. The editor selected as a sample the opening of "The Children" by Patrick Lane:

> The children are singing.
> Hear them as they rise out of the deep hollows,
> the tangles of wildwood and wandering vines.
> They are lifting from the shadows
> where the black creek water flows
> over mud and stones. They have left behind
> the green whip of a snake
> thrown like a thin necklace into the trees . . .

Grain is digest-sized, professionally printed, 144 pgs. Circulation is 1,500, with 1,100 subscriptions of which 100 are libraries. They receive about 700 submissions of poetry/year, use 80-140 poems. Subscription: $19.95 (Canadian), $23.95 for US, $25.95 for other foreign destinations. **Sample: $6.95 plus IRC. Submit maximum of 8 poems, typed on 8½×11 paper, single-spaced, one side only. No previously published poems or simultaneous submissions. Cover letter required. Include "the number of poems submitted, address (with postal or zip code) and phone number. Submissions accepted by regular post only." Send SASE (or SAE and IRC) for guidelines or request via e-mail or website. Reports in 4-6 months. Pays $30+/poem plus 2 copies. Buys first North American serial rights.** Holds an annual Short Grain Contest. Entries are either prose poems (a lyric poem written as a prose paragraph or paragraphs in 500 words or less), dramatic monologues, or postcard stories (also 500 words or less). Prizes in each category, $500 first, $300 second, $200 third and honorable mentions. All winners and honorable mentions receive regular payment for publication in *Grain*. Entry fee of $20 allows up to two entries in the same category, and includes a one-year subscription. Additional entries are $5 each. Entries are normally accepted between September 1 and January 31. The poem "The Old Order/Night/The White Planet" by Lorna Crozier (published in

Grain) received a Gold Medal from the Canadian National Magazine Awards. The editor comments, "Only work of the highest literary quality is accepted. Read several back issues."

GRAND STREET (III), 131 Varick St., Room 906, New York NY 10013, is a quarterly magazine publishing poetry, fiction, nonfiction and art. **"We have no writer's guidelines, but publish the most original poetry we can find—encompassing quality writing from all schools."** They have published poetry by John Ashbery, Nicholas Christopher, Fanny Howe, Robert Kelly, August Kleinzahler, Hilda Morley, Michael Palmer and Charles Simic. **Sample postpaid: $15. Submit 5 poems at a time. Publishes theme issues. Reports in 2 months.** Work published in *Grand Street* has been included in the 1992, 1993, 1994 and 1995 volumes of *The Best American Poetry*.

GRASSLANDS REVIEW (I, II), P.O. Box 626, Berea OH 44017, founded 1989, editor Laura B. Kennelly, is a magazine **"to encourage beginning writers and to give creative writing students experience in editing fiction and poetry; using any type of poetry; shorter poems stand best chance."** They have recently published poetry by Steve Sneyd, Cher Holt-Fortin, Gerald Gullickson, Mary Winters, Laurie Calhoun and Wendy Battin. As a sample the editor selected these lines from "***" by Simon Perchik:

> —*it's easy to be lost in winter, the water*
> *almost ice, the sky almost ice, the sun*
> *almost ice and the boat listing*
> *changing color in total silence*
> *except the old iron keel*
> *somewhere at the bottom must think it hears*
> *birdsong and answers, keeps answering.*

GR is 80 pgs., digest-sized, professionally printed, photocopied, saddle-stapled with card cover. They accept 60-70 of 500 submissions received. Press run is 300. Subscription (2 issues): $8 for individuals, $20 institutions. **Sample postpaid: $3. Submit only during October and March, no more than 5 poems at a time. No previously published poems or simultaneous submissions. Short cover letter preferred. Send #10 SASE for response. Editor comments on submissions "sometimes." Reports in 10-12 weeks. Sometimes sends prepublication galleys. Pays 2 copies.**

GRAYWOLF PRESS (V), 2402 University Ave., Suite 203, Saint Paul MN 55114, phone (612)641-0077, founded 1975, poetry editor Fiona McCrae, **does not read unsolicited mss.** They have recently published poetry by Jane Kenyon, Vijay Seshadri, John Haines, Carl Phillips, Eamon Grennan, Tess Gallagher, Linda Gregg, Sophie Cabot Black and Dana Gioia. **Sometimes sends prepublication galleys. Pays 7½-10% royalties, 10 author's copies, advance negotiated.** Their book *The Misunderstanding of Nature*, by Sophie Cabot Black, received the Poetry Society of America's Norma Farber First Book Award. In conjunction with *Agni* magazine (see listing in this section), they also publish a new annual series introducing emerging poets, called "Take Three." Graywolf Press does not take direct submissions for this series.

‡THE GREEN HAT (I, II), P.O. Box 8023, Des Moines IA 50301, founded 1995, editor Guillaume Williams, is an annual designed to publish **"poets who have material that is difficult to market** due to length, theme, darkness, or any other reason." **They want "well-crafted poetry that leaves the reader's ability for interpretation. Strong forms are OK. No limit to length or subject, except no short poems (6 lines or less), no preaching, no cute poetry, and no rhymes (unless strict forms)."** The editor says *The Green Hat* is about 70 pgs., digest-sized, professionally printed and flat-spined with stock cover, no art or ads. Press run is 500-700. Single copy: $8. **Submit 3 poems at a time, double-spaced. Previously published poems and simultaneous submissions OK. Cover letter preferred. Seldom comments on rejections. Publishes theme issues. Send SASE for upcoming themes. Reports in 1-4 weeks. Sometimes sends prepublication galleys. Pays 1 copy, sometimes 2. Acquires first or one-time rights.** The best poem each issue (selected by panel) may be subtitled on the cover of the magazine and the author of the poem will receive $50. The editor says, "We like poetry that doesn't spell it out. Thought provoking material is desired and things rich in images. If you get material returned that an editor liked but didn't publish, we want to see it."

THE CHAPBOOK INDEX, located before the Geographical Index, lists those publishers who consider chapbook manuscripts. A chapbook, a small volume of work, is often a good middle step between magazine and book publication.

‡**GREEN HILLS LITERARY LANTERN (II)**, P.O. Box 375, Trenton MO 64683, editors Jack Smith and Ken Reger, poetry editor Joe Benevento, is the annual journal of the North Central Missouri Writer's Guild and is open to short fiction and poetry of "exceptional quality." **They want "the best poetry, in any style, preferably understandable. No haiku, limericks or anything over 3 pages."** They have recently published poetry by Jim Thomas, Peter Desy and Hugh Fox. As a sample the editor selected these lines from "Exotic Dancer" by Stephanie Dickinson:

> *The racks of elk branch over the men.*
> *Cigarettes glow in the eyes of prongtails,*
> *Javelina, moose. The mounted birds swirl like shawls:*
> *An African gray with shellacked beak, a macaw,*
> *A golden vulture. . . .*

Green Hills is 120 pgs., 5½ × 8½, neatly printed and perfect-bound with matte card cover. They receive work by more than 200 poets a year and publish 2-3 poems by about 20% of the poets submitting—less than 10% of all poetry received. Press run is 225. Subscription or **sample postpaid: $5.95. Submit 7-8 poems at a time. No previously published poems; simultaneous submissions OK but not preferred. Cover letter with list of publications preferred. Often comments on rejections. Send SASE for guidelines. Reports in 3 months. Always sends prepublication galleys. Pays 1-2 copies. Acquires one-time rights.** The editor says, "Read the best poetry and study the market."

GREEN MOUNTAINS REVIEW (II), Johnson State College, Johnson VT 05656, phone (802)635-2356 ext. 350, founded 1975, poetry editor Neil Shepard, appears twice a year and includes poetry (and other writing) by well-known authors and promising newcomers. **"We publish quality work; formal or free verse, realistic or surrealistic, narrative-based or language poetry."** They have published poetry by Galway Kinnell, Derek Walcott, Maxine Kumin, Stephen Dunn, David Mura, Larry Levis and David St. John. *GMR* is digest-sized, flat-spined, 150-200 pgs. Of 600 submissions they publish 30 authors. Press run is 1,500 for 200 subscribers of which 30 are libraries. Subscription: $12/year. **Sample postpaid: $7. Submit no more than 5 poems at a time. No simultaneous submissions. Reads submissions September 1 through May 15 only. Editor sometimes comments on rejection slip. Publishes theme issues. Send SASE for guidelines and upcoming themes. Reports in 2-3 months. Pays 1 copy plus 1-year subscription. Acquires first North American serial rights.** Send books for review consideration. Poetry published in *GMR* has been selected for inclusion in *The Best American Poetry 1994* and *Pushcart Prize* anthologies.

GREENHOUSE REVIEW PRESS (V), 3965 Bonny Doon Rd., Santa Cruz CA 95060, founded 1975, publishes a series of poetry chapbooks and broadsides. **"Unsolicited mss are not accepted."** Send SASE for catalog to buy samples.

GREEN'S MAGAZINE (II); CLOVER PRESS (V), P.O. Box 3236, Regina, Saskatchewan S4P 3H1 Canada, founded 1972, editor David Green. *Green's Magazine* is a literary quarterly with a balanced diet of short fiction and poetry. They publish **"free/blank verse examining emotions or situations." They do not want greeting card jingles or pale imitations of the masters.** They have recently published poetry by Mary Balazs, Lyn Lifshin, Ruth Moon Kempher, Geoff Stevens and Fr. Thomas Kretz. As a sample the editor selected these lines from "The Calvinist" by Kenneth C. Steven:

> *The heron is a presbyterian minister*
> *Standing gloomy in his long grey coat*
> *Looking at his own reflection in a Sabbath loch.*
>
> *Every now and again, pronouncing fire and brimstone*
> *He snatches at an unsuspecting trout*
> *And stands with a lump in his throat.*

The magazine is 100 pgs., digest-sized, typeset on buff stock with line drawings, matte card cover, saddle-stapled. Circulation is 300. Subscription: $12. **Sample postpaid: $4. Submit 4-6 poems at a time. The editor prefers typescript, complete originals. No simultaneous submissions. "If © used, poet must give permission to use and state clearly the work is unpublished."** Time between acceptance and publication is 3 months. **Comments are usually provided on rejected mss. Send SASE for guidelines. (IRCs for US queries and/or mss.) Reports in 2 months. Pays 2 copies. Acquires first North American serial rights.** Occasionally reviews books of poetry in "up to 150-200 words." Send books for review consideration. "Would-be contributors are urged to study the magazine first."

THE GREENSBORO REVIEW; GREENSBORO REVIEW LITERARY AWARDS; AMON LINER POETRY AWARD (II), English Dept., Room 134, McIver Bldg., University of North Carolina, Greensboro NC 27412, phone (910)334-5459, fax (910)339-3281, e-mail clarkj@fagan.uncg.edu, founded 1966, editor Jim Clark. *TGR* appears twice yearly and showcases well-made verse in all styles and forms, though shorter poems (under 50 lines) seem preferred. They have published poetry by Stephen Dobyns, Askold Melnyczuk, Steven Cramer and Gail Mazur. As a sample the poetry editor selected these lines from "Leaving Fargo" by Michael Evans:

> *. . . and you count your steps away*
> *through waves of red dust*
>
> *knowing how quickly cramps will come*
> *on the long ride home, her panicked eyes dark*
> *and searching for an open place to jump,*
> *ready to abandon every room she's ever known*
> *for anything as kind as disgrace.*

The digest-sized, flat-spined magazine, 120 pgs., colored matte cover, professional printing, uses about 25 pgs. of poetry in each issue, about 2.5% of the 2,000 submissions received each year. Circulation is 500 for 300 subscribers of which 100 are libraries. **Sample postpaid: $4. "Submissions (of no more than 5 poems) must arrive by September 15 to be considered for the Winter issue (acceptances in December) and February 15 to be considered for the Summer issue (acceptances in May). Manuscripts arriving after those dates will be held for consideration with the next issue." No simultaneous submissions. Cover letter not required but helpful. Include number of poems submitted. Reports in 2-4 months. Always sends prepublication galleys. Pays 3 copies. Acquires first North American serial rights.** They offer the Amon Liner Poetry Award for the best poem appearing in the magazine. They also sponsor an open competition for the Greensboro Review Literary Awards, $250 for both poetry and fiction each year. Deadline: September 15. Send SASE for guidelines.

‡GREY MATTER (II), P.O. Box 780, St. Petersburg FL 33731, first issue Fall 1996, is a quarterly. **"We seek thought-provoking poetry. We prefer poetry that is intense, incisive, and bursting with energy. Use rich metaphors! No hackneyed themes or doggerel."** They have recently published poetry by Peggy Des Autels. Asked for a sample, they say, "We believe that art is inimitable. To provide sample lines would be misleading, since nothing we ever accept will look like anything we've accepted before." *Grey Matter* is 64 pgs., professionally printed and saddle-stapled with original artwork and a heavy textured stock cover. They accept less than 5% of the poetry received. Press run is 500. Subscription: $12. **Sample postpaid: $4. Submit 4 poems at a time. No previously published poems; simultaneous submissions OK. Cover letter preferred.** Time between acceptance and publication is 6-12 months. **Poems are circulated to an editorial board. Send SASE for guidelines. Reports within 4 months. Sometimes sends prepublication galleys. Pays 1 copy. Acquires one-time rights.** They also include short reviews of other magazines. The reviews are staff-written and less than 200 words. The editor says, "We prefer multiple layered poetry with both fresh, provocative metaphors and philosophical depth. We believe that in words lies power. Art is the only way to combat the insanity and violence of a world gone amuck. If you care about something, then you should write about it!"

GROVE ATLANTIC (V), 841 Broadway, New York NY 10003. Grove Press and Atlantic Monthly Press merged in February 1993. **They currently do not accept unsolicited mss.**

GUERNICA EDITIONS INC.; ESSENTIAL POET SERIES, PROSE SERIES, DRAMA SE-RIES; INTERNATIONAL WRITERS (IV-Regional, translations, ethnic/nationality), P.O. Box 117, Toronto, Ontario M5S 2S6 Canada, founded 1978, poetry editor Antonio D'Alfonso. "We wish to bring together the **different and often divergent voices that exist in Canada and the U.S. We are interested in translations. We are mostly interested right now in poetry and essays on pluriculturalism.**" They have published work by Hélène Dorion, Yves Préfontaine and Suzanne Jacob (Quebec); Alda Merini and Maria Luisa Spaziani (Italy); Gianna Patriarca, Joseph Maviglia and Raymond Filip (Canada); and Maria Mazziotti Gillan, Rachel Guido de Vries and Peter Carravetta (USA). **Query with 1-2 pgs. of samples. Send SASE (Canadian stamps only) or SAE and IRCs for catalog.** The editor comments, "We are interested in promoting a pluricultural view of literature by bridging languages and cultures. Besides our specialization in international translation, we also focus on the work of Italian, Italian/Canadian and Italian/American writers."

GUILD PRESS; FULL CIRCLE SERIES (I, IV-Ethnic), Dept. PM, P.O. Box 22583, Robbinsdale MN 55422-0583, founded 1978, senior editor Leon Knight, **"the leading publisher of minority authors in Minnesota," wants poems to 40 lines max., nothing sexually graphic.** They have published poetry by George Clabon, Hazel Clayton Harrison and Nancy Ellen Williams (Big Mama). As a sample the editor selected these lines (poet unidentified):

> *I thought poetry*
> *made a difference*
> *. . .*
> *But photography*
> *doesn't alter sunsets:*

> *poetry does not*
> *restrain the wind*

The Full Circle Series are **annual anthologies of 35-50 poets. Individual collections are published "by invitation only" to poets who have appeared in the "open-invitation" anthologies. Send SASE for guidelines. Pays 1 copy.**

GULF COAST: A JOURNAL OF LITERATURE AND FINE ART (II), Dept. of English, University of Houston, Houston TX 77204-3012, founded 1986, contact Poetry Editors, is published twice a year in the winter and summer. While the journal features work by a number of established poets, editors are also interested in "providing a forum for new and emerging writers who are producing well-crafted work that takes risks, intensifying the accepted conventions for poetry—whether formally inventive or focused on a form's inherent strengths—with an acute awareness of its own language." Each issue includes poetry, fiction, essays, interviews, and color reproductions of work by Houston artists. They have recently published poetry by Kamala Das, Heather McHugh, Kevin Young, John Koethe and Amy Gerstler. As a sample we selected these lines from "Passion Fruit" by Daniel Bosch:

> Blueberries
>
> *Eye-blue,*
> *Staring from the bowl—*
> *Blind pupils,*
> *Hard nipples*
> *In cream cold*
> *As dew.*

The editor says *Gulf Coast* is 140 pgs., 6×9, offset, perfect-bound. Single copy: $7; subscription: $12 for 1 year, $22 for 2 years. **Submit up to 4 poems at a time. No previously published poems; simultaneous submissions OK. Cover letter with previous publications, "if any," and a brief bio required. Does not read submissions May through July. Send SASE for guidelines. Reports in 2-6 months. Pays copies. Returns rights upon publication.**

GULF STREAM MAGAZINE (II), English Dept., Florida International University, North Miami Campus, North Miami FL 33181, phone (305)940-5599, founded 1989, editor Lynne Barrett, associate editors Andrew Goldman and Maidel Barrett, is the biannual literary magazine associated with the creative writing program at FIU. They want **"poetry of any style and subject matter as long as it is of high literary quality."** They have published poetry by Gerald Costanzo, Naomi Shihab Nye, Jill Bialosky and Catherine Bowman. The handsome magazine is 90 pgs., digest-sized, flat-spined, printed on quality stock with glossy card cover. They accept less than 10% of poetry received. Press run is 750. Subscription: $7.50. **Sample postpaid: $4. Submit no more than 5 poems. No simultaneous submissions. Reads submissions September 15 through April 30 only. Editor comments on submissions "if we feel we can be helpful." Publishes theme issues. Send SASE for guidelines. Reports in 2-3 months. Pays 2 free subscriptions. Acquires first North American serial rights.**

GUT PUNCH PRESS (III), P.O. Box 105, Cabin John MD 20818, founded 1987, editor Derrick Hsu, publishes 1-2 paperbacks/year. **They want "free verse with an innovative edge and possibly a sense of humor. No language school or formal narrative style."** They have published poetry collections by Richard Peabody, Sunil Freeman and Rose Solari, and an anthology of African-American poetry edited by Alan Spears. No poems previously published in book form or simultaneous submissions. Time between acceptance and publication is 1 year. **Replies to mss (if invited) in 3 months. Pays royalties ("determined on an individual basis") and 50 author's copies. For sample books, send SASE for list and order form.** Most books are $7.95 postpaid.

‡HABERSHAM REVIEW (III, IV-Regional), P.O. Box 10, Demorest GA 30535, fax (706)776-2811, founded 1991, poetry editor Dr. Stephen R. Whited, is a biannual, general interest, regional journal published by Piedmont College. **"While we are interested in publishing regional poets, we will publish a good poem no matter where the poet lives. We accept all styles, and we prefer a range of subject matter."** They have recently published poetry by Judson Mitcham, R.T. Smith, Paul Ramsey, William Miller and Simon Perchik. As a sample we selected these lines from "When I Survey the Wondrous Cross" by David Bottoms:

> *A heavy odor of flowers*
> *rode the fans,*
> *and I sat with my bare feet dangling over a bench.*
> *Light from an open window fell across the face*
> *of a brown guitar, dust twisting like worms in that light,*
> *as the pail of water*
> *slid across the splintered floor.*

HR is about 100 pgs., 6¾×10, perfect-bound, offset, with color art and photographs on the cover, some b&w art and photographs inside, and ads. It receives 250 poems a year, accept 40. Press run is 1,000 for 300 subscribers of which 10% are libraries, 50-100 shelf sales. Subscription: $12. **Sample postpaid: $6. Make checks payable to Piedmont College. Submit up to 5 poems at a time. No previously published poems or simultaneous submissions. Cover letter preferred. Reads submissions September through May only.** Time between acceptance and publication is 1-2 years, "in some cases." Send SASE for guidelines. **Reports in 3-6 months. Pays 5 copies. Acquires first rights. Requires acknowledgment if reprinted elsewhere.** Staff reviews books of poetry in 200-500 words, single or multi-book format. Poets may send books for review consideration.

HAIGHT ASHBURY LITERARY JOURNAL (II, IV-Social issues, themes), 558 Joost Ave., San Francisco CA 94127, phone (415)221-2017, founded 1979-1980, editors Joanne Hotchkiss, Alice Rogoff and Will Walker, is a newsprint tabloid that appears 1-3 times a year. They use **"all forms and lengths, including haiku. Subject matter sometimes political, but open to all subjects. Poems of background—prison, minority experience—often published, as well as poems of protest and of Central America. Few rhymes."** They have published poetry by Joyce Odam, Jack Micheline, Edgar Silex, Lonnie Hull Dupont, Bill Shields and Ina Cumpiano. As a sample the editors selected these lines from "Pa—ece—" by Arlene Biala:

> When you lie awake nights straining
> to put her face in a place to define
> all those words, you pick up a pen
> and bleed her expression onto the page.

The tabloid has a photo of its featured poet on the cover, uses graphics, ads, 16 pgs., circulation 2,000-3,000. $35 for a lifetime subscription, which includes 3 back issues. $12 for 4-issue subscription. **Sample postpaid: $3. Make checks payable to Alice Rogoff. Submit up to 6 poems. Prefers poems under 2 pages long. "Please type one poem to a page, put name and address on every page and include SASE." No previously published poems. Each issue changes its theme and emphasis. Send SASE for guidelines and upcoming themes. Reports in 2-6 months. Pays 3 copies. Rights revert to author except for reprints in future anthologies.** An anthology of past issues, *This Far Together*, is available for $13. *HAL* received a 1995 American Literary Magazine Special Merit Award for Editorial Content.

HAIKU HEADLINES: A MONTHLY NEWSLETTER OF HAIKU AND SENRYU (IV-Form), 1347 W. 71st St., Los Angeles CA 90044-2505, phone (213)778-5337, founded 1988, editor/publisher Rengé/David Priebe. *HH*, "America's only monthly publication dedicated to the genre," uses **haiku and senryu only. The editor prefers the 5/7/5 syllabic discipline, but accepts irregular haiku and senryu which display pivotal imagery and contrast.** They have recently published haiku by Dorothy McLaughlin, Jean Calkins, Günther Klinge, George Knox and Mark Arvid White. Here are examples of haiku and senryu by Rengé:

> Low clouds gathering   Catching a moth
> over the ocean . . . sunbeams   and setting it free outdoors
> glare and disappear.   . . . gold dust in my hand.

The newsletter is 8 pgs., 8½ × 11, corner-stapled and punched for a three-ring binder. "Each issue has a different color graphic front page. The back page showcases a Featured Haiku Poet with a photo-portrait, biography, philosophy and six of the poet's own favorite haiku." *HH* publishes 80-90 haiku/senryu a month, including, on the average, work from 6 newcomers. They have 225 subscribers of which 3 are libraries. Single copy: $1.75 US, $2 Canada, $2.50 overseas; subscription: $21 US, $24 Canada, $30 overseas. **Haiku/senryu may be submitted with 12 maximum/single page. Unpublished submissions from subscribers will be considered first. Nonsubscriber submissions will be accepted only if space permits and SASE is included. Reports in about 2 months. Pays subscribers half price rebates for issues containing their work—credits applicable to subscription. Nonsubscribers are encouraged to prepay for issues containing their work.** Monthly Readers' Choice Awards: The Awards Kitty (average $50-75—contributions of postage stamps and money by the voters) is shared by the top three favorites. The "First Timer" with the most votes receives an Award of Special Recognition ($5). *HH* sponsors an annual contest (prizes $100, $75, $50) and publishes the results in a calendar book, *Timepieces: Haiku Week At-A-Glance*, which the selected contributors can purchase at half the market price. The contest is open to the public and accepts entries from April 1 through July 31. Write for details.

HALF TONES TO JUBILEE (II), English Dept., Pensacola Junior College, 1000 College Blvd., Pensacola FL 32504, phone (904)484-1418, founded 1986, faculty editor Walter Spara, is an annual literary journal featuring poetry and short fiction. They have published poetry by R.T. Smith, Sue Walker, Larry Rubin and Simon Perchik. As a sample we selected these lines from "Penpal Who Has Not Written" by Andrea Hollander Budy:

> You are the one I've never met who
> wrote so splendidly when I needed you

> *and I am the one who, after awhile, let*
> *years grow like a row of taverns*
> *between receiving and giving*
> *back. . . .*

HTTJ is 100 pgs., digest-sized, perfect-bound with matte card cover, professionally printed. They receive 1,000 submissions/year, use 50-60. Press run is 500. Subscription: $5. **Sample: $5. Submit 5 poems at a time. No previously published work or simultaneous submissions. SASE mandatory. Cover letter with bio and/or publication history preferred. Reads submissions August 1 through May 15 only. Reports in 2-3 months, faster when possible. Pays 1 copy. Acquires first rights.** *HTTJ* sponsors an annual poetry competition, $300 first prize, $200 second, $100 third. Entry fee: $2/poem. Send SASE for rules, deadlines. In addition to numerous awards from the Florida Press Association, *Half Tones to Jubilee* has received two national awards, a first place with merit from the American Scholastic Press Association, and first place, Southern division, literary magazine competition, Community College Humanities Association.

HAMMERS; DOUBLESTAR PRESS (III), 1718 Sherman, #203, Evanston IL 60201, founded 1989, editor Nat David. *Hammers*, "an end of millennium irregular poetry magazine," appears at least twice a year. Many of the poets they have published are from the Chicago area, although each issue also includes the work of poets from a variety of other geographical regions. **They want "honest, well-written poetry from the depths of the poet's universe and experience, which is cognizant of our interconnectedness."** They have published poetry by Duffy Childress, John Dickson, Lucy Anderton, Albert Huffstickler and T. Kilgore Splake. As a sample the editor selected these lines from "one breath" by Andy Nettles:

> *And I drift into a dream*
> *where it is my hand she's holding*
> *like a soft morning squash*
> *and I notice she is my mother then*
> *she is my daughter, and*
> *then she is my sister*
> *and I'm twisting sweet in her hand.*

Hammers is 88 pgs., 6⅞ × 8½, professionally printed and saddle-stapled with matte card cover. Single copy: $5; subscription: $15 for 4 issues. **Sample postpaid: $6. Submit 5-10 poems at a time. Editor seldom comments on submissions. Reports ASAP. Pays 1 copy.** In 1999, the editor intends to publish in book form *The Best of Hammers*.

HANDSHAKE EDITIONS (V); CASSETTE GAZETTE (II), Atelier A2, 83 rue de la Tombe Issoire, Paris, France 75014, phone 33-1-4327-1767, fax 33-1-4320-4195, e-mail jim_haynes_fm@msn.com, founded 1979. *Cassette Gazette* is an audiocassette issued "from time to time. We are interested in **poetry dealing with political/social issues and women/feminism themes."** Poets published include Ted Joans, Yianna Katsoulos, Judith Malina, Elaine Cohen, Amanda Hoover, Jayne Cortez, Roy Williamson and Mary Guggenheim. **Pays in copies. Handshake Editions does not accept unsolicited mss for book publication.** Jim Haynes, publisher, says, "I prefer to deal face to face."

HANGING LOOSE PRESS (V); HANGING LOOSE (I, II, IV-Teens/students), 231 Wyckoff St., Brooklyn NY 11217, founded 1966, poetry editors Robert Hershon, Dick Lourie, Mark Pawlak and Ron Schreiber. **The press does not accept unsolicited book mss, but welcomes work for the magazine,** which appears 3 times/year. The magazine has published poetry by Paul Violi, Donna Brook, Kimiko Hahn, Ron Overton, Jack Anderson and Frances Phillips. *Hanging Loose* is 96-120 pgs., flat-spined, offset on heavy stock with a 2-color glossy card cover. One section contains **poems by high-school-age poets. The editor says it "concentrates on the work of new writers." Sample postpaid: $8.50. Submit 4-6 "excellent, energetic" poems. No simultaneous submissions. "Would-be contributors should read the magazine first." Reports in 1-12 weeks. Pays small fee and 3 copies.** Poetry published in *Hanging Loose* has been included in the 1993, 1995 and 1996 volumes of *The Best American Poetry*.

‡**HANGMAN BOOKS (I)**, 2 May Rd., Rochester, Kent ME1 2HY England, founded 1982, editor Jack Ketch, publishes selected books of poetry on a cooperative basis. **They want "personal" poetry, "underground" writing, "none rhyming, none political, bla bla bla."** They have published poetry by Chris Broderick and Neil Sparkes. As a sample the editor selected these lines from "dead funny" by Billy Childish from his book, *Big Hart and Balls*:

> *and with every poem i rite*
> *my fame grows*
> *another nail in my coffin*
> *people feel embarrassed for me*
> *everything i utter becomes a cliche*

> *when oh when the people ask*
> *will billy shut up?*

When submitting a ms, send sufficient IRCs for return. Editor always sends prepublication galleys. 60% of press run belongs to poet.

‡HARBOUR PUBLISHING (IV-Regional), P.O. Box 219, Madeira Park, British Columbia V0N 2H0 Canada, founded 1972, president Howard White, publishes poetry collections by **"Canadian authors—citizens or permanent residents—with an emphasis on West Coast themes."** They have recently published collections by Patrick Lane, Tom Wayman, Anne Cameron and Peter Trower. They say their books are typically 80 pgs., perfect-bound. **Canadian poets should query first, with 15 sample poems and a cover letter with brief bio and publication credits. Previously published poems and simultaneous submissions OK. Seldom comments on rejections. Replies to queries and mss (if invited) in 3-6 months. Pays standard industry royalties.** They say, "If Canadian poets want to buy a Harbour catalog to get a better idea of the titles we publish, please send $3 and an 8½×11 SASE to our address with your request."

HARCOURT BRACE & COMPANY; HB CHILDREN'S BOOKS; GULLIVER BOOKS; BROWNDEER PRESS; JANE YOLEN BOOKS (V, IV-Children), 525 B St., Suite 1900, San Diego CA 92101, phone (619)699-6810. HB Children's Books, Gulliver Books, Browndeer Press and Jane Yolen Books publish hardback and trade paperback books for children. They have published books of children's poetry by Jane Yolen, Arnold Adoff, James Dickey, e.e. cummings, Lee Bennett Hopkins and Carl Sandburg. **Unsolicited material is no longer accepted.**

HARD ROW TO HOE; MISTY HILL PRESS (I, IV-Nature/rural/ecology), P.O. Box 541-I, Healdsburg CA 95448, phone (707)433-9786. *Hard Row to Hoe,* taken over from Seven Buffaloes Press in 1987, editor Joe E. Armstrong, is a "book review newsletter of literature from rural America with a section reserved for short stories (about 2,000 words) and **poetry featuring unpublished authors. The subject matter must apply to rural America including nature and environmental subjects. Poems of 30 lines or less given preference, but no arbitrary limit. No style limits. Do not want any subject matter not related to rural subjects."** As a sample the editor selected "Neighborly Exchanges" by Donna Kalchik:

> *Place across the road*
> *has a cow and a windmill*
> *we have apples*
> *and a dozen chickens.*
> *Meeting in the middle*
> *we agree on*
> *eggs for milk*
> *water for apple cider*

HRTH is 12 pgs., magazine-sized, side-stapled, appearing 3 times a year, 3 pgs. reserved for short stories and poetry. Press run is 300. Subscription: $7/year. **Sample postpaid: $2. Submit 3-4 poems at a time. No simultaneous submissions. Previously published poems OK only if published in local or university papers. Send SASE for guidelines. Editor comments on rejections "if I think the quality warrants." Pays 2 copies. Acquires one-time rights.** Reviews books of poetry in 600-700 words. Open to unsolicited reviews. Poets may also send books for review consideration. *Hard Row to Hoe* was selected by *Small Press Review* as one of the 10 best newsletters in the US.

HARP-STRINGS POETRY JOURNAL; EDNA ST. VINCENT MILLAY AWARD; ELIZA-BETH B. BROWNING SONNETS AWARD; ROBERT FROST BLANK VERSE AWARD (II); POETS' FORUM MAGAZINE (I), P.O. Box 640387, Beverly Hills FL 34464, founded 1989, editor Madelyn Eastlund. *Harp-Strings* appears 3 times/year. **They want poems of "14-80 lines, narratives, lyrics, ballads, sestinas, rondeau, redouble, blank verse. Nothing 'dashed off,' trite, broken prose masquerading as poetry."** Occasionally they have a profile and selection of poems from one featured poet. They have recently published poetry by Walter Griffin, Patricia Higginbotham, Norman Kraeft and June Owens. As a sample the editor selected these lines from "Legend" by Sharon Kourous:

> *There is no gold in winter*
> *there the colors are stark.*
> *The fragile thrust of lace,*
> *skeletoned where fold lies dark.*
> *Long fingers of shadow,*
> *earth's pulse below the heart.*

Harp-Strings is 40 pgs., digest-sized, saddle-stapled, professionally printed on quality colored matte stock with matte card cover. She accepts 5-10% of poems received. Press run is 125 for 75 subscribers. Subscription: $15. **Sample postpaid: $6. Submit 3-5 poems at a time. Cover letters that provide**

information about poet or poem ("a few interesting lines to use in contributor's notes") welcome.
Reports in 2-3 weeks. Pays 1 copy. Acquires one-time rights. "I am interested in seeing poems
that have won awards but have not been published." Sponsors 3 contests each year: Elizabeth B.
Browning Sonnets Award (Shakespearean or Petrarchan Sonnet, deadline March 15); Edna St. Vincent
Millay Award (narrative from 36 to 80 lines, deadline July 15); Robert Frost Blank Verse Award
(deadline November 15). Poems must be unpublished and not have won awards of more than $10.
Entry fee for each contest: $2/poem, $5/3 poems. Cash awards of $10-40 and publication. They also
publish the quarterly *Poets' Forum Magazine*, which includes poet profiles; instruction on poetry
forms and patterns; information on submitting work, organizations for poets and entering contests.
PFM also contains an 8-page supplement entitled "Just Poetry," which wants poems "no longer than
24 lines and no more than 45 characters across." Single copy: $4.50; subscription: $16. (For both
Harp-Strings and *Poets' Forum*, make checks payable to Madelyn Eastlund.) Submit 3-5 poems
at a time. No simultaneous submissions. "We are especially pleased to see poems in recognized
forms. Stanley Kunitz once said, 'Poetry today has become easier to write but harder to remember.'
We want poetry to remember, poetry that haunts, poetry the reader wants to read again and again."

**THE HARTLAND POETRY QUARTERLY; HARTLAND PRESS (II, IV-Children,
themes)**, Dept. PM, 168 Fremont, Romeo MI 48065, phone (810)752-5507, e-mail dtbock@aol.com,
founded 1989, contact David Bock. **"Prefer 24 lines or less; no style restrictions; no pornography—
none—nada—nil! Looking for serious poems by Viet Nam veterans and I mean serious—don't
send the one-and-only angry poem—I got that stuff coming out of my ears. Very, very open to
good children's poems written only by children under 15 for a special 'coming out' part of the
magazine."** They have published poetry by Loriann Zimmer, T. Kilgore Splake and Laurence W.
Thomas. Their quarterly is digest-sized, spine-stapled, 25-30 pgs. They accept about 15% of 300-500
poems received/year. Press run is 500 for 70 subscribers of which 15 are libraries, 300 shelf sales.
Subscription: $8. **Sample postpaid: $1. Submit 3 poems at a time. Include bio with submission.
Publishes theme issues occasionally. Reports in 8-10 weeks. Sometimes sends prepublication
galleys. Pays 2 copies.** Reviews books of poetry. **They publish 2 chapbooks/year of poets already
published in the quarterly. Pays 20 copies.** The editor says, "Write about what you have lived. Read,
read, write, write—repeat cycle 'till death. Support as many small publications as you can afford."

THE HARVARD ADVOCATE (IV-Specialized: university affiliation), Dept. PM, 21 South
St., Cambridge MA 02138, phone (617)495-0737, founded 1866, is a quarterly literary magazine,
circulation 4,000, that publishes **poetry, fiction and art only by those affiliated with Harvard
University; open to outside submissions of essays. Sample: $4. In submitting state your exact
relationship to Harvard. Does not pay.** Reviews books, including poetry.

HAUNTS (IV-Science fiction/fantasy, horror), Nightshade Publications, P.O. Box 8068, Cran-
ston RI 02926-0068, phone (401)781-9438, fax (401)943-0980, is a "literary quarterly geared to those
fans of the 'pulp' magazines of the 30s, 40s and 50s, with tales of **horror, the supernatural and the
bizarre. We are trying to reach those in the 18-35 age-group."** They use free verse, light verse
and traditional, about **12-16 poems a year.** Circulation: 2,750. **Sample: $4.95 plus $1 postage. Send
a maximum of 3 poems. Cover letter including "brief introduction of the writer and the work
submitted" required. Send SASE for guidelines. Pays $3/poem.**

HAWAII PACIFIC REVIEW (II), 1060 Bishop St., Honolulu HI 96813, founded 1986, editor
Elizabeth Fischel, is an annual literary journal "publishing quality poetry, short fiction and personal
essays from writers worldwide. **Our journal seeks to promote a world view that celebrates a variety
of cultural themes, beliefs, values and viewpoints. Although we do publish beginning poets on
occasion, we do not publish amateurish poetry. We wish to further the growth of artistic vision
and talent by encouraging sophisticated and innovative poetic and narrative techniques."** They
have published poetry by Robert Cooperman and Mary Kay Rummel. As a sample the editor selected
these lines from Rummel's "Stations of the Cross":

> As I type through rivers of pulp
> The desktop meets me at the waist.
> I am the vertical shaft.

> We finish our crosses. A poor place
> to hang a life whether with yeasted strips
> of bread, cotton pieces or a plastic pen-
> to hang so long and miss the resurrection.

HPR is 80-120 pgs., 6×9, professionally printed on quality paper, perfect-bound, with coated card
cover; each issue features original artwork. Mostly free verse, poems here tend to be insightful, informative and well-made with an emphasis on cultural diversity. They receive 800-1,000 poems, accept 30-
40. Press run is approximately 1,000 for 200 shelf sales. Single copy: $5-6. **Sample postpaid: $4. No**

previously published poems; simultaneous submissions OK. Cover letter with 5-line professional bio including prior publications required. Seldom comments on rejections. Send SASE for guidelines. Reports within 3 months. Pays 2 copies. Acquires first North American serial rights. The editor says, "We'd like to receive more experimental verse. Many of the poems we receive are more personal therapy than true art. Good poetry is eye-opening; it investigates the unfamiliar or reveals the spectacular in the ordinary. Good poetry does more than simply express the poet's feelings; it provides both insight and unexpected beauty."

HAYDEN'S FERRY REVIEW (II), Box 871502, Arizona State University, Tempe AZ 85287-1502, phone (602)965-1243, founded 1986, managing editor Salima Keegan, is a handsome literary magazine appearing twice a year. They have published poetry by Dennis Schmitz, Raymond Carver, Maura Stanton, Ai, and David St. John. *HFR* is 6×9, 120 pgs., flat-spined with glossy card cover. Press run is 1,000 for 100 subscribers of which 30 are libraries, 500 shelf sales. They accept about 3% of 5,000 submissions annually. Subscription: $10. **Sample postpaid: $6. "No specifications other than limit in number (6) and no simultaneous submissions. We would like a brief bio for contributor's note included." Submissions circulated to two poetry editors. Editor comments on submissions "often." Send SASE for guidelines. Reports in 8-10 weeks of deadlines. Deadlines: February 28 for Spring/Summer issue; September 30 for Fall/Winter. Sends contributors galley proofs. Pays 2 copies.**

HAYDEN'S FERRY
R E V I E W

Mimi Jensen, Ariana-Sophia Kartsonis,
Alexander S. Pushkin, Jewell Parker Rhodes, Jim Simmerman

Unless for a theme issue, the covers of *Hayden's Ferry Review* are not representative of the work inside. And, like most of the covers for the semiannual literary magazine, the artwork for their 17th issue was chosen for its artistic merit alone. Managing editor Salima Keegan says, "The painting captures a luminous quality that makes this image memorable. It's bright, colorful and striking—a real eye-catcher." Published by Student Publications at Arizona State University, *HFR* publishes about 35 pages of poetry in each issue, as well as fiction and art, and sees the magazine as a "vehicle for new and emerging poets and fiction writers to find an audience for their work." The cover artwork, an oil on canvas entitled "The First Time," is by San Francisco-based artist Mimi Jensen.

THE HEARTLANDS TODAY (II, IV-Regional, themes), Firelands College, 901 Rye Beach Rd., Huron OH 44839, phone (419)433-5560, fax (419)433-9696, founded 1990, editors Deb Benko and David Shevin. *The Heartlands Today* is an annual publication of the Firelands Writing Center at Firelands College. They want work by **Midwestern writers about the Midwest Heartlands, "writing and photography that is set in the Midwest today and deals revealingly and creatively with the issues we face—good writing and art that documents our lives." Each issue has a specific theme.** They have published poetry by Alberta Turner, David Baker, Chris Llewellyn and James Bertolino. The editors describe it as 160 pgs., 6×9, perfect-bound with 30-40 b&w photos. They accept 10-20% of the poetry received. Press run is 850-900. Single copy: $8.50. **Sample postpaid: $5. Submit up to 5 poems at a time. Simultaneous submissions OK. Cover letter with brief bio required. Reads submissions January 1 to July 1 only. Often comments on rejections. Send SASE for guidelines and upcoming themes. Reports in 2 months once reading period begins. Pays $10 and 2 copies. Buys first or second rights.** They also sponsor an annual chapbook contest. Send up to 10 poems ("a unified whole") with a $10 reading fee; writer receives a critique and a copy of the magazine. Winner receives $100 and publication in *The Heartlands Today*.

HEAVEN BONE MAGAZINE; HEAVEN BONE PRESS; HEAVEN BONE PRESS INTERNATIONAL CHAPBOOK COMPETITION (II, IV-Spiritual, nature/rural/ecology), P.O. Box 486, Chester NY 10918, phone (914)469-9018, e-mail 71340.520@compuserve.com, founded

1986, poetry editor Steve Hirsch, publishes poetry, fiction, essays and reviews with **"an emphasis on spiritual, metaphysical, esoteric and ecological concerns."** They have published poetry and fiction by Charles Bukowski, Marge Piercy, Kirpal Gordon, Diane di Prima and Michael McClure. As a sample the editor selected these lines from "Message of Hope" by G. Sutton Breiding:

> The screech owl's call
> Is vertical: a tower
> Rippling in the mist,
> A door of oracles
> Hung between night
> And dawn that opens
> And shuts softly
> In the white places
> Of sleep.

Heaven Bone is 96 pgs., magazine-sized, saddle-stapled, using b&w art, photos and ads, on recycled bond stock with glossy 4-color recycled card cover. Of 500-800 poems received they accept 18-30. They have a press run of 2,500. Subscription: $16.95. **Sample postpaid: $6. Submit 3-10 poems at a time. "I will not read submissions without SASEs."** Simultaneous submissions and previously **published poems OK, "if notified."** Time between acceptance and publication is 8 months. **Occasionally publishes theme issues. Send SASE for upcoming themes. Reports in 2 weeks to 6 months. Sometimes sends prepublication galleys. Pays 2 copies. Acquires first North American serial rights.** Reviews books of poetry. Open to unsolicited reviews. Poets may also send books for review consideration. The press sponsors the annual Heaven Bone Press International Chapbook Competition which awards $100 plus publication to an original, unpublished poetry ms of 30 pgs. or less. Requires $10 reading fee. Send SASE for guidelines. Editor advises, "Please be familiar with the magazine before sending mss. We receive too much religious verse. Break free of common 'poetic' limitations and speak freely with no contrivances. No forced end-line rhyming please. Channel the muse and music without being an obstacle to the poem."

‡HECATE'S LOOM MAGAZINE (IV-Psychic/occult), P.O. Box 5206, Station B, Victoria, British Columbia V8R 6N4 Canada, phone (604)478-0401, fax (604)478-9287, e-mail loom@islandnet.com, website http://www.hecate.com, founded 1986, publishing editor Yvonne Owens. *Hecate's Loom*, "Canada's International Pagan Magazine," is a quarterly "dedicated to the creative expression of Paganism. **We want poetry that relates directly to our subject matter: Paganism, Wicca, Goddess Worship and Shamanism."** They have recently published poetry by Robin Skelton, Margaret Blackwood and Kerry Slavens. The magazine is 60 pgs., 8½ × 11, neatly printed and saddle-stapled with coated paper cover with full-color art and b&w photos, graphics and ads inside. They receive about 200 poems a year, accept approximately 20%. Press run is 2,000 for 600 subscribers, 1,200 shelf sales. Single copy: $5.25; subscription: $18 Canadian, $24 US, $28 US overseas. **Sample postpaid: $7.25. Submit 2 poems at a time. Previously published poems "rarely" accepted; simultaneous submissions OK, if notified. Cover letter required.** Time between acceptance and publication is usually 8 months. **Seldom comments on rejections. Publishes theme issues. Send SASE (or SAE and IRC) for guidelines and upcoming themes. Information can also be obtained via e-mail or website. Reports in 2 months. Pays 1 copy. Acquires first rights.** Reviews related books of poetry in about 300 words, single format. Open to unsolicited reviews. Poets may also send books for review consideration.

HELICON NINE EDITIONS (V); MARIANNE MOORE POETRY PRIZE (II), 3607 Pennsylvania Ave., Kansas City MO 64111, phone (816)753-1090, founded 1977, editor Gloria Vando Hickok. Helicon Nine, formerly a literary magazine, now publishes winners of the annual Marianne Moore Poetry Prize. **The editor reads no unsolicited mss for Helicon Nine Editions.** They have published poetry by Joyce Carol Oates, Grace Paley, Ellen Gilchrist and James Dickey. As a sample the editor selected these lines from "The instruction of Clotilde" by Regina deCormier from her book, *Hoofbeats on the Door*:

> Dragging his reluctant shadow, François
> leaves the stone paved courtyard of his house
> at dawn. His cloak lifts with the wind
> of his step, the long toes of his shoes
> curl, and point to Heaven. Light is
> just beginning to spool off the face
> of Our Lady of Paris and a bronze cock
>
> is crowing goodbye. Evening will find him
> fifteen kilometres southeast of Paris,
> a blue rug over his knees.

The Marianne Moore Poetry Prize awards $1,000 and publication for an unpublished poetry ms of at least 50 pgs. **Manuscripts are not returned, and there is a $15 reading fee for all contest entries. Deadline for entry: May 1.** Send SASE for guidelines.

HELIKON PRESS (V), 120 W. 71st St., New York NY 10023, founded 1972, poetry editors Robin Prising and William Leo Coakley, **"tries to publish the best contemporary poetry in the tradition of English verse."** As a sample the editors selected these lines from *Selected Poems & Ballads* by Helen Adam:

> *Towers of atoms fall and rise*
> *Where gigantic Adam lies.*

"We read (and listen to) poetry and ask poets to build a collection around particular poems. We print fine editions illustrated by good artists. Unfortunately we cannot encourage submissions."

HELLAS: A JOURNAL OF POETRY AND THE HUMANITIES; THE HELLAS AWARD; THE ALDINE PRESS, LTD.; THE NEW CLASSICISTS (II, IV-Form), 304 S. Tyson Ave., Glenside PA 19038, phone (215)884-1086, founded 1988, editor Gerald Harnett. *Hellas* is a semiannual published by Aldine Press that wants poetry of **"any kind but especially poems in meter. We prize elegance and formality in verse, but specifically encourage poetry of the utmost boldness and innovation, so long as it is not willfully obscurantist; no ignorant, illiterate, meaningless free verse or political poems."** They have published poetry by Hadas, Steele, Moore, Butler, Kessler, Gioia and many others. As a sample we selected these lines from "Seed" by Charley Custer:

> *Within the hard damp dark, marooned*
> *in rot between dead root and weed*
> *through every bitter winter wound*
> *and solstice, is the seed.*

Hellas is 172 pgs., 6×9, flat-spined, offset, using b&w art. Press run is 1,000. Subscription: $14. **Sample postpaid: $8.75. Submit 3-5 poems at a time. They will not consider simultaneous submissions or previously published poems. Editor comments on rejections "happily if requested. If I don't understand it, I don't print it. On the other hand, we don't want obvious, easy, clichéd or sentimental verse."** Send SASE for guidelines. **Reports in 3-4 months. Pays 1 copy. Acquires first North American serial rights.** The *Hellas* Award ($200) is open to *Hellas* subscribers only and is awarded annually to the finest poem entered in the contest. Poems may be submitted to both *Hellas* and the contest simultaneously at any time throughout the year, but the annual deadline is December 31. Winner is published in spring issue of *Hellas*. Enclose SASE if submission is to be returned. The New Classicists is a Society of friends of the Aldine Press that publishes a quarterly newsletter for members. In addition to *Hellas*, the press publishes Lyrica, an ongoing series of metrical poetry chapbooks, in conjunction with sponsoring The Lycidas Award offered to the best chapbook of that series. They also plan to publish The New Classicists, "the only permanent and ongoing series of new books of metrical poetry." In addition, they sponsor the *Hellas* readings, held at various locations in Philadelphia, New York and elsewhere. Send SASE for guidelines. Their flyer says, **"*Hellas* is a lively and provocative assault on a century of modernist barbarism in the arts. A unique, Miltonic wedding of *paideia* and *poiesis*, engaging scholarship and original poetry, *Hellas* has become the forum of a remarkable new generation of poets, critics and theorists committed to the renovation of the art of our time . . . Meter is especially welcome, as well as rhymed and stanzaic verse. We judge a poem by its verbal artifice and its truth. Lines should not end arbitrarily, diction should be precise: We suggest that such principles can appear 'limiting' only to an impoverished imagination. To the contrary, we encourage any conceivable boldness and innovation, so long as it is executed with discipline and is not a masquerade for self-indulgent obscurantism. . . . We do not print poems about Nicaragua, whales or an author's body parts. We do specifically welcome submissions from newer authors."**

HEN'S TEETH (V), P.O. Box 855, Golden CO 80402-0855, founded 1988, editor Janice H. Mikesell, expects to publish a book every 2 years but **will not be open for submissions. "I publish material that I have written or co-edited only. Unsolicited material, unless accompanied by a SASE, will not be returned."** She has published *Women Houses & Homes: an anthology of prose, poetry and photography*, $8 plus $1 p&h, a 52-page, saddle-stapled book, cut with a roof-line top, professionally printed with a cover photograph of a "painted lady" Victorian house and now in its fifth printing. As a sample the editor selected these lines from her second book, *A Survivor's Manual: a book of poems*:

> *I ask you this*
> *remember me*
> *I used to be your wife*

> *be sure that I'll remember you*
> *as the man who*
> *stole my life*

That book is a 52-page, perfect-bound paperback with an arresting cover photo (also $8 plus $1 p&h), now in its second printing.

‡**THE HERB NETWORK (IV-Specialized)**, P.O. Box 12937, Albuquerque NM 87195, founded 1995, editor Kathleen O'Mara, is a quarterly newsletter of information for herbal enthusiasts. **They want poetry related to herbs or plants—real or folklore. Short poems to 250 words.** The newsletter is 12 pgs., 8½×11, neatly printed on plain white paper with a few b&w graphics. The issue we received included recipes, information about herbs used by midwives, an article focusing on lavender, book reviews and classified ads. Press run is 2,500 for 2,000 subscribers. Subscription: $20/year. **Sample postpaid: $5. Submit 1-3 poems at a time, typed double-spaced, one poem/page, name and address on each. Previously published poems and simultaneous submissions OK. Cover letter preferred. Send SASE for guidelines. Reports in 3-6 months. Sometimes sends prepublication galleys. Pays by barter, offering free advertisements or copies. Acquires first or one-time rights.**

HIGH PLAINS LITERARY REVIEW (III), 180 Adams St., Suite 250, Denver CO 80206, phone (303)320-6828, founded 1986, editor Robert O. Greer, associate poetry editor Ray Gonzalez, appears 3 times/year using **"high quality poetry, fiction, essays, book reviews and interviews."** The format is 135 pgs., 70 lb. paper, heavy cover stock. Subscription: $20. **Sample postpaid: $4. Pays $10/ published page for poetry.**

HIGH PLAINS PRESS (IV-Regional), P.O. Box 123, Glendo WY 82213, phone (307)735-4370, founded 1985, poetry editor Nancy Curtis, considers books of **poetry "specifically relating to Wyoming and the West, particularly poetry based on historical people/events or nature. We're mainly a publisher of historical nonfiction, but do publish one book of poetry every year."** They have published poetry by Peggy Simson Curry, Robert Roripaugh and Mary Alice Gunderson. As a sample she quoted these lines from the book *No Roof But Sky* by Jane Candia Coleman. The poem is "Geronimo photographed at Ft. Sill (1905)":

> Bring me the elusive images
> of my life, and I will smile for you—
> over and over—an exchange of illusions
> like the dying change into light.

Query first with 3 sample poems (from a 50-poem ms). Reports in 2 months, publication in 18-24 months. Always sends prepublication galleys. Pays 10% of sales. Buys first rights. Catalog available on request; sample books: $5. Their book, *The Red Drum: Poetry of the American West*, also by Jane C. Coleman, won the Wrangler Award for "accuracy and literary merit in portraying the West" in the poetry category from the National Cowboy Hall of Fame in 1995.

HIGH/COO PRESS; MAYFLY (IV-Form), 4634 Hale Dr., Decatur IL 62526, phone (217)877-2966, founded 1976, editors Randy and Shirley Brooks. High/Coo is a small press publishing nothing but **haiku in English.** "We publish haiku poemcards, minichapbooks, anthologies and a bibliography of haiku publications in addition to paperbacks and cloth editions and the magazine *Mayfly*, evoking emotions from contemporary experience. We are not interested in orientalism nor Japanese imitations." **They publish no poetry except haiku.** They have published haiku by Virgil Hutton, Lee Gurga and Wally Swist. As a sample the editors selected this haiku by Bill Pauly:

> country field—
> home run rolling
> past the headstones

Mayfly is 16 pgs., 3×5, professionally printed on high-quality stock, saddle-stapled, one haiku/page. It appears in January and August. They publish 32 of an estimated 1,800 submissions. Subscription: $8. **Sample postpaid: $4; or send $17 (Illinois residents add 7½% tax) for the *Midwest Haiku Anthology* which includes the work of 54 haiku poets.** A Macintosh computer disk of haiku-related stacks is available for $10 postpaid. **Submit no more than 5 haiku/issue. No simultaneous submissions or previously published poems. Send SASE for guidelines. Pays $5/poem; no copies.** High/Coo Press **considers mss "by invitation only."** Randy Brooks says, "Publishing poetry is a joyous work of love. We publish to share those moments of insight contained in evocative haiku. We aren't in it for fame, gain or name. We publish to serve an enthusiastic readership. **Please note that**

---

we have changed our policy of requiring contributors to be subscribers, so submissions are open from all writers."

HIGHLIGHTS FOR CHILDREN (IV-Children), 803 Church St., Honesdale PA 18431, founded 1946, appears every month using **poetry for children ages 2-12. They want "meaningful and/or fun poems accessible to children of all ages. Welcome light, humorous verse. Rarely publish a poem longer than 16 lines, most are shorter. No poetry that is unintelligible to children, poems containing sex, violence or unmitigated pessimism."** They have recently published poetry by Bobbi Katz, Myra Cohn Livingston, Eileen Spinelli and Carl Sandburg. As a sample the editor selected "Instead of Buying You a Valentine, I Looked Out My Kitchen Window" by Barbara Crooker:

> In February, trees are bare,
> snowflakes lace the frosted air
> and make the ground a clean white sheet
> of paper, scrawled by tiny feet
> of juncoes, titmice, chickadees,
> who write their names with practiced ease,
> and on a branch of snowy pine,
> two cardinals sit—a valentine.

It is generally 42 pgs., magazine-sized, full-color throughout. They purchase 6-10 of 300 submissions/ year. Press run is 3.3 million for approximately 2.8 million subscribers. Subscription: $26.04 (one year; reduced rates for multiple years). **Submit typed ms with very brief cover letter. Please indicate if simultaneous submission. Editor comments on submissions "occasionally, if ms has merit or author seems to have potential for our market." Reports "generally within 1 month." Always sends prepublication galleys. Payment: "money varies" plus 2 copies. Buys all rights.** The editor says, "We are always open to submissions of poetry not previously published. However, we purchase a very limited amount of such material. We may use the verse as 'filler,' or illustrate the verse with a full-page piece of art. Please note that we do not buy material from anyone under 16 years old."

HILLTOP PRESS (V, IV-Science fiction), 4 Nowell Place, Almondbury, Huddersfield, West York- shire HD5 8PB England, founded 1966, editor Steve Sneyd, publishes **"mainly science fiction poetry nowadays,"** but does not accept unsolicited mss. **Query (with SAE/IRC) with proposals for relevant projects.** Publications include *War of the Words*, humorous science fiction verse from the 30s to the 70s, including John Brunner, A. Vincent Clarke and C.S. Yond (John Christopher); *The Fantastic Muse*, reprinting a 1938 article and 1939 poem by science fiction giant Arthur C. Clarke; and *"AE—The Seven Wonders of the Universe"* by Mike Johnson. As a sample the editor selected these lines from "Spaceman" by Dave Calder:

> set free from the old migrations
> where will you go, exile, nomad
>
> i will wander the stars, which are perhaps
> the summer pasture of my species' time
>
> to fill myself with the fresh wonders
> i feel my memory is hungry for.

The ongoing Data Dump series, up to #13 at the end of 1995, gives bibliographical information on science fiction collections and anthologies. 4 pgs., A5 each. All but the latest issues are out of print, but photostat reprints can be supplied—#1-11 for $10 postpaid; #12, #13 for $1.50 postpaid each. (Checks payable to S. Sneyd. US orders: will also accept $ bills or small denomination, unused US stamps). "My advice for beginning poets is (a) persist—don't let any one editor discourage you. 'In poetry's house are many mansions,' what one publication hates another may love; (b) be prepared for the possibility of long delays between acceptance and appearance of work—the small press is mostly self-financed and part time, so don't expect it to be more efficient than commercial publishers; (c) *always* keep a copy of everything you send out, and put your name and address on *everything* you send."

HIPPOPOTAMUS PRESS (IV-Form); OUTPOSTS POETRY QUARTERLY; OUTPOSTS ANNUAL POETRY COMPETITION (II), 22 Whitewell Rd., Frome, Somerset BA11 4EL En- gland, phone/fax 01373-466653, *Outposts* founded 1943, Hippopotamus Press founded 1974, poetry editor Roland John, who explains, "*Outposts* **is a general poetry magazine that welcomes all work either from the recognized or the unknown poet. The Hippopotamus Press is specialized, with an affinity with Modernism. No Typewriter, Concrete, Surrealism."** They have published in *OPQ* poetry by John Heath-Stubbs, Peter Dale and Elizabeth Jennings. *Outposts* is 70-100 pgs., digest- sized, flat-spined, litho, in professionally set small type, using ads. Of 60,000 poems received he uses about 300. Press run is 3,000 for 2,800 subscribers of which 10% are libraries, 2% of circulation through shelf sales. Subscription: $32. **Sample postpaid: $8. Submit 5 poems at a time. "IRCs must**

accompany US submissions." **Simultaneous submissions and previously published poems OK. Cover letter required. Reports in 2 weeks plus post time. Sometimes sends prepublication galleys. Pays $8/poem plus 1 copy. Copyright remains with author.** Staff reviews books of poetry in 200 words for "Books Received" page. Also uses full essays up to 4,000 words. Send books for review consideration, attn. M. Pargitter. The magazine also holds an annual poetry competition. Hippopotamus Press publishes 6 books a year, averaging 80 pgs. **For book publication query with sample poems. Simultaneous submissions and previously published poems OK. Reports in 6 weeks. Pays 10% royalties plus 20 paper copies, 6 cloth. Send for book catalog to buy samples.**

HIRAM POETRY REVIEW (I, II), P.O. Box 162, Hiram OH 44234, founded 1967, poetry editor Hale Chatfield, is a semiannual with occasional special supplements. **"We favor new talent—and except for one issue in two years, read *only* unsolicited mss."** They are interested in **"all kinds of high quality poetry"** and have published poetry by Grace Butcher, David Citino, Michael Finley, Peter Wild, Jim Daniels, Peter Klappert and Harold Witt. As a sample the editor selected these lines from "Three Musics" by William Johnson:

> *Grief has a sound*
> *the way snow ticks*
> *and falls away*
> *from the metal light pole.*

There are 30 pgs. of poetry in the professionally printed, digest-sized, saddle-stapled magazine (glossy cover with b&w photo). Circulation is 400 for 300 subscriptions of which 150 are libraries. They receive about 7,500 submissions/year, use 50, have up to a 6-month backlog. Although most poems appearing here tend to be lyric and narrative free verse under 50 lines, exceptions occur (a few longer, sequence or formal works can be found in each issue). Single copy: $4; subscription: $8. **Sample: free! No simultaneous submissions. "Send 4-5 fresh, neat copies of your best poems." Reports in 2-6 months. Pays 2 copies plus year's subscription. Acquires first North American serial rights; returns rights upon publication.** Reviews books of poetry in single or multi-book format, no set length. Send books for review consideration.

HOLIDAY HOUSE, INC. (V, IV-Children), Dept. PM, 425 Madison Ave., New York NY 10017, phone (212)688-0085, founded 1936, editor-in-chief Regina Griffin, is a trade children's book house. They have published hardcover books for children by Myra Cohn Livingston. They publish 3 books a year averaging 32 pages. **However, they are currently not accepting poetry submissions.**

THE HOLLINS CRITIC (II), P.O. Box 9538, Hollins College, Roanoke VA 24020-1538, phone (703)362-6317, fax (540)362-6642, founded 1964, editor John Rees Moore, appears 5 times yearly, publishing critical essays, poetry and book reviews. **They use a few short poems in each issue, interesting in form, content or both.** They have recently published poetry by Susan E. Brown, E.F. Wersalitz, Devon Miller Duggar and Jennifer Bates. As a sample the editor selected these lines from "My Tarzan" by Susann Bick:

> *All those serene Madonna and Child paintings*
> *   in the art books were wrong.*
> *Slowly, slowly, like spring*
> *   creeping into chill, grey Ohio,*
> *We became acquainted*
> *   during the long nights*
> *(when once you were awake for fourteen straight*
> *   hours).*
> *I learned to write while holding you to my*
> *   breast with one hand.*
> *Outside: ice and withered red dahlias.*
>
> *Now, in another snapshot, you are four.*
> *   Naked in the locust tree,*
> *You are my Tarzan.*

The Hollins Critic is 20 pgs., magazine-sized. Circulation is 500. **Sample: $1.50. Submit up to 5 poems, none over 35 lines, must be typewritten. Cover letter preferred. No submissions via fax. Reports in 6 weeks (slower in the summer). Pays $25/poem plus 5 copies.** Open to unsolicited reviews. Poets may also send books for review consideration. Traditionally, verse here has been open as to form and style with poems that please the mind, eye and senses. As the magazine is occasionally overstocked, your best bet is to send for a sample copy and inquire as to whether editors are reading unsolicited submissions.

HENRY HOLT & COMPANY (V), 115 W. 18th St., New York NY 10011, **accepts no unsolicited poetry.**

HOME PLANET NEWS (II), Dept. PM, P.O. Box 415, Stuyvesant Station, New York NY 10009, phone (718)769-2854, founded 1979, editors Enid Dame and Donald Lev, is a tabloid (newsprint) journal, appearing 3-4 times a year presenting a "lively, eclectic and comprehensive view of contemporary literature." **They want "honest, well-crafted poems, open or closed form, on any subject, but we will not publish any work which seems to us to be racist, sexist, ageist, anti-semitic or has undue emphasis on violence. Poems under 30 lines stand a better chance. We lean somewhat toward poetry with urban sensibility but are not rigid about this. Do not sacrifice craft for message."** They have published poetry by Alicia Ostriker, Tuli Kupferberg, Denise Duhamel, Will Inman, Andrew Glaze, Robert Peters, Carl Solomon and Rose Romano. As a sample the editors selected these lines from "Entered Collage" by Lorraine Schein:

> I am the ephemerist
> collecting myself, I disperse my thoughts.
> The wind blows this paper
> Out of my hand

They use approximately 13 full 11×16 pgs. of poetry in each 24-page issue. Circulation is 1,000 for 400 subscribers of which 8 are libraries. Of 1,200 submissions/year, they use about 50-60. Publication could take one year from acceptance. Subscription: $8/year. **Sample postpaid: $3. Submit 3-5 poems, typed double-spaced, with SASE. No previously published poems or simultaneous submissions. Cover letter welcome. "We now only read poetry manuscripts between February 1 and May 31." Reports within 4 months. Pays 3 copies and year's subscription. All rights revert to author.** Reviews books of poetry. Open to unsolicited reviews. Poets may also send books for review consideration. "We cosponsor 'Day of the Poet,' a poetry festival and contest which takes place each October in Ulster County, New York." Poetry by Daniel Berrigan published in *Home Planet News* appeared in a *Pushcart Prize* anthology.

‡**HOME TIMES (I)**, P.O. Box 16096, West Palm Beach FL 33416, phone (561)439-3509, founded 1988, editor/publisher Dennis Lombard, is a monthly "independent, conservative, pro-Christian, pro-Jewish," 20-page newsprint tabloid of local, national and world news and views, including information in the areas of home and family, arts and entertainment, and religion. **They want poetry that is "humorous or spiritual—not 'religious'; for a general audience."** As a sample we selected these lines from "Heritage" by Paul Swope:

> And, overwhelmingly, I realize
> That, trying to be different,
> I have become my father
> Then, relieved, I remember
> That as he grew older,
> he seemed quite intelligent
> And before he died
> We agreed on almost everything
> My son is a different story . . .

The editor says they receive about 200 poems a year, accept 2-3%. Press run is 5,000. Single copy: $1; subscription: $12/year. **Sample: $3. Submit 3 poems at a time. Previously published poems and simultaneous submissions OK.** Time between acceptance and publication is 1-6 months. **Sometimes comments on rejections. Send SASE for guidelines. Reports in 2-4 weeks. Pays $5 "generally"; a 6-month subscription, if requested; and 3 copies. Buys one-time rights.** The editor says, "*Home Times* is very different! Please read guidelines and sample issues."

‡**HOOTENANNY (II)**, 62 N. Seventh St. 3-R, Brooklyn NY 11211, e-mail drkeith@mailbox.syr. edu, website http://web.syr.edu/~drkeith/hootenanny.html, founded 1994, editors David Keith and Ken Weathersby, appears twice a year. "Our contributors tend to be artists and writers. The content reflects this. It's a fine arts/literary jambalaya, or hootenanny. **We have a penchant for prose poems and short short stories (one- to two-pagers). We want poems with strong voice—ones that look good on the page and sound good to say out loud."** They have recently published poetry by Lawson Fusao Inada, W.T. Pfefferle and David Breeden. As a sample the editors selected these lines from "Baudelaire's Ablutions" by Roger Fanning:

> Poetry jolts awake the lucky few. I praise
> the mirror gazing mighty poet Baudelaire,
> my hero, a fop full of compulsions,
> a perfectionist to whom a single
> tweezered nosehair brought tears of joy.

The editor says *Hootenanny* is a limited edition, handmade collectible—about 100 pgs., $8\frac{1}{2} \times 11$, with hand binding and handmade artwork—"very visual, very tactile." They receive 50-100 poems a year, accept 5-10%. Press run is 200 for 5 subscribers, 50-60 shelf sales. "In spite of our limited circulation, we distribute nationwide—in bookstores in New York City, Boston, Pittsburgh, Syracuse and Dallas—and have a distributor in Paris, France. Subscription: $25. **Sample postpaid: $10. Make checks** payable to David Keith. Submit 3-5 poems at a time "by e-mail in plain ASCII format or as a Word 6.0 document for Windows; or by snail mail on a good clean copy. 3.5 floppy also desirable—MS Word 6.0. Note: Submissions may be used for either the print or the web version." No previously published poems; simultaneous submissions OK. Cover letter preferred. Poems are circulated to an editorial board. "A new group of readers is assembled for each issue. Two to five readers read all submissions. Editors make final choice. Seldom comments on rejections. Publishes theme issues. Send SASE for guidelines and upcoming themes or obtain information via website. Reports in 4-6 weeks. Pays 1 copy. Acquires first North American serial rights. David Keith adds, "A hootenanny is a festival, a hoedown. Everyone who shows up picks up an object and makes some noise."

‡HOPEWELL REVIEW (IV-Regional), 47 S. Pennsylvania St., Suite 701, Indianapolis IN 46204-3622, is an annual publication using poems and short stories **by residents of Indiana. "Writers should send no more than three poems and/or one short story with a manuscript-sized SASE and a brief biography. Poems of 40 lines or less will stand best chance of publication."** Simultaneous submissions OK if so noted. **Deadline: March 15. Send SASE for guidelines. Pays $35 for each accepted poem.** One poem will be selected by a nationally recognized juror, for a $500 cash award of excellence.

HOPSCOTCH: THE MAGAZINE FOR GIRLS; BOYS' QUEST (IV-Children), P.O. Box 164, Bluffton OH 45817-0164, phone (419)358-4610, founded 1989, editor Marilyn B. Edwards. *Hopscotch* is a bimonthly magazine for **girls 6-12. "No length restrictions. In need of short traditional poems for various holidays and seasons. (Limit to 21 lines if possible.) However, we do not want Halloween-related material. Nothing abstract, experimental."** They have published poetry by Lois Grambling, Judy Nichols, Leila Dornak, Judith Harkham Semas and Maggie McGee. As a sample we selected these lines from "First Frost" by Glenn DeTurk:

> *The sugary white glaze*
> *Glistens in the morning sun.*
> *The whole world seems to be waiting,*
> *For a new season has begun.*

The editor describes *Hopscotch* as "full-color cover, 50 pgs. of 2-color inside, 7×9, saddle-stapled." They use about 30-35 of some 2,000 poems received/year. Press run is 11,000 for 10,000 subscribers of which 7,000 are libraries, 200 to inquiring schools and libraries. Subscription: $15. **Sample postpaid: $3. Submit 3-6 poems/submission. Cover letter preferred; include experience and where published. Publishes theme issues. Send SASE for upcoming themes.** Themes include Dogs (October/November 1996), Post Office (December/January 1997), "Sight"-Seeing-Eyes (February/March 1997), Birds (April/May 1997), The West (June/July 1997), Sports (August/September 1997), Teeth (October/November 1997) and Cooking (December/January 1998). **Reports in 2-4 weeks. Pays $10-40. Buys first American serial rights.** The few poems in this children's magazine occasionally address the audience, challenging young girls to pursue their dreams. To see how, order a sample copy (or check one out at the library) because it is too easy for poets who write children's verse to forget that each magazine targets a specific audience . . . in a specific way. They also publish *Boys' Quest*, a bimonthly magazine for **boys 6-13.** Similar in format to *Hopscotch*, the magazine premiered in June/July 1995. **Upcoming themes include: Birds (October/November 1996), Dogs (December/January 1997), Cowboys (February/March 1997) and Cars (April/May 1997). Send SASE for details.**

HOUGHTON MIFFLIN CO. (V), 222 Berkeley St., Boston MA 02116, founded 1850, poetry editor Peter Davison. Houghton Mifflin is a high-prestige trade publisher that puts out both hardcover and paperback books, but **poetry submission is by invitation only and they are not seeking new poets at present.** They have published poetry books by Donald Hall, May Swenson, Rodney Jones, Geoffrey Hill, Galway Kinnell, Thomas Lux, Erica Funkhouser, William Matthews, Margaret Atwood and Andrew Hudgins. **Always sends prepublication galleys. Authors are paid 10% royalties on hardcover books, 6% royalties on paperbacks (minimum), $1,000 advance and 12 author's copies.**

‡HOUSE OF ANANSI PRESS (II, IV-Regional), 1800 Steeles Ave. W., Concord, Ontario L4K 2P3 Canada, phone (905)660-0611, fax (905)660-0676, e-mail anansi@irwin-pub.com, website http://www.irwin-pub.com/irwin/anansi, founded 1967, publisher Michael Davis, editor Martha Sharpe, publishes literary fiction and poetry **by Canadian writers. "We seek to balance the list between well-known and emerging writers, with an interest in writing by Canadians of all backgrounds. We publish Canadian poetry only, and poets must have a substantial publication record—if not in books, then definitely in journals and magazines of repute. No children's poetry and no poetry by previously unpublished poets."** They have published *Two Minutes for Holding* by Douglas Burnet Smith and *More Watery Still* by Patricia Young. As a sample they selected these lines from "The Ecstasy of Skeptics" in the book *The Ecstasy of Skeptics* by Steven Heighton:

This tongue
is a moment of moistened dust, it must learn
to turn the grit of old books
into hydrogen, and burn
The dust of the muscles must burn
down the blood-fuse of the sinews, . . .

Their books are generally 96-144 pgs., trade paperback with French sleeves, a matte finish cover and full-color cover art. **Canadian poets should query first with 10 sample poems (typed double-spaced) and a cover letter with brief bio and publication credits. Previously published poems and simultaneous submissions OK. Poems are circulated to an editorial board. Often comments on rejections. Replies to queries within 3 months, to mss (if invited) within 4 months. Pays 8-10% royalties, a $500 honorarium and 10 author's copies (out of a press run of 1,000).** To learn more about their titles, check their website or write to the press directly for a catalog. They say, "We strongly advise poets to build up a publishing résumé by submitting poems to reputable magazines and journals. This indicates three important things to us: One, that he or she is becoming a part of the Canadian poetry community; two, that he or she is building up a readership through magazine subscribers; and three, it establishes credibility in his or her work. There is a great deal of competition for only three or four spots on our list each year—which always includes works by poets we have previously published."

HOUSEWIFE-WRITER'S FORUM (IV-Women, humor), P.O. Box 780, Lyman WY 82937, phone (307)782-7003, founded 1988, editor/publisher Emma Bluemel, is a magazine of "prose, poetry, information and open forum communication for and by housewives or any woman or man who writes while juggling a busy schedule. **We have no specifications as to form, subject, style or purpose. Length maximum 30 lines. We publish both serious poetry and humorous. Nothing pornographic, but erudite expression is fine."** As a sample she selected these lines from "Off Limits" by Katherine H. Brooks:

I used to save a lot of stuff.
Till Mother hollered "That's enough!"
And made me have, all day, a fear
That something nice would disappear.
I hurried home from school, to see
What damage had been done to me,
And when I went to find the rocks
I'd hidden underneath my socks,
I saw it—almost in a flash—
That all my things were in the trash.

Emma Bluemel describes the magazine as "a small market for women who aspire to write for larger women's markets or support each other in the quest for finding time and energy to write." It is 48 pgs., desktop-published, using some art, graphics and ads, appearing bimonthly. Press run is 2,000. **Sample postpaid: $3. "Simultaneous submissions are OK." Send SASE for guidelines. Reports in 2 months. Pays 1 copy plus $1-2/poem. Buys first-time rights.** She holds an annual contest with $4/poem fee, June 1 deadline. *Housewife-Writer's Forum* received a 1st place award for magazine editing from Wyoming Media Professionals. The editor adds, "I like to see poems that have a strong central purpose and use the language to express it beautifully, powerfully. I also like to see poems that make me laugh."

HOWLING DOG (V), 2913 Woodcock Court, Rochester MI 48306, founded 1985, poetry editor Wipee Zippie. *Howling Dog*, a literary journal, is **not accepting unsolicited manuscripts at this time.**

HQ: THE HAIKU QUARTERLY; THE DAY DREAM PRESS (II), 39 Exmouth St., Kingshill, Swindon, Wiltshire SN1 3PU England, phone 01793-523927, founded 1990, editor Kevin Bailey, is "a platform from which new and established poets can speak and/or experiment with new forms and ideas." They want **"any poetry of good quality."** They have published poetry by Peter Redgrove, Alan Brownjohn, James Kirkup and Cid Corman. As a sample the editor selected these lines from "Copenhagen" by Tom Lowenstein:

It was winter in Europe.
I thump up the pillows and
lay Rilke on the bedside table.
The snow drifts at random
through the aspen branches.

The editor says *HQ* is 48-64 pgs., A5, perfect-bound with art, ads and reviews. They accept approximately 5% of poetry received. Press run is 500-600 for 500 subscribers of which 30 are libraries. Subscription: £9 UK, £12 foreign. **Sample postpaid: £2.50. No previously published poems or**

simultaneous submissions. Cover letter and SASE (or SAE and IRCs) required. Time between acceptance and publication is 3-6 months. **Often comments on rejections. Reports "as time allows." Pays 1 copy.** Reviews books of poetry in about 1,000 words, single format. Open to unsolicited reviews. Poets may also send books for review consideration.

HRAFNHOH (IV-Form, religious); BLACK EAGLE (IV-Ethnic, translations), 32 Strŷd Ebeneser, Pontypridd, CF 37 5PB Wales via GB, founded 1987, editor Joseph Biddulph, *Hrafnhoh* is a small press magazine **seeking "metrical verse."** They use **"poetry in traditional verse forms with a Christian inspiration and purpose, with an active concern for metrical technique and conveying a serious message in an evocative and entertaining style."** They have published poetry by John Waddington-Feather, M.A.B. Jones, Joe Keysor and many others. The editor describes *Hrafnhoh* as 24 pgs., digest-sized, typeset, illustrated with carefully-researched heraldic illustrations and other sketches. He accepts about 1 of 6-10 poems received, but is not always able to publish even if accepted. Press run is 100-500. *Hrafnhoh* now includes a supplement, *Black Eagle*, which seeks **short, preferably metrical verse on the living experience of Africa or the African diaspora, or translations of African languages in English, French, Spanish or Creole. Sample copy free worldwide. Submit up to 7 poems at a time. Simultaneous submissions and previously published poems OK. Publishes theme issues. Reports as soon as possible. Pays up to 10 copies, "depending on circumstances."** The editor says, "Almost all unsolicited manuscripts are in one form—free verse—and without substance, i.e., without a definite purpose, message or conclusion. I am anxious to obtain verse with a strong technique, particularly on Pro-Life and Christian subjects."

HU (HONEST ULSTERMAN) (II, IV-Regional), 49 Main St., Greyabbey, County Down BT22 2NF United Kingdom, founded 1968, editor Tom Clyde, is a literary magazine appearing 3-4 times a year using **"technically competent poetry and prose and book reviews. Special reference to Northern Irish and Irish literature. Lively, humorous, adventurous, outspoken."** They have published poetry by Seamus Heaney, Paul Muldoon, Gavin Ewart, Craig Raine, Fleur Adcock and Medbh McGuckian. The editor describes it as "75-100 pgs., A5 (digest-sized), photolithographic, phototypeset, with photographs and line drawings. Occasionally color covers." Press run is 1,000 for 350 subscribers. Subscription: $28. **Sample postpaid: $7. "Potential contributors are strongly advised to read the magazine before submitting their work." Submit 6 poems at a time.** Editor comments on submissions "occasionally." **Publishes theme issues. Theme for September 1996 issue was "Writing from the (Ulster) Borders." Send SASE (or SAE and IRCs) for upcoming themes. Pays "a nominal fee"** plus 2 copies. Reviews books of literary and cultural interest in 500-1,000 words, single or multi-book format. Open to unsolicited reviews. Poets may also send books for review consideration. They also publish occasional poetry pamphlets.

HUBBUB (III), 5344 SE 38th Ave., Portland OR 97202, founded 1983, editors L. Steinman and J. Shugrue, appears once a year. *Hubbub* is designed "to feature a multitude of voices from interesting contemporary American poets. **We look for poems that are well-crafted, with something to say. We have no single style, subject or length requirement and, in particular, will consider long poems. No light verse."** They have published poetry by Madeline DeFrees, William Matthews, Cecil Giscombe, Carolyn Kizer, Agha Shahid Ali and Alice Fulton. The editors describe *Hubbub* as 60-65 pgs., 5½ × 8½, offset, perfect-bound, cover art only, usually no ads. They receive about 1,200 submissions/year, use approximately 2%. Press run is 350 for 100 subscribers of which 12 are libraries, about 150 shelf sales. Subscription: $5/year. **Sample postpaid: $2.65 (volumes 1-8), $3.15 (volumes 9 and 11), $6.25 (volume 10, 12 and following). Submit 3-6 typed poems (no more than 6). No previously published poems or simultaneous submissions. Send SASE for guidelines. Reports in 2-4 months. Pays 2 copies. Acquires first North American serial rights.** "We review two to four poetry books a year in short (3-page) reviews; all reviews are solicited. We do, however, list books received/recommended." Send books for consideration. Outside judges choose poems from each volume for two awards: Vi Gale Award ($100) and Adrienne Lee Award ($50). There are no special submission procedures or entry fees involved.

THE HUDSON REVIEW (III), 684 Park Ave., New York NY 10021. *The Hudson Review* is a high-quality, flat-spined quarterly, considered one of the most prestigious and influential journals in the nation. Editors welcome all styles and forms. However, competition is extraordinarily keen, especially since poems compete with prose. **Sample postpaid: $7. Nonsubscribers may submit poems only between April 1 and July 31. "Simultaneous submissions are returned unread." Reports in 6-8 weeks. Always sends prepublication galleys. Pays 50¢/line for poetry.** Work published in this review has also been included in the 1993 and 1994 volumes of *The Best American Poetry*.

THE HUNTED NEWS; THE SUBOURBON PRESS (I, II), P.O. Box 9101, Warwick RI 02889, founded 1990, editor Mike Wood. *The Hunted News* is an annual "designed to find good writers and give them one more outlet to get their voices heard." As for poetry, the editor says, **"The poems that**

need to be written are those that need to be read." They do not want to see "the poetry that does not need to be written or which is written only to get a reaction or congratulate the poet." As a sample the editor selected these lines (poet unidentified):

> Birds who strike window panes with
> a heavy thud
> are misinformed.
> They've been sabotaged by outmoded
> weather charts
> In miniscule and mugging ways
> they resemble our finest actors
> Bury them in sand . . .
> and wait.

The editor says *THN* is 25-30 pgs., 8½ × 11, photocopied, unstapled. "I receive over 200 poems per month and accept perhaps 10%." Press run is 150-200. **Sample free with SASE. Previously published poems OK; no simultaneous submissions. Always comments on rejections. Send SASE for guidelines. Reports in 1 month. Pays 1 copy, more on request.** "I review current chapbooks and other magazines and do other random reviews of books, music, etc. Word count varies." The editor says, "I receive mostly beginner's poetry that attempts to be too philosophical, without much experience to back up statements, or self-impressed 'radical' poems by poets who assume that I will publish them because they are beyond criticism. I would like poets to send work whose point lies in language and economy and in experience, not in trite final lines, or worse, in the arrogant cover letter."

HURRICANE ALICE (IV-Feminist), 207 Lind Hall, 207 Church St. SE, Minneapolis MN 55455, founded 1983, acquisitions editor Toni McNaron, is a quarterly feminist review. Poems should be **"infused by a feminist sensibility (whether the poet is female or male)."** They have published poetry by Alice Walker, Ellen Bass, Patricia Hampl, Nellie Wong, Pauline Brunette Danforth and Marcella Taylor. As a sample the editor selected these lines from "Living Without Horses" by Judith Barrington:

> Living without horses
> is like breathing into the lungs
> but never further;
> never deep into the great cavity below
> where horses of emerald and blue
> fill the void with their squeals,
> their thudding feet,
> their waltzes into deep space.

The magazine is a "12-page folio with plenty of graphics." Circulation is 500-1,000, of which 350 are subscriptions and about 50 go to libraries. Single copy: $1.95; subscription: $12 (or $10 low-income). **Sample postpaid: $2.50. Considers simultaneous submissions.** Send SASE for upcoming themes. **Reports in 3-4 months and time to publication is 3-6 months. Pays 5-10 copies.** Reviews books of poetry. The editor says, "Read what good poets have already written. If someone has already written your poem(s), listen to the message. Spare the trees."

HYACINTH HOUSE PUBLICATIONS; BROWNBAG PRESS; PSYCHOTRAIN; THE CROWBAIT REVIEW (II), P.O. Box 120, Fayetteville AR 72702-0120, founded 1989, contact Shannon Frach. *Brownbag Press*, *The Crowbait Review* and *PsychoTrain* are semiannual magazines. *Brownbag Press* seeks "forceful writing full of spark and vigor for a widely diverse, intelligent, fairly left-of-center audience." *PsychoTrain* uses "bizarre, avant-garde material with a delightfully psychotic edge. Heady and chaotic." *The Crowbait Review* is a poetry-only publication "using a wide stylistic mix, from the abrasive and gut-level to the deliciously surreal. It comes out more often than our other publications and is cheaper to produce, hence allowing us to publish far more poetry than we used to. This is a zine in the rawest sense of the word; do not expect to see a perfect-bound, coffee-table edition. Please send camera-ready copy for this magazine." The editors want **poetry that is "avant-garde, confessional, contemporary, erotic, experimental, gay/lesbian, pagan/occult or punk. Also Dada, surrealism and decadent writing at its best. Stop sending us rhyming poetry, mainstream poetry, academic poetry. We are interested in free verse. Don't send traditional 'horror' or vampire poetry. We're looking for what would typically be considered 'underground' or 'alternative' writing. People who send us material that isn't in some way twisted, bizarre or weird are wasting both our time and theirs. We're seeing far too much 'straight' writing. Be bold. Morbid humor is always a plus here. We prefer two-fisted, dynamic, very intense poetry. Don't be afraid to show us street language from any culture."** They have recently published poetry by Andrew Lucariello, Marty Evans, Lawrence Carradini, Noelle Kocot, Kimberly J. Bright and C.F. Roberts. As a sample the editors selected these lines from "condoms are doggie bags of soul" by Randal Seyler:

> . . . she tilts her head back at the neck
> laughs like christ on the cross

like jekyll taking a crap . . .
her hand crouched on my thigh like a spider
waiting for a love letter

Brownbag is 24 pgs. and **PsychoTrain** is 20 pgs., magazine-sized. Both are photocopied and stapled with card covers. **The Crowbait Review** is 14 pgs., photocopied and stapled. Press run for each is 300 for 100 subscribers, 125 shelf sales. **Sample postpaid: $4 for Brownbag, $4 for PsychoTrain, $2 for The Crowbait Review. "Make checks out to Hyacinth House Publications. Cash is also OK." Submit 4-8 poems at a time. Previously published poems and simultaneous submissions OK.** Time between acceptance and publication is 1 year or more. **Often comments on rejections. Send SASE for guidelines. Reports in "2 weeks to 8 months—depends on the backlog. We do not pay." Acquires one-time rights.** "Please, *always* tell us whether or not your submissions are disposable. If you send 4-8 poems, we have a better overview of your material, but are not overwhelmed. We'd prefer to see each poem on a separate sheet. Don't send us long poems; if a poem runs over a single standard-sized page, the chances of its acceptance diminish dramatically. Finally, always include a SASE. We are getting an alarming number of submissions arriving without return postage—submissions which are promptly used for kindling, as are any queries or correspondence arriving without the courtesy of an enclosed SASE." Hyacinth House also has **a chapbook series. "Presently we're using solicited material only**—please don't send us unsolicited chapbook mss at this time. We will be doing approximately seven chapbooks this year, all from authors who have first appeared in our magazines. We don't take chapbook submissions 'out of the blue'—we like to know who we're working with." Hyacinth House Publications also sponsors the Richard A. Seffron Memorial Poetry Prize. "This is an ongoing competition with an annual deadline of May 1. Winners receive chapbook copies and a small cash prize. Send SASE for details and any queries concerning the Seffron Prize. Do not even *think* about submitting without first acquiring guidelines." Previous winners of the Seffron Prize include Noelle Kocot and Marty Evans. The editors say, "We may end up having to reject your submissions, but we'll still respect you in the morning. We encourage both new and established 'name' writers to submit here. Anyone sending us material should be aware that we don't like pretentious, windy, overly-serious poetry; we also dislike smarmy, trite rhymes about God and family. Send those to your hometown newspaper, not us. Also, please be aware that when you submit to one Hyacinth House publication, you're submitting to them all. If you submit to **Brownbag**, but the piece would work better in **PsychoTrain** or **The Crowbait Review**, that's where it's going."

HYPHEN MAGAZINE (II), P.O. Box 10481, Chicago IL 60610-0481, phone/fax (312)465-5985 (but no faxed submissions), e-mail ingebret@interaccess.com, founded 1991, appears 3 times a year (in April, August and December). "*Hyphen* presents new fiction, poetry, art and ideas in an accessible and appealing format, seeking to demystify art by building bridges and exploring common ground." As for poetry, the editors say they have **"no formal or subject restrictions; usually limited to 1-2 pages in length. We usually publish 1 or 2 performance poems each issue—but performance poems should read as well on the page as on the stage.** *Hyphen* **looks for poems that have immediacy, accessibility and craft; poems that break your heart, take your breath away, and blow the top right off your head. Please don't submit sentimental or inspirational poems, light comic verse, bad rhyming verse, violent or demeaning erotica, or, generally speaking, bad poetry of any kind. To really get an idea of the kind of poetry we publish, take this publisher's advice and** *order a sample copy.* **It's a good idea; it works."** They have recently published poetry by Luis Rodriguez, Duane Locke, Dwight Okita and Rane Arroyo. As a sample the editors selected these lines from "The Non-Stick Gospels, or Everything I Know I Learned Talking Out Of Church," by Jim Banks:

You're born a chunk of raw id in a kennel full of authority figures.
God's cops use choke-holds to coerce your voluntary love.
The market is an illusion, but you continue to buy and sell.
You didn't ask yourself in, you can't kick yourself out.
If you're not allergic to this, you're addicted to that.
You keep forgetting to panic.

Hyphen is 72 pgs., 8½ × 11, offset and saddle-stapled with 2-color slick paper cover with photo. The interior includes b&w art, photos, graphics and ads. They receive 500-600 poems a year, accept about 30. Press run is 1,500 for 250 subscribers. Single copy: $4.95; subscription: $14/year, $25/2 years. **Sample postpaid: $6. Guidelines are found in the magazine. Submit no more than 6 poems at a time (name and address on each sheet) with brief bio (75 words or less). No previously published poems; simultaneous submissions OK ("but we're not crazy about them"). E-mail welcome. "Don't use the ease of e-mail to dump your life's work on us; follow our guidelines for paper submissions." Poems are circulated to an editorial board. Seldom comments on rejections. Reports in 3-4 months. Pays 2 copies. Acquires first North American serial rights and retains rights to anthologize.** Reviews books and other media in the "Aftershock" section, in 200-300 words. Open to unsolicited reviews. Poets may also send books for review consideration. *Hyphen* plans to have a web version on the Internet soon; e-mail editor for details.

‡I.E. MAGAZINE, A JOURNAL OF LITERATURE AND THE ARTS (II), P.O. Box 73403, Houston TX 77273-3403, phone (713)901-2750 (voice mail, can only return calls collect), founded 1990, managing editor Yolande Gottlieb, poetry editor Milt McLeod, appears quarterly with some additional supplements. *i.e. magazine* contains poetry, fiction, nonfiction, science fiction, fantasy, play reviews with photos, translations and art. **"We are committed to furthering excellence in literature and the arts." They want "well-crafted, though-provoking poetry that is crisp, vivid and imaginative; poetry of irresistible brilliance, writing that makes a difference."** They have recently published poetry by André de Korvin, Michael Lieberman, A.B. Telyachenk and Martina Reisz. As a sample we selected these lines from "Dancing in the Eye" by Larry L. Fontenot:

> Air is elastic, stretches to hold almost everything:
> the curse of long distance, the failure of conversation,
> the howl of a stray dog hunkered down by the back door
> just ahead of the hurricane.
> Along the creek line moaning trees sway,
> birds stumble like words chasing lovers.

i.e. magazine is 40-48 pgs., 5½ × 8½, professionally printed on coated stock, saddle-stitched, with b&w photos and graphics. They receive about 500 poems a year, accept 12-15/issue. Press run is 1,000 for 200 subscribers of which 10 are libraries, 100 shelf sales. Single copy: $4.50; subscription: $20. **Sample postpaid: $6. Submit 3-5 poems at a time, 2 copies of each with name, address and phone number. No previously published poems or simultaneous submissions. Cover letter required with brief bio, photo (for publication) and publication credits, if any. "Please label envelopes with genre." Disk (3.5 IBM compatible) and e-mail submissions OK.** Time between acceptance and publication is 2-12 months. **Seldom comments on rejections. Send SASE for guidelines. Reports in 1-4 months. Pays $1-2 (as funds permit) plus 1 copy. Acquires first rights.** Reviews books and chapbooks of poetry. Open to unsolicited reviews. Poets may also send books for review consideration. Sponsors annual poetry and poetry chapbook contests. Send SASE for details. The editors say, "We advise new poets to read as much contemporary poetry as possible, small literary magazines, contemporary anthologies, prestigious magazines. See what is being published everywhere." (Yolande Gottlieb is also the poetry editor for *A Poet's Journey*, see listing in this section.)

ICE COLD WATERMELON (IV-Ethnic, erotica, gay/lesbian), 2394B Adina Dr., Atlanta GA 30324, founded 1990, editors M. Christopher Young and Simoné, is an annual journal of memory and prophecy. **"Interested solely in poignant, economical poetry with voice and character using innovative imagery. Want to see brave poetry with an edge, that gives us a peek into the mystical experience of persons of color. Erotica/gay/lesbian writings especially encouraged. Do not want to see anything that tries too hard. No academic or 'selfish' personal poetry. Nothing trite or mundane."** As a sample the editors selected the poem "Yes" by M. Christopher Young:

> hey man,
> yeah, you
>
> the brother over there
> yeah, him, the one with
> the empty, outstretched hand
>
> he is speaking to you
> right this very minute
>
> can you hear what he is saying?

The editors describe it as 50-65 pgs., digest-sized, professionally printed. They accept about 150 of 500 submissions received annually. Press run is 200 with 5 library subscriptions. "Most copies distributed free to other editors, publishers and writing institutions." Subscription: $10 for 2 years. **Submit 5 poems, typed. Send SASE for guidelines. Reports in 8-10 weeks, up to 18-month backlog. Pays 2 copies.** They say, "What we want is writing that is empowered by spirit, magic and secrets. In your writing, we want you to have no qualms about telling the cultural truths as you know them and allowing our readers to share those experiences with you."

‡ICON; HART CRANE AWARD (II), Kent State University-Trumbull, 4314 Mahoning Ave., NW, Warren OH 44483-1998, phone (216)847-0571, e-mail lynchm@lyceum.trumbull.kent.edu, website http://www.trumbull.kent.edu/icon.html/, founded 1966, is a biannual, "eclectic" literary and art magazine. **"We prefer short lyric poems, although all forms are considered. Originality and innovation are appreciated. Sentimental or angst-ridden poems should send themselves elsewhere."** They have recently published poetry by Gay Brewer and William Greenway. The editor says *Icon* is 48-60 pgs., saddle-stapled with b&w photos and graphics. They receive 1,200 poems a year, publish about 90. Press run is 500 for 75 subscribers of which 15 are libraries, 400 distributed free to students. Single copy: $4; subscription: $6. **Sample postpaid: $2. Submit 5 poems at a time. No**

previously published poems; simultaneous submissions OK. Cover letter preferred. Reads submissions September 15 through April 15 only. Poems are circulated to an editorial board. Often comments on rejections. Reports in 2-6 months. Pays 2 copies. They also offer the Hart Crane Award, an annual poetry award of $100. The winner is published in the spring issue. Send SASE for details.

THE ICONOCLAST (II), 1675 Amazon Rd., Mohegan Lake NY 10547-1804, founded 1992, editor/publisher Phil Wagner, is a general interest literary publication appearing 8 times/year "for those who find life absurd and profound." **They want "poems that have something to say—the more levels the better. Nothing sentimental, religious, obscure or self-absorbed. Our poetry is accessible to a thoughtful reading public."** *The Iconoclast* is 28 pgs., 5½ × 8½, double-stapled, typeset and photocopied on 20 lb. white paper, with b&w art, graphics and ads. They receive about 1,000 poems a year, use 5%. Press run is 500 for 240 subscribers. Subscription: $12 for 8 issues. **Sample postpaid: $1.75. Submit 3-4 poems at a time. Previously published poems and simultaneous submissions OK, though they say "previously published and simultaneous submissions must be demonstrably better than others."** Time between acceptance and publication is 1-6 months. **"Poems are subject to the extremely fallible judgments of the editor-in-chief." Often comments on rejections. Reports in 2-4 weeks. Pays 1 copy, 40% discount on extras. Acquires one-time rights.** Reviews books of poetry in 250 words, single format.

THE IDIOT (IV-Humor), 1706 S. Bedford St., Los Angeles CA 90035, founded 1993, editor Sam Hayes, is a biannual humor magazine. "We mostly use fiction, articles and cartoons, but **will use anything funny, including poetry. Nothing pretentious."** They have recently published poetry by Lactose Jones, Harry Lime and Brian Campbell. As a sample the editor selected these lines from "The Waste Receptacle" by Joe Deasy:

> *Cerebus, why do you prevent me from opening my mail?*
> *The cries of the debt*
> *10 little monkeys jumpin' on the bed.*
> *One fell off. Oh, haven't we all.*

The Idiot is 48 pgs., 5½ × 8½, professionally printed and staple-bound with glossy cover. They receive about 30 submissions a year, accept 3-4. Press run is 300. Single copy: $3. **Sample postpaid: $5. Previously published poems and simultaneous submissions OK. Seldom comments on rejections. Reports in 2-6 months. Pays 1 copy. Acquires one-time rights.** The editor says, "If it ain't funny, don't send it! I mean it! We're talkin' belly laughs, damn it!"

UNIVERSITY OF ILLINOIS PRESS (III), 1325 S. Oak St., Champaign IL 61820, founded 1918, poetry editor Laurence Lieberman, publishes **collections of individual poets, 65-105 pgs. Submissions by invitation only.** They have published collections of poetry by Mark Doty, Debora Greger, Alice Fulton, Len Roberts, Michael Harper, Miller Williams, Lorna Goodison, Stephen Berg, Dave Smith, Sydney Lea and David Wagoner. **Offers royalty contract and 10 copies.**

‡ILLYA'S HONEY (I, II), 432 Greenridge, Coppell TX 75019-5717, phone (214)462-7186, e-mail swbrodie@aol.com, founded 1994, editor Stephen W. Brodie, is a quarterly journal of poetry and b&w artwork, occasionally using very short stories. **"All subjects and styles of poetry are welcome. Poems can be up to 60 lines and should be interesting, imaginative and thought-provoking. Different is good. No forced rhyme or overly religious verse, please."** They have recently published poetry by Liza Bachman, Clebo Rainey, Julie Irsch and Douglas Spangle. As a sample the editor selected these lines from "The Werewolf's Daughters" by Bob Zordani:

> *another flawless bloom who fills her field*
> *with song. My daughters waltz about the town*
> *so carelessly they will not guess whose voice*
> *has bid them dance, whose tune will deem them ripe,*
> *whose undulating claws will gleam like death*
> *personified and carve them into ghosts . . .*

Illya's Honey is 50-60 pgs., 5½ × 8½, desktop-published and saddle-stitched with glossy card cover and b&w artwork throughout. They receive about 2,000 poems a year, use approximately 125. Press run is 250 for 80 subscribers, 50 shelf sales. Subscription: $18. **Sample postpaid: $5. Submit 5 poems at a time. Previously published poems and simultaneous submissions OK. Cover letter preferred. Seldom comments on rejections. Send SASE for guidelines or obtain via e-mail. Reports in 2 months, sometimes sooner. Sometimes sends prepublication galleys. Payment is publication. Contributors must purchase a copy if they want to see their work in print.**

IMAGO: NEW WRITING; CITY OF BRISBANE POETRY AWARD (II, IV-Regional), School of Media & Journalism, Q.U.T., GPO Box 2434, Brisbane 4001 Queensland, Australia, fax (07)3864-1810, founded 1988, appears three times a year, publishing "the best **Australian writing,**

placing particular emphasis on Queensland writing and culture, but also welcoming submissions from overseas. Poems preferably short—up to about 50 lines, most from 12-25 lines. Our main criterion is good writing." They have recently published poetry by Tom Shapcott, Nancy Cato and Philip Hammial. As a sample the editor selected these lines from "Far and Near" by David Malouf:

> ... We are held
> by this; the coins in our pockets, amalgam fillings,
> gold that laps a finger gravely compliant
> as the magnet tilts and tugs us
> down. A flair for technology and faith is what keeps us
> above earth's instant muddle, but never far and not for long.

Imago is 160 pgs., digest-sized, with glossy card cover. They accept about 10% of 500 poems from about 150 writers. Press run is 1,000 for 450 subscribers of which 36 are libraries. Subscription: $A21 in Australia; $A28, overseas (airmail). **Sample postpaid: $A9.50. Submit 6-8 poems at a time. "A brief biography (few lines) of the writer accompanying the submission saves time if the work is accepted. We have a Notes on Contributors column." Comments if requested. Reports in 1-6 months. Never sends prepublication galleys "unless specifically asked for by contributor." Pays $30-40 plus 1 copy. Buys first Australian serial rights. They publish the winning poems of the City of Brisbane Poetry Award (annual).** Reviews books of poetry in 600 words—"usually commissioned. Unsolicited reviews would have to be of books relevant to *Imago* (Queensland or writing)." Send books for review consideration.

THE IMPLODING TIE-DYED TOUPEE; BURNING LLAMA PRESS (II, IV-Form/style), 82 Ridge Lake Dr., Columbia SC 29209-4213, founded 1993, editors Keith Higginbotham and T.R. Combs, is a biannual outlet "for people who dare to take language to its outer limits. We prefer sounds and juxtapositions of images over 'meaning.' " They want **"Dada, surrealism, experimental, language poetry, found poetry, collaborative poetry—anything unusual. No traditional poetry, light verse, blood and guts, academic, confessional or inspirational poetry."** They have recently published poetry by Susan Smith Nash, Richard Kostelanetz, Sheila E. Murphy and Nathan Whiting. As a sample the editors selected "Hilt" by John M. Bennett:

> Better lamping's what I
> need   or your face
> pillowed   a conference of
> hair   like the phone's
> dust   my pants just billowed
>
> Lace hanging like my speech milk

The Imploding Tie-Dyed Toupee is 40 pgs., digest-sized, photocopied and saddle-stapled with card stock cover and bizarre graphics coupled with intriguing visual poems. "On the average, we accept one poem per 200 received." Press run is 200 for 20 subscribers, various shelf sales. Subscription: $16 for 4 issues. **Sample postpaid: $4. Submit 3-10 poems at a time. No previously published poems or simultaneous submissions. "Everyone, no matter how 'well known,' should have the decency or professional courtesy to include a cover letter or some kind of personal communication. Otherwise, we consider the poet to be arrogant. Poets should also always include a SASE."** Time between acceptance and publication varies. **Seldom comments on rejections. Send SASE for guidelines. Reports within 3 months. Pays 1 copy. Acquires first North American serial rights.** "Open to short reviews of magazines; surreal reviews of TV shows." Poets may also send books for review consideration. The editors add, "Do the unexpected with language."

‡IMPLOSION: A JOURNAL OF THE BIZARRE AND ECCENTRIC (II), Box 533653, Orlando FL 32853, e-mail smudge21@aol.com, founded 1995, editor Cynthia Conlin, is a quarterly journal of short fiction, artwork, photography, poetry and nonfiction. "*Implosion* explores the unusual side of human existence. **We want anything that is truly bizarre and eccentric—as the title implies. No poetry over one page long. Nothing with a moral or some overt moralistic message nor anything in the style of a bad episode of *Star Trek*.**" As a sample the editor selected these lines by "Frank":

> The conservative side of society
> Is easily entertained,
> Simply satisfied with watered-down whisky

---

‡   **THE DOUBLE DAGGER** before a listing indicates that the listing is new in this edition. New markets are often the most receptive to submissions.

> *And dry humor.*
> *With this knowledge*
> *I should open a club.*
> *Bill Cosby would have the audience*
> *Rolling in the aisles, laughing,*
> *Where I could pick their pockets and purses.*

Implosion is about 60 pgs., 8½ × 11, saddle-stapled with full-color glossy cover and lots of photographs and artwork. They receive more than 500 poems a year, accept approximately 5%. Press run is 5,000 for 200 subscribers, a few thousand shelf sales. Single copy: $4.95; subscription: $14/year. **Sample postpaid: $5. Submit no more than 5 poems at a time. Previously published poems and simultaneous submissions OK. Cover letter preferred—"tell us a little about yourself, your prior publishing history, and what makes you different from everyone else in the world."** Time between acceptance and publication is 3-6 months. **Often comments on rejections. Send SASE for guidelines or request via e-mail. Reports in 6-12 weeks. Sometimes sends prepublication galleys. Pays 2 copies. Acquires one-time rights.** Staff reviews books of poetry in about 200 words. Poets may send books for review consideration. The editor says, " 'Bizarre' doesn't mean incoherent."

IMPLOSION PRESS; IMPETUS (I, II, IV-Erotica, women), 4975 Comanche Trail, Stow OH 44224-1217, phone/fax (216)688-5210, e-mail impetus@aol.com, founded 1984, poetry editor Cheryl Townsend, publishes *Impetus*, a "somewhat" quarterly literary magazine, chapbooks, special issues. The editor would like to see **"strong social protest with raw emotion. No topic is taboo. Material should be straight from the gut, uncensored and real. Absolutely no nature poetry or rhyme for the sake of rhyme, oriental, or 'Kissy, kissy I love you' poems. Any length as long as it works. All subjects OK, providing it isn't too rank.** *Impetus* **is now publishing annual erotica and all female issues. Material should reflect these themes."** They have published poetry by Ron Androla, Kurt Nimmo, Lyn Lifshin and Lonnie Sherman. As a sample the editor selected these lines from "Gunshy" by B. Arcus Shoenborn:

> *Instead,*
> *I hid in my bedroom.*
> *Soaked between blooded sheets,*
> *I explored immaculate concepts.*
> *Then my white heart severed;*
> *It gushed rivers of angry rapists.*
> *One flagged a revolver;*
> *he held it to my head and said,*
> *I'd live, but couldn't tell.*

The 7½ × 9 magazine is photocopied from typescript, saddle-stapled. Press run is about 1,000, with 300 subscriptions. Generally a 3-month backlog. Subscription: $15 for 4 issues; $20 for 4 issues plus chapbooks. **Sample postpaid: $5; make checks payable to Cheryl Townsend. Submit 3-8 poems at a time. The editor says, "I prefer shorter, to-the-point work." Include name and address on each page. Previously published work OK if it is noted when and where. "I always like a cover letter that tells me how the poet found out about my magazine." No submissions via e-mail. Send SASE for guidelines. Usually reports within 3 months. Pays 1 copy. Acquires first or one-time rights.** In her comments on rejections, the editor usually refers poets to other magazines she feels would appreciate the work more. Reviews books of poetry. Open to unsolicited reviews. Poets may also send books for review consideration. Implosion Press now hosts "The Last Friday Poetry Readings" at Borders Books & Music in Fairlawn, Ohio, "The First Friday Poetry Readings" at Cheryl's Daily Grind in Akron, Ohio, and will be touring cities with Borders inviting local *Impetus* poets to read. They also host "Notes from the Underground" on WAPS 91.3 FM radio in Akron, Ohio. The editor says, "Bear with the small press. We're working as best as we can and usually harder. We can only do so much at a time. Support the small presses!"

IMPROVIJAZZATION NATION (I), 5308 65th Ave., SE, Lacey WA 98513, phone (360)456-1683, fax (360)456-8982, e-mail rotcod@halcyon.com, website http://www.math.duke.edu/~priley/ination/.nathtml, founded 1991, editor Dick Metcalf. *Improvijazzation Nation* is a quarterly "devoted to networking; prime focus is tape/music reviews, includes quite a bit of poetry." **They want "experimental, visual impact and non-establishment poetry, no more than 15 lines. No hearts and flowers, shallow, epic."** They have published poetry by John M. Bennett, Joan Payne Kincaid and Anthony Lucero. The editor says *IN* is 20 pgs., 8½ × 11, photocopied, no binding. They receive 50-100 poems a year, use approximately 50%. Press run is 100. Single copy: $2.25; subscription: $8 for 4 issues. **Sample postpaid: $2.50. Submit 3 poems at a time. Previously published poems and simultaneous submissions OK. "Fax OK, e-mail is better." Often comments on rejections. Reports within a week or two. "No payment, no contributor's copies, no tearsheets; poets must buy the issue their work appears in. The one exception is that any contributor who furnishes a valid e-mail address will receive an ASCII copy of the entire magazine, if requested."** Reviews books of poetry. Also accepts short essays/commentary on the use of networking to void commercial music markets, as well as material of interest to musical/artist improvisors.

IN YOUR FACE! (I), P.O. Box 174, Manasquan NJ 08736, founded 1992, editors Gina Grega and Ronda Matthews, is a quarterly that publishes art, poetry, essays and reviews, "whatever strikes our fancy and knocks the wind out of us." **They want "anything bold, confrontational, risky and/or risqué, funny, political, personal, sexual, unpretentious, honest, real-life language. No PC multicultural whinings, phony pseudo-emotionalism, rhyming poems, unintelligible manifestos filled with 50-cent words. No women-hating spewage."** They have recently published poetry by Maggie Jaffe, Kimberly Bright, Ken Pell, Kerry Knudsen and Joanne Holdridge. As a sample the editor selected this poem, "When She Went To Florida," by Brent Askari:

> When she went to Florida
> my soul wailed like
> a hammond organ
> played by an epileptic
> during a power surge

IYF! is 50-60 pgs., 5½×8½, saddle-stapled, with colored card cover, b&w art and ads. They receive about 1,500 pieces a year, accept 10-15%. Press run is 350 for 100 subscribers. Subscription: $16. **Sample postpaid: $4. Make checks payable to Gina Grega. Submit no more than 5 pgs. at a time. Previously published poems and simultaneous submissions OK. "Be friendly, drop us a note, not a pretentious bio! SASE with appropriate postage a must. Also, if you don't want your writings returned, let us know." Often comments on rejections. Send SASE for guidelines. Reports in 2-3 months. Pays 1-2 copies.** Reviews books, chapbooks, 'zines, "whatever else we can get our hands on," in roughly 75-100 words each. Open to unsolicited reviews. Poets may also send books for review consideration. The editor says, "*In Your Face!* isn't afraid to offend. We look for gut-punching work—not big names. We especially encourage beginners as they haven't been polished by the cold, impersonal 'name' magazines and are usually still humble enough to send a 'hi' with their submissions. We *recommend* that contributors see a copy of our publication, but this is not a requirement."

INDEFINITE SPACE (II), P.O. Box 40101, Pasadena CA 91114, founded 1992, editors Marcia Arrieta and Kevin Joy, is a poetry journal published annually or biannually, "depending on finances." **They want "experimental, minimalistic, imagistic, philosophical poetry not exceeding two pages. No rhyming poetry."** They have published poetry by Hugh Fox, Jeffery, John M. Bennett and Sheila E. Murphy. As a sample the editors selected these lines from "Latitude" by Spencer Selby:

> Does not know
> this ship sprung up on soil
> to verify delivery
> at the entrance
> of world ruins
> I have never reached.

Indefinite Space is 32-40 pgs., 5½×8½, neatly printed and saddle-stapled with matte card cover with b&w art, no ads, poems appearing one to a page. Press run is 125-150 for 20 subscribers of which 5 are libraries. Subscription: $7. **Sample postpaid: $4. "Please make checks payable to editors." No previously published poems; simultaneous submissions OK. Seldom comments on rejections. Send SASE for guidelines. Reports usually within a month. Pays 1 copy. Rights remain with poet.**

INDIA CURRENTS (IV-Ethnic, regional), P.O. Box 21285, San Jose CA 95151-1285, phone (408)274-6966, e-mail editor@indiacur.com, website http://www.indiacur.com/indiacur/, founded 1987, editor Arvind Kumar, is a monthly magazine about Indian culture in the U.S. They want **"poetry that offers an insight into India, Indians, Indian Americans; very brief works stand a better chance of acceptance."** They do not want "poetry that exploits mystery or exoticism about India or long poems (over 300 words). Readership is 70% Indian, 30% non-Indian." They have published poetry by Chitra Divakaruni. It is 136 pgs., 8½×11, offset, newsprint, saddle-stitched. They receive 50-75 submissions a year, "accept fewer than 12." Press run is 24,000 for 4,000 subscribers. Rest distributed free at stores, restaurants and libraries. Single copy: $1.95; subscription: $19.95. **Sample postpaid: $3. Previously published poems and simultaneous and e-mail submissions OK. Cover letter with brief bio and background required.** Time between acceptance and publication is 6-12 months. **Send SASE for guidelines. Reports in 3 months.** Reviews books of poetry in 300 words maximum. Open to unsolicited reviews. Poets may also send books for review consideration. The editor says, "*India Currents* has a heavy tilt in favor of arts. We feel that arts can contribute to global understanding and peace by bringing it about at a personal level. America needs to learn about India just as India needs to learn about America."

INDIANA REVIEW (II), Indiana University, 316 N. Jordan Ave., Bloomington IN 47405, phone (812)855-3439, founded 1982, editor Shirley Stephenson, is a biannual of prose, poetry and visual art. "In general the *Review* **looks for fresh, original poems of insight, poems that are challenging without being obtuse. We'll consider all types of poems—free verse, traditional, experimental. Reading a sample issue is the best way to determine if *IR* is a potential home for your work. Any subject matter is acceptable if it is written well."** They have recently published poetry by Philip Levine, Taslimā Nāsreen, Sherman Alexie, Charles Simic, Mark Strand and Alberto Rios. As a sample the editor selected these lines from "Dull Weather" by Lucie Brock-Broido:

> *Rises, sets, by my own hand, dog days end.*
> *Even my self reminds me of you.*
>
> *I cannot refrain from Ruin.*
> *Your boys practice violence, even in peculiar*
>
> *Heat. They are hairless, clean as copper*
> *Coins made in a New England mint, doomed*
>
> *To be spent.*

The magazine uses about 50-70 pgs. of poetry in each issue (6×9, flat-spined, 200 pages, color matte cover, professional printing). They receive about 8,000 submissions/year of which they use about 60. The magazine has 1,000 subscriptions of which 120 are libraries. **Sample postpaid: $7. Submit 3-5 poems at a time, do not send more than 8-10 pages of poetry per submission. Pays $5/page ($10 minimum/poem), plus 2 copies and remainder of year's subscription. Buys first North American serial rights only. "We try to respond to manuscripts in 2-3 months. Reading time is often slower during summer and holiday months."** This magazine's reputation continues to grow in literary circles. It is generally accepted now as one of the best publications, featuring all styles, forms and lengths of poetry (much of it exciting or tense). Brief book reviews are also featured. Send books for review consideration. Poetry published in *IR* has also been selected for inclusion in *The Best American Poetry 1996*.

INDIGO MAGAZINE: THE SPANISH-CANADIAN PRESENCE IN THE ARTS (IV-Foreign languages, translations, themes), Room 252, Atkinson College, York University, North York, Ontario M3T 1P3 Canada, phone (416)736-2100, ext. 6632, founded 1989, editor-in-chief Prof. Margarita Feliciano, appears twice a year using **"poetry to be thematically of Hispanic contents if written in French or English (not the case if written in Spanish)."** They have published poetry by Rafael Barreto-Rivera and Rosemary Sullivan. As a sample the editor selected these lines (poet unidentified):

> *I was born on this lip of stone*
> *Jutting out over the jungle*
> *I've never wanted to go down.*
> *As a child I would run to the edge to catch the birds*
> *or follow the lizards with my hand along the ledges.*

It is approximately 150 pgs., professionally printed, flat-spined, with glossy card cover. "I accept 50% of submissions (about 40)." Press run 300 for 50 subscribers. Subscription: $25. **Cover letter, including background on the poet, required with submissions. Price of sample, payment, reporting time not given. The editor says she always comments on rejections.** Open to unsolicited reviews.

INKSLINGER (I, IV-Subscription), 8661 Prairie Rd. NW, Washington Court House OH 43160-9490, founded 1993, publisher/editor Nancy E. Martindale, appears 3 times/year (in March, July and November) to "provide an additional market for poets and to further the poetic arts." **They want poetry from subscribers only. Any subject, any format, no longer than 30 lines. "No porn or erotica. Also no translations or foreign language poetry."** They have recently published poetry by Geraldine Zeigler, Ryan Trauman, Katherine Brooks and A.M. Roman. As a sample the editor selected the poem "Relationship" by Scott Stolsenberg:

> *Fragments of a broken dream*
> *Fall through a shattered mind*
> *A thousand hopes and wishes*
> *A treasure lost to time*
> *I only wish we could have known*
> *If it was meant to be*
> *What could have been will never pass*
> *We drift the lonely sea*

Inkslinger is 20 pgs., digest-sized, saddle-stapled with 60 lb. colored paper cover. They receive 200-300 poems a year, accept 54 or more if short in length. Subscription: $12/year, $23/2 years, $35/3 years. **Sample postpaid: $4. "Purchase of a 1-year subscription is required to submit at present** time—hoping to change this policy soon." **Send no more than 5 poems at a time. Previously published poems OK if author still owns copyright; no simultaneous submissions.** Time between acceptance and publication is 1 month. "Poems arriving too late for one issue will be held for the next issue's consideration. Poems are judged according to imagery, style, creativity, originality and sincerity (5 points each). Poems with most points are accepted. One(s) with the highest is named 'Editor's Choice' and poet receives $10." **Seldom comments on rejections. Send SASE for guidelines. Reports in 5 months maximum. Pays no money at present (except to "Editor's Choice"), "but hoping to pay soon." Poets retain all rights.** The editor says, "Novices and experienced poets welcome. We're small, but open. *Always read guidelines first.* Failure to meet even one will result in unread, returned manuscripts."

INSECTS ARE PEOPLE TWO; PUFF 'N' STUFF PRODUCTIONS (I, IV-Specialized), P.O. Box 146486, Chicago IL 60614-6400, phone (312)772-8686, founded 1989, publisher H.R. Felgenhauer, an infrequent publication focusing solely on **"poems about insects doing people things and people doing insect things."** The first issue was a collection of the publisher's own poems. The second edition contains "better than 50 poems by 40 poets, one short story and one novella." As a sample the publisher selected these lines from a poem of his own, "Resist and You Will be Destroyed":

> *Geometrical abstraction of space-vehicle-ness sprouts conquest.*
> *Inferior species succumb to superior weapons, transport and*
> *communication systems blistering through onion skinned civilizations.*
> *They were bigger and better and all around us; we expanded right*
> *into their hoary mouths, razor sharp venom spouting ruin . . .*

Insects is 8½×11, stapled down the side, with card cover, b&w art and graphics. Press run is 400. **Sample postpaid: $5. Previously published poems and simultaneous submissions OK. Often comments on rejections. Reports "immediately." Pay varies.** Open to unsolicited reviews. Poets may also send books for review consideration. **Puff 'N' Stuff Productions publishes 1 chapbook/year. Replies to queries and mss in 10 days. Pay is negotiable.** H.R. Felgenhauer says, "Hit me with your best shot. Never give up—editors have tunnel-vision. The *BEST* mags you almost *NEVER* even hear about. Don't believe reviews. Write for yourself. Prepare for failure, not success."

THE INTERCULTURAL WRITER'S REVIEW; THE INTERCULTURAL WRITER'S ASSOCIATION (I, IV-Membership); MERLANA'S MAGICKAL MESSAGES (I, IV-Spirituality/inspirational, psychic/occult); PAGAN PASSIONS (I, IV-Erotica); NAVARRO PUBLICATIONS (IV-Anthology), P.O. Box 1107, Dept. PM, Blythe CA 92226-1107, phone (888)922-0835, managing editor Marjorie E. Navarro, consultant and art director Richard LeJose Navarro. *The Intercultural Writer's Review*, first published in April 1995, is the official publication of The Intercultural Writer's Association and is published quarterly. **They welcome poetry on any subject, up to 45 lines in length.** Short stories and articles, up to 2,500 words, are also used. They have recently published work by Rose Marie Hunola, James McGarry, Toni L. Briggs and Beryl Abdullah Khabeer. The editor describes *TIWR* as digest-sized with soft cover. **"Membership is not necessary for publication; however, members will be considered first."** The membership fee is $34/year and includes "a subscription and no-fee members' contests, discounts on extra copies and independently published poetry chapbooks." **Sample postpaid: $8.50. Make checks or money orders payable to Navarro Publications. Payment is in contributor's copies for members, tearsheets for nonmembers.** Their publication *Merlana's Magickal Messages*, first published in March 1995, is "a metaphysical, spiritual, New Age publication" which appears in March, July and October. **"We prefer uplifting material with a magickal message for our reader's spirit from the spirit of the author. We want poetry up to 45 lines.** We also use short stories (up to 2,500 words) and articles (up to 1,500 words). **It is best to send for a sample issue before submitting. And there is a reading fee of $2 for six poems, $3 for each article or short story."** They have recently published work by Jaunita Torrence-Thompson, Molly Moonwind, Vesna Dye, Bill Coffman and Vicki Henricksen. As a sample the editor selected these lines from "Specters in a Park" by Pete McGovern:

> *We walked this way one*
> *glad September*
> *You kissed me . . . There!*
> *D'you Remember?*
> *Oh my heart quickened that long ago*
> *Your undying words . . . I love you so!*

The editor says *MMM* is desktop-published. **Sample postpaid: $7. Make checks or money orders payable to Navarro Publications. Occasionally publishes theme issues. Theme for October 1997 issue is "A Salute to the Goddess" (deadline May 18, 1997). Reading fee for this issue is $3. Reports "as soon as possible." Pays in copies.** Their latest publication, *Pagan Passions* (first issue scheduled for May 1997), is a journal of **pagan erotica**–containing short stories, articles and poetry. **"No taboos—send me work you wouldn't send elsewhere." Requires reading fee of $4 for up to 6 poems. Pays 1 copy.** Navarro Publications is also planning one poetry anthology and three poetry chapbooks in 1997. Sponsors an annual poetry contest and an ongoing poetry chapbook contest. Send SASE for details. "We also offer short-run book publishing. Information is available for this and our literary services for a SASE." The editor says, "In all our endeavors we seek originality and conciseness. Read *Poet's Market* listings *carefully* and send for sample copies to avoid sending material not suitable for various markets. Doing so saves on postage and helps the already overworked and underpaid editors tremendously!"

INTERIM (II), Dept. of English, University of Nevada at Las Vegas, Las Vegas NV 89154, phone (702)895-3458, founded in Seattle, 1944-55, revived 1986. Editor and founder A. Wilber Stevens, associate editors James Hazen, Joseph B. McCullough and Timothy Erwin, English editor John Heath-Stubbs. Member CLMP, New York. Indexed in *Index of American Periodical Verse*. Biannual magazine, **publishing the best poetry it can find, no specific demands in form, new and established writers.** They have published poetry by William Stafford, Richard Eberhart, Diane Wakoski, Stephen Stepanchev and Anca Vlasopolos. As a sample we selected these lines from "Winter's Tale" by Charlotte F. Otten:

> Her voice is silent now,
> sunk deep into the tap root of her brain.
> A stroke that struck her throat
> blizzarded all sound.
> Words swirl around her like an early snow
> clinging to unfallen leaves.

Interim is 48 pgs., 6×9, professionally printed and saddle-stapled with coated card cover. Press run is 600. Individual subscription: $8/year, $13/two years, $16/three years; libraries: $14/year. **Sample copy: $5. Submit 4-6 poems at a time, SASE and brief biographical note. No simultaneous submissions. Reports in 3 months. Sometimes sends prepublication galleys. Pays 2 contributor's copies and a 2-year subscription.** *Interim* acquires copyright. Poems may be reprinted elsewhere with a permission line noting publication in *Interim*. Starting short poetry review. Send books for review consideration.

INTERNATIONAL BLACK WRITERS; BLACK WRITER MAGAZINE (I, IV-Ethnic), P.O. Box 1030, Chicago IL 60690, phone (312)409-2292, founded 1970, executive director Mable Terrell. *BWM* is a "quarterly literary magazine to showcase new writers and poets and provide educational information for writers. **Open to all types of poetry.**" The editor describes it as 30 pgs., magazine-sized, offset printing, with glossy cover. Circulation is 1,000 for 200 subscribers. Subscription: $19/year. **Sample postpaid: $1.50. Reports in 10 days,** has 1 quarter backlog. **Pays 10 copies. For chapbook publication (40 pgs.), submit 2 sample poems and cover letter with short bio. Simultaneous submissions OK. Pays copies. For sample chapbook, send SASE with bookrate postage.** They offer awards of $100, $50 and $25 for the best poems published in the magazine and present them to winners at annual awards banquet. *IBW* is open to all writers.

INTERNATIONAL OLYMPIC LIFTER (IOL) (IV-Specialized), P.O. Box 65855, Los Angeles CA 90065, founded 1973, poetry editor Dale Rhoades, is a bimonthly "for the serious weight lifter, coach, administrator and enthusiast." **They want poetry about olympic-style weight lifting—occasionally use poetry about nature, the environment or health. "We prefer balanced meter rhyming, 10-16 lines."** Press run is 3,000 for 2,700 subscribers of which approximately 5% are libraries. Subscription: $25. **Sample postpaid: $4.50. No previously published poems; simultaneous submissions OK. Reports "immediately." Pays $10-25.** The editor says, "Know your market. Often we get poems on body building, power lifting, running or aerobics which are all foreign to olympic lifting. Purchase a copy to understand our requirements."

INTERNATIONAL POETRY REVIEW (II, IV-Translations), Dept. of Romance Languages, UNC-Greensboro, Greensboro NC 27412, phone (910)334-5655, fax (910)334-5358, founded 1975, editor Mark Smith-Soto, is a biannual primarily publishing **translations of contemporary poetry with corresponding originals (published on facing pages) as well as original poetry in English.** They have published work by Jasha Kessler, Lyn Lifshin, Pureza Canelo, Jaime Sabines and Fred Chappell. As a sample the editor selected these lines from "Poema de Invierno" by Chilean poet Jorge Teillier:

> En la casa ha empezado la fiesta.
> Pero el niño sabe que la fiesta está en otra parte,
> y mira por la ventana buscando a los desconocidos
> que pasará toda la vida tratando de encontrar.

translated as "Winter Poem" by Mary Crow:

> In the house the party has begun.
> But the child knows the party is somewhere else,
> and he looks out the window searching for the strangers

he will spend his whole life trying to find.

IPR is 100 pgs., 5½×8½, professionally printed and perfect-bound with 2-3 color cover. "We accept 5% of original poetry in English and about 30% of translations submitted." Press run is 500 for 250 subscribers of which 100 are libraries. Subscription: $10 individuals, $15 institutions. **Sample post-paid: $5. Submit no more than 5 pages of poetry. No previously published poems; simultaneous submissions OK. Seldom comments on rejections. Send SASE for guidelines. Reports in 2-4 months. Pays 1 copy. All rights revert to authors and translators.** Occasionally reviews books of poetry. Open to unsolicited reviews. Poets may also send books for review consideration. The editor says, "We strongly encourage contributors to subscribe. We prefer poetry in English to have an international or cross-cultural theme."

INTERNATIONAL QUARTERLY (II, IV-Translations), P.O. Box 10521, Tallahassee FL 32302-0521, phone (904)224-5078, fax (904)224-5127, e-mail vbrock@mailer.fsu.edu, website http://mailer.fsu.edu/~vbrock/, founded 1993, editor-in-chief Van K. Brock. **"We welcome outstanding writing in all genres, in original English and in translation, quality work that transcends cultural givens. No one-dimensional views of people or place, work that is amateurish or lacks complexity." They are also interested in work addressing international concerns.** They have recently published work by S a adi Yusuf, David Bottoms and Miroslav Holub. As a sample the editor selected these lines by Anna Akhmatova, translated by Judith Hemschemeyer:

> *I came here without a child, without a knapsack,*
> *Without so much as a walking stick,*
> *Accompanied only by the ringing voice*
> *Of yearning.*

IQ is 200 pgs., 7½×10, offset, perfect-bound, with full-color artwork on the coated card cover and an 8-page, 4-color insert. They receive about 800 mss/year, accept a quarter. Press run is 5,000 for 1,000 shelf sales. Single copy: $10; subscription: $30/year. **Sample postpaid: $6. Submit no more than 8 poems, name on each. No previously published poems; simultaneous submissions OK. Cover letter welcomed. Accepts submissions, requests for information, or any sort of query via phone, fax or e-mail.** Time between acceptance and publication is 3-9 months. Poems go from multiple readers to poetry editor to editorial board and editor-in-chief. **Often comments on rejections. Send SASE for upcoming themes or request via e-mail. Reports within 4 months. Pays 2 copies plus subscription for poets. Acquires first serial rights.** Reviews books of poetry. Open to unsolicited reviews; query first. Poets may also send books for review consideration. Sponsors an annual contest called Crossing Boundaries. Awards $500 in each of 4 categories: poetry, fiction, nonfiction and "Crossing Boundaries." Send SASE for guidelines. The editor says, "Writers who have not published elsewhere are welcome to submit, but rarely have the polish necessary to be published in *IQ*."

INTERTEXT (III, IV-Translations), 2633 E. 17th Ave., Anchorage AK 99508-3207, founded 1982, editor Sharon Ann Jaeger, publishes "full-length collections by poets of demonstrated achievement" and is "devoted to producing lasting works in every sense. We specialize in poetry, translations and short works in the fine arts and literary criticism. **We publish work that is truly excellent—no restrictions on form, length or style. Cannot use religious verse. Like both surrealist and realist poetry, poetry with intensity, striking insight, vivid imagery, fresh metaphor, musical use of language in both word sounds and rhythm. Must make the world—in all its dimensions—come alive."** To give a sense of her taste she says, "I admire the work of Sarah Kirsch, William Stafford, Eavan Boland, António Ramos Rosa, Gary Snyder, W.S. Merwin, Bob Perelman and Rainer Maria Rilke." Forthcoming: *Karasuyama Poems* by Brenda Jaeger and two collections by Burmese poet Kyi May Kaung. As a sample the editor selected these lines by James Hanlen from *17 Toutle River Haiku*:

> *I would paint a black*
> *cloud tied to roots; river rock*
> *floating on sunlight.*

Query first with 3-5 samples and SASE sent by first-class mail. Simultaneous queries OK. She says, **"Cover letter optional—the sample poems are always read first—but no form letters, please. If sample poems are promising, then the complete book ms will be requested." Always sends prepublication galleys. Pays 10% royalty after costs of production, promotion and distribution have been recovered.** The editor says, "As we may move into electronic publishing and multimedia in the future, Intertext will be even more selective. Please do not send a complete manuscript unless we specifically ask to see it. Intertext is not grant-supported, and each poet published represents a heavy investment of time, money, and life moments on the part of the staff."

INTRO (IV-Students), AWP, Tallwood House, MS 1E3, George Mason University, Fairfax VA 22030, founded 1970, publications manager Gwyn McVay. See Associated Writing Programs in the Organizations Useful to Poets section of this book. **Students in college writing programs belonging to AWP may submit to this consortium of magazines publishing student poetry, fiction and plays.**

They are open as to the type of poetry submitted except they do not want "non-literary, haiku, etc." As to poets they have published, they say, "In our history, we've introduced Dara Wier, Carolyn Forché, Greg Pope, Norman Dubie and others." Circulation 9,500. **All work must be submitted by the writing program. Programs nominate *Intro* works in the fall. Ask the director of your writing program for more information.**

INVERTED-A, INC.; INVERTED-A HORN (I), 401 Forrest Hill, Grand Prairie TX 75051, phone (214)264-0066, founded 1977, editors Amnon Katz and Aya Katz, is a very small press that evolved from publishing technical manuals for other products. "Our interests center on freedom, justice and honor." *Inverted-A Horn* is a periodical, magazine-sized, offset, usually 9 pages, which appears irregularly; circulation is 300. **Submissions of poetry for *Horn* and chapbooks are accepted. They publish 1 chapbook/year. The editors do not want to see anything "modern, formless, existentialist."** As a sample, they quote the following lines by Mike Pettingill:

> *"I sing! I sing!" the sorry wraith replied,*
> *"Though lost our life our hatred keeps us there,*
> *"To share for aye our own abject despair.*
> *"Should living man gain Trove for which we vied,*
> *"It would defeat the cause for which we died;*
> *"Nor man nor God could ere that pain repair."*

Queries are reported on in 1 month, mss in 4 months. Simultaneous submissions are OK. Pay is one free copy and a 40% discount on further copies. Samples: "A recent issue of the *Horn* can be had by merely sending a SASE with postage for 2 ounces (subject to availability)." The editor says, "I strongly recommend that would-be contributors avail themselves of this opportunity to explore what we are looking for. Most of the submissions we receive do not come close."

IOTA (II), 67 Hady Crescent, Chesterfield, Derbyshire S41 0EB Great Britain, phone 01246-276532, founded 1988, editor David Holliday, is a quarterly wanting **"any style and subject; no specific limitations as to length, though, obviously, the shorter a poem is, the easier it is to get it in, which means that poems over 40 lines can still get in if they seem good enough. No concrete poetry (no facilities) or self-indulgent logorrhea."** They have recently published poetry by R.V. Bailey, Lee Duke, Michael Facherty, Sophie Hannah, Sanjeev Richhariya and David Starkey. As a sample the editor selected this poem, "In Camera," by Kinborough Hutton:

> *"Don't you," the dictator said,*
> *stopping in his troubled walk along the parquet,*
> *wheeling round between the heroic bronzes,*
> *"Don't you sometimes get appalled*
> *at the burden of all those lives out there, locked together,*
> *never free of each other, each thinking he's the whole world?"*

Iota is 36 pgs., printed from typescript, saddle-stapled, with colored paper cover. They publish about 200 of 4,000 poems received. Their press run is 400 with 200 subscribers of which 6 are libraries. **Subscription: $10 (£6). Sample postpaid: $2 (£1) "but sometimes sent free." Submit 4-6 poems at a time. The editor prefers name and address on each poem, typed, "but provided it's legible, am happy to accept anything."** He considers simultaneous submissions, but previously published poems **"only if outstanding." First report in 1-3 weeks (unless production of the next issue takes precedence) but final acceptance/rejection may take up to a year. Pays 2 copies. Acquires first British serial rights only. Editor usually comments on rejections, "but detailed comment only when time allows and the poem warrants it."** Reviews books of poetry in about 200 words, single or multi-book format. Open to unsolicited reviews. Poets may also send books for review consideration. He says, "I am after crafted verse that says something; self-indulgent word-spinning is out. All editors have their blind spots; the only advice I can offer a beginning poet is to find a sympathetic editor (and you will only do that by seeing their magazines) and not to be discouraged by initial lack of success. Keep plugging!"

UNIVERSITY OF IOWA PRESS; THE IOWA POETRY PRIZES (III), 119 West Park Rd., 100 Kuhl House, Iowa City IA 52242-1000. The University of Iowa Press offers annually The Iowa Poetry Prizes **for book-length mss (50-150 pgs.) by poets who have already published at least one full-length book in an edition of at least 500 copies. Two awards are given each year of $1,000 plus publication with standard royalty contract.** (This competition is the only way in which this press accepts poetry.) **Mss are received annually in February and March only. Mss are screened by a panel of poets and final judging is done by the press's editorial staff. All writers of English are eligible, whether citizens of the US or not. Poems from previously published books may be included only in mss of selected or collected poems, submissions of which are encouraged. Simultaneous submissions OK if press is immediately notified if the book is accepted by another publisher. No reading fee is charged, but stamped, self-addressed packaging is required or mss**

will not be returned. "These awards have been initiated to encourage poets who are beyond the first-book stage to submit their very best work."

THE IOWA REVIEW (II), Dept. PM, 308 EPB, University of Iowa, Iowa City IA 52242, phone (319)335-0462, founded 1970, editor David Hamilton (first readers for poetry and occasional guest editors vary), appears 3 times a year. The editor says, "We simply look for poems that at the time we read and choose, we admire. **No specifications as to form, length, style, subject matter or purpose.** There are around 30-40 pgs. of poetry in each issue and currently we like to give several pages to a single poet. Though we print work from established writers, we're always delighted when we discover new talent." *IR* is 200 pgs., professionally printed, flat-spined. They receive about 5,000 submissions/year, use about 100. Editors of this influential journal do seem open to all styles and lengths, with most poems falling into the lyric free verse category. Diction, for the most part, is accessible although some examples show degrees of experimentation with form. In all, poems evoke intriguing situations or ideas. Circulation is 1,200-1,300 with 1,000 subscribers of which about half are libraries. Subscription: $18. **Sample postpaid: $6. Submit 3-6 poems at a time. Reads submissions September 1 through May 1 only.** Time between acceptance and publication is "around a year. Sometimes people hit at the right time and come out in a few months." **Occasionally comments on rejections or offers suggestions on accepted poems. Reports in 1-4 months. Pays $1 a line, 2-3 copies and a year's subscription. Buys first North American serial rights.** Poetry published in *The Iowa Review* has also been included in the 1992, 1993, 1994, 1995 and 1996 volumes of *The Best American Poetry* and the *Pushcart Prize* anthology for 1994. The editor advises, "That old advice of putting poems in a drawer for nine years was rather nice; I'd at least like to believe the poems had endured with their author for nine months."

IOWA WOMAN (IV-Women), P.O. Box 680, Iowa City IA 52244, founded 1979, poetry editor Debra Marquart. "We are a literary quarterly publishing fiction, essays and poetry of interest to women. This is a literary magazine that has received national recognition for editorial excellence. We are publishing work **by women, about women and for women. Prefer contemporary poetry that is clear and concise. Prefer narrative and lyric. No greeting card verse.**" They have published poetry by Lyn Lifshin, Alice Friman and Enid Shomer. As a sample the editor selected these lines by Maria S. Wickwire:

> She forgot and forgot, releasing
> small things with infinite patience and love
> gently pulling threads from the tapestry she had kept so long in place.

> As she forgot the foxes, they came out from the trees
> and leaned their soft noses into her palms.
> All the forgotten birds came down in a flock, returning their wordless songs.

Iowa Woman is elegantly printed, 48 pgs., magazine-sized, 4-color cover with "original cover art and illustrations." Of 2,000 poems received "I accept about 30." Press run is 2,500 for subscriptions and national newsstand sales. **Sample postpaid: $6. Submit 4-5 poems at a time. No simultaneous submissions. Send SASE for guidelines. Pays 2 copies and $5/poem. Buys first rights.** Reviews books of poetry in 500-1,000 words. Open to unsolicited reviews. Poets may also send books to Book Editor for review consideration. "No guarantee that books sent will be reviewed; this is at the discretion of our reviewers." They hold an annual poetry contest with first-place prize of $100. $10 entry fee, 3 poems, for non-subscribers. Contest guidelines available after May. Deadline: December 31. The editor says, "We would like to receive more poetry from minority women about their life experiences."

IRON PRESS; IRON (II), 5 Marden Terrace, Cullercoats, North Shields, Tyne & Wear, NE30 4PD England, phone (0191)2531901, founded 1973, poetry editors Peter Mortimer, Jenny Lewis and David Stephenson, "publishes contemporary writing both in magazine form (*Iron*) and in individual books. Magazine concentrates on poetry, the books on prose and drama." They are **"open to many influences, but no 19th century derivatives please, or work from people who seem unaware anything has happened poetically since Wordsworth."** Peter Mortimer says, "Writing is accepted and published because when I read it I feel the world should see it—if I don't feel that, it's no good. What's the point of poetry nobody understands except the poet?" The poets they have published include John Whitworth, Richard Kostelanetz and Sharon Olds. *Iron* is 8¼ × 7¾, professionally printed in small type, 1-3 columns, flat-spined, using b&w photos and graphics, three-color glossy card cover, about 50 pgs. of poetry in each issue. Circulation is 1,000 for 600 subscribers of which 50 are libraries. **Sample postpaid: $10 (bills only, no checks), or £4. Submit a maximum of 5 poems. "Just the poems—no need for long-winded backgrounds. The poems must stand by themselves. For return of poems, a SAE with IRCs is essential." Always comments on rejections** "provided poets keep to our maximum of 5 poems per submission." **Reports in "2 weeks maximum." Pays £10/page.** Staff reviews books of poetry. Send books for review consideration % Val Laws, Reviews Editor. They do not invite poetry submissions for books, which they commission themselves. The editor advises, "Don't start submitting work too soon. It will only waste your own and editors' time. Many writers turn out a few dozen poems, then rush them off before they've learnt much of the craft, never mind the art." And about his occupation as editor, this journalist, poet, playwright and humorist says, "Small magazines and presses contain some awful writing, which is inevitable. They also contain a kind of truth which the large commercial organizations (over-burdened with marketing men, accountants and financial advisors) have long forgotten. And the good writing in small presses more than compensates for the awful."

ISRAEL HORIZONS (IV-Ethnic), 224 W. 35th St., Suite #403, New York NY 10001, founded 1952, poetry consultants Rochelle Ratner and Jon Shevin. A quarterly Socialist-Zionist periodical which **uses poetry reflecting Israeli and Jewish culture and concerns.** *Israel Horizons* reflects the Israeli left and the Zionist peace camp in Israel, including but not exclusively *Mapam* and the National Kibbutz (*Artzi*) Federation; it deals with current challenges to Israeli Society and the world Jewish community from a Socialist-Zionist perspective and examines questions confronting democratic socialism in our day. It includes editorial comments, regular columns on various topics and book and film reviews. It has an international readership with readers in the U.S., Israel, Canada and 22 other countries. The publication is 8½ × 11, 32-40 pgs. Press run is 5,000. Subscription: $15/year. **Sample: $3 and SASE. Reports in 3-6 months. Pays 2 copies.**

ITALIAN AMERICANA (IV-Ethnic), URI/CCE, 80 Washington St., Providence RI 02903-1803, fax (401)277-5070, founded 1974, editor Carol Bonomo Albright, poetry editor Dana Gioia, appears twice a year using **8-10 poems "on Italian-American subjects, no more than 3 pgs. No trite nostalgia; no poems about grandparents."** As a sample the editor selected these lines from "Late Evening in Cheyenne" by Ned Condini:

> *Nocturnal warmths of spring are in the air,*
> *echoing our eager youth, a rare*
> *marriage of constellations in the sky.*
> *This aged wine burns, and I want you to drink it*
> *with me, feel it rush down your thirsty throat,*
> *and thus bewitched, on tantalizing days*
> *of loss, forget for this glory your cross.*

It is 150-200 pgs., 7 × 9, professionally printed, flat-spined. Press run is 1,000 for 900 subscribers of which 175 are libraries, 175 shelf sales, the rest individual adult subscribers. Subscription: $15. **Sample postpaid: $7.50. Submit 3 poems at a time. No previously published poems or simultaneous submissions. Cover letter not required "but helpful." Name on first page of ms only. Do not submit mss in July, August or September. Occasionally comments on rejections. Reports in 4-6 weeks. Acquires first rights.** Reviews books of poetry in 600 words, multi-book format. Poets may send books for review consideration to Prof. John Paul Russo, English Dept., University of Miami, Coral Gables FL 33124. The editor says, "Single copies of poems for submissions are sufficient."

ITALICA PRESS (IV-Bilingual/foreign language), 595 Main St., #605, New York NY 10044-0047, phone (212)935-4230, fax (212)838-7812, e-mail italica@aol.com, founded 1985, publishers Eileen Gardiner and Ronald G. Musto, is a small press publisher of **English translations of Italian works** in Smyth-sewn paperbacks, averaging 175 pgs. They have published *Guido Cavalcanti, The Complete Poems*, a dual-language (English/Italian) book with English translation and introduction by Marc Cirigliano, and *Women Poets of the Italian Renaissance*, a dual-language anthology, edited by Laura Anna Stortoni and translated by Laura Anna Stortoni and Mary Prentice Lillie. **Query with 10 sample translations of medieval and Renaissance Italian poets. Include cover letter, bio and list of publications. Simultaneous submissions OK, but translation should not be "totally" previously published. No submissions via fax or e-mail; however, queries via fax or e-mail are OK. Reports on queries in 3 weeks, on mss in 3 months. Always sends prepublication galleys. Pays 7-15% royalties plus 10 author's copies. Buys English language rights. Sometimes comments on rejections.**

‡JACARANDA (II), Dept. of English, California State University-Fullerton, Fullerton CA 92634, phone (714)773-3163, fax (714)448-5954, founded 1985, editor Cornel Bonca, is a biannual, "serious

---

ALWAYS include a self-addressed, stamped envelope (SASE) when sending a ms or query to a publisher within your own country. When sending material to other countries, include a self-addressed envelope and International Reply Coupons (IRCs), available for purchase at many post offices.

literary magazine publishing poetry, fiction, reviews, interviews and art." **They want "serious literary work only; no specifications on form, length or style—although we've never published inspirational verse, genre fiction that seems unaware of its own conventions, or anything that isn't scrupulously attentive to the effects of language."** They have recently published poetry by Heather McHugh, Carolyn Forché, Craig Raine and Charles Bukowski. As a sample the editor selected these lines from "Memento Mori" by Billy Collins:

> There is no need for me to keep a skull on my desk,
> to stand with one foot up on the ruins of Rome,
> or to wear a locket with a sliver of a saint's bone.
> It is enough to realize that every common object
> in this small sunny room will outlive me—
> the mirror, radio, bookstand and rocker.

Jacaranda is 120-160 pgs., perfect-bound, with 4-color covers and occasional color art inside. They receive about 3,000 poems a year, accept about 2%. Press run is 1,500 for 450 subscribers of which 50 are libraries, 500-600 shelf sales. Subscription: $12/year. **Sample postpaid: $6. Submit up to 4 poems at a time. No previously published poems; simultaneous submissions OK. Cover letter preferred. Poems are circulated to an editorial board. "We have at least three people read each submission. If one or more of these like it, it goes before the editorial board for serious consideration. Seldom comments on rejections. Send SASE for guidelines. Reports in 2-3 months. Pays 3 copies, plus discount on additional copies. Acquires first rights.** Reviews books of poetry in 500-5,000 words. Open to unsolicited reviews. Poets may also send books for review consideration. Sponsors biannual poetry contest. Prizes: $200 first prize, $100 second prize, $50 third prize, $25 six honorable mentions. All submissions must be previously unpublished. Reading fee: $3/poem. Deadlines: November 15 and May 10. Send SASE for details. Most recent judge was Carolyn Forché.

JACKSON HARBOR PRESS (V), RR1, Box 107AA, Washington Island WI 54246-9722, founded 1993, editor/publisher William Olson, was scheduled to publish 1 chapbook in 1996. They have published *Island Verse* by William Olson, *Tam O' Shanter* by Robert Burns and William Olson and *Robin Song*, an anthology. **They are currently unable to accept unsolicited submissions**, but say that "perhaps we will be able to open our door to regional poets in one or two years."

JACKSON'S ARM (III), % Sunk Island Publishing, Box 74, Lincoln LN1 1QG England, phone (01522)575660, fax (01522)520394, e-mail 100074.140@compuserve.com, founded 1985, editor Michael Blackburn, is a small press publisher of poetry chapbooks and translations. **"No specifications as to subject or style. The poetry I want to publish should be vigorous and imaginative, with a firm grasp of everyday realities. Nothing bland, safe or pretentious."** The press publishes occasional chapbooks, books, cards and cassettes. However, the editor says **he does not usually accept unsolicited submissions. Pays in copies: 10% of print run.** Also sponsors the annual Jackson's Arm Poetry Pamphlet Competition for 16 pgs. of poetry. Winning collection is published. Two runners-up receive £25 each. Send SASE (or SAE and IRCs) for details. Mr. Blackburn advises, "Read everything you can, in particular *contemporary* poets and writers. Get hold of all the 'small' poetry magazines you can, as well as the more commercial and prestigious."

JANUS, A JOURNAL OF LITERATURE; COLLINGS HOUSE PRESS (III), P.O. Box 376, Collingswood NJ 08108, editor David Livewell, appears semiannually in the spring and fall. The editor says, **"We seek well-crafted verse in forms that are necessary to the content. Both metrical and free verse are considered."** They have recently published poetry by Anthony Hecht, Thomas Kinsella, Louis McKee, Louis Simpson, Robin Skelton and David Slavitt. As a sample the editor selected these lines from "Ruisdael and Constable in South Jersey" by Claude Koch:

> Then resurrection's commonplace
> Rolls from the heart its blinding stone
> Carapace of casual dread,
> And Janus-eyed, and from the dead,
> We take the common vision home.

Janus is 48 pgs., 5½×8½, neatly printed and saddle-stapled, with colored card cover and b&w graphics. They receive approximately 800 poetry submissions a year, accept about 16. Press run is 500. Subscription: $7, $8 for institutions. **Submit 3-5 poems at a time. "Submissions cannot be returned." Include SASE for response. No previously published poems or simultaneous submissions. Cover letter and short bio required. Poems are circulated to an editorial board. Often comments on rejections. Reports in 2-3 months. Pays in copies.** "We review books of poetry and other books of literary merit." Open to unsolicited reviews and essays provided "they are serious and relevant to contemporary poetry." The editor says, "We do not want to discourage submissions, but since we publish so few unsolicited poems, it is important that authors submit their very best work. In particular, we do not see enough attention paid to the intricacies of meter and form."

JAPANOPHILE (IV-Form, ethnic), P.O. Box 223, Okemos MI 48864-0223, phone (517)669-2109, e-mail japanlove@aol.com, website http://voyager.net/japanophile, founded 1974, poetry editor Earl R. Snodgrass, is a literary quarterly about Japanese culture (not just in Japan). Issues include articles, photos, art, a short story and **poetry. They want haiku or other Japanese forms ("they need not be about Japanese culture") or any form if the subject is about Japan, Japanese culture or American-Japanese relations. (Note: Karate and ikebana in the US are examples of Japanese culture.)** They have recently published poetry by Renee Leopold, Nancy Corson Carter, Jean Jorgensen, Mimi Walter Hinman and reprints of Bashō. As a sample the editor selected this haiku (poet unidentified):

> first snowstorm
> our old cat rediscovers
> the warm airduct

There are 10-15 pgs. of poetry in each issue (digest-sized, about 58 pgs., saddle-stapled). They have a circulation of 800 with 200 subscriptions of which 30 are libraries. They receive about 500 submissions a year, use 70, have a 2-month backlog. **Sample postpaid: $4. Summer is the best time to submit. Cover letter required; include brief bio and credits if any. Send SASE for guidelines or request via e-mail. Reports in 2 months. Pays $1 for haiku and up to $15 for longer poems.** Open to unsolicited reviews. Poets may also send books for review consideration, attn. Vada L. Davis. They also publish books under the Japanophile imprint, but so far only one has been of poetry. Query with samples and cover letter (about 1 pg.) giving publishing credits, bio. The editor says, "This quarterly is out as each season begins. Poems that name or suggest a season, and are received two or three months before the season, get a good look."

JEWISH CURRENTS (II), 22 E. 17th St., Suite 601, New York NY 10003-1919, phone (212)924-5740, founded 1946, editor Morris U. Schappes, is a magazine appearing 11 times a year that publishes **poetry on Jewish subjects and themes, including translations from the Yiddish and Hebrew** (original texts should be submitted with translations). The editor says it is 48 pgs., 5×8, offset, saddle-stapled. Press run is 2,600 for 2,500 subscribers of which about 10% are libraries. Subscription: $30/year. **Sample postpaid: $2. Submit 1 poem at a time, typed, double-spaced, with SASE. No previously published poems or simultaneous submissions. Cover letter required. Publishes theme issues.** Time between acceptance and publication is 2 years. **Seldom comments on rejections. Send SASE for guidelines and upcoming themes. Reports in 6-12 months. Always sends prepublication galleys. Pays 6 copies plus 1-year subscription.** Reviews books of poetry.

JEWISH SPECTATOR (IV-Religious), 4391 Park Milano, Calabasas CA 91302, phone (818)591-7481, fax (818)591-7267, e-mail jewishspec@aol.com, founded 1935, editor Robert Bleiweiss. *Jewish Spectator* is a 68-page Judaic scholarly quarterly that **welcomes poetry on Jewish themes.** Subscribers: 1,400. **No simultaneous submissions or previously published poems. Cover letter with brief bio (2-3 lines) required. Reports in 6 weeks. Returns mss only with SASE. Pays 2 copies.** Open to unsolicited reviews. Poets may also send books for review consideration.

JEWISH VEGETARIANS NEWSLETTER; JEWISH VEGETARIANS OF NORTH AMERICA (I, IV-Religious, specialized), 6938 Reliance Rd., Federalsburg MD 21632, phone (410)754-5550, founded 1983, editor Eva R. Mossman. *Jewish Vegetarians Newsletter* is a quarterly publication of the Jewish Vegetarians of North America, a nonprofit organization. It is designed to promote vegetarianism within the Judaic tradition and includes various articles, recipes and short book reviews. **They want poetry that is "Jewish related and/or about vegetarianism, veganism, animal rights and/or the environment."** As a sample the editor selected these lines from "The Festival of Fruit" by Louis Berman, in honor of the Jewish Holiday Tu B'Shevat ("Tu B'Shevat is a kind of springtime Thanksgiving."):

> When Springtime warms the earth
> And lengthens the daylight hours
> This is the sign of promise
> That the earth is awakening from its wintry sleep
> And will again become fruitful.

The newsletter is 16 pgs., $8\frac{1}{2} \times 11$, printed on recycled paper and saddle-stapled. Press run is 1,200 for 700 subscribers. Subscription: $12/year. **Sample available free with #10 SAE and 2 first-class stamps. Submit 2 poems at a time. Previously published poems and simultaneous submissions OK. Cover letter required. "Please include permission to print." Often comments on rejections. Send SASE for upcoming themes. Reports in no more than 3 months. "We do not pay for literary contributions."** However, copies are available free for the cost of postage and all poetry remains the property of the author. The editor says, "We encourage everyone to obtain a sample issue."

JEWISH WOMEN'S LITERARY ANNUAL; JEWISH WOMEN'S RESOURCE CENTER (IV-Ethnic, women), 9 E. 69th St., New York NY 10021, phone (212)751-9223, fax (212)935-3523, founded 1994, editor Henny Wenkart, publishes poetry and fiction **by Jewish women. They want "poems by Jewish women on any topic, but of the highest literary quality."** They have recently published poetry by Alicia Ostriker, Lyn Lifshin, Grace Herman, Enid Dame and Lesléa Newman. As a sample the editor selected these lines from "Definition of a Desert" by Helen Papell:

> All I hold are stones tuned
> and turned by the river,
> faceless.
> I ask Miriam How do I know if any?
>
> She says The definition of a desert
> is you have to wait
> until it breaks itself open.

The annual is 160 pgs., 6×9, perfect-bound with a laminated card cover, b&w art and photos inside. They receive about 500 poems a year, publish approximately 15%. Press run is 1,000. **Sample postpaid: $5. No previously published poems. Prefers to receive submissions by "snail mail." Poems are circulated to an editorial board. Often comments on rejections. Reports in 3-5 months. Pays 3 copies. Rights remain with the poet.** The Jewish Women's Resource Center holds a monthly workshop, sponsors occasional readings and **also publishes a few books of poetry.** "We select only one or two manuscripts a year out of about 20 submitted. But although authors then receive editing help and publicity, they bear the cost of production. Members of the workshop we conduct and poets published in our annual receive first attention." The editor says, "It would be helpful, but not essential, if poets would send for a sample copy of our annual before submitting."

THE JOHNS HOPKINS UNIVERSITY PRESS (V), 2715 N. Charles St., Baltimore MD 21218, founded 1878, editor-in-chief Eric Halpern. "One of the largest American university presses, Johns Hopkins is a publisher mainly of scholarly books and journals. We do, however, publish short fiction and poetry in the series Johns Hopkins: Poetry and Fiction, edited by John Irwin on 10% royalty contracts. **Unsolicited submissions are not considered.**"

THE JOURNAL (III), Dept. of English, Ohio State University, 164 W. 17th Ave., Columbus OH 43210, phone (614)292-4076, fax (614)292-7816, founded 1972, co-editors Kathy Fagan and Michelle Herman, appears twice yearly with reviews, essays, quality fiction and poetry. **"We're open to all forms; we tend to favor work that gives evidence of a mature and sophisticated sense of the language."** They have recently published poetry by Brigit Kelly, Lucia Perillo, Timothy Liu and Heather McHugh. The following sample is from the poem "The Helmet of Mambrino" by Linda Bierds:

> I would know that tumble often, that
> explorer's slide, belief to belief, conviction
> to its memory, to conviction. Once I placed
> my marker-coin on Mt. Whitney's double, lost in a mist,
> convinced I had climbed to the highest land. Once
> I charted a lake from opal air.

The Journal is 6×9, professionally printed on heavy stock, 80-120 pgs., of which about 50 in each issue are devoted to poetry. They receive about 4,000 submissions/year, use 200, and have a 3- to 6-month backlog. Press run is 1,500. Subscription: $8. **Sample: $5. No submissions via fax. On occasion editor comments on rejections. Pays 2 copies and an honorarium of $25-50 when funds are available. Acquires all rights. Returns rights on publication.** Reviews books of poetry. Contributing editor David Citino advises, "However else poets train or educate themselves, they must do what they can to know our language. Too much of the writing that we see indicates that poets do not in many cases develop a feel for the possibilities of language, and do not pay attention to craft. Poets should not be in a rush to publish—until they are ready." (Also see Ohio State University Press/*The Journal* Award in Poetry.)

JOURNAL OF ASIAN MARTIAL ARTS (IV-Specialized), 821 W. 24th St., Erie PA 16502-2523, phone (814)455-9517, fax (814)838-7811, founded 1991, editor-in-chief Michael A. DeMarco, is a quarterly "comprehensive journal on Asian martial arts with high standards and academic approach." **They want poetry about Asian martial arts and Asian martial art history/culture. They have no restrictions provided the poet has a feel for, and good understanding of, the subject. They don't want poetry showing a narrow view. "We look for a variety of styles from an interdisciplinary approach."** As a sample we selected the opening lines from "Kensei" by Berrien C. Henderson:

> He approaches last.
> A zephyr gusts and swirls about him.
> His **gi** flaps and pops in the wind.
> Brow furrowed and jet hair shining, he stands

> *As tranquil as a distant mountain*
> *While his topknot swings ever so gently.*

The editor says the journal is 128 pgs., 8½ × 11, perfect-bound, with soft cover, b&w illustrations, computer and hand art and ads. Press run is 6,000 for 1,000 subscribers of which 50 are libraries, the rest mainly shelf sales. Single copy: $9.75; subscription: $32 for 1 year, $55 for 2 years. **Sample postpaid: $10. Previously published poems OK; no simultaneous submissions. Cover letter required. Often comments on rejections. Send SASE for guidelines. Reports in 1-2 months. Sometimes sends prepublication galleys. Pays $1-100 and/or 1-5 copies on publication. Buys first and reprint rights.** Reviews books of poetry "if they have some connection to Asian martial arts; length is open." Open to unsolicited reviews. Poets may also send books for review consideration. The editor adds, "We offer a unique medium for serious poetry dealing with Asian martial arts. Any style is welcome if there is quality in thought and writing."

"The discipline of the lines captures the freedom of being, and that delicate balance is what we strive for in each issue," says Editor Sander Zulauf of the cover artwork for this issue of the *Journal of New Jersey Poets*. "This particular cover was chosen for its clarity and sensitivity of line, conveying the fragility of the natural subject matter." The regional biannual journal, published by the County College of Morris in Randolph, New Jersey, is devoted solely to poetry and accepts work from current and former New Jersey residents. The cover art is by James Gwynne, an artist and Professor of Fine Art at the County College of Morris.

JOURNAL OF NEW JERSEY POETS (II, IV-Regional), English Dept., County College of Morris, Randolph NJ 07869-2086, phone (201)328-5471, fax (201)328-5425, founded 1976, editor Sander Zulauf. This biannual periodical uses poetry from **current or former residents of New Jersey. They want "serious work that is regional in origin but universal in scope." They do not want "sentimental, greeting card verse."** Poets recently published include Amiri Baraka, X.J. Kennedy, Brigit Pegeen Kelly, Kenneth Burke, Gerald Stern, Renée and Ted Weiss, and Michael Bugeja. As a sample the editor selected these lines from "In My Universe There is No Hope (A Poem of Joy)" by Joe Weil:

> *In my universe, there is no hope,*
> *only an old blue-gray cat,*
> *dreaming its version*
> *of valhalla—birds swift, but not overly so,*
> *familiar well-marked laps, the scent of catnip*
> *wafting every breeze.*
> *Soon, I'll be nearing an exit I always miss.*

The journal is published in Summer (May) and Winter (December), and is digest-sized, offset, with an average of 64 pgs. Press run is 900. Subscription: $7/year, $12/2 years. **Sample: $4. There are "no limitations" on submissions; SASE required. Faxed submissions will not be returned. Reports in 3-6 months.** Time between acceptance and publication is within 1 year. **Pays 2 copies/published poem. Acquires first North American serial rights.** Only using solicited reviews. Send books for review consideration. "We plan to offer brief reviews of 100-150 words."

JOURNAL OF POETRY THERAPY (IV-Specialized), Dept. PM, Human Sciences Press, 233 Spring St., New York NY 10013-1578, phone (212)620-8000 or (800)221-9369, founded 1987. **Poetry**

mss should be sent to journal editor, Dr. Nicholas Mazza, School of Social Work, Florida State University, Tallahassee FL 32306-2024. They use **"poems that could be useful in therapeutic settings, prefer relatively short poems; no sentimental, long poems."** They have published poetry by Ingrid Wendt and Virginia Bagliore. As a sample the editor selected these lines from "all too often, love " by Elaine Preston:

> *like our hunger*
> *in the house where we warmed our fingers*
> *and laughed against cracks in walls*
> *long since plastered shut against the cold*

"The *Journal* is devoted to the use of the poetic in health, mental health education and other human service settings." The quarterly is 64 pgs., digest-sized, flat-spined, using 3-6 pgs. for poetry. They accept approximately 10% of 100 poems received. There are 500 subscriptions. Subscription: $42 (US), $49 (international) for individuals; $155 (US), $180 (international) for institutions. **Write publisher for free sample. Submit maximum of 3 poems, 4 copies of each with name on only 1 of them. Include SASE. Editor "occasionally" comments on rejections. Pays 1 copy.**

JOURNAL OF THE AMERICAN MEDICAL ASSOCIATION (JAMA) (II, IV-Specialized, themes), 515 N. State, Chicago IL 60610, phone (312)464-2417, fax (312)464-5824, founded 1883, associate editor Charlene Breedlove, has a "Poetry and Medicine" column and publishes **poetry "in some way related to a medical experience, whether from the point-of-view of a health care worker or patient, or simply an observer. No unskilled poetry."** They have recently published poetry by Aimée Grunberger and Jack Coulehan. As a sample the editor selected these lines from "Storm in the Morning" by Floyd Skloot:

> *All I have to do is wait here.*
> *Yes, I know I do not know where*
> *I am now, so I must be near*
> *the source of peace. Across the years*
> *to this bed blazed by a long skein*
> *of dreams, I find myself at ease.*

JAMA, magazine-sized, flat-spined, with glossy paper cover, has 360,000 subscribers of which 369 are libraries. They accept about 7% of 550 poems received/year. Subscription: $66. **Sample free. No previously published poems; simultaneous submissions OK, if identified. "I always appreciate inclusion of a brief cover letter with, at minimum, the author's name and address clearly printed. Mention of other publications and special biographical notes are always of interest." Publishes theme issues.** Theme issues include managed care, medical education, ethics/human rights, allergy and immunology, and science reporting. **Pays up to 3 copies. "We ask for a signed copyright release, but publication elsewhere is always granted free of charge."**

‡JOYFUL NOISE: THE JOURNAL OF CHRISTIAN POETRY (IV-Religious), P.O. Box 401, Bowling Green KY 42102, editor Jim Erskine, appears quarterly. **They want "poetry with a Christian outlook, any style—free verse, rhyme, haiku, etc. Maximum length: 25 lines."** The journal is 24 pgs., 8½×11, saddle-stapled with a card stock cover and a few b&w graphics. Single copy: $6; subscription: $20/year. **Sample postpaid: $5. Submit no more than 3 poems at a time. "Simultaneous submissions OK, but previously *un*published poems preferred." Reports in 1 month. Pays copies. Also awards 3 Editor's Choice Awards ranging from $10-25.** The editor says, "Avoid political, social, New Age and broad, universal topics—love, brotherhood, peace, etc. We think the smaller in scope and more personal your subject, the better the poem."

JUGGLER'S WORLD (IV-Specialized), % Ken Letko, College of the Redwoods, 883 W. Washington Blvd., Crescent City CA 95531-8361, phone (707)464-7457, founded 1982, literary editor Ken Letko, is a quarterly magazine, **using poems about juggling. "Only restriction is that all content is focused on juggling."** They have recently published poetry by Siv Cedering, Anita Endrezze, Barbara Goldberg, Robert Hill Long, Lucien Stryk and Margo Wilding. As a sample the editor selected these lines from "American Juggler on Grafton Street, Dublin, October 1988" by Pat Boran:

> *Quiet as Bohr's*
> *celebrated model of the atom,*
> *the balls seem held there*
> *in space and time*
> *for our scrutiny.*

> *Even the raindrops*

JW is 40 pgs., magazine-sized, professionally printed on glossy stock and saddle-stapled, with 2-color glossy paper cover. They receive 50-100 poetry submissions/year, use 4-8 poems. Press run is 3,500, circulated to more than 3,000 jugglers in more than 20 countries. Subscription: $30. **Sample: $8. They will consider previously published poems. Editor sometimes comments on rejections, suggesting** some revision. **Reports in 1-4 months. Pays 1 copy. Acquires first or one-time rights.** The editor urges poets to "provide insights and remember that the theme is always juggling!"

‡**JUNCTION PRESS (II)**, P.O. Box 40537, San Diego CA 92164, phone (619)282-0371, fax (619)282-0297, founded 1991, publisher Mark Weiss, aims to publish "overlooked non-mainstream poetry." The press publishes 2 paperback books of poetry a year. **They want "modern or postmodern work, any form or length. No academic, Iowa school or formal poetry."** They have recently published poetry by Susie Mee, Richard Elman and Rochelle Owens. They say their books are typically 72-96 pgs., 5½ × 8½, offset and perfect-bound with coated covers with graphics. **Query first with 10-15 pgs. of poetry and a cover letter (bio unnecessary). Previously published poems OK; no simultaneous submissions. Often comments on rejections. Replies to queries in 6 months, to mss (if invited) "immediately." Pays 100 copies (out of a press run of 1,000).** The publisher says, "While I don't dismiss the possibility of finding a second Rimbaud, please note that all of my authors have been in their 50s and have written for many years."

JUNIPER PRESS; NORTHEAST; JUNIPER BOOKS; THE WILLIAM N. JUDSON SERIES OF CONTEMPORARY AMERICAN POETRY; CHICKADEE; INLAND SEA SERIES; GIFTS OF THE PRESS (III, IV-Form), 1310 Shorewood Dr., La Crosse WI 54601, e-mail juniperpr @aol.com, founded 1962, poetry editors John Judson and Joanne Judson, is one of the oldest and most respected programs of publishing poetry in the country. *Northeast* is a semiannual little magazine, digest-sized, saddle-stapled. **"Poets published in our books have first appeared in *Northeast* and are invited to submit mss. Any other book mss sent will be returned without being read." Reports in 2-4 months.** A subscription to *Northeast*/Juniper Press is $33/year ($38 for institutions), which brings you 2 issues of the magazine and the Juniper Books, Chickadees, WNJ Books and some gifts of the press, a total of about 5-8 items. (Or send SASE for catalog to order individual items; orders can be placed via e-mail. **Sample postpaid: $2.50.**) The Juniper Books are perfect-bound books of poetry; the WNJ Books are letterpress poetry books by one author; Chickadees are 12-24 pgs. each, in wrappers; Inland Sea Series is for larger works; Gifts of the Press are usually given only to subscribers or friends of the press. "Please read us before sending mss. It will aid in your selection of materials to send. If you don't like what we do, please don't submit."

JUST ABOUT HORSES (II, IV-Animals), 14 Industrial Rd., Pequannock NJ 07440, founded 1975, editor Stephanie Macejko, is a magazine which appears 6 times/year and provides information about both the model horse hobby and real horses. **"Our magazine contains information on model horses and real horses. Any style of poetry will be read as long as the style suits the subject matter."** *Just About Horses* is 40 pgs., digest-sized, saddle-stapled, professionally printed on glossy paper with b&w and color photos. Press run is 15,000 for 12,500 subscribers. Subscription: $12. **Sample postpaid: $2.50.**

KALEIDOSCOPE: INTERNATIONAL MAGAZINE OF LITERATURE, FINE ARTS, AND DISABILITY (IV-Specialized, themes), 326 Locust St., Akron OH 44302, phone (216)762-9755, fax (216)762-0912, founded 1979, editor-in-chief Dr. Darshan C. Perusek, consulting poetry editor Christopher Hewitt. *Kaleidoscope* is based at United Disability Services, a nonprofit agency. **Poetry should deal with the experience of disability but not limited to that when writer has a disability. "*Kaleidoscope* is interested in high-quality poetry with vivid, believable images and evocative language. Works should not use stereotyping, patronizing or offending language about disability."** They have recently published poetry by Margaret Robison, Sheryl L. Nelms, Sandra J. Lindow and Barbara Seaman. As a sample they offer these lines from "Lake Superior Wind Chimes" by David A. Heinlein:

> Big green rhododendron leaves
> Rattle in the wind.
> Up high, cirrus.
> My Aikido calligraphy
> On weathered board
> Hangs from the cypress.

Circulation 1,500, including libraries, social service agencies, health-care professionals, universities and individual subscribers. Single copy: $5; subscription: $9 individual, $14 agency. **Sample: $4. Submit photocopies with SASE for return of work. Limit 5 poems/submission. Previously published poems and simultaneous submissions OK, "as long as we are notified in both instances." Cover letter required.** All submissions must be accompanied by an autobiographical sketch. **Deadlines: March and August 1. Publishes theme issues. Send SASE for upcoming themes. Theme for 1997 is "Disability and the Visual Arts"—July 1997 (deadline March 1997). Reports in 3 weeks; acceptance or rejection may take 6 months. Pays $10-125. Rights return to author upon publication.** Staff reviews books of poetry. Send books for review consideration to Gail Willmott, senior editor.

KALLIOPE, a journal of women's art (IV-Women, translations, themes), 3939 Roosevelt Blvd., Jacksonville FL 32205, phone (904)381-3511, founded 1978, editor Mary Sue Koeppel, is a literary/visual arts journal published by Florida Community College at Jacksonville; the emphasis is on women writers and artists. The editors say, **"We like the idea of poetry as a sort of artesian well—there's one meaning that's clear on the surface and another deeper meaning that comes welling up from underneath. We'd like to see more poetry from Black, Hispanic and Native American women. Nothing sexist, racist, conventionally sentimental. We will have one special theme issue each year. Write for specific guidelines."** Poets published include Elisavietta Ritchie, Marge Piercy, Martha M. Vertreace, Enid Shomer and Tess Gallager. As a sample the editor selected the following lines by Ruth Moon Kempher:

> But I sail hot, sail cold, depending
> not on externals, but on that queer greed
> driving, from sea to street
>   on to dark hedgerows
> shadowed alleys, like a creature
> chased, like Cinderella
> shoes in hand.

Kalliope calls itself "a journal of women's art" and publishes fiction, interviews, drama and visual art in addition to poetry. The magazine, which appears 3 times a year, is 7¼×8¼, flat-spined, handsomely printed on white stock, glossy card cover and b&w photographs of works of art. Average number of pages is 80. Poems here are lively, celebratory and varied in form, style and length. The circulation is 1,500, of which 400-500 are subscriptions, including 100 library subscriptions, and 800 are copies sold on newsstands and in bookstores. Subscription: $12.50/year or $22/2 years. **Sample: $7. Poems should be submitted in batches of 3-5 with brief bio note, phone number and address. No previously published poems. SASE required. Because all submissions are read by several members of the editing staff, response time is usually 3-4 months. Publication will be within 6 months. Criticism is provided "when time permits and the author has requested it." Send SASE for guidelines and upcoming themes. Pays $10 or subscription. Acquires first publication rights.** Reviews books of poetry, "but we prefer groups of books in one review." Open to unsolicited reviews. Poets may also send books for review consideration. They sponsor the Sue Saniel Elkind Poetry Contest. 1996 judge was Joy Harjo. First prize: $1,000; runners up published in *Kalliope*. Deadline: October 15. Send SASE for details. The editor says, "*Kalliope* is a carefully stitched patchwork of how women feel, what they experience, and what they have come to know and understand about their lives . . . a collection of visions from or about women all over the world. Send for a sample copy, to see what appeals to us, or better yet, subscribe! We have increased our circulation and can pay our contributors a bit."

KANSAS QUARTERLY/ARKANSAS REVIEW (II, IV-Regional), (formerly just *Kansas Quarterly*), Dept. of English and Philosophy, P.O. Box 1890, Arkansas State University, State University AR 72467, editor Norman Lavers, now published under the combined name of *Kansas Quarterly/Arkansas Review*, the magazine will "seek to continue the fine 25-year tradition of the *Kansas Quarterly*. But there will be changes in format and emphasis. *KQ/AR* will publish almost entirely fiction and creative nonfiction. Each issue will publish, at most, the poetry of two or three people. (An occasional all-poetry issue may also be published.) And, since part of *KQ/AR*'s funding comes from the Arkansas State University Delta Studies Project, the magazine will preserve a corner to showcase the art and culture of the lower Mississippi Delta." **They are "wide open" as far as submission guidelines, but seek "quality. We just want good work." Send SASE for details.**

KARAMU (II), Dept. of English, Eastern Illinois University, Charleston IL 61920, phone (217)581-5614, founded 1966, editor Peggy Brayfield, is an annual whose "goal is to provide a forum for the best contemporary poetry and fiction that comes our way. We especially like to print the works of new writers. **We like to see poetry that shows a good sense of what's being done with poetry currently. We like poetry that builds around real experiences, real images and real characters and that avoids abstraction, overt philosophizing and fuzzy pontifications. In terms of form, we prefer well-structured free verse, poetry with an inner, sub-surface structure as opposed to, let's say, the surface structure of rhymed quatrains. We have definite preferences in terms of style and form, but no such preferences in terms of length or subject matter. Purpose, however, is another thing. We don't have much interest in the openly didactic poem. If the poet wants to preach against or for some political or religious viewpoint, the preaching shouldn't be so strident that it overwhelms the poem. The poem should first be a poem."** They have published poetry by David Bond, Mary McDaniel, Pamela Donald and Karen Subach. As a sample the editor selected these lines from "We Begin Here" by Steven Blaski:

> Your death broke into you as if it were a door
> of glass that you smashed your body through.
> Still, each night I followed you to the rooms

> *of my ravaged childhood, where you wore*
> *the hellish body that performed in the freak show*
> *of intensive care . . .*

The format is 120 pgs., 5×8, matte cover, handsomely printed (narrow margins), attractive b&w art. The most recent issue carries 60 pgs. of poetry. They receive submissions from about 300 poets each year, use 40-50 poems. Never more than a year—usually 6-7 months—between acceptance and publication. They have a circulation of 350 with 300 subscribers of which 15 are libraries. **Sample: $5; 2 recent issues: $6. Poems—in batches of no more than 4-6—may be submitted to Peggy Brayfield. "We don't much care for simultaneous submissions. We read September 1 through June 30 only, for fastest decision submit February through May. Poets should not bother to query. We critique a few of the better poems. We want the poet to consider our comments and then submit new work." Publishes theme issues occasionally. Submissions on the theme "Humor" may be submitted between September and November, 1996, for publication Spring 1997. Pays 1 copy. Acquires first serial rights.** The editor says, "Follow the standard advice: Know your market. Read contemporary poetry and the magazines you want to be published in. Be patient."

KATYDID BOOKS (V), 1 Balsa Rd., Santa Fe NM 87505, founded 1973, editors/publishers Karen Hargreaves-Fitzsimmons and Thomas Fitzsimmons, publishes 3 paperbacks and 3 hardbacks/year. "We publish three series of poetry: Asian Poetry in Translation, European Writing in Translation, and American Poets." They have published poetry by Makoto Ooka, Shuntaro Tanikawa and Ryuichi Tamura. **However, they are currently not accepting submissions.**

KAWABATA PRESS; SEPIA POETRY MAGAZINE (I, II, IV-Anthology), Knill Cross House, Millbrook, Torpoint, Cornwall, United Kingdom, founded 1977, poetry editor Colin David Webb, publishes **"nontraditional poetry, prose and artwork (line only), open to all original and well thought-out work. I dislike rhymes, traditional poems and 'genre' stories. I want original and thought-provoking material."** *Sepia* is published 3 times a year in an inexpensively produced, 32-page, digest-sized, saddle-stapled format, photoreduced from typescript, with narrow margins and bizarre drawings. They receive 250 submissions/year, use 50-60. Press run is 150 for 75 subscribers of which 5-6 are libraries. Subscription: £2 ($5) a year. **Sample: 75p. ($2). Submit 6 poems at a time, typed. Prefers not to use previously published poems. Simultaneous submissions OK. "Letter with poems is polite." Reports in 10 days. Sometimes sends prepublication galleys. Pays free copy.** Reviews books of poetry in 50-100 words. Open to unsolicited reviews. Poets may also send books for review consideration. Under the imprint of Kawabata Press, Colin Webb also publishes anthologies and collections. **However, publication of these has been temporarily suspended. Query with 6-10 poems and "maybe a brief outline of intent." Poet gets 50% of profits (after cost of printing is covered) and 4 copies.** A book catalog of Kawabata Press publications is on the back of *Sepia*, for ordering copies. The editor **always comments on rejections** and advises, "Strike out everything that sounds like a cliché. Don't try any tricks. Work at it, have a feeling for what you write, don't send 'exercise' pieces. Believe in what you send."

‡KAYA PRODUCTION; MUAE: A JOURNAL OF TRANSCULTURAL PRODUCTION (IV-Ethnic/nationality), 8 Harrison St., Suite 3, New York NY 10013, phone (212)966-4798, fax (212)966-3987, e-mail kaya@panix.com, website http://www.kaya.com, founded 1994, editorial director Lawrence Chua, associate editor Sunyoung Lee. *Muae* is an annual journal that combines "innovative creative writing, poetry, photo-essays, scholarly research and investigative journalism on Asian and Asian diasporic culture and society." The editor says their premier issue was 272 pgs., $7\frac{1}{4} \times 9$, perfect-bound with color and b&w illustrations. They accept 10% of poetry received. Press run is 2,500. **Sample postpaid: $19.95. Make checks payable to Kaya Production. Previously published poems and simultaneous submissions OK. Cover letter required. Publishes theme issues. Send SASE for guidelines and upcoming themes or request via e-mail. Reports within 4 months. Always sends prepublication galleys. Pay 1 copy and small honorarium.** Kaya Production is a "publisher of a wide range of experimental and more traditional poetry." They publish 3 paperbacks and 1 hardback/year. Format is determined on a book-by-book basis. "Kaya is committed to a high production quality in addition to a high literary standard." **They want experimental as well as more traditional types of poetry. Replies to queries in 1-2 months, to mss in 4 months. Pays (for books) 7-9% royalties plus an advance and 10 author's copies.** Kaya Production received a 1995 Gregory Kolovakos Seed Grant from the Council of Literary Magazines and Presses for outstanding new presses.

KELSEY REVIEW (IV-Regional), Mercer County Community College, P.O. Box B, Trenton NJ 08690, phone (609)586-4800, fax (609)586-2318, e-mail schore@mccc.edu, founded 1988, editor-in-chief Robin Schore, is an annual published by Mercer County Community College. It serves as "an outlet for literary talent **of people living and working in Mercer County, New Jersey only."** They have **no specifications as to form, length, subject matter or style, but do not want to see poetry**

about **"kittens and puppies."** As a sample the editor selected these lines from "Dancing at the Cash Machine" by A. Tobias Grace:

> Music fills the warm summer night,
> Turning the light from the street lamps to crystal,
> Shimmering bright against the blackness,
> Sounding fine,
> An open jeep,
> Night all mine,
> Six big speakers, two amps and all,
> Drawing attention like shots from a pistol,
> Demanding rhythm and no slackness.

Kelsey Review is 86 glossy pgs., 7×11, with paper cover and line drawings; no ads. They receive about 60 submissions a year, accept 6-10. Press run is 1,750. All distributed free to contributors, area libraries and schools. **Submit no more than 6 poems at a time, typed. No previously published poems or simultaneous submissions. Deadline: May 1. Always comments on rejections. May request information via e-mail or fax. Reports in May of each year. All rights revert to authors.**

THE KENYON REVIEW (II), Kenyon College, Gambier OH 43022, phone (614)427-5208, fax (614)427-5417, e-mail kenyonreview@kenyon.edu, founded 1939, editor David Lynn, is a triquarterly review containing poetry, fiction, criticism, reviews and memoirs. It is **one of the country's leading literary publications.** Under David Lynn's editorship, this magazine continues to blossom, featuring all styles and forms, lengths and subject matters—a real openness. But this market is more closed than others because of the volume of submissions typically received during each reading cycle. Issues contain work by such poets as Cyrus Cassells, Judith Ortiz Cofer, Joy Harjo, Richard Howard, Josephine Jacobsen, Alicia Ostriker, Sherod Santos and Quincy Troupe. The elegantly printed, flat-spined, 7×10, 180-page review has a circulation of 4,000 with 3,200 subscriptions of which 1,100 are libraries. They receive about 3,000-4,000 submissions a year, use 50-60 (about 50 pgs. of poetry in each issue), have a 1-year backlog. The editor urges poets to read a few copies before submitting to find out what they are publishing. **Sample postpaid: $8. Unsolicited submissions are read from September 1 through March 31** *only.* **Writers may contact by phone, fax or e-mail, but may submit mss by mail only. Reports in 3 months. Pays $15/page for poetry, $10/page for prose. Buys first North American serial rights.** Reviews books of poetry in 2,500-7,000 words, single or multi-book format. "Reviews are primarily solicited—potential reviewers should inquire first." Poetry published in *The Kenyon Review* was also selected for inclusion in the 1992, 1993, 1994 and 1996 volumes of *The Best American Poetry* and several *Pushcart Prize* anthologies.

KINESIS (II), P.O. Box 4007, Whitefish MT 59937-4007, e-mail kinesis@eworld.com, founded 1992. *Kinesis* is a monthly that calls itself "the literary magazine for the rest of us" and includes fiction, poetry, essays and reviews. **They want any type of poetry—"as long as it moves."** They have published poetry by Lucy Shaw, John Leax, Ross Talarico, Simon Perchik and Rick Newby. As a sample the editor selected these lines from "Leaving the Hospital" by Pamela McClure:

> . . . I notice that it is the middle of summer where I step out
>
> and the ambulance is announcing its arrival
> and the nurses are announcing their arrival
> and the flutter of my father's pulse
>
> announces its set of exercises
> in his wrist. . . .

Kinesis is 48 pgs., 8½×11, printed on recycled paper and saddle-stitched with spot color and artwork, graphics and ads inside. They accept about 10% of the poetry received. Press run is 2,000 for 1,600 subscribers of which 10 are libraries, 500 shelf sales. Single copy: $3; subscription: $20. **Sample postpaid: $4. Previously published poems and simultaneous submissions OK. Send SASE for guidelines. Reports in 1 month. Pays 5 copies and a subscription. Acquires one-time rights.** Reviews books of all kinds in 1,000-2,000 words and offers a page of "Book Briefs" in addition. Poets may also send books for review consideration. They sponsor an annual "If It Moves . . . Contest" for both poetry and fiction. $10 reading fee covers 3 poems or 1 story. All entrants receive a year's

---

MARKET CATEGORIES: (I) Beginning; (II) General; (III) Limited; (IV) Specialized; (V) Closed.

subscription. Poetry winners receive prizes of $200, $100 and $50 (fiction: $200, $100 and $50) in addition to publication. Send SASE for details.

‡**KINGFISHER (V, IV-Anthologies, children)**, Elsley House, 24-30 Great Titchfield St., London W1P 7AD United Kingdom, phone (0171)631-0878, fax (0171)323-4694, is the children's imprint of Larousse plc and publishes very little poetry. "We currently have five titles in print, anthologies of verse for children either on particular themes or for particular age-groups, compiled by leading British poets. Our *Poems For The Very Young*, compiled by Michael Rosen, was the Gold Medal Winner of The National Parenting Publications Awards. The anthologies contain published work except in a few rare instances. **Because our anthologies are compiled by outside editors, we do not accept unsolicited poetry.**"

KIOSK (II), 306 Clemens Hall, SUNY, Buffalo NY 14260, phone (716)645-2578, founded 1985, editor Lia Vella, poetry editor Charlotte Pressler, is an annual literary magazine using **poetry of "any length, any style, especially experimental."** They have recently published poetry by Raymond Federman, Sheila Murphy, Lyn Lifshin, Carl Dennis and Charles Bernstein. As a sample the editor selected these lines by Seth Frechie:

> The intent
> to say it without awkwardness,
> "I _____"
> A grave uttering,
> the gravity—

The editor describes *Kiosk* as flat-spined, digest-sized. Of 400 poems they accept 10-15. **Sample free (if available) with SAE and 6 first-class stamps. Submit poems in batches of three. Cover letter not required, "but we suggest one be included." Reads submissions September 1 through April 30 only. Reports within 4 months. Pays in copies.**

KITCHEN TABLE: WOMEN OF COLOR PRESS (V, IV-Women/feminism, lesbian, ethnic, political), P.O. Box 40-4920, Brooklyn NY 11240-4920, phone (718)935-1082, fax (718)935-1107, founded 1981, is "the only publisher in North America committed to producing and distributing the **work of women of color of all racial/cultural heritages, sexualities and classes.**" They publish flat-spined paperback collections and anthologies. **"Unfortunately, because we are severely undercapitalized and understaffed, we receive far more manuscripts than we can respond to and cannot, at this time, give the manuscripts the attention they deserve."** They publish an average of one book of poetry every other year and have published three anthologies, two of which contain poetry. All books are published simultaneously in hardback for library sales. **Write for catalog to purchase samples.** The editors say, "We are particularly interested in publishing work by women of color which would generally be overlooked by other publishers, especially work by American Indian, Latina, Asian-American and African-American women who may be working class, lesbian, disabled or older writers."

ALFRED A. KNOPF (V), 201 E. 50th St., New York NY 10022, poetry editor Harry Ford. Over the years Knopf has been one of the most important and distinguished publishers of poetry in the United States. **"The list is closed to new submissions at this time."**

KONOCTI BOOKS (V), 23311 County Rd. 88, Winters CA 95694, phone (916)662-3364, founded 1973, editor/publisher Noel Peattie, **publishes poetry by invitation only.**

KRAX (II, IV-Humor); RUMP BOOKLETS (V), 63 Dixon Lane, Leeds, Yorkshire LS12 4RR England, founded 1971, poetry editors Andy Robson et al. *Krax* appears twice yearly, and they want poetry which is **"light-hearted and witty; original ideas. Undesired: haiku, religious or topical politics, $1,000 bills." 2,000 words maximum. All forms and styles considered.** As a sample the editor selected these lines from "Global Warming" by Paul McDonald:

> The seagulls are bigger
> than we imagine, and the ocean less blue . . .
> it's just that, as the years go by,
> it takes us less and less time to reach it.

Krax is 6×8, 48 pgs. of which 30 are poetry, saddle-stapled, offset with b&w cartoons and graphics. They receive up to 1,000 submissions/year of which they use 6%, have a 2- to 3-year backlog. Single copy: £2 ($4); subscription: £7.50 ($15). **Sample: $1 (75p). "Submit maximum of 6 pieces. Writer's name on same sheet as poem. SASE or SAE with IRC encouraged but not vital." No previously published poems or simultaneous submissions. Brief cover letter preferred. Reports within 2 months. Pays 1 copy.** Reviews books of poetry (brief, individual comments; no outside reviews). Send books for review consideration. *Rump Booklets* are miniature format, 3×4, 16-page collections. **They are not currently accepting work in this series. Send SASE for catalog.** The editor says,

"Before sending your poems, always add your address to the piece—we can't always place everyone's pseudonym."

KUMQUAT MERINGUE; PENUMBRA PRESS (I, II), P.O. Box 5144, Rockford IL 61125, phone (815)968-0713, e-mail moodyriver@aol.com, founded 1990, editor Christian Nelson, appears approximately 2 times/year using **"mostly shorter poetry about the small details of life, especially the quirky side of love and sex. Not interested in rhyming, meaning of life or high-flown poetry."** They have recently published works by Gina Bergamino, T. Kilgore Splake, Antler, Monica Kershner, Lynne Douglass and Ianthe Brautigan. As a sample the editor selected these lines from "Leaping Lizards" by Emile Luria:

> *After we made love . . . Kate said,*
> *"You're so weird, really,*
> *Even weirder than I thought."*
> *And I thought, could she taste the salt,*
> *Feel the sea lapping on my back?*
> *I went to sleep wondering*
> *About dinosaurs and lungfish*
> *And the deepest reaches of the sea*

It is 40-48 pgs., digest-sized, "professionally designed with professional typography and nicely printed." Press run is 600 for 250 subscribers. Subscription: $8 (3 issues). **Sample postpaid: $4. "We like cover letters but prefer to read things about who you are, rather than your long list of publishing credits. Previously published and simultaneous submissions are OK, but please let us know." Often comments on submissions. "E-mail address is only for those who want to say 'Hi.' " Send SASE for guidelines. Usually reports in 2 months. Pays 1 copy. Acquires one-time rights.** The magazine is "dedicated to the memory of Richard Brautigan." The editor advises, "Read *Kumquat Meringue* and anything by Richard Brautigan to get a feel for what we want, but don't copy Richard Brautigan, and don't copy those who have copied him. We just want that same feel. We also have a definite weakness for poems written 'to' or 'for' Richard Brautigan. Reviewers have called our publication iconoclastic, post-hip, post-beat, post-antipostmodern; and our poetry, carefully crafted imagery. When you get discouraged, write some more. Don't give up. Eventually your poems will find a home. We're very open to unpublished writers, and a high percentage of our writers had never been published anywhere before they submitted here."

KUUMBA (IV-Ethnic, gay/lesbian, love/romance/erotica), Box 83912, Los Angeles CA 90083-0912, phone (310)410-0808, fax (310)410-9250, e-mail newsroom@blk.com, website http://www.blk.com/blk, founded 1991, editor Mark Haile, is a biannual poetry journal of the black lesbian and gay community. **They want subject matter related to black lesbian and gay concerns.** "Among the experiences of interest are: coming out, interacting with family and/or community, substance abuse, political activism, oral histories, AIDS and intimate relationships." **They do not want to see "gay only subjects that have no black content, or black only subjects with no gay content."** They have published poetry by David Frechette, Assotto Saint, Sabrina Sojourner and Eric S. Booth. As a sample we selected these lines from "The Sweetest Taboo" (for Gene) by Richard D. Gore:

> *Forbidden,*
> > *But I loved you anyway*
> *Dark, smouldering, and sweet*
> > *Luminous Black skin and Sloe-eyes. . .*

Kuumba is 48 pgs., 8½ × 11, offset and saddle-stitched, with b&w cover drawing and ads. They receive approximately 500 poems a year, accept about 25%. Press run is 3,000 for 750 subscribers of which 25 are libraries, 2,000 shelf sales. Subscription: $7.50/year. **Sample postpaid: $4.50. Make checks payable to BLK Publishing Company. Submit 3 poems at a time. No previously published poems; simultaneous submissions OK, if notified. Cover letter preferred. Seldom comments on rejections. Send SASE for guidelines. Reports in 6 weeks. Pays 5 copies. Acquires first North American serial rights and right to anthologize.** The editors add, "Named for one of the Nguzo Saba (Seven Principles) which are celebrated at Kwanzaa, Kuumba means creativity." This poetry journal is not only dedicated to the celebration of the lives and experiences of black lesbians and gay men, but it is also intended to encourage new and experienced writers to develop their poetic craft.

LACTUCA (II, IV-Translations), 159 Jewett Ave., Jersey City NJ 07304-2003, phone/fax (201)451-5411, e-mail lactuca@aol.com, founded 1986, editor/publisher Mike Selender, appears 0-3 times a year. **"Our bias is toward work with a strong sense of place, a strong sense of experience, a quiet dignity and an honest emotional depth. Dark and disturbing writings are preferred over safer material. No haiku, poems about writing poems, poems using the poem as an image, light poems or self-indulgent poems. Readability is crucial. We want poetry that readily transposes between the spoken word and printed page. First English language translations are welcome provided that the translator has obtained the approval of the author."** They have published poetry by Sherman Alexie, Joe Cardillo, Christy Beatty and Kathleen ten Haken. As a sample the editor selected these lines from "The Jaws of Factory" by Peter Bakowski:

> In war or prison there is fear,
> here it is the slow death:
> Danny's lost an arm last week,
> David's got crow's feet under his eyes
> and he's only 24. . .

Lactuca is 72 pgs., digest-sized, saddle-stapled, laser printed or offset on 24 lb. bond with matte card cover, no ads. They receive "a few thousand poems a year of which less than 5% are accepted." Circulation 500 for 100 subscriptions, 200 store sales. Subscription: $10/3 issues, $17/6 issues. **Sample postpaid: $4. "Query before submitting work to find out if we're accepting new submissions." Queries accepted via e-mail. Submit 4-5 poems at a time. "We do not print previously published material nor do we accept simultaneous submissions. We comment on rejections when we can. However the volume of mail we receive limits this." Reports within 3 months, "usually within one." Always sends prepublication galleys. Pays 2-5 copies "depending on length." Acquires first rights.** Reviews books of poetry. Open to unsolicited reviews. Poets may also send books for review consideration. He says, "The purpose of *Lactuca* is to be a small literary magazine publishing high-quality poetry, fiction and b&w drawings. Much of our circulation goes to contributors' copies and exchange copies with other literary magazines. *Lactuca* is not for poets expecting large circulation. Poets appearing here will find themselves in the company of other good writers."

‡**LACUNAE MAGAZINE (I)**, P.O. Box 827, Clifton Park NY 12065, e-mail lacunaemag@aol.com, founded 1994, editor Pamela Hazelton, is a bimonthly featuring comics, fiction, poetry, music, reviews and interviews. "*Lacunae* is *the* showplace to feature independent talent." The magazine's content is aimed at **"mature audiences" and ranges from humor to horror to science fiction to crime. They do not want romance.** They have recently published poetry by Hart D. Fisher, Jaime Hill, James Russell and Sean Kelley McKeever. *Lacunae* is 48 pgs., 6¾ × 10¼, professionally printed and saddle-stapled with full-color glossy cover and b&w art inside. They receive 100-200 poems a year, accept 20-30%. Press run is about 5,000 for 50 subscribers, approximately 3,000 shelf sales. Single copy: $2.50; subscription: $14/year. **Sample postpaid: $3.25. Submit up to 10 poems at a time. Previously published poems and simultaneous submissions OK. Cover letter required. E-mail submissions OK.** Time between acceptance and publication is 1-4 months. **Poems are circulated to an editorial board. Always comments on rejections. Publishes theme issues. Send SASE for guidelines and upcoming themes. Reports in 2-6 weeks. Pays 5-10 copies.** Reviews books of poetry. Open to unsolicited reviews. Poets may also send books for review consideration to Attn: Reviews. "Include price and address [with review copy] for ordering direct." Sponsors contest. Send SASE for details.

LAKE SHORE PUBLISHING; SOUNDINGS (I, IV-Anthology), 373 Ramsay Rd., Deerfield IL 60015, phone (847)945-4324, founded 1983, poetry editor Carol Spelius, is an effort "to put out decent, economical volumes of poetry." **Reading fee: $1/page. They want poetry which is "understandable and *moving*, imaginative with a unique view, in any form. Make me laugh or cry or think. I'm not so keen on gutter language or political dogma—but I try to keep an open mind. No limitations in length."** They have recently published poetry by Bob Mills, Constance Vogel and Dona Goldman. The editor selected these sample lines from "Slow Miracle" by Christine Swanberg:

> There were times when walking here
> would not have been enough, times
> my restless spirit needed an ocean,
> not this river, serene and simple.

The first 253-page anthology, including over 100 poets, is a paperback, at $7.95 (add $1 mailing cost), which was published (in 1985) in an edition of 2,000. It is flat-spined, photocopied from typescript, with glossy, colored card cover with art. *Soundings II* is scheduled for early 1996. **Submit 5 poems at a time, with $1/page reading fee, and a cover letter telling about your other publications, biographical background, personal or aesthetic philosophy, poetic goals and principles. Simultaneous submissions OK. Any form or length. "Reads submissions anytime, but best in fall." Send SASE for upcoming themes. Reports within 8 months. Pays 1 copy and half-price for additional copies. "All rights return to poet after first printing." The editor will read chapbooks, or full-length collections, with the possibility of sharing costs** if Lake Shore Publishing likes the book ($1/page reading fee). "I split the cost if I like the book." She advises, "I'm gathering poems for a small anthology, *Love Gone Away*, and a collection of poems for children." **Sample copy of anthology or random choice of full-length collections to interested poets: $5.**

THE LAMP-POST (I, II, IV-Religious, form/style), 29562 Westmont Court, San Juan Capistrano CA 92675-1221, founded 1977, senior editor James Prothero, is the quarterly publication of the Southern California C.S. Lewis Society and "echoes his thoughts in scholarly essays, informal essays, fiction and poetry as well as reviews. **We look for (1) formal, (2) literary quality poetry with (3) an**

orthodox Christian slant. Will look at free verse, but prefer formal." They have recently published poetry by John Brugaletta, Paul Willis and Joe Christopher. As a sample the editor selected these lines from "Prayer: After George Herbert" by Geoff Pope:

> *Prayer—the Church's compass, preface to bliss,*
> *Body battery, heaven's zeal-stamped mail,*
> *Silo, well, invisible kiss,*
> *Worship's gentle sibling, the heart's mended sail;*
>
> *Shouts dispelling capital doubts, simply*
> *Something disarming for the world to see; . . .*

The Lamp-Post is 32 pgs., digest-sized, professionally printed and saddle-stapled with card cover and b&w line drawings. They receive 100 poems a year, use about 20. Press run is 300 for 250 subscribers of which 5 are libraries. Subscription: $12, $8 students, seniors and libraries. **Sample postpaid: $3. For subscriptions and sample back issues, write to Edie Dougherty, managing editor/secretary, 1212 W. 162nd St., Gardena CA 90247. Previously published poems accepted "cautiously." No simultaneous submissions. Cover letter not required, "but we like them." No SASE, no reply.** Time between acceptance and publication is about 1 year. **Sometimes comments on rejections. Send SASE for guidelines. Reports in 6-8 weeks. Pays 3 copies. Acquires first serial or reprint rights.** Reviews books of poetry "if the poet is a Lewis scholar or the poetry has some connection to C.S. Lewis." Open to unsolicited reviews. Poets may also send books for review consideration and scholarly articles to M.J. Logsdon, 119 Washington Dr., Salinas CA 93905. The editor says, "We exist to echo the thought of C.S. Lewis in contemporary writing. Quality, literary poetry only, please. Read John Donne, George Herbert, Gerard Manley Hopkins and Francis Thompson and give us that sort of formal, literary and Christian quality—**no 'inspirational' please**; inspire us with quality and depth."

‡LANDFALL: NEW ZEALAND ARTS AND LETTERS (IV-Regional), University of Otago Press, P.O. Box 56, Dunedin, New Zealand, phone 0064 3 479 8807, fax 0064 3 479 8385, founded 1947, originally published by Caxton Press, then by Oxford University Press, now published by University of Otago Press, appears twice a year (in May and November). They say, "Apart from occasional commissioned features on aspects of international literature, *Landfall* focuses primarily on **New Zealand literature and arts.** It publishes new fiction, poetry, commentary, and interviews with New Zealand artists and writers, and reviews of New Zealand books." Subscription: $39.95 NZ for 2 issues for New Zealand subscribers, $30 A for Australian subscribers, $30 US for other overseas subscribers. **Pays (for poetry) $15 NZ/printed page and 1 copy. New Zealand poets should write for further information.**

PETER LANG PUBLISHING, INC. (IV-Translations), 275 Seventh Ave., 28th Floor, New York NY 10001, phone (212)647-7700, fax (212)647-7707, editor Owen Lancer, publishes primarily scholarly monographs in the humanities and social sciences. List includes **critical editions of great poets of the past. Submit descriptive cover letter and *curriculum vita*.**

LATEST JOKES NEWSLETTER (IV-Humor), P.O. Box 23304, Brooklyn NY 11202-0066, phone (718)855-5057, editor Robert Makinson. *LJN* is a monthly newsletter of humor for TV and radio personalities, comedians and professional speakers. **They want "short humorous verse that can be used by a public speaker to liven up a speech.** Short jokes for speakers are even more needed. **Seasonal material is not needed. Standard literary verse, professorial type material, is not wanted."** Sample: $3 and 1 first-class stamp. Submit maximum 3 poems at a time. Reports in 3 weeks. Pays $1-3.

THE LAUREATE LETTER; WRITERS GAZETTE (I), 899 Williamson Trail, Eclectic AL 36024-6131, founded 1993, editor Brenda Williamson. *The Laureate Letter* is a sporadically published newsletter open to submissions of poetry. **They want "simple, easy to understand poems which stretch the mind to remember their lives, the hopes of others and the dreams that exist amongst us. Any form, but prefer titled, 16 lines maximum. No jibberish or extremely mushy garbage."** As a sample the editor selected the poem "Spider," by Kimberly L. Coulter:

> *A spider is like a nightmare*
> *crawling into your mind in the dark of night*
> *tickling your senses*
> *Like a memory you are scared of*
> *And try to kill.*

They receive 1,500-2,000 poems a year, accept 25%. Press run is 250. Single copy: $2. **Sample postpaid: $2 plus #10 SASE. Submit 3 poems at a time. Previously published poems and simultaneous submissions OK.** Time between acceptance and publication is 1-2 months. **Send SASE for guidelines. Reports in 1-4 weeks "most of the time." No pay in cash or copies, but no fee required for publication. Acquires one-time rights.** They also publish *Writers Gazette*. Founded in 1980, the publication appears 4 times/year and is designed "for writers, by writers, about writing." It includes poetry, fiction, nonfiction, art, cartoons, occasional photos, and sometimes contains market listings, contest information and news on related writing subjects. **They want poems of "any style, subject or length, but prefer short verses of under 24 lines. Always looking for shorter poems of 4-12 lines. New writers are always encouraged and regularly published, even children."** They have recently published poetry by Carl Dietrich, Ann Boger and Denise Clinton. As a sample the editor selected these lines from "Reflection" by Paul Devine:

> . . . I stare at the crack in the mirror
> distorting the true reflection
> I've been looking for all my life.

The editor says **WG** is approximately 16 pgs., 8½×11, with some ads. They receive 1,200 poems a year, accept 10%. Press run is 500 for 250 subscribers. Subscription: $15. **Sample postpaid: $4. Previously published poems and simultaneous submissions OK. Seldom comments on rejections. Send SASE for guidelines. Reports in 1-2 months. No pay in cash or copies. Acquires one-time rights.** Reviews books and chapbooks of poetry. Poets may also send books for review consideration. The editor says, "I read everything that crosses my desk and reply as soon as possible. Be creative and unusual. Don't query—send entire manuscripts. Also, we check for SASE before ever considering poems. If authors cannot consider sending SASE, we cannot consider their work."

LAUREL REVIEW (III); GREENTOWER PRESS (V), Dept. of English, Northwest Missouri State University, Maryville MO 64468, phone (816)562-1265, founded 1960, co-editors William Trowbridge, David Slater and Beth Richards. **LR** is a literary journal appearing twice a year using **"poetry fiction, and creative nonfiction of the highest literary quality."** They have published poetry by Patricia Goedicke, Paul Zimmer, Miller Williams, Albert Goldbarth, David Citino and Nancy Willard. As a sample the editors selected these lines from "Wheel" by Jim Simmerman:

> Don't fall in love before you've made the wheel
> your study. See how it crushes and churns
> unsullied on to the next disaster.
> See how it burns like the hoop an animal
> learns to leap through for its supper. Study
> the heart and its demolition derby.

This handsome journal (128 pgs., 6×9) features excellent poems—usually more than 20 each issue— in all styles and forms. Press run is 900 for 400 subscribers of which 53 are libraries, 100 shelf sales. Subscription: $8/year. **Sample postpaid: $5. Submit 4 poems at a time. No previously published poems or simultaneous submissions. Reads submissions September 1 through May 31 only. Editor "does not usually" comment on submissions. Reports in 1 week to 4 months. Always sends prepublication galleys. Pays 2 copies plus 1-year subscription. Rights revert to author upon publication.** Greentower Press **does not accept unsolicited mss.**

THE LEADING EDGE (I, IV-Science fiction/fantasy), 3163 JKHB, Provo UT 84602, e-mail tle@byu.edu (correspondence only, no submissions), website http://humanities.byu.edu/tle/theleadinge dge.html, executive editor Alex Grover. **The Leading Edge** is a magazine appearing 2 times a year. They want **"high quality poetry related to science fiction and fantasy. We accept traditional science fiction and fantasy poetry, but we like innovative stuff. No graphic sex, violence or profanity."** They have published poetry by Michael Collings, Ann K. Schwader and Bruce Boston. As a sample the editor selected this poem, "The Spectra of Galaxies (A Zen Joke)," by Alyce Wilson:

> A man with a telescope
> reduces the universe
> to one red-shifted line
> on a piece of graph paper.
>
> Folds it in his pocket, forgets it.
>
> On laundry day, he cleans
> galaxies out of the lint filter.
> And at last, he understands.

The editor describes the magazine as 140 pgs., 6×9, using art. They accept about 15 out of 150 poems received/year. Press run is 500, going to 100 subscribers (10 of them libraries) and 300 shelf sales. Single copy: $3.95; subscription: $11.85. **Sample postpaid: $4.50. Submit 1 or more poems with name and address at the top of each page. No simultaneous submissions or previously published poems. Cover sheet with name, address, phone number, length of poem, title and type of poem preferred. Send SASE for guidelines. Reports in 3-4 months. Always sends prepublication galleys. Pays $10 for the first 1-4 typeset pages, $4.50 for each additional page; plus 2 contributor's copies. Buys first North American serial rights.** They say, "Poetry is given equal standing with fiction and is not treated as filler, but is treated as art."

CLOSE-UP

Feedback is important even after publication

Poet Susan Ludvigson joined a "small group of aspiring writers" very early in her writing career, and her writing group, which has changed much of its membership over the years, remains an invaluable source of support and inspiration. "I think belonging to a group can be very important. I know it's not for everybody and some even say you ought to get to a place in your writing where there is no longer a need, but I can't imagine not needing this feedback."

A good writing group, she says, can give you constructive criticism as well as the encouragement to submit your work. "My group meets once a week and in some ways is very social, but when it comes to poetry we're very serious. These are

Susan Ludvigson

really supportive people, but they are also tough critics."

Her first group encouraged her to send her work to small magazines and to target regional publications. Taking their advice, Ludvigson began submitting work and found quick acceptance in the *South Carolina Review*. She marks this as "her first real publication" and since then her poems have appeared in *The Georgia Review*, *The Gettysburg Review*, *Michigan Quarterly Review*, *The Ohio Review*, *Poetry*, and many others.

She is also the author of seven poetry collections and several chapbooks. Her most recent book, *Trinity*, was published by Louisiana State University Press in the fall of 1996. LSU Press is also the publisher of five of her other books: *Everything Winged Must be Dreaming*, 1993; *To Find the Gold*, 1990; *The Beautiful Noon of No Shadow*, 1987; *The Swimmer*, 1984; and *Northern Lights*, 1981.

Although she does not consciously impose a structure on her books, most contain three clearly-defined sections each relating in a different way to an overriding theme. *Trinity* follows a structure similar to her earlier books, but its spiritual and personal nature makes it a departure for her. Inspired by the legend of Mary Magdalene, the first section, "The Gospel According to Mary Magdalene," was published on its own in *The Gettysburg Review* and received the magazine's award for best poem in 1995. Other sections in the book include a series of poems from God to Emily Dickinson and the Faust story told from a woman's point of view. "That section," she says, "is about me and the devil."

Most of the time, Ludvigson does not discover a theme for a book until after most of the poems are written. Sometimes she doesn't have enough poems for

CLOSE-UP, *Ludvigson*

"Lasting"

When the first radio wave music escaped Earth's ionosphere, it literally did become eternal. Music, in this century, has been converted from sound into the clarity of pure light. Radio has superseded the constraints of space.

Art & Physics, by Leonard Shilain

Imagine Vivaldi suddenly falling
on the ears of a woman
somewhere beyond Alpha Centauri,
her planet spun into luminescence
aeons from now. She might be
much like us, meditating
on the body, her lover murmuring
to the underside of her breast
before its heaviness suspends,
for a moment, the lift and pause
of his breath. A music she almost knows
drifts through centuries, startling,
augmenting her pleasure.
When earth is particles of dust,
Orson Wells may still strike fear
into the hearts of millions
who wake one morning, unaware
that light has arrived
as an audible prank. Ezra Pound might rasp
his particular madness from an Italy
still alive in arias that shower
into the open windows
of a world youthful as hope.
When books are no longer even ashes,
and no heart beats in any space
near where we were, suns
may intersect, and some of our voices
blend into choirs, the music of the spheres
adrift among new stars.

(from *Everything Winged Must be Dreaming*, 1993, LSU Press)

CLOSE-UP, *continued*

an entire collection, but has a group of poems that seem to go together well. These she publishes as a chapbook. For instance, *The Wisconsin Women*, a group of poems based on a series of newspaper reports from a turn-of-the-century Wisconsin newspaper, was first published as a chapbook but later included in *Northern Lights*.

With so many publications, it comes as no surprise that, for most of her writing life, Ludvigson has kept a fairly rigid writing schedule. She tries to write everyday and alternates between one- and two-hour morning writing sessions, though she'll write longer if the writing is going well. She encourages writers to stick to a schedule and try to make writing part of their daily routine.

Ludvigson was born in northern Wisconsin, but moved south, first to Charlotte, North Carolina, and later to Rock Hill, South Carolina, where she teaches English and creative writing at Winthrop University. Although she did not begin writing seriously until after she was married and her son was born, her career took off quickly once she began to submit her work. She is the recipient of numerous awards and grants including National Endowment for the Arts Fellowships, a Guggenheim Fellowship and a Fulbright Fellowship. The Fulbright landed her in Yugoslavia where she toured the country and met Yugoslavian poets, most of whom were eager to find translators for their work.

Europe continues to hold particular interest for Ludvigson, and she and her second husband are part owners of a house in southern France, where she spends part of the year. Not only has her work been influenced by her Midwestern roots, her current Southern landscape and her experiences in Europe, but she has also become well-acquainted with the differences between how the American and European cultures view writers and other artists.

"Writing by nature is lonely, especially in our culture because it's not valued here in the way it is in Europe. It's nice to be in countries where, when people ask you what you do and you tell them you are a poet, you feel an immediate sense of appreciation from them. Here, when I'm asked that question, I usually say 'I teach.' If I say I'm a poet, they ask me if there is any money in it and, if not, why do I do it?"

Europe also appeals to Ludvigson because, there, the past is very present. "We're such a young country. In France, we live very near Roman and medieval ruins. You feel a very strong sense of the centuries there."

While some of Ludvigson's work deals with historical subjects, it is the characters from history, she says, that fascinate her. In particular, one of her favorite and highly acclaimed poems, from *To Find the Gold*, is based on the life of sculptor Camille Claudel, whose tumultuous relationship with Rodin overshadowed her life and work. Ludvigson saw an exhibition of Claudel's work in Paris and was moved to tears. Later she researched Claudel's life through biographies and personal letters.

"It was the longest poem I had ever done and it scared me to death. I worked on it every day and it was very uncomfortable. Certain stories just connect with you and your imagination. Something happens in a writer's psyche when certain things come along. There is a connection and the best work can come out of that connection."

CLOSE-UP, *Ludvigson*

However, Ludvigson warns new writers not to try to start a poem with an idea. "Ideas can be the death of a poem. Eighty percent of the time I don't know what the poem will be until I have written it." Trusting the unconscious part of your brain is an important part of the creative process, she says.

In fact, Ludvigson teaches a course called "The Creative Process and the Arts," and another version of the course called "The Intuitive Way of Knowing." In her courses she looks at the creative process in all areas of the arts and even the sciences. Participants listen to guest speakers and read diaries of creative people as well as discuss their own creative processes. From this work, Ludvigson says she's found that writers, artists, architects, painters—anyone who uses creativity to solve a problem—learn to tap into the unconscious and trust it.

"Dreams provide some of the easiest access to the unconscious. They contain a wealth of images and insights that can lead to creative work." She says it's a process of learning to let go of the conscious and bring what you've learned in the unconscious back so you can use it.

Sometimes a biography or story will inspire Ludvigson, but most of the time, she says, her poems start with a single line or phrase. "The usual impetus comes in a line. I read poetry and nonfiction and in the middle of reading, a line will come to me. Often it's not really anything to do with what I'm reading. Something about reading, though, sets my mind in the right direction. That line, whether I end up using it or not, will set the rhythm of the poem."

Her main piece of advice for new writers is to become as well-read as possible. No one ever went wrong studying the poets of the past, like Donne and Yeats, she says. On the other hand, read contemporary poets to balance this. It's important to know what's out there and to be aware of what magazines are publishing right now.

Although, by all standards, Ludvigson's career has been very successful, she admits she made mistakes as a beginning writer. As many eager new writers do, she sent her first work to an anthology in which all writers were accepted and published in a volume which they in turn could buy. She cautions new writers about these quick-publishing schemes and also against publishing too soon. She says she regrets publishing her first book (which she published under another surname) before she was really ready to be published. Take the time, she says, to learn the craft before you become eager for publication.

On the other hand, recognize when you are ready, she says. "There does come a point when people are very good, but they fear sending things out. The best way to conquer that fear is to have several batches of work ready to go out. Have in mind where you will send the next poem so you don't spend a lot of time agonizing over publication."

—*Robin Gee*

THE LEDGE POETRY AND FICTION MAGAZINE (II), 64-65 Cooper Ave., Glendale NY 11385, founded 1988, editor-in-chief/publisher Timothy Monaghan, co-editors George Held and Laura M. Corrado. **"Our purpose is to publish the best poems we receive. We publish poetry by well-known and little-known poets."** Recent contributors include Robert Cooperman, Elliot Richman, Elisavietta Ritchie, Will Inman and Carolyn E. Campbell. As a sample the editor-in-chief selected the opening lines of "Widower" by Ben Wilensky:

> She is thick and fat and hairy,
> And there are so many juicy things sticking out of her body,
> It would take me a week to lick the platter clean.
> She reminds me of my former wife,
> Although my wife was bigger and stronger
> And more poisonously endowed.

The Ledge is 144 pgs., digest-sized, typeset and perfect-bound with b&w glossy cover. They accept 5% of poetry submissions. Circulation is 1,000, including 200 subscribers. Subscription: $15 for 2 years (4 issues), $9 for 1 year (2 issues). **Current issue postpaid: $5. Submit 3-5 poems at a time. No previously published work. Simultaneous submissions OK. Do not submit mss in July or August. "Submissions received during those months will be returned unread." Reports in 3 months. Pays 2 copies. Acquires one-time rights.** *The Ledge* sponsors an annual poetry chapbook contest, as well as annual poetry and fiction awards competitions. Send SASE for details. Timothy Monaghan says: "We like strong, visceral poetry, but are open to submissions of any kind. Excellence is our only criterion."

LEFT CURVE (II, IV-Social issues), P.O. Box 472, Oakland CA 94604-0472, phone/fax (510)763-7193, founded 1974, editor Csaba Polony, appears "irregularly, about every 10 months." **They want poetry that is "critical culture, social, political, 'post-modern,' not purely formal, too self-centered, poetry that doesn't address in sufficient depth today's problems."** They have published poetry by Errol Miller, Luis J. Rodriguez and Hasan Dewran. As a sample the editor selected these lines by Christos Tsiokas:

> The great God money has dominion all over this globe. West, East. North,
> South. Air, fire, water, earth. I could walk this planet, roam the last desert,
> sail the lost sea searching for my Authentic Man. And find instead
> Only Narcissus gazing into my reflection.

The editor describes it as "about 120 pgs., offset, flat-spined, Durosheen cover." Press run is 2,000 for 200 subscribers of which 50 are libraries, 1,500 shelf sales. Subscription: $25/3 issues (individuals). **Sample postpaid: $8. Submit up to 5 poems at a time. Cover letter stating "why you are submitting" required. Publishes theme issues. Send SASE for guidelines and upcoming themes. Reports in 3-6 months. Pays 3 copies.** Open to unsolicited reviews. Poets may also send books for review consideration.

‡**L'EPERVIER PRESS (V)**, 1326 NE 62nd, Seattle WA 98115, founded 1977, editor Robert McNamara, is a "small press publisher of contemporary American poetry in perfect-bound and casebound books." **Currently not accepting submissions.** He has published books by Bruce Renner, Linda Bierds, Frederic Will and Paul Hoover. The press publishes 2 poetry books each year, 6×9 with an average page count of 64, some flat-spined paperbacks and some hardcovers. *Second Sun*, by Bill Tremblay, is handsomely printed on heavy buff stock, 81 pgs., with glossy card cover in grey, yellow and white; there is a b&w landscape photo on the front cover and a photo of the author on the back; the book is priced at $6.95.

LIBERTY HILL POETRY REVIEW (II), P.O. Box 426967, San Francisco CA 94142-6967, founded 1994, editor Ken Butler, is a biannual designed to publish local and national poets, both experienced writers and talented newcomers. **They want "well-crafted free verse which exhibits a thorough knowledge of and love for language and content. Poetry that is carefully thought-out with proper punctuation, spelling and grammar. No subject matter is taboo, except those which promote racism, homophobia, and the humiliation of any race, gender or orientation. No prose poetry, no haiku; visual and verbal gymnastics are discouraged."** They have recently published poetry by Simon Perchik, William Doreski, Errol Miller, CB Follett and Rose Marie Hunold. As a sample the editor selected these lines from "To Garcia Lorca" by Maggie Schold:

> You, Garcia Lorca, I love the sound of your name
> I love the sound of watermelons, crunch and swish
> of biting into firm flesh, you have such firm
> flesh, Garcia Lorca, if that is truly your name.

LHPR is 56 pgs., digest-sized, attractively designed, saddle-stapled with matte card stock cover. They receive about 2,200 poems a year, accept 75%. Press run is 250. Single copy: $4; subscription: $7. **Sample postpaid: $3. Submit up to 5 typed poems of no more than 60 lines in length. Include name and address on each page. SASE required. Simultaneous submissions OK if noted. No** previously published poems. **Cover letter encouraged. Reads submissions August through September (for Fall/Winter issue) and January through February (for Spring/Summer issue). Often comments on rejections. No backlog.** "We like to start fresh each time." **Send SASE for guidelines. Reports in 2-8 weeks. Pays 2 copies. Acquires one-time rights.** The editor says, "Above all, please support your local small presses and readings. Read as much poetry as you write. And always read a copy of the magazine to which you are submitting."

LIBIDO: THE JOURNAL OF SEX AND SEXUALITY (II, IV-Erotica, humor, gay/lesbian/ bisexual), P.O. Box 146721, Chicago IL 60614-6721, phone (312)275-0842, fax (312)275-0752, e-mail rune@mcs.com, website http://www.indrd.com/libido, founded 1988, editors Marianna Beck and Jack Hafferkamp, is a quarterly. **"Form, length and style are open. We want poetry of any and all styles as long as it is erotic and/or erotically humorous. We make a distinction between erotica and pornography. We want wit, not dirty words."** They have published poetry by Stuart Silverman, Alan Isler, Lani Kaahumanu, Anne MacNaughton, Chocolate Waters, Robert Perchan, Bruce Lennard and Bill Vickers. As a sample the editors selected these lines by Ralph Tyler:

>'Twas brillig in that cheap hotel
>The looking glass had cataracts
>All mimsey were the bureau drawrs
>The paper was a glimpse of hell
>"Come to my arms, my beamish boy"
>Her scarlet mouth invited him.

Libido is 88 pgs., digest-sized, professionally printed, flat-spined, with 2-color varnished card cover. They accept about 5% of poetry received. Press run is 9,500 for 3,500 subscribers, 3,500 shelf sales and 1,500 single issues by mail. Subscription: $30 in US, $40 in Canada and Mexico (US funds), $50 in Europe and $60 elsewhere. **Sample postpaid: $8. Submit 2-3 poems at a time. Cover letter including "a one-sentence bio for contributors' page" required with submission. "Please, no handwritten mss and do not submit via fax or e-mail." Reports in 4-6 months. Pays $0-25 plus 2 copies.** Send books for review consideration "only if the primary focus is love/eroticism."

LIBRA PUBLISHERS, INC. (I), 3089C Clairemont Dr., Suite 383, San Diego CA 92117, phone (619)571-1414, poetry editor William Kroll, publishes two professional journals, *Adolescence* and *Family Therapy*, plus books, primarily in the behavorial sciences but also some general nonfiction, fiction and poetry. "At first we published books of poetry on a standard royalty basis, paying 10% of the retail price to the authors. Although at times we were successful in selling enough copies to at least break even, we found that we could no longer afford to publish poetry on this basis. Now, unless we fall madly in love with a particular collection, **we offer professional services to assist the author in self-publishing."** They have published books of poetry by Martin Rosner, William Blackwell, John Travers Moore and C. Margaret Hall. **Prefers complete ms but accepts query with 6 sample poems, publishing credits and bio. Replies to query in 2 days, to submissions in 2-3 weeks. Mss should be double-spaced. Sometimes sends prepublication galleys. Send 9 × 12 SASE for catalog. Sample books may be purchased on a returnable basis.**

THE LICKING RIVER REVIEW (II), Dept. of Literature and Language, Northern Kentucky University, Highland Heights KY 41099, founded 1991, is an annual designed "to showcase the best writing by Northern Kentucky University students alongside work by new or established writers from the region or elsewhere." **They have no specifications regarding form, subject matter or style of poetry. "No long poems (maximum 60 lines)."** They have recently published poetry by Ron Wallace, Jim Barnes, Ann Struthers, Jack Meyers, Allison Joseph and William Greenway. The review is 96 pgs., 7 × 10, offset on recycled paper and perfect-bound with a 16-page artwork inset (all art solicited). They accept 5% of the poetry received. Press run is 1,500. Single copy and **sample postpaid: $5. Submit no more than 4 poems at a time. No previously published poems or simultaneous submissions. Reads submissions September through January.** Poems are circulated to an editorial board. **Reports in up to 6 months. Pays in copies. Rights revert to author.** Requests acknowledgment if poem is later reprinted.

LIGHT (II), Box 7500, Chicago IL 60680, founded 1992, editor John Mella, is a quarterly of **"light and occasional verse, satire, wordplay, puzzles, cartoons and line art." They do not want "greeting card verse, cloying or sentimental verse."** As a sample the editor selected "The Cow's Revenge" by X.J. Kennedy:

>Obligingly, the mild cow lets us quaff
>The milk that she'd intended for her calf,
>But takes revenge: In every pint she packs
>A heavy cream to trigger heart attacks.

The editor says *Light* is 32 pgs., stapled, including art and graphics. Single copy: $5; subscription: $16. **Sample postpaid: $4. Submit 1 poem on a page with name, address, poem title and page** number on each page. **No previously published poems or simultaneous submissions. Seldom comments on rejections. Publishes theme issues. Send #10 SASE for guidelines and upcoming themes. Reports in 3 months or less. Always sends prepublication galleys. Pays 2 copies to domestic contributors, 1 copy to foreign contributors.** Open to unsolicited reviews; query first. Poets may also send books for review consideration.

LIGHT AND LIFE MAGAZINE; EVANGEL (IV-Religious), Dept. PM, Free Methodist Church of North America, P.O. Box 535002, Indianapolis IN 46253-5002, phone (317)244-3660. *Light and Life*, editor Doug Newton, is a religious monthly magazine. **"Poems are used only as they relate to an article in the magazine. No 'fillers' or descriptive poems are used. We are looking for short, well-written devotional or inspirational pieces and poetry . . . offering unique insights into the great themes of the Bible. Poems should rhyme and flow with a recognizable rhythm pattern. Avoid obscure allusions and unfamiliar language. Maximum length: 20 lines. Each submission should be typed on plain white paper, double-spaced, at least 1" margin on all sides, no erasable bond, name, address and telephone number on each ms, each submission on a separate sheet of paper, even if they are short pieces." Send SASE for guidelines. Reports in 4-6 weeks. Pays $10/ poem, "even short ones." Buys first rights.** They also conduct annual writing contests with varying rules and prizes (send SASE for rules December through March). *Evangel*, editor Carolyn Smith, **is a weekly 8-page paper for adults using nature and devotional poetry, 8-16 lines, "free verse or with rhyme scheme."** The circulation is 35,000; it is sold in bulk to Sunday schools. **Sample for 6×9 SASE. SASE required with submissions. Simultaneous submissions OK. Reports in 1 month. Pays $10.** The editor advises, "Do not write abstractions. Use concrete words to picture concept for reader."

LILITH MAGAZINE (IV-Women, ethnic), 250 W. 57th St., Suite 2432, New York NY 10107, phone (212)757-0818, fax (212)757-5705, e-mail lilithmag@aol.com, founded in 1976, editor-in-chief Susan Weidman Schneider, poetry editor Alicia Ostriker, "is an independent magazine with a Jewish feminist perspective" which uses **poetry by Jewish women "about the Jewish woman's experience. Generally we use short rather than long poems. Run 4 poems/year. Do not want to see poetry on other subjects."** They have published poetry by Irena Klepfisz, Lyn Lifshin, Yael Messinai, Sharon Neemani, Marcia Falk and Adrienne Rich. It is glossy, magazine-sized. "We use colors. Page count varies. Covers are very attractive and professional-looking (one has won an award). Generous amount of art. It appears 4 times a year, circulation about 10,000, about 5,000 subscriptions." Subscription: $18 for 4 issues. **Sample postpaid: $5. Send no more than 3 poems at a time; advise if simultaneous submission. Editor "sometimes" comments on rejections. Send SASE for guidelines.** She advises: "(1) Read a copy of the publication before you submit your work. (2) Be realistic if you are a beginner. The competition is *severe*, so don't start to send out your work until you've written for a few years. (3) Short cover letters only. Copy should be neatly typed and proofread for typos and spelling errors."

LILLIPUT REVIEW (II, IV-Form), 282 Main St., Pittsburgh PA 15201-2807, founded 1989, editor Don Wentworth, is a tiny (4½×3.6 or 3½×4¼), 12- to 16-page magazine, appearing irregularly and **using poems in any style or form no longer than 10 lines.** They have published poetry by Albert Huffstickler, Lonnie Sherman, Lyn Lifshin and charlie mehrhoff. As a sample the editor selected "your body" by scarecrow:

> each piece a shining eye
> examining
> the rest of the explosion.

LR is laser-printed on colored paper and stapled. Press run is 250. **Sample: $1 or SASE. Make checks payable to Don Wentworth. Submit no more than 3 poems at a time.** Currently, every fourth issue is a broadside featuring the work of one particular poet. **Send SASE for guidelines. Reports usually within 2 months. Pays 2 copies/poem. Acquires first rights.** Editor comments on submissions "occasionally—always at least try to establish human contact." He started the Modest Proposal Chapbook Series in 1994, publishing 1-2 chapbooks/year, 18-24 pgs. in length. **Chapbook submissions are by invitation only. Query with standard SASE. Sample chapbook: $2.50.** Recent chapbook publications include *Color & Light* by Lyn Lifshin and *Inhaling the Dead* by Steven Doering. The editor says, "A note above my desk reads 'Clarity & resonance, not necessarily in that order.' The perfect little poem for *LR* is simple in style and language and elusive/allusive in meaning and philosophy. *LR* is open to all short poems in both approach and theme, including any of the short Eastern forms, traditional or otherwise."

LIMESTONE: A LITERARY JOURNAL (II), Dept. of English, 1215 Patterson Office Tower, University of Kentucky, Lexington KY 40506-0027, phone (606)257-6993, founded as *Fabbro* in 1979, as *Limestone* in 1986, editor Morris Grubbs, is an annual seeking **"poetry that matters, poetry that shows attention to content and form. We're interested in all poetics, but we do watch for quality of thought and a use of language that will wake up the reader and resonate in his/her**

mind." They have published poetry by Wendell Berry, Guy Davenport, Michael Cadnum, Noel M. Valis and James Baker Hall. It is 6×9, perfect-bound, offset. They accept 5-10 of 100-150 poems submitted annually. Press run is 500 for 30 subscriptions (20 of them libraries). **Sample postpaid: $3. Simultaneous submissions OK. Submit 1-10 pgs. at a time. Reports in 3-6 months. Pays 3 copies.** "If you're considering publication," the editor advises, "read as much poetry as possible. Listen carefully. Work over your poems till you're sick of them. The lack of such care shows up in many of the mss we receive."

LIMITED EDITIONS PRESS; ART: MAG (III), P.O. Box 70896, Las Vegas NV 89170, phone (702)734-8121, founded 1982, editor Peter Magliocco, "have become, due to economic and other factors, more limited to a select audience of poets as well as readers. We seek to expel the superficiality of our factitious culture, in all its drive-thru, junk-food-brain, commercial-ridden extravagance—and stylize a magazine of hard-line aesthetics, where truth and beauty meet on a vector not shallowly drawn. Conforming to this outlook is an operational policy of **seeking poetry from solicited poets primarily, though unsolicited submissions will be read, considered and perhaps used infrequently. Sought from the chosen is a creative use of poetic styles, systems and emotional morphologies other than banally constricting.**" They have recently published poetry by T. Anders Carson, Arlene Mandell, John Grey, Joseph Shields and Mark Sonnenfeld. As a sample the editor selected these lines from "For Sad Songs and Salvation" by Errol Miller:

> The thin closed furrow of childhood,
> the plows of another spring unearthing an author
> cresting with the Jordan, some seedy immature novelist
> from make-believe pounding on the glass door of the Aircastle
> as inaccessible the world turns and sips mint juleps
> and pulls closed the yellow shades of sanity.

ART: MAG, appearing in 1-2 large issues of 100 copies/year, is limited to a few poets. **Sample copies are the price of a regular issue, $5 or more, postpaid. Submit 5 poems at a time with SASE.** "Submissions should be neat and use consistent style format (except experimental work). Cover letters are optional." **No previously published poems; simultaneous submissions OK. Sometimes comments on rejections. Publishes theme issues. Send SASE for guidelines and upcoming themes. Reports within 3 months. Pays 1 copy. Acquires first rights.** Staff occasionally reviews books of poetry. Send books for review consideration. The press also occasionally publishes chapbooks (such as *Non-Parables*, by Peter Magliocco), "along with other possibly 'aesthetic surprises' (such as original art sketchbooks for patrons, etc.), but these aren't strictly scheduled." The editor says, "The mag is seeking a futuristic aestheticism where the barriers of fact and fiction meet, where interplanetary travel is a given, and a stellar Neo-Earth is created in the 21st century, as well as in our poetic consciousness of what we and poetry will become."

LINCOLN SPRINGS PRESS (II), 32 Oak Place, Hawthorne NJ 07506, founded 1987, editor M. Gabrielle, publishes 1 paperback and 1 hardback book of poetry each year. They have published poetry by Maria Mazziotti Gillan, Justin Vitiello and Abigail Stone. **Query first with sample poems and cover letter with brief bio and publication credits. Send SASE for response. No previously published poems; simultaneous submissions OK. Accepts submissions October through April. Seldom comments on rejections. Replies to queries in 2-4 weeks, to mss in 2-3 months. Always sends prepublication galleys. Pays 15% royalties.**

LINES N' RHYMES (I), 5604 Harmeson Dr., Anderson IN 46013, phone (317)642-1239, founded 1989, editor Pearl Clark, appears every other month using **"some 4-line poetry, most between 12-20 lines. I like poems concerning life, belief in God's guidance. Nothing pornographic or occult."** They have published poetry by Ainsley Jo Phillips, Pearl Mary Wilshaw, Dr. Harry Snider and Kae Jaworski. As a sample the editor selected these lines from "The Cardinal" by Rosina Clifford:

> We know who owns the garden—
> Just listen to him sing!
> The faithful watchman caretaker
> who dresses like a king.

It is photocopied on 6 legal-sized colored sheets, sometimes 5. Press run is 70, 3-5 shelf sales. Subscription: $7/6 issues. **Sample: $2. Submit 3 poems at a time.** "A brief cover letter is OK but not

---

USE THE GENERAL INDEX to find the page number of a specific publisher.
Also, if a publisher from last year's edition is not included in this edition, the General Index will tell you why.

essential. I receive 170 poems/year—accept 70%. I pay nothing for poetry used. I award 'Editor's Choice' to two poets/issue at $2. I give preference to subscribers. However, I also use poetry from non-subscribers." Previously published poems and simultaneous submissions OK. Reviews books of poetry and comments in current issue. Open to unsolicited reviews. Poets may also send books for review consideration. She holds a contest for humorous poetry (4-6 lines) each September with 3 prizes of $5 each, open only to subscribers.

LINES REVIEW (III, IV-Regional), Edgefield Rd., Loanhead, Edinburgh EH20 9SY Scotland, founded 1952 ("the oldest continuing Scottish literary magazine"), editor Tessa Ransford. *LR* is a quarterly which **gives priority to poets living in Scotland** and, the editor says, "is generally receiving too much from elsewhere at present. **I like to accept from 4-6 poems in traditional page format, though with energy and intelligence in use of language, form and content. No unusual typography, concrete, sensation-seeking, nostalgic, dully descriptive or fanatically political poetry.**" They have published poetry by David Grubb, Martin Bennett, Alan Riach, Stewart Conn and Robin Fulton. *LR* is known for well-written, thoughtful, lucid poetry that is intelligible to the educated reader. Press run is 750 for 500 subscribers of which 100 are libraries, 100 shelf sales. **Sample postpaid: £3 sterling. Submit 4-6 poems at a time. No previously published poems. Cover letter required; include information relevant to the work. "Double spacing helps, and clear indication whether a page break is or is not also a stanza break, and careful attention to punctuation—that it is as it will be printed." Reports in 2-3 weeks. Pays £10/page plus 1 copy.** Includes "good review section." *LR* often has special issues devoted, for example, to poetry from Glasgow, Japan, America, Canada and Italy. They also publish translations. Tessa Ransford is also director of Scottish Poetry Library (see listing under Organizations) and offers a School of Poets and Critical Service through the library.

‡LINGO: A LANGUAGE ART JOURNAL (I, IV-Form/style), 217 S. Blvd. #4, Richmond VA 23220, founded 1995, editor Kara J. West, is a quarterly publication of both language poetry and poetry about language. "Our purpose is to take language to a point where it is broken and undeniably whole at the same time." **They want language-oriented, experimental work, "anything that challenges the conventional uses of language. No sentimental, rhyming, confessional poetry; no greeting card or light verse."** They have recently published poetry by Denver Butson and Jeremy Markowitz. As a sample the editor selected these lines from Butson's poem "Textual Marriage":

> Do me that love
> She lies on the hay
> as a tree, tree
> and I lie on her
> where birds and wind
> the rain drops off the roof
> Sing though they know
> while the rain pours outside

Lingo is 12-24 pgs., 8½×11 (folded lengthwise), photocopied and unbound with line drawings. To be distributed, the journal is folded down to 4×5½ and stapled. Press run is 500. Subscription: $8/year. **Sample postpaid: $2. Make checks payable to Kara J. West. Submit 2-4 poems at a time. Previously published poems and simultaneous submissions OK. Cover letter preferred. "Include a brief philosophy of poetry and language in cover letter." Often comments on rejections. Send SASE for guidelines. Reports in 1-3 months. Pays 5 copies. Acquires first and reprint rights.** Reviews books of language-oriented poetry. Open to unsolicited reviews. Poets may also send books for review consideration. Poetry published here has also been selected for inclusion in *The Best American Poetry 1996*. The editor says, "*Lingo* is interested in de-solving language into art. Send us your visceral celebrations of language, your vivid exploitations."

LINQ (II), c/o English Dept., James Cook University, Townsville, Queensland 4811 Australia, phone (077)815097 or (077)814451, fax (077)815655, e-mail jcu.linq@jcu.edu.au, founded 1971, administrator Tina Langford. *LiNQ* is a 100-page biannual which "aims to publish works of a high literary standard, encompassing a wide and varied range of interest." **They do not want to see "overtly naive and self-consciously subjective poetry."** They have recently published poetry by Mark O'Connor, Alison Croggon, Aileen Kelly, Eve Stafford and Rebecca Edwards. As a sample they selected these lines from "Sign Me In" by Peter Porter:

> The private truth I kept within
> Grew as a cancer undisclosed,
> My books were bound in my dead skin,
> My patent brilliances opposed
> The ordinariness of life: I said
> I'll show up brighter when I'm dead.

They receive about 250 poems a year, use approximately 20/edition. Press run is 350 for 160 subscribers of which 30 are libraries, 180 shelf sales. Single copy: $10 (within Australia), $15 (overseas); subscription: $20 individual (within Australia), $25 institution (within Australia), $30 overseas (for individual and institution). Since the journal is published in May and October, all subscriptions are due by November 1. **Sample back issue postpaid: $6 (Australian). Poems must be typed, one to a page, and contain title, page number and writer's name and address. No previously published poems; simultaneous submissions OK. Cover letter with brief bio required. Submissions via fax or e-mail OK. Submission deadlines: September 30 (May edition) and April 30 (October edition). Send SASE (or SAE and 3 IRCs) for return of work. Author retains copyright.** The editors say, "*LiNQ* aims for a broadly based sympathetic approach to creative work, particularly from new and young Australian writers."

LINTEL (II), P.O. Box 8609, Roanoke VA 24014-2311, phone (540)982-2265, founded 1977, poetry editor Walter James Miller, who says, **"We publish poetry and innovative fiction of types ignored by commercial presses. We consider any poetry except conventional, traditional, cliché, greeting card types, i.e., we consider any artistic poetry."** They have published poetry by Sue Saniel Elkind, Samuel Exler, Adrienne Wolfert and Edmund Pennant. As a sample the editor selected these lines by Nathan Teitel:

> loneliness
> is a Mexican earring
> and fear
> a crushed cigarette

The book from which this was taken, *In Time of Tide*, is 64 pgs., digest-sized, professionally printed in bold type, flat-spined, hard cover stamped in gold, jacket with art and author's photo on back. Walter James Miller asks that you **query with 5 sample poems. Reads submissions January and August only.** He replies to the query within a month, to the ms (if invited) in 2 months. **"We consider simultaneous submissions if so marked and if the writer agrees to notify us of acceptance elsewhere." Ms should be typed. Always sends prepublication galleys. Pays royalties after all costs are met and 100 copies. Buys all rights. Offers usual subsidiary rights: 50%/50%. To see samples, send SASE for catalog and ask for "trial rate" (50%).** The editor says, "Form follows function! We accept any excellent poem whose form—be it sonnet or free verse—suits the content and the theme. We like our poets to have a good publishing record in literary magazines, before they begin to think of a book."

‡LINWOOD PUBLISHERS (II), P.O. Box 371819, Decatur GA 30037-1819, phone (800)827-1920, founded 1982, poetry editor Bernard Chase, was "organized as an independent small press, primarily to publish the poetry of known, unknown and little known poets." They have published in both paper and hardback editions. The editor says he is interested in **"quality poetry of any form."** They have published poetry by Simon Perchik, Carl Lindner, Barbara Unger, T.S. Wallace, George Gott, Isabella Pupurai Matsikidze, Barbara Crooker, Betty Schilling, Gary Fort and Steve Wilson. As a sample the editor selected these lines from "True Priests" by Klaus Luthardt, from his book *When Love Had a Face*:

> There walk among us, without priestly robes,
> Those who lead us from despair
> Into the light where joy resides.
> Their consecration needs no pontiff.
> Response became their sacred ritual
> As they grew out of childhood
> And took their place among us.

They will consider unsolicited submissions of book mss. **It is your option whether to query first, send samples or complete mss. Your cover letter should give publication history and bio. They try to reply to queries within 1 month, to mss within a year. They prefer typed mss. Simultaneous submissions OK. Contracts are for 5-10% royalties and author's copies (negotiated). Send 7×10 SAE with 3 ozs. postage for catalog.** "Sample copies of our publications can be purchased directly from the publisher." Bernard Chase advises, "Feel no intimidation by the breadth, the depth of this craft of which you have chosen to become a part. Although we are very open to beginners, we do not as a rule respond with comments, suggestions or criticisms."

‡THE LISTENING EYE (II), Kent State Geauga Campus, 14111 Claridon-Troy Rd., Burton OH 44021, phone (216)286-3840, founded 1970 for student work, 1990 as national publication, editor Grace Butcher, is an annual publication of poetry, short fiction, creative nonfiction and art that welcomes both new and established poets and writers. **They want "high literary quality poetry. Prefer shorter poems (less than two pages) but will consider longer if space allows. Any subject, any style. No trite images or predictable rhyme."** They have published poetry by William Stafford, Walter McDonald and Timothy Russell. As a sample the editor selected the final stanza from "Yet Another Poem about Death" by Alois Zimmerman:

> These then are the characters

for our basketful of weather.
We're leaving for grandma's house.
Our bones already know the plot.

The Listening Eye is 52-60 pgs., 5½ × 8½, professionally printed and saddle-stapled with card stock cover with b&w art. They receive about 200 poems a year, accept approximately 5%. Press run is 300. Single copy: $3. **Sample postpaid: $3.50. Make checks payable to Kent State University. Submit 4 poems at a time. Previously published poems occasionally accepted; no simultaneous submissions. Cover letter preferred. Reads submissions January 1 through April 15.** Time between acceptance and publication is 4-6 months. **Poems are circulated to the editor and two assistant editors who read and evaluate work separately, then meet for final decisions. Seldom comments on rejections. Write for guidelines. Reports in 3 months. Pays 2 copies. Acquires first or one-time rights.** Also awards $30 to the best sports poem. Write for details.

LITERAL LATTÉ; LITERAL LATTÉ POETRY AWARDS (II), 61 E. Eighth St., Suite 240, New York NY 10003, phone (212)260-5532, e-mail litlatté@aol.com, founded 1994, editor Jenine Gordon, is a bimonthly tabloid of "pure prose, poetry and art," distributed free in coffeehouses and bookstores in New York City, and by subscription. **They are "open to all styles of poetry—quality is the determining factor."** They have published poetry by Allen Ginsberg, Carol Muske and John Updike. As a sample we selected these lines from "O.R." by Roberta Swann:

I watched a boy so pale he disappeared
into the sandbox. His name was Alexander.
He was the Sisyphus of kids, scooping
up dirt, climbing out and over to a step,
dumping and tamping it down, tumbling back
into the box and starting again.

LL is 24-28 pgs., 11 × 17, neatly printed, newsprint, with b&w art, graphics and ads. They receive about 2,000 poems a year, accept approximately 2%. Press run is 20,000 for distribution in over 200 bookstores and coffeehouses. Subscription: $15. **Sample postpaid: $5. No previously published poems; simultaneous submissions OK. Cover letter with bio and SASE required.** Time between acceptance and publication is 6 months. **Often comments on rejections. Send SASE for guidelines or request via e-mail. Reports in 2-3 months. Pays 10 copies and 3 subscriptions (2 gift subscriptions in author's name). All rights return to author upon publication.** They also sponsor the *Literal Latté* Poetry Awards, an annual contest for previously unpublished work. Entry fee: $10 for 3 poems (or buy a subscription and the entry fee for 3 poems is included). A past contest was judged by Carol Muske and offered $500 in awards, and publication. Send SASE for current details.

LITERARY FRAGMENTS; CEDAR BAY PRESS (I, II), P.O. Box 751, Beaverton OR 97075-0751, e-mail editor@cedarbay.com, website http://www.teleport.com/~cedarbay/index.html, founded 1980, editor Susan Roberts, is a printed and electronic quarterly "contemporary authors showcase" **open to all forms, lengths, styles and subjects of poetry as well as short stories.** As a sample the editor selected this poem, "Essentials," by Diana Watanabe:

The pierced heart
The pulsating pain
The provoked waves of poignant feelings
Mental polarity struggling for identity
Searching for trust. . . a trust in the process.

The editor says *LF* is 48-80 pgs., 8½ × 11, saddle-stitched, with b&w art/graphics and display ads. They receive approximately 1,500 poems a year. Press run is 3,500, largely distributed free to various distant points. **Sample postpaid: $6 for current issue and guidelines. Send SASE for guidelines alone. Submit 10 or more poems with SASE. Previously published poems and simultaneous submissions OK. Prefers text on PC-DOS compatible disk. E-mail submissions also OK.** Time between acceptance and publication is 6 months. **Usually comments on rejections. Reports in 3-6 months. Pays $5 and up. Acquires one-time rights.** "Poems of notable merit are also published in 'Best of' anthology." Reviews books of poetry in 350-1,200 words, single or multi-book format. Open to unsolicited reviews. Poets may also send books for review consideration. Cedar Bay Press (formerly Sauvie Island Press) publishes chapbooks in print and electronic format. Send $2 for information or view website. The editor says, "*Literary Fragments* is growing and getting a new face-lift and the staff is growing by two new editors. Things are very exciting."

THE LITERARY REVIEW: An International Journal of Contemporary Writing (III), Fairleigh Dickinson University, 285 Madison Ave., Madison NJ 07940, phone/fax (201)443-8564, e-mail tlr@fdu.edu, website http://www.cais.com/aesir/fiction/tlr, founded 1957, editor-in-chief Walter Cummins, a quarterly, seeks **"work by new and established poets which reflects a sensitivity to literary standards and the poetic form." No specifications as to form, length, style, subject matter or purpose.** They have recently published poetry by Robert Cooperman, Gary Fincke, R.S. Thomas, Jeff

Worley and Beth Houston. The magazine is 128 pgs., 6×9, flat-spined, professionally printed with glossy color cover, using 20-50 pgs. of poetry in each issue. Circulation is 2,500 with 900 subscriptions of which one-third are overseas. They receive about 1,200 submissions/year, use 100-150, have a 6- to 12-month backlog. Poems appearing here show careful attention to line, image and form—largely lyric free verse. Editors of recent issues also seem particularly open to translations. **Sample postpaid: $5, request a "general issue." Submit no more than 5 poems at a time, clear typed. Simultaneous submissions OK. At times the editor comments on rejections. Publishes theme issues. Send SASE for upcoming themes or request via e-mail. Reports in 2-3 months. Always sends prepublication galleys. Pays 2 copies. Acquires first rights.** Reviews books of poetry in 500 words, single format. Open to unsolicited reviews. Poets may also send books for review consideration. They advise, "Read a general issue of the magazine carefully before submitting."

LITERATURE AND BELIEF (II, IV-Religious), 3076-E Jesse Knight Humanities Building, Brigham Young University, Provo UT 84602, phone (801)378-3073, founded 1981, editor Richard H. Cracroft, is the "biannual journal of the Center for the Study of Christian Values in Literature." **It uses "carefully crafted, affirmation poetry in the Judeo-Christian tradition."** They have published poetry by Ted Hughes, Donnel Hunter, Leslie Norris, William Stafford and Susan Elizabeth Howe. It is handsomely printed and flat-spined. Single copy: $5 US, $7 outside US. **Submit 3-4 poems at a time. No previously published poems.** They conduct an annual contest with $150 first prize for poetry. Deadline: May 15.

‡**LITTERATURA MAGAZINE (I)**, P.O. Box 18092, Chicago IL 60618, e-mail Johnnyd827@aol. com or litteratur@aol.com, founded 1995, editor/publisher J. Dolsen, is a bimonthly showcasing unpublished authors and poets. **They are open to "just about every type of poetry." However, they do not want to see "anything that would be objectionable to a member of a typical family."** They have recently published poetry by Adrian Robert Ford, Richard F. Hay Sr., Helen T. Morris and Gary Elton Warrick. As a sample we selected these lines from "Fire Dance" by Elizabeth Smaha:

> Dancing in the moonlight
> the fire glowing upon her skin.
> She reaches up to the sky
> trying to wrap her fingers
> around the stars.

LM is about 44 pgs., 5½×8½, photocopied and saddle-stapled with paper cover. They publish 30-35 poems/issue. Press run is approximately 200 for more than 25 subscribers. They also publish a 16-page sample copy version of the magazine which is distributed free to local libraries and coffeehouses. Subscription: $15/year. **Sample postpaid: $3. Make checks payable to J. Dolsen. Submit 3 poems at a time with SASE. Previously published poems and simultaneous submissions OK. "Cover letters are OK, but not solicited." Seldom comments on rejections. Send SASE for guidelines or request via e-mail. Pays 3 copies. Acquires first or one-time rights.** Sponsors contest. Send SASE for details.

LITTLE RIVER PRESS (V), 10 Lowell Ave., Westfield MA 01085, phone (413)568-5598, founded 1976, editor Ronald Edwards, publishes **"limited editions of poetry collections, chapbooks and postcards of New England poets."** They have published poetry by Steven Sossaman, Wanda Cook and Frank Mello. **However, they currently do not accept unsolicited submissions.**

LIVINGSTON PRESS (V), University of West Alabama, Station 22, Livingston AL 35470, founded 1981, editor Joe Taylor, publishes 4-6 paperbacks and 4-6 hardbacks each year. They have published *Synchronized Swimming* by Stephen Corey, *Lizard Fever* by Eugene Walter, *Speaking in Tongues* by Charles Ghigna and *Flight from Valhalla* by Michael J. Bugeja. **However, they are currently not accepting unsolicited submissions. Interested poets should query. They pay 5% royalties and author's copies.** Send SASE for catalog.

‡**THE LOCKHART PRESS (II)**, Box 1366, Lake Stevens WA 98258, phone (206)335-4818, founded 1982, poetry editor Russell A. Lockhart, Ph.D., began as a publisher of fine handmade hardbound books, now expanding to chapbooks and paperbacks, is interested in, **but not limited to, "poetry having its origin in or strongly influenced by dreams." No specifications as to form, length or style.** All handmade editions include special readings by the poets on tape. Limited deluxe editions cost $75 or more. As a sample the editor selected these lines from Marc Hudson's *Journal for an Injured Son*:

> My boy also is a swimmer, for whom desire
> annihilates distance. He is my dolphin, my little Odysseus.
> Death could not steal from his eyes
> the dawn of his homecoming.

Query with 5 samples, usual bio and credits information. Replies to query in 2 weeks, reports

on submission (if invited) in 3 months. Ms should be clear in any form—simultaneous submissions or disks compatible with Macintosh OK. Sometimes comments on rejections. Contract is for 15% royalties (after cost recovery) plus 10 copies (handmade), 100 copies (trade). Buys all rights. Return negotiable. To see a sample, you may ask for one on approval.

LODESTAR BOOKS (V, IV-Children/teen), 375 Hudson St., New York NY 10014, phone (212)366-2627, fax (212)366-2011, affiliate of Dutton's Children's Books, a division of Penguin USA, founded 1980, editorial director Virginia Buckley, is a trade publisher of **juvenile and young adult nonfiction, fiction and picture books.** "We are not currently accepting unsolicited submissions."

‡LONDON MAGAZINE (II), 30 Thurloe Place, London SW7 England, founded 1954, poetry editor Alan Ross, is a literary and art monthly using **poetry "the best of its kind."** Editors seem open to all styles and forms, including well-made formal works. Some of the best poems in England appear here. It is a $6 \times 8\frac{1}{2}$, perfect-bound, elegant-looking magazine, with card cover, averaging about 150 pages six times a year. They accept about 150 of 2,000 poems received each year. Press run is 5,000 for 2,000 subscribers. Subscription: £28.50 or $67. **Sample postpaid: £4.75. Cover letter required with submissions. Reports "very soon." Pays £20/page. Buys first British serial rights.** Reviews books of poetry in up to 1,200 words. Open to unsolicited reviews. Poets may also send books for review consideration. Alan Ross says, "Quality is our only criterion."

LONDON REVIEW OF BOOKS (III), 28 Little Russell St., London WC1A 2HM England, fax (071)404-3337, founded 1979, editor Mary-Kay Wilmers, is published 24 times a year, mostly reviews and essays but some poems. They have published some of the most distinguished contemporary poets, such as Ted Hughes, Tony Harrison, James Fenton, Frederick Seidel and Thom Gunn. As a sample we selected the opening stanza of "The Metronomic Moon" by Michael Young:

> In other years I would say, how pretty they are,
> The cherries outside our house.
> This autumn I see the first leaves
> Writhe from the green into the yellow and
> From the yellow into what seems a frantic red
> Before they corkscrew to their conclusion
> When the morning wipers scrape them from the windscreens
> To drop them in the dog shit on the pavement
> Their beauty has not brought them mercy.

The paper has a circulation of 17,000 with 14,000 subscriptions. **Sample: £2.15 in UK, $2.95 in US and Canada—excluding postage. Submit 3 poems at a time. "Poems should be typed, double-spaced, on one side of the paper only. Please send cover letter and enclose SAE (and IRCs)."** No previously published poems. Considers simultaneous submissions. Always sends prepublication galleys. Pays £50/poem.

LONE WILLOW PRESS (III), P.O. Box 31647, Omaha NE 68131-0647, founded 1993, editor Dale Champy, publishes 2-3 chapbooks a year. **"We publish chapbooks on single themes and we are open to all themes. The only requirement is excellence. However, we do not want to see doggerel or greeting card verse."** They have recently published *Gay, Some Assembly Required* by Brian E. Bengtson and *Tishku, After She Created Men* by Marjorie Power. As a sample the editor selected these lines from "Living in the Vows" in *The Abbey Poems* by Fredrick Zydek:

> You must learn to pile your temptations
> like coins saved for a rainy day.
> You must let the will go. Let it float
> like a wonderful balloon
> through the celestial machinery.

That book is 20 pgs., digest-sized, neatly printed on gray paper and saddle-stapled with a light, gray card stock cover. **Query first with 5 sample poems and cover letter with brief bio and publication credits. Previously published poems OK; no simultaneous submissions.** Time between acceptance and publication is 6 months. **Seldom comments on rejections. Send SASE for guidelines. Replies to queries in 1 month, to mss (if invited) in 2-3 months. Pays 25 author's copies. "We also pay a small royalty if the book goes into a second printing."** For a sample chapbook, send $7.95 in check or money order. The editor says, "If you don't know the work of Roethke, DeFrees and Hugo, don't bother sending work our way. We work with no more than two poets at a time."

LONG ISLAND QUARTERLY (IV-Regional), P.O. Box 114, Northport NY 11768, founded 1990, editor and publisher George Wallace, is a quarterly using **poetry by people on or from Long Island. "Surprise us with fresh language. No conventional imagery, self-indulgent confessionalism, compulsive article-droppers."** They have published poetry by Edmund Pennant and David Ignatow. As a sample the editor selected this poem, "The Willow," by William Heyen:

Crazy Horse counted the leaves of willows along the river.
He realized one leaf for each buffalo,
& the leaves just now appearing in the Moon of Tender Grass
were calves being born. If he could keep the trees
from the whites, the herds would seed themselves.
He watched the buffalo leaves for long, & long,
how their colors wavered dark & light in the running wind.
If he could keep his rootedness within this dream,
he could shade his people to the end of time.

LIQ is a handsome publication whose clean design (28 pgs., digest-sized, saddle-stapled, professionally printed on quality stock with matte card cover) enhances the image-based, mostly lyric free verse inside. Most contributions show attention to craft and structure. Press run is 250 for 150 subscribers of which 15 are libraries, 50-75 shelf sales. Subscription: $15. **Sample postpaid: $4. Submit 3 poems at a time. Name and address on each page. Cover letter including connection to Long Island region required. Submissions without SASE are not returned. Responds in 3 months. Sometimes sends prepublication galleys. Pays 1 copy.** Sponsors an annual open poetry competition with deadline of March 31. The winner and runners up are awarded cash prizes. Entrants may send up to 5 original, unpublished poems for consideration. No restrictions on theme or length. Entry fee: $5. No mss will be returned. Winners announced 2 months after closing date. For competition results, include SASE. Send submissions to: Long Island Quarterly Poetry Prize at the above address. The editor advises: "(1) Go beyond yourself; (2) Don't be afraid to fictionalize; (3) Don't write your autobiography—if you are worth it, maybe someone else will."

LONG ISLANDER; WALT'S CORNER (II), 322 Main St., Huntington NY 11743, phone (516)427-7000, fax (516)427-5820, founded 1838 by Walt Whitman, poetry editor George Wallace, is a weekly newspaper, 25,000 circulation, using **unrhymed poetry up to 20 lines "grounded in personal/social matrix; no haiku, inspirational."** They have published poetry by David Ignatow, David Axelrod and R.B. Weber. As a sample the editor selected these lines from "Sleepless at Christmas" by L. Dellarocca:

It's another kind of light that seethes here,
this wrenched wrenched orphanage of hearts.
Death touched men who've come to worship night,
god of bottles and mouths.

It is "48 pgs., newsprint." They use 52 of about 1,000 poems submitted each year. Subscription: $18. **Sample postpaid: $2.50. Submit 3 poems at a time. Simultaneous submissions OK. "Cover letter should be simple, not effusive. SASE missing? Then it's going in the garbage." Editor "normally" comments on rejections. Pays 1 copy.** Staff reviews books of poetry. Send books for review consideration.

LONG SHOT (III), P.O. Box 6238, Hoboken NJ 07030, founded 1982, edited by Danny Shot and Nancy Mercado, is, they say, "writing from the real world." They have published poetry by Adrienne Rich, Gregory Corso, Miguel Algarin, Pedro Pietri, Allen Ginsberg, Amiri Baraka and June Jordan. As a sample the editors selected these lines from "High Holy Days Magazine" by R.E. Sherwin:

Gd gets off cheap. Throw
the world a Jew, now and then,
to keep their minds off
the fucked up universe. Or
what passes for minds. Or worlds.

Long Shot is 224 pgs., flat-spined, professionally printed with glossy card cover using b&w photos, drawings and cartoons. It comes out twice a year. Press run is 2,000. Subscription: $22 for 2 years (4 issues). **Sample: $8. No previously published poems; simultaneous submissions OK. Reports in 2 months. Pays 2 copies.** Unlike other publishers, Danny Shot says they receive "too many requests for writer's guidelines. Just send the poems."

‡THE LONGNECK (I, II), P.O. Box 659, Vermillion SD 57069, phone (605)624-4837, fax (605)624-5562, founded 1993, poetry editor Michael Tidemann, assistant editor J.D. Erickson, is an annual publication of the Northbank Writers Group. "We publish established and new authors side by side." **They want poetry with "fresh, strong imagery, both visually and intellectually. No tired, ineffectual meanderings or greeting card work."** They have recently published poetry by Joseph Ditta, Corrine DeWinter and Norma Wilson. As a sample the editor selected these lines from "The Cold Dark Age Ahead" by Errol Miller:

Oh Lord, we are all innocent and guilty, framed
by someone Else's uniform method
of loveliness and loneliness,
enacting the same selfsame play

over and over among the sawbriar and the thorn

The Longneck is 48 pgs., 11 × 17, professionally printed on 50# white paper with b&w photos, illustrations and ads. They receive about 250 poems a year, use approximately 25%. Press run is 1,000 for 700-800 shelf sales. Single copy: $3. **Sample postpaid: $4.95. Submit 5 poems at a time, name and address on each page. Previously published poems and simultaneous submissions OK. Cover letter with brief bio preferred. Submission deadline: February 1. Poems are circulated to an editorial board. Often comments on rejections. Send SASE for guidelines. Reports in 3-6 months. Pays 2 copies. Acquires first or one-time rights.** The editor says, "Read and write a lot of poetry. Bloom late if that's the way it is—share your work—listen to your critics. Find your images and then fine-tune them. As we are an annual publication with volunteer staff, please be patient in having your work returned. If we take an extended period to return your work, that is good news. It means we are seriously considering your work."

‡**THE LONSDALE: THE INTERNATIONAL QUARTERLY OF THE ROMANTIC SIX (IV-Specialized)**, VIP Meguro 802, 4-1-16, Shimo-Meguro, Meguro-Ku, Tokyo 153 Japan, phone/fax (+81-3)5721-9979, founded 1993, editor Michael L. Jabri-Pickett, is a quarterly journal devoted to the works of William Blake, William Wordsworth, Samuel Taylor Coleridge, Lord Byron, Percy Bysshe Shelley and John Keats. **"Content must be relevant to one of the six writers with which the publication is devoted. Poems of any length and style may be considered, but no haiku."** *The Lonsdale* is 16 pgs., 8½ × 11, professionally printed and saddle-stitched. They receive 10-20 poems a year, "to date none have been published." Press run is 1,500, most distributed free to museums and libraries throughout the UK. Single copy: $10; subscription: $19/year. **Sample free. Make checks payable to Michael L. Jabri-Pickett. Submit 3 poems at a time, typed double-spaced, one poem/page. No previously published poems or simultaneous submissions. Cover letter required. Reports in 4-6 weeks. Pays 30 copies.** Reviews anything of relevance; limitless word count, single or multi-book reviews. Open to unsolicited reviews. Poets may also send related books for review consideration.

LOOM PRESS (III), P.O. Box 1394, Lowell MA 01853-1394, founded 1978, editor/publisher Paul Marion, is a small press publisher of books with **an emphasis on publishing poets from New England.** Poets recently published include Eric Linden, Bunrith Sath, Stan Berstein and Rhina Espaillat. Books are usually perfect-bound, 6 × 9, with an average page count of 64. **Sample postpaid: $10. Writers should query first for book publication, sending cover letter, credits, 5 sample poems and bio. "Do not send book-length mss."** Queries will be answered in 1 month, mss reported on in 3 months. Simultaneous submissions will be considered. Time to publication is 12-18 months. **The editor comments on mss "when time allows." Always sends prepublication galleys. Pays royalties of 10%, plus 5% of print run.** The editor says, "Please support the small publishers who make poetry available. We are especially interested in poems that address issues related to place and history and American culture."

LOONFEATHER; LOONFEATHER PRESS (II, IV-Regional), P.O. Box 1212, Bemidji MN 56619-1212, phone (218)751-4869, founded 1979, poetry editors Betty Rossi, Elmo Heggie and Marshall Muirhead, is a small press publisher of the literary magazine *Loonfeather* appearing 2 times a year, **"primarily but not exclusively for Minnesota writers. Prefer short poems of not over 42 lines, accepts some traditional forms if well done, no generalizations on worn-out topics."** They have published poetry by Spencer Reece, Joyce Penchansky, Thom Ward and Mary Winters. As a sample the editors selected these lines from "The Owl" by Malcolm Moos:

Who was it that I saw moving through the language of the rain?
Was it my grandmother, lingering?
Something heard and forgotten, deep in the forest of my body,
something I am always trying to remember. . . .

Loonfeather is 48 pgs., 5½ × 8½, saddle-stapled, professionally printed in small type with matte card cover, using b&w art and ads. Single copy current issue: $5; back issues: $2.50, subscription: $7.50/year. **Submission deadlines January 31 and July 31 for May and November publications. Publishes theme issues occasionally. Send SASE for upcoming themes. Pays 2 copies.** Loonfeather Press publishes a limited number of quality poetry books. They recently published *Feast* by Carol Ann Russell and *Notes of an Ancient Chinese Poet* by Philip Dacey. **Query with 2-3 sample poems, cover letter and previous publications. "Please do not query until after January 1997." Replies to queries in 6 months.** Time between acceptance and publication is 1-1½ years. **Pays 10% royalties.**

LOTHROP, LEE & SHEPARD BOOKS (V), 1350 Avenue of the Americas, New York NY 10019, founded 1894, editor-in-chief Susan Pearson. **"We do not accept unsolicited mss."**

LOTUS POETRY SERIES; NAOMI LONG MADGETT POETRY AWARD (IV-Ethnic), P.O. Box 21607, Detroit MI 48221, phone (313)861-1280, fax (313)861-4740, founded 1972, editor

Naomi Long Madgett. "With one exception of a textbook, we publish books of **poetry by individual authors,** although we have published three anthologies. We occasionally sponsor readings. **Most, but not all, of our authors are black."** Their most recent anthology is *Adam of Ifé: Black Women in Praise of Black Men.* They have recently published poetry by Adam David Miller, Robert Chrisman and Alvin Aubert. As a sample we selected these lines from "Thinking About Medusa" from *Walking North* by Beverly V. Head:

> she must have been lonely
> watching all those possible lovers
> turn into beautiful stone
> horror painted perfectly
> across their faces. . .

Submit 5-10 sample poems, typed. Poems previously published in magazines OK; no simultaneous submissions. Time between acceptance and publication is 12-18 months. **Poems are circulated to an editorial board. "Senior editor reads manuscripts first, then passes on the best with names removed to other editors." Seldom comments on rejections. Response is usually within 6 weeks. SASE required for response. Pays 10% royalties plus author's copies. Poets are not expected to contribute to the cost of publication. "Copies may be ordered from our catalog, which is free upon request. We do not give samples."** They also sponsor the Naomi Long Madgett Poetry Award. The award goes to a manuscript by an African-American poet who is 60 years of age or older. Interested persons may write for details. The editor says, "Beginners should read a great deal of contemporary poetry and recognize what is and what is not usually being done. That does not rule out experimentation, but styles of bygone eras and imitation of other poets' styles are discouraged."

LOUISIANA LITERATURE; LOUISIANA LITERATURE PRIZE FOR POETRY (II, IV-Regional), SLU-792, Southeastern Louisiana University, Hammond LA 70402, phone (504)549-5022, fax (504)549-5021, editor David Hanson, appears twice a year. They say they **"receive mss year round although we work through submissions more slowly in summer. We consider creative work from anyone though we strive to showcase our state's talent. We appreciate poetry that shows firm control and craft, is sophisticated yet accessible to a broad readership. We don't use highly experimental work."** They have published poetry by Sue Owen, Catharine Savage Brosman, Diane Wakoski, Claire Bateman, Kate Daniels, Elton Glaser, Sandra Nelson, Gray Jacobik, Al Maginnes and Judy Longley. As a sample the editor selected these lines from "Four Coffees" by Jody Bilyeu:

> In his grandparents' shallow, ancient pond
> he discovered among cattails
> and swamped Sudan grass a hundred baby
> fish and yanked some into a kitchen strainer,
> rapt by their slippery blackness,
> their writhing, the fact that some had legs.

The magazine is 100 pgs., 6¾×9¾, flat-spined, handsomely printed on heavy matte stock with matte card cover. Single copies: $5 for individuals; subscription: $10 for individuals, $12.50 for institutions. **Submit up to 5 poems at a time. Send cover letter, including bio to use in the event of acceptance. No simultaneous submissions. Enclose SASE specifying whether work is to be returned or discarded. No submissions via fax. Publishes theme issues. Upcoming theme is Louisiana Nature Writing (date not set). Send SASE for details. Sometimes sends prepublication galleys. Pays 2 copies.** Open to unsolicited reviews. Poets may also send books for review consideration; include cover letter. The Louisiana Literature Prize for Poetry offers a $400 award. Send SASE for guidelines. The editor says, "It's important to us that the poets we publish be in control of their creations. Too much of what we see seems arbitrary."

LOUISIANA STATE UNIVERSITY PRESS (V), P.O. Box 25053, Baton Rouge LA 70894-5053, phone (504)388-6294, fax (504)388-6461, founded 1935, poetry editor L.E. Phillabaum, is a highly respected publisher of collections by poets such as Lisel Mueller, Margaret Gibson, Fred Chappell and Henry Taylor. **Currently not accepting poetry submissions; "fully committed through 1998."**

THE LOUISVILLE REVIEW (II, IV-Children/teen), Dept. PM, 315 Bingham Humanities, University of Louisville, Louisville KY 40292, phone (502)852-6801, founded 1976, faculty editor Sena Jeter Naslund, appears twice a year. **They use any kind of poetry except translations, and they have a section of children's poetry (grades K-12).** They have published poetry by Richard Jackson, Jeffrey

---

THE SUBJECT INDEX, located before the General Index, can help you select markets for your work. It lists those publishers whose poetry interests are specialized.

Commitment and courage get poetry published

"I think anything done on a serious level, whether it's architecture or child raising or poetry, requires a person to push himself and to keep going when he feels like stopping, to try to excel when he feels like sliding by," says Max Garland. "I think poetry is like that, but I don't think it's special in the person who is a poet or that an artist has some special courage that he should be saluted for. I think all endeavors someone attempts at the deepest level require the same kind of courage. Every emotional relationship, every aspect of a regular person's working life requires acts and moments of courage if he wants to do it with his full self. Creativity is like that—it's no exception."

Max Garland

Over the years, Garland has viewed poetry from three different windows: as a student, a struggling poet and an instructor. Poetry first took hold of him during his undergraduate years at Western Kentucky University where he obtained a degree in English. However, the academic view toward poetry at the time didn't sit well with Garland. "To me, there was something almost unnatural, the way poems were talked about and analyzed in universities— thought of as assignments. When I was in college in the late '60s and early '70s, it was the time of the study of the great dead writers, and as someone who had ambitions of being a living one, the university didn't seem like the place to be."

So Garland returned to his rural hometown of Paducah, Kentucky, and began to live the life that interested him. "The people I wanted to write about, the kind of language I wanted to use, made it necessary for me to go back home and live there as an adult and work every day for a long, long time and understand poetry from that perspective."

For ten years, Garland lived in Paducah and worked as a mail carrier on the same route his grandfather had run for 25 years. He spent his free time on his poems, trying to perfect a voice which was more representative of the language around him. "The reading of William Stafford's poetry influenced me to think I could write with a voice closer to a speaking voice than I had understood was possible," he says.

Stafford's influence also led Garland to his first publication in **Plainsong**, the literary journal of Western Kentucky University. Garland submitted work to the journal because he recognized in the poems it published something similar to his own poetry. The journal also offered beginning poets the chance to be seen along-

CLOSE-UP, *Garland*

"The Nap Situation"

I wake up with the intelligence of moss,
and not the brightest of mosses at that.
I study the stitching of the bedsheets
with a drowsy version of awe. I notice
the shifting patterns of lint held
in the sunlight. Only minutes away
from the seamlessness of sleep
and already there's an autumn chill,
a tangle of shadows, a passel of dying
leaves at the windowpane. I'm un-
prepared for the profusion of things,
each with its own little spirit, its own
little spiel. The boundary between sloth
and pointless attention to detail
grows murky. A pencil rests uneasily
on a sill. A book stifles a cough.
A geranium pauses for emphasis.
The longer I'm awake, the more
they arrive, the separate things,
the particulars, with their hats
in their hands like mendicants,
like babies on the doorstep,
like penniless relatives
with stories so farflung and desolate
I'd need a heart of stone
not to listen.

CLOSE-UP, *continued*

side such well established names as Stafford, Coleman Barks and William Matthews.

However, there were times when Garland went long periods without submitting work. "At various stages, I was trying to work on learning to write and just thought I wasn't ready. I felt the need to just work on the writing and let it sit for awhile. Then, eventually, the need would arise and the poems would make their way out. But I have always been leery of trying to rush publishing and finding a place for everything."

Not all of Garland's work found a place, and he, like many other writers, received "countless" rejection letters. But the rejection of his work didn't diminish his enthusiasm and, in fact, gave Garland the chance to view his poetry more objectively and see its faults. "A lot of people try to figure out the angle that will provide them with publication or a career without devoting themselves to deepening their writing, expanding their writing, taking it to another level. All and all, the best course for being taken seriously as a poet is to write better. And, with regard to publishing, it might be that writing well is the best advice."

Though Garland says he is thankful some of his early work was rejected, for him, finding the time to write, to improve his work, isn't the tough part of being a poet—it's finding the courage to maintain the habit of writing. And through this courage and commitment to his work, Garland gained the confidence to submit poems to publications more national in scope. Eventually, he saw his work published in *The Carolina Quarterly*, *Chicago Review*, *The Georgia Review*, *The Gettysburg Review*, *The Iowa Review* and *Poetry*. Despite Garland's commitment, however, writing began to take second place to his job as a mail carrier and the financial security it offered.

So he left the postal service, took his savings and enrolled in the Iowa Writers' Workshop. "For a long time I liked having the writing part of my life separate and having a job that was really unconnected," says Garland. "But after awhile, I felt the separateness too much and wanted my life to be more integrated. So I resigned from a job I basically had for life and went after an M.F.A. in Creative Writing."

While working on his M.F.A., Garland began compiling his work into a book. However, the collection, which contained poems from his time in Paducah and work he had written while at the Workshop, wasn't completed until close to the end of his stay at Iowa. Then, in 1990, Garland applied for and won a poetry fellowship from the University of Wisconsin in Madison, where he worked as a visiting writer/lecturer for six years. He now teaches full-time at the University of Wisconsin-Eau Claire.

Around the same time he arrived in Madison, Garland began to submit his book to "first book" competitions and to a few university presses. But, being fully aware of how tough a first book of poetry is to publish, Garland focused his efforts on the competitions. He submitted the book to 25 competitions in all—continually changing the book with each rejection. "I would take some poems out. I would add some poems if I had written anything new that seemed to fit. I would constantly rearrange and try to improve it," Garland says. "Then [with] letter after letter coming back, it became discouraging. It didn't become discouraging because of the writing. I was going to write whether I published a

CLOSE-UP, *Garland*

book or not. I was going to write even if I was a mailman *all* my life."

In 1994, all of Garland's rearranging and patience paid off when his collection of poems won the Juniper Prize sponsored by the University of Massachusetts Press. The book, entitled *The Postal Confessions*, was published by the press in 1995. "I think the reason I had some trouble getting the book published early on is that it probably wasn't finished," he says. "And that is what I always thought when I was having trouble publishing—these poems aren't far enough along and I have to go back to the drawing board."

With the first press run of *The Postal Confessions* practically selling out in less than a year, Garland is very pleased with his book's success. But, he says, success is more than sales. "Just having all the poems between covers and being able to give them to people without having to make copies, that is success for me. Whether you are doing this for thousands of people and posterity or to tell one person what life means to you, I think, given all of the things one could spend time doing, poetry is not a waste of time.

"Poetry is the language of the interior, the language of the human heart. In a time and culture in which we are bombarded with superficial language, political manipulation, cartoon-like renderings of the human condition, and the good old-fashioned sales pitch, it seems important that there still be a means of reaching past that, reaching toward something complex and mysterious. The more babble that surrounds us, the more necessary poetry becomes."

—*Chantelle Bentley*

Skinner, Maura Stanton, Richard Cecil, Roger Weingarten and Greg Pape. *TLR* is 200 pgs., flat-spined, 6×8¾. They accept about 10% of some 700 pieces received a year. **Sample postpaid: $4. "Poetry by children must include permission of parent to publish if accepted. In all of our poetry we look for the striking metaphor, unusual imagery and fresh language. We do not read in summer. Poems are read by 3 readers; report time is 1-2 months and time to publication is 2-3 months." Pays 1 copy.**

LOW-TECH PRESS (V), 30-73 47th St., Long Island City NY 11103, founded 1981, editor Ron Kolm, has published work by Hal Sirowitz, John Yau and Jennifer Nostrand. As a sample the editor selected these lines (poet unidentified):

> They firebombed
> the dinner table
> taking us completely
> by surprise.

"I am only interested in short poems with clear images. Since almost nobody gets paid for their work, I believe in multiple submissions and multiple publishings. Even though we only publish solicited mss, I respond right away to any mail the press receives."

LUCIDITY; BEAR HOUSE PUBLISHING (I), Route 2, Box 94, Eureka Springs AR 72632-9505, phone (501)253-9351, founded 1985, editor Ted O. Badger. *Lucidity* is a quarterly of poetry. **Submission fee required—$1/poem for "juried" selection by a panel of judges or $2/poem to compete for cash awards of $15, $10 and $5. Other winners paid in both cash and in copies. In addition, the editor invites a few guest contributors to submit to each issue. Contributors are encouraged to subscribe or buy a copy of the magazine.** The magazine is called *Lucidity* because, the editor says, "I have felt that too many publications of verse lean to the abstract in content and the obscure in style." They are **"open as to form. 36-line limit due to format. No restriction on subject matter except that something definitive be given to the reader. We look for poetry that is life-related and has clarity and substance." Purpose: "to give a platform to poets who can impart their ideas with clarity." He does not want "religious, nature or vulgar poems."** Recently published poets include Janice Braud, Marta Boswell, Emily Moore, Janet A. Sullivan and Laurence Thomas. As a sample of the type of verse sought, the editor offers these lines by Junette Fabian:

> *Your shirts*
> *swell on the line*
> *you hung for me last week;*
> *I run to hug you but the wind*
> *has stilled.*

The magazine is 76 pgs., digest-sized, photocopied from typescript, saddle-stapled, with matte card cover. It's a surprisingly lively small press magazine featuring accessible narrative and lyric poetry, with almost equal space given to free and formal verse. Press run is 350 for 190 subscribers. Subscription: $10. **Sample postpaid: $2.50. Submit 3-6 poems at a time. Simultaneous submissions OK.** Time between acceptance and publication is 3 months. **Send SASE for guidelines. Reports in 2-3 months. Buys one-time rights.** Bear House Press is a self-publishing arrangement by which poets can pay to have booklets published in the same format as *Lucidity*, prices beginning at 100 copies of 32 pgs. for $224. Publishes 10 chapbooks/year. The editor says, "Small press journals offer the best opportunity to most poets for publication."

LUNA BISONTE PRODS; LOST AND FOUND TIMES (IV-Style), 137 Leland Ave., Columbus OH 43214-7505, founded 1967, poetry editor John M. Bennett, may be the zaniest phenomenon in central Ohio. John Bennett is a publisher (and practitioner) of **experimental and avant-garde writing**, sometimes sexually explicit, and art in a bewildering array of formats including the magazine, *Lost and Found Times*, postcard series, posters, chapbooks, pamphlets, labels and audiocassette tapes. You can get a **sampling of Luna Bisonte Prods for $6. Numerous reviewers have commented on the bizarre *Lost and Found Times,*** "reminiscent of several West Coast dada magazines"; "This exciting magazine is recommended only for the most daring souls"; "truly demented"; "Insults . . . the past 3,000 years of literature"; "revolution where it counts, in the dangerous depths of the imagination," etc. Bennett wants to see **"unusual poetry, naive poetry, surrealism, experimental, visual poetry, collaborations—*no* poetry workshop or academic pabulum."** He has recently published poetry by I. Argüelles, G. Beining, B. Heman, R. Olson, J. Lipman, B. Porter, C.H. Ford, P. Weinman, E.N. Brookings, F.A. Nettelbeck, D. Raphael, R. Crozier, S. Sollfrey, M. Andre, N. Vassilakis, S.E. Murphy, T. Taylor, F. Doctorovich and A. Ackerman. As a sample, the editor selected these lines from a poem by Jim Leftwich:

> *destroy the motives to desire by despairing of the lips. the tool*
> *raged in the essay. the road is a flaccid car. time is the choir of*
> *thumbs, halo of a shoe. I hear the mad haddock lurking in its*
> *wrappers. altogether creatures of the magnificent stage. this*
> *lesser lesson of utter sincerity. and it may be that you will obtain*
> *the raw bandana, the rare bandana. moonstream through the*
> *periscope in a gnostic breeze. invoked triage, vanilla jar. cave*

The digest-sized, 52-page magazine, photoreduced typescript and wild graphics, matte card cover with graphics, has a circulation of 350 with 75 subscribers of which 30 are libraries. Subscription: $25 for 5 numbers. **Sample postpaid: $6. Submit anytime—preferably camera-ready (but this is not required). Reports in 1-2 days. Pays copies. All rights revert to authors upon publication.** Staff reviews books of poetry. Send books for review consideration. **Luna Bisonte also will consider book submissions:** query with samples and cover letter (but "keep it brief"). **Chapbook publishing usually depends on grants or other subsidies and is usually by solicitation.** He will also consider subsidy arrangements on negotiable terms. The editor says, "I would like to see more experimental and avant-garde material in Spanish and Portuguese, or in mixtures of languages."

LUNA NEGRA (I), Box 26, % Office of Campus Life/Student Activities or English Dept., Kent State University, Kent OH 44240, phone (216)672-2676, editor Dr. Jentoft, is a student-run, biannual literary and art magazine of the KSU main campus, **open to all forms of poetry and prose.** The editor says it is 40-50 pgs., 5½×8½, with art and photography throughout. They receive 400-450 poems a year, accept 40 or 50. Press run is 2,000, most distributed to KSU students. **Submit no more than 3 poems at a time. Simultaneous submissions OK. Reads submissions September 1 through March 30 only. Seldom comments on rejections. Reports in 1 month or so ("depending on school calendar"). Pays 1 copy. "All rights revert to author immediately after publication."** The editor adds, "We are also interested in any b&w reproducible artwork or photographs."

THE LUTHERAN JOURNAL (IV-Religious), Dept. PM, 7317 Cahill Rd., Edina MN 55439, phone (612)941-6830, editor The Rev. Armin U. Deye, is a family quarterly, 32 pgs., circulation 125,000, for Lutheran Church members, middle age and older. They use **poetry "related to subject matter,"** traditional, free verse, blank verse. Sample free for SASE. **Simultaneous submissions OK. Pays.**

LYNX, A JOURNAL FOR LINKING POETS; AHA BOOKS; INTERNATIONAL TANKA SPLENDOR AWARD (IV-Form), P.O. Box 1250, Gualala CA 95445, e-mail ahabooks@men.org, website http://www.faximum.com/aha!poetry, founded as *APA-Renga* in 1986, later the name was changed to *Lynx* "to link an endangered species of poetry with an endangered animal and to inspire the traditional wit of renga," says Jane Reichhold, who co-edits the publication with Werner Reichhold. *Lynx*, published 3 times a year (February, June and October) "is **based on the ancient craft of renga, linked verse with origins in Zen and Japanese culture, and now publishes both renga and tanka.** A renga is a non-narrative series of linked images as a group effort. Tanka is the most popular poetry form in Japan and the oldest continued form." As a sample the editor selected this renga excerpt by Jane Reichhold, T.B., Kenneth C. Leibman and Tundra Wind:

> *panty hose   as she crosses her legs   she whispers*
> *from the back room   a sigh*
> *on the table   her letter punctuated   with a teardrop*
> *from the apartment upstairs   a lullaby*

Lynx is 90 pgs., 4½×11, neatly printed and comb-bound with card cover. It also publishes essays, book reviews, articles, interviews, experimental linked forms, linked prose, art, commentaries and "whatever encourages poets to link ideas." They currently have 300 subscribers. Subscription: $15 US and Canada, $20 elsewhere. **Sample postpaid: $4, includes guidelines. Make checks payable to AHA Books. Submit 1 renga and/or 6-10 tanka at a time.** *Lynx* **encourages submissions by those experienced and experimenting with collaborative forms. Subscribers participate in ongoing renga, start trends and otherwise determine the content. All submissions should include a brief bio with the title of the work. E-mail submissions are welcome. E-mail information requests are welcome if the receiver can retrieve attached files. Most information is available on the website. "Please send us copies that do not need to be returned." Include SASE for reply. Editor responds to all who submit. Reports in 1 week.** AHA Books also sponsors the International Tanka Splendor Award. Winning entries will be published in *Tanka Splendor*. Deadline: September 30. Send SASE for details.

LYNX EYE; SCRIBBLEFEST LITERARY GROUP (I), 1880 Hill Dr., Los Angeles CA 90041-1244, founded 1994, co-editors Pam McCully and Kathryn Morrison. *Lynx Eye* is the quarterly publication of the ScribbleFest Literary Group, a new organization dedicated to the development and promotion of the literary arts. *Lynx Eye* is **"dedicated to showcasing visionary writers and artists, particularly new voices." Each issue contains a special feature called Presenting, in which an unpublished writer of prose or poetry makes his/her print debut. They have no specifications regarding form, subject matter or style of poetry, but poems should be 30 lines or less.** They have recently published poetry by Whitman McGowan, Margery Snyder, Sarah Bean and Antler. As a sample we selected these lines from "I Got So Lost I Should Have Left Home Yesterday" by Ashira Belsey:

> *Look, I got off at the wrong exit,*
> *Sue me*
> *So I stopped at a 7-11 and the clerk*
> *Never heard of the street.*

Lynx Eye is about 120 pgs., 5½×8½, perfect-bound with b&w artwork. They receive about 2,000 poetry submissions a year and have space for about 75. Press run is 250-500 for 100 subscribers, 100 shelf sales. Single copy price varies from $5 to $7.50. Subscription: $20/year. **Sample postpaid: $5. No previously published poems; simultaneous submissions OK. Name, address and phone number on each piece. Always comments on rejections. Send SASE for guidelines. Reports in 2-3 months. Pays $10/piece and 3 copies. Buys first North American serial rights.**

THE LYRIC (II), 307 Dunton Dr. SW, Blacksburg VA 24060-5127, founded 1921 ("the oldest magazine in North America in continuous publication devoted to the publication of **traditional poetry**"), poetry editor Leslie Mellichamp, uses about 65 poems each quarterly issue. **"We use rhymed verse in traditional forms, for the most part, with an occasional piece of blank or free verse. 40 lines or so is usually our limit. Our themes are varied, ranging from religious ecstasy to humor to raw grief, but we feel no compulsion to shock, embitter or confound our readers. We also avoid poems about contemporary political or social problems—grief but not grievances, as Frost put it. Frost is helpful in other ways: If yours is more than a lover's quarrel with life, we're not your best market. And most of our poems are accessible on first or second reading. Frost again: Don't hide too far away."** They have published poetry by Anne Barlow, Tom Riley, Michael J. Bugeja, Rhina P. Espaillat, Richard Moore, Barbara Loots, Alfred Dorn, Sharon Kourous, Gail White, Neill Megaw and Alice Mackenzie Swaim. The editor selected these sample lines from "The Days of Night" by R.H. Morrison:

> *Why do you punctuate your life with days*
> *and rank the blatant noon above night's gleams?*
> *Night is the cradle of our hopes and dreams*
> *that rise from sleep and go their glittering ways.*

The Lyric is 36 pgs., digest-sized, professionally printed with varied typography, matte card cover. It has a circulation of 850 with 800 subscriptions of which 290 are libraries. They receive about 5,000 submissions/year, use 250, have an average 3-month backlog. Subscription: $12 US, $14 Canada and other countries (in US funds only). **Sample postpaid: $3. Submit up to 5 poems at a time. No previously published poems; simultaneous submissions OK. "Cover letters often helpful, but not required." Send SASE for guidelines. Reports in 2 months (average). Pays 1 copy, and all contributors are eligible for quarterly and annual prizes totaling over $800.** Leslie Mellichamp comments, "Our raison d'être has been the encouragement of form, music, rhyme and accessibility in poetry. We detect a growing dissatisfaction with the modernist movement that ignores these things and a growing interest in the traditional wellsprings of the craft. Naturally, we are proud to have provided an alternative for 75 years that helped keep the true roots of poetry alive."

M.I.P. COMPANY (IV-Foreign language, erotica), P.O. Box 27484, Minneapolis MN 55427, phone (612)546-7578, fax (612)544-6077, e-mail mp@mip.com, website http://www.mip.com, founded in 1984, contact Michael Peltsman, publishes 3 paperbacks/year. **They only publish Russian erotic poetry and prose written in Russian.** They have published poetry collections by Mikhail Armalinsky and Aleksey Shelvakh. **No previously published poems; simultaneous submissions OK. Replies to queries in 1 month. Seldom comments on rejections.**

‡M.O.O.N. MAGAZINE; MOON SHADOW PUBLICATIONS (I, IV-Membership/subscription); "FINISH THIS POEM CONTEST" (I), 2404 75th St., Kenosha WI 53143, phone/fax (414)658-2520, founded 1992, editor/publisher B.C. Mullikin. *M.O.O.N. Magazine* (Muse Odyssey Orbital News), a quarterly appearing in January, April, July and October, "was created as an alternative answer for poets, writers and artists who are seeking to be published and promoted. *M.O.O.N.* is an open format, literary and art membership publication." **They want to see "more humorous poetry and free verse relating to contemporary issues, 25 lines or less. We do not want to see submissions promoting any form of discrimination or containing pornographic content."** They have recently published poetry by Martha Calloway, Irma Wassall, Jane Stuart and William T. Masonis. As a sample the editor selected the poem, "SCHhhh . . . ," by Bonnie Dupree:

> Sally Saw Six
> .38 Cal. Shells,
> Down by the
> Sea Shore.

M.O.O.N. is about 20 pgs., 8½ × 11, saddle-stitched, colored card cover with artwork, b&w cartoons and drawings, and ads. They receive about 300 poems a year, accept 50%. Press run is 300 for 50 subscribers. Subscription: $20. **Sample (including guidelines) postpaid: $6. Nonmember submissions, if selected, will be published one time only. For future submissions to be considered, contributors must then become a member by purchasing a subscription. Submit 3-6 poems at a time. Previously published poems OK; no simultaneous submissions. Cover letter preferred.** Time between acceptance and publication is 3-6 months. **Seldom comments on rejections. Send SASE for guidelines only. Reports in 1-3 months. Sometimes sends prepublication galleys. Pays 1 copy. Acquires one-time rights.** Reviews books of poetry in their "Moon Market" section. Open to unsolicited reviews. Poets may send books for review consideration to Attn: Madame Zonka. They also sponsor the "Finish This Poem Contest." First Place: $50, Second Place: $25, and Third Place: 6-month subscription (2 issues). The three top winners, and a select group of honorable mentions, also receive publication in *M.O.O.N.*. The contest is open to everyone. Entry fee: $5 for the first poem, $1 each additional. Each entrant receives a copy of *M.O.O.N.* containing the contest results. Send SASE for details. The editor says, "Be bold, original and explore new ideas."

MACFADDEN WOMEN'S GROUP; TRUE CONFESSIONS; TRUE ROMANCES; TRUE LOVE; TRUE STORY; SECRETS; MODERN ROMANCES (I), Dept. PM, 233 Park Ave. S., New York NY 10003, phone (212)979-4800. **Address each magazine individually; do not submit to Macfadden Women's Group.** Each of these romance magazines uses poetry—usually no more than 1 poem/issue. **Their requirements vary; readers should study them individually and write for guidelines.** These mass-circulation magazines (available on newsstands) are a very limited market, yet a possible one for beginners—especially those who like the prose contents and are tuned in to their editorial tastes.

THE MACGUFFIN (II), Schoolcraft College, 18600 Haggerty Rd., Livonia MI 48152-2696, phone (313)462-4400 ext. 5292, fax (313)462-4558, founded 1983, editor Arthur Lindenberg, who says, "*The MacGuffin* is a literary magazine which appears three times each year, in April, June and November. We publish the best poetry, fiction, nonfiction and artwork we find. We have no thematic or stylistic biases. **We look for well-crafted poetry. Long poems should not exceed 300 lines. Avoid pornography, trite and sloppy poetry. We do not publish haiku, concrete or light verse."** They have published poetry by Kathleen Ripley Leo, Stephen Dunning, Jim Daniels and Daniel James

Sundahl. As a sample the editor selected these lines from "Neruda" by Peter Brett:

> The women pass like calendar days
> leaving in mind the aftertaste of
> mango, papaya days with high fore-
> heads and astonished eyes . . .

The MacGuffin is 144 pgs., digest-sized, professionally printed on heavy buff stock, with matte card cover, flat-spined, with b&w illustrations and photos. Circulation is 600, of which 215 are subscriptions and the rest are local newsstand sales, contributor copies and distribution to college offices. Single copy: $4.50; subscription: $12. **Sample postpaid: $4. "The editorial staff is grateful to consider unsolicited manuscripts and graphics." Writers should submit no more than 5 poems of no more than 300 lines; poems should be typewritten. "We discourage simultaneous submissions." Prefers submissions to be sent through the mail. Publishes theme issues. Send SASE for guidelines and upcoming themes or request via fax. Mss are reported on in 10-12 weeks and the publication backlog is 6 months. Pays 2 copies,** "occasional money or prizes." Poetry published in *The MacGuffin* has been selected for inclusion in *Pushcart Prize* anthologies. The editor says, "We will always comment on 'near misses.' Writing is a search, and it is a journey. Don't become sidetracked. Don't become discouraged. Keep looking. Keep traveling. Keep writing."

MACMILLAN PUBLISHING CO.; SCRIBNER; ATHENEUM, 1230 Avenue of the Americas, New York NY 10020. Prefers not to share information.

MAD RIVER PRESS (V), State Road, Richmond MA 01254, phone (413)698-3184, founded 1986, editor Barry Sternlieb, publishes 3 broadsides and 1 chapbook/year, **"all types of poetry, no bias," but none unsolicited.** They have published poetry by Gary Snyder, Hayden Carruth, W.S. Merwin, Louise Glück, Linda Gregg and Richard Wilbur. Call or write for information.

‡MADAME BULL'S TAVERN (I, II), Box 60369, U. of A. Postal Outlet, Edmonton, Alberta T6G 2S6 Canada, phone (403)439-6816, founded 1995, editors Annette Cannell, Jocko, Tom Emmens and Gail Sídonie Sobat, is a biannual literary magazine "with publicly-engaged poetry, genre fiction (with a strong literary grounding), topical essays and staff reviews." **They want "any form of poetry, up to 100 lines. Prefer poetry with some form of narrative. Subject matter: urban, social, political. Prefer poetry that has something to say, and it should have, where possible, public and personal dimensions. No purely personal or purely experimental poetry. No purely formal exercises."** They have recently published poetry by S.K. Kelen, Anna Mioduchowska and Matt Santateresa. As a sample the editors selected these lines from "The moon of magpies quarrelling" by Alice Major:

> The moon of magpies quarrelling
> shimmers in the pale sky of early morning
> like a court reporter's screen. It records
> the magpies' proceedings—litigious birds
> with ermine draped across their shoulders,
> their bellies drooped in prosperous curves.

The editors describe *MBT* as 64 pgs., digest-sized, high-quality photocopied and saddle-stapled with offset card stock cover and some graphics. They accept 10% of the material received. Press run is 200. Single copy: $6. **Submit 5-8 poems at a time. Cover letter preferred. Poems are screened by two readers and narrowed down for the five-person editorial board. Often comments on rejections. Send SASE (or SAE and IRCs) for guidelines. Reports in 2-4 months. Pays 1 copy. Acquires first North American serial rights.** Staff reviews books of poetry. Poets may send books for review consideration. The editors add, "We like to see writers who know how to think, as well as how to feel. Poets we enjoy are able to see beyond themselves and engage the surroundings and issues of their time. And it never hurts to be able to tell a good story and so begin to create the new myths for our society."

THE MADISON REVIEW; PHYLLIS SMART YOUNG PRIZE IN POETRY (II), Dept. of English, Helen C. White Hall, University of Wisconsin, 600 N. Park St., Madison WI 53706, phone (608)263-0566, founded 1978, poetry editor Michelle Ephraim, want **poems that are "smart and tight, that fulfill their own propositions. Spare us: love poems, religious or patriotic dogma, light verse. We'd like to see poetry in ethnic/nationality, form/style, gay/lesbian, humor (not light verse, though), political, social issues and women/feminism categories."** They have published work by Lise Goett, Lisa Steinman and Richard Tillinghast. As a sample the editors selected these lines from "Gulls" by Jerry Mirskin:

> Now it's the sharp and damp smell of gasoline
> and now the sun, the full theater of the sun
> torching the town, so the windows
> of the houses along the shore burn like glasses of tea.

The Madison Review is published in May and December, with 15-20 poems selected from a pool of

750. **Sample back issue postpaid: $2.50. Submit maximum of 6 poems. No simultaneous submissions. Usually reports in 4 months, may be longer in summer. Pays 2 copies. "We do appreciate a concise cover letter with short bio information."** The Phyllis Smart Young Prize in Poetry (formerly the Felix Pollak Prize in Poetry) is for $500 and publication in *TMR*, for "the best group of three unpublished poems submitted by a single author." Send SASE for rules before submitting for prize or see announcement for guidelines in *AWP* or *Poets & Writers* magazines. Submissions must arrive during September—winner announced December 15. The editor says, "Contributors: Know your market! Read before, during and after writing. Treat your poems *better* than job applications!"

THE MAGAZINE OF SPECULATIVE POETRY (IV-Science fiction), P.O. Box 564, Beloit WI 53512, founded 1984, editors Roger Dutcher and Mark Rich, is an irregularly published magazine that features **"the best new speculative poetry. We are especially interested in narrative form, but interested in variety of styles, open to any form, length (within reason), purpose. We're looking for the best of the new poetry utilizing the ideas, imagery and approaches developed by speculative fiction and will welcome experimental techniques as well as the fresh employment of traditional forms."** They have published poetry by Brian Aldiss, Jane Yolen, William Stafford, Ron Ellis and S.R. Compton. As a sample Roger Dutcher chose these lines from "Time Machines" by Steve Rasnic Tem:

> *The Big Bang tide sends us chasing*
> *each of our moments through space*
> *trying to escape the collapse*
> *and our own heat-death*
> *when all time runs backward*
> *and we leap from our graves*

The digest-sized magazine, 20-24 pgs., is offset from professional typesetting, saddle-stapled with matte card cover. They accept less than 10% of some 500 poems received/year. Press run is 100-200, going to nearly 100 subscribers of which 4 are libraries. Subscription: $11. **Sample postpaid: $3.50. Submit 3 poems at a time, double-spaced. No previously published poems or simultaneous submissions. "We like cover letters but they aren't necessary. We like to see where you heard of us; the name of the poems submitted; a statement if the poetry ms is disposable; a big enough SASE; and if you've been published, some recent places." Editor comments on rejections "on occasion." Send SASE for guidelines. Reports in 1-2 months. Pays 3¢/word, minimum $3, plus copy. Buys first North American serial rights.** Reviews books of speculative poetry. Query on unsolicited reviews. Send speculative poetry books for review consideration.

MAGIC CHANGES (IV-Themes), P.O. Box 5892, Naperville IL 60567-5892, phone (312)213-7410, e-mail sennett@cig.mot.com, founded 1978, poetry editor John Sennett, is published every 18 months, in an unusual format. Photocopied from typescript on many different weights and colors of paper, magazine-sized, stapled along the long side (you read it both vertically and horizontally), taped flat spine, full of fantasy drawings, pages packed with poems of all varieties, fiction, photos, drawings, odds and ends—including reviews of little magazines and other small press publications. It is **intended to make poetry (and literature) fun—and unpredictable. Each issue is on an announced theme.** *Magic Changes* **is divided into sections such as 'The Order of the Celestial Otter,' 'State of the Arts,' 'Time,' 'Music' and 'Skyscraper Rats.' A magical musical theme pervades."** They have published poetry by Sue Standing, Caleb Bullen, Hugh Ogden, Lauren Sennett, Chris Robbins, Kaela Sennett, Patricia A. Davey and Walt Curtis. As a sample the editor selected these lines from his poem "Mourning Friend":

> *Did I hear*
> *The dying dove's song?*
>
> *Today,*
> *I promise myself*
> *To listen to pace:*
>
> *Footsteps*
> *Wind in cracks*
> *Wings*

There are about 100 pgs. of poetry/issue. Circulation is 500 for 28 subscriptions of which 10 are libraries. **Sample postpaid: $7 US, $10 foreign. Submit 3-5 poems anytime. Send SASE for upcoming themes. The editor sometimes comments on rejections and offers criticism for $5/page of poetry. Reports in 4 months. Pays 1 or 2 copies. Acquires first North American serial rights.** Reviews books of poetry in "usually about 500 words." Open to unsolicited reviews. Poets may also send books for review consideration.

‡MAIL CALL (IV-Specialized: Civil War); DISTANT FRONTIER PRESS, P.O. Box 5031, South Hackensack NJ 07606, phone (201)296-0419, e-mail mailcall1@aol.com, founded 1990, managing editor Anna Pansini, appears 6 times a year with the purpose of "keeping the spirit of the Civil War soldier alive." **They want poetry with unique Civil War themes in first or third person.** *Mail Call* is 8 pgs., 8½×11, offset printed on colored paper and corner stapled. They receive about 100 poems a year, accept approximately 15. Press run is 500 for 450 subscribers of which 5 are libraries. Subscription: $24.95/year. **Sample postpaid: $5. "We prefer contributors order a writer's packet for $5 which includes a sample copy before submitting, but it is not required." Previously published poems and simultaneous submissions OK. Cover letter optional.** "If poet is a descendant of a Civil War soldier or a member of any Civil War organizations, please provide details for publication." Time between acceptance and publication is 6-12 months. **Often comments of rejections. Send SASE for guidelines. Reports in 6-12 months. Pays 2 copies, but "open to negotiation."** Distant Frontier Press publishes book excerpts, narratives, diary entries, poems and editorial think pieces. Send SASE for details. The editor says, "Don't make a Civil War movie into a poem. Write with feeling from your heart."

THE MALAHAT REVIEW (II); LONG POEM PRIZES (II, IV-Form), P.O. Box 1700, MS 8524, University of Victoria, Victoria, British Columbia V8W 2Y2 Canada, phone (604)721-8524, founded 1967, editor Derk Wynand, is "a high quality, visually appealing literary quarterly which has earned the praise of notable literary figures throughout North America. Its purpose is to publish and promote poetry and fiction of a very high standard, both Canadian and international. **We are interested in various styles, lengths and themes. The criterion is excellence.**" They have published poetry by Erin Mouré, Susan Musgrave and Tom Wayman. As a sample the editor selected these lines from "How Were the People Made?" by Marilyn Bowering:

> They were made from pictures that were altered,
> and altered again.
> They were made from paintings
> by a child with an imaginary friend.
> They were made from a single shoe in the middle of the road.
> They were made from expectations.

They use 50 pgs. of poetry in each issue, have 1,500 subscribers of which 300 are libraries. They use about 100 of 2,000 submissions received/year, have no backlog. Topics and length in this handsome publication are particularly open, though editors show a distinct taste for free verse exhibiting craft and focus. Subscription: $35 Canadian (or US equivalent). **Sample postpaid: $8 US. Submit 5-10 poems, addressed to Editor Derk Wynand. The editors comment if they "feel the ms warrants some attention even though it is not accepted." Send SASE (or SAE and IRC) for guidelines. Reports within 3 months. Pays $25 per poem/page plus 2 copies and reduced rates on others.** Reviews books of poetry. The Long Poem Prizes of $400, plus publication and payment at their usual rates (entry fee is a year's subscription), is for a long poem or cycle 5-15 pgs. (flexible minimum and maximum), deadline March 1 of alternate years (1997, 1999, etc.).

‡MALEVOLENCE; MALEVOLENCE PUBLICATIONS (I, II), P.O. Box 55, Willoughby OH 44094-0055, founded 1995, editor Jennifer Helms. *Malevolence*, a quarterly publication, "was created to exhibit art and poetry in a professional way from those who are very talented and, perhaps, unknown." **They want all styles and genres—"humorous to bizarre to dark work. Please, no blatant, sappy rhymes or preachy religious verse."** They have recently published poetry by Kat Blackbird, John Benson and Tina Reigel. As a sample the editor selected these lines from "Soul Deep" by Donna Taylor Burgess:

> Curiosity drove me to unzip his flesh
> and see what's inside
> I wanted him without
> within
> deep
> soul deep

Malevolence is 70-80 pgs., digest-sized and saddle-stapled with full-color cover, b&w illustrations and ads inside. They receive 500 poems a year, publish 25%. Press run is 200 for 40 subscribers, 50 shelf sales. Subscription: $9. **Sample (including guidelines) postpaid: $3.50. Previously published poems and simultaneous submissions OK. Cover letter preferred. "I am not impressed with long lists of publishing credits. The poetry should speak for itself. I want to know about you, not your awards." Often comments on rejections. Publishes theme issues. Send SASE for upcoming themes. Reports in 3-4 weeks. Pays 2 copies.** Malevolence Publications publishes **2 chapbooks/year** by "those who might not otherwise get a chance. Most chapbooks are taken from poets who have been published in *Malevolence* magazine." Chapbooks are usually 10-25 pgs., digest-sized and saddle-stapled with card cover. **"Send 5-7 sample poems, specifying that they are for chapbook consideration. We will send an information sheet in return if accepted." Replies in 1 month. Pays 50 author's copies (out of a press run of 150).** The editor says, "I read everything, so don't be afraid to submit. I've been on your end as well, so I know how it feels. Don't choke—give it a shot. There is such a race in the poetry world for 'what will sell,' that true genius has been pushed aside. It's not about running after the Almighty Dollar. It's about being uninhibited and putting yourself down on paper."

THE MANHATTAN REVIEW (II, IV-Translations), 440 Riverside Dr., Apt. 45, New York NY 10027, phone (212)932-1854, founded 1980, poetry editor Philip Fried, tries **"to publish American and foreign writers, and we choose foreign writers with something valuable to offer the American scene. We like to think of poetry as a powerful discipline engaged with many other fields. We want to see ambitious work. Interested in both lyric and narrative. Not interested in mawkish, sentimental poetry.** We select high-quality work from a number of different countries, including the U.S." They have recently published poetry by Wistawa Szymborska, Baron Wormser, D. Nurkse, Julia Mishkin and Penelope Shuttle. As a sample the editor selected these lines by Adam Zagajewski:

> The shoes of Auschwitz, in pyramids
> high as the sky, groan faintly:
> Alas, we outlived mankind, now
> let us sleep, sleep:
> We have nowhere to go.

The *MR* is now "an annual with ambitions to be semiannual." The magazine is 64 pgs., digest-sized, professionally printed with glossy card cover, photos and graphics. Press run is 500 for 85 subscribers of which 35 are libraries. It is also distributed by Bernhard DeBoer, Inc. and Fine Arts Distributors. They receive about 300 submissions/year, use few ("but I do read everything submitted carefully and with an open mind"). "I return submissions as promptly as possible." Single copy: $5; subscription: $10. **Sample: $6.25 with 6 × 9 envelope. Submit 3-5 pgs. at a time. No simultaneous submissions. Cover letter with short bio and publications required. Editor sometimes comments "but don't count on it." Reports in 10-12 weeks. Pays copies.** Staff reviews books of poetry. Send books for review consideration. Philip Fried advises, "Don't be swayed by fads. Search for your own voice. Support other poets whose work you respect and enjoy. Be persistent. Keep aware of poetry being written in other countries."

‡MANIFOLD (I); THE ENTRENCHED PRESS (V), P.O. Box 11, Elizabethtown PA 17022-0011, phone (717)361-9258, founded 1994, editors/co-founders David Frechard and Douglas Baker. *Manifold* is a quarterly publication for writers, poets and photographers. **They do not want to see whimsical, rhyming poetry.** They have recently published poetry by Allen Ginsberg, Paco and Kerry Shawn Keys. As a sample they selected these lines from "The Last Poem" by James P. Goertel:

> The places that call to me
> like distant Meccas through a phone
> are just postcards I keep pinning on a wall
> reminders
> that I am a stranger in this too familiar land.

Manifold is 35-45 pgs., digest-sized, attractively printed on bond paper and saddle-stapled with heavy card cover with b&w photo or illustration. They receive work from 150-200 poets a year, accept about 50 poems. Press run is 500 for 25 subscribers, 50 shelf sales. Subscription: $10. **Sample postpaid: $2.95. Make checks payable to The Entrenched Press. Submit 5 poems at a time. No previously published poems or simultaneous submissions. Cover letter preferred. SASE required. Poems are circulated to an editorial board. Seldom comments on rejections. Reports in 3-6 months. Pays 5 copies. Acquires first rights.** The Entrenched Press publishes chapbooks by **invitation only**. The editors say, "We are looking for writing that aims at the heart of it all—good or bad, positive or negative—which is presented creatively, either surreal or simplistic, so that the reader may gain insight."

MANKATO POETRY REVIEW (II), Box 53, English Dept., Mankato State, Mankato MN 56001, phone (507)389-5511, founded 1984, editor Roger Sheffer, is a semiannual magazine that is **"open to all forms of poetry. We will look at poems up to 60 lines, any subject matter."** They have published poetry by Edward Micus, Judith Skillman and Walter Griffin. As a sample the editor chose the following lines from a poem by Richard Robbins:

> Sage connects to lava rock mile by mile.
> West of Atomic City, blue flowers
> in the craters of the moon.

The magazine is 5 × 8, typeset on 60 lb. paper, 30 pgs., saddle-stapled with buff matte card cover printed in one color. It appears usually in May and December and has a circulation of 200. Subscription: $5/year. **Sample postpaid: $2.50. Submit 3-5 poems at a time. However, do not submit mss in summer (May through August). No previously published poems or simultaneous submissions. Cover letter required. Send SASE for guidelines. Reports in about 2 months; "We accept only what we can publish in next issue." Pays 2 copies.** The editor says, "We're interested in looking at longer poems—up to 60 lines, with great depth of detail relating to place (landscape, townscape)."

MANNA; MANNA FORTY, INC. (I, IV-Nature/ecology, religion, psychology/science), Box 548, Rt. 1, Sharon OK 73857-9761, phone (405)254-2660, founded 1986, literary format 1991, editor Richard D. Kahoe. As their "Mission Statement" says: "*manna*, a quarterly literary-professional journal, advances and publishes interests of manna forty, inc., a not-for-profit corporation. *manna* promotes ideals of a holistic view of truth and beauty, expressed in poetry, appropriate prose and pen sketches. It focuses on nature (natural living, ecology, environmental issues), religion (Christian and ecumenical) and psychology (and related sciences), and especially the interfaces of these areas." **They are open to all styles of poetry up to 50 lines, "but prefer shorter (under 25 lines) and will be publishing no more than 35% free verse." They want poetry related to religion, nature and psychology. "Prefer integrating two or three of these areas. No mushy sentimentality, highly obscure verse or doggerel (except possibly in short humorous context)."** They have recently published poetry by C. David Hay, Marian Ford Park and Howard F. Stein. As a sample the editor selected this poem, "Divorce," by R.D. Holt:

> *I guess I did well*
> *To escape from my hell*
> *But I think that when push comes to shove,*

> *Though I hated her ways,*
> *I still long for the days*
> *When the crowd at least thought I was loved.*

manna is 8 pgs., 8½ × 11, desktop-published and professionally printed on 70 lb. recycled stock, with line drawings. Press run is 350 for 100 subscribers of which 6 are libraries, 200 distributed free to community groups and to contributors. Subscription: free ("donation encouraged"). **Sample available for 1 first-class stamp. "Contributors who can are asked (but not required) to make donation toward costs, generally $7.50-15, depending on length of poem." Previously published poems and simultaneous submissions OK. SASE and cover letter required. "Prefer to receive 2-6 poems on separate pages." Deadlines: February 15, May 15, August 15 and November 15. Publication appears one month later. Comments on rejections with SASE. Publishes occasional theme issues. Send SASE for guidelines and subscribe for upcoming themes. Themes are announced 1 issue in advance. Reports in 1-3 months. Pays at least 2 copies but for minimal donation pays 5 copies direct to poet, 10 mailed to addresses provided by poet.** The editor says, "Poets and prose contributors should observe our subject guidelines. Beginners are encouraged, but we prefer poems not to *sound* like beginners."

MANOA: A PACIFIC JOURNAL OF INTERNATIONAL WRITING (II), 1733 Donaghho Rd., Honolulu HI 96822, website http://www2.hawaii.edu/uhpress/Journals/MA/MAHome.html, founded 1989, poetry editor Frank Stewart, appears twice a year. **"We are a general interest literary magazine, open to all forms and styles. We are not for the beginning writer, no matter what style. We are not interested in Pacific exotica."** They have published poetry by John Updike, Norman Dubie, Walter Pavlich and Eugene Ruggles. It is 200 pgs., 7 × 10, offset, flat-spined using art and graphics. They accept about 2% of 3,000 submissions received/year. Press run is 2,000 for 1,000 subscribers of which 30 are libraries, 700 shelf sales. Subscription: $20/year. **Sample postpaid: $10. Submit 3-5 poems at a time. Send SASE for guidelines. Reports in 6 weeks. Always sends prepublication galleys. Pay "competitive" plus 2 copies. Seldom comments on rejections.** They review current books and chapbooks of poetry. Open to unsolicited reviews. Poets may also send books for review consideration, attn. reviews editor. This magazine, one of the most exciting new journals in recent years, has become well known for the quality and diversity of its verse. It has also received a Design Excellence Award from the American Association of University Presses and Best Journal of the Year Award from the Council of Editors of Learned Journals. Poetry published in *Manoa* has also been selected for inclusion in the 1995 and 1996 volumes of *The Best American Poetry*. The editor says, "We welcome the opportunity to read poetry submissions from throughout the country. We are not a regional journal, but we do feature work from the Pacific Rim, national and international, especially in our reviews and essays. We are not interested in genre or formalist writing for its own sake, or picturesque impressions of the region."

MANUSHI (II), C/202, Lajpat Nagar 1, New Delhi 110024 India, phone 6839158 or 6833022, founded 1978, editor Madhu Kishwar, is a bimonthly "journal about women and society." **They look for "good poetry with social relevance." They do not want poetry "which makes no point."** They have published poetry by Archana Verma, Indu Jain and Amrita Pritam. As a sample the editor selected these lines (poet unidentified):

> *Today, once again*
> *She crumpled a poem,*
> *Lit the fire with it,*
> *And put up the water for tea*

Manushi is 44 pgs., approximately 8 × 10½, offset, saddle-stapled with glossy full-color cover. "We receive a considerable number of poems, accept about 10%." **No previously published poems or simultaneous submissions. Cover letter required. Often comments on rejections. Reports "fairly soon." Pays "as many copies as author requires."**

‡MANY MOUNTAINS MOVING; MANY MOUNTAINS MOVING LITERARY AWARDS (II), 420 22nd St., Boulder CO 80302, phone (303)545-9942, fax (303)444-6510, founded 1994, co-editors Naomi Horii and Marilyn Krysl. Appearing 3 times a year, *Many Mountains Moving* is "a literary journal of diverse contemporary voices that welcomes fiction, poetry, nonfiction, and art from writers and artists of all walks of life. We publish the world's top writers as well as emerging talents."-**They are open to any style of poetry, but they do not want "Hallmark-y" poetry.** They have recently published poetry by Robert Bly, Lorna Dee Cervantes, Allen Ginsberg and Adrienne Rich. As a sample they selected these lines from "Ghost Sickness" by Luis Alberto Urrea:

> *I saw the dead nodding sugar skulls.*
> *They danced dark alleys bright*
> *from burning.*
> *Children licked the letters of their names*
> *from glassy candy foreheads. Whorehouse poets*
> *whispered sly reports*
> *to ice cream suited gunmen.*

The attractive journal is about 200 pgs., 6×9, web offset and perfect-bound with full-color cover and b&w art and photos inside. They receive 3,000 poems a year, accept about 2%. Press run is 2,000 for 400 subscribers. Single copy: $6.50; subscription: $18/year, $15/year for students and teachers. **Submit 3-10 poems at a time, typed with SASE. No previously published poems; simultaneous submissions OK. Cover letter preferred. Poems are circulated to an editorial board. "Poems are first read by several readers. If considered seriously, they are passed to the poetry editor for final decision." Seldom comments on rejections. Publishes theme issues occasionally. Send SASE for guidelines. Reports in 1-4 weeks, "if we are seriously considering a submission, we may take longer." Sometimes sends prepublication galleys. Pays 3 copies, additional copies available at a discount of $3/copy. Acquires first North American serial rights and "rights to publish in a future edition of the** *Best of Many Mountains Moving Anthology.*" They sponsor the annual Many Mountains Moving Literary Awards which awards $200 plus publication in the categories of poetry, fiction and essay. Entry fee: $14 (includes subscription). Send SASE for details. Poetry published in *Many Mountains Moving* has also been included in *The Best American Poetry 1996*. The editors say, "Although we have featured a number of established poets, we encourage new writers to submit. However, we recommend that poets read through at least one issue to familiarize themselves with the type of work we generally publish."

MARK: A LITERARY JOURNAL (II), 2801 W. Bancroft SU1501, Toledo OH 43606, first appeared 1967-69, then resumed 1978, editors change every 1-2 years, 1996-1997 editors Jennifer Kohout and Mike Donnelly, is an annual journal of fiction, poetry, photographs and sketches. **"We're tired of the same old romance/love poems. Give us something with substance. Politically irresponsible work (racist, sexist, heterosexist, anti-choice) has no place with us."** As a sample the editor selected these lines from "flood wall revisited" by Robin Murray:

> *At least you're not a dike, he said.*
> *Did he mean*
> *I couldn't keep the flood of water*
> *from innundating the hems*
> *of my rolled up jeans?*

Mark is 70 pgs., digest-sized, saddle-stapled, professionally printed, with matte card cover. Single copy: $3. (Make checks payable to University of Toledo.) **Submit 6 poems at a time. "We appreciate brief cover letters with name, address, date and titles of work submitted. We accept submissions all year round; manuscripts received after January 31 are held for the following year's issue." Editor comments "very rarely." Pays 2 copies. Acquires first serial rights.**

‡MAROVERLAG (V), Riedingerstr. 24, 86153 Augsburg Germany, phone 0821/416033, founded 1970, editor Lothar Reiserer. **Maroverlag publishes paperbacks and some hardcover books of poetry, one a year, averaging 80 pages.** The books are in German, but they have published a number of English and American poets (for example, Charles Bukowski, La Loca and Raymond Carver). **They are currently not accepting unsolicited submissions.**

MARYLAND POETRY REVIEW; MARYLAND STATE POETRY AND LITERARY SOCIETY (I, II), P.O. Drawer H, Catonsville MD 21228, founded 1985, edited by Rosemary Klein, "is interested in promoting the literary arts in Maryland as well as nationally and internationally. **We are interested in strong, thoughtful poetry with a slight bias to free verse. All submissions are read carefully.** *MPR* is open to good poets who have not published extensively as well as to those who have." They have published poetry by Celia Brown, Elisabeth Stevens, Josephine Jacobsen, Enid Shomer and Joseph Somoza. As a sample the editor selected these lines from "The Fool's Dark Lantern" by Michael Fallon:

> Like a fly that spins
> in wounded circles on the sill
> his thoughts revolve around a single thought:
> there is only so much time
> in which to know

MPR is 75 pgs., 7×11, professionally printed in small type on quality eggshell stock, saddle-stapled with a glossy b&w card cover. It appears twice a year in double issues (Spring/Summer and Fall/Winter). In the past they have done special issues on confessional, Irish, Hispanic and Australian poetry. **Query about possible future special issues.** Subscription and Maryland State Poetry and Literary Society membership is $17 ($12 for students and senior citizens; $20 for member and spouse; $25 for institutions). **Sample postpaid: $8. Submit no more than 5 poems at a time with brief bio. No simultaneous submissions. "We read submissions only in January, April and September but accept all year." Send SASE for guidelines and upcoming themes. Reports in 3-6 months. Pays 1 copy.** Book reviews are generally solicited. Send books for review consideration, attn. Robert Cooperman. MSPLS sponsors the Maryland State Poetry and Literary Society's Annual Poetry and Fiction Contest for poetry of any length and fiction to 2,500 words. Entry fee: $3/poem or four for $10, $3/story. Contest runs from January 1 through May 31. Cash prizes and magazine publication. They also sponsor the Michael Egan Memorial Poetry Contest for poetry of any length. Entry fee: $3/poem. Contest runs from September 1 through October 28. Cash prizes and magazine publication. Send SASE for guidelines.

‡**MARYLAND REVIEW (II)**, Dept. of English and Modern Languages, Wilson Hall, UMES, Princess Anne MD 21853, phone (410)651-6552, fax (410)651-6550, founded 1986, is an annual literary journal of poetry and short fiction. *"MR* is looking for insightful work, historical or contemporary in perspective." **They want all kinds of poetry. "Special emphasis on black literature, entertaining, original themes, believable characters, widely appealing. Nothing that is clearly autobiographical."** They have recently published poetry by Errol Miller and Stephen Cushman. As a sample the editor selected these lines from "Sieve" by Steven Duplij:

> Turning over pages of streets split
> Of alien cities' warped bodies,
> I asked the Shadow over them swirling
> Whence execution of dreams comes.
>
> The meaning bespattered cuts off the meeting
> With blows of beggars and lashes of gods . . .

The editor says *MR* is 100-200 pgs., 6×9, typeset in Aldus PageMaker and professionally bound with 1-6 pgs. of graphics or art, no ads. They receive 50-100 poems a year, accept 10-30%. Press run is 500-1,000 for 75-100 subscribers of which 15 are libraries. Subscription: $6 for 1 year, $11.50 for 2 years. **Sample (including guidelines) postpaid: $6. Submit 2-5 poems at a time. No previously published poems; simultaneous submissions OK. Cover letter with brief bio (no more than 75 words) required. "All text must be in laser quality/scannable type. Manuscripts submitted on Macintosh or PC disks should be written using Macwrite. Wordperfect, or MS Word. Hard copy should accompany disks. Reads submissions September through May only. Reports in up to 1 year, average 6 months. Sometimes sends prepublication galleys. Pays 2 copies. Acquires first serial rights only.** The editor says they want "writing that broadens the reader's sensitivities to aspects of the human experience. The writing should be substantive—not flippant or 'empty' i.e., much said about nothing. Racial minority writers are particularly encouraged to share their work with *MR*."

‡**MASONIA ROUNDUP (I)**, 200 Coolwell Rd., Madison Heights VA 24572, founded 1990, editors Ardis and Dan Mason, is a quarterly "personal magazine of general interest written by real people about what has happened to them, their thoughts and ideas." **They want humor, short poetry (up to 30 lines), and family/children-oriented work. "Nothing too profound."** As a sample the editors selected these lines from "Hearts of Time" by Marsh Reizenstein:

> Today she is young at heart
> Free in spirit
> Love does its magical wonders
> A child holds in her hand the power
> Turning the clock of age back
> Great-grandmother and child.

Masonia Roundup is 16 pgs. (including cover), 7×8½ (four 8½×14 sheets folded in half), photocopied and unbound. They receive about 100 poems a year, accept 4-8. Press run is 150 for 92 subscribers. Subscription: $5. **Sample postpaid: $1.50. Make checks payable to Ardis or Dan Mason. Submit**

10 poems at a time, typed with SASE. Previously published poems and simultaneous submissions OK. Cover letter preferred. Time between acceptance and publication is 6 months to 1 year. Seldom comments on rejections. Send SASE for guidelines. Reports in 1-2 months. Pays 2 copies. Acquires first or one-time rights. Staff reviews books of poetry. Poets may also send books for review consideration.

THE UNIVERSITY OF MASSACHUSETTS PRESS; THE JUNIPER PRIZE (II), P.O. Box 429, Amherst MA 01004-0429, phone (413)545-2217, fax (413)545-1226, website http://www.vyne. com/umasspress/, founded 1964. The press offers an annual competition for the Juniper Prize, in alternate years to first and subsequent books. In 1996 the prize was for a subsequent book: mss whose authors have had at least one full-length book or chapbook of poetry published or accepted for publication. In 1997 only "first books" will be considered: mss by writers whose poems may have appeared in literary journals and/or anthologies but have not been published, or been accepted for publication, in book form. They have published *Cities and Towns: Poems* by Arthur Vogelsang, *The Postal Confessions* by Max Garland, and *Little-Known Sports* by Vern Rutsala. "Poetry books are approximately $14 for paperback editions and $24 for cloth." **Submissions must not exceed 60 pgs. in typescript (generally 50-55 poems). Include paginated contents page. A list of poems published or slated for publication in literary journals and/or anthologies must also accompany the ms. Such poems may be included in the ms and must be identified. "Mss by more than one author, entries of more than one ms simultaneously or within the same year, and translations are not eligible." Entry fee: $10 plus SASE for return of ms or notification. Entries must be postmarked not later than September 30.** The award is announced in April/May and publication is scheduled for the following spring. The amount of the prize is $1,000 and is in lieu of royalties on the first print run. Poet also receives 12 copies in one edition or six copies each if published in both hardcover and paperbound editions. **Fax or send SASE for guidelines and/or further information to the above address. Entries are to be mailed to Juniper Prize, University of Massachusetts, Amherst MA 01003.**

THE MASSACHUSETTS REVIEW (II), Memorial Hall, University of Massachusetts, Amherst MA 01003, phone (413)545-2689, founded 1959, editors Paul Jenkins and Mary Heath. Mostly free verse, all lengths and topics, appears here, with emphasis in recent issues on narrative work. An interesting feature: Editors run poems with long-line lengths in smaller type, to fit on the page without typographical interruption (as in other journals). They have published poetry by Marge Piercy, Michael Benedikt and Eavan Boland. The editors describe this quarterly as offset (some color used in art sections), 6×9. They receive about 2,500 poems a year, use about 50. Press run is 1,600 for 1,100-1,200 subscribers of which 1,000 are libraries, the rest for shelf sales. Subscription: $15 (US), $20 outside US, $17 for libraries. **Sample postpaid: $5.75. No simultaneous submissions or previously published poems. Read submissions October 1 through June 1 only. Send SASE for guidelines. Reports in 6 weeks. Pays minimum of $10, or 35¢/line, plus 2 copies.** Work published in this review has been included in *The Best American Poetry 1995.*

MATTOID (II), School of Literature & Journalism, Deakin University, Geelong, Victoria, Australia 3217, fax (052)272484, founded 1977, contact Dr. Brian Edwards, appears 3 times/year. **"No special requirements but interesting complexity, quality, experimentation. No naive rhyming verse."** They have published poetry by Lauris Edmond, Kevin Hart and Judith Rodriguez. It is 200 pgs., flat-spined with 2-color cover. They receive about 800 poems a year, publish 10-15%. Press run is 650 for 400 subscribers of which 10 are libraries, 50-100 shelf sales. **Sample postpaid: $15 overseas. Publishes theme issues. Send SASE (or SAE and IRC) for upcoming themes. Reports in 2-3 months. Pays 2 copies.** Reviews books of poetry in 1,000-2,000 words, single format.

MATURE YEARS (IV-Senior citizen, religious), P.O. Box 801, 201 Eighth Ave. S., Nashville TN 37202, phone (615)749-6292, founded 1954, editor Marvin W. Cropsey, is a quarterly. "The magazine's purpose is to help persons understand and use the resources of Christian faith in dealing with specific opportunities and problems related to aging. **Poems are usually limited to sixteen lines and may, or may not, be overtly religious. Poems should not poke fun at older adults, but may take a humorous look at them. Avoid sentimentality and saccharine. If using rhymes and meter, make sure they are accurate."** As a sample the editor selected these lines by Carole Johnston:

> What is winter
> but a large and cold
> secret that somehow
> keeps me warm . . . for
> I know where sweet
> daffodils lie sleeping.
> I know the graves of
> six brave crocuses

> *and the tulip colors*
> *of next spring.*

MY is 112 pgs., magazine-sized, perfect-bound, with full-color glossy paper cover. Circulation 70,000. **Sample postpaid: $3.95. Submit season and nature poems for spring during December through February; for summer, March through May; for fall, June through August; and for winter, September through November. Send SASE for guidelines. Reports in 2 months; sometimes a year's delay before publication. Pays 50¢-$1/line upon acceptance.**

THE MAVERICK PRESS; SOUTHWEST POETS SERIES ANNUAL CHAPBOOK CONTEST (II, IV-Regional, themes), Rt. 2 Box 4915, Eagle Pass TX 78852-9604, phone (210)773-1836, founded 1991, editor Carol Cullar, publishes a biannual of "outstanding Texas writers and other mavericks whose works represent the contemporary scene. Each issue is individually named (i.e., the April 1996 issue was titled *Jack Rabbit*)." They are **looking for "strong, uncluttered figurative language to 100 lines. No diatribes on current events or political posturings, no smut."** They have recently published poetry by Errol Miller, Gina Tabasso, Jo LeCoeur and Duane Locke. As a sample the editor selected these lines from "The View She Promised" by Larry L. Fontenot:

> *. . . The hawk sears the sky,*
> *its shadow lost in the blur of flight.*
> *Its cry promises her the next journey.*
> *She leaves her old voice at the top of the view,*
> *trades tongue for talon,*
> *feels the breeze of rising wings. . . .*

The editor says it is 74 pgs., 5½×8½, saddle-stapled. Cover is an original block print by the editor, inside illustrations include b&w line drawings or block prints by contributors. They receive 1,000-2,000 poems a year, accept 4-8%. Press run is 250 for 100 subscribers of which 12 are libraries, 120 shelf sales. Subscription: $13.50. **Sample postpaid: $7.50. Submit up to 6 poems at a time. "Author's name and address must appear on every page submitted. Prefer standard size paper and envelopes 6×9 or larger." No previously published poems; simultaneous submissions OK with notification up front and a phone call if ms is accepted elsewhere. Cover letter with brief bio required.** Time between acceptance and publication is a year and a half maximum. **"All entries are sorted into Texans/Non-Texans, then read impartially. Outstanding pieces are reread and resorted later with slight consideration made to Texas writers. Final selections are made after consultation with Rio Bravo Literary Arts Council." Often comments on rejections. Criticism provided, if requested. Fee negotiated on a job-by-job basis, minimum $25. Publishes one theme issue each year. Send SASE for guidelines and upcoming themes. Theme for November 1996: "Taboos." Reports in 6-8 weeks. Sometimes sends prepublication galleys. Pays 1 copy. All rights retained by authors.** They also sponsor the Southwest Poets Series Annual Chapbook Contest, for residents of Arizona, California (Southern), Colorado, Nevada, New Mexico, Oklahoma, Texas and Utah. Entry fee: $10, includes copy of winning chapbook published in February of following year. Deadline: October 31. Write for details. The editor says, "We are looking for strong, uncluttered, figurative language and prefer free verse, although the exception is considered. I would like to see more poems that 'push the envelope'—test the limits of what is poetic. Main criterion is excellence. Beginners: Presentation is important, but content is paramount."

MAYAPPLE PRESS (III, IV-Regional, women), P.O. Box 5473, Saginaw MI 48603-0473, phone (517)793-2801, e-mail kerman@tardis.svsu.edu, website http://www.cris.com/~JKerman, founded 1978, publisher/editor Judith Kerman, publishes **"women's poetry, Great Lakes regional poetry"** in chapbooks. **They want "quality contemporary poetry rooted in real experience and strongly crafted. No greeting card verse, sentimental or conventional poetry."** They have recently published *Blues for Port City* by David Lunde. **Sample postpaid: $6. Query with 5-6 samples. Check *Poets & Writers* for open times.** "We are not likely to publish unless poet accepts a *primary* role in distribution. Reality is only poets themselves can sell unknown work." **Usually sends prepublication galleys. Pays 5% of run. Publishes on "cooperative" basis.** "Generally poet agrees to purchase most of the run at 50% of cover price." Editor **"sometimes comments (very briefly)" on rejections.** She says, "Poets must create the audience for their work. No small press 'white knight' can make an unknown famous (or even sell more than a few books!)."

> **THE GEOGRAPHICAL INDEX**, located before the Subject Index, can help you discover the publishers in your region. Publishers often favor poets (and work) from their own areas.

MEADOWBROOK PRESS (IV-Anthologies, children, humor), 18318 Minnetonka Blvd., Deephaven MN 55391, founded 1975, contact Children's Poetry Editor. Meadowbrook Press publishes one anthology a year as part of a series of funny poetry books for children. **They want humorous poems aimed at children ages 6-12. Length limit: 45 lines. "Poems should be fun, light and refreshing. We're looking for new, hilarious, contemporary voices in children's poetry that kids can relate to."** They have published poetry by Shel Silverstein, Jack Prelutsky, Jeff Moss and Bruce Lansky. As a sample the editor selected "The Burp" (anonymous):

> Pardon me for being so rude.
> It was not me, it was my food.
> It got so lonely down below,
> it just popped up to say hello.

Their first two anthologies are *Kids Pick the Funniest Poems* and *A Bad Case of the Giggles*. Forthcoming will be *Miles of Smiles*. **"Submit your best work." One poem to a page, name and address on each. Include SASE with each submission. Previously published poems and simultaneous submissions OK. Cover letter required "just to know where the poet found us."** Time between acceptance and publication is 1-2 years. **Poems are tested in front of grade school students before being published. Send SASE for guidelines. Pays $50-100 for each poem published.**

‡**MEDICINAL PURPOSES LITERARY REVIEW; POET TO POET, INC. (I, II)**, 86-37 120th St., #2D, Richmond Hill NY 11418, phone (718)776-8853, e-mail scarptp@usa.pipeline.com, founded 1994, executive editor Robert Dunn, managing editor Thomas M. Catterson, poetry editor Leigh Harrison. *Medicinal Purposes* appears 3 times a year and **wants "virtually any sort of quality poetry (3 poems or 100 lines, whichever comes first). Please, no pornography, gratuitous violence or hate mongering."** They have recently published poetry by D.H. Melhem, Rhina P. Espaillat, W.R. Elton, Chocolate Waters and t. kilgore splake. As a sample they selected these lines from "A Misaligned Melodrama" by Sestina Turner:

> For a bottomless jackpot oft-times follows an evil deed
> Performed at the saw mill, the cliff's edge, the railroad track.
> Sardonic, sadistic chuckles bombarded the ears of our
>   heroine,
> As she thought of all the places she'd have rather been at
>   5:15.
> Alas! There is no tougher taskmaster than a full service
>   mortgage—
> One slip and you fall prey to the eager hands of some villain.

Medicinal Purposes is 60 pgs., 8½ × 5½ (landscape format), professionally printed and perfect-bound with card stock cover with b&w illustration, b&w illustrations also inside. They receive 800 poems a year, accept 10%. Press run is 1,000 for 120 subscribers, 30% shelf sales. Subscription: $16/year. **Sample postpaid: $6. Make checks payable to Poet to Poet. Submit 3 poems at a time, typed with SASE. No previously published poems or simultaneous submissions. Cover letter preferred.** Time between acceptance and publication is 4-16 months. **Often comments on rejections. Send SASE for guidelines. Reports in 3 months. Always sends prepublication galleys. Pays 2 copies. Acquires first rights.** They also produce a poetry/folk music public access cable show called "Poet to Poet." The editors say, "Poetry cannot be created out of a vacuum. Read the work of others, listen to performances, and most important—Get A Life! Only then do you stand a chance of finding your own voice."

MEDIPHORS (I, II, IV-Health concerns), P.O. Box 327, Bloomsburg PA 17815-0327, founded 1992, editor Eugene D. Radice, M.D. *Mediphors* is a biannual literary journal of the health professions that publishes literary work in medicine and health, including poetry, short story, humor, essay, drawing, art/photography. **They want "fresh insights into illness and those caregivers with the burden and joy of working in the fields of medicine and health. Optimism in the face of adversity and overwhelming sorrow. The day-to-day feelings of healthcare workers in diverse settings from hospitals in cities to war zones in military hot spots."** As a sample the editor selected these lines from "The Horn of Africa" by Michael H. Lythgoe:

> In the villages, voices long dehydrated,
> Grope to compose lyrical lines,
> Rumors of virtues among the villainy.
> Oral poems trickle as a serum,
> Sustaining drips
> Of life for skin and bones.

Mediphors is 72 pgs., 8½ × 11, offset and saddle-stapled with color cover and b&w art, graphics and photos throughout. They receive about 2,000 poetry submissions a year, accept approximately 100. Press run is 900 for 300 subscribers of which 20 are libraries, 200 shelf sales. Single copy: $6.95; subscription: $15. **Sample postpaid: $5.50. Submit "2 copies of each poem that we can keep; 6 poems maximum, 30 lines each. We do not accept previously published poems or simultaneous**

$6.00

Medicinal
Purposes

A Literary Review ®

Winter 1996

The goal *Medicinal Purposes* has for its covers is not only to catch the readers' attention, but to keep hold of it, "at least for a couple of months," says Robert Dunn, executive editor and cover illustrator. "The incongruity of the elements depicted in this cover reflects the diversity of the material inside, the sense of 'anything can happen and usually does.' " The New York-based journal appears three times a year and focuses on "reading pleasure." And while it publishes prose, line drawings and crossword puzzles, poetry is "paramount to *Medicinal Purposes*—it is our lover, our shield, and occasionally our weapon. . . . if there weren't any poetry in this world, there wouldn't be a *Medicinal Purposes*."

submissions, and it is upsetting to find out that this has occurred when we accept a poem." **Cover letter not required "but helpful."** Time between acceptance and publication is 10-12 months. **Seldom comments on rejections. Send SASE for guidelines. Reports in 1-3 months. Pays 2 copies. "We require authors to sign a very tight contract for first North American serial rights that makes them legally responsible for plagiarism, libel, copyright infringement, etc."** The editor says, "Our goal is to place in print as many new authors as possible, particularly those working within the health/medical fields (such as doctors, nurses, technologists, therapists, etc.). We encourage unsolicited manuscripts."

MELLEN POETRY PRESS (II), (formerly The Edwin Mellen Press), P.O. Box 450, Lewiston NY 14092-0450, phone (716)754-2266, fax (716)754-4056, e-mail mellen@ag.net, founded 1973, poetry editor Patricia Schultz, is a scholarly press. "We do not have access to large chain bookstores for distribution, but depend on direct sales and independent bookstores." **They pay 2 copies, no royalties. "We require no author subsidies. However, we encourage our authors to seek grants from Councils for the Arts and other foundations because these add to the reputation of the volume." They want "original integrated work—living unity of poems, preferably unpublished, encompassable in one reading."** They have published poetry by W.R. Elton and Albert Cook. Their books are 64 pgs., 6×9, softcover binding, no graphics. Price: $12.95. **Submit 30-60 sample poems with cover letter including bio and publications. "We do not print until we receive at least 100 prepaid orders. Successful marketing of poetry books depends on the author's active involvement.** We send out up to 15 free review copies to journals or newspapers, the names of which may be suggested by the author. An author may (but is not required to) purchase books to make up the needed 100 prepublication sales." The editor says, "We seek to publish volumes unified in mood, tone, theme."

‡**MELTING TREES REVIEW (I, II); COUNTERCULTURE PRESS (V)**, 2026 Mt. Meigs Rd. #2, Montgomery AL 36107, founded 1995, editor Mike Catalano, associate editor Suzanne Catalano. *Melting Trees Review*, "The Peoples' Park of Poetry," appears quarterly and "encourages the ethnic, the disillusioned, and the anarchistic to explore their different drummers." **They want "free verse, vivid imagery; risk-taking and ethnic work; apocalyptic and anarchistic poetry. No academic work; prose chopped into poetry; boring, obscure or rhyming poetry."** They have recently pub-

lished poetry by Morton Marcus, Willie James King, Tanaya C. Hilton and Clay Koontz. As a sample they selected these lines from associate editor Suzanne Catalano's poem "The American Dream":

> People fought Vivian Malone unmercifully
> Who was there to protect?
> The footsteps of Rosa Parks
> Forced from her seat haunts us all

The issues we received are 22 pgs., 8½×11, photocopied and side-stapled with b&w cover and border art. However, the format has changed to 52 pgs., digest-sized, saddle-stapled with card stock cover. They publish 10-15% of poetry received. Press run is 250. **Sample postpaid: $3. Make checks payable to Mike Catalano. Submit 3-5 typed poems at a time. No previously published poems or simultaneous submissions. Cover letter preferred. Poems are circulated to a three-member editorial board. "Unanimous concensus needed for acceptance." Always comments on rejections. Send SASE for guidelines. Reports in 2-3 weeks. Pays 1 copy. Acquires first rights.** Reviews books and chapbooks of poetry in 100-500 words, single format. Open to unsolicited reviews. Poets may also send books for review consideration. Counterculture Press is a publisher of poetry chapbooks that "the reader would not only read twice, but tell their friends about." They publish **2 chapbooks/year.** Chapbooks are usually 44-52 pgs., saddle-stapled with b&w artwork. **"At the present time, however, Counterculture Press publishes by invitation only."** Sample chapbooks available for $4. The editors say, "In our opinion, there is too much unimaginative, formalistic poetry. Our readers want bite. Few mainstream poets take risks anymore. We disdain the so-called Poetry Expansive Movement bringing poetry back to the dark ages with its restrictive rhymes and strait-jacket syntax. Also, submissions without SASE end up in the shredder, unread."

MENNONITE PUBLISHING HOUSE; PURPOSE; STORY FRIENDS; ON THE LINE; WITH (IV-Religious, children), 616 Walnut Ave., Scottdale PA 15683-1999, phone (412)887-8500. **Send submissions or queries directly to the editor of the specific magazine at address indicated.** The official publisher for the Mennonite Church in North America seeks also to serve a broad Christian audience. **Each of the magazines listed has different specifications, and the editor of each should be queried for more exact information.** *Purpose*, editor James E. Horsch, a "monthly in weekly parts," circulation 14,000, is **for adults of all ages, its focus: "action oriented, discipleship living."** It is 5⅜×8⅜, with two-color printing throughout. **They buy appropriate poetry up to 12 lines.** *Purpose* uses 3-4 poems/week, receives about 2,000/year of which they use 150, has a 10- to 12-week backlog. **Send guidelines and free sample. Mss should be typewritten, double-spaced, one side of sheet only. Simultaneous submissions OK. Reports in 6-8 weeks. Pays $7.50-20/poem plus 2 copies.** *On the Line*, edited by Mary C. Meyer, another "monthly in weekly parts," is **for children 10-14,** a "story paper that reinforces Christian values," circulation 6,500. It is 7×10, saddle-stapled, with 2-color printing on the cover and inside, using art and photos. **Sample free with SASE. Wants poems 3-24 lines. Submit poems "each typed on a separate 8½×11 sheet." Simultaneous submissions and previously published poems OK. Reports in 1 month. Pays $10-25/poem plus 2 copies.** *Story Friends*, edited by Rose Mary Stutzman, is for **children 4-9,** a "story paper that reinforces Christian values," also a "monthly in weekly issues," circulation 6,900, uses **3-12 lines. Send SASE for guidelines/sample copy. Pays $5-10.** *With*, Editorial Team, Box 347, Newton KS 67114, phone (316)238-5100, is for **"senior highs, ages 15-18,"** focusing on helping "high school youth make a commitment to Christ in the context of the church amidst the complex and conflicting values they encounter in their world," circulation 5,800, uses **poetry dealing with youth in relation to their world, nature and light verse. Poems should be 4-50 lines. Pays $10-25.**

MERLYN'S PEN: THE NATIONAL MAGAZINES OF STUDENT WRITING, GRADES 6-12 (IV-Students, young adults), Dept. PM, Box 1058, East Greenwich RI 02818, phone (401)885-5175, founded 1985, editor R. Jim Stahl, one for grades 6-9, the other ("senior edition") for grades 9-12. Each edition is 40 pgs., magazine-sized, professionally printed with glossy paper, color cover. Press run is 40,000 for 38,000 subscriptions of which 5,000 are libraries. Subscription: $21. **Sample postpaid: $3. Send SASE for guidelines. Reports in 3 months. Pays 3 copies plus $5-10/ piece.**

‡MERRIMACK BOOKS; PALACE CORBIE; CONSEQUENTIAL INEBRIATION (II), P.O. Box 83514, Lincoln NE 68501-3514, e-mail wedwards@unlgrad1.unl.edu, website http://www.para-net.com/~palace_corbie, founded 1986, editor/publisher Wayne Edwards. *Palace Corbie* is an annual fiction and poetry anthology. **They want nontraditional poetry containing misery, angst and anguish. No rhyming poetry.** The editor says *Palace Corbie* is 224 pgs., 5½×8½, perfect-bound with 4-color cover. They receive approximately 1,000 poems a year, accept less than 1%. Press run is 1,000. Single copy: $9.95. **Sample postpaid: $6. Make checks payable to Merrimack Books. Previously published poems OK if noted; no simultaneous submissions. Seldom comments on rejections. Send SASE for guidelines. Reports in 1 month. Sometimes sends prepublication galleys. Pay varies, but "usually 1 copy." Acquires one-time rights.** Merrimack Books looks for "unusual emotive poems" and publishes 1-2 paperbacks and **3-5 chapbooks a year**. Chapbooks are usually 32-44 pgs. and saddle-stitched. **Submit entire ms. Replies in 1 month.** Merrimack Books also publishes *Consequential Inebriation*, a punk zine using "lots of poetry." Send SASE for more information.

MICHIGAN QUARTERLY REVIEW (III), Dept. PM, 3032 Rackham Bldg., University of Michigan, Ann Arbor MI 48109, phone (313)764-9265, founded 1962, editor-in-chief Laurence Goldstein, is "an interdisciplinary, general interest academic journal that publishes mainly essays and reviews on subjects of cultural and literary interest." They use **all kinds of poetry except light verse. No specifications as to form, length, style, subject matter or purpose.** They have published poetry by Tess Gallagher, Robert Hass, Amy Gerstler and Cathy Song. As a sample the editor selected these lines by Donald Hall:

> *Daylilies go from the hill; asters return; maples redden again*
> *as summer departs for winter's virtuous deprivation.*
> *When we stroll the Pond Road at nightfall, western sun stripes*
> *down through dust raised by a pickup ten minutes ago:*
> *vertical birches, hilly road, sunlight slant and descending.*

The *MQR* is 160 pgs., 6×9, flat-spined, professionally printed with glossy card cover, b&w photos and art. They receive 1,500 submissions/year, use 30, have a 1-year backlog. Circulation is 2,000, with 1,500 subscriptions of which half are libraries. Single copy: $5; subscription: $18. **Sample postpaid: $2.50. They prefer typed mss. No previously published poems or simultaneous submissions. Publishes theme issues. Reports in 4-6 weeks. Always sends prepublication galleys. Pays $8-12/page. Buys first rights only.** Reviews books of poetry. "All reviews are commissioned." Poetry published in the *Michigan Quarterly Review* was also selected for inclusion in the 1992, 1994 and 1995 volumes of *The Best American Poetry*. Laurence Goldstein advises, "There is no substitute for omnivorous reading and careful study of poets past and present, as well as reading in new and old areas of knowledge. Attention to technique, especially to rhythm and patterns of imagery, is vital."

MID-AMERICAN REVIEW; JAMES WRIGHT PRIZE FOR POETRY (II, IV-Translations), Dept. of English, Bowling Green State University, Bowling Green OH 43403, phone (419)372-2725, founded 1980, editor-in-chief George Looney, appears twice a year. **"Poetry should emanate from strong, evocative images; use fresh, interesting language; and have a consistent sense of voice. Each line must carry the poem, and an individual vision should be evident. We encourage new as well as established writers. There is no length limit."** They have published poetry by Stephen Dunn, Catherine Sasanov, Albert Goldbarth, Naomi Shihab Nye, Greg Pape, David Baker, Martín Espada and Frankie Paino. As a sample the editor selected these lines from "Conversations With Air" by Al Maginnes:

> *. . . Now we are silent*
> *before those angels, listening*
> *for the rustle of scaled wings, the conversations*
> *with air that all flight, all language*
> *finally is. Between blows of the chisel,*
> *those sculptors listened and were answered.*

The review is 200 pgs., offset printed, flat-spined, using line drawings, laminated card cover. They receive over 1,000 mss a year, use 60-80 poems. Press run is 1,000. Single copy: $7; subscription: $12. **Sample postpaid: $5. Reads submissions September 1 through May 30 only. Send SASE for guidelines. Sometimes sends prepublication galleys. Pays $10/printed page plus 2 copies. Rights revert to authors on publication.** Reviews books of poetry. Open to unsolicited reviews. Poets may also send books to Andrea Van Vorhis, reviews editor, for review consideration. **They also publish chapbooks in translation** and award the James Wright Prize for Poetry to a ms published in regular editions of *MAR*, when funding is available.

MIDDLE EAST REPORT (IV-Regional, ethnic, themes), 1500 Massachusetts Ave. NW, Suite 119, Washington DC 20005, phone (202)223-3677, founded 1971, editor Geoff Hartman, is "a magazine on contemporary political, economic, cultural and social developments in the Middle East and North Africa and U.S. policy toward the region. We occasionally publish **poetry that addresses political or social issues of Middle Eastern peoples.**" They have published poetry by Dan Almagor (Israeli) and Etel Adnan (Lebanese). It is 48 pgs., magazine-sized, saddle-stapled, professionally printed on glossy stock with glossy paper cover, 4 issues/year. Press run is 7,500. Subscription: $32. **Sample postpaid: $6 domestic; $8 airmail overseas. Simultaneous submissions and previously published poems OK.** "We key poetry to the theme of a particular issue. Could be as long as 6 months between acceptance and publication." **Editor sometimes comments on submissions. Reports in 6-8 weeks. Pays 3 copies.**

MIDLAND REVIEW (II), English Dept., Morrill Hall, Oklahoma State University, Stillwater OK 74078, phone (405)744-9474, founded 1985, is a literary annual that publishes "poetry, fiction, essays, ethnic, experimental, women's work, contemporary feminist." The editors say, **"style and form are open." They do not want "long or religious poetry."** They have published poetry by Amy Clampitt, William Stafford, Bill Knott, Tom Lux and Richard Kostelanetz. As a sample, the editors selected these lines by James Doyle:

> The pressured houses squat
> beneath a black sky. Smoke
> passes back and forth between
> them down the street. Gilled
> animals swim the thin odors
> home, calling themselves planets . . .

Midland Review is 100-120 pgs., digest-sized, with photography, artwork and ads. Circulation is 500 for 470 subscribers. Single copy: $6. **Sample postpaid: $5. Writers should submit 3-5 poems at a time, typed ms in any form. "We no longer read during the summer (May 1 through August 31)."** Time between acceptance and publication is 6-12 months. **Reports in 3-6 months. Pays 1 copy.**

MIDSTREAM: A MONTHLY JEWISH REVIEW (IV-Ethnic), 110 E. 59th St., New York NY 10022, phone (212)339-6040, editor Joel Carmichael, is an international journal appearing monthly except February/March, June/July and August/September, when it is bimonthly. **They want short poems with Jewish themes or atmosphere.** They have published poetry by Yehuda Amichai, James Reiss, Abraham Sutzkever, Liz Rosenberg and John Hollander. The magazine is 48 pgs., approximately 8½×11, saddle-stapled with colored card cover. Each issue includes 4 to 5 poems (which tend to be short, lyric and freestyle expressing seminal symbolism of Jewish history and Scripture). They receive about 300 submissions/year, use 5-10%. Circulation: 10,000. Single copy: $3; subscription: $21. **Submit 3 poems at a time. Publishes theme issues. Reports in 3 months. Pays $25/poem. Buys all rights.**

MIDWEST POETRY REVIEW (II), P.O. Box 20236, Atlanta GA 30325-0236, phone (404)350-0714, founded 1980, editor/publisher John K. Ottley, Jr., is a quarterly, with no other support than subscriptions, contest entry fees and an occasional advertisement. **They are looking for "quality accessible verse. Great imagery with powerful adjectives and verbs. Poetry that opens the door to the author's feelings through sensory descriptions.** We are attempting to encourage the cause of poetry by purchasing the best of modern poetry. **No jingly verses or limericks. 40-line limit. Any subject is considered, if handled with skill and taste. No pornography."** They have recently published poetry by Heywood Anderson, Miriam Bevers, Daniel Brodsky, Patricia Fain Hutson, Flori Ignoffo, Mariana Warner, Pearl Mary Wilshaw and Mary Zachmeyer. As a sample the editor selected these lines from "View from the Summit" by Nancy Niemeyer Graham:

> The world beneath this airy brow has yet to hear
> the childish babble of a star, to dream
> of stammered words from distant spheres
> or learn the cryptic language of the moon.
> On this cloudy peak I have perceived the lyrics
> of the wind, clocked the countless rhythms
> of the rain, and heard the august chariots of God
> wheel across the attic of the sky.

MPR is 40 pgs., professionally printed in Univers type, digest-sized, saddle-stapled with matte card cover. Subscription: $20 ($25 Canadian, $30 foreign, both in US funds). **Submit 5 poems at a time. Send SASE and $1 for guidelines. Reports in 3-4 weeks. Pays $5-20/poem. Buys first rights.** They have varied contests in each issue, with prizes ranging from $10-250, with "unbiased, non-staff judges for all competitions." Contests have entry fees. Send SASE for details. A 20-point self-analysis survey to assist poets in analyzing their own work is offered free to new subscribers.

THE MIDWEST QUARTERLY (II), Pittsburg State University, Pittsburg KS 66762, phone (316)235-4689, e-mail smeats@pittstate.edu, founded 1959, poetry editor Stephen Meats, "publishes articles on any subject of contemporary interest, particularly literary criticism, political science, philosophy, education, biography and sociology, and each issue contains a **section of poetry** usually **15 poems in length.** I am interested in **well-crafted, though not necessarily traditional poems that explore the inter-relationship of the human and natural worlds in bold, surrealistic images of a writer's imaginative, mystical experience. 60 lines or less (occasionally longer if exceptional)."** They have recently published poetry by Walter McDonald, David Ray, Rita Signorelli-Pappos, Lyn Lifshin, Jeanne Murray Walker and William Kloefkorn. As a sample the editor selected these lines from "The Ox" by George Eklund:

> Ox, my dying flower,
> my wooden ship with sails ablaze
> my cannon of symphonies
> my destroyer of geometry and the atomic clock.

> *Your mind sings in the last famine of the crows*
> *you have suckled Allah, the Buddah and the Christ*
> *and the psychopathic generals who squat*
> *in jungles and in the toilets of Washington.*

The magazine is 130 pgs., digest-sized, flat-spined, matte cover, professionally printed. A nice mix of poems appears here, most of it free verse with room for an occasional formal or narrative piece. Circulation is 650, with 600 subscribers of which 500 are libraries. They receive approximately 4,200 poems annually; publish 60. "My plan is to publish all acceptances within 1 year." Subscription: $12. **Sample: $3. Mss should be typed with poet's name on each page, 10 poems or fewer. No previously published poems; simultaneous submissions OK. Publishes theme issues occasionally. Reports in 1 month, usually sooner. "Submissions without SASE cannot be acknowledged." Pays 3 copies. Acquires first serial rights. Editor comments on rejections "if the poet or poems seem particularly promising."** Reviews books of poetry by *MQ* published poets only. He says, "Keep writing; read as much contemporary poetry as you can lay your hands on; don't let the discouragement of rejection keep you from sending your work out to editors."

MIDWEST VILLAGES & VOICES (V, IV-Regional), 3220 Tenth Ave. S., Minneapolis MN 55407, phone (612)822-6878, founded 1979, is a cultural organization and small press publisher of **Midwestern poetry and prose**. They have published books of poetry by Ethna McKiernan, Florence Chard Dacey, Kevin FitzPatrick and Sue Doro. Forthcoming: a collection of poetry and prose by Irene Paull. As a sample here are lines from Dacey's poem "Necklace":

> *Layer upon layer*
> *of bone, bead,*
> *wood and stone,*
> *heavier than your body,*
> *breathing, sinister,*
> *raised*
> *at great cost*
> *from the cave below the tree,*
> *as common as your life,*
> *strung that tightly,*
> *as large as a shroud.*

The flat-spined books are generally 48+ pgs., professionally printed with glossy card covers, selling for $5-12. **"We encourage and support Midwestern writers and artists. However, at this time submissions are accepted by invitation only. Unsolicited submissions are not accepted."**

MIDWIFERY TODAY (IV-Specialized: childbirth), P.O. Box 2672, Eugene OR 97402-0223, phone (541)344-7438, fax (541)344-1422, e-mail midwifery@aol.com, founded 1986, editor Jan Tritten, is a quarterly that "provides a voice for midwives and childbirth educators. **We are a midwifery magazine. Subject must be birth or profession related.**" They do not want poetry that is "off subject or puts down the subject." As a sample the editor selected these lines by Karen Hope Ehrlich:

> *you get to keep the baby*
> *not the midwife*
> *she is a fickle lover*
> *merged and passing*

MT is 56 pgs., 8½×11, offset, saddle-stapled, with glossy card cover with b&w photo and b&w photos, artwork and ads inside. They use about 1 poem/issue. Press run is 5,000 for 3,000 subscribers, 1,000 shelf sales. Subscription: $35. **Sample postpaid: $9. No previously published poems or simultaneous submissions. Cover letter required.** Time between acceptance and publication is 1-2 years. **Seldom comments on rejections. Publishes theme issues. Send SASE for writer's guidelines and upcoming themes. Reports in 2-6 weeks. Pays 2 copies. Acquires first rights.** The editor says, "With our publication *please* stay on the subject."

MILKWEED EDITIONS (II), 430 First Ave. N., Suite 400, Minneapolis MN 55401-1743, phone (612)332-3192, founded 1979, poetry editor Emilie Buchwald. Three collections published annually. **Unsolicited mss are only accepted from writers who have previously published a book-length collection of poetry or a minimum of 6 poems in commercial or literary journals.** One of the leading literary presses in the country, Milkweed publishes some of the best poets composing today in well-made, attractively designed collections. Published books of poetry include: *The Phoenix Gone, The Terrace Empty* by Marilyn Chin; *Firekeeper* by Pattiann Rogers; and *The Long Experience of Love* by Jim Moore. **Submit 60- to 200-page ms. Include SAS postcard for notification of ms arrival. Unsolicited mss read in January and June; please include return postage. Send submissions to Poetry Readers. Send SASE for guidelines. Reports in 1-6 months.** Catalog available on request, with $1.50 in postage.

MIND IN MOTION: A MAGAZINE OF POETRY AND SHORT PROSE (I, II), P.O. Box 1118, Apple Valley CA 92307, phone (619)248-6512, founded 1985, editor Céleste Goyer, is a quarterly wanting poetry **"15-60 lines. Explosive, provocative. Images not clichéd but directly conveyant of the point of the poem. Use of free association particularly desired. We encourage free verse, keeping in mind the essential elements of rhythm and rhyme. Traditional forms are acceptable if within length restrictions. Meaning should be implicit, as in the styles of Blake, Poe, Coleridge, Stephen Crane, Emily Dickinson, Leonard Cohen. Not interested in sentimentality, emotionalism, simplistic nature worship, explicit references.** *MIM* **is known for thoughtful poetry that explores the timeless themes of philosophy and human nature."** She has recently published poetry by Robert E. Brimhall, Karl Lorenzen, Nathan Whiting, Charlie Mehrhoff and H.R. Felgenhauer. As a sample she selected these lines from "Just Turn the Other Cheek" (poet unidentified):

> *Just lay down the gun there son*
> *and pick up instead the flag to*
> *bear bravely into the sullen skies*
> *as your generation lies trampled*
> *into the dirt by the greed and ego*
> *of its betters made more possible*
> *while masquerading in the name of*
> *mother and country, because after*
> *all everyone is equal.*

MIM is 54 pgs., digest-sized, saddle-stapled, photocopied from photoreduced typescript with a heavy matte cover with b&w drawing. Of approximately 2,400 poems/year she accepts about 200. Press run is 525 for 350 subscribers. Subscription: $14. **Sample postpaid: $3.50 (overseas: $4.50, $18/year). Submit 6 poems at a time. Unpublished works only. Simultaneous submissions OK, if notified. "Please have name and address on each poem. We also use dates of composition; it would help if these were provided with submissions."** Editor usually comments on rejected mss. Send SASE for guidelines. **Reports in 1-6 weeks. Pays 1 copy "when financially possible." Magazine is copyrighted; all rights revert to author.** "Please do not submit further material until your last submission has been responded to. Please be patient and don't overwhelm the editor."

MIND MATTERS REVIEW (III), 2040 Polk St., #234, San Francisco CA 94109, founded 1988, phone (415)775-4545, editor Carrie Drake, poetry editor Lorraine A. Donfor **(and submissions should be sent directly to her at 2837 Blue Spruce Lane, Silver Spring MD 20906)**, is a "literary annual with emphasis on use of science as a tool for responsible organization of information; analysis of the role of language in consciousness, knowledge and intelligence; and social criticism particularly of metaphysics. Also includes book reviews, poetry, short stories, art and essays." They want **"short poems for fillers. Would like to see inspirational poetry; but open to satire and contemporary subjects that reflect the struggle between the 'inner voice' and external pressures; poetry on social issues. Rhythm important, but rhyme isn't."** They have published poetry by T.N. Turner. As a sample the editor selected these lines by Barbara Zeolla:

> *There is no shelter from their thoughts*
> *Or the images of faces*
> *Reflected in the glass.*
> *They are there and yet*
> *   not there at all.*

MMR is magazine-sized, desktop-published, includes graphics, sketches, b&w photos. Subscription: $15 US, $20 foreign. **Sample postpaid: $3.50. Poets are encouraged to buy a copy before submitting. Submit 3 poems at a time. No simultaneous submissions; previously published poems OK. Cover letter required; include publishing credits and note if submissions have been previously published or accepted for publication elsewhere. Publishes theme issues. Send SASE for guidelines and upcoming themes. Sometimes sends prepublication galleys. Pays 1 copy.** Staff reviews books of poetry. Send books for review consideration to David Castleman, 512 Tamalpais Dr., Mill Valley CA 94941. The editor says, "Poetry should reflect the deeper layers of consciousness, its perceptions, observations, joys and sorrows; should reflect the independence of the individual spirit. Should not be 'trendy' or 'poetic' in a forced way."

‡MIND PURGE (I, II), NT Box 5471, Denton TX 76203, e-mail jivan@anet-dfw.com, founded 1994, editors Jason Hensel and Cheryl Doughty, is a biannual literary and art magazine publishing poetry, short fiction, one-act plays, short screenplays, essays, book reviews and art. **They want poetry that is "well-crafted, insightful, imagistic. No specifications as to form, length, subject matter or style. However no greeting card verse, hackneyed themes or poetry that says nothing or goes nowhere."** They have recently published poetry by Cannon, Ben Omhart and Christopher Stolle. As a sample the editors selected these lines from "Boquillas" by Chad Forbes:

> *And we rode to Boquillas in the back of a rusted brown truck*
> *that snaked up the gravel road. A Mexican child who was probably*

five stood on the open tailgate and swayed at fifty with one hand gripping,
worrying us Americans until someone said, "He's here to keep us from falling."

Mind Purge is 36-52 pgs., 7×8½, neatly printed and saddle-stapled with matte card stock cover with b&w photo and b&w photos inside. They receive about 100 poems a year, accept approximately 10%. Press run is 100 for 10 subscribers. Single copy: $3; subscription: $5. **Sample postpaid: $2. Make checks payable to Jason Hensel. Submit up to 5 poems at a time, name and address on each page. No previously published poems or simultaneous submissions. Cover letter preferred. Seldom comments on rejections. Reports within 3 months. Pays 1 copy.** Reviews books of poetry in 200 words, single format. Open to unsolicited reviews. Poets may also send books for review consideration. Jason Hensel's advice: "Don't give up, just keep submitting. And read, not only poetry, but everything you can get your hands on."

THE MINNESOTA REVIEW (II), English Dept., East Carolina University, Greenville NC 27858-4353, phone (919)328-6388, founded 1960, editor Jeffrey Williams, is a biannual literary magazine wanting **"poetry which explores some aspect of social or political issues and/or the nature of relationships. No nature poems, and no lyric poetry without the above focus."** As a sample the editors selected the opening lines from "In Historic Perspective" by Charlotte Mayerson:

> *Without the women of the Holocaust*
> *Who saw their children ripped asunder*
> *I could not go on.*
> *Without the women*
> *Of eighteen hundred and five*
> *Who bore eight children and raised five*
> *I would go under. . . .*

TMR is 200 pgs., digest-sized, flat-spined, with b&w glossy card cover and art. Mostly free verse (lyric and narrative), poems here tend to have strong themes and powerful content, perhaps to coincide with the magazine's subtitle: "a journal of committed writing." Circulation: 1,500 for 800 subscribers. Subscription: $12 to individuals, $24 to institutions. **Sample postpaid: $7.50. Address submissions to "Poetry Editor" (not to a specific editor). Cover letter including "brief intro with address" preferred. Publishes theme issues. Send SASE for upcoming themes. Theme for Fall 1996: "The White Issue." Reports in 2-4 months. Pays 2 copies. Acquires all rights. Returns rights upon request.** Reviews books of poetry in single or multi-book format. Open to unsolicited reviews.

‡MINORITY LITERARY EXPO (IV-Membership, ethnic), 216 Avenue T, Pratt City, Birmingham AL 35214-5308, phone (205)798-9083, founded 1990, editor/publisher Kervin Fondren, is an annual literary professional publication featuring minority poets, novices and professionals. **"Organization membership open to all minority poets nationally. I want poems from minority poets that are holistic and wholesome, less than 24 lines each, no vulgar or hate poetry accepted, any style, any form, any subject matter. Poetry that expresses holistic views and philosophies is very acceptable. Literary value is emphasized. Selected poets receive financial awards, certificates, honorable mentions, critiques and special poetic honors." No fee is charged for inclusion.** As a sample the editor selected these lines from his poem "Rain and Pain":

> *Do I Dare*
> *As A Man*
> *Dance in My Backyard*
> *In the Rain*

"We will focus on human/social issues and education-oriented facets through 1997." Send SASE for guidelines and upcoming themes. Pays 1-3 copies. They also sponsor an annual poetry chapbook contest and an annual "Analyze the Poem" contest. Send SASE for details. The editor says, "We seek novices and unpublished poets to breathe the new life every poetry organization needs."

‡MINOTAUR PRESS; MINOTAUR (II), 95 Harbormaster Rd., #11, South San Francisco CA 94080, e-mail 102552.1253@compuserve.com, founded 1974, editor Jim Gove. *Minotaur* is a "small press literary quarterly **with emphasis on contemporary and experimental styles. Must be relevant. No rhymed and/or traditional verse."** They have recently published poetry by Judson Crews, Mark Weber, Alan Catlin, Will Inman, Hugh Fox and Duane Locke. As a sample the editor selected these lines from "The Tsar is Terrible" by David Lincoln Fisher:

> *The Tsar is terrible; jadelike,*
> *skinny, blacker*
> *than anthracite, over his face*
> *eyes go skidding, like a stalled motorbike.*
> *A foreign guest sat down,*
> *bashed to the head like a nail.*
> *Homeric drums, the windowed stars,*
> *on the moonlit window sill an aluminum bird.*

The editor describes it as digest-sized, offset, saddle-stapled, "stock cover—cover graphics—sometimes use interior graphics, but rarely." They publish about 5 of 100 poems received. Press run is 300 for 200 subscribers of which 30 are libraries. Subscription: $18. **Sample postpaid: $3.50. "Submissions via e-mail are encouraged." Send SASE for guidelines. Submit 4-8 poems at a time with name and address on each page. Sends prepublication galleys "with exception of submissions via e-mail." Reports in 3-6 weeks, faster for e-mail submissions. Pays 1 copy. They also award a $50 prize for the best poem in each issue by a subscribing poet. However, "you do not need to subscribe to be published." Editor comments on submissions "if requested only."** Open to unsolicited reviews. The editor says, "Subscribe to the magazines that publish your work. Few poetry magazines run in the black. We would like to see more experimental, leading edge, borderline poetry."

MIORITA: A JOURNAL OF ROMANIAN STUDIES (IV-Ethnic), Dept. of Linguistics, University of Rochester, Rochester NY 14627, phone (716)275-8053, is an irregular scholarly publication, 100 pgs., digest-sized, circulation 200, focusing on **Romanian culture and using some poetry by Romanians or on Romanian themes. Sample: $5. Pays copies.** Reviews books of poetry "occasionally; must be Romanian-connected."

THE MIRACULOUS MEDAL (IV-Religious), 475 E. Chelten Ave., Philadelphia PA 19144-5785, phone (215)848-1010, founded 1928, editor Rev. John W. Gouldrick, C.M., is a religious quarterly. **"Poetry should reflect solid Catholic doctrine and experience. Any subject matter is acceptable, provided it does not contradict the teachings of the Roman Catholic Church. Poetry must have a religious theme, preferably about the Blessed Virgin Mary."** They have published poetry by Gladys McKee. The editor describes it as 32 pgs., digest-sized, saddle-stapled, 2-color inside and cover, no ads. *The Miraculous Medal* is no longer circulated on a subscription basis. It is used as a promotional piece and is sent to all clients of the Central Association of the Miraculous Medal. Circulation is 340,000. **Sample and guidelines free for postage. Poems should be a maximum of 20 lines, double-spaced. No simultaneous submissions or previously published poems. Reports in 6 months to 3 years. Pays 50¢ and up/line, on acceptance. Buys first North American rights.**

MISSISSIPPI MUD (III), 1505 Drake Ave., Austin TX 78704, phone (512)444-5459, founded 1973, editor Joel Weinstein, is an irregular publication that features fiction, poetry and artwork that "portray life in America at the twilight of the 20th century." As for poetry **they want "lively, contemporary themes and forms, free verse preferred." They do not want "anything stodgy, pathetic or moralistic; the self-consciously pretty or clever; purely formal exercises."** They have published poetry by Ivan Arguelles, Christy Sheffield Sanford and Simon Perchik. *MM* is 52 pgs., 11 × 17, saddle-stitched, with 4-color glossy paper cover, full-page graphics and display ads. They receive 100-200 poems a year, accept less than 10%. Press run is 1,500 for 150 subscribers of which 16 are libraries, 1,000 shelf sales, about 200 distributed free to galleries, museums and critical media. Subscription: $25 for 4 issues. **Sample postpaid: $6. Submit no more than 6 poems at a time. No previously published poems; simultaneous submissions OK.** Time between acceptance and publication is a year or more. **Seldom comments on rejections. Reports in 4-6 months. Pays $25 and 2 copies. Buys first North American serial rights.**

MISSISSIPPI REVIEW (II), University of Southern Mississippi, Box 5144, Hattiesburg MS 39406-5144, phone (601)266-4321, editor Frederick Barthelme, managing editor Rie Fortenberry. Literary publication for those interested in contemporary literature. Poems differ in style, length and form, but all have craft in common (along with intriguing content). **Sample: $8. Query before submitting. Does not read manuscripts in summer. Pays copies.**

MISSOURI REVIEW (II), 1507 Hillcrest Hall, University of Missouri, Columbia MO 65211, phone (314)882-4474, fax (314)884-4671, founded 1978, poetry editor Greg Michalson, general editor Speer Morgan, is a quality literary journal, 6 × 9, 208 pgs., which appears 3 times a year, **publishing poetry features only—6-12 pages for each of 3 to 5 poets/issue.** By devoting more editorial space to each poet, *MR* provides a fuller look at the work of some of the best writers composing today. However, the number of poets whose work appears here has decreased significantly, limiting your chances in a prestigious market where competition has become even keener than in the past. **Sample: $7. Submit 6-12 poems at a time. "Poets should submit only unpublished work." No simultaneous submissions. Reports in 8-10 weeks. Sometimes sends prepublication galleys. Pays $125-250/feature. Buys all rights. Returns rights "after publication, without charge, at the request of the authors."** Reviews books of poetry. "Short, inhouse reviews only." Awards the Tom McAfee Discovery Feature once or twice a year to an outstanding young poet who has not yet published a book; poets are selected from regular submissions at the discretion of the editors. Also offers the Editors' Prize Contest in Poetry. Deadline: October 15. $750 first prize and publication. Three finalists named in addition. Write for details. The editors add, "We think we have enhanced the quality of our poetry section and increased our reader interest in this section. We remain dedicated to publishing at least one younger or emerging poet in every issue."

MR. COGITO PRESS (V), Pacific University, 2518 NW Savier, Portland OR 97210, founded 1973, poetry editors John M. Gogol and Robert A. Davies, **publishes collections by invitation only.** Send SASE for catalog to buy samples. The press formerly published *Mr. Cogito* magazine; however, the magazine has been discontinued.

‡**MOBIUS (I, II)**, P.O. Box 674, St. Clair Shores MI 48080, fax (810)774-4772, founded 1982, editor Jean Hull Herman, assistant editor Joanna Linsalata. They look for "the informed mind responding to the challenges of reality and the expression of the imagination in poetry with intelligence and wit. **Poets should say significant, passionate things about the larger world outside themselves and use all the resources of our language and art. Open to meter, rhyme, dramatic and narrative structures, traditional as well as free verse and all that pleases the ear as well as the soul. General topics include response to art and to nature; the philosophical questions; love and romance; relationships; war; the events of and thoughts about everyday life; science and technology; and humor (for which the editor has a weakness). Shorter poems as well as longer ones will be considered."** They have recently published poetry by Gary Blankenburg, Ace Boggess, R.L. Cook, Robert Cooperman, Louise Heck-Rabi, Lenore A. Reiss, Aline Soules and N. Anne Highlands Tiley. As a sample the editor selected these lines from "Icefall" by Jerry H. Jenkin:

> *I watched the astronauts' brief walk in space*
> *along a slender boom. I thought of them*
> *as aphids, stiff and white upon a stem—*
> *unexpectedly devoid of grace.*
> *A hemisphere of earth, blue, white, and green,*
> *floated to their side, a vast contour.*
> *I contemplated how some hours before*
> *I'd fallen on the steps and across.*

Mobius is published twice a year, at Memorial Day and Thanksgiving. It is magazine-sized, 60 pgs., professionally printed, saddle-stapled with matte card cover. Subscription: $12/year. **Sample postpaid: $8. No submissions via fax; correspondence OK. Send SASE for guidelines. "Response time is two weeks to two months, as editor does read submissions all year round. Printed authors receive one copy free. Editor will comment on all rejections."**

MOCKINGBIRD; ROBERT FRANCIS MEMORIAL PRIZE (II), P.O. Box 761, Davis CA 95617, founded 1994, co-editors C.G. Macdonald and Joe Aimone (with frequent guest editors as well). *Mockingbird* is a biannual journal of poetry and reviews. **They are looking for "craft and inspiration; also we value clarity and intensity. We want form, but not witless conformity; innovation, but not convenient ignorance of tradition."** They have recently published poetry by Sandra McPherson, Annie Finch, Charles Rafferty, Hugh Fox and Rigoberto Gonzalez. As a sample the editors selected these lines from "Orthodox Christmas Eve" by Gail White:

> *The incense rises like the church's breath*
> *into a frosty world. This night of birth*
> *raises and tosses me on tides of love.*
> *But tides recede—I know this moment's worth.*
> *If unbelief were only more like faith,*
> *if only our emotions were enough.*

Mockingbird is 48 pgs., 5½×8½, photocopied from desktop-published originals and saddle-stapled with matte card cover with b&w art. They receive about 1,000-1,200 poems a year and publish about 50-60 (not counting a few solicited works). Press run is 250 for 125 subscribers of which 4 are libraries, 20 shelf sales. Subscription: $7.50 for 1 year, $12 for 2 years. **Sample postpaid: $4. Submit no more than 5-6 pages of poetry at a time. No previously published poems or simultaneous submissions. Cover letter preferred. Sometimes comments on rejections. Send SASE for guidelines. Reports usually within 2 months, "3-4 months on acceptances and near misses." Pays 1 copy. Acquires first serial rights. Requests acknowledgment if work is reprinted elsewhere.** Reviews books and chapbooks of poetry as well as other magazines in up to 1,500 words. Open to unsolicited reviews. Poets may also send books for review consideration. They also sponsor the Robert Francis Memorial Prize which awards a total of $350 to one first place winner and two seconds. The contest runs from July 4 to Halloween. Entry fee: $2/poem. An $8 entry includes a one-year subscription. Send SASE for details. The editor says, "We are a unique magazine. Reading a sample copy could be very helpful to submitting poets. We are eclectic but especially interested in formal poetry, West Coast and other marginalized writers, wit, and a flair for the vernacular. We encourage real world referents, especially to the natural, personal, sensual and political worlds."

MODERN BRIDE (IV-Love/romance), 249 W. 17th St., New York NY 10011, phone (212)337-7000, executive editor Mary Ann Cavlin, a slick bimonthly, occasionally buys **poetry pertaining to love and marriage. Pays $30-40 for average short poem.**

MODERN HAIKU; FOUR HIGH SCHOOL SENIOR SCHOLARSHIPS (IV-Form, students), P.O. Box 1752, Madison WI 53701-1752, phone (608)233-2738, founded 1969, poetry editor Robert Spiess, "is the foremost international journal of English language haiku and criticism. We are devoted to publishing only the very best haiku being written and also publish articles on haiku and have the most complete review section of haiku books. Issues average over 100 pages." **They want "contemporary haiku in English (including translations into English) that incorporate the traditional aesthetics of the haiku genre, but which may be innovative as to subject matter, mode of approach or angle of perception, and form of expression. Haiku only. No tanka or other forms."** They have recently published haiku by Wally Swist, Phyllis Walsh, Cor van den Heuvel and Michael Dylan Welch. As a sample the editor selected this haiku (poet unidentified):

> muttering thunder—
>   the bottom of the river
>   scattered with clams

The digest-sized magazine appears 3 times a year, printed on heavy quality stock with cover illustrations especially painted for each issue by the staff artist. They receive 12,000-14,000 submissions/year, use 800. There are over 260 poems in each issue. Circulation 650. Subscription: $16.25. **Sample postpaid: $5.50. Submit on "any size sheets, any number of haiku on a sheet; but name and address on each sheet." Include SASE. No previously published haiku or simultaneous submissions. Send SASE for guidelines. Reports in 2 weeks. Pays $1/haiku (but no contributor's copy). Buys first North American serial rights.** Staff reviews books of haiku in 350-1,000 words, single format. Send books for review consideration. They offer four annual scholarships for the best haiku by high school seniors. Scholarships range from $200-500 (total $1,400). Deadline is in early March. Send SASE for rules. The editor says, "Haiku achieve their effect of felt-depth, insight and intuition through juxtaposition of perceived entities, not through intellective comment or abstract words."

‡MODERN WORDS (IV-Gay/lesbian), 350 Bay St., #100, Box 325, San Francisco CA 94133, press founded 1984, journal 1994, editor/publisher Garland Richard Kyle. *Modern Words*, "a thoroughly queer international literary journal," appears twice a year. **"*Modern Words* is eclectic and no specific theme or style is required. While submissions do not have to be homosexual-themed, work should be original and reflect the diversity of our voices. Non-American-born writers and international-themed work is especially encouraged."** They have recently published poetry by Gavin Geoffrey Dillard, Blaine Marchand, Gerry Gomez Pearlberg and Jules Mann. As a sample we selected these lines from "Moribundo" by Michael Gregg Michaud:

> Daisies maybe. Some irises.
> But I decide no. He was a rodeo cowboy.
> He never liked flowers anyway. And
> he'll think something is wrong.
> His eyes shut.
> Again and again.
> And they will again
> until they stay.

Modern Words is about 110 pgs., 4½ × 7, professionally printed and perfect-bound with 2-color coated card cover with b&w photo and b&w photos of the authors inside. They receive 500-1,000 poems a year, use less than 10%. Press run is 1,000 for 100 subscribers of which 6 are libraries, 25-50% shelf sales. Subscription: $25 for 3 issues, $100 for lifetime. **Sample postpaid: $10. Submit no more than 10 pgs. of poetry at a time. No previously published poems; simultaneous submissions OK. Cover letter preferred. Seldom comments on rejections. Send SASE for guidelines. Reports "promptly." Always sends prepublication galleys. Pays 2 copies. Acquires first serial rights.**

THE CHAPBOOK INDEX, located before the Geographical Index, lists those publishers who consider chapbook manuscripts. A chapbook, a small volume of work, is often a good middle step between magazine and book publication.

MOKSHA JOURNAL; VAJRA PRINTING & PUBLISHING OF YOGA ANAND ASHRAM (IV-Spiritual), 49 Forrest Pl., Amityville NY 11701-3307, phone/fax (516)691-8475, founded 1984, is a "small press publisher of **spiritual and/or philosophical literature, nonfiction and poetry pertaining to the concept of 'Moksha,'** defined by Monier-Williams as a 'liberation, release' (A Sanskrit-English Dictionary, 1899). **Perspectives include, but are not limited to: Yoga, various schools of Buddhism, Sufism, Mystical Christianity, etc.**" *Moksha Journal* appears twice a year, regularly using poetry, and is 50-70 pgs., 5¼×8¼, offset, litho. Press run is 400-500 for that many subscribers. Subscription: $8. **Sample: $4. Submit up to 5 poems at a time. Simultaneous and fax submissions OK. Reports in 4-6 weeks. Pays 2 copies.** The press publishes perfect-bound paperbacks, including *Ways of Yoga* and *Rtu* by Gurani Anjali. Yoga Anand Ashram is a not-for-profit organization "dedicated singularly to community education through each person's realization of the highest goal of human existence as realized through the practice of Yoga."

‡**THE MOODY STREET REVIEW (II)**, 205 E. 78th St., Apt. 19L, New York NY 10021, founded 1988, editor David Gibson, appears once annually, publishes **"poetry of literary type, with strong sensory/concrete imagery and metaphorical meaning(s). I don't appreciate the work of naive poets, who are not familiar with the poetic traditions of the 20th century, i.e., symbolism, imagism, objectivism, projective verse, beat generation, etc."** They have published poetry by Arthur Winfield Knight, Joy Walsh and George Bowering, and translations of Nicanor Parra, Raymond Radiguet and Federico Garcia Lorca. As a sample the editor selected these lines by Jane Hohenberger:

> A person has a heart in pieces
> not three whole hearts like an octopus, only one
> red fist beats in the birdcage of this body
> maybe where the breath goes
> The small heart is not decoration
> and when he took it from her zoo
> to wear as an earring
> She fell like steam rising
> came down like rain
> she came down tiny like steam rising
> to rain.

The editor says *MSR* is typically 50-70 pgs., 8½×11, photocopied with a hand-printed cover, with b&w artwork in drawings, linoleum prints and photographs. They receive 100 submissions of poetry/month, "publish no more than 10-15% of all material received. **I like to get an overview of a poet's work, so send at least a half-dozen poems. All submissions shall be answered in 6 months' time. All bets are off after that date. If curious, query for immediate response."** Pays 2 copies, more at a 30% discount. **Acquires one-time rights.** The editor says, "My advice to submittors is just to send their work. I'll know if I do or don't like it right away. They don't have to query for samples or guidelines. The work stands for itself. I would like to receive more work from American authors living abroad, of their poetry and experiences (journals) in places as varied as France, Latin America, Africa and Germany."

‡**MOOSE BOUND PRESS (I)**, P.O. Box 111781, Anchorage AK 99511-1781, founded 1995, editor Sonia Walker, publisher Robert L. Walker, publishes a quarterly journal which appears under various titles. "We provide positive and energetic poetry, short stories and essays; and promote creative writing, literacy and family reading. Our reading audience includes elementary school children to senior citizens. Therefore, we ask that material sent be something **the entire family can enjoy reading. Our tastes are general and eclectic**." They have recently published poetry by Lyn Lifshin, Michael Lizza, C. David Hay and Diana Kwiatkowski Rubin. As a sample they selected these lines from "Winter Jazz" by Patrick Flavin:

> Winter
> idly waiting
> strums cattails, taps milkweed
> pods, blows trumpeting white snow dunes—
> the blues

The journal we received, entitled *The Snowy Trail*, was 147 pgs., 8½×11, spiral-bound with b&w clip art, photos and drawings inside. Press run is 500 for 100 subscribers of which 20 are libraries, 200 shelf sales. Subscription: $24/year. **Sample postpaid: $8. Make checks payable to Sonia Walker. Submit 5 poems at a time, no more than 30 lines each, 1 poem to a page. Previously published poems and simultaneous submissions OK. Cover letter preferred.** Time between acceptance and publication is 3-6 months. **Often comments on rejections. Publishes theme issues. Send SASE for guidelines and upcoming themes. Reports in 2-4 weeks. "No payment other than publication." Acquires one-time rights.** Sponsors an Editor's Choice Award. They also publish a quarterly newsletter which contains poetry, general interest articles and announcements of themes for future editions of their quarterly journals. The newsletter is included with the cost of an annual subscription. The editor says, "Moose Bound Press encourages and is receptive to new writers of all ages. Do not be afraid of rejection—MBP believes there is a poem or story that wants to be shared and enjoyed by the reading world."

WILLIAM MORROW AND CO. (V), 1350 Avenue of the Americas, New York NY 10019, phone (212)261-6500, publishes poetry on standard royalty contracts **but accepts no unsolicited mss. Queries with samples should be submitted through an agent.**

(m)ÖTHÊR TØÑGUÉ PRESS (I, II), 290 Fulford-Ganges Rd., Salt Spring Island, British Columbia V8K 2K6 Canada, founded 1990, editor/publisher Mona Fertig, holds an annual poetry chapbook contest for the best international ms of poetry and the best Canadian ms of poetry. For each category, the winner receives $300 plus publication of a "beautiful limited edition chapbook." **Send 15 pgs. of unpublished poetry with short bio and $20 entry fee. SASE (or SAE with IRCs) must be included. Mss will not be returned. Send SASE (or SAE with IRCs) for details. Deadline: November 30.** Past winners are Elizabeth Biller of California and Shannon Bailey of British Columbia, Canada.

MOVING PARTS PRESS (V), 10699 Empire Grade, Santa Cruz CA 95060-9474, phone (408)427-2271, fax (408)458-2810, founded 1977. Poetry editor Felicia Rice says they are a "fine arts literary publisher using letterpress printing and printmaking to produce handsome and innovative books, broadsides and prints in limited editions." Moving Parts has recently published books of poetry by Francisco X. Alarcón, Elba Rosario Sánchez, Nathaniel Mackey and Henri Michaux. As a sample here are the opening lines of "On a Darkening Road" by Robert Lundquist from *Before-the-Rain*:

> This evening the tide is low,
> Ducks walk through bunched beds of kelp
> Looking for insects.

They do not accept unsolicited mss. Pay 10% of the edition in copies. The book *De Amor Oscuro/ Of Dark Love* received one of 18 international design awards from among the "600 Best Designed Books in the World" exhibit mounted by Stiftung Buchkunst at the Leipzig Book Fair.

‡THE MPF MUSE LETTER; MISSOURI POETS AND FRIENDS (I, IV-MEMBERSHIP/ SUBSCRIPTION), P.O. Box 2701, Springfield MO 65801-2701, organization founded 1986, publication founded 1988, editor James C. Stone. *The MPF Muse Letter* appears bimonthly and is "a working poet's newsletter with articles on the art and craft of poetry, publishing contacts and contests—and poetry just for the joy of it." **They want any form or style of poetry, preferrably 32 lines or less. "I love beautiful language that sings, concrete images, and ideas pregnant with possibility. No porn or tacky language. I detest sexist/racist crap and prefer not to see sentimentalist, sermonizing, or political poetry unless with a twist, satire or irony."** They have recently published poetry by Dorothy Brown, Tom Padgett, Wanda Sue Parrott and Lee Ann Russell. As a sample the editor selected these lines from his own poem "At The Beach: The Spider Approaches":

> Back home she is staring at the carpet
>   as though some loved one
>   is buried beneath the floorboards
> And it is silent
>   save for the sounds of unforgiveness.

MPF is 16-20 pgs., 5½×8½, photocopied and saddle-stapled with paper cover. They receive about 50 poems a year, use approximately 90%. Press run is 100 for 51 subscribers. Subscription: $6. **Sample postpaid: $1. Make checks payable to Missouri Poets and Friends. "Subscribers and members of Missouri Poets and Friends are, by necessity, first choice; nonsubscribers will still have about a 30% chance of being accepted." Submit 3 poems at a time. Previously published poems OK; no simultaneous submissions. Cover letter preferred. Often comments on rejections. Send SASE for guidelines. Reports in about 1 month. Pays 1 copy/poem. Acquires first or one-time rights.** Sponsors a bimonthly contest for members/subscribers only. Entry fee: $1 for up to 2 poems. Contest guidelines listed in the journal. They also publish an annual anthology for members. Members of Missouri Poets and Friends are automatically members of the National Federation of State Poetry Societies, Inc. The editor says, "Be concrete—even abstract poetry needs solid images (visual, smell, sensual). Be strange or weird—say something new and exciting. Be childlike—honest, truthful, even if it's not my truth, make it yours."

MS. MAGAZINE (V), 230 Park Ave., 7th Floor, New York NY 10169, founded 1972, is a bimonthly "feminist source of national and international news, politics, arts, scholarship and book reviews." **They are currently not accepting unsolicited poetry.** They have published poetry by Alice Walker, Maya Angelou and May Swenson. Circulation is 150,000. Single copy: $5.95 (available on newsstands); subscription: $30. They say, "Due to the volume of the material received, we cannot accept, acknowledge or return unsolicited poetry or fiction. We cannot discuss queries on the phone and cannot be held responsible for manuscripts sent to us."

MUDDY RIVER POETRY REVIEW (I, II), 89 Longwood Ave., Brookline MA 02146, phone (617)277-5667, founded 1995, editor Zvi A. Sesling, associate editors Michael D. Sesling and Lawrence Spiegel, is a semiannual poetry publication seeking a broad range of subjects and styles. **They prefer free verse, one page in length.** "No inspirational verse. No pornography or explicit sexual content. Rhyming poetry only if exceptional." They have recently published poetry by Sam Cornish, Taylor Graham and Jean Hull Herman. They prefer not to provide a sample "so poets are not influenced, misled or intimidated." The editor says *MRPR* is 48-60 pgs., stapled. They receive about 500 poems an issue, accept 10-20%. Subscription: $10/year, $18/2 years. **Sample: $5. No previously published poems; simultaneous submissions OK, if indicated. Cover letter with bio required. Reads submissions February 15 through May 15 and September 15 through November 15. Often comments on rejections. Send SASE for guidelines. Reports in 1 month. Pays 1 copy (20% discount on additionals). Acquires first rights.** The editor says, "First-timers, don't be afraid to submit. Rejection only reflects what the editor is looking for, not your talent!"

MUDFISH; BOX TURTLE PRESS (I, II), 184 Franklin St., New York NY 10013, phone (212)219-9278, founded 1983, editor Jill Hoffman. *Mudfish*, published by Box Turtle Press, is a journal of poetry and art that appears once a year and is looking for **free verse with "energy, intensity, and originality of voice, mastery of style, the presence of passion."** They have recently published poetry by Charles Simic, Jennifer Belle, Hal Sirowitz, Doug Dorph and John Ashbery. As a sample the editor selected these lines from "Quince" by Shannon Hamann:

> When you're God, eternity is already over,
> but at the Cloisters, Jenny gives me
> a quince she plucked from a tree in the courtyard,
> her eyes like eightballs, eyes
> that could heat Russia, shining with the mischief
> of every woman who ever offered a boy fruit . . .

Press run is 1,200. **Sample copies are available for $10 plus $2.50 shipping and handling. Submit 4-6 poems at a time. They will not consider simultaneous submissions or previously published poems. Reports from "immediately to 3 months." Sends prepublication galleys. Pays 1 copy.** Sponsors the Mudfish Poetry Prize Award: $500. Submit up to 3 poems for $10, $2 for each additional poem. Deadline: November 12. Write for further guidelines.

‡MURDEROUS INTENT (IV-Mystery), Madison Publishing Company, P.O. Box 5947, Vancouver WA 98668-5947, phone (360)695-9004, fax (360)693-3354, e-mail madison@teleport.com, website http://www.teleport.com/~madison, founded 1994, editor Margo Power, is a quarterly magazine of mystery and suspense which uses mystery-related poetry, limericks and such as fillers. **The editor says all poetry (including humorous verse) must be mystery-related and must easily entertain. They do not want poetry with "deep, convoluted meaning" and the shorter the work, the better. "Four-liners are always good though we occasionally buy a longer, ballad-type poem—always mystery-related."** The editor says *Murderous Intent* is 64 pgs., 8½×11, saddle-stapled, with 2-color cover and b&w interior including art, graphics and ads. Press run is 4,500; 15% subscribers, 85% shelf sales. Single copy: $5; subscription: $18. **Sample postpaid: $6.24. Make checks payable to Madison Publishing Company. Submit 6-10 poems at a time. Previously published poems and simultaneous submissions OK. Cover letter preferred.** "If accepted, we would like poetry sent on a 3.5 disk." Time between acceptance and publication can be 1-2 years, "usually less." **Seldom comments on rejections. Reports in 2-3 months. Sometimes sends prepublication galleys. Pays $2 and 1 copy. Buys first or one-time rights.**

‡MUSE OF FIRE (I, II), 21 Kruse Rd., Port Angeles WA 98362-8900, founded 1996, editor/publisher Tim Scannell, is a bimonthly newsletter. **"All forms welcome: lyric, fixed form, humor. No taboos. Craftsmanship is the only requirement."** *Muse Of Fire* is 6 pgs., 8½×11, unbound with b&w clip art. Press run is 50. Single copy: $1; subscription: $3/year. **Sample available for #10 SASE. Previously published poems and simultaneous submissions OK. Cover letter required. Seldom comments on rejections. Send SASE for guidelines. Reports in 1 week. Pays 1 copy. Acquires one-time rights.** The editor says, "There are nine musae and so nine grand areas for poetry. Write in all nine areas, in every traditional and untraditional form! And, remember, words become a poem only after eight to twelve revisions."

MUSE PORTFOLIO (II), 25 Tannery Rd., Unit Box 8, Westfield MA 01085-4800, founded 1992, editor Haemi Balgassi, appears 2-4 times a year. *Muse Portfolio* is a "casual magazine for sincere, eloquent, earnest writers who crave forum to share work with others." **They want poetry of "any structure, formal or free, 50 lines maximum. Poetry with writing themes welcome. No forced rhymes, nothing profane.** We also publish short stories and nonfiction, as well as cartoons and art sketches." They have recently published poetry by Frederick Moe and Addie Lacoe. As a sample the editor selected these lines from "Portrait of the Mother" by Mary Rudbeck Stanko:

> *Out of the dark canvas of her smile*
> *flows fisherman's lace,*
> *a hairnet for a weary lady*
> *draped*
> *in gracious folds about her stateliness*

Muse Portfolio is 40 pgs., 5½ × 8½, saddle-stapled, printed on 20 lb. paper with heavier stock cover, b&w artwork, occasional ads. They receive about 300 poems/year, accept 5%. Press run is 150 for 100 subscribers. Subscription: $5. **Sample postpaid: $2.50. Submit up to 3 poems at a time. Previously published poems and simultaneous submissions OK. Cover letter required. "Include a biographical paragraph—need not list published credits if author prefers to write something else." Seldom comments on rejections. Send SASE for guidelines. Reports in 3-4 months. Pays 1 copy. Acquires one-time rights.** The editor says, "Please remember to include a SASE with submissions."

MUSICWORKS (IV-Themes), 179 Richmond St. W., Toronto, Ontario M5V 1V3 Canada, phone (416)977-3546, founded 1978, editor Gayle Young, is a triannual journal of contemporary music. The editor says, **"The poetry we publish only relates directly to the topics discussed in the magazine or relates to contemporary sound poetry—*usually* it is poetry written by the (music) composer or performers we are featuring."** Poets published include bpnichol, Colin Morton and Jackson Mac Low. The magazine is 64 pgs., 8½ × 11, with b&w visuals, b&w photography, some illustrative graphics and scores and accompanied by 60-minute cassette. Circulation is 1,600, of which 500 are subscriptions. Price is $5/issue or $11 for the magazine plus CD. **Sample postpaid: $15 for magazine and CD. Considers simultaneous submissions. They report on submissions within 2 months, and there is no backlog before publication. The magazine pays Canadian contributors variable rate.**

THE MUSING PLACE (IV-Specialized: poets with a history of mental illness), 2700 N. Lakeview, Chicago IL 60614, phone (312)281-3800 ext. 2465, fax (312)281-8790, founded 1986, editor Linda Krinsky, is a biannual magazine **"written and published by people with a history of mental illness. All kinds and forms of poetry are welcome."** As a sample the editor selected these lines from "Why Must I Be Poor?" by Gracian Vital:

> *Wrapped in elegance,*
> *I was born*
> *Queenly to behold*
> *But when you see my*
> *Pocketbook*
> *I fold.*

The editor says *The Musing Place* is 32 pgs., 8½ × 11, typeset and stapled with art also produced by people with a history of mental illness. They receive about 100 poems/year, publish about 40. Press run is 1,000. Single copy: $2. **No previously published poems; simultaneous submissions OK. Cover letter required. "Poets must prove and explain their history of mental illness."** Time between acceptance and publication is 6 months to 1 year. **"The board reviews submissions and chooses those that fit into each issue of the publication. All submissions are kept for possible publication in future issues." Seldom comments on rejections. Reports within 6 months. Pays "negotiable" number of contributor's copies.**

MY LEGACY (I); OMNIFIC (I); FELICITY (I, IV-Themes); THE BOTTOM LINE, HC-13, Box 21-AA, Artemas PA 17211-9405, phone (814)458-3102, editor/publisher Kay Weems. *My Legacy* is a quarterly of poetry and short stories using **36-line, sometimes longer, poems, "anything in good taste" with an Editor's Choice small cash award for each issue. No contributor copies.** Subscription: $12/year; $3.50/copy. *Omnific*, a **"family-type" quarterly publishes poetry only, 36 lines, sometimes longer; readers vote on favorites, small cash award or copy to favorites. Send SASE for guidelines. No contributor copies.** Subscription: $16/year; $3.50/copy. *Felicity,* founded 1988, is a bimonthly newsletter for contests only, 30-40 pgs. They offer 10 contests/flyer including a bimonthly theme contest, 36 lines. Other contests may be for theme, form, chapbook, etc. Entry fees vary. Send SASE for guidelines and upcoming themes. Payment for contest winners is small cash award and/or publication. No work is returned. They consider simultaneous submissions and previously published poems. All winning entries including honorable mentions are printed in the newsletter which also publishes market and other contest listings. Subscription: $16/year; $2.50/copy. She also publishes an annual **Christmas anthology. Poetry only, published/unpublished, 36 lines maximum, Christmas themes. Address to "Christmas Anthology." Deadline: August 31.** *The Bottom Line,* founded 1988, is a monthly newsletter listing over 50 publications and contests for writers, reproducing guidelines of still others. Information is presented in chronological order by deadline date, and then in alphabetical order. Circulation 200-300. Subscription: $21/year; $2.50/copy.

MYSTERY TIME (I, IV-Mystery); RHYME TIME (IV-Subscribers), P.O. Box 2907, Decatur IL 62524, poetry editor Linda Hutton, founded 1983, is a semiannual containing 3-4 pages of **humorous**

poems about mysteries and mystery writers in each issue. As a sample the editor selected the poem "Gut Instinct" by Jessica J. Frasca:

> *"Great Scot!" declared Holmes with a look of surprise.*
> *"It's the cook's fault he's dead?" Disbelief in his eyes.*
> *Watson's head nodded, the cook turned and fled.*
> *"Alimentary, my dear Holmes," was all that he said.*

Mystery Time is 44 pgs., digest-sized, stapled with heavy stock cover. They receive up to 15 submissions a year, use 4-6. Circulation 100. **Sample: $4. Submit 3 poems at a time, "typed in proper format with SASE." Previously published poems OK. Does not read mss in December. Guidelines available for #10 SASE. Pays $5 on acceptance.** Hutton's other publication, *Rhyme Time*, is a quarterly newsletter **publishing only the work of subscribers. No length limit or style restriction.** Subscription: $24. **Sample: $4.** Cash prize of $5 awarded to the best poem in each issue. She also sponsors an annual poetry contest that awards a $10 cash prize for the best poem in any style or length. Submit typed poem with SASE. No entry fee; one entry/person. Deadline: November 1.

THE MYTHIC CIRCLE; THE MYTHOPOEIC SOCIETY (II, IV-Fantasy), P.O. Box 6707, Altadena CA 91001, editor Tina Cooper. *The Mythic Circle* is a "writer's workshop in print," appearing 2-3 times a year, publishing fantasy short stories and poems. **They want "poetry, particularly traditional poetry, with a mythic or fairy-tale theme."** They have published poetry by Angelee Anderson and Gwyneth Hood. They receive approximately 100 poetry submissions/year, accept 10%. Press run is 230 for 200 subscribers. Subscription: $18/year for non-members of sponsoring organization, The Mythopoeic Society; $13/year for members. **Sample postpaid: $6.50. No previously published poems or simultaneous submissions.** Time between acceptance and publication is 2 years. **Seldom comments on rejections. Send SASE for guidelines. Reports in 2-4 months. Pays 1 copy for 3 poems.** The editor says, "Subscribers are heavily favored, since they provide the critical review which our authors need in their letters of comment."

NADA PRESS; BIG SCREAM (II, IV-Form/style), 2782 Dixie SW, Grandville MI 49418, phone (616)531-1442, founded 1974, poetry editor David Cope. *Big Scream* appears annually and is **"a brief anthology of mostly 'unknown' poets. We are promoting a continuation of objectivist tradition begun by Williams and Reznikoff. We want objectivist-based short works; some surrealism; basically short, tight work that shows clarity of perception and care in its making."** They have published poetry by Antler, Richard Kostelanetz, Andy Clausen, Allen Ginsberg, John Steinbeck, Jr., Jim Cohn and Marcia Arrieta. *Big Scream* is 35 pgs., magazine-sized, xerograph on 60 lb. paper, side-stapled, "sent gratis to a select group of poets and editors." They receive "several hundred (not sure)" unsolicited submissions/year, use "very few." Press run is 100. Subscription to institutions: $6/year. **Sample postpaid: $6. Submit after July. Send 10 pgs. No cover letter. "If poetry interests me, I will ask the proper questions of the poet." Simultaneous submissions OK. Comments on rejections "if requested and ms warrants it." Reports in 1-14 days. Sometimes sends prepublication galleys. Pays as many copies as requested, within reason.** The editor advises: "Read Pound's essay, 'A Retrospect,' then Reznikoff and Williams; follow through the Beats and NY School, especially Denby & Berrigan, and you have our approach to writing well in hand. I expect to be publishing *BS* regularly 10 years from now, same basic format."

NASSAU REVIEW (III), English Dept., Nassau Community College, Garden City NY 11530-6793, phone (516)572-7792, founded 1964, managing editor Dr. Paul A. Doyle, is an annual "creative and research vehicle for Nassau College faculty and the faculty of other colleges." **They want "serious, intellectual poetry of any form or style. No light verse or satiric verse." Submissions from adults only. "No college students; graduate students acceptable."** They have published poetry by Patti Tana, Dick Allen, Louis Phillips, David Heyen and Simon Perchik. As a sample the editor selected these lines from "Chekhov, For Beginners" by Barbara Novack:

> *Chekhov said*
> *throw out the first three pages;*
> *it takes that long*
> *to get to the beginning.*
>
> *And I may say*
> *put aside the first three decades*
> *sweep away their debris*
> *cast off versions of the self . . .*

NR is about 150 pgs., digest-sized, flat-spined. They receive 700-800 poems/year, use approximately 20-25. Press run is 1,200 for about 1,200 subscribers of which 600 are libraries. **Sample free. Submit only 3 poems at a time. No previously published poems or simultaneous submissions. Reads submissions October 1 through March 1 only. Reports in 3-6 months. Pays copies.** They sponsor occasional contests with $100 or $200 poetry awards, depending on college funding. Well-edited and visually appealing, *Nassau Review* tends to publish free verse emphasizing voice in well-crafted lyric and narrative forms. The editor says, "Each year we are more and more overwhelmed by the number of poems submitted, but many are of an amateur quality."

THE NATION; "DISCOVERY"/THE NATION POETRY CONTEST (III), 72 Fifth Ave., New York NY 10011, founded 1865, poetry editor Grace Schulman. *The Nation*'s **only requirement for poetry is "excellence,"** which can be inferred from the list of poets they have published: Marianne Moore, Robert Lowell, W.S. Merwin, Maxine Kumin, Donald Justice, James Merrill, Richard Howard, May Swenson, Amy Clampitt, Edward Hirsch and Charles Simic. The editor chose this sample from a poem in *The Nation*, 1939, by W.B. Yeats:

> Like a long-legged fly upon the stream
> His mind moves upon silence.

Pay for poetry is $1/line, not to exceed 35 lines, plus 1 copy. The magazine co-sponsors the Lenore Marshall Prize for Poetry which is an annual award of $10,000 for the outstanding book of poems published in the US in each year. For details, write to the Academy of American Poets, 584 Broadway, #1208, New York NY 10012. They also co-sponsor the "Discovery"/*The Nation* Poetry Contest ($200 each plus a reading at The Poetry Center, 1395 Lexington Ave., New York NY 10128. Deadline: mid-February. Send SASE for application). Poetry published in *The Nation* has been included in the 1993 and 1995 volumes of *The Best American Poetry*.

NATIONAL ENQUIRER (II, IV-Humor), Lantana FL 33464, filler editor Kathy Martin, is a weekly tabloid which uses **short poems, most of them humorous and traditional rhyming verse. "We want poetry with a message or reflection on the human condition or everyday life. Avoid sending obscure or 'arty' poetry or poetry for art's sake. Also looking for philosophical and inspirational material. Submit seasonal/holiday material at least 3 months in advance. No poetry over 8 lines will be accepted."** Submit 1-5 poems at a time. Requires cover letter from first-time submitters; include name, address, social security and phone numbers. **"Do not send SASE; filler material will not be returned."** Pays $25 after publication; original material only. Buys first rights.

NATIONAL FORUM: THE PHI KAPPA PHI JOURNAL (III), 129 Quad Center, Mell St., Auburn University AL 36849-5306, phone (334)844-5200, founded 1915, editor James P. Kaetz, is the quarterly of Phi Kappa Phi using **quality poetry.** As a sample the editor selected these lines from "Visiting Hours" by Molly Tamarkin:

> The rip of rip-stop nylon against barbed wire,
> the flash of headlights, and the drifting snow
> suggest it's time. The faint light casts shadows
> with the wintry air of permanence,
> and the fisherman, packing up his tackle,
> appears grossly overshadowed by a cottonwood.

NF is 48 pgs., magazine-sized, professionally printed, saddle-stapled, with full-color paper cover and two-color interior. They publish about 20 poems of 300 received a year. Their press run is 120,000 with 117,000 subscriptions of which 300 are libraries. Subscription: $25. **Submit 3-5 poems at a time, including a biographical sketch with recent publications. Reads submissions approximately every 3 months. Reports about 4 months after submission. Pays 10 copies.**

NATURALLY: NUDE RECREATION FOR ALL AGES; EVENTS UNLIMITED PUBLISHING CO. (IV-Specialized), P.O. Box 317, Newfoundland NJ 07435-0317, phone/fax (201)697-8313, website www.tiac.net/users/acon/evl.html, founded 1981, editor/publisher Bern Loibl. *Naturally* is a quarterly magazine devoted to family nudism and naturism. **They want poetry about the naturalness of the human body and nature, any length.** As a sample the editor selected these lines by Bill Beattie:

> The churches call it "sinful" but their
>   logic's kind of odd,
> Since the Bible says that we were made
>   the image of our God.
> The Pagans called it "skyclad" and the
>   hippies "being free";
> If I had to call it anything,
>   I'd call it being . . . me.

Naturally is 48 pgs., 8½ × 11, printed on glossy paper and saddle-stitched with b&w and full-color photos throughout. They receive about 30 poems a year, use 5-10. Press run is 13,000 for 5,500 subscribers, 6,500 shelf sales. Single copy: $5.95; subscription: $19.95. **Sample postpaid: $6.95. Previously published poems and simultaneous submissions OK. Often comments on rejections. Reports in 2 months. Pay is negotiable. Buys first North American serial or one-time rights.**

NAZARENE INTERNATIONAL HEADQUARTERS; STANDARD; LISTEN; BREAD; TEENS TODAY; HERALD OF HOLINESS (IV-Religious, children), 6401 The Paseo, Kansas City MO 64131, phone (816)333-7000. Each of the magazines published by the Nazarenes has a separate editor, focus and audience. *Standard*, circulation 177,000, is a weekly **inspirational "story paper" with Christian leisure reading for adults. Send SASE for free sample and guidelines. Uses a poem each week. Submit maximum of 5 poems, no more than 50 lines each. Pays 25¢ a line.** For *Listen, Bread, Teens Today* and *Herald of Holiness*, write individually for guidelines and samples.

NEBO: A LITERARY JOURNAL (II), English Dept., Arkansas Tech University, Russellville AR 72801-2222, phone (501)968-0256, founded 1982, poetry editor Michael Ritchie, appears in May and December. Regarding poetry they say, **"We accept all kinds, all styles, all subject matters and will publish a longer poem if it is outstanding. We are especially interested in formal poetry."** They have published poetry by Jack Butler, Turner Cassity, Wyatt Prunty, Charles Martin, Julia Randall and Brenda Hillman. *Nebo* is 50-70 pgs., digest-sized, professionally printed on quality matte stock with matte card cover. Press run "varies." **Sample postpaid: $6. Submit 3-5 poems at a time. Simultaneous submissions OK. "Please no offbeat colors." Cover letter with bio material and recent publications required. Do not submit mss between May 1 and August 15. Editor comments on rejections "if the work has merit but requires revision and resubmission; we do all we can to help." Reports at the end of November and February respectively. Pays 1 copy.** Staff reviews books of poetry. Send books for review consideration.

THE NEBRASKA REVIEW; TNR AWARDS (II), Creative Writing Program, ASH 212, University of Nebraska, Omaha NE 68182-0324, phone (402)554-2771, fax (402)554-3436, e-mail aizenberg @fa-cpacs.unomaha.edu, founded 1973, co-editor Art Homer, poetry editor Susan Aizenberg, is a semiannual literary magazine publishing fiction and poetry with occasional essays. The editors want **"lyric poetry from 10-200 lines, preference being for under 100 lines. Subject matter is unimportant, as long as it has some. Poets should have mastered form, meaning poems should have form, not simply 'demonstrate' it."** They don't want to see **"concrete, inspirational, didactic or merely political poetry."** They have recently published poetry by Erin Belieu, Michael Bugeja, Stuart Dybek and Roger Weingarten. As a sample, they selected these lines from "Crickets" by Pamela Stewart:

> *In every small place the eye, toe, or caught breath turns,*
> *crickets are singing. From that shin*
> *just above the ground they fling an edge of sound*
> *straight through what's left of wilderness.*
> *It swings out across the trees and yards,*
> *up to the warm sills of September.*

The magazine is 6×9, nicely printed, 60 pgs., with flat-spined, glossy card cover. It is a publication of the Writer's Workshop at the University of Nebraska. Some of the most exciting, accessible verse is published in this magazine. All styles and forms are welcome here, although relatively few long poems are used. Circulation is 500, of which 380 are subscriptions and 85 go to libraries. Single copy: $5; subscription: $9.50/year. **Sample postpaid: $3.50. Submit 4-6 poems at a time. "Clean typed copy strongly preferred." Reads open submissions January 1 through April 15 only. Reports in 3-4 months.** Time between acceptance and publication is 3-6 months. **Pays 2 copies and 1-year subscription. Acquires first North American serial rights.** Submissions for The Nebraska Review Awards are read from September 1 through November 30. The TNR Awards of $500 each in poetry and fiction are published in the spring issue. Entry fee: $9, includes discounted subscription. You can enter as many times as desired. Deadline: November 30. The editor says, "Your first allegiance is to the poem. Publishing will come in time, but it will always be less than you feel you deserve. Therefore, don't look to publication as a reward for writing well; it has no relationship."

NEDGE (II), P.O. Box 2321, Providence RI 02906, founded 1969, editor Henry Gould, is a biannual published by The Poetry Mission, a nonprofit arts organization. It includes poetry, fiction, reviews and essays. **They want work that "exhibits originality, talent, sincerity, skill and inspiration."** As a sample the editor selected these lines from "Library Termites" by Pete Lee:

> *the workers*
> *devour Marx*
> *and Steinbeck*
> *swarm over*
> *Upton Sinclair*

The purpose of *Nedge* is "to aim toward a Rhode Island literary standard, both local and international in scope." Circulation is 300. **Sample postpaid: $5. No simultaneous submissions. SASE required. Reports in 2-5 months. Pays 1 copy.**

NEGATIVE CAPABILITY; NEGATIVE CAPABILITY PRESS; EVE OF ST. AGNES COMPETITION (III), 62 Ridgelawn Dr. E., Mobile AL 36608-2465, fax (334)344-8478, founded 1981, poetry editor Sue Walker. *Negative Capability* is a tri-quarterly of verse, fiction, commentary, music and art. The press publishes broadsides, chapbooks, perfect-bound paperbacks and hardbacks. They want **both contemporary and traditional poetry. "Quality has its own specifications—length and form."** They have published poetry by John Brugaletta, Marge Piercy, John Updike, Carolyn Page, Vivian Shipley and Diana Der Hovanessian. As a sample Sue Walker selected these lines from "First Blood" by Jack Coulehan:

> *Your old wound has opened up*
> *again—children holding on*
> *and letting go, the ghosts*
> *of parents, both the dead*
> *and nearly dead, the pricks*
> *of being close to fifty—*
> *no wonder you sit keening*
> *on the bed, almost empty.*

The editor says, "Reaching irritably after a few facts will not describe *Negative Capability.* Read it to know what quality goes to form creative achievement. Shakespeare had negative capability, do you?" In its short history this journal has indeed achieved a major prominence on our literary scene. It is an elegantly printed, flat-spined, digest-sized format of 200 pgs., glossy card color cover with art, circulation 1,000. About 60 pgs. of each issue are devoted to poetry. They receive about 1,200 unsolicited submissions/year, use 350. Single copy: $5; subscription: $15. **Sample postpaid: $4. Submit 3-5 poems at a time. Reads submissions September 1 through May 30 only. Send SASE for guidelines and upcoming themes. Reports in 6-8 weeks. Pays 1 copy. Acquires first rights.** Reviews books of poetry. Negative Capability Press has recently published *Little Dragons*, by Michael Bugeja and *The Mouse Whole*, by Richard Moore. **For book publication, query with 10-12 samples and "brief letter with major publications, significant contributions, awards. We like to know a person as well as their poem." Replies to queries in 3-4 weeks, to submissions (if invited) in 6-8 weeks. Payment arranged with authors. Editor sometimes comments on rejections.** They offer an annual Eve of St. Agnes Competition with major poets as judges. Send SASE for details. The editor says, "Poets should keep abreast of current books, know who the contemporary poets are and learn from them. Reading stimulates the muse."

NERVE (I, II), P.O. Box 124578, San Diego CA 92112-4578, founded 1994, editor/publisher Geoffrey N.T. Young, appears 3 times a year. "We publish about 10 poems per issue along with a couple short stories." **They are "open to anything that is well-crafted. No poem will be rejected on the basis of form alone—all styles welcome." However, they do not want to see "Hallmark greeting card type verse."** They have recently published poetry by Errol Miller, John Grey, Pete Lee and Michael Estabrook. As a sample they selected these lines from "In This House" by Charles G. Lauder, Jr.:

> *The floorboards creak as if they were as pregnant as you*
> *or as you wish to be swelling with memories*
> *like a trunk burgeoning between its thirtieth and thirty-first year*
> *a concentric circle of pulp jamming the arm of the sofa*
> *into yesterday's views history like the commodity it is*
> *another futon teetering on the end of the juggler's nose*

nerve is 32-40 pgs., 5½×8½, photocopied from desktop originals and saddle-stapled with card cover. They receive about 300 poems a year, accept approximately 10%. Press run is 300. Subscription: $5. **Sample postpaid: $2. Make checks payable to Geoffrey N.T. Young. Submit up to 5 poems at a time, with SASE. No previously published poems or simultaneous submissions. Cover letter not required, but "it never hurts to include one." Seldom comments on rejections. Reports in 2-6 months. Pays 3 copies. Rights return to poet upon publication.** Staff reviews books of poetry, chapbooks and other magazines. Reviews are generally kept to fewer than 200 words. Send books for review consideration. The editor says, "Read a lot. Write a lot. Practice your craft. Research the markets. Above all, always have faith in yourself and your potential to be brilliant."

‡NERVE COWBOY (I, II); LIQUID PAPER PRESS (V), P.O. Box 4973, Austin TX 78765, founded 1995, editors Joseph Shields and Jerry Hagins. *Nerve Cowboy* is a biannual literary journal featuring contemporary poetry, short fiction and b&w drawings. **The editors are "open to all forms, styles and subject matter. We want to see poetry of experience and passion which can find that raw nerve and ride it. No rhyming, no 'curtains flapping in the wind' poetry; no overly academic verse."** They have recently published poetry by Will Inman, Mark Weber, Gerald Locklin, Patrick McKinnon, Laurel Speer and Ron Androla. As a sample the editors selected these lines from "Hickory Street Breakfast Blues" by Albert Huffstickler:

> *I think*
> *when I die*

it will just
be for a little
then I'll
wake up standing
beside a road
in the morning
light.

Nerve Cowboy is 40-52 pgs., 7×8½, attractively printed and saddle-stapled with matte card cover with b&w cover art. They currently accept 5-10% of the submissions received. Press run is 200-300 for 30 subscribers. Subscription: $14 for 4 issues. **Sample postpaid: $4. Make checks payable to Joseph Shields or Jerry Hagins. Submit 3-5 poems at a time, name on each page. Previously published poems and simultaneous submissions OK. Informal cover letter with bio credits. Seldom comments on rejections. Send SASE for guidelines. Reports in 2-4 weeks. Sometimes sends prepublication galleys. Pays 1 copy and 25% off any additional copies. Acquires first or one-time rights.** Liquid Paper Press also plans to publish **1-2 chapbooks/year starting in 1997 but will not be accepting unsolicited chapbook mss in the foreseeable future.** Chapbooks will be 16 pgs., 5½×8½, photocopied with some b&w drawings. Send SASE for a list of available titles.

NEW COLLAGE MAGAZINE (II), 5700 N. Tamiami Trail, Sarasota FL 34243-2197, phone (941)359-5605, founded 1970, poetry editor A. McA. Miller. *New CollAge* provides "a forum for contemporary poets, both known and undiscovered. We are **partial to fresh slants on traditional prosodies and poetry with clear focus and clear imagery. No greeting card verse. We prefer poems shorter than five single-spaced pages. We like a maximum of 3-5 poems per submission.**" They have published poetry by Peter Meinke, Yvonne Sapia, Lola Haskins, J.P. White, Peter Klappert, Peter Wild, Stephen Corey and Malcolm Glass. The editor selected these sample lines from "The Palm at the Edge of the Bay" by Daniel Bosch:

I would need a ship to moore here, really,
if I were to earn this girth of fibrous hemp,
round-waisted, tall, leaning a head
into the corner a cross-breeze walls itself against . . .

The magazine appears 2 times a year, 28-32 pgs. of poetry in each issue, circulation 500 with 200 subscriptions of which 30 are libraries. They receive about 5,000 poems/year, use 90. Subscription: $6. **Sample: $2. No simultaneous submissions. Publishes theme issues. Send SASE for upcoming themes. Reports in 6 weeks. Pays 2 copies. Editor sometimes comments on rejections.** "We review books and chapbooks in 1,000-2,000 words." Editor "Mac" Miller advises, "Sending a ms already marked 'copyright' is absurd and unprofessional. Mss may be marked 'first North American serials only,' though this is unnecessary. Also, quality is the only standard. Get a sample issue to see our taste."

THE NEW CRITERION (III), The Foundation for Cultural Review, Inc., 850 Seventh Ave., New York NY 10019, poetry editor Robert Richman, is a monthly (except July and August) review of ideas and the arts, which uses **poetry of high literary quality**. They have published poetry by Donald Justice, Andrew Hudgins, Elizabeth Spires and Herbert Morris. It is 90 pgs., 7×10, flat-spined. Poems here truly are open, with structured free verse and formal works highlighted in the issues we critiqued. Much of it was excellent, and book reviews were insightful. **Sample postpaid: $4.75. Cover letter required with submissions. Reports in 2-3 months. Pays $2.50/line ($75 minimum).** Poetry published in this review was selected for inclusion in the 1992 and 1994 volumes of *The Best American Poetry*. The editor says, "To have an idea of who we are or what we stand for aesthetically, poets should consult back issues."

NEW DIRECTIONS PUBLISHING CORPORATION (V, IV-Translations), 80 Eighth Ave., New York NY 10011, phone (212)255-0230, founded 1936, contact poetry editor. New Directions is "a small publisher of 20th-Century literature with an emphasis on the experimental," publishing about 36 paperback and hardback titles each year. **"We are looking for highly unusual, literary, experimental poetry. We can't use traditional poetry, no matter how accomplished. However, we are not accepting submissions at this time."** They have published poetry by William Carlos Williams, Ezra Pound, Denise Levertov, Jerome Rothenberg, Robert Creeley, Michael McClure, Kenneth Rexroth, H.D., Robert Duncan, Stevie Smith, David Antin, Hayden Carruth, George Oppen, Dylan Thomas, Lawrence Ferlinghetti, Jimmy Santiago Baca, Rosmarie Waldrop and Gary Snyder. **To see samples, try the library or purchase from their catalog (available), local bookstores or their distributor, W.W. Norton.** New Directions advises, "Getting published is not easy, but the best thing to do is to work on being published in the magazines and journals, thus building up an audience. Once the poet has an audience, the publisher will be able to sell the poet's books. Avoid vanity publishers and read a lot of poetry."

NEW EARTH PUBLICATIONS (IV-Spiritual, political, translations), 1921 Ashby Ave., Berkeley CA 94703, phone (510)549-0176, founded 1990, editors Clifton Ross and Dave Karoly, publishes **"books (up to 96 pgs.; query if longer) dealing with the struggle for peace and justice, revolutionary anarchism, quality poetry, prose and translations. Some publications are author subsidized."** They publish 1-2 paperbacks, 2-3 chapbooks/year. **Reports on queries in 2 weeks, on mss in 6 weeks. Sometimes sends prepublication galleys.**

NEW ENGLAND REVIEW (II), Middlebury College, Middlebury VT 05753, phone (802)388-3711 ext. 5075, e-mail nereview@mail.middlebury.edu, founded 1978, editor Stephen Donadio. *New England Review* is a prestigious literary quarterly, 160 pgs., 6×9, flat-spined, elegant make-up and printing on heavy stock, glossy cover with art. All styles and forms are welcome in this carefully edited publication. Poets published include Toi Derricotte, Albert Goldbarth, Norman Dubie, Philip Booth and Carol Frost. Sample copies or subscriptions may be ordered through the University Press of New England, 23 S. Main St., Hanover NH 03755; (800)421-1561. Subscription: $23. **Sample postpaid: $7. Submit no more than 6 poems at a time. Address submissions to Poetry Editor. No previously published poems. "Brief cover letters are useful. All submissions by mail. Questions by e-mail OK." Reads submissions September 1 through May 31 only. Response times can be exceptionally slow here, far exceeding published limits of 6-8 weeks. Always sends prepublication galleys. Pays 2 copies.** Also features essay-reviews. Publishers may send books for review consideration. Work published in this review was included in the 1992, 1993 and 1994 volumes of *The Best American Poetry.*

NEW ERA MAGAZINE (I, IV-Religious, teen/young adult), 50 E. North Temple St., Salt Lake City UT 84150-0001, phone (801)240-2951, fax (801)240-5997, founded 1971, managing editor Richard M. Romney, appears monthly. *New Era* is an "official publication for youth of The Church of Jesus Christ of Latter-day Saints; it contains feature stories, photo stories, fiction, news, etc." **They want "short verse in any form, particularly traditional—must pertain to teenage LDS audience (religious and teenage themes). No sing-songy doggerel, gushy love poems or forced rhymes."** As a sample the editor selected these lines from "Walls" by Dorothy Karen Patterson:

> All those walls,
> See how they crumble
> At the touch of the hand
> Of love.

> Like sandcastles,
> Melted by the kiss of the sea,
> My fortress falls
> With each warm word
> And gentle look.

New Era is 52 pgs., approximately 8 × 10½, 4-color offset, saddle-stitched, quality stock, top-notch art and graphics, no ads. They receive 200-300 submissions, purchase 2-5%. Press run is 220,000 for 205,000 subscribers, 10,000 shelf sales. Single copy: $1.50; subscription: $8/year. **Sample: $1.50 plus postage. Send no more than 5 poems at one time. No previously published poems or simultaneous submissions.** Time between acceptance and publication is a year or longer. "We publish one poem each month next to our photo of the month." **Sometimes comments on rejections. Publishes 1-2 theme issues each year, one of which is geographically themed (LDS youth in one country). Theme for the July 1997 issue: "Anniversary of Arrival of Mormon Pioneers in Utah." Theme deadlines are 6 months minimum to 1 year in advance. Send SASE for writer's guidelines and upcoming themes. Reports in 6-8 weeks. Sometimes sends prepublication galleys. Pays $10 minimum. "LDS church retains rights to publish again in church publications—all other rights returned."** They also offer an annual contest—including poetry—for active members of the LDS church between ages 12-23. Poetry entries should consist of one entry of 6-10 different original poems (none of which exceeds 50 lines) reflecting LDS values. Deadline: January. Winners receive either a partial scholarship to BYU or Ricks College or a cash award. Send SASE for rules. The editor says, "Study the magazine before submitting. We're a great market for beginners, but you must understand Mormons to write well for us. Just because a subject is noble or inspirational doesn't mean the poetry automatically is noble or inspirational. Pay attention to the craft of writing. Poetry is more than just writing down your thoughts about an inspirational subject. Poetry needs to communicate easily and be readily understood—it's too easy to mistake esoteric expression for true insight."

‡**NEW FRONTIERS OF NEW MEXICO (II)**, P.O. Box 1299, Tijeras NM 87059, phone (505)281-1990, fax (505)281-2300, founded 1993, editor/publisher Wally Gordon, is a quarterly publication of "poetry, fiction, journalism and commentary dealing with New Mexico and the Southwest." **They want poems under 60 lines, light verse and "prefer, but do not require, a Southwestern theme. No touristic poems about sunsets and blue skies."** They have recently published poetry by Lyn Lifshin, Wayne Hogan, Jay Udall and Francis DiPietro. As a sample the editor selected these lines from "Loneliness is not silent" by Diana L. Martinez:

> Loneliness is not silent
> Its screams compound
> And bounce violent
> Down
> Halls that shriek you're gone.

The editor says *New Frontiers* is 32 pgs., 8 × 11, with 2-color cover, photos, cartoons and drawings inside. They receive about 400 poems a year, use approximately 50. Press run is 3,000 for 1,000 subscribers of which 25 are libraries, 1,000 shelf sales. Subscription: $9.50/year. **Sample postpaid: $2.95. Simultaneous submissions OK. Cover letter including brief bio with publication credits preferred. Seldom comments on rejections. Send SASE for guidelines. Reports in 2 months. Pays up to $25 and 1 copy. Buys first North American serial rights, "but will consider republication if not in competing magazine."** Sponsors an annual contest in collaboration with PEN. Send SASE for details. The editor says, "Poets in the Southwest sometimes think scenery is an appropriate subject in and of itself. It's not—unless the writer puts something unusual in the scene."

NEW HOPE INTERNATIONAL (III), 20 Werneth Ave., Gee Cross, Hyde, Cheshire SK14 5NL United Kingdom, founded 1969, editor Gerald England, includes *"NHI Writing,* **publishing poetry, short fiction, artwork, literary essays and reports. All types of poetry from traditional to avant-garde, from haiku to long poems, including translations (usually with the original).** *NHI Review* **carries reviews of books, magazines, cassettes, CDs, records, PC software, etc. Special Edition Chapbooks with a theme or individual collections also included."** They have recently published poetry by Linda Chase, Alison Grayhurst, Nigel McLoughlin, Albert Russo and Vittoria Vaughn. As a sample the editor selected these lines from "A Bit of Fresh" by Hélène Sonn:

> A bit of freshness—let it splash!
> Let the bud explode and split
> In two, engendering new
> Breath, with a new right to fight—for survival,
> New wings to rise with the revival.
>
> Yes! Yes! A bit of fresh!

The digest-sized magazine, 36-40 pgs., is printed offset-litho from computer typesetting, saddle-stapled, color card cover, using b&w artwork. Press run is 600 for 300 subscribers of which 25 are libraries. £20 for 6 issues (*NHI Writing, NHI Review* and **S.E. Chapbooks** as published). **Sample postpaid: £4. Make checks payable to Gerald England. "Non-sterling cheques no longer accepted. Payment by International Giro (available from Post Offices worldwide) preferred. Currency notes to the sterling equivalent accepted as a last resort." Put name and address on each sheet; not more than 6 at a time; simultaneous submissions** *not* **encouraged. Cover letter required. Translations should include copy of original. Full guidelines available for IRC (3 for airmail). Send 1 IRC for reply if return of mss not required. Reports "usually fairly prompt, but sometimes up to 4 months." Always sends prepublication galleys. Pays 1 copy. Acquires first British serial rights.** Staff reviews books of poetry. Send books for review consideration. **For chapbooks, query first.** The editor advises, "Long lists of previous publications do not impress; perceptive, interesting, fresh writing indicative of a live, thinking person makes this job worthwhile."

NEW HORIZONS POETRY CLUB (II, IV-Membership), Box 5561, Chula Vista CA 91912, phone (619)474-4715, founded 1984, poetry editor Alex Stewart (also president of the California Federation of Chaparral Poets). This organization offers poetry contests of various sorts for experienced writers, publishing winners in an anthology. They also offer newsletters and critiques and publish anthologies of members' poetry. Membership (includes 4 newsletters): $12.50/year. They have published poetry by Alice Mackenzie Swaim, Glenna Holloway, Pegasus Buchanan and Patricia Laurence. Prizes in their Annual Poetry Day Contest are "$250 and down. We offer other cash awards, prizes and trophies, and certificates for honorable mentions. 'Mini-manuscript' winners are offered trophies, cash prizes and free anthologies." Entry fees are $5/2 poems, $10/5 poems. **"We expect poets to know technique, to be familiar with traditional forms and to be able to conform to requirements regarding category, style and length and to show originality, imagery and craftsmanship. Nothing**

amateurish, trite or in poor taste." Alex Stewart offers critiques at reasonable rates. (Discounts on critiques and books to members.) She says, "Poets need to study technique before *rushing to get published! (Where* is what counts!)* The current trend seems to be a wide range of traditional forms and comprehensible free verse. The sonnet is making a comeback!" NHPC publishes 2 books annually in the NHPC Poets' Series (4 poets/book). (Book list, including *The Poet's Art*, the editor's complete handbook on the craft of poetry writing, available on request.)

THE NEW LAUREL REVIEW (II, IV-Translations), 828 Lesseps St., New Orleans LA 70117, phone (504)947-6001, founded 1971, editor Lee Meitzen Grue, "is an annual independent nonprofit literary magazine dedicated to fine art. Each issue contains poetry, translations, literary essays, reviews of small press books, and visual art." They want **"poetry with strong, accurate imagery. We have no particular preference in style. We try to be eclectic. No more than 3 poems in a submission."** They have published poetry by Jane McClellan, Kalamu Ya Salaam, Melody Davis, Sue Walker and Keith Cartwright. The *Review* is 6×9, laser printed, 115 pgs., original art on cover, accepts 30 poems of 300 mss received. It has a circulation of 500. Single copy: $9. **Sample (back issue) postpaid: $7. No simultaneous submissions. Submit 3-5 poems with SASE and a short note with previous publications. Reads submissions September 1 through May 30 only. Guidelines for SASE. Reports on submissions in 3 months, publishes in 8-10 months. Pays contributor's copies. Acquires first rights.** Reviews books of poetry in 1,000 words, single or multi-book format. The editor advises, "Read our magazine before submitting poetry."

NEW LETTERS; NEW LETTERS POETRY PRIZE (II), University of Missouri-Kansas City, Kansas City MO 64110, phone (816)235-1168, fax (816)235-2611, founded 1934 as *University Review*, became *New Letters* in 1971, managing editor Bob Stewart, editor James McKinley, "is dedicated to publishing the best short fiction, best contemporary poetry, literary articles, photography and artwork by both established writers and new talents." They want **"contemporary writing of all types—free verse poetry preferred, short works are more likely to be accepted than very long ones."** They have published poetry by Joyce Carol Oates, Hayden Carruth, John Frederick Nims, Louise Glück, Louis Simpson, Vassar Miller and John Tagliabue. The 6×9, flat-spined, professionally printed quarterly, glossy 2-color cover with art, uses about 40-45 (of 120) pgs. of poetry in each issue. Circulation is 1,845 with 1,520 subscriptions of which about 40% are libraries. They receive about 7,000 submissions/year, use less than 1%, have a 6-month backlog. Poems appear in a variety of styles exhibiting a high degree of craft and universality of theme (rare in many journals). Subscription: $17. **Sample postpaid: $5. Send no more than 6 poems at a time. No previously published poems or simultaneous submissions. Short cover letter preferred. "We strongly prefer original typescripts and we don't read between May 15 and October 15. No query needed." Reports in 4-10 weeks. Pays a small fee plus 2 copies. Occasionally James McKinley comments on rejections.** The New Letters Poetry Prize of $750 is given annually for a group of 3-6 poems, entry fee $10 (check payable to New Letters Literary Awards). Send SASE for entry guidelines. Deadline: May 15. They also publish occasional anthologies, selected and edited by McKinley. Work published in *New Letters* appeared in *The Best American Poetry 1992*.

NEW METHODS: THE JOURNAL OF ANIMAL HEALTH TECHNOLOGY (IV-Animals), P.O. Box 22605, San Francisco CA 94122-0605, phone (415)664-3469, founded as *Methods* in 1976, poetry editor Ronald S. Lippert, AHT, is an irregular 4-page newsletter, "a networking service in the animal field, active in seeking new avenues of knowledge for our readers, combining animal professionals under one roof." They want poetry which is **"animal related but not cutesy, two pages maximum."** They receive about 50 poems a year, accept 5. Press run is 5,000 for 4,000 subscribers of which 100 are libraries. Subscription: $32. **Sample: $3.20. A listing of all back issues and the topics covered is available for $5, and there is a 20% discount on an order of 12 or more mixed copies. No previously published poems or simultaneous submissions. Dated cover letter required. Everything typed, double-spaced with one-inch margins. Often comments on rejections. Send SASE for guidelines. Reports in 2-4 weeks. Pays negotiable number of copies.** Reviews books of poetry "pertaining to our subject matter."

‡**NEW NATIVE PRESS (III)**, P.O. Box 661, Cullowhee NC 28723, phone (704)293-9237, founded 1979, publisher Thomas Rain Crowe, is a publisher of "new, original and innovative work by American and foreign authors with an emphasis on translated material." They publish 2 paperbacks/year. **They want lyric poetry and translations. "No one-dimensional rhymed metric, confessional, political or issue-oriented poetry."** They have recently published poetry by Philip Daughtry, Ken Wainio and John Lane. As a sample the publisher selected these lines from his own poem "Learning to Dance":

> *. . . I have given up the toys of my childhood and my ambitions for old age*
> *and have moved deep within the walls of her silver skin.*
> *I am through with my love of suffering and the words that describe that love.*
> *I am going to carry on a magnificent affair with the wind*

from the inside of her body, where we both sleep.

Books are typically 80 pgs., offset and perfect-bound with glossy 120 lb. cover with graphics. **Query first with 10 sample poems and cover letter with brief bio and publication credits. Previously published poems and simultaneous submissions OK.** Time between acceptance and publication is 6 months to 1 year. **Always comments on rejections. Reports in 2 weeks. Pays copies, "amount varies with author and title."** The publisher says, "Manuscripts for books accepted are most often solicited—with the possible exception of rare talent and translations. I am always looking for unique and original voices using language experimentally and symbolically."

NEW ORLEANS POETRY JOURNAL PRESS (III), 2131 General Pershing St., New Orleans LA 70115, phone (504)891-3458, founded 1956, publisher/editor Maxine Cassin, co-editor Charles deGravelles. **"We prefer to publish relatively new and/or little-known poets of unusual promise or those inexplicably neglected—'the real thing.' "** They do not want to see **"cliché or doggerel, anything incomprehensible or too derivative, or workshop exercises. First-rate lyric poetry preferred (not necessarily in traditional forms)."** They have published books by Vassar Miller, Everette Maddox, Charles Black, Raeburn Miller and Martha McFerren. Their most recent book is *Illuminated Manuscript* by Malaika Favorite. As a sample the editor selected these lines from "Missing Z and Nola" in *Hanoi Rose* by Ralph Adamo:

Nobody owns the bright blue dawn for long.
You can be there day after day, raking it in,
and still there'll be a palm under your token,
and the palm won't be yours. And the animal
you traded power with will contrive to be
given away. In the barracks where the last
detachment waits, beauty won't show her face.

Query first. They do not accept unsolicited submissions for chapbooks, which are flat-spined paperbacks. **The editors report on queries in 2-3 months, mss in the same time period, if solicited. Simultaneous submissions will possibly be accepted. Sometimes sends prepublication galleys. Pays copies, usually 50-100.** Ms. Cassin does not subsidy publish at present and does not offer grants or awards. For aspiring poets, she quotes the advice Borges received from his father: "1) Read as much as possible! 2) Write only when you *must*, and 3) Don't rush into print!" As a small press editor and publisher, she urges poets to read instructions in *Poet's Market* listings with utmost care! She says, "No poetry should be sent without querying first! Publishers are concerned about expenses unnecessarily incurred in mailing manuscripts. *Telephoning is not encouraged.*"

NEW ORLEANS REVIEW (II), Box 195, Loyola University, New Orleans LA 70118, phone (504)865-2295 or 865-2286, fax (504)865-2294, e-mail adamo@beta.loyno.edu., founded 1968, editor Ralph Adamo. They have published poetry by Jimmy Carter, and a special section on the life and work of the late poet Everette Maddox. *New Orleans Review* publishes **"lyric poetry of all types**, fiction that is strongly voiced and essays." It is 100 pgs., perfect-bound, elegantly printed with glossy card cover. Circulation is 750. **Sample postpaid: $10. Submit 3-6 poems at a time. No previously published work. Brief cover letter preferred. Reports in 3 months. Acquires first North American serial rights.**

THE NEW PRESS LITERARY QUARTERLY; THE NEW PRESS POETRY CONTEST (II), 63-44 Saunders St., Suite 3, Rego Park NY 11374-2039, phone (718)459-6807, fax (718)275-1647, founded 1984, poetry editor Evie-Ivy, is a quarterly magazine using poems **"less than 100 lines, accessible, imaginative. No doggerel, sentimentality."** They now include a multilingual section for poetry. **They want poems in Spanish, Italian, Portuguese and French, accompanied by their English versions/translations. Each poem must list the author's and translator's names and addresses.** They have published poetry by Allen Ginsberg, Lawrence Ferlinghetti, Louise Jaffe, Mary Winters, D.H. Melhem, Les Bridges and Gina Bergamino. As a sample the editor selected these lines by R. Nikolas Macioci:

a conversation he has
with himself as he thinks now
of hinges he must oil
before old doors will open
quietly onto another year's
garden and the scent
of newly spaded soil.

It is magazine-sized, 40-48 pgs., desktop-published, with glossy cover, saddle-stapled. They accept about 10% of 500-1,000 poems received/year. Press run is 2,000 for 350 subscribers. Subscription: $15/year, $29/2 years (add $5/year for overseas). **Sample postpaid: $5.50. "Payable by check or money order in U.S. funds only." Submit 3 poems at a time. "Include name and address on the top of each page." Publishes theme issues. Send SASE for upcoming themes. Reports in 4 months.**

Always sends prepublication galleys. Pays 2 copies. Acquires first-time rights. The New Press Poetry Contest is annual, deadline is July 1, entry fee of $5 for up to 3 poems or 100 lines, has prizes of $200, $75 and five 2-year subscriptions. Also sponsors quarterly essay and fiction contests. Send 10 (essays) and 22 (fiction) double-spaced pgs. maximum with entry fee of $5 and SASE. Prize is $100. They also sponsor poetry readings in Brooklyn, Queens and Manhattan. Send SASE for details.

THE NEW QUARTERLY (II, IV-Regional), ELPP University of Waterloo, Waterloo, Ontario N2L 3G1 Canada, phone (519)885-1211, ext. 2837, founded 1981, managing editor Mary Merikle, is a "literary quarterly—new directions in Canadian writing." For the poetry they want, the editors have **"no preconceived conception—usually Canadian work, poetry capable of being computer typeset—4½″ line length typeset lines. No greeting card verse."** The editor describes it as 120 pgs., flat-spined, 6×8½, with a photograph on the cover, no graphics or art, some ads. Of 2,000 poems received/year, they use 100. Press run is 600 for 300 subscriptions (10 of them libraries) and additional shelf sales. Subscription: $18 ($23 for US or overseas subscriptions). **Sample postpaid: $5 Canadian, $5 US. Submit no more than 5 poems at a time. Cover letter with short bio required. Send SASE for guidelines. Reports in 3-6 months. Pays $20/poem.**

THE NEW RENAISSANCE (I, IV-Translations, bilingual), 9 Heath Rd., Arlington MA 02174, founded 1968. *the new renaissance* is "intended for the 'renaissance' person—the generalist, not the specialist. Publishes the best new writing and translations. Offers a forum for articles of public concern, features established as well as emerging visual artists and writers, and highlights reviews of small press books and other books of merit. **We are open to traditional as well as other types of poetry and usually receive samples of every kind during our submission periods."** They have recently published poetry by Stephen Booker, Joan Colby and Allen C. Fisher, and translations of Mario Luzi (by Laura Anna Stortoni) and Domokos Szilagyi (by Len Roberts). As a sample of the poetry they're publishing, the editor selected these lines from "The Ghosts of Hannibal's Elephants" by Ann Struthers:

> The ghosts of Hannibal's elephants rise up
> like mist after centuries in the Alpine ice,
> come crashing down the mountains,
> trumpet wildly, capture the Colosseum,
> ride up the steps overlooking the Forum
> and speak from Julius Caesar's balcony.

tnr is flat-spined, professionally printed on heavy stock, glossy, color cover, 144-186 pgs., using 24-40 pgs. of poetry in each issue. They receive about 750 poetry submissions/year, use 15-20, have about a 1½- to 2-year backlog. Usual press run is 1,600 for 710 subscribers of which approximately 132 are libraries. Subscriptions: $21/3 issues US, $22 Canada, $24 all others. **"We're an unsponsored, independent small litmag. All poetry submissions are tied to our Awards Program for best poetry published in a 3-issue volume. Entry fee $15 for nonsubscribers, $10 for subscribers, for which they may receive either of the following: 2 back issues or a current issue." Submit 3-6 poems at a time, "unless a long poem—then one." No previously published poems "unless magazine's circulation was under 300"; simultaneous submissions OK, if notified. Reads mss January through March, and September and October. Send SASE for guidelines. Reports in 3-6 months. Pays $13-20, more for the occasional longer poem, plus 1 copy. Buys all rights. Returns rights provided** *tnr* **retains rights for any** *tnr* **collection, anthology, etc.** Reviews books of poetry. The Awards Program gives 3 prizes of $250, $125 and $50. The editor says, "We believe that poets should not only be readers but lovers of poetry. We're looking for 'literalists of the imagination—imaginary gardens with real toads in them.' Our range is from traditionalist poetry to post-modern, experimental (the latter only occasionally, though) and street poetry. We also like the occasional 'light' poem and, of course, have an emphasis on translations. We're especially interested in the individual voice. We aren't interested in greeting card verse or prose set in poetic forms. If you're querying us about anything, please include a SASE. We won't answer unless there is one."

THE NEW REPUBLIC (II), 1220 19th St. NW, Washington DC 20036, phone (202)331-7494, founded 1914, poetry editor Mark Strand. *The New Republic*, a weekly journal of opinion, is magazine-sized, printed on slick paper, 42 pgs., saddle-stapled with 4-color cover. Subscription: $69.97/year. **Back issues available for $3.50 postpaid. Include SASE with submissions. Always sends prepublication galleys. They provide no payment information.** Poetry published in *The New Republic* has also been included in the 1993, 1994 and 1995 volumes of *The Best American Poetry*.

NEW RIVERS PRESS; MINNESOTA VOICES PROJECT, INC. (II, IV-Regional, translations), 420 N. Fifth St., Suite 910, Minneapolis MN 55401, founded 1968, publishes collections of poetry, translations of contemporary literature, collections of short fiction, and is also involved in publishing **quality literary material. Write for free catalog or send SASE for guidelines/inquiries. Pays 25 copies.** New and emerging authors living in Iowa, Minnesota, North and South Dakota, and Wisconsin are eligible for the Minnesota Voices Project. Book-length mss of poetry, short fiction, novellas or familiar essays are all accepted. **Send SASE for entry form. Winning authors receive a stipend of $500 plus publication by New Rivers. Second and subsequent printings of works will allow 15% royalties for author. Postmark deadline: April 1.**

‡**NEW SPIRIT PRESS; POEMS THAT THUMP IN THE DARK/SECOND GLANCE MAGAZINE (II)**, 82-34 138 St., #6F, Kew Gardens NY 11435, phone (718)847-1482, e-mail newspirit@gnn.com, website http://members.gnn.com/newspirit/, founded 1991, editor Ignatius Graffeo. *Poems That Thump in the Dark/Second Glance* appears 3 times a year and publishes poetry, poetry book reviews and poetry magazine reviews. **They want "all styles and forms of fine crafted poetry on mythology, folklore, gothic, erotica, humor, history, contemporary people and/or experiences; poetry with good metaphors, form and feeling. No greeting card verse, cascading stanzas, political ravings, gratuitous violence or sex."** They have recently published poetry by Stephen Dunn, Colette Inez, Donna Masini and William Pitt Root. As a sample the editor selected these lines from "Vulcan & Venus" by LindaAnn Loschiavo:

> *The first time he saw Venus Vulcan loved.*
> *She was a flower, petals arching back,*
> *Intent on showing off its pollen tease.*
> *Without her in his life he'd be a dead sea*
> *That's drying up. Without her as his wife,*
> *The god of fire suspects he will amount*
> *To merely supervisor of the clowns.*
> *His smithy's flames were never this intense.*
> *Those passions of extremity, he knows,*
> *Have rendered subsequent existence pale,*
> *Her image driven into him, hard nailed.*

It is 72 pgs., digest-sized, laser-printed and saddle-stapled with heavy card cover with b&w art, b&w graphics and ads inside. Press run is 300 for 100 subscribers of which 10 are libraries, 30 shelf sales. Subscription: $20. **Sample postpaid: $6. Make checks payable to New Spirit Press. Submit 4 poems at a time. No previously published poems; simultaneous submissions OK. Cover letter including brief bio, publication credits and SASE preferred. "Windows/IBM compatible diskette submissions OK."** Time between acceptance and publication is up to 1 year. **Seldom comments on rejections. Send SASE for guidelines. Reports in 3-6 months. Pays 1 copy plus 33% discount on additional copies.** Staff reviews books and magazines of poetry in 3,000 words. Poets may send books for review consideration. New Spirit Press also publishes chapbooks through their quarterly chapbook contests. The winner receives 50 copies of chapbook. Submit mss of 16-20 pgs. Deadlines: March 31, June 30, September 30 and December 31. Entry fee: $10, includes copy of winning chapbook. Send SASE for guidelines.

‡**NEW STATESMAN (II)**, Foundation House, Perseverance Works, 38 Kingsland Rd., London E2 8DQ England, phone (0171)739-3211, fax (0171)739-9307, contact Poetry Editor, is a weekly general interest publication containing "left of centre politics and the arts." **They want exciting poetry. "We sometimes publish poems specifically written for children. No boring, flat verse; fascist, sadistic or junkie trash."** They have recently published poetry by Ted Hughes, Edwin Morgan, Sujata Bhatt, Paul McCartney and Robert Creeley. As a sample they selected these lines from "The Shop" by Martin Evans:

> *If only they sold*
> *bottles of sleep,*
> *in shades of wandering green,*
> *grey and open blue,*
> *stacked in shops*
> *with sliding shelves*
> *and cloudy windows. . . .*

The editor says it is 48 pgs., A4, with drawings and photos. They receive 2,000 poems a year, accept about 150. Press run is 35,000 for 25,000 subscribers. Subscription: £50. **Sample (including guidelines) postpaid: $3 US. Submit up to 6 poems at a time, typed with SASE (or SAE and IRCs). No previously published poems or simultaneous submissions. Cover letter preferred.** Time between acceptance and publication is up to 1 year. **Reports within 2 months. Sometimes sends prepublication galleys. Pays £80/page plus 1 copy. Buys first rights.**

‡**NEW THOUGHT JOURNAL (II, IV-Inspirational)**, 2520 Evelyn Dr., Kettering OH 45409, phone/fax (513)293-9717, e-mail ntjmag@aol.com, founded 1993, editor/publisher Jeffrey M. Ohl, is a quarterly art and literary magazine including stories (fiction and nonfiction), poetry, art and reviews "focusing on arts, humanities, metaphysics, creativity, transformation, personal growth and spiritual themes." **They want poetry of any form, any length, but "subject matter to be inspirational,**

CLOSE-UP

Coming of age with fellow poets

Gerald Stern is, undeniably, one of today's grand masters. In addition to publishing eight books of poetry, including Lamont Poetry Prize winner *Lucky Life* (Houghton Mifflin, 1977), *Bread Without Sugar* (Norton, 1992), and *Odd Mercy* (Norton, 1995), Stern has written a number of essays and taught for nearly 14 years at the University of Iowa—considered the "Rome of the workshop." In spite of his time at Iowa, however, Stern has mixed feelings about what an aspiring writer can hope to gain from the workshop experience.

© 1994 Martin J. Desht

Gerald Stern

"The main good of workshops is that they create a community where people can suffer together, weep on each other's shoulders, exchange books and such. They also give quick access to the current modes in writing so somebody doesn't have to learn everything by himself. They provide encounters with other people and challenges to your own presumptions, forcing you out into the open. These are the good things about workshops, and I applaud these things. The bad things are obvious: They create a normative procedure; they assume anything can be taught; they perhaps subvert, really unintentionally, the radical, loud, original processes that might exist in somebody and tame them, domesticate them—I say perhaps, and to some degree."

Stern himself did not attend a workshop, but instead "came of age" with two fellow poets, Jack Gilbert and Richard Hazley, in his native Pennsylvania during the late '40s and early '50s. "We met in the evening and in the afternoon, the three of us. We talked about what we had read that day. We recited poems to each other. But we never examined each other's poems—that was a private thing. If we learned to write in common, it was by reading and by studying the lives of other writers and imitating them."

Stern and his comrades went to New York and then to Paris, where Stern attempted to emulate his romantic concept of the working poet. "I would read a chapter from *Paradise Lost* and a chapter from the Scriptures, then fondle a statue I had—a reproduction of a Michelangelo. Then I'd almost lock myself to my desk, as we heard Yeats did, and write for four hours. Sometimes one line would come, sometimes twenty. That was my schooling."

Although Stern believes travel is important to his poetry, he doesn't think the lack of travel precludes a person from writing. "I've benefited from it, and my poetry is based on multiculturalism. But that's one way, and there are other ways. Everybody does what they want to do. You don't have to travel, but you write a different kind of poetry. In general, it's good to know languages—because you can learn things from foreign languages of inestimable value—it's good to experience

CLOSE-UP, *Stern*

things outside the place where you live, where the newspaper says 'World News on Page 3.' Besides, things get in the air. Things are in magazines, and of course there is instant communication—television, interviews and such, so people today have access to cultural ideas."

While aspiring writers often approach a poet of Stern's caliber for the secret to success, he maintains that "everybody's got to find his or her own way." Stern's way includes writing all the time, every day. "I just have a driving need to do it. When I was writing in Paris I didn't enjoy writing. I liked the idea of being a poet, but it was very painful for me to write and I would use any excuse to leave my desk, whether it was to see some friends, have lunch, go to the museum, read a book, whatever."

"Leaf"

He picked a leaf, there just had to be
a little drama wherever he went, he put it
in the left pocket with the number two pencil
and the set of keys; it was a little wet,
which made it diaphanous, and when he pressed it
inside his book though it had started to dry
and even shrink it still could be supple and even
give off a little knowledge. Half way across
to his second house he held it in his mouth
the way an ape does; this was another drama
and he wasn't even accountable; the taste
was nothing, only looking for his keys
he swallowed a little juice. Where he put it
down and how he looked at it later when
he walked out for his oranges he would remember
while sitting beside his lamp with a paper napkin
under his coffee and eating a little and turning
the light into the wall, the heavy stem
like a trunk, the branches upturned, the stunted ones,
as in all leaves, half-glistening, the tree
that lay on the floor, he swept up or he scattered.

It wasn't until after Stern turned 40 that he found his voice, and with it the recognition, the publications, the acclaim. Although Stern had been writing for some 20 years before this, he acknowledges that people can, nevertheless, come late to poetry. "I see a lot of people of an advanced age—not 18, but 30, 40, 50—who are just discovering poetry. This is especially true for women, who put in time in other activities, like child rearing and husband rearing, before they have a chance to develop themselves. But there's no reason in the world why they—women and men—can't become important poets, or great poets."

Like poems, people take all kinds of directions. At the heart of the matter is the writing itself. Stern identifies two things that make a poem interesting. "First, if it's well organized and in an interesting form, with useful and efficient langu-

CLOSE-UP, *continued*

age, lovely language. Second, if it's important or has to be said—if it changes thought, or changes feeling, or changes the language, or changes life, or the life of the poet, or is a discovery. In other words, the truth.''

While Stern considers "the truth" as the more important of the two, he stresses the significance of form. "For me, when I read a poet, what makes me close the book, tear up the page, throw it away, and not continue is the absence of form. I'm not thinking in terms of quatrains or strophes or perfectly organized pentameter, although I love those things. The form I speak of has to do with the language being absolutely right, which means two things: it has to effectively say what it wants to say—what it means, what it needs to say—and it's got to say it beautifully. But the one is not an adornment or an illustration of the other. They are intermingled.''

Accomplishing this, of course, requires a great deal of dedication. "You have to be a grind. You have to pay attention to details, be a worker. Then, from time to time, you're touched by the muse. But you never know when you're going to be touched. I never know. And you can't teach someone to be touched by the muse. It's arrogant to assume you can do that.''

Reading Stern's poetry, it is difficult to believe he doesn't have direct access to the muse. He describes his poetry as "associative," and indeed, each poem is, to borrow a line from Wallace Stevens (a poet Stern admires and has been compared to), a "blissful liaison" of history, intellect, culture, nostalgia, and emotion that can leave the reader stunned by the enormity—by the power—of his words.

Surprisingly perhaps, Stern does not start with a map of the completed poem. "I almost never know where I'm going. I start with music, with sound. I start with an idea, with language. Often, it's the last line that defines the poem for me. It's as if the poem doesn't occur as a complete thought or unit or entity until the last line is written. On the other hand, the poem is going on, and it's going in a certain direction. Part of it is unconscious, or if not unconscious, indescribable verbally. And then, when the last line occurs, it puts a mouth on these faces that just had eyes and noses.

"You know, poetry is self-generating. An act of will. You want to be a poet? Then believe it, but you can't do it with one foot in the water. There's no halfway—give up your life or not, period. Then, if you're going to do it, read madly. Reading is training for the poet. And find some companions who also write. You need a community. You can't do it alone.''
—*Michelle Moore*

moving readers to change the world and/or the way they look at the world, to bring people together. No hatred or negativity, nothing prejudicial.'' They have recently published poetry by T. Kilgore Splake, Mary Winters, Daniel Green and Caron Andregg. As a sample the editor selected the first stanza of "A Thousand Years of War" by James Scofield:

> He is a boy, with a club, pounding the sand.
> A howling, whirling, divided, dervish boy,
> chasing birds at rest, while waves charge the shore,
> manes flying, collapsing then on the gull scarred sand.
> A thousand years of war in this beast most innocent.

NTJ, subtitled "The Beat of a Thousand Drummers," is about 36 pgs., 8½×11, offset and saddle-stitched with a high quality 4-color glossy cover and b&w photos, illustrations and ads inside. They receive about 400 poems a year, accept 100-150. Press run is 3,000 for 2,500 shelf sales. Single copy: $3.50; subscription: $14. **Sample (including guidelines) postpaid: $4. Submit 4 poems at a time. Previously published poems and simultaneous submissions OK. Cover letter preferred; include "background, author biography—inspiration for poem." Seldom comments on rejections. Reports upon publication by sending 2 copies to the author. Acquires one-time rights.** Open to unsolicited reviews.

NEW WELSH REVIEW (II, IV-Ethnic), Chapter Arts Centre, Market Rd., Cardiff CF5 1QE Wales, United Kingdom, phone 0222-665529, founded 1988, editor Robin Reeves. *NWR* is a literary quarterly publishing articles, short stories and poems. The editor describes it as an average of 100 pgs., glossy paper in three colors, laminated cover, using photographs, graphics and ads. Their press run is 1,100. Subscription: £15. **Sample postpaid: £4.20. Submit poems double-spaced. No simultaneous submissions or previously published poems. Reports in 3 months. Publication within 1-7 months.** Reviews books of poetry.

NEW WRITER'S MAGAZINE (I, II, IV-Humor, writing), P.O. Box 5976, Sarasota FL 34277-5976, phone (941)953-7903, e-mail newriters@aol.com, founded 1986, editor George J. Haborak, is a bimonthly magazine "for aspiring writers, and professional ones as well, to exchange ideas and working experiences." **They are open to free verse, light verse and traditional, 8-20 lines, reflecting upon the writing lifestyle. "Humorous slant on writing life especially welcomed." They do not want poems about "love, personal problems, abstract ideas or fantasy."** *NWM* is 28 pgs., 8½×11, offset, saddle-stapled, with glossy paper cover, b&w photos and ads. They receive about 300 poems a year, accept approximately 10%. Press run is 5,000. Subscription: $15 for 1 year, $25 for 2 years. **Sample postpaid: $3. Submit up to 3 poems at a time. No previously published poems or simultaneous submissions.** Time between acceptance and publication is 1 year maximum. **Send SASE for guidelines or request via e-mail. Reports in 1-2 months. Pays $5/poem. Buys first North American serial rights.** Each issue of this magazine also includes an interview with a recognized author, articles on writing and the writing life, tips and markets.

NEW YORK QUARTERLY (II), P.O. Box 693, Old Chelsea Station, New York NY 10113, founded 1969, poetry editor William Packard, appears 3 times/year. They seek to publish "a cross-section of the best of contemporary American poetry" and, indeed, **have a record of publishing many of the best and most diverse of poets**, including W.D. Snodgrass, Gregory Corso, James Dickey and Judson Jerome. It appears in a 6×9, flat-spined format, thick, elegantly printed, glossy color cover. Subscription: $15. **Submit 3-5 poems at a time; include SASE. Reports within 2 weeks. Pays copies.**

THE NEW YORKER (III, IV-Translations, humor), 20 W. 43rd St., New York NY 10036, founded 1925, poetry editor Alice Quinn, circulation 640,000, uses **poetry of the highest quality (including translations). Sample: $2.95 (available on newsstands). Mss are not read during the summer. Replies in 6-8 weeks. Pays top rates.** Poems appearing in *The New Yorker* have also been selected for inclusion in the 1992, 1993, 1994, 1995 and 1996 volumes of *The Best American Poetry*.

NEWSLETTER INAGO (I), P.O. Box 26244, Tucson AZ 85726-6244, phone (520)294-7031, founded 1979, poetry editor Del Reitz, is a monthly newsletter. **"Free verse and short narrative poetry preferred although other forms will be read. Rhymed poetry must be truly exceptional (nonforced) for consideration. Due to format, 'epic' and monothematic poetry will not be considered. Cause specific, political or religious poetry stands little chance of consideration. A wide range of short poetry, showing the poet's preferably eclectic perspective is best for *NI*. No haiku, please."** They have recently published poetry by Chloe Heuch, Rose Marie Hunold, Elizabeth Zibas, Holly Lalena Day, Simon Perchik, Albert Huffstickler, L. Lee Abelard, Catherine Merritt, Anne Simon and Kirsten Fox. As a sample the editor selected these lines from "Feathers And Strings" by Mark J. Isham:

> The Bell-Ringer and the Elephant Man
> were pissing away another afternoon
> in a West Hollywood bar
> Safe from paparrazzi and People
>   Magazine
> Hunched over another round
> mumbling about feathers and strings
> and the unbearable lightness of being
> Charles Bukowski would've been proud
> Tom Waits too

NI is 4-5 pgs., corner-stapled. Their press run is approximately 200 for that many subscriptions. **No** price is given for the newsletter, but the editor suggests a donation of $3.50 an issue or $17.50 annually ($3.50 and $21 Canada, £8 and £21 UK). (All checks must be made payable to Del Reitz.) Submit 10-15 poems at a time. "Poetry should be submitted in the format in which the poet wants it to appear, and cover letters are always a good idea." They consider simultaneous submissions and previously published poems. Editor sometimes comments on rejections. Send SASE for guidelines. Reports ASAP (usually within 2 weeks). Pays 4 copies. The first and second audio anthologies of poetry (on audiotapes) are now available. These anthologies present selections from the poetry published in *Newsletter Inago* during the first and second five years, respectively. Write for current price and details.

NEXT PHASE; PHANTOM PRESS PUBLICATIONS (II), 5A Green Meadow Dr., Nantucket Island MA 02554, phone (508)325-0411, founded 1989, poetry editor Holly Day and **submissions should go directly to her at University of Tampa, P.O. Box 1041, 401 W. Kennedy Blvd., Tampa FL 33606.** *Next Phase* is a fiction magazine that appears 3 times a year and includes poetry, commentary, interviews and book reviews. **They prefer "positive, inspirational work with an emphasis on environmental and social issues." They do not want to see work over two pages long . . . "and please no depressing poetry!"** They have published poetry by Allen Ginsberg and John Grey. As a sample the editor selected these lines from "Silences" by Diane Thiel:

> In a small boat distance changes
> the world becomes big and wild again
> the weather is more than words
> but what you live your life by
>
> We who numb ourselves with noise
> need to listen for the silences

Next Phase is 48 pgs., 8½ × 11, saddle-stitched with a 4-color semi-glossy paper cover; b&w photos, art and graphics inside. They receive about 150 poetry submissions a year, publish about 20. Press run is 1,700 for 200 subscribers, 1,500 shelf sales. Single copy: $3.95; subscription: $16 for 2 years. **Sample postpaid: $4. Previously published poems and simultaneous submissions OK. Cover letter required.** Time between acceptance and publication is 1-2 years. **Seldom comments on rejections. Send SASE for guidelines. Reports in 6 weeks. Pays 2 copies. Acquires one-time rights.** "We review small press books only." Send books for review consideration to Charlie Cockett, Box 1239, Torrington WY 82240.

NEXUS (II), WO16A Student Union, Wright State University, Dayton OH 45435, phone (513)873-5533, founded 1967, editor Tara L. Miller. "*Nexus* is a student operated magazine of mainstream and street poetry; also essays on environmental and political issues. **We're looking for truthful, direct poetry. Open to poets anywhere. We look for contemporary, imaginative work.**" *Nexus* appears 3 times a year—fall, winter and spring, using about 40 pgs. of poetry (of 80-96) in each issue. They receive 1,000 submissions/year, use 30-50. Circulation 1,000. **For a sample, send a 10 × 15 SAE with 5 first-class stamps and $5. Submit 4-6 pgs. of poetry with bio. Reads submissions September through May only.** Simultaneous submissions OK, "but due to short response time we want to be told it's a simultaneous submission." Editor sometimes comments on rejections. Send SASE for guidelines. **Reports in 15-20 weeks except summer months. Pays 2 copies. Acquires first rights.**

NIGHT ROSES (I, IV-Teen/young adult, love/romance, nature, students, women/feminism); MOONSTONE BLUE (I, IV-Anthology, science fiction/fantasy), P.O. Box 393, Prospect Heights IL 60070-0393, phone (847)392-2435, founded 1986, poetry editor Allen T. Billy, appears 2-4 times a year. "*Moonstone Blue* is a science fiction/fantasy anthology, but we have no set dates of publication. We do an issue every 14-24 months as items, time and funds allow. We look for women/feminism themes for our *Bikini* series." For *Night Roses* they want "**poems about dance, bells, clocks, nature, ghost images of past or future, romance and flowers (roses, wildflowers, violets, etc.). Do not want poems with raw language.**" They have published poetry by Judith Beckett, M. Riesa Clark, Joan Payne Kincaid, Lyn Lifshin and Alice Rogoff. As a sample the editor selected these lines from "The Antique Tea Pot" by Betty Rawlinson:

> The antique tea pot,
> once part of cherished set
> stored on a shelf out of reach,
> and so its useful years past.

Night Roses is 44 pgs., saddle-stapled, photocopied from typescript on offset paper with tinted matte card cover. Press run is 200-300. Subscription: $10 for 3 issues. **Sample postpaid: $3.50 for** *Night Roses*, **$3 for** *Moonstone Blue*. **Submit no more than 8 poems at a time.** "Desire author's name and address on all sheets of ms. If previously published—an acknowledgment must be provided by author with it." **No simultaneous submissions;** some previously published poems used. "I prefer submissions between March and September." Reports in 6-12 weeks. "Material is accepted for current issue and 2 in progress." Sometimes sends prepublication galleys. Pays 1 copy. Acquires first or reprint rights. Staff reviews books of poetry. Send books for review consideration. The editor says, "We are more interested in items that would be of interest to our teen and women readers and to our readership in the fields of dance, art and creative learning. We are interested in positive motives in this area."

NIGHT SONGS (IV-Horror), 4998 Perkins Rd., Baton Rouge LA 70808-3043, founded 1991, editor Gary William Crawford, is a quarterly newsletter that publishes "supernatural horror poetry in the great tradition of supernatural verse. Poems that modernize themes explored in the poetry of Poe, Baudelaire, H.P. Lovecraft." **They want "horror poetry in a variety of forms. However, not interested in strict imitations of such poets as Edgar Allan Poe or H.P. Lovecraft. In general, themes of terror and darkness, madness and death should be present. Poems that explore the underlying horror of civilization."** They have published poetry by Bruce Boston, Lisa Lepovetsky, Keith Allen Daniels and Joey Froehlich. As a sample the editor selected these lines from "The Morning of Interment" by June Miller:

> The human step creeps closer, almost silent
> but at first tread great wings outspread,
> three glittering jet projectiles shoot the sky
> soaring, arcing over shore and ocean,
> black against the sun.

Night Songs is 6 pgs., 8½×11, neatly photocopied with line drawings and stapled at the corner. They receive about 30 poems/month, use approximately 5. Press run is 75 for 45 subscribers. Subscription: $3/year. **Sample postpaid: $1. Submit 3 poems at a time. No previously published poems or simultaneous submissions. Cover letter required.** Time between acceptance and publication is 6 months. **Often comments on rejections. Reports in 2 weeks. Always sends prepublication galleys. Pays $1/poem. Buys first rights.**

NIGHTSUN (II), Dept. of English, Frostburg State University, Frostburg MD 21532, phone (301)689-4221 or 4208, founded 1981, editor Douglas DeMars, is a literary annual of poetry, fiction and interviews. **They want "highest quality poetry." Subject matter open. Publishes mostly free verse. Prefers poems not much longer than 40 lines. Not interested in the "extremes of sentimental, obvious poetry on the one hand and the subjectless 'great gossamer-winged gnat' school of poetry on the other."** They have published poetry by Diane Wakoski, Philip Dacey, Walter McDonald, David Citino, Stephen Perry and Robert Cooperman. Interviews include Lucille Clifton, Sharon Olds, Galway Kinnell, Stephen Dobyns, Maxine Kumin, Marvin Bell and Marge Piercy. As a sample the editor selected these lines from "Looking Into the Ether" by Dina Coe:

> I close the door on the highways
> lit like an underground:
> arteries of the same rough heart
> that has born two to climb
> towards bedtime in the window
> of Earth's obtuse dark.

Nightsun is 68 pgs., 6×9, printed on 100% recycled paper and perfect-bound with card cover, b&w print on front. This attractive journal features well-known poets alongside relative newcomers. Editors take free verse mostly with attention paid to line, stanza and shape of poem. They accept about 1% of poetry received. **Subscription/sample postpaid: $6.50. Submit 3-5 poems at a time. No simultaneous submissions. Do not submit mss during summer months. Reports within 2-3 months. Pays 2 copies. Acquires first rights. "Contributors encouraged to subscribe."**

NIMROD: INTERNATIONAL JOURNAL OF CONTEMPORARY POETRY AND FICTION; RUTH G. HARDMAN AWARD: PABLO NERUDA PRIZE FOR POETRY (I, II), University of Tulsa, 600 S. College, Tulsa OK 74104-3189, phone/fax (918)631-3080, founded 1956, editor-in-chief Francine Ringold, "is an active 'little magazine,' part of the movement in American letters which has been essential to the development of modern literature. *Nimrod* publishes 2 issues per year: an awards issue in the fall featuring the prize winners of our national competition and a thematic issue each spring." **They want "vigorous writing that is neither wholly of the academy nor the streets, typed mss."** They have recently published poetry by Wendy Wirth-Brock, Jan Beatty, Ruth Schwartz and Terry Ehret. The 6×9, flat-spined, 160-page journal, full-color glossy cover, professionally printed on coated stock with b&w photos and art, uses 50-90 pgs. of poetry in each issue. It is an extraordinarily lovely magazine with one of the best designs in the lit world. Poems in non-award issues range from formal to freestyle with several translations. They use about 1% of the 2,000 submissions they receive each year, have a 3- to 6-month backlog. Circulation 3,500, 500 subscriptions of which 100 are public and university libraries. Subscription: $15/year inside USA; $18 outside. **Sample postpaid: $8 for a recent issue, $6.95 for an issue more than 2 years old. Submit**

up to 10 poems at a time." Send SASE for upcoming themes. Reports in 3 weeks to 1 month. Pays $5/page up to $25 and 2 copies plus reduced cost on additional copies. "Poets should be aware that during the months that the Ruth Hardman Awards Competition is being conducted, reporting time on non-contest manuscripts will be longer." Send business-sized SASE for guidelines and rules for the Ruth G. Hardman Award: Pablo Neruda Prize for Poetry ($1,000 and $500 prizes). Entries accepted January 1 through April 1 each year with $15 entry fee for which you get one copy of *Nimrod* or a $20 subscription order for which you receive 2 issues plus credit for entry fee. This annual poetry contest is considered one of the most prestigious in the publishing world, and your material is still considered for publication if you lose in the contest! Poetry published in *Nimrod* has been included in *The Best American Poetry 1995*.

96 INC (I, II); BRUCE P. ROSSLEY LITERARY AWARDS (IV-Regional), P.O. Box 15559, Boston MA 02215, founded 1992, editors Julie Anderson, Nancy Mehegan and Andrew Dawson. *96 Inc* is a biannual literary magazine that focuses on new voices, "connecting the beginner to the established, a training center for the process of publication." **They want all forms and styles of poetry, though "shorter is better."** They have recently published poetry by Jennifer Barber, Hope Steele and Ellen Summers. As a sample the editors selected these lines from "the funeral" by Jacinta Taitano Martens:

> i watch my mother from the dining room
> (not that we ever used it for dining)
> i watch her make another pot of rice,
> fry more lumpia and warm the pansit.
> she is grieving the way our women do.
> they cry, they wipe their eyes, they laugh
> and they cook.

96 Inc is 38-50 pgs., 8½×11, saddle-stapled with coated card cover and b&w photos and graphics. They receive "a few hundred" submissions a year, accept 10%. Press run is 3,000 for 400 subscribers of which 50 are libraries, 1,500 shelf sales. Single copy: $4; subscription: $13. **Sample postpaid: $5.50. No previously published poems; simultaneous submissions OK.** Time between acceptance and publication is 1 year. **Poems are circulated to an editorial board. Often comments on rejections. Send SASE for general guidelines. Reports in 6 months. Pays $20-75 (depending on funding) and 4 copies. Copyright reverts to author 2 months after publication.** Occasionally, staff reviews books of poetry. Send books for review consideration, attn: Mark Wagner. The Bruce P. Rossley Literary Awards are given to previously under-recognized writers (of poetry or fiction) in the state of Massachusetts. Writers can be nominated by anyone familiar with their work. Send SASE for further information. The editors add, *"96 Inc* is an artists' collaborative and a local resource. It often provides venues and hosts readings in addition to publishing a magazine."

NINETY-SIX PRESS (V, IV-Regional), Furman University, Greenville SC 29613-0438, founded 1991, editors William Rogers and Gilbert Allen, publishes 1-2 paperback books of poetry/year. "The name of the press is derived from the old name for the area around Greenville, South Carolina—the Ninety-Six District. The name suggests our interest in the writers, readers and culture of the region. In 1994, we published an anthology of South Carolina poetry, including the work of more than 40 poets. **We currently accept submissions by invitation only. At some point in the future, however, we hope to be able to encourage submissions by widely published poets who live in South Carolina."** They have recently published *Fly with the Puffin* by Dorothy Thompson and *Paying the Anesthesiologist* by Starkey Flythe. As a sample the editors selected these lines from "Who Can Show the Child as She Is?" in *Learning to Dance* by William Aarnes:

> Truth is, she's just too ridiculous,
> my daughter standing naked in her pool,
> her swimming suit tossed into the grass,
> and over her head the tilted hose spouting
> a putto's wing. She commands, imperious:
> "Take your shorts off; take them off now!"

That book is 58 pgs., 6×9, professionally printed and perfect-bound with coated stock cover. **For a sample, send $10.**

‡NITE-WRITER'S INTERNATIONAL LITERARY ARTS JOURNAL (I), 3101 Schieck St., Suite 100, Pittsburgh PA 15227-4151, phone (412)882-2259, founded 1993, editor/publisher John A. Thompson Sr., is a quarterly open to beginners as well as professionals. *Nite-Writer's* is " 'dedicated to the emotional intellectual' with a creative perception of life." **They want strong imagery and accept free verse, avant-garde poetry, haiku and senryu. Open to length and subject matter. No porn or violence.** They have recently published poetry by Lyn Lifshin, Rose Marie Hunold, Peter Vetrano, Carol Frances Brown and Richard King Perkins II. As a sample we selected these lines from "Argument" by Julia McSweeney:

> *With a single flick*
> *of a deftly turned phrase*
> *She spread his anger*
> *across the table*
> *And set it for dinner,*
> *Using only the finest silver.*

The editor says the journal is 30-50 pgs., 8½ × 11, laser-printed, stock cover with sleeve, some graphics and artwork. They receive approximately 1,000 poems a year, use 10-15%. Press run is about 100 for more than 60 subscribers of which 10 are libraries. Single copy: $6; subscription: $20. **Sample postpaid (when available): $4. Previously published poems and simultaneous submissions OK. Cover letter preferred. "Give brief bio, state where you heard of us, state if material has been previously published and where. Always enclose SASE if you seek reply and return of your material."** Time between acceptance and publication is within 1 year. **Always comments on rejections. Send SASE for guidelines. Reports in 2-4 weeks.** The editor says, "Don't be afraid to submit your material. Take rejection as advice—study your market. Create your own style and voice, then be heard. 'I am a creator, a name beneath words' (from my poem, 'unidentified-Identified')."

NO EXIT (II), 52175 Central Ave., South Bend IN 46637-3807, founded 1994, editor Mike Amato, is a quarterly forum "for the experimental as well as traditional excellence." **The editor says he wants "poetry that takes chances in form or content. Form, length, subject matter and style are open. No bad rhyme nor poetry that's unsure of why it was written."** They have published poetry by Errol Miller, Simon Perchik and Michael Casey. As a sample the editor selected these lines from "Water" by John Bradley:

> *Raymond or Roman or Ramona, nursing on the breast of this woman*
> *who cannot swim, swims in a river that is endless and warm. The toaster*
> *sputters as a fat drop of water strikes it. The mother strokes the child's*
> *soft head and murmurs:* The ashtray, it's full of water again. How are we
> ever going to know your name?

NE is 32 pgs., saddle-stapled, digest-sized, card cover with art. They accept 10-15% of the submissions received. Press run is less than 500 for 65 subscribers of which 6 are libraries. Subscription: $12. **Sample postpaid: $4. No previously published poems; simultaneous submissions OK.** Time between acceptance and publication can vary from 1 month to 1 year. **Sometimes comments on rejections,** "if the poem strikes me as worth saving." **Send SASE for guidelines. Reports in 6-8 weeks. Pays 1 copy plus 4-issue subscription. Acquires first North American serial rights.** Reviews books of poetry. "Also looking for articles, critical in nature, on poetry/poets." Open to unsolicited reviews. Poets may also send books for review consideration. The editor says, "Don't let rejection keep you from submitting again. Presentation means something; namely, that you care about what you do. I'm amazed at the number of submissions I get that don't have the writer's name on them. And it takes a powerful piece of work for me to overlook spelling and other like errors. Don't take criticism, when offered, personally. I'll work with you if I see something solid to focus on."

‡NO RØSES REVIEW (II), 1322 N. Wicker Park, Chicago IL 60622, founded 1992, editors Carolyn Koo and Davis McCombs, is a biannual publication of **"progressive, non-conventional and experimental poetry."** They have recently published poetry by Barbara Guest, Clark Coolidge and Rosmarie Waldrop. The review is 60-80 pgs., 5½ × 8½, photocopied and perfect-bound with a printed cover. They receive about 780 poems a year, accept approximately 10%. Press run is 250 for 20 subscribers, 70 shelf sales. Subscription: $12. **Sample postpaid: $6. Submit 3-5 poems at a time, on 10 pgs. maximum. No previously published poems or simultaneous submissions. Cover letter preferred. Seldom comments on rejections. Send SASE for guidelines. Reports in 1-3 months. Pays 2 copies. Acquires first North American serial rights.** Also sponsors an annual poetry contest with prizes of $100 and $50. Reading fee: $6 for up to 4 poems. Deadline: May 15. Send SASE for details. The review has received a Gregory Kolavakos Seed Grant and an Illinois Arts Council Literary Award and poetry published in the review has been included in the 1993, 1994 and 1996 volumes of *The Best American Poetry.*

NOCTURNAL LYRIC, JOURNAL OF THE BIZARRE (I, IV-Horror), P.O. Box 115, San Pedro CA 90733-0115, phone (310)519-9220, founded 1987, editor Susan Moon, is a quarterly journal "featuring bizarre fiction and poetry, primarily by new writers." **They want "poems dealing with the bizarre: fantasy, death, morbidity, horror, gore, etc. Any length. No 'boring poetry.' "** They have recently published poetry by Skylar Hamilton and Michael Shrum. As a sample the editor selected these lines from "For Less than a Minute" by Rebecca Meiser:

> *For less than a minute, I pictured*
> *you dead. Stone cold hands,*
> *bone white flesh, eyes*
> *lolling upwards to stare*

at the ravens circling above you. . . .

NL is 40 pgs., digest-sized, photocopied, saddle-stapled, with trade ads and staff artwork. They receive about 200 poems a year, use approximately 35%. Press run is 250 for 40 subscribers. Subscription: $10. **Sample postpaid: $3, $2 for back issues. Make checks payable to Susan Moon. Submit up to 4 poems at a time. Previously published poems and simultaneous submissions OK. Seldom comments on rejections. Reports in 4-6 months. Pays 50¢ "discount on subscription" coupons. Acquires one-time rights.** The editor says, "Please send us something really wild and intense!"

NOMAD'S CHOIR (II), % Meander, P.O. Box 232, Flushing NY 11385-0232, founded 1989, editor Joshua Meander, is a quarterly. **"Subjects wanted: love poems, protest poems, mystical poems, nature poems, poems of humanity, poems with solutions to world problems and inner conflict. 9-30 lines, poems with hope. Simple words, careful phrasing. Free verse, rhymed poems, sonnets, half-page parables, myths and legends, song lyrics. No curse words in poems, little or no name-dropping, no naming of consumer products, no two-page poems, no humor, no bias writing, no poems untitled."** They have published poetry by Brenda Charles, Joseph Gourdji, Dorothy Wheeler and Jeff Swan. As a sample the editor selected these lines from "Love's Giant Piano" by Connie Goodman:

> *Walk a giant piano . . .*
> *Destination, the stars*
> *Along love's entrancing melody;*
> *The night, it is ours.*

Nomad's Choir is 10 pgs., 8½ × 11, typeset and saddle-stapled with 3 poems/page. They receive 150 poems/year, use about 50. Press run is 400, all distributed free. Subscription: $5; **per copy: $1.25. Make checks payable to Joshua Meander. Reports in 6-8 weeks. Pays 1 copy.** The editor says, "Stick to your guns; however, keep in mind that an editor may be able to correct a minor flaw in your poem. Accept only minor adjustments. Go to many open poetry readings. Respect the masters. Read and listen to other poets on the current scene. Make pen pals. Start your own poetry journal. Do it all out of pure love."

THE NORTH; THE POETRY BUSINESS; SMITH/DOORSTOP PUBLISHING (III), The Studio, Byram Arcade, Westgate, Huddersfield HD1 1ND England, phone 01484 434840, fax 01484 426566, founded 1986, editors Peter Sansom and Janet Fisher, is a small press and magazine publisher of contemporary poetry. **"No particular restrictions on form, length, etc. But work must be contemporary, of a high standard, and must speak with the writer's own authentic voice. No copies of traditional poems, echoes of old voices, poems about the death of poet's grandfather, poems which describe how miserable the poet is feeling right now."** They have published poetry by Robert Hershon, Paul Violi, Joan Jobe Smith and John Harvey. As a sample the editors selected these lines from "Swimming the English Channel" by Susan Bright:

> *I did not intend to be a theater.*
> *I do not like the man in the basement who controls me.*
> *I do not want to be a house, a hotel, a car.*
> *I do not like being exposed!*

The North is "⅔ A4 format, 48-52 pgs., offset litho, graphics, ads, colored card cover, staple-bound." It appears 2 times/year. Press run is 600 for 400 subscriptions. Subscription: £10 (£12 US rate). **Submit up to 6 poems at a time. Poems should be typed with writer's name and address on each page. "We'll accept poems previously published in the U.S. but not the U.K." Pays 2 copies.** Smith/Doorstop publishes 6 perfect-bound paperbacks/year. **For book consideration, submit 6 sample poems and brief cover letter with bio and previous publications. Responds to queries in 1 month, to mss in 3 months. Pays 20 copies.** They hold an annual book (perfect-bound, laminated) competition. Write for full details. The editors say, "Read plenty of poetry, contemporary and traditional. Attend workshops, etc., and meet other writers. Keep submitting poems, even if you fail. Build up a track record in magazines before trying to get a book published."

NORTH AMERICAN REVIEW (III), University of Northern Iowa, Cedar Falls IA 50614, phone (319)273-6455, founded 1815, poetry editor Peter Cooley, is a slick magazine-sized bimonthly of general interest, 48 pgs. average, saddle-stapled, professionally printed with glossy full-color paper cover, **publishing poetry of the highest quality.** They have published poetry by Francine Sterle,

---

† **THE DOUBLE DAGGER** before a listing indicates that the listing is new in this edition. New markets are often the most receptive to submissions.

Cynthia Hogue and Marvin Bell. The editor says they receive 15,000 poems a year, publish 20-30. Press run is 6,400 for 2,200 subscribers of which 1,100 are libraries, some 2,800 newsstand or bookstore sales. Subscription: $18. **Sample postpaid: $4. No simultaneous submissions or previously published poems. Send SASE for guidelines. Reports in 1-2 months, as much as a year between acceptance and publication. Always sends prepublication galleys. Pays 50¢/line and 2 copies.** Work published in the *North American Review* has been included in the 1992, 1995 and 1996 volumes of *The Best American Poetry*.

NORTH DAKOTA QUARTERLY (III), Box 7209, University of North Dakota, Grand Forks ND 58202-7209, fax (701)777-3650, founded 1910, poetry editor Jay Meek, is a literary quarterly published by the University of North Dakota that includes material in the arts and humanities—essays, fiction, interviews, poems and visual art. **"We want to see poetry that reflects an understanding not only of the difficulties of the craft, but of the vitality and tact that each poem calls into play."** Poets recently published include John Allman, Lorna Crozier, Martin Espada and Leslie Andrienne Miller. As a sample, the poetry editor selected lines from "Carving Your Future" by Douglas Woodsum:

> . . . I don't sell knives,
> I sell pardons, and relics, and talismans. I sell hope,
> belief, faith, self-esteem. I save marriages
> and battered kids. I sell knives out of a wooden
> booth I've pulled behind my pickup from Fryburg, Maine,
> to West Point, Mississippi.

The poetry editor says *North Dakota Quarterly* is 6×9, about 200 pgs., perfect-bound, professionally designed and often printed with full-color artwork on a white card cover. You can find almost every kind of poem here—avant-garde to traditional. Typically the work of about 10 poets is included in each issue. Circulation of the journal is 850, of which 650 are subscriptions. Subscription: $20/year. **Sample postpaid: $5. Submit 5 poems at a time, typed, double-spaced. No previously published poems or simultaneous submissions. Reporting time is 4-6 weeks and time to publication varies. Always sends prepublication galleys. Pays 2 copies and a year's subscription.** The press does not usually publish chapbooks.

NORTHEAST ARTS MAGAZINE; BOSTON ARTS ORGANIZATION, INC. (III), P.O. Box 6061, J.F.K. Station, Boston MA 02114, founded 1990, editor/president Mr. Leigh Donaldson, is a biannual using **poetry that is "honest, clear, with a love of expression through simple language, under 30 lines. Care for words and craftsmanship are appreciated."** They have published poetry by S.P. Lutrell, Eliot Richman, Elizabeth R. Curry and Alisa Aran. As a sample the editor selected these lines by Martina Fischer:

> This golden necklace dropped
> into a Venice canal
> will kill a man
> in New York City. . .

It is 32 or more pgs., digest-sized, professionally printed with 1-color coated card cover. They accept 20-25% of submissions. Press run is 500-1,000 for 150 subscribers of which half are libraries, 50 to arts organizations. An updated arts information section and feature articles are included. Subscription: $10. **Sample postpaid: $4.50. Reads submissions September 1 through February 28 only. "A short bio is helpful." Send SASE for guidelines. Reports in 2-3 months. Pays 2 copies. Acquires first North American serial rights.**

NORTHEASTERN UNIVERSITY PRESS; SAMUEL FRENCH MORSE POETRY PRIZE (III), Northeastern University, 360 Huntington Ave., 416 CP, Boston MA 02115. The Samuel French Morse Poetry Prize, % Prof. Guy Rotella, Editor, Morse Poetry Prize, English Dept., 406 Holmes, Northeastern University, Boston MA 02115, for book publication (ms 50-70 pgs.) by Northeastern University Press and an **award of $500. Entry fee: $10. Deadline of August 1 for inquiries, September 15 for single copy of ms. Ms will not be returned. Open to US poets who have published no more than 1 book of poetry.**

THE NORTHERN CENTINEL (II), 115 E. 82nd St., Suite 8B, New York NY 10028-0872, founded 1788, poetry editors Ellen Rachlin and Lucie Aidinoff, is a newspaper appearing 6 times/year focusing on "political/cultural essays and analyses on matters of national interest." **They publish 2 poems each issue.** They have recently published poetry by Molly Peacock, Allen Ginsberg and Martin Tucker. It is 20-24 pgs., 11×17, offset on newsprint, with b&w artwork, photos, engravings, woodcuts, political cartoons and ads. Press run is 20,000. Subscription: $15. **Sample postpaid: $2.50. No previously published poems; simultaneous submissions OK. Cover letter with SASE required.** Time between acceptance and publication is up to a year. **Seldom comments on rejections. Reports within 3 months. Pays $40 plus 1 copy.**

NORTHERN PERSPECTIVE (II), Northern Territory University, Darwin NT 0909 Australia, phone (089)466124, fax (089)466151, e-mail cameronj@darwin.ntu.edu.au, founded 1977, managing editor Dr. Jim Cameron, appears twice a year. This liberal arts journal is 115-125 pgs., magazine-sized, using a full-color cover, professionally printed. Press run is 800 for 420 subscribers of which 20 are libraries, including university and public libraries in the US, UK, Europe and Africa; 300 shelf sales. **Sample postpaid: $7.50 AUD. Submit 3 poems at a time, in March and September. Editor often comments on rejections. Reports "hopefully within 10 weeks." Pays minimum of $20 AUD/poem.** Reviews books of poetry in 300-500 words. "Review articles are 1,500-2,500 words. *NP* reviews are *not* solicited; review articles, however, may be submitted."

NORTHWEST LITERARY FORUM; IRVINGTON PRESS (II, IV-Form), 3439 NE Sandy Blvd. #143, Portland OR 97232, e-mail forumnw@aol.com, founded 1992, editor Ce Rosenow, is a quarterly publication of poetry, short fiction, interviews, short plays and essays. **They are open to all types of poetry (except translations) and even have a special section for haiku and related forms.** They have recently published poetry by Taylor Graham, Errol Miller and Lyn Lifshin. As a sample the editors selected these lines from "Braiding/Ribbons of Hope" by Victoria Lena Manyarrows:

>   *some say treaties are made to be broken*
>   *and braiding is out of fashion*
>   *but i'll still braid your ribbons of hope*
>   *joining those strands of strength & years*
>   *weaving us together as one*

NLF is 40 pgs., 5½×8½, offset printed and saddle-stapled with card cover and b&w cover art. Press run is 150. Subscription: $15. **Sample postpaid: $4. No previously published poems or simultaneous submissions.** Time between acceptance and publication is 1-3 months. **Seldom comments on rejections. Reports in 1 month. Acquires first North American serial rights.** Does not review books of poetry, but lists publications received with ordering information. Poets may send books for listing consideration.

NORTHWEST REVIEW (II), 369 PLC, University of Oregon, Eugene OR 97403, phone (503)346-3957, founded 1957, poetry editor John Witte. They are "seeking excellence in whatever form we can find it" and use **"all types" of poetry.** They have published poetry by Alan Dugan, Olga Broumas, William Stafford and Richard Eberhart. *NR*, a 6×9, flat-spined magazine, appears 3 times/year and uses 25-40 pgs. of poetry in each issue. They receive 3,500 submissions/year, use 4%, have up to a 4-month backlog. Press run is 1,300 for 1,200 subscribers of which half are libraries. **Sample postpaid: $4. Submit 6-8 poems clearly reproduced. No simultaneous submissions. The editor comments "whenever possible" on rejections. Send SASE for guidelines. Reports in 8-10 weeks. Pays 3 copies.** Poetry published in this review has been included in *The Best American Poetry 1994*. The editor advises poets to "persist."

NORTHWOODS PRESS; NORTHWOODS JOURNAL: A MAGAZINE FOR WRITERS; C.A.L. (II), P.O. Box 298, Thomaston ME 04861-0298, phone (207)354-0998, Northwoods Press founded 1972, C.A.L. (Conservatory of American Letters) 1986 and *Northwoods Journal* 1993. *Northwoods Journal* is a quarterly literary magazine. **"The journal is interested in all poets who feel they have something to say and who work to say it well. We have no interest in closet poets, or credit seekers. All poets seeking an audience, working to improve their craft and determined to 'get it right' are welcome here. Please request submission guidelines (with SASE) before submitting."** Subscription: $12/year, free to C.A.L. members. **Sample: $5. Deadlines are the 1st of April, July, October and January for seasonal publication. Reports within 2 weeks after deadline, sometimes sooner. Pays $5/page, average, on acceptance.** "For book-length poetry manuscripts, submit to Northwoods Press, designed for the excellent *working poet* who has a following which is likely to create sales of $3,000 or more. Without at least that much of a following and at least that level of sales, no book can be published. Request 15-point poetry program. **Please do not submit book-length manuscripts until you have read our guidelines." Northwoods Press will pay a minimum of $250 advance on contracting a book.** C.A.L. is a nonprofit tax-exempt literary/educational foundation; up to 4 anthologies of poetry and prose are published each year. **There is a $1 (cash—no checks) reading fee for each poetry submission to their anthologies, which goes to readers, not to the publisher. Poets are paid $5/page on acceptance, shorter poems pro-rata page rate. "Payment is advance against 10% royalties on all sales we can attribute to the influence of the author. To be considered for our next anthology, send #10 SASE and request guidelines for Next Anthology."** Robert Olmsted regards his efforts as an attempt to face reality and provide a sensible royalty-contract means of publishing many books. He says, "If you are at the stage of considering book publication, have a large number of poems in print in respected magazines, perhaps previous book publication, and are confident that you have a sufficient following to insure very modest sales, send 8½×11 SASE (3 oz. postage) for descriptions of the Northwoods Poetry Program and C.A.L." His advice is, "Poetry must be non-trite, non-didactic. It must never bounce. Rhyme, if used at all, should be subtle. One phrase should tune the ear in preparation for the next. They should flow and create an emotional response." Bob Olmsted "rarely" comments on rejections, but he offers commentary for a fee, though he says he "strongly recommends *against* it." Membership in C.A.L. is $24 a year, **however, membership is not required.** Members receive the quarterly *Northwoods Journal* plus 10% discount on all books and have many services available to them. C.A.L. sponsors an annual writers' conference with no tuition, only a $20 registration fee. The *Northwoods Journal* now sponsors "the only no compromise poetry contest in the country." Unpublished poems only. Send SASE for contest guidelines.

W.W. NORTON & COMPANY, INC. (III), 500 Fifth Ave., New York NY 10110, phone (212)354-5500, founded 1925, poetry editor Jill Bialosky. W.W. Norton is a well-known commercial trade publishing house that publishes only original work in both hardcover and paperback. **They want "quality literary poetry"; no "light or inspirational verse."** They have recently published books by Rita Dove, Marilyn Hacker, Joy Harjo, Martin Espada, Stephen Dunn and Eavan Boland. W.W. Norton publishes approximately 10 books of poetry each year with an average page count of 64. They are published in cloth and flat-spined paperbacks, attractively printed, with two-color glossy card covers. **Unsolicited submissions are accepted, but authors should query first, sending credits and 15 sample poems plus bio. Simultaneous submissions will be considered if the editor is notified. Norton will consider only poets whose work has been published in quality literary magazines. They report on queries in 2-3 weeks and mss in 4 months. Catalog is free on request.** W.W. Norton also published an attractive anthology of cowboy poets, entitled *Between Earth and Sky: Poets of the Cowboy West*, edited by Anne Heath Widmark. The anthology showcases the work of 12 well-known cowboy poets, including Buck Ramsey, Wallace McRae, Paul Zarzyski and Sue Wallis. For a close-up look at a cowboy poet, also see the interview with Wallace McRae in the *1996 Poet's Market*.

NOSTALGIA: A SENTIMENTAL STATE OF MIND (II), P.O. Box 2224, Orangeburg SC 29116, founded 1986, poetry editor Connie Lakey Martin, appears spring and fall using **"nostalgic poetry, style open, prefer *non* rhyme, but occasional rhyme OK, relatively short poems, never longer than one page, no profanity, no ballads."** *Nostalgia* is 24 pgs., digest-sized, offset typescript, saddle-stapled, with matte card cover. Press run is 1,000. Subscription: $8. **Sample postpaid: $5.** **"Most poems selected from contest."** There are contests in each issue with award of $100 and publication for outstanding poem, publication and 1-year subscription for Honorable Mentions. Entry fee of $5 reserves future edition, covers 3 entries. Deadlines: June 30 and December 31 each year. **No previously published poems or simultaneous submissions. Guidelines available for SASE. Sometimes sends prepublication galleys. All rights revert to author upon publication.** Reviews books of poetry. Open to unsolicited reviews. Poets may also send books for review consideration. Connie Martin says, "I offer criticism to most rejected poems, but I suggest sampling before submitting. More poets seem to be sampling and getting a better idea of what type of poetry I use. That's great. Sending a poem to a publisher without sampling is like dropping a message in a bottle and tossing it out to sea. Don't you care where it lands?"

NOW AND THEN (IV-Regional, themes), ETSU, P.O. Box 70556, Johnson City TN 37614-0556, phone (423)929-5348, fax (423)929-6340, e-mail woodsidjatetsu-tn.edu, founded 1984, editor-in-chief Jane Woodside, poetry editor Linda Parsons, is a regional magazine that covers Appalachian issues and culture. **The editor specifically wants poetry related to the region. Previous issues have focused on Appalachian politics, storytelling, the Civil War, education, sports, the Scottish-Appalachian connection, New Writing, media, family and community, tourism, and activism. "We want genuine, well-crafted voices, not sentimentalized stereotypes."** They have published poetry by Fred Chappell, Rita Quillen, Michael Chitwood, Jim Wayne Miller and George Ella Lyon. As a sample the editor selected these lines from "For the Cutover Woods of Dixie" by Errol Miller:

> *O Lord of the Long Nap, something*
> *is moving in my net, fermenting, ruling over me,*
> *something sweet and sour like Dixie's*
> *lingering dreams. There is festering within me*
> *a sense of history, of myself, of the earth, of all*
> *the great structures of commerce boarded up,*
> *that reverse momentum where the wind*
> *sways through the trees for a while before*
> *the workmen come to silence the music.*

Now and Then appears three times a year and is 42 pgs., magazine-sized, saddle-stapled, professionally printed, with matte card cover. Its press run is 2,000 for 900 members of the Center for Appalachian Studies and Services, of which 200 are libraries. They accept 6-10 poems an issue. Center membership is $15; the magazine is one of the membership benefits. **Sample: $4.50 plus $1.50 postage. They will consider simultaneous submissions; they occasionally use previously published poems. Submit up to 5 poems, with SASE and cover letter including "a few lines about yourself for a contributor's note and whether the work has been published or accepted elsewhere."** Deadlines: March

1, July 1 and November 1. **Publishes theme issues. Send SASE for guidelines and upcoming themes. Editor prefers fax or e-mail to phone calls. Reports in 4 months. Sometimes sends prepublication galleys. Pays $10/poem plus 2 copies. Acquires all rights.** Reviews books of poetry in 750 words. Open to unsolicited reviews. Poets may also send books for review consideration to Sandy Ballard, book review editor, Dept. of English, Carson-Newman College, Box 2059, Jefferson City TN 37760.

NUTHOUSE; TWIN RIVERS PRESS (I, IV-Humor), P.O. Box 119, Ellenton FL 34222, press founded 1989, magazine founded 1993, editor D.A. White. *Nuthouse*, "amusements by and for delightfully diseased minds," appears every 6 weeks using humor of all kinds, including homespun and political. **They simply want "humorous verse; virtually all genres considered."** They have published poetry by Holly Day, Daveed Garstenstein-Ross and Don Webb. The editor says *Nuthouse* is 12 pgs., digest-sized and photocopied from desktop-published originals. They receive about 100 poems a year, usually accept about 25. Press run is 100 for 50 subscribers. Subscription: $5/5 issues. **Sample postpaid: $1. Previously published poems and simultaneous submissions OK.** Time between acceptance and publication is 6-12 months. **Often comments on rejections. Reports within 1 month. Pays 1 copy/poem. Acquires one-time rights.**

NV MAGAZINE; HOMELESS PUBLICATIONS (I), 4360 E. Main #242, Ventura CA 93003, founded 1994, editor Heather Woodward, is a bimonthly magazine "dedicated to publishing unknown talent in the USA. **We like to see solid, well thought-out poetry; mostly free verse, all subjects. No rhyme. No greeting card verse. Please don't send anything fashionable or trendy, mundane or mainstream."** The editor says they work mainly with unpublished artists. As a sample the editor selected these lines from her own poetry:

>   mirrors reflect the sweat
>   glistening on fingers
>   pulling hair biting lips
>   fingers
>   thin and dainty
>   handkerchiefs

The editor says *NV* is 50-100 pgs., 8×11, with 100 lb. glossy color cover, b&w text with lots of graphics. She says, "75% of what we receive is poetry. 40% we accept." Their press run is 1,900. Subscription: $25. **Sample postpaid: $5, $3.50 with 8×12 SASE. No previously published poems or simultaneous submissions. Cover letter required.** "No SASE = destruction." Time between acceptance and publication is 6 months. **Always comments on rejections. Send SASE for guidelines. Reports in 3 months. Pays 5 copies. "We retain all periodical rights to what we publish for one year after publication (at which time they revert to the author), and reprint, electronic and anthology rights for the duration of the copyright."** The editor says, "We are particularly interested in poets who incorporate graphics into their writing. We also like liberal and/or opinionated work. We are hard to offend. The more bizarre, left-wing or right-wing, the better."

THE OAK (I); PHANTASM (I, IV-Fantasy, horror, mystery); THE ACORN (I, IV-Children); THE GRAY SQUIRREL (I, IV-Senior citizens), 1530 Seventh St., Rock Island IL 61201, phone (309)788-3980, poetry editor Betty Mowery. *The Oak*, founded 1990, is a "publication for writers with poetry and fiction (no more than 500 words)." They want poetry **"no more than 32 lines. No restrictions as to types and style, but no pornography."** *The Oak* appears 6 times/year and now includes *Phantasm*, founded 1993, which publishes **soft horror, fantasy and mystery.** They take more than half of about 100 poems received each year. Press run is 250, with 10 going to libraries. Subscription: $10. **Sample: $2. Submit 5 poems at a time. Simultaneous submissions and previously published poems OK. Reports in 1 week.** *"The Oak does not pay in dollars or copies but you need not purchase to be published."* **Acquires first or second rights.** *The Oak* holds an Orange Blossom Poetry Contest February 1 through August 1. *The Acorn*, founded 1988, is a "newsletter for young authors and teachers or anyone else interested in our young authors. **Takes mss from kids K-12th grades. Poetry no more than 32 lines.** It also takes fiction of no more than 500 words." It appears 4 times/year and "we take well over half of submitted mss." Press run is 100, with 6 going to libraries. Subscription: $10. **Sample postpaid: $2. Submit 5 poems at a time. Simultaneous submissions and previously published poems OK. Reports in 1 week.** *"The Acorn does not pay in dollars or copies but you need not purchase to be published."* **Acquires first or second rights. Young authors, submitting to *The Acorn*, should put either age or grade on manuscripts.** Founded 1991, *The Gray Squirrel* appears 6 times/year. **Takes poetry of no more than 20 lines only from poets 60 years of age and up.** Press run is about 100. Six issues: $10. **Sample: $2. Submit 5 poems at a time. Reports in 1 week. Acquires first and second rights.** *The Gray Squirrel* sponsors the Minnie Chezum Memorial Contest December through May. Editor Betty Mowery advises, "Beginning poets should submit again as quickly as possible if rejected. Study the market: don't submit blind.

Always include a SASE or rejected manuscripts will not be returned. Please make checks for *all* publications payable to *The Oak*."

OASIS BOOKS; OASIS (III), 12 Stevenage Rd., London SW6 6ES England, founded 1969, editor/ publisher Ian Robinson. *Oasis* is a bimonthly magazine of short fiction and poetry as well as occasional reviews and other material. **"No preference for style or subject matter; just quality. No long poems;** *Oasis* **is a very short magazine. Also, usually no rhyming poetry."** They have published poetry by John Ash, Lee Harwood, George Evans and Roy Fisher. The editor says *Oasis* is international A5 size, litho, folded sheets. They receive 500-600 poems a year, use about 4 or 5. Press run is 500 for 400 subscribers of which 10 are libraries. **Sample postpaid: $2.50. Submit up to 6 poems at a time. Previously published poems sometimes OK; simultaneous submissions OK "if work comes from outside the U.K."** Include SAE and 4 IRCs for return. Seldom comments on rejections. **Reports in 1 month. Pays 4 copies.** Staff reviews books of poetry. Send books for review consideration. Oasis Books publishes 2-3 paperbacks and 2-3 chapbooks/year. **Replies to queries and mss in 1 month. For sample books or chapbooks, write for catalog.** Ian Robinson says, "One IRC is not enough to ensure return airmail postage; four will, provided manuscript is not too thick. No return postage will ensure that the ms is junked."

‡OATMEAL AND POETRY; VOYAGER PUBLISHING (I, IV-SUBSCRIBERS), P.O. Box 2215, Dept. PM, Stillwater MN 55082-2215, founded 1994, editor Demitra Flanagan. A quarterly magazine of short stories and verse "from the country side of life, *Oatmeal and Poetry* is a product of a dream; to keep alive the integrity and beauty of traditional, metric poetry as an art form." **They want "traditional rhyme and form poetry; sonnets, haiku, senryu and tanka; poetry with strong use of meter and rhyme combined with visualization, metaphor, etc.; country and family themes; poems should be no longer than 30 lines. Free and blank verse are considered, but must be exceptional to be published. No experimental garble dealing with overly explicit sexual connotations; no satanic or cult themes; no profanity."** They have recently published C. David Hay, Terri Warden and Najwa Salam Brax. As a sample the editor selected these lines from "Wintergreen" by Kay Karras:

> You take me back to the days when I,
> A barefoot girl 'neath an azure sky
> Came to hunt in the cooling breeze
> The wintergreen berries and wintergreen leaves.
> I see in your happy eyes the smile
> Making me wonder all the while
> As the years flit by and I cease to be,
> Will you look for me here
> By the wintergreen tree?

Oatmeal and Poetry is 36 pgs., 8½ × 11, desktop-published and saddle-stapled with parchment cover and b&w art, photos and graphics inside. They receive more than 3,000 poems a year, publish 50-60 poems/issue. Press run is 500. Subscription: $18. **Sample postpaid: $4.50. Make checks payable to Voyager Publishing. There is a $1/poem reading fee for nonsubscribers. Submit 3 poems at a time, typed or legibly printed. One poem to a page (3/page for haiku/senryu/tanka) with name and address on each page. "Submissions which do not include SASE or required fee will be discarded without response." Previously published poems OK; no simultaneous submissions. Cover letter preferred.** Time between acceptance and publication is 2 months to 1 year. **Poems are circulated to an editorial board. Seldom comments on rejections. Publishes theme issues. Send SASE for guidelines and upcoming themes. Reports in 2 weeks to 3 months. Pays 1 copy. Acquires first North American serial or reprint rights.** Reviews chapbooks of poetry. Open to unsolicited reviews. Poets may also send books for review consideration with $3 reading fee. They include "The Network Muse" classified section in *Oatmeal and Poetry*. It publishes market and contest listings. They also sponsor quarterly contests plus an annual anthology contest. Send SASE for details. The editor says, "All submissions are considered for publication based on their own merit. The best way to see what will get published is to obtain a copy of our journal. Because we are a family magazine, we do not consider any works which are profane, or excessively violent."

OBLATES (IV-Religious, spirituality/inspirational), Missionary Association of Mary Immaculate, 15 S. 59th St., Belleville IL 62223-4694, phone (618)233-2238, editor Christine Portell, is a bimonthly magazine circulating free to 500,000 benefactors. **"We use well-written, perceptive traditional verse, average 16 lines. Avoid heavy allusions. Good rhyme and/or rhythm a must. We prefer a reverent, inspirational tone, but not overly 'sectarian and scriptural' in content. We like to use seasonal material. We like traditional poetry (with meter) and are always on the lookout for good Christmas poetry."** They have recently published poetry by Jean Conder Soule, Carlton J. Duncan and Claire Puneky. *Oblates* is 20 pgs., digest-sized, saddle-stapled, using color inside and on the cover. **Sample and guidelines for SAE and 2 first-class stamps. Submit not more than 2 poems**

at a time. **Considers simultaneous submissions.** Time to publication "is usually within 1 to 2 years." **Editor comments "occasionally, but always when ms 'just missed or when a writer shows promise.' " Reports within 4-6 weeks. Pays $30 plus 3 copies. Buys first North American serial rights.** She says, "We are a small publication very open to mss from authors—beginners and professionals. We do, however, demand professional quality work. Poets need to study our publication, **and to send no more than one or two poems at a time. Content must be relevant to our older audience to inspire and motivate in a positive manner."**

OFFERINGS (I, IV-Students), P.O. Box 1667, Lebanon MO 65536-1667, founded 1994, editor Velvet Fackeldey, is a poetry quarterly. **"We accept traditional and free verse from established and new poets, as well as students. Prefer poems of less than 30 lines. No erotica."** They have recently published poetry by Michael Estabrook, Kent Braithwaite, Jocelyne Kamerer and Robert Hentz. As a sample the editor selected these lines from "The Proper Forms" by Robert Cooperman:

> *It was the night I learned*
> *that instead of my big-boned father*
> *there was only a teacup*
> *balanced on a table's edge*
> *just before the world's worst earthquake*
> *and all the sacred prayer shawls*
> *couldn't refit the shards of his heart.*

Offerings is 50-60 pgs., digest-sized, neatly printed (one poem to a page) and saddle-stapled with paper cover. They receive about 500 poems a year, accept approximately 25%. Press run is 100 for 75 subscribers, 25 shelf sales. Single copy: $5; subscription: $16. **Sample postpaid: $3. Submit typed poems with name and address on each page. Students should also include grade level. SASE required. No previously published poems or simultaneous submissions. Seldom comments on rejections. Send SASE for guidelines. Reports in 1 week. Acquires first rights.** The editor says, "We are unable to offer payment at this time (not even copies) but hope to be able to do so in the future. We welcome beginning poets."

OFFICE NUMBER ONE (I, IV-Form), 1708 S. Congress Ave., Austin TX 78704, e-mail onocding us@aol.com, founded 1988, editor Carlos B. Dingus, appears 2-4 times/year. *ONO* is a "humorous, satirical zine of news information and events from parallel and alternate realities." In addition to stories, they want **limericks, 3-5-3 or 5-7-5 haiku and rhymed/metered quatrains. "Poems should be short (2-12 lines) and make a point. No long rambling poetry about suffering and pathos."** As for a sample, the editor says, "No one poem provides a fair sample." *ONO* is 12 pgs., 8½×11, computer set in 10 pt. type, saddle-stitched, with graphics and ads. They use about 20 poems a year. Press run is 2,000 for 75 subscribers, 50 shelf sales, 1,600 distributed free locally. Single copy: $1.85; subscription: $8.82/6 issues. **Sample postpaid: $2. Submit up to 5 pgs. of poetry at a time. Previously published poems and simultaneous submissions OK. E-mail submissions also OK. "Will comment on rejections if comment is requested." Publishes theme issues occasionally. Send SASE for guidelines and upcoming themes or request via e-mail. Reports in 1-2 months. Pays "23¢"** and 1 copy. Buys "one-time use, and use in any *ONO* anthology." The editor says, "Say something that a person can use to change his life."

THE OGALALA REVIEW (II), P.O. Box 628, Guymon OK 73942-0628, founded 1989, is an annual journal of poetry, fiction, creative nonfiction and translation. **No longer interested in reviews or scholarly articles. "We use both formal and free verse. We don't use light verse, inspirational poetry, or any work that relies on typographical gimmicks."** They have recently published poetry by Enid Shomer, Naton Leslie and David Citino. As a sample the editors selected these lines from "The Sundial" by Rainer Maria Rilke (translated by Carol Babylon):

> *Seldom does the chill of moist decay*
> *reach beyond the shadows in the garden—*
> *(where the drops hear one another fall in solemn*
> *counterpoint)—to the column*
> *choked with coriander and marjoram*
> *that counts the hours of the summer day*

Format for *The Ogalala Review* varies, but the most recent issue we received was 120 pgs., digest-sized, perfect-bound, with glossy cover. "The average issue has three longish prose pieces and a dozen pages of poetry." They receive about 2,000 poems a year, use about 2%. Subscription: $10. **Sample postpaid: $5. "We don't care whether poets submitting to us have published before, but we don't like to receive work from people who seem to have read nothing new since the Victorian Period. We hate reading long résumés; if poets insist on mentioning their credits, they should limit the list to two or three." Include name and address on each poem. Simultaneous submissions OK, "but writers must notify us promptly of acceptance elsewhere. We do not normally consider previously published work." For translations, include written permission from copyright holder** or statement that the work is in public domain. Include SASE for response. Reports in 4 months or less. Pays 2 copies. Acquires first serial rights only. The editors add, "Because the magazine is under new staff, we suggest people who haven't seen it recently order a sample or a subscription."

THE OHIO REVIEW (II); OHIO REVIEW BOOKS (V), 209C Ellis Hall, Ohio University, Athens OH 45701-2979, phone (614)593-1900, founded 1959, editor Wayne Dodd, attempts "to publish the best in contemporary poetry, fiction and reviews" in the *Review* and in chapbooks, flat-spined paperbacks and hardback books. They use **"all types"** of poetry and have published poems by David Baker, William Matthews, Lynn Emanuel and Robin Behn. As a sample the editor selected these lines from "Alba" by Pamela Kircher:

> The lovers rise from bed and leave
> the fire banked in ashes,
> stars dim and disappearing
> as night unpins and drops
> its faded cloth.

The Ohio Review appears 2 times/year in a professionally printed, flat-spined format of 200 pgs., matte cover with color and art, circulation 3,000, featuring about 28 poets/issue. One of the respected "credits" in the literary world, this magazine tends to publish mostly lyric and narrative free verse with an emphasis on voice. Content, structure and length seem open, and voices tend to complement each other, evidence of careful editing. Moreover, you'll find top-name writers appearing with relative newcomers. They receive about 3,000 submissions/year, use 1% of them, and have a 6- to 12-month backlog. Subscription: $16. **Sample postpaid: $6. Reads submissions September 15 through March 30 only. Editor sometimes comments on rejections. Send SASE for guidelines. Reports in 1 month. Always sends prepublication galleys. Pays $1/line for poems and $5/page for prose plus copies. Buys first North American serial rights.** Reviews books of poetry in 5-10 pgs., single or multi-book format. Send books to Robert Kinsley for review consideration. **They are not currently accepting unsolicited submissions of book mss. Query with publication credits, bio.** Work published in *The Ohio Review* has been included in *The Best American Poetry* (1992 and 1993) and *Pushcart Prize* anthologies.

OHIO STATE UNIVERSITY PRESS/THE JOURNAL AWARD IN POETRY (II), 180 Pressey Hall, 1070 Carmack Rd., Columbus OH 43210-1002, phone (800)437-4439, fax (614)292-2065, poetry editor David Citino. Each year *The Journal* (see listing also in this section) selects for publication by Ohio State University Press for the Ohio State University Press/Journal Award **one full-length (at least 48 pgs.) book ms submitted during September, typed, double-spaced, $15 handling fee (payable to OSU).** Send SASE for return of ms; self-addressed, stamped postcard for notification of ms receipt. **Some or all of the poems in the collection may have appeared in periodicals, chapbooks or anthologies, but must be identified. Along with publication,** *The Journal* **Award in Poetry pays $1,000 cash prize from the Helen Hooven Santmyer Fund "in addition to the usual royalties."** Each entrant receives a subscription (2 issues) to *The Journal*.

OLD CROW REVIEW (III), P.O. Box 662, Amherst MA 01004-0662, e-mail tkelley@ais.smith.edu, founded 1990, editors John Gibney and Tawnya Kelley, is a biannual magazine with mythic concerns, "visions or fragments of visions of a new myth." It includes novel fragments, short stories, poems, essays, interviews, photography and art. **They have no specifications regarding form, length, subject matter or style of poetry.** They have published poetry by Simon Perchick, Patricia Martin and Pat Schneider. As a sample the editors selected these lines from "The Density of Her Gaze" by Christopher Jones:

> I have never seen my mother, but I
> can feel sometimes when she goes by,
> crouched down in a taxicab.
>
> She hides from me, has always hidden.
> I know my mother only through blurry spy
> photographs and the density of her gaze.

Old Crow is 100 pgs., digest-sized, neatly printed and perfect-bound with card cover. They receive about 1,000 submissions a year, accept 2-3%. Press run is 500. Subscription: $9/year. **Sample postpaid: $5. (A portion of the sale price from each review goes to Food For All, a nonprofit organization benefiting the hungry and homeless.) Submit 3-6 poems at a time. Previously published poems and simultaneous submissions OK. Cover letter with brief bio (for Contributor's Notes) required. Reads submissions February 1 through July 30 and October 1 through December 15. Poems are screened by editorial assistants then the editorial board then the editor-in-chief (John Gibney). Seldom comments on rejections. Reports in 1 month. Pays 1 copy. Copyright reverts to poet at publication.** Open to unsolicited reviews. The editors say, "Long live the new flesh!"

THE OLD RED KIMONO (I, II), P.O. Box 1864, Rome GA 30162, phone (706)295-6312, founded 1972, poetry editor Jon Hershey, a publication of the Humanities Division of Floyd College, has the "sole purpose of putting out a magazine of original, high-quality poetry and fiction. *ORK* **is looking for submissions of 3-5 short poems. Poems should be very concise and imagistic. Nothing sentimental or didactic."** They have recently published poetry by Walter McDonald, Peter Huggins, Midred Greear, John C. Morrison, Jack Stewart, Kirsten Fox and Al Braselton. The magazine is an annual, circulation 1,400, 72 pgs., 8½×11, professionally printed on heavy stock with b&w graphics, colored matte cover with art, using approximately 40 pgs. of poetry (usually 1 or 2 poems to the page). They receive 1,000 submissions/year, use 60-70. **Reading period is September 1 through March 1. Reports in 3 months. Pays copies. Acquires first publication rights.**

THE OLIVE PRESS PUBLICATIONS (V), Box 99, Los Olivos CA 93441-0099, phone/fax (805)688-2445, founded 1979, editor Lynne Norris, is a general small press publisher for whom "poetry is an incidental effort at this time. We specialize in local and family history." They have previously published *It Don't Hurt to Laugh*, a collection of cowboy poetry by Jake Copass.

OLYMPIA REVIEW; ZERO CITY PRESS; ZERO CITY POETRY WEB ZINE; THE HAWK (III), 3430 Pacific Ave. SE, Suite A-6254, Olympia WA 98501, e-mail mmichael@art.net, website http://www.CRUZIO.com/~zerocity/, founded 1992, editor Michael McNeilley, managing editor Stephanie Brooks, appears at least twice annually, publishing "the best available contemporary writing, without regard for rules, conventions or precedent. **No taboos, beyond reasonably good taste; style and talent, significance and artistry are our only criteria. Seldom use rhyme. Nothing incidental, religious or sentimental. Prefer poems under 50 lines or so."** They have published poetry by Charles Bukowski, Ronald Wallace, Hayley R. Mitchell, Albert Huffstickler, Errol Miller, Virgil Hervey, Antler, Colt Townsend, John Forrest Glade, Matt Dennison and Lyn Lifshin. As a sample the editor selected this haiku by A.C. Missias:

> surprising cool breeze
> disturbs the grass shadow
> on an open book

The editor says *OR* is 60-100 pgs., digest-sized, flat-spined, with 2-color coated card cover, art, graphics, photos and ads. Press run is 750-1,000. Subscription: $12.95 for 4 issues. **Sample postpaid: $4.50. Submit up to 6 poems at a time. Previously published poems ("tell us where") and simultaneous submissions OK. Cover letter and short bio required.** *OR* **prefers submissions by regular mail. Seldom comments on rejections. Send SASE for guidelines or request via e-mail. Reports in 1-12 months. Pays 1 copy. Acquires first North American serial or one-time rights.** Reviews books of poetry and magazines in up to 700 words, single or multi-book format. Zero City Press publishes 1-2 chapbooks/year in varied formats; authors selected from those published in *OR*. They also publish a periodic broadside "using work representative of the quality found in the *Olympia Review*" and an annual anthology. Pays 3 copies. *Zero City Poetry WebZine*, contact co-editors Michael McNeilley and J.J. Webb at zcity@cruzio.com, publishes poetry and art, and hosts the Small Press Bulletin Board, with submission and ordering information on a variety of small press publications, and links to Internet poetry sites around the world. "*Zero City* attracted more than 1,000 readers in its first month of operation, billing itself as 'ground zero for explosive poetry.' " Recently published writers include B.Z. Niditch, John Grey, C.E. Nelson, Janet Bernichon and Meredyth Smith. Regular mail for *Zero City* can be addressed to the *Olympia Review* above. *The Hawk* (http://www.cruzio.com/~hawk), is "an arts and literary eZine for the world wide web, accepting submissions of fiction up to 5,000 words, poetry, essays, reviews and graphics." It has published writers such as Robert Anton Wilson, Nick Herbert, Ralph Abraham, Christopher Herold and Robert Sward, and has a quarterly circulation in excess of 20,000. **Reports in 1 week to 8 months. Pays $5-10/published piece.** Contact editor J.J. Webb or fiction editor Michael McNeilley at hawk@cruzio.com, or write *The Hawk*, 240A Sylvan Way, Boulder Creek CA 95006. Michael McNeilley advises poets to "start with the classics, to see where poetry has been. Then read more poetry, and fiction, in the little magazines, where today's writing is found. Develop your own voice, write a clean line, edit mercilessly and you may help determine where poetry is going. Read an issue, see firsthand what we're up to, then submit."

ON SPEC: THE CANADIAN MAGAZINE OF SPECULATIVE WRITING (IV-Regional, science fiction/fantasy), P.O. Box 4727, Edmonton, Alberta T6E 5G6 Canada, e-mail onspec@freen et.edmonton.ab.ca, founded 1989, is a quarterly featuring Canadian science fiction writers and artists. **They want work by Canadian poets only and only science fiction/speculative poetry. 100 lines maximum.** They have published poetry by Alice Major and Eileen Kernaghan. *On Spec* is 96 pgs., digest-sized, offset printed on recycled paper and perfect-bound with color cover, b&w art and ads inside. They receive about 100 poems a year, accept approximately 5%. Press run is 1,750 for 800 subscribers of which 10 are libraries, 600 shelf sales. Single copy: $4.95; subscription: $19.95 (both in Canadian funds). **Sample postpaid: $6. Submit no more than 5 poems at a time, in "competition format" (author's name should not appear on the ms). No previously published poems or simulta-**

neous submissions. **Cover letter with poem titles and 2-sentence bio required.** Time between acceptance and publication is 6 months. **Poems are circulated to an editorial board. Seldom comments on rejections. Send SASE or e-mail for guidelines. Reports in 5 months maximum. Pays $15/poem and 1 copy. Acquires first North American serial rights.**

‡**ONCE UPON A WORLD (IV-Science fiction/fantasy)**, 646 W. Fleming Dr., Nineveh IN 46164-9718, founded 1988, editor Emily Alward. **"All poetry submitted should relate to science fiction or fantasy in concept and/or imagery. This does not mean it has to be 'about' space travel or dragons. None with a nihilistic outlook, extremely avant-garde style or formats."** They have published poetry by John Grey, W. Gregory Stewart and Laura Vess. As a sample the editor selected these lines from "Instant Icons" by Gary Every:

> I remember watching Neil Armstrong
> step onto the moon
> as my family gathered around
> the electronic oracle at my grandfather's
> summer lodge outside Detroit. The television
> newscaster narrated events as they unfolded,
> the Stars and Stripes unfurled,
> but I was 9 years old and unimpressed.
> It was lame compared to Sunday Afternoon
> Science Fiction Theatre . . .

Once Upon A World is 80-100 pgs, magazine-sized, with heavy card stock colored covers, spiralbound. They accept 5-10 of 50 submissions received. Press run is 120. **Sample postpaid: $8.50. Checks payable to Emily Alward. Reports in 1-4 months. Pays 1 copy. "We strongly recommend purchase of a copy before submitting both to give some idea of the content and tone and to help keep the magazine solvent. But this is not a requirement."** The editor says, "Our major interest is in presenting science fiction and fantasy *short* stories with well-worked-out alternate world settings and an emphasis on ideas and/or character interaction. We use poetry for fillers. Where possible we try to match a poem with an adjacent story that it somewhat resembles in subject matter or tone. As the editor's major interest is fiction, she does not feel qualified to give in-depth critiques of poetry."

ONIONHEAD; ARTS ON THE PARK, INC. (THE LAKELAND CENTER FOR CREATIVE ARTS); WORDART, THE NATIONAL POETS COMPETITION; ESMÉ BRADBERRY CONTEMPORARY POETS PRIZE (II), 115 N. Kentucky Ave., Lakeland FL 33801-5044, phone (941)680-2787, editors Susan Crawford, Dot D. Davis, K.C. Jarrett and Brenda Patterson. Arts on the Park founded 1979; *Onionhead* founded 1988. *Onionhead* is a literary quarterly. **"Our focus is on provocative political, social and cultural observations and hypotheses. Controversial material is encouraged. International submissions are welcome. We have no taboos, but provocation is secondary to literary excellence. No light verse please."** They have published poetry by Jessica Freeman, Arthur Knight, Lyn Lifshin, B.Z. Niditch and A.D. Winans. As a sample we selected these lines from "Paying Back Karma" by Jo Ann Lordahl:

> This bed I made
> will haunt me
>
> Until I burn it
> bury it, or defuse it.

The magazine is 40-50 pgs., digest-sized, photocopied from typescript, saddle-stapled with glossy card cover. They use 100 of 2,500 submissions received/year. Press run is 250. Complimentary distribution to universities, reviews and libraries worldwide. Subscription: $8 US, $16 other. **Sample postpaid: $3. Submit 3-8 poems at a time, maximum 60 lines each. No previously published poems or simultaneous submissions. Short cover letter preferred. Poet's name and title of poems should appear in the upper right-hand corner of each page. Poem "should be submitted exactly as you intend it to appear if selected for publication." SASE required for return of material.** Poems are reviewed by an Editorial Board. **"Rarely"** comments on rejections. **Reports in 10 weeks. If accepted, poems will normally appear within one year. Pays 1 copy. Acquires first serial and electronic rights.** WORDART, The National Poets Competition, established 1983, is open to all American authors. Cash awards, "including the prestigious Esmé Bradberry Contemporary Poets Prize and chapbook, are announced at a reading and reception during the first part of March." $8 reading fee. For guidelines and specific dates send SASE to the sponsoring organization, Arts on the Park, Inc., at the above address.

ONTHEBUS; BOMBSHELTER PRESS (II), P.O. Box 481266, Bicentennial Station, Los Angeles CA 90048, founded 1975, *ONTHEBUS* editor Jack Grapes, Bombshelter Press poetry editors Jack Grapes and Michael Andrews. *ONTHEBUS* uses **"contemporary mainstream poetry—no more than 6 poems (10 pgs. total) at a time. No rhymed, 19th Century traditional 'verse.' "** They have published poetry by Charles Bukowski, Albert Goldbarth, Ai, Norman Dubie, Kate Braverman, Stephen Dobyns, Allen Ginsberg, David Mura, Richard Jones and Ernesto Cardenal. As a sample Jack Grapes selected these lines from "A Significant Poet" by Michael Andrews:

> Tu Fu knew what I found out—
> a poet that leaves his poems to unborn children
> is planting dandelions on his grave.
> Pissing on your grave won't make the roses grow.
> For all the difference the poem will make
> it is better to dig an honest trench.

ONTHEBUS is a magazine appearing 2 times/year, 275 pgs., offset, flat-spined, with color card cover. Press run is 3,500 for 600 subscribers of which 40 are libraries, 1,200 shelf sales ("500 sold directly at readings"). Subscription: $28 for 3 issues; Issue #8/9, special double issue: $15. **Sample postpaid: $12. Guidelines are printed on the copyright page of each issue. Submit 3-6 poems at a time. Simultaneous submissions and previously published poems OK, "if I am informed where poem has previously appeared and/or where poem is also being submitted. I expect neatly typed, professional looking cover letters with list of poems included plus poet's bio. Sloppiness and unprofessional submissions do not equate with great writing." Do not submit mss between November 1 and March 1 or between June 1 and September 1. Submissions sent during those times will be returned unread. Reports in "anywhere from 2 weeks to 2 years." Pays 1 copy. Acquires one-time rights. No comments on rejections.** Reviews books of poetry in 400 words (chapbooks in 200 words), single format. Open to unsolicited reviews. Poets may also send books for review consideration. This exciting journal seems a cross between *The Paris Review* and *New York Quarterly* with a distinct West Coast flavor that puts it in a league of its own. Editor Jack Grapes jam-packs each issue with dozens upon dozens of poems, mostly free verse (lyric, narrative, dramatic)—some tending toward avant-garde and some quite accessible—that manages somehow to reach out and say: "Read Me." Poetry published in *ONTHEBUS* has been included in *The Best American Poetry 1993*. Bombshelter Press publishes 4-6 flat-spined paperbacks and 5 chapbooks/year. **Query first. Primarily interested in Los Angeles poets. "We publish very few unsolicited mss." Reports in 3 months. Pays 50 copies.** They also publish the *ONTHEBUS* Poets Anthology Series. Send SASE for details. Jack Grapes says, "My goal is to publish a democratic range of American poets and insure they are read by striving to circulate the magazine as widely as possible. It's hard work and a financial drain. I hope the mag is healthy for poets and writers, and that they support the endeavor by subscribing as well as submitting."

OPEN HAND PUBLISHING INC. (V), P.O. Box 22048, Seattle WA 98122-0048, phone (206)323-2187, fax (206)323-2188, founded 1981, publisher P. Anna Johnson, is a "literary/political book publisher" bringing out flat-spined paperbacks as well as cloth cover editions about African-American and multicultural issues." They have published *Puerto Rican Writers at Home in the USA*, "an anthology of seventeen of the most well-known Puerto Rican writers"; *Where Are the Love Poems for Dictators?* by E. Ethelbert Miller; and *Stone on Stone/Piedra Sobre Piedra*, a bilingual anthology edited by Zoë Anglesey. As a sample the editor selected "Kira's Tanka" from *Old Woman of Irish Blood* by Pat Andrus:

> Fragrant pea blossom,
> why do your scent and color
> wake me at sunrise?
> Daughter's breath sweet after birth.
> Her small body light rose tones.

They do not consider unsolicited mss. Send SASE for catalog to order samples.

‡OPEN UNISON STOP; PM PRESS (II), 427 SW Madison, Suite 136, Corvallis OR 97333, founded 1990, editors Michael Spring and p. notzka. *open unison stop* is an annual magazine publishing poems, short (short) stories, parts-of-novels, essays with a literary bent, copy-ready art/photography and reviews from all fronts, quarters, movements and schools writing in English. **"Prefer poems around 35 lines or less, but will consider longer poems if exceptional. Open to all forms/styles. Editors prefer strong imagery, rich language and explorative verse, original twists in vision and metaphor. No didactic, greeting card, cliché-ridden verse."** They have recently published poetry

---

ALWAYS include a self-addressed, stamped envelope (SASE) when sending a ms or query to a publisher within your own country. When sending material to other countries, include a self-addressed envelope and International Reply Coupons (IRCs), available for purchase at many post offices.

by christian gholson, B.Z. Niditch, Sonya Hess, Sheila E. Murphy, Errol Miller, Richard Kostelanetz and Sean Brendan-Brown. As a sample the editors selected these lines from "Voyage of the Self that Dreams" by Carolyn Stoloff:

> *springs creak as the dreaming self escapes*
> *its skin to glide up the road, any road:*
> *water, air . . . past tense dobermans,*
> *past listerine lights, to board the dream*

open unison stop is 20 pgs., 4¼ × 11, photocopied from laser printed master sheets on ordinary paper with b&w illustrations. They accept about 2% of the submissions received. Subscription: $10, includes at least 2 issues, as well as any broadsides or chapbooks PM Press may publish. **Sample postpaid: $3. No previously published poems or simultaneous submissions. "No SASE sees the submission directly to the door and into the street." Reports in 1 day to 3 months. Always sends prepublication galleys. Pays 1 copy.** PM Press solicits mss for chapbooks from regular contributors of *open unison stop.* The editors advise, "Read, read, read. Write and rewrite often. Be patient and persistent with your craft and vision."

ORACLE POETRY; ASSOCIATION OF AFRICAN WRITERS; RISING STAR PUBLISHERS (I, IV-Ethnic), 2105 Amherst Rd., Hyattsville MD 20783, phone (301)422-2665, fax (301)422-2720, founded 1989, editorial director Obi Harrison Ekwonna. *Oracle Poetry* and *Oracle Story* appear quarterly using works **"mainly of African orientation; must be probing and must have meaning—any style or form. Writers must have the language of discourse and good punctuation. No gay, lesbian or erotic poetry."** As a sample the editor selected these lines from "War of 1968" by Greggette Soto:

> *Twenty-three years ago*
> *A son went off to war*
> *It wasn't to fight*
> *Communism in Vietnam*
> *But to fight*
> *Racism in his own backyard.*

Membership in the Association of African Writers is $20/year. *Oracle Poetry* is 46 pgs., digest-sized, saddle-stapled, print run 500. Subscription: $20/year. **No previously published poems or simultaneous submissions. "Poets may submit materials by fax; however, we prefer submissions by disk in WordPerfect 5.1, or in copies." Reports in 4-6 weeks. Pays 1 copy. Acquires first North American serial rights.** Reviews books of poetry. Sponsors contests. Send SASE for details. The editor says, "Read widely, write well and punctuate right."

ORBIS: AN INTERNATIONAL QUARTERLY OF POETRY AND PROSE (II); RHYME INTERNATIONAL COMPETITION FOR RHYMING POETRY (IV-Form), 199 The Long Shoot, Nuneaton, Warwickshire CV11 6JQ England, founded 1968, editor Mike Shields, considers **"all poetry so long as it's genuine in feeling and well executed of its type."** They have published poetry by Sir John Betjeman, Ray Bradbury, Seamus Heaney and Naomi Mitchison, as well as a US issue including Bukowski, Levertov, Piercy, Stafford and many others, "but are just as likely to publish absolute unknowns." The quarterly is 64 pgs., 6 × 8½, flat-spined, professionally printed with glossy card cover. They receive "thousands" of submissions/year, use "less than 5%." Circulation is 1,000 with 600 subscriptions of which 50 are libraries. Single copy: £3.95 ($6); subscription: £15 ($28). **Sample postpaid: $2 (or £1). Submit 1 poem/sheet, typed on 1 side only. No bio, no query. Enclose IRCs for reply, not US postage. Reports in 1-2 months. Pays $10 or more/acceptance plus 1 free copy. Each issue carries £50 in prizes paid on basis of reader votes. Editor comments on rejections "occasionally—if we think we can help.** *Orbis* is completely independent and receives no grant-aid from anywhere." They sponsor the Rhyme International Competition for Rhyming Poetry. The competition has 2 categories (open class, any rhyming poem up to 50 lines; strict form class) with prizes averaging £500 in each class each year (at least 60% of fees received); minimum entry fee £5 (or $10). They claim to be "the only competition in the world exclusively for rhymed poetry." Write for entry form. Deadline: September 30.

ORCHISES PRESS (III), P.O. Box 20602, Alexandria VA 22320-1602, founded 1983, poetry editor Roger Lathbury, is a small press publisher of literary and general material in flat-spined paperbacks and in hardcover. **"Although we will consider mss submitted, we prefer to seek out the work of poets who interest us." Regarding poetry he states: "No restrictions, really; but it must be technically proficient and deeply felt. I find it increasingly unlikely that I would publish a ms unless a fair proportion of its contents has appeared previously in respected literary journals."** He has recently published poetry by L.S. Asekoff and Lia Purpura. Asked for a sample, he says, "I find this difficult, but . . ." (from Fred Dings's "Redwing Blackbirds"):

> *Tonight, as I look at the cold sky*
> *and its flock of blue-white scars,*

> *I can't yet turn from Orion's red star*
> *whose trembling red light has traveled for years*
> *to die now into any eyes that will hold it.*

He publishes about 4 flat-spined paperbacks of poetry a year, averaging 96 pgs., and some casebound books. **Submit 5-6 poems at a time. Poems must be typed. When submitting, "tell where poems have previously been published." Brief cover letter preferred. Reports in 1 month. Pays 36% of money earned once Orchises recoups its initial costs and has a "generous free copy policy."**

OREGON EAST (II, IV-Regional), Hoke Center, Eastern Oregon State College, La Grande OR 97850, phone (541)962-3787, founded 1950, editor changes yearly, is the "literary annual of EOSC, 50% of magazine open to off-campus professional writing." Their preferences: **"Eclectic tastes in poetry with the only requirement being literary quality work for off-campus submissions. Chances of publication are better for short poems (one page) than longer ones. Northwest themes welcome. No 'greeting card' verse."** They have recently published poetry and fiction by Jessica Mills, R.S. Kromwall, Kerri Brostrom, Christine Grey and Mark Shadle. It is approximately 100 pgs., 6×9, flat-spined, book format, typeset, with end papers, using graphics and b&w art. Content tends toward free verse lyrics. Editors try to give readers an overview of art in each issue, from poetry to prose to graphics. "We also publish short one-act plays." Circulation is 1,000 (300 off-campus) with 100 subscribers of which 30-40 are libraries. Single copy: $5. **Submit only 3-5 typed poems at a time. No simultaneous submissions. All submissions must be accompanied by SASE and cover letter with brief bio and phone number. Reads submissions September 1 through March 1 only. Notification by June. Send SASE for upcoming themes. Sometimes sends prepublication galleys. Pays 2 copies. Acquires all rights. Returns rights "with condition that *Oregon East* may reprint in any upcoming anthology."** The editor says, "Be fresh. Be daring. Your words should come to life on the page as they're read. We want poetry we can see and feel."

ORTALDA & ASSOCIATES (V), 1208 Delaware St., Berkeley CA 94702-1407, founded 1985, poetry editor Floyd Salas, director/editor Claire Ortalda, publishes quality flat-spined paperbacks of poetry but **is not accepting submissions at this time.** They have published poetry by Czeslaw Milosz, Robert Hass, Ishmael Reed, Gary Soto, Jack Micheline and Carolyn Kizer. As a sample Claire Ortalda selected these lines by Floyd Salas:

> *There is no honor among thieves*
> *He will bleed me down to serum for his vein*
> *and pop me into his arm*
> *He will sell me to the fence*
> *at the corner grocery store*

OSIRIS, AN INTERNATIONAL POETRY JOURNAL/UNE REVUE INTERNATIONALE (II, IV-Translations, bilingual), P.O. Box 297, Deerfield MA 01342-0297, phone (413)774-4027, founded 1972, poetry editor Andrea Moorhead, is a semiannual that **publishes contemporary poetry in English, French and Italian without translation and in other languages with translation, including Polish, Danish and German.** They want poetry which is **"lyrical, non-narrative, multi-temporal, post modern, well crafted. Also looking for translations from non-IndoEuropean languages."** They have recently published poetry by Ingrid Swanberg, Charles Cantalupo, Tahar Bekri (France) and Madeleine Gagnon (Québec). As a sample the editor selected this poem by Eugenio de Andrade, translated from the Portuguese by Alexis Levitin:

> *To make a boat from a word*
> *is the whole of my task*
> *or from flowering flax a mirror*
> *where the light of a face falls*
> *extravagant.*

Osiris is 40 pgs., 6×9, saddle-stapled with graphics and photos. There are 15-20 pgs. of poetry in English in each issue of this intriguing publication. They have a print run of 500 and send 50 subscription copies to college and university libraries, including foreign libraries. They receive 200-300 unsolicited submissions/year, use 12. Single copy: $6; subscription: $12. **Sample postpaid: $3. Submit 4-6 poems at a time. Include short bio and SASE with submission. "Translators should include a letter of permission from the poet or publisher as well as copies of the original text." Reports in 1 month. Sometimes sends prepublication galleys. Pays 5 copies.** If you translate poems from other countries or want to gain an international perspective on the art, you should send for a sample copy. Two poems published in *Osiris* have received Honorable Mentions from *The Pushcart Prize*. The editor advises, "It is always best to look at a sample copy of a journal before submitting work, and when you do submit work, do it often and do not get discouraged. Try to read poetry and support other writers."

THE OTHER SIDE MAGAZINE (III, IV-Political, religious, social issues), 300 W. Apsley St., Philadelphia PA 19144, phone (215)849-2178, founded 1965, poetry editor Rod Jellema, is a "magazine (published 6 times a year) concerned with **social justice issues from a Christian perspective. The magazine publishes 1-2 poems per issue. Submissions should be of high quality and must speak to and/or reflect the concerns and life experiences of the magazine's readers. We look for fresh insights and creative imagery in a tight, cohesive whole. Be warned that only 0.5% of the poems reviewed are accepted. Seldom does any published poem exceed 40-50 lines. We do not want to see pious religiosity, sentimental schlock or haiku."** They have recently published poetry by Kathleen Norris, Paul Ramsey, Carol Hamilton and John Knoepfle. *The Other Side* is magazine-sized, professionally printed on quality pulp stock, 64 pgs., saddle-stapled, with full-color paper cover, circulation 13,000 to that many subscriptions. Subscription: $29.50. **Sample postpaid: $4.50. Submit 3-5 poems at a time. No simultaneous submissions. No previously published poems. Editor "almost never" comments on rejections. Send SASE for guidelines. Pays $15 plus 4 copies and free subscription.**

OTIS RUSH; LITTLE ESTHER BOOKS (III), P.O. Box 21, North Adelaide 5006 South Australia, founded 1987, editor Ken Bolton. *Otis Rush*, appearing every 4 to 10 months, is a journal of "new writing, mostly poetry, some prose, plus writing on Australian visual art and occasional literary reviews." **They want "new, self-conscious, stylistically aware poetry."** They have recently published poetry by Harry Mathews, Tony Towle, Jenny Bornholdt and Gregory O'Brien. The editor says *OR* is 120-150 pgs., offset, perfect-bound, with some ads and art. Press run is 500 for about 100 subscribers of which 15 are libraries, 200 shelf sales. Single copy: $15; subscription: $40 Australian, $60 overseas. **Sample postpaid: $14. Submit 3-6 poems at a time. Previously published poems and simultaneous submissions OK. Cover letter required. Often comments on rejections. Send SASE for guidelines. Reports in 2 months.** Little Esther Books publishes 1-6 paperbacks/year. **Replies to queries in 1 month, to mss in 3-4 months. Pays 10% royalties and 15 author's copies.**

OTTER (IV-Regional), Parford Cottage, Chagford, Devon TQ13 8JR United Kingdom, founded 1988, editor Christopher Southgate, appears 3 times/year using **poetry by contributors associated with the County of Devon, "poems concerned with local community and issues—social, political, religious—and/or in strict forms."** They have published poetry by Lawrence Sail, Ron Tamplin, Harry Guest and Jane Beeson. As a sample, here are lines from "The Yellow and Green Daughter" by Sandra McBain:

> She dances like a daffodil
> or wind driven forsythia
> like a petal whirled in water

It is digest-sized, 48 pgs., stapled with glossy card cover, professionally printed. They accept about 25% of 400-500 poems/year. Press run is 400 for 70 subscribers of which 5 are libraries. Subscription: £6.50. **Sample postpaid: £2.50 (or $6 US; dollar checks OK). Submit up to 5 poems at a time. "Those not resident in Devon should indicate in their cover letter their connection with the county." Editor always comments on rejections. Reports within 3 months. Pays 1 copy.**

OUR FAMILY (IV-Religious), Box 249, Battleford, Saskatchewan S0M 0E0 Canada, phone (306)937-7771, fax (306)937-7644, founded 1949, editor Nestor Gregoire, o.m.i., is a monthly religious magazine **for Roman Catholic families. "Any form of poetry is acceptable. In content we look for simplicity and vividness of imagery. The subject matter should center on the human struggle to live out one's relationship with the God of the Bible in the context of our modern world. We do not want to see science fiction poetry, metaphysical speculation poetry, or anything that demeans or belittles the spirit of human beings or degrades the image of God in him/her as it is described in the Bible."** They have published poetry by Nadene Murphy and Arthur Stilwell. *Our Family* is 40 pgs., magazine-sized, glossy color paper cover, using drawings, cartoons, two-color ink. Circulation 10,000 of which 48 are libraries. Single copy: $1.95; subscription: $15.98 Canada/$21.98 US. **Sample postpaid: $2.50. Send SASE or SAE with IRC or personal check (American postage cannot be used in Canada) for writer's guidelines and upcoming themes. Will consider poems of 4-30 lines. Simultaneous submissions OK. Reports within 1 month after receipt. Pays 75¢-$1/ line.** The editor advises, "The essence of poetry is imagery. The form is less important. Really good poets use both effectively."

OUTERBRIDGE (II), English A324, The College of Staten Island, 2800 Victory Blvd., Staten Island NY 10314, phone (718)982-3640, founded 1975, editor Charlotte Alexander, publishes "the most crafted, professional poetry and short fiction we can find (unsolicited except special features—to date rural, urban and Southern, promoted in standard newsletters such as *Poets & Writers, AWP, Small Press Review*), interested in newer voices. **Anti loose, amateurish, uncrafted poems showing little awareness of the long-established fundamentals of verse; also anti blatant PRO-movement writing when it sacrifices craft for protest and message. Poems usually 1-4 pgs. in length."** They have published poetry by Walter McDonald, Thomas Swiss and Naomi Rachel. As a sample the editor selected these lines from "How to Imagine Deafness" by Kim Roberts:

> *Darken your ears until the tunnels*
> *with their intricate clockwork*
> *are sheathed in pitchy calm.*
> *Hum a little blue, to yourself,*
> *but keep it secret.*

The digest-sized, flat-spined annual is 100 pgs., about half poetry, circulation 500-600, 150 subscriptions of which 28 are libraries. They receive 500-700 submissions/year, use about 60. **Sample postpaid: $5. Submit 3-5 poems only, anytime except June and July. Include name and address on each page. "We dislike simultaneous submissions and if a poem accepted by us proves to have already been accepted elsewhere, a poet will be blacklisted as there are many good poets waiting in line." Cover letter with *brief* bio preferred. Reports in 2 months. Pays 2 copies (and offers additional copies at half price). Acquires first rights.** The editor says, "As a poet/editor I feel magazines like *Outerbridge* provide an invaluable publication outlet for individual poets (particularly since publishing a book of poetry, respectably, is extremely difficult these days). As in all of the arts, poetry—its traditions, conventions and variations, experiments—should be studied. One current 'trend' I detect is a lot of mutual backscratching which can result in very loose, amateurish writing. Discipline!"

OUTREACH: FOR THE HOUSEBOUND, ELDERLY AND DISABLED (IV-Senior citizens, specialized: disabled, religious), 7 Grayson Close, Stocksbridge, Sheffield S30 5BJ England, phone (0114)288-5346, editor Mike Brooks, founded 1985, is a quarterly using **"semi-religious poetry and short articles; cowboy, humor, love and romance, mystery, senior citizen and spirituality/inspired poetry. This is a magazine for the housebound, elderly and disabled who need cheering up, not made more depressed or bored!"** As a sample, here are lines from "Stairs to God" by Helen S. Rice:

> *Prayers are the stairs*
> *We must climb every day,*
> *If we would reach God*
> *There is no other way.*

Outreach is photocopied from typescript on ordinary paper, folded and saddle-stapled. **Send SAE with IRC for upcoming themes.**

OUTRIDER PRESS (I, IV-Women/feminism, gay/lesbian/bisexual), 1004 E. Steger Rd., Suite C-3, Crete IL 60417-1362, founded 1988, president Phyllis Nelson, publishes 1-2 novels/anthologies/chapbooks annually. **They want "poetry dealing with the terrain of the human heart and plotting inner journeys; growth and grace under pressure. No bag ladies, loves-that-never-were, please."** As a sample the editor selected these lines from "Elegy" in *Listen to the Moon* by Whitney Scott:

> *He slipped*
> *Away,*
> *Gently as the rustle of silk*
> *He so favored in his shirts.*

That chapbook is 16 pgs., digest-sized, photocopied from typescript with matte card cover, $5. **Submit 3-5 poems at a time. Include name, address and phone/fax number on every poem. Simultaneous submissions OK, if specified. Cover letter preferred. Responds to queries in 3 months, to submissions in 6 months. Sometimes sends prepublication galleys. Pays 1 copy.** The editor notes, "Outrider Press published its first original trade paper novel, *Dancing to the End of the Shining Bar*, by Whitney Scott, in January, 1994, and its first anthology, *Prairie Hearts: Women's Writings on the Midwest*, in mid-1996." The press is affiliated with the Feminist Writers Guild, an 18-year-old organization open to all who support feminist writing.

‡"OVER THE BACK FENCE" MAGAZINE (IV-Regional), P.O. Box 756, Chillicothe OH 45601, phone (614)772-2165, fax (614)773-7626, founded 1994, senior editor Barbara Brickey Jividen, is a quarterly regional magazine "serving eighteen counties in southern Ohio. *Over The Back Fence*" has a wholesome, neighborly style that is appealing to readers from young adults to seniors." **They want rhyming or free verse poetry, 24 lines or less; open to subject matter, "but seasonal works well"; friendly or inspirational work. "Since most of our readers are not poets, we want something simple and likeable by the general public. No profanity, please."** As a sample the editor selected these lines from her poem "Birth Of Spring":

> *The heartbeat of a new season*
> *pounds beneath the earth,*
>
> *as frozen rains begin to thaw*
> *and pulsate through the veins*
> *of unborn flowers.*

The editor says it is 68 pgs., published on high gloss paper, saddle-stapled with b&w and color illustrations and photos, includes ads. They receive less than 200 poems a year, publish 4-10. Press run is 15,000 for about 2,000 subscribers, 40% shelf sales. Single copy: $2.95; subscription: $9.97/ year. **Sample postpaid: $4. Make checks payable to Back Fence Publishing, Inc. Submit up to 4 poems at a time. Previously published poems and simultaneous submissions OK, "if identified as such." Cover letter preferred. "Since we prefer reader-submitted poetry, we would like for the cover letter to include comments about our magazine or contents."** Time between acceptance and publication is 6-12 months. **Seldom comments on rejections. "We do not publish theme issues, but do feature specific Ohio counties quarterly. Send or call for specific areas." Send SASE for guidelines. Reports in 1-3 months. Pays 10¢/word, $25 minimum. Buys one-time North American print rights.** The editor says, "While we truly appreciate the professional poet, most of our published poetry comes from beginners or amateurs. We strive for reader response and solicit poetry contributions through the magazine."

THE OVERLOOK PRESS; TUSK BOOKS (V), 149 Wooster St., New York NY 10012, phone (212)477-7162, founded 1972, are trade publishers with about 8 poetry titles. They have published *Disappearances* by Paul Auster, *After a Lost Original* by David Shapiro and, most recently, *The Boy in the Well* by Daniel Mark Epstein. Tusk/Overlook Books are distributed by Viking/Penguin. **They publish on standard royalty contracts with author's copies. They "are no longer accepting poetry submissions."**

OVERVIEW LTD. POETRY (I, II), P.O. Box 211, Wood-Ridge NJ 07075, fax (201)778-5111, founded 1990, editor Joseph Lanciotti, is a biannual publication of **"plain good poetry, 10-40 lines."** As a sample the editor selected these lines from "Bridgeport Baseball" by Laura L. Koenig:

> All teams dissolve in the outfield.
> It's all heads up and everyone runs
> regardless of whose game it comes from,
> which
> one of the three
> being played in the park tonight.
> and it's not a big park;
> they're back to back.
> and side to side.
> It's baseball season
> in Bridgeport.

Overview Ltd. is 24 pgs., digest-sized, professionally printed and saddle-stapled with matte card cover. Press run is 500 for 150 subscribers, 250 shelf sales. **Sample postpaid: $5. Submit 3-4 poems at a time. No previously published poems; simultaneous submissions OK. Cover letter required. Submit by mail (with SASE) only." Send SASE for guidelines "*before* submitting." Reports in 3 months. Pays 1 copy plus $5-15.** The editor says, "*Overview Ltd.* is published only when a sufficient amount of good poetry has been submitted."

OWEN WISTER REVIEW (II), Box 4238, University Station, Laramie WY 82071-4238, fax (307)766-4027, e-mail owr@uwyo.edu, founded 1979, is the biannual literary and art magazine of the University of Wyoming. **They have no specifications regarding form, length, subject matter or style of poetry.** As a sample the editor selected these lines by Stephanie Studer:

> It is hot. Motionless air sits in my room
> and lungs, heavy with anticipation.
> Her skin shines intermittently red,
> reflecting the flash-fade of the sign outside my window.
> She is too far away. I will never
> touch her.

The editor says *OWR* is 76-92 pgs., 6×9, professionally printed and perfect-bound with art on the cover and inside; no ads. They receive more than 500 submissions a year, accept 4-6%. Press run is 500. Single copy: $5; subscription: $15. **Sample postpaid: $3.50. No previously published poems; simultaneous and e-mail submissions OK. Cover letter required. May query by e-mail or fax; must include mailing address. Reads submissions September 1 through March 31 only. Poems are circulated to an editorial board. Often comments on rejections. Send SASE for guidelines. Reports in 2-3 months. Pays 1 copy and 10% discount on additional copies. Acquires first rights.**

OWL CREEK PRESS; OWL CREEK PRESS POETRY PRIZE; GREEN LAKE CHAPBOOK PRIZE (II), 1620 N. 45th St., Seattle WA 98103, founded 1979, poetry editor Rich Ives. "Owl Creek Press is a nonprofit literary publisher. Selections for publication are based solely on literary quality." They publish full-length poetry books, chapbooks, anthologies. **"No subject or length limitations. We look for poetry that will endure."** They have published poetry by Angela Ball, Art Homer and

Laurie Blauner. As a sample here are the opening lines of "Ordinance on Returning" by Naomi Lazard:

> *We commend you on your courage.*
> *The place you have chosen to revisit*
> *is as seductive as ever.*
> *It has been in that business for centuries.*

Owl Creek Press **accepts books and chapbooks for publication only through its two annual contests.** The Owl Creek Press Poetry Prize selects 1-3 books for publication. Mss should be a minimum of 50 typed pages and should include an acknowledgments page for previous publications. Deadline: February 15; entry fee: $15; winners receive $750 and 10 copies of published book. The Green Lake Chapbook Prize chooses 1-3 chapbooks for publication. Mss should be under 40 pages and should include an acknowledgments page for previous publications. Deadline: August 15; entry fee: $10; winners receive 5 copies of published chapbook and a cash prize of $500 as an advance against royalties. Additional payment for reprinting. Send SASE for additional information on the contests. The editor says, "It is clear that many would-be poets do not read enough. A hungry mind is a valuable asset. Feed it."

OXFORD MAGAZINE (II), 261 Bachelor Hall, Miami University, Oxford OH 45056, phone (513)529-1954, fax (513)529-1392, founded 1984, appears annually, in the spring. **"We are open in terms of form, content and subject matter. We have eclectic tastes, ranging from New Formalism to Language poetry to Nuyorican poetry."** They have published poetry by Eve Shelnutt, Denise Duhamel and Walter McDonald. It is 100-120 pgs., 6×9, professionally printed and flat-spined. Press run is 500. **Sample postpaid: $5. Submit 3-5 poems at a time. No previously published poems. Simultaneous submissions OK, with notification. Cover letter with a short (one or two-line) bio required. Submission deadline: January 1. Pays copies. Buys first North American serial rights.**

‡**OXFORD POETRY; THE RICHARD ELLMANN PRIZE (I, II)**, Magdalen College, Oxford, Oxon 0X1 4AU England, founded 1983, co-editor Sinead Garrigan, appears 3 times a year. *Oxford Poetry*, designed to promote "new" poets, includes poetry, interviews, reviews and features. **They want "good poetry—not too long, any subject matter, any style except 'therapy' poetry."** They have recently published poetry by Seamus Heaney, Peter Reading, John Fuller and Jamie McKendrick. The editor says *Oxford Poetry* is about 52 pgs., A5 format, with colored card cover and ads on the back and inside covers. They receive about 800 poems a year, use approximately 70. Press run is 500 for 100 subscribers of which 20 are libraries, 200 shelf sales. Single copy: £2.40. **Sample postpaid: £2. Submit 4-6 poems at a time. No previously published poems; simultaneous submissions OK. Cover letter with brief bio required. Poems are circulated to an editorial board. Seldom comments on rejections. Send SASE (or SAE and IRCs) for guidelines. Reports in 6 months maximum. Pays 1 copy.** Reviews 2 new collections (first publication) in each issue. Poets may send books for review consideration. The Richard Ellmann Prize (established by Seamus Heaney) is awarded to the best poem in 3 issues. They also hold a translation competition in every second issue. Prize: £25. Send SASE (or SAE and IRCs) for details.

OXFORD UNIVERSITY PRESS, 198 Madison Ave., New York NY 10016. See listing in Publications Useful to Poets.

OXYGEN (II), 535 Geary St. #1010, San Francisco CA 94102-1633, phone (415)776-9681, founded 1991, editor Richard Hack, is a "spirited, independent literary magazine" which appears 3-4 times a year and is designed "to seek and celebrate beauty, truth and justice in well-crafted verse and prose." **They want poetry that is "ambitious, vivid, exploring sensitive areas of life; any form or mode or length (1-20 pgs.); grassroots, community focus; spiritual; progressive without cliché; Joycean; Blakean; Juan Ramón Jiménez; darkside, low life OK. We also like translations, but be sure to include original text. We generally stay away from light verse (unless very clever), so-called experimental writing, and post-mod theorizing."** They have recently published poetry by Hafiz, Devreaux Baker, Sal Salasin and Janet Fujimoto. As a sample the editor selected these lines from "The Beach" by Victor Martinez:

> *When finally the black mold of dread*
> *is burnt away, and a hand on your shoulder*
> *smacks of the impending fire,*
> *you know you've been cleansed, and can once again*
> *go home to the open window: the stamp of blue*
> *happiness, that was always there.*

Oxygen is 64 pgs., 8½×11, set in PageMaker, perfect-bound with slick cover, about 4 graphics each issue. They receive about 1,200 poems a year, publish approximately 2%. Press run is 600 for 50 subscribers, 250 shelf sales. Subscription: $14 (libraries $25; foreign $30). **Sample postpaid: $4 (Request from distributor: Bernhard DeBoer, Inc., 113 E. Centre St., Nutley NJ 07110). Submit up to 12 poems at a time with 2-4 lines for possible contributor's note. Previously published** poems and simultaneous submissions OK, "but let us know if previously published and where." Seldom comments on rejections (but will provide editorial commentary and consultation for a fee: $25 minimum, per-hour basis). Send SASE for general writer's guidelines. Reports within 2 months generally, "often 3-4 weeks." Pays 2 copies. All rights revert to contributors. Occasionally reviews books of poetry or other magazines. Open to unsolicited reviews. Poets may also send books for review consideration. The editor's advice: "Love words and rhythm. Educate yourself as much as possible in literature and experience. Eschew stand-up comedy posing as literature and declarative prose claiming to be poetry. Avoid evasive cynicism and flatness. Develop your spiritual life. Feel gratitude to society, acknowledge interdependence, love sharing."

PABLO LENNIS (I, IV-Science fiction/fantasy), 30 N. 19th St., Lafayette IN 47904, founded 1976, editor John Thiel, appears irregularly, is a **"science fiction and fantasy fanzine preferring poems of an expressive cosmic consciousness or full magical approach. I want poetry that rhymes and scans and I like a good rhythmic structure appropriate to the subject. Shorter poems are much preferred. I want them to exalt the mind, imagination, or perception into a consciousness of the subject. Optimism is usually preferred, and English language perfection eminently preferable. Nothing that is not science fiction or fantasy, or which contains morbid sentiments, or is perverse, or does not rhyme or contains slang."** They have published poetry by Sean McCormack, Don Meyerowitz, Deborah Kolodui and David C. Bryan. As a sample the editor selected these lines from "Wizard's Sestina" by Lynn Tait:

> A raging war of tides against the night,
> Blue, blazing trails no man may ever see,
> Irregular distortions of the light
> Like lasers bouncing aimlessly and free
> Towards an upward plateau where the white
> Of wizards flourish, ghosts there guard the key.

It is 22 pgs., magazine-sized, photocopied from typescript, side-stapled, using fantastic ink drawings and hand-lettering. "I get maybe fifty poems a year and have been using most of them." Press run is "up to 100 copies." Subscription: $20/year. **Sample postpaid: $2. No previously published poems or simultaneous submissions. Send SASE for guidelines. Reports "at once. I generally say something about why the poetry was not used, if it was not. If someone else might like it, I mention an address." Pays 1 copy, 2 if requested.** Reviews books of poetry if they are science fiction or fantasy. Open to unsolicited reviews. Poets may also send books for review consideration. The editor says, "Poetry is magic. I want spells, incantations, sorceries of a rhythmic and rhyming nature, loftily and optimistically expressed, and I think this is what others want. People buy poetry to have something that will affect them, add new things to their lives. If they want something to think about, they get prose. See how much magic you can make. See how well-liked it is."

‡PACIFIC COAST JOURNAL; FRENCH BREAD AWARDS; FRENCH BREAD PUBLI-CATIONS (II), P.O. Box 355, Campbell CA 95009-0355, e-mail paccoastj@aol.com, founded 1992, editor Stillson Graham. *PCJ* is a quarterly "unprofessional" literary magazine. **They want "offbeat poetry, visual poetry, poetry that is aware of itself. We don't rule out rhyming poetry, but rarely do we accept it. And no greeting card verse."** They have recently published poetry by Joan Payne Kincaid, Errol Miller and Hugh Fox. As a sample the editor selected these lines by Steve Teal:

> i see your humanity
> trapped gray
> in a television box
> your history flickers
> in images; hot pinks . . .
> and fragmented sentences . . .

PCJ is 56 pgs., 5½ × 8½, photocopied and saddle-stitched with a card stock cover and b&w photos and artwork. They receive 400-500 poems a year, accept approximately 15%. Press run is 200 for 75 subscribers, 25 shelf sales. Single copy: $3; subscription: $12. **Sample postpaid: $2.50. Submit 4 poems at a time. No previously published poems; simultaneous submissions OK. Cover letter preferred.** Time between acceptance and publication is 6-12 months. **Seldom comments on rejections. Send SASE for guidelines or request via e-mail. Reports in 2-3 months. Pays 1 copy. Acquires one-time rights.** Reviews novels, short story collections and chapbooks of poetry in 1,500 words, single format. Open to unsolicited reviews (and pays $5 if accepted). Poets may also send books for review consideration. They also sponsor the French Bread Awards for short fiction/poetry. Entry fee: $6 for a group of up to 4 poems (no longer than 8 pgs. total). First prize: $50. Second prize: $25. Deadline: August 1. Send SASE for details. French Bread Publications also occasionally publishes short story collections, short novellas, and chapbooks of poetry. Books are similar to the journal in format. **Query first with 5 sample poems, a cover letter and a list of credits for all the poems in the ms. Replies to queries in 1-2 months, to mss (if invited) in 2-3 months. Pays royalties and 50**

author's copies (out of a press run of 500). The editor says, "Most poetry looks like any other poetry. We want experiments in what poetry is."

PAINTED BRIDE QUARTERLY (II), 230 Vine St., Philadelphia PA 19106, editors Kathy Volk Miller and Marion Wrenn, founded 1973, appears quarterly. **"We have no specifications or restrictions. We'll look at anything."** They have published poetry by Robert Bly, Charles Bukowski, S.J. Marks and James Hazen. "*PBQ* aims to be a leader among little magazines published by and for independent poets and writers nationally." The 80-page, digest-sized, perfect-bound magazine uses 40 pgs. of poetry/issue, receiving over 1,000 submissions/year and using under 150. Neatly printed, it has a circulation of 1,000, 850 subscriptions, of which 40 are libraries. Subscription: $16. **Sample postpaid: $6. Submit no more than 6 poems, any length, typed; only original, unpublished work. "Submissions should include a** *short* **bio." Editors seldom comment on rejections. They have a 6- to 9-month backlog. Pays 1-year subscription, 1 half-priced contributor's copy and $5/accepted piece.** Publishes reviews of poetry books. "We also occasionally publish critical essays." Sponsors annual poetry contest and chapbook competition. Entry fee required for both. Send SASE for details. Poetry published in *PBQ* has been included in *The Best American Poetry 1995*.

PALANQUIN/TDM; PALANQUIN POETRY SERIES (II), Dept. of English, University of South Carolina-Aiken, 171 University Pkwy., Aiken SC 29801, fax (803)641-3461, e-mail phebed@aik en.sc.edu, founded 1988, editor Phebe Davidson, publishes a pamphlet series 6 times a year featuring one poet/issue. **They do not want "sentimental, religious, consciously academic" poetry.** They have recently published poetry by Dorothy Perry Thompson, Gregory Jerozal, Danny Romero, Mary Winters and Janet Krauss. As a sample the editor selected these lines by Joe Weil:

> *Above the above ground swimming pools*
> *In backyards of Elizabeth*
> *Gnats swarm at dusk*
> *And always the same girl stands*

The pamphlet we received, featuring poems by Janet Krauss, is professionally printed on heavy paper. Press run is 150 for 80 subscribers. Subscription: $10. **Sample postpaid: $1. Submit 5-10 poems at a time with bio and SASE. No previously published poems. "I read January through March for the following year." Reports in 2-3 months. Pays 25 copies.** *Palanquin* also holds an annual chapbook contest, deadline May 1. Include 20-25 pgs. of poetry (single poems may be previously published), bio, $10 reading fee. SASE for results only.

PALO ALTO REVIEW (I, II, IV-Themes), 1400 W. Villaret Blvd., San Antonio TX 78224, phone (210)921-5255 or 921-5017, fax (210)921-5115, e-mail eshull@accd.edu, founded 1992, editors Ellen Shull and Bob Richmond, is a biannual publication of Palo Alto college. "We invite writing that investigates the full range of education in its myriad forms. Ideas are what we are after. The *Palo Alto Review* is interested in connecting the college and the community. We would hope that those who attempt these connections will choose startling topics and find interesting angles from which to study the length and breadth of ideas and learning, a lifelong pursuit." The review includes articles, essays, memoirs, interviews, book reviews, fiction and poetry. **They want "poetry which has something to say, literary quality poems, with strong images, up to 50 lines. No inspirational verse, haiku or doggerel."** They have published poetry by Diane Glancy, Wendy Bishop, Lyn Lifshin and Ruth Daigon. As a sample we selected the opening lines of "A Sentence On Buck Creek" by Barbara Van Noord:

> *Buck Creek froze in winter and we skated*
> *before the snows fell, far, far*
> *beyond the farmhouse, beyond*
> *the little vineyard, into no man's land*
> *further than we had ever gone before,*
> *brushing aside the past, leaving*
> *just broken stencils in the nubbly ice,*
> *white glide lines like a trail of bread crumbs. . .*

PAR is 60 pgs., 8½ × 11, professionally printed on recycled paper and saddle-stapled with matte card cover with art; b&w photos, art and graphics inside. They publish about 8 poems in each issue (16 poems/year). Press run is 700 for 400 subscribers of which 10 are libraries, 200 shelf sales. Subscription: $10. **Sample postpaid: $5. Submit 3-5 poems at a time. No previously published poems; simultaneous submissions OK. Poems are read by an advisory board and recommended to editors, who sometimes suggest revisions. Always comments on rejections. "Although we frequently announce a theme, the entire issue will not necessarily be dedicated to the theme." Send SASE for guidelines and upcoming themes. Reports in 1-3 months. Pays 2 copies. Acquires first North American serial rights. "Please note poems as first published in** *Palo Alto Review* **in subsequent printings."** The editors say there are no requirements for submission, "though we recommend the reading (purchase) of a sample copy."

THE PANHANDLER (II), Dept. PM, English Dept., University of West Florida, Pensacola FL 32514-5751, phone (904)474-2923, founded 1976, editor Dr. Laurie O'Brien appears twice a year, using **poetry "grounded in experience with strong individual 'voice' and natural language. Any subject, no 'causes.' Length to 200 lines, but prefer 30-100. No self-consciously experimental, unrestrained howling, sophomoric wailings on the human condition."** They have published poetry by Malcolm Glass, Lyn Lifshin, Donald Junkins, David Kirby and Joan Colby. As a sample here is the first stanza of "York, Maine" by Leo Connellan:

> Through the Cutty Sark motel room 21 picture window now
> the gray waves coming into York Beach like
> an invasion of plows pushing snow. Tomorrow
> the sun will scratch its chin and bleed along the skyline
> but today everything is gray poached in a steam of fog.

The handsomely printed magazine is 64 pgs., digest-sized, flat-spined, large type on heavy eggshell stock, matte card cover with art. Circulation is 500 for 100 subscribers of which 10 are libraries and 200 complimentary copies going to the English department and writing program. Subscription: $5. **Sample postpaid: $2. No simultaneous submissions. Submit maximum of 7 poems, typewritten or letter-perfect printout. Reports in 4-6 months.** Time between acceptance and publication is 6-12 months. **Pays 2 copies.** They sponsor a national chapbook competition each year, October 15 through January 15. Competition awards $100 plus 50 copies. Submit 24-30 pgs. with $7 reading fee. Send SASE for details. The editor advises: "(1) Take care with ms preparation. Sloppy mss are difficult to evaluate fairly. (2) Send only poems you believe in. Everything you write isn't publishable; send finished work."

PANJANDRUM BOOKS; PANJANDRUM POETRY JOURNAL (III, IV-Translations), 6156 Wilkinson Ave., North Hollywood CA 91606, founded 1971, editor Dennis Koran, associate editor David Guss. **The press publishes a distinguished list of avant-garde books. They are interested in translations (especially European) of modern poetry, surrealism, dada and experimental poetry and accept book-length mss only with SASE; query first. Cover letter listing previous publications is required.** *Panjandrum Poetry Journal* is published occasionally. **Submit no more than 10 poems at a time. No simultaneous submissions.** Staff also reviews books of poetry. Send books for review consideration to Dennis Koran.

PANTHEON BOOKS INC., 201 E. 50th St., New York NY 10022. Prefers not to share information.

‡PAPER BOAT MAGAZINE; PAPER BOAT PRESS (I, II), P.O. Box 2615, Poulsbo WA 98370, founded 1995, editor Maura Alia Bramkamp, publisher Paul Bramkamp. *Paper Boat* is a biannual literary magazine. "We aim to publish fresh, new poetry, short-short fiction, personal essays and b&w artwork. We have a slight Pacific Northwest bias—but are open to all. **We like the original, quirky, catch-you-off-guard poems; favor narrative free verse, but are open to other forms. One-page poems have a better chance due to space limitations. No greeting card or religious verse, no haiku, no tiresome pseudo-porn, no violence."** They have recently published poetry by Jana Harris, Diane Glancy, James Snydal and Lyn Lifshin. As a sample the editor selected these lines from "File Clerk Days" by John Gorski:

> Baskets filling
> with six-digit requisitions
> for me to file
> so they can be pulled and filed again,
> paper shuttling endlessly
> between desk and folder.
> All day I attend
> to the numerical sequence
> of the University's purchases.
> This is why I studied Shakespeare
> and the major English poets.

PB is 42-64 pgs., 8½ × 11, saddle-stapled, glossy card cover with b&w photos, artwork and cartoons. In 1995, they received 4,000 poems, accepted about 1.5%. Press run is 250 for 50 subscribers. Subscription: $8, $18/year overseas. **Sample postpaid: $4. Make checks payable to Paper Boat Press. Submit 3-5 poems at a time. Very rarely accepts previously published poems; no simultaneous submissions. Cover letter including bio required. Reads submissions September 1 through December 1 and February 1 through May 1.** Seldom comments on rejections. Publishes theme issues from time to time. **Send SASE for guidelines and upcoming themes. Reports in 1-6 months. Pays 1-2 copies, offers 40% discount on additional copies. Acquires first North American serial rights.** Paper Boat Press **publishes chapbooks through its biennial contest only. "We aim to publish new voices as well as those that have 'been around.' We seek fresh, original, surprising poetry."** Chapbooks are usually 20-25 pgs., digest-sized, saddle-stapled, card cover with art. Submit up to 24 pgs., of original poetry with acknowledgement page, bio and SASE. Entry fee: $10. Winner receives $200; publication and 50 copies of chapbooks. Winner announced in Fall/Winter issue; chapbook published the following Spring. Deadline: March 15, 1998. Send SASE for information. The editor says, "Do not bombard us with inquiries after submitting. We take our time to select quality work. Please be patient. You may send a postcard if you haven't heard from us in six months. Also, we strongly encourage poets to order a sample to get a feel for the magazine. We've had too many people submit one bizarre thing after another without ever reading us."

A biannual literary magazine based in Poulsbo, Washington, **Paper Boat** publishes short-short fiction, personal essays and b&w artwork, but is "driven" by poetry. **PB** looks for clear, fresh voices; publishes work by both well-known and emerging poets; and has a bias toward writers from the Pacific Northwest. The cover for their inaugural issue was selected for its "sense of celebration," Editor Maura Alia Bramkamp says. "We felt the linocut [entitled 'Tango'] represented the theme of our publication in its directness. Both the publisher and I are drawn to the stark yet detailed images provided by woodprints and linocuts." The linocut was created by Janette K. Hopper, who teaches art at Columbia Basin College in Pasco, Washington.

THE PAPER SALAd POETRY JOURNAL (II), P.O. Box 520061, Salt Lake City UT 84152-0061, founded 1990, editor R.L. Moore, is an annual using **"poetry by poets who work rigorously on their poetry, who make every poem an attempt at the 'perfect' poem, and who know that the meaning of a poem is always secondary to the music of the poem."** Note: *PAPER SALAd* will not be accepting submissions between June 1997 and January 1998. They have published poetry by Richard Cronshey, Lyn Lifshin, Christien Gholson and Gayle Elen Harvey. As a sample the editor selected this untitled poem by Steven B. Edmonds:

> Nature opens above-around-within us
> Green canopy,
> Umbrella hung in the human head,
> Halo of a planet cooled & coddled by a mother of cloud.
> What delicacy there is in this good common sense,
> One thing threaded to another, and We, quilted tight,
> Stitched & centered—the focal eye that is the fabric.

The editor describes it as 80-110 pgs., flat-spined, digest-sized. Press run is 400. **Sample: $7.25 ("An additional dollar will help with postage, but is optional"). Submit no more than 6 poems at a time, one poem to a page, name and address on each. "Submissions without a SASE get tossed." A $1.50/item coupon toward *PAPER SALAd* stuff will be given to each poet who submits work on disk. "All poems in one file, please. IBM compatible, WordPerfect preferred. Please also include a hard copy of each poem." Seldom comments on rejections. Replies within 2 months. Pays 1 copy.** The editor says, "I don't really feel that a poem has to be *about* anything at all. In fact it's often the poem that tries to be *about* something that ends up failing. It starts to feel forced or too intentional. I think it's more important for a poem to draw the reader into a space or situation that is both familiar and yet new. I personally like poetry that has a bit of a surreal edge to it, but that doesn't mean the weirder the better. All poems must arise out of the genuine experience of existence to be of any value. I feel the best poetry helps to draw attention to the tension between the mundane and the ascensional."

PAPIER-MACHE PRESS (IV-Themes, anthologies, women), 135 Aviation Way, #14, Watsonville CA 95076-2064, phone (408)763-1420, fax (408)763-1421, founded 1984, acquisitions editor

Shirley Coe, is a small press publisher of anthologies, poetry and short fiction in perfect-bound and casebound books. **Their anthologies typically "explore a particular aspect of women's experience, such as aging, parental relationships, work or body image."** They have published poetry by Sue Saniel Elkind, Lynn Kozma, Patti Tana, Ruth Daigon, Barbara Sperber and Janet Carncross Chandler. As a sample the editor selected these lines from "Mothers and Daughters" by Maude Meehan, published in *Washing the Stones: Selected Poems 1975-1995*:

> There is a cord between us
> not yet cut
> On it we move
> like tightrope walkers
> novices
> uncertain of the net

They publish 1-2 poetry collections and one anthology each year. Poetry collections contain at least 120 poems and are accepted in July and August only. Each anthology contains 30-40 poems, and submissions are accepted only when a particular theme has been announced (watch *Poets & Writers Magazine* for announcements). Send SASE for guidelines. Simultaneous submissions must be identified as such. Cover letter required; include name, address, phone and fax numbers (if available) as well as length and subject of submission. No submissions via fax. They report on mss in 3-4 months. Always sends prepublication galleys. Royalties, modest advances and several copies are negotiated for both individual collections and work accepted for anthologies. Send SASE for catalog to buy samples; books typically cost $8-14. "Papier-Mache's primary objective is to publish anthologies, poetry and fiction books by, for and about midlife and older women and about the art of women and men aging. We select well-written, accessible material on subjects of particular importance to women, develop attractive, high quality book formats and market them to an audience that might not otherwise buy books of poetry. We take particular pride in our reputation for dealing with our contributors in a caring, professional manner."

‡**PAPYRUS (III, IV-Ethnic/nationality)**, P.O. Box 270797, West Hartford CT 06127-0797, founded 1994, editor Ginger Whitaker, is a quarterly "writer's 'craftletter' featuring the Black experience," published by Papyrus Literary Enterprises, Inc. It includes articles on the art of writing; fiction, nonfiction and poetry; marketplace news; and literary notes for the serious beginning writer. **They want African-American-centered poetry, but will accept good work by anyone. Shorter works preferred, but nothing against any ethnic group.** They have recently published poetry by Lyn Lifshin, Lenard D. Moore and Simon Perchik. As a sample we selected these lines from "I Know the Grandmother One Had Hands" by Jaki Shelton Green:

> I know the grandmother one had hands
> but they were always in bowls
> folding, pinching, rolling the dough
> making the bread
> I know the grandmother one had hands
> but they were always under water
> sifting rice
> bluing clothes
> starching lives . . .

Papyrus is 20 pgs., 8½ × 11, printed in 2 colors and saddle-stitched. They receive about 25 poems a year, publish approximately 50%. Press run is 2,000 for 500 subscribers, 200 shelf sales. Single copy: $2.20; subscription: $8/year. **Sample postpaid: $1. Submit up to 5 poems at a time. No previously published poems or simultaneous submissions. Work may be submitted on a 3.5 disk, with 2 hard copies.** "Macintosh users should submit files in ClarisWorks, Microsoft Word, WordPerfect or MacWrite II. IBM users should submit files saved in ASCII." **Poems are reviewed by 2 senior editors and an independent poetry consultant. Often comments on rejections. Send SASE for guidelines. Reports in 1 month. Pays $10-25 and 2 copies. Buys first rights.**

MARKET CATEGORIES: (I) Beginning; **(II)** General; **(III)** Limited; **(IV)** Specialized; **(V)** Closed.

PARABOLA: THE MAGAZINE OF MYTH AND TRADITION (IV-Spirituality, themes), 656 Broadway, New York NY 10012, phone (212)505-9037, fax (212)979-7325, e-mail parabola@pani x.com, founded 1976, is a quarterly "devoted to the exploration of the quest for meaning as expressed in the myths, symbols, and tales of the world's spiritual traditions. **We very rarely publish poetry, and only use material** *directly* **related to one of our upcoming themes. Please send SASE for current list."** They have recently published poetry by Kenneth Koch, James Laughlin and Mary Oliver, and translations by Sam Hamill. Almost all of the poetry they have published has been reprints. *Parabola* is 128 pgs., 6½×10, professionally printed and perfect-bound with full-color, semi-glossy paper cover and b&w art and photos inside. More than half the publication contains articles, stories and poetry; the rest is book reviews and ads. They receive 120-150 poetry mss a year, accept 1-2 original poems, 2-4 reprints. Press run is 40,000. Subscription: $20. **Sample postpaid: $6 current issue, $8 back issue. Previously published poems and simultaneous submissions OK. Cover letter required. "State to which theme you are submitting, and please make separate submissions if you have work for more than one theme."** No unsolicited mss via e-mail. However, queries and short mss are OK by fax. **Send SASE for general guidelines and upcoming themes or request via e-mail. Reports in 3-6 months. Payment varies, but includes complimentary copy. Author retains rights.** Reviews nationally available books, including related books of poetry, in 500 words, single format. Open to unsolicited reviews. Poets may also send related books for review consideration, attn: Book Review Editor.

PARADISE PUBLICATIONS (I, IV-Cowboy), P.O. Box 9084, Wichita Falls TX 76310, founded 1992, editor Leah Galligar, publishes 3-4 perfect-bound paperback books of poetry each year. **"We are looking for cowboy poetry and poetry with an old-fashioned, Western flair. We would also like to see submissions from cow girls and Western poetry from a woman's point of view."** They have published poetry by D.L. Chance and Sharon Chance. As a sample the editor selected this poem, "TEXAS #2," by D.L. Chance:

> The French tourguide became unusually distressed
> when the rich Texan gazed at the Eiffel, unimpressed.
> "Well, I have to admit it's the BIGGEST I've seen yet,
> but what matters, Pierre, is how many BARRELS does she get?"

Query first with 1 sample poem and cover letter with brief bio and publication credits. No previously published poems; simultaneous submissions OK. Replies to queries in 1 month. Pays 10% royalties and 2 author's copies. Send $5 for sample copies of their books.

PARADOX; PARADOX PUBLICATIONS (II), P.O. Box 643, Saranac Lake NY 12983, e-mail zbodah@ocvaxa.cc.oberlin.edu, founded 1991, editor Rev. Dan Bodah, appears 1-2 times/year. "*Paradox* thrives on diversity and raw electricity. *Paradox* is exempt from stopping at railroad crossings. I like poetry with *power*, no matter which genre. However, I wish to see no light verse. From now on, all issues will be theme issues." They have published poetry by Maurice Kenny, John M. Bennett, Rochelle Owens and Susan Smith Nash. As a sample the editor selected these lines from "Resurgence" by Jake Berry:

> Suddenly I'm nauseous and run for the door.
> Outside and vomiting I see frogs like
> crucifixes rising out of the ground, drifting
> toward the sun where they explode in a
> sweet crimson rain of mother horns.

The editor says *Paradox* varies between digest-sized and magazine-sized and is photocopied, hand-assembled, and often individually decorated. "Audiotapes are included with #3 onwards." Press run is 200 for 3 subscribers, 25-50 shelf sales. Single copy: $5; subscription: $15 for 4 issues. **Sample postpaid: $4. No previously published poems; simultaneous submissions OK.** Time between acceptance and publication is 6-12 months. **Seldom comments on rejections. Send SASE for upcoming themes. Reports in 2-8 weeks. Pays 1-2 copies. Acquires first rights.** Paradox Publications **also** publishes 1 chapbook/year. "I can only be swayed to publish unsolicited book mss if they are really good and I feel I can do them justice and/or handle the project. Poets can feel free to send an entire ms without a prior query." **Replies in 2-4 weeks. Pays royalties and 10 author's copies. For sample chapbook, send $3.**

PARAMOUR MAGAZINE (I, II, IV-Erotica), P.O. Box 949, Cambridge MA 02140-0008, phone/ fax (617)499-0069, founded 1993, poetry editor John Mulrooney, publisher/editor Amelia Copeland, is a quarterly devoted to "literary and artistic erotica," including short fiction, poetry, photography, illustration and reviews. **They want erotic poetry—"crude, humorous, sweet, all OK. Nothing navel-contemplative."** They have published poetry by Lyn Lifshin, Corwin Ericson, John Cantey Knight and Cheryl Townsend. *Paramour* is 36 pgs., 9×12, printed 2-color on recycled paper and saddle-stapled with paper cover and b&w photos throughout. Much of the content is sexually explicit. They receive 400-500 poems a year, accept approximately 10%. Press run is 12,000 for 250 subscribers, about 8,000 shelf sales. Single copy: $4.95; subscription: $18. **Submit no more than 10 poems each quarter. Include name, address and phone number on every page. Previously published poems OK, "only if published in obscure publications." Simultaneous submissions OK, "but you must inform us of which publications." Written work will not be returned. Send SASE for guidelines. Reports in 4 months. Pays 3 copies plus a 1-year subscription. Acquires first or second rights.**

THE PARIS REVIEW; BERNARD F. CONNORS PRIZE (III), 45-39 171 Place, Flushing NY 11358, phone (718)539-7085, founded 1952, poetry editor Richard Howard. (**Submissions should go to him at 541 E. 72nd St., New York NY 10021**). This distinguished quarterly (circulation 11,000, digest-sized, 200 pgs.) has published many of the major poets writing in English. Though form, content and length seem open, free verse—some structured, some experimental—tends to dominate recent issues. Because the journal is considered one of the most prestigious in the world, competition is keen and response times can lag. Subscription: $34 (US); $42 (outside US). **Sample: $11. Study publication before submitting.** The Bernard F. Connors prize of $1,000 is awarded annually for the best previously unpublished long poem (over 200 lines). **All submissions must be sent to the 541 E. 72nd St., New York NY 10021 address.** Poetry published in *The Paris Review* was selected for inclusion in the 1992, 1993, 1994, 1995 and 1996 volumes of *The Best American Poetry*.

PARNASSUS LITERARY JOURNAL (I, II), P.O. Box 1384, Forest Park GA 30051-1384, phone (404)366-3177, founded 1975, edited by Denver Stull: "Our sole purpose is to promote poetry and to offer an outlet where poets may be heard. **We are open to all poets and all forms of poetry, including Oriental, 24-line limit, maximum 3 poems.**" They have published poetry by Alice Mackenzie Swaim, Diana Kwiatkowski Rubin, Ruth Schuler, T.K. Splake, William J. Vernon and H.F. Noyes. As a sample the editor selected "Gossip" by Jan Brevet:

> Gossip begins from a very small shoot.
> But oh how bitter the taste of the fruit!
> Perhaps the uprooting is almost ahead
> Of the lightning strokes by which it is spread.
> Take care it explodes with a jolt-making force
> In the face of the starter . . . it buries the source.

PLJ, published 3 times a year, is 84 pgs., photocopied from typescript, saddled-stapled, with an occasional drawing. They receive about 1,500 submissions/year, of which they use 350. Currently have about a 1-year backlog. Press run is 300 for 200 subscribers of which 5 are libraries. Circulation includes Japan, England, Greece, India, Korea, Germany and Netherlands. Single copy: $5.25; subscription: $15 US, $16.50 Canada, $22.50 overseas. **Sample: $4.50. Make checks or money orders payable to Denver Stull. Include name and address on each page of ms. "I am dismayed at the haphazard manner in which work is often submitted. I have a number of poems in my file containing no name and/or address. Simply placing your name and address on your envelope is not enough." Previously published poems OK; no simultaneous submissions. Cover letter including something about the writer preferred. "Definitely" comments on rejections. "We do not respond to submissions or queries not accompanied by SASE." Reports within 1 week. Pays 1 copy. Acquires all rights. Returns rights.** Readers vote on best of each issue. Also conducts a contest periodically. Staff reviews books of poetry by subscribers only. The editor advises: "Write about what you know. Study what you have written. Does it make sense? A poem should not leave the reader wondering what you are trying to say. Improve your writings by studying the work of others. Be professional."

PARNASSUS: POETRY IN REVIEW; POETRY IN REVIEW FOUNDATION (V), 205 W. 89th St., #8F, New York NY 10024-1835, phone (212)362-3492, fax (212)875-0148, founded 1972, poetry editor Herbert Leibowitz, provides "comprehensive and in-depth coverage of new books of poetry, including translations from foreign poetry. **We publish poems and translations on occasion, but we solicit all poetry. Poets invited to submit are given all the space they wish; the only stipulation is that the style be non-academic.**" They have published work by Alice Fulton, Eavan Boland, Ross Feld, Debora Greger, William Logan, Tess Gallagher, Seamus Heaney and Rodney Jones. They do consider unsolicited essays. In fact, this is an exceptionally rich market for thoughtful, insightful, technical essay-reviews of contemporary collections. However, it is strongly recommended that writers study the magazine before submitting. **Multiple submissions disliked. Cover letter required. Send SASE for upcoming themes. Reports on essay submissions within 4-10 weeks (response takes longer during the summer). Pays $25-250 plus 2 gift subscriptions—contributors can also take one themselves. Editor comments on rejections—from 1 paragraph to 2 pages.** Send for a sample copy (prices of individual issues can vary) to get a feel for the critical acumen needed to place here. Subscriptions are $27/year, $46/year for libraries; they have 1,100 subscribers, of which 550 are libraries. The editor comments, "Contributors should be urged to subscribe to at least one literary magazine. There is a pervasive ignorance of the cost of putting out a magazine and no sense of responsibility for supporting one."

PARTING GIFTS; MARCH STREET PRESS (II), 3413 Wilshire, Greensboro NC 27408, website http://users.aol.com/marchst/msp.html, founded 1987, editor Robert Bixby. **"I want to see everything.** I'm a big fan of Jim Harrison, C.K. Williams, Amy Hempel and Janet Kauffman." He has published poetry by Eric Torgersen, Lyn Lifshin, Elizabeth Kerlikowske and Russell Thorburn. *PG* is 50 pgs., digest-sized, photocopied, with colored matte card cover, appearing twice a year. Press run is 200. Subscription: $8. **Sample postpaid: $4. Submit in groups of 3-10 with SASE. No previously published poems, but simultaneous submissions OK. "I like a cover letter because it makes the transaction more human. Best time to submit mss is early in the year."** Send SASE for guidelines. **Reports in 1-2 weeks. Sometimes sends prepublication galleys. Pays 1 copy.** March Street Press **publishes chapbooks; $10 reading fee.**

PARTISAN REVIEW (II, IV-Translations, themes), Dept. PM, 236 Bay State Rd., Boston MA 02215, phone (617)353-4260, founded 1934, editor Edith Kurzweil, editor-in-chief William Phillips, is a distinguished quarterly literary journal using **poetry of high quality. "Our poetry section is very small and highly selective. We are open to fresh, quality translations but submissions must include poem in original language as well as translation. We occasionally have special poetry sections on specified themes."** They have published poetry by John Hollander, Czeslaw Milosz, Donald Revell and Rosanna Warren. The journal is 160 pgs., 6×9, flat-spined. Circulation is 8,200 for 6,000 subscriptions and shelf sales. **Sample postpaid: $7.50. Submit maximum of 6 poems at a time. No simultaneous submissions. Reports in 2 months. Pays $50 and 50% discount on copies.** Work published in this review has also been selected for inclusion in *The Best American Poetry 1995*.

PASQUE PETALS; SOUTH DAKOTA STATE POETRY SOCIETY, INC. (I, IV-Regional, subscribers), 521 N. Maple, Watertown SD 57201, founded 1926, editor Cynthia A. Stupnik. This is the official poetry magazine for the South Dakota State Poetry Society, Inc., but it is open to nonmembers. **Those not residents of SD are required to subscribe when (or before) submitting. They use "all forms. 44-line limit, 50-character lines. Count titles and spaces. Lean toward SD and Midwest themes. No rough language or porno—magazine goes into SD schools and libraries."** As a sample they selected this poem, "The Errol Flynn Look-Alike," by Barbara Stevens:

> *His tongue was as smooth as honey on a spoon.*
> *Went from job to job,*
> *Fooled everyone at first meeting*
>   *talked great projects completed by others.*
> *Fooled his wife all the time,*
> *she grew fat and comfortable*
>   *He left her*
>   *for a size five.*

PP appears 8 times a year and is 16-20 pgs., digest-sized, using small b&w sketches. Circulation is 250 to members/subscribers (16 to libraries). Subscription: $20/year. **Sample postpaid: $2. Submit 3 poems at a time, 1 poem (or 2 haiku)/page, seasonal material 3 months ahead. Send SASE for guidelines. Reports in 3 months. Has a 2- to 3-month backlog. Pays nonmembers only 1 copy. Acquires first rights.** Reviews books of poetry by members only. Offers $5 prize for the best poem in every issue. They also sponsor a yearly contest with 10 categories. Entry fees vary. Prizes total $600. Send SASE for details.

PASSAGER: A JOURNAL OF REMEMBRANCE AND DISCOVERY (I, II, IV-Senior citizen, themes), School of Communications Design, University of Baltimore, 1420 N. Charles St., Baltimore MD 21201-5779, phone (410)837-6026, founded 1989, editors Kendra Kopelke, Mary Azrael and Ebby Malmgren. *Passager* is published quarterly and publishes fiction, poetry and interviews that give voice to human experience. **"We seek powerful images of remembrance and discovery from writers of all ages. One of our missions is to provide exposure for new older writers; another is to function as a literary community for writers across the country who are not connected to academic institutions or other organized groups."** The journal is 32 pgs., 8×8, printed on white linen and saddle-stitched. Includes photos of writers. **Sample postpaid: $4. Submit 3-5 poems at a time, each 30 lines maximum; fiction, 3,000 words maximum. "We like clean, readable typed copy with name, address and phone number on each page."** Simultaneous submissions acceptable if notified. No reprints. **"We prefer cover sheets because it makes it personal. However, we hate pushy cover letters, 'I'm sure you'll find your readers will love my story.' "** Does not read mss June through August. Occasionally does special issues. Send SASE for guidelines and upcoming themes. **Reports in 3 months. Pays 2 copies and 1 year's subscription.** They sponsor an annual spring poetry contest for new poets over 50 years old, with 1st, 2nd and 3rd prizes; honorable mentions; and publication in *Passager*.

PASSAGES NORTH (II), College of Arts & Sciences, 358 Magers Hall, Northern Michigan University, Marquette MI 49855, phone (906)227-2715, founded 1979, poetry editor Anne Youngs, is a semiannual magazine containing fiction, poetry, essays, interviews and visual art. **"The magazine publishes quality work by established and emerging writers."** They have published poetry by William Matthews, Thomas Lux, Jo Anne Rawson, Michael Collier, Lisa Sewell, Nancy Willard, Mark Halliday, Nancy Eimers and John Rybicki. As a sample the editor selected these lines from "Totally" by Tony Hoagland:

> For example, it is autumn here.
> The defoliated trees look frightened
> at the edge of town,
>
> as if the train they missed
> had taken all their clothes.
> The whole world in unison is turning
> toward a zone of nakedness and cold.
>
> But me, I have this strange conviction
> that I am going to be born.

Passages North is 100 pgs., perfect-bound. Circulation is at 1,000 "and growing." Single copy: $6; subscription: $10 for 1 year, $18 for 2 years, add $10 for international mail. **Prefers groups of 4-6 poems, typed single-spaced. Simultaneous submissions OK, if writer agrees to telephone** *Passages North* **immediately when work accepted elsewhere. Reads submissions September through May only. Reports in 6-8 weeks, delay to publication is 6 months. Pays copies.**

PATH PRESS, INC. (IV-Ethnic), 53 W. Jackson Blvd., Suite 724, Chicago IL 60604-3610, phone (312)663-0167, fax (312)663-5318, e-mail bjjIII@aol.com, founded 1969, president Bennett J. Johnson, executive vice president and poetry editor Herman C. Gilbert, is a small publisher of books and poetry primarily **"by, for and about African-American and Third World people." The press is open to all types of poetic forms except "poor quality." Submissions should be typewritten in manuscript format. Writers should send sample poems, credits and bio.** The books are "hardback and quality paperbacks."

‡PAVEMENT SAW (III); PAVEMENT SAW PRESS (II), 7 James St., Scotia NY 12302, founded 1992, editors David Baratier and Tara Pauliny. *Pavement Saw*, which appears annually, **wants "poetry on any subject, especially work. Length: 1 or 2 pages. No poems that tell, no work by a deceased writer and no translations."** They have recently published poetry by Jendi Reiter, Gian Lombardo, Timothy Russell and Simon Perchik. The editor says *PS* is 56 pgs., 6×9, perfect-bound. They receive 7,500-9,000 poems a year, publish less than 1%. Press run is 500 for about 250 subscribers, about 250 shelf sales. Single copy: $3.50; subscription: $6. **Sample postpaid: $3. Make checks payable to David Baratier. Submit 5 poems at a time. "No fancy typefaces." No previously published poems or simultaneous submissions. Cover letter required. Seldom comments on rejections. Send SASE for guidelines. Reports in 3-6 months. Sometimes sends prepublication galleys. Pays 2 copies. Acquires first rights.** The press also occasionally publishes books of poetry ("most are by authors who have been published in the journal") and sponsors an annual chapbook contest. **For consideration in the contest, submit up to 32 pgs. of poetry with a cover letter and $6 entry fee. The winner will receive $500, publication of the chapbook, and 25 copies. Each entrant will receive a copy of the winning chapbook provided a 9×12 SAE with $2.16 postage is supplied. Deadline: December 15. Send SASE for complete details.**

PEARL; PEARL CHAPBOOK CONTEST (II), 3030 E. Second St., Long Beach CA 90803-5163, phone (310)434-4523 or (714)968-7530, founded 1974, poetry editors Joan Jobe Smith, Marilyn Johnson and Barbara Hauk, is a literary magazine appearing three times a year. **"We are interested in accessible, humanistic poetry that communicates and is related to real life. Humor and wit are welcome, along with the ironic and serious. No taboos stylistically or subject-wise. Prefer poems up to 35 lines, with lines no longer than 10 words. We don't want to see sentimental, obscure, predictable, abstract or cliché-ridden poetry. Our purpose is to provide a forum for lively, readable poetry, the direct, outspoken type, variously known as 'neo-pop' or 'stand-up,' that reflects a wide variety of contemporary voices, viewpoints and experiences—that speaks to** *real* **people about** *real* **life in direct, living language, profane or sublime."** They have recently published poetry by Edward Field, Donna Hilbert, Hayley R. Mitchell, Todd Moore, Fred Voss and Charles Webb. As a sample the editor selected these lines from "How I Learned to Kiss" by Myra Shapiro:

> A movie actress taught me. She crept inside
> a bed to warm a man who had a chill;
> he was an outlaw but she had to
> save his life, her body had to do that.
> Her hair, her breasts, her vivid
> darkened mouth opening towards him . . .

Pearl is 96 pgs., digest-sized, perfect-bound, offset, with laminated cover. Their press run is 600 with 100 subscriptions of which 7 are libraries. Subscription: $15/year. **Sample postpaid: $6. Submit 3-5 poems at a time. "Handwritten submissions and unreadable dot-matrix printouts are not acceptable." No previously published poems; simultaneous submissions OK. "Cover letters appreciated." Guidelines available for SASE. Reports in 6-8 weeks. Sometimes sends prepublication galleys. Pays 2 copies. Acquires first serial rights.** Each issue contains the work of 60-70 different poets and a special 10- to 15-page section that showcases the work of a single poet. "We sponsor an annual chapbook contest, judged by one of our more well-known contributors. Winner receives publication, $500 and 50 copies. Entries accepted during the months of May and June. There is a $10 entry fee, which includes a copy of the winning chapbook." Send SASE for complete rules and guidelines. Recent chapbooks include *Monsters and Other Lovers* by Lisa Glatt, *The Wave He Caught* by Rick Noguchi, *How the Sky Fell* by Denise Duhamel, *The Old Mongoose and Other Poems* by Gerald Locklin and *Das 1st Alles: Charles Bukowski Recollected*, edited by Joan Jobe Smith. The editors add, "Advice for beginning poets? Just write from your own experience, using images that are as concrete and sensory as possible. Keep these images fresh and objective, and always listen to the music. . . ."

‡**THE PEARL (I, II)**, English Dept., University of Massachusetts at Lowell, University Ave., Lowell MA 01854, phone (508)934-4182, founded 1989, is an annual publication designed "to enlighten the readers to other ideas and forms of thinking. **Poetry should be no longer than 50 lines. We accept various styles and forms, but please avoid abstractions. Writing must be well-written and proofed.**" The editor says *The Pearl* is 150 pgs., perfect-bound with a limited number of art pgs. They receive about 150 poems a year, accept approximately 25%. Press run is 200. **Sample postpaid: $4. Make checks payable to University of Massachusetts. Submit 3 poems at a time—2 copies of each, 1 without name or identifying marks. Previously published poems and simultaneous submissions OK. Cover letter with bio preferred. Reads submissions September 1 through January 1 for April publication. Poems are circulated to an editorial board. Seldom comments on rejections. Send SASE for guidelines. Reports in 2-3 months. Pays 2 copies. Acquires first or one-time rights.** The editor says, "We publish thought-provoking literature which leaves the reader with a sensation of having gained wisdom. *The Pearl* is a student-run organization with changing editors and staffs so if you get rejected once, please submit again."

PEGASUS (II), 525 Ave. B, Boulder City NV 89005, founded 1986, editor M.E. Hildebrand, is a poetry quarterly "for serious poets who have something to say and know how to say it using sensory imagery." **Submit 3-5 poems, 3-40 lines. Avoid "religious, political, pornographic themes."** They have published poetry by John Grey, Stan Moseley, Gayle Elen Harvey, Robert K. Johnson and Elizabeth Perry, who provides the opening lines of "The Meeting Hour" as a sample:

> Before Dawn drops
> her luminous petals
> I wake and listen
> for your muted voice
> to break the silence
> of our worlds
> like rustlings
> in the deep woods.

Pegasus is 32 pgs., digest-sized, saddle-stapled, offset from typescript with colored paper cover. Publishes 10-15% of the work received. Circulation 200. Subscription: $15. **Sample postpaid: $5. Previously published poems OK, provided poet retains rights, but no simultaneous submissions. Send SASE for guidelines. Reports in 2 weeks. Publication is payment. Acquires first or one-time rights.**

THE PEGASUS REVIEW (I, II, IV-Themes), P.O. Box 88, Henderson MD 21640-0088, phone (410)482-6736, founded 1980, is a 14-page (counting cover) pamphlet entirely in calligraphy, illustrated on high-quality paper, some color overlays. Editor Art Bounds says, "This magazine is a bimonthly, **based on specific themes. Write to request list of upcoming themes. Because of the calligraphic format, open to all styles, but brevity is the key. Uses poetry not more than 24 lines (the shorter the better); fiction that is short short (about 2½ pages would be ideal); essays and cartoons. All material must pertain to indicated themes only. Would like to see various forms rather than just free verse.**" Poets published include C. David Hay, Thelma Schiller, Ella Cavis and M.J. Vassallo. As a sample the editor selected these lines from "Art" by L.A. Evans:

> Next to the ruddy glow
> of the eternal fire
> I place my small lump of coal
> inside is my heart.

Press run is 160 for 150 subscribers, of which 4 are libraries. Subscription: $10. **Sample: $2.50.**

Submit 3-5 poems with name and address on each page. "Previously published poems OK, if there is no conflict or violation of rights agreement. Simultaneous submissions OK, but author must notify proper parties once specific material is accepted. Brief cover letter with specifics as they relate to one's writing background welcome." Query if additional information is needed. Reports within a month, often with a personal response. Pays 2 copies. Occasional book awards throughout the year. Also issues a writer's calendar—in calligraphy—with motivational sayings and writing advice ($8 plus $2.50 p&h). The editor advises, "Follow all published guidelines carefully and accurately. Try to become familiar with most of the publications through a sample copy, a library copy or, possibly, a subscription. Many small presses are falling to the wayside. But new ones appear to come up. Overall they need support of both their subscribers as well as contributors. I urge each and every writer to either join or start a writers group. The benefits can be most rewarding. Above all, market your work and study your markets through such publications as *Poet's Market*, *International Directory of Small Presses and Literary Magazines* and the numerous writing magazines available. It pays to do your homework."

THE PEKING DUCK; O PATO, INC. (II), P.O. Box 331661, Corpus Christi TX 78463-1661, e-mail info@evolute.org, website http://www.evolute.org, founded 1993, editor Edward Cossette. *The Peking Duck* is "a mendicant publication with the aim of promoting experimental or other 'offbeat' forms of writing." **They have no specific guidelines regarding form, length, subject matter or style of poetry—"good work is good work."** They have published poetry by B.Z. Niditch, Lyn Lifshin, Arlene Mandrell and Errol Miller. As a sample we selected these lines from "A Different Kind of Surrender" by William J. Vernon:

> This morning, fog breaking, I pause
> at windows, watching pine boughs
> droop with cones. Out there like dreams,
>
> the world makes designs,
> leaving patterns in lines
> so distinct, I imagine,
> tracing them to their source.

The Peking Duck is currently in a state of "flux" and will only appear in its "physical" format once a year. Any additional issues will exist in an electronic, computer-based version. In its "physical" format, *The Peking Duck* is 12 pgs., 8½ × 11, offset printed in 2 colors on 70 lb. glossy paper, saddle-stapled, drawings and graphics throughout. They receive 200-300 poems a year, accept approximately 5%. **Sample postpaid: $2. "We are particularly interested in work that takes advantage of the electronic medium. Poets are encouraged to submit work it html format and to make hypertext links, graphics and sound files a part of the work." Send SASE for guidelines.** The editor says, "Read an issue first! Much perfectly 'good' work gets passed over because it doesn't mesh with our outlook/style. Published poets are relentless: submitting often, writing always."

PELICAN PUBLISHING COMPANY (V, IV-Children, regional), Box 3110, Gretna LA 70054-3110, founded 1926, editor-in-chief Nina Kooij, is a "moderate-sized publisher of cookbooks, travel guides, regional books and inspirational/motivational books," which accepts **poetry for "hardcover children's books *only*, preferably with a regional focus. However, our needs for this are very limited; we do fewer than 5 juvenile titles per year, and most of these are prose, not poetry."** They have published *Santa's Christmas Surprise*, by Robert Bernardini. As a sample the editor selected these lines from *An Iron Night Before Christmas* by Kirwan Blazek:

> As cute as a devil,
> In Aran and green,
> Stood ould Father Christmas
> Looking ever so keen.

They are currently not accepting unsolicited mss. Query first with 2 sample poems and cover letter including "work and writing backgrounds, plot summary and promotional connections." No previously published poems or simultaneous submissions. Reports on queries in 1 month, on mss (if invited) in 3 months. Always sends prepublication galleys. Pays royalties. Buys all rights. Returns rights upon termination of contract. These are 32-page, large-format (magazine-sized) books with illustrations. Two of their popular series are prose books about Gaston the Green-Nosed Alligator by James Rice and Clovis Crawfish by Mary Alice Fontenot. They have a variety of books based on "The Night Before Christmas" adapted to regional settings such as Cajun, prairie, and Texas. Typically their books sell for $14.95. **Write for catalog to buy samples.** The editor says, "We try to avoid rhyme altogether, especially predictable rhyme. Monotonous rhythm can also be a problem."

PEMBROKE MAGAZINE (II), Box 60, Pembroke State University, One University Dr., Pembroke NC 28372-1510, founded 1969 by Norman Macleod, edited by Shelby Stephenson, is a heavy (252 pgs., 6 × 9), flat-spined, quality literary annual which has published poetry by Fred Chappell, Stephen

Sandy, A.R. Ammons, Barbara Guest and Betty Adcock. Press run is 500 for 125 subscribers of which 100 are libraries. **Sample postpaid: $5. Sometimes comments on rejections. Reports within 3 months. Pays copies.** Stephenson advises, "Publication will come if you write. Writing is all."

PEN AND INK MAGAZINE (I, II), P.O. Box 130574, Ann Arbor MI 48113-0574, founded 1994, editor Peter D. MacKay, is a semiannual magazine designed "to provide a forum for both new and established poets. *Pen and Ink* **is interested in all forms of poetry, including free verse, experimental and traditional styles. We prefer short to moderate length poems. Diversity is the key—many styles, forms and subjects from many writers.**" They have published poetry by Junette Fabian, Winnie E. Fitzpatrick, Eric Bernreuter, Helen E. Rilling, T.N. Turner, Jane Taylor Overton, Todd Weiss, Bruce E. Massis, M.Q. Thorburn and Taylor Reese. As a sample the editor selected this complete poem, "Hibernation," by Joy Hewitt Mann:

> My need to write is dormant
> as I sleep between my winter words,
> praying spring will come to melt
> the ice that seals this unlit cave.

Pen and Ink is 40-52 pgs., digest-sized, neatly printed and saddle-stapled with light card stock cover. They accept 10-15% of the poetry received. Press run is 100-150. Subscription: $9. **Sample postpaid: $5. Include name, address and phone number on every page of submission. No previously published poems or simultaneous submissions. A SASE (or SAE and IRCs) must be included for response. Send SASE for guidelines. Reports in 1-3 months. Pays 1 copy. Acquires first rights.**

PENNINE INK (I, II), % Mid Pennine Arts, MP The Gallery, Yorke St., Burnley BB11 3JJ Great Britain, founded 1985, appears annually ("hopefully more frequently") using mainly poems, a few short prose items and a few b&w illustrations. They want **"poetry up to 40 lines maximum. Consider all kinds."** As a sample the editor selected these lines from "Bandit Player" by Derek Woodcock:

> Racy lights moved the bar wall
> as the girl, all high-tech poise,
> switched on menus, shot coins down chutes,
> her face, I imagined, warmed by coals,
> sweetened by a line of grapes.
> The black-eyed Cleopatra flaunted tokens,
> played for time, sipped the final snakebite.

The editor says it is 48 pgs., A5, with b&w illustrated cover, a few small local ads and 3 or 4 b&w graphics. They receive about 400 items a year, use approximately 40. Press run is 350. **Submit up to 6 poems at a time. Previously published poems and simultaneous submissions OK. Cover letter preferred. Seldom comments on rejections.** Reviews small press poetry books in about 200 words. The editor adds, "Prose, poetry and illustrations should be accompanied by a suitable stamped, addressed envelope (SASE or SAE with IRCs) for return of work. Contributors wishing to purchase a copy of *Pennine Ink* should enclose £1.50 per copy plus postage and packing."

PENNINE PLATFORM (II), Ingmanthorpe Hall Farm Cottage, Wetherby, W. Yorkshire LS22 5EQ England, phone 0937-584674, founded 1973, poetry editor Brian Merrikin Hill, appears 3 times a year. The editor wants **any kind of poetry but concrete ("lack of facilities for reproduction"). No specifications of length, but poems of less than 40 lines have a better chance. "All styles—effort is to find things good of their kind. Preference for religious or sociopolitical awareness of an acute, not conventional kind."** They have published poetry by Elizabeth Bartlett, Anna Adams, John Ward, Ian Caws, John Latham and Geoffrey Holloway. As a sample the editor selected these lines from "A Vision of Cabez De Vaca" by Cal Clothier:

> Blanched to a skin manned by bones,
> we have blood and our breathing
> to prove we are men, and the hungry light
> jerking our eyes. We are down to mercy,
> gratitude, love, down to humanity.

The 6×8, 48-page journal is photocopied from typescript, saddle-stapled, with matte card cover with graphics, circulation 400, 300 subscriptions of which 16 are libraries. They receive about 300 submissions/year, use about 30, have about a 6-month backlog. Subscription: £7 for 3 issues (£10 abroad; £25 if not in sterling). **Sample postpaid: £2. Submit up to 6 poems, typed. Reports in about a month. No pay. Acquires first serial rights. Editor occasionally comments on rejections.** Reviews books of poetry in 2,500 words, multi-book format. Open to unsolicited reviews. Poets may also send books for review consideration. They would like to see more sociopolitical themes in traditional forms, less free verse. Brian Hill comments, "It is time to avoid the paradigm-magazine-poem and reject establishments—ancient, modern or allegedly contemporary. Small magazines and presses often publish superior material to the commercial hyped publishers."

PENNSYLVANIA ENGLISH (II), Penn State-Erie, Erie PA 16563, phone (814)824-2000, founded 1988 (first issue in March, 1989), poetry editor John Coleman, is "a journal sponsored by the Pennsylvania College English Association." They want poetry of **"any length, any style."** The journal is magazine-sized, saddle-stapled, and appears twice a year. Press run is 300. Subscription: $15, which includes membership in PCEA. **Submit 4-5 typed poems at a time. Do not submit mss in the summer. They consider simultaneous submissions but not previously published poems. Reports in 1 month. Pays 2 copies.**

‡**PENNY DREADFUL PRESS; THE PENNY DREADFUL REVIEW (I, IV-Erotica, form/style)**, 4210 Park Ave., Nashville TN 37209-3650, phone (615)297-1056, founded November 1993, "maximum domineditrix" Ms. Penelope Dreadful, assistant editor and factotum C Ra McGuirt. *The Penny Dreadful Review* is now a quarterly publication of eclectic tastes. "Our motto: Where Poe Meets Bukowski. We accept poetry, short prose, cartoons and b&w photographs. As before, Penny likes **very personal, dark, funny, erotic and/or experimental material; concrete character-driven work preferred.**" They have recently published poetry by Steven McDaris, Michael Estabrook, Janet Kuypers and Pete Lee. As a sample the editors selected "this is how I came to love" by John Knoll:

> i killed mom
> when dad found out
> he was very angry
> & said he'd never be my lover again
> i grew more & more despondent
> i couldn't even watch t.v.

The Penny Dreadful Review is 48 pgs., 5½ × 8½, photocopied and center-stapled. Press run is 500. Single/sample copy: $3; 4-issue subscription: $10/year. **Previously published poems and simultaneous submissions OK. Cover letter preferred. "Tell us a little about yourself; communication is its own reward. We will consider any amount of material, but please include sufficient postage for its return if desired and at the least a SASE for our editorial response. We also accept submissions by e-mail as well as information requests."** Time between acceptance and publication is no more than 6 months. **Often comments on rejections. "We try for same day response." Pays at least 1 copy. All rights remain with poets.** Penny's Dreadful Catalogue, which includes guidelines as well as a complete listing of all chapbooks and back issues of *PDR*, is available for 2 first-class stamps on a SASE.

‡**PENNYWHISTLE PRESS (II)**, 105 E. Marcy St., Suite 123, Santa Fe NM 87501, phone/fax (505)982-0066, e-mail pnywhistle@aol.com, founded 1986, managing editor Jeanie C. Williams, publisher Victor di Suvero, "was started as a way to present the work of notable poets to the reading public. Known for its Poetry Chapbook Series, which currently features 18 titles by some of the strongest voices of our time: Francisco X. Alarcón, Dennis Brutus, Joyce Jenkins, Jerome Rothenberg, Suzanne Lummis, Judyth Hill and Sarah Blake, the Press has recently expanded its line-up by branching out into the anthology market with the publication of *Saludos! Poemas de Nuevo Mexico*, a bilingual collection of 66 poets presenting their diverse views of this unusual tricultural state, which is also a state of being. Poets in this collection run the spectrum from N. Scott Momaday, Luci Tapahonso and Carolyn Forché to Janet Holmes, Reneé Gregorio and Keith Wilson." The press also has recently released a new series entitled Sextet, "an anthology of poetry comprised of six chapbooks by new and established voices." They publish 2 paperbacks and 6 chapbooks a year. **They want poetry with "deep, rich imagery; confessional, solid, strong and experimental—generally one page in length." No rhyme.** As a sample the editor selected these lines from "A Love Song from the Chimayó Landfill" by Janet Holmes from the anthology, *Saludos! Poemas de Nuevo Mexico*:

> . . . I had merely
> two bags of garbage to heave into the heap,
> a minor offering beside that of the men
> emptying their truckbeds with shovels. They
> were happy, too; yes, everyone was laughing,
> as if it were Fiesta, not the dump. I wanted to tell you:
> this is how you make me feel, my darling.

Chapbooks are usually 32 pgs., 5¼ × 8⅜, perfect-bound; anthologies are about 200 pgs., 6 × 9, perfect-bound. **Submit 10 poems at a time. Previously published poems and simultaneous submissions OK. Cover letter preferred. Poems are circulated to an editorial board. "Reviewed by four members of editorial board and then submitted to managing editor and publisher for approval." Always comments on rejections. Replies to queries in 2-4 months, to mss in 1 month. Pays $100** honorarium and 25 author's copies (out of a press run of 1,500). Write to obtain samples of books or chapbooks.

PEOPLENET DISABILITY DATENET (I, IV-Specialized: disabled people, love/romance), P.O. Box 897, Levittown NY 11756-0911, phone (516)579-4043, e-mail mauro@chelsea.ios.com, website: http://chelsea.ios.com/~mauro, founded 1987, editor/publisher Robert Mauro, is now a home page (formerly published as a newsletter) **for disabled people focusing on dating, love and relationships.** The editor wants **"poetry on relationships, love and romance only. The length should remain 10 lines or less. We publish beginners, new poets. Prefer free verse, a lot of good imagery—and very little rhyme."** As a sample the editor selected these lines from his poem "When All That Blooms Are Roses":

> *Mornings are not mornings*
> *when all that blooms are roses:*
> *dewy petals opening, blushing*
> *in the wind; a hand*
> *plucks a flower, a finger*
> *touches a bud that didn't*
> *bloom and never will.*

PeopleNet DisAbility DateNet appears only on the World Wide Web at the above website. **Submit 3 poems at a time via e-mail only. Poems should be neatly typed with name and address. No simultaneous submissions. Editor comments on good but rejected mss. Reports "immediately." Acquires first rights.** He says, "We want to publish poems that express the importance of love, acceptance, inner beauty, the need for love and relationship, and the joy of loving and being loved."

PEP PUBLISHING; LOVING MORE (I, IV-Specialized: "ethical multiple relationships"), P.O. Box 6306, Ocean View HI 96737-6306, fax (808)929-9831, e-mail ryam@aol.com, website http://www.wp.com/lovemore, founded 1984, editor Ryam Nearing. *Loving More* is a quarterly that "publishes articles, letters, poems, drawings and reviews related to **polyfidelity, group marriage and multiple** *intimacy*." They use "relatively short poems, though a quality piece of length would be considered, but topic relevance is essential. Please no swinger or porno pieces. Group marriage should not be equated with group sex." It is 40 pgs., magazine-sized, few ads. Circulation is 1,500. Subscription: $49 a year. **Sample: $6 to poets. Submit up to 10 poems at a time. Ms should be "readable." Considers simultaneous submissions.** Time between acceptance and publication is 2-6 months. **Editor comments on rejections "sometimes—if requested." Publishes theme issues. Themes for Fall 1996 and Winter 1997 are Men's and Women's Issues (deadline October 1) and Spirituality/Politics of Loving More (deadline January 1), respectively. Send SASE for upcoming themes. Responds "ASAP." Pays 1 copy.** Open to unsolicited reviews. Poets may also send books for review consideration. The editor says, "We're always looking for good poetry related specifically to our topic. Our readers love it when we find some to include. Writers should read our publication before submitting, and I emphasize no swinger or porno pieces will be published."

PEQUOD: A JOURNAL OF CONTEMPORARY LITERATURE AND LITERARY CRITICISM (III), Dept. of English, New York University, 19 University Place, Room 200, New York NY 10003, contact poetry editor, is a semiannual literary review publishing **quality poetry, fiction, essays and translations.** They have published poetry by Sam Hamill, Donald Hall and John Updike. It is 200 pgs., digest-sized, professionally printed, flat-spined with glossy card cover. Subscription: $12. **Sample postpaid: $5. Reads submissions September 15 through April 15 only. Always sends prepublication galleys.** Poetry published in *Pequod* has also been included in the 1993 and 1995 volumes of *The Best American Poetry*.

‡PERCEPTIONS (I, IV-Erotica), P.O. Box 2210, Livermore CA 94550, e-mail airsafe@inreach.com, founded 1987, editor Alexandra Lloyd, is a quarterly "journal of imaginative sensuality" published by The Sensuous SIG, a Mensa special interest group. **They want "short, sensual poems. Nothing nonsensual or longer than 30-40 lines."** The journal is 52 pgs. (including cover), $5\frac{1}{2} \times 8\frac{1}{2}$, saddle-stitched with nude photos in b&w and various b&w graphics. Press run is 250 for 150 subscribers. Subscription: $14/year. **Sample postpaid: $4. Previously published poems and simultaneous sub-**

USE THE GENERAL INDEX to find the page number of a specific publisher.

Also, if a publisher from last year's edition is not included in this edition, the General Index will tell you why.

missions OK. Cover letter preferred. Publishes theme issues. Send SASE for guidelines and upcoming themes. Reports "ASAP." Rarely sends prepublication galleys. Pays 1 copy.

‡PERCEPTIONS (IV-Women), 73 Eastcombe Ave., London SE7 7LL England, founded 1982, poetry editor Temi Rose, is a "small prize-winning **women's poetry magazine for the promotion and development of women's consciousness of peace and hope and freedom to be.**" They have published poetry by Chocolate Waters, Lyn Lifshin and Edna Kovacs. As a sample the editor selected these lines by Marcia Arrieta:

> *eyes like birds*
> *and hips for babies*
> *a woman who is*
> *not afraid to wander*
> *into mountains alone*

Perceptions is 30 pgs., digest-sized, photocopied from typescript with printed cover and comes out 3 times a year. They publish about 360 of 3,000 poems received/year. Press run is 300 for 50 subscribers of which 3 are libraries. Subscription: $21. **Sample postpaid: $7. They consider simultaneous submissions and previously published poems. Guidelines available for SASE. Reports in 1-3 months. Pays 1 copy.**

‡PEREGRINE: THE JOURNAL OF AMHERST WRITERS & ARTISTS (II); AWA CHAP-BOOK SERIES (V), P.O. Box 1076, Amherst MA 01004-1076, phone (413)253-3307, fax (413)253-7764, *Peregrine* founded 1983, Amherst Writers & Artists Press, Inc., 1987, poetry editor Janet Sadler. **Open to all styles, forms and subjects except greeting card verse.** They have published poetry by Jane Yolen, Martin Espada and Barbara Van Noord. As a sample the editors selected these lines from "Western State Hospital 1" by Barbara Ganzel:

> *I am not a believer.*
> *But I have been touched.*
> *The hills rocked me in heat like a cradle.*
> *And the blue sky, from horizon*
> *to as far as I could see*
> *rang, really*
> *rang like bells.*

Peregrine is 70 pgs., digest-sized, professionally printed, with matte card cover. Each issue includes at least one poem in translation and one or two poems by children. Their press run is 500. **Sample postpaid: $4. "We may hold poems for several months, so we encourage simultaneous submissions." Pays 2 contributor's copies.** Sponsors occasional contest. Write for guidelines.

PERIVALE PRESS; PERIVALE POETRY CHAPBOOKS; PERIVALE TRANSLATION SE-RIES (II, IV-Translations, anthology), 13830 Erwin St., Van Nuys CA 91401-2914, phone (818)785-4671, fax (818)904-0512, founded 1968, editor Lawrence P. Spingarn, publishes **Perivale Poetry Chapbooks, Perivale Translation Series**, anthologies. The collections by individuals are usually translations, but here are some lines by R.L. Barth from "Da Nang Nights: Liberty Song" in *Forced-Marching to the Styx*:

> *In sudden light we choose*
> *Lust by lust our bar:*
> *And whatever else we lose,*
> *We also lose the war.*

They publish an average of one 20-page saddle-stapled chapbook, one perfect-bound (20-70 pgs.) collection, one anthology per year, all quality print jobs. Send SASE for catalog. Perivale publishes both on **straight royalty basis (10%, 10 author's copies) usually grant supported, and by subsidy, the author paying 100%, being repaid from profits, if any. "Payment for chapbooks accepted is 60-100 free copies of press run.** Authors should agree to promote books via readings, talk shows, orders and signings with local bookshops. **Contributors are encouraged to buy samples of chapbooks, etc., for clues to editor's tastes." Samples of previous poetry chapbooks: $5.75 postpaid.** (Barth title out of print.) Latest title: *Positions* by Sheila Hellman. **To submit, query first, with sample of 5 poems, cover letter, bio, previous books. Do not submit mss from June 15 to September 1. Reports in 6 weeks. Always sends prepublication galleys.** Spingarn, a well-known, widely published poet, offers criticism for a fee, the amount dependent on length of book. Sponsors a poetry chapbook contest. Winner receives $100 plus 60 copies of chapbook. Reading fee: $12. Send SASE for details. The editor advises, "Contributors should read samples and guidelines thoroughly before submitting. Also, we would like to see poems with less self-involvement (fewer poems that open with 'I') and a wider world view."

PERMAFROST: A LITERARY JOURNAL (II, IV-Regional), %English Dept., P.O. Box 755720, University of Alaska Fairbanks, Fairbanks AK 99775, founded 1977, is an annual publication. *Perma-*

frost publishes poems, short stories, creative nonfiction and b&w drawings, photographs and prints. "We survive on both new and established writers, and hope and expect to see your best work. **We publish any style of poetry provided it is conceived, written and revised with care. While we encourage submissions about Alaska and by Alaskans, we also encourage and welcome poems about anywhere and from anywhere.** We have published work by Wendy Bishop, John Haines, Naomi Shihab Nye, Peggy Shumaker, Leslie Fields, John Morgan and Patricia Monaghan." The journal is 100-125 pgs., 4×6, professionally printed, flat-spined, with b&w graphics and photos. Subscription: $7. **Sample postpaid: $5. Submit 3-10 poems, typed, single or double-spaced, and formatted as they should appear. Considers simultaneous submissions. Deadline: March 15. Does not accept submissions between April 1 and August 1. Editors comment only on mss that have made the final round. Send SASE for further guidelines. Return time is 1-3 months. Journal is distributed in the fall. Pays 2 copies; reduced contributor rate on additional copies.** *Permafrost* also sponsors the Midnight Sun Poetry Chapbook Contest and an annual fiction contest. Send SASE for guidelines. Contest entry fees: $10, includes a subscription to the journal. Deadline: March 15.

PERMEABLE PRESS; PUCK: THE UNOFFICIAL JOURNAL OF THE IRREPRESSIBLE

(III), 47 Noe St. #4, San Francisco CA 94114-1017, phone (415)648-2175, founded 1984, editor Brian Clark, associate editor Stan Henry. *Puck* is a triannual designed to "provoke thought, dialog. Contents: reviews, stories, essays, poems." **As for poetry they want "radical reinterpretations of the 'accepted.' No restrictions as to style, length, etc. No love poems."** They have published poetry by B. Subraman and Hugh Fox. As a sample they selected these lines from "Tarot of Nature" by Susan Luzarro:

> *Yesterday the queen of wands came to me. She was painted with honey-colored locks*
> *to perpetuate the myth that nature, like christ, was blonde.* Lay me down, *she said.*
> Do not reverse me & I will offer you this sunflower, beneath it—a promise—the
> bud of an unknown flower. I spit on the solace of nature, *I said*, give me a happy life.

The editors describe *Puck* as 80 pgs., 8½×11, offset and saddle-stapled with color covers. They accept 1% or less of poetry received. Press run is 8,000. Single copy: $6.50; subscription: $17/3 issues. **Previously published poems OK; no simultaneous submissions. Cover letter required. "SASE must be big enough to accommodate return of all material submitted." Send SASE for guidelines. Reports in 1-4 weeks. Pays 2 copies. Acquires first North American serial or reprint rights. "Subsequent publication should mention *Puck*."** They add, "Current issue contains 30 (out of 80) pages of reviews. We review anything, everything." Permeable Press also publishes 6 paperbacks and **3 chapbooks/year. Query first with sample poems and cover letter with brief bio and publication credits. Replies to queries in 1 month, to mss in 1-2 months. Pays 50 author's copies for chapbooks.**

PERSEA BOOKS (V), 171 Madison Ave., Suite 1103-04, New York NY 10016, phone (212)779-7668, fax (212)689-5405, editor Michael Braziller, publishes books of **"serious" poetry.** They have published poetry by Thylias Moss, Paul Blackburn and Wayne Koestenbaum. They publish 1-2 books of poetry/year. **However, they are not reading unsolicited mss until November 1997. "We are committed to future books of poets we are already publishing."**

PETERLOO POETS (II), 2 Kelly Gardens, Calstock, Cornwall PL18 9SA Great Britain, founded 1977, poetry editor Harry Chambers. They publish collections of "well-made" poetry (rhyming and free verse) under the Peterloo Poets imprint: flat-spined paperbacks, hardbacks and poetry cassettes. They have published *Undark* by John Glenday and *Safe as Houses* by U.A. Fanthorpe (both Poetry Book Society Recommendations). As a sample we selected these lines from "In the Pub" as published in *Masterclass* by Brian Waltham:

> *Out here the two of us yell*
> *Above the yell above the jukebox.*
> *We need words that reach, but the*
> *Words we need make no sense*
> *Unless they're said quietly*
> *Or said by needful arms or*
> *By a hand tracing the*
> *Curve of a cheek.*

Query with 10 sample poems, bio and list of publications. Considers simultaneous submissions and previously published poems if they have not been in book form. Always sends prepublication galleys. Pays 10% royalties, $100 advance (for first volume, $200 for subsequent volumes) and 12 copies. Editor "normally, briefly" comments on rejections. Sponsors an annual open poetry competition. First prize: £3,000 sterling; second prize: £1,000 sterling; four other prizes totaling £1,100 sterling. Send IRC for entry form and rules.

PETRONIUM PRESS (V, IV-Regional), 1255 Nuuanu Ave., 1813, Honolulu HI 96817, founded 1975, editor Frank Stewart. Petronium is a small press publisher of poetry, fiction, essays and art— **"primarily interested in writers in and from Hawaii, but will publish others under special circumstances.** Interested in fine printing, fine typography and design in limited editions." They publish chapbooks, trade books, limited editions, broadsides and "other ephemera," but they **"are not accepting unsolicited material at this time."** They publish 3-6 poetry chapbooks/year, with an average page count of 32, flat-spined paperbacks. The editor says, **"Query letters are welcome, with SASE."** He replies to queries within 3 weeks and reports on mss in the same amount of time. He has **"no special requirements," but will not accept photocopied mss or disks. "Payment of authors is negotiated differently for each book." Buys all rights. Returns rights by request. The editor does not comment on rejections "unless the material is exceptionally good."** He says, "We are not really for beginners nor, in general, for people outside the Pacific region. We are not strict regionalists, but believe in nurturing first the writers around us. Beginning writers might do well to look for publishers with this same philosophy in their own cities and states rather than flinging their work to the wind, to unknown editors or to large publishing houses. All writers should consider supporting quality publishing in their own region first." Some of Petronium's books are distributed by the University of Hawaii Press (2840 Kolowalu St., Honolulu HI 96822) and may be obtained from them; "send for their literature catalog or ask for our titles specifically."

PHASE AND CYCLE (II); PHASE AND CYCLE PRESS (V), 3537 E. Prospect, Fort Collins CO 80525-9774, phone (970)482-7573, founded 1988, poetry editor Loy Banks. *Phase and Cycle* is a poetry magazine published semiannually. **"We look for short to moderate-length poems of all kinds, especially those that set out 'the long perspectives open at each instance' (Larkin). We are looking for poetry that will pass technical inspection in the academic community. Also, we prefer poetry that is largely accessible rather than deliberately 'difficult'."** They have recently published poetry by Jane McClellan, Martin Kich, Christian Knoeller, Mark Johnston and George Held. As a sample the editor selected these lines from "Annunciation" by Paul Willis:

> The words that come to us we do not choose.
> Nor do best apples loosing from the bough
> indent the earth by her command and choice.
> They patter down in providential place.

The magazine is 48-52 pgs., digest-sized, saddle-stapled. **Sample postpaid: $1. Submit 4-7 poems at a time. "A brief bio note may accompany poems." No simultaneous submissions or previously published poems. Editor sometimes comments on rejections. Send SASE for guidelines. Reports in 5-10 weeks. Pays 2 copies. Acquires first rights only.** Poets may send books for review consideration. Phase and Cycle Press has published two poetry chapbooks, *Breathing In The World* by Bruce Holland Rogers and Holly Arrow and *Out of Darkness* by Mary Balazs. **"At present we accept inquiries only. No book manuscripts."**

PHILOMEL; PHILOMATHEAN SOCIETY (II), Box 7, College Hall, University of Pennsylvania, Philadelphia PA 19104-6303, phone (215)898-8907, founded in 1813, editor Mr. E.C. Morales. *Philomel* is a literary annual using **"any kind of poetry, no more than 300 words or 3 pgs. per poem."** They also use stories, essays and "witty recipes." As a sample they selected these lines from "Tender is the Night" by David Perry Jones:

> Sweep, sweep; the agony settles shoulder-dust deep in the stillness
> Of still bolder enmity:
> Red-thundered eyes scream shrill shelter in the pelting.
> Weep, weep; unsated escalation
> Clears the wiry field; the carpet rims and folds; two minarets afire
> Seethe; black-stones scathe, defile the evening sky . . .

Philomel comes out each spring. It is 64 pgs., 6×9, flat-spined, with matte card cover. Poems are selected by a committee of the Philomathean Society. Press run is 1,500 for 20 subscribers of which 3 are libraries, 1,400 distributed free to the university community. **Sample postpaid: $5. Submit up to 3 poems at a time. Deadline for submissions: February 1, annually. Pays 3 or more copies.**

PHILOMEL BOOKS (III), 200 Madison Ave., New York NY 10016, phone (212)951-8700, an imprint founded in 1980, editorial director Patricia Gauch. Philomel Books publishes 15-20 hardbacks and 5-7 chapbooks/year. They say, "Since we're a children's book imprint, **we are open to individual poem submissions—anything suitable for a picture book. However, publication of poetry collections is usually done on a project basis—we acquire from outside through permissions, etc. Don't usually use unpublished material.**" They have published poetry by Edna St. Vincent Millay and Walt Whitman. **Query first with 3 sample poems and cover letter including publishing history. Previously published poems and simultaneous submissions OK. Replies to queries in 1 month, to mss in 2. Pay is negotiable.**

PHOEBE (II), George Mason University, 4400 University Dr., Fairfax VA 22030, phone (703)993-2915, founded 1970, poetry editor Graham Foust, is a literary biannual **"looking for imagery that will make your thumbs sweat when you touch it."** They have recently published poetry by C.K. Williams, Mark Doty, Cornelius Eady, Michael Palmer, Leslie Scalapino and Gillian Conoley. As a sample the editor selected these lines from "Semantics of Longing" by Leslie Bumstead:

> Was he superb in speech
> class? Even at parties with women dangling
> hunger on their brilliant clavicles, he must
> forever look for the just and longest
> word (it's Samson through the trees
> of high heels) . . .

Circulation is 3,000, with 30-35 pgs. of poetry in each issue. Subscription: $12/year; $6/single issue. *Phoebe* receives 4,000 submissions/year. **Submit up to 5 poems at a time; submission should be accompanied by SASE and a short bio. No simultaneous submissions. Reports in 2-3 months. Pays copies.** Work published in *Phoebe* was selected for inclusion in *The Best American Poetry 1993*.

‡PHOENIX PRESS (V), 22 Pintail Dr., Pittsburgh PA 15238, founded 1982, poetry editors Heywood Ostrow and Robert Julian, publishes 2-3 books a year **but accepts no unsolicited mss.** They have published poetry by Robert Julian and Sebastian Barker. As a sample here are the opening lines from *XII* by George Barker:

> Ah most unreliable of all women of grace
> in the breathless hurry of your leave taking
> you forgot, you forgot for ever, our last embrace

‡PICA (I), 165 N. Ashbury Ave., Bolingbrook IL 60440, founded 1995, editor Lisa Green, appears 3 times/year. *PICA* is a literary zine for **experimental, avant-garde and contemplative fiction essays and poetry. They want "witty, contemplative free verse. No religion, no preaching morality, no traditional, predictable rhyming schemes."** *PICA* is 40-50 pgs., $5\frac{1}{2} \times 8\frac{1}{2}$, saddle-stitched with colored paper cover. They receive about 30 poems a year, accept 25-30%. Press run is 100 for 20 subcribers, 40 shelf sales. Subscription: $10/year. **Sample postpaid: $4. Make checks payable to Lisa Green-PICA. Submit up to 10 poems at a time. Previously published poems OK; no simultaneous submissions. "Please send a cover letter if you have a list of credits, and be prepared to send a 25-word bio upon request."** Time between acceptance and publication is 6 months. **Often comments on rejections. Send SASE for guidelines. Reports in 6-8 weeks. Sometimes sends prepublication galleys. Pays 3 copies or subscription. Acquires one-time rights.** The editor says, "Please, please read a copy of *PICA*, or any other mag, before you submit. And show me, don't tell me. Assume your audience is smarter than you."

‡PIEDMONT LITERARY REVIEW; PIEDMONT LITERARY SOCIETY (I, II, IV-Form), Rt. 1, Box 1014, Forest VA 24551, founded 1976; poetry editor William Reuben Smith, 3750 Woodside Ave., Lynchburg VA 24503 (and **poetry submissions should go to his address**). If you join the Piedmont Literary Society, $15 a year, you get the quarterly *Review* and a quarterly newsletter containing much market and contest information. William Smith says, **"I consider all types of poems—am partial to rhyme—up to 42 lines. Each issue has a special section for oriental forms with an emphasis on haiku."** Each also includes short fiction. He does *not* want: **"smut or overly sentimental verse."** *PLR* has published poetry by Harold Witt, Joseph Awad, Sharon Kourous and Tom Riley. As a sample the editor selected these lines by Jeanne Heath Heritage:

> —you gazed upon my son,
> reached out with icy fingers, touched my hand
> In sorrow far too deep for tears, you bowed your head
> and then for me, for your own son and mine,
> for all the children lost out in the rain;
> high in the sodden silence of the sky
> I heard your scream

The quarterly is digest-sized, saddle-stapled, offset from typescript, matte card cover, using b&w graphics, with 40-50 pgs. of poetry in each issue, circulation 300 with 200 subscriptions of which 10 are libraries. It's a well-established publication with well-made formal and free verse poems. **Sample postpaid: $4, or $3 prepublication. Submit 3-5 poems at a time. Editor often comments on rejections. Send SASE for guidelines. Reports within 3 months. Pays 1 copy. Acquires first rights.** Briefly reviews "a few" books of poetry, "mostly contributors' books," in accompanying newsletter which contains current market information. They also sponsor occasional contests. The editor says he is "interested only in poetry which communicates to the thoughtful reader, with special interest in established verse forms and free verse. Not interested in experimental verse."

PIG IRON; KENNETH PATCHEN COMPETITION (II, IV-Themes), Dept. PM, P.O. Box 237, Youngstown OH 44501, phone (216)747-6932, founded 1975, poetry editor Jim Villani, is a literary annual devoted to special themes. They want **poetry "up to 300 lines; free verse and experimental; write for current themes."** Forthcoming themes: The Family: Tradition & Possibility and Jazz Tradition. **They do *not* want to see "traditional" poetry.** They have published poetry by Wayne Hogan, Laurel Speer, Louis McKee, Lloyd Mills, Marian Steele, Hugh Fox and John Pyros. As a sample the editor selected these lines by Joan Kincaid:

> I'm yelling my goose call
> bahonk bahonk
> to make her laugh
> because there are no geese
> when we're surprised
> by an eerie screech-purr
> echoing across the dark water
> I bahonk again
> and a white swan launches
> into the night a song
> I've never heard.

Pig Iron is 128 pgs., magazine-sized, flat-spined, typeset on good stock with glossy card cover using b&w graphics and art, no ads, circulation 1,000. They have 200 subscriptions of which 50 are libraries. Single copy: $10.95. Subscription: $9/1 year, $16/2 years. **Sample postpaid: $4. No simultaneous submissions. Send SASE for guidelines. Reports in 3 months.** Time between acceptance and publication is 12-18 months. **Pays $5/poem plus 2 copies. Buys one-time rights.** They sponsor the annual Kenneth Patchen Competition. Send SASE for details. The editor says, "We want tomorrow's poetry, not yesterday's."

PIKEVILLE REVIEW (II), Humanities Dept., Pikeville College, Pikeville KY 41501, phone (606)432-9234, founded 1987, editor James Alan Riley, who says: **"There's no editorial bias though we recognize and appreciate style and control in each piece. No emotional gushing."** *PR* appears once yearly, accepting about 10% of poetry received. Press run is 500. **Sample postpaid: $3. No simultaneous submissions or previously published poems. Editor sometimes comments on rejections. Send SASE for guidelines. Pays 5 copies.** They also sponsor contests.

PINCHGUT PRESS (V), 6 Oaks Ave., Cremorne, Sydney, NSW 2090 Australia, phone (02)9908-2402, founded 1948, publishes **Australian poetry but is not currently accepting poetry submissions. Send SASE for catalog to order samples.**

‡PINE PRESS (III), RD1 Box 530, Landisburg PA 17040-9739, founded 1978, editor Kerry Shawn Keys, publishes "the finest poetry, especially by younger, less published poets." They publish 2 paperbacks and 3 chapbooks a year under Pine Press or Redtail Books. **They have no particular poetry needs except they do not want poetry "written for the marketplace."** They have recently published poetry by Craig Czury, Gerald Stern, J.C. Todd and H.T. As a sample the editor selected these lines from "Saint Christopher's Monkey" by Andrew Zecs:

> Now I remember my dreams. I race to
> stop the shooting of a wolf
> but am entangled by the bear behind me.
> The young crow asks me for food, he knows
> less about animals than he used to.

Books are usually 32-64 pgs., 5½ × 8½, laser-printed, hand-sewn with flat spine, linen-style cover with artwork. **Send complete ms (25 pgs. maximum) with SASE. Previously published poems and simultaneous submissions OK. Cover letter required.** Time between acceptance and publication is 1 year. **Poems are circulated to an editorial board. "Submissions are sent to five readers from different regions of the world." Seldom comments on rejections. Replies in 4 months. Pays $5 honorarium and 75 copies, additional copies available at 50% off list price.** The editor says, "No advice, no scene, just let the daimons in and provide the tongue, the breath, the pen."

THE PIPE SMOKER'S EPHEMERIS (I, IV-Specialized), 20-37 120th St., College Point NY 11356-2128, editor/publisher Tom Dunn, who says, "The *Ephemeris* is a limited edition, irregular quarterly **for pipe smokers and anyone else who is interested in its varied contents.** Publication costs are absorbed by the editor/publisher, assisted by any contributions—financial or otherwise—that readers might wish to make." **They want poetry with themes related to pipes and pipe smoking.** Issues range from 76-96 pgs., and are 8½ × 11, offset from photoreduced typed copy, saddle-stitched, with colored paper covers and illustrations. The editor has also published collections covering the first and second 15 years of the *Ephemeris*. **Cover letter required with submissions; include any credits. Pays 1-2 copies.** Staff also reviews books of poetry. Send books for review consideration.

PIRATE WRITINGS; PIRATE WRITINGS PUBLISHING (I, II, IV-Science fiction/fantasy, mystery), 53 Whitman Ave., Islip NY 11751, founded 1992, editor/publisher Edward J. McFadden. *Pirate Writings: Tales of Fantasy, Mystery & Science Fiction* is a quarterly magazine "filled with fiction, poetry, art and reviews by top name professionals and tomorrow's rising stars." **They want all forms and styles of poetry "within our genres—literary (humorous or straight), fantasy, science fiction, mystery/suspense and adventure. Best chance is 20 lines or less. No crude language or excessive violence. No pornography, horror, western or romance. Poems should be typed with exact capitalization and punctuation suited to your creative needs."** They have recently published poetry by Nancy Springer and John Grey. As a sample the editor selected these lines from "The Long Cellar" by Jane Yolen:

> Jack Dogherty knew a merrow
> could drink any man of Ennis
> under the pub table
> and still find strength
> to crawl back to the sea.

Pirate Writings is 72 pgs., magazine-sized and saddle-stapled with a full-color cover, interior spot color and b&w art throughout. They receive about 150 poetry submissions a year, use approximately 15-25 poems. Subscription: $15 for 4 issues, $25 for 8 issues. **Sample postpaid: $4.99. Simultaneous submissions OK. Cover letter required; include credits, if applicable. Often comments on rejections. Send SASE for guidelines. Reports in 1-2 months. Pays 1-2 copies. Acquires first North American serial rights. Also "reserves the right to print in anthology."** Query regarding reviews of chapbooks. Pirate Writings Publishing **publishes chapbooks through various arrangements.** Published: *Moorhaven Fair* by Richard Novak. **Query first. Replies to queries in 1 month, to mss in 2 months. Poets may have to share publication costs. For sample chapbooks, write for flier.** Pirate Writings Publishing has also published *The Poe Pulpit*, stories and poems in the Poe tradition, and *Thoughts of Christmas*.

PITT POETRY SERIES; UNIVERSITY OF PITTSBURGH PRESS; AGNES LYNCH STARRETT POETRY PRIZE (II), 127 N. Bellefield Ave., Pittsburgh PA 15260, founded 1968, poetry editor Ed Ochester, publishes **"poetry of the highest quality; otherwise, no restrictions—book mss minimum of 48 pages." Poets who have previously published books should query. Simultaneous submissions OK. Always sends prepublication galleys.** They have published books of poetry by Richard Garcia, Larry Levis, Sharon Doubiago, Robley Wilson and Liz Rosenberg. Their booklist also features such poets as Peter Meinke, Leonard Nathan, Sharon Olds, Ronald Wallace, David Wojahn and Belle Waring. **"Poets who have not previously published a book should send SASE for rules of the Starrett competition ($15 handling fee), the *only* vehicle through which we publish first books of poetry." The Starrett Prize consists of cash award of $3,000 and book publication.**

THE PITTSBURGH QUARTERLY; THE SARA HENDERSON HAY PRIZE (II), 36 Haberman Ave., Pittsburgh PA 15211-2144, phone (412)431-8885, founded 1990, editor Frank Correnti, who says, **"Our first criterion is good writing with the variety of content that is common to a broad community interest. Generally, writing with narrative and real-life elements. We don't want doggerel or most rhyme."** They have published poetry by Marc Jampole, Ellen Smith, Kristin Kovacic, Robert Cooperman and Lynne Hugo de Courcy. As a sample the editor selected these lines from "Tender Meat" by June Hopper Hymas:

> . . . the sounds and the smells of the lives of the poet
> and the poet's ancestors. I haven't thought
>
> to ask my children if they talk to janitors or sometimes feel
> like sawdust: null brown bits, cellulose without form.
>
> Tonight is a hot night; when you hung up on me,
> I did not call you back. I am reclaiming myself.

It is 76 pgs., digest-sized, professionally printed, saddle-stapled with matte card cover. Press run is 700 for 250 subscribers of which 10 are libraries, 300 shelf sales. Subscription: $12 ($14 Canadian). **Sample postpaid: $5. "We will reply by letter to queries." Editor often comments on submissions. Reports in 3-4 months. Pays 2 copies. Acquires first North American serial rights.** Published books are reviewed as space is available, 1-2/issue. Accepts reviews of 4-6 pages, double-spaced. Send books for review consideration. "We are responding in part to the network of writers whose crafted creativity made the magazine possible, but we also are attempting to provide a readership that will connect more strongly to the community of poets and writers through this quarterly." *The Pittsburgh Quarterly* now sponsors an annual prize for poetry: The Sara Henderson Hay Prize. Entry requires current subscription or renewal and is limited to 3 poems up to 100 lines each. Deadline: July 1. Winner receives a cash award and publication of the winning poem in the fall issue.

PIVOT (II), 250 Riverside Dr., #23, New York NY 10025, phone (212)222-1408, founded 1951, editor Martin Mitchell, is a poetry annual that has published poetry by Philip Appleman, William Matthews, Eugene McCarthy, Craig Raine, W.D. Snodgrass and Robert Wrigley. As a sample the editor selected "January Thaw" by X.J. Kennedy:

> *Beware. This seamless inverness of ice*
> *Cloaking the brick walk and the treacherous street*
> *Might, in a plot that sweeps you off your feet,*
> *Induce paralysis.*
>
> *Some gray, malignant growth, it lies immune*
> *To clouded skies till, slicing through the cold,*
> *One ray of sun, inserted, breaks its hold*
> *Like a good scalpel freeing up a brain.*

Pivot is a handsome, 6×9, flat-spined, professionally printed magazine with glossy card cover. Press run is 1,200. Single copy: $5. **Submit 3-7 poems at a time. Brief cover letter preferred. Reads submissions January 1 through June 1 only. Reports in 2-4 weeks. Sometimes sends prepublication galleys. Pays 2 copies.**

THE PLACE IN THE WOODS; READ, AMERICA! (I, IV-Children), 3900 Glenwood Ave., Golden Valley MN 55422, phone (612)374-2120, founded 1980, editor and publisher Roger A. Hammer, publishes *Read, America!*, a quarterly newsletter for reading coordinators. They want **"poems for children that are understandable, under 500 words, unusual views of life. Also, foreign-language poems with English translation. Nothing vague, self-indulgent, erotic. No navel introspection."** As a sample we selected these lines from "Circus" by Eugene C. Baggott:

> *Did you ever watch the bareback riders*
> *As they lovingly groomed their steeds?*
> *Or the trapeze artist practice his catch*
> *While hanging by his knees?*

Read, America! is 8 pgs., magazine-sized, professionally printed on yellow paper. "Pages 1-4 are distributed free to some 10,000 programs. Four additional pages go only to readers who support us as subscribers." Most poems appear in the "Subscribers only" insert but poets do not have to be subscribers to submit. Subscription: $20. **No previously published poems; simultaneous submissions OK. Cover letter "optional and appreciated for insight into poet's background and interests or goals." Always comments on rejections. Pays $10 on publication. Buys all rights.**

PLAINSONG (I, II), Box 8245, Western Kentucky University, Bowling Green KY 42101, phone (502)745-5708, founded 1979, poetry editors Frank Steele, Elizabeth Oakes and Peggy Steele, is an occasional poetry journal. "Our purpose is to print the best work we can get, from known and unknown writers. This means, of course, that we print what we like: poems about places, objects, people, moods, politics, experiences. **We like straightforward, conversational language, short poems in which the marriage of thinking and feeling doesn't break up because of spouse-abuse (the poem in which ideas wrestle feeling into the ground or in which feeling sings alone—and boringly—at the edge of a desert). Prefer poems under 20 lines in free verse—brief, understated lyrics that depend on the image combined with an intimate, conversational voice. No limits on subject matter, though we like to think of ourselves as humane, interested in the environment, in peace (we're anti-nuclear), in the possibility that the human race may have a future."** They have published poetry by Robert Bly, Ted Kooser, Judy Kronenfeld, Laurie Lamon, David Till and Angie Estes. The magazine is 48-56 pgs., 6×9, professionally printed, flat-spined, color matte card cover with photos and graphics. They use about 100 of the 2,000 submissions received each year. Press run is 600 with 250 subscriptions of which 65 are libraries. Subscription: $7. **Sample postpaid: $3.50. Submit 5-6 poems at a time. "We prefer poems typed, double-spaced. Simultaneous submissions can, of course, get people into trouble, at times." Publishes theme issues occasionally. Send SASE for guidelines. Reports "within a month, usually." Pays copies.** Staff reviews books of poetry. Send books for review consideration to Frank Steele. The editor says, "We receive too many poems in 'the schoolroom voice'—full of language that's really prose. We'd like to see more poems with a voice that feels something without being sentimental or melodramatic."

PLAINSONGS (II), Dept. of English, Hastings College, Hastings NE 68902-0269, phone (402)463-2402 or 461-7352, founded 1980, editor Dwight C. Marsh, is a poetry magazine that **"accepts manuscripts from anyone, considering poems on any subject in any style but free verse preferred. Regional poems encouraged."** They have recently published poetry by Robert Cooperman, Thomas Gribble, Edward Lynskey, John Sokol, Laura L. Sullivan and Rex Walton. As a sample the editor selected these lines from "Mother Lode," a *Plainsongs* Award poem by Laura L. Sullivan:

> *. . . As latecomer, I strip*
> *mined the last of you until your teeth were chalk;*

> *until the brittle reeds that had been your bones*
> *bowed and bent with weary breasts I left*
> *shrivelled and dry; until those hollowed bones*
> *could shatter like Sunday china at the lightest brush*
> *with the ground; . . .*

Plainsongs is 40 pgs., digest-sized, set on laser in Times font, printed on thin paper and saddle-stapled with one-color matte card cover with generic black logo. The magazine is supported by the English Dept. of Hastings College and financed primarily by subscriptions, which cost $9 for 3 issues/year. The name suggests not only its location on the Great Plains, but its preference for the living language, whether in free or formal verse. It is committed to poems only, to make space without visual graphics, bio or critical positions. **Sample copies: $3. Submit up to 6 poems at a time with name and address on each page. Ms deadlines are August 15 for fall issue; November 15 for winter; March 15 for spring. Notification is mailed about 5 weeks after deadlines. Pay is 2 copies and a year's subscription, with 3 award poems in each issue receiving small monetary recognition (currently $25). "A short essay in appreciation accompanies each award poem." Acquires first rights.**

PLANET: THE WELSH INTERNATIONALIST (III), P.O. Box 44, Aberystwyth, Dyfed, Wales, phone 01970-611255, fax 01970-623311, founded 1970, editor John Barnie, is a bimonthly cultural magazine, "centered on Wales, but with broader interests in arts, sociology, politics, history and science." **They want "good poetry in a wide variety of styles. No limitations as to subject matter; length can be a problem."** They have published poetry by J.K. Gill and R.S. Thomas. As a sample the editor selected these lines from "On Home Beaches" by Les Murray:

> *Back, in my fifties, fatter than I was then,*
> *I step on the sand, belch down slight horror to walk*
> *a wincing pit edge, waiting for the pistol shot*
> *laughter. Long greening waves cash themselves, foam change*
> *sliding into Ocean's pocket. She turns: ridicule looks down,*
> *strappy, with faces averted, or is glare and families.*

Planet is 120 pgs., A5 size, professionally printed and perfect-bound with glossy color card cover. They receive about 300 submissions a year, accept approximately 5%. Press run is 1,400 for 1,150 subscribers of which about 10% are libraries, 200 shelf sales. Single copy: £2.50; subscription: £12 (overseas: £13). **Sample postpaid: £3.56. No previously published poems or simultaneous submissions. Do not submit via fax. SASE or SAE with IRCs essential for reply.** Time between acceptance and publication is 6-10 months. **Seldom comments on rejections. Send SASE (or SAE and IRCs if outside UK) for guidelines. Reports within a month or so. Pays £25 minimum. Buys first serial rights only.** Reviews books of poetry in 700 words, single and multi-book format. Open to unsolicited reviews. Poets may also send books for review consideration.

PLANTAGENET PRODUCTIONS (V), Westridge, Andover Rd., Highclere, Nr. Newbury, Royal Berkshire RG 20 9 PJ England, founded 1964, director of productions Miss Dorothy Rose Gribble. Plantagenet issues cassette recordings of poetry, philosophy and narrative (although they have issued nothing new since 1980). Miss Gribble says, "Our public likes classical work . . . We **have published a few living poets, but this is not very popular with our listeners, and we shall issue no more."** They have issued cassettes by Oscar Wilde, Chaucer and Pope, as well as Charles Graves, Elizabeth Jennings, Leonard Clark and Alice V. Stuart. The recordings are issued privately and are obtainable only direct from Plantagenet Productions; write for list. Miss Gribble's advice to poets is: "If intended for a listening public, let the meaning be clear. If possible, let the music of the words sing."

THE PLASTIC TOWER (II), P.O. Box 702, Bowie MD 20718, founded 1989, editors Carol Dyer and Roger Kyle-Keith, is a quarterly using **"everything from iambic pentameter to silly limericks, modern free verse, haiku, rhymed couplets—we like it all! Only restriction is length—under 40 lines preferred. So send us poems that are cool or wild, funny or tragic—but especially those closest to your soul."** They have published poetry by "more than 400 different poets." As a sample we selected these lines from "the realist" by W. Gregory Stewart:

> *. . . says*
> *that his cup is half-full*
> *if he has been filling it,*
> *and that it is half-empty*

THE SUBJECT INDEX, located before the General Index, can help you select markets for your work. It lists those publishers whose poetry interests are specialized.

if he has been drinking from it.
he knows
the difference between
politics and government,
and does not confuse
truth with fact.

It is 38-54 pgs., digest-sized, saddle-stapled; "variety of typefaces and b&w graphics on cheap photo-copy paper." Press run is 200. Subscription: $8/year. Copy of current issue: $2.50. **"We'll send a back issue free for a *large* (at least 6×9) SAE with 75¢ postage attached." Submit no more than 10 poems at a time. Previously published poems and simultaneous submissions OK. Editors comment on submissions "often." Send SASE for guidelines. Reports in 3-4 months. Pays 1 copy.** Open to unsolicited reviews. Poets may also send books for review consideration. Roger Kyle-Keith says, *"PT* is an unpretentious little rag dedicated to enjoying verse and making poetry accessible to the general public as well as fellow poets. We don't claim to be the best, but we try to be the nicest and most personal. And we really, genuinely love poetry—just like you! And always remember (never forget?) your poems are important. Rejection and acceptance slips aren't. Don't let those cruddy pieces of paper define your life. Most, ours included, aren't worth the paper on which they're printed. So sing and shout and laugh and cry and stop on by *The Plastic Tower.*"

THE PLAZA (II, IV-Bilingual), U-Kan, Inc., Yoyogi 2-32-1, Shibuya-ku, Tokyo 151, Japan, phone 81-3-3379-3881, fax 81-3-3379-3882, e-mail u-kan@u-kan.co.jp, website http://u-kan.co.jp/~u-kan, founded 1985, poetry editors Roger Lakhani and Mari Tochiya, is a quarterly which "represents a borderless forum for contemporary writers and artists" and includes poetry, fiction and essays published simultaneously in English and Japanese. **They want "highly artistic poetry dealing with being human and interculturally related. Nothing stressing political, national, religious or racial differences.** *The Plaza* is edited with a global view of mankind." They have published poetry by Morgan Gibson, Sharon Scholl and Catherine Buckaway. As a sample the editors selected these lines from "Dialectic of the Deep" by Richard Alan Bunch:

Sand:

*Where do you come from
o sea that slaps the land?*

*And who is your mother o
sea of essential things?*

*What do you chart with your olive
eyes o main of the north country?*

Sea:

*From a trailing wind and dreams
of a wife of night.*

*A siege of mutual love, naked
as now, who refuses none.*

*Ashes of butterflies
who stirrup like the phoenix.*

The Plaza is 48 pgs., A5, professionally printed and saddle-stapled with card cover. Submissions (and its covers) are illustrated with artistic b&w drawings. They receive about 2,500 poems a year, accept approximately 4%. Press run is 7,000 for 4,800 subscribers of which 460 are libraries (including 160 overseas), 1,500 shelf sales. Single copy: 380 yen; subscription: 1,500 yen. **Sample available for 5 IRCs (for overseas airmail). No previously published poems; simultaneous submissions OK. Cover letter required.** "Please include telephone and fax numbers with submissions. As *The Plaza* is a bilingual publication in English and Japanese, it is sometimes necessary, for translation purposes, to contact authors. Japanese translations are prepared by the editorial staff." Seldom comments on rejections. **Reports within 1 month. Pays 10 copies plus an additional 10 if self-translated into Japanese.** Reviews books of poetry, usually in less than 500 words. Open to unsolicited reviews. Poets may also send books for review consideration. Roger Lakhani says, *"The Plaza* focuses not on human beings but humans being human in the borderless world. It is not international, but intercultural. And it is circulated all over the world—in the American continents, Oceania, Asia, the Middle East, Europe and Africa."

PLAZM MAGAZINE; PLAZM MEDIA (I, II), P.O. Box 2863, Portland OR 97208-2863, phone (503)222-6389, fax (503)235-9666, founded 1991. *Plazm Magazine* is published 4 times a year by Plazm Media, "a cooperative dedicated to free expression." **They want experimental poetry. Nothing "rudimentary."** They have published poetry by Dan Raphael, Jay Marvin and Bill Shields. As a sample the editor selected these lines by Laura Winter:

rolled
up tight
as a potato bug
the fiddle head
is edible
and

won't
run away

The editor says *Plazm* is 9 × 12, printed offset litho and saddle-stitched, with "much art and design." Press run is 7,500 for 250 subscribers of which 10 are libraries, most shelf sales. Subscription: $16 for 4 issues. **Sample postpaid: $6. Previously published poems OK (but not preferred). Simultaneous submissions also OK. SASE and biographical statement required. Poems are circulated to an editorial board. Often comments on rejections. Send SASE for guidelines. Reports in 3-4 months. Pays 3 copies and a subscription.** Reviews books of poetry in 25-250 words. Open to unsolicited reviews. Poets may also send books for review consideration.

‡**PLEIADES (II)**, Dept. of English and Philosophy, Central Missouri State University, Warrensburg MO 64093, phone (816)543-4425, fax (816)543-8006, founded as *Spring Flight* in 1939, reestablished in its present format in 1990, general editor R.M. Kinder. *Pleiades*, a semiannual journal which publishes poetry, fiction, literary criticism, belles lettres (occasionally) and reviews. It is open to all writers and emphasizes cultural diversity. **They want "avant-garde, free verse and traditional poetry, and some quality light verse. Nothing pretentious, didactic or overly sentimental."** They have recently published poetry by William Doreski, Bosley Wilder and Katharyn Howd Machan. As a sample the editor selected these lines from "Thoughts on Clearing Out the Ice Tray" by John Ditsky:

> *All those random forms! Those crystal*
> *forming and reforming at the random whims*
> *of temperature produced these chunks*
> *And shavings, brittle and cold and old.*
> *Shake them loose into a glass, and then*
> *Pour Vodka over them. As you watch*
> *a slush ensues. And moves and eddies*
> *As it melts like mush of glaciers calving.*

The editor says *Pleiades* is 120 pgs., 5½ × 8½, perfect-bound with a heavy coated cover and b&w cover art. They receive about 400 poems a year, accept approximately 10%. Press run is 300, about 200 distributed free to educational institutions and libraries across the country, about 100 shelf sales. Single copy: $5.50; subscription: $10. **Sample postpaid: $3.50. Make checks payable to Pleiades Press. Submit 3-5 poems at a time. No previously published poems; simultaneous submissions OK. Cover letter with brief bio preferred.** Time between acceptance and publication can be up to 1 year. **Each poem published must be accepted by 2 readers and approved by the general editor. Seldom comments on rejections. Send SASE for guidelines. Reports in 3-4 months. Pays a small honorarium ("when funds allow") and 1 copy. Acquires first North American serial rights.**

PLOUGHSHARES (III), Emerson College, 100 Beacon St., Boston MA 02116, phone (617)824-8753, founded 1971. **The magazine is "a journal of new writing edited on a revolving basis by professional poets and writers to reflect different and contrasting points of view."** Editors have included Carolyn Forché, Gerald Stern, Rita Dove, Chase Twichell and Marilyn Hacker. They have published poetry by Donald Hall, Li-Young Lee, Robert Pinsky, Brenda Hillman and Thylias Moss. The triquarterly is 250 pgs., 5½ × 8½, circulation 6,000. They receive approximately 2,500 poetry submissions/year. Since this influential magazine features different editors with each issue, content varies. The issue edited by Carolyn Forché, for example, displays a variety of styles and forms with strong voices and messages. As always with prestigious journals, competition is keen. Response times can be slow because submissions are logged inhouse and sent to outside guest editors. Subscription: $19 domestic; $24 foreign. **Sample postpaid: $8.95 current issue, $6 back issue. "We suggest you read a few issues before submitting." Simultaneous submissions acceptable. Do not submit mss from April 1 to July 31. Reports in 3-5 months. Always sends prepublication galleys. Pays $50 minimum per poem, $25/printed page per poem, plus 2 contributor copies and a subscription.** Work published in *Ploughshares* appears in the 1992, 1993, 1994, 1995 and 1996 volumes of *The Best American Poetry*.

THE PLOWMAN (I, II), Box 414, Whitby, Ontario L1N 5S4 Canada, phone (905)668-7803, founded 1988, editor Tony Scavetta, appears 3 times/year using **"didactic, eclectic poetry; all forms. We will also take most religious poetry except satanic and evil."** As a sample the editor selected these lines from his own poetry:

> *The Word of God*
> *Sharper than a two edged sword*
> *Rip and tear*
> *The eyes of your children*
> *Like a fish-hook*
> *Same Holy Spirit*
> *Gives you everlasting Life*
> *Through Jesus Christ*

My Lord and Saviour

The Plowman is a 56-page, newsprint tabloid which accepts 70% of the poetry received. Press run is 15,000 for 1,200 subscribers of which 500 are libraries. Single copy: $7.50; subscription: $10. **Sample free. Previously published poems and simultaneous submissions OK. Cover letter required. No SASE necessary. Always comments on rejections. Guidelines available free. Reports in 1 week. Always sends prepublication galleys.** Reviews books of poetry. They offer monthly poetry contests. Entry fee: $2/poem. 1st prize: 50% of the proceeds; 2nd: 25%; 3rd: 10%. The top poems are published. "Balance of the poems will be used for anthologies." **They also publish 125 chapbooks/year. Replies to queries and mss in 1 week. Requires $25 reading fee/book. Pays 20% royalties.**

THE PLUM REVIEW (II), P.O. Box 1347, Philadelphia PA 19105-1347, founded 1990, editors Mike Hammer and Christina Daub, managing editor Karen Faul, appears twice a year. **"We are open to original, high quality poetry of all forms, lengths, styles and subject matters. Our only criterion is excellence."** They have recently published poetry by Robert Bly, Donald Hall, David Ignatow, Linda Pastan, Elizabeth Spires, Diane Wakoski, Marie Howe and Billy Collins. As a sample the editors selected these lines from "For Char Gardner, Preparing Her Art" by Henry Taylor:

> *All this, you understand, is mere example.*
> *You might be hoarding bits of twine or bark,*
> *peeling the labels from antique tin cans,*
> *or breeding chickens toward imagined plumage.*
> *Somehow the ingredients will find you.*

The Plum Review is approximately 120 pgs., professionally printed and flat-spined. Editors seem to favor well-made free verse, emphasizing voice and line. Press run is 1,500. **Sample postpaid: $7. Submit up to 5 poems at a time. "Absolutely no simultaneous submissions. Include a brief bio indicating previous publications and/or awards." Sometimes comments on rejections. Reports in 1-2 months. Pays 1 copy.** They welcome unsolicited reviews (up to 15 pgs., single or multi-book format) of recently published books of poetry and interviews with prominent poets. Poets may also send books for review consideration. They sponsor a reading series and creative writing workshops for the elderly and the handicapped. *The Plum Review* also has an annual poetry competition which awards $500 to the best poem(s). Deadline: February 28, 1997. Submit up to 3 poems with SASE and $5 entry fee. All entries will be considered for publication. No simultaneous submissions. No previously published poems. This magazine says that it is "so delicious"—a takeoff on William Carlos Williams's famous lyric "This Is Just To Say"?—and it is, too, featuring the best work of top-name poets and relative newcomers. In addition, *The Plum Review* was awarded a grant from the Council of Literary Magazines and Presses for outstanding content and design.

POCAHONTAS PRESS, INC.; MANUSCRIPT MEMORIES (V), P.O. Drawer F, Blacksburg VA 24063-1020, phone (540)951-0467, e-mail mchollim@vtvmi.vt.edu, founded 1984, president Mary C. Holliman, publishes chapbook collections of poetry, but **is temporarily not considering new mss** "because I am trying to finish those already accepted." Inquire before submitting. **Prefers Appalachian-related themes and authors only. "Most of the poetry books I have published have been subsidized to some extent by the author. So far one of those authors' books has sold enough copies that the author has received a significant reimbursement for his investment. We continue to market all of our books as aggressively as possible. The idea is to make a profit for both of us (though we have yet to do so)."** She has published books by Leslie Mellichamp, Lynn Kozma, Mildred Nash, Preston Newman and Elaine Emans. As a sample the editor selected these lines by Cecil J. Mullins:

> *In the East, time has been divorced*
> *From things. No clocks hem the hours*
> *In, and time, not being firmly forced,*
> *Slops around.*

Submit 8-10 poems at a time. Always sends prepublication galleys. Pays 10% royalties on all sales receipts, 10 free copies of book, and any number of copies at 50% for resale or "whatever use author wishes. If author helps with printing costs, then an additional percentage of receipts will be paid." She offers editorial critiques for $40/hour. Mary Holliman adds, "There's much more good poetry being written than is getting published, and I only wish I could publish more of it. We are planning to try a new marketing technique—single-fold notecards with one poem from a collection per card, perhaps 3 poem/cards (2 each in a set of 6). The full collection and how to order will be given on the back of each card."

POEM; HUNTSVILLE LITERARY ASSOCIATION (II), English Dept., University of Alabama at Huntsville, Huntsville AL 35899, founded 1967, poetry editor Nancy Frey Dillard, appears twice a year, consisting entirely of poetry. **"We are particularly open to traditional as well as non-traditional forms, but we favor work with the expected compression and intensity of good lyric poetry and a high degree of verbal and dramatic tension. We welcome equally submissions from estab-**

lished poets as well as from less known and beginning poets. **We do not accept translations, previously published works or simultaneous submissions. We prefer to see a sample of 3-5 poems at a submission, with SASE. We generally respond within a month. We are a nonprofit organization and can pay only in copy to contributors. Sample copies are available at $5."** They have published poetry by Robert Cooperman, Andrew Dillon and Scott Travis Hutchison. As a sample the editor selected these lines from "Mister Varsey" by Sally Jo Sorensen:

> With the myths
> his methods excelled:
> The Odyssey, for instance,
> became more than just the same old song
> about some guy who'd left his wife and kid
> for the guys. Mr. Varsey fetched a bow
> out of his great, fabled closet
> and asked the gentlemen of the class—
> as he called them—to see who might be
> Penelope's true suitor. None could
> match the task, so he exclaimed
> blind Homer walks again!
> until I raised my hand

Poem is a flat-spined, 4⅜ × 7¼, 90-page journal that contains more than 60 poems (mostly lyric free verse under 50 lines) generally featured one to a page on good stock paper with a clean design and a classy matte cover. Circulation is 400 (all subscriptions of which 90 are libraries). Overall, it's a good market for beginners and experienced poets who pay attention to craft.

POEMS & PLAYS; THE TENNESSEE CHAPBOOK PRIZE (II), English Dept., Middle Tennessee State University, Murfreesboro TN 37132, phone (615)898-2712, founded 1993, editor Gay Brewer, is an annual "eclectic publication for poems and short plays," published in April. **They have no restrictions on style or content of poetry.** They have recently published poetry by Stephen Dobyns, Philip Levine, Charles Bukowski and David Citino. As a sample the editor selected these lines from "The Day Before" by Stephen Dunn:

> Then something sudden, massive, conclusive,
> Something gene-driven that comes deeply
> from your father, perhaps even tinged
> with his goodness, and you're gone.

Poems & Plays is 88 pgs., 6 × 9, professionally printed and perfect-bound with coated color card cover and art. "We received 1,550 poems for our third issue (Spring/Summer 1996), published 30." Press run is 550. Subscription: $10 (2 issues). **Sample postpaid: $6. No previously published poems or simultaneous submissions (except for chapbook submissions). Reads submissions October 1 through January 15 only. "Work is circulated among advisory editors for comments and preferences. All accepted material is published in the following issue." Usually comments on rejections. Reports in 1-2 months. Pays 1 copy. Acquires first publication rights only.** "We accept chapbook manuscripts (of poems or short plays) of 24 pages for The Tennessee Chapbook Prize. The winner is printed as an interior chapbook in *Poems & Plays* and receives 50 copies of the issue. SASE and $10 fee (for one copy of the issue) required. Dates for contest entry are the same as for the magazine (October 1 through January 15). Past winners include Maureen Micus Crisick, David Stark, Steven Sater and Angela Kelly. The 1996 chapbook competition drew 114 manuscripts from 35 states, Canada, England and Guam."

POET LORE; JOHN WILLIAMS ANDREWS NARRATIVE POETRY COMPETITION (II), The Writer's Center, 4508 Walsh St., Bethesda MD 20815, phone (301)654-8664, founded 1889, managing editor Sunil Freeman, executive editors Philip Jason and Geraldine Connolly, is a quarterly dedicated "to the best in American and world poetry and objective and timely reviews and commentary. We look for **fresh uses of traditional form and devices, but any kind of excellence is welcome. The editors encourage narrative poetry and original translations of works by contemporary world poets."** They have published poetry by Sharon Olds, John Balaban, William Heyen, Walter McDonald, Reginald Gibbons and Howard Nemerov. *Poet Lore* is 6 × 9, 80 pgs., perfect-bound, professionally printed with matte card cover. Circulation includes 600 subscriptions of which 200 are libraries. Editors are open to all styles (as long as the work is well-crafted and insightful), leaning toward lyric and narrative free verse with an emphasis on voice. They receive about 3,000 poems/year, use about 125. Single copy: $5.50; subscription: $15. **Sample postpaid: $4. Submit typed poems, author's name and address on each page. Reports in 3 months. Pays 2 copies.** Reviews books of poetry. Open to unsolicited reviews. Poets may also send books for review consideration. Sponsors the John Williams Andrews Narrative Poetry Competition for unpublished poems of 100 lines or more. The annual competition awards $350 and publication in *Poet Lore*. Deadline: November 30. Send SASE for entry form and guidelines. Poetry published in *Poet Lore* has also been selected for inclusion in *The Best American Poetry 1994*.

POET MAGAZINE; COOPER HOUSE PUBLISHING INC.; JOHN DAVID JOHNSON MEMORIAL POETRY AWARDS; IVA MARY WILLIAMS INSPIRATIONAL POETRY AWARDS; AMERICAN COLLEGE & UNIVERSITY POETRY AWARDS; AMERICAN HIGH SCHOOL POETRY AWARDS; THE AMERICAN LITERARY MAGAZINE AWARDS (II), P.O. Box 5646, Shreveport LA 71135, founded 1984, managing editor Peggy Cooper, editor Joy Hall, poetry editor Michael Hall. "*Poet* is one of the largest commercial publishers of poetry in the U.S. and is **open to submissions from writers at all levels of experience.**" Michael Hall says, **"I look for poems that display wit, knowledge and skill . . . verse that employs arresting images, poems that make the reader think or smile or even sometimes cry."** They have published poetry by Lewis Turco and H.R. Coursen. As a sample the editor selected the opening stanzas of "Marshwind Song" by Patricia A. Lawrence:

> The music of the marsh has my heart pinned
> To tidal flats and skittle dancing crabs.
> A hanging gull is tossed on beats of wind.
>
> Her lonely mewing, plaintive, swordlike, stabs
> Each note that wells to fullness like a tide
> Until she streaks the sky. A talon grabs
>
> Another note that haunts me . . .

Poet is magazine-sized, professionally printed, 56-80 pgs. with glossy cover, saddle-stitched. Of about 7,000-10,000 submissions, they use a little fewer than 5%. Subscription: $24/year. Subscribers receive free the giant "Forms of Poetry" poster. **Sample copy of *Poet*, postpaid: $6.50 or "call your book-store where you can purchase it for $5.50 ($6.50 Canada) if it's in stock. If it's not in stock, ask them to order it through Fine Print Distributors."** For guidelines, send 3 loose first-class stamps with request. Submit 5 poems at a time. Previously published poems and simultaneous submissions OK. Editor sometimes comments on rejections. Reports within 3-6 months. Pays 1 copy. Reviews books of poetry. Open to unsolicited reviews. Poets may also send books for review consideration to Joy Hall, P.O. Box 22047, Alexandria VA 22304. John David Johnson Memorial Poetry Awards (prizes of $50, $25, $12.50, special merit and honorable mention awards, award certificates, publication and a copy of the magazine in which the winning poems appear to all winners. Entry fee: $5/poem. March 1 and September 1 deadlines). Iva Mary Williams Inspirational Poetry Awards (prizes of $50, $25, $12.50, special merit and honorable mention awards, award certificates, publication and a copy of the magazine in which the winning poems appear to all winners. Entry fee: $5/poem. February 1 and August 1 deadlines). American College & University Poetry Awards (prizes of $100, $50, $25, each divided equally between winning student and teacher, special merit and honorable mention awards, award certificates, publication and copy of the magazine in which the winning poems appear to all winners. No entry fee. Rules and official entry forms may be requested with 4 loose first-class stamps). American High School Poetry Awards (certificates, publication and copy of the magazine in which the winning poems appear to all winners. No entry fee. Rules and official entry forms may be requested with 4 loose first-class stamps). The American Literary Magazine Awards are engraved plaques, award certificate and free advertising in *Poet Magazine*. All contestants receive a gift. $35 entry fee/title. Deadline: December 31. Send 2 loose first-class stamps with request for rules and entry form.

‡POET PAPERS; THE RECORD SUN (II, IV-Subscribers), P.O. Box 8025, Northridge CA 91327-8025, founded 1969. *The Record Sun* is a 4- to 12-page quarterly tabloid which uses **quality poetry, mostly by its subscribers. Sample: $5. Poet Papers publishes collections of poetry, mostly solicited.** *Always* **send SASE if you want a reply.**

POETIC PAGE (I, II); OPUS LITERARY REVIEW (II), P.O. Box 71192, Madison Heights MI 48071-0192, phone (810)548-0865, e-mail poeticpage@aol.com., *Poetic Page* founded 1989, *Opus Literary Review* founded 1993, editor Denise Martinson. *Poetic Page* appears quarterly. **Each issue has a contest, $1/poem fee, prizes of $30, $20, $10 and $5. About 90% of the poetry published is that of contest winners, and the rest is invitational only. "All forms are used except explicit sex, violence and crude. 30 lines."** They have published poetry by MacDonald Carey, Alice Mackenzie Swaim, T.N. Turner, T. Kilgore Splake, Glenna Holloway and John Grey. As a sample the editor selected the ending to "Infected" by Corrine DeWinter:

> There is nothing
>   I could have done
> to pull the arrow
> from its target.

> *But now I can tell*
> *you and you and you*
>   *almost how it feels*
> *to be a vine*
> *clinging*
> *to something solid.*

Poetic Page is 32-36 pgs., magazine-sized, saddle-stapled with coated card cover, desktop-published. Press run is 250-350, sent to libraries, universities, editors and subscribers. Subscription: $20. **Sample postpaid: $4. Simultaneous submissions and previously published poems OK. Prefers cover letter. E-mail is for information only. No submissions. Publishes theme issues. Send SASE for guidelines and upcoming themes. Nonsubscribers receive 1 copy.** The editor says, "We look for poetry that has something to say. No trite rhyme. Only the very best poems are selected each issue. First place is featured on its own page. We now use more articles, tidbits, poet interactions and fillers. We pay copies for articles and cover art, but must be of the highest quality. We ask poets to send us copies of their poetry books for our 'Review' section. Just because we are listed under the I category, does not mean that we are an easy magazine to be published in. We want poetry that is well written, poetry that demands to be read. Send your best." **Opus Literary Review** is a biannual. **No specifications as to form, length, style, subject matter or purpose.** They have published poetry by Rudy Zenker, Leonard Cirino, Laurel Speer, Robert S. King, Lyn Lifshin, Pearl Bloch Segall, John Grey and Patricia A. Lawrence. As a sample the editor selected these lines from "A Moment of Rest for a Drag-line Operator" by Janice L. Braud:

> *Bury him with hardhat, steel-toed shoes.*
> *He'll need them again*
> *perhaps to scoop out habitation space*
> *in airless asteroid millennia away*
> *or fence the flow of milky way debris*
> *to power man-made turbine stars with*
> *Big-Bang energy.*
> *Dig him a hole he would be proud of.*

Opus Literary Review is desktop-published with matte cover. Subscription: $10. **Sample postpaid: $5. No previously published poems or simultaneous submissions "unless of exceptional quality." Cover letter required. Editor often comments on rejections. Send SASE for guidelines. All accepted poets receive one copy and are listed with bio. Acquires first rights.** The editor says: "We want poetry that will last the ages. Poetry that is intelligent, well thought out. If you want to write a poem about a flower, go ahead. But make that flower unique—surprise us. Give us your best work. But beginners beware, no trite rhyme here. However, we will publish a well-written rhyme if the rhyme is the poem, not the word endings. Free verse is what we prefer."

POETIC SPACE: POETRY & FICTION (I), P.O. Box 11157, Eugene OR 97440, founded 1983, editor Don Hildenbrand, is a nonprofit literary magazine with emphasis on contemporary poetry, fiction, reviews (including film and drama), interviews, market news and translations. Accepts poetry and fiction that is **"well-crafted and takes risks. We like poetry with guts. Would like to see some poetry on social and political issues. We would also like to see gay/lesbian poetry and poetry on women's issues. Erotic and experimental OK." Prefers poems under 1,000 words.** They have published poetry by Crawdad Nelson, Ed Meek, Kell Robertson, Ray Barker, Kit Knight and Lynda S. Silva. As a sample the editor selected these lines by Olga Broumas and T. Begley:

> *As in Heaven*
> *women care for fresh game*
> *we pick up the nude sounds*
>
> *what can heart do to splash on their bodies*
> *what do these things that I am feeling mean*
> *whose hand is holding on*

The magazine is 30 pgs., 8½×11, saddle-stapled, offset from typescript and sometimes photoreduced. It is published twice a year. They use about 25% of the 200-300 poems received/year. Press run is 800 with 50 subscribers of which 12 are libraries. Single copy: $4; subscription: $7 for 2 issues, $13 for 4 issues. **Send SASE for list of available back issues ($4). Ms should be typed, double-spaced, clean, name/address on each page. "Submissions without SASE will not be considered." Simultaneous submissions and previously published poems OK. Editor provides some critical comments. Send SASE for guidelines. Reports in 2-4 months. Pays 1 copy, but more can be ordered by sending SASE and postage.** Reviews books of poetry in 500-1,000 words. Open to unsolicited reviews. Poets may also send books for review consideration. They have published an *Anthology: 1987-1991 Best of Poetic Space*, $5. Also publishes one chapbook each spring. Their first chapbook was *Truth Rides to Work and Good Girls*, poetry by Crawdad Nelson and fiction by Louise A. Blum ($5 plus $1.50 p&h). Don Hildenbrand says, "We like poetry that takes risks—original writing that gives us a new, different perspective."

‡POETICAL HISTORIES (IV-Regional, style), 27 Sturton St., Cambridge CB1 2QG United Kingdom, founded 1985, editor Peter Riley, is a "small press publishing **poetry only."** They publish **poetry that is "British, modernist,"** not **"experimental, translated, homely."** They have recently published poetry by J.H. Prynne, Douglas Oliver, Denise Riley and Nicholas Moore. **They publish 8-10 hand-printed chapbooks/year averaging 8 pgs. each.** *PH* is also a contact address for The Cambridge Conference of Contemporary Poetry, which takes place annually in late April.

POETRY; THE MODERN POETRY ASSOCIATION; BESS HOKIN PRIZE; LEVINSON PRIZE; OSCAR BLUMENTHAL PRIZE; EUNICE TIETJENS MEMORIAL PRIZE; FREDERICK BOCK PRIZE; GEORGE KENT PRIZE; UNION LEAGUE PRIZE; J. HOWARD AND BARBARA M.J. WOOD PRIZE; RUTH LILLY POETRY PRIZE (III), 60 W. Walton St., Chicago IL 60610-3380, founded 1912, editor Joseph Parisi, "is the oldest and most distinguished monthly magazine devoted entirely to verse," according to their literature. "Founded in Chicago in 1912, it immediately became the international showcase that it has remained ever since, publishing in its earliest years—and often for the first time—such giants as Ezra Pound, Robert Frost, T.S. Eliot, Marianne Moore and Wallace Stevens. *Poetry* has continued to print the major voices of our time and to discover new talent, establishing an unprecedented record. There is virtually no important contemporary poet in our language who has not at a crucial stage in his career depended on *Poetry* to find a public for him: John Ashbery, Dylan Thomas, Edna St. Vincent Millay, James Merrill, Anne Sexton, Sylvia Plath, James Dickey, Thom Gunn, David Wagoner—only a partial list to suggest how *Poetry* has represented, without affiliation with any movements or schools, what Stephen Spender has described as 'the best, and simply the best' poetry being written." Although its offices have always been in Chicago, *Poetry*'s influence and scope extend far beyond, throughout the US and in over 45 countries around the world. Asked to select 4 lines of poetry "which represent the taste and quality you want in your publication" Joseph Parisi selected the opening lines of "The Love Song of J. Alfred Prufrock" by T.S. Eliot, which first appeared in *Poetry* in 1915:

> *Let us go then, you and I,*
> *When the evening is spread out against the sky*
> *Like a patient etherized upon a table;*
> *Let us go, through certain half-deserted streets . . .*

Poetry is an elegantly printed, flat-spined, 5½×9 magazine. They receive over 75,000 submissions/year, use 300-350, have a 9-month backlog. Circulation 7,500, 6,000 subscriptions of which 53% are libraries. Single copy: $3; subscription: $27, $30 for institutions. **Sample postpaid: $4.50. Submit no more than 4 poems at a time. Send SASE for guidelines. Reports in 2-3 months—longer for mss submitted during the summer. Pays $2 a line. Buys all rights. Returns rights "upon written request."** Reviews books of poetry in 750-1,000 words, multi-book format. Open to unsolicited reviews. Poets may also send books to Stephen Young, associate editor, for review consideration. This is probably the most prestigious poetry credit in the publishing business. Consequently, competition here is extraordinarily keen with more poems received in a year than there are people in some cities in your state. Yet Joseph Parisi is one of the most efficient (and discerning) editors around, and he does much to promote poetry. This is a magazine that you can buy straight off the newsstand to get a feel for the pulse of poetry each month. Eight prizes (named in heading) ranging from $200 to $1,500 are awarded annually to poets whose work has appeared in the magazine that year. *Only verse already published in Poetry is eligible for consideration and no formal application is necessary. Poetry* also sponsors the Ruth Lilly Poetry Prize, an annual award of $75,000, and the Ruth Lilly Collegiate Poetry Fellowship, an annual award of $15,000 to undergraduates to support their further studies in poetry/creative writing. Work published in *Poetry* was also selected for inclusion in the 1992, 1993, 1994, 1995 and 1996 volumes of *The Best American Poetry*.

POETRY & AUDIENCE (I, II), School of English, University of Leeds, Leeds, West Yorkshire LS2 9JT England, founded 1953, editors Alex Goody and Carolyn Fyffe. *P&A* appears 2 times/year and accepts work from new and established poets. **"We do not discriminate against any form of poetry although there is a general move towards a more lyrical style. This said, we have and will continue to publish even the most obscure poetic forms."** They have published poetry by Carol Ann Duffy, Geoffrey Hill and Tony Harrison. As a sample the editors selected these lines from "Palm Reading" by Sonya Ardan:

> *I fill time—write to you*
> *Of Spain in the full fever*
> *Of its Easter, how it divides*
> *Its cities by color (the suffering*
> *Of a blue Virgin against the bitterness*
> *Of White) and how there's silence*

CLOSE-UP

Poets, take your roles as town criers seriously

Inspired by the Black Arts Movement of the 1960s, Sapphire was reading her work in public for years before she ever considered publishing it. "Poetry reading was part of what was called 'speak-outs,' public forums. These were issues-oriented. We were sharing our work through oral performance but it was on a consciousness-raising level. I wasn't thinking that much about getting published.

"Readings are a very important part of my work. I can't envision what kind of artist I'd be if I was not reading. There's something about the immediacy of reading to an audience. You can feel the power of the poem when you present it in public."

Photo by Becket Logan

Sapphire

That's why Sapphire encourages writers to become involved in readings. "Take chances, expose yourself. You may meet editors, and you'll broaden your audience." Sapphire did broaden *her* audience. In fact, her first publications resulted from one of her readings. After reading her work at a coffeehouse, she was approached by two editors, one from a magazine called *Azalea* and the other from *Heresies*. She placed poems in both publications.

Since then her work, much of it characterized by its gutsy, honest and challenging depiction of the world, has appeared in numerous publications, including *Amaranth Review*, *Brooklyn Review*, *Common Lives/Lesbian Lives*, *Conditions* and *Seems*. Her work has also been included in anthologies such as *Women on Women: An Anthology of Lesbian Short Fiction* (Plume, 1990), *Loving in FEAR: An Anthology of Lesbian and Gay Survivors of Childhood Sexual Abuse* (Queer Press, 1991), *Life Notes: Personal Writings by Contemporary Black Women* (W.W. Norton, 1994) and *High Risk 2* (Plume, 1994).

She even met the editor of her first collection of poetry, *American Dreams*, published by High Risk Books/Serpent's Tail in 1994, at a reading held as part of the Outright Conference, a gay and lesbian event in San Francisco. "I was at a reading at City Lights [bookstore] when an editor came up and asked if I'd like to submit to an anthology she was working on. She later became my editor on *American Dreams*, so you could say that book started as a reading, too."

Besides participation in readings, Sapphire says beginning writers should seek publications that focus on themes found in their work. Many opportunities exist and it's a matter of sending to publications most interested in the type of work you do. "Look for journals that are speaking to the same things you are. If you are a woman poet living in Iowa and you learn of a journal publishing the work

CLOSE-UP, *Sapphire*

of Midwestern women, there's a flag waving for you. Try it."

She also says writers should not delay the pursuit of publication. "This is the opposite of what you usually hear, but I don't agree that you have to be 'ready.' I don't know what 'ready' really means. Some people in their newness may be creating their best work. I say send it out, send it high, send it low, send it to a friend, don't wait for it to be 'perfect.'"

This is not to say poets can't benefit from working on their craft. Sapphire has attended several writing workshops and has studied at the Omega Institute in Rhinebeck, New York. In doing so, she has worked with Sharon Olds, Carolyn Forché and Marge Piercy. She says working closely with other writers has worked well for her, and she urges beginning writers to seek such opportunities.

> One time when I was a little girl living on an army base
> I was in a gymnasium & the general walked in.
> & the general is like god or the president if you believe.
> The young woman who was supervising the group of
> children I was with said,
> "Stand up everybody! The general's here!"
> Everybody stood up except for me.
> The woman looked at me & hissed,
> "Stand up for the general."
> I told her, "My father's in the army not me."
> & I remained seated.
> & throughout 38 years of
> bucking & winging
> grinning & crawling
> brown nosing & begging
> there has been a quiet
> 10 year old in me
> who has remained seated.
> She perhaps is the real American Dream.

(excerpt from "American Dreams," the title poem of Sapphire's book, *American Dreams*, 1994, published by High Risk Books/Serpent's Tail)

Not long ago, Sapphire received an M.F.A. in Writing from Brooklyn College. That more formal learning experience was also a good one, she says, but it differs from writing groups and workshops in important ways. "You work with the same people for two years, but you do not choose whom you are working with. It's not always as supportive [as a writing group], but you learn to deal with a diverse group of people. That's what all this talk about multiculturalism is about—it's calling on us to be more flexible as humans, to learn to deal with people from different backgrounds, who look different.

"Poet Gwendolyn Brooks has said 'I don't think school is a place for you to feel comfort,' and she's right. School is a place to come and feel challenged, but not threatened. Your ideas should be questioned but you should be given the tools

CLOSE-UP, *continued*

to put them back together again. At school I still saw the tragedy of old ideas—sexism, racism. I did encounter negative things, but it only made me more determined to work to end them."

It's clear from many of the poems included in *American Dreams* that Sapphire takes her own advice seriously. Notice the excerpt from the title poem on the previous page. Sapphire often exposes herself on a very personal level. Some poems even deal with her experiences with childhood sexual abuse.

When asked if writing this work was painful, she says, "The hard part was living it. Hearing about others' experiences is very hard and painful, too. But in the actual writing, the pain, whether lived or shared with humanity, is transformed or transmuted. You're not reliving it in the writing. I think 'transcend' is the best word for what happens in the writing of these experiences."

Poetry does not replace the actual therapeutic process, she says. Other types of writing are more helpful, and journal writing has become a very important tool in the process. She may draw from her journal for her poems, but she says at that point, the work becomes art, not therapy.

In addition to her journal, Sapphire often gets ideas for poems from everyday events. "I'm a real urban dweller. I've lived in New York City since the 1970s and right now I live on Lenox Avenue in Harlem. I'm very much affected by people's daily news. I hear what happens. I have my own internal agenda, of course, but that internal reality is affected strongly by the external reality."

Sapphire also pays close attention to the way women's stories are told in the media. Her poem "for jennifer, marla, tawana & me" deals not only with real women who have been victims of violence, sexism and racism, but also with the media's depiction of these women. News coverage of sensational trials is splashed on the front pages of newspapers across the country. This draws attention to certain issues, she says, but it can and often does exploit the victims of these crimes.

She notes that racism has a way of seeping into the language in subtle ways, and she tries to expose that in her writing as well. It bothers her that when African-Americans are charged with violent crimes they are often referred to as "animals or beasts" in the press, while killers who happen to be white are not similarly labeled. Her poem "Wild Thing" deals with this issue. She noticed that mass murderer Jeffrey Dahmer was called "a troubled human being" while the group of boys who beat and raped a female jogger in Central Park were called "wild animals." She wanted to explore this difference in how the media treats African-Americans. "I'm definitely not saying what they did was not horrible, but why not call them vicious killers which is what they were? In my work I try to appropriate the media voice in order to expose and, hopefully, change it."

Poets, she says, should see poetry as a tool for revealing the truth. "Every artist defines what he or she does differently. For me, I see myself in part as an internal poet, centering on the self, but the other part of me is literally slapped in the face by what's happening around me. I took a course once with Allen Ginsberg in which he said poets were like the griots in Africa or the town criers in England, calling out the news. I definitely see the poet's role as one of town crier." And poets should not be afraid, she says, to "cry out the news."

—Robin Gee

Press run is 200-300 for 50 subscribers of which 10 are libraries. Subscription: £10 (overseas). **Sample: £2. Submit 4 poems at a time. "Please double or at least use 1.5 spacing for all lines with triple-line spacing of stanzas. Please give birth date and place in any correspondence as well as previous publications, if applicable. We require work to be previously unpublished and not simultaneously submitted. We will often try to include constructive comments in the event of a rejection." Replies in 2 months. Pays 1 copy.** Open to unsolicited reviews. Poets may also send books for review consideration.

‡THE POETRY CONNEXION (III), % Austin Straus, producer, P.O. Box 29154, Los Angeles CA 90029-0154. **"The Poetry Connexion" is a radio program, usually live; poets coming to the Los Angeles area make contact several months in advance and send work with SASE just as though the program were a press. "We are especially interested in poets who are planning to do readings in the Los Angeles area. Please notify us at least 1-3 months in advance for consideration as a guest on our program. Always include at least 6 poems, cover letter and vita in any submission. Also include your latest book, if you have one. Do not submit unpublished mss. SASE required for return of submission."** The program is heard on Friday mornings of each week from 9:30 to 10 a.m. PST. Its purpose is "to broaden the audience, reading and listening, for poetry in the Southern California area which continues to experience a cultural 'boom' of sorts. **We are volunteer Pacifica Radio broadcasters and do not pay."** The producer adds, "We have a preference for the 'serious' poet who has published in recognized magazines. The poet may not necessarily have a book but must be on the verge of publishing, participating in workshops, readings, residencies, etc. We are also always most interested in poets whose lives are as committed and intense as their work."

‡POETRY DIGEST (II), P.O. Box 7692, Port St. Lucie FL 34985-7692, founded 1991, editor John DeStefano, is a national magazine of contemporary poetry which appears 3 times a year. **They want "high quality poetry by new and established writers. We are open to all forms of contemporary poetry, up to 100 lines. Individuality as well as a skillful crafting with respect to the art must be evident in the framework of the poem. No nature poems, 'sticky' love poems or light verse. And nothing abstract or political."** They have recently published poetry by Brendan Galvin, Alfred Dorn, H.R. Coursen, Gerald Locklin, Stuart Friebert, Sanford Pinsker, Walter McDonald and Len Krisak. *POETRY Digest* is 40-48 pgs. (80 pgs. in their Spring/Summer double issue), $5\frac{3}{4} \times 8\frac{3}{4}$, offset printed and perfect-bound with textured matte cover printed in 2 colors. (Subscribers receive free display/classified ad space for their published chapbooks.) They receive 3,000-3,500 poems a year, accept 35-40%, and publish 40-50 poems in each issue, 80 poems in a double issue. Press run is 450 for 250 subscribers. Subscription: $14.75. **Sample postpaid: $6.75. Make checks payable to John DeStefano. Submit 5-8 poems at a time. No previously published poems; simultaneous submissions OK. Cover letter with brief bio preferred. Seldom comments on rejections. Reports "usually within 15 days." Always sends prepublication galleys. Pays 1 copy.** The editor publishes reviews of books by contributors, and issues feature occasional articles, essays, commentary and interviews—all focusing on contemporary poets and poetry.

POETRY EAST (II), Dept. of English, DePaul University, 802 W. Belden Ave., Chicago IL 60614, phone (312)325-7487, founded 1980, editor Richard Jones, "is a biannual international magazine publishing poetry, translations and reviews. We suggest that authors look through back issues of the magazine before making submissions. **No constraints or specifications; we are open to both traditional forms and free verse."** They have published poetry by Tom Crawford, Thomas McGrath, Denise Levertov, Galway Kinnell, Sharon Olds and Amiri Baraka. The digest-sized, flat-spined journal is 100 pgs., professionally printed with glossy color card cover. They use 60-80 pgs. of poetry in each issue. They receive approximately 4,000 submissions/year, use 10%, have a 4-month backlog. Circulation 1,200, 250 subscriptions of which 80 are libraries. Single copy: $8; subscription: $12. **Sample postpaid: $5. Reports in 4 months. Pays copies. Editors sometimes comment on rejections.** Open to unsolicited reviews. Poets may also send books for review consideration. This is one of the best-edited and designed magazines being published today. Award-winning editor Richard Jones assembles an exciting array of accessible poems, leaning toward lyric free verse with room for narrative and otherwise well-structured poems in all traditions. He occasionally schedules theme issues and selects poems accordingly. Because competition is keen, response times can exceed stated limits, particularly in the spring. Work published in *Poetry East* has been included in *The Best American Poetry 1993*.

THE POETRY EXPLOSION NEWSLETTER (THE PEN) (I), P.O. Box 4725, Pittsburgh PA 15206, phone (412)683-0712, founded 1984, editor Arthur C. Ford, is a "quarterly newsletter dedicated to the preservation of poetry." Arthur Ford wants **"poetry—40 lines maximum, no minimum. All forms and subject matter with the use of good imagery, symbolism and honesty. Rhyme and non-rhyme. No vulgarity."** He has published poetry by Veona Thomas and Rose Robaldo. *The Pen* is 12-16 pgs., saddle-stitched, mimeographed on both sides. He accepts about 80 of 300 poems received.

Press run is 450 for 350 subscribers of which 5 are libraries. Subscription: $15. **Send $4 for sample copy and more information. Submit maximum of 5 poems at a time. Include $1 reading fee. (Make checkes payable to Arthur C. Ford.) Also include large SASE if you want work returned. Simultaneous submissions and previously published poems OK. Publishes theme issues. "We announce future dates when decided. June's issue is usually full of romantic poetry." Send SASE for upcoming themes. Editor comments on rejections "sometimes, but not obligated." Pays 1 copy.** He will criticize poetry for 15¢ a word. Open to unsolicited reviews. Poets may also send books for review consideration. The editor comments: "Even though free verse is more popular today, we try to stay versatile."

POETRY HARBOR; NORTH COAST REVIEW (I, II, IV-Regional), P.O. Box 103, Duluth MN 55801-0103, phone (218)728-3728, founded 1989, director Patrick McKinnon. Poetry Harbor is a "nonprofit, tax-exempt organization dedicated to fostering literary creativity through public readings, publications, radio and television broadcasts, and other artistic and educational means." Its main publication, *North Coast Review*, is a regional magazine appearing 3 times a year with **poetry and prose poems by and about Upper Midwest people, including those from Minnesota, Wisconsin, North and South Dakota, and the upper peninsula of Michigan. "No form/style/content specifications, though we are inclined toward narrative, imagist poetry. We do not want to see anything from outside our region, not because it isn't good, but because we can't publish it due to geographics."** They have recently published poetry by Mark Vinz, Joe Paddock, Susan Hauser and Jim Northrup. As a sample the editor selected these lines from "Rolling Up Sidewalks" by William Borden:

> I imagine the sidewalks rolled to each corner
> like sardine can lids
> each evening at sundown by old men
> underpaid but loyal, in blue uniforms
> a bit shabby and threadbare. They start at one corner
> and wiggle their calloused fingers into the crack
> between curb and cement. No one tries it, so no one knows it's easy.

NCR is 56 pgs., 7×8½, offset and saddle-stapled, paper cover with various b&w art, ads at back. They receive about 500 submissions a year, use 100-150. Press run is 1,000 for 200 subscribers of which 20 are libraries, 300 shelf sales. Two-year subscription: $19.50. **Sample postpaid: $3.50. Submit 3-5 pgs. of poetry, typed single-spaced, with name and address on each page. Previously published poems and simultaneous submissions OK, if noted. Cover letter with brief bio ("writer's credits") required. "We read three times a year, but our deadlines change from time to time. Write to us for current deadlines for our various projects." Send SASE for guidelines. Reports in 1-5 months. Pays $10 plus copies. Buys one-time rights.** Poetry Harbor also publishes 1 perfect-bound paperback of poetry and 4-8 chapbooks each biennium. "Chapbooks are selected by our editorial board from the pool of poets we have published in *North Coast Review* or have worked with in our other projects. **We suggest you send a submission to *North Coast Review* first. We almost always print chapbooks and anthologies by poets we've previously published or hired for readings."** Anthologies include *Poets Who Haven't Moved to St. Paul* and *Days of Obsidian, Days of Grace*, selected poetry and prose by four Native American writers. Complete publications list available upon request. Poetry Harbor also sponsors a monthly reading series ("poets are paid to perform"), a weekly TV program (3 different cable networks regionally), various radio programming, a prison workshop series and other special events. They say, "Poetry Harbor is extremely committed to cultivating a literary community and an appreciation for our region's literature within the Upper Midwest. Poetry Harbor projects are in place to create paying, well-attended venues for our region's fine poets. Poets are now OK to people up here, and literature is thriving. The general public is proving to us that they *do* like poetry if you give them some that is both readable and rooted in the lives of the community."

POETRY IN MOTION; NATIONAL POET'S ASSOCIATION (I, IV-Membership), P.O. Box 173, Dept. PM, Bayport MN 55003-0173, phone (612)779-6952, e-mail poim@aol.com, founded 1992, editor Nadia Giordana. *Poetry in Motion* is a quarterly publication "dedicated to showcasing the finest work of emerging poets, writers, artists and photographers from across the U.S. and abroad." Each issue includes poetry, short stories, cartoons, artwork, book reviews and articles. **"Approximately 60% of the material published is by members of the National Poet's Association; 40% is written by nonmembers. Nonmembers must pay a $1 per page reading fee."** They are open to all kinds of poetry, including humorous poems and haiku, 32 lines maximum. They have published poetry by Clyde Wallin Jr., James S. McLellan, Sara L. Holt and Nancy S. Young. As a sample we selected these lines from "Clavicle" by Sharon F. Suer:

> Fractured—and an oddly pleasant discomfort,
> like the wet sponge inside your head with a cold
> or the unrest in every muscle with the flu,
> so that you just want to stretch your limbs
> in a whole-body yawn. Or the fatigue so intense

that it hurts, every cell trying hard to lie down.
Poetry in Motion is 48 pgs., 8½×11, professionally printed with 4-color cover on heavy stock and numerous ads from local supporters. Press run is 3,000. Membership/subscription: $19.99 (4 issues of *Poetry in Motion* and 4 issues of the NPA Newsletter). **Sample postpaid: $5. Submit work typed single-spaced, 1 poem (or 3 haiku) to a page, name and address on each. Cover letter (with "interesting information about yourself") required. Nonmembers must include reading fee. Send large SASE for guidelines or request via e-mail. "We may keep material for up to three months if it is being seriously considered for publication." Pays 1 copy/accepted piece.** Reviews books of poetry. Send books for review consideration. They also publish chapbooks and illustrations, and an occasional full-sized anthology. Send SASE for details. The editor says, "Membership does not insure publication. All material submitted by members and nonmembers alike is judged and chosen solely on its own merit. Since we publish poetry and stories on a wide variety of subjects, it is always a good idea to review a sample copy to get an idea of what is likely to get published. Please, nothing excessively profane or violent."

POETRY IRELAND REVIEW; POETRY IRELAND (II, IV-Regional), Bermingham Tower, Upper Yard, Dublin Castle, Dublin 2, Ireland, phone 353.1.6714632, fax 353.1.6714634, e-mail poetry @iol.ie, founded 1979, administrator Niamh Morris, **the magazine of Ireland's national poetry organization "provides an outlet for Irish poets; submissions from abroad also considered. No specific style or subject matter is prescribed. We strongly dislike sexism and racism."** They have recently published poetry by Seamus Heaney, Michael Longley, Denise Levertov, Medbh McGuckian and Charles Wright. Occasionally publishes special issues. The 6×8 quarterly uses 60 pgs. of poetry in each issue, circulation 1,200, with 800 subscriptions of which 120 are libraries. They receive about 2,000 submissions/year, use 10%, have a 2-month backlog. Single copy: IR£5; subscription: IR£20 Ireland and UK; IR£28 overseas (surface). **Sample postpaid: $10. Submit up to 8 poems at a time. No previously published poems or simultaneous submissions.** Time between acceptance and publication is 1-3 months. **Seldom comments on rejections. Send SASE (or SAE with IRCs) for guidelines. Reports in 6-8 weeks. Pays IR£10/poem or 1-year subscription.** Reviews books of poetry in 500-1,000 words. *PIR* is published by Poetry Ireland, an organization established to "promote poets and poetry throughout Ireland." Poetry Ireland offers readings, an information service, library and administrative center, and a bimonthly newsletter giving news, details of readings, competitions, etc. for IR£6/year. They also sponsor an annual poetry competition. Send SASE (or SAE with IRCs) for details. The editors advise, "Keep submitting: Good work will get through."

POETRY KANTO (II), Kanto Gakuin University, Kamariya-cho, Kanazawa-Ku, Yokohama 236, Japan, founded 1984, editor William I. Elliott. *Poetry Kanto* is a literary annual published by the Kanto Poetry Center, which sponsors an annual poetry conference. It publishes **well-crafted original poems in English and in Japanese.** The magazine publishes **"anything except pornography, English haiku and tanka, and tends to publish poems under 30 lines."** They have recently published work by A.D. Hope, Peter Robinson, Naomi Shihab Nye, Nuala Ni Dhomhnaill and Les Murray. As a sample the editor selected these lines by Chris Wallace-Crabbe:

> *But here, in the serene glass,*
> *hairy tussocks are wearing rhinestones*
> *and the sun appears hunched*
>
> *behind a strip of pewter cloudbank*
> *while the big moon-face*
> *sits on an old rooftree, hoping to set.*

The magazine is digest-sized, nicely printed (the English poems occupy the first half of the issue, the Japanese poems the second), 60 pgs., saddle-stapled, matte card cover. Circulation is 700, of which 400 are complimentary copies sent to schools, poets and presses; it is also distributed at poetry seminars. The magazine is unpriced. **Interested poets should query from October through December with SAE and IRCs before submitting. Then, if query is accepted, submit 3-5 poems. No previously published poems or simultaneous submissions. Often comments on rejections. Reports on mss in 1-2 weeks. Pays 3-5 copies.** The editor advises, "Read a lot. Get feedback from poets and/or workshops. Be neat, clean, legible and polite in submissions. *SAE with International Reply Coupons absolutely necessary when requesting sample copy.*"

THE POETRY MISCELLANY (II), English Dept., University of Tennessee at Chattanooga, Chattanooga TN 37403, phone (423)755-4629, e-mail suobodni@aol.com, founded 1971 (in North Adams, MA), poetry editor Richard Jackson. "We publish new and established writers—poems, interviews, essays, translations. We are truly a miscellany: **We look at all schools, types, etc.**" They have published poetry by William Matthews, Marvin Bell, Paula Rankin, Tomaž Šalmun and Donald Justice. As a sample the editor selected these lines from "Elvis Poem" by Regina Wilkins:

> *But the big things come into your life*

> *only through the little things that give you identity.*
> *That's when things like Love become real.*
> *We spent a lot of the fifty dollars in the Snack Bar.*
> *We spent a little more at the souvenir shop.*
> *The preacher at grandfather's funeral said he could*
> *explain the Bible as plainly as if he had spoken*
> *to Paul himself. I knew when Janis turned down*
> *the Elvis impersonator he'd hit on me. So everything was*
> *back to normal. The world wasn't ending.*
> *And we had ten dollars left, which was enough.*

The 16-page tabloid appears annually, professionally printed, with black ink on grey paper. Circulation is 750 for 400 subscriptions of which 100 are libraries. They receive about 10,000 submissions/year, use 20, have a 6-12 month backlog. Subscription: $5. **Sample postpaid: $2.50. Submit 3-4 clear copies/submission. Editor "rarely" comments on rejections. Send SASE for guidelines. Reports in 3-4 months. Pays 2 copies. Also publishes chapbooks.** Sometimes holds contests "when grants allow."

POETRY MOTEL; SUBURBAN WILDERNESS PRESS BROADSIDES (I, II), 1228 E. Third St., Duluth MN 55805, founded 1984, editors Patrick McKinnon, Bud Backen, Ed Gooder and Ellen Seitz-Ryan aim **"to keep the rooms clean and available for these poor ragged poems to crash in once they are through driving or committing adultery." They want "poems that took longer than 10 minutes to author." No other specifications.** They have recently published poetry by Robert Peters, Willie Smith, Albert Huffstickler, Ron Androla, Serena Fusek, Tony Moffeit and Todd Moore. As a sample they selected this poem, "Manitowoc" by Carolyn Ahrens:

> *I did what my father told me to do.*
> *I parked the car off*
> *to an angle, shined the brights*
> *and waited. He told me never*
> *to get too close; they can kick you to death*
> *in their dying. And if they come through*
> *the windshield, duck.*

Poetry Motel appears "every 260 days" as a 7×8½ digest, with wallpaper cover, circulation 1,000 (to 600 subscribers), 52 pgs. of poetry, prose, essays, literary memoirs and reviews. They receive about 1,500 submissions/year, take 150, have a 3- to 24-month backlog. **Sample: $6.95. Submit 3-5 pgs. of poetry at a time, with SASE. Simultaneous submissions OK. Informal cover letter with bio credits required. Reports in 1-10 weeks. Pay varies.** Reviews books of poetry. Open to unsolicited reviews. Poets may also send books for review consideration. They advise, "Poets should read as much poetry as they can lay their hands on. And they should realize that although poetry is no fraternal club, poets are responsible for its survival, both financially and emotionally. Join us out here—this is where the edge meets the vision. We are very open to work from 'beginners.' "

POETRY NEW YORK: A JOURNAL OF POETRY AND TRANSLATION (II, IV-Transla-tions, themes), P.O. Box 3184, Church Street Station, New York NY 10008, e-mail tunguska@tribeca .iso.com, founded 1985, editors Burt Kimmelman, Tod Thilleman and Emmy Hunter, is an annual. They have published poetry by Wanda Coleman, Jerome Rothenberg, Enid Dame, Amiel Alcalay and Ann Lauterbach, and translations of Mallarme, Hesiod and Makoto Ooka. As a sample the editors selected these lines from "The Second Month of Separation" by Corinne Robins:

> *I don't hear or see,*
> *an ocean and your drugs are*
> *in between.*
> *The beautiful garbage birds fly the island ferry,*
> *and ocean planes criss-cross*
> *while I dream you grow beyond closed doors.*

The editors describe it as 80 pgs., 6×9, perfect-bound. They accept about 20% of "blind submissions." Press run is 500 for 300 shelf sales. **Some issues are on themes. "Query us first to see whether we are currently reading manuscripts. If so, send no more than five poems per submission." Editor comments on submissions "at times." Send SASE for guidelines and upcoming themes or request**

THE GEOGRAPHICAL INDEX, located before the Subject Index, can help you discover the publishers in your region. Publishers often favor poets (and work) from their own areas.

via e-mail, "with mailing address for reply." Reports in 3-4 months. Pays 1 copy. They sometimes sponsor readings. Work published in *Poetry New York* has been included in the 1993 and 1994 volumes of *The Best American Poetry*.

POETRY NORTHWEST (II), University of Washington, 4045 Brooklyn Ave. NE, JA-15, Seattle WA 98105, phone (206)685-4750, founded 1959, editor David Wagoner, is a quarterly. The magazine is 48 pgs., 5½×8½, professionally printed with color card cover. It features all styles and forms. For instance, lyric and narrative free verse has been included alongside a sonnet sequence, minimalist sonnets and stanza patterns—all accessible and lively. They receive 10,000 poems/year, use 160, have a 3-month backlog. Circulation 1,500. Subscription: $15. **Sample postpaid: $4. Occasionally comments on rejections. Reports in 1 month maximum. Pays 2 copies. Awards prizes of $500, $100, $50 and $50 yearly, judged by the editors.** Poetry published here has also been included in *The Best American Poetry 1996*.

‡POETRY NOTTINGHAM INTERNATIONAL; LAKE ASKE MEMORIAL OPEN POETRY COMPETITION (II); NOTTINGHAM POETRY SOCIETY; QUEENIE LEE COMPETITION (IV-Membership/subscription), 39 Cavendish Rd., Long Eaton, Nottingham NG10 4HY England, founded 1941, editor Martin Holroyd. Nottingham Poetry Society meets monthly for readings, talks, etc., and publishes quarterly its magazine, *Poetry Nottingham International*, which is open to submissions from anyone. **"We wish to see poetry that is intelligible to and enjoyable by the intelligent reader. We do not want any party politics or religious freaks. Poems not more than 30 lines in length."** They have published poetry by Bert Almon, William Davey and Nikolas Macioci from the US. As a sample the editor selected these lines from "Half-Term" by Maurice Rutherford:

> And if you've ever wondered what goes on
> inside the heads of men who sit on seats
> and ogle passers-by, come, sit with me,
> it's marvelous . . . fantastic's more the word!
> I chose at will, make this one rich, that poor . . .

There are 40 pgs. of poetry in each issue of the 6×8 magazine, professional printing with occasional essays, glossy art paper cover. They receive about 1,500 submissions/year, use 120, usually have a 1- to 3-month backlog. Circulation 325 for 200 subscriptions of which 20 are libraries. Subscriptions: £4 overseas ($60 for 2 years US); per copy: £2 ($8 US). **Sample postpaid: $8 or £1.75. Submit 3 poems at any time, not more than 30 lines each, not handwritten, and previously unpublished. Send SAE and 3 IRCs for stamps. No need to query but requires cover letter. Reports "within 2 months plus mailing time." Pays 1 copy.** Staff reviews books of poetry, but space allows only listings or brief review. Send books for review consideration. **Nottingham Poetry Society publishes collections by individual poets who are members of Nottingham Poetry Society.** The Lake Aske Memorial Open Poetry Competition offers cash prizes, annual subscriptions and publication in *Poetry Nottingham*. Open to all. The Queenie Lee Competition is for members and subscribers only, offers a cash prize and publication. The editor says they would like to see "more traditional forms. No disjointed prose under the guise of free verse."

POETRY OF THE PEOPLE (I, IV-Humor, love, nature, fantasy, themes), P.O. Box 298, Micanopy FL 32667, phone (352)374-1805, founded 1986, poetry editor Paul Cohen. *Poetry of the People* is a leaflet that appears 3 times a year. **"We take all forms of poetry but we like humorous poetry, love poetry, nature poetry and fantasy. No racist or highly ethnocentric poetry will be accepted. I do not like poetry that lacks images or is too personal or contains rhyme to the point that the poem has been destroyed." They are also accepting poetry written in French and Spanish.** They have recently published poetry by Max Lizard, Prof. Jerry Reminick, Ian Ayers and Noelle Kocot. The format for *Poetry of the People* varies from 8-32 pgs., 5½×8 to 5½×4⅜, stapled, sometimes on colored paper. Issues are usually theme oriented. It has a circulation between 300 and 2,300. Copies are distributed to Gainesville residents for 25¢ each. **Samples: $4 for 11 pamphlets. "Please send donations, the magazine bank account is overdrawn. Suggested donation: $2." Submit up to 10 poems at a time. Cover letter with biographical information required with submissions.** "I feel autobiographical information is important in understanding the poetry." Poems returned within 6 months. Editor comments on rejections "often." Send SASE for upcoming themes. Takes suggestions for theme issues. Sometimes sends prepublication galleys. Pays 10 copies. Acquires first rights. He advises, "Be creative; there is a lot of competition out there."

POETRY WALES; SEREN PRESS (II, IV-Ethnic), 2 Wyndham St., First Floor, Bridgend, Mid-Glamorgan CF31 1EF Wales, founded 1965. *Poetry Wales*, a 72-page, 248×177mm quarterly, circulation 1,000, has a primary interest in **Welsh and Anglo-Welsh poets but also considers submissions internationally. Send submissions (with SAE and IRC) to Richard Poole, editor, Glan-y-Werydd, Llandanwg, Harlech LL46 2SD Wales.** Overseas subscription: £18/year. **Sample: £2.50. Submit 6**

poems at a time. No previously published poems. One-page cover letter required; include name, address and previous publications. SASE or SAE with IRC must be included for reply. Publishes theme issues. Send SASE (or SAE and IRC) for upcoming themes. Pays. Staff reviews books of poetry. Send books for review consideration to Amy L. Wack, reviews editor, Wyndham Street address. Seren Press publishes books of **primarily Welsh and Anglo-Welsh poetry**, also biography, critical works and some fiction, distributed by Dufour Editions, Inc., Box 449, Chester Springs PA 19425. They have received several Welsh Arts Council "Book of the Year" Prizes. The editor says, "We would like to see more formal poetry."

POETRY WLU (I, II), Dept. of English, Wilfrid Laurier University, Waterloo, Ontario N2L 3C5 Canada, phone (519)884-1970, ext. 3308, founded 1979, editorial contact E. Jewinski, is an annual literary magazine (published every March) "with emphasis on *all* poetry and *all* prose *under* 1,000 words. **20-30 lines are ideal; but all kinds and lengths considered.**" As a sample the editor selected the opening lines from "Katherine's Eye" by Bruce Bond:

> *It's the faithfulness that fools us,*
> *how its fine red vein*
> *slips under the living seam*

> *When Katherine lost her glass eye*
> *in the deep-end of her uncle's pool,*
> *her brothers scouted the blue*

Poetry WLU is 6½×8, saddle-stapled, typeset, with matte card cover using b&w art. They receive about 100-120 submissions a year, use approximately 15-20%. Press run is 300. **Sample postpaid: $5. Submit 5 poems at a time. "We strongly discourage simultaneous submissions." Cover letter preferred. Reads submissions September 1 through January 30 only. "When the editorial board has time, comments are made." Reports in 6-8 months. Pays 1 copy.** Staff reviews books of poetry.

POETS AT WORK (I, IV-Subscribers), VAMC 325 New Castle Rd., Box 113, Butler PA 16001, founded 1985, editor/publisher Jessee Poet, **all contributors are expected to subscribe.** The editor says, **"Every poet who writes within the dictates of good taste and within my twenty-line limit will be published in each issue. I accept all forms and themes of poetry, including seasonal and holiday, but no porn, no profanity."** He has recently published poetry by Jaye Giammarion, Katherine Krebs, Ann Gasser, Warren Jones and Ralph Hammond. As a sample he selected his poem "An Old Romance":

> *I almost loved you . . . did you know?*
> *Sometimes you still disturb my dreams.*
> *A summer romance long ago*
> *I almost loved you . . . did you know?*
> *We danced to music soft and low*
> *Just yesterday . . . or so it seems*
> *I almost loved you . . . did you know?*
> *Sometimes you still disturb my dreams.*

Poets at Work, a bimonthly, is generally 36-40 pgs., magazine-sized, saddle-stapled, photocopied from typescript with colored paper cover. Subscription: $18. **Sample: $3. Submit 5-10 poems at a time. Simultaneous submissions and previously published poems OK. Reports within 2 weeks. Pays nothing, not even a copy.** "Because I publish hundreds of poets, I cannot afford to pay or give free issues. Every subscriber, of course, gets an issue. Subscribers also have many opportunities to regain their subscription money in the numerous contests offered in each issue. Send SASE for flyer for my separate monthly and special contests." He also publishes chapbooks. Send SASE for details. The editor adds, "These days even the best poets tell me that it is difficult to get published. I am here for the novice as well as the experienced poet. I consider *Poets at Work* to be a hotbed for poets where each one can stretch and grow at his or her own pace. Each of us learns from the other, and we do not criticize one another. The door for poets is always open, so please stop by; we probably will like each other immediately."

‡THE POET'S ATTIC (II), P.O. Box 34273, Philadelphia PA 19101, e-mail 72604,1154@compuser ve.com, website http://ourworld.compuserve.com/homepages/The_Attic, founded 1993, editor William Rothwell, co-editor Kelly Marie Johnston, assistant editor Ray Reeves. *The Poet's Attic* is a monthly publication designed "to expose 'closet' poets that seek a medium for expression." **They welcome young and new writers. "Open to content, enjoy universality. But no verse crippled by conservatism. No teenage angst. No painful rhyme scheme. No poems over 100 lines. Otherwise, we receive you with open arms."** They have recently published poetry by Edward Francis, Kalyani Broderick and Patrick Kelly. As a sample the editor selected these lines from "Diving the Arc" by Katherine Wilding-Hepner (winner of their annual contest):

> *the palace of his arms*

> *chest like a yogi's*
> *legs enfolded*
> *light and blood*
> *come pouring out*
> *in a glass blower's fantasy . . .*

The Poet's Attic is 16 pgs., 5½×8½, photocopied and saddle-stitched with different front and back covers each month, various b&w graphics (including a few nude photos) "to fit the poems," and ads every other month. They receive about 1,000 poems a year, accept approximately 630. Press run is 500 for 100 subscribers, 350 shelf sales. Single copy: $2; subscription: $14/year ($8 for 6 months). **Sample postpaid: $2.55. Make checks payable to William Rothwell. Submit 3-5 poems at a time. No previously published poems; simultaneous submissions OK. Cover letter preferred; include "places of previous publication, mention poems you liked in our last issue, etc." Poems are read by each of the editors. Seldom comments on rejections. Brief guidelines are included inside the magazine or can be obtained via website. Reports in 2-6 weeks. Pays 1 copy.** They also sponsor an annual contest with a $500 first prize, $100 second prize, and various one-year subscriptions thereafter. Reading fee: $2/poem. Deadline: October 15. Send SASE for details.

POET'S FANTASY (I, IV-Fantasy), Dept. PM, 227 Hatten Ave., Rice Lake WI 54868-2030, founded 1991, publisher/editor Gloria Stoeckel, is a bimonthly designed "to help the striving poet see his/her work in print." **They want sonnets, haiku and humorous free verse, 4-16 lines. "I accept good, clean poetry. Looking for poems of fantasy, but not exclusively. No profanity or sexual use of words."** They have published poetry by earl jay perel and Gary Michael Lawson. As a sample we selected these lines from "Speechio" by Jane Stuart:

> *You unblinking told me I was curtains*
> *and the rabbit jumped again against*
> *the mirror.*
>
> *The nothingness of being isn't anything*
> *to write home about*
> *and my heart rings with less than true*
> *de facto.*

Poet's Fantasy is 36 pgs., digest-sized, computer-generated and laser-printed, photocopied and saddle-stapled with colored paper cover, graphics and ads. They receive approximately 200 poems a year, accept about 90%. Press run is 300 for 250 subscribers. Subscription: $18/year; foreign $24/year. **Sample postpaid: $4. Submit 3-5 poems at a time. No previously published poems or simultaneous submissions. Often comments on rejections. Send SASE for guidelines. Reports within 2 weeks. Pays coupon for $3 off subscription price or greeting card order. (Poets must purchase copy their work is in.) Acquires first North American serial rights.** "I do book reviews if poet sends a complimentary copy of the book and a $3 reading fee. Reviews are approximately 200 to 300 words in length." She holds contests in each issue and also creates greeting cards for poets. "They use verse they wrote and can design their own cover." Send SASE for details.

‡THE POET'S GUILD (I, II), P.O. Box 161236, Sacramento CA 95816-1236, founded 1995, editor Mr. Laverne Frith, associate editor Joyce Odam, appears bimonthly. **They want "original poetry that clearly demonstrates an understanding of craft. All styles accepted." However, they do not want to see "poetry which is overtly religious, erotic, inflammatory or demeans the human spirit."** They have recently published poetry by Lyn Lifshin, Ann Menebroker, Jane Blue, Taylor Graham and Geoff Stevens. *The Poet's Guild* is 32-40 pgs., digest-sized, printed on recycled paper and saddle-stapled with a card stock cover with original pen art, interior clip art, and a decorative paper centerfold. They receive 1,800-2,000 poems a year, accept approximately 10%. Press run is 200 for 50-100 shelf sales. Single copy: $3; subscription: $16. Send subscription requests to Gary Elton Warrick, publisher, 5836 North Haven Dr., North Highlands CA 95660. **Submit 2-5 poems at a time, maximum 45 characters/line. Previously published poems "occasionally" accepted with publication credits; no simultaneous submissions. Cover letter required; include SASE and 3-5 lines of biographical information and credits. Often comments on rejections. Send SASE for guidelines. Reports in 3 months. Pays 1 copy. Acquires first (or occasionally reprint) rights.** Also awards $50 to the best poem (as voted by subscribers) written by a subscriber and published in the magazine during the current calendar year.

‡A POET'S JOURNEY; ASTRA PRESS (I), P.O. Box 9873, The Woodlands TX 77387-6873, founded 1996, poetry editor Yolande Gottlieb, is a biannual that publishes "poetry, translations, short articles on the life and poetry of famous poets and short-shorts about poetics." **They want "imaginative, well constructed, outstanding poetry; 8-36 lines maximum; open on form or subject matter and style. (We will consider a longer poem if asked.) No religious, juvenile or greeting card verse."** They have recently published poetry by Budd Powel Mahan and A.B. Telyachenko. The editor says *APJ* is 26-40 pgs., digest-sized, color card cover. Press run is 150. Subscription: $8.50. **Sample postpaid: $4.50. Make checks payable to "Magazine." Submit 3-5 poems at a time. Reading fee: $1 per poem. Previously published poems and simultaneous submissions OK. Cover letter including bio and publication credits (if any) required. "Poems must be typed, one poem/page with name, address and phone." Seldom comments on rejections. Send SASE for guidelines. Reports in 2-8 weeks. Pays 1 copy. Acquires first rights.** Awards $20, $10, $5 and 3 honorable mentions to the best poems in each issue. Astra Press is a small press that "poets pay to have booklets published for them. We start at $150 for 50 books of 34 pages or less." The editor says, "We ask poets to read good poetry; good contemporary poetry will broaden their perspective. We hope they grow confident in their craft by writing daily if possible. Seek poetry groups and participate in their programs." Yolande Gottlieb is also the managing editor for *i.e. magazine*. See listing in this section.

POETS ON: (II, IV-Themes), 29 Loring Ave., Mill Valley CA 94941, phone (415)381-2824, e-mail poetsonlne@aol.com, founded 1976, poetry editor Ruth Daigon, is a poetry semiannual, **each issue on an announced theme (such as *Poets On: Regrets*). "We want well-crafted, humanistic, accessible poetry. We don't want to see sentimental rhymed verse. Length preferably 40 lines or less, or at the very most 80 lines (2-page poems)."** They have published poetry by Marge Piercy, Charles Edward Eaton, Walter Pavlich, Barbara Crooker and Lyn Lifshin. As a sample the editor selected these lines from "A Way of Saying" by Robert Funge in *Poets On: Remembrance*:

> So we have named the Wind, that we may have
> a way of saying what it is that moves
> between us, as between all things that move
> and through all that are still. And this we call
> Touch, this thing like wind that we can know
> only by what it moves. And we have named ourselves
> Man and Woman, to have soft words to call
> each other, who like the wind are known
> more by how we move the things we touch.

Poets On: is 48 pgs., digest-sized, professionally printed, matte card cover with b&w graphics. They use about 5% of the 3,000 submissions they receive each year, have a 2- to 3-month backlog. Daigon tends to accept strong and well-structured lyric free verse, although you are apt to find any style or form with exciting or insightful content. Circulation is 450, 350 subscriptions of which 125 are libraries. Subscription: $8. **Sample postpaid: $5. Query with SASE for upcoming themes and deadlines. Submit up to 4 poems (40 lines or less). Requests for information via e-mail OK, but submit poems through the mail. No previously published poems; simultaneous submissions OK, if "notified well in advance whether poem is accepted elsewhere." No handwritten mss. Include short bio with writing background. "It's a good idea to read the magazine before submitting poetry." Submit only September 1 through December 1 or February 1 through May 1. Reports in 2-3 months. Pays 1 copy. Editor sometimes comments on rejections.** She has designed a rejection slip that has several categories explaining why your work didn't make it into the magazine, and yet she'll often add a comment to encourage good work. Daigon says, "We are not interested in poetry that is declamatory, sloganeering, bathetic or opaque. Nor are we concerned with poetry as mere word-games or technical exercises."

‡**THE POET'S PAGE (I)**, P.O. Box 372, Wyanet IL 61379, founded 1994, editor/publisher Ione K. Pence, is a quarterly "for poets and all who love poetry." **They want poetry of "any subject, any length, any style, but we are not interested in shock poetry or vulgarities."** They have recently published poetry by Lyn Lifshin, Taylor Reese, Jean Harmon and Duane Locke. *TPP* is 40 pgs., digest-sized and saddle-stapled with colored card stock cover. Subscription: $10. **Sample postpaid: $3. No previously published poems; simultaneous submissions OK, "but we must be notified immediately if work is accepted elsewhere. Also, without a SASE or SAE and IRC, submissions go directly into our wastebasket with no response of any kind to the submitter."** Time between acceptance and publication is 9-12 months. **Send SASE for guidelines. Reports within a month. Pays copies.** All rights retained by authors.

POETS. PAINTERS. COMPOSERS; COLIN'S MAGAZINE (II), 10254 35th Ave. SW, Seattle WA 98146, phone (206)937-8155, founded 1984, editor Joseph Keppler, who says "*Poets. Painters. Composers.* is an avant-garde arts journal which appears once or twice a year and publishes poetry, drawings, scores, criticism, essays, reviews, photographs and original art. **If poetry, music or art is submitted, the work should be somehow extraordinary, not what other magazines already have published too much of.**" The journal is magazine-sized, 86 pgs. Each cover has an original painting on it. Mr. Keppler says, "each odd-numbered issue appears in an 8½ × 11 format; each even-numbered issue changes format: No. 2, for example, is published as posters; No. 4 appears on cassettes. No. 6 has incorporated an exhibition, a gallery and a series of sculptures as part of its content. No. 7 will be a print issue featuring poetry, art and criticism. No. 8 will be a radio issue involving art specifically for radio communication." Circulation is 300, no subscriptions. Each issue of the magazine carries an individual price tag. A copy of *Poets. Painters. Composers.* No. 5 is $50. **Sample of No. 3 available for $21.50 postpaid. "Contributors' poetry receives great care. All material is returned right away unless (a) it's being painstakingly examined for acceptance into the journal or (b) it's being considered as right for some other way of publishing it or (c) we died." Contributors receive 1 copy. Acquires one-time rights.** "We prefer short (500-800 word) reviews unless we already have asked for a longer piece from a poet/reviewer because of his or her interest in the book."

POET'S REVIEW (I, IV-Subscribers); THEME POETRY (IV-Themes), P.O. Box I, 806 Kings Row, Varnell GA 30756, phone (706)694-8441, founded 1988, publisher Bob Riemke, is a monthly booklet, using **poetry by subscribers** and making cash awards monthly and annually on basis of votes by subscribers. **"Prefer rhyme. Short poems, 44 lines or less. Open to limericks and humor. Any subject. No porn! No foreign languages."** They have published poetry by Helen Webb, Ashley Anders and J. Alvin Speers. *PR* is 28 pgs., digest-sized, photocopied from typescript with paper cover. Subscription: $36. **Sample postpaid: $4. Submit 1 typed poem at a time. "Subscribers are sent a ballot along with their monthly booklet to vote for the poems they believe to be the best." Monthly prizes are $75, $50 and $25, plus 7 honorable mentions. "All $75 winners are presented to the subscribers again at the end of the year and compete for a $500, $250 and $100 prize."** 30-50 poems are printed each month along with the names of winners for the previous month. They also publish *Theme Poetry*, "a monthly magazine for poems with a theme." **They want poems under 40 lines dealing with the specific theme for the month. "No porn or foreign languages." Send SASE for guidelines and upcoming themes.**

POETS' ROUNDTABLE; POETS' STUDY CLUB OF TERRE HAUTE; POETS' STUDY CLUB INTERNATIONAL CONTEST (I, IV-Membership), 826 S. Center St., Terre Haute IN 47807, phone (812)234-0819, founded in 1939, president/editor Esther Alman. Poets' Study Club is one of the oldest associations of amateur poets. It publishes, every other month, *Poets' Roundtable*, a newsletter of market and contest information and news of the publications and activities of its members in a mimeographed, 10-page bulletin (magazine-sized, stapled at the corner), circulation 2,000. They have also published an occasional chapbook-anthology of poetry by members "but do not often do so." **Dues: $6/year. Sample free for SASE. Uses short poems by members only. Simultaneous submissions and previously published poems OK.** They offer an annual Poets' Study Club International Contest, open to all, with no fees and cash prizes—a $25 and $15 award in 3 categories: traditional haiku, serious poetry, light verse. Deadline: February 1. Also contests for members only each two months. "We have scheduled criticism programs for members only."

‡**POINT JUDITH LIGHT (IV-Form/style)**, P.O. Box 6145, Springfield MA 01101, phone (413)746-3294, founded 1992, editor Patrick Frank, is a biannual publishing individual haiku/senryu, sequences and essays on Eastern philosophy and creativity theory. They want **haiku/senryu "which explore the relation of the poet to his/her environment and which focus on life as truly lived; 17 syllables maximum."** They have recently published haiku/senryu by H.F. Noyes, Tom Clausen and Douglas Johnson. As a sample the editor selected these haiku/senryu by Allan T. Summers and JW McMillan respectively:

> disembodied voices, darkness, light
> express train jolts

> Asian grocery store
> fresh and dry produce rice and spice
> and much, more more

PJL is desktop-published in a newsletter format, 20 pgs. maximum. Press run is 300. Subscription: $6/year. **Sample postpaid: $3. Previously published poems OK; no simultaneous submissions. Send 20 haiku/senryu maximum. Submissions should be typed. Cover letter with bio required.** "I want to have some knowledge of the poet behind the work." **Send SASE for guidelines. Reports within 6 months. Pays 1 copy. Acquires first or one-time rights.** The editor says, "Focus on the aspects of life that are immediately before you. Be yourself. Follow your intuition and be willing to explore and experiment. With James J.Y. Liu, I see poetry as a vehicle to explore external and internal worlds, as well as the language in which it is written. I am particularly interested in promoting the development of haiku/senryu sequencing in English. I am also exploring the connection between haiku, Eastern philosophy and creativity theory. Children's haiku are welcome. Politically relevant haiku are welcome, if they are imagistic and grounded in concrete experience. I also publish sports-related haiku."

THE POINTED CIRCLE (II), 705 N. Killingsworth, Portland OR 97217, phone (503)978-5230, fax (503)978-5050, e-mail rstevens@pcc.edu, founded 1980, advisor Rachel Stevens, is an annual. **They want poems "under 60 lines, mostly shorter. One-page poems on any topic of any form."** They have published poetry by Judith Barrington, Lyn Lifshin and Barbara Drake. As a sample the editor selected this poem, "Solitary Cheating," by Anne Ellsworth:

> Alone at night,

348 Poet's Market '97

> *my mother would play solitaire,*
> *believing if she won the game,*
> *her cheating husband would return,*
> *manipulating hearts and spades,*
> *drinking wine and shuffling cards,*
> *cheating.*

It is 80 pgs., professionally printed and flat-spined, with b&w glossy card cover. Press run is 200. **Sample postpaid: $3.50. No simultaneous submissions. Cover letter required. Submit mss from December 1 through February 15 only. "Place name, address, etc., on cover sheet only, listing titles of submissions. Limit 6 poems/poet. All submissions are read anonymously by student editorial staff; notification about June 1 for submissions received by February 15." Send SASE for guidelines. Pays 1 copy. Acquires one-time rights.**

PORTABLE WALL (V), 215 Burlington, Billings MT 59101, phone (406)256-3588, founded 1977, publisher Daniel Struckman. He publishes, as Ezra Pound described, **"words that throw the object on to the visual imagination and that induce emotional correlations by the sound and rhythm of the speech."** He has published poetry by Dave Thomas and Joe Salerno. As a sample he selected these lines by Kathleen Taylor:

> *Lightning rams down*
> *a cloud-clotted sky;*
> *the red moon is wasted.*

PW, published irregularly, is 60 pgs., saddle-stapled, on heavy tinted stock with 2-color matte card cover. Press run is 400. Subscription: $18 for 4 issues. **Sample postpaid: $6.50. Currently not accepting poetry submissions.** The editor says, "I have more poetry than I can print."

PORTLAND REVIEW (II), Box 751-SD, Portland State University, Portland OR 97207, phone (503)725-4533, founded 1954, is a literary annual published by Portland State University 3 times a year. **"Experimental poetry welcomed. No poems over 3 pages. No rhyming poetry."** The annual is magazine-sized, about 128 pgs. They accept about 30 of 300 poems received each year. Press run is 500 for 100 subscribers of which 10 are libraries. **Sample: $5. Simultaneous submissions OK. Send SASE for guidelines. Pays 1 copy.**

POST-INDUSTRIAL PRESS (III), P.O. Box 265, Greensboro PA 15338, founded 1989, publishes 1-3 paperbacks/year. They have published poetry by Georges Perec and Johannes Poethen. **No simultaneous submissions. Replies to queries in 1 month.**

POTATO EYES; NIGHTSHADE PRESS (II), P.O. Box 76, Troy ME 04987-0076, phone (207)948-3427, founded 1988, editors Roy Zarucchi and Carolyn Page, is a semiannual literary arts journal **"with a focus on writers who write about the land and/or quality of life close to the earth. We now accept submissions from throughout the U.S., also from Canada, Australia, England, Ireland and Brazil, although much of our poetry is from Appalachian states."** They have recently published poetry by Daniel Lusk, Barbara Presnell, Jack Coulehan, Julie Kate Howard and Elizabeth Cohen. As a sample the editors selected these lines from "You Never Get To The Horizon" by Ava Leavell Haymon, published in her chapbook *Built in Fear of Heat*:

> *In the delta, you're ringed by horizons.*
> *The great plowed land is flat as Holland*
> *and all the trees were cut down with the Indians.*
> *The taste of dust in your mouth there*
> *is flavored always by cotton poison.*
> *The air must have tasted like that*
> *in Berlin, between the wars.*

PE is 100 pgs., 5½×8½, flat-spined, professionally printed, with block cut matte paper cover. Circulation is 800. Subscription: $11 ($14 Canadian). **Sample postpaid: $6 (back issue $5), or $7 Canadian. The editors say, "those who submit receive a handwritten rejection/acceptance. We are open to any form other than rhymed, in batches of 3-5, but we tend to favor poetry with concrete visual imagery, solid intensity and compression. We respect word courage and risk-taking, along with thoughtful lineation. We prefer rebellious to complacent poetry. We prefer a cover letter with brief bio along with SASE." Reports in 1-2 months. Pays 1 copy. Acquires first North American serial rights.** Reviews books of poetry. Open to unsolicited reviews. Poets may also send books for review consideration. Nightshade Press is the imprint under which they publish about 5 books/chapbooks a year, each 24-48 pgs. or longer, "usually with block print or pen-and-ink covers, endsheets and recycled 60 lb. text, 80 lb. covers. **Selections come from competitions, mainly, but a few may be from poets who appear first in our magazine." Send SASE for catalog and information and/ or send $5 for sample chapbook.** They advise, "Beginning poets should devour as much good poetry as possible in order to delineate their own style and voice. Look for a match between substance and sound. We reject fluff but respect poetry that is multi-layered and which makes a definite statement."

POTES & POETS PRESS, INC.; ABACUS (III), 181 Edgemont Ave., Elmwood CT 06110, phone (203)233-2023, press founded in 1981, magazine in 1984, editor Peter Ganick. The press publishes avant-garde poetry in magazine form under the *Abacus* imprint, one writer per issue. The P+Pinc books are perfect-bound and range from 80-120 pgs. in trade editions. **In addition to avant-garde, they want experimental or language-oriented poetry, not too much concrete poetry. No** *"New Yorker* **magazine,** *Ploughshares* **magazine, mainstream poetry."** They have published poetry by Ron Silliman, Jackson Mac Low, Charles Bernstein, Leslie Scalapino, Carla Harryman and Rachel Blau Du Plessis. *Abacus* is 12-18 pgs., magazine-sized, photocopied, no graphics; it appears every 6 weeks. Circulation is 150, of which 40 are subscriptions and 10 go to libraries. Price per issue is $4; subscription: $26/year. **Sample postpaid: $4.50. Simultaneous submissions are OK. Pay is 10 copies. Unsolicited submissions are accepted for book publication. Writers should "just send the manuscript."** *However, they rarely accept mss from authors new to the press.* The press publishes 2 flat-spined paperback books of poetry/year with an average page count of 100.

POTPOURRI (II), P.O. Box 8278, Prairie Village KS 66208, phone (913)642-1503, fax (913)642-3128, founded 1989, poetry editor Terry Hoyland, haiku editor Robert G. Duchouquette, is a quarterly magazine "to publish works of writers, **including new and unpublished writers. We want strongly voiced original poems in either free verse or traditional. Traditional work must represent the best of the craft. No religious, confessional, racial, political, erotic, abusive or sexual preference materials unless fictional and necessary to plot or characterization. No concrete/visual poetry (because of format)."** They have recently published poetry by X.J. Kennedy, David Ray, Richard Moore, Pattiann Rogers and Tess Gallagher. As a sample the editor selected these lines from "Upon Learning of His Wife's Cancer" by Glen Enloe:

> *After that, his eyes,*
> *like blown-glass floats,*
> *caught the summer print*
> *of her cotton dress*
> *nestled in saffron,*
> *colandered through curtains.*

It is 68 pgs. Press run is 1,500 for 675 subscribers. Subscription: $15. **Sample postpaid: $4.95. Submit no more than 3 poems at a time, one to a page, length to 75 lines (approximately 30 preferred). Submit seasonal themes 6 months in advance. Address haiku and related forms to Robert G. Duchouquette. Send SASE for guidelines. Reports in 8-10 weeks at most. Pays 1 copy. Acquires first North American serial rights.** The David Ray Poetry Award ($100 or more, depending upon grant monies) is given annually for best of volume. Another new annual award is sponsored by the Council on National Literatures and offers $100 and publication in *Potpourri* for selected poem or short story; alternating years (1997 poetry). Send SASE for official guidelines. Deadline: June 30, 1997. *Potpourri* received the 1995 Jack Henry Pyramid of Arts Award. The editors advise, "Keep your new poems around long enough to become friends with them before parting. Let them ripen, and, above all, learn to be your own best editor. Read them aloud, boldly, to see how they ripple the air and echo what you mean to say. Unrequited love, favorite pets and descriptions that seem to be written for their own sake find little chance here."

POULTRY, A MAGAZINE OF VOICE (IV-Humor), P.O. Box 4413, Springfield MA 01101, phone (413)736-4216, founded 1979, editors Jack Flavin, Brendan Galvin and George Garrett, is a biannual tabloid of **"parody, satire, humor and wit, particularly of the modern literary scene." They do not want to see "serious" poetry.** They have recently published poetry by David R. Slavitt, Drew Dunphy, Stan Blair, Neill Megaw and Klipschutz. As a sample the editors selected these lines from "Poet Lariats (A.R. Ammons)" by J. Patrick Lewis:

> *In vain: does he unravel*
> *the lint trap from his navel:*
> *but praise: when he examines*
> *his colon:*
> > A.R. Ammons

The 11½×17 tabloid, 8 pgs., unstapled, professionally printed on newsprint, uses b&w photos, graphics, drawings. Press run is 500 for 250 subscribers of which 35 are libraries. Subscription: $6/13 issues ($5/libraries). **Sample postpaid: $3. Submit 5-6 poems at a time. Simultaneous submissions OK; "rarely" uses previously published poems. Pays 10 copies. Acquires first rights.** Jack Flavin calls for "a little more humor and light, please, in the deadly serious (and oftentimes deadly) business of being a poet, a writer and getting published. Beginning poet? Get it down while it's hot, let it cool and consider it with a cold eye a bit later. Learn to write by doing it, if you're lucky, under the watchful eye and with encouragement from a good critic."

PRAIRIE FIRE (III), 100 Arthur St., Room 423, Winnipeg, Manitoba R3B 1H3 Canada, phone (204)943-9066, fax (204)942-1555, founded 1978, editor Andris Taskans, is a quarterly magazine of new writing including fiction, poetry and reviews. **They want "poetry that articulates a connection between language and ethics, an aesthetic of writing 'from the body,' and open to the nuances of orality, ethnic and racial differences and feminism. No haiku, sonnets or other rhyming forms, nor political or religious treatises in verse form."** They have published poetry by Di Brandt, Katharine Bitney and Kristjana Gunnars. As a sample the editor selected these lines from "talking 3 a.m." by Patrick Friesen:

> it's 3 a.m. and I remember the fall of white silk from my love's shoulders
>   the mole on her left arm her slender thighs
> remembering again and again what matters losing the rest in small
>   blowouts of the brain and the radio's noise
> I want to say something about love how it's flesh only for a while how
>   it's words for a long time

Prairie Fire is 128 pgs., 6×9, offset, perfect-bound, glossy card cover, illustrations and ads. They receive 400-500 submissions (average 6 poems each), accept approximately 2%. Press run is 1,600 for 1,200 subscribers of which 100 are libraries, 150 shelf sales. Single copy: $8.95; subscription: $24 Canadian, $28 US. **Sample postpaid: $9 Canadian. Submissions should be typed, double-spaced, one poem to a page, name and address on each page, no more than 6 poems at a time. No previously published poems or simultaneous submissions. Cover letter required. Include other publications, brief biographical information, list of poems submitted, name, address and phone number. Reads submissions September 1 through June 30 only.** Time between acceptance and publication is 1 year. **Seldom comments on rejections. Publishes theme issues. Send SASE (or SAE and IRC) for guidelines and upcoming themes. Reports in 3-4 months. Pays $30 for first page, $25 for each additional page, plus 1 copy. Buys first Canadian serial rights only.** Staff reviews books of poetry in 500-2,000 words, single or multi-book format. Send books for review consideration. The editor says, "Be patient!"

THE PRAIRIE JOURNAL (II); PRAIRIE JOURNAL PRESS (IV-Regional, themes), P.O. Box 61203, Brentwood Post Office, 217-3630 Brentwood Rd. NW, Calgary, Alberta T2L 2K6 Canada, founded 1983, editor A. Burke, who wants to see **poetry of "any length, free verse, contemporary themes (feminist, nature, urban, non-political), aesthetic value, a poet's poetry." Does not want to see "most rhymed verse, sentimentality, egotistical ravings. No cowboys or sage brush."** They have published poetry by Mick Burrs, Lorna Crozier, Mary Melfi, Art Cuelho and John Hicks. *Prairie Journal* is 7×8½, 40-60 pgs., offset, saddle-stitched with card cover, b&w drawings and ads, appearing twice a year. They accept about 4% of the 500 or so poems they receive a year. Press run is 600 per issue, 200 subscriptions of which 50% are libraries, the rest are distributed on the newsstand. Subscription: $6 for individuals, $12 for libraries. **Sample postpaid: $6 ("Use postal money order"). No simultaneous submissions or previously published poems. Guidelines available for postage (but "no U.S. stamps, please"—get IRCs from the Post Office). "We will not be reading submissions until such time as an issue is in preparation (twice yearly), so be patient and we will acknowledge, accept for publication or return work at that time."** Sometimes sends prepublication galleys. **Pays $10-50 plus 1 copy. Acquires first North American serial rights.** Reviews books of poetry "but must be assigned by editor. Query first." **For chapbook publication, Canadian poets only (preferably from the region) should query with 5 samples, bio, publications. Responds to queries in 2 months, to mss in 6 months.** Payment in modest honoraria. They have published *Voices From Earth*, selected poems by Ronald Kurt and Mark McCawley, and *In the Presence of Grace*, by McCandless Callaghan. "We also publish anthologies on themes when material is available." A. Burke advises, "Read recent poets! Experiment with line length, images, metaphors. Innovate."

THE PRAIRIE PUBLISHING COMPANY (III, IV-Regional), Dept. PM, Box 2997, Winnipeg, Manitoba R3C 4B5 Canada, phone (204)885-6496, founded 1963, publisher Ralph E. Watkins, is a "small press catering to regional market, local history, fantasy, poetry and nonfiction," with flat-spined paperbacks. They want **"basically well-crafted poems of reasonable length" and do not want to see "the work of rank amateurs and tentative and time-consuming effort."** They have published collections of poetry by Brian Richardson and Brian MacKinnon. Their books are 6×9, handsomely produced, using b&w photos and art along with the poems, glossy card covers. They publish about 1

THE CHAPBOOK INDEX, located before the Geographical Index, lists those publishers who consider chapbook manuscripts. A chapbook, a small volume of work, is often a good middle step between magazine and book publication.

a year, 68 pgs. **Samples available at a 20% discount—send SASE or SAE and IRC for catalog. Query with samples. Simultaneous submissions OK. Do not submit mss during summer. Responds to queries in 6 weeks.** Nancy Watkins notes, "Robert E. Pletta's point that most poets need to do more reading is well taken. We would endorse this suggestion."

PRAIRIE SCHOONER; STROUSSE PRIZE; SLOTE PRIZE; FAULKNER AWARD; HUGH J. LUKE AWARD; STANLEY AWARD; READERS' CHOICE AWARDS (II), 201 Andrews, University of Nebraska, Lincoln NE 68588-0334, phone (402)472-0911, founded 1927, editor Hilda Raz; "one of the oldest literary quarterlies in continuous publication; publishes poetry, fiction, personal essays, interviews and reviews." **They want "poems that fulfill the expectations they set up." No specifications as to form, length, style, subject matter or purpose.** They have published poetry by Albert Goldbarth, Rafael Campo, Toi Derricotte, Alicia Ostriker, Dave Smith and Marcia Southwick. As a sample the editor selected these lines from "How to Get in the Best Magazines" by Eleanor Wilner:

> it is time to write
> the acceptable poem—
> ice and glass, with its splinter
> of bone, its pit
> of an olive,
> the dregs
> of the cup of abundance,
> useless spill of gold
> from the thresher, the dust
> of it filling the sunlight, the chum
> broadcast on the black waters
> and the fish
>   —the beautiful, ravenous fish—
> refusing to rise.

The magazine is 6×9, flat-spined, 176 pgs. and uses 70-80 pgs. of poetry in each issue. They receive about 4,800 mss (of all types)/year from which they choose 300 pgs. of poetry. Press run is 3,100. Single copy: $7.75; subscription: $22. **Sample postpaid: $5. Submit 5-7 poems at a time. No simultaneous submissions. "Clear copy appreciated." Considers mss from September through May only. Publishes theme issues. Send SASE for guidelines. Reports in 3-4 months; "sooner if possible." Always sends prepublication galleys. Pays copies. Acquires all rights. Returns rights upon request without fee.** Reviews books of poetry. Open to unsolicited reviews. Poets may also send books for review consideration. One of the most influential magazines being published today (often named as such in independent surveys of creative writers), this publication is genuinely open to excellent work in any form: lyric, narrative, dramatic, traditional, etc. Send only your best work, as competition is keen. Brief reviews are an excellent way to break into the journal. Editor Hilda Raz also promotes poets whose work has appeared in her pages by listing their continued accomplishments in a special section (even when their work does not concurrently appear in the magazine). The $500 Strousse Prize is awarded to the best poetry published in the magazine each year. The Slote Prize for beginning writers ($500), Hugh J. Luke Award ($250), the Stanley Award for Poetry ($500) and six other *PS* prizes are also awarded, as well as the Faulkner Award for Excellence in Writing ($1,000). Also, each year 5-10 Readers' Choice Awards ($250 each) are given for poetry, fiction and nonfiction. Editors serve as judges. Poetry published in *PS* has also been selected for inclusion in *The Best American Poetry 1996*. Hilda Raz comments, "*Prairie Schooner* receives a large number of poetry submissions; we're not unusual. We don't have time to comment on mss, but the magazine's reputation is evidence of our careful reading. We've been dedicated to the publication of good poems for a very long time and have published work early in the career of many successful poets."

PRAIRIE WINDS (II), Box 536, Dakota Wesleyan University, 1200 W. University Ave., Mitchell SD 57301, phone (605)995-2814, editor Howard F. Gunston, is an annual of poetry, fiction, short essays, photos and art. **They are open to all forms, lengths, styles and subjects of poetry except pornographic.** They have published poetry by Simon Perchik, Aaron Kramer, David Ignatow and Henry Hughes. The editor says *PW* is 50-60 pgs., 7½×9¼, offset, bound, gloss litho, no ads. They accept approximately 25% of the poetry received each year. Press run is 500 for 50 subscribers of which 10 are libraries. The rest are distributed free to professors and students. **Sample postpaid: $2. Submit 5-10 poems at a time. No previously published poems; simultaneous submissions OK. Cover letter required. "We are an annual, published in spring. All submissions must arrive by January 4." Reads submissions January 4 through 31 only. Seldom comments on rejections. Send SASE for guidelines. Reports by end of February. Pays 1 copy.**

PRAKALPANA LITERATURE; KOBISENA (I, IV-Bilingual, form), P-40 Nandana Park, Calcutta 700034, West Bengal, India, phone (91)(033)478-2347, *Kobisena* founded 1972, *Prakalpana*

Literature press founded 1974, magazine 1977, editor Vattacharja Chandan, who says, "We are small magazines which publish only *Prakalpana* (a mixed form of prose and poetry), Sarbangin (whole) poetry, experimental b&w art and photographs, essays on Prakalpana movement and Sarbangin poetry movement, letters, literary news and very few books on Prakalpana and Sarbangin literature. **Purpose and form: for advancement of poetry in the super-space age, the poetry must be really experimental and avant-garde using mathematical signs and symbols and visualizing the pictures inherent in the alphabet (within typography) with sonorous effect accessible to people. That is Sarbangin poetry. Length: within 30 lines (up to 4 poems). Prakalpana is a mixed form of prose, poetry, essay, novel, story, play with visual effect and it is not at all short story as it is often misunderstood. Better send 6 IRCs to read *Prakalpana Literature* first and then submit. Length: within 16 pages (up to 2 prakalpanas) at a time. Subject matter: society, nature, cosmos, humanity, love, peace, etc. Style: own. We do not want to see traditional, conventional, academic, religious, mainstream and poetry of prevailing norms and forms."** They have recently published poetry by Dilip Gupta, Rachael Z. Ikins, Bill West and Babloo Roychowdhury. As a sample the editor chose these lines by Norman J. Olson:

> *12345678901234567890123456789012345678901234567890*
> *Bisecting the coastal equation is a raft of*
> *///infections/// anti-logic///*
> *numero-logic//push the right keys//&&&*
> *&&&&&Fat beetles are grazing on the sky!!!!!*

Prakalpana Literature, an annual, is 120 pgs., $7 \times 4\frac{1}{2}$, saddle-stapled, printed on thin stock with matte card cover. *Kobisena*, which also appears once a year, is 16 pgs., digest-sized, a newsletter format with no cover. Both are hand composed and printed by letterpress. Both use both English and Bengali. They use about 10% of some 400 poems received/year. The press run is 1,000 for each, and each has about 450 subscriptions of which 50 are libraries. **Samples: 15 rupees for *Prakalpana*, 4 rupees for *Kobisena*. Overseas: 6 IRCs and 3 IRCs respectively or exchange of avant-garde magazines. Submit 4 poems at a time. Simultaneous submissions and previously published poetry OK. Cover letter with short bio and small photo/sketch of poet/writer/artist required; camera-ready copy ($4 \times 6\frac{1}{2}$) preferred.** Publication within a year. **After being published in the magazines, poets may be included in future anthologies with translations into Bengali/English if and when necessary. "Joining with us is welcome but not a pre-condition."** Editor comments on rejections "if wanted." **Send SAE with IRC for guidelines. No reporting time given. Sometimes sends prepublication galleys. Pays 1 copy.** Reviews books of poetry, fiction and art, "but preferably experimental books." Open to unsolicited reviews. Poets, writers and artists may also send books for review consideration. He says, "We believe that only through poetry, fiction and art, the deepest feelings of humanity as well as nature and the cosmos can be best expressed and conveyed to the peoples of the ages to come. And only poetry can fill up the gap in the peaceless hearts of dispirited peoples, resulted from the retreat of god and religion with the advancement of hi-tech. So, in an attempt, since the inception of Prakalpana Movement in 1969, to reach that goal in the avant-garde and experimental way we stand for Sarbangin poetry. And to poets and all concerned with poetry we wave the white handkerchief saying (in the words of Vattacharja Chandan), 'We want them who want us.' "

THE PRESBYTERIAN RECORD (IV-Inspirational, religious), 50 Wynford Dr., North York, Ontario M3C 1J7 Canada, phone (416)441-1111, fax (416)441-2825, founded 1876, is "the national magazine that serves the membership of The Presbyterian Church in Canada (and many who are not Canadian Presbyterians). We seek to stimulate, inform, inspire, to provide an 'apologetic' and a critique of our church and the world (not necessarily in that order!)." **They want poetry which is "inspirational, Christian, thoughtful, even satiric but *not* maudlin. No 'sympathy card' type verse a la Edgar Guest or Francis Gay. It would take a *very* exceptional poem of epic length for us to use it. Shorter poems, 10-30 lines, preferred. Blank verse OK (if it's not just rearranged prose). 'Found' poems. Subject matter should have some Christian import (however subtle)."** They have recently published poetry by Margaret Avison, Joan Dower Kosmachuk, Fredrick Zydek, Robert C. Jones, T.M. Dickey and Charles Cooper. The magazine comes out 11 times a year. Press run is 64,000. Subscription: $15. **Submit 3-6 poems at a time; seasonal work 6 weeks before month of publication. Simultaneous submissions OK; rarely accepts previously published poems. Poems should be typed, double-spaced. Pays $20-50/poem. Buys one-time rights.** Staff reviews books of poetry. Send books for review consideration. *The Presbyterian Record* has won several Canadian Church Press Awards.

PRESCOTT STREET PRESS (V, IV-Regional), Box 40312, Portland OR 97240-0312, founded 1974, poetry editor Vi Gale: **"Poetry and fine print from the Northwest."** Vi Gale says, "Our books and cards are the product of many hands from poet, artist, printer, designer, typesetter to bookstore and distributor. Somewhere along the line the editor/publisher [herself] arranges to pay one and all in the same way. Sometimes we have had grant help from the NEA and also from state and metropolitan arts organizations. But most of our help has come from readers, friends and the poets and artists themselves. Everyone has worked very hard. And we are immodestly pleased with our labors! **We are not a strictly regional press, although the poets I take on are connected with the Northwest in some way when we bring out the books. We are currently overstocked with poetry through 1998.**" Vi Gale publishes a series of postcards, notecards, paperback and hardback books of poetry in various artistic formats with illustrations by nationally known artists. Send SASE for catalog to order copies. As a sample, here are lines by Rolf Aggestam from a postcard:

> *muttering. cold*
> > *hands split fresh kindling*
> > *damn*
> *what a life. you are far away.*
> > *in the darkness we used to call*
> *each other forth*
> > *with fingers and a few small words.*
> *we created a little border*
> > *between darkness and darkness.*

Considers simultaneous submissions. Sometimes sends prepublication galleys. "We pay all of our poets. A modest sum, perhaps, but we pay everyone something."

PRESS GANG PUBLISHERS (III, IV-Regional, women, lesbian), #101-225 E. 17th Ave., Vancouver, British Columbia V5V 1A6 Canada, phone (604)876-7787, fax (604)876-7892, e-mail pgangpub@portal.ca, founded 1975, managing editor Barbara Kuhne, publishes 1 perfect-bound paperback book of poetry a year. **"We give priority to Canadian women's work. Nothing sexist, racist, homophobic."** They have published books of poetry by Chrystos and Joanne Arnott. As a sample the editor selected these lines from Chrystos's poem "Savage Eloquence":

> *Big Mountain*
> *you old story you old*
> *thing you fighting over nothing everything*
> *how they work us*
> *against one another   They mean to kill us*
> *all   Vanishing is no joke   they mean it*

Query first with sample poems and cover letter with brief bio and publication credits. E-mail queries OK. Previously published poems and simultaneous submissions OK. "U.S. postage cannot be used to return manuscripts from Canada. Send international postal coupons." Time between acceptance and publication is 9-12 months. **Seldom comments on rejections. Replies to queries in 1 month, to mss (if invited) in 4-6 months. Pays 8-10% royalties and 20 author's copies.** To see what type of work Press Gang publishes, "ask your local bookstore to order books from Inland Book Co., our U.S. distributor."

PRESS HERE (IV-Form), P.O. Box 4014, Foster City CA 94404, phone (415)571-9428, e-mail WelchM@aol.com, founded 1989, editor/publisher Michael Dylan Welch (who is also editor/publisher of *Woodnotes*), publishes 3 chapbooks a year. "Press Here was founded to publish fine books of haiku and related forms. Its goal is to present new and established voices through a variety of high-quality publications. Available books include informative interviews with established haiku poets, individual poetry collections and broad-ranging anthologies. **I wish to see manuscripts of poetry, or essays and interviews, related to haiku, senryu or tanka. I am also interested in concrete poetry. Not interested in longer poetry."** They have recently published work by William J. Higginson, Sono Uchida, Lee Gurga and Virginia Brady Young. As a sample the editor selected these lines of his own:

> *all my books collect dust*
> *except the one of love poems*
> *you gave me that day*
> *when the spring rains*
> *kept us indoors*

Query first with sample poems and cover letter. Previously published poems OK; no simultaneous submissions. "Queries are acceptable via e-mail, but snail-mail queries are preferred, especially if a catalog is desired." Always comments on rejections. Replies to queries in 1 month, to mss (if invited) in 6-9 months. Pays author's copies. For sample books, write for catalog.

THE PRESS OF THE NIGHTOWL (V), 320 Snapfinger Dr., Athens GA 30605, phone (706)353-7719, founded 1965, owner Dwight Agner, publishes 1-2 paperbacks and 1-2 hardbacks each year. They have published poetry by Paul Zimmer, Stephen Corey, Mary Anne Coleman and C.K. Williams. **However, they are currently not accepting unsolicited poetry submissions. Pays author's copies. Sample books may be ordered directly from the publisher or located through bookstores.**

THE PRESS OF THE THIRD MIND (IV-Form), 65 E. Scott St., Loft 6P, Chicago IL 60610, phone (312)337-3122, founded 1985, poetry editor "Badly Steamed Lard (anagram of Bradley Lastname)," is a small press publisher of artist books, poetry and fiction. **"We are especially interested in found poems, Dada, surrealism, written table-scraps left on the floors of lunatic asylums by incurable psychotics, etc."** They have published poetry by Anthony Stark, Jorn Barger, Tom Vaultonberg, Kevin Riordan and Eric Forsburg. As a sample the editor selected these lines from "Blind Trail With Wings (for Phillip Lamantia)" by Paul Grillo:

> An unidentified heart explodes packed with lava
> With blood of violins and undersea brambles
> I see the beautiful Swimmer unfolding himself
> Weighted down with Death's dark sequins
> His wide skirts billowing over the arches
> Embracing the angels of empty subways
> Who scratch the opposite side of the pearl into song

They have a press run of 500-1,000 with books often going into a second or third printing. **Sample postpaid: $5. For book publication submit up to 20 sample poems. Simultaneous submissions OK, if noted. "Cover letter is good, but we don't need to know everything you published since you were age 9 in single-spaced detail." Send SASE for upcoming themes. "Authors are paid as the publication transcends the break-even benchmark."** In 1995, the press released an 80-page anthology entitled *Empty Calories* and published a deconstructivist novel about the repetition complusion called *The Squeaky Fromme Gets the Grease*.

PRIMAVERA (II, IV-Women), P.O. Box #37-7547, Chicago IL 60637, phone (312)324-5920, founded 1975, co-editor Ruth Young, is "an irregularly published but approximately annual magazine of poetry and fiction reflecting **the experiences of women. We look for strong, original voice and imagery, generally prefer free verse, fairly short length, related, even tangentially, to women's experience."** They have published poetry by Lynne Hugo de Courcy, Sagaree Sengupta, Anita N. Feng and Denise Dumars. As a sample the editors selected these lines by Diane Seuss Brakeman:

> Unfasten your belt. Let your stomach out.
> Let it lower. Let it grow. Unbraid the braid.
> Shake your hair out. Blow your nose. Spit.

The elegantly printed publication, flat-spined, generously illustrated with photos and graphics, uses 30-35 pgs. of poetry in each issue. They receive over 1,000 submissions of poetry/year, use 32. Circulation is 1,000. Single copy: $10. **Sample postpaid: $5. Submit no more than 6 poems anytime, no queries. No simultaneous submissions. Editors comment on rejections "when requested or inspired." Send SASE for guidelines. Reports in 1-2 months. Pays 2 copies. Acquires first-time rights.**

PRINCETON UNIVERSITY PRESS; LOCKERT LIBRARY OF POETRY IN TRANSLATION (IV-Translations, bilingual), 41 William St., Princeton NJ 08540, phone (609)258-4900. "In the Lockert Library series, we publish simultaneous cloth and paperback (flat-spine) editions for each poet. Clothbound editions are on acid-free paper, and binding materials are chosen for strength and durability. Each book is given individual design treatment rather than stamped into a series mold. We have published a wide range of poets from other cultures, including well-known writers such as Hölderlin and Cavafy, and those who have not yet had their due in English translation, such as Ingeborg Bachmann and Faiz Ahmed Faiz. Manuscripts are judged with several criteria in mind: the ability of the translation to stand on its own as poetry in English; fidelity to the tone and spirit of the original, rather than literal accuracy; and the importance of the translated poet to the literature of his or her time and country." The editor says, "All our books in this series are heavily subsidized to break even. We have internal funds to cover deficits of publishing costs. We do not, however, publish books chosen and subsidized by other agencies, such as AWP." **Simultaneous submissions OK if you tell them. Cover letter required. Send mss only during respective reading periods stated in guidelines. Send SASE for guidelines to submit. Reports in 2-3 months.**

PRISM INTERNATIONAL (II), Dept. of Creative Writing, University of British Columbia, Vancouver, British Columbia V6T 1Z1 Canada, phone (604)822-2514, fax (604)822-3616, e-mail prism@u nixg.ubc.ca, website http://www.arts.ubc.ca/crwr/prism/prism.html, founded 1959, executive editors Sara O'Leary and Tim Mitchell. "*Prism* is an international quarterly that publishes poetry, drama, short fiction, imaginative nonfiction and translation into English in all genres. We have no thematic or stylistic allegiances: Excellence is our main criterion for acceptance of mss. **We want fresh, distinctive poetry that shows an awareness of traditions old and new. We read everything."** They have recently published poetry by Floyd Skloot, William Logan, Karen Connelly and Tom Wayman. As a sample the editors selected these lines from "Psalm 17" by April Bulmer:

> His trousers folded to the knee. I lift his narrow foot from the
> basin. For a moment—my hand firm around the high arch. His
> ankles pale as new trees in winter. His shoes like broken bark.

> *I take the little scissors in my grasp. They open like the beak of*
> *a young bird. Clippings fall like new moons from a thin horizon.*

> *I have come so far not to speak of my heart, the way you held*
> *it—only briefly—and it arched in the light. The small bones*
> *shifting at your touch.*

Prism is 80 pgs., 6×9, elegantly printed, flat-spined with original color artwork on a glossy card cover. Circulation to 1,000 subscribers of which 200 are libraries. They receive 1,000 submissions/year, use 80, have a 2- to 4-month backlog. Subscription: $16. **Sample postpaid: $5. Submit a maximum of 6 poems at a time, any print so long as it's typed. No previously published poems or simultaneous submissions. Cover letter with brief introduction and previous publications required. "Translations must be accompanied by a copy of the original. Poets may submit by e-mail, or through our website. Include the poem in the main body of the message." Send Canadian SASE or SAE with IRCs for guidelines. Reports in 2-4 months. Pays $20/printed page plus subscription; plus an additional $10/printed page to selected authors for publication on the World Wide Web. Editors sometimes comment on rejections.** *Prism International* is known in literary circles as one of the top journals in Canada. The editors say, "While we don't automatically discount any kind of poetry, we prefer to publish work that challenges the writer as much as it does the reader. We are particularly looking for poetry in translation."

PRISONERS OF THE NIGHT; MKASHEF ENTERPRISES (V, IV-Psychic/occult, science fiction/fantasy, horror, erotica)

P.O. Box 688, Yucca Valley CA 92286-0688, poetry editor Alayne Gelfand. *Prisoners of the Night*, founded 1987, **focusing on vampire erotica, uses poetry that is "erotic, unique, less horrific and more romantic, non-pornographic, original visions of the vampire."** Poets who have appeared recently in *POTN* include Tippi M. Blevins, Corrine DeWinter, Bobbi Sinaha-Morey, Elizabeth Wein, John Grey and Wendy Rathbone. As a sample the editor selected these lines from "Nosferatu Appears As A Black Hole" by Ann K. Schwader:

> *Like the dark, they are always*
> *with us: dull gravity's*
> *grimmest children,*
> *Schwarzchild sirens*
> *haunting horizons of dream.*

The intent of *POTN* is "to show the erotic, the romantic, rather than the horrific aspects of the vampire." It is 70-90 pgs., magazine-sized, perfect-bound, with color cover, produced by high-speed photocopying. Most poems are illustrated. It appears annually, usually in August. Of over 300 poems received/year they use between 10 and 20. It has an initial press run of 3,000, but each issue is kept in print. **Sample postpaid: $15 each (for #1-4), $12 (#5), $9.95 each (#6-9). Note: The editor is currently not accepting submissions as the August 1997 issue will feature the work of poet Wendy Rathbone. However, beginning in September 1997, she will be accepting submissions for the 1998 issue. Send SASE for guidelines. Submit no more than 6 poems at a time. No simultaneous submissions or previously published poems, "unless they've only appeared in your own chapbook." Editor sometimes comments on rejections. Reports "within 1 month." Pays $5/poem plus 1 copy. Buys first serial rights.** *POTN* wants unusual visions of the vampire, not stereotypical characterizations. The editor says, "Be original! Find new ways of saying things, explore the infinite possibilities of words and images. Do not rely on stereotypical visions of the vampire; the use of clichés is the quickest road to rejection. I'm not looking for your typical 'count' or 'countess,' no loners in ruined castles. I'm looking for the unusual image and sharp word usage. I want you to make my heart race with both the structure and subject of your poem. Non-rhyming, unstructured poems much prefered."

THE PROSE POEM (II, IV-Form)

610 Clyde Court, San Marcos TX 78666-2840, phone (512)353-4998, founded 1990, editor Steve Wilson, is an annual using **prose poems only. "I hope and pray the author knows what prose poetry is before submitting to me. For me 'prose poems' run from margin to margin, with no line breaks, and use intense, compact language."** They have published poetry by Linda Nemec Foster, Barry Silesky, Ray Gonzalez, Tom Whalen, Harriet Zinnes, Robert Bly and George Myers, Jr. The editor describes *TPP* as 60 pgs., professionally printed with card stock cover, saddle-stapled. Most selections are one paragraph or a few small ones, each about (or under) 200 words. Press run is 200. **Sample postpaid: $3. Submissions accepted October 1 through December 31. Reports 3 months after deadline. Pays 1 copy. Acquires first North American serial rights.** Staff reviews books of poetry. Send books for review consideration. The editor says, "*TPP* is a journal focusing on one particular genre and publishing only the best work done in that genre. This does not mean an author cannot experiment. I encourage it. It also does not mean I don't want to see work from new writers. Please send, but only your best. I publish this magazine with my own money, so sales are very important. If you think prose poetry matters and like the idea of a journal dedicated to it, please help me keep it going by sending great work and subscribing."

PROSETRY: NEWSLETTER FOR, BY AND ABOUT WRITERS (I), The Write Place, P.O. Box 117727, Burlingame CA 94011, phone (415)347-7613, e-mail prosetry@aol.com, editor P.D. Steele, founded 1986. *Prosetry* is a monthly newsletter featuring "new and newly published poets and prose writers with a 'guest writer' column each month. Our purpose is to provide writers with up-to-date information regarding markets, conferences and contests. To help get the juices flowing, to get the writer's work in the hands of an editor, and to offer the poet a forum in which to 'show their wares.' " *Prosetry* is 4 pgs., 8½ × 11, printed on heavy bond paper and 3-hole punched for home binding. Single copy: $2; subscription: $12/year. **Sample for 2 first-class stamps. Invites new writers. Send up to 3 poems, no more than 20 lines, English only. No profanity. Requires 2-line bio plus latest credits ("tell us if you've never been published"). Publishes theme issues. Send SASE for guidelines and upcoming themes. Themes for February, May and December are Love, Spring and Holidays, respectively. "All deadlines are first of month." Reports in less than 1 month. Pays one-year subscription. Acquires one-time rights; release required.** Reviews books of poetry in 150 words. Open to unsolicited reviews. Poets may also send books for review consideration. "For 'guest writer' column we would prefer information relevant to the beginning or newly published writer/ poet." Also publishes "How-to" *CLIPS©* for writers, $2.50 each. Free list for SASE. The editor says, "I'd like to receive less morose poetry and more humor."

PROVINCETOWN ARTS; PROVINCETOWN ARTS PRESS (II), 650 Commercial St., Provincetown MA 02657-1725, phone (508)487-3167, fax (508)487-8634, founded 1985, editor Christopher Busa, is an elegant annual using quality poetry. "*Provincetown Arts* focuses broadly on the artists and writers who inhabit or visit the tip of Cape Cod and seeks to stimulate creative activity and enhance public awareness of the cultural life of the nation's oldest continuous art colony. Drawing upon a century-long tradition rich in visual art, literature and theater, *Provincetown Arts* publishes material with a view towards demonstrating that the artists' colony, functioning outside the urban centers, is a utopian dream with an ongoing vitality." They have published poetry by Bruce Smith, Franz Wright, Sandra McPherson and Cyrus Cassells. As a sample the editor selected these lines from "Sky of Clouds" by Susan Mitchell:

> And after heavy rains, when the egrets
> settle on the gardens, cramming
> their beaks with the shrill
> cries of the frogs, I think
> I could do that too, I could be gorgeous and cruel.

PA is 170 pgs., 8¾ × 11⅞, flat-spined with full-color glossy cover. Press run is 10,000 for 500 subscribers of which 20 are libraries, 6,000 shelf sales. **Sample postpaid: $10. Submit up to 3 typed poems at a time. "We discourage simultaneous submissions." All queries and submissions should be via regular mail. Reads submissions September 1 through February 1. Send SASE for guidelines. Reports in 2-3 months. Sometimes sends prepublication galleys. Pays $25-100/poem plus 2 copies. Buys first rights.** Reviews books of poetry in 500-3,000 words, single or multi-book format. Open to unsolicited reviews. Poets may also send books for review consideration. The Provincetown Arts Press has published 4 volumes of poetry. The Provincetown Poets Series includes *At the Gate* by Martha Rhodes and *Euphorbia* by Anne-Marie Levine which was a finalist in the 1995 Paterson Poetry Prize. *Provincetown Arts* has also had work published in *Pushcart Prize XVIII, Pushcart Prize XX* and in *The Best American Poetry* (1991 and 1993, respectively).

PSYCHOPOETICA (II, IV-Specialized: psychologically-based), Dept. of Psychology, University of Hull, Hull HU6 7RX England, founded 1979, co-editors Dr. Geoff Lowe and Trevor Millum, uses **"psychologically-based poetry."** That is not a very narrow category, though many of the poems in *Psychopoetica* are explicitly about psychology or psychological treatment. But most good poetry is in some sense "psychologically based," as the editors seem to recognize in these comments (from their guidelines): **"We prefer short, experimental, rhymed and unrhymed, light verse, haiku, etc., (and visual poems). We will read and consider any style, any length, providing it's within the arena of 'psychologically-based' poetry. We're not too keen on self-indulgent therapeutic poetry (unless it's good and original), nor sweetly inspirational stuff. We like poetry that has some (or all!) of the following: humor, vivid imagery, powerful feelings, guts and substance, originality, creative style, punch or twist, word-play, good craftsmanship, etc."** Published poets include Sheila E. Murphy, Wes Magee, R. Nikolas Macioci, Allen Renfro, Vi Vi Hlavsa and John Brander. The magazine appears 4 times/year, circulating to "several hundred and increasing." It is A4, perfect-bound. **Sample: £1.50 ($3). Submit a maximum of 6 poems at a time. Previously published poems ("state where and when") and simultaneous submissions OK. Publishes theme issues. Send SASE (or SAE and IRC) for guidelines and upcoming themes. Theme for an upcoming issue is Introducing Poetry (brief introductions to accompany each poem). Editor usually comments on rejections. Pays 1 copy.** Occasionally reviews books of poetry in 25 words, single format. Open to unsolicited reviews. Poets may also send books for review consideration. They say, "Careful presentation of work is most important. But we continue to be impressed by the rich variety of submissions, especially work that shifts boundaries. Also, we now welcome interesting juxtapositions of words and graphics."

THE PUCKERBRUSH PRESS; THE PUCKERBRUSH REVIEW (I, IV-Regional), 76 Main St., Orono ME 04473-1430, phone (207)866-4868 or 581-3832, press founded 1971, *Review* founded 1978, poetry editor Constance Hunting, is a "small press publisher of a literary, twice-a-year magazine focused on Maine and of flat-spined paperbacks of literary quality." The editor **looks for freshness and simplicity, but does not want to see "confessional, religious, sentimental, dull, feminist, incompetent, derivative"** poetry. They have recently published *Claiming* by Patricia Ranzoni and *To a Vanished World* by Lee Sharkey. As a sample the editor selected these lines from "Not a Navigable River" by Muska Nagel:

> *flow seaward, seaward*
> *my river, filled to the brink—*
> *(but no king's horses, no more*
> *will ever come to drink).*

For the review, submit 5 poems at a time. For book publication, query with 10 samples. Prefers no simultaneous submissions. Offers criticism for a fee: $100 is usual. Pays 10% royalties plus 10 copies.

PUDDING HOUSE PUBLICATIONS; PUDDING MAGAZINE: THE INTERNATIONAL JOURNAL OF APPLIED POETRY; PUDDING HOUSE WRITING COMPETITIONS; PUDDING HOUSE BED & BREAKFAST FOR WRITERS; OHIO POETRY THERAPY CENTER & LIBRARY (II, IV-Political, social issues, popular culture), 60 N. Main St., Johnstown OH 43031, phone (614)967-6060, founded 1979, editor Jennifer Bosveld, provides "a sociological looking glass through poems that provide 'felt experience' and share intense human situations. Speaks for the difficulties and the solutions. Additionally a forum for poems and articles by people who take poetry arts into the schools and the human services." They publish *Pudding* every several months, also chapbooks, anthologies, broadsides. They **"want experimental and contemporary poetry—what hasn't been said before. Speak the unspeakable. Don't want preachments or sentimentality. Don't want obvious traditional forms without fresh approach. Long poems happily considered too, as long as they aren't windy. Interested in receiving poetry on popular culture and rich brief narratives, i.e. 'virtual journalism.' "** They have published poetry by Lowell Jaeger, Edward Boccia and Jane Elsdon. The editor selected these sample lines from "Dustbowl Prophet" by Wilma Elizabeth McDaniel:

> *Like all the men in the Meade family*
> *Uncle John's hands were farmer rough and big as shovels.*

Pudding **is a literary journal with an emphasis on poetry arts in human service.** They use about 80 pgs. of poetry in each issue—5½ × 8½, 80 pgs., offset composed on IBM 1st choice, circulation 1,500, 1,400 subscriptions of which 50 are libraries. Subscription (3 issues): $18. **Sample postpaid: $6.75. Submit 4-10 poems at a time with SASE. "Submissions without SASEs will be discarded." No simultaneous submissions. Previously published submissions** *respected* **but include credits. Likes cover letter. Sometimes publishes theme issues. Send SASE for guidelines and upcoming projects. Reports on same day (unless traveling). Pays 1 copy—to featured poet $10 and 4 copies. Returns rights "with** *Pudding* **permitted to reprint."** Staff reviews books of poetry. Send books for review consideration. **For chapbook publication, no query. $5 reading fee. Send complete ms and cover letter with publication credits and bio. Editor often comments, will critique on request for $3/page of poetry or $50 an hour in person.** Jennifer Bosveld shares, "Editors have pet peeves. I won't respond to postcards or on them. I require envelopes, not postcards. Don't individually-fold rather than group-fold poems. I don't like cover letters that state the obvious." The Pudding Writing Competitions are for single poems (deadline September 30, fee $2/poem) and for chapbook publication (deadline June 30, $9 entry fee). Pudding House Bed & Breakfast for Writers offers "luxurious rooms with desk and all the free paper you can use" as well as free breakfast in large comfortable home ½ block from post office. Location of the Ohio Poetry Therapy Center and Library. $65 single or double/night, discounts available. Reservations recommended far in advance. Send SASE for details.

PUEBLO POETRY PROJECT (IV-Regional), Dept. PM, 1501 E. Seventh St., Pueblo CO 81001, phone (719)584-3401, founded 1979, director Tony Moffeit, **publishes poets from the Pueblo area only. If you qualify, inquire.**

PUERTO DEL SOL (II, IV-Translations, regional), Box 3E, New Mexico State University, Las Cruces NM 88003-0001, phone (505)646-2345 or 3517, founded 1972 (in present format), poetry editor Kathleene West. "We publish a literary magazine twice per year. Interested in poems, fiction, essays, photos, originals and translations from the Spanish. Also (generally solicited) reviews and dialogues between writers. We want **top quality poetry, any style, from anywhere. We are sympathetic to Southwestern writers, but this is not a theme magazine. Excellent poetry of any kind, any form."** They have recently published poetry by Judith Sornbergern, Ana Castillo, Marilyn Hacker,

Virgil Suarez and Lois-Ann Yamanaka. As a sample the editor selected these lines from "And Seeing It" by Valerie Martínez:

> Orange, orange. And the hand arching up
> to hold it. The woman's hand, the arching.
> Up. And the star exploding, seeing it
> where it wasn't, a telescope on the night sky.
> The thermonuclear flash. The explosion.

The 6×9, flat-spined, professionally printed magazine, matte card cover with art, has a circulation of 1,250, 300 subscriptions of which 25-30 are libraries. 40-50 pgs. are devoted to poetry in each 150-page issue, which also includes quite a lot of prose. They use about 50 of the 800 submissions (about 6,000 poems) received each year to fill up the 90 pgs. of poetry two issues encompass. "Generally no backlog." You won't find many literary journals as attractive as this one. It has an award-caliber design (from the selection of fonts to the use of rules and type-size to enhance content). Furthermore, the journal features readable, thought provoking verse in all styles including translations. It's an exceptional publication. One-year subscription (2 issues): $10. **Sample copy: $7. Submit 3-6 poems at a time, 1 poem to a page. Simultaneous submissions OK. Cover letter welcome. Reads mss September 1 to March 1 only. Offers editorial comments on most mss. Reports in 3-6 months. Sometimes sends prepublication galleys. Pays 2 copies.** In the past this publication was awarded a NEA Literary Magazine Grant. The editor says, "We're looking for poems that are risk-taking and honest."

PURDUE UNIVERSITY PRESS; VERNA EMERY POETRY PRIZE (II), 1532 S. Campus Courts-E, West Lafayette IN 47907-1532, phone (317)494-2038, founded 1960. They select 1 book/year to publish through the Verna Emery Poetry Prize. They have published poetry by Jim Barnes, editor of *Chariton Review*, and Fleda Brown Jackson, whose book, *Fishing With Blood*, won the GLCA New Writers Award. **There is a reading fee. Those interested are urged to send SASE for guidelines as particulars vary from year to year.**

PYGMY FOREST PRESS; SEMI-DWARF QUARTERLY (II), P.O. Box 591, Albion CA 95410, phone (707)937-2347, founded 1987, editor/publisher Leonard Cirino, publishes flat-spined paperbacks. **"Forms of any kind/length to 96 pgs., subject matter open; especially ecology, prison, asylum, Third World, anarchist to far right. Prefer Stevens to Williams. I like Berryman, Roethke, William Bronk; dislike most 'Beats.' Open to anything I consider 'good.' Open to traditional rhyme, meter, but must be modern in subject matter. Also open to translations."** He has published *From Beirut* by Mahmoud Darwish, translated by Stephen Kessler; *Pagan Fishing & Other Poems* by Walt McLaughlin; *Where the Four Winds Blow* (including epitaphs) by Phillipe Soupault, translated by Pat Nolan; *The Circle & The Line* by Victoria Bouroncle; *Lessons of A Radical Finitude* by Michael McIrwin; and *Inside the Boar's Circle* by Stephen Miller. As a sample the editor selected these lines from "Exile" by John P. Freeman, published in his book *Illusion on the Louisiana Side*:

> Then everything is once more as it always was,
> standing near you in a field to watch a flight
> of geese calling in a dialect
> only your blood can know.

Submit 10-15 poems with bio, acknowledgements, publications. Simultaneous submissions and previously published material OK. Reports on queries in 1-3 weeks, submissions in 2-4 weeks. Usually pays 20% of run ("if author typesets on IBM compatible")—about 30-50 copies. Buys first rights. He comments on "almost every" ms. Leonard Cirino says, "I am basically an anarchist. Belong to no 'school.' I fund myself. Receive no grants or private funding. Generally politically left, but no mainline Stalinist or Marxist. Plan to publish 1-3 books yearly." Also publishes *Semi-Dwarf Quarterly* which accepts poetry, stories, translations, memoirs, essays and b&w art. Send SASE for details.

PYX PRESS; MAGIC REALISM (II, IV-Fantasy); SHILLELAGH (II, IV-Horror, fantasy); WRITER'S KEEPER (I, II, IV-Writing), P.O. Box 922648, Sylmar CA 91392-2648, founded 1990. *Magic Realism* editors C. Darren Butler and Julie Thomas, appears quarterly using poetry of **"depth and imagination.** *Magic Realism* **subverts reality by shaping it into a human mold, bringing it closer to the imagination and to the subconscious. Inner reality becomes empirical reality. We always need good short poems of 3-12 lines."** It is 80 pgs., digest-sized, typeset, offset or xerographically printed, with card cover using b&w art. They use 5-15 poems/issue. Press run is 600-800 for 200 subscribers. **Sample postpaid: $5.95. Previously published poems and simultaneous submissions OK. Send #10 SASE for guidelines. Reports in 2-6 months. Always sends prepublication galleys. Pays $3/magazine page on acceptance for poetry and 1 copy. Buys first North American serial or one-time rights and nonexclusive reprint rights; also needs worldwide Spanish language rights for translation which appears 1-2 years after English edition. Editor rarely comments.** The editor says, "I am looking for literary work based in exaggerated realism. Fantasy should permeate the reality, give it luster. My needs are somewhat flexible. For example, I occasionally publish genre work, or glib fantasy of the sort found in folktales and fables." *Shillelagh*, editors C. Darren Butler and Lisa S. Laurencot, appears irregularly (1-2 times/year) using **"bizarre, horrific short-shorts and poetry. We are most interested in dreamy, surreal, decadent poetry; intensely imaginative and bizarre works. We try to publish material in any form or category that promotes a sense of wonder or terror or awe, work that transforms the mind and the experience of living. Horror and comedy are closely related. For this reason, we also accept comedic or absurd work when they fit thematically with the magazine." No obscene, gory, gratuitous, pornographic or trite poetry. Also, no vampires, werewolves, or other horror clichés.** The editor says *Shillelagh* is 48 pgs., digest-sized, xerographically printed, saddle-stapled with b&w cover and art, ads also included. They use approximately 20 poems/issue. Press run is 400 for 80 subscribers. Subscription: $10.95 for 3 issues. **Sample postpaid: $4.50. Previously published poems and simultaneous submissions OK. Send SASE for guidelines. Reports in 2-6 months. Pays 1 copy. Acquires first North American serial rights; reprint rights optional.** *Writer's Keeper*, editor C. Darren Butler, is a quarterly publishing poetry, fiction and nonfiction **pertaining to writing. Accepts poetry to 30 lines, any style. "Humorous works especially needed."** *WK* is 2-6 pgs., 8½ × 11, photocopied, corner-stapled. They receive 600-800 submissions a year, accept approximately 2%. Press run 800-1,000 for 40 subscribers, 80% are distributed free. Subscription: $5. **Sample postpaid: $1.25 or free for #10 SASE. Previously published poems and simultaneous submissions OK. Send SASE for guidelines. Reports in 3 months, "occasionally longer, often sooner." Pays $1 plus contributor's copy and 3-issue subscription. Acquires first North American serial rights.** All three magazines review books of poetry, chapbooks and magazines in ¼ to ½ page as space permits. Poets may send books for review consideration. Pyx Press publishes books and chapbooks. "Generally poets we publish first appear in *Magic Realism* or *Shillelagh*." Send SASE for catalog.

THE QUARTERLY (II), 650 Madison Ave., Suite 2600, New York NY 10022, phone (212)888-4769, founded 1987, editor Gordon Lish, is a literary quarterly publishing poetry, fiction and humor. **They want poetry of the "highest standards."** They have published poetry by Sharon Olds, Bruce Beasley, Jack Gilbert and Thomas Lynch. It is 256 pgs., digest-sized, flat-spined, with matte cover. Circulation: 15,000. Subscription: $30. **"Do not submit a batch of poems folded separately!" Sends prepublication galleys. Pays contributor's copies.** The editor says, "Don't apply unless your work is worth your life."

QUARTERLY REVIEW OF LITERATURE POETRY BOOK SERIES; QRL PRIZE AWARDS (II, IV-Subscription, translation), 26 Haslet Ave., Princeton NJ 08540, founded 1943, poetry editors T. Weiss and R. Weiss. After more than 35 years as one of the most distinguished literary journals in the country, *QRL* now appears as the *QRL Poetry Book Series*, in which 4-6 books, chosen in open competition, are combined in one annual volume, each of the 4-6 poets receiving $1,000 and 100 copies. The resulting 300- to 400-page volumes are printed in editions of 3,000-5,000, selling in paperback for $12, in hardback for $20. Subscription—2 paperback volumes containing 10 books: $20. **Manuscripts may be sent for reading during the months of November and May only. The collection need not be a first book. It should be 50-80 pgs. if it is a group of connected poems, a selection of miscellaneous poems, a poetic play or a work of poetry translation, or it can be a single long poem of 30 pgs. or more. Some of the individual poems may have had magazine publication. Also considers simultaneous submissions. Manuscripts in English or translated into English are also invited from outside the US. Only one ms may be submitted per reading period and must include a SASE. Reports in 4-6 weeks. They always send prepublication galleys.** "Since poetry as a thriving art must depend partly upon the enthusiasm and willingness of those directly involved to join in its support, the editors require that **each ms be accompanied by a subscription to the series."**

QUARTERLY WEST (II), 317 Olpin Union, University of Utah, Salt Lake City UT 84112, phone/fax (801)581-3938, founded 1976, co-editors M.L. Williams and Lawrence Coates, poetry editors Sally Thomas and Margot Schilpp. *Quarterly West* is a semiannual literary magazine that **seeks "original and accomplished literary verse—free or formal. No greeting card or sentimental poetry."** Also **publishes translations.** They have recently published poetry by Stephen Dunn, Robert Pinsky and Eavan Boland. *QW* is 220 pgs., 6 × 9, offset with 4-color cover art. They receive 750-1,000 submissions

---

MARKET CONDITIONS are constantly changing! If you're still using this book and it is 1998 or later, buy the newest edition of *Poet's Market* at your favorite bookstore or order directly from Writer's Digest Books.

a year, accept less than 1%. Press run is 1,100 for 500 subscribers of which 300-400 are libraries. Subscription: $11 for 1 year, $20 for 2 years. **Sample postpaid: $6.50. Submit 3-5 poems at a time. No previously published poems; simultaneous submissions OK, with notification. Seldom comments on rejections. Send SASE for guidelines. Reports in 1-6 months. Pays $15-100. Buys all rights. Returns rights with acknowledgement and right to reprint.** Reviews books of poetry in 1,000-3,000 words. Open to unsolicited reviews. Poets may also send books for review consideration.

QUEEN OF ALL HEARTS (IV-Religious), 26 S. Saxon Ave., Bay Shore NY 11706, phone (516)665-0726, founded 1950, poetry editor Joseph Tusiani, is a magazine-sized bimonthly that uses **poetry "dealing with Mary, the Mother of Jesus—inspirational poetry. Not too long."** They have published poetry by Fernando Sembiante and Alberta Schumacher. The professionally printed magazine, 48 pgs., heavy stock, various colors of ink and paper, liberal use of graphics and photos, has approximately 4,000 subscriptions at $17/year. Single copy: $2.50. **Sample postpaid: $3.** They receive 40-50 submissions of poetry/year, use 2/issue. **Submit double-spaced mss. Reports within 3-4 weeks. Pays 6 copies (sometimes more) and complimentary subscription. Sometimes editor comments on rejections.** His advice: "Try and try again! Inspiration is not automatic!"

ELLERY QUEEN'S MYSTERY MAGAZINE (IV-Mystery), 1540 Broadway, New York NY 10036-4039, founded 1941, appears 11 times a year, primarily using short stories of mystery, crime or suspense. **"We also publish short limericks and verse pertaining to the mystery field."** As a sample the editor selected these lines from "Coffee Olé" by Marie E. Truitt:

> *But once he married, breakfasts were the nastiest of scenes;*
> *On making coffee, Wifie didn't know a hill of beans.*
> *The bitter taste! . . . the inch-deep dregs! . . . he couldn't take much more!*
> *It went from bad to mega-bad, till Fred let out a roar:*
> *"I've had enough! It's Splitsville! There's just no other course!*
> *And I hold within this cup, my Dear, the grounds for our divorce!"*

EQMM is 160 pgs., 5×7¾, professionally printed newsprint, flat-spined with glossy paper cover. Subscription: $34. **Sample: $2.95 (available on newsstands). No previously published poems; simultaneous submissions OK. Include SASE with submissions. Reports in 3 months. Pays $5-50 plus 3 copies.**

QUEEN'S QUARTERLY: A CANADIAN REVIEW (II, IV-Regional), Queen's University, 184 Union St., Kingston, Ontario K7L 3N6 Canada, phone (613)545-2667, founded 1893, editor Boris Castel, is "a general interest intellectual review featuring articles on science, politics, humanities, arts and letters, extensive book reviews, some poetry and fiction. **We are especially interested in poetry by Canadian writers. Shorter poems preferred."** They have published poetry by Evelyn Lau, Sue Nevill and Raymond Souster. There are about 12 pgs. of poetry in each issue, 6×9, 224 pgs. Circulation is 3,500. They receive about 400 submissions of poetry/year, use 40. Subscription: $20 Canadian, $25 US for US and foreign subscribers. **Sample postpaid: $6.50 US. Submit no more than 6 poems at a time. No simultaneous submissions. Reports in 1 month. Pays usually $50 (Canadian)/poem, "but it varies,"** plus 2 copies.

‡RACS/RENT-A-CHICKEN SPEAKS (I, II), P.O. Box 1501, Wappingers Falls NY 12590-8501, phone (914)297-9307, founded 1994, editor Garth Coogan, is a quarterly of "serious contemporary literature for students, educators and the adult public." **They have no specifications regarding form or subject, although they do not want to see "light verse."** Poetry up to 125 lines welcome. They have recently published poetry by Joe Malone, Simon Perchik and Nancy Means Wright. As a sample the editor selected these lines from "Riverwind Magnolias" by Lyn Lifshin:

> *you pulled me*
> *down toward the bench*
> *pulled my hand*
> *to where you*
> *were least shy*

RACS is 40-50 pgs., 5½×8½, photocopied and saddle-stapled with colored card stock cover. They receive about 400 poems a year, publish about 165. Press run is 300, more than 100 distributed free to small press editors. Single copy: $3.75. **Sample postpaid: $5. Submit up to 12 poems at a time. Previously published poems and simultaneous submissions OK, if fully noted. Cover letter preferred.** Time between acceptance and publication is 3-9 months. **Frequently edits work and returns edited form to poet for publication approval. Always comments on rejections. Send SASE for guidelines. Reports within 10 weeks. Sometimes sends prepublication galleys. Pays 3 copies. Acquires one-time rights.** The editor says, "*RACS* is striving to be a mode of inexpensive publication of contemporary poetry and occasionally publishes what it calls a Minichap (a short chapbook), incorporated as part of a regular issue of the magazine."

RADCLIFFE QUARTERLY (IV-Specialized: alumnae), 10 Garden St., Cambridge MA 02138, phone (617)495-8608, editor Diane Sherlock, is an alumnae quarterly that **publishes alumnae and college-related poets.** *RQ* is magazine-sized, with glossy full-color paper cover. They receive about 50 poems/year, use 3 poems/issue. Press run is 35,000. **Samples free to anyone. No pay.** Reviews books of poetry in 250 words, single format. The Dean's office sponsors a contest for poets, winners printed in the quarterly. Must be a Radcliffe student to enter.

RADIANCE: THE MAGAZINE FOR LARGE WOMEN (I, IV-Women), P.O. Box 30246, Oakland CA 94604, phone/fax (510)482-0680, e-mail radmag2@aol.com, founded 1984, publisher/ editor Alice Ansfield, appears quarterly. **"Keeping in mind that our magazine is geared toward large women, we look for poetry from women of any size and men who don't accept society's stereotypical standards of beauty and weight—but who celebrate women's bodies, sexuality, search for self-esteem and personal growth."** As a sample she quotes "Homage to My Hips" by Lucille Clifton:

> *these hips are big hips*
> *they need space to*
> *move around in.*
> *they don't fit into little*
> *petty places. these hips*
> *are free hips.*
> *they don't like to be held back.*
> *these hips have never been enslaved,*
> *they go where they want to go*
> *they do what they want to do.*
> *these hips are mighty hips.*
> *these hips are magic hips.*
> *i have known them*
> *to put a spell on a man and*
> *spin him like a top!*

Radiance is 60 pgs., magazine-sized, professionally printed on glossy stock with full-color paper cover, saddle-stapled, 2-color graphics, photos and ads. Circulation is 10,000 for 4,000 subscriptions, 2,500 selling on newsstands or in bookstores, 1,000 sent as complimentary copies to media and clothing stores for large women. Subscription: $20/year. **Sample postpaid: $3.50. Submit double-spaced, typed ms. Editor usually comments on rejections. Send SASE for guidelines. Reports in 4-6 months. Pays $10-30 plus contributor's copy. Buys one-time rights.** Reviews related books of poetry in 500-800 words.

RAG MAG; BLACK HAT PRESS (I, II), P.O. Box 12, Goodhue MN 55027, phone (612)923-4590, founded 1982, poetry editor Beverly Voldseth, accepts **poetry of "any length or style. No pornographic SM violent crap."** They have recently published poetry by Nancy Cox, Franz K. Baskett, Lyle Daggett and Kris Bigalk. As a sample the editor selected these lines from "Home" by Stephanie Pershing Buehler:

> *We unlock the last door home,*
> *changing time at Murdo.*
> *These yellow plains familiar backyard grass*
> *and each South Dakota rest area*
> *a room in the place I live.*
> *Then mountains,*
> *milk in the refrigerator,*
> *and mail on the table,*
> *as if, on this journey, we had never left.*
> *Even the clock is wound.*
> *It is this time too in Murdo.*

Rag Mag, appearing twice a year, is 80-112 pgs., perfect-bound, 6×9, professionally printed in dark type with ads for books, matte colored card cover. The editor says she accepts about 10% of poetry received. Press run is 250 for 80 subscriptions of which 8 are libraries. Subscription: $10. **Sample postpaid: $6. "Send 3-9 of your best with brief bio. Something that tells a story, creates images, speaks to the heart." Name and address on each page. SASE required for return of work or response. Previously published poems and simultaneous submissions OK, "but please acknowledge both." Publishes theme issues. Theme for October 1997 issue is "Families." Submissions accepted April through June 1997. Send SASE for guidelines and upcoming themes. Pays 1 copy. Acquires first or one-time rights.** Reviews books of poetry. Open to unsolicited reviews. Poets may also send books for review consideration. **They may publish chapbook or paperback collections of poetry under the imprint of Black Hat Press. Query first. Simultaneous submissions and previously printed material OK. Reports in 6 weeks. Detailed comments provided "sometimes."**

Financial arrangements for book publication vary. They have recently published *Boom Town* by Diane Glancy and *Poems of Saisseval* by Pierre Garnier.

‡**RAMBUNCTIOUS PRESS; RAMBUNCTIOUS REVIEW (II, IV-Regional)**, 1221 W. Pratt, Chicago IL 60626, founded 1982, poetry editors Mary Alberts, Richard Goldman, Beth Hausler and Nancy Lennon. *Rambunctious Review* appears once yearly. They want **"spirited, quality poetry,** fiction, photos and graphics. **Some focus on local work, but all work is considered."** As a sample the editors selected these lines from "I Grew Up in Arles" by Anne Valdez:

> *I grew up in Arles, South Chicago,*
> *The town where Vincent lived*
> *I never knew the tavern/cafe/bars*
> *But I knew the trees and houses*
> *And people with spider-jointed fingers.*

RR is 48 pgs., 7×10, handsomely printed and saddle-stapled. They receive 500-600 submissions a year and use 50-60. They have a circulation of about 500 with 200 subscriptions. **Sample postpaid: $4. Will consider simultaneous submissions. No submissions accepted June 1 through August 31. No queries. Occasionally comments on mss. Publishes theme issues. Reports in 9 months. Pays 2 copies.** They run annual contests in poetry, fiction and short drama.

RANGER RICK MAGAZINE (III, IV-Children, nature/ecology), 8925 Leesburg Pike, Vienna VA 22184, founded 1967, senior editor Deborah Churchman, is a monthly nature magazine for children aged 6-12. **They want "short, funny verses for children about nature and the environment. Must be accurate. No religious, preachy or difficult poetry."** They have published poetry by John Ciardi and Charles Ghigna. *RR* is 48 pgs., 8×10, saddle-stitched, glossy paper with numerous full color photos. They receive 100-200 submissions/year, "may accept one." Press run is 900,000. Subscription: $15. **Sample postpaid: $2. Submit up to 5 poems at a time. Previously published poems OK; no simultaneous submissions.** Time between acceptance and publication is 2-5 years. **Seldom comments on rejections. Publishes theme issues. Send SASE for guidelines and upcoming themes. Reports in 2 months. Always sends prepublication galleys. Pays $5/line plus 2 copies. Buys all rights. Return is "negotiable."** The editor says, "Think: Will kids understand these words? Will it hook them? Will an 8-year-old want to read this instead of playing Nintendo?"

RARACH PRESS (V), 1005 Oakland Dr., Kalamazoo MI 49008, founded 1981, owner Ladislav Hanka, is a "small bibliophilic press specializing in hand-printing, hand-binding with original artwork. The material is either in Czech or, if English, dealing with environmentalist subject matter." He has printed books of poetry by Richard Neugebauer, Ben Mitchell and Rainer Maria Rilke. As a sample the editor selected these lines from "Wildness" by Jim Armstrong:

> *We were far from the road, and in those places*
> *where silence grew like a root: anonymous flowers*
> *opened themselves. Deer tracks marked off absence.*
> *A stump crumbled. A caddis fly clung to a stone.*
> *It was routine—but a kind of organization*
> *unlike our own, and we yearned for it.*

The editor says, "Authors tend to be friends, acquaintances or dead. They are given a portion of the books or a portion of sales after the fact. **I do not care to receive unsolicited mss.** I pity the lot of you. I fully expect most of my books to eventually be taken apart and sold for the artwork when they pass from the present collector of bibliophilia to some philistine. This means the poetry will be lost . . . I really sell my books for the price of the binding and artwork."

RARITAN QUARTERLY (III), Dept. PM, 31 Mine St., New Brunswick NJ 08903, phone (908)932-7887, founded 1982, editor Richard Poirier. **"We publish very little poetry. We publish *almost* no unsolicited poetry, so it would be misleading to encourage submissions."** They have published poetry by J.D. McClatchy, James Merrill, Richard Howard and Robert Pinsky. It is 150 pgs., 6×9, flat-spined, with matte card cover, professionally printed. The few poems appearing here (including sequences and translations) tend toward free verse. Press run is 4,000 for 3,500 subscribers of which 800 are libraries. Subscription: $16. **Sample postpaid: $5. Pays $100/submission if accepted.** Reviews recent poetry books and chapbooks. Poetry published in this quarterly was included in *The Best American Poetry 1992*.

‡**RATTLE (II)**, 13440 Ventura Blvd. #200, Sherman Oaks CA 91423, phone (818)788-3232, fax (818)788-2831, founded 1994, editor Alan C. Fox, is a biannual poetry publication which also includes interviews with poets, essays on poetry and brief reviews of poetry books. **They want "high quality poetry of any form, 4 pages maximum. Nothing boring or unintelligible."** They have published poetry by Charles Bukowski, William Stafford, Charles Webb and Ai. As a sample the editor selected these lines from "The Fun" by Ruth Bavetta:

was always where I wasn't,
in the other room, behind the paisley curtains,
on the bigger Ferris wheel,
out in the backyard while I was washing cups.
It was always just before my Currie's Mile Hi cone
or just after I left the party.

Rattle is 100-128 pgs., 5½ × 8½, neatly printed and perfect-bound with two-color coated card cover. They receive about 700 poems a year, accept approximately 140. Press run is 650. Subscription: $16 for 2 years. **Sample postpaid: $5. Make checks payable to Alan C. Fox. Submit 5 poems at a time. Previously published poems and simultaneous submissions OK. Cover letter with brief bio preferred. Reads submissions September 1 through May 31 only. Seldom comments on rejections. Reports in 3-5 months. Pays 2 copies. Rights revert to authors upon publication.** Welcomes short essays on poetry and one-page book reviews. Poets may also send books for review consideration.

RAW DOG PRESS; POST POEMS (II, IV-Humor), 151 S. West St., Doylestown PA 18901-4134, phone (215)345-6838, founded 1977, poetry editor R. Gerry Fabian, "publishes Post Poems annual—a postcard series. **We want short poetry (3-7 lines) on any subject. The positive poem or the poem of understated humor always has an inside track. No taboos, however. All styles considered. Anything with rhyme had better be immortal.**" They have published poetry by Charles Rossiter, Lyn Lifshin, John Grey, Glen G. Coats and the editor, R. Gerry Fabian, who selected his poem, "Arc Welder," as a sample:

After years of burning
he pressed his lips against hers
and sealed out any doubt.

Submit 3-5 poems at a time. Send SASE for catalog to buy samples. The editor "always" comments on rejections. Pays copies. Acquires all rights. Returns rights on mention of first publication. Sometimes reviews books of poetry. He says he will offer criticism for a fee; "if someone is desperate to publish and is willing to pay, we will use our vast knowledge to help steer the ms in the right direction. We will advise against it, but as P.T. Barnum said . . . . Raw Dog Press welcomes new poets and detests second-rate poems from 'name' poets. We exist because we are dumb like a fox, but even a fox takes care of its own." The editor also says, "I get more poems that do not fit my needs. At least one quarter of all poets waste their postage because they do not read the requirements."

RE:AL—THE JOURNAL OF LIBERAL ARTS (II, IV-Bilingual, translations, humor), (formerly *REAL [Re Arts & Letters]*), Dept. PM, Box 13007, Stephen F. Austin State University, Nacogdoches TX 75962, phone (409)468-2028, e-mail real@titan.sfasu.edu, founded 1968, editor W. Dale Hearell, is a "Liberal Arts Forum" using short fiction, drama, reviews and interviews; contains editorial notes and personalized "Contributors' Notes"; printed in the winter and summer. They "hope to use from 15 to 35 pages of poetry per issue, one poem per page (typeset in editor's office). Last two issues had submissions from thirty-eight states, Great Britain, Italy and Israel." **They receive between 10-35 poems/week. "We presently do not receive enough formal or witty/ironic pieces. We need a better balance between open and generic forms. We're also interested in critical writings on poems or writing poetry and translations with a bilingual format (permissions from original author)."** As a sample the editor selected these lines from "Within the Womb of This Mountain" by Jenna Fedock:

We will not see him again,
"Lord have mercy,"
but only in the black box wedged in an aisle,
heavy lid crushing our heads. We chant
"Vichnaya pamyat, Vichnaya pamyat, Vichnaya pamyat,"
trying to cast it off—but cannot.

It is handsomely printed, "reserved format," perfect-bound with line drawings and photos. Simply one of the most readable literary magazines published today, *RE:AL* welcomes all styles and forms that display craft, insight and accessibility. Circulation approximately 400, "more than half of which are major college libraries." Subscriptions also in Great Britain, Ireland, Italy, Holland, Puerto Rico, Brazil and Canada. **Sample postpaid: $5. Submit original and copy. "Editors prefer a statement that ms is not being simultaneously submitted; however, this fact is taken for granted when we receive a ms." Writer's guidelines for SASE. They acknowledge receipt of submissions and strive for a 1-month decision. Submissions during summer semesters may take longer. "We will return poems rather than tie them up for more than a one-issue backlog (6-9 months)." Pays copies.** Reviews are assigned, but queries about doing reviews are welcome.

REALITY STREET EDITIONS (V), 4 Howard Court, Peckham Rye, London SE15 3PH United Kingdom, phone (0171)639-7297, e-mail 100344.2546@compuserve.com, is the joint imprint of Reality Studios and Street Editions, editors Ken Edwards and Wendy Mulford. They publish 4 paperbacks/

CLOSE-UP

Editor says opportunities abound in Canberra, Australia

"Writing Poetry"

new laid pavers creak
need sand between cracks
to pack their separateness
broad brooms pushing back and forth
filling   cushioning
then patient hand-brushes
to coax grains between spaces
hourglass trickling
forming a seamless whole

Sally Clarke

Enormous opportunities exist for aspiring poets in Canberra, says Sally Clarke, speaking of Austra-lia's capital, located southwest of Sydney. Clarke, who is managing editor of *Redoubt*, the University of Canberra's semiannual literary magazine, says opportunities for writers include an array of "really good poets giving workshops," regular local readings, a Word Festival every two years (the next is scheduled for March of 1997), and a variety of events sponsored by the Canberra Centre for Writing, which attracts a number of prominent writers.

Clarke herself is deeply involved in Canberra's "very active writing scene." Besides serving as president of the Fellowship of Australian Writers, a cross-continent organization founded in the 1930s, she teaches creative and autobio-graphical writing at the University of the Third Age, an educational institution for seniors—in addition to her role as managing editor of a literary magazine.

That Clarke works on *Redoubt* in a voluntary capacity attests to the "enormous loyalty" the magazine has generated since its debut in January of 1988, 200 years after the arrival of the First Fleet, an important event in Australia's unique literary history. It was the "polite" speech of the military administrators and the more "vulgar" speech of the convicts they transported that combined with "the many dialects of the initial settlers carried here from all over England" to create a distinc-tively Australian "voice" that is evident in poetry and literature, Clarke says.

There is also the country's impressive landscape—"the large island with the arid center"—which insures that "the bush experience is never very far from the poetic expression," although, she admits, "this can be an idealistic realization, considering that many of us live in cities."

Language, landscape, and the commingling of European, Asian, and Aborigi-nal cultures are all important to Australian verse, and Clarke notes that "with all this to draw on, the writing of poetry can only benefit." She says these aspects and others make Australian poetry "applicable to any Western country."

CLOSE-UP, *Clarke*

And Australian writers have found publication outside their homeland.

Clarke's own experience in writing poetry came relatively late in life. In fact, it wasn't until after her children were grown and had children of their own that she returned to the course work she abandoned at 20 to complete a B.A. in Professional Writing with a major in Literary Studies at the University of Canberra (then the Canberra College of Advanced Education). She went on to complete a M.A. in English and has since published two books of history and community writing, in addition to short stories, articles, reviews and, of course, poetry.

Obviously, Clarke does not view age as a barrier. "I know many people who started writing poetry late in their lives. When older, you often have more time, *and* all that life experience to call on. I say, go for it."

Her advice for writers of all ages is "to just keep at it," and she encourages writers to consider attending workshops or joining groups. "It is inspirational to be with like-minded people, but you need a real connection with each other. Find people whose work you admire and whose judgment you trust—and get them to assess some of your work and comment on ways you may improve."

Clarke says it is also important to read what other people are writing and publishing to keep up with what is currently being done. However, it is equally important to "learn to trust your inner voice," to tap in to "the unique, individual, unusual view of life that is especially yours" and then "observe, take time to notice. Once you're in this mode things start to hit you, that is, the small incidents will trigger some comment in your mind. Then you need to disconnect to get at what it is you want to express. Trust your instincts, let your mind wander around the subject. See where the original thought takes you."

At *Redoubt*, Clarke not only seeks work from Australians, but she also encourages submissions from both new and established writers overseas. "A literary magazine such as ours, which declares itself interested in the fresh and the original, has a broad range of material it will consider. We accept work on a continual basis, and it is sent to the editors for assessment. If it is rejected, the author will be advised fairly quickly. If it is being considered for the next issue, there will be a delay in replying."

Presentation, of course, is important. Like most editors, Clarke wants poetry manuscripts neatly typed on good quality, white paper. And, like most *overseas* editors, she recommends sending large enough self-addressed envelopes with International Reply Coupons of sufficient value for responses to inquiries or to have work returned. Final selections for her publication are usually made in March and September for May and November issues, and, at present, the rate of pay for overseas writers is contributor's copies, due to the difficulties of foreign exchange.

While submission details can seem bothersome, they are important to follow. Most important, however, is that you "don't leave your precious work to languish in some bottom drawer," says Clarke. "You need to get your work out there for some evaluation. Bear in mind that it is unlikely that you will ever have a book of your poems published unless you can say that others have considered your work of enough worth to put it in their publications. So, *do* submit."

—*Michelle Moore*

year. They have recently published *Out of Everywhere*, an anthology of innovative poetry by women in North America and the United Kingdom; it is edited by Maggie O'Sullivan and includes Susan Howe, Barbara Guest, Lyn Hejinian, Denise Riley and 26 others. **However, they currently do not accept unsolicited mss.** Their US distributor is Small Press Distribution, 1814 San Pablo Ave., Berkeley CA 94302.

THE RED CANDLE PRESS; CANDELABRUM (II), 9 Milner Rd., Wisbech PE13 2LR England, phone 01945-581067, founded 1970, editor M.L. McCarthy, M.A., administrative editor Helen Gordon, B.A., was "founded to encourage poets working in **traditional-type verse, metrical unrhymed or metrical rhymed.** We're more interested in poems than poets: that is, we're interested in what sort of poems an author produces, not in his or her personality." They publish the magazine, *Candelabrum*, twice yearly (April and October), occasional postcards, paperbound staple-spined chapbooks and occasional poetry leaflets. For all of these they want **"good-quality metrical verse, with rhymed verse specially wanted. Elegantly cadenced free verse is acceptable. No weak stuff (moons and Junes, loves and doves, etc.) No chopped-up prose pretending to be free verse. Any length up to about 50 lines for *Candelabrum*, any subject, including eroticism (but not porn)—satire, love poems, nature lyrics, philosophical—any subject, but nothing racist or sexist."** They have recently published poetry by Andrea Abraham, Leo Yankevich, John Gurney, Ann Keith, M.L. McCarthy and Peter G.P. Thompson. The editors offer these lines by Paul Look as a sample:

> The moon runs down the rivers of its streets,
> Washing all colour from the ones I meet.
> Malicious voices, delicate and slow,
> Reveal the truths I never wished to know.

The digest-sized magazine, staple-spined, small type, exemplifies their intent to "pack in as much as possible, wasting no space, and try to keep a neat appearance with the minimum expense." They get in about 44 pgs. (some 60 poems) in each issue. They receive about 2,000 submissions/year, use approximately 5% of those, sometimes holding over poems for the next year or longer. Circulation: 900 with 700 subscriptions of which 22 are libraries. **Sample: $4 in bills only; checks not accepted. "Submit anytime. IRCs essential for reply and please check the weight if you wish your ms returned. Each poem on a separate sheet please, neat typescripts or neat *legible* manuscripts. *Please* no dark, oily photostats, no colored ink (only black or blue). Author's name and address on each sheet, please." No simultaneous submissions. Reports in about 2 months. Pays 1 contributor's copy.** Occasional reviews of books of poetry. Send books for review consideration. They occasionally publish poetry pamphlets of 12-24 pgs. **"at our invitation to the poet, and at our expense. We pay the author a small royalty-advance, but he/she keeps the copyright."** The editor comments, "Traditional-type poetry is much more popular here in Britain, and we think also in the United States, now than it was in 1970, when we founded *Candelabrum*. We **always welcome new poets, especially traditionalists, and we like to hear from the U.S.A. as well as from here at home.** General tip: Study the various outlets at the library, or buy a copy of *Candelabrum*, or borrow a copy from a subscriber, before you go to the expense of submitting your work. The Red Candle Press regrets that, because of bank charges, it is unable to accept dollar cheques. However, it is always happy to accept U.S. and Canadian dollar bills."

RED CEDAR REVIEW (II), 17C Morrill Hall, Dept. of English, Michigan State University, East Lansing MI 48824, editor Laura Klynstra, founded 1963, is a literary biannual which uses poetry— **"any subject, form, length; the only requirement is originality and vision." The editor encourages work "that shows careful thought and unification of imagery."** They have published poetry by Margaret Atwood, Diane Wakoski, Jim Harrison and Stuart Dybek. As a sample the editor selected these lines from "Late-Night Groceries/Let's Call This The Scarf" by Matthew Thorburn:

> Tells you she's from Italy.
> When she asks where you're from you stretch
> out your hand to make a map of Michigan,
> point to the center of your palm. Here.

ALWAYS include a self-addressed, stamped envelope (SASE) when sending a ms or query to a publisher within your own country. When sending material to other countries, include a self-addressed envelope and International Reply Coupons (IRCs), available for purchase at many post offices.

> She slips off her sandal,
> puts her foot up on the counter.
> I'm from here, *pointing*
> to the show curve of her arch.

The review is 120 pgs., digest-sized. They receive about 500 submissions/year, use 20. Press run is 400 for 200 subscribers of which 100 are libraries. Single copy: $5; subscription: $10. **Sample post-paid: $2.50. Submit up to 4 poems at a time. Submit only previously unpublished works. Simultaneous submissions are discouraged. Reports in 1-4 months. Pays 2 copies. Editor sometimes comments on rejections. Send SASE for submission guidelines.**

RED DANCEFLOOR PRESS (III); RED DANCEFLOOR (V), P.O. Box 4974, Lancaster CA 93539-4974, e-mail dubpoet@aol.com, founded 1989, editor David Goldschlag, publishes full-length books, chapbooks and poetry audiotapes. **"No restrictions on form, length or subject matter. We want poetry that is well thought out—not a first draft. If you send us rhyme it should have a specific purpose and work."** They have recently published poetry by Michael C Ford, Laurel Ann Bogen, Annie Reim and Gary Walton. As a sample the editor selected the poem "Love Songs of The Young Couple, The Dumb Job" by Sean Thomas Daugherty:

> The dreary tumult of rain brightens
> with the sound of you in the shower,
> the lather of soap on your breasts
> I watch as I shave—
> careful not to circumsize my chin!
> Does every weekday morning toll
> toward this? A few joyful minutes
> stretched across years.

He says, The author may want to get a copy of a book, chap or tape before submitting. (Send SAE with first-class stamp for catalog.) **"We openly accept submissions for books, chaps and tapes, but** *please* **query first with 10 samples and a cover letter explaining which area of our press you are interested in. Listing credits in a cover letter is fine, but don't go crazy." Queries and submissions welcome via e-mail.** The press also publishes the magazine, *Red Dancefloor*. However, the magazine has suspended publication until further notice.

RED HERRING POETS; MATRIX; RED HERRING PRESS; RED HERRING CHAPBOOK SERIES; CHANNING-MURRAY FOUNDATION (IV-Membership), 1209 W. Oregon St., Urbana IL 61801, phone (217)344-1176, founded 1975, director of Red Herring Poets Ruth S. Walker. The Red Herring Poets is a workshop that publishes its members' work, after they have attended at least 5 meetings, in their annual magazine, *Matrix*, and, for those who have been members for at least 2 years and given 2 public readings, one chapbook/year.

‡RED OWL MAGAZINE (I, II), 35 Hampshire Rd., Portsmouth NH 03801-4815, phone (603)431-2691, founded 1995, editor Edward O. Knowlton, is a biannual magazine of poetry and b&w art. **"Ideally, poetry here might stress a harmony between nature and industry; add a pinch of humor for spice. Nothing introspective or downtrodden. Sometimes long poems are OK, yet poems which are 10 to 20 lines seem to fit best."** They have recently published poetry by Lyn Lifshin and John Binns. As a sample the editor selected these lines from "Skippy" by Colby Dorian:

> I'm a guest.
> I'm a pest;
> I'll try to rob your nest . . .
> It's the high school head from Harvard High.
> Would you care to smell a pie?

Red Owl is 36 pgs., 8½ × 11, neatly photocopied in a variety of type styles and spiral-bound with a heavy stock cover and b&w art inside. "Out of a few hundred poems received, roughly one third are considered." Press run is 100 for 65 subscribers, 5 shelf sales. Subscription: $20. **Sample (including brief guidelines) postpaid: $10. Makes checks payable to Edward O. Knowlton. Submit 4 poems at a time. No previously published poems or simultaneous submissions. Cover letter preferred. Seldom comments on rejections. Reports in 3 weeks to 3 months. Pays 1 copy.** The editor says, "Try and be bright; hold your head up. Yes, there are hard times in the land of plenty, yet we might try to overshadow them. . . ."

RED RAMPAN' PRESS; RED RAMPAN' REVIEW; RED RAMPAN' BROADSIDE SERIES (V), 4707 Fielder St., Midland TX 79707-2817, phone (915)697-7689, founded 1981, poetry editor Larry D. Griffin. *RRR* is an "eclectic review quarterly." The editor says it is 48-60 pgs., 6×9, with a press run of 300, **"presently not accepting poetry** and only using staff-written reviews."

THE REDNECK REVIEW OF LITERATURE (II, IV-Regional), P.O. Box 0654, Pocatello ID 83204-0654, phone (208)232-4263, founded 1975, editor Penelope Reedy, is a semiannual magazine publishing poetry, fiction, drama and essays **dealing with the contemporary West. The editor wants to see "any form, length or style." She does not want "ethereal ditties about nothing; the obscure."** She has recently published poetry by Jean Toyama, Ford Swetnam and Laurel Speer. As a sample the editor selected these lines from "Breaking Them to Run" by Dave McCain:

> Figure eight them
> because unless
> you cross them up a lot
> they never learn
> to change leads
> under your direction
> without stumbling.

The magazine, which appears in the spring and fall each year, is magazine-sized, offset, perfect-bound, some advertising. Circulation is 500, of which 200 are subscriptions and 100-150 are newsstand sales. **Sample postpaid: $10. Writers should submit "3 poems at a time, letter quality—don't like simultaneous submissions. Please send SASE with *enough* postage to return mss." Criticism is sometimes given. Rejected mss are reported on in 3 months, and no accepted mss are held beyond 3 issues. Publishes theme issues. Send SASE for upcoming themes. Pays 1 copy.** Reviews books of poetry. The editor says, "Rethink what 'the West' means to American culture—as a concept rather than merely a geographical area. Lighten up—share your poems and write a new one tomorrow."

REDOUBT (II), Faculty of Communication, University of Canberra, P.O. Box 1, Belconnen, ACT 2616, Australia, phone 06-201-2945, fax 06-201-5300, founded 1988, managing editor Sally Clarke, is a biannual literary magazine of fiction, poetry, reviews, articles and graphics which publishes new and established writers. **In poetry, they want "the immediate image, the fresh metaphor. Work preferably under 25 lines. No doggerel, long narrative, limerick or other light entertainment."** They have published poetry by Charles Bukowski, Coral Hull and David Linwood. As a sample the editor selected these lines from "Sylvia Plath in a Bikini," a 17-line poem by Kevin Densley:

> "Sylvia Plath in a Bikini"
> —I've had this title in my mind
> for a long time now.
> I got it from a picture
> of (no surprises here!) Sylvia Plath in a bikini,
> a picture I saw whilst flicking through
> a book about her life.

Redoubt is about 130 pgs., approximately 7 × 10, professionally printed and perfect-bound with coated card cover with b&w photo and b&w photos and illustrations inside. They receive about 500 poetry submissions a year, accept about 10%. Press run is 300-400 for 150 subscribers of which 20 are libraries, 50 shelf sales. Single copy: A$8.50; subscription: A$16 posted in Australia, A$20 abroad. **Sample postpaid: A$8. No previously published poems; simultaneous submissions OK. Name on every page. Cover letter with brief bio and SASE (or SAE and IRCs) required. Reads submissions March 1 through November 30 only. Seldom comments on rejections. Send SASE for guidelines; SAE and IRCs if outside Australia. Reports anywhere from 2 weeks to 6 months. Pays $10 Australian and 1 copy. "Because of difficulties with exchange rates and transfer of monies, overseas contributors will be given a one-year subscription in lieu of payment."** Reviews books of poetry in about 500 words. Open to unsolicited reviews. Poets may also send books for review consideration. The editor says, "Keep it short. Aim for a single image. Don't try to be funny unless you are very experienced at humour. Don't send originals and keep copies of everything."

‡REED (II), c/o English Dept., San Jose State University, One Washington Square, San Jose CA 95192-0090, founded 1946, is an annual general literary magazine including SJSU student work, Bay Area work, and work from around the US. **They want "any high quality work. No form or content restrictions. We particularly welcome regional/California/Bay Area material."** They have recently published poetry by Rose Marie Hunold, Lyn Lifshin and Mary Winters. *Reed* is 120 pgs., 5¼ × 8, professionally printed and perfect-bound with 2-color coated card cover and b&w art inside. They receive about 300 poems a year, publish 25-30. Press run is 500. **Submit 3-5 poems at a time. No previously published poems or simultaneous submissions. Reads submissions August 1 through November 1 only. Poems are circulated to an editorial board. Seldom comments on rejections. Reports in November and December. Pays 1 copy.**

REFLECT (IV-Form/style), 3306 Argonne Ave., Norfolk VA 23509, founded 1979, poetry editor W.S. Kennedy. They use **"spiral poetry: featuring an inner-directed concern with sound (euphony), mystical references or overtones, and objectivity—rather than personal and emotional poems. No love poems, pornography, far left propaganda; nothing overly sentimental."** They have published poetry by B.Z. Niditch, Lyn Lifshin, Joe Malone, Ruth Wildes Schuler and Stan Proper. As a sample the editor selected these lines from "April Sashays in Lime Heels" by Edward C. Lynskey:

> April sashays across ashy mews,
> in lime heels and lilac breath,
> swells sappy stalks, and shoos
> winter north, the killing guest.

> Hyacinths blush and daffodils
> blink as a wisp of apple smoke
> curlicues through screens until
> kale yards wakes in a rainy soak.

The quarterly is 48 pgs., digest-sized, saddle-stapled, typescript. Subscription: $8. **Sample postpaid: $2. Submit 4 or 5 poems at a time. All submissions should be *single-spaced* and should fit on one typed page. No previously published poems or simultaneous submissions. Editor sometimes comments on rejections. Guidelines available for SASE. Reports within a month. No backlog. Pays 1 copy to nonsubscribers, 2 copies to subscribing contributors. Acquires first rights.** Occasionally reviews books of poetry in 50 words or more.

RENDITIONS: A CHINESE-ENGLISH TRANSLATION MAGAZINE (IV-Translations), Research Center for Translation, CUHK, Shatin, NT, Hong Kong, editor Dr. Eva Hung, appears twice a year. **"Contents exclusively translations from Chinese, ancient and modern."** They also publish a paperback series of Chinese literature in English translation. They have published translations of the poetry of Gu Cheng, Shu Ting, Mang Ke and Bei Dao. *Renditions* is magazine-sized, 150 pgs., flat-spined, elegantly printed, all poetry with side-by-side Chinese and English texts, using some b&w and color drawings and photos, with glossy card cover. Annual subscription: $20; 2 years: $36; 3 years: $50 (US). **Sample postpaid: $13. Publishes theme issues. Reports in 2 months. Pays "honorarium" plus 2 copies. Use British spelling. They "will consider" book mss, for which they would like a query with sample translations. Books pay 10% royalties plus 10 copies. Mss usually not returned. Editor sometimes comments on rejections.**

REPORT TO HELL (I), P.O. Box 44089, Calabash NC 28467, founded 1993, co-editors P. Saur and M. O'Shaughnessy, appears every 2-3 months and features poetry, stories and essays **"on discontent, misery and angst (plus the occasional glimmer of hope)." They want poetry that is "dark but not necessarily morbid; thoughtful without clichés. Nothing flowery or bland."** They have recently published poetry by Tom Churm, M. Estabrook, John Grey and Ian Griffin. As a sample the editors selected these lines from "deal" by Michael O'Shaughnessy:

> i wished for wings
> and awoke with two, both broken.
> and bleeding gills.

The editors say *RTH* is 40-60 pgs., digest-sized, simple type, photocopied and staple-bound with graphics included. They accept "much" of the poetry received. Press run is 200 for 30 subscribers. Subscription: $10 for 6 issues. **Sample postpaid: $2. Make checks payable to Paul Saur. Previously published poems and simultaneous submissions OK. Cover letter with brief bio required. Often comments on rejections. Reports within 3-4 weeks. Pays 1 copy.** Reviews books of poetry in 100 words or less. Open to unsolicited reviews. Poets may also send books for review consideration. The editors hope to also publish chapbooks in the future.

RESPONSE (IV-Ethnic, students), 27 W. 20th St., 9th Floor, New York NY 10011, phone (212)620-0350, fax (212)929-3459, e-mail response@panix.com, founded 1966, poetry editor Yigal Schleifer, is a "contemporary Jewish review publishing poetry, fiction and essays **by students and young adult authors." The only specification for poetry is that it be on a Jewish theme and have some significant Jewish content.** They have published poetry by Sharon Kessler, Sue Saniel Elkind and Shulamith Bat-Yisrael. As a sample the editor chose these lines from "Old Nazis Don't Die (They Move To South America)" by Sylvia Warsh:

> The jungles of Brazil teem
> with a new strain of
> European animal, serpents of
> such camouflage that their own
> Bavarian mothers would not
> recognize them,
> insects that thrust hard
> consonants into a victim's
> heart and suck him dry,
> then use his shell
> for a livingroom.

They look for "creative, challenging and chutzapadik writing" from young writers. The quarterly is 120 pgs., 6×9, professionally printed on heavy stock, flat-spined, with a glossy "varnished" cover with artwork. Circulation 1,600 with 600 subscribers of which 30% are libraries. 1,000 distributed through bookstores and newsstands. Subscription: $20 ($12 for students); $25 for institutions. **Sample postpaid: $6. Cover letter with bio and previous publications required with submissions.** Time between acceptance and publication is 6 months. **Reports in about 2 months. Pays 2 copies/poem published. Acquires all rights.** Occasionally reviews books of Jewish poetry. Open to unsolicited reviews. Poets may also send books for review consideration.

REVIEW: LATIN AMERICAN LITERATURE AND ARTS (IV-Ethnic, regional, translations), Dept. PM, 680 Park Ave., New York NY 10021, phone (212)249-8950 ext. 366, founded 1967, managing editor Daniel Shapiro, is a biannual magazine which serves as a "major forum for Latin American literature in English translation and articles on Latin American visual and performing arts." **They want contemporary Latin American poetry.** They have published poetry by Jose A. Mazzotti, Mateo Rosas de Oquendo and Gregorio de Matos. As a sample the editor selected these lines from "The Forest" by Mariela Dreyfus, translated from the Spanish by Alfred J. MacAdam:

> Dark, I wander amid the uncertain
> I avoid the traces of the human
> silence is the king in this forest
> here, where only your breath protects me in winter.

It is 100 pgs., 8½×11, with b&w photos of Latin American art. They receive 50-100 submissions, accept the work of 1-2 poets. Press run is 10,000 for 6,000 subscribers of which 500 are libraries. Subscription: $18 for individuals, $27 for institutions, $28 for international. Two-year subscription: $32 for individuals, $52 for institutions, $54 for international. **Sample postpaid: $9. Query before submitting work. Previously published poems and simultaneous submissions OK. Cover letter required. Reports in 2-3 months. Pays $100-300.** Reviews books of poetry by Latin Americans. The *Review* is published by the Americas Society, a not-for-profit organization.

‡REVISTA/REVIEW INTERAMERICANA (IV-Ethnic, regional), Inter-American University of Puerto Rico, Box 5100, San Germán, Puerto Rico 00683, phone (809)264-1912 ext. 7229 or 7230, editor Anibal José Aponte. The *Revista/Review* is a bilingual scholarly journal oriented to **Puerto Rican, Caribbean and Hispanic American and inter-American subjects, poetry, short stories and reviews.** Press run is 750. **Submit at least 5 poems in Spanish or English, blank verse, free verse, experimental, traditional and avant-garde, typed double-spaced. No simultaneous submissions. Cover letter with brief personal data required. Pays 2 copies.** Open to unsolicited reviews. The editor says, "It is very difficult to really get the feel of a poet's merit when only one or two poems are submitted."

RHINO (I), 1808 N. Larrabee, Chicago IL 60614, founded 1976, editors Kay Meier and Don Hoffman, "is an annually published poetry journal. **We seek well-crafted work with fresh insights and authentic emotion by known or new writers, poems which show careful attention to form and contain surprise. Poems no longer than 3 pgs. double-spaced.**" They have published poetry by John Dickson, Marcellus Leonard and Robert Edwards. The editors chose as a sample the opening lines of "Grandma and the Latch-Key Child" by Carol L. Gloor:

> In 1916 my Irish grandma clutches
> her needlepoint satchel on the heaving
> ferry from Ellis Island. She has escaped
> the starched convent, and the wheeling
> seagull air screams fish, sweat and hope.
> She doesn't know in four years she will marry
> the Midwest and a man
> she doesn't love.

Rhino is a 96-page journal, digest-sized, matte card cover with art, offset from typescript on high-quality paper. They receive 1,000 submissions a year, use 50-70. Press run is 300 for 200 subscribers of which 10 are libraries. **Sample: $6 plus $1.30 postage. Submit 3-5 double-spaced poems with $3 reading fee. Submissions are accepted year-round. Decisions are made in late December. Pays 1 copy. Acquires first rights only.**

THE RIALTO (II), 32 Grosvenor Rd., Norwich, Norfolk NR2 2PZ England, founded 1984, poetry editors John and Rhiannon Wakeman, want **"poetry of intelligence, wit, compassion, skill, excellence, written by humans. We seek poetry that works in its own terms, regardless of form or subject. Potential contributors are strongly advised to read *The Rialto* before submitting."** They have recently published poetry by Simon Armitage, Carol Ann Duffy, Peter Redgrove, Hans Magnus Enzensberger, Les Murray and Jenny Joseph. As a sample the editors selected these lines from "Lyric" by the late Frank Redpath:

Something is happening that never, ever,
Happened to anyone before, he thought.
This is the moment when the sudden river
Breaks through the rocks to flow and end the drought.
  Sitting straight-backed upon the bedside chair,
  She took pins from her lips and fixed her hair. . . .

The Rialto, which appears 3 times a year, is 48 pgs., magazine-sized, saddle-stapled, beautifully printed on glossy stock with glossy b&w card cover, using b&w drawings. "U.S.A. subscription is now £16. **Single issue to U.S.A. is £6 sterling. Payment in sterling only." Submit up to 6 poems with SAE and IRCs. No simultaneous submissions or previously printed poetry. Editor "only rarely" comments on rejections. Reports within 3 months. Pays £10/poem.** *The Rialto* has been called "the poets' choice" among U.K. literary magazines and has received a special grant for "excellence" from the Arts Council of Great Britain. Also, a *The Rialto* selection, Jenny Joseph's poem "In Honor of Love," won the Forward Prize for best individual poem of 1995. The editors add, "We would like to receive more poetry that confronts contemporary political issues with compassion and art, without hysteria."

RIO GRANDE PRESS; SE LA VIE WRITER'S JOURNAL (I, IV-Themes), P.O. Box 71745, Las Vegas NV 89170, founded 1987, editor Rosalie Avara. *Se La Vie Writer's Journal* is a quarterly journal with articles and cartoons about poetry and writing and monthly contests in poetry and quarterly contests in poetry, essays and short stories. Prizes are $5-25 for poems, entry fee $5 for 3 poems. Publishes 70% of mss received/quarter, **"dedicated to encouraging novice writers, poets and artists; we are interested in original, unpublished mss that reflect the 'life' theme (La Vie). Poems are judged on originality, clarity of thought and ability to evoke emotional response."** They have recently published poetry by Marian Ford Park, Robert Gaurnier and Angie Monneus. *SLVWJ* is 64 pgs., digest-sized, photocopied from typescript, with blue cover, saddle-stapled. **Sample postpaid: $4. Publishes theme issues. Send SASE for guidelines and upcoming themes.** Staff reviews books of poetry. Send books for review consideration. Also publishes several poetry/short story anthologies annually. "No fee or purchase necessary to enter contests and be published." Cash prizes. Send SASE for guidelines.

RIVELIN GRAPHEME PRESS (II), The Annexe Kennet House, 19 High St., Hungerford, Berkshire RG170NL England, founded 1984, poetry editor Snowdon Barnett, publishes **only poetry. Query first with biographical information, previous publications and a photo, if possible. If invited, send book-length manuscript, typed, double-spaced, photocopy OK. Payment is 20 copies of first printing up to 2,000, then 5% royalties on subsequent printings.**

RIVER CITY; HOHENBERG AWARD (II), English Dept., Memphis State University, Memphis TN 38152, phone (901)678-2651, founded 1980, editor Dr. Paul Naylor. *River City* publishes fiction, poetry, interviews and essays. Contributors have included John Updike, Marvin Bell, Philip Levine, Maxine Kumin, Robert Penn Warren, W.D. Snodgrass, Mary Oliver, Fred Busch, Beth Bentley, Mona Van Duyn and Peter Porter. The biannual is 100 pgs., 6×9, perfect-bound, professionally printed with two-color matte cover. Publishes 40-50 pgs. of poetry in each issue. Circulation 1,000. Subscription: $9. **Sample postpaid: $5. Submit no more than 5 poems at a time. Does not send mss June through August. Reports in 2-12 weeks. Pays 2 copies (and cash when grant funds available).** The $100 Hohenberg Award is given annually to the best fiction or poetry selected by the staff. Poetry published here has also been included in *The Best American Poetry 1996*.

‡**RIVER OAK REVIEW (II)**, P.O. Box 3127, Oak Park IL 60303, founded 1993, is a biannual literary magazine publishing high quality short fiction, creative nonfiction and poetry. **Regarding work, they say, "quality is primary, but we probably wouldn't publish poems longer than 100 lines or so."** They have recently published poetry by Phil Dacey, Kathleen Norris, Mary Swander and Stuart Friebert. *ROR* is 112 pgs., 6×9, neatly printed and perfect-bound with 2-color glossy card cover with b&w art. They receive 1,500-2,500 poems a year, publish 1-2%. Press run is 1,000 for 500 subscribers, 200 shelf sales. Single copy: $6; subscription: $12. **Sample postpaid: $5. Make checks payable to River Oak Arts. Submit 4 poems at a time. No previously published poems; simultaneous submissions OK if notified. Cover letter preferred. Poems are circulated to readers, then an editorial board, then the editor. Seldom comments on rejections. Send SASE for guidelines. Reports in 3 months.**

✝ **THE DOUBLE DAGGER** before a listing indicates that the listing is new in this edition. New markets are often the most receptive to submissions.

Always sends prepublication galleys. Pays $10-25 and 2 copies. Buys first North American serial rights. They also sponsor a poetry contest in December with an award of $500. Send SASE for guidelines. The editor says, "Our advice? Read literary magazines; read new poetry books; only submit if it's excellent."

RIVER STYX MAGAZINE; BIG RIVER ASSOCIATION (II), 3207 Washington Ave., St. Louis MO 63103-1218, founded 1975, senior editors Michael Castro and Quincy Troupe, editor Richard Newman, is "an international, multicultural journal publishing both award-winning and previously undiscovered writers. We feature poetry, short prose, interviews, fine art and photography." They want **"excellent poetry—original, energetic and well-crafted."** They have recently published work by Marilyn Hacker, Gary Soto, Rita Dove, Allen Ginsberg, Yusef Komunyakaa, Maura Stanton and Joy Harjo. As a sample the editor selected these lines from "Talking to a Writer" by Lucinda Roy:

> O, she said, if only we were virgins!
> Mountains would arch beneath us like the vertebrae of cats,
> our mouths would reveal our tongues, naked as peeled
> bananas, and the sweet museum of our sheets
> would convene delight!

River Styx appears 3 times a year. The editor describes it as 70-100 pgs., with color cover. They accept less than 5% of 3,000 mss received a year. **Sample postpaid: $7. Submit 3-5 poems at a time, "legible copies with name and address on each page." Reading period is May 1 through November 30. Guidelines available for SASE. Editor sometimes comments on rejections. Reports in 3-5 months, publication within a year. Pays 2 copies. Buys one-time rights.** Poetry published in *River Styx* has been selected for inclusion in the 1994 and 1996 volumes of *The Best American Poetry* and *Best of The Small Presses*.

RIVERRUN (II), Glen Oaks Community College, Centreville MI 49032-9719, founded 1974, poetry editor David Bainbridge, is a literary biannual, using **30-40 magazine-sized pages of poetry in each issue—"no prejudices. We try to give each issue its own distinct, admittedly subjective personality. Best bet is to see the attitude and themes portrayed in the most recent guidelines."** As a sample the editor selected these opening lines from "One That Will Do to Swell a Progress" by Robert R. Hentz:

> Our game over, we were ready to go
> When he said, "It's discouraging to know
> That you are mediocre and will never do
> Anything of extraordinary value
> Like the composer who knows in his heart
> He is no Beethoven or Mozart."

They receive 1,000 poems/month, use up to 240/year. Press run is 850. **Sample postpaid: $5. Submit 3-6 poems at a time. Previously published poems and simultaneous submissions OK. Publishes theme issues. Send SASE for upcoming themes. Reports ASAP (usually 2 weeks to 1 month). Pays 1 copy.** The editor says, "We proudly publish an extremely broad range of individuals well-known to small press circles and beyond (for instance, t. Winter-Damon, Bruce Boston, Stuart Friebert, Tom Riley, Lyn Lifshin and Denise Dumars), but we also pride ourselves on devoting occasional space to local poets and as-yet-unpublished poets."

RIVERSIDE QUARTERLY (II, IV-Science fiction/fantasy), Box 12085, San Antonio TX 78212, phone (210)734-5424, founded 1964, editor Leland Sapiro, poetry editor Sheryl Smith **(and submissions should go directly to her at 515 Saratoga #2, Santa Clara CA 95050)**. *Riverside Quarterly* is **"aimed at the literate reader of science fiction and fantasy. If you've been reared on 'Startrek,' then *RQ* is not for you. We have no specific subject matter or style preferences. Length: 50 lines maximum. No didactic or 'uplifting' verse."** They have published poetry by George Gott, Sue Saniel Elkind, Julia Thomas, Edward Mycue and Denise Dumars. As a sample the editor selected these lines from "Ymir's Mirror/Eiseley's Glass" by Ace Pilkington:

> From the skull in the stone
> Eye sockets scrape the sky:
> Both are wayward worlds
> Aglint with stars.
> Black, bleak caverns
> Where the lightning grows

RQ is 68 pgs., approximately 5×8, offset, saddle-stapled with paper cover and b&w art. They receive about 1,100 poems a year, accept approximately 3%. Press run is 1,200 for 550 subscribers of which 200 are libraries. Subscription: $8. **Sample postpaid: $2.50. No previously published poems or simultaneous submissions. Cover letter recommended.** Time between acceptance and publication is 15 months. **Usually comments on rejections. Reports in 10 days. Always sends prepublication galleys. Pays 4 copies. Acquires all rights; rights released to contributor after publication.** "We print reviews of books, movies and magazines—no maximum length." They say, "We advise all contributors (of poetry or prose) to read a copy or two (available at any major public or college library) before sending a ms."

RIVERSTONE, A PRESS FOR POETRY (II), 1184A MacPherson Dr., West Chester PA 19380-3814, founded 1992, publishes 1 or 2 chapbooks a year through an annual contest. They have published chapbooks by Gia Hansbury, Jefferson Carter, Marcia Hurlow and Cathleen Calbert. As a sample the editor selected these lines from Calbert's "When Forever Began":

> He's leaning to me and gently whispering, "dear,
> I love you madly," and I'm thinking, why that?
> Wanting to be loved sanely for a change,
> wishing I could stop writing fragments to friends
> in a strange, rhythmic scrawl: I am crazy about him.
> We're mad for each other. Can you get me out of here?

That's from the chapbook *My Summer as a Bride*, which won the 1995 Riverstone Poetry Chapbook Award. It is 28 pgs., digest-sized, attractively printed on 80 lb. paper and hand-sewn with dark red endleaves and a grey card stock cover with matching dark red ink. **To be considered for the contest, submit $8 reading fee and chapbook ms of 20-24 pgs., "including poems in their proposed arrangement, title page, contents and acknowledgments." Previously published poems OK. Include 6×9 SASE for notification and copy of the winning chapbook. Send SASE for guidelines. Contest deadline: June 30 postmark. Winner receives publication, 50 author's copies and a cash prize when possible (in 1996 it was $100).** Sample chapbooks can be ordered from the press for $5 postpaid.

RIVERWIND (II, IV-Regional), General Studies, Hocking College, Nelsonville OH 45764, phone (614)753-3591 ext. 2363, founded 1982, poetry editor J.A. Fuller, is a literary annual publishing **mainly writers from Appalachia.** In addition, one feature poet is published in each issue with a selection of 10-15 poems. They want **"work from serious writers. We are most open to work with serious content, though humor may be the vehicle. Do not want to see poetry from those who view it as a 'hobby.' We have not published limericks."** They have published poetry by Naton Leslie, Gloria Ruth, Charles Semones, John Aber and Greg Anderson. As a sample the editor selected these lines from "Scrub Pines" by Amy Newman:

> Seasons are full of it:
> the buds return in a time they call
> particular to a tree
> or out of their dirt in the pushing green
> a silent child in a corner.

Riverwind is 80-120 pgs., 7×7, flat-spined, offset, with 2-color semiglossy card cover. Of 500 poems received they accept approximately 60. Press run is 500. Single copy: $2.50. **Sample back issue postpaid: $1. Submit 3-5 poems at a time. No previously published poems or simultaneous submissions. Reads submissions September 15 through June 15 only. Submissions received after June 15 will be considered for the following year. Reports in 1-4 months. Pays 2 copies.** Reviews books of poetry.

ROCKET PRESS (II), P.O. Box 672, Water Mill NY 11976-0672, e-mail rocketusa@delphi.com (don't send poems by e-mail), founded 1993, editor Darren Johnson, features "styles and forms definitely for the 21st century." **The editor wants "experimental and eccentric poetry and original ideas expressed in 'a true voice.' I don't want to see hero worship-type poems that drop names. Don't use the words 'poem,' 'love' or 'ode.' "** They have recently published poetry by Ben Ohmart, Albert Huffstickler and Cheryl Townsend. As a sample the editor selected poem "The Bovine Photograph" by Brandon Freels:

> At the art museum
> we both stood in front of the
> bovine photograph.
>
> "It's sexy," Kris said.
> "I think it's just a sexy photo!"
>
> "Look at those thighs!"
> Someone in the background
> mumbled.
>
> "You know,"
> I said. "It is kind of sexy."

Rocket Press is a newspaper tabloid, 20 pgs., professionally printed, with a circulation over 2,000. They receive about 1,000 poems a year, accept 1-2%. Press run is 2,000 for 200 subscribers of which

2 are libraries, 400 shelf sales. Subscription: $5. **Sample postpaid: $1.50. Submit 3 poems at a time. No previously published poems; simultaneous submissions OK.** Time between acceptance and publication is 3 months to 1 year. **Often comments on rejections. "Subscribers get fuller critiques." Reports in less than 3 months. Pays 1 copy. Acquires one-time rights.** Editor includes his own blurb reviews "of anything cool." Send books for review consideration. They also sponsor an annual poetry competition. Submit 3 poems with SASE and $1 reading fee. Deadline: September 1. The editor says, "Poets are a lot better at buying samples than fiction writers and it's probably more important for a poet to see what's contemporary, what's 'out there.' You can't write 'modern' poetry while only reading Yeats. Poetry is ever-changing."

THE ROCKFORD REVIEW; ROCKFORD WRITERS' GUILD (I, II), P.O. Box 858, Rockford IL 61105, founded 1971, editor David Ross, is a publication of the Rockford Writers' Guild which appears 3 times/year, **publishing their poetry and prose, that of other writers throughout the country and contributors from other countries.** *RR* seeks experimental or traditional poetry of up to 50 lines. **"We look for the magical power of the words themselves, a playfulness with language in the creation of images and fresh insights on old themes, whether it be poetry, satire or fiction."** They have published poetry by Russell King, David Koenig and Christine Swanberg. As a sample the editor selected these lines by Olivia Diamond:

> *The chill will nip us all in the end*
> *even fragile stems we brace in vases.*
> *The tips of petals curl in and bend*
> *toward the ground in stiff embraces.*

TRR is 50 pgs., digest-sized, flat-spined, glossy cover with b&w photos. Circulation is 750. Single copy: $5; subscription: $15 (3 issues plus the Guild's monthly newsletter, *Write Away*). **Considers simultaneous submissions. Reports in 4-6 weeks. Pays 1 copy. Acquires first North American serial rights.** They offer Editor's Choice Prizes of $25 for prose, $25 for poetry each issue. The Rockford Writers' Guild is a nonprofit, tax-exempt corporation established "to encourage, develop and nuture writers and good writing of all kinds and to promote the art of writing in the Rockford area." They offer lectures by Midwest authors, editors and publishers, and workshops. Membership: $25/year. Write for further information.

ROCKY MOUNTAIN REVIEW OF LANGUAGE AND LITERATURE (IV-Membership, translations), Boise State University English Dept., Boise ID 83725, phone (208)385-1233, fax (208)385-4373, e-mail aaswidma@idbsu.idbsu.edu, founded 1947, editor Jan Widmayer, poetry editor Marcia Southwick. **Contributors to the literary quarterly must be members of Rocky Mountain Modern Language Association. Poetry should be "generally relatively short" and may be in English or other modern languages.** The review has published poetry by Scott P. Sanders and David Faldet and translations of Antonio Cisneros, David Huerta and Viktor Bokov. As a sample we selected these lines from "Bitches on the Bright Side" by Constance Merritt:

> *Say what you will, there's something to be said*
> *For desperate calls unanswered, meals alone,*
> *Keeping corners, and lying late in bed.*
>
> *For bodies over-full but seldom nourished,*
> *For cold and rain that's carried in the bone.*
> *Say what you will, there's something to be said*

The 224-page, 6×9, flat-spined semiannual publishes work of interest to college and university teachers of literature and language. Circulation of the review is 1,100-1,200, all membership subscriptions. They accept a few ads from other journals and publishers. **Contributors are not paid and do not receive extra copies; contributors must be RMMLA members. Poets should submit 2 copies, *without author's name.*** **They report on submissions in 1-2 months and publish usually within 6 months but no more than 1 year after acceptance.**

‡ROLLING PENNY REVIEW (I), P.O. Box 42, Woodbury CT 06798, founded 1994, editor C.W. Strode, appears "as often as possible." **They want both experimental and traditional work— "anything well-crafted with an emphasis on image and metaphor. No hate messages."** The editor says *RPR* is 10 pgs., digest-sized and saddle-stapled, with 20 lb. bond cover. They also do occasional broadsheets. They receive 1,000 poems a year, accept 30-50%. Press run is 10-100. Submit 3 poems at a time. Previously published poems and simultaneous submissions OK. Cover letter preferred, "can be informal." Time between acceptance and publication is 6 months. **Often comments on rejections. Also offers criticism for a fee (hourly rate). Publishes theme issues. Send SASE for guidelines and upcoming themes. Reports in 3 months. Pays 1 copy. Acquires one-time rights.** Occasionally includes short reviews of other small press magazines. The editor says, "Donations are encouraged— art is meant to be shared, but it must be supported." As for writing, he says, "Be yourself. Listen to your own voice. Become a student and let your desire be a motivation."

THE ROMANTIST (IV-Fantasy), Saracinesca House, 3610 Meadowbrook Ave., Nashville TN 37205, phone (615)834-5069, poetry editor Steve Eng, founded 1977, is an "irregular literary magazine of nonfiction articles on fantasy, imaginative and romantic literature, using **lyrical poetry—prefer fantasy content. No homespun, gushy, trite verse with forced rhyme.**" They have published poetry by Donald Sidney-Fryer, Joey Froehlich, Stephanie Stearns and Margo Skinner. The editor says *The Romantist* is 100-152 pgs., magazine-sized, letterpress or offset, perfect-bound with b&w illustrations and ads. Press run is 300 numbered copies for 150 subscriptions of which 30 are libraries. **Sample postpaid: $15. Submit no more than 3 poems at a time, double-spaced. No previously published poems or simultaneous submissions. Cover letter required.** Time between acceptance and publication may be as long as 2-3 years. **Editor sometimes comments on rejections. Reports in 1 month. Contributors may purchase a copy for 50% of its price. Acquires all rights.** Open to unsolicited reviews. Poets may also send books for review consideration. The editor says, "Too much contemporary poetry is easy to write and hard to read. We resist the depressed, carefully jaded tone so often fashionable. We prefer lyric verse that reflects some knowledge of traditions of poetry, though we do not require the slavish adherence to any school."

RONSDALE PRESS (II, IV-Regional), 3350 W. 21st Ave., Vancouver, British Columbia V6S 1G7 Canada, founded 1988, director Ronald B. Hatch, publishes 3 flat-spined paperbacks of poetry/year—**by Canadian poets only—classical to experimental**. They have published *Phantoms in the Ark* by A.F. Moritz, *Two Shores/Deux rives* by Thuong Vuong-Riddick, and *Burning Stone* by Zoë Landale. As a sample the director selected these lines from "The Process" in *The Edge of Time* by Robin Skelton:

> *Begin with listening—the voice*
> *elsewhere and here, a gleam of brown,*
> *its movements fluent and its flying leaps*
> *the sudden judgement of a heart in shock*
> *at precipices we'd not thought to find.*

Query first, with sample poems and cover letter with brief bio and publication credits. Previously published poems and simultaneous submissions OK. Often comments on rejections. Replies to queries in 2 weeks, to mss in 2 months. Pays 10% royalties and 10 author's copies. Write for catalog to purchase sample books. The director adds, "Confessional poetry or even first-person poetry is very difficult to write well."

ROOM OF ONE'S OWN (II, IV-Women), P.O. Box 46160 Station D, Vancouver, British Columbia V6J 5G5 Canada, founded 1975, is a quarterly using **"poetry by and about women, written from a feminist perspective. Nothing simplistic, clichéd. Short fiction also accepted."** It is 128 pgs., digest-sized. Press run is 1,000 for 420 subscribers of which 50-100 are libraries, 350 shelf sales. Subscription: $20 ($30 US or foreign). **Sample: $7 plus postage or IRCs. "We prefer to receive 5-6 poems at a time, so we can select a pair or group."** Include bio note. **No simultaneous submissions. The mss are circulated to a collective, which "takes time." Publishes theme issues. Send SASE or SAE with 1 IRC for guidelines and upcoming themes. Reports in 6 months. Pays honorarium plus 2 copies. Buys first North American serial rights.** "We solicit reviews." Send books for review consideration, attn. book review editor.

ROSEBUD (II, IV-Themes), P.O. Box 459, Cambridge WI 53523, phone (608)423-9690, founded 1993, editor Rod Clark, is an attractive quarterly "for people who enjoy writing." The editor says it is "a writer's feast for the eye, ear and heart" which has rotating themes/departments. **They want contemporary poetry with "strong images, real emotion, authentic voice; well crafted, literary quality. No inspirational verse."** As a sample we selected these lines from "Silk" by Anne Giles Rimbey:

> *I would write a letter to a lover today*
> *on apricot paper with a cream fountain pen.*
> *I pretend I am curled in a quilt of dark wool*
> *and lean against the window. Raindrops like moonstones*
> *leak down the pane. I tell a tale in velvet lines*
> *of yellow flames and turquoise silk scarves, sandalwood*
> *and drums. For you, I dance soft dances on skin rugs.*

Rosebud is 128 pgs., 7×10, offset printed and perfect-bound with duotone coated card cover, art, graphics and ads. They receive about 700 poems a year, accept approximately 10%. Press run is 6,000 for 1,500 subscribers of which 300 are libraries, 4,000 shelf sales. Subscription: $19. **Sample postpaid: $6.50. Submit 3-5 poems at a time. Previously published poems and simultaneous submissions OK. Often comments on rejections. Send SASE for guidelines and explanation of themes/departments. Reports in 10 weeks. Pays $45/piece and 2 copies. Buys one-time rights.** Each year they also award 3 prizes of $150 for work published in the magazine. The editor says, "We are seeking stories, articles, profiles and poems of love, alienation, travel, humor, nostalgia and unexpected revelation. And something has to 'happen' in the pieces we choose."

THE ROUND TABLE: A JOURNAL OF POETRY AND FICTION (II), P.O. Box 18673, Rochester NY 14618, phone (716)244-0623, founded 1984, poetry editors Alan Lupack and Barbara Lupack. "We publish a journal of poetry and fiction. **However, we are publishing more chapbooks which substitute for our regular issues of** *TRT.* **Virtually all of our publications focus on the Arthurian legends. Few restrictions on poetry—except high quality. We like forms if finely crafted. Very long poems must be exceptional.**" They have published poetry by Kathleene West, John Tagliabue, Wendy Mnookin and Paul Scott. *The Round Table*, now published irregularly, is 64 pgs., digest-sized, perfect-bound, professionally printed (offset) with matte card cover. Circulation is 125 for 75 subscribers of which 3 are libraries. Subscription: $7.50. **Sample postpaid: $5. "We like to see about 5 poems at a time (but we read whatever is submitted)." Cover letter required. Simultaneous submissions OK. "But we expect to be notified if a poem submitted to us is accepted elsewhere. Quality of poetry, not format, is most important thing. We try to report in 3 months, but—especially for poems under serious consideration—it may take longer." Pays copies.** "Some years we will publish a volume of Arthurian poetry by one author."

‡**ROUTE ONE; MEMO (I)**, P.O. Box 1375, Mendocino CA 95460, founded 1991, poetry editor William James Kovanda. *Route One* is the centerfold of *Memo*, a bimonthly springboard for writers. The editor says, **"Essentially, I am moved by free form verse. However, I accept other versification if the residual effect of the piece produces thought provocation."** He has recently published poetry by Del Reitz, John Brander, Esther Leiper and Richard Weekley. *Memo* is a tabloid paper covering "politics, religion, various gripes, wishes, sexual matters, hates and loves. We are open to all forms of writing, but poetry is only published in *Route One*." The editor says he receives 250-600 poems a year and accepts 20-25 poems each issue. Press run is 7,000, most distributed free. Subscription: $30. **Sample postpaid: $2.50. Submit 5 poems at a time** *with $3 reading fee.* **Previously published poems and simultaneous submissions OK. Often comments on rejections. Occasionally publishes theme issues. Send SASE for guidelines and upcoming themes. Reports in 2-4 weeks. Generally pays 2 copies. If 3 or more poems are accepted, pays $10 and 2 copies. Or, if a "Featured Poet," pays $20. Buys one-time rights.** The editor says, "Don't buy into any literary scene. Fads in anything come and go but originality stays. Your development as a writer comes from sticking to a plan and working out the kinks. This takes years, sometimes a lifetime. Remember, always be yourself, never a slave to what's hot and what's not. Keep this in mind: Reading is essential."

‡**THE RUGGING ROOM; RUGGING ROOM BULLETIN (IV-Specialized: rug hooking/ fiber arts)**, 10 Sawmill Dr., Westford MA 01886-2236, founded as a press in 1983, periodical in 1987, poetry editor Jeanne H. Fallier, publisher of "how-to books **related to traditional rug hooking and related subjects of interest to people in fiber crafts." Verses of a philosophical theme or concerning nature are acceptable if they refer to hand works, wool or fibers, the therapeutic value of hand-made fiber crafts, etc. They accept "very short poems related to fiber arts (especially hooking) crafts—not more than ½ page." Want more traditional forms.** They have recently published poetry by Paula Richards and B. Kim Meyer. The *Rugging Room Bulletin* is a newsletter, 8-16 pgs., 8½×11, appearing 4 times a year, printed on white stock, with b&w illustrations, ads and graphics. Circulation 300 but widespread, coast to coast. Subscription: $12; $15 Canadian (in US funds). **Sample postpaid: $2.50. Simultaneous submissions OK. Cover letter explaining what inspired your poem required. Publishes theme issues. Send SASE for upcoming themes. Reports within about 2 weeks. Pays 3 copies plus 1-year subscription. Contributors are also expected to buy 1 copy. Acquires all rights. Returns rights after publication, by arrangement.** Staff reviews related books of poetry. Send books for review consideration.

THE RUNAWAY SPOON PRESS (I, IV-Form), Box 3621, Port Charlotte FL 33949-3621, phone (941)629-8045, founded 1987, editor Bob Grumman, is a "photocopy publisher of chapbooks of otherstream poetry & illumagery." He publishes **"visual poetry, textual poetry mixed with visual matter, verbo-visual collages, infra-verbal poetry and burning poodle poetry. No work in which politics is more important than aesthetics. Standard free-verse is way too traditional for my press."** He has recently published the following books of poetry: *Text Blocks* by John Byrum and *dislimitation* by Arue Rautenberg. As a sample the editor selected this passage by Jake Berry:

> beyond
> Hyperion,
> Hydrogen
>
> *"meet me with*
> *gold*
> Monday at dawn"

The books are usually about $4 \times 5\frac{1}{2}$, printed on good stock with matte card covers. He prints about 10 a year averaging 48 pgs. **Simultaneous submissions and previously published poems OK. Editor comments on submissions "always." Sometimes sends prepublication galleys. Pays 25% of first edition of 100. Acquires all rights. Releases rights to author(s) upon publication. Sample books available for $3 apiece.** The editor says, "If you show me in your cover letter that you've read at least *one* of the poets I've published, it'll be a huge plus for you."

RURAL HERITAGE (I, IV-Rural, humor), 281 Dean Ridge Lane, Gainesboro TN 38562-5039, phone (615)268-0655, founded 1975, editor Gail Damerow, **uses poetry related to draft animal power, livestock, rural living, Americana. "Traditional meter and rhyme only. Poems must have touch of humor or other twist. Please, no comparisons between country and city life and no religious, political or issues-oriented material."** As a sample the editor selected this poem, "He Should've Bought a Horse," by John M. Floyd:

> An old Kansas farmer named Ben
> Had a mule kick him square in the chin.
> As he whipped out his gun,
> He saw three mules, not one,
> And the middle one kicked him again.

RH is magazine-sized, bimonthly, using b&w photos, graphics and ads, 4-6 poems/issue. Circulation 3,000. Subscription: $19. **Sample postpaid: $6. Submit no more than 3 poems at a time, one/page. "Previously published poems are OK if we are told where and when. Simultaneous submissions must be withdrawn before we publish."** Time between acceptance and publication is 4-6 months. "We often group poems by theme, for example gardening, threshing and so forth according to season. Verse may also be coupled with an article of similar theme such as maple sugaring, mule teams, etc." **Publishes theme issues. Theme for January 1997 is Winter (deadline October 1); March 1997 is Spring Planting (deadline December 1). Send SASE for guidelines. Reports ASAP. Pays on publication, $5 and up (depending on length) and 2 copies.** The editor says, "We receive too much modern poetry, not enough traditional, not enough humor. We get too much image poetry (we prefer action) and most poems are too long—we prefer 12 lines or less."

SACHEM PRESS (II, IV-Translations, bilingual), P.O. Box 9, Old Chatham NY 12136-0009, founded 1980, editor Louis Hammer, a small press publisher of poetry and fiction, both hardcover and flat-spined paperbacks. **No new submissions, only statements of projects, until January 1997. Submit mss January through March.** The editor wants to see **"strong, compelling, even visionary work, English-language or translations."** He has published poetry by Cesar Vallejo, Yannis Ritsos, 24 leading poets of Spain (in an anthology), Miltos Sahtouris and himself. As a sample, he selected the following lines from his book *Poetry at the End of the Mind*:

> If the only paper you had
> was the flesh on your back
> between your shoulder blades
> what would you write
> with the motion of your body?

The paperbacks average 120 pgs. and the anthology of Spanish poetry contains 340 pgs. Each poem is printed in both Spanish and English, and there are biographical notes about the authors. The small books cost $6.95 and the anthology $11.95. **Royalties are 10% maximum, after expenses are recovered, plus 50 author's copies. Rights are negotiable.** Book catalog is free "when available," and poets can purchase books from Sachem "by writing to us, $33\frac{1}{3}$% discount."

ST. ANDREW PRESS (IV-Religious), P.O. Box 329, Big Island VA 24526, fax (804)299-5949, founded 1986, poetry editor Ray Buchanan, is a "small press publisher of religious material (worship materials, lyrics and music, etc.), **specializing in meditations, lifestyle, church renewal, spirituality, hunger, peace and justice issues." Any form or style up to 64 lines on subjects listed. "No profanity for shock value only; no sickeningly sweet idealism."** They say they will publish 1-2 chapbooks and flat-spined paperbacks, averaging 64 pgs., each year. They have recently published *Silence and the Gift* by Richard Beale. **Submit 4-6 samples, bio, other publications. Simultaneous and fax submissions and previously published poems OK. Reports in 2-4 weeks. Payment is usually $10 minimum, averages more.** The editor says, "We are looking forward to doing more with poetry in the next couple of years. The amount we do will be largely determined by quality of submissions we receive. Poetry is not accepted if it is too 'sing-song' with trite rhymes, if it could be rewritten in paragraphs as prose, or if it is so 'stream-of-consciousness' that no one could possibly follow the thought or get any meaning from it."

ST. ANTHONY MESSENGER (IV-Religious), 1615 Republic St., Cincinnati OH 45210-1298, phone (513)241-5615, is a monthly 56-page magazine, circulation 325,000, for Catholic families, mostly with children in grade school, high school or college. In some issues, they have a **poetry page**

which uses poems appropriate for their readership. Their poetry needs are limited but poetry submissions are always welcomed. As a sample here is "A Valentine for Darby" by Jean M. Syed:

> Why do I love you, my potbellied love?
> Not for your pregnant form or shiny pate.
> Were these on tender those decades ago,
> would I have been so indiscriminate
> as to let you win my heart? No princess
> from passion ever took a frog to mate.

"Submit seasonal poetry (Christmas/Easter/nature poems) several months in advance. Submit a few poems at a time; do not send us your entire collection of poetry. We seek to publish accessible poetry of high quality." Send regular SASE for guidelines and 9 × 12 SASE for free sample. Pays $2/line on acceptance. Buys first North American serial rights. *St. Anthony Messenger* poetry occasionally receives awards from the Catholic Press Association Annual Competition.

ST. JOSEPH MESSENGER AND ADVOCATE OF THE BLIND (I, IV-Religious), 541 Pavonia Ave., P.O. Box 288, Jersey City NJ 07303, founded 1898, poetry editor Sister Ursula Maphet, C.S.J.P, is semiannual, (16 pgs., 8 × 11). They want **"brief but thought-filled poetry; do not want lengthy and issue-filled."** Most of the poets they have used are previously unpublished. They receive 400-500 submissions/year, use 50. There are about 2 pgs. of poetry in each issue. Circulation 18,000. Subscription: $5. **Editor sometimes comments on rejections. Publishes theme issues. Send SASE for guidelines, free sample and upcoming themes. Reports within 2 weeks. Pays $5-20/poem and 2 copies.**

ST. MARTIN'S PRESS, 175 Fifth Ave., New York NY 10010. Prefers not to share information.

SALMON RUN PRESS (III), P.O. Box 231081, Anchorage AK 99523-1081, founded 1991, editor/publisher John E. Smelcer, publishes 2-3 books/year. They want **"quality poetry by established poets, any subject, any style. No poetry that is not representative of the highest achievement in the art."** They have recently published Galway Kinnell, Ursula K. Le Guin, X.J. Kennedy, John Haines, Molly Peacock, Denise Levertov and Denise Duhamel. As a sample the editor selected these lines from Kinnell's "The Burn":

> Twelve years ago I came here
> to wander across burnt land,
> I had only begun to know
> the kind of pain others endure,
> I was too full of sorrows.

Their books are flat-spined and professionally printed on heavy, natural-colored paper. **Query first with sample poems and cover letter with brief bio. Previously published poems and simultaneous submissions OK. Usually comments on rejections. Replies to queries within 1-3 weeks, to mss in 1-2 months. Pays 10% royalties, sometimes advances and a negotiable number of author's copies.** They also sponsor a pamphlet series ("by invitation only") and an annual poetry contest for book-length mss of 48-96 pgs. $10 reading fee and SASE required. Entries must be postmarked by December 30. The winning ms will be published in book form and nationally distributed.

SALT LICK; SALT LICK FOUNDATION, INC.; SALT LICK PRESS; SALT LICK SAMPLERS; LUCKY HEART BOOKS (II), B416-Riggecrest, 1900 Hwy. 6 West, Waco TX 76712, phone (817)741-9144, founded 1969, editor James Haining, publishes "new literature and graphic arts in their various forms." They have published poetry by Robert Creeley, Charles Olson, Michael Lally, David Searcy, Julie Siegel, Paul Shuttleworth, Wm. Hart, Robert Slater, Gerald Burns and Sheila Murphy. The magazine-sized journal, 100 pgs., saddle-stapled, matte cover, experimental graphics throughout, appears irregularly. They receive 400-600 poems/year, use 1-2%. Press run is 1,000. **Sample postpaid: $6. Reports in 1-6 weeks. Pays copies. To submit for book publication under the Lucky Heart Books imprint, send 20 samples, cover letter "open." Simultaneous submissions OK. Always sends prepublication galleys. Pays copies.**

SAMSARA (I, IV-Specialized: suffering/healing), P.O. Box 367, College Park MD 20741-0367, founded 1993, editor R. David Fulcher, is a biannual publication of poetry and fiction dealing with suffering. **"All subject matter should deal with suffering/healing."** They have published poetry by John Grey and Corrine DeWinter. As a sample we selected these lines from DeWinter's "Glissando":

> All that separates the living
> and the grey cloaked director is one
> hand, one heart, one move.
> Rolling them into one you found
> easier said than done.

Samsara is 80 pgs., 8½ × 11, neatly typeset and stapled down the side with a colored card stock cover and b&w art. They receive about 150 poems a year, accept approximately 7%. Press run is 200 for 35 subscribers. Single copy: $5.50. **Reprints acceptable if 3 years since publication; simultaneous submissions OK, but "if it is a simultaneous submission, a cover letter should be provided explaining this status."** Seldom comments on rejections. **Send SASE for guidelines. Reports in 1-2 months. Pays 1 copy. Acquires first North American serial rights.** The editor says, "Make me feel anguish, pain and loss—and then some hope—and you'll probably get into *Samsara*."

SAN FERNANDO POETRY JOURNAL; KENT PUBLICATIONS, INC. (I, IV-Social issues), 18301 Halsted St., Northridge CA 91325, founded 1978, poetry editors Richard Cloke, Shirley Rodecker and Lori Smith. *San Fernando Poetry Journal* uses **poetry of social protest.** According to Richard Cloke, "Poetry, for us, should be *didactic* in the Brechtian sense. **It must say something, must inform, in the tenor of our time.** We follow Hart Crane's definition of poetry as architectural in essence, building upon the past but incorporating the newest of this age also, including science, machinery, sub-atomic and cosmic physical phenomena as well as the social convulsions wrenching the very roots of our present world." **Send SASE for guidelines which explain this more fully.** For example, we quote this passage for its general usefulness for poets: "In some, the end-line rhyming is too insistent, seeming *forced;* in others the words are not vibrant enough to give the content an arresting framework. Others do not have any beat (cadence) at all and some are simply not well thought out—often like first drafts, or seem like prose statements. Please try reworking again to get some energy in your statement. If your poetry is to succeed in impelling the reader to act, it must electrify, or at least command interest and attention." **They welcome new and unpublished poets.** As a sample the editor selected this poem, "Paradise Lost," by Marian Steele:

> Adam trod the earth enraptured
> When he was nearly alone on a younger land.
> His name was Muir . . . Bartram . . . Burroughs . . .
>   Audubon.
> It was not so long ago.
> We have seen to it;
> Whether in Saudi desert,
> Flaming Brazilian rain forest,
> In Detroit's blighted back streets
> Or South Bronx alleyways,
> In the belches from redbrick smokestack,
> Recoilless rifle, naval Big Gun,
> Or even Three-Mile-Island-Chernobyl—
> We have remodeled our planet
> In our own image.

The flat-spined quarterly, photocopied from typescript, uses 100 pgs. of poetry in each issue. They use about 300 of the 1,000 submissions (the editor rightly prefers to call them "contributions") each year. Press run is 400 for 350 subscribers of which 45 are libraries. **Sample postpaid: $2.50. No specifications for ms form. Simultaneous submissions OK. Reports in 1 week. Pays copies.** The press, under its various imprints, also publishes a few collections by individuals. **Query with 5-6 pgs. of samples.**

SANDPIPER PRESS (V), P.O. Box 286, Brookings OR 97415-0028, phone (541)469-5588, founded 1979, is a small press publisher of large print books. They have published *Poems from the Oregon Sea Coast*; *Unicorns for Everyone*, which includes some poetry; and *Walk With Me*, a book of prayers and meditations. However, **they currently do not accept unsolicited poetry.**

SANSKRIT (I), UNC Charlotte, Cone University Center, Charlotte NC 28223, phone (704)547-2326, founded 1965, editor Scott Hubbard, is a literary annual using **poetry. "No restrictions as to form or genre, but we do look for maturity and sincerity in submissions. Nothing trite or sentimental."** They have recently published poetry by Kimberleigh Luke-Stallings, Duane Locke, Stella Hastie and Makyo. As a sample the editor selected these lines by Christy Beatty:

> If your father's taking lithium and your nana
> won't let the shades up and the caterpillars
> in your backyard are ablaze at some slight
> fault of your own, if there exists urban
> atrocity and decay that don't quite touch you
> yet infect your daily media intake
> Fight back.
> Change your name.

Their purpose is "to encourage and promote beginning and established artists and writers." It is 60-65 pgs., 9×12, flat-spined, printed on quality matte paper with heavy matte card cover. Press run is 3,500 for about 100 subscriptions of which 2 are libraries. **Sample postpaid: $6. Submit no more than**

5 poems at a time. Simultaneous submissions OK. Cover letter with biographical information and past publications required. Reads submissions September through October only. Editor comments on submissions "infrequently." Reports in 6-8 weeks. Pays 1 copy.

SANTA BARBARA REVIEW (II), 104 La Vereda Lane, Santa Barbara CA 93108-2508, founded 1993, editor Patricia Stockton Leddy, is a literary arts journal appearing 3 times a year publishing poetry, fiction and essays, including essays on poetry. **They want poetry with "lively, concrete imagery. Show us connections between things we had previously thought disparate. Nothing self-indulgent. No therapeutic diatribes, doggerel or epics. We're also not interested in abstract explanations of what life is about."** They have published poetry by Tess Gallagher, Chana Bloch, Stephen Ratcliffe, Marilyn Chandler and John Sanford. As a sample the editor selected these lines from "Lost By Way of Tchin-Tabarden" by Susan Rich (winner of "The Phenomena of Place" Contest):

> Nomads are said to know their way by an exact spot in the sky,
> the touch of sand to their fingers, granules on the tongue.
>
> But sometimes a system breaks down. Why am I traveling
> this road to Zinder, where really there is no road?

SBR is 160 pgs., 6×9, professionally printed and perfect-bound with b&w coated card cover and b&w illustrations inside. They use 12-18 poems each issue. Press run is 1,000 for 200 subscribers of which 10 are libraries, 75% shelf sales. Single copy: $7; subscription: $16/1 year. **Sample postpaid: $5. Submit 3-5 poems at a time. No simultaneous submissions. Reads submissions September 1 through March 31 only. Often comments on rejections. Send SASE for guidelines. Reports in 2-3 months. Pays 2 copies. Acquires one-time rights.** Sponsors "The Phenomena of Place" contest for poems not more than 28 lines. Awards $100 to winning poem. Reading fee: $1/poem. Deadline: December 16. Send SASE for details. The editor says, "The first thing we look for in any submission, whether it is a photograph, essay, poem or story, is voice. Other than a desire to avoid topics for their news value or political correctness, we have no taboo relative to subject matter. So far as length is concerned, make every image, word or trope count."

SANTA MONICA REVIEW (III), Santa Monica College, 1900 Pico Blvd., Santa Monica CA 90405, phone (310)450-5150, founded 1988, editor Lee Montgomery, appears twice a year publishing fiction and poetry, but is **not interested in traditional forms**. They have recently published poetry by Milton Katselas, Scott Anderson, T.M. McNally, Cynthia Shearer, Maya Sonenberg, Eve Wood and Anna Mortál. Single copy: $7; subscription: $12/year. **No submission information provided.** Poetry published in this review has been included in *The Best American Poetry 1993*.

SARABANDE BOOKS, INC.; THE KATHRYN A. MORTON PRIZE IN POETRY (II), 2234 Dundee Rd., Suite 200, Louisville KY 40205, phone (502)458-4028, fax (502)458-4065, e-mail sarabandeb@aol.com, founded 1994, editor-in-chief Sarah Gorham, publishes books of poetry and short fiction. **They want "poetry of superior artistic quality. Otherwise no restraints or specifications."** They have recently published poetry by Jane Mead, Richard Frost and Sharon Bryan. **Query with 10 sample poems during the month of September only. No fax submissions. SASE must always be enclosed. Previously published poems OK if acknowledged as such. Simultaneous submissions OK "if notified immediately of acceptance elsewhere." Seldom comments on rejections. Replies to queries in 3 months, to mss (if invited) in 6 months. Pays 10% royalties and author's copies.** The Kathryn A. Morton Prize in Poetry is awarded to a book-length ms submitted between January 1 and February 15. $15 handling fee and entry form required. Send SASE for guidelines beginning in November. Winner receives a $2,000 cash award, publication and a standard royalty contract.

SATURDAY EVENING POST (IV-Humor), 1100 Waterway Blvd., Indianapolis IN 46202, phone (317)636-8881, founded 1728 as the *Pennsylvania Gazette*, since 1821 as *The Saturday Evening Post*, Post Scripts editor Steve Pettinga, P.O. Box 567, Indianapolis IN 46206. *SEP* is a general interest, mass circulation bimonthly with emphasis on preventive medicine, using *"humorous light verse only. No more than 100 words per poem. Stay away from four-letter words and sexually graphic subject matter. No experimental verse (haiku, etc.). Morally, the *Post* is an anachronism of the*

ALWAYS include a self-addressed, stamped envelope (SASE) when sending a ms or query to a publisher within your own country. When sending material to other countries, include a self-addressed envelope and International Reply Coupons (IRCs), available for purchase at many post offices.

early 50s; most of its readers are elderly. Other than that, anything goes, as long as it's in good taste." Subscription: $13.97. **Payment is $15 for all rights.**

SATURDAY PRESS, INC. (V), Box 884, Upper Montclair NJ 07043, phone (201)256-5053, founded 1975, editor Charlotte Mandel. "Saturday Press, Inc., is a nonprofit literary organization." They have published books of poetry by Janice Thaddeus, Jean Hollander, Anne Carpenter, Anneliese Wagner and Doris Radin. **However, "We do not plan to read manuscripts in the foreseeable future."**

SCARP (II); FIVE ISLANDS PRESS (IV-Regional), School of Creative Arts, University of Wollongong, Northfields Ave., Wollongong Australia 2522, phone (042)213867, fax (042)213301, founded 1981, editor Ron Pretty. *Scarp*, which appears twice a year, is a publication of poetry, prose fiction and new art. It also contains articles and reviews. Both new and established writers are encouraged to contribute. **"Not restricted by genre or form or subject matter or style or purpose, however we would prefer not to publish anything of an epic length."** They have published poetry by Opal Palmer Adisa, Graham Rowlands, Andy Kissane and Charlotte Clutterbuck. As a sample the editor selected these lines from "Birthdays" by Deb Westbury:

> *Champagne corks could break windows*
> *and dent the ceiling,*
> *they could make a great noise*
> *and come all over the carpet.*
>
> *Now I hold the bottle*
> *between my knees and make a face;*
> *and gently ease it out*
> *anticipating a small, discreet*
> *explosion in my palm.*

Scarp is 72-84 pgs., A4 landscape format, perfect-bound, color card cover, b&w art and photography, some (mainly local) ads. There's a different flavor to poetry down under, but it is still mostly free verse bordering sometimes on what US poets would call the avant garde. Other poems are well-crafted and accessible, and the magazine is an odd rectangular shape but handsome and artistically designed. "*Scarp 25* received about 1,500 poems from 200 contributors. We published 17 poems from these." Press run is 1,000 for approximately 650 subscribers of which 100 are libraries. **Sample postpaid: $A10. Submit no more than 5 poems at a time. No simultaneous submissions or poems previously published in Australia. Reads submissions February through April (June issue) and July through August (October issue). Seldom comments on rejections. Send SASE (or SAE and IRC) for guidelines. Reports in 1-4 months. "Material that is clearly unsuitable we send back within a month; but material that has some chance of inclusion is kept to be considered after entries close at the beginning of May and September each year. The best way to avoid delays is to submit in March and/or August each year." Pays "at least" $A40 plus subscription.** However, overseas contributors receive 2 copies plus a 2-year subscription. **Buys first Australian rights only.** Staff reviews books of poetry in 300-1,000 words, single or multi-book format. Five Islands Press publishes poetry by Australian poets only. However, "We publish poetry from all over the world in *Scarp*." The editor says, "We're looking for poetry and prose that leaps off the page at you, and that usually means there's a lot of life in the language."

SCAVENGER'S NEWSLETTER; KILLER FROG CONTEST (IV-Science fiction/fantasy, horror, mystery, writing), 519 Ellinwood, Osage City KS 66523-1329, phone (913)528-3538, may seem an odd place to publish poems, but its editor, Janet Fox, uses 1-2 every month. The *Newsletter* is a **booklet packed with news about science fiction and horror publications. Janet prefers science fiction/fantasy, horror and mystery poetry and will read anything that is offbeat or bizarre. Writing-oriented poetry is occasionally accepted but "poems on writing must present fresh ideas and viewpoints. Poetry is used as filler so it must be 10 lines or under. I like poems with sharp images and careful craftsmanship."** Recently published poets include Dan Buck, Melissa Cannon, Margaret Macigewski and Brian Maycock. As a sample she selected this poem, "Beyond Suwanee," by Marge Simon:

> *drowning man in greenwood shadows*
> *mouth forms protest loam flecks sparkle*
> *sequined design of moonlight droplets*
> *frothcarpet chantilly microcosms dance*
> *on viscous mirrorshards of face*

Scavenger's Newsletter is 28 pgs., printed at a quick printing shop for 950 subscribers. **Subscription: $15.50/year; $7.75/6 months. Sample copy plus guidelines for $2; guidelines alone for SASE. Submit 3-6 poems at a time. Previously published poems and simultaneous submissions OK (if informed)—reprints if credit is given.** At last report was "accepting about 1 out of 20 poems submitted. I have changed my policy of closing from September to April due to overstock to staying open even when I have somewhat of a backlog. I am currently reading selectively. I put the notice 'reading selectively due to overstock' on my guidelines, so writers will realize that I will be accepting very little during this period." Reports in 1 month or less. Pays $2 on acceptance plus one copy. Buys one-time rights. Staff reviews science fiction/fantasy/horror and mystery chapbooks, books and magazines only. Send materials for review to either: Jim Lee, 801 - 26th St., Windber PA 15963 or Steve Sawicki, 186 Woodruff Ave., Watertown CT 06795. "I hold an annual 'Killer Frog Contest' for horror so bad or outrageous it becomes funny. There is a category for horror poetry. Has been opening April 1, closing July 1 of each year. Prizes are $25 each in four categories: poetry, art, short stories and short short stories, plus the 'coveted' Froggie statuette." The last contest had no entry fee but entrants wanting the anthology pay $3.50 (postpaid). Winners list available for SASE.

SCIENCE FICTION POETRY ASSOCIATION; STAR*LINE (IV-Science fiction, horror); THE RHYSLING ANTHOLOGY (V), 1412 NE 35th St., Ocala FL 34479, founded 1978, editor Margaret Simon, the Association publishes *Star*Line*, a bimonthly newsletter and poetry magazine. They are **"open to all forms—free verse, traditional forms, light verse—so long as your poetry shows skilled use of the language and makes a good use of science fiction, science, fantasy, horror or speculative motifs."** The Association also publishes *The Rhysling Anthology*, a yearly collection of nominations from the membership "for the best science fiction/fantasy long and short poetry of the preceding year." The magazine has published poetry by Bruce Boston, Thomas Disch, Denise Dumars, John M. Ford, Robert Frazier and Steve Rasnic Tem. As a sample we selected these lines from "Threshold-Haunting" by karen verba:

> atoms virulently mobilized, screaming hindrance
> shattered like proverbs on the periphery of matter.
> feeling pain, an illusion of solidity—
> fearfully pacified by those sins
> we possessively clutch to ourselves
> in imagined conflict between the mystical & the mundane.

The digest-sized magazine and anthology are saddle-stapled, photocopied, with numerous illustrations and decorations. They have 250 subscribers (1 library) paying $13 for 6 issues/year. **Sample postpaid: $2.** Send requests for copies/membership information to John Nichols, Secretary-Treasurer, 6075 Bellevue Dr., North Olmstead OH 44070. **Submissions to *Star*Line* only.** They receive 200-300 submissions/year and use about 80—**mostly short (under 50 lines). Send 3-5 poems/submission, typed. No simultaneous submissions, no queries. Brief cover letter preferred. Submit in November. Reads submissions November 1 through December 31. Publishes theme issues. They have one all-horror issue each year. Send SASE for upcoming themes. Reports in a month. Pays 5¢/line plus 1¢/word and a copy. Buys first North American serial rights.** Reviews books of poetry "within the science fiction/fantasy field" in 50-500 words. Open to unsolicited reviews. Poets may also send books for review consideration to Todd Earl Rhodes, 735 Queensbury Loop, Winter Garden FL 34787-5808. A copy of *The Rhysling Anthology* is $3.

SCOP PUBLICATIONS, INC. (II, IV-Regional), Box 376, College Park MD 20740, phone (301)422-1930, founded 1977, president Stacy Tuthill, publishes approximately 2 paperbacks/year as well as an occasional anthology. They want **"book-length regional manuscripts. No restrictions as to length or form but want well-crafted modern poetry with vivid imagery and skillful use of language with regard to sense impressions and fresh insights."** They have published poetry by Ann Darr, Barbara Lefcowitz and Elisavietta Ritchie. **For sample book, send $5.** Interested poets should **query with sample poems. Previously published poems and simultaneous submissions OK. Cover letter should include a short biography and recent credits. Seldom comments on rejections. Replies to queries in 6 weeks, to mss in 2-3 months. Pays copies.**

SCORE MAGAZINE; SCORE CHAPBOOKS AND BOOKLETS (II, IV-Form), 1015 NW Clifford St., Pullman WA 99163, phone (509)332-1120, poetry editors Crag Hill and Spencer Selby, is a small press publisher of **visual poetry** in the annual magazine *Score*, booklets, postcards and broadsides. They want **"poetry which melds language and the visual arts such as concrete poetry; experimental use of language, words and letters—forms. The appearance of the poem should have as much to say as the text. Poems on any subject; conceptual poetry; poems which use experimental, non-traditional methods to communicate their meanings."** They don't want "traditional verse of any kind—be it free verse or rhymed." They have recently published poetry by Stephen-Paul Martin, A.L. Nielsen, Jonathan Brannen, Larry Eigner and Gregory St. Thomasino. They say that it is impossible to quote a sample because "some of our poems consist of only a single word— or in some cases no recognizable words." **We strongly advise looking at a sample copy before submitting if you are not familiar with visual poetry.** *Score* is 48-72 pgs., magazine-sized, offset, saddle-stapled, using b&w graphics, 2-color matte card cover. Press run is 200 for 25 subscribers (6 of them libraries) and about 40 shelf sales. **Sample postpaid: $10.** Previously published poems OK "if noted." No simultaneous submissions. Send SASE for guidelines. **Pays 2 copies.** Open to unsolicited reviews. Poets may also send books for review consideration. **For chapbook consideration send entire ms. No simultaneous submissions. Almost always comments on rejections. Pays 25% of the press run.** They subsidy publish "if author requests it."

SCREAM PRESS; ETHEREAL DANCES (II); POET OF THE WEEK (III), P.O. Box 2056, Cupertino CA 95015, founded 1987, editor of *Ethereal Dances* Sara Hyatt Boyd, editor of *Poet Of The Week* Anthony Boyd. *Ethereal Dances* is "a journal featuring writers and poets in an artistically simple way." *Poet Of The Week* (formerly *Whisper*) features a new poet every weekend on the World Wide Web, and includes not only the text of the poems, but a photo of each poet, a small biography, and even audio recordings. They have recently published Lyn Lifshin, Errol Miller and Bob Hostetler. As a sample the editors selected these lines from "war paint" by Jenifer Bartels (published in *Ethereal Dances*):

> Earth's paint splatters and splashes
>   drips and dribbles
>   and the Artist made a wonderful mistake
> when he spilled the ocean blue into your eyes.

and these lines from "Echo" by Jill DiMaggio (published in *Poet Of The Week*):

> memory is but a quiet
> melodic rebirth that keeps
> slipping through my mind
> like a phantom

Ethereal Dances is a triannual, 20 pgs., 5½ × 8½, laser printed, saddle-stapled, color paper, cover artwork. *Poet Of The Week* does not appear in print, but rather as a "Web Page" on the Internet. Sara Hyatt Boyd receives about 400 poems a year for *Ethereal Dances*. She accepts approximately 15%. Anthony Boyd receives about 2,500 poems a year for *Poet Of The Week*. He accepts approximately 4%. **Sample postpaid: $2 (for *Ethereal Dances*). Submit 3-5 poems at a time, 1 poem to a page. Previously published poems OK if noted; no simultaneous submissions. Reports in 1 month. Acquires first or one-time rights (printed and electronic).** Anthony Boyd says, "Those of you who read and loved our magazine, *Whisper*, will be happy to know that while we're no longer publishing it, back issues are archived on our website, and issues 6-8 are still available in print for $2 each. *Poet Of The Week* is basically *Whisper* in a new format, so whatever you would have felt appropriate for *Whisper* is fine for *Poet Of The Week*. However, due to a flood of submissions, I am no longer able to make comments on rejections. If you are online, you may send e-mail to whisper@zoom.com, and you may visit Scream Press America at http://www.zoom.com/~whisper/ and Scream Press Europe at http://www.jsp.fi/~whisper/."

‡SEAM (II), 1 Horncastle Rd., Louth, Lincolnshire LN11 9LB Great Britain, founded 1994, editors David Lightfoot and Robert Etty, appears twice a year (in January and July) to publish "good contemporary poetry." **They want "any poetry that engages the reader. Short rather than long. Sequences welcome. Nothing derivative; no self-therapy."** They have recently published poetry by Vernon Scannell, U.A. Fanthorpe, Hugo Williams and John Harvey. *Seam* is 64 pgs., A6 (4 × 5¾), perfect-bound with b&w cover photo. They receive about 2,000 poems a year, accept approximately 5%. Press run is 210 for 150 subscribers of which 5 are libraries, 50 shelf sales. Subscription: £6/year. **Sample postpaid: £3, £4 overseas. Submit 5-6 poems at a time; each poem on 1 sheet of paper (A4 size). No previously published poems or simultaneous submissions. Seldom comments on rejections. Reports in 2-3 weeks. Pays 1 copy.** Staff reviews books of poetry. Send books for review consideration to Sam Gardiner, 82 Milton Rd., Grimsby DN33 1DE United Kingdom. The editors say, "First, read, read, read what *is* being published. Second, subscribe."

‡SEASONS OF THE MUSE; CALLIOPE PRESS (I), 2 Jasmine Court, Millbrae CA 94030, first issue Spring 1996, editor/publisher Dawn Zapletal, appears quarterly "with the seasons, to give new and established poets a showcase for their work." **They want poetry of all types; "free verse, haiku, rhyme—24 lines or less preferred. No religious, political or pornographic work."** The editor says *SOTM* is 4-6 pgs., 8½ × 11, corner stapled, with cover graphics. "No samples or subscriptions available. Only published poets receive copies." **Submit 4 poems at a time with $1 reading fee, "stamps or cash only. No checks, please." Previously published poems and simultaneous submissions OK. Send addressed postal card for reply. Does not return material. Poems are circulated to a 3-member editorial board. Decisions must be unanimous for acceptance. Always comments on rejections. Reports in 1 week to 1 month. Pays $1 plus 1 copy.** Sponsors an Editor's Choice Award in each issue. The best poem from each issue receives $5. The editor says, "Write what you feel. Honesty is a must. No vague inaccessible poetry."

SEATTLE REVIEW (II), Padelford Hall, Box 354330, University of Washington, Seattle WA 98195, phone (206)543-9865, founded 1978, poetry editor Colleen McElroy, appears in the fall and spring using **"contemporary and traditional" poetry.** They have published poetry by William Stafford,

Tess Gallagher, Marvin Bell and Walter McDonald. As a sample the editor selected these lines from "Car Mechanic Blues" by Jan Wallace:

> He lords his wrench over me like
> a magic wand. His ease with grease, the way
> he calms the speeding idle should convince
> me, this man's got the power. He wants
> to show me how the sparks fire. I say,
> No thanks, I'll get the book.

The review is 110 pgs., professionally printed, flat-spined, with glossy card cover. Press run is 800 for 250 subscribers of which 50 are libraries, 400 shelf sales. Single copy: $5; subscription: $9. **Sample postpaid: $3. Reads submissions September 1 through May 31 only. Send SASE for guidelines. Reports in 2-6 months. Pay "varies, but we do pay" plus 2 copies.** The editors offer these "practical suggestions: Cover letters with submissions do help. A cover letter provides something about the author and tells where and for what s/he is submitting. And don't let those rejection letters be cause for discouragement. Rejections can often be a matter of timing. The journal in question may be publishing a special issue with a certain theme (we've done a number of themes—'all-fiction,' 'all-poetry,' 'Asian-American,' 'environmental hazards,' 'Beauty and the Beasts,' etc.). Also, editorial boards do change, and new editors bring their individual opinions and tastes in writing. Good poetry will eventually be published if it is circulated."

SECOND AEON PUBLICATIONS (V), 19 Southminster Rd., Roath, Cardiff CF2 S4T Wales, phone 01222-493093, founded 1966, poetry editor Peter Finch, is a "small press concerned in the main with **experimental literary works.**" He has published poetry by Bob Cobbing and himself. **Does not accept unsolicited mss. Pays copies.** Reviews poetry as a freelancer for a broad range of publications.

SEEMS (II), P.O. Box 359, Lakeland College, Sheboygan WI 53082-0359, phone (414)565-1276, fax (414)565-1206, founded 1971, published irregularly (31 issues in 24 years). This is a handsomely printed, nearly square ($7 \times 8\frac{1}{4}$) magazine, saddle-stapled, generous with white space on heavy paper. Two of the issues are considered chapbooks, and the editor, Karl Elder, suggests that a way **to get acquainted would be to order** *Seems #14, What Is The Future Of Poetry?* **for $5**, consisting of essays by 22 contemporary poets, and "If you don't like it, return it and we'll return your $5." *Explain That You Live: Mark Strand with Karl Elder* (#29) is available for $3. There are usually about 20 pgs. of poetry/issue. Elder has recently used poetry by David Elliott, Pete Lee, Daniel Smith, Theodora Todd and Richard Welin. He said it was "impossible" to select four illustrative lines. The magazine has a print run of 350 for 200 subscriptions (20 libraries) and sells for $4 an issue (or $16 for a subscription—four issues). There is a **1- to 2-year backlog. "People may call or fax with virtually any question, understanding that the editor may have no answer." Reports in 1-3 months. Pays 1 copy. Acquires North American serial rights. Returns rights upon publication.** The editor says, "We'd like to consider more prose poems."

SEGUE FOUNDATION; ROOF BOOKS; SEGUE BOOKS (V), 303 E. Eighth St., New York NY 10009, phone (212)674-0199, fax (212)254-4145, president James Sherry, is a small press publisher of avant-garde and experimental poetry, literary criticism, and film and performance texts. Most of their books are flat-spined paperbacks, some hardcover. They have published books by Jackson MacLow, Charles Bernstein, Ron Silliman, Leslie Scalapino and Diane Ward, but **they do not consider unsolicited mss. Query first.**

SENECA REVIEW (II, IV-Translations), Hobart and William Smith Colleges, Geneva NY 14456-3397, phone (315)781-3349, founded 1970, editor Deborah Tall, is a biannual. **They want "serious poetry of any form, including translations. No light verse. Also essays on contemporary poetry."** They have published poetry by Seamus Heaney, Rita Dove, Denise Levertov, Stephen Dunn and Hayden Carruth. *Seneca Review* is 100 pgs., 6×9, professionally printed on quality stock and perfect-bound with matte card cover. You'll find plenty of free verse here—some accessible and some leaning toward experimental—with the emphasis on voice, image and diction. All in all, poems and translations complement each other and create a distinct editorial mood each issue. They receive 3,000-4,000 poems a year, accept approximately 100. Press run is 1,000 for 500 subscribers of which half are libraries, about 250 shelf sales. Subscription: $8/year, $15/2 years. **Sample postpaid: $5. Submit 3-5 poems at a time. No simultaneous submissions or previously published poems. Reads submissions September 1 through May 1 only. Reports in 6-12 weeks. Pays 2 copies.** Poetry published in *Seneca Review* has also been included in *The Best American Poetry 1994.*

SENSATIONS MAGAZINE (I, IV-Membership/subscription, themes), 2 Radio Ave., A5, Secaucus NJ 07094, founded 1987, founder David Messineo. **Subscription required before submission of material, but this is among the top 10 paying poetry markets in the US.** However, interested poets should contact them for submission and payment details. *Sensations Magazine* is an unusual mix of contemporary poetry, contemporary fiction and historical research. **"We encourage diversity: Buy back issue, see types and themes of published poems, and send something different."** As a sample, the founder selected these lines from "The Pearl Eater" by Melanie Pimont:

> *Night creatures shiver in their burrows*
> *as darkness flies over the earth. A raven croaks.*
> *Its wings beat above and my ears feel*
> *the weight of its passage. Even the shadows*
> *have fled. Hurry, light the round lanterns.*
> *Hang paper moons from tree branches. Shoot*
> *fireworks high into the sky. Scare the sky dragon.*
> *Make it loose light upon this world again.*

Sensations is "desktop-published with elegance and respect for the written word." Subscription: $12 "to start. **We send SASE for your poetry submission once you have subscribed, so don't send poetry until** *after* **you have subscribed. Check (or International Money Order) must be made payable to David Messineo. If you send material without a SASE, you will receive no response."** Previously published poems OK. Theme for April 1997 issue is "almost anything goes, 120 lines or less (no profanity)." Deadline: February 1, 1997. Pays up to $125/poem minus the difference between the amount of a paid subscription and the cost of the issue in which work appears. **Acquires one-time publication rights.** The founder says, "Funds raised go into costs of publication and research—editors are unpaid volunteers. Have doubts? Name five independent, non-grant-funded publications you submitted to back in 1987 that are still around. We have beaten the odds of failure and are looking forward to our Fifteenth Anniversary Issue in 2002 (we even advance planned all issues, deadlines, and themes between now and then). *Sensations Magazine* is unlike any other literary magazine you've seen. We will treat you with respect and remarkable courtesy, and ask your professionalism in return by following our submission requirements in full. For those of you who tried us before, we strongly encourage you to revisit. Why not prepare a SASE right now and send it to the address above, while we're on your mind? We look forward to hearing from you, and will respond within a week or two of your inquiry."

SEQUOIA (II), Storke Publications Building, Stanford University, Stanford CA 94305, phone (415)497-7703, founded 1892, poetry editor Carlos Rodriguez, appears annually. They have published poetry by Susan Howe, Seamus Heaney, Adrienne Rich, Rita Dove and James Merrill. As a sample the editor selected these lines from "The Amish Visit Pella, Iowa" by Keith Ratzlaff:

> *to be healed of themselves,*
> *the curves their bones take.*
> *They come because the chiropractor*
> *works in the open the way they do:*
> *hard and with his hands.*

Sequoia is 80-100 pgs., 6×9, professionally printed, flat-spined, with matte card cover with art. They publish a small percentage of hundreds of unsolicited submissions. Their press run is 500 with 200 subscriptions, of which half are libraries. Subscription: $10. **Sample postpaid: $5. Submit up to 9 typed poems at a time. They do not consider simultaneous submissions or previously published poems. Reads submissions September 15 through June 1. Reports in "2 months or more." Pays 2 copies.**

SERPENT & EAGLE PRESS (V), RD#1, Box 29B, Laurens NY 13796, phone (607)432-2990, founded 1981, poetry editor Jo Mish. "Our aim is to print fine limited letterpress editions of titles worth printing in all subject areas." Their chapbooks are elegantly designed and printed on handmade paper with hand-sewn wrappers. **However, they are currently not accepting poetry submissions.**

SEVEN BUFFALOES PRESS; AZOREAN EXPRESS; BLACK JACK; VALLEY GRAPE-VINE; HILL AND HOLLER ANTHOLOGY SERIES (IV-Rural, regional, anthologies), Box 249, Big Timber MT 59011, founded 1973, editor Art Coelho, who writes, "I've always thought that rural and working class writers, poets and artists deserve the same tribute given to country singers." These publications all express that interest. For all of them Art Coelho wants **poetry oriented toward rural and working people, "a poem that tells a story, preferably free verse, not longer than 50-100 lines, poems with strong lyric and metaphor, not romantical, poetry of the heart as much as the head, not poems written like grocery lists or the first thing that comes from a poet's mind, no ivory tower, and half my contributors are women."** He has published poetry by R.T. Smith, James Goode, Leo Connellan and Wendell Berry. *The Azorean Express* is 35 pgs., 5½×8½, side-stapled. It appears twice a year. Circulation 200. **Sample postpaid: $6.75. Submit 4-8 poems at a time. No simultaneous submissions. Reports in 1 month. Pays 1 copy.** *Black Jack* is an anthology series on Rural America that uses rural material from anywhere, especially the American West; *Valley Grapevine* is an anthology on central California, circulation 750, that uses rural material from central

CLOSE-UP

Listening to "the instrument of the world's passion"

With 20 titles under his belt—including the 1982 American Book Award winner *Life Supports*—William Bronk has chiseled a permanent mark in the rather small stone of "Great American Poets." Although he's been publishing poetry for almost 50 years, not until the early '80s did Bronk receive long-warranted recognition, mostly because he was not part of any poetry "school" or "movement" that became popularized in the '50s, '60s and '70s. He's been hailed as "one of our finest poets" by *The New York Times Book Review*, "one of the most solid and unfrivolous contemporary poets" by *Kirkus Reviews*, and "our most significant poet" by *The Nation*.

William Bronk

Photo by Don Prues

Bronk's is a forthright poetry of questions and propositions that reaches right down the reader's throat and grabs the gut with what *Village Voice* calls "a speed and agility that cut to the core of knotty matters." Often called "philosophical," "speculative," "skeptical," "despairing," and even "religious," Bronk's poems seem less like poetry and more like a recording of Bronk's interior monologue (*"What else but the mind / senses the final uselessness of the mind?"* asks the voice in "The Mind's Limitations Are Its Freedoms"), all without sounding confessional, arrogant or schizophrenic.

His philosophy of composition is as rare as his poetry. He claims he doesn't compose: "I feel the poems come to me ready made, and that's not theoretical, that's experience." Writing poems is a matter of listening, waiting for the poems when they call him. "Frequently I wake up in the morning and there a poem is beside me in the bed. Or maybe in the night if I wake up or while I'm doing something during the day and then it's 'Oh, there's a poem right there.' I might tell myself, 'Oh, now, come off it, that's not a poem.' But then I can't get it out of my head. It is insistent. It's as though something were saying, 'Okay, now here's the first line.' "

Perhaps because writing poetry is more receptivity than work for Bronk, he is suspicious of those deliberately trying to make themselves poets. A poem can't be forced or fashioned. He says, "The poet W.H. Auden believed if you are a poet you go to your desk in the morning and write poetry. That was his system at Oxford. Everyday he would write and show his work to his teacher, who would say, 'I like this line in that one and that line in this one.' Together the two would make up a poem of the selected lines. Is that poetry? To me, that's homemade poetry, and if you read Auden's work from that time you'll see how awkward it

CLOSE-UP, *Bronk*

sounds. Sure, Auden was talented and came up with a lot of good lines, but I don't work that way. I have never forced myself to sit down and write a poem. The poem is somehow always there; it lets me know when it wants me."

"The Poems: All Concessions Made"

The poems, (are they?) (such as they are), stay
with me or seem to. I turn away
sometimes, pretending alone, to do something else.
It is as though they wait—as if there.
I find them there. Their brief and still suspense
is the pause of performers, hearing applause on the stage.
The pause confirms them, of course, but they need me
to resume, are confident I mean to return.
Coming back, (I do) I find them there.
They are waiting for me. Well, we have to go on.
For no reason except that we started once.
That isn't a reason. It isn't reasonable.
We concede so much. What don't we concede?
I wish I had something; and the poems are there.

While Bronk insists he is just a vessel through which the poems flow (*"If anything at all, I am / the instrument of the world's passion and not / the doer or the done to"*), he does not discredit his formal instruction. "Of course you can acquire abilities and craft and so on. I'm not against poetry writing courses. The instruction I got from my teacher [poet and writer Sidney Cox], even though I sometimes disagreed with it, got me to think about the issues. I then took my own positions on them, which is what everyone must do. I would not in any way dismiss my experiences in writing courses. But they did not make me a poet."

What, then, makes Bronk a poet? "I have no secrets," he says. "A person doesn't become a writer by wanting to be a writer. That doesn't mean there's anything wrong with wanting to be a writer, but desire alone won't do it. You either are a writer, I think, or you are not a writer." In Bronk's world, persistence, dedication, and even publication won't certify you as a poet; you must have a poetic propensity and foster it. "One can be an undeveloped poet or a genuine poet who hasn't taken advantage of his talents, but simply working to be a poet will not get you there. It may get you published, probably will get you published if you try hard enough, but as far as I'm concerned, that doesn't mean it works, doesn't mean you've become a poet."

If this poet-as-vessel bit seems much too odd, consider that Bronk rarely rewrites, evident in the spotlessness of his notebook, which has been likened to the sheets on which Mozart composed. Sound too silly, too much like waiting for that old, inspiring muse? Well Bronk's poems are a far cry from traditional muse-inspired poetry—no mawkish love poems, no lofty language, no hyperbolic mumbo-jumbo—and Bronk wouldn't call whatever offers him poems a muse. In fact, he doesn't know what to name it. But he can't deny the process. "What I'm

CLOSE-UP, *continued*

talking about," he says, "is the feel of the experience. It is *as though* it happens as I've told you. I feel it's not my mind that does the making."

And what does he think about books like **Poet's Market** that give unpublished poets tips for breaking into print? "You want me to tell young writers that to be a poet you've got to work hard at what you do, that you've got to write so many hours a week, that you've got to rewrite and rewrite to keep perfecting your work. Well, that's not how poetry works for me," he says. "What younger poets are interested in is, 'How do I get published?' and I say that it doesn't matter whether they get published at all." Sounds contradictory coming from a man who first published in **The New Yorker** back in 1949. "I got published there," he modestly proclaims, "because I met the editor a while before in Connecticut. I think it was a kind of indulgence that he publish the poem. I don't think he thought much of my poetry. After that, I sent something out only after I was asked for it." A practice he continues to this day.

How can one gauge the merits of one's poetry, if publication does not confirm a poet? Bronk admits that's difficult to answer, but he wants to make it clear there's more to poetry than publication. "If I sent most journals poems without my name on them they'd immediately get tossed in the trash pile. So if getting published is what's important, the one sure way to do it is to get to know the right people, make sure they know your name. But suppose, then, you do get published. Would you really consider yourself a poet? You can worry about being published as a personal validation, but if you are writing poetry only to get published, you belong in some other kind of writing."

Bronk's unique writing practice poses many questions: Does he intentionally focus on a particular metaphor? Does he interpret poems? Does a particular scene or memory spark him to think, "I'll write about that"? Or do all poems merely come to him, as he says, "ready made"? "Believe it or not, the poem itself comes to me, as is, words and all. The idea comes later," he says. "Many times I have rejected the poem as it comes to me, or at least resisted it. I'll tell myself, 'I don't think that's right.' But if it's really a poem it won't go away. It keeps nudging."

Bronk says he doesn't quite realize what he's written until after the words are on the page. "I always write the poem before I write the title. I keep looking at the poem and say to myself, 'Well, what's this about?' In time I find a title that fits. Often, when a poem is more than a few lines, I come to find there are various elements in it that I first never noticed. It amazes me. Frequently I ask, 'How did I hit on those words?' and I have no answer."

Ultimately, then, why does Bronk write? "I write for the poem because the poem is there," he insists. "The relationship is not between me and the reader; the relationship is between me and the poems. The essayist Walter Benjamin once said, 'No poem was ever written for the reader and no picture was ever painted for the viewer.' He's right. Art is about a private relationship between the artist and the work."

—*Don Prues*

*All excerpts come from *Life Supports: New & Collected Poems*, North Point Press, 1982.

California; *Hill and Holler*, Southern Appalachian Mountain series, takes in rural mountain lifestyle and folkways. **Sample of any postpaid: $6.75. Seven Buffaloes Press does not accept unsolicited mss but publishes books solicited from writers who have appeared in the above magazines.** Art Coelho advises, "Don't tell the editor how great you are. This one happens to be a poet and novelist who has been writing for 30 years. Your writing should not only be fused with what you know from the head, but also from what you know within your heart. Most of what we call life may be some kind of gift of an unknown river within us. The secret to be learned is to live with ease in the darkness, because there are too many things of the night in this world. But the important clue to remember is that there are many worlds within us."

THE SEWANEE REVIEW; AIKEN TAYLOR AWARD FOR MODERN POETRY (III), University of the South, Sewanee TN 37383-1000, phone (615)598-1246, founded 1892, thus being our nation's oldest continuously published literary quarterly, editor George Core. Fiction, criticism and poetry are invariably of the **highest establishment standards. Most of our major poets appear here from time to time.** *SR* has published poetry by William Logan, Howard Nemerov and Barry Spacks. Each issue is a hefty paperback of nearly 200 pgs., conservatively bound in matte paper, always of the same typography. Truly a magazine open to all styles and forms, issues we critiqued featured formal sequences, metered verse, structured free verse, sonnets, and lyric and narrative forms—all accessible and intelligent. Circulation: 3,200. **Sample: $6.25. Reports in 1-4 weeks. Pays 70¢/line.** Also includes brief, standard and essay-reviews. The Aiken Taylor Award for Modern Poetry is awarded by *The Sewanee Review* and its publisher, the University of the South in Sewanee, TN, "for the work of a substantial and distinguished career." Poetry published in *The Sewanee Review* was also selected for inclusion in *The Best American Poetry 1992*.

SHAMAL BOOKS (IV-Ethnic, anthologies), Dept. PM, GPO Box 16, New York NY 10116, phone (718)622-4426, founded 1976, editor Louis Reyes Rivera. Shamal Books is a small press whose purpose is **"to promote the literary efforts of African-American and Caribbean writers, particularly those who would not otherwise be able to establish their literary credentials as their concerns as artists are with the people."** The press publishes individual and "anthological" books and chapbooks, mostly flat-spined paper texts. They have published poetry by SeKou Sundiata, Sandra Maria Esteves and Rashidah Ismaili. The editor wants to see **"poetry that clearly demonstrates an understanding of craft, content and intent as the scriptural source of the word guiding and encouraging the intellect of the people." He does not consider unsolicited submissions of individual mss, but will look at work only while anthologies are open. Submit 2 sample poems. Mss should be "neat and single-spaced." Cover letter "leaning toward personal goals and poetic principles" required. Replies to queries within 2 months. Royalties for book authors are 15%.** The editor says that he will subsidy publish "delicately—depends on resources and interest in work." His projects include "an international anthology; drama; prison anthology; books on language as a weapon; a collectivized publisher's catalog of Third World presses working out of NYC." His advice to poets: "Certainly to study the craft more and to research more into the historical role that has been the hallmark of poetry across class and caste conscious lines that limit younger perspectives. Not to be as quick to publish as to be in serious study, then while looking to publish, looking as well into collective ventures with other poets for publication and distribution. Above all, *read!*"

SHARING THE VICTORY (IV-Spirituality/inspirational, sports), 8701 Leeds Rd., Kansas City MO 64129, phone (816)921-0909, founded 1959, editor John Dodderidge, assistant editor Will Greer, managing editor Kevin Harlan. This monthly magazine is published September through May by the Fellowship of Christian Athletes. **They want free verse on themes of interest to Christian athletes (high school and college, male and female).** As a sample they selected these lines by Aileen L. Myers:

> *I am more than*
> *skill and conditioning*
> *More because*
> *I am a child of a loving God,*
> *who created me in His spiritual image,*
> *loves me for myself*
> *and promises me the eternal Victory.*

They use 2-3 poems/year. Press run is 50,000. **Sample available for $1 with 8½ × 11 SASE (first-class stamps for 3 ozs.). Reads submissions July 1 through March 1 only.** Time between acceptance and publication averages 3-4 months. **Guidelines available free. Reports in 2 weeks. Pays $25-50. Buys first or second rights.**

SHATTERED WIG REVIEW (II), 425 E. 31st, Baltimore MD 21218, phone (410)243-6888, founded 1988, contact Sonny Bodkin, is a semiannual using **"liquid, messy poetry, oozing the stuff of life. No frustrated English professor poetry."** They have recently published poetry by John M.

Bennett, Cynthia Hendershot, Sheila Murphy and Dan Raphael. As a sample the editor selected these
lines by Chris Toll:

> *A 10,000-year-old white man rules the world*
> *when he needs a new heart,*
> *he murders a 16-year-old boy*
> *His tanks may rumble through the cities*
> *My crack dealers will fight back to back with my crystal healers*
> *Every cell in my body knows the new world is coming*

SHW is approximately 70 pgs., 8½ × 8½, photocopied, side-stapled with card stock covers with original
artwork, art and graphics also inside. They receive about 10 submissions/week, accept about 20%.
Press run is 300 for 100 subscribers of which 10 are libraries, 100 shelf sales. Subscription: $9 for 2
issues. **Sample postpaid: $4. Previously published poems and simultaneous submissions OK.
Seldom comments on rejections. Reports within a month. Pays 1 copy. Acquires one-time rights.**
Occasionally reviews books of poetry in 100 words. Open to unsolicited reviews. Poets may also send
books for review consideration. The editor says there are no requirements for contributors except "that
the contributor include us in their nightly prayers."

HAROLD SHAW PUBLISHERS; WHEATON LITERARY SERIES (V), P.O. Box 567,
Wheaton IL 60189, phone (630)665-6700, founded 1967, literary editor Lil Copan, is "small publisher
of the Wheaton Literary Series and Northcote Books, **works of Christian and literary merit** including
fiction, poetry, literary criticism and original prose" in flat-spined paperback and hardback books.
They have published poetry by Madeleine L'Engle, John Leax, Sister Maura Eichner and Luci Shaw.
They publish on a 10/5% royalty basis or a flat fee. They publish a volume in the Wheaton Literary
Series approximately every 2 years. "Our work reflects **a Christian evangelical world-view**, though
this need not be explicit. In the future we may publish an anthology, rather than single poets." **However,
they are currently still not accepting poetry submissions.**

SHEILA-NA-GIG (II), 23106 Kent Ave., Torrance CA 90505, founded 1990, editor Hayley R.
Mitchell. *Sheila-na-gig* appears once a year as a large general issue using **"all forms (particularly
free verse), styles and subject matter—length, I generally don't publish poems over three pages
(don't ramble!). No religious or ultra traditional verse, please."** They have recently published work
by Lyn Lifshin, Gerald Locklin, Michael McNeilley, Alan Catlin, Denise Duhamel, Paul Weinman
and Charles Webb. As a sample the editor selected these lines by Terry Wolverton:

> *My lover, steering wheel in hand,*
> *stared into narrow streets*
> *with the eyes of a dark bird,*
> *"Which way," she cawed, "which way?"*
> *But mine glowed with the blankness*
> *of a woman swaying from a noose, . . .*

Sheila-na-gig is 100-150 pgs., digest-sized, flat-spined, photocopied from laser prints with matte card
cover. Subscription: $7 yearly, $12 for two years. **Sample postpaid: $7 for current issue ($5/$3 for
older back issues). Cover letter preferred with submissions.** Include SASE, brief bio and note
stating whether poems are previously published or simultaneous submissions. **1997 Deadline:
May 31.** "I'll begin reading submissions on June 1, and will report in 6-8 weeks. Submit up to
5 poems, and/or short stories (1-10 pgs.), and/or b&w artwork (5×7 and easy to reproduce)." **Pays
copies. Acquires first rights.** Sponsors an annual poetry contest. Submit 3 poems with SASE and $5
entry fee. $50 first prize, copies, and publication of runners-up. Also sponsors an annual chapbook
contest. Submit 20-24 poems (25 pgs. maximum) with SASE and $10 entry fee. Prize: $100, publication
and 100 copies. Deadline for both contests is June 30. Work in *Sheila-na-gig* has been nominated for
inclusion in *Pushcart Prize XIX: Best of the Small Presses (1994-95 edition)*. The editor says, "I
encourage new poets with new styles and a strong voice, and look especially for poets not afraid to
speak out on issues of sexuality, politics, human rights and feminist issues. Looking for poetry on the
edge. If in doubt, order a back issue. Please make all checks payable to Hayley R. Mitchell. Thank
you for your interest in and support of *Sheila-na-gig*."

SHENANDOAH (II), Troubadour Theater, 2nd Floor, Washington and Lee University, Lexington
VA 24450-0303, founded 1950, editor R.T. Smith, managing editor Lynn L. Leech. Published at
Washington and Lee University, it is a quarterly literary magazine which has recently published poetry
by Mary Oliver, Margaret Gibson, Rodney Jones, Brendan Galvin and Reginald Shepherd. As a sample
the editor selected "The Ghost Orchid" by Michael Longley:

> *Added to its few remaining sites will be the stanza*
> *I compose about leaves like flakes of skin, a colour*
> *Dithering between pink and yellow, and then the root*
> *That grows like coral among shadows and leaf-litter.*
> *Just touching the petals bruises them into darkness.*

The magazine is 120 pgs., 6×9, perfect-bound, professionally printed with full-color cover. Generally, it is open to all styles and forms but leans toward lyric and narrative free verse with an emphasis on voice. Circulation is 1,900. Subscription: $11/year, $18/2 years, $25/3 years. **Sample postpaid: $3.50. All submissions should be typed on one side of the paper only. Your name and address must be clearly written on the upper right corner of the ms. Include SASE. Reads submissions September 1 through May 30. Reports in 3 months. Payment includes a check, one-year subscription and one copy. Buys first publication rights.** Staff reviews books in 7-10 pages, multi-book format. Send books for review consideration. Some reviews are solicited. A prize is given for the best poetry, fiction and nonfiction published in the calendar year. Poetry published in *Shenandoah* has been included in *The Best American Poetry 1993*.

SHIP OF FOOLS (II); SHIP OF FOOLS PRESS (V), Box 1028, University of Rio Grande, Rio Grande OH 45674-9989, phone (614)992-3333, founded 1983, editor Jack Hart, advisory editor Gina Pellegrino-Pines, review editor James Doubleday, is "more or less quarterly." They want **"coherent, well-written, traditional or modern, myth, archetype, love—most types. No concrete, incoherent or greeting card poetry."** They have published poetry by Rhina Espaillat, Carolyn Page, Denver Stull and T. Kilgore Splake. As a sample the editors selected these lines from "Following the Reaper" by Nancy Haas:

> *I am here again;*
> *Gathering the heads*
> *With their wide astonished eyes*
> *And the hands*
> *With their silent fluttering fingers.*

They describe *Ship of Fools* as digest-sized, saddle-stapled, offset printed with cover art and graphics. Press run is 250 for 41 subscribers of which 6 are libraries. Subscription: $7 for 4 issues. **Sample postpaid: $2. No previously published poems or simultaneous submissions. Cover letter preferred. Often comments on rejections. Reports in 2-4 weeks. "If longer than six weeks, write and ask why." Pays 1 copy.** Reviews books of poetry. Ship of Fools Press publishes chapbooks but does not accept unsolicited mss.

SHOFAR (IV-Children, ethnic, religious), 43 Northcote Dr., Melville NY 11747-3924, founded 1984, publisher/editor Gerald H. Grayson, is a magazine **for Jewish children 9-13**, appearing monthly October through May (double issues December/January and April/May). It is 32 pgs., magazine-sized, professionally printed, with color paper cover. Their press run is 17,000 with 16,000 subscriptions of which 1,000 are libraries. Subscription: $14.95. **Sample: $1.01 postage and 9×12 SAE. They will consider simultaneous submissions and "maybe" previously published poems. Send SASE for guidelines. Submit holiday theme poems at least 4 months in advance. Reports in 6-8 weeks. Pays 10¢/word plus 5 copies. Buys first North American serial rights.**

SIDESADDLE (IV-Cowgirl, regional, women), 111 W. Fourth St., Suite 300, Fort Worth TX 76102, phone (817)336-4475, founded 1979, is the annual publication of the National Cowgirl Hall of Fame and Western Heritage Center and is designed to honor cowgirls and Western women. **"All poetry must be cowgirl or Western poetry."** They have published poetry by Keith Avery, Georgie Sicking and Betty Solt. *SideSaddle* is 92 pgs., 8½×11, professionally printed on slick stock and saddle-stitched with a laminated full-color cover. Inside it features Western women and includes both b&w and full-color art and photos. **Sample postpaid: $6. Previously published poems and simultaneous submissions OK. Cover letter required. Poems are circulated to an editorial board. Always comments on rejections. Reports "ASAP."** Includes related book features/reviews within each issue. Open to unsolicited reviews. Poets may also send related books for review consideration.

‡SIDEWALKS (I, II), P.O. Box 321, Champlin MN 55316, founded 1991, editor Tom Heie, is a semiannual anthology of poetry, short prose and art, published to promote the work of emerging and published writers and artists. **They want "poetry that uses strong, original images and language, showing attention to craftsmanship, but not self-conscious; poetry that shows insight. No porno, kinky sex or rhyming verse."** They have recently published poetry by Mark Vinz, Jay Meek, Michael Dennis Browne and Kenneth Pobo. As a sample the editor selected the last stanza of "The Winter Heart" by Mary Kay Rummel:

> *She searches for the bear, remembering*
> *how she'd watched her roll down the road*
> *on round haunches. She knows they both*
> *will wake with lust some morning*
> *will walk on the ice in shoes of fire.*

Sidewalks is 76-80 pgs., 5½×8½, professionally printed and perfect-bound with matte card cover and b&w art. They receive 600-800 poems a year, accept approximately 10%. Press run is 300 for 100 subscribers, 50 shelf sales. Single copy: $6; subscription: $9. **Sample postpaid: $5. Submit 3-6** poems at a time, name and address on each. **No previously published poems or simultaneous submissions. Cover letter preferred. Deadlines: May 31 and December 31. Three readers read and vote on submissions; then a group meets to select the best work. Seldom comments on rejections. Send SASE for guidelines. Reports 1 month after deadline. Pays 1 copy. Acquires first rights.** The editor says, "Sidewalks [are] those places where a child first meets the world, [a] place of discovery, of myth, power, incantation . . . a world in itself, places we continue to meet people, ignoring some, smiling at others, preoccupied, on our way somewhere, . . . [places] where we pass with just a glance or smile or protectively turn up our collar on a windy day, . . . paths to and from neighbors, to the corner grocery . . . paths that bring us home."

SIERRA NEVADA COLLEGE REVIEW (I), P.O. Box 4269, Incline Village NV 89450, founded 1990, editor June Sylvester, is an annual literary magazine featuring poetry and short fiction by new writers. **They want "high quality, image-oriented poems that suggest or surprise; no limit on length, style, etc. No light verse, sloppy sentiment, purposeful obscurity, clichés or cuteness."** They have published poetry by Marisella Veiga, Ivanov Y. Reyez, Colleen O'Brien and B.Z. Nidith. As a sample the editor selected these lines from "The Book of Ruth" by Margaret Almon:

> I must not dream of anger.
> Placing a kernel
> in the bend of his knee,
> willing it to sprout into tangles
> around his throat—
> tangles like the ones in my hair
> that break the comb.
> Placing a sheaf beneath his bed,
> his body becoming a field of bruises.

The editor says *SNCR* is approximately 75 pgs., with cover art only. "We receive approximately 500 poems a year and accept approximately 50." Press run is 500. Subscription: $5/year. **Sample postpaid: $2.50. Submit 5 poems at a time. No previously published poems; simultaneous submissions OK. Include brief bio. Reads submissions September 1 through April 1 only. Often comments on rejections. Reports in 3 weeks to 3 months. Pays 2 copies.** The editor says, "We delight in publishing the unpublished or underpublished writer. We look specifically for subtlety and skill."

SILHOUETTE; HARDING STEDLER AWARD (I) (formerly *Shawnee Silhouette*), Shawnee State University, 940 Second St., Portsmouth OH 45662, phone (614)355-2300, founded 1985, editor Judith Allen, appears 3 times/year (winter, spring and summer) publishing poetry, artwork and photography, and occasionally sponsoring a poetry contest. **They want "any subject done in good taste; blank and free verse conventional forms; 28 lines including spaces."** They have recently published poetry by Rod Farmer, John Engle, Jr., Juanita Mays-Hipple and Ken Pell. As a sample the editor selected these lines by Sue Lonny:

> In the Dark
> One night I woke to hear a poem
> shaken loose in sleep,
> I copied words in darkness
> I later could not read.
> Perhaps because the piece was lost
> It was my finest work,
> and I will spend a poet's life
> remembering the words.

Silhouette is 48 pgs., digest-sized, offset from WordPerfect 6.0 with Laser writer Plus, utilizing a variety of typestyles, with b&w drawings and photographs, saddle-stapled, matte card cover with b&w photo. Single copy: $2.50; subscription: $6/year. **Send 3 poems at a time, typed double-spaced. No simultaneous submissions.** Time between acceptance and publication is 3 months. **Reports in 3 months. Pays 2 copies.** Sponsors the Harding Stedler Award, an annual award given to the best poem published in *Silhouette* in a given year. The editor says, "We are interested only in quality material and try to provide a diversity of styles and topics in each issue."

SILVER APPLES PRESS (V), P.O. Box 292, Hainesport NJ 08036, phone (609)267-2758, founded 1982, poetry editor Geraldine Little. "We're a very small press with very limited funds. Published our

---

MARKET CATEGORIES: (I) Beginning; **(II)** General; **(III)** Limited;
(IV) Specialized; **(V)** Closed.

first chapbook in 1988; open contest for same. We plan to publish randomly, as things turn us on and as funds permit—pamphlets, chapbooks, a set of postcards. **We are over-committed at present. Not currently accepting unsolicited poetry submissions. Watch *Poets & Writers* for announcements.**" They publish **"first-class poetry by experienced poets. No greeting card verse, soupy sentimental verse or blatantly religious verse.**" They have published *Contrasts in Keening: Ireland* by Geraldine C. Little, *Abandoned House* by Susan Fawcett and *The Verb to Love* by Barbara Horton. As a sample the editor selected these lines from *Keeping Him Alive* by Charlotte Mandel:

> We do not cut it down.
> In winter,
> within the bitter scrabble
> of bared, practiced branches,
> the dead tree, too, promises.

‡THE SILVER WEB: A MAGAZINE OF THE SURREAL (I, IV-Science fiction, horror), P.O. Box 38190, Tallahassee FL 32315, founded 1989, editor Ann Kennedy, is a semiannual publication featuring fiction, poetry, art and thought-provoking articles. **They want "works ranging from speculative fiction to dark tales and all weirdness in between; specifically works of the surreal. We are looking for well-written work that is unusual and original. No genre clichés, that is, no vampires, werewolves, zombies, witches, fairies, elves, dragons, etc. Also no fantasy, sword and sorcery. Poems must use standard poetic conventions whether free verse or rhyming.**" They have recently published poetry by Glenna Holloway, Simon Perchik, Tippi N. Blevins and Jacie Ragan. As a sample we selected these lines from "Empty House" by Fabian Peake:

> You walk the pavement
> of my street in your
> scuffed black shoes,
> dragging behind you
> (on lengths of string
> tied to your belt),
> a hundred paintbrushes
> dancing like drumsticks . . .

The editor says *The Silver Web* is 64 pgs., 8½ × 11. They receive 10-20 poems a week, accept 10-20 a year. Press run is 1,000 for more than 200 subscribers. Single copy: $4.95; subscription: $10. **Sample postpaid: $5.95, $6.95 Canada and overseas. Submit up to 5 poems at a time. Previously published poems OK, but note previous credit. Simultaneous submissions also OK. Reads submissions January 1 through September 30 only. Seldom comments on rejections. Send SASE for guidelines. Reports in 4-6 weeks. Always sends prepublication galleys. Pays $5-20 and 2 copies. Buys first or one-time rights.** Poetry published in *The Silver Web* has also been included in *The Rhysling Anthology* and *The Year's Best Fantasy and Horror.*

SILVER WINGS (IV-Religious, spirituality/inspirational), P.O. Box 1000, Pearblossom CA 93553-1000, phone (805)264-3726, founded 1983, published by Poetry on Wings, Inc., poetry editor Jackson Wilcox. "As a committed Christian service we produce and publish *Silver Wings*, a quarterly poetry magazine. We want **poems with a Christian perspective, reflecting a vital personal faith and a love for God and man. Will consider poems from 3-20 lines. Quite open in regard to meter and rhyme.**" They have recently published poetry by Elva McAllaster, Mary Ann Henn, Hugh Alexander and C. David Hay. As a sample the editor selected this poem, "The Heaven Road," by Marian Ford Park:

> I've soared the skies on silver wings
> That glistened with the dew;
> I've sailed my craft of jeweled lakes
> That mirrored Heaven's blue.
> I've roamed the hills and combed
> The dales and through the darkness trod
> The path of pain, but I've survived
> To touch the hand of God.

The magazine is 32 pgs., digest-sized, offset with cartoon-like art. They receive 1,500 submissions/year, use 260. Circulation is 450 with 300 subscribers, 50 shelf sales. Subscription: $7. **Sample postpaid: $2. Submit typed ms, double-spaced. No previously published poems; simultaneous submissions OK.** Time between acceptance and publication can be up to 2 years. **Send SASE for guidelines and upcoming themes. Reports in 3 weeks, providing SASE is supplied. Pays 1 copy plus subscription. "We occasionally offer an award to a poem we consider outstanding and most closely in the spirit of what *Silver Wings* seeks to accomplish." Acquires first rights.** The editor says, "We have felt that the state of secular poetry today is thrashing in a stagnant pond out of which it cannot extract itself. We want to lift our poetry to a high road where God's sunlight is shining. We even encourage poets with little ability but having an upward mobile commitment."

SILVERFISH REVIEW; SILVERFISH REVIEW PRESS; GERALD CABLE POETRY CONTEST (II), P.O. Box 3541, Eugene OR 97403, phone (503)344-5060, founded 1979, poetry editor Rodger Moody, is a biannual (June and December) literary magazine. **"The only criterion for selection of poetry is quality. In future issues** *Silverfish Review* **also wants to showcase the short short story."** They have recently published poetry by Chelsey Minnis, Denise Duhamel, Dick Allen, Ivan Arguelles, Gary Young, Robert Gregory, Kevin Bowen, Richard Jones, Floyd Skloot and Judith Skillman. As a sample the editor selected these lines by Lauren Mesa:

> *This one, the tall boy with brown hair,*
> *the wicker creel's strap slung*
> *across his crest, is Great-Uncle Mickey,*
> *Michelangelo Cipolla, the uncle*
> *who dressed as Santa the years*
> *my mother was a child.*

The magazine is 48 pgs., digest-sized, professionally printed in dark type on quality stock, matte card cover with art. There are 30-34 pgs. of poetry in each issue. They receive about 1,000 submissions of poetry/year, use 20, have a 6- to 12-month backlog. Circulation is 1,000. Subscription for institutions: $12; for individuals: $8. **Sample: $4, single copy orders should include $1.50 for p&h. Submit at least 5 poems to editor. No simultaneous submissions. Reports in about 2-6 months. Pays 2 copies and one-year subscription, plus small honorarium when grant support permits.** Reviews books of poetry. Open to unsolicited reviews. Poets may also send books for review consideration. Silverfish Review Press sponsors the Gerald Cable Poetry Contest. A $1,000 cash award and publication by SRP is awarded annually to the best book-length ms or original poetry by an author who has not yet published a full-length collection. No restrictions on the kind of poetry of subject matter; translations not acceptable. A $15 reading fee must accompany the ms; make checks payable to Silverfish Review Press. **Send SASE for rules.**

SING HEAVENLY MUSE! (IV-Feminist), Box 13320, Minneapolis MN 55414, founded 1977, editorial circle fosters "the work of women poets, fiction writers and artists. The magazine is **feminist in an open, generous sense: We encourage women to range freely, honestly and imaginatively over all subjects, philosophies and styles. We do not wish to confine women to women's subjects,** whether these are defined traditionally, in terms of femininity and domesticity, or modernly, from a sometimes narrow polemical perspective. We look for explorations, questions that do not come with ready-made answers, emotionally or intellectually." For poetry they have **"no limitations except women's writing or men's writing that reflects awareness of women's consciousness."** They have published poetry by Alexis Rotella, Jill Breckenridge and Amirh Bahati. The editor selected these sample lines from "Sons of Soweto" by June Jordan:

> *Words live in the spirit of her face*
> *and that sound will no longer yield . . .*
> *she will stand under the sun!*
> *She will stay!*

The magazine appears once a year in a 6×9, flat-spined, 125-page format, offset from typescript on heavy stock, b&w art, glossy card color cover. They receive 1,500 submissions/year, use 50-60. Press run is 1,000 for 275 subscribers of which 50 are libraries. Single copy: $8 plus $2 p&h; subscription: $15 for 2 issues, $20 for 3 issues ($16 low income), $38 for 6 issues. **Sample postpaid: $4. "Copies are also available in bookstores nationwide that carry small press women's literature." Submit 3-5 poems at a time, name and address on each page. No simultaneous submissions. Editors sometimes comment on rejections. Send SASE for guidelines, information about upcoming reading periods and themes. Reports in 4-5 months. Pays "usually $25 plus 2 copies."**

SINGULAR SPEECH PRESS (IV-Form), 10 Hilltop Dr., Canton CT 06019-2139, phone/fax (860)693-6059, e-mail dondwilson@aol.com, founded 1976, editor Don D. Wilson. "Singular Speech Press presents examples of our many real poets—probably our most unsupported artists. **And so we publish at least 6 mss per annum, 40-96 pages. We have few biases, are enamored of both free and formal verse, are gladdened by unknown and well-known poets; however, we cannot stomach prosaic or confessional poetry. We have recently decided to concentrate on formal poetry, for diverse reasons, partly to simplify, because we are inundated by vers libre, partly because we believe it's time to support again the time-honored sonnet, et al."** They have recently published Geraldine Little's *No Home to Return to But This*, Penny Harter's *Grandmother's Milk*, Louise Kennelly's *Tracking God in Italy*, Carol Poster's *Surrounded by Dangerous Things* and Gray Burr's *Afterliver*. As a sample here are six lines from "In the Coorong" in *All I Have Is a Fountain* by R.H. Morrison:

> *The pure rose will crave its countering thorn,*
> *a somber, jagged note must rive our tunes,*
> *some lifted form break up the level plain.*
> *This peace in its antithesis was born;*

what calms us is unpinned behind those dunes:
the sea's turmoil, the sea's rage, the sea's pain.

‡**SINISTER WISDOM (IV-Lesbian, feminist)**, P.O. Box 3252, Berkeley CA 94703, founded 1976, editor Akiba Onáda-Sikwoia, is a lesbian feminist journal. The editor says, **"We want poetry that reflects the diversity of lesbian experience—lesbians of color, Third World, Jewish, old, young, working class, poor, disabled, fat, etc.—from a lesbian and/or feminist perspective. No heterosexual themes. We will not print anything that is oppressive or demeaning to women, or which perpetuates negative stereotypes."** The journal has published work by Gloria Anzaldúa, Sapphire and Betsy Warland. As a sample the editor chose the following lines from Minnie Bruce Pratt's poem "#67 To Be Posted on 21st Street, Between Eye and Pennsylvania":

Like a movie, sudden threat
Predictable. I get so tired of this disbelief.
My tongue, faithful in my mouth, said: Yes, we are.
the shout: Lesbians. Lesbians. Trying to curse
us with our name. Me louder: That's what we are.

The editor says the quarterly magazine is 128-144 pgs., digest-sized, flat-spined, with photos and b&w graphics. Circulation is 3,500 of which 1,000 are subscriptions and 100 go to libraries; newsstand sales and bookstores are 1,500. Single copy: $6; subscription: $20 US, $25 foreign. **Sample postpaid: $7.50. No simultaneous submissions.** Time between acceptance and publication is 6 months to 1 year. **Publishes theme issues. Send SASE for upcoming themes. Reports in up to 9 months. Pays 2 copies.** Reviews books of poetry in 500-1,500 words, single or multi-book format. The editor says they would like "anything *other* than love poetry."

‡**THE SIREN (II)**, Campus Box 1514, Eckerd College, 4200 54th Ave. S., St. Petersburg FL 33711, e-mail siren@eckerd.edu, founded 1993, is the annual, nationally-distributed literary magazine of Eckerd College which publishes high-quality poetry, fiction and color and b&w artwork. **"We want to see poems of a wide range of content, length and tone from poets who pay particular attention to craft (particularly line, stanza and voice). Nothing sentimental or cliché, nor poems that are needlessly obscure or Beat."** They have recently published poetry by Kathryn Stripling Byer, Fred Chappell and R.T. Smith. As a sample the editor selected these lines from "First Snake in Five Years" by Robert Wrigley:

After all, the rattler's half asleep
under the sun and a cool spring breeze,
a green so true he looks to be pure
chlorophyl himself, his taper of rattles closing
on a nub red and swollen
as an in-grown nail . . .

The editor says *Siren* is 100 pgs., perfect-bound with full-color cover and art. "We receive 200-300 poems a year and usually accept 1%." Press run is 1,400 for 800 shelf sales. **Sample postpaid: $6. Submit 4 poems at a time. No previously published poems or simultaneous submissions. Cover letter required. Reads submissions September 1 through January 15 only. Poems are first read by a staff of 20. Final decisions are made by an editorial board. Seldom comments on rejections. Send SASE for guidelines. Reports in 6 weeks. Pays 1 copy. Acquires first rights.** Staff reviews books of poetry and fiction in 900 words, single format. Poets may send books for review consideration. The editor says, "Editors favor authors who have studied other poets as well as their craft."

SISTER VISION PRESS (IV-Ethnic, women), P.O. Box 217, Station E, Toronto, Ontario M6H 4E2 Canada, phone (416)595-5033, founded 1985, managing editor Makeda Silvera, publishes 8-10 paperbacks/year. They want **"poetry that reflects our lives as women of color; not restricted by form or length."** They have published poetry by ahdri zhina mandiela and Ramabai Espinet. As a sample the editor selected these lines from "Crebo" in Espinet's book *Nuclear Seasons*:

My hands had wrinkles
But rims grew around my eyes
My skin became ebony and rose
And my tongue grew long beyond words

Submit a sample of work, to a maximum of 10 pages. Previously published poems and simultaneous submissions OK. Cover letter required. Replies to queries in 1 month, to mss (if invited) in 2 months. Pays 10% royalties and 10 author's copies. Write for samples. They say, "Know the publisher you are submitting mss to. This saves the poet and publisher time, money and energy."

SISTERS TODAY (II, IV-Spirituality/inspirational), The Liturgical Press, Collegeville MN 56321; send submissions to: poetry editor Sister Mary Virginia Micka, C.S.J., 1884 Randolph, St. Paul MN 55105. *Sisters Today* has been published for about 60 years. Though it is a Roman Catholic magazine, **poetry may be on any topic, but "should clearly be *poems*, not simply *statements* or**

prayers." They want "short poems (not over 25 lines) using clean, fresh images that appeal to the reader's feelings in a compelling way." They do not want poetry that depends "heavily on rhyme, verbal 'tricks' or excessive capitalization, manipulation of spacing, etc." *ST*, appearing 6 times/year, is 80 pgs., 6 × 9, saddle-stapled, professionally printed with matte card cover. They receive about 50 poems/month, accept 3-4. Press run is 4,000. Subscription: $20 US; $22 foreign. **Sample postpaid: $3.50 (Send to: Sister Mary Anthony Wagner, O.S.B., Editor, *Sisters Today*, St. Benedict's Convent, St. Joseph MN 56374). Submit up to 5 poems at a time. No simultaneous submissions. Original poems much preferred. They require "each poem typed on a separate standard-size typing sheet, and each page must carry complete legal name, address and social security number typed in the upper right corner. Manuscripts without SASE will not be returned."** Time between acceptance and publication is 6-12 months. **Send SASE to Collegeville, MN address (above) for guidelines. Reports within 1-2 months. Pays $10/poem and 2 copies. Buys first rights.**

‡**SITUATION (II)**, 10402 Ewell Ave., Kensington MD 20895, e-mail mdw@gwis2.circ.gwu.edu, founded 1991, contact Mark Wallace, appears 4 times a year and is interested in "**innovative work that explores how writing creates, dismantles, or restructures the possibility of identity. A poetry of situation. Works involving questions of race, class, gender or sexual preference are all encouraged.**" They want experimental or avant-garde poetry; "**less likely to accept poetry in traditional forms.**" They have recently published poetry by Charles Bernstein, Sterling Plumpp, Joan Retallack and Stephen-Paul Martin. As a sample we selected these lines from "Plaid Into Conquest" by Connie Deanovich:

> *the matador imagines*
> *that even an American woman*
> *in a plaid bikini*
> *who was basted with water*
> *from the River Nile*
> *would match the vivaciousness*
> *of his cape*
> *and would similarly use on him*
> *ancient movements of seduction*

Situation is 24 pgs., 7 × 8½, neatly printed on bond paper, saddle-stapled, no cover. They receive about 200 submissions a year, accept 15%. Press run is 200 for 100 subscribers of which 5 are libraries. Subscription: $10. **Sample postpaid: $3. Make checks payable to Mark Wallace. Submit 7 poems at a time. No previously published poems; simultaneous submissions OK. Cover letter required. "All submissions must be accompanied by SASE."** Time between acceptance and publication is usually 6 months. **Seldom comments on rejections. Send SASE for guidelines. Reports in 3 months. Sometimes sends prepublication galleys. Pays 2 copies. Acquires first rights.**

SIVULLINEN (V), Kaarelantie 86 B 28, 00420 Helsinki, Finland, founded 1985, editor Jouni Waarakangas, is a biannual publication of drawings, graphics, poems and short stories—**publishes all kinds of poetry. However, "due to enormous amount of poetry submissions received, I have enough poems for a few issues."** They have published poetry by Timothy Hodor, Ana Christy and Norman J. Olson. As a sample we selected these lines from "Better To" by Wendell Metzger:

> *lie in bed*
> *and be awake*
> *than sit before a TV*
> *get sleepy*

The editor says *Sivullinen* is copied and varies between 28-56 pgs., A4 size and A5 size. They accept about 20% of poetry received. Press run is 500. **Sample postpaid: $2-4. When open to submissions, they accept 3-5 poems at a time. Previously published poems and simultaneous submissions OK.** Time between acceptance and publication is 3 months to 1 year. **Reports in 3-10 weeks. Pays 1 copy.**

‡**SKIPPING STONES: A MULTICULTURAL CHILDREN'S MAGAZINE (IV-Children/ teen, ethnic/nationality)**, P.O. Box 3939, Eugene OR 97403, phone (541)342-4956, founded 1988, editor Arun Toké, is a "nonprofit magazine published bimonthly during the school year (5 issues) that encourages cooperation, creativity and celebration of cultural and environmental richness." **They want poetry by youth under 18; 30 lines maximum on "nature, multicultural and social issues, family, freedom . . . uplifting." No work by adults.** As a sample we selected these lines from "Two Voices: Mother and Daughter" by Tara Ashcraft, age 15, from St. Paul, Minnesota:

> *The daughter of mine,*
> The mother of mine,
>
> *Has a beautiful face,*
> Has a beautiful face,

That lights up with wonder and awe.
That is always wondering about me.

But I just don't understand,
But sometimes she just doesn't understand,

Why it's so hard to be a mother,
What it's like to be a daughter, . . .

SS is 8½ × 11, saddle-stitched, printed on recycled paper. They receive 500-1,000 poems a year, accept about 10%. Press run is 3,000 for 1,700 subscribers. Subscription: $20. **Sample postpaid: $5. Submit up to 3 poems at a time. No previously published poems; simultaneous submissions OK. Cover letter preferred. "Include your cultural background, experiences and what was the inspiration behind your creation."** Time between acceptance and publication is 3-9 months. Poems are circulated to a 3-member editorial board. **"Generally a piece is chosen for publication when all the editorial staff feel good about it." Seldom comments on rejections. Publishes theme issues. Send SASE for guidelines and upcoming themes. Reports in 2-4 months. Pays 1 copy, offers 25% discount on 4 or more. Acquires all rights. Returns rights after publication, but "we keep reprint rights."** Sponsors Annual Youth Honor Awards for 7-16 year olds. Entry fee: $3, includes free issue containing the winners. *Skipping Stones* received a 1995 Golden Shoestring Award from Ed Press.

SKYLARK (I, II, IV-Themes), Purdue University Calumet, 2200 169th St., Hammond IN 46323, phone (219)989-2262, founded 1972, editor-in-chief Pamela Hunter, poetry editor Christine Shrader, is "a fine arts annual, **one section (about 25 pages) of which is devoted to a special theme."** They are looking for **"fresh voices, original images, concise presentation and honesty; poems up to 25 lines; narrative poems to 75 lines. No horror, nothing extremely religious, no pornography."** They are also interested in receiving more prose poems and more well-crafted surrealistic poems. They have recently published poetry by Mary Driscoll, Richard Fein, Harding Stedler and Lois Greene Stone. As a sample the editor selected these lines from "Havling Mondays" by William Cannon:

On Mondays, the bag of time like some
diaphanous epiphany billows out
behind me all my days on earth,
trails out like so much 'what's the use'
catching on door knobs and shrubbery,

Skylark is 100 pgs., magazine-sized, professionally printed, perfect-bound, with matte card cover. Press run is 900-1,000 for 50 subscriptions of which 12 are libraries. Single copy: $7. **Sample postpaid: $5. Submit 3-5 poems at a time. "Cover letter encouraged. No simultaneous submissions. Inquire (with SASE) as to annual theme for special section."** The theme for 1997 is "Home." **Do not submit mss between June 1 and November 1. Reports in 4 months. Pays 1 copy. Acquires first rights. Editor may encourage rejected but promising writers.** She says she would like to receive "poems with better editing, greater coordination of form and content, and sharper, more original imagery."

SLANT: A JOURNAL OF POETRY (II), Box 5063, University of Central Arkansas, Conway AR 72035-0001, phone (501)450-5107, founded 1987, editor James Fowler, is an annual using *only* poetry. They use **"traditional and 'modern' poetry, even experimental, moderate length, any subject on approval of Board of Readers; purpose is to publish a journal of fine poetry from all regions of the United States. No haiku, no translations."** They have recently published poetry by Philip Dacey, Vivian Shipley and Daniel Tobin. As a sample the editor selected these lines from "Spring" by Leonard Nathan:

Spring and the old apple tree
in bloom—you feel years younger,
as do your enemies.

They come at you laughing, singing,
shooting at the sky, hair
crowned with apple blossoms.

Slant is 125 pgs., professionally printed on quality stock, flat-spined, with matte card cover. They publish about 70-80 poems of the 1,400 received each year. Press run is 250 for 70-100 subscribers. **Sample postpaid: $10. Submit no more than 5 poems of moderate length. "Put name and address top of each page." No simultaneous submissions or previously published poems. Editor comments on rejections "on occasion." Allow 3-4 months from November 15 deadline for response. Pays 1 copy.** The editor says, "I would like to see more formal verse."

THE SLATE (II), P.O. Box 581189, Minneapolis MN 55458-1189, phone (612)871-8532, founded 1994, first issue published in April of 1995, appears 3 times/year and is designed "to promote the written word as an art form." **The editors have no restrictions regarding form, length or subject of poetry.** They say *The Slate* is 100 pgs., 6×9, perfect-bound. Press run is 1,500. **Simultaneous submissions OK. All four editors read everything and then discuss it. Often comment on rejections. Send SASE for guidelines and upcoming themes. Pays 2 copies. Acquires all rights. Returns rights upon publication of next issue.** Current issue: $6. **Sample: $4.95.**

SLATE & STYLE (IV-Specialized: blind writers), Dept. PM, 2704 Beach Dr., Merrick NY 11566, phone (516)868-8718, fax (516)868-9076, editor Loraine Stayer, is a **quarterly for blind writers available on cassette, in large print and Braille,** "including articles of interest to blind writers, resources for blind writers. Membership/subscription is $10 per year, all formats. Division of the National Federation of the Blind." **Poems may be "5-35 lines. Prefer contributors to be blind writers, or at least writers by profession or inclination, but prefer poems** *not* **about blindness. No obscenities. Will consider all forms of poetry including haiku. Interested in new talent."** They have published poetry by Stephanie Pieck, Louise Hope Bristow, Janet Wolff and Ken Volonte. As a sample we selected these lines from "April" by Marie Grant:

> April is a woman
> This is how I know:
> She's provocative and flirty,
> And promises too much.
> She giggles in the rosy dawn
> By noon her tears are falling.
> She wept when March departed,
> Greeted May with a harlot's kiss.

The print version is 28-32 pgs., magazine-sized, stapled, with a fiction and poetry section. Press run is 200 for 160 subscribers of which 4-5 are libraries. Subscription: $10/year. **Sample postpaid: $2.50. Submit 3 poems once or twice a year. No simultaneous submissions or previously published poems. Cover letter preferred.** "On occasion we receive poems in Braille. I prefer print, since Braille slows me down. Typed is best." **Do not submit mss in July. Editor comments on rejections "if requested." Send SASE for guidelines. Reports in "2 weeks if I like it." Pays 1 copy.** Reviews books of poetry. Open to unsolicited reviews. Poets may also send books for review consideration. They offer an annual poetry contest. Entry fee: $5/poem. Deadline: May 1. Write for details. Loraine Stayer says, "Poetry is one of the toughest ways to express oneself, yet ought to be the easiest to read. Anything that looks simple is the result of much work."

SLIGHTLY WEST (II), CAB 320, The Evergreen State College, Olympia WA 98505, phone (360)866-6000 ext. 6879, founded 1985, editors Sarah Dougherty and Melia Luoto, is a biannual designed "to give a boost to new or struggling writers and to promote art throughout the community." **They are open to all types, forms and styles of poetry. "No fluff. We are taking only the upper crust of submissions."** They have recently published poetry by Cari Alhstrom, Matt Schwartz, Pamela Brookman and Mark Peters. As a sample the editors selected these lines "Untitled" by Scott Caughron:

> He calls his friends from the pickup
> and suddenly my peace is invaded
> by loud dirty apes pounding themselves
> on the head, barking lies and war cries
> bringing barbecue in mechanic fingers
> bragging of the day's kill
> to blackeyed women with sagging breasts
> in yellowed lace haltertops that hang
> from one shoulder pulled by a scrofulous
> baby tyrant with snot bubbling slowly down
> into his screaming mouth

The editors say *SW* is 50-60 pgs., perfect-bound with cover and inside artwork. They receive 700-1,000 submissions a year, accept approximately 15%. Press run is 1,500 for 55 subscribers of which 5 are libraries; 1,000 distributed free to local community. Subscription: $5. **Sample postpaid: $2.50. Submit 3 poems at a time. Previously published poems and simultaneous submissions OK. Cover letter required. "They allow the poet to become more recognizable, not just a poem but a person behind the words. We have a selections board of 5-10 poets and writers who critique and comment on submissions." Often comments on rejections. Send SASE for guidelines. Reports in 1 month. Pays 1 copy. Acquires one-time rights.** The editors say, "We have been established for 10 years as just a 'school' magazine. Currently we are upgrading our requirements for poetry submissions. We encourage beginners to send poetry. We will return manuscripts with comments *only if SASE enclosed.*"

SLIPSTREAM (II, IV-Themes), Box 2071, New Market Station, Niagara Falls NY 14301-0071, phone (716)282-2616 (after 5pm, EST), founded 1980, poetry editors Dan Sicoli, Robert Borgatti and Livio Farallo. *Slipstream* is a "small press literary mag that is about 90% poetry and 10% fiction/

prose, some artwork. The editors like **new work with contemporary urban flavor. Writing must have a cutting edge to get our attention. We like to keep an open forum, any length, subject, style. Best to see a sample to get a feel. Like city stuff as opposed to country. Like poetry that springs from the gut, screams from dark alleys, inspired by experience." No "pastoral, religious, traditional, rhyming" poetry.** They have recently published poetry by Michael McNeilley, Elizabeth Balestrieri, Angela Consolo Mankiewicz, Gailmarie Pahmeier, Gerald Locklin, Joan Jobe Smith, Charles Bukowski, B.D. Love and E.R. Baxter III. As a sample the editors selected these lines from "Dr. Zhivago" by Chris Mortenson:

> Men no longer live for their country
> unless they are something
> less than human
> and they do not die for it unless
> they are in some way
> already dead.

Slipstream appears 1-2 times a year in a $7 \times 8\frac{1}{2}$ format, 80-100 pgs., professionally printed, saddle-stapled, using b&w photos and graphics. It contains mostly free verse, some stanza patterns. They receive over 2,500 submissions of poetry/year, use less than 10%. Press run is 500 for 400 subscribers of which 10 are libraries. Subscription: $15 for 2 issues and 2 chapbooks. **Sample postpaid: $6. Editor sometimes comments on rejections. Publishes theme issues. Send SASE for guidelines and upcoming themes. Reports in 2-8 weeks, "if SASE included." Pays copies.** Annual chapbook contest has December 1 deadline. Reading fee: $10. Submit up to 40 pgs. of poetry, any style, previously published work OK with acknowledgments. Winner receives $500 and 50 copies. All entrants receive copy of winning chapbook and an issue of the magazine. Past winners have included Gerald Locklin, Serena Fusek, Robert Cooperman, Kurt Nimmo, David Chorlton, Richard Amidon, Sherman Alexie, and most recently, Katharine Harer for her book *Hubba Hubba*. Dan Sicoli advises, "Do not waste time submitting your work 'blindly.' Sample issues from the small press first to determine which ones would be most receptive to your work."

SMALL POND MAGAZINE OF LITERATURE (II), P.O. Box 664, Stratford CT 06497, phone (203)378-4066, founded 1964, editor Napoleon St. Cyr, a literary triquarterly that features poetry . . . "and anything else the editor feels is original, important." Poetry can be **"any style, form, topic, except haiku, so long as it is deemed good, but limit of about 100 lines."** Napoleon St. Cyr wants **"nothing about cats, pets, flowers, butterflies, etc. Generally nothing under 8 lines."** Although he calls it name-dropping, he "reluctantly" provided the names of Marvin Soloman, Marilyn Johnson, Richard Kostelanetz, Fritz Hamilton and Emilie Glen as poets published. The magazine is 40 pgs., digest-sized, offset from typescript on off-white paper, with matte card cover, saddle-stapled, artwork both on cover and inside. Circulation is 300, of which about a third go to libraries. Subscription: $9 (for 3 issues). **Sample postpaid: $2.50 for a random selection, $3.50 current. Guidelines are available in each issue.** The editor says he doesn't want 60 pages of anything; **"dozen pages of poems max." Name and address on each page. No previously published poems or simultaneous submissions. Brief cover letter preferred.** Time between acceptance and publication is within 3-18 months. **Reports in 10-45 days (longer in summer). Pays 2 copies. Acquires all rights. Returns rights with written request including stated use. "One-time use per request."** Staff reviews books of poetry. Send books for review consideration. All styles and forms are welcome here. The editor usually responds quickly, often with comments to guide poets whose work interests him. He says, "I would like to receive more good surreal verse."

‡SMALL PRESS GENRE ASSOCIATION (SPGA); THE GENRE WRITER'S NEWS (IV-Membership, science fiction/horror/fantasy/mystery/westerns), P.O. Box 6301, Concord CA 94524, phone (510)254-7442 or 7053, president/treasurer Joe Morey, vice president John B. Rosenman, secretary Cathy Hicks. The association publishes a quarterly digest with emphasis on aiding members, advice columns, short poetry, art, reviews and short fiction; provides a poetry commentary service for members only; and publishes a yearly anthology of members' work. **They don't want to see "religious, highly sentimental, pornographic, racial or political poetry."** They have recently published poetry by Jacie Ragan, John Grey, Herb Kauderer and Charlotte H. Deskins. As a sample they selected these lines from "Bodies of Light" by Wendy Rathbone:

> The finest men are tendrils
> and shadows and chameleons
> They live sideways in the steeped liquid
> of fantasy formed from tense
> and accentuated will

Send all poetry submissions to poetry editor Bobbi Sinha-Morey, 30 Canyon View Dr., Orinda CA 94563. Staff reviews books of poetry in 200-500 words, single format. The Small Press Genre Association promotes "excellence in writing, illustration, calligraphy, editing, and publication of material related to the literary genres of fantasy, sword and sorcery, horror, western, mystery, weird, or science fiction." Membership is open to any writer, poet, artist, editor, publisher or calligrapher. Dues are $25 for US members, $30 for members outside US. For more information or to join, send SASE to Cathy Hicks, SPGA Secretary, 2131 S. 227th Dr., Buckeye AZ 85326-3872.

THE SMITH; THE GENERALIST PAPERS (II), 69 Joralemon St., Brooklyn NY 11201-4003, founded 1964, editor Harry Smith, publishes 3 to 5 books yearly. They have published *Poems New & Selected 1962-1992* by Lloyd Van Brunt and *Your Heart Will Fly Away* by David Rigsbee. As a sample the editor selected these lines from "Hawk Forever in Mid-Dive" in Lance Lee's *Wrestling with the Angel*:

> Her feet on the patio are leaves blown
> over flagstones. Aimed at her head,
> beak thrust out wings angled severely
> a hawk hangs frozen in mid-air,
> fanned to permanent fire in her sky.

"Send 3-6 poem sampling with query. No jingles, no standard academic verse. The decision process is relatively slow—about three months—as many mss are offered. Readers' reports are often passed along and the editor often comments." Always sends prepublication galleys. Pays 15% royalties, $500 advance, 10 copies. Send SASE for catalog or send $2 for a "slightly irregular" book ("with bumped corners or a little dust"). *The Generalist Papers*, appearing 6 times/year, consists of lively critical commentaries on contemporary writing—more candor than you will find in most reviews. Subscription: $12. **Sample postpaid: $2.** Harry Smith received a Poor Richard Award, a lifetime achievement award for distinguished contribution to small press publishing from the Small Press Center. He advises, "Revert to earlier models. *Avoid* university wordshops where there are standard recent models leading to standard mod verse. A close reading of *The Pearl Poet* will be more nourishing than all the asparagus of John Ashbery or Robert Bly."

GIBBS SMITH, PUBLISHER; PEREGRINE SMITH POETRY COMPETITION (III), P.O. Box 667, Layton UT 84041-0667, phone (801)544-2958 or 544-9800, fax (801)544-5582, founded 1971, poetry series established 1988, poetry editor Gail Yngue. **They want "serious, contemporary poetry of merit."** They have published books of poetry by David Huddle, Angie Estes and Carol Frost. Books are selected for publication through competition for the Peregrine Smith Poetry Prize of $500 plus publication. **Entries are received in April only and require a $15 reading fee and SASE. Mss should be 48-64 typewritten pgs.** "We publish only one unsolicited poetry ms per year—the winner of our annual Peregrine Smith Poetry Contest. For guidelines to the contest, we prefer that interested poets send a request with SASE through the mail. However, they can request guidelines through fax and telephone." The winner of the 1995 contest was Harvey Hix's *Perfect Hell*. The judge and general editor for the series is Christopher Merrill.

SMITHS KNOLL (I, II), 49 Church Rd., Little Glemham, Woodbridge, Suffolk IP13 0BJ England, founded 1991, co-editors Roy Blackman and Michael Laskey, is a magazine appearing 3 times a year. They look for **poetry with honesty, depth of feeling, lucidity and craft.** As a sample the editors selected these lines from "At the End of the Killing Line" by Peter Wyton:

> Places I seldom go, if I can help it: 1. Upstairs,
> where there are people in suits. 2. The opposite end
> of the killing line, where pigs are individually
> stampeded through a channel, underneath a rusted stile,
> where the man stands with the fag hanging from his lip,
> one eye closed, the long mallet arcing over and down.

The editors say it is 60 pgs., A5, offset-litho, perfect-bound, with card cover. They receive 5,000-7,000 poems a year, "accept about one in thirty." Press run is 450 for 300 subscribers. Single copy: £3.50; subscription: £10 for 3 issues (outside UK). **Submit up to 5 poems at a time. "We would consider poems previously published in magazines outside the U.K." No simultaneous submissions. Poems only. Doesn't commission work. "Cover letters should be brief: name, address, date, number of poems sent (or titles). We don't want life histories or complete publishing successes or what the poems are about. Constructive criticism of rejections where possible." Tries to report within 1 month (outside UK). Pays £5 plus 1 copy/poem.**

SNAKE RIVER REFLECTIONS (II), 1863 Bitterroot Dr., Twin Falls ID 83301, phone (208)734-0746, e-mail william@magiclink.com, editor William White, appears 10 times a year using **short poems, up to 30 lines, any topic.** As a sample we selected these lines from "The Wall" by C. David Hay:

> Could tears but wash the pain away
> And heal a nation's scar,
> That men may find a better way
> Than futile acts of war.

Pray their death was not in vain—
A lesson to recall;
A future world without the need
Of names upon a Wall.

It is 8 pgs. (2 8½ × 11 sheets folded), printed on colored paper and saddle-stapled. Press run is 100-300. Subscription: $8.50/10 issues. **Sample postpaid: 30¢. Submit 10-15 poems at a time. No previously published poems or simultaneous submissions. Cover letter encouraged. Send SASE for guidelines. Pays 1 copy. Acquires first North American serial rights.** Reviews books of poetry. Send books for review consideration.

SNOWY EGRET (II, IV-Nature), P.O. Box 9, Bowling Green IN 47833, founded 1922 by Humphrey A. Olsen, editor Philip Repp. **They want poetry that is "nature-oriented: poetry that celebrates the abundance and beauty of nature or explores the interconnections between nature and the human psyche."** As a sample of published poetry they selected the opening lines of "In a Climax Forest" by Conrad Hilberry:

> *The wooden past grows larger, I grow less*
> *and less convincing in this sullen air*
> *that wants a wind to stir its emptiness.*

Snowy Egret appears twice a year in a 48-page, magazine-sized format, offset, saddle-stapled, with original graphics. Of the 500 poems received they accept about 20. Their press run is 800 for 500 subscribers of which 50 are libraries. **Sample postpaid: $8. Send #10 SASE for writer's guidelines. Reports in 1 month. Always sends prepublication galleys. Pays $4/poem or $4/page plus 2 copies. Buys first North American or reprint rights.** Open to unsolicited reviews. Poets may also send books for review consideration.

SOCIAL ANARCHISM (IV-Political, social issues, women/feminism), 2743 Maryland Ave., Baltimore MD 21218, phone (410)243-6987, founded (Vacant Lots Press) 1980, poetry editor Howard J. Ehrlich, is a biannual using about 6 pgs. of poetry in each issue which **"represents a political or social commentary that is congruent with a nonviolent anarchist, antiauthoritarian and feminist perspective."** They have published poetry by Earl Coleman, John Sokol, E.C. Archibeque, Richard Ballon, Barbara F. Stout, Deirdre V. Lovecky, Joel Lewis and Steven Hill. As a sample we selected these lines from "The Painted Soldier" by Lynn Olson:

> *He lay flat on the dirt road*
> *flat where the thick, wide tires of our trucks*
> *had pressed him out thin against the dirt road*
> *flat where the wide treads of our tanks*
> *had pressed him out thinner on the dirt road. . . .*

SA is 112 pgs., digest-sized. Print run is 1,500. **Sample postpaid: $4. Submit up to 5 poems at a time. Considers simultaneous submissions. Cover letter with short (3-sentence) bio required. Reports in 4-6 weeks. Pays 3 copies.** Query regarding book reviews.

THE SOCIETY OF AMERICAN POETS (SOAP); IN HIS STEPS PUBLISHING COMPANY; THE POET'S PEN (I, IV-Religious, membership), P.O. Box 85, Tifton GA 31793, phone/fax (912)382-5377, founded 1984, editor Dr. Charles E. Cravey. *The Poet's Pen* is a literary quarterly of poetry and short stories. In His Steps publishes religious and other books and publishes music for the commercial record market. **"Open to all styles of poetry and prose—both religious and secular. No gross or 'X-rated' poetry without taste or character."** They have recently published poetry by James Pecquet, Claudette Clarke and Kelly Martin. As a sample the editor selected these lines from "Beyond My Blindness" by Mark Anthony Grubb:

> *Beyond my vision and many light years away,*
> *A galaxy is affected by things that I say.*
> *For I am one unit in the motion and flow,*
> *In a sea of creation that continues to grow.*

The Poet's Pen uses **poetry primarily by members and subscribers.** (Membership: $25/year.) **Submit 3 poems at a time, include name and address on each page. "Submissions or inquiries will not be responded to without a SASE. We do stress originality and have each new poet and/or subscriber sign a waiver form verifying originality."** Simultaneous submissions OK; previously published poems OK, if permission from previous publisher is included. Publishes seasonal/theme issues. Send SASE for upcoming themes. Sometimes sends prepublication galleys. Query for book publication. 60/40 split of pay. Editor "most certainly" comments on rejections. Sponsors several contests each quarter which total $250-500 in cash awards. Editor's Choice Awards each quarter, prizes $25, $15 and $10. President's Award for Superior Choice has a prize of $50; deadline is November 1. They also publish a quarterly anthology that has poetry competitions in several categories with prizes of $25-100. The editor says, "We're looking for poets who wish to unite in fellowship with our growing family of poets nationwide. We currently have over 850 poets and are one of the nation's largest societies, yet small enough and family operated to give each of our poets individual attention and pointers."

SOJOURNERS (IV-Religious, political), 2401 15th St. NW, Washington DC 20009, phone (202)328-8842, fax (202)328-8757, founded 1975, poetry editor Rose Berger, appears 6 times/year, "with approximately 40,000 subscribers. **We focus on faith, politics and culture from a radical Christian perspective. We publish 1-3 poems/month depending on length. All poems must be original and unpublished. We look for seasoned, well-crafted poetry that reflects the issues and perspectives covered in our magazine. Poetry using non-inclusive language (any racist, sexist, homophobic poetry) will not be accepted."** As a sample the editor selected these lines by David Abrams:

> *An eagle against a clear sky,*
> *A snake coming off a rock,*
> *A skiff in the center of a lake,*
> *And the Spirit slipping into bodies.*

The editor describes *Sojourners* as 52 pgs., offset printed. It appears bimonthly. Of 400 poems received/ year, they publish 6-8. Press run is 50,000 for 40,000 subscribers of which 500 are libraries, 2,000 shelf sales. Subscription: $30. **Sample postpaid: $3.95. Submit no more than 3 poems at a time. Cover letter with brief bio required. Editor comments on submissions "sometimes." Publishes theme issues. Send SASE for guidelines and upcoming themes. Reports in 4-6 weeks. Pays $15-25/poem plus 5 copies. "We assume permission to grant reprints unless the author requests otherwise."** Staff reviews books of poetry in 600 words, single or multi-book format.

SOLO FLYER; SPARE CHANGE POETRY PRESS (I), 2115 Clearview NE, Massillon OH 44646-2003, e-mail mccoy@eznets.canton.oh.us, Spare Change Poetry Press founded 1979, editor David B. McCoy. *Solo Flyer* is a 4-page flyer appearing 2-5 times/year featuring the work of a single poet in each issue. They want **poetry using punctuation and capitalization. "Like to see poems with a common theme and more prose poems."** As a sample the editor selected "Absences" by Ruth V. Tams-Fuquen:

> *Wordless*
> *we walked that hotel's midnight garden.*
> *The blossom you laid on my palm*
>
> *spoke*
> *for the song you hummed,*
>
> *suggested*
> *the words you chose*
> *not to sing.*

The flyers are folded 8½ × 11 sheets of colored paper. **Sample free with #10 SASE. Previously published material OK. Submissions and requests accepted via e-mail. Pays 20-25 copies.** The editor says, "Mail submissions without SASE are not read."

SONORA REVIEW (II), Dept. of English, University of Arizona, Tucson AZ 85721, phone (520)626-8383 or 621-1836, founded 1980, address all work to Poetry Editor, is a semiannual literary journal that publishes "non-genre" fiction and poetry. **The editors want "quality poetry, literary concerns. Translations welcome. No dull, well-crafted but passionless poetry or swooping and universal sentiment. Experimental work welcome."** They have published poetry by Jane Miller, Christopher Davis, Barbara Cully and Rosmarie Waldrop. As a sample, the editors chose the following lines by Joshua Clover:

> *Across the tracks her scalp took on the feel*
> *of a cigarette foil's papered side. Snow*
> *hair & boots. The most wasted man around*
> *would persuade his lover to waste him even more*
> *in the pause I woke into.*

Sonora Review is a handsome magazine, 130 pgs., 6 × 9, professionally printed on heavy off-white stock, flat-spined, with 2-color glossy card cover. Recent issues have tended to include lyric and

---

USE THE GENERAL INDEX to find the page number of a specific publisher. Also, if a publisher from last year's edition is not included in this edition, the General Index will tell you why.

narrative free verse, with some metered poetry, translations and sequences rounding out selections. Circulation is 650, of which 250 are subscriptions and 45 go to libraries. Subscription: $12/year, $24/ 2 years. **Back issue available for $6 postpaid. Poets should submit typed copy; simultaneous submissions OK. "Brief cover letter helpful but optional." Publishes theme issues. Send SASE for upcoming themes. Reporting time is 2 months and time to publication 6 months. Sometimes sends prepublication galleys. Pays 2 copies.** Send books for review consideration. The magazine also sponsors annual poetry awards. Send #10 SASE for deadlines and guidelines. In the past, contributors to *Sonora Review* have been listed in *Best of the West*, *Pushcart Prize*, *O. Henry* and *Best American Poetry* anthologies.

SOUTH ASH PRESS (I, II), 2311 E. Indian School Rd., Phoenix AZ 85016, founded 1991, publisher Chuck Hadd Jr., is a monthly poetry magazine sustained and distributed by community advertisers. **They want "well-crafted poems by beginning and established poets. 75 lines maximum."** They have published poetry by Denis Johnson. As a sample the publisher selected these lines from "Traveling Between Storms" by Albino Carrillo:

> *Thunder is what wakes us all,*
> *the taste like salt and meat*
> *lingering as we pull on our clothes.*
> *And just before the evening's spent*
> *to wander with the gray constellations.*
> *To know this blackness, to know it well.*

South Ash Press is 12 pgs., magazine-sized, saddle-stapled with card cover with b&w photo, numerous ads on same pages as poems. They receive about 1,500 poems a year, publish about 250. Each issue includes a number of poems by a "Featured Poet." Press run is 2,000, distributed free through advertisers. Subscription: $20/year. **Sample postpaid: $2. Submit up to 5 poems at a time. One poem to a page including name and address. No previously published poems; simultaneous submissions OK. "We do not provide critiques and/or advice." Reports in 3-4 months. Pays 1 copy. Acquires first rights.**

SOUTH CAROLINA REVIEW (II), English Dept., 801 Strode Tower, Clemson University, Box 341503, Clemson SC 29634-1503, phone (803)656-5404 or 656-3457, fax (803)656-1345, founded 1968, managing editor Frank Day, is a biannual literary magazine "recognized by the *New York Quarterly* as one of the top 20 of this type." They will consider **"any kind of poetry as long as it's good. No stale metaphors, uncertain rhythms or lack of line integrity. Interested in seeing more traditional forms. Format should be according to new MLA Stylesheet."** They have published poetry by Pattiann Rogers, J.W. Rivers and Claire Bateman. It is 200 pgs., 6×9, professionally printed, flat-spined and uses about 8-10 pgs. of poetry in each issue. Reviews of recent issues back up editorial claims that all styles and forms are welcome; moreover, poems were accessible and well-executed. Circulation is 600, for 400 subscribers of which 250 are libraries. They receive about 1,000 unsolicited submissions of poetry/year, use 10, have a 2-year backlog. **Sample postpaid: $10. Submit 3-10 poems at a time in an "8×10 manila envelope so poems aren't creased." No previously published poems or simultaneous submissions. "Editor prefers a chatty, personal cover letter plus a list of publishing credits." Do not submit during June, July, August or December. Publishes theme issues. Reports in 6-9 months. Pays copies.** Staff reviews books of poetry.

SOUTH DAKOTA REVIEW (II, IV-Regional, themes), University of South Dakota, Vermillion SD 57069, phone (605)677-5229 or 677-5966, founded 1963, editor Brian Bedard, is a "literary quarterly publishing poetry, fiction, criticism, essays. **When material warrants, an emphasis on the American West; writers from the West; Western places or subjects; frequent issues with no geographical emphasis; periodic special issues on one theme, or one place or one writer. Looking for originality, some kind of sophistication, significance, craft—i.e., professional work. Nothing confessional, purely descriptive, too filled with self-importance."** They use 10-15 poems/issue, "receive tons, it seems." Press run is 650-900 for 450 subscribers of which half are libraries. Subscription: $18/year, $30/2 years. **Sample postpaid: $4. Editor comments on submissions "rarely." Reports in 4-6 weeks. Pays 1 copy/page. Acquires first and reprint rights.** They have a distinct bias against personal or confessional poems, and generally publish free verse with a strong sense of place, a strong voice and a universal theme. Read the magazine—it's attractive and well-edited—to get a feel for the type of poetry that succeeds here. The editor advises, "Find universal meaning in the regional. Avoid constant 'I' personal experiences that are not of interest to anyone else. Learn to be less self-centered and more objective."

THE SOUTHERN CALIFORNIA ANTHOLOGY; ANN STANFORD POETRY PRIZES (III), c/o Master of Professional Writing Program, WPH 404, University of Southern California, Los Angeles CA 90089-4034, phone (213)740-3252, founded 1983, is an "annual literary review of serious contemporary poetry and fiction. **Very open to all subject matters except pornography. Any form,**

style OK." They have recently published poetry by Robert Bly, Donald Hall, Maxine Kumin, John Updike, Denise Levertov and Amiri Baraka. As a sample the editor selected these lines from "The Rivers of Paris" by James Ragan:

> *The boulevards are the rivers wind owes*
> *to the eyes' reflections, light*
> *to the panes transparent*
> *in the domes of air wind weaves along Sacre Coeur*

The anthology is 144 pgs., digest-sized, perfect-bound, with a semi-glossy color cover featuring one art piece. A fine selection of poems distinguish this journal, and it has an excellent reputation, well-deserved. The downside, if it has one, concerns limited space for newcomers. Circulation is 1,500, 50% going to subscribers of which 50% are libraries, 30% are for shelf sales. **Sample postpaid: $5.95. No simultaneous submissions or previously published poems. Submit 3-5 poems between September 1 and January 1. All decisions made by mid-February. Send SASE for guidelines. Reports in 4 months. Pays 3 copies. Acquires all rights.** The Ann Stanford Poetry Prizes ($750, $250 and $100) have an April 15 deadline, $10 fee (5 poem limit), for unpublished poems. Include cover sheet with name, address and titles and SASE for contest results. All entries are considered for publication, and all entrants receive a copy of *SCA*.

SOUTHERN HUMANITIES REVIEW; THEODORE CHRISTIAN HOEPFNER AWARD (II, IV-Translations), 9088 Haley Center, Auburn University, Auburn AL 36849-5202, co-editors Dan Latimer and Virginia M. Kouidis, founded 1967, is a literary quarterly **interested in poems of any length, subject, genre. Space is limited, and brief poems are more likely to be accepted. "Translations welcome."** This journal continues to gain influence and prestige in the literary world by publishing a wide variety of verse that displays careful attention to image, theme, craft and voice. They have published poetry by Eamon Grennan, Donald Hall, Brendan Galvin, Mary Ruefle, Hayden Carruth, Robert Morgan and Fred Chappell. *SHR* is 100 pgs., 6×9, circulation 700. Subscription: $15/year. **Sample: $5. "Send 3-5 poems in a business-sized envelope. Avoid sending faint computer printout." No previously published poems or simultaneous submissions. Reports in 1-2 months, possibly longer in summer. Always sends prepublication galleys. Pays 2 copies. Copyright reverts to author upon publication.** Reviews books of poetry in approximately 750-1,000 words. Send books for review consideration. Sponsors the Theodore Christian Hoepfner Award, a $50 award for the best poem published in a given volume of *SHR*. The editors advise, "For beginners we'd recommend study and wide reading in English and classical literature, and, of course, American literature—the old works, not just the new. We also recommend study of or exposure to a foreign language and a foreign culture. Poets need the reactions of others to their work: criticism, suggestions, discussion. A good creative writing teacher would be desirable here, and perhaps some course work too. And then submission of work, attendance at workshops. And again, the reading: history, biography, verse, essays—all of it. We want to see poems that have gone beyond the language of slippage and easy attitudes."

SOUTHERN POETRY REVIEW; GUY OWEN POETRY PRIZE (II), Advancement Studies, Central Piedmont Community College, Charlotte NC 28235, phone (704)342-6002, editor Ken McLaurin, founded 1958, a semiannual literary magazine "with emphasis on effective poetry. **There are no restrictions on form, style or content of poetry; length subject to limitations of space."** They have published work by Linda Pastan, Judith Ortiz Cofer, David Ray, Stephen Sandy, Betty Adcock and Walter McDonald. As a sample the editor selected these lines from "The Last Image" by Heather Burns:

> *I hold onto it with dissolving hands.*
> *The bed is wet from nightsweating.*
> *A vapor has entered the room.*
> *It smells like ocean foam and salt.*
> *It is warm, like another skin.*
> *Whose face have I touched besides my own?*

Southern Poetry Review is 78 pgs., 6×9, handsomely printed on buff stock, flat-spined with textured, one-color matte card cover. Circulation is 1,000. Subscription: $8/year. **Sample postpaid: $2. Queries answered with SASE. Submit no more than 3-5 poems at a time. Reads submissions September 1 through May 31 only. Pays 1 copy. Acquires first-time rights.** Staff reviews books of poetry. Send books for review consideration. This is the type of literary magazine to settle back with in a chair and read, particularly during dry creative spells, to inspire one's muse. It is recommended as a market for that reason. It's a tough sell, though. Work is read closely and the magazine reports in a timely manner. There is a yearly contest, the Guy Owen Poetry Prize of $500, to which the entry fee is an $8 subscription; submission must be postmarked in April.

THE SOUTHERN REVIEW (II), 43 Allen Hall, Louisiana State University, Baton Rouge LA 70803, phone (504)388-5108, founded 1935 (original series), 1965 (new series), poetry editors James Olney and Dave Smith, "is a literary quarterly which publishes fiction, poetry, critical essays and book reviews, with emphasis on contemporary literature in the U.S. and abroad, and with special interest in Southern culture and history. Selections are made with careful attention to craftsmanship and technique and to the seriousness of the subject matter." By general agreement this is one of the most distinguished of literary journals. Joyce Carol Oates, for instance, says, "Over the years I have continued to be impressed with the consistent high quality of *SR*'s publications and its general 'aura,' which bespeaks careful editing, adventuresome tastes and a sense of thematic unity. *SR* is characterized by a refreshing openness to new work, placed side by side with that of older, more established, and in many cases highly distinguished writers." The editors say, **"We are interested in any variety of poetry that is well crafted, though we cannot normally accommodate excessively long poems (say 10 pgs. and over)."** They have recently published poetry by Norman Dubie, Margaret Gibson, Seamus Heaney, Yusef Komunyakaa, Susan Ludvigson and Robert Penn Warren. The beautifully printed quarterly is massive: 6¾×10, 240 pgs., flat-spined, matte card cover. They receive about 10,000 submissions of poetry. All styles and forms seem welcome, although accessible lyric and narrative free verse appear most often in recent issues. Press run is 3,100 for 2,100 subscribers of which 70% are libraries. Subscription: $20. **Sample postpaid: $6. "We do not require a cover letter but we prefer one giving information about the author and previous publications." Prefers submissions of 1-4 pgs. Send SASE for guidelines. Reports in 2 months. Pays $20/printed page plus 2 copies. Buys first North American serial rights.** Staff reviews books of poetry in 3,000 words, multi-book format. Send books for review consideration. Work published in this review has been included in the 1995 and 1996 volumes of *The Best American Poetry*.

SOUTHWEST REVIEW; ELIZABETH MATCHETT STOVER MEMORIAL AWARD (II), 307 Fondren Library West, Box 374, Southern Methodist University, Dallas TX 75275, phone (214)768-1037, founded 1915, editor Willard Spiegelman. *Southwest Review* is a literary quarterly that publishes fiction, essays, poetry and interviews. "It is hard to describe our preference for poetry in a few words. We always suggest that potential contributors read several issues of the magazine to see for themselves what we like. But some things may be said: We demand **very high quality in our poems; we accept both traditional and experimental writing, but avoid unnecessary obscurity and private symbolism; we place no arbitrary limits on length but find shorter poems easier to fit into our format than longer ones. We have no specific limitations as to theme."** They have recently published poetry by Adrienne Rich, Amy Clampitt, Albert Goldbarth, Leonard Nathan, Molly Peacock and Charles Wright. The journal is 6×9, 144 pgs., perfect-bound, professionally printed, with matte text stock cover. They receive about 1,000 unsolicited submissions of poetry/year, use 32. Poems tend to be lyric and narrative free verse combining a strong voice with powerful topics or situations. Diction is accessible and content often conveys a strong sense of place. Circulation is 1,500 with 1,000 subscriptions of which 600 are libraries. Subscription: $20. **Sample postpaid: $6. No simultaneous submissions or previously published work. Publishes theme issues. Send SASE for guidelines. Reports within a month. Always sends prepublication galleys. Pays cash plus copies.** The $150 Elizabeth Matchett Stover Memorial Prize is awarded annually for the best poem, chosen by editors, published in the preceding year. Poetry published in *Southwest Review* has been included in the 1993, 1994 and 1995 volumes of *The Best American Poetry*.

SOU'WESTER (II), Box 1438, Southern Illinois University, Edwardsville IL 62026, phone (618)692-3190, founded 1960, managing editor Fred W. Robbins, poetry editor Nancy Avdoian, appears twice a year. **"We like poetry with imagery and figurative language that has strong associations and don't care for abstract poetry. We have no particular preference for form or length."** They have published poetry by Marnie Bullock, Susan Swartwont and Bruce Guernsey. As a sample the editor selected the final stanzas of "The Gleaners" by William Jolliff:

> And even when their too-large coats are soaked
> with winter rains, I envy those children,
> the birds we were, kicking their buckles
>
> through the muddy dark. It would be a fair trade,
> a fair swap, for the work we turn to now,
> each grey and brittle season, seeking, digging,
>
> kicking the stalks for a blessing.

There are 30-40 pgs. of poetry in each 6×9, 100-page issue. The magazine is professionally printed, flat-spined, with textured matte card cover, circulation 300, 500 subscriptions of which 50 are libraries. They receive some 3,000 poems (from 600 poets) each year, use 36-40, have a 4-month backlog. Subscription: $10 (2 issues). **Sample postpaid: $5. Simultaneous submissions OK. Does not read during August. Rejections usually within 4 months. Pays 2 copies. Acquires all rights. Returns rights. Editor comments on rejections "usually, in the case of those that we almost accept."** He says, "Read poetry past and present. Have something to say and say it in your own voice. Poetry is a very personal thing for many editors. When all else fails, we may rely on gut reactions, so take whatever hints you're given to improve your poetry, and keep submitting."

THE SOW'S EAR POETRY REVIEW (II), 19535 Pleasant View Dr., Abingdon VA 24211-6827, phone (540)628-2651, founded 1988, managing editor Larry Richman, graphics editor Mary Calhoun, is a quarterly. **"We are open to many forms and styles, and have no limitations on length. We try to be interesting visually, and we use graphics to complement the poems. Though we publish some work from our local community of poets, we are interested in poems from all over. We publish a few by school-age and previously unpublished poets."** They have recently published poetry by Tony Barnstone, Helen Frost and Debra Markquart. As a sample the editors selected these lines from "How Stories Would Change Us" by Kathryn Winograd:

> *I could tell it so simply,*
> *children in a creek playing, sunlight*
> *breaking over them, those glints of gold.*
> *Or how for once it seemed he was almost*
> *happy, the boy we always hated as children hate—*
> *blind and animal—this day playing beside us*

TSE is 32 pgs., 8½×11, saddle-stapled, with matte card cover, professionally printed. They accept about 100 of 2,000 poems submitted. Press run is 800 for 700 subscribers of which 15 are libraries, 20-40 shelf sales. Subscription: $10. **Sample postpaid: $3.50. Submit up to 5 poems at a time. No previously published poems; simultaneous submissions OK if you tell them promptly when work is accepted elsewhere. Enclose brief bio. Reports in 3-6 months. Pays 1 copy. Buys first publication rights.** Most prose (reviews, interviews, features) is commissioned. They offer an annual contest for unpublished poems, with fee of $2/poem, prizes of $500, $100 and $50, and publication for 15-20 finalists. For contest, submit poems in September/October, with name and address on back of each poem. Submissions of 5 poems/$10 receive a subscription. Include SASE for notification. 1995 Judge: Rodney Jones. They also sponsor a chapbook contest in March/April with $10 fee, $500 prize and publication; second and third prizes of $100. Send SASE for chapbook contest guidelines.

‡SPACE AND TIME (I, II, IV-Science fiction/fantasy, horror), 138 W. 70th St. (4B), New York NY 10023-4468, founded 1966, poetry editor Lawrence Greenberg, is a biannual that publishes "primarily science fiction/fantasy/horror; some related poetry and articles. **We do not want to see anything that doesn't fit science fiction/fantasy/weird genres."** They have recently published poetry by Lyn Lifshin, Susan Spilecki, Mark Kreighbaum and Cynthia Tedesco. As a sample we selected these lines from "Polarion" by Jessica Amanda Salmonson:

> *Fear, O Cruel Daughters,*
> *The return of Spring;*
> *Drink the salty waves*
> *That were dreamy towers of gleaming ice*
> *between curtains of rainbows.*
> *Weep, O Cruel Daughters*
> *When Polarion melts into*
> *diluvian madness.*

The issue of *Space and Time* we received was about 100 pgs., 5½×8½, perfect-bound. However, they are reformatting to 64 pgs., 8½×11, web press printed on 50 lb. stock and saddle-stitched with glossy card cover and interior b&w illustrations. They receive about 500 poems a year, accept 5%. Press run is 2,000 for 200 subscribers of which 10 are libraries, 1,200 shelf sales. Single copy: $5; subscription: $10. **Sample postpaid: $6.25. Submit up to 4 poems at a time. No previously published poems or simultaneous submissions.** Time between acceptance and publication is 3-9 months. **Often comments on rejections. Poets may send SASE for guidelines "but they won't see more than what's here." Reports in 2-6 weeks, "longer if recommended." Pays 1¢/word ($5 minimum) plus 2 copies. Buys first North American serial rights.**

SPARROW: THE YEARBOOK OF THE SONNET (IV-Form), 103 Waldron St., West Lafayette IN 47906, founded 1954, editor/publisher Felix Stefanile, appears every October. **We are noted for our devotion to the publication of formal, contemporary sonnets. We occasionally publish other types of structured verse, but only rarely, and only when the poem seems to compel us to take it. No subject restrictions. We don't publish poems in poor taste."** They have recently published poetry by X.J. Kennedy, R.S. Gwynn, Jared Carter and John Haines. As a sample the editor selected these lines from "With Our Boots On" by Dessa Ewing:

> *My life seems like those country western songs:*
> *some man in black keeps walkin' out the door*
> *and in the honky tonk some woman wrongs*
> *the last good man in town and takes the floor*
> *two steppin' with her husband's cousin's son.*

Sparrow is about 100 pgs., 8½×11, attractively printed, perfect-bound with light card cover, using occasional graphics only by invitation. They receive about 2,000 mss a year, use less than 1%. Press run is 650 for about 400 subscribers of which about 50 are libraries, 200 shelf sales. Single copy: $6. Sample back issue postpaid: $5. Submit 4-5 poems at a time, typed on 8½×11 bond paper. One poem to a page with name and address on each. "We consider previously published poems only now and then." No simultaneous submissions. No material returned without SASE. "We have a very cynical attitude toward long cover letters." Reads submissions January through September. Seldom comments on rejections. "We are not in the business of offering criticism or advice." Send SASE with all queries. Reports in 6 weeks. Sometimes sends prepublication galleys. Pays $3 a sonnet plus 1 copy. Buys first and non-exclusive reprint rights. "We also offer a $25 prize for the best sonnet each issue." Staff reviews books of poetry. Send books for review consideration. The editor says, "We are now essentially a 'new' magazine with a fine, old name. We pride ourselves on our liveliness and our currency. We also publish scores of musical settings for sonnets, by special arrangement with the composer. We are really not a market for beginners and the MFA degree does not impress us."

‡**SPILLWAY (II)**, P.O. Box 6000-337, Huntington Beach CA 92646, founded 1991, editor Mifanwy Kaiser, associate editor B. Lynne Zika, is a biannual journal "celebrating writing's diversity and power to affect our lives. **Open to all voices, schools and tendencies: Confessional, neo-narrative, deep image, new formalist, language, political, etc. We usually do not use writing which tells instead of shows, or writing which contains general, abstract lines not anchored in images."** They have recently published poetry by Richard Jones, Jack Grapes, Charles Bukowski, Stellasue Lee and James O'Hern. *Spillway* is about 100 pgs., digest-sized, attractively printed, perfect-bound, with 2-color card cover. Press run is 600. Subscription: $10. **Sample (including guidelines) postpaid: $6. Make checks payable to Spillway, Mifanwy Kaiser. Submit 3-6 poems at a time, 10 pages total. Previously published work ("say when and where") and simultaneous submissions ("say where also submitted") OK. Cover letter including brief bio required. "No cute bios—we need professional ones." Submission deadlines: March 27 for Spring/Summer issue, August 27 for Fall/Winter issue. Reports in 2 weeks to 6 months. Pays 1 copy. Acquires one-time rights.** Reviews books of poetry in 500 words maximum. Poets may also send books for review consideration. The editors say, "We have no problem with simultaneous or previously published submissions. Poems are murky creatures—they shift and change in time and context. It's exciting to pick up a volume, read a poem in the context of all the other pieces and then find the same poem in another time and place. And, we don't think a poet should have to wait until death to see work in more than one volume. What joy to find out that more than one editor values one's work. Our responsibility as editors, collectively, is to promote the work of poets as much as possible—how can we do this if we say to a writer you may only have a piece published in one volume and only one time?"

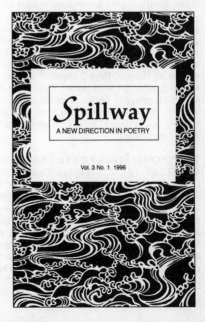

As described in *Spillway*'s subtitle, "A New Direction in Poetry," the editors focus on the motion and movement of poetry. This idea has also been translated into the images on the journal's covers. "We believe motion (rhythm) and careful attention to image convey the emotion—the deep voice—of the poem," says Mifanwy Kaiser, editor of the California-based biannual. "We think this cover represents not only the deep voice of the individual poems, but also the larger landscape created by all the poems taken together." The cover illustration was originally created by Founding Editor Stephanie Hager. Since then, however, the image has been revised by Gregory Watters Images in Atlanta, Georgia.

SPINDRIFT (II), Shoreline Community College, 16101 Greenwood Ave., Seattle WA 98133, phone (206)546-5864, founded 1962, faculty advisor varies each year, currently Carol Orlock, is **open to all varieties of poetry except greeting card style.** They have recently published poetry by Lyn Lifshin, Mary Lou Sanelli, James Bertolino, Edward Harkness and Richard West. *Spindrift*, an annual, is 125 pgs., handsomely printed in an 8″ square, flat-spined. Circulation is 500. Single copy: $6.50. **Sample postpaid: $5. "Submit 2 copies of each poem, 6 maximum. Include cover letter with biographical information. We accept submissions until February 1—report back in March." Send SASE for guidelines. Pays 2 copies. Acquires first serial rights.** The editors advise, "Read what the major contemporary poets are writing. Read what local poets are writing. Be distinctive, love the language, avoid sentiment."

THE SPIRIT THAT MOVES US; THE SPIRIT THAT MOVES US PRESS (II); EDITOR'S CHOICE (IV-Anthology), P.O. Box 720820-PM, Jackson Heights, Queens NY 11372-0820, phone (718)426-8788, founded 1974, poetry editor Morty Sklar. *"The Spirit That Moves Us* will be continuing its *Editor's Choice* series and publishing regular issues only occasionally. *Editor's Choice* consists of selections from other literary magazines and small presses, where we choose from nominations by the editors of those magazines and presses." They have published poetry by Barbara Unger, Darryl Holmes, Yala Korwin, Rhina Espaillat and Rita Dove. As a sample the editor selected these lines from "Just Off The Queen Elizabeth, New York City, 1948" by Joan Dobbie:

> *"I called out the only two words*
> *I could think of in English,*
> *'GO AWAY!'*
> *I meant for the children to come,*
> *I was longing to touch them."*

They offer *Patchwork of Dreams: Voices from the Heart of the New America*, an anthology in which the above poem appears, as a sample for $8 plus $1 postage (regularly $12 plus $1.50 postage). **"We are in a lull, and behind in getting our publications out. Please wait until 1997 before querying. Publishes theme issues. Send SASE in 1997 for upcoming themes and time frames. Sometimes sends prepublication galleys.** The editor's advice: "Write what you would like to write, in a style (or styles) which is/are best for your own expression. Don't worry about acceptance, though you may be concerned about it. Don't just send work which you think editors would like to see, though take that into consideration. Think of the relationship between poem, poet and editor as personal. You may send good poems to editors who simply do not like them, whereas other editors might."

SPITBALL; CASEY AWARD (IV-Sports), 5560 Fox Rd., Cincinnati OH 45239, phone (513)385-2268, founded 1981, poetry editor William J. McGill, is "a unique literary magazine devoted to poetry, fiction and book reviews *exclusively* **about baseball.** Newcomers are very welcome, but remember that you have to know the subject. We do and our readers do. Perhaps a good place to start for beginners is one's personal reactions to the game, *a* game, a player, etc. and take it from there." The 96-page, digest-sized quarterly is computer typeset and perfect-bound. They receive about 1,000 submissions/year, use 40—very small backlog. "Many times we are able to publish accepted work almost immediately." Circulation is 1,000, 750 subscriptions of which 25 are libraries. Subscription: $16. **Sample postpaid: $5. "We are not very concerned with the technical details of submitting, but we do prefer a cover letter with some bio info. We also like batches of poems and prefer to use several of same poet in an issue rather than a single poem." Publishes theme issues. Send SASE for upcoming themes. Pays 2 copies.** "We encourage anyone interested to submit to *Spitball*. We are always looking for fresh talent. Those who have never written 'baseball poetry' before should read some first probably before submitting. Not necessarily ours. We sponsor the Casey Award (for best baseball book of the year) and hold the Casey Awards Banquet every January. Any chapbook of baseball poetry should be sent to us for consideration for the 'Casey' plaque that we award to the winner each year."

THE SPOON RIVER POETRY REVIEW (III, IV-Regional, translations); EDITORS' PRIZE CONTEST (II), 4240/English Dept., Illinois State University, Normal IL 61790-4240, phone (309)438-7906, founded 1976, poetry editor Lucia Getsi, is a "poetry magazine that features newer and well-known poets from around the country and world." Also features **one Illinois poet/issue** at length for the magazine's Illinois Poet Series. **"We want interesting and compelling poetry that operates beyond the ho-hum, so-what level, in any form or style about anything; language that is fresh, energetic, committed, filled with a strong voice that grabs the reader in the first line and never lets go. Do not want to see insipid, dull, boring poems, especially those that I cannot ascertain why they're in lines and not paragraphs; poetry which, if you were to put it into paragraphs, would become bad prose." They also use translations of poetry.** They have recently published poetry by Frankie Paino, Marilyn Krysl, Kurt Leland, Tim Seibles, Dave Smith, Elaine Terranova, Roger Mitchell and Stuart Dybek. As a sample Lucia Getsi selected these lines by Kay Murphy:

> *This is as close as I can come to make what she says true:*
> *Inside, my uncle has his hand inside my aunt's blue dress.*
> *The fields are burning with a want I don't yet understand.*
> *The orchard has simply given up, as my cousin has.*

SRPR has moved to a twice a year, double issue format. It is digest-sized, laser set with card cover using photos, ads. They accept about 2% of 1,000 poems received/month. Press run is 1,500 for 500 subscriptions (100 of them libraries) and shelf sales. Subscription: $14. **Sample: $9. "No simultaneous submissions unless we are notified immediately if a submission is accepted elsewhere. Include name and address on every poem." Do not submit mss May 1 through September 1. Editor comments on rejections "many times, if a poet is promising." Reports in 2 months. Pays a year's subscription. Acquires first North American serial rights only.** Staff reviews books of poetry. Send books for review consideration. Sponsors the Editor's Prize Contest for previously unpublished work. One poem will be awarded $500 and published in the fall issue of *SRPR*, and two finalists will receive $50 each and publication in the fall issue. Entry fee: $15, including 1-year subscription. Write for details. Recent winners were Marilyn Krysl and E.C. Hinsey. *The Spoon River Poetry Review* has received several Illinois Arts Council Awards and is one of the best reads in the poetry-publishing world. Editor Lucia Cordell Getsi jampacks the journal with poems of varied styles and presents them in a handsome, perfect-bound product. You'll want to order a sample issue to get a feel for this fine publication. Work published in this review has also been included in *The Best American Poetry 1993*.

‡**SPOUT MAGAZINE (II)**, 28 W. Robie, St. Paul MN 55107, e-mail colb0018@gold.tc.umn.edu, founded 1989, editors John Colburn and Michelle Filkins, appears approximately 3 times a year providing "a paper community of unique expression." **They want "poetry of the imagination, poetry that surprises. We enjoy the surreal, the forceful, the political, the expression of confusion." No light verse, archaic forms or language.** They have recently published poetry by John M. Bennett, Lyn Lifshin, William E. Harrold and Jeffrey Little. As a sample the editor selected these lines by Paul Kremsreiter:

> *I think we're all walking zombies*
> *In a web of weariness*
> *In a glove filled with frosting.*

The editor says *Spout* is 40 pgs., 8½ × 11, saddle-stapled, card stock cover is different color each issue. They receive about 400-450 poems a year, accept 15%. Press run is 200-250 for 35-40 subscribers, 100-150 shelf sales. Single copy price: $3; subscription: $12. **Sample postpaid: $4. Submit up to 6 poems at a time. Previously published poems and simultaneous submissions OK. Cover letter preferred. "Poems incorporating artwork are welcomed."** Time between acceptance and publication is 2-3 months. **Poems are circulated to an editorial board. "Poems are reviewed by two of three editors, those selected for final review are read again by all three." Seldom comments on rejections. Send SASE for guidelines. Reports in 1-3 months. Pays 1 copy.**

SPRING: THE JOURNAL OF THE E.E. CUMMINGS SOCIETY (IV-Specialized), 33-54 164th St., Flushing NY 11358-1442, phone (718)353-3631, editor Norman Friedman, is an annual publication designed "to maintain and broaden the audience for Cummings and to explore various facets of his life and art." **They want poems in the spirit of Cummings, primarily poems of one page or less. Nothing "amateurish."** They have published poetry by John Tagliabue, Ruth Whitman, M.L. Rosenthal, William Jay Smith and Theodore Weiss. As a sample the editor selected these lines from "The Whip" by Robert Creeley:

> *I spent a night turning in bed,*
> *my love was a feather, a flat*
>
> *sleeping thing. She was*
> *very white*
>
> *and quiet, and above us on*
> *the roof, there was another woman . . .*

Spring is 100-120 pgs., 5½ × 8½, offset and perfect-bound with light card stock cover. Press run is 700 for 200 subscribers of which 15 are libraries, 450 shelf sales. Subscription or **sample postpaid: $15. No previously published poems or simultaneous submissions. Cover letter required. Reads submissions January through March. Seldom comments on rejections. Reports in 6 months. Pays 1 copy.** "Contributors are encouraged to subscribe."

STAND MAGAZINE; NORTHERN HOUSE (I, II, IV-Translations), 179 Wingrove Rd., Newcastle on Tyne NE4 9DA England. US Editors: Daniel Schenker and Amanda Kay, 122 Morris Rd., Lacey's Spring AL 35754. *Stand*, founded by editor Jon Silkin in 1952, is a highly esteemed literary quarterly. Jon Silkin seeks more subscriptions from US readers and also hopes "that the magazine would be seriously treated as an alternative platform to American literary journals." He wants

"verse that tries to explore forms. No formulaic verse." They have published poems by such poets as Peter Redgrove, Elizabeth Jennings and Barry Spacks. *Library Journal* calls *Stand* "one of England's best, liveliest and truly imaginative little magazines." Among better-known American poets whose work has appeared here are Robert Bly, William Stafford, Michael Mott, Angela Ball and Naomi Wallace. Poet Donald Hall says of it, "among essential magazines, there is Jon Silkin's *Stand*, politically left, with reviews, poems and much translation from continental literature." In its current format it is 6×8, flat-spined, 84 pgs., professionally printed in 2 columns, small type, on thin stock with glossy cover, using ads. Circulation is 4,500 with 2,800 subscriptions of which 600 are libraries. Subscription: $25. **Sample postpaid: $7. Cover letter required with submissions, "assuring us that work is not also being offered elsewhere." Publishes theme issues. Always sends prepublication galleys. Pays £25/poem (unless under 6 lines) and 1 copy (⅓ off additional copies). Buys first world serial rights for 3 months after publication. If work(s) appear elsewhere *Stand*/Northern House must be credited.** Reviews books of poetry in 3,000-4,000 words, multi-book format. Open to unsolicited reviews. Poets may also send books for review consideration. Northern House (13 Queen's Terrace, Newcastle on Tyne NE2 2PJ England) "publishes mostly small collections of poetry by new or established poets. The pamphlets often contain a group of poems written to one theme. Occasionally larger volumes are published, such as the full-length collection by Sorley Maclean, translated by Iain Crichton Smith."

STAPLE (II), Gilderoy East, Upperwood Rd., Matlock, Bath DE4 3PD United Kingdom, phone 0629-583867 and 0629-582764, founded 1982, co-editor Bob Windsor. This literary magazine appears 4 times a year including supplements. **"Nothing barred: Evidence of craft, but both traditional and modernist accepted; no totally esoteric or concrete poetry."** They have recently published poetry by Donna Hilbert, Jennifer Olds, Michael Daugherty, Paul Munden and Adèle Geras. As a sample they selected these lines from "Flint" by Kenneth C. Steven:

> ... *Where drums of high water roll the rocks*
> *Shining things are skipped up dancing*
> *Grey as wolves.*
>
> ... *Men chipped arrowtips, fine and perfect*
> *As a wren's beak, so thin you could see the sky*
> *Through the milky tip.*

Staple is professionally printed, flat-spined, 80 pgs., with card cover. Of 10,000 poems received/year they accept about 2%. Their press run is up to 800 with 350 subscriptions. Subscription: £15 (sterling only). **Sample postpaid: £3. Submit 6 poems at a time. They do not consider simultaneous submissions or previously published poems. Cover letter preferred. Editors sometimes comment on rejections. Submission deadlines are end of February, June and November. Response in up to 3 months. Sometimes sends prepublication galleys. Pays overseas writers complimentary copies.** Send SASE (or SAE with IRC) for rules for their open biennial competitions (£1,200 in prizes) and for *Staple First Editions* monographs (sample postpaid: $10). Recently published monographs include *An Extra Half-Acre* by Jennifer Olds. They also produce (to order) poetry postcards of poetry *published* in the magazine. The editor says, "We get too many short minimalist pieces from America. More developed pieces preferred."

STATE STREET PRESS (II), P.O. Box 278, Brockport NY 14420, phone (716)637-0023, founded 1981, poetry editor Judith Kitchen, "publishes **chapbooks of poetry (20-24 pgs.) usually chosen in an anonymous competition**. State Street Press hopes to publish emerging writers with accomplished manuscripts and to offer a format for established writers who have a collection of poems that work together as a chapbook. We also occasionally publish full-length books including translations (query before sending). We want **serious traditional and free verse. We are not usually interested in the language school of poets. We ask only that the poems work as a collection, that the chapbook be more than an aggregate of poems—that they work together.**" They have recently published poetry by Naomi Shihab Nye, Dionisio Martinez, Diane Swan, Patricia Hooper, Jan Beatly, Pamela Stewart, Kath Anderson and Joe Survant. As a sample the editor selected these lines from "Botany" by Kathleen Wakefield:

> *Each day I watch the blossoms close,*
> *then open skyward, as if aspiring to something.*
> *By night, the moth mullein, named*
> *for beast and flower, practices its cool white deceit*
> *by which its stationary blooms in darkness*
> *endlessly repeat.*

Chapbooks are beautifully designed and printed, 6×9, 30 pgs., with textured matte wrapper with art. **Send SASE for guidelines and chapbook contest rules. There is a $10 entry fee, for which you receive one of the chapbooks already published. Simultaneous submissions encouraged. Reads submissions March 15 through May 15. Always sends prepublication galleys. Pays copies and** small honorarium. **Authors buy additional copies at cost, sell at readings and keep the profits.** Judith Kitchen comments, "State Street Press believes that the magazines are doing a good job of publishing beginning poets and we hope to present published and unpublished work in a more permanent format, so we do reflect the current market and tastes. We expect our writers to have published individual poems and to be considering a larger body of work that in some way forms a 'book.' We have been cited as a press that prints poetry that is accessible to the general reader. We have become one of the most well-known chapbook series. Our authors have gone on to win many major national poetry awards as well as Whiting Foundation Fellowships and other honors. Our books receive national reviews."

THE STEELHEAD SPECIAL (I), P.O. Box 219, Bayside CA 95524, phone (707)445-1907, founded 1991, editor Crawdad Nelson, publisher Joseph Shermis, is a bimonthly "Northwest working-class cultural and literary review." They want **"fresh, working-class, rugged, bold poetry. Nothing weepy, clichéd, sentimental."** They have published poetry by Joe Smith, Sharon Doubiago and John Colburn. As a sample the editor selected these lines from "The Throat" by L.J. Cirino:

> This morning, walking down the ridge,
> the throat of the river, beautifully
> bloody, washed out and purpled the sea . . .

It is 40 pgs., 8½×11, newsprint, saddle-stapled, with art and graphics. They receive 500-600 poems a year, accept 10-20/issue. Press run is 3,000 for 200 subscribers, rest distributed free to the general public and fishermen. Single copy: $1; subscription: $12. **Sample postpaid: $2. Submit 6 poems at a time. Previously published poems and simultaneous submissions OK. Often comments on rejections. Publishes theme issues. Reports in 1-8 weeks. Pays 1-2 copies; "discounts to poets on larger orders."** Open to unsolicited reviews. Poets may also send books for review consideration. Crawdad Nelson says, "We see lots of good poetry. Hope to see more. Nothing bogged down in bourgeois ennui, please. Vitality helps, but stay alert. We need more *lyrical*, less broken prose. Subscriptions encouraged."

STERLING HOUSE PUBLISHER (I), The Sterling Building, 440 Friday Rd., Pittsburgh PA 15209, phone (412)821-6211, fax (412)821-6099, founded 1988, owner Cynthia Shore-Sterling. **"Sterling House offers both straight and co-op publishing. We publish approximately 25 collections of poetry each year, poetry in all its variety of styles and forms. We are also open to foreign translations."** As a sample the owner selected these lines from Sheila Fiscus's poem "Thoughts From The Throne" from her book *Just A Housewife*:

> As I sit naked on the porcelain throne,
> My life files by, a procession of household care products.
> But what of my heart, my soul, my joy of living?
> Are they to be flushed into the sewer
> By consummate daily tasks?

They will consider simultaneous submissions and unsolicited mss of 25-60 poems throughout the year. For further information, send SASE for catalog and guidelines. Sample: $5.95 (includes shipping). They are presently developing the Sterling Foundation.

THE WALLACE STEVENS JOURNAL (II, IV-Specialized), Liberal Studies, Clarkson University, Box 5750, Potsdam NY 13699-5750, fax (315)268-3983, e-mail duemer@craft.camp.clarkson.edu, founded 1977, poetry editor Prof. Joseph Duemer, appears biannually using **"poems about or in the spirit of Wallace Stevens or having some relation to his work. No bad parodies of Stevens' anthology pieces."** They have published poetry by Elizabeth Spires, Jorie Graham, Charles Wright, X.J. Kennedy and Robert Creeley. As a sample the editor selected these lines from "A World Without Desire" by Michael G. Gessner:

> Occurred tonight for an hour only,
> An hour spent around the back porch
> Where I was sent from the family, exiled
> From myself. It was a world of order,
> Order and presence, the final meaning
> Of forms conversing through the night
> As large as all thought must be
> This house a ragged piece of locale

THE SUBJECT INDEX, located before the General Index, can help you select markets for your work. It lists those publishers whose poetry interests are specialized.

> *Torn adrift in the space of a dark mind.*

The editor describes it as 80-120 pgs., 6×9, typeset, flat-spined, with cover art on glossy stock. They accept 10-15 poems of 200-300 received. Press run is 900 for 600 subscribers of which 200 are libraries. Subscription: $15. **Sample postpaid: $4. Submit 3-5 poems at a time. "We like to receive clean, readable copy. We generally do not publish previously published material, though we have made a few exceptions to this rule. No fax or e-mail submissions, though requests for information are fine." Reports in 4-10 weeks. Always sends prepublication galleys. Pays 2 copies. Acquires all rights. Returns rights with permission and acknowledgment.** Staff reviews books of poetry. Send books for review consideration "only if there is some clear connection to Stevens." *The Wallace Stevens Journal* is published by the Wallace Stevens Society. The editor says, "Brief cover letters are fine, even encouraged. Please don't submit to *WSJ* if you have not read Stevens. We like parodies, but they must *add* a new angle of perception. Most of the poems we publish are not parodies but meditations on themes related to Wallace Stevens and those poets he has influenced. Those wishing to contribute might wish especially to examine the Spring 1993 issue, devoted to prose and poetry by American poets."

STICKS; STICKS PRESS (III, IV-Form), P.O. Box 399, Maplesville AL 36750-0399, press founded 1989, journal 1991, editor/publisher Mary Veazey. *Sticks*, appearing irregularly, **publishes "the best short poems of experienced/established poets. All styles, subjects. Preferred length: 10 lines or less; width: 50 spaces per line."** She has published poetry by X.J. Kennedy and Richard Kostelanetz. As a sample the editor selected this poem, "Open Affection" by Rosemary Klein:

> *It is no disaster to feel*
> *an open affection for life.*
> *The wider my gaze the more*
> *I see myself coming and going.*

The magazine is a 4¼×5½, saddle-stapled or saddle-sewn booklet, professionally printed on acid-free paper, 32 pgs. Press run is 500. Permanent mailing list in lieu of subscriptions. **Sample issue $3; sewn binding by request. Submit up to 3 poems at a time. "No guidelines, just be a master of the short poem." Does not comment on rejections. Reports in 3 months or less. Pays 2 copies. Acquires first North American serial rights.** The editor says, "*Sticks* is more mini-anthology than serial, since it often reveals a subtle thematic undercurrent and appears *only* when money for printing and a number of excellent small poems converge. *The Oxford Book of Short Poems* is the touchstone here; write the poem that will outlast us all; historically many such poems have been brief."

STILL WATERS PRESS (II, IV-Women), 459 S. Willow Ave., Galloway NJ 08201-4633, phone (609)652-0545, founded 1989, editor Shirley Warren, is a "small press publisher of poetry chapbooks and poet's handbooks (contemporary craft). Especially interested in **works by, for and about women. We prefer poetry firmly planted in the real world, but equally mindful of poetry as art. The transformation from pain to perseverance, from ordinary to extraordinary, from defeat to triumph, pleases us. But we reject Pollyanna poetry immediately. Nothing sexist, in either direction, nothing sexually erotic. No rhymed poetry unless you're a master of form who can meticulously avoid strange manipulations of syntax simply to achieve end-rhyme. No patriarchal religious verse. Preferred length: 4 lines to 2 pages per poem. Form: no restrictions—we expect content to dictate the form."** They have published poetry by Linda Milstein and Susan Cavanaugh. The press publishes 4-8 chapbooks a year, averaging 28 pgs. Sample chapbooks: $5; writer's guide booklets: $3. **Send SASE for guidelines, then query. Simultaneous submissions and previously published poems OK. Always sends prepublication galleys. Pays 10% of the press run. Royalties on 2nd and subsequent press runs. Acquires first or reprint rights.** They hold 2 annual contests, each with $10 reading fee; send SASE for detailed guidelines. The editor says, "Read other poets, contemporary and traditional. Attend workshops, establish rapport with your local peers, attend readings. Keep your best work in circulation. Someone out there is looking for you."

STONE SOUP, THE MAGAZINE BY YOUNG WRITERS AND ARTISTS; THE CHIL-DREN'S ART FOUNDATION (IV-Children), P.O. Box 83, Santa Cruz CA 95063, phone (408)426-5557, fax (408)426-1161, e-mail editor@stonesoup.com, founded 1973, editor Ms. Gerry Mandel. *Stone Soup* publishes **writing and art by children through age 13; they want to see free verse poetry but no rhyming poetry, haiku or cinquain.** As a sample the editor selected this poem, "Nightfall," by 7-year-old Jaiva Larsen:

> *When the blackberry moon rises*
> *And the sky flies by like ocean waves*
> *And the chill of the evening*
> *Flies through your heart*
> *Run home*
> *Run home*

Stone Soup, published 5 times a year, is a handsome 6×8¾ magazine, professionally printed on heavy stock with 4 full-color art reproductions inside and a full-color illustration on the coated cover, saddle-stapled. A membership in the Children's Art Foundation at $26/year includes a subscription to the magazine, each issue of which contains an Activity Guide. The editor receives 5,000 poetry submissions/year and only uses 20. There are 4 pgs. of poetry in each issue. Circulation is 20,000; 13,000 in subscriptions, 5,000 to bookstores, 2,000 other. **Sample postpaid: $4.50. Submissions can be any number of pages, any format, but not simultaneous. Criticism will be given when requested. "We prefer submissions by mail because we need an SASE in order to respond. Submissions that arrive via fax or e-mail will receive a response only if they are accepted." Send SASE for guidelines. Reports in 1 month. Pays $10 and 2 copies plus discounts. Buys all rights. Returns rights upon request.** Open to reviews by children. Children through age 13 may also send books for review consideration. *Stone Soup* has received both Parents' Choice and Edpress Golden Lamp Honor Awards.

STORMLINE PRESS, INC. (V), Box 593, Urbana IL 61801, phone (217)328-2665, founded 1985, publisher Raymond Bial, is an independent press publishing fiction, poetry and photography, **with emphasis upon the rural Midwest. They accept submissions "only by invitation. Do not send unsolicited manuscripts. Query in November and December only with SASE. We publish both established and new poets, but in the latter case prefer to publish those poets who have been working some years to master their craft."** The press publishes 1-2 books each year with an average page count of 48-64. They are 6×9, some flat-spined paperbacks and some hardcover.

STORY LINE PRESS (V); NICHOLAS ROERICH POETRY PRIZE FOR UNPUBLISHED FIRST BOOK OF POETRY (II), Three Oaks Farm, 27006 Gap Road, Brownsville OR 97327-9718, phone (541)466-5352, Story Line Press founded 1985, poetry editor Robert McDowell. Story Line Press publishes each year the winner of the Nicholas Roerich Poetry Prize for an Unpublished First Book of Poetry ($1,000 plus publication and a paid reading at the Roerich Museum in New York City; a runner-up receives a full Story Line Press Scholarship to the Wesleyan Writers Conference in Middletown, CT [see listing in Conferences and Workshops section]; $15 entry and handling fee). Deadline for submissions: October 15. Send SASE for complete guidelines. The press also publishes books about poetry and has published collections by such poets as Colette Inez, Rita Dove, Bruce Bawer, Louis Simpson, Frederick Morgan and George Keithley. **They consider unsolicited mss only for the Nicholas Roerich Poetry Prize competition. Always sends prepublication galleys.**

STRAIGHT; STANDARD PUBLISHING CO. (IV-Religious, teens), 8121 Hamilton Ave., Cincinnati OH 45231, editor Heather E. Wallace. Standard is a large religious publishing company. *Straight* is a weekly take-home publication (digest-sized, 12 pgs., color newsprint) **for teens. Poetry is *by* teenagers, any style, religious or inspirational in nature. No adult-written poetry.** As a sample the editor selected "Our Savior's Love" by Rustie Hill:

> I know the anger locked in you is wear-
> ing out your heart.
> I know you hit because you hurt and
> need a brand new start.
> Despite the fact you hurt me, I still love
> you even now;
> My Lord said, "Love thy neighbor," and
> His love has shown me how.

Teen author must include birthdate and social security number. Submit 1-5 poems at a time. Simultaneous submissions OK. Time between acceptance and publication is 9-12 months. **Publishes theme issues. Guidelines and upcoming themes available for SASE. Reports in 4-6 weeks. Pays $10/poem plus 5 copies. Buys first or reprint rights.** The editor says, "Many teenagers write poetry in their English classes at school. If you've written a poem on an inspirational topic, and your teacher's given you an 'A' on it, you've got a very good chance of having it published in *Straight*."

STREET PRESS (V), P.O. Box 772, Sound Beach NY 11789-0772, founded 1974, editor Graham Everett. Street Press publishes an occasional limited edition book of poetry. Recent publications: *Minus Green Plus* by Graham Everett, *Limousine to Nowhere* by Jim Tyack and *Endless Staircase* by Sandy McIntosh. **They are currently not accepting poetry submissions.** Send SASE for a list of available titles.

STRUGGLE: A MAGAZINE OF PROLETARIAN REVOLUTIONARY LITERATURE (I, II, IV-Political, science fiction/fantasy, workers' social issues, women/feminism), P.O. Box 13261, Detroit MI 48213-0261, founded 1985, editor Tim Hall, is a "literary quarterly, content: the struggle of the working people and all oppressed against the rich. Issues such as: racism, poverty, aggressive wars, workers' struggle for jobs and job security, the overall struggle for a non-exploitative society, a genuine socialism." The **poetry and songs they use are "generally short, any style, subject matter must criticize or fight against the rule of the billionaires. We welcome experimentation**

devoted to furthering such content." They have recently published poetry by Kimberly Sonnich, Lee Dennard, Michael Swift, Laurie Calhoun and Albert Marcowitz. As a sample the editor selected this excerpt from "Pulpit Bullies" by Ray Pence:

> Pulpit bullies
> breathing fascist fire
> stoked by racist brimstone,
> fanning the flames
> of intolerant ideology
> with flag-draped rhetoric,
> striving to divide the working class
> like so many loaves and fishes.

Struggle is 36 pgs., digest-sized, photocopied, occasional photos of artwork, short stories and short plays as well as poetry and songs. Subscription: $10 for 4 issues. **Sample postpaid: $2.50. Submit 8 poems at a time. Checks must be payable to "Tim Hall—Special Account." Accepted work usually appears in the next issue. Editor tries to provide criticism "with every submission." Tries to report in 3-4 months. Pays 2 copies.** Tim Hall says, "Show passion and fire. Formal experiments, traditional forms both welcome. Especially favor: works reflecting rebellion by the working people against the rich; works against racism, sexism, militarism, imperialism; works critical of our exploit-ative culture; works showing a desire for—or fantasy of—a non-exploitative society; works attacking the Republican New Stone Age and the Democrats' surrender to it."

STUDENT LEADERSHIP JOURNAL (IV-Students, religious), Dept. PM, P.O. Box 7895, Madison WI 53707-7895, phone (608)274-4823 ext. 425 or 413, editor Jeff Yourison, is a **"magazine for Christian student leaders on secular campuses. We accept a wide variety of poetry. Do not want to see trite poetry. Also, we accept little rhymed poetry; it must be very, very good."** As a sample the editor selected the last stanzas of "A bird in the church" by Luci Shaw:

> and high and low and up again, through the sun's
> transfixing shafts, her wings test gravity
> in a bewilderment of interior air, opening
> and closing on her feathered restlessness
> until, as though coming home, she settles
>
> on the arm of the crucifix. Having found
> a nesting tree (even thine altars, O Lord!),
> she lodges at last, at the angle
> where vertex and horizon meet, resting
> in the steady pain of Christ's left eye.

Student Leadership is a quarterly, 32 pgs., magazine-sized, 2-color inside, 2-color covers, with no advertising, 70% editorial, 30% graphics/art. Press run is 8,000 going to college students in the US and Canada. Subscription: $16. **Sample postpaid: $3. No simultaneous submissions. Previously published poems OK. "Would-be contributors should read us to be familiar with what we pub-lish." Best time to submit mss is March through July ("We set our year's editorial plan"). Editor "occasionally" comments on rejections. Send SASE for guidelines. Reports in 2-3 months.** Time between acceptance and publication is 1-24 months. **Pays $25-50/poem plus 2 copies. Buys first or reprint rights.** He says, "Try to express feelings through images and metaphor. Religious poetry should not be overly didactic, and it should never moralize!"

STUDIO, A JOURNAL OF CHRISTIANS WRITING (II, IV-Religious, spirituality), 727 Peel St., Albury, New South Wales 2640 Australia, founded 1980, publisher Paul Grover, is a small press literary quarterly "with contents **focusing upon the Christian striving for excellence in poetry,** prose and occasional articles relating Christian views of literary ideas." **In poetry, the editors want "shorter pieces but with no specification as to form or length (necessarily less than 3-4 pages), subject matter, style or purpose. People who send material should be comfortable being published under this banner: *Studio, A Journal of Christians Writing.*"** They have published poetry by John Foulcher and other Australian poets. *Studio* is 36 pgs., digest-sized, professionally printed on high-quality recycled paper, saddle-stapled, matte card cover, with graphics and line drawings. Circulation is 300, all subscriptions. Subscription: $40 (Aud) for overseas members. **Sample available (airmail from US) for $8 (Aud). Submissions may be "double-spaced, typed copy or simultaneous." Name and address must appear on the reverse side of each page submitted. Cover letter required; include brief details of previous publishing history, if any. Reporting time is 2 months and time to publication is 9 months. Pays 1 copy. Acquires first Australian rights.** Reviews books of poetry in 250 words, single format. Open to unsolicited reviews. Poets may also send books for review consideration. The magazine conducts a biannual poetry and short story contest. The editor says, "Trend in Australia is for imagist poetry and poetry exploring the land and the self. Reading the magazine gives the best indication of style and standard, so send a few dollars for a sample copy before sending your poetry. Keep writing, and we look forward to hearing from you.''

STUDIO ONE (II), P.O. Box 1558, St. Joseph MN 56374, founded 1976, editor changes yearly. *Studio One* is an annual literary and visual arts magazine designed as a forum for local, regional and national poets/writers. **They have no specifications regarding form, subject matter or style of poetry submitted. However, poetry no more than 2 pages stands a better chance of publication.** They have recently published poetry by Yuko Taniguchi and Larry Schug. As a sample the editor selected these lines from "Waiting Room" by Erin Marsh:

> Then we saw the hallowed light
> and the whisper was gone
> creating a pain
> that could be heard
> by all

The editor says *Studio One* is 50-80 pgs., soft cover, typeset. It includes 1-3 short stories, 22-30 poems and 10-13 visual art representations. They receive 250-400 submissions a year. No subscriptions, but a **sample copy can be obtained by sending a SASE with no less than $2 postage. Previously published poems and simultaneous submissions OK. Deadline: February 16 for spring publication. Seldom comments on rejections. Send SASE and note if you want material returned.** *Studio One* received the 1995 Medalist Award from The Columbia Scholastic Press Association, Columbia University.

‡SUBLIME ODYSSEY (IV-Love/romance), 200 Park Ave. #45, Yuba City CA 95991, founded 1995, editor Dana Miner, appears 2-3 times a year and promotes "the writing and appreciation of classic love poetry." **They want "love poetry of great beauty, tenderness, imagination and creativity; prefer poems of no more than one page, but longer works of high quality are accepted. No profanity, pornography, erotica or blasphemy; no negative or homosexual work. No gripping, bitter poetry; no third-rate greeting card verse."** They have recently published poetry by Robert S. King and Joanna Scott. As a sample the editor selected these lines from "Blessed With Shining Light" by Kimberly Anne Schure:

> Subtle thy beauty, gentle thy love
> As sweet as a summer breeze embrace
> Trembling the delicate petals and the dove.
> Beautiful thy heart and thy soul, in every trace
> Warming my heart as the glaring sun,
> Brilliant, blinding: such in One.

Sublime Odyssey is 35-45 pgs., 8½×11, photocopied and side-stapled with b&w cover illustration. They accept about 10% of poems received. Press run varies. **Submit 10 poems at a time. "Poets must have at least 6 acceptable poems to gain entry in any future issues." No previously published poems or simultaneous submissions. Cover letter preferred. Reads submissions January 1 through May 31 only.** Time between acceptance and publication is 1-6 months. **Seldom comments on rejections. Regarding guidelines the editor says, "Guidelines won't help my contributors—they either have the material or not. Just send material if you think it meets my needs." Reports in 1-3 weeks. Pays 1 copy. Acquires first rights.** The editor adds, *"Sublime Odyssey* is a platform for serious writers of love and romantic fantasy poetry, and any poet pursuing this path should have the necessary heart and soul to do it well. Bitterness and negativity have no place here. Beauty and imagination are the qualities I want most."

SUB-TERRAIN; ANVIL PRESS (II, IV-Social issues, political, form/style), P.O. Box 1575, Bentall Centre, Vancouver, British Columbia V6C 2P7 Canada, phone (604)876-8710, founded 1988, poetry editor Paul Pitre. Anvil Press is an "alternate small press publishing *Sub-Terrain*—a socially conscious literary quarterly whose aim is to produce a reading source that will stand in contrast to the trite and pandered—as well as broadsheets, chapbooks and the occasional monograph." They want **"work that has a point-of-view; work that has some passion behind it and is exploring issues that are of pressing importance (particularly that with an urban slant); work that challenges conventional notions of what poetry is or should be; work with a social conscience. No bland, flowery, uninventive poetry that says nothing in style or content."** As a sample the editor selected these lines from "Skin Dogs" by Helen Baker:

> The bodies are buried, but
> not the images:
> the school girl left
> squirming in a trash bag, a
> two-year-old cut open
> with the top of a tin
>
> Skin dogs; skinners

other cons call them. . . .

Sub-Terrain is 40 pgs., 7½×10½, offset, with a press run of 3,000. Subscription: $15. **Sample post-paid: $4. Submit 4-6 poems at a time. They will consider simultaneous submissions, but not previously published poems. Reports in 8-10 weeks. Pays money only for solicited work; for other work, 4-issue subscription. Acquires one-time rights for magazine. "If chapbook contract, we retain right to publish subsequent printings unless we let a title lapse out-of-print for more than 1 year."** Staff occasionally reviews small press poetry chapbooks. Sponsors Last Poems Poetry Contest for "poetry that encapsulates North American experience at the close of the 20th Century"; information for SASE (or SAE and IRC). **For chapbook or book publication submit 4 sample poems and bio, no simultaneous submissions. "We are willing to consider mss. But I must stress that we are a co-op, depending on support from an interested audience. New titles will be under-taken with caution. We are not subsidized at this point and do not want to give authors false hopes—but if something is important and should be in print, we will do our best."** Editor provides **brief comment and more extensive comments for fees.** He says, "Poetry, in our opinion, should be a distillation of emotion and experience that is being given back to the world. Pretty words and fancy syntax are just that. Where are the modern day writers who are willing to risk it all, put it all on the line? Young, new writers: Show it all. The last thing the world needs is soppy, sentimental fluff that gives nothing and says nothing."

SULFUR MAGAZINE (II, IV-Translations), % Dept. of English, Eastern Michigan University, Ypsilanti MI 48197, phone (313)483-9787, founded 1981, poetry editor Clayton Eshleman, is a physi-cally gorgeous and hefty (250 pgs., 6×9, flat-spined, glossy card cover, elegant graphics and printing on quality stock) biannual that has earned a distinguished reputation. They have published poetry by John Ashbery, Ed Sanders, Gary Snyder, Jackson MacLow, Paul Blackburn and the editor (one of our better-known poets). As a sample the editor selected "Irish" by Paul Celan, translated by Pierre Joris:

> Give me the right of way
> across the grain ladder of your sleep,
> the right of way
> across the sleep trail,
> The right, for me to cut peat
> along the heart's hillside,
> tomorrow.

Published at EMU, *Sulfur* has a circulation of 2,000, using approximately 100 pgs. of poetry in each issue. They use 15-20 of 600-700 submissions received/year. Free verse dominates here, much of it leaning toward the experimental. Subscription: $14. **Sample postpaid: $7. "We urge would-be contributors to *read* the magazine and send us material only if it seems to be appropriate."** Editor comments "sometimes, if the material is interesting." **Reports in 2-3 weeks. Pays $35-45/ contributor.** Reviews 10-20 poetry books/issue. Open to unsolicited reviews. Poets may also send books for review consideration. Poetry published in *Sulfur* has also been selected for inclusion in *The Best American Poetry 1996*. Clayton Eshleman says, "Most unsolicited material is of the 'I am sensitive and have practiced my sensitivity' school—with little attention to language as such, or incor-poration of materials that lead the poem into more ample contexts than 'personal' experience. I fear too many young writers today spend more time on themselves, without deeply engaging their *selves*, in a serious psychological way—and too little time breaking their heads against the Blakes, Stevens and Vallejos of the world. That is, writing has replaced reading. I believe that writing is a form of reading and vice versa. Of course, it is the quality and wildness of imagination that finally counts—but this 'quality' is a composite considerably dependent on assimilative reading (and translating, too)."

SULPHUR RIVER LITERARY REVIEW (II), P.O. Box 19228, Austin TX 78760-9228, founded 1978, reestablished 1987, editor/publisher James Michael Robbins, is a semiannual of poetry, prose and artwork. **They have "no restrictions except quality." They do not want poetry that is "trite or religious or verse that does not incite thought."** They have published poetry by Walt McDonald, Lyn Lifshin, Laurel Speer, Albert Huffstickler and Gerald Burns. As a sample the editor selected these lines from "The Small Credo" by Harland Ristau:

> living
> is believing
> what we did
> what is not done.
> believing wrapped
> with ribbons of hope,
> the dream we wake from,
> living is believing
> spirit will mend,
> mend all things,
> bandaged by mercy,

> with time moored
> to a heart knowing
> when to come home.

SRLR is digest-sized, perfect-bound, with glossy cover. They receive about 1,000 poems a year, accept about 5%. Press run is 400 for 200 subscribers, 100 shelf sales. Subscription: $10. **Sample postpaid: $6. No previously published poems or simultaneous submissions. Often comments on rejections. Reports in 1 month. Sometimes sends prepublication galleys. Pays 2 copies.** The editor says, "Poetry is, for me, the essential art, the ultimate art, and any effort to reach the effect of the successful poem deserves some comment other than 'sorry.' This is why I try to comment as much as possible on submissions, though by doing so I risk my own special absurdity. So be it. However, there can be no compromise of quality if the poem is to be successful or essential art."

SUMMER STREAM PRESS (II), P.O. Box 6056, Santa Barbara CA 93160-6056, phone (805)962-6540, founded 1978, poetry editor David D. Frost, publishes a series of books (Box Cars) in hardcover and softcover, each presenting 6 poets, averaging 70 text pgs. for each poet. "The mix of poets represents many parts of the country and many approaches to poetry. The poets previously selected have been published, but that is no requirement. We welcome traditional poets in the mix and thus offer them a chance for publication in this world of free-versers. **The six poets share a 15% royalty. We require rights for our editions worldwide and share 50-50 with authors for translation rights and for republication of our editions by another publisher. Otherwise all rights remain with the authors.**" They have published poetry by Virginia E. Smith, Sandra Russell, Jennifer MacPherson, Nancy Berg, Lois Shapley Bassen and Nancy J. Wallace. To be considered for future volumes in this series, **query with about 12 sample poems, no cover letter. Replies to query in 6 months, to submission (if invited) in 1 year. Previously published poetry and simultaneous submissions OK. Editor usually comments on rejections. Always sends prepublication galleys.** He says, "We welcome both traditional poetry and free verse. However, we find we must reject almost all the traditional poetry received simply because the poets exhibit little or no knowledge of the structure and rules of traditional forms. Much of it is rhymed free verse."

THE SUN (II), 107 N. Roberson St., Chapel Hill NC 27516, phone (919)942-5282, founded 1974, editor Sy Safransky, is "a monthly magazine of ideas. Noted for honest, personal work that's not too obscure or academic. **We avoid traditional, rhyming poetry, as well as limericks, haiku and religious poetry. We're open to almost anything else: free verse, prose poems, short and long poems.**" They have published poetry by Alison Luterman, David Budbill, Carolyn Acree, Lyn Lifshin and Lou Lipsitz. As a sample the editor selected these lines from "Nudging A Poem" by Robert Bly:

> To nudge a poem along toward its beauty.
> Is that selfishness? Is it something silly?
>
> Do others love poems as I do? Longing
> To find you in a phrase, and be close
> There, kissing the walls and the door frame.
> Happy in the change of a single word.

The Sun is 40 pgs., magazine-sized, printed on 50 lb. offset, saddle-stapled, with b&w photos and graphics. Circulation is 27,000 for 25,000 subscriptions of which 50 are libraries. They receive 3,000 submissions of poetry/year, use 36, have a 1- to 3-month backlog. Subscription: $32. **Sample postpaid: $3.50. Submit no more than 6 poems. Poems should be typed and accompanied by a cover letter. Previously published poems and simultaneous submissions OK, but should be noted. Send SASE for guidelines. Reports within 3 months. Pays $50-200 on publication plus copies and subscription. Buys first serial or one-time rights.** *The Sun* received an *Utne Reader* Award for General Excellence.

SUN DOG: THE SOUTHEAST REVIEW (II), 406 Williams Bldg., English Dept., Florida State University, Tallahassee FL 32306, phone (904)644-4230, founded 1979, poetry editor Russ Franklin. "The journal has a small student staff. We publish two magazines per year of poetry, short fiction and essays. As a norm, we usually accept about 12 poems per issue. **We accept poetry of the highest caliber, looking for the most 'whole' works. A poet may submit any length, but because of space, poems over 2 pages are impractical. Excellent formal verse highly regarded.**" They have published poetry by David Bottoms, David Kirby, Peter Meinke and Leon Stokesbury. *SD* is 100 pgs., 6×9, flat-spined with a glossy card cover, usually including half-tones, line drawings and color art when budget allows. Press run is 1,250. Subscription: $8 for 2 issues. **Sample postpaid: $4. Submit 2-5 poems at a time, typed, single-spaced. If simultaneous submission, say so. No previously published poems. Editor will comment briefly on most poems, especially those which come close to being accepted. Send SASE for guidelines. Reports in 3 months. Pays 2 copies. Acquires first North American serial rights.** *SD* sponsors the Richard Eberhart Prize in Poetry. This is an annual award given to the best unpublished poem of no fewer than 30 lines and no more than 100. The winner receives $300 and publication in *Sun Dog*. Submit 1 poem only and SASE for results to the Richard Eberhart Prize at the above address. No entry fee or form is required. Submission deadline: September 15. Winner will be announced on December 31.

SUNSTONE (II), 331 S. Rio Grande St., Suite 206, Salt Lake City UT 84101-1136, founded 1974, poetry editor Dixie Partridge, appears 8 times a year. *Sunstone* publishes "scholarly articles of interest to an open, Mormon audience; personal essays; fiction; and poetry." **They want "both lyric and narrative, poetry that engages the reader with fresh, strong images, skillful use of language and a strong sense of voice and/or place. No didactic poetry, sing-song rhymes or in-process work."** They have published poetry by R.A. Christmas, Susan Howe, Anita Tanner, Robert Rees and Niranjan Mohanty. As a sample the editor selected these lines from "A Trip to the Sea" by Philip White:

> At our backs the sun burned,
> and the gulls crossed it, hung
> trembling on the wind, turned,
> crossed again, their bodies
> on crooked wings falling and falling
> into the circle of flames.

Sunstone is 96 pgs., 8½ × 11, professionally printed and saddle-stapled with a semi-glossy paper cover. They receive more than 400 poems a year, accept 40-50. Press run is 10,000 for 8,000 subscribers of which 300 are libraries, 700 shelf sales. Subscription: $32 for 8 issues. **Sample postpaid: $4.95. No previously published poems or simultaneous submissions.** Time between acceptance and publication is a year or less. **Seldom comments on rejections. Send SASE for guidelines. Reports in 3 months. Pays 3 copies. Acquires first North American serial rights.** Reviews books of poetry. Open to unsolicited reviews. Poets may also send books for review consideration. The editor says, "Poetry does not have to be Mormon related at all. Most of it is not. We've published poems rooted strongly in place, narratives seeing life from another time or culture, poems on religious belief or doubt—a wide range of subject matter."

SURPRISE ME (I, IV-Spirituality, subscribers), P.O. Box 1762, Claremore OK 74018-1762, founded 1994, editor Lynda Nicolls. A biannual, *Surprise Me* recently changed to a subscribers-only format and **now only publishes work submitted by subscribers.** *"Surprise Me* is founded on the hope of providing a home for those souls who believe life's purpose is to serve Truth and Beauty. Our main interests are religion, mysticism, nature, art, literature, music, dance, relationships, love and peace. **We are open on form, length and style to all kinds of poetry. Profanity, intolerance and pro-violence are not welcome."** They have recently published poetry by C. David Hay, Gail Spaulding, Leah Smith and Eugene Adams. As a sample the editor selected these lines from her poem "On the Wings of Migrating Geese":

> And even as I stand behind this window,
> icy rain crawling down its fogged glass,
> you are flying South on the wings of migrating geese,
> you are floating away under the wings of blowing leaves,
> to return, someday, on the wings of butterflies,
> to smile, one day, in the wings of red poppies.

Surprise Me is 16-20 pgs., 8½ × 11, professionally printed by offset lithography on colored paper with b&w artwork and saddle-stapled. They receive about 1,000 poems a year, use approximately 10%. Press run is 50. Single copy: $6; subscription: $12 individual in US; $14 institution in US; $14 Canada and Mexico; $16 overseas. **Submit no more than 6 double-spaced pages at a time, name and address at the top of each page. Previously published poems and simultaneous submissions OK. Cover letter with brief bio required.** "Submissions without cover letters (or at least a note) are **too impersonal for me.** Submissions without SASE or IRCs will usually not receive a response." Time between acceptance and publication is about 2 years. **Seldom comments on rejections. Send SASE for guidelines. Reports ASAP. Pays 1 copy. Acquires one-time rights.** "We may review contributors' books and magazines in the future. Please query before sending books for review consideration." Open to unsolicited reviews. The editor says, "I don't like much of what is being currently published, because it lacks spirituality and often has shock value as its motive. I'm glad to see that rhyming poetry is making a comeback. I would advise beginners to read a lot—perhaps Yeats, Jeffers, Frost, Eliot, Whitman and Dickinson—and to remember that editorial comments (bad or good) are only one person's opinion. If one editor thinks your work is garbage, another editor may call it a treasure."

SYCAMORE REVIEW (II), Dept. of English, Purdue University, West Lafayette IN 47907, phone (317)494-3783, fax (317)494-3780, e-mail sycamore@expert.cc.purdue.edu, website http://www.sla.p urdue.edu/academic/engl/sycamore, founded 1988 (first issue May, 1989), editor-in-chief Rob Davidson, poetry editor changes each year; submit to Poetry Editor. "We accept personal essays, short fiction, drama, translations and **quality poetry in any form. We aim to publish many diverse styles of**

poetry from formalist to prose poems, narrative and lyric." They have recently published poetry by Tom Andrews, Philip Dacey, Denise Levertov, Thylias Moss, Lee Upton, Dean Young and Liliana Ursu. The magazine is semiannual in a digest-sized format, 160 pgs., flat-spined, professionally printed, with matte, color cover. Press run is 1,000 for 500 subscribers of which 50 are libraries. Subscription: $10; $12 outside US. **Sample postpaid: $7. Submit 3-6 poems at a time. Name and address on each page. No previously published poems except translations; simultaneous submissions OK, if notified immediately of acceptance elsewhere. No submissions accepted via fax or e-mail. Cover letters not required but invited; include phone number, short bio and previous publications, if any. "We read September 1 through May 1." Guidelines available for SASE. Reports in 4 months. Pays 2 copies.** Staff reviews books of poetry. Send books to editor-in-chief for review consideration. The editor says, "Poets who do not include SASE do not receive a response."

TAK TAK TAK (V, IV-Themes), BCM Tak, London WC1N 3XX England, founded 1986, editors Andrew and Tim Brown, appears occasionally in print and on cassettes. **"No restrictions on form or style. However, we are currently not accepting poetry submissions. Each issue of the magazine is on a theme (e.g., 'Mother Country/Fatherland,' 'Postcards from Paradise'), and** *all* **contributions must be relevant. If a contribution is long it is going to be more difficult to fit in than something shorter. Write for details of subject(s), etc., of forthcoming issue(s)."** They have published poetry by Michael Horovitz, Karl Blake, Keith Jafrate, Ramona Fotiade and Paul Buck. The editors describe it as "100 pgs., A5, photolithographed, board cover, line drawings and photographs, plus cassette of spoken word, music, sounds." Press run is 1,000. **Sample postpaid to US: £7.06 airmail (without cassette), £8.11 airmail (with cassette).** The editors say, "Poetry is just one of the many creative forms our contributions take. We are equally interested in prose and in visual and sound media."

TALISMAN: A JOURNAL OF CONTEMPORARY POETRY AND POETICS; TALISMAN HOUSE PUBLISHERS (III), P.O. Box 3157, Jersey City NJ 07303-3157, phone (201)938-0698, founded 1988, editor Edward Foster, appears twice a year. "Each issue centers on the poetry and poetics of a *major* contemporary poet and includes a selection of new work by other important contemporary writers. **We are particularly interested in poetry in alternative (***not*** academic) traditions. We don't want traditional poetry."** They have published poetry by William Bronk, Gerrit Lansing, Leslie Scalapino, Gustaf Sobin, Will Alexander and Susan Howe. As a sample the editor selected the following lines from "Opening Day" by Ann Lauterbach:

> *Locally a firm disavowal within the drift.*
> *Shaman of discourse said*
> *Or could have said*
> *These logics go teasingly forward*
> *Into capacities, and then the then.*

Talisman is 268 pgs., digest-sized, flat-spined, photocopied from computer printed Baskerville type, with matte card cover. "We are inundated with submissions and lost track of the number long ago." Their press run is 1,000 with "substantial" subscriptions of which many are libraries. Subscription: $11 individual; $15 institution. **Sample postpaid: $6. Reporting time varies. Always sends prepublication galleys. Pays 1 copy. Acquires first North American serial rights.** Reviews books of poetry in 500-1,000 words, single format. Talisman House Publishers produces "distinguished" books of poetry, fiction and essays. Send SASE for more information.

TAMAQUA (II, IV-Themes), C120, Parkland College, 2400 W. Bradley Ave., Champaign IL 61821-1899, phone (217)351-2380, founded 1989, editor-in-chief Bruce Morgan, is a biannual literary/arts journal **"of** *high* **quality. No restrictions on poetry, but it must be intelligently and professionally done."** They have recently published poetry by Ray Young Bear and Gwendolyn Brooks. As a sample the editor selected these lines from "Meeting, at a Party, a Woman with an Artificial Larynx" by Conrad Hilberry:

> *"How do you do," she said, her lips and tongue*
> *shaping the words but the voice flat, metallic,*
> *a wire on which the other voices hung*
> *like laundry flapping. I thought I heard a click*
> *where a thought ended.*

Tamaqua is 160-256 pgs., digest-sized, offset and perfect-bound with 4-color coated card cover, b&w (and occasional color) art and photos inside. They receive 2,000-3,000 poems/year, accept approximately 50. Press run is 1,500 for 400 subscribers of which 50 are libraries, 750 shelf sales. Subscription: $12/year. **Sample postpaid: $7. Submit 3-7 poems at a time. Prefers poems typed on bonded paper. No previously published poems; simultaneous submissions OK, "if noted in cover letter and contacted immediately if accepted elsewhere." Cover letter required. "All submissions are juried anonymously; only managing editor knows identity of writer before selection."** Seldom comments on rejections. Publishes theme issues. Send SASE for guidelines. Theme for Winter

1996 issue is "European Voices." Deadline: November 15, 1995. Reports in 4 months. Pays $10-20 plus copies. Acquires first North American serial rights. Reviews books of poetry in both single and multi-book format, no minimum length. Open to unsolicited reviews, but prefers "meditative review." Poets may also send books for review consideration, attn. Seth Mendelowitz. The editor says, "Nothing replaces knowledge of your market; hence *study* **Tamaqua** and similar magazines to discern the difference between good, solid, intelligent literature/art and that which is not."

TAMPA REVIEW (III), Dept. PM, University of Tampa, 401 W. Kennedy Blvd., Tampa FL 33606-1490, phone (813)253-3333 ext. 6266, founded 1964 as *UT Poetry Review*, became *Tampa Review* in 1988, editor Richard Mathews, poetry editors Kathryn Van Spanckeren and Donald Morrill, is an elegant semiannual of fiction, nonfiction, poetry and art (not limited to US authors) wanting **"original and well-crafted poetry written with intelligence and spirit. We do accept translations, but no greeting card or inspirational verse."** They have recently published poetry by Alberto Rios, Naomi Shihab Nye, Jim Daniels, Denise Levertov and Stephen Dunn. As a sample, the editors selected these lines from "Little Love Story" by Richard Chess:

> Their love was earth into which they dug
> uncovering one civilization after another
> some say that before the surprise
> of the next war, they found.
> the road that leads to Eden, beheld its flaming gate.

TR is 78-96 pgs., 7½×10½ flat-spined, with a matte card color cover. They accept about 50-60 of 2,000 poems received a year. Their press run is 500 with 175 subscriptions of which 20 are libraries. **Sample postpaid: $5. Submit 3-7 poems at a time. No previously published poems or simultaneous submissions. Unsolicited mss are read between September and December. Reports by mid-February. Sometimes sends prepublication galleys. Pays $10/printed page plus 1 copy and 40% discount on additional copies. Buys first North American serial rights.** Poetry published in *Tampa Review* has been included in *The Best American Poetry 1995*.

TAPROOT LITERARY REVIEW (I), 302 Park Rd., Ambridge PA 15003, phone (412)266-8476, founded 1986, editor Tikvah Feinstein, is an annual contest publication, open to beginners. In addition to contest, each year guest poets are selected; payment in copies. Writers published include Robert Johnson, George Kalamaras, Elizabeth Cappo, Mary Pogge and B.Z. Niditch. As a sample the editor selected these lines from "Of Love" by Elizabeth R. Curry:

> after especially the small things:
> shoelaces, patched shirts, broken watches, little rings:
>
> After all this I see in dreams six million pairs of eyes
> made beautiful by the obsessive love that created them,
> like the luminous glances of a kitten,
> and this shining hope in an animal child willing to love
> reminds me of what our history has forever lost.

The review is approximately 95 pgs., printed by offset on white stock with one-color glossy cover, art and no ads. Circulation is 500, sold at bookstores, readings and through the mail. Single copy: $5.50. **Sample postpaid: $5. There is a $10 entry fee for up to 5 poems, "no longer than 30 lines each." Nothing previously published or pending publication will be accepted. Cover letter with general information required. "We cannot answer without a SASE." Submissions accepted between September 1 and December 31. Publishes theme issues. Send SASE for upcoming themes. Sometimes sends prepublication galleys. All entrants receive a copy of *Taproot*; enclose $2 for p&h.** Send books for review consideration. The editor says, "We publish the best poetry we can in a variety of styles and subjects, so long as its literary quality and speaks to us."

TAR RIVER POETRY (II), English Dept., East Carolina University, Greenville NC 27858-4353, phone (919)328-6046 or 328-6467, fax (919)328-4889, founded 1960, editor Peter Makuck, associate editor Luke Whisnant. **"We are not interested in sentimental, flat-statement poetry. What we would like to see is skillful use of figurative language."** They have recently published poetry by Susan Elizabeth Howe, Naomi Shihab Nye, Emily Grosholz, Paul Zimmer, Laurence Lieberman, Vern

---

THE GEOGRAPHICAL INDEX, located before the Subject Index, can help you discover the publishers in your region. Publishers often favor poets (and work) from their own areas.

Rutsala, Elizabeth Dodd, Philip Dacey, Brendan Galvin and Sharon Bryan. As a sample the editors selected this poem, "Piano at Midnight," by Michael Mott:

> You stop your walk along the beach.
> Someone is playing Scarlatti.
>
> The night is dark about the lighted window.
> The vast sea settles quietly.
>
> Someone also is playing for everyone awake.
> All debts are cancelled. All are free.

Tar River appears twice yearly and is 60 pgs., digest-sized, professionally printed on salmon stock, some decorative line drawings, matte card cover with photo. They receive 6,000-8,000 submissions/year, use 150-200. Press run is 900 for 500 subscribers of which 125 are libraries. Subscription: $10. **Sample: $5.50. Submit 3-6 poems at a time. "We do not consider previously published poems or simultaneous submissions. Double or single-spaced OK. Name and address on each page. We do not consider mss during summer months." Reads submissions September 1 through April 15 only. Editors will comment "if slight revision will do the trick." Send SASE for guidelines. Reports in 4-6 weeks. Pays 2 copies. Acquires first rights.** Reviews books of poetry in 4,000 words maximum, single or multi-book format. This is an especially good market for intelligent, concisely written book reviews. Poets may also send books for review consideration. **Tar River** is an "all-poetry" magazine that accepts dozens of poems in each issue, providing the talented beginner and experienced writer with an excellent forum that features all styles and forms of verse. Frequently contributors' works are included in the **Anthology of Magazine Verse & Yearbook of American Poetry**. Poetry published in **Tar River** was also selected for inclusion in **The Best American Poetry 1994**. The editors advise, "Read, read, read. Saul Bellow says the writer is primarily a reader moved to emulation. Read the poetry column in **Writer's Digest**. Read the books recommended therein. Do your homework."

"TEAK" ROUNDUP (I, IV-Subscribers), West Coast Paradise Publishing, #5-9060 Tronson Rd., Vernon, British Columbia V1T 6L7 Canada, phone (604)545-4186, fax (604)545-4194, editors Yvonne and Robert G. Anstey. **"Teak" Roundup** is an international quarterly **open to the work of subscribers only.** They publish work from authors and poets across North America and beyond. West Coast Paradise Publishing also publishes books and chapbooks. Send SASE for catalog. As a sample the editors selected these lines from Robert G. Anstey's poem "Song In The Trellises Of Love":

> I have long been entrenched in the facade
> of warm and friendly hands but they
> retreated as I blossomed in the sun
>
> now the slow echo of the summer reaches me
> and light in spears of colour sing
> a rhapsody in the trellises of love.

TR was recently purchased by West Coast Paradise Publishing from Aardvark Enterprises but continues to accept work from **subscribers only.** Subscription (in Canadian currency): $17, $24 overseas. **Sample: $5, $8 overseas. Submit 3-5 poems at a time. SASE (or SAE with IRC) required for response. Send SASE for guidelines and upcoming themes. No payment. "It is our goal to become a paying market when circulation makes it feasible."**

TEARS IN THE FENCE (II), 38 Hodview, Stourpaine, Nr. Blandford Forum, Dorset DT11 8TN England, phone 01258-456803, founded 1984, general editor David Caddy, poetry editor Sarah Hopkins, is a "small press magazine of poetry, fiction, interviews, articles, reviews and graphics. **We are open to a wide variety of poetic styles. Work of a social, political, ecological and feminist awareness will be close to our purpose. However, we like to publish a balanced variety of work." The editors do not want to see "didactic rhyming poems."** They have published poetry by Joan Jobe Smith, Martin Stannard, Ann Born and Catherine Swanson. As a sample they selected the following lines from "From a Gloucestershire Window" by Brian Hinton:

> Look, the manor house blazes red, its complex windows on fire
> with history, blind mirrors in which we disappear, over wrought
> gates that we can never enter. My mother, orphaned here, inspired
> me with tales of forced church on Sunday, bowing to the court

Tears in the Fence appears 3 times/year. It is 84 pgs., A5, "docu-tech printed" on 110 gms. paper and perfect-bound with matte card cover and b&w art and graphics. It has a press run of 450, of which 262 go to subscribers. Subscription: $15 for 3 issues. **Sample: $5. Writers should submit 6 typed poems with IRCs. Cover letter with brief bio required. Publishes theme issues. Send SASE (or SAE and IRC) for upcoming themes. Reports in 3 months.** Time to publication is 8-10 months "but can be much less." **Pays 1 copy.** Reviews books of poetry in 2,000-3,000 words, single or multi-book format. Open to unsolicited reviews. Poets may also send books for review consideration. The magazine is informally connected with the East Street Poets literary promotions, workshops and publications. They also sponsor an annual pamphlet competition open to poets from around the world. The editor says, "I think it helps to subscribe to several magazines in order to study the market and develop an understanding of what type of poetry is published. Use the review sections and send off to magazines that are new to you."

THE TENNESSEE QUARTERLY (II), Dept. of Literature and Language, Belmont University, 1900 Belmont Blvd., Nashville TN 37212-3757, phone (615)383-7001, first issue Spring 1994, co-editor Anthony Lombardy, appears 3 times/year (in the fall, winter and spring). *"The Tennessee Quarterly* publishes poems, short fiction, essays of general interest as well as of broad literary-critical and theoretical reach, translations, and articles of art theory and criticism." **They want poetry of "any form, subject or style, but we favor language highly marked whether by metrical form or rhetorical figure."** They have published poetry by Peter Russell, Emily Grosholz and Richard Moore and a translation by Dana Gioia. As a sample the editor selected the last stanza of "In the Shield of Athena" by Greg Williamson:

> And so envision shrouds of grief, the gem
> Of naked beauty, and the knucklebone
> Of hate; such things as on the face of them
> Would blind the eye or turn the heart to stone.

The Tennessee Quarterly is 60-100 pgs., 6×9, professionally printed on quality stock and flat-spined with light matte card cover. They receive 4,000-5,000 poems a year, accept about 50. Press run is 500 for 200 subscribers, 100 shelf sales. Subscription: $15/year. **Sample postpaid: $5. No previously published poems or simultaneous submissions. Reads submissions September 1-June 15 only.** Time between acceptance and publication is 6 months. **Seldom comments on rejections. Reports usually within a month. Pays 2 copies. Acquires first North American serial rights.** Reviews books of poetry in up to 2,000 words. Open to unsolicited reviews. Poets may also send books for review consideration.

‡10TH MUSE (II), 33 Hartington Rd., Newtown, Southampton, Hants SO2 0EW England, founded 1990, editor Andrew Jordan, is an occasional publication of poetry, prose, book reviews and b&w artwork. They are **"particularly interested in absurd landscape poetry, fields on stilts, ridiculous scenery and placelessness generally. In authentic poetics a speciality—no sincere poems, please."** They have published poetry by Peter Redgrove, Sheila E. Murphy and Belinda Subraman. As a sample the editor selected these lines from "Photograph of Wittey Court, Worcestershire" by Melaine Byfield:

> Know the price
> And the doing
> And the ruin
> I stood on the brink of the ha-ha
> and laughed

10th Muse is 48 pgs., A5, photocopied, saddle-stapled, with card cover, no ads. Press run is 200 for 24 subscribers of which 3 are libraries. "U.S. subscribers—send $10 in bills for 2 issues, $5 for single copy." **Often comments on rejections. Reports in 2-3 months. Pays 1 copy.** Staff reviews books of poetry. Send books for review consideration. The editor says, "Poets should read a copy of the magazine first."

TESSERA (IV-Women, regional, bilingual, themes, translations), 350 Stong, York University, 4700 Keele St., North York, Ontario M3J 1P3 Canada, phone (416)736-2100, founded 1984, revived 1988, contact Lianne Moyes, appears twice a year: **"feminist literary theory and experimental writing by women in French and English, preference to Canadians."** It is 94 pgs., digest-sized, professionally printed, with glossy card cover. Subscription: $18 plus $6 postage for individuals; $24 plus $6 postage for institutions. **Sample postpaid: $13. Submit 4 poems at a time. Simultaneous submissions and previously published poems ("sometimes") OK. Editor comments on submissions "sometimes." Publishes theme issues. Theme for Volume 21 is "Symbolic Violence and the Avant Garde." Pays $10/page.** The editor says, "I appreciate a cover letter introducing the poetic project the poems come out of. I also appreciate poets who have done a bit of research and are familiar with the kinds of texts we publish."

TESSERACT PUBLICATIONS (I), P.O. Box 505, Hudson SD 57034-0505, phone (605)987-5070, fax (605)987-5071, founded 1981, publisher Janet Leih. **"All my books are subsidized publications. Payment is ⅓ in advance, ⅓ when book goes to printer, balance when book is complete. I help my poets with copyright, bar codes, listings and whatever publicity I can get for them. I have a number of mailing lists and will prepare special mailings for them, work with competent proofreaders, artists and a capable reviewer." Sometimes sends prepublication galleys.** They have helped publish books of poetry by Helen Eikamp, Gertrude Johnson, Fern Stuefen, Wanda Todd and Ellis Ovesen. As a sample Janet Leih selected these lines by Lois Bogue:

Last night northern lights
shimmered in silent glory
across starry spaces.
Suddenly I was a child
sky-watching with my father.

They also hold occasional contests. Send SASE (55¢ postage) for information. Janet Leih adds, "I publish a catalog of books by South Dakota writers and take their books on consignment to fill orders. The catalog is modest at this time but the hope is to expand to a larger catalog and distribute it more widely."

TEXAS TECH UNIVERSITY PRESS (V, IV-Series), P.O. Box 41037, Lubbock TX 79409-1037, phone (806)742-2982, founded 1971, editor Judith Keeling, publishes volumes of poetry in 2 categories only: **First-Book Poetry Series**: "Winning and finalist mss in an annual competition conducted by Poetry Editor Robert A. Fink who surveys literary journals throughout the year and normally invites 12 poets to submit mss for consideration in the competition"; and **Invited Poets Series**: "Collections invited from established poets whose work continues to appear in distinguished journals." Most recently published: *An Animal of the Sixth Day* by Laura Fargas and *Anna and the Steel Mill* by Deborah Burnham. **Does not read unsolicited manuscripts. Books published on royalty contracts.**

‡TEXTSHOP (I), Dept. of English, University of Regina, Regina, Saskatchewan S4S 0A2 Canada, founded 1993, editor Andrew Stubbs, is an annual "collaborative writing journal" that **seeks "experimental, postmodern poetry; one page in length, or sequences up to five pages. No thematic poetry."** They have recently published poetry by Bruce Bond and Judith Miller. As a sample the editor selected these lines from "Connections" by Rienzi Crusz:

Come summer
and the family is back
to its sun beginnings;
suck the sweet rambuttan,
let the mango juice run down your shirt

Textshop is 36 pgs., 7½ × 10, saddle-stapled with coated card cover and lots of shaded boxes used for graphic effects. They receive 75-100 poems a year, accept approximately 20%. Press run is 250 for 25 subscribers of which 15 are libraries, 200 shelf sales. Single copy: $3.50. **Sample free. Submit 5 poems at a time. Previously published poems OK; no simultaneous submissions. Cover letter with capsule bio required. Reads submissions January through April. Poems are circulated to an editorial board. Always comments on rejections. Reports in 1 month. Pays 1 copy.** At the end of each issue, in sections titled "Reflections," the editors also include written commentary regarding the work published in the issue.

TEXTURE; TEXTURE PRESS (II, IV-Form/style), 3760 Cedar Ridge Dr., Norman OK 73072, fax (405)364-3627, founded 1989, editor Susan Smith Nash, is an annual ("approximately") of experimental and innovative writing: poetry, criticism, fiction and reviews. **They want "innovative or experimental poetry which openly addresses difficult philosophical, theoretical or linguistic issues. No dull, sterile, derivative work."** They have published poetry by Robert Kelly, Rochelle Owens, Cydney Chadwick, Valerie Fox and Douglas Messerli. As a sample the editor selected these lines from "Prime Sway: A Transduction of Sor Juana's Primero Suento, 1692" by John M. Bennett:

PYRAMID, wall, furnace tears
nascent slumber, Ah Ceiling walking
vanes and obelisks pumped the thigh . . .

texture is 100 pgs., 8½ × 11, offset and perfect-bound with colored matte card cover. They receive 1,000 poems a year, accept approximately 20%. Press run is 1,000 for 300 subscribers of which 15 are libraries. Single copy: $8; subscription: $10 for 2 issues. **Sample postpaid: $6. No previously published poems or simultaneous submissions. Cover letter required. Reads submissions October 1 through May 15 only. Poems are circulated to an editorial board. Seldom comments on rejections. Reports in 3-6 months. Pays 1 copy. Acquires first rights.** Includes book briefs of 50 words and reviews of 250-500 words. Open to unsolicited reviews. Poets may also send books for review consideration. texture press also publishes books, chapbooks and miniatures. **"Query first and explain the critical grounding of the work. texture likes to publish a critical accompaniment to help readers locate the text within the current literary scene and understand how to read it."** Replies to queries in 2 months, to mss (if invited) in 6 months. **Payment is negotiated.** The editor says, "Feel free to experiment, to mangle text, and to ironize the cultural verities by juxtaposing them with the words of sages, philosophers, or your favorite great aunt."

THALIA: STUDIES IN LITERARY HUMOR (I, IV-Subscribers, humor), Dept. of English, University of Ottawa, Ottawa, Ontario K1N 6N5 Canada, phone (613)230-9505, fax (613)565-5786, e-mail jtaverni@aixl.uottawa.ca, editor Dr. J. Tavernier-Courbin, appears twice a year using **"humor**

(literary, mostly). **Poems submitted must actually be literary parodies."** The editor describes it as 7×8½, flat-spined, "with illustrated cover." Press run is 500 for 475 subscribers. Subscription: $20 for individuals, $22 for libraries. **Sample postpaid: $8 up to volume 11, $15 and $20 for volume 12-15 respectively (double issues). Contributors must subscribe. Simultaneous submissions OK but *Thalia* must have copyright. Will authorize reprints. "Queries via phone, fax or e-mail OK. However, submissions must be in hard copy." Editor comments on submissions. Reports in 3-4 months.** Reviews books of poetry. "Send queries to the editor concerning specific books."

THEMA (II, IV-Themes), Thema Literary Society, P.O. Box 74109, Metairie LA 70033-4109, founded 1988, editor Virginia Howard, is a triannual literary magazine **using poetry related to specific themes. "Each issue is based on an unusual premise. Please, please send SASE for guidelines before submitting poetry to find out the upcoming themes. Upcoming themes (and submission deadlines) include: 'Too proud to ask' (11-1-96), 'Scrawled in a library book' (3-1-97), 'Eureka!' (7-1-97) and 'An unexpected guest' (11-1-97). No scatologic language, alternate life-style, explicit love poetry."** They have recently published poetry by Eileen Spinelli, Nora Ruth Roberts, James Penha and Nancy G. Westerfield. As a sample the editor selected these lines by Binnie Pasquier:

> I spend the bulk of time
> swimming in subconscious clutter
> and collective illusions
> of the past . . .

Thema is 200 pgs., digest-sized, professionally printed, with matte card cover. They accept about 8% of 400 poems received/year. Press run is 500 for 270 subscribers of which 30 are libraries. Subscription: $16. **Sample postpaid: $8. Submit up to 3 poems at a time. All submissions should be typewritten and on standard 8½×11 paper. Submissions are accepted all year, but evaluated after specified deadlines. Editor comments on submissions. Pays $10/poem plus 1 copy. Buys one-time rights.**

THE THIRD ALTERNATIVE (II, IV-Science fiction/fantasy, horror); ZENE: THE SMALL PRESS GUIDE, 5 Martins Lane, Witcham, Ely, Cambridgeshire CB6 2LB England, founded 1994, editor Andy Cox. *The Third Alternative* is a quarterly of **"cutting-edge horror, dark fantasy and science fiction, often transcending such genres to explore the slipstream, the interface of genre and mainstream writing." They want "well-crafted, literary, powerful poems, usually 40 lines maximum, from imaginative to disturbing. Translations welcome. Not keen on rhyming poetry or haiku."** They have published poetry by Sheila E. Murphy, Bruce Boston, Andrew Darlington and Steve Sneyd. As a sample the editor selected these lines from "The Birth of Hieronymous Bosch" by David Chorlton:

> A bell drips
> from a shivering tower. The leading
> melts in coloured windows
>
> and glass
> rains onto the silky wings
> of bats circling in crepuscular panic.

The Third Alternative is 60 pgs., A5, litho printed on coated paper and saddle-stitched with b&w coated card cover and b&w graphics. They accept less than 10% of the poetry received. Press run is 450 for 25 subscribers ("and rising"). Subscription: £9, $22 USA. **Sample postpaid: £2.50, $6 USA. Previously published poems OK; no simultaneous submissions. Cover letter required.** Time between acceptance and publication is 2-3 issues. **Always comments on rejections. Reports in 1 month. Pays 1 copy. Acquires first British serial rights.** Andy Cox is also the editor of *Zene: The Small Press Guide*, a quarterly which lists "detailed contributor's guidelines of small press, independent and semi-pro markets worldwide, plus articles, news, views, interviews and reviews. Every issue carries a number of reviews of poetry publications, plus articles on various types of poetry." Poets may send books for review consideration to the above address. *Zene* is 36 pgs., A5, litho printed on coated paper and saddle-stitched. Single copy: £1.95, $4.50 USA; subscription: £7, $16.60 USA.

‡THIRD COAST (II), Dept. of English, Western Michigan University, Kalamazoo MI 49008-5092, phone (616)387-2675, website http://www.wmich.edu/thirdcoast, founded 1995, contact poetry editors, is a biannual national literary magazine of poetry, prose, creative nonfiction and translation. **They want "excellence of craft and originality of thought. Nothing trite."** They have recently published poetry by Dean Young, Alice B. Fogel, David Clewell and Alison Hawthorne Deming. As a sample we selected these lines from "Action at a Distance" by Alane Rollings:

> Turn off the light; let's see how the sky affects us.
> With your cheekbone two inches from my forehead,
> tell me the mass and circumference of the universe
> and how at home you are in its basic emptiness. I can't do without
> these revelations, though they sound so disconsolate in your mouth.

Third Coast is 140 pgs., 6×9, professionally printed and perfect-bound with a 4-color cover with art. They receive about 2,000 poems a year, accept 3-5%. Press run is 1,100 for 150 subscribers of which 20 are libraries, 350 shelf sales. Single copy: $6; subscription: $11 for 1 year, $20 for 2 years, $29 for 3 years. **Submit 3-5 poems at a time. No previously published poems; simultaneous submissions OK. Cover letter preferred. Reads submissions September 1 through May 1 only. Poems are circulated to assistant poetry editors and poetry editors; poetry editors make final decisions. Seldom comments on rejections. Send SASE for guidelines. Reports in 1-2 months. Pays 2 copies and one-year subscription. Acquires first rights.**

As a literary magazine with an eclectic balance of taste in literature and art, *Third Coast* selects cover images that reflect the balance it tries to achieve in its content. "We selected the painting 'Butterfly' partially for its literary allusion to 'Madame Butterfly' and partially because the editors felt the painting captured the tension between beauty and risk which corresponds with our magazine's mission," says Theresa Coty O'Neil, managing editor of the biannual published by Western Michigan University's Graduate Creative Writing Program. *Third Coast* publishes poetry, prose, creative nonfiction and translation, but poetry fills half of the magazine's pages. The cover artwork, an oil on canvas, was created by California-based artist Erin Scott and appeared courtesy of the Joyce Petter Gallery in Douglas, Michigan.

THE THIRD HALF LITERARY MAGAZINE; K.T. PUBLICATIONS (I, II), 16, Fane Close, Stamford, Lincolnshire PE9 1HG England, founded 1987, editor Mr. Kevin Troop. *TTH* appears "as often as possible each year." K.T. Publications also publishes up to 6 other books, with a Minibooks Series, for use in the classroom. The editor wants **"meaningful, human and humane, funny poems up to 40 lines. Work which** *says* **something without being obscene."** They have published poetry by Lee Bridges (Holland), Ann Keith (Amsterdam), Toby Litt (Prague) and Edmund Harwood, Michael Newman, Louise Rogers and Steve Sneyd (Britain). As a sample the editor selected this poem, "Fly," by Esther Gress (Denmark):

> *Like a butterfly*
> *we often fly in vain*
> *against the window pane*
> *and see not*
> *like the butterfly*
> *the open door*
> *to the sky*

TTH is up to 100 pgs., A5, perfect-bound, illustrated, printed on white paper with glossy cover. Press run is over 200. Individual booklets vary in length and use colored paper and card covers. **Submit 6 poems at a time. No simultaneous submissions. Cover letter and suitable SAE required. Reports ASAP. Pays 1 copy. "Procedure for the publication of books is explained to each author; each case is different.** *The Third Half* is priced at £2.50 each, £2.95 by post in UK, £4 overseas; two subsequent issues for £4.25 and three issues for £6.25 plus suitable SAEs, including postage and handling."

13TH MOON (II, IV-Women), English Dept., University at Albany, 1400 Washington Ave., Albany NY 12222, phone (518)442-4181, founded 1973, editor Judith Johnson, is a feminist literary magazine appearing yearly (one double issue) in a 6×9, flat-spined, handsomely printed format with glossy card cover, using photographs and line art, ads at $200/page. Beyond a doubt, a real selection of forms and styles is featured here. For instance, in recent issues free verse has appeared with formal work, concrete poems, long poems, stanza patterns, prose poems, a crown of sonnets and more. Press run is 2,000 for 690 subscribers of which 61 are libraries, 700 shelf sales. Subscription: $10. **Sample**

postpaid: $10. Submit 3-5 poems at a time. No previously published work or simultaneous submissions. Reads submissions September 1 through May 30 only. Publishes theme issues. Send SASE for guidelines and upcoming themes. Themes include "special issues on women's poetics, one focusing on poetry, one on narrative forms." Pays 2 copies. Acquires first North American serial rights.

THISTLEDOWN PRESS LTD. (IV-Regional), 633 Main St., Saskatoon, Saskatchewan S7H 0J8 Canada, founded 1975, editor-in-chief Patrick O'Rourke, is "a literary press that specializes in **quality books of contemporary poetry by Canadian authors. Only the best of contemporary poetry that amply demonstrates an understanding of craft with a distinctive use of voice and language. Only interested in full-length poetry mss with 53-71 pgs. minimum.**" They recently published *Wormwood Vermouth, Warpphistory* by Charles Noble and *Saved by the Telling* by Eva Tihanyi. **Do not submit unsolicited mss.** Canadian poets must **query first with letter, bio and publication credits. Submission guidelines available upon request. Replies to queries in 2-3 weeks, to submissions (if invited) in 3 months. No authors outside Canada. No simultaneous submissions. "Please submit quality laser-printed or photocopied material." Always sends prepublication galleys. Contract is for 10% royalty plus 10 copies.** They comment, "Poets submitting mss to Thistledown Press for possible publication should think in 'book' terms in every facet of the organization and presentation of the mss: Poets presenting mss that *read* like good books of poetry will have greatly enhanced their possibilities of being published. We strongly suggest that poets familiarize themselves with some of our poetry books before submitting a query letter."

THOUGHTS FOR ALL SEASONS: THE MAGAZINE OF EPIGRAMS (IV-Form, humor), % editor Prof. Em. Michel Paul Richard, 478 NE 56th St., Miami FL 33137-2621, founded 1976, "is an irregular serial: **designed to preserve the epigram as a literary form; satirical.** All issues are commemorative." **Rhyming poetry and nonsense verse with good imagery will be considered although most modern epigrams are prose.** Prof. Richard has published poetry by Jack Hart and offers this sample:

> Beware a cause: it is our fate
> To turn into the things we hate

TFAS is 84 pgs., offset from typescript with full-page illustrations, card cover, saddle-stapled. The editor accepts about 20% of material submitted. Press run is 500-1,000. There are several library subscriptions but most distribution is through direct mail or local bookstores and newsstand sales. Single copy: $4.75 plus $1.50 postage. **Submit at least one full page of poems at a time, with SASE. Simultaneous submissions OK, but not previously published epigrams "unless a thought is appended which alters it." Editor comments on rejections. Publishes one section devoted to a theme. Send SASE for guidelines. Reports in 1 month. Pays 1 copy.**

THREE CONTINENTS PRESS INC. (III, IV-Ethnic, translations), P.O. Box 38009, Colorado Springs CO 80937-8009, phone (719)579-0977, fax (719)576-4689, founded 1973, poetry editor Donald Herdeck. "**Published poets only welcomed and only non-European and non-American poets . . . We publish literature by creative writers from the non-western world (Africa, the Middle East, the Caribbean and Asia/Pacific)—poetry *only* by non-western writers or good translations of such poetry if original language is Arabic, French, African vernacular, etc.**" They have published poetry by Derek Walcott, Khalil Hawi, Mahmud Darwish, Julia Fields, Hilary Tham, Houda Naamani and Nizar Kabbani. They also publish anthologies and criticisms focused on relevant themes. As a sample the editor selected these lines from "Fear," published in *Fan of Swords* by Muhammad al-Maghut:

> On these cloudy days
> I am afraid to awaken one morning and find no birds left,
> no single flower tucked into a braid,
> no friend in any coffee house.
> I fear being chained to the wash-stand
>   or chimney
> being sprayed by bullets
> while the toothbrush is still in my mouth.
> Hurry up, Mother, ask the bedouins
>   for a leatherbound charm or special weed
> to protect me from this fear.

Query with 4-5 samples, bio, publication credits. Replies to queries in 5-10 weeks, to submissions (if invited) in 4-5 weeks. Sometimes sends prepublication galleys. Offers 10% royalty contract (5% for translator) with $100-200 advance plus 10 copies. Buys worldwide English rights. Send SASE for catalog to buy samples.

‡**360 DEGREES (II)**, 980 Bush St., Suite 404, San Francisco CA 94109, founded 1993, managing editor Karen Kinnison, is a quarterly review, containing literature and artwork, "that is more like a museum than a magazine, preserving the best from our times so readers in the future will seek us as a rare source." **They say they have "no real limits" on poetry, "only the limits of the submitter's imagination." However, they do not want to see "greeting card verse, simplified emotions or religious verse."** They have recently published poetry by Nancy Willard, Sean Brendan-Brown, Julia Gilberte Rhodes and Rochelle Holt. As a sample the editor selected these lines from "it is a concept I don't understand" by Mark Sonnenfeld:

> walk away to wonderful wonderful volumes
> the beginning
> planets have gone this way
> do realize
> this isn't Kansas

360 Degrees is 40 pgs., digest-sized, neatly printed and saddle-stapled with a 4-page full-color art insert. They receive about 500 poems a year, accept about 50. Press run is 500 for 100 subscribers. Subscription: $15. **Sample postpaid: $5. Submit 3 poems at a time. No previously published poems; simultaneous submissions OK. Cover letter preferred. Seldom comments on rejections. Send SASE for guidelines. Reports within 1 month. Pays $5/poem and 2 copies. Buys first rights.** The editor says, "Most of the poems we accept not only show mastery of words, but present new ideas. The mastery of language is something we expect from freelancers, but the content of the idea being expressed is the selling point."

THE THREEPENNY REVIEW (II), P.O. Box 9131, Berkeley CA 94709, phone (510)849-4545, fax (510)849-4551, founded 1980, poetry editor Wendy Lesser, "is a quarterly review of literature, performing and visual arts, and social articles aimed at the intelligent, well-read, but not necessarily academic reader. Nationwide circulation. **Want: formal, narrative, short poems (and others); do not want: confessional, no punctuation, no capital letters. Prefer under 50 lines but not necessary. No bias *against* formal poetry, in fact a slight bias in favor of it."** They have published poetry by Thom Gunn, Frank Bidart, Seamus Heaney, Czeslaw Milosz and Louise Glück. There are about 9-10 poems in each 36-page tabloid issue. They receive about 4,500 submissions of poetry/year, use 12. Press run is 10,000 for 8,000 subscribers of which 300 are libraries. Subscription: $16. **Sample: $6. Send 5 poems or fewer/submission. Do not submit mss June-September. Send SASE for guidelines. Reports in 2-8 weeks. Pays $100/poem. Buys first serial rights.** Open to unsolicited reviews. "Send for review guidelines (SASE required)." Work published in this review has also been included in the 1993, 1994 and 1995 volumes of *The Best American Poetry*.

THRESHOLD BOOKS (IV-Spirituality, translations), RD #4, Box 600, Dusty Ridge Rd., Putney VT 05346, phone (802)254-8300, fax (802)257-2779, founded 1981, poetry editor Edmund Helminski, is "a small press dedicated to the publication of quality works in metaphysics, poetry in translation and literature with some spiritual impact. **We would like to see poetry in translation of high literary merit with spiritual qualities by established authors. We specialize in publication of poetry with Sufi tradition."** Published books of poetry include *Love Is A Stranger* by Rumi and *Doorkeeper Of The Heart* by Rabia. As a sample the editor selected these lines by Jelaluddin Rumi, translated by John Moyne and Coleman Barks:

> We've given up making a living.
> It's all this crazy love poetry now.
>
> It's everywhere. Our eyes and our feelings
> Focus together, with our words

That comes from a collection, *Open Secret, Versions of Rumi*, published in a beautifully printed, flat-spined, digest-sized paperback, glossy color card cover, 96 pgs. Per copy: $10. **Query with 10 poems, bio, publication credits and SASE. Previously published poems and simultaneous submissions OK; disks compatible with IBM and hard copy preferred. Replies to queries and submissions (if invited) in 1-2 months. Publishes on 7% contract plus 10 copies (and 50% discount on additional copies). Send SASE for catalog to buy samples.**

TIA CHUCHA PRESS (II), P.O. Box 476969, Chicago IL 60647-2304, phone (312)252-5321, fax (312)252-5388, founded 1989, president Luis J. Rodriguez. They publish 2-4 paperbacks a year, **"multicultural, lyrical, engaging, passionate works informed by social, racial, class experience. Evocative. Poets should be knowledgeable of contemporary and traditional poetry, even if experimenting."** They have published poetry by Marvin Tate, Lisa Buscani and Andres Rodriguez. As a sample the editor selected these lines from "Poem for the Unnamed" from *Crossing With the Light* by Dwight Okita:

> They say if you don't
> name a child when it is born,

> *it will start crawling north,*
> *unable to be pulled back*
> *by the string of its name.*

Submit complete ms of 48 pages or more with SASE ("unless you don't want the manuscript returned"). Simultaneous submissions OK, if notified. Only original, unpublished work in book form. "Although, we like to have poems that have been published in magazines and/or chapbooks." Deadline: June 30. Do not submit via fax. Reads submissions during the summer months. They say, "We are known for publishing the best of what is usually spoken word or oral presentations of poetry. However, we like to publish poems that best work on the page. Yet, we are not limited to that. Our authors come from a diversity of ethnic, racial and gender backgrounds. Our main thrust is openness, in forms as well as content. We are cross-cultural, but we don't see this as a prison. The openness and inclusiveness is a foundation to include a broader democratic notion of what poetry should be in this country."

TICKLED BY THUNDER: THE MAGAZINE THAT SET FICTION FREE (I, II, IV-Subscribers), 7385 129th St., Surrey, British Columbia V3W 7B8 Canada, e-mail larry_lindner@mindlink .bc.ca, website http://mindlink.bc.ca/Larry.Lindner/Thunder.html, founded 1990, publisher/editor Larry Lindner, appears 4 times/year, using poems about **"fantasy particularly, about writing or whatever. Prefer original images and thoughts. Keep them short (up to 40 lines)—not interested in long, long poems. Nothing pornographic, childish, unimaginative. Welcome humor and inspirational verse."** They have recently published poetry by Laleh Dadpour Jackson and Helen Michiko Singh. As a sample the editor selected these lines (poet unidentified):

> *So she put a monkee in his tea*
> *marshmallows on the side . . .*

It is 16-20 pgs., digest-sized, published on Macintosh. 5,000 distributed free in Vancouver. Subscription: $12 for 4 issues. **Sample postpaid: $2.50. Send SASE (or SAE and IRC) for guidelines. Include 3-5 samples of writing with queries. Cover letter required with submissions; include "a few facts about yourself and brief list of publishing credits." Reports in 2-3 months. Pays 5¢/ line to $2 maximum. Buys first rights. Editor comments on rejections "99% of the time."** Reviews books of poetry in up to 300 words. Open to unsolicited reviews. Poets may also send books for review consideration. They also offer a poetry contest 4 times/year. Deadlines: the 15th of February, May, August and October. Entry fee: $5 for 1 poem; free for subscribers. Prize: cash, publication and subscription. They also offer a chapbook contest. Send SASE (or SAE and IRC) for details.

TIGHT; TIGHT PRESS (II), P.O. Box 1591, Guerneville CA 95446, founded 1990, editor Ann Erickson, appears 4 times/year. *"tight uses experimental poetry, post-LANGUAGE, surrealist, microchunks of experience."* They have recently published poetry by Cydney Chadwick, Susan Smith Nash, Ken Harris, Paul Weidenhoff, Darrel Pritchard, Jim McCrary, Pat Nolan, Nancy Ibsen, jake berry, Gregory Vincent St. Thomasino and John M. Bennet. As a sample the editor selected these lines from "The Blue Image" by Richard Paul Schmonsees:

> *I lay on the bed as still as the night itself,*
> *as I watch a blue image speaking to me from the tin*
> *ceiling. It says,—Let me tell you a story son. Then I*
> *hear shot guns outside in the silent rain, and sirens,*
> *far off. Then it hovers for a moment, and freezes as if a*
> *holograph. Then there is the sound as if someone were*
> *placing a needle on the groove of a recording, and the blue*
> *image's message repeats. Let me tell you a story son. The*
> *sirens. This goes on all night long until dawn.*

tight is 60 pgs., 8½ × 11, photocopied from typescript. **Sample postpaid: $5. Checks must be payable to Ann Erickson. Reports in 2 months. Pays 1 copy. Acquires one-time rights. tight press has discontinued printing chapbooks.**

TIGHTROPE (II); SWAMP PRESS (V), 323 Pelham Rd., Amherst MA 01002-1654, founded 1977, chief editor Ed Rayher. Swamp Press is a small press publisher of poetry and graphic art in limited edition, letterpress chapbooks. *Tightrope*, appearing 1-2 times a year, is a literary magazine of varying format. Circulation 300, 150 subscribers of which 25 are libraries. Subscription: $10 for 2 issues. **Sample of *Tightrope* postpaid: $6. Submit 3-6 poems at a time. No simultaneous submissions.** Time between acceptance and publication is 6-12 months. **Sometimes comments on rejections. Send SASE for guidelines. Reports in 2 months. Pays "sometimes" and provides 2 contributor's copies. Acquires first rights.** Reviews books of poetry in one paragraph, single format. Swamp Press has published books by Edward Kaplan, editor Ed Rayher, Alexis Rotella (miniature, 3 × 3, containing 6 haiku), Sandra Dutton (a 4 foot long poem), Frannie Lindsay (a 10 × 13 format containing 3 poems), Andrew Glaze, Tom Haxo, Carole Stone and Steven Ruhl. **The editor is not presently accepting unsolicited submissions for chapbook publication but when he publishes chapbooks he pays 5-**

10% of press run and, if there is grant money available, an honorarium (about $50). Send SASE for catalog.

TIMBER CREEK REVIEW (II, IV-Humor); WORDS OF WISDOM (I, IV-Humor), 612 Front St. East, Glendora NJ 08029-1133, founded 1981, editor J.M. Freiermuth. Both magazines appear quarterly using **"primarily short stories, but occasionally short, pithy poetry. The stuff that brings a smile to the reader's face on the first reading. No blank verse or blank thought. No religious."** *Words of Wisdom* **is more open to work by beginning writers.** The editor has recently published poetry by Darcy Cummings, Daniel Green, Celestine W. Liu, John M. Floyd, Robert H. Deluty, Errol Miller and Taylor Graham. *TCR* and *WOW* are similar in format. They are 60-84 pgs., 5½ × 8½, photocopied, saddle-stapled with color paper covers and some graphics. They publish 10% of the 600-700 submissions received. Press runs are 130-150 for 70-120 subscribers. For either magazine a subscription is $12. **Sample postpaid: $3. Make checks payable to J.M. Freiermuth. Simultaneous submissions OK. Cover letter required; "include names of lit mags author subscribes to." No submissions accepted December 1 through January 31. Seldom comments on rejections. Reports in 1-3 months. Pays 1 copy. Acquires one-time rights.** The editor says, "Stop watching TV and read a book of poetry."

TIMBERLINE PRESS (V), 6281 Red Bud, Fulton MO 65251, phone (573)642-5035, founded 1975, poetry editor Clarence Wolfshohl. "We do limited letterpress editions with the goal of blending strong poetry with well-crafted and designed printing. **We lean toward natural history or strongly imagistic nature poetry but will look at any good work. Also, good humorous poetry. Currently, still not accepting submissions because we have a good backlog of mss to publish—enough for the next 2-3 years."** They have recently published the books *The Vertical River* by Walter Bargen and *Blowing Reeds* by Wally Swist. As a sample the editor selected these lines from "Morning News" published in Ray's *Pigeons in the Chandeliers* by Judy Ray:

> Trees obscured the thunderheads
> so yesterday's bolt came from
> sunshine, flinging racquets from
> startled tennis grip,
>   whipcrack
> breaking sky-blue china.

Sample copies may be obtained by sending $5, requesting sample copy, and noting you saw the listing in *Poet's Market.* **Reports in under 1 month. Pays "50-50 split with author after Timberline Press has recovered its expenses."**

TIME OF SINGING, A MAGAZINE OF CHRISTIAN POETRY (I, IV-Religious, themes), P.O. Box 149, Conneaut Lake PA 16316, founded 1958-1965, revived 1980, editor Charles A. Waugaman, managing editor Lora Hill. "The viewpoint is **unblushingly Christian—but in its widest and most inclusive meaning.** Moreover, it is believed that the vital message of Christian poems, as well as inspiring the general reader, will give pastors, teachers, and devotional leaders rich current sources of inspiring material to aid them in their ministries. We tend to have a Fall/Christmas issue, a Lent/Easter one, and a Summer one. But **we do have themes quite often. We tend to value content, rather than form; prefer short poems for practical reasons."** They have recently published poetry by Elva McAllaster, Ralph Seager, Ken Siegelman, Frances P. Reid, John Charles Cooper, Barbara Mitchell, Edith Lovejoy Pierce and Nancy James. As a sample the editor selected these lines from "Buttonbush" by Tony Cosier:

> We sat at our shaded height so quietly so long
> The heron we'd scared forgot us and came back.
> It wafted over cattails and watercress aimed at a stump
> And in its reflection grazed a spray of stars.

Time of Singing is 40 pgs., digest-sized, offset from typescript with decorative line drawings scattered throughout. Besides their 3 scheduled issues, they will also be publishing 1-2 bonus issues a year. The bonus issues will *not* be theme based. They receive over 500 submissions/year, use about 210. Circulation is 350 with 150 subscriptions. Single copy: $6; subscription: $15 US, $18 Canada, $27 overseas. **Sample: $3. Prefers about 5 poems at a time, double-spaced. No simultaneous submissions; previously published poems OK, but not encouraged.** Time between acceptance and publication is 6 months to 1 year. **Editor frequently comments with suggestions for improvement for publication. Send SASE for guidelines and upcoming themes. Reports in 1-2 months. Pays 1 copy plus 25¢/line ($1 minimum to $4 maximum/poem). Reserves right to reprint poems in other formats. "We tend to be traditional. We like poems that are aware of grammar.** Collections of uneven lines, series of phrases, preachy statements, unstructured 'prayers,' and trite sing-song rhymes usually get returned. We look for poems that 'show' rather than 'tell.' "** They also publish chapbooks of poets of the editor's selection and offer contests, "generally one for each scheduled issue on a given subject related to our theme. Send SASE for rules."

TOMORROW MAGAZINE (II), P.O. Box 148486, Chicago IL 60614-8486, e-mail audrelv@tezcat .com, founded 1982, editor Tim W. Brown, is a biannual magazine appearing in January and July. "We focus roughly half on poets from Chicago, half from elsewhere. We prefer work that falls between the 'academic' and 'underground' extremes of the literary spectrum." **They want "free verse strong in image and emotion. No formalist and academic poetry, Hallmark verse, or religious poetry."** They have published poetry by Richard Kostelanetz, Lyn Lifshin, Hugh Fox and Antler. As a sample, the editor selected these lines from "Poem" by Jim Tyack:

. . . *Who else could live in those eyes*
they are quite unhouse-like and I plod and sweep fluttering
insects and leaves off the water's shimmering surface
as you drift away somewhere praying to the snow-covered

Andes or a tree in the backyard where you become an expert
at divining deeper meaning from the common place.

TM is 32 pgs., 8½×11, custom-bound, with card stock cover, b&w cover photo. They receive about 300 mss/year, usually accept 10-12%. Press run is 300 for 200 shelf sales. **Sample postpaid: $5. Send no more than 5-6 poems at one time. No previously published poems; simultaneous submissions OK. Cover letter with brief bio welcome. "Querying by e-mail is fine, but we prefer submissions on paper through the post."** Time between acceptance and publication is 6-9 months. **Seldom comments on rejections. Send SASE for guidelines. Reports in 3 weeks to 3 months. Pays 1 copy. Acquires first rights. Requests acknowledgment when reprinting in anthologies or collections.** The editor says, "There are too many tribes in poetry. At *Tomorrow* we like to think we have a pluralistic outlook."

TOUCH (IV-Religious, teens, themes), P.O. Box 7259, Grand Rapids MI 49510, phone (616)241-5616, founded 1970, poetry editor Carol Smith: "Our magazine is a 24-page edition written **for girls 7-14 to show them how God is at work in their lives and in the world around them. *Touch* is theme-oriented. We like our poetry to fit the theme of each issue. We send out a theme update biannually to all our listed freelancers. We prefer short poems with a Christian emphasis that can show girls how God works in their lives."** They have published poetry by Janet Shafer Boyanton and Iris Alderson. As a sample we selected "Shall I Compare Myself to Others?" by May Richstone:

Better not. Such comparisons
Most likely would become a strain—
My betters could make me envious,
The lesser tend to make me vain.

Much better compare
Yesterday's me
With the tomorrow's
I hope to be.

Touch is published 10 times a year, magazine-sized. They receive 150-200 submissions of poetry/ year, use 2 poems in each issue, have a 6-month backlog. Circulation is 15,800 for 15,500 subscribers. Subscription: $12.50 US, $15 Canada, $20 foreign. **Sample and guidelines free with 8×10 SASE. Poems must not be longer than 20 lines—prefer much shorter. Simultaneous submissions OK. Query with SASE for theme update. Reports in 2 months. Pays $10-15 and copies.**

TOUCHSTONE (I, II), Viterbo College, La Crosse WI 54601-4797, phone (608)791-0271, fax (608)791-0367, e-mail eng_ruppel@viterbo.edu, founded 1950, moderator Richard Ruppel, is a literary quarterly publishing poetry, short stories and artwork. As a sample the editor selected these lines from "Outbound" by Kate Larkin:

Beware of the Park Street exit
Where corners cross
And weepy people
Stare, pasty-faced.

The magazine is 48 pgs., digest-sized, saddle-stapled, with semi-glossy card cover. Press run is 1,200 for 100 subscribers of which 25 are libraries. Subscription: $15. **Sample postpaid: $7.50. Cover letter required; include "a note of origination" (i.e. that the work is original). "Poets may submit via**

THE CHAPBOOK INDEX, located before the Geographical Index, lists those publishers who consider chapbook manuscripts. A chapbook, a small volume of work, is often a good middle step between magazine and book publication.

fax, e-mail or snail-mail." Reads submissions August 1 through March 1 only. Send SASE for guidelines. Reports in 2 months. Pays 1 copy.

TOUCHSTONE LITERARY JOURNAL; TOUCHSTONE PRESS (III, IV-Translations), P.O. Box 8308, Spring TX 77387-8308, founded 1975, poetry editor William Laufer, is an annual publishing **"experimental or well-crafted traditional form, including sonnets, and translations. No light verse or doggerel."** They have published poetry by Walter Griffin, Thomas Amherst Perry, Paul Ramsey and Janice Whittington. As a sample the editor selected these lines from "Blue Prefect" by John Marvin:

> We had spoken of stance in circumstance
> soul on ice rowan martin pueblo tet
> like the semblance of an image
> nature can't betray what it hasn't promised
> mccarthy johnson king kennedy
> of notion ocean of estimation nation
> robinson hair columbia
> grant that we would stand
> in stony silence gazing forth
> tool in hand prepared for the new day

Touchstone is 100 pgs., digest-sized, flat-spined, professionally printed in small, dark type with glossy card cover. Subscription: $7. **Sample postpaid: $4. Submit 5 poems at a time. "Cover letter telling something about the poet piques our interest and makes the submission seem less like a mass mailing." Sometimes sends prepublication galleys. Pays 1 copy.** Reviews books of poetry. Open to unsolicited reviews. Poets may also send books for review consideration, to Review Editor. Touchstone Press also **publishes an occasional chapbook. Send SASE for chapbook submission guidelines.** "We previously published a book-length epic, *Kingdom of the Leopard: An Epic of Old Benin* by Nigerian poet chi chi layor. We are open to new projects. Query first, with SASE. Absolutely no mail is answered without SASE."

TOWER POETRY SOCIETY; TOWER (II), Dundas Public Library, 18 Ogilvie St., Dundas, Ontario L9H 2S2 Canada, phone (905)648-4878, founded 1951, editor-in-chief Joanna Lawson. "The Tower Poetry Society was started by a few members of McMaster University faculty to promote interest in poetry. We publish *Tower* twice a year and a few chapbooks. We want **rhymed or free verse, traditional or modern, but not prose chopped into short lines, maximum 40 lines in length, any subject, any comprehensible style.**" They have published poetry by June Walker and Helen Fitzgerald Dougher. The editor selected these sample lines by Tony Cosier:

> From forging brass he took to forging soul,
> gave up plowing soil to plow his skull,
> ripped open the eye that never closed again
> and took for tongue the howl of the beast in pain.

Tower is 40 pgs., digest-sized. Circulation is 250 for 60 subscribers of which 8 are libraries. They receive about 400 unsolicited submissions of poetry/year, use 30, no backlog. Subscription: $8 including postage; $9.50 abroad. **Sample postpaid: $3. Submit no more than 4 poems at a time. Reads submissions during February or August. Reports in 2 months. Pays 1 copy.** The editor advises, "Read a lot of poetry before you try to write it."

TOWNSHIPS SUN (IV-Rural/ecological, regional), 7 Conley St., P.O. Box 28, Lennoxville, Quebec J1M 1Z3 Canada, phone (819)566-7424, founded 1972, editor Patricia Ball, is a monthly newspaper in English "concerned with **history of townships, English community, agriculture and ecology and using poetry on these themes. Only poems about the area and people of Quebec ever accepted. Others need not submit."** The tabloid has a press run of 1,500 for 1,200 subscribers of which 20 are libraries, and 280 shelf sales. Subscription: $15/year Canada, $20/year outside Canada. **Sample postpaid: $2. Pays $10-30 plus 1 copy. "Will publish poems specifically about townships, townshippers, or of specific interest to townshippers."** Staff reviews books of poetry.

TRESTLE CREEK REVIEW (II,IV-Regional), English Dept. North Idaho College, 1000 West Garden, Coeur d'Alene ID 83814, phone (208)769-3384, fax (208)769-3431, founded 1982-83, poetry editor Chad Klinger et al, is a "2-year college creative writing program production. Purposes: (1) expand the range of publishing/editing experience for our small band of writers; (2) expose them to editing experience; (3) create another outlet for serious, beginning writers. **We're fairly eclectic but prefer poetry on the Northwest region, particularly the innermountain West (Idaho, Montana, etc.). We favor poetry strong on image and sound, and country vs. city; spare us the romantic, rhymed clichés. We can't publish much if it's long (more than 2 pgs.)."** They have recently published poetry by Jesse Bier, Walter Griffin, Lance Olsen and Mary Winters. As a sample Chad Klinger selected these lines by Laurinda Lind:

> From the air, how much
> The Intermountain West
> Must look like a railroad playset:
> Making cruciform shadows over
> Brigham Young's redoubt,
> The pilot dreams above snap-in hills
> Whose crests go M for Montpelier,
> S for Soda Springs.

TCR is a 57-page annual, digest-sized, professionally printed on heavy buff stock, perfect-bound, matte cover with art. Circulation is 500 for 6 subscribers of which 4 are libraries. This publication is well-designed and features both free and formal verse by relative newcomers. The editors receive unsolicited poetry submissions from about 100 persons/year, use 30. **Sample: $4. Submit before March 1 (for May publication), no more than 5 pgs. No simultaneous submissions or previously published poems. Reports by March 30. Pays 2 copies.** The editor advises, "Be neat; be precise; don't romanticize or cry in your beer; strike the surprising, universal note. Know the names of things."

TRIQUARTERLY MAGAZINE; TRIQUARTERLY BOOKS (II), 2020 Ridge Ave., Evanston IL 60208-4302, phone (708)491-7614, founded 1964, editors Reginald Gibbons and Susan Hahn, is one of the most respected and visually appealing journals produced in the United States. Editors accept a wide range of verse forms and styles of verse (long poems, sequences, etc.) **with the emphasis solely on excellence,** and some issues are published as books on specific themes. They have published poetry by Tom Sleigh, Albert Goldbarth, Linda McCarriston, Pattiann Rogers and Theodore Weiss. *TriQuarterly*'s three issues per year are 200 pgs., 6×9, professionally printed and flat-spined with b&w photography, graphics, glossy card cover. There are about 40 or more pgs. of poetry in each issue. They receive about 3,000 unsolicited submissions of poetry/year, use 60, have about a year backlog. Press run is 5,000 for 2,000 subscribers of which 35% are libraries. Single copy: $11.95; subscription: $24; **Sample postpaid: $5. No simultaneous submissions. Reads submissions October 1 through March 31 only. Sometimes works with poets, inviting rewrites of interesting work. Reports in 3 months. Always sends prepublication galleys. Pays 2 copies, additional copies available at a 40% discount. Acquires first North American serial rights.** "We *suggest* prospective contributors examine sample copy before submitting." Reviews books of poetry "at times." Send books for review consideration. Work appearing in *TriQuarterly* has been included in *The Best American Poetry* (1993, 1994 and 1995) and the *Pushcart Prize* anthology. TriQuarterly Books welcomes **queries with up to 10 sample pages of poetry, "but we cannot consider unsolicited manuscripts."** Send SASE for additional information.

TROUT CREEK PRESS; DOG RIVER REVIEW POETRY SERIES; BACKPOCKET PO-ETS (II), 5976 Billings Rd., Parkdale OR 97041-9610, phone (541)352-6494, e-mail lfh42@aol.com, founded 1981, poetry editor Laurence F. Hawkins, prefers **"visceral poetry with cerebral undertones or vice versa. Shorter poems (to 30 lines) but will consider longer. Will also consider book or chapbook publication. No restrictions on form or content. No pornography or religious verse."** They have published poetry by Judson Crews, Gerald Locklin, Arthur Winfield Knight, Wilma Elizabeth McDaniel, Nathaniel Tarn and Sam Silva. As a sample the editor selected these lines from "Toccata" by Elvira Bennet:

> What I am touched by
> heals me of wounds I
> hardly knew I had.
> What you touch you heal.
> In our sensitive
> carapace, sealing
> in, turning out, we
> are all wounds, all cures.

Backpocket Poets is a series of 4×5¼ chapbooks, professionally printed, 26-32 pgs., saddle-stapled or perfect-bound with matte card cover, selling for $2.50-4 each, a drawing or photo of the author on the back. The Dog River Review Poetry Series consists of digest-sized, professionally printed, saddle-stapled chapbooks up to 56 pgs. with matte card covers, selling for $3-6. **For book publication by Trout Creek Press, submit complete ms of up to 44 pgs. Replies to queries immediately, to submissions in 1-2 months. No simultaneous submissions. Editor sometimes comments on rejections. Always sends prepublication galleys for chapbooks. No payment until "material costs recovered. We also publish individual authors on cassette tape."** Send SASE for catalog to buy samples.

TUCUMCARI LITERARY REVIEW (II), 3108 W. Bellevue Ave., Los Angeles CA 90026, founded 1988, editor Troxey Kemper, assistant editor Neoma Reed, appears every other month. **"Prefer rhyming and established forms, 2-100 lines, but the primary goal is to publish good work. No talking**

animals. No haiku. No disjointed, fragmentary, rambling words or phrases typed in odd-shaped staggered lines trying to look like poetry. The quest here is for poetry that will be just as welcome many years later as it is now." They have recently published poetry by Elizabeth Dabbs, Fontaine Falkoff, Marian Ford Park, Ruth Daniels, Wilma Elizabeth McDaniel, Andy Peterson, Harvey Stanbrough, Jim Dunlap and Walter Kuchinsky. As a sample the editor selected a triolet, "Leaving the Mississippi" by Brooke Howard:

> He'd loved this river, calm and gleaming;
> He cursed it now, his life an ache.
> For years of grain in acres streaming,
> He'd loved this river, calm and gleaming;
> But flooded homes, his daughter screaming,
> Afloat, then gone—no more he'd take!
> He'd loved this river, calm and gleaming;
> He cursed it now, his life an ache.

The magazine is 48 pgs., digest-sized, saddle-stapled, photocopied from typescript, with card cover. Their press run is 150-200. Subscription: $12, $20 for overseas. **Sample: $2, $4 for overseas. Submit no more than 4 poems at a time. Considers simultaneous submissions and previously published poems. Send SASE for guidelines. Reports within 1 month. Pays 1 copy. Acquires one-time rights.** This magazine is inexpensively produced but contains some good formal poems. If you're looking to place a particular sonnet or villanelle, try Troxey Kemper's magazine. He reports quickly, by the way, and may comment on rejections. The editor says, "Writing is welcomed from amateurs, in-betweens and professors/scholars. Oddly, some of the work by amateurs is more interesting than erudite, obscure allusions to Greek/Roman mythology personages and events—more honest, earnest and heart-felt. The main measure of acceptability is: It is interesting? Is it good? What counts is what it *says* not whether the work is handwritten on 3-hole lined notebook paper or presented on expensive computer-generated equipment/paper which often is very difficult to read."

TURKEY PRESS (V), 6746 Sueno Rd., Isla Vista CA 93117-4904, founded 1974, poetry editor Harry Reese along with his wife, Sandra Reese, "is involved with publishing contemporary literature, producing traditional and experimental book art, one-of-a-kind commissioned projects and collaborations with various artists and writers. **We do not encourage solicitations of any kind to the press. We seek out and develop projects on our own."** They have published poetry by Thomas Merton, James Laughlin, Sam Hamill, Edwin Honig, Glenna Luschei, Tom Clark, Michael Hannon, Keith Waldrop, David Ossman, Peter Whigham, Jack Curtis, Kirk Robertson and Anne E. Edge.

TURNSTILE (II), 175 Fifth Ave., Suite 2348, New York NY 10010, founded 1988, is a biannual literary magazine publishing poetry, fiction, essays, art, interviews, novel excerpts and plays. **They want poetry that is "well-crafted, with a strong sense of line, form and sound."** They have published poetry by James Applewhite, Kevin Pilkington, Robert Morgan and Dabney Stuart. The editors describe it as 128 pgs., 6×9, 55 lb. paper. Circulation: 3,000. Subscription: $12. **Sample postpaid: $6.50. "Send no more than 4 poems at one time. Refer to the guidelines in the front of our magazine." Often comments on rejections. Reports in 2-3 months. Pays 5 copies.**

‡TWILIGHT ENDING (I), 21 Ludlow Dr., Milford CT 06460-6822, phone (203)877-3473, founded 1995, editor/publisher Emma J. Blanch, appears 3 times a year publishing "poetry and short fiction of the highest caliber." They have featured the work of poets from the US, Canada, England and India. **They want "poems with originality in thought and in style, reflecting the latest trend in writing, moving from the usual set-up to a vertical non-conformist approach, some following Kerouac's form, having none of the required punctuation. We prefer unrhymed poetry, however we accept rhymed verse if rhymes are perfect. We look for the unusual approach in content and style."** The editor says *TE* is 5½×8½, "elegantly printed on white linen with one poem per page (12-30 lines)." They receive 1,500 poems a year, accept 10%. Press run is 100 for 50 subscribers of which 25 are libraries. **Sample postpaid: $5 US, $6 Canada, $6.50 England, $7.50 India. Make checks payable to Emma J. Blanch. Submit 3-4 poems at a time. No previously published poems or simultaneous submissions ("including poems submitted to contests"). "When accepted, poems and fiction will not be returned so keep copies." Submission postmark deadlines: December 30 for Winter issue, April 30 for Spring/Summer issue, September 30 for Fall issue. No backlog, "all poems are destroyed after publication." Often comments on rejections. Send SASE for guidelines. Reports in 1 week. Pays nothing—not even a copy. Acquires first rights.** The editor says, "If editing is needed, suggestions will be made for the writer to rework and resubmit a corrected version. The author always decides; remember that you deal with experts."

TWISTED (IV-Horror, fantasy), P.O. Box 1249, Palmetto GA 30268-1249, phone (770)463-1458, founded 1985, editor/publisher Christine Hoard, uses **poetry of "horror/dark fantasy; humor OK. Form and style open. Not more than 1 page long."** They have recently published poetry by Gary

William Crawford, Holly Day and Wayne Edwards. As a sample the editor selected these lines by Ann K. Schwader:

> black aftertaste
> rusted to blood on my tongue
> a smothered
> scream somewhere & me wondering
> if I'm not
> having my nightmare
> who is

Christine Hoard describes *Twisted* as "150 pgs., magazine-sized, offset, vellum bristol cover, much art, some ads, 60 lb. matte paper. I receive a lot of poetry submissions, use 30-50 per issue." Press run is 300 for single-copy sales. **Sample postpaid: $6. Make checks payable to Christine Hoard. "Don't submit more than four poems at a time. You should see a sample copy to get a 'feel' for what we publish." No simultaneous submissions. Editor sometimes comments on rejections. Send SASE for guidelines. Reports within 3 months. "We're not always an open market. We usually close when we're overstocked or preparing the next issue." Pays 1 copy.** She says, "Poets of science fiction, horror, fantasy will be pleased to know there are several markets in the small press and some organizations are available to offer support and market information."

2 AM MAGAZINE; 2 AM PUBLICATIONS (IV-Science fiction/fantasy, horror), P.O. Box 6754, Rockford IL 61125-1754, e-mail p.anderson2/@genie.geis.com, founded 1986, editor Gretta McCombs Anderson, is a quarterly that wants **"fantasy, science fiction, heroic fantasy, horror, weird; any form, any style; preferred length is 1-2 pgs. We want poetry that leaves an after-image in the mind of the reader."** They have published poetry by Mark Rich, G.N. Gabbard, Bruce Boston and Robert Frazier. The editor describes it as 68 pgs., magazine-sized, offset on 60 lb. stock, cover printed on glossy stock, illustrations "by leading fantasy artists" and ads. Circulation 2,000 with 350 subscriptions. Single copy: $4.95; subscription: $19/year. **Sample postpaid: $5.95. Submit no more than 5 poems at a time. "Prefer original poems no more than 2 pages in length. Please type all manuscripts."** Time between acceptance and publication is 6-12 months. **Editor "sometimes" comments on rejections. Send SASE for guidelines. Reports in 2 months. Always sends prepublication galleys. Pays 5¢/line or $1 minimum plus 1 copy, 40% discount for more. Buys one-time rights.** Reviews books of poetry in 250 words, single format. Open to unsolicited reviews. Poets may also send books for review consideration, attn. Irwin Chapman. Gretta M. Anderson advises, "Read widely, be aware of what's already been done. Short poems stand a good chance with us. Looking for mood-generating poetry of a cosmic nature, poems with extended imagery that work on multiple levels. Not interested in self-indulgent poetry."

‡256 SHADES OF GREY; BLACK GRANITE PUBLICATIONS (I, II), P.O. Box 555, Eau Claire WI 54702, phone (715)831-9263, fax (715)835-1121, e-mail blkgrnt@primenet.com, website http://www.primenet.com/~blkgrnt, founded January 1995, publisher Clifford J. Kurkowski, is a monthly "stepping stone magazine for new writers and poets. Established writers always welcome." **They want "original poetry from sonnets to free verse."** They have recently published poetry by Aloha Brown, Louis Simpson, James Snydal, Daniel Green, Frank Smoot, Simon Perchik and Bruce Taylor. As a sample the publisher selected these lines from "Birds In Art" by Christian P. Knoeller:

> Painters present preen before their work,
> signing autographs, dressed to match
> the plumage they have rendered. If life imitates
> art, will they soon take wing to distant
> forests or settle here instead, captioned
> on a perfectly illusory perch?

256 Shades of Grey is 50-100 pgs., 8½×11, tape-bound with colored covers with b&w art. They receive 400-600 poems a year, accept approximately 70%. Press run is 500 for 200 subscribers of which 40 are libraries, 100 shelf sales. Single copy: $1.50; subscription: $20/year. **Sample postpaid: $3.50. Make checks payable to Black Granite Publications. Submit 6 poems at a time. Previously published poems and simultaneous submissions OK. Cover letter with brief bio and credits preferred. Deadlines are the 5th of each month. Seldom comments on rejections. Reports within 2 months. Sometimes sends prepublication galleys. Pays 1 copy.** Reviews books of poetry. Send books for review consideration. The publisher says, "In order to write poetry effectively writers must peer into their own souls and ponder about the demons inside themselves."

TYRO PUBLISHING (I, II), 194 Carlbert St., Sault Ste. Marie, Ontario P6A 5E1 Canada, phone (705)253-6402, fax (705)942-3625, founded 1984, editor Stan Gordon. They only consider full-length mss for book publication. Published works include: *The Book of Cries* by Bruce Bedell, *On a Mound a Sleeping Leopard* by Anna Livig, and *Vision at Delphi* by Nancy Fisher. **Query first with at least**

6 sample poems. Mss should be in standard format. Send SASE for guidelines and further information. Always sends prepublication galleys.

ULTRAMARINE PUBLISHING CO., INC. (II), P.O. Box 303, Hastings-on-Hudson NY 10706-1817, phone (914)478-1339, fax (914)478-1365, founded 1974, editor C.P. Stephens, who says, "We mostly distribute books for authors who had a title dropped by a major publisher—the author is usually able to purchase copies very cheaply. We use existing copies purchased by the author from the publisher when the title is being dropped." Ultramarine's list includes 250 titles, 90% of them cloth bound, one-third of them science fiction and 10% poetry. **The press pays 10% royalties. "Distributor terms are on a book-by-book basis, but is a rough split." Authors should query before making submissions; queries will be answered in 1 week. No queries/submissions via fax. Simultaneous submissions OK, but no disks.**

‡**UNDERWHICH EDITIONS (V)**, Box 262, Adelaide St. Station, Toronto, Ontario M5C 2J4 Canada, and, in western Canada, 920 Ninth Ave. N., Saskatoon, Saskatchewan S7K 2Z4 Canada, founded 1978, editors Karl Jirgens, Lucas Mulder, Jill Robinson, Susan Andrews Grace, Steven Ross Smith and Paul Dutton are "dedicated to presenting in diverse and appealing physical formats, new works by contemporary creators, **focusing on formal invention and encompassing the expanded frontiers of musical and literary endeavor**" in chapbooks, pamphlets, flat-spined paperbacks, posters, cassettes, records and anthologies. They have recently published poetry by Paul Dutton, Kristjana Gunnars and Gerry Shikatani. As a sample the editors selected these lines from "Year of the Rush" by Gerry Gilbert:

> *manly mammal hums greensleeves*
> *to orange & scarlet wing insignifier*
> *fat black hockey bird*
> *sounding off on a bullrush*
> *free tweets*
> *& a warble right from the shoulder*

They are currently not accepting poetry submissions. "We have all the mss we can handle for the foreseeable future."

THE UNFORGETTABLE FIRE (IV-Women/feminism), 530 Riverside Dr. #5G, New York NY 10027, founded 1991, editor Jordan O'Neill, is a biannual publication of poetry, short short stories, book reviews and "activist activities" **written by, for and about women. They want relatively short poetry that is "women oriented, activist oriented. Nothing book-length. No haiku nor any poetry which advocates violence, racism, sexism or homophobia."** They have published poetry by Lyn Lifshin, Elisavietta Ritchie, Linda Wasmer Smith and Mary Sue Koeppel. As a sample the editor selected these lines from "the flower woman" by Cara Andrichak:

> *saw her today*
> *silent on the staircase.*
> *The flower woman,*
> *on her arm*
> *the purple appeared again*
> *as bright as the petunias*
> *she's growing on her windowsill.*

The editor says *The Unforgettable Fire* is 30-40 pgs., 8½ × 11, with art, graphics and ads. They receive 200-300 poems a year, accept 50-60%. Press run is 3,000 for 1,200 subscribers of which 15 are libraries. Subscription: $10. **Sample back issue postpaid: $5. Previously published poems and simultaneous submissions OK. Include short bio, "about author and work." Often comments on rejections. Send SASE for guidelines and upcoming themes. Reports in 1-2 months. Pays 2 copies.** Reviews related books and magazines, usually in 500 words or less. Open to unsolicited reviews. Poets may also send books for review consideration. They hope to sponsor a poetry contest in 1996. Send SASE for details. The editor says, "I believe it's important to read, read, read what is out there. Big and small publications are incredibly valuable to writers, and writers should read publications (including *The Unforgettable Fire*) before submitting to them. Also read guidelines carefully."

UNITY MAGAZINE; DAILY WORD (IV-Religious), Unity School of Christianity, 1901 NW Blue Pkwy., Unity Village MO 64065, founded 1889. "Unity periodicals are devoted to spreading the truth of practical Christianity, the everyday use of Christ's principles. The material used in them is constructive, friendly, unbiased as regards creed or sect, and positive and inspirational in tone. We suggest that prospective contributors study carefully the various publications before submitting material. **Sample copies are sent on request; please send 6 × 9 SASE. Complimentary copies are sent to writers on publication. We accept mss only with the understanding that they are original and previously unpublished. Mss should be typewritten in double space. Unity School pays on acceptance, buying first North American serial rights.** *Unity Magazine* is a monthly journal that publishes "articles and **poems that give a clear message of Truth and provide practical, positive help in meeting human needs for healing, supply and harmony. Only 1 or 2 poems are published each month. We pay $50."** *Daily Word* is a "monthly manual of daily studies" which "buys a limited number of short devotional articles and poems. **We pay a $30 minimum for poetry and $50 a page for prose."**

UNMUZZLED OX (IV-Themes, bilingual/foreign language), 105 Hudson St., New York NY 10013, phone (212)226-7170, or Box 550, Kingston, Ontario K7L 4W5 Canada, founded 1971, poetry editor Michael Andre, is a tabloid literary biannual. **Each edition is built around a theme or specific project.** The editor says, "The chances of an unsolicited poem being accepted are slight since I always have specific ideas in mind." Contributors have been Allen Ginsberg, Robert Creeley and Denise Levertov. As a sample the editor selected these lines from "CL" by Daniel Berrigan:

> Let's be grandiose, it's a game
> Let's climb a balcony
> Let's issue a manifesto
>
> Why, we're turning things on their head
> we're making history
> we're—
>
> Harmless.

He is assembling material for issues titled *Poems to the Tune*, "simply poems to old tunes, a buncha contemporary *Beggar's Opera*. The other is tentatively called *The Unmuzzled Ox Book of Erotic Verse*. **Only unpublished work will be considered, but works may be in French as well as English."** Subscription: $20.

THE URBANITE; URBAN LEGEND PRESS (II, IV-Horror, fantasy, themes), P.O. Box 4737, Davenport IA 52808-4737, founded 1991, editor Mark McLaughlin, appears 3 times a year "to promote literate, character-oriented and entertaining fiction and poetry in the genre of surrealism." **Each issue is based on a particular theme. Send SASE for details. They want contemporary fantasy/surrealism (maximum 2 pages/poem). No "slice-of-life, sentimental, gore, porn, Western, haiku or rambling rants against society."** They have recently published poetry by Marni Griffin, Rhonda Eikamp and Shawn Mlekush. As a sample the editor selected the peom "Home Birth (twice a day)" by Joy Golisch:

> Every poem is
> giving birth
> squatting in my chair
> groaning and screaming
> until happily
> I've turned myself inside out
> making something
> that grows apart from me
>
> I lay back on the rug
> panting
> white and black spotted child
> fluttering
> on my empty abdomen.

The Urbanite is 64-92 pgs., 8½ × 11, saddle-stitched or perfect-bound with 2-color coated card cover. They receive about 500 poems a year, accept less than 10%. Press run is 500. Subscription: $13.50 for 3 issues. **Sample postpaid: $5. Submit only 3 poems at a time. No previously published poems or simultaneous submissions. Cover letter required. Sends checklist reply form, but sometimes comments on rejections. Send SASE for guidelines and upcoming themes. Reports within 1 month, sometimes longer. Pays $10/poem and 2 copies. Buys first North American serial rights and nonexclusive rights for public readings.** ("We hold readings of the magazine at libraries and other venues.") Print rights revert to the writer after publication. In addition to the magazine, Urban Legend Press **publishes one or more chapbooks a year. Interested poets should "submit to the magazine first, to establish a relationship with our readers."** A copy of Joy Golisch's chapbook, *Surfing with Monkeys and Other Diversions*, is available from the press for $4.

URBANUS MAGAZINE; URBANUS PRESS (III), P.O. Box 192921, San Francisco CA 94119-2921, founded 1987, editor Peter Drizhal, which appears 2-3 times/year, is a journal of fiction, poetry, features and art—with an urban emphasis. **"Seeks post-modernist, experimental and mainstream poetry—with a social slant."** They have published poetry by Yusef Komunyakaa, Isabel Nathaniel, Clarence Major, Charles Fort, Anna Enquist and Denise Duhamel. As a sample the editors selected these lines from "And What Do You Get" by Heather McHugh (which also appears in *The Best American Poetry 1995*):

> Excise the er from exercise. Or from
> example, take the ex out: now it's bigger;
> to be lonely, take the amp out
> and replace it with an i. Take am or me
> away from name
> and suddenly there's not
> much left, the name's one of the many names

The 64-page, digest-sized, perfect-bound magazine uses approximately 50 of the 5,000 submissions they receive annually. Circulation is 1,200. Subscription: $12 ($15 institutions). **Sample postpaid: $5. Submit 3-5 poems (under 40 lines each) at a time. No previously published poems or simultaneous submissions. Reports in 3-12 weeks.** Time between acceptance and publication is 4-18 months. **Pays $10/poem or $5/page, plus 5 copies.** Poetry published in *Urbanus* has been selected for inclusion in the 1994 and 1995 volumes of *The Best American Poetry*. The editor says, "We do not actively seek haiku, *very rarely* accept rhymed verse, and with few exceptions, would rather not see conversational narrative poetry—or for that matter, the 'classic' chopped prose poem (though we *are* guilty of having published this sort, and will, without apologies, publish it again; suffice to say, this approach doesn't very often hold our interest . . .); we also have a bias against poetry littered with similes ('it is like this/it is like that'). *Urbanus Magazine* solicits much of its writing, and generally speaking, we are a very difficult market to break into; but talented newcomers are always welcome."

US1 WORKSHEETS; US1 POETS' COOPERATIVE (II), %Postings, P.O. Box 1, Ringoes NJ 08551-0001, founded 1973, is a literary annual, 20-25 pgs., 11½×17, circulation 500, which uses **high quality poetry and fiction. "We use a rotating board of editors; it's wisest to query when we're next reading before submitting. A self-addressed, stamped postcard to the secretary will get our next reading period dates."** They have recently published poetry by Alicia Ostriker, Elizabeth Anne Socolow, Jean Hollander, Frederick Tibbetts, Lois Marie Harrod, James Haba, Charlotte Mandel and David Keller. **"We read a lot but take very few. Prefer complex, well-written work." Sample: $5. Submit 5 poems at a time. Include name, address and phone number in upper right-hand corner. No simultaneous submissions; rarely accepts previously published poems. Requests for sample copies, subscriptions, queries, back issues, and all mss should be addressed to the secretary, % POSTINGS (address at beginning of listing). Sometimes sends prepublication galleys. Pays 1 copy.**

UTAH STATE UNIVERSITY PRESS (V), Logan UT 84322-7800, phone (801)797-1362, founded 1972, editor John R. Alley, publishes poetry but is **not open for submissions.**

VEGETARIAN JOURNAL; THE VEGETARIAN RESOURCE GROUP (IV-Specialized, children/teens), P.O. Box 1463, Baltimore MD 21203, founded 1982. The Vegetarian Resource Group is a small press publisher of nonfiction. *VJ* is a bimonthly, 36 pgs., 8½×11, saddle-stapled and professionally printed with glossy card cover. Circulation is 20,000. **Sample: $3. "Please no submissions of poetry from adults; 18 and under only."** The Vegetarian Resource Group offers an annual contest for ages 18 and under, $50 savings bond in 3 age categories for the best contribution on any aspect of vegetarianism. "Most entries are essay, but we would accept poetry with enthusiasm." Deadline: May 1 postmark. Send SASE for details.

VEHICULE PRESS; SIGNAL EDITIONS (III, IV-Regional), P.O. Box 125 Station Place du Parc, Montreal, Quebec H2W 2M9 Canada, phone (514)844-6073, fax (514)844-7543, poetry editor Michael Harris, publisher Simon Dardick, is a "literary press with poetry series, Signal Editions, **publishing the work of Canadian poets only.**" They publish flat-spined paperbacks and hardbacks. Among the poets they have recently published are Peter Dale Scott, Doug Beardsley, John Reibetonz, Rhea Tregébor, Susan Glickman and Jan Conn. As a sample they selected these lines by Carla Hartsfield:

> Isn't it possible men
> are jealous of women?
> How we root ourselves
> in autonomy. Like trees
> women can be both things:
> wound and tourniquet.

They publish Canadian poetry which is **"first-rate, original, content-conscious." However, they are booked until 1999."**

‡**VERBAL EXPRESSION (I)**, 7 Pleasant St., Oxford MI 48371, founded January 1995, appears quarterly and is **"open to all types of poetry."** As a sample the editor selected this poem, "Angel Tears," by Jon Camfield:

> *And the rain fell down here,*
> *Maybe not over the horizon,*
> *Maybe not a mile away,*
> *but it fell down here,*
> *here I am living,*
> *here it matters*
> *that the rain*
> *fell down.*

The editor says *VE* is 32 pgs., 5½×8½, photocopied and staple-bound with graphics, cover art and ads. They receive about 100 poems a year, accept 30-40. Press run is 500 for 400 subscribers. Single copy: $2.50; subscription: $9. Make checks payable to Pleasant Publishing. **Submit up to 5 poems at a time, name and address on each page. Previously published poems and simultaneous submissions OK. Cover letter preferred.** Time between acceptance and publication is 3-9 months. **Reports in 1 month. Pays 1 copy. Acquire one-time rights.**

VERSE (III), English Dept., College of William and Mary, P.O. Box 8795, Williamsburg VA 23187-8795, founded 1984, editors Brian Henry and Nancy Schoenberger, is "an international poetry journal which also publishes interviews with poets, articles about poetry and book reviews." They **want "no specific kind; we look for high quality poetry. Our focus is not only on American poetry, but on all poetry written in English, as well as translations."** They have published poetry by Seamus Heaney, James Merrill, John Ashbery, Charles Simic, Medbh McGuckian, Simon Armitage, A.R. Ammons, Iain Crichton Smith, Robert Pinsky and Carolyn Kizer. *Verse* is published 3 times/year. It is 128-256 pgs., digest-sized, professionally printed and perfect-bound with card cover. They receive 5,000 poems a year, accept about 100. Press run is 1,000 for 600 subscribers of which 150 are libraries, 200 shelf sales. Subscription: $15 for individuals, $21 for institutions. **Sample postpaid: $5. Submit up to 5 poems at a time. No previously published poems; simultaneous submissions OK. Cover letter required.** Time between acceptance and publication is 3-9 months. **Reports in 2 months. Often comments on rejections. Publishes theme issues. Send SASE for upcoming themes. Usually sends prepublication galleys. Pays 2 copies.** Open to unsolicited reviews. Poets may also send books for review consideration. Poetry published in this journal has appeared in *The Best American Poetry 1992*.

VERVE (II, IV-Themes), P.O. Box 3205, Simi Valley CA 93093-3205, founded 1989, editor/publisher Ron Reichick, editor Marilyn Hochheiser, associate editors Virginia Anderson and Margie Davidson, is published twice a year and **"open to contemporary poetry of any form which fits the theme of the issue; we look for fresh metaphor, unique ideas and language and vivid imagery that informs."** They have published poetry by Marge Piercy, Carol Muske, Denise Levertov, Alberto Rios and Quincy Troupe. As a sample the editors selected these lines from "A Glass of Sea Water Or A Pinch of Salt" by Philip Levine:

> *In the city at the end of the world*
> *everyone goes about in finery.*
> *Our mothers flash their shoulders and breasts*
> *at all hours, our fathers make their music,*
> *the long moaning notes of the sea at rest.*
> *Beyond the viaduct, I could be the sea spume*
> *riding toward shore, you could be the hum*
> *of the clouds at play, if only there were time.*

Verve is approximately 40 pgs., digest-sized, saddle-stitched, using bios of each contributor. Press run is 750 for 100 subscribers of which 3 are libraries. **Sample postpaid: $3.50. Submit up to 5 poems, 2 pgs. maximum/poem; "36 lines or less has best chance." Simultaneous submissions OK, if noted. Publishes theme issues. Send SASE for guidelines and upcoming themes. Sometimes sends prepublication galleys. Pays 1 copy. Acquires first rights.** Staff reviews books of poetry in 250 words, single format. Send books for review consideration. They also sponsor 2 annual contests, each having prizes of $100, $50 and $25. Entry fee: $2/poem. Deadlines: April 1 and October 1. The editor advises, "Read a copy of *Verve* before you submit. Read good contemporary poetry—then write. Listen to criticism, but follow your instinct *and* the poem. *Then*—keep submitting."

VIGIL; AMMONITE; VIGIL PUBLICATIONS (II, IV-Themes), 12 Priory Mead, Bruton, Somerset BA10 ODZ England, founded 1979, poetry editor John Howard Greaves. *Vigil* appears 2 times a year. They **want "poetry with a high level of emotional force or intensity of observation. Poems should normally be no longer than 35 lines. Color, imagery and appeal to the senses should be important features. No whining self-indulgent, neurotic soul-baring poetry."** They have recently published poetry by Michael Newman, Peter de Rous, Jennifer Friesen and Ayn Cates. As a sample we selected the poem "Night's Colours" by Hilary Mellon:

> *You make me dress*

and leave this naked darkness
before green shades of day
can wake your fears

though knowing that for you
I'll wear night's colours
my stockings shiny as tears

The digest-sized magazine is 40 pgs., saddle-stapled, photoreduced typescript, with colored matte card cover. They accept about 60 of 200 submissions received. Press run is 250 for 85 subscriptions of which 6 are libraries. Subscription: £4.50. **Sample postpaid: £2. Submit no more than 6 poems at a time. Send SASE (or SAE and IRC) for upcoming themes. Sometimes sends prepublication galleys. Pays 2 copies. Editor sometimes comments on rejections.** *Ammonite* appears twice a year with **"myth, image and word towards the secondary millenium . . . a seedbed of mythology for our future, potently embryonic."** Single copy: £1.75 (UK), £2.50 (overseas); subscription: £3.50 (UK), £5 (overseas). **Query regarding book publication by Vigil Publications.** The editor offers "appraisal" for £7.50 for a sample of a maximum of 12 poems.

VIKING PENGUIN, 375 Hudson St., New York NY 10014. Prefers not to share information.

THE VILLAGER (II), Dept. PM, 135 Midland Ave., Bronxville NY 10708-1800, phone (914)337-3252, founded 1928, editor Amy Murphy, poetry editor Mae Aiello, a publication of the Bronxville Women's Club for club members and families, professional people and advertisers, circulation 750, in 9 monthly issues, October through June. **Sample postpaid: $1.25. Submit 1 poem at a time, "unless it is very short."** They use one page or more of poetry/issue, **prefer poems less than 20 lines, "in good taste only." Send seasonal (Thanksgiving, Christmas, Easter) 3 months in advance. SASE required. Pays 2 copies. They copyright material but will release it to author on request.**

THE VINCENT BROTHERS REVIEW (II, IV-Themes), 4566 Northern Circle, Riverside OH 45424-5733, founded 1988, editor Kimberly A. Willardson, is a journal appearing 3 times a year. **"We look for well-crafted, thoughtful poems that shoot bolts of electricity into the reader's mind, stimulating a powerful response. We also welcome light verse and are thrilled by unusual, innovative subjects and styles. We do not accept previously published poems, simultaneous submissions or any type of bigoted propaganda. Sloppy mss containing typos and/or unintentional misspellings are automatically rejected.** *TVBR* publishes 2 theme issues/year—poets should send us a SASE to receive details about our upcoming themes."** They have recently published poetry by Gerald England, Richard Kostelanetz, Jack Lent and Michelle Whitley Turner. As a sample the editor selected these lines from "Mountains on the Moon" by David Garrison:

Midnight. So cold
that breathing pulls
crystals into your throat
and burns your lungs;
so clear that you see mountains
on the full moon, hear ice
cracking on the river.

TVBR is 88 pgs., digest-sized, perfect-bound, professionally printed with matte card cover. Press run is 350. "We have 200 subscribers, 10 of which are libraries." Subscription: $12. **Sample postpaid: $6.50. Submit no more than 6 poems at a time, name and address on each page. Cover letter preferred; include recent publication credits and note "where author read or heard about** *TVBR*. **We do not read in December." Editor "often" comments on rejections. Send SASE for guidelines. Reports in 3-4 months (after readings by editor and 2 associate editors). Always sends prepublication galleys. Pays 2 copies for poems printed inside the journal. Pays $10 for poems printed on "Page Left" (the back page). "For 'Page Left,' we look for the unusual—concrete poems, wordplay, avant-garde pieces, etc." Acquires one-time rights.** Reviews books of poetry in 3,500 words maximum, single or multi-book format. Open to unsolicited reviews. Poets may also send books for review consideration. The editor advises, *"Don't* send your poetry to a magazine you haven't read. Subscribe to the little magazines you respect—they contain the work of your peers and competitors. Proofread your poetry carefully and read it aloud before sending it out."

MARKET CONDITIONS are constantly changing! If you're still using this book and it is 1998 or later, buy the newest edition of *Poet's Market* at your favorite bookstore or order directly from Writer's Digest Books.

VIRGIN MEAT (IV-Horror), 2325 West Ave. K-15, Lancaster CA 93536, phone (805)722-1758, e-mail virginmeat@aol.com, founded 1986. *VM* is a computerized, interactive magazine of gothic horror. Prints fiction, poetry, art, .SND Sound and .MooV Quick Time movies. **Guidelines are available by request from e-mail or for a SASE. Sample postpaid: $5 (Macintosh only). Simultaneous and previously published poems OK.** Submissions without a SASE or to the e-mail address will not be read. **Reports in 4 months. Pays 1 copy. Reviews anything with a cover price.**

THE VIRGINIA QUARTERLY REVIEW; EMILY CLARK BALCH PRIZE (III), 1 West Range, Charlottesville VA 22903, phone (804)924-3124, fax (804)924-1397, e-mail jco7e@virginia.edu, founded 1925, is one of the oldest and most distinguished literary journals in the country. **It uses about 15 pgs. of poetry in each issue, no length or subject restrictions.** Issues have largely included lyric and narrative free verse, most of which features a strong message or powerful voice. The review is 220 pgs., digest-sized, flat-spined, circulation 4,000. **Send SASE for submission details; do not request via e-mail or fax. Pays $1/line.** They also sponsor the Emily Clark Balch Prize, an annual prize of $500 given to the best poem published in the review during the year. Poetry published here has been included in *The Best American Poetry 1993*.

VIRTUE: THE CHRISTIAN MAGAZINE FOR WOMEN (IV-Religious), 4050 Lee Vance View, Colorado Springs CO 80918-7102, editor Jeanette Thomason, associate editor Debbie Colclough, editor-at-large Nancie Carmichael, founded 1978, is a Christian magazine, appearing 6 times a year, to **"encourage and integrate biblical truth with daily living."** As for poetry, they look for **"rhythmic control and metric effects, whether free or patterned stanzas; use of simile and metaphor; sensory perceptions, aptly recorded; and implicit rather than explicit spiritual tone."** As a sample the editor selected these lines from "Bending" by Barbara Seaman:

> *Down on my knees again, Lord*
> *and undignified as ever,*
> *(how to mop mud with grace?)*
> *attempting to confine the exuberance*
> *of yesterday's rain to the kitchen only . . .*

Virtue is 80 pgs., magazine-sized, saddle-stapled, with full-color pages inside as well as on its paper cover. Press run is 115,000. Single copy: $3.95; subscription: $16.95. **Sample postpaid: $3. Submit "no more than 3 poems, each on separate sheet, typewritten; notify if simultaneous submission."** Time between acceptance and publication is 3-9 months. **Send SASE for guidelines. Reports in approximately 2 months. Pays $20-40/poem and 1 copy. Buys first rights.**

VOICES INTERNATIONAL (II), 1115 Gillette Dr., Little Rock AR 72227, phone (501)225-0166, editor Clovita Rice, is a quarterly poetry journal. **"We look for poetry with a new focus, memorable detail and phrasing, and significant and haunting statement climax, all of which impel the reader to reread the poem and return to it for future pleasure and reference."** As a sample the editor selected "And the Gulf Pulls" by Ella Cavis:

> *me like a magnet that never lets go,*
> *as she once clutched Masefield.*
> *I must see the white flounces of her frock,*
> *jewelry of shells she wears and casts off,*
> *flight of pelicans above*
> *emulating her smoothness on windless days,*
> *and people playing in her precinct,*
> *bathers huddling close to shore,*
> *as if they know they are specks*
> *in sweeping water.*

It is 32-40 pgs., 6×9, saddle-stapled, professionally printed with b&w matte card cover. Subscription: $10/year. **Sample postpaid (always a back issue): $2. Prefers free verse but accepts high quality traditional. Limit submissions to batches of 5, double-spaced, 3-40 lines (will consider longer if good). No simultaneous submissions. Cover letter preferred; include personal data.** Publishes an average of 18 months after acceptance. **Send SASE for guidelines. Pays copies.** The editor says, "Too many poets submit poetry without studying a copy to become familiar with what we are publishing. Our guidelines help poets polish their poems before submission."

VOICES ISRAEL (I, IV-Anthology); REUBEN ROSE POETRY COMPETITION (I); MONTHLY POET'S VOICE (IV-Members), P.O. Box 5780, 46157 Herzlia Israel, founded 1972, *Voices Israel* editor Mark L. Levinson, with an editorial board of 7, is an annual anthology of poetry in English coming from all over the world. **You have to buy a copy to see your work in print. Submit all kinds of poetry (up to 4 poems), each no longer than 40 lines, in seven copies.** They have published poetry by Yehuda Amichai, Eugene Dubnov, Alan Sillitoe and Gad Yaacobi. As a sample the editor selected these lines from "Are You the Moon?" by Aaron Anthony Vessup:

You fed me flowery melodies, jazzy stanzas scored against the weight
of gravity and thistled puberty, my feet found an itching suspending
their soles called forth like the braying and bleating sounds of morning
unctuous, prophetic, in relentless song. Their reward.

The annual **Voices Israel** is 6½×9⅜, offset from laser output on ordinary paper, approximately 121 pgs., flat-spined with varying cover. Circulation 350. Subscription: $15. **Sample back copy postpaid: $10. Contributor's copy: $15 airmail. Previously published poems OK, "but please include details and assurance that copyright problems do not exist." No simultaneous submissions. Cover letter with brief biographical details required with submissions. Deadline end of February each year. Reports in fall.** Sponsors the annual Reuben Rose Poetry Competition. Send poems of up to 40 lines each, plus $5/poem to P.O. Box 236, Kiriat Ata, Israel. Poet's name and address should be on a separate sheet with titles of poems. *The Monthly Poet's Voice*, a broadside edited by Ezra Ben-Meir, **is sent only to members of the Voices Group of Poets in English.** The *Voices Israel* editor advises, "We would like to see more humorous but well constructed poetry. We like to be surprised."

VOL. NO. MAGAZINE (II, IV-Themes), 24721 Newhall Ave., Newhall CA 91321, phone (805)254-0851, founded 1983, poetry editors Richard Weekley, Jerry Danielsen and Don McLeod. "*Vol. No.* publishes lively, concise, unafraid works. Vivid connections. **Each issue has a theme. Theme for August 1997 is "All In A Day's Work." Send SASE for details. No trivial, clichéd or unthoughtout work. Work that penetrates the ozone within. One-page poems have the best chance.**" They have published poetry by Octavio Paz, Anne Marple, Jane Hirshfield and Julian Pulley. The editors selected these sample lines by William Stafford:

> *We stand for hours where sunlight tells us*
> *it forgives. A golden shaft pours down.*
> *The air waits. A cardinal sings and sings.*
> *We stand for hours.*

Vol. No. is a digest-sized, saddle-stapled, 32-page annual, circulation 300. They receive about 600 unsolicited submissions of poetry/year, use 60, have a 6-month backlog. Subscription: $10 (2 issues). **Sample postpaid: $5. Submit limit of 6 poems. Simultaneous submissions OK. Reports in 1-5 months. Pays 2 copies.**

THE VOYANT; HOLLOW MAN PUBLISHING (II), Box 414, 20384 Fraser Highway, Langley, British Columbia V3A 4G1 Canada, e-mail petrus@mpersandsfu.ca, founded 1994, editors Robert Ivins and Jamie Scott, appears annually. "*The Voyant* is an avant-garde arts mag with an emphasis on poetry and intermedia art. We publish poetry, music scores, drawings, photographs, essays, criticism and original art. Our journal is highly visual, covering intermedia and fringe arts. We publish some str8 lit. We are especially interested in computer technology and how it interfaces with the arts. Only the wildest, boldest artists need submit." As each issue will be in a different format, there are no subscription rates. The Winter 1996 issue appears on the World Wide Web. **Query for cost of sample. Submit up to 10 poems at a time. Cover letter "appreciated." Previously published poems and simultaneous submissions OK. Comments on rejections "where time and merit allow." Send SASE (or SAE and IRC) for guidelines. Reports "as soon as humanly possible." Usually pays in copies. Acquires first North American serial or one-time rights.** Hollow Man Publishing may, in the future, publish chapbooks of outstanding material. Robert Ivins says, "The Voyant embodies the spirit of revolution and discovery. He induces madness in himself in order to bring to his people knowledge of the unknown, and this is what we are attempting to do with *The Voyant*. We retain a strong interest in poets of the West Coast and Canada, but will publish material from anywhere in the world. We publish innovative work whether in form or content, but not experimental for experiment's sake."

W.I.M. PUBLICATIONS (WOMAN IN THE MOON); THE SPIRIT; 2 CROW'S MAGIC (I, IV-Gay/lesbian, women/feminism), Dept. PM, P.O. Box 2087, Cupertino CA 95015-2087, phone/fax (408)738-4623 (press * to fax), e-mail 02071@mercuryfhda.edu., founded 1979, poetry editor Dr. SDiane Bogus, who says, "We are a small press with trade press ambitions. We publish poetry, New Age and reference books. **We pay royalties. We prefer a query and a modest track record.**" She wants poetry by **"gay, black, women, prison poets, enlightened others—contemporary narrative or lyric work, free verse OK, but not too experimental for cognition. We prefer poems to be a page or less if not part of long narrative. No obviously self-indulgent exercises in the psychology of the poet. No sexual abuse themes. No gross sexual references. No hate poems."** In addition to her own work, she has published poetry by Merilene M. Murphy and I. Lillian Randolph. As a sample she selected these lines from "His Life" in *The Book of Lives* by Sherrylynn Posey:

> *I had 4 maybe 5 lovers*
> *in my life*
> *one of them*
> *lied to me*

Dr. Bogus publishes 2-4 chapbooks and flat-spined paperbacks a year each averaging 48-100 pages. Press run is 250-1,000. **Submit full ms of poems, typed, 1 to a page. Include cover letter with statement of "vision and poetics, theme selection of the work, poetic mentors, track record and $35 reading fee. New poets must take poetry test ($10 plus free critique). Submit between January 1 and April 30 each year. We acknowledge submissions upon receipt. No submissions via fax or e-mail. However, we do not mind queries by these means. Send $5.01 for guidelines/catalog. We report at end of reading season, July through August 7. Simultaneous submissions and previously published poems OK. Authors are asked to assist in promo and sales by providing list of prospective readers and promotional photos. To established authors we pay 7-10% royalties after costs; others 5-8%. We may take advanced orders. We will accept subscriptions for a book in production at retail price. We fill orders author has provided and others our promo has prompted."** W.I.M. subsidy publishes under the imprint 2 Crow's Magic. Write for details. They also publish the quarterly newsletter, *The Spirit*. It features reviews, poetry, stories, news from the press and winner announcements. Subscription: $22. They sponsor 3 poetry contests/year: The T. Nelson Gilbert Poetry Prize (January 1 through May 31), Pat Parker Memorial Poetry Award (March 1 through May 31) and the Poetry Lottery (one poet wins every 3 months; submissions are good for two chances). Write for guidelines. They also offer a writer's grant of $300 or less for writers wishing to advance their careers. Write for information. W.I.M. also offers a self-publishing and consultation criticism service for a fee. Bogus says, "W.I.M. promotes readings for its poets and encourages each poet who submits with a personal letter which discusses her or his strengths and weaknesses. Often we allow repeat submissions. Also, we welcome a tape of the poet reading from the submitted manuscript."

‡WAKE FOREST UNIVERSITY PRESS (IV-Bilingual/foreign language, ethnic/nationality), P.O. Box 7333, Winston-Salem NC 27109, phone (910)759-5448, fax (910)759-4691, e-mail cmjones@wfu.edu, founded 1976, director and poetry editor Dillon Johnston. **"We publish only poetry from Ireland and bilingual editions of French poetry in translation. I am able to consider only poetry written by Irish poets or translations of contemporary French poetry. I must return, unread, poetry from American poets."** They have published *Captain Lavender* by Medbh McGuckian, *Collected Poems* by John Montague, *The Hudson Letter* by Derek Mahon, and *The Brazen Serpent* by Eiléan Ní Chuilleanáin. As a sample the editor selected the poem "The White Garden" by Michael Longley from his book, *The Ghost Orchid*:

> So white are the white flowers in the white garden that I
> Disappear in no time at all among lace and veils.
> For whom do I scribble the few words that come to me
> From beyond the arch of white roses as from nowhere,
> My memorandum to posterity? Listen. 'The saw
> Is under the garden bench and the gate is unlatched.'

Query with 4-5 samples and cover letter. No simultaneous submissions. Replies to queries in 1-2 weeks, to submissions (if invited) in 2-3 months. Sometimes sends prepublication galleys. Publishes on 10% royalty contract with $500 advance, 6-8 author's copies. Buys North American or US rights. They say, "Because our press is so circumscribed, we get few direct submissions from Ireland. Our main problem, however, is receiving submissions from American poets, whom we do not publish because of our very limited focus here. I would advise American poets to read listings carefully so they do not misdirect to presses such as ours work that they, and I, value."

WARTHOG PRESS (II), 29 S. Valley Rd., West Orange NJ 07052, phone (201)731-9269, founded 1979, poetry editor Patricia Fillingham, publishes books of poetry **"that are understandable, poetic."** They have published *From the Other Side of Death* by Joe Lackey, *Wishing for the Worst* by Linda Portnay, and *Hanging On* by Joe Benevento. **Query with 5 samples, cover letter "saying what the author is looking for" and SASE. Simultaneous submissions OK. Ms should be "readable." Comments on rejections, "if asked for. People really don't want criticism." Pays copies, but "I would like to get my costs back."** Patricia Fillingham feels, "The best way to sell poetry still seems to be from poet to listener."

WASCANA REVIEW (II), Dept. of English, University of Regina, Regina, Saskatchewan S4S 0A2 Canada, phone (306)585-4302, fax (306)585-4827, e-mail wallka@leroy.uregina.ca, founded 1966, editor Kathleen Wall, appears twice a year publishing contemporary poetry and short fiction along with critical articles on modern and post-modern literature. **"We look for high-quality literary poetry of all forms, including translations. No haiku or doggerel. No long poems. No concrete poetry."** They have published poetry by Stephen Heighton, Robert Cooperman, Cornelia Hoogland and Eugene Dubnov. The editor says *WR* is a trade-sized paperback, 75-100 pgs., no art/graphics, no ads. They receive about 200-300 submissions a year, accept under 10%. Press run is 400 for 192 subscribers of which 134 are libraries, 100 shelf sales. Subscription: $10/year, $12 outside Canada. **Sample postpaid: $5. No previously published poems or simultaneous submissions. Cover letter required. SASE or SAE and IRCs necessary for return of mss.** "Poems are read by at least two individuals who make comments and/or recommendations. Poetry editor chooses poems based on these comments. Poets may request information via e-mail. But no faxed or e-mailed submissions, please." Often comments on rejections. Reports within 6 months. Pays $10/page and 2 copies. Buys first North American serial rights. Reviews books of poetry in both single and multi-book format. The editor says, "*WR* will be featuring special issues from time to time. Poets should watch for news of these in upcoming editions."

WASHINGTON REVIEW; FRIENDS OF THE WASHINGTON REVIEW OF THE ARTS, INC. (II), P.O. Box 50132, Washington DC 20091-0132, phone (202)638-0515, founded 1974, literary editor Joe Ross, is a bimonthly journal of arts and literature published by the Friends of the Washington Review of the Arts, Inc., a nonprofit, tax-exempt educational organization. **They publish local Washington metropolitan area poets as well as poets from across the US and abroad. "We have eclectic tastes but lean with more favor toward experimental work."** *WR* is tabloid-sized, using 2 of the large pgs. each issue for poetry, saddle-stapled on high-quality newsprint. Circulation is 2,000 with 700 subscribers of which 10 are libraries. **Sample postpaid: $2.50. Cover letter with brief bio required with submissions. Pays 5 copies.** Reviews books of poetry in 1,000-1,500 words, single format—multi-book "on occasion." Open to unsolicited reviews. Poets may also send books for review consideration.

WASHINGTON WRITERS' PUBLISHING HOUSE (IV-Regional), P.O. Box 15271, Washington DC 20003, phone (202)543-1905, founded 1975. An editorial board is elected annually from the collective. "We are a poetry publishing collective that publishes outstanding poetry collections in flat-spined paperbacks by **individual authors living in the greater Washington DC area (60-mile radius, excluding Baltimore) on the basis of competitions held once a year.**" They have recently published poetry by Laura Brylawski-Miller, Myra Sklarew, Ann Darr, Barbara Lefcowitz, Maxine Clair, Ann Knox, Nan Fry and Naomi Thiers. As a sample the editors selected these lines from "Bomb Document" in *Come Looking* by Dan Johnson:

> Some day, when you are the last to leave,
> the call came, the calm threat
> of a learned man with an accent
> who was once merely a strange boy
> without a name.

Send SASE for guidelines and a brochure of published poets to: Barri Armitage, Secretary, 13904 North Gate Dr., Silver Spring MD 20906. Pays copies. Poets become working members of the collective.

WATER MARK PRESS (V), 138 Duane St., New York NY 10013, founded 1978, editor Coco Gordon, proposes "to publish regardless of form in archival editions with handmade paper and hand done elements in sewn, bound books, broadsides, chapbooks and artworks. **I use only avant-garde material.**" **Currently they do not accept any unsolicited poetry.** They have published poetry by Carolyne Wright and Alison Knowles. The editor selected this sample from "After Eden" by Michael Blumenthal:

> Once again the invasion of purpose
> into gesture: the stem towards the vase,
> the hands towards the dreaded morning music
> of predictability, Indian paintbrush fades

That's from a collection of his poetry, *Sympathetic Magic*, 96 pgs., flat-spined, with art by Theo Fried, printed on archival, matte card cover with colored art, $9; hardbound $40. **Note: Please do not confuse Water Mark Press with the imprint Watermark Press, used by other businesses.**

WATERWAYS: POETRY IN THE MAINSTREAM (I, IV-Themes); TEN PENNY PLAYERS (IV-Children/teen/young adult); BARD PRESS (V), 393 St. Paul's Ave., Staten Island NY 10304-2127, phone (718)442-7429, fax (718)442-4978, e-mail 72713.3625@compuserve.com, founded 1977, poetry editors Barbara Fisher and Richard Spiegel, "publishes **poetry by adult poets in a magazine that is published 11 times a year. We do theme issues** and are trying to increase an audience for poetry and the printed and performed word. The project produces performance readings in public spaces and is in residence year round at the New York public library with workshops and readings. We publish the magazine *Waterways*, anthologies and chapbooks. **We are not fond of haiku or rhyming poetry; never use material of an explicit sexual nature.** We are open to reading material from people we have never published, writing in traditional and experimental poetry forms. While we do 'themes,' sometimes an idea for a future magazine is inspired by a submission so we try to remain open to poets' inspirations. Poets should be guided however by the fact that we are children's and animal rights advocates and are a NYC press." They have recently published poetry by Ida Fasel, Kit Knight, Terry Thomas and Will Inman. As a sample the editors selected these lines from "The Way of Art" by Albert Huffstickler:

> It seems to me that,
> paralleling the paths of action, devotion, etc.,
> there is a path called Art
> and that the sages of the East would have recognized
> Faulkner, Edward Hopper, Beethoven, William Carlos Williams,
> and addressed them as equals.

Waterways is 40 pgs., 4¼×7, photocopied from various type styles, saddle-stapled, using b&w drawings, matte card cover. They use 60% of poems submitted. Circulation is 150 with 58 subscriptions of which 12 are libraries. Subscription: $20. **Sample postpaid: $2.60. Submit less than 10 poems for first submission. Simultaneous submissions OK. No submissions via fax. Send SASE for guidelines for approaching themes.** "Since we've taken the time to be very specific in our response, writers should take seriously our comments and not waste their emotional energy and our time sending material that isn't within our area of interest. Sending for our theme sheet and for a sample issue and then objectively thinking about the writer's own work is practical and wise. Without meaning to sound 'precious' or unfriendly, the writer should understand that small press publishers doing limited editions and all production work inhouse are working from their personal artistic vision and know exactly what notes will harmonize, effectively counterpoint and meld. Many excellent poems are sent back to the writers by *Waterways* because they don't relate to what we are trying to create in a given month or months. Some poets get printed regularly in *Waterways*; others will probably never be published by us, not because the poet doesn't write well (although that too is sometimes the case) but only because we are artists with opinions and we exercise them in building each issue. Manuscripts that arrive without a return envelope are not sent back." **Editors sometimes comment on rejections. Reports in less than a month. Pays 1 copy. Acquires one-time publication rights.** They hold contests for children only. **Chapbooks published by Ten Penny Players are "by children and young adults only—and not by submission; they come through our workshops in the library and schools. Adult poets are published by us through our Bard Press imprint, by invitation only. Books evolve from the relationship we develop with writers who we publish in *Waterways* and whom we would like to give more exposure."** The editors advise, "We suggest that poets attend book fairs. It's a fast way to find out what we are all publishing."

WAYNE STATE UNIVERSITY PRESS (V), 4809 Woodward Ave., Detroit MI 48201-1309, phone (313)577-4606, fax (313)577-6131, founded 1941, director Arthur B. Evans, publishes 1 paperback book of poetry/year. They have published poetry by Ruth Whitman and Jim Daniels. **However, they are currently not accepting unsolicited submissions. Query first with sample poems and cover letter with brief bio and publication credits. Previously published poems OK; no simultaneous submissions.** They currently have a 2- to 3-year backlog. **"Two peer reviews are required. If favorable, the project is recommended to an edit board, which must approve all books published." Seldom comments on rejections. Replies to queries in 1 week, to mss (if invited) in 2 months. Pays 6-10% royalties and 6 author's copies.**

WEBSTER REVIEW (II, IV-Translations, regional), English Dept., St. Louis Community College—Meramec, 11333 Big Bend Rd., St. Louis MO 63122-5799, founded 1974, poetry editors Robert Boyd and Greg Marshall, is a literary annual. They want **"no beginners. We are especially interested in translations of foreign contemporary poetry and in the work of Missouri authors."** They have published poetry by Georgi Belev, Antony Oldknow, Bruce Bond, Jane Schapiro and Ernest Kroll. As a sample the editor selected these lines from "That Day I Died" by James Finnegan:

> This is my story of how I died and didn't.
> My body paralyzed suddenly
> while swimming in the Black River,
> you can find it on any map of Missouri,
> I sank on my back to the riverbed. Eyes open
> awash with all of the world above and around me, . . .

Webster Review is 128 pgs., digest-sized, flat-spined, professionally printed with glossy card cover. They receive about 1,500 poems/year, use 90. Press run is 1,000 with 500 subscribers of which 200 are libraries. Single copy/subscription: $5. **Sample free for SASE. Submit 3-6 poems at a time. No previously published poems, simultaneous submissions OK, but not encouraged. Editors comment on rejections "if time permits." Reports "within 2 months, usually." Contributors receive 2 copies.**

WESLEYAN UNIVERSITY PRESS (III), 110 Mt. Vernon, Middletown CT 06459, phone (203)344-7918, founded 1957, editor Suzanna Tamminen, is one of the major publishers of poetry in the nation. They publish 4-6 titles/year. They have published poetry by James Dickey, Joy Harjo, James Tate and Yusef Komunyakaa. **Send query and SASE. Considers simultaneous submissions. Send SASE for guidelines. Responds to queries in 6-8 weeks, to mss in 2-4 months. Pays royalties plus 10 copies.** Poetry publications from Wesleyan tend to get widely (and respectfully) reviewed.

WEST BRANCH (II), Bucknell Hall, Bucknell University, Lewisburg PA 17837, founded 1977, is a literary biannual, using **quality poetry.** Free verse is the dominant form—lyric, narrative and dramatic—occasionally longer than one page, much of it accessible with the emphasis on voice and/or powerful content. They have published poetry by D. Nurkse, Deborah Burnham, Jim Daniels, Anneliese Wagner, Betsy Sholl, David Citino, Barbara Crooker and David Brooks. It is 100-120 pgs., digest-sized, circulation 500. One-year subscription: $7. Two years (4 issues): $11. **Sample: $3. "We do not consider simultaneous submissions. Each poem is judged on its own merits, regardless of subject or form. We strive to publish the best work being written today."** Reports in 6-8 weeks. **Pays copies and subscription to the magazine. Acquires first rights.** Reviews books and chapbooks of poetry but only those by writers who have been published in *West Branch*.

WEST COAST LINE (II, IV-Regional), 2027 EAA, Simon Fraser University, Burnaby, British Columbia V5A 1S6 Canada, phone (604)291-4287, website http://www.sfu.ca/west-coast-line/WCL.ht ml, founded 1990, editor Roy Miki. *West Coast Line* is published 3 times a year and **"favors work by both new and established Canadian writers, but it observes no borders in encouraging original creativity.** Our focus is on contemporary poetry, short fiction, criticism and reviews of books." They have published poetry by Monty Reid, Daphne Marlatt, Erin Mouré, Bruce Andrews, Gerry Shikatani and Hiromi Goto. As a sample the editor selected these lines from *"Flesh, Song*(e) *et Promenade"* by Nicole Brossard, translated by Lola Lemire Tostevin:

> *revocable words*
> *culture caught red-handed*
> *this truly biographical nuance*
> *of shoulders and knees*
> *amidst the arguments*
> *in a yes the lightning* I

The magazine is handsomely printed on glossy paper, 6×9, flat-spined, 144 pgs. They accept about 20 of the 500-600 poetry mss received each year. Approximately 26 pages of poetry/issue. Press run is 800 for 500 subscribers of which 350 are libraries, 150 shelf sales. Single copy: $10; subscription: $20. **No simultaneous submissions or previously published poetry.** Time between acceptance and publication is 2-8 months. **Publishes theme issues.** Their most recent special issue featured new innovative poetry from Britain and Ireland. **Send SASE for guidelines. Reports in 6-8 weeks. Sends prepublication galleys on request. Pays approximately $8 (Canadian)/printed page plus a one-year subscription. Mss returned only if accompanied by sufficient Canadian postage or IRC.** The editor says, "We have a special concern for contemporary writers who are experimenting with, or expanding the boundaries of, conventional forms of poetry, fiction and criticism. That is, poetry should be formally innovative."

WEST OF BOSTON (II), Box 2, Cochituate Station, Wayland MA 01778, phone (508)653-7241, press founded 1983, poetry editor Norman Andrew Kirk, wants to see **"poetry of power, compassion, originality and wit—and talent, too. Poetry that reveals the nature of life from the religious to the sensual, from personal exposures to universal truths. No subject is taboo so long as it is authentic and/or passionate."** They have published poetry by Mary K. Leen, R. Nikolas Macioci, Errol Miller, Lyn Lifshin and Barry Spacks. As a sample the editor selected these lines from "Leaves of an Autumn Past" by Lynda S. Silva:

> *you remember . . .*
>
> *we had that old*
> *painted-lady house*
> *with a bathroom*
> *red tile and chrome,*
>
> *an Indian woman, nude,*
> *touched with silver, . . .*

They are now accepting submissions for a new publication of previously unpublished poems, also called *West of Boston*. Depending on submissions, it will be an annual or semiannual, perfect-bound on high quality paper. **Submit no more than 10 poems at a time. Include a brief bio and SASE with submission. All contributors will receive 1 copy.** Subscription available for $10/issue. **For book or chapbook submission, query with 5-10 sample poems, credits and bio. Simultaneous submissions and previously published poems OK.** Editor "sometimes" comments on rejected mss. Sometimes sends prepublication galleys. **Pays 10% of press run.**

WEST WIND WRITERS & ARTISTS PROJECT (II, IV-Anthology), (formerly *West Wind Review*), English Dept., Southern Oregon State College, Ashland OR 97520, phone (541)552-6581, e-mail westwind@tao.sosc.osshe.edu, founded 1982, publishes an annual anthology each spring, editor and title of anthology change yearly. **They are "looking for sensitive but strong verse that celebrates**

CLOSE-UP

"American-Irish" poet says, "Stick to your guns"

Beyond finding their own voices, setting high standards for their work, and persisting until they "break through" the often elusive poetry marketplace, Julie O'Callaghan suggests poets face a more awesome challenge, a challenge that touches the heart of why poets write in the first place. "The most difficult task for a poet," she says, "is to have the chutzpa and strength to continue writing poems in a world that isn't interested in poetry."

Fortunately for O'Callaghan, while few Irish people will turn off the TV to read a book of poetry, "poetry in Ireland enjoys a residual respect—part fear, part admiration—which means its edge is still a cutting one." Born in Chicago, Illinois, but a resident of Ireland since 1974, O'Callaghan says this

Julie O'Callaghan

respect for poetry, coupled with the country's high standard of poetry, makes Dublin, Ireland, a locale that suits her temperamentally as a poetic base.

"To write in a country where one may bump into Seamus Heaney on the street or Thomas Kinsella in the supermarket is an exhilarating experience," she says. "But if the standard is bracingly high, the scale is pleasantly small and the sense of a poet as an individual, rather than part of a faculty or movement, is still possible."

A distinctive feature of O'Callaghan's poetry is its accessibility. Her poems seem to conceal acute observations with a playfulness and immediacy that make them very readable. She says her poems are "a manifestation of homesickness," and by writing poems that sound American and familiar, also "a cure for it."

Another feature of O'Callaghan's work linked to her unique perspective as a foreigner is her ability to capture dialect and colloquialism. She acknowledges that her distance from the United States has made her more aware of what is distinctive about its language. "I hear American English clearer for the distance," she says. "The Irish have a very exciting way of using English because it has been distilled through Gaelic. But I have to resist picking up Irish phrases and ways of saying things, or my poems would get caught between American and Irish English, which to my ear sounds strange."

But a poet doesn't have to move away to realize what makes his native language unique—he only has to use his imagination, says O'Callaghan. "Poets have a reputation for being able to make the unfamiliar seem familiar, which suggests they have a particular gift for detaching themselves imaginatively from their daily environment." And while she admits this is easier to achieve at a

CLOSE-UP, *O'Callaghan*

"THE LONG ROOM GALLERY
Trinity College Dublin"

There is nothing to breathe
here in the Gallery
except old years.
The air from today
goes in one lung
and 1783 comes out the other.
As for the topic of spirits,
stand perfectly still
and you will feel them
carousing near your ear.
Tourists down below
think they've seen a ghost
when they spot you
floating through bookcases
over their heads.
On a creaky wooden balcony
you tunnel through centuries,
mountains of books
rising into the cumulus.
You could scale a ladder
up the rockface of knowledge
or search the little white slips
stuck in books
for a personal message
from Swift.
Ancient oxygen,
antique dust particles,
petrified wood . . .
Who are you kidding?
You belong down there:
baseball caps, chewing gum, videos.

(commissioned by Trinity College Closet Press for the Trinity College Library; reprinted by permission of author Julie O'Callaghan)

CLOSE-UP, *continued*

geographical distance, "it is by no means impossible to achieve a comparable result while remaining at home."

O'Callaghan, who works part-time in Dublin's Trinity College Library, stresses the importance of reading other poets' work, and lists as her favorite poets Marina Tsvetaeva, Patrick Kavanagh, Robert Frost, Frank O'Hara, John Berryman, Philip Larkin, Pablo Neruda and Shakespeare. "The poet I've felt closest to in spirit for most of the years I've been writing is James Schuyler," she says. "I love his sad/funny/beautiful poems, a description which also fits another favorite, [Scottish poet] W.S. Graham." She says reading the work of these poets has made her very humble about her own work, but it also shows her how "to find a voice of my own and stick to it regardless of what the poetic fashions are."

Actually, O'Callaghan advises beginning poets to avoid following fashions. "Stick to your guns," she says. "Don't fall into the trap of trying to sound like today's fashionable poets, because nothing will look more dated tomorrow." She also urges new poets to set their standards high. "Don't mistake mediocre poetry for the real thing—poets who at first seem discouragingly brilliant are far better company than those whose standards are more attainable merely because they aim less high."

The author of three books of poetry (*What's What*, Bloodaxe Books, 1991; *Taking My Pen for a Walk*, Orchard Books, 1988; and *Edible Anecdotes*, Dolmen Press, 1983), O'Callaghan is a multifaceted and prolific writer of poems for children and adults. Her work has also appeared in numerous periodicals, including *Atlanta Review*, *HU* (*The Honest Ulsterman*) and *Poetry Ireland Review*. She is slotted as both an American and an Irish poet by publishers and reviewers, and that suits her just fine.

"On the one hand, I'm delighted to have been included in anthologies such as *The New Younger Irish Poets* [Blackstaff Press, 1991] and *Ireland's Women* [W.W. Norton & Company, 1995], but I am equally happy to be marketed by my publishers as an American," she says. "*The Times Literary Supplement* assigned my books to their American poetry specialist, while *The Village Voice* included me on their list of recommended Irish poets. Perhaps I am a mid-Atlantic poet or, quite literally, an American-Irish one."

While it is difficult to classify O'Callaghan as either an American or an Irish poet, it is equally difficult to categorize her work. She doesn't view herself as writing a certain type of poetry, but admits she is *viewed* ("or, perhaps, I should say *reviewed*") as such. "I am thought of by reviewers as essentially a composer of poetry monologues," she says, "and it is true that I have written a considerable number of monologues. But in recent years I have tried to concentrate on more directly lyrical poems, both personal—scenes from a life—and imaginary—scenes from the life of a Court Lady in Heian Japan."

O'Callaghan's poems for children resulted from an editorial decision rather than a creative one. "Mostly I just write the poems and later decide which ones would suit high school readers and which work better for adults," she says. "In fact, all of the poems in my first children's collection, *Taking My Pen for a Walk*, were written for adults originally. Fortunately, my resident critic [her husband, Irish poet and critic Dennis O'Driscoll] pointed out to me that a group of poems

CLOSE-UP, *O'Callaghan*

I had written would be great for teenagers."

She says that, while some poems seem more suitable for adults than for children, she agrees with the poet W.H. Auden, who said, "There are no good poems which are only for children." As she says, "Sometimes I read a few children's poems during an adult poetry reading without causing any obvious resentment, or regression to childish behavior, on the part of the audience."

O'Callaghan notes that readings are prevalent in Ireland, ranging from individual readings by established poets to group readings by emerging poets, with the occasional reading by a visiting poet. Festivals held in Kilkenny, Listowel, Sligo, Bangor and Galway are important outlets for beginning poets, since they all feature well-attended readings, and "a number of poetry careers in Ireland have been launched from the stage rather than the page," she says.

Having been there once herself, O'Callaghan understands the struggle beginning poets face when seeking outlets for their work. "In my experience, it is almost impossible for a beginning poet to know which editors will respond positively to their particular style of writing. As a new poet, I sometimes found larger magazines more encouraging than smaller ones."

The good news, she says, is that once a new poet breaks through the magazine market, other outlets become open to him. "Once I had begun to publish regularly in magazines, the market for my poems began to expand in the sense that a magazine appearance might lead to a radio interview which might in turn lead to a poetry reading or a commission to review a book or produce a poem for a limited edition. In literature, as in life, one thing leads to another. . . ."

—Roseann S. Biederman

all aspects of men's and women's experiences, both exalted and tragic. We are looking to print material that reflects ethnic and social diversity." They have recently published poetry by Simon J. Ortiz and Lawson F. Inada. As a sample the editor selected these lines from "Terminus" by Patrick Bernard:

> *Loss: public and game show obvious.*
> *A timid, lurking hope in three parts,*
> *Twelve steps to peace*
> *(all of them reckless and expensive)*

The anthology is usually 224 pgs., digest-sized, handsomely printed and flat-spined. They receive about 1,200 submissions/year, publish 50-60 poems, 10 short stories and 16 pgs. of art. Press run is 600. Sample "at current year's price. We take submissions—limit of 5 poems not exceeding 50 lines. Manuscripts should have poet's name and address on each page." No previously published poems; simultaneous submissions OK. Cover letter required; include brief bio and publication credits. No e-mail submissions. Deadline: December 1 for publication in late May or early June. Send SASE for guidelines or request via e-mail. Reports in 2-3 months after deadline. Pays 1 copy. Offers $25 awards for each category.

WESTERLY; PATRICIA HACKETT PRIZE (II), Centre for Studies in Australian Literature, University of Western Australia, Nedlands 6907, Australia, phone (09)380-2101, fax (09)380-1030, e-mail westerly@uniwa.uwa.edu.au, founded 1956, editors Dennis Haskell and Delys Bird. *Westerly* is a literary and cultural quarterly publishing quality short fiction, poetry, literary critical, socio-historical articles and book reviews. "No restrictions on creative material. Our only criterion [for poetry] is literary quality. We don't dictate to writers on rhyme, style, experimentation, or anything else. We are willing to publish short or long poems. We do assume a reasonably well read, intelligent audience. Past issues of *Westerly* provide the best guides. Not consciously an academic magazine." They have published work by Edwin Thumboo, Jean Kent, Diane Fahey, Brian Turner and Kirpal

Singh. The quarterly magazine is 144 pgs., 5½×8½, "electronically printed," with some photos and graphics. Press run is 1,000. Single copy: $8 (Aus.) plus overseas postage via surface mail; subscription: $38 (Aus.)/year or $10 by e-mail. **Sample: $8 (Aus.) surface mail, $12 (Aus.) airmail. Submit up to 6 poems at a time. "Please do not send simultaneous submissions. Covering letters should be brief and nonconfessional."** Time between acceptance and publication is 3 months. **Publishes occasional theme issues. Theme for December 1996 is Australian/Jewish writing. Reports in 2-3 months. Minimum pay for poetry is $30 plus 1 copy. Buys first publication rights; requests acknowledgment on reprints.** Reviews books of poetry in 500-1,000 words. Open to unsolicited reviews. Poets may also send books to Reviews Editor for review consideration. The Patricia Hackett Prize (value approx. $500) is awarded in March for the best contribution published in *Westerly* during the previous calendar year. The advice of the editors is: "Be sensible. Write what matters for you but think about the reader. Don't spell out the meanings of the poems and the attitudes to be taken to the subject matter—i.e. trust the reader. Don't be swayed by literary fashion. Read the magazine if possible before sending submissions. Read, read, read literature of all kinds and periods."

WESTERN HUMANITIES REVIEW (II), Dept. of English, 3500 LNCO, University of Utah, Salt Lake City UT 84112, phone (801)581-6168, fax (801)585-5167, founded 1947, managing editor Amanda Pecor, is a quarterly of poetry, fiction and a small selection of nonfiction. **They want "quality poetry of any form, including translations."** They have published poetry by Philip Levine, Bin Ramke, Lucie Brock-Broido, Timothy Liu and Rachel Wetzsteon. As a sample we selected these lines from "Storm on Fishing Bay" by John Drury:

> *What's hard to explain*
> *darkens the prospect of happiness—*
> *like wind picking up off shore*
> *where four people retreat, separately.*
>
> *Darkened, the prospect of happiness*
> *falls back to a hunting lodge*
> *where four people retreat, separately*
> *latching shutters, brewing coffee, gazing.*

WHR is 96-125 pgs., 6×9, professionally printed on quality stock and perfect-bound with coated card cover. They receive about 700 submissions a year, accept less than 10%, publish approximately 60 poets. Press run is 1,100 for 1,000 subscribers of which 900 are libraries. Subscription: $20 to individuals in the US. **Sample postpaid: $6. "We do not publish writer's guidelines because we think that the magazine itself conveys an accurate picture of our requirements." No previously published poems; simultaneous submissions OK. Reads submissions September 1 through May 31 only.** Time between acceptance and publication is 1-3 issues. **Managing editor Amanda Pecor makes an initial cut ("eliminating only a few submissions"), then the poetry editor makes the final selections. Seldom comments on rejections. Occasionally publishes special issues. Reports in 1-6 months. Pays $50/poem and 2 copies. Acquires first serial rights.** They also offer an annual spring contest for Utah poets. Prize is $250. Poetry published in this review has been selected for inclusion in the 1992, 1993 and 1995 volumes of *The Best American Poetry*.

WESTERN PRODUCER PUBLICATIONS; WESTERN PEOPLE (IV-Regional), P.O. Box 2500, Saskatoon, Saskatchewan S7K 2C4 Canada, phone (306)665-3500, founded 1923, managing editor Michael Gillgannon. *Western People* is a magazine supplement to *The Western Producer*, a weekly newspaper, circulation 100,000, which uses **"poetry about the people, interests and environment of rural Western Canada."** As a sample the editor selected the entire poem "sky so heavy and low" by Marilyn Cay:

> *it is November in Saskatchewan*
> *the sky so heavy and low*
> *I can feel the weight of it*
> *on my chest*
> *the days so short and getting shorter*
> *I can touch the sides of them*
> *at midday*

The magazine-sized supplement is 16 pgs., newsprint, with color and b&w photography and graphics. They receive about 300 submissions of poetry/year, use 60-70. **Sample free for postage (2 oz.)—and ask for guidelines. One poem/page, maximum of 3 poems/submission. Name, address and telephone number in upper left corner of each page. Reports within 2 weeks. Pays $15-50/poem.** The editor comments, "It is difficult for someone from outside Western Canada to catch the flavor of this region; almost all the poems we purchase are written by Western Canadians."

‡**WESTERN TALES (IV-Regional, cowboy)**, P.O. Box 33842, Granada Hills CA 91394, founded 1993, publisher Dorman Nelson, editor Mariann Kumke, is a quarterly publication of western genre

fiction, poetry, pen and ink drawings, and event listings. **They want poetry of any length on nature, romance, animals, adventure; Native American and cowboy poetry, or any work pertaining to the "factual, mythical Wild West."** As a sample we selected this poem, "What a Cowboy's Got," by Carrie S. Walker:

> Boots, tight jeans, a vest and a hat
> It doesn't get much better than that!
> Your country music, your horse and a rope
> You're a cowboy now, at least you hope.
>
> You've got your woman, you've got your beer,
> if that don't work, you've got your tears.
> But no matter what happens to that,
> you've always got:
> Boots, tight jeans, a vest and a hat!

Western Tales is 98 pgs., 8½ × 11, attractively printed and perfect-bound with full-color cover and b&w illustrations inside. They receive 400-500 poems a year, accept 75. Press run is 6,000 for 1,500 subscribers. Single copy: $4.95; subscription: $16/year. **Sample postpaid: $6. Submit up to 3 poems at a time with SASE. Seldom accepts previously published poems; simultaneous submissions OK. Often comments on rejections. Send SASE for guidelines. Reports in 3 months. Pays $25 and 1 copy. Acquires first or one-time rights.**

WESTVIEW: A JOURNAL OF WESTERN OKLAHOMA (II), 100 Campus Dr., SOSU, Weatherford OK 73096, phone (405)774-3168, founded 1981, editor Fred Alsberg, is a quarterly that is **"particularly interested in writers from the Southwest; however, we are open to work of quality by poets from elsewhere. We publish free verse and formal poetry."** They have published poetry by Mark Sanders, Michael McKinney, Alicia Ostriker and James Whitehead. As a sample the editor selected these lines from "Learning from Mother" by Holly Hunt:

> I will tell you that my mother was smart,
> a wire-cutting wit that could snap everything
> midair and bring pause to all voices there.
> And in that pause would form a certain space
> in every thought, when she would say something
> so accurate that all ears would leap,
> heads tilted to the Common Philosophy Lady

Westview is 44 pgs., magazine-sized, saddle-stapled, with glossy card cover in full-color. They use about 25% of 100 poems received/year. Press run is 1,000 for 500 subscribers of which about 25 are libraries, 150 shelf sales. Subscription: $10. **Sample postpaid: $4. Submit 5 poems at a time. Cover letter including biographical data for contributor's note required with submissions. "Poems on computer disk are welcome so long as they are accompanied by the hard copy and the SASE has the appropriate postage." Editor comments on submissions "when close." "Mss are circulated to an editorial board; we usually respond within 2-3 months." Pays 1 copy.**

WEYFARERS; GUILDFORD POETS PRESS (II), 9, White Rose Lane, Woking, Surrey GU22 7JA United Kingdom, phone (01483)762614, founded 1972, administrative editor Margaret Pain, poetry editors Margaret Pain, Martin Jones and Jeffery Wheatley. They say, "We publish *Weyfarers* magazine three times a year. All our editors are themselves poets and give their spare time free to help other poets." They describe their needs as **"all types of poetry, serious and humorous, free verse and rhymed/metered, but mostly 'mainstream' modern. Excellence is the main consideration. NO hard porn, graphics, way-out experimental. Any subject publishable, from religious to satire. Not more than 40 lines."** They have recently published poetry by Kenneth Pobo and Deborah Ann Register (US), Hélène Sonn (France) and Barbara Dickinson. As a sample the editors selected these lines from "Bosnia" by Kenneth C. Steven:

> . . . . We live nothing but slow days and soft evenings,
> Damp grass underfoot in the first light,
> A garden singing with birds.
>
> How can I believe in a war
> On the other side of these mountains
> Out of sight, out of earshot?
>
> How can I put my hand in these wounds,
> Feel the marks of the nails and the spear?

The digest-sized, saddle-stapled format contains about 28 pgs. of poetry (of a total of 32 pgs.). They use about 125 of 1,200-1,500 submissions received each year. The magazine has a circulation of "about 300," including about 200 subscribers of which 5 are libraries. **Sample (current issue) postpaid: $5** in cash US or £1.60 UK. Submit no more than 6 poems, one poem/sheet. No previously published or simultaneous submissions. Closing dates for submissions are end of January, May and September. Sometimes comments briefly, if requested, on rejections. Pays 1 copy. Staff reviews books of poetry briefly, in newsletter sent to subscribers. "We are associated with Surrey Poetry Center, which has an annual Open Poetry Competition. The prize-winners are published in *Weyfarers*." Their advice to poets is, "Always read a magazine before submitting. And read plenty of modern poetry."

‡WHETSTONE (I, II), Dept. of English, University of Lethbridge, 4401 University Drive, Lethbridge, Alberta T1K 3M4 Canada, editor Lori Leister, is a biannual encouraging all forms of submissions. They predominantly publish poetry and short fiction, but are also open to "essays, artwork and other forms of expression. All submissions must be original and unpublished." *Whetstone* is 80 pgs., digest-sized, perfect-bound, professionally printed in boldface type with 2-color matte card cover. Circulation is 500 with 200 subscriptions of which 25 are libraries. Subscription: $12 for 1 year, $22 for 2 years (Canadian funds only). Sample postpaid: $7. Submit up to 6 poems, any length of poetry OK. Cover letter including brief bio required. Editor sometimes comments on rejections. "Submissions which do not have a SASE, or SAE with IRC, will not be returned or commented on." Send SASE for guidelines. Pays 1 copy. "*Whetstone* also runs periodic features and contests. Regulations are specific and writers should request information before submitting."

WHETSTONE; WHETSTONE PRIZE (II), P.O. Box 1266, Barrington IL 60011-1266, phone (847)382-5626, fax (847)382-3685, editors Sandra Berris, Marsha Portnoy, Jean Tolle and Julie Fleenor, is an annual. "We emphasize quality more than category and favor the concrete over the abstract, the accessible over the obscure. We like poets who use words in ways that transform them and us." They have recently published poetry by Shulamith Wechter Caine, Jeff Gundy, Pearl Karrer and Louis Phillips. As a sample an editor selected these lines from "To Bette" by Anna Stoessinger:

> Strange, how light plays the body
> as if it could be tuned,
> that you might be whole again,
> the late afternoon sun encircling you
> in small immediate waves
> as if casting a sculpture.

It is 96 pgs., digest-sized, professionally printed, flat-spined with matte card cover. Press run is 700 for 100 subscribers of which 5 are libraries, 350 shelf sales. Sample postpaid: $3. Reports in 1-4 months. Always sends prepublication galleys. Pays 2 copies plus a monetary amount that varies. Buys first North American serial rights. Awards the Whetstone Prize of $500 for the best poetry or fiction in each issue, and additional prizes as well. *Whetstone* received two Illinois Arts Council 1995 Literary Awards and received an Honorable Mention for editorial content from the 1995 American Literary Magazine Awards.

WHISKEY ISLAND MAGAZINE (II), English Dept., Cleveland State University, Cleveland OH 44115, phone (216)687-2056, founded 1978, student editors change yearly, is a biannual magazine publishing poetry, fiction and an interview with a poet/writer each issue. They want "advanced writing." They have recently published poetry by Vivian Shipley, Kathleene West, Claudia Rankine, Patricia Smith and Dennis Saleh. As a sample the editor selected these lines from "January Thaw" by Teresa Fanelli:

> Winter trees spike through
> the season's fruitless preservation,
> fall remains like thin memory.
> Jumbo cardinals perch and leap,
> from brittle limbs bluejays drop
> and screech, splinters of icefall
> spatter on the ground,
> where broken branches
> lie beneath the glaze.

Whiskey Island Magazine is 86-104 pgs., 5½×8½, professionally printed and perfect-bound with light card stock cover and b&w art. They receive 1,000-1,500 poetry mss a year, accept approximately 6%. Press run is 1,200 for 200 subscribers of which 20 are libraries, about 120 shelf sales. Subscription:

---

‡   **THE DOUBLE DAGGER** before a listing indicates that the listing is new in this edition. New markets are often the most receptive to submissions.

$12. **Sample postpaid: $6. Submit no more than 10 pgs. of poetry at a time. Include name, address and phone number on each page. No previously published poems. Cover letter with brief bio required. Poems are circulated to an editorial committee. Send SASE for guidelines. Reports within 3 months. Pays 2 copies.** In 1995 and 1996, they held a contest for both poetry and fiction. Query regarding contest for 1997. The editor says, "Always type everything. Always include SASEs and your name and address for contact. Keep trying. Rejection, like acceptance, is subjective and often arbitrary."

WHITE EAGLE COFFEE STORE PRESS (II); FRESH GROUND (II, IV-Anthology), P.O. Box 383, Fox River Grove IL 60021-0383, phone (847)639-9200, e-mail wecspress@aol.com, founded 1992, is a small press publishing 5-6 chapbooks/year. **"Alternate chapbooks are published by invitation and by competition. Author published by invitation becomes judge for next competition."** They are **"open to any kind of poetry. No censorship at this press. Literary values are the only standard. Generally not interested in sentimental or didactic writing."** They have published poetry by Annie Davidovicz, Peter Blair, Martha M. Vertreace, James Plath, Leilani Wright and Jill Peláez Baumgaertner. As a sample the editor selected these lines from "Hot Saws" by Paul Andrew E. Smith:

> It's a metallic taste she has, sweet,
> my teeth are numb, my cheek bones.
> Yes, by God in the treetops,
> I'm beginning to see how these are
> necessary skills, this lumberjacking.

Sample postpaid: $5.95. Submit complete chapbook ms (20-24 pgs.) with a brief bio, 125-word statement that introduces your writing and $10 reading fee. Previously published poems and simultaneous submissions OK, with notice. No electronic submissions. Competition deadlines: March 30 for spring contest; September 30 for fall contest. Send SASE for guidelines. "Each competition is judged by either the author of the most recent chapbook published by invitation or by previous competition winners." **Seldom comments on rejections. Reports 3 months after deadline. All entrants will receive a copy of the winning chapbook. Winner receives $150 and 25 copies.** *Fresh Ground* is an annual anthology that features "some of the best work of emerging poets. **We're looking for edgy, crafted poetry.** *Fresh Ground* is published in September. Poems for this annual are accepted during May through June." They say, "Poetry is about a passion for language. That's what we're about. We'd like to provide an opportunity for poets of any age who are fairly early in their careers to publish something substantial. We're excited by the enthusiasm shown for this new press and by the extraordinary quality of the writing we've received."

WHITE PINE PRESS (V); THE WHITE PINE POETRY PRIZE (II), 10 Village Square, Suite 28, Fredonia NY 14063, founded 1973, editor Dennis Maloney, managing director Elaine LaMattina. White Pine Press publishes poetry, fiction, literature in translation, essays—perfect-bound paperbacks. **"At present we are accepting unsolicited mss only for our annual competition, The White Pine Poetry Prize. This competition awards $500 plus publication to a book-length collection of poems by a US author. Entry fee: $15. Deadline: December 1. Send SASE for details."** They have recently published poetry by Marjorie Agosin, Sam Hamill, John Brandi and Gene Zeiger. **Send $1 for catalog.**

JAMES WHITE REVIEW: A GAY MEN'S LITERARY QUARTERLY; THE DAVID LINDAHL PRIZE FOR POETRY (IV-Gay), Box 3356, Butler Quarter Station, Minneapolis MN 55403, phone (612)339-8317, founded 1983, poetry editor Clif Mayhood, associate poetry editor William Reichard, **uses all kinds of poetry by gay men.** They have recently published poetry by Robert Peters, Reginald Shepherd and Len Blanchard. They receive about 1,400 submissions/year, use 100, have a 6-week backlog. Press run is 4,000 for 1,500 subscribers of which 50 are libraries. Subscription: $14/year (US). **Sample postpaid: $3. Submit up to 8 poems or 250 lines. A poem can exceed 250 lines, but it "better be very good." Send SASE for guidelines. Reports in 4 months. Pays $10/poem and 2 copies.** Reviews books of poetry. Sponsors The David Lindahl Prize for Poetry which awards $500 to the best poem published in each calendar year.

WHITE WALL REVIEW (I), 63 Gould St., Toronto, Ontario M5B 1E9 Canada, phone (416)977-9924, founded 1976, editors change every year, is an annual using **"interesting, preferably spare art. No style is unacceptable. Should poetry serve a purpose beyond being poetry and communicating a poet's idea? Nothing boring, self-satisfied, gratuitously sexual, violent or indulgent."** They have recently published poetry by R.L. Cook and K.G. Sambrano. As a sample the editor selected this poem, "Violets," by Mary-Alice Seibel:

> After long
> Frozen weeks
> When fields lay
> As empty and dry
> As the moon

> This miracle
> Of blue violets
> The sky seeping out of
> The earth.

WWR is between 144-160 pgs., digest-sized, professionally printed and perfect-bound with glossy card cover, using b&w photos and illustrations. Press run is 500. Subscription: $9 in Canada, $9.50 in US and elsewhere. **Sample postpaid: $8. Submit up to 5 poems at a time with a $5 reading fee. "Please do not submit between January and August of a given year." Cover letter required; include short bio. Reports "as soon as we can (usually in April or May). We comment on all mss, accepted or not." Pays 1 copy.** They say, "Poets should send what they consider *their best work*, not everything they've got."

WHOLE NOTES; WHOLE NOTES PRESS (I, II, IV-Children, translations), P.O. Box 1374, Las Cruces NM 88004-1374, *WN* founded 1984, Whole Notes Press founded 1988, editor Nancy Peters Hastings. *WN* appears twice a year. Whole Notes Press publishes 1 chapbook/year by a single poet. **WN tends toward close observation of the natural world, the beauty of nature and a poetry which affirms the human spirit. "All forms will be considered."** Under Whole Notes Press, they have published chapbooks by Keith Wilson (*The Way of the Dove*), Robert Dorsett (*Threshold*) and Roy Scheele (*To See How it Tallies*). As a sample the editor selected these lines from "Snow Geese" by Elsie Wear Stockwell:

> I saw this once . . .
>
> a snow goose circling,
> flapping
> round its wounded mate
> from bloody dawn
> to umber dusk.

WN is 32 pgs., digest-sized, "nicely printed," staple bound, with a "linen 'fine arts' cover." They accept about 10% of some 800 submissions/year. Press run is 400 for 200 subscriptions of which 10 are libraries. Subscription: $6. **Sample postpaid: $3. Submit 4 poems at a time. Some previously published poems used; no simultaneous submissions. Reports in 2-3 weeks. Pays 2 copies. For 20-page chapbook consideration, submit 3-5 samples with bio and list of other publications. Pays 25 copies of chapbook. Editor sometimes comments on rejections.** The editor says, "In the fall of each even-numbered year I edit a special issue of *WN* that features writing by young people (under 21). Overall, we'd like to see more translations and more poems about rural experiences."

THE WICAZO SA REVIEW (IV-Ethnic), 3755 Blake Court N., Rapid City SD 57701-4716, phone (605)341-3228, founded 1985, poetry editor Elizabeth Cook-Lynn, is a "scholarly magazine, appearing twice a year, devoted to the developing of Native American Studies as an academic discipline and using **poetry of exceptional quality."** They have published poetry by Simon Ortiz, Joy Harjo, Gray Cohoe and Earle Thompson. As a sample the editor chose these lines by Ray Young Bear:

> With the Community's great "registered" Cottonwood
> Smoldering under an overcast sky
> no one will believe we are here
> in the middle & deepest part
> of the flood

TWSR is 80-120 pgs., magazine-sized, professionally printed on heavy glossy stock and saddle-stapled with b&w glossy card cover. They use only 3-4 poems/issue. Once in a while they "feature" an exceptional poet. Press run is 600. **Sample postpaid: $10. Cover letter required including credits and tribal enrollment affiliation. Pays 3 copies.** Reviews books of poetry. Open to unsolicited reviews and literary criticism essays. Poets may also send books for review consideration.

WILDWOOD JOURNAL (IV-Specialized: college affiliation); THE WILDWOOD PRIZE IN POETRY (II), T.H.S. Wallace, Arts 213, 1 HACC Dr., Harrisburg PA 17110-2999, phone (717)780-2487. *Wildwood Journal*, an annual, is **open only to students, alumni and faculty of Harrisburg Area Community College. Sample copy: $5.** The Wildwood Prize, however, is open to any poet, $500 annually, $5 reading fee made payable to HACC. Final selection for the prize is made by a distinguished poet (in 1996: Barbara Crooker) who usually remains anonymous until the winner is announced. Poems are accepted between October 15 and November 30. Rules available for SASE.

THE WILLIAM AND MARY REVIEW (II), Campus Center, College of William and Mary, P.O. Box 8795, Williamsburg VA 23187-8795, phone (804)221-3290, fax (804)221-3451, e-mail review@m ail.wm.edu, founded 1962, editor Forrest Pritchard, poetry editors Seth Archer and Brian Waniewski, is a 112-page annual, **"dedicated to publishing new work by established poets as well as work by new and vital voices."** They have published poetry by Dana Gioia, Robert Morgan, Cornelius Eady,

Amy Clampitt, Elizabeth Alexander, Robert Hershon, Diane Ackerman, Agha Shahid Ali, Bruce Weigl, Robert Bly and Phyllis Janowitz. They accept 15-20 of about 5,000 poems submitted/year. Press run is 3,500. They have 250 library subscriptions, about 500 shelf sales. **Sample postpaid: $5.50. Submit 1 poem/page, batches of no more than 6 poems. Cover letter required; include address, phone number, past publishing history and brief bio note. Reads submissions September 15 through February 15 only. Reports in approximately 4 months. Always sends prepublication galleys. Pays 5 copies.** Open to unsolicited reviews. Poets may also send books to poetry editors for review consideration.

WILLOW REVIEW; COLLEGE OF LAKE COUNTY READING SERIES (II), College of Lake County, 19351 W. Washington St., Grayslake IL 60030-1198, phone (847)223-6601, ext. 2956, fax (847)223-9371, founded 1969, edited by Paulette Roeske. **"We are interested in poetry and fiction of high quality with no preferences as to form, style or subject."** They have recently published poetry by Lisel Mueller, Lucien Stryk, David Ray, Louis Rodriguez, John Dickson and Garrett Hongo and interviews with Gregory Orr, Diane Ackerman and Li-Young Lee. As a sample the editor selected these lines from "The Remedy" by Richard Jones:

> I pour my bowl of soup,
> and recite this poem,
> this magic,
> this incantation cleaving sickness from
> health. I fold the two knives of my hands
> in prayer and say grace,
> asking to live
> a while longer in this body,
> which I bless at every meal,
> crossing it with one hand
> and feeding it with another.

The review is an 88-page, flat-spined annual, 6×9, professionally printed with a 4-color cover featuring work by an Illinois artist. Editors are open to all styles, free verse to form, as long as each poem stands on its own as art and communicates ideas. Circulation is 1,000, with distribution to bookstores nationwide. Subscription: $13 for 3 issues, $20 for 5 issues. **Sample back issue: $4. Submit up to 5 poems or short fiction/creative nonfiction up to 4,000 words. "We read year round but response is slower in the summer months." Sometimes sends prepublication galleys. Pays 2 copies. Acquires first North American serial rights. Prizes of $150 are awarded to the best poetry and short fiction/creative nonfiction in each issue.** The reading series, 4-7 readings/academic year, has included Angela Jackson, Ellen Bryant Voigt, Thomas Lux, Charles Simic, Gloria Naylor, David Mura, Galway Kinnell, Lisel Mueller, Amiri Baraka, Stephen Dobyns, Heather McHugh, Linda Pastan, Katha Pollitt, Tobias Wolff, William Stafford and others. One reading is for contributors to *Willow Review*. Readings are usually held on Thursday evenings, for audiences of about 150 students and faculty of the College of Lake County and other area colleges and residents of local communities. They are widely publicized in Chicago and suburban newspapers.

WILLOW SPRINGS (II, IV-Translations), 526 Fifth St., MS-1, Eastern Washington University, Cheney WA 99004-2431, phone (509)623-4349, founded 1977. "We publish quality poetry and fiction that is imaginative, intelligent, and has a concern and care for language. **We are especially interested in translations from any language or period."** They have published poetry by Denise Levertov, Carolyn Kizer, Michael Burkard, Russell Edson, Dara Wier, Thomas Lux, Madeline DeFrees, Hayden Carruth, Al Young, Odysseas Elytis, W.S. Merwin, Olga Broumas, Kay Boyle and Lisel Mueller. *Willow Springs*, a semiannual, is one of the most visually appealing journals being published. It is 128 pgs., 6×9, professionally printed, flat-spined, with glossy 4-color card cover with art. They use 1-2% of some 4,000 unsolicited poems received each year. Editors seem to prefer free verse with varying degrees of accessibility (although an occasional formal poem does appear). Circulation is 1,500 for 700 subscribers of which 30% are libraries. Subscription: $10.50/year, $20/2 years. **Sample postpaid: $5.50. Submit September 15 through May 15 only. "We do not read in the summer months." Include name on every page, address on first page of each poem. Brief cover letter saying how many poems on how many pages preferred. No simultaneous submissions. Send SASE for guidelines. Reports in 1-3 months. Pays 2 copies, others at half price, and cash when funds available. Acquires all rights. Returns rights on release.** Reviews books of poetry and short fiction in 200-500 words. Open to unsolicited reviews. Poets may also send books for review consideration. They have annual poetry and fiction awards ($100 and $250 respectively) for work published in the journal.

WIND PUBLICATIONS; WIND MAGAZINE (II), P.O. Box 24548, Lexington KY 40524, phone (606)885-5342, *Wind Magazine* founded in 1971, editor/publisher Charlie G. Hughes. "Although we publish poets of national repute, we are friendly toward beginners who have something to say and do so effectively and interestingly. **No taboos, no preferred school, form, style, etc. Our interests are inclusive.** Competition is keen; send only your best." *Wind* appears twice a year and is about 100 pgs., digest-sized, perfect-bound, containing approximately 40% poetry, also short fiction, essays and reviews ("Editor's Choice"). "We accept about 1% of submissions." Subscription: $10/year. **Sample postpaid: $3.50. Submit no more than 5 poems. No simultaneous submissions. "Cover letter optional; short bio desirable." Editor comments on submissions which are near misses. Reports in 6-8 weeks, publication within 1 year. Sometimes sends prepublication galleys. Pays 1 contributor's copy plus discount on extras. "Your submission is understood to guarantee Wind Publications first North American serial rights and anthology reprint rights only."** Wind Publications sponsors a yearly chapbook competition. Reading fee: $10. Send SASE for chapbook guidelines.

THE WINDLESS ORCHARD; THE WINDLESS ORCHARD CHAPBOOKS (II), English Dept., Indiana University, Fort Wayne IN 46805, phone (219)483-6845, founded 1970, poetry editor Robert Novak, is a "shoestring labor of love—chapbooks only from frequent contributors to magazine. Sometimes publish calendars." They want **"heuristic, excited, valid non-xian religious exercises. Our muse is interested only in the beautiful, the erotic and the sacred."** *The Windless Orchard* appears irregularly, 50 pgs., digest-sized, offset from typescript, saddle-stapled, with matte card cover with b&w photos. There are about 35 pgs. of poetry in each issue (**with a regular section of autobiographical poems on being age 17**). They receive about 3,000 submissions of poetry/year, use 200, have a 6-month backlog. The editors say they have 100 subscribers of which 25 are libraries, a press run of 300, total circulation: 280. Subscription: $10. **Sample postpaid: $4. Submit only 3 poems or 10 haiku at a time. Considers simultaneous submissions. Reports in 1 day to 4 months. Pays 2 copies. Chapbook submissions by invitation only to contributors to the magazine. Poets pay costs for 300 copies, of which The Windless Orchard Chapbook Series receives 100 for its expenses. Sample: $4. Editors sometimes comment on rejections.** They advise, "Memorize a poem a day, do translations for the education."

‡THE WIND-MILL (IV-Specialized: genealogy, ethnic), % Rainbow City, P.O. Box 8445, Berkeley CA 94707-8445, editor Helen B. Harvey, is a semiannual publication featuring articles, poetry, reviews, art and photos relating to genealogy and family history. "The purpose of *Wind-Mill* is to provide a friendly, relaxed forum for sharing information about family history research and, in particular, information about German/Dutch (Ostfriesen, East Frisian/North German) culture, history and ethnic traditions." Subscription: $12/year. **Sample postpaid: $6 plus SASE. Submit up to 3 poems, 30 lines maximum each. "Send SASE along with any material that you wish to be returned to you or if you want a response." Submission deadlines: March 1 for Spring/Summer issue; September 1 for Autumn/Winter issue. Pays 1 copy.** They are also interested in reviews of computerized genealogy software; beginning German or Plattdeutsch language instruction programs; reviews of books, tapes and other items related to genealogy research; German/Ostfriesen immigration patterns; amusing anecdotes about ancestors; and specific biographies of or details about individuals. Send SASE for details. The editor advises, "Please obtain and study a sample issue prior to submitting anything for publication."

WINDSOR REVIEW (II), English Dept., University of Windsor, Windsor, Ontario N9B 3P4 Canada, phone (519)253-4232, ext. 2332, fax (519)973-7050, e-mail uwrevu@uwindsor.ca, founded 1966, poetry editor John Ditsky, appears twice a year. **"Open to all poetry but no epics."** They have published poetry by Ben Bennani, Walter McDonald, Larry Rubin and Lyn Lifshin. As a sample the editor selected these lines (poet unidentified):

> *talking to white wolves*
> *talking to the first*
> *white wolves ever*
> *telling of how things are*
> *in his world.*

It is professionally printed, 100 pgs., digest-sized. They accept about 15% of 500 poems received/year. Press run is 400. Subscription: $19.95 (+7% GST) individuals, $29.95 (+7% GST) institutions (Canadian); $19.95 individuals, $29.95 institutions (US). **Sample postpaid: $7. Submit 5-10 poems at a time. Queries via e-mail OK. No e-mail submissions. Reports in 6 weeks.**

‡WINEBERRY PRESS (V, IV-Regional), 3207 Macomb St. NW, Washington DC 20008-3327, phone (202)363-8036 or (416)964-2002, founded 1983, founder and president Elisavietta Ritchie, publishes anthologies and chapbooks of poems by **Washington area poets but is not currently accepting unsolicited mss.** She has published poetry by Judith McCombs, Elizabeth Follin-Jones and Beatrice Murphy. As a sample Elisavietta Ritchie selected these lines from "Through The Looking Glass" by Maxine Combs, included in *Swimming Out Of The Collective Unconscious*:

> *I drop a carton*

in someone else's shopping cart,
kneel to comfort a weeping child
I mistake for my own . . . . We start
swimming out of the collective unconscious
and end by resembling our lovers.

WISCONSIN ACADEMY REVIEW (IV-Regional), 1922 University Ave., Madison WI 53705, phone (608)263-1692, founded 1954, poetry editor Faith B. Miracle, "distributes information on scientific and cultural life of Wisconsin and provides a forum for **Wisconsin (or Wisconsin background) artists and authors." They want "good lyric poetry; traditional meters acceptable if content is fresh. No poem over 65 lines."** They have published poetry by Credo Enriquez, Jean Feraca, Felix Pollak, Ron Wallace, Sara Rath and Lorine Niedecker. As a sample we selected these lines from "J L Jones" by Art Madson:

Running before the wind
on canvas wings,
on lifting hands, empty spirits,
I try, like flying fish
sailing the Pacific,
to transcend my element.

Wisconsin Academy Review is a 52-page quarterly, magazine-sized, professionally printed on glossy stock, glossy card color cover. Press run is 1,800 for 1,500 subscribers of which 100 are libraries. They use 3-6 pgs. of poetry/issue. Of over 150 submissions of poetry/year, they use about 24, have a 6- to 12-month backlog. **Sample postpaid: $3. Submit 5 pgs. maximum, double-spaced, with SASE. Must include Wisconsin connection if not Wisconsin return address. Editor sometimes comments on rejections. Reports in 10-12 weeks. Always sends prepublication printouts. Pays 3 copies.** Staff reviews books of poetry with Wisconsin connection only. Send related books for review consideration. The editor says, "We would like to receive good traditional forms—not sentimental rhymes."

UNIVERSITY OF WISCONSIN PRESS; BRITTINGHAM PRIZE IN POETRY; FELIX POLLAK PRIZE IN POETRY (II), 114 N. Murray St., Madison WI 53715-1199, Brittingham Prize inaugurated in 1985, poetry editor Ronald Wallace. The University of Wisconsin Press publishes primarily scholarly works, but they offer the annual **Brittingham Prize and now the Felix Pollak Prize, both $1,000 plus publication. These prizes are the only way in which this press publishes poetry. Send SASE for rules. For both prizes, submit between September 1 and October 1, unbound ms volume of 50-80 pgs., with name, address and telephone number on title page. No translations. Poems must be previously unpublished in book form. Poems published in journals, chapbooks and anthologies may be included but must be acknowledged. There is a non-refundable $15 reading fee which must accompany the ms. (Checks to University of Wisconsin Press.) Mss will *not* be returned. Enclose SASE for contest results.** Qualified readers will screen all mss. Winners will be selected by "a distinguished poet who will remain anonymous until the winners are announced in mid-February." Past judges include Mona Van Duyn, Charles Wright, Gerald Stern, Mary Oliver, Donald Finkel, Donald Justice, Lisel Mueller, Henry Taylor, Carolyn Kizer and Philip Levine. Winners include David Kirby, Lisa Zeidner, Stefanie Marlis, Judith Vollmer, Renée A. Ashley, Tony Hoagland, Stephanie Strickland, Lisa Lewis, David Clewell, Bob Hicok and Lynn Powell. The editor says, "**Each submission is considered for both prizes (one entry fee only).**"

WISCONSIN REVIEW; WISCONSIN REVIEW PRESS (II), Box 158, Radford Hall, University of Wisconsin-Oshkosh, Oshkosh WI 54901, phone (414)424-2267, founded 1966, editor Elisa Derickson, is published 3 times/year. "**In poetry we publish mostly free verse with strong images and fresh approaches. We want new turns of phrase.**" They have published poetry by Laurel Mills, Joseph Bruchac, Kenneth Frost, Paul Marion, Dionisio Martinez, Stephen Perry, Margaret Randall, David Steingass, Brian Swann and Peter Wild. As a sample the editor selected these lines from "Early Morning of Another World" by Tom McKeown:

After squid and cool white wine there is
no sleep. The long tentacles uncurl
out of the dark with all that was left behind.
Promises expand promises. A frayed mouth
loses its color in the dawn.

The *Review* is 48-64 pgs., 6×9, elegantly printed on quality white stock, glossy card cover with color art, b&w art inside. They receive about 1,500 poetry submissions/year, use about 75. They use 30-40 pgs. of poetry in each issue. Press run is 2,000 for 50 subscribers of which 30 are libraries. Single copy: $3; subscription: $8. **Sample postpaid: $2. Submit mss September 15 through May 15. Offices checked bimonthly during summer. Editor requests no more than 4 poems/submission, one poem/page, single-spaced with name and address of writer on each page. Simultaneous submissions OK, but previously unsubmitted works preferable. Cover letter also preferred; in-**

clude brief bio. Send SASE for guidelines. Reports within 1-4 months. Pays 2 copies.

THE WISHING WELL (IV-Membership, women/feminism, lesbian/bisexual), P.O. Box 713090, Santee CA 92072-3090, phone (619)443-4818, founded 1974, editor/publisher Laddie Hosler, is a "contact magazine for **women who love women** the world over; members' descriptions, photos, letters and poetry published with their permission only; resources, etc., listed. I publish writings only for and by members so membership is required." 1-2 pgs. in each issue are devoted to **poetry, "which can be 6″ to full page—depending upon acceptance by editor, 3″ width column."** It is 7 × 8½ offset press from typescript, with soft matte card cover. It appears bimonthly and goes to 800 members. **A sample is available for $5. Membership in** *Wishing Well* **is $35 for 3-5 months, $60 for 5-7 months, $120 for 15 months. Membership includes the right to publish poetry, a self description (exactly as you write it), to have responses forwarded to you, and other privileges.** Reviews books of poetry. Personal classifieds section, members and/or nonmembers, $1/word.

WITNESS (II, IV-Themes), Oakland Community College, Orchard Ridge Campus, 27055 Orchard Lake Rd., Farmington Hills MI 48334, phone (810)471-7740, founded 1987, editor Peter Stine, is a biannual journal of poetry, fiction and essays which often publishes special issues centered around themes. **They want "poetry that highlights the role of the writer as witness to his/her times. No real specifications, except nothing concrete or wildly experimental."** They have published poetry by John Balaban, Mary Oliver, Alicia Ostriker and Mark Doty. As a sample we selected the opening lines of "Omaha" by Steve Langan, published in the special issue on American cities:

> City no one's said it best about;
> city that ignores its river,
> its young, its elderly, its myths.

> I sat in its taverns for five years,
> my pledge not to miss a day —
> that pledge got me nowhere . . .

Witness is 192 pgs., 6 × 9, professionally printed and perfect-bound with coated card cover with full-color photo and b&w photos inside. They receive about 500 poems a year, accept approximately 5%. Press run is 2,800 for 400 subscribers of which 60 are libraries, 1,200 distributed to bookstores. Subscription: $12/year. **Sample postpaid: $7; upcoming special issues are announced inside. No previously published poems; simultaneous submissions OK. Cover letter required. Seldom comments on rejections. Reports in 2-3 months. Pays $10/page. Buys first serial rights.** Poetry published here has also been included in the 1992, 1994 and 1995 volumes of *The Best American Poetry*.

WOLSAK AND WYNN PUBLISHERS LTD. (II), Box 316, Don Mills Post Office, Don Mills, Ontario M3C 2S7 Canada, phone (416)222-4690, founded 1982, poetry editor Maria Jacobs, publishes 5 flat-spined literary paperbacks/year (56-100 pgs.). They have recently published collections of poetry by Richard Harrison and Polly Fleck. Here is a sample from *Cantos From A Small Room* by Robert Hilles:

> Some mornings I wake to an opera on the radio
> and I think of her hand raised to me
> and how small I was as I kissed it and she
> smiled and I knew that her defeat was mine too that
> there is little that the living can share with the dying.

The books are handsomely printed. **Sample: $10 US or $12 Canadian. Send sample poems with query, bio, publications. No simultaneous submissions. Reports on queries in 4 months. Always sends prepublication galleys. Pays 10% royalties. Buys first rights.** Maria Jacobs says, "W&W prefers not to prescribe. We are open to *good* writing of any kind."

WOMEN'S EDUCATION DES FEMMES (IV-Regional, women/feminism), 47 Main St., Toronto, Ontario M4E 2V6 Canada, phone (416)699-1909, fax (416)699-2145, e-mail cclon@web.apc. org, founded 1982, editor Christina Starr, poetry editor Catherine Lake, is a quarterly using **"feminist poetry, about women, written by Canadian women only."** They have recently published poetry by Susan Ioannou and Sylvie Bourassa. As a sample the editor selected these lines by Mary Rudbeck Stanko:

> Hidden within a metaphor of eyes
> your glance became the character of windows,
> a place where mirrors refracted
> subdued and ghostly rays
> which we mistook for ornaments of shade.

The editor describes it as 48 pgs., magazine-sized, web offset, saddle-stapled, with one-color cover. Subscription: $17 individual, $30 institution. **Sample postpaid: $2.50. Submit 3-6 poems at a time. Publishes theme issues. Send SASE for upcoming themes or request via e-mail. Reports in 2-3** months. **Pays $25/poem plus 2 copies.** Occasionally reviews books of poetry. Open to unsolicited reviews.

WOMEN'S STUDIES QUARTERLY; THE FEMINIST PRESS AT CUNY (V, IV-Women, feminist, bilingual), Dept. PM, 311 E. 94th St., New York NY 10128, phone (212)360-5790. *Women's Studies Quarterly*, founded 1972, publisher Florence Howe, is a nonfiction quarterly publishing **"poetry that focuses on current issues of importance to women; emphasis on education or activism preferable."** They have published poetry by Mila Aguilar. The editor describes it as 5½ × 8½, 150-200 pgs. Their press run is 1,500. **Sample postpaid: $22. "Although poetry is included in each issue, the poems are chosen by the guest editor."** The Feminist Press publishes primarily both historical and contemporary fiction and nonfiction (12-15 titles/year), but it also publishes some poetry, such as the series, *The Defiant Muse,* bilingual volumes (Hispanic, French, Italian and German) of poetry by women from the Middle Ages to the present.

WOMENWISE (III, IV-Women/feminism, health concerns), 38 S. Main St., Concord NH 03301-4817, founded 1978, run by an editorial committee, is "a quarterly newspaper that deals specifically with issues relating to women's health—research, education, and politics." They want **"poetry reflecting status of women in society, relating specifically to women's health issues."** They do not want "poetry that doesn't include women or is written by men; poetry that degrades women or is anti-choice." As a sample we selected these lines from "Two Days Before My Stroke" by Margaret Robison:

> Whatever happens, we'll always have this, *I said,*
> *wondering at the melodrama of my words.*
> *We stood at the boat rail, eyes filled with ocean.*
> *Neither of us understood the dream that had waked her*
> *in the night, with a voice that said:* Tell Margaret
> to feel the energy that spirals through you, into her
> and back again. This will be only for a little while . . .

Women Wise is a tabloid newspaper, 12 pgs., printed on quality stock with b&w art and graphics. Press run is 3,000. Subscription: $10/year. **Sample: $2.95. Submissions should be typed double-spaced. Reads submissions March, June, September and December only. Publishes theme issues. Send SASE for upcoming themes. Reporting time and time to publication varies. Pays 1-year subscription. Acquires first North American serial rights.** Staff reviews books of poetry in "any word count," single format. They say they often receive mss with no SASE. "We throw them away. Please remember that we are a nonprofit organization with limited resources." The editor adds, "We receive a great deal of badly written free verse. We would appreciate receiving more poetry in traditional form, as well as more poetry in free verse written with skill and care."

‡WOODEN HEAD REVIEW; NON COMPOS MENTIS PRESS (II), 240 Thompson Ave., East Liverpool OH 43920, founded 1994, editor/publisher Mark Hartenbach. *Wooden Head Review* is a biannual journal containing poetry, b&w artwork and very short or "flash" fiction. **They want "street level, honest, surreal, outsider, insane poems; also Dada/Beat, experimental and visual poetry. No academic or rhyming work."** They have recently published poetry by Charles Plymell, Gerald Locklin, Mark Weber, Steve Richmond and John M. Bennett. As a sample the editor selected these lines from "poem for the 21st century" by ron androla:

> In early 90s we dissolve uranium, pack faster cigarettes, pity
> mass indiscriminate murderers, burn poets in hell-fire ignorance
> & declare art be moderately commercial & significant to billionaires
> thumbs of society pinch aids-infested pimples popping into citizens'
> wounds who petition the lord with public prayer

WHR is 44 pgs., digest-sized, saddle-stapled with b&w art. They receive about 2,000 poems a year, accept approximately 10%. Press run is 300. **Sample postpaid: $4. Make checks payable to Mark Hartenbach. Submit 5-10 poems at a time. Previously published poems OK. No simultaneous submissions. Cover letter preferred. "We would like to know about writers, what motivates their art. No lengthy credits."** Seldom comments on rejections. **Reports in approximately 2-3 months. Pays 1 copy. Acquires first or one-time rights.** Non Compos Mentis Press

---

ALWAYS include a self-addressed, stamped envelope (SASE) when sending a ms or query to a publisher within your own country. When sending material to other countries, include a self-addressed envelope and International Reply Coupons (IRCs), available for purchase at many post offices.

publishes 6 chapbooks a year. They also publish poetry in broadsides and on postcards. Chapbooks are usually 20-30 pgs., digest-sized with card stock cover and b&w art. **"Chapbook submissions are generally selected from previous contributors, friendships with poets and collaborations." Replies to queries in 2 weeks, mss in 1-2 months. Pays 30 author's copies (out of a press run of 100). For sample chapbooks, send $2.**

WOODLEY MEMORIAL PRESS; THE ROBERT GROSS MEMORIAL PRIZE FOR POETRY (IV-Regional), English Dept., Washburn University, Topeka KS 66621, phone (913)234-1032, founded 1980, editor Robert Lawson, publishes 1-2 flat-spined paperbacks a year, **collections of poets from Kansas or with Kansas connections, "terms individually arranged with author on acceptance of ms."** They have recently published *Looking for the Pale Eagle* by Stephen Meats and *Killing Seasons* by Christopher Cokinos. As a sample the editor selected these lines from "Crows" in *Gathering Reunion* by David Tangeman:

> *A wintering of crows descended to roost*
> *in sheltering mulberries that, row by row,*
> *shield from north wind the clapboard house*
> *situated hard on the eastern section road.*
>
> *Their dark presence in the windbreak*
> *invaded the goosedown comforter and*
> *sent gloom into the sleeping floorboards*

Samples may be individually ordered from the press for $5. Replies to queries in 2 weeks, to mss in 2 months. Time between acceptance and publication is 1 year. Send SASE for guidelines for Robert Gross Memorial Poetry and Fiction Prize ($100 and publication).

WOODNOTES (I, IV-Form), 248 Beach Park Blvd., Foster City CA 94404, phone (415)571-9428, e-mail welchm@aol.com, founded 1989, editor Michael Dylan Welch (who is also editor/publisher of Press Here). *Woodnotes* is published quarterly. **"We want to see striking and engaging haiku, senryu, tanka and haibun. We don't want to see unrelated forms."** They have recently published work by Jeff Witkin, Cherie Hunter Day, Helen K. Davie and Ronan. As a sample the editor selected this piece of his own:

> *clicking off the late movie . . .*
> *the couch cushion*
> *reinflates*

The editor says *Woodnotes* is 44-56 pgs., 5½×8½, offset printed and saddle-stapled with cover art and some interior illustrations. They receive about 4,000 poems a year, accept approximately 12%. Press run is 300 for 240 subscribers of which 8 are libraries. Subscription: $16. **Sample postpaid: $5. Inquire about international rates. "We accept no more than two poems per person per issue."** No previously published poems or simultaneous submissions. Cover letter preferred. Queries and submissions accepted via e-mail. Often comments on rejections. Reports usually in 1-2 weeks. Acquires first North American serial rights. There is no payment, other than the best poem in each issue receives $10.** They review haiku-related poetry books in anywhere from 100 to 1,000 words. Reviews are usually assigned or done by the editors, but they are open to unsolicited reviews. Poets may also send books for review consideration. The editor says, "Haiku in English is a brief, one-breath form of poetry using objective words to convey heightened subjective feeling about nature and human nature. Read William J. Higginson's *Haiku Handbook*, Cor van den Heuvel's *The Haiku Anthology* and Bruce Ross's *Haiku Moment* for a good introduction to haiku and examples in English. We welcome submissions from beginning and advanced haiku poets."

WORCESTER REVIEW; WORCESTER COUNTY POETRY ASSOCIATION, INC. (II, IV-Regional), 6 Chatham St., Worcester MA 01609, phone (508)797-4770, founded 1973, managing editor Rodger Martin. *WR* appears annually with emphasis on poetry. **New England writers are encouraged to submit, though work by other poets is used also. They want "work that is crafted, intuitively honest and empathetic, not work that shows the poet little respects his work or his readers."** They have published poetry by Kathleen Spivack, Bruce Weigl and Walter McDonald. As a sample the editor selected these lines from "At the Conservatory of Flowers" by Chris Gompert:

> *In the snug greenhouse air, water drips down leaves*
> *of* Quisqualis Indicia—*Rangoon Creeper vine*
> *that rambles overhead. Lapping at my feet*
> *are heart-shaped Brazilian Prayer Plants. I stop,*
> (To be a real flower, you must be a sunflower) . . .

WR is 160 pgs., 6×9, flat-spined, professionally printed in dark type on quality stock with glossy card cover. Press run is 1,000 for 300 subscribers of which 50 are libraries, 300 shelf sales. Subscription: $20 (includes membership in WCPA). **Sample postpaid: $5. Submit maximum of 5 poems at a time. "I recommend 3 or less for most favorable readings." Simultaneous submissions OK "if** indicated." Previously published poems "only on special occasions." Editor comments on rejections "if ms warrants a response." Send SASE for guidelines. Reports in 4-6 months. Pays 2 copies. Buys first rights. They have an annual contest for poets who live, work, or in some way (past/present) have a Worcester County connection. The editor advises, "Read some. Listen a lot."

‡**THE WORD WORKS; THE WASHINGTON PRIZE (II)**, P.O. Box 42164, Washington DC 20015, founded 1974, poetry editors Karren Alenier, J.H. Beall, Hilary Tham and Robert Sargent, "is a nonprofit literary organization publishing contemporary poetry in single author editions usually in collaboration with a visual artist. We sponsor an ongoing poetry reading series, educational programs, the Capital Collection—publishing metropolitan Washington D.C. poets, and the Washington Prize— an award of $1,000 for a book-length manuscript by a living American poet." Previous winners include *Tipping Point* by Fred Marchant, *Stalking the Florida Panther* by Enid Shomer, *Farewell to the Body* by Barbara Moore, *Sun, Moon, Salt* by Nancy White and *The CutOff* by Jay Rogoff. Submission open to any American writer except those connected with Word Works. Send SASE for rules. Entries accepted between February 1 and March 1. Postmark deadline is March 1. They publish perfect-bound paperbacks and occasional anthologies and want **"well-crafted poetry, open to most forms and styles (though not political themes particularly). Experimentation welcomed."** As a sample the editors selected these lines from "Crossing the Border" by Linda Lee Harper:

> *If you look carefully,*
> *you will see the tail of those*
> *who trekked out before you.*
> *The messages they send back*
> *. . . tell you nothing is impossible*
> *to offend if you whittle time down*
> *to exquisite trivialities,*
> *each essential outrage . . .*
> *like a charm to ward off good luck,*
> *to fend off reasonable compromise*
> *or precipitous retreat.*

"We want more than a collection of poetry. We care about the individual poems—the craft, the emotional content and the risks taken—but we want manuscripts where one poem leads to the next. We strongly recommend you read the books that have already won the Washington Prize. Buy them, if you can, or ask for your libraries to purchase them. (Not a prerequisite.) **Currently we are only reading unsolicited manuscripts for the Washington Prize."** Simultaneous submissions OK, if so stated. Always sends prepublication galleys. Payment is 15% of run (usually of 500). Send SASE for catalog to buy samples. Occasionally comments on rejections. Their anthology, *The Stones Remember: Native Israeli Poetry*, was a recipient of the Witter Bynner Foundation Award and was selected as an "Outstanding Book" by *Choice* magazine. The editors advise, "Get community support for your work, know your audience and support contemporary literature by buying and reading the small press."

WORDSONG; BOYDS MILLS PRESS (IV-Children/teen/young adult), 815 Church St., Honesdale PA 18431, phone (800)949-7777, founded 1990, editor-in-chief Dr. Bernice E. Cullinan, is the imprint under which Boyds Mills Press (a *Highlights for Children* company) publishes books of poetry for children of all ages. **"Wordsong encourages quality poetry which reflects childhood fun, moral standards and multiculturalism. We are not interested in poetry for adults or that which includes violence or sexuality or promotes hatred."** They have recently published *Where Is the Night Train Going?*, bedtime poems by Eileen Spinelli, and *Baseball, Snakes and Summer Squash*, poems about growing up by Donald Graves. As a sample the editor selected these lines from "Wings" by Spinelli:

> *I have no wings*
> *With which to fly*
> *But I can sail*
> *The sweeping sky*
> *And I can soar*
> *Above the sea*
> *On borrowed wings*
> *Of poetry.*

"Wordsong prefers original work but will consider anthologies and previously published collections. We ask poets to send collections of 30-50 poems with a common theme; please send complete book manuscripts, not single poems. We buy all rights to collections and publish on an advance-and-royalty basis. Wordsong guarantees a response from editors within one month of our receiving submissions or the poet may call us toll free to inquire. Please direct submissions to Beth Troop, manuscript coordinator." Always sends prepublication galleys. Wordsong's *Inner Chimes* received the International Reading Association Teachers' Choice Award. Dr. Cullinan says, "Poetry lies at the heart of the elementary school literature and reading program. In fact, poetry lies right at the heart of children's language learning. Poetry speaks to the heart of a child. We are anxious to find poetry that deals with imagination, wonder, seeing the world in a new way, family relationships, friends, school, nature and growing up."

WORKS MAGAZINE (IV-Science fiction), 12 Blakestones Rd., Slaithwaite, Huddersfield, Yorks HD7 5UQ United Kingdom, phone/fax 01484 842324, founded 1989, editor Dave W. Hughes, is a biannual using "speculative and imaginative fiction and poetry favoring science fiction." They want "**surreal/science fiction poetry. Nothing more than 50 lines. No romance or general work.**" They have published poetry by Andy Darlington, Steve Sneyd, Paul Weinman and Brian Aldiss. The editor says *Works* is 40 pgs., A4, stitched with glossy cover. They receive about 150 poems/year, use 36. Press run is 400 for 200 subscribers of which 4 are libraries, 50 shelf sales. Single copy: £2 (£4.50 for US); 4-issue subscription: £7.50 (£14 US). **No simultaneous submissions. Cover letter required. Disk submissions acceptable: IBM (5¼ or 3½-inch) or Atari 520ST (3½-inch); ASCII files only. Seldom comments on rejections. Send SASE (or SAE and IRC) for guidelines. Reports within a month. Pays 1 copy.** The editor says, "Study the market."

WoRM fEASt!; TAPE WoRM; VIDEO WoRM; KNIGHTMAYOR PRODUCTIONS (II), P.O. Box 519, Westminster MD 21158-0519, *WoRM fEASt!*, an underground monthly, founded 1989, editor Llori Steinberg. *Tape WoRM* is an audio magazine with music, poetry, comedy and more. *Video WoRM* is a video endeavor with movies, visual art, animation, music videos, news events and more. Send SASE for details. For *Wf* they want "**as strange as humanoids can get; no traditional verse, no rhyme (unless it's way off the keister), no haiku, no love poems unless one-sided and morbid/ dark and unusually sickening; and no Christian poetry.**" They have published poetry by Gregory K.H. Bryant, Robert Howington, C.F. Roberts, Bill Shields and Vinnie Van Leer. The editor says *Wf* is usually 32 pgs., saddle-stitched, format size varies, with artwork and photos. "The digest is different every time." Press run is 500. Subscription: $25 for *Tape WoRM;* $20 for *WoRM fEASt!*, when available. **Sample postpaid: $5 (make all checks and any other forms of payment to Llori Steinberg). Submit 1 poem at a time. Previously published poems OK. Cover letter with SASE required;** "don't have to be professional, just state the facts and why you're interested in submitting." **Publishes theme issues. Send SASE for guidelines and upcoming themes. "We report as quickly as we can." Sometimes sends prepublication galleys. Pays 1 copy of *WoRM fEASt!* No payment on *Tape WoRM*; contact for submission guidelines.** Reviews books of poetry. Open to unsolicited reviews. Send books to Llori Steinberg for review consideration. "Sometimes we publish chapbooks for poets' personal use. They buy and they sell." Cost is $100 for 100 chapbooks of under 25 pgs. each. Sponsors contests. Send SASE for details. The editor says, "**We want everything— *Video WoRM* and *Tape WoRM* especially—from serious to sick, profound to profane, from sane to insane, from graceful to gory—get it?**"

WORMWOOD REVIEW PRESS; THE WORMWOOD REVIEW; THE WORMWOOD AWARD (II), P.O. Box 4698, Stockton CA 95204-0698, phone (209)466-8231, founded 1959, poetry editor Marvin Malone. "The philosophy behind *Wormwood*: (i) avoid publishing oneself and personal friends, (ii) avoid being a 'local' magazine and strive for a national and international audience, (iii) seek unknown talents rather than establishment or fashionable authors, (iv) encourage originality by working with and promoting authors capable of extending the existing patterns of Amerenglish literature, (v) avoid all cults and allegiances and the you-scratch-my-back-and-I-will-scratch-yours approach to publishing, (vi) accept the fact that magazine content is more important than format in the long run, (vii) presume a literate audience and try to make the mag readable from the first page to the last, (viii) restrict the number of pages to no more than 40 per issue since only the insensitive and the masochistic can handle more pages at one sitting, (ix) pay bills on time and don't expect special favors in honor of the muse, and lastly and most importantly (x) don't become too serious and righteous." They want "**poetry and prose poetry that communicate the temper and range of human experience in contemporary society; don't want religious poetry and work that descends into bathos; don't want imitative sweet verse. Must be original; any style or school from traditional to ultra experimental, but *must* communicate; 3-600 lines.**" They have published poetry by Ron Koertge, Gerald Locklin, Charles Bukowski and Edward Field. As a sample the editor selected these lines by Peter Bakowski:

> *Store-front Santas*
> *clanging their bells,*
> *forcing the homeless*
> *to beg a little louder.*

Wormwood is a digest-sized quarterly, offset from photoreduced typescript, saddle-stapled. Yellow pages in the center of each issue feature "one poet or one idea." Press run is 700 for 500 subscribers of which 210 are libraries. Subscription: $12. **Sample postpaid: $4. Submit 2-10 poems on as many pages. No previously published poems or simultaneous submissions. Send SASE for guidelines.**

Reports in 2-8 weeks. Pays 2-10 copies of the magazine or cash equivalent ($6-30). Acquires all rights. Returns rights on written request, without cost, provided the magazine is acknowledged whenever reprinted. Reviews books of poetry. For chapbook publication, no query; send 40-60 poems. "Covering letter not necessary—decisions are made solely on merit of submitted work." Reports in 1-2 months. Pays 35 copies or cash equivalent ($105). Send $4 for samples or check libraries. They offer the Wormwood Award to the Most Overlooked Book of Worth (poetry or prose) for a calendar year, judged by Marvin Malone. Comments on rejections if the work has merit. The editor advises, "Have something to say. Read the past and modern 'master' poets. Absorb what they've done, but then write as effectively as you can in your own style. If you can say it in 40 words, do *not* use 400 or 4,000 words."

‡**THE WRITE WAY (I, IV-Writing); TAKING CARE OF YOURSELF (I, IV-Health concerns); ANN'S ENTERPRISES**, 810 Overhill Rd., Deland FL 32720-1440, founded 1988, editor Ann Larberg. *TWW* is a quarterly using **poems of up to 20 lines on the theme of writing.** As a sample the editor selected "Limerick Lamentation" by Donna Bickley:

> Composing a limerick's not easy
> Although my attempts make me queasy,
> I jot down a line, I stretch for a rhyme.
> Reaching as far as it pleases me.

TWW is an 8-page newsletter with articles on writing and ads. Single copy: $3; subscription: $12. **Sample free with SASE. Must include $1 reading fee and SASE with submissions (up to 5 poems). Do not submit in summer. Reads submissions January 1 through June 30. Publishes theme issues. Send SASE for upcoming themes. Reports in 6 weeks. Pays 2 copies.** Open to unsolicited reviews. Poets may also send books for review consideration. They hold contests quarterly and publish an annual holiday poetry edition with cash awards. *Taking Care of Yourself*, a 4-page newsletter of well-being, is also published quarterly and **accepts 1-2 short poems/issue on the theme of health. Sample free with SASE. Pays copies.**

THE WRITER; POET TO POET (I, II), 120 Boylston St., Boston MA 02116-4615, founded 1887. This monthly magazine for writers has a quarterly instructional column, "Poet to Poet," to which poets may submit previously unpublished work for possible publication and comment. Subscription: $28 (introductory offer: 5 issues for $10). Single copy: $3.50 back issues; $2.50 newsstand. **Submit no more than 3 poems, no longer than 30 lines each, not on onion skin or erasable bond, name and address on each page, one poem to a page. Send SASE for guidelines only; do not send SASE with submission. There is no pay and mss are not acknowledged or returned.** Acquires first North American serial rights.

WRITERS' CENTER PRESS; THE FLYING ISLAND; WRITERS' CENTER OF INDIANAPOLIS (II, IV-Regional), P.O. Box 88386, Indianapolis IN 46208, phone (317)929-0625, founded 1979, executive director Jim Powell. Writers' Center Press publishes *The Flying Island*, a biannual of fiction, poetry, reviews and literary commentary by those **living in or connected to Indiana. They want poetry of high literary quality; no stylistic or thematic restrictions.** They have published poetry by Jared Carter, Alice Friman, Yusef Komunyakaa and Roger Mitchell. As a sample the editor selected these lines from "Snapshot: Father Washing the Dog" by Karen I. Jaquish:

> The reek of Sergeant's Flea Soap stings.
> Our dog is lathered into placid acceptance.
> You glance up, toss that famous grin
> given to strangers and Kodak cameras.

TFI, a 24-page tabloid, includes artwork, graphics and photography. They receive about 1,000 poems a year, accept approximately 5%. Press run is 1,000 for 500 subscribers. **Submit 3 poems at a time. Previously published poems OK, but not encouraged. Simultaneous submissions OK, if so advised. Brief bio required. Often comments on rejections. Send SASE for guidelines. Reports in 3-6 months. Pays $5 minimum for previously unpublished work. Buys first North American serial rights.** Staff reviews books of poetry. Send books for review consideration. The center sponsors frequent contests for members through its quarterly newsletter and open readings. They advise, "Balance solitary writing time by getting involved in a writing community. We frequently recommend rejected writers join a poetry workshop."

WRITER'S DIGEST (IV-Writing, humor); WRITER'S DIGEST WRITING COMPETITION (II), 1507 Dana Ave., Cincinnati OH 45207, phone (513)531-2222, founded 1921, assistant editor Amanda Boyd, is a monthly magazine for writers—fiction, nonfiction, poetry and drama. "All editorial copy is aimed at helping writers to write better and become more successful. **Poetry is included in 'The Writing Life' section of *Writer's Digest* only. Preference is given to short, light verse concerning 'the writing life'—the foibles, frenzies, delights and distractions inherent in being a writer. Serious verse is acceptable; however, no poetry unrelated to writing. Please avoid**

the trite or maudlin." **Preferred length: 4-20 lines.** The magazine has published poetry by Charles Ghigna. As a sample the editors selected this poem, "Mixed Messages," by Lois McBride Terry:

> *"As a poet, you're no Poe."*
> *"At prose, you're certainly not a pro."*
> *"Your movie script is nondescript.*
> *(And sadder still, your comic strip.)"*
> *The only line they don't reject:*
> *"Enclosed is my subscription check."*

They use a maximum of 2 short poems/issue, about 15/year of the 1,500 submitted. *Writer's Digest* has a circulation of 240,000. Subscription: $27. **Sample postpaid: $3.50. Do not submit to Michael Bugeja, poetry columnist for the magazine. Submit to Amanda Boyd, assistant editor, each poem on a separate page, no more than 8/submission. Previously published poems and simultaneous submissions OK if acknowledged in cover letter. Editor comments on rejections "when we want to encourage or explain decision." Send SASE for guidelines and/or reply. Reports in 3-6 weeks. Always sends prepublication galleys. Pays $15-50/poem plus 1 copy.** Poetry up to 32 lines on any theme is eligible for the annual Writer's Digest Writing Competition. Watch magazine for information, or send a SASE for a copy of the contest's rules. Deadline: May 31. (Also see Writer's Digest Books under Publications Useful to Poets.)

WRITER'S EXCHANGE; R.S.V.P. PRESS (I); NEW MARKETS, Box 394, Society Hill SC 29593-0394, phone (803)378-4556, founded 1983, editor Gene Boone, is a quarterly newsletter of articles on any aspect of writing, poetry and artwork with a special emphasis on beginners. He wants **"poetry to 24 lines, any subject or style. I also consider short poems such as haiku, tanka, senryu and other fixed forms. I like writing that is upbeat, positive, enlightening or inspiring, especially humorous poetry. I will not consider material that is anti-religious, racist or obscene."** He has recently published poetry by Victor Chapman, Diane L. Krueger, Sarah Jensen and Teresa A. Goldwater. As a sample he selected these lines (poet unidentified):

> *A hurried world, spinning too fast*
> *Modern technology replaces dreams*
> *With skyscraper nightmares*
> *God watches as we dance at Satan's feet.*

WE is 24 pgs., digest-sized, saddle-stitched, with a colored paper cover. He accepts about half or more of the poetry received. Press run is 250. Subscription: $10. **Sample postpaid: $2. Submit 3-10 poems at a time. "I prefer typed mss, one poem per page, readable. Poets should always proofread mss before sending them out. Errors can cause rejection." No simultaneous submissions. Previously published poetry OK. Cover letter required; list "prior credits, if any, and other details of writing background."** Time between acceptance and publication is 4 months. **Send SASE for guidelines. Reports in 2-4 weeks. Pays 1 copy. Acquires one-time rights.** Staff reviews books of poetry. Send books for review consideration. They offer cash awards for quarterly contests sponsored through the magazine. Send SASE for current rules. In 1995 they began publishing *New Markets*, a newsletter featuring information on small press and New Age markets. Send SASE for details. The editor says he comments on rejections, "if I feel it will benefit the poet in the long run, never anything too harsh or overly discouraging." His advice to poets: "Support the small press publications you read and enjoy. Without your support these publications will cease to exist. The small press has given many poets their start. In essence, the small press is where poetry lives!"

WRITERS' FORUM (II, IV-Regional), Dept. PM, University of Colorado, Colorado Springs CO 80933-7150, founded 1974, poetry editor Victoria McCabe. *Writers' Forum*, an annual, publishes both beginning and well-known writers, giving **"some emphasis to contemporary Western literature**, that is, to representation of living experience west of the 100th meridian in relation to place and culture. We collaborate with authors in the process of revision, reconsider and frequently publish revised work. We are open to **solidly crafted imaginative work that is verbally interesting and reveals authentic voice. We would like to see more formal work, nicely executed."** They have published poems by William Stafford, David Ray, Kenneth Fields, Harold Witt and Judson Crews. The annual is 225 pgs., digest-sized, professionally printed with matte card cover, flat-spined, using 40-50 pgs. of poetry in each issue. They use about 25 of 500 submissions of poetry/year. Circulation 800 with 100 subscriptions of which 25 are libraries. **The list price is $8.95 but they offer it at $5.95 to readers of *Writer's Digest*. Submit 3-5 poems at a time with SASE. No previously published poems; simultaneous submissions OK, if acknowledged. Reads submissions September 1 through March 15. Reports in 3 months. Pays 1 copy. Acquires all rights, but returns them.**

WRITERS FORUM; AND MAGAZINE (IV-Form), 89A Petherton Rd., London N5 2QT England, phone (0171)226-2657, founded 1963, editor Bob Cobbing, is a small press publisher of experimental work including sound and visual poetry in cards, leaflets, chapbooks, occasional paperbacks and a magazine. **"Explorations of 'the limits of poetry' including 'graphic' displays, notations for**

sound and performance, as well as semantic and syntactic developments, not to mention fun."
They have recently published poetry by Lawrence Upton, Robert Sheppard and Patricia Farrell, Serge
Segay, Rea Nikonova and Bill Griffiths. As a sample the editor selected these lines by Maggie O'Sulli-
van:

> hey-go-merry-go-higgledy Hurling
> REMEMBRANCER - (herited . here/it'd . here it is .
> heretic . heresies . here she is . here her is . in
> her it .) -
>
> Inheritances
> In Here She Dances

The magazine is published "irregularly" and uses "very little unsolicited poetry; practically none."
Press run "varies." **Submit 6 poems at a time. "We normally don't publish previously published
work." Work should generally be submitted camera-ready. Pays 2 copies, additional copies at
half price.** Under the imprint Writers Forum they publish 12-18 books a year averaging 28 pgs.
**Samples and listing: $5. For book publication, query with 6 samples, bio, publications. Pays 12
copies, additional copies at half price.** The editor says, "We publish only that which surprises and
excites us; poets who have a very individual voice and style."

WRITER'S JOURNAL (I, II), P.O. Box 25376, St. Paul MN 55125, phone (612)730-4280, founded
1980, poetry editor Esther M. Leiper. *Writer's Journal* is a bimonthly magazine "for writers and poets
that offers advice and guidance, motivation, inspiration, to the more serious and published writers and
poets." Esther Leiper has 2 columns: "Esther Comments," which specifically critiques poems sent in
by readers, and "Every Day with Poetry," which discusses a wide range of poetry topics, often—but
not always—including readers' work. She says, **"I enjoy a variety of poetry: free verse, strict forms,
concrete, Oriental. But we take nothing vulgar, preachy or sloppily written. Since we appeal to
those of different skill levels, some poems are more sophisticated than others, but those accepted
must move, intrigue or otherwise positively capture me.** 'Esther Comments' is never used as a
negative force to put a poem or a poet down. Indeed, I focus on the best part of a given work and
seek to suggest means of improvement on weaker aspects. **Short is best: 25-line limit, though *very*
occasionally we use longer. 3-4 poems at a time is just right."** They have published poetry by
Lawrence Schug, Diana Sutliff and Eugene E. Grollmes. As a sample the editor selected these lines
from "an unidentified author we'd love to hear from":

> I am with Haysie again on God's ranch,
> It is not yet dawn; we ride west
> over the mountains. His face is in shadow
> but I know it is Haysie because
> I have loved his shadow so.

Writer's Journal is 64 pgs. (including paper cover), magazine-sized, professionally printed, using 4-
5 pgs. of poetry in each issue, including columns. Circulation is 51,000. They receive about 400
submissions/year of which they use 30-40 (including those used in Esther's columns). **Sample postpaid: $4. No query. Reports in 4-5 months. Pays 25¢/line.** The magazine also has quarterly poetry
contests for previously unpublished poetry. Deadlines: February 28, April 15, August 15 and November
30. Reading fee for each contest: $2 first poem, $1 each poem thereafter.

WRITER'S LIFELINE (I), P.O. Box 1641, Cornwall, Ontario K6H 5V6 Canada, phone (613)932-
2135, fax (613)932-7735, founded 1974, editor Stephen Gill, published 3 times a year, containing
articles and information useful to writers, **poetry** and book reviews. **"We prefer poems on social
concerns. We avoid sex."** As a sample the editor selected these lines from his poem, "Bigotry":

> It grows
> on the babel of confusion
> in the lap of
> the blinding dust of vanity
> by the arrogant prince of ignorance.

WL is 36-40 pgs., digest-sized, saddle-stitched with 2-color paper cover, printed in small type, poems
sometimes in bold or italics. Circulation is 1,500. Subscription: $18. **Sample postpaid: $3. Publishes
theme issues. Send SASE for guidelines and upcoming themes. Responds in 1 month. Pays 3
copies. Acquires first North American serial rights.** Reviews books of poetry in 500-1,500 words.
"We need book reviews." Query if interested.

WRITER'S WORLD; MAR-JON PUBLICATIONS (III), 204 E. 19th St., Big Stone Gap VA
24219-1322, phone (540)523-0830, fax (540)523-5757, founded 1990, editor Gainelle Murray, poetry
editor Diane L. Krueger (**submissions should go directly to her at 17 Oswego Ave., Rockaway NJ
07866, phone (201)627-0439, fax (201)627-3314**). *Writer's World* is a bimonthly literary publication
presenting poetry, articles and columns on writing. **They want "avant-garde, free verse, light verse,**

traditional, 12-16 lines. **No erotica nor anything mentioning violence, abortion or drug abuse."**
They have published poetry by Joyce Carbone, Denise Martinson, William J. White and Arthur C.
Ford. As a sample the editor selected the opening lines of "The Poet" by Linda J. Crider:

> Bits of memory
> Ideas and dreams,
> Running in sunlight
> Dancing in moonbeams
> Floating through tomorrow
> On gossamer wings.

WW is 24 pgs., 8½×11, typeset and saddle-stapled with glossy paper cover, clip art and ads. They
receive 300-500 poems a year, accept approximately 15%. Press run is 3,600 for 3,100 subscribers of
which 2% are libraries. Single copy: $4.50; subscription: $15. **Sample: $3.50 and 9×12 SAE with
$1.01 postage. Submit 3-5 poems at a time, none untitled. Previously published poems OK; no
simultaneous submissions. Cover letter required. "Submissions without name and address on
each page and a SASE will not be read or returned." Poets may submit work and requests via
fax.** Time between acceptance and publication is 6-12 months. **Often comments on rejections. Send
SASE for guidelines and upcoming themes. Reports in 2 months. Pays $5 for poetry used on the
front cover; all others receive 2 copies. Buys one-time rights.** The editor says, "We have a critique
service with subscribers given reduced rates. Write for more information."

‡**WRITES OF PASSAGE (I, IV-Teens)**, 817 Broadway, 6th Floor, New York NY 10003, phone
(212)473-7564, e-mail wpusa@aol.com, website http://www.writes.org, founded 1994, editor/publisher
Laura Hoffman, is a biannual literary journal for teenagers across the country. **They only publish
poems by teenagers (12-19). "We accept all topics and forms, but do not want poems longer than
3 pages."** As a sample the editor selected these lines from "One Last Breath" by Nathan Mackin:

> Used to be a good son,
> white shirt and tie,
> but found myself drowning,
> while others passed by,
> drowning in the drug
> of a loving hate,
> drowning in myself,
> guilty minds, too late.

Writes of Passage is 100 pgs., 5½×8½, professionally printed and perfect-bound with semiglossy
color cover. They receive about 2,000 poems a year, accept about 100. Press run is 2,500 for 400
subscribers of which 100 are libraries, 1,500 shelf sales. Subscription: $12. **Sample postpaid: $6.
Make checks payable to Writes of Passage USA, Inc. Submit up to 5 poems at a time. Previously
published poems OK; no simultaneous submissions. Cover letter with brief bio (2-3 lines) preferred. Three editors review poems. Seldom comments on rejections. Send SASE for guidelines
or request via e-mail. Reports in 6-8 weeks. Sometimes sends prepublication galleys. Pays 2
copies.** Writes of Passage USA is a nonprofit educational organization dedicated to providing teenagers
with a forum for their creative writing. In addition to publishing the literary journal, they also occasionally conduct workshops and organize readings. The editor says, "We also accept tips and advice on
writing poetry by authors and educators."

WRITING FOR OUR LIVES; RUNNING DEER PRESS (I, II, IV-Women), 647 N. Santa
Cruz Ave., The Annex, Los Gatos CA 95030-4350, founded 1991, editor/publisher Janet McEwan,
appears twice a year. "*Writing For Our Lives* serves as a vessel for poems, short fiction, stories,
letters, autobiographies and journal excerpts from the life stories, experiences and spiritual journeys
of women." They want **poetry that is "personal, women's real life, life-saving, autobiographical,
serious—but don't forget humorous, silence-breaking, many styles, many voices. Women writers
only, please."** They have recently published poetry by Sylvia Berta Alaniz, Louise V. Jeffredo, Sandy
J. Austin, River Wolton and Mildred Tremblay. As a sample the editor selected these lines from
"Interview With the Reluctant Woman" by Marilyn Manzanita:

> After that his pulse faded.
> I held his hand,
> the hand that brushed my nipple hours before.
> It was cold.
>
> He died about 5 AM.
>
> Forgive me if I can't recall every detail . . .

Writing For Our Lives is 80 pgs., 5¼×8¼, printed on recycled paper and perfect-bound with matte
card cover. They receive about 400 poems a year, accept approximately 5%. Press run is 1,000.
Subscription: $11.50 individuals, $14 institutions. **Sample postpaid: $6.50. Submit 1-5 typed poems**

with name and phone number on each page. Previously published poems ("sometimes") and simultaneous submissions OK. Include 2 self-addressed stamped envelopes; "at least one of them should be sufficient to return manuscripts if you want them returned." Closing dates are February 15 and August 15. Usually reports in 1-3 days, occasionally longer. "As we are now shaping 2-4 issues in advance, we may ask to hold certain poems for later consideration over a period of 18 to 24 months." Seldom comments on rejections. Send SASE for guidelines. Pays 2 copies, discount on additional copies and discount on 1-year subscription. Acquires first world-wide English language serial (or one-time reprint) rights. The editor says, "Our contributors and circulation are international."

WYRD (IV-Psychic/occult), P.O. Box 624, Monroeville PA 15146-0624, founded 1986, "editrix" Goldie Brown, is a quarterly now publishing only poetry. They want **poetry about magick, the occult, mystical experiences, nature or spirituality—no longer than 45 lines.** They have recently published poetry by Fletcher de Wolf, Victor Anderson, Brian Walker and Crayton Divination Moody. As a sample the editor selected these lines from "Rainbow Eclipse" by jon Eric:

> Temple of the Golden Sun
> Silver Moon, Brazen Twin
> Garden of the Emerald Earth
> Turquoise Sea, Indigo Sky
> Chalice of the Violet Flame
> Ruby Blood, Umbar Flesh

WYRD is 16 pgs., 8½×11, side stapled, with art and graphics. They receive about 200 poems a year, use approximately 40%. Press run is 150 for 100 subscribers. Subscription: $20. **Sample postpaid: $5. Submit 2 poems at a time. No previously published poems; simultaneous submissions OK. Cover letter required. Reports in 2 months. Pays 1 copy.** Reviews related books of poetry in 150-200 words, single format.

XANADU; POETIMES; LONG ISLAND POETRY COLLECTIVE (II), % LIPC, P.O. Box 773, Huntington NY 11743, founded 1979, editors Lois V. Walker, Mildred Jeffrey, Sue Kain and Weslea Sidon, is an annual publishing "serious poems and an occasional, adventuresome essay on contemporary poetry or critical theory." They want **"well-crafted quality poems. Nothing inspirational, obscene or from beginners."** They have published poetry by Philip Dacey, Diana Chang, Simon Perchik, Louis David Brodsky and Ioanna-Veronika Warwick. As a sample the editors selected these lines from "Sex, Genetics, The Sea" by Charles Entrekin:

> Like falling backwards in time
> toward something I don't comprehend,
> if I run forward, if I stand still,
> what I see has no name,
> slouches away if I look at it,
> yet feel in the touch of bones . . .

The editors describe the journal as 55-65 pgs., no ads, no graphics. Press run is 300 for 100 subscribers of which 5 are libraries. **Sample postpaid: $7. No previously published poems; simultaneous submissions OK. Poems must be typed. Seldom comments on rejections. Send #10 SASE for guidelines. Reports in 2 weeks to 4 months. Pays 1 copy. Acquires first North American serial rights.** The Long Island Poetry Collective also publishes *Poetimes*, a bimonthly newsletter edited by Binnie Pasquier that includes an extensive calendar of poetry events on Long Island, contests, market listings and poetry by its members. Subscription: $18/year, includes membership in LIPC and subscription to *Xanadu*. They say, "We would be glad to look at more quality post-modernist and formalist poetry."

XIB; XIB PUBLICATIONS (II), P.O. Box 262112, San Diego CA 92126-2112, phone (619)298-4927, fax (619)278-5101, founded 1990, editor tolek, appears irregularly, usually annually, publishing poetry, short fiction and b&w artwork and photos. **They want poetry of any form, length, subject, style or purpose. "Prefer 'quirky' things, however."** They have published poetry by Christine C. Brown, Sheila E. Murphy and Judson Crews. As a sample the editor selected these lines from "Scarecrow" by Arthur G. Gottlieb:

> My fingers tremble on the bolt,
> but if I let him in, the ravens
> will eat my eyes in revenge.

xib is 60 pgs., 6½×8½, photocopied on heavy bond, saddle-stapled, 12 pt. gloss mimeo cover, 80% illustrated with art and photos, some ads. They receive about 3,000 poems a year, use approximately 3%. Press run is 500 for 50 subscribers of which a third are libraries, 350 shelf sales. Subscription: $10 for 2 issues and a chapbook. **Sample postpaid: $5, back issues $4; make checks payable to tolek. Submit 5-7 poems at a time. Previously published poems and simultaneous submissions OK. Cover letter preferred. "Work sent without a cover letter will be read but may be returned without comment." Fax submissions OK. Seldom comments on rejections. "Guidelines, broad-**

sides and tearsheets available for SASE." Reports in 3-5 weeks. Pays 1 copy. Acquires one-time rights. xib publications **publishes 1-2 chapbooks/year, "irregularly and arbitrarily. Please do not query or submit with chapbook intent. Most chaps form out of friendly joint-efforts."** Press run for chapbooks is about 75-100. Authors receive half; the rest goes to subscribers, reviewers and trades. The editor says, "Cover letters tell me by their content how formal/informal the submission is, and how I respond to it. People show their personality, I show mine."

‡XIQUAN PUBLISHING HOUSE; THE PARADOXIST LITERARY MOVEMENT JOURNAL; THE PARADOXIST MOVEMENT ASSOCIATION (IV-Form), 2456 S. Rose Peak Dr., Tucson AZ 85710-6122, founded 1990, editor Florentin Smarandache. *The Paradoxist Literary Movement Journal* is an annual journal of "avant-garde poetry, experiments, poems without verses, literature beyond the words, anti-language, non-literature and its literature, as well as the sense of the non-sense; revolutionary forms of poetry." They want **"avant-garde poetry, 1-2 pages, any subject, any style (lyrical experiments). No classical, fixed forms."** They have published poetry by Teresinka Pereira, Titu Popescu, Ion Rotaru, Michéle de LaPlante and Claude LeRoy. As a sample here is "Dear Deer" from *Nonpoems* by the editor:

> - Hear, here!
>   Buy, by
>   our hour,
>   four fore
>   pears pairs!
> - Sun son,
>   no! Know
>   two, too!
> - Hi! Hie!

The editor says *TPLM* is 52 pgs., digest-sized, offset, soft cover. Press run is 500. "It is distributed to its collaborators, U.S. and Canadian university libraries and the Library of Congress as well as European, Chinese, Indian and Japanese libraries." **No previously published poems or simultaneous submissions. Do not submit mss in the summer. "We do not return published or unpublished poems or notify the author of date of publication." Reports in 3-6 months. Pays 1-2 copies.** Xiquan Publishing House also publishes 2 paperbacks and **1-2 chapbooks/year, including translations. The poems must be unpublished and must meet the requirements of the Paradoxist Movement Association. Replies to queries in 1-2 months, to mss in 3-6 months. Pays 50 author's copies. Inquire about sample books.** They say, "We mostly receive traditional or modern verse, but not avant-garde (very different from any previously published verse). We want anti-literature and its literature, style of the non-style, poems without poems, non-words and non-sentence poems, very upset free verse, intelligible unintelligible language, impersonal texts personalized, transformation of the abnormal to the normal. Make literature from everything; make literature from nothing!"

YALE UNIVERSITY PRESS; THE YALE SERIES OF YOUNGER POETS COMPETITION (III), P.O. Box 209040, New Haven CT 06520-9040, founded 1919, poetry editor (Yale University Press) Richard Miller. The Yale Series of Younger Poets Competition is **open to poets under 40 who have not had a book previously published. Submit ms of 48-64 pgs. in February. Entry fee: $15. Send SASE for rules and guidelines.** Poets are not disqualified by previous publication of limited editions of no more than 300 copies or previously published poems in newspapers and periodicals, which may be used in the book ms if so identified. Previous winners include Richard Kenney, Carolyn Forché and Robert Hass.

‡THE YALOBUSHA REVIEW (II), P.O. Box 186, University MS 38677, e-mail yalobush@sunset.backbone.olemiss.edu, founded 1995, poetry editor J.E. Pitti, is an annual literary magazine of the University of Mississippi. **They want "high quality, professional material. No limericks, long prose poems or poems over 10 pages."** As a sample the editor selected these lines from "The Weather of Escape" by David Powell:

> And leaving around the curve of Africa,
> you throw one wink in an arc edged
> with expense startlingly full and bare
> to return will last like moths.

The Yalobusha Review is about 100 pgs., 5½ × 8½, perfect-bound with matte card cover. They receive about 200 poems a year, accept approximately 10%. Press run is 500. **Sample postpaid: $6. Submit 6 poems at a time. No previously published poems; simultaneous submissions OK. Short cover letter preferred. Reads submissions October 1 through March 1. Poems are circulated to an editorial board. Seldom comments on rejections. Send SASE for guidelines. Reports in up to 6 months. Pays 2 copies.** Also gives an Editor's Choice Award of $100 for the best fiction and poetry of the issue.

YANKEE MAGAZINE; YANKEE ANNUAL POETRY CONTEST (II), P.O. Box 520, Dublin NH 03444-0520, phone (603)563-8111, founded in 1935, poetry editor (since 1955) Jean Burden. Though it has a New England emphasis, the poetry is not necessarily about New England or by New Englanders, and it has a national distribution of more than 700,000 subscribers. They want to see **"high quality contemporary poems in either free verse or traditional form. Does not have to be regional in theme. Any subject acceptable, provided it is in good taste. We look for originality in thought, imagery, insight—as well as technical control."** They do not want poetry that is "cliché-ridden, banal verse." They have published poetry by Maxine Kumin, Liz Rosenberg, Josephine Jacobsen, Nancy Willard, Linda Pastan, Paul Zimmer and Hayden Carruth. As a sample the editor selected these lines from "Waking" by Joan LaBombard:

> But blood's in thrall to the world
> and the body's bound
> by its clocks and invisible pulleys—
> sun plucking at bedclothes,
> a mockingbird's ultimatum.
> I reenter the world's cage, the house
> of my daylight body.
> My blood discovers its old riverbed,
> and my name remembers me.

The monthly is 6×9, 144 pgs., professionally printed, saddle-stapled, using full-color and b&w ads and illustrations, with full-color glossy paper cover. They receive over 30,000 submissions a year, accept about 50-60 poems, use 4-5 poems/monthly issue. Subscription: $22. **Submit no more than 6 poems up to 30 lines each, free verse or traditional. No simultaneous submissions or previously published poems.** "Cover letters are interesting if they include previous publication information." Submissions without SASE "are tossed." Editor comments on rejections "only if poem has so many good qualities it only needs minor revisions." Reports in 2-3 weeks. Approximately 18-month backlog. Pays $50/poem, all rights; $35, first magazine rights. Sponsors an annual poetry contest judged by a prominent New England poet and published in the February issue, with awards of $150, $100 and $50 for the best 3 poems in the preceding year. Jean Burden advises, "Study previous issues of *Yankee* to determine the kind of poetry we want. Get involved in poetry workshops at home. Read the best contemporary poetry you can find."

YARROW, A JOURNAL OF POETRY (II), English Dept., Lytle Hall, Kutztown State University, Kutztown PA 19530, founded 1981, editor Harry Humes, appears twice a year. They have published poetry by Gibbons Ruark, Jared Carter, William Pitt Root and Fleda Brown Jackson. It is 40 pgs., 6×9, offset. Press run is 350. Subscription: $5/2 years. **Reports in 1-2 months. Pays 2 copies plus 1-year subscription.** Poetry published in *Yarrow* was also selected for inclusion in a *Pushcart Prize* anthology.

YEFIEF (II), P.O. Box 8505, Santa Fe NM 87504-8505, phone (505)753-3648, fax (505)753-7049, e-mail arr@ifm.com, founded 1993, editor Ann Racuya-Robbins, is an annual designed "to construct a narrative of culture at the end of the century." **They want "innovative visionary work of all kinds."** They have published poetry by Michael Palmer, Simon Perchik and Carla Harryman. As a sample the editor selected these lines from "Tendons, Paragraphs and Milky Way" by Nicole Brossard, translated by Susanne de Lotbiniere-Harwood:

> Everything was within range of the gaze, autumn, the century and the narrative. Truth alone
>   was missing.

Yefief is 176 pgs., 7×9, offset and perfect-bound with color coated card cover and b&w photos, art and graphics inside. Press run is 1,000. Single copy: $7.95. **Submit 3-6 poems at a time. Previously published poems and simultaneous submissions OK. Reports in 6-8 weeks. Pays 2-3 copies.** Open to unsolicited reviews. Poets may also send books for review consideration.

YESTERDAY'S MAGAZETTE (I, IV-Senior citizens), Independent Publishing Co., P.O. Box 15126, Sarasota FL 34277, editor and publisher Ned Burke, founded 1973. This bimonthly magazine is for *"all* nostalgia lovers. *YM* believes that everyone has a yesterday and everyone has a memory to share. Nothing fancy here . . . just 'plain folks' relating their individual life experiences. **We are always seeking new and innovative writers with imagination and promise, and we would like to see more 40s, 50s and 60s pieces."** As a sample here are lines from "The Backyard Pump" by J.E. Coulbourn:

> With two small hands you'd
> grasp the monster's tail
> And try to pump the water in the pail,
> But if his darned esophagus got dry
> No water came no matter how you'd try.

YM is 28 pgs., magazine-sized, saddle-stapled, professionally printed on good stock with glossy color cover. A year's subscription is $15 or 2 years for $25. **Sample: $3. Submissions for "Quills, Quips, & Quotes" (their poetry page) should be "thoughtful, amusing, or just plain interesting for our 'plain folks' readers. No SASE is required as short items are generally not returned nor acknowledged, unless requested by the contributor." Pays copies.**

YOUNG VOICES MAGAZINE; YOUNG VOICES (V, IV-Children), P.O. Box 2321, Olympia WA 98507, phone (360)357-4683, founded 1988, director Steve Charak, poetry editor Emma Russell, is "a magazine of **creative work of elementary through high school students. The age limit is rigid."** It appears every other month. Press run is 2,000 for 1,000 subscribers of which 100 are libraries. Membership/subscription: $20 for 1 year, $35 for 2 years. **Sample postpaid: $4. Query first. No longer accepting unsolicited poetry submissions.** The magazine is published by Young Voices, a nonprofit organization which also offers local workshops for children and publishes a newsletter on children's writing and creativity for parents and teachers. Send SASE for details. Steve Charak says, "Revise. Remember that in a poem, every word counts. Forget about the need to rhyme. Instead, put feeling into each word."

ZEITGEIST (II), P.O. Box 1568, Eureka MT 59917, phone (406)296-3197, fax (406)296-3198, founded 1990, publisher/editor John S. Slack, appears 4 times/year. For poetry, **"best is 1 page or less dealing with personal relationships to world and others. Focused ideas. Disturbing or provocative imagery welcomed. No same old love-death-suicide stuff, graphic sex and/or gratuitous profanity. No blatantly didactic stuff. We want poems that contain truth."** They have recently published poetry by Paul Hadella, Thomasine Reed and Lyn Lifshin. As a sample the editor selected these lines from "Border Town" by Jill Buckner:

> She is seamless, shameless
> and will roll you
> on a bed so coarse welts form
> on the skin, Guatemalan blankets
> whirling around and around.

Zeitgeist is 20-28 pgs., 5×8, offset printed and saddle-stapled. They accept about 10% of poems submitted. Press run is 200 for 40 subscribers of which 3 are libraries. Subscription: $12. **Sample postpaid: $3. Submit up to 10 poems at a time. Previously published poems and simultaneous submissions OK. Cover letter with 3-4 publishing credits preferred.** "A 3-line bio would help us get a feel of who you are." **Editor often comments on rejections. Send SASE for guidelines. Reports in 1-6 months. Pays "each issue in which poet appears."** Open to unsolicited reviews. The editor says, "Keep your eyes, ears and nose open, along with your mind. Don't take rejection personally. Sometimes it takes a while to find your audience. Strive for truth, write lots and send the best."

ZEPHYR PRESS; GLAS: NEW RUSSIAN WRITING (III, IV-Translations), 13 Robinson St., Somerville MA 02145-3698, founded 1980, editors Ed Hogan and Leora Zeitlin. **"We are now publishing very little poetry, and exclusively Russian and Eastern European poetry in translation."** An example publication is *The Complete Poems of Anna Akhmatova*, translations by Judith Hemschemeyer. Their catalog lists books of poetry by Sue Standing, Anne Valley Fox and Miriam Sagan. **Query with 5 sample translations. Simultaneous submissions OK.** "We will respond only if interested." **Pays 10% of press run or by royalty, depending upon the particular project.** Zephyr Press is the North American editorial office for *Glas*. They are particularly interested in translations of living 20th Century Russian poets. Queries submitted to Zephyr are passed on to the publisher in Russia.

ZOLAND BOOKS INC. (III), 384 Huron Ave., Cambridge MA 02138, phone (617)864-6252, founded 1987, publisher Roland Pease, is a "literary press: fiction, poetry, photography, gift books, books of literary interest." **They want "high-quality" poetry, not sentimental.** They have recently published poetry by Joseph Torra, Alice B. Fogel, James Laughlin, William Corbett, Karen Fiser, Patricia Smith and Sam Cornish. They publish 8-10 books/year, flat-spined, averaging 104 pgs. **Query with 5-10 sample poems, bio, publications and SASE. Editor does not comment on submissions. Sometimes sends prepublication galleys. Pays 5-10% royalties plus 5 copies. Buys all rights.**

ZUZU'S PETALS QUARTERLY ONLINE (II), (formerly *Zuzu's Petals Annual*), P.O. Box 156, Whitehall PA 18052, phone (610)821-1324, e-mail: zuzu@epix.net, website http://www.hway.net/ zuzu/index.htm, founded 1992, editor T. Dunn. "We publish high quality fiction, essays, poetry and reviews on our award winning website, which was The NCSA/Mosaic Pick of the Week and is featured in The Whole Internet Catalog Select. Becoming an internet publication allows us to offer thousands of helpful resources and addresses for poets, writers, editors and researchers, as well as to greatly expand our readership. **Free verse, blank verse, experimental, visually sensual poetry, etc. are especially welcome here. We're looking for a freshness of language, new ideas and original expression. No 'June, moon and spoon' rhymed poetry. No light verse. I'm open to considering more feminist, ethnic, alternative poetry, as well as poetry of place."** They have published poetry by

Max Greenberg, Gayle Elen Harvey, Timothy Russell and Sandra Nelson. As a sample the editor selected these lines from Jean-Paul DeVellard:

> *Now I must learn to draw*
> *all over again*
> *struggle to lay claim*
> *to the perfect and last*
> *for all time depiction*
> *of your soft and faithful*
> *universal mouth*

ZPQO averages 70-100 pgs., using full-color artwork, and is an electronic publication available free of charge on the internet. "Many libraries, colleges, and coffeehouses offer access to the internet for those without home internet accounts." They receive about 3,000 poems a year, accept approximately 10%. **A copy of *Zuzu's Petals Poetry Buffet*, a sample of writing from the past 4 years is available for $5. Submit up to 4 poems at a time. Previously published poems and simultaneous submissions OK. "Cover letters are not necessary. The work should speak for itself." Submissions via e-mail are welcome, as well as submissions in ASCII (DOS IBM) format on 3½ disks OK. Seldom comments on rejections. Send SASE for guidelines. Reports in 2 weeks to 2 months. Acquires one-time electronic rights. Back issues are archived on their website.** Staff reviews books of poetry in approximately 200 words. Send books, galleys or proofs for review consideration. They also sponsor twice-yearly poetry contests. Entry fee: $2/poem, any style, length or subject. Deadlines are the first of March and September. 40% of proceeds goes to prize winners: 25% to first prize, 10% to second, 5% to third. Free critiques to honorable mentions. The remaining 60% of proceeds goes towards the publication and allows them to expand their writers' resources on the internet. The editor says, "Read as much poetry as you can. Support the literary arts: Go to poetry readings, read chapbooks and collections of verse. Eat poetry for breakfast, cultivate a love of language, then write!"

Contests and Awards

The opportunities for poets to receive recognition and get work published are growing via the route of contests and awards. And while this section of *Poet's Market* is considerably smaller than Publishers of Poetry, it contains more than two dozen new entries within its 140 "markets."

Here you will find a wide range of competitions—everything from contests with modest prizes sponsored by state poetry societies, colleges or even cities to prestigious awards offered by private foundations. Among the various contests and awards included in this section are those that offer publication in addition to their monetary prizes. And as Poet Max Garland discovered, contests are a more viable means of getting a first book of poetry published. (See the interview with Garland on page 240.) But even if publication is not included, the publicity generated upon winning some of these contests can make your name more familiar to editors.

SELECTING CONTESTS

Whether you're submitting one poem to a quarterly contest sponsored by a journal or an entire manuscript to an award offered by a book publisher, you should never submit to contests and awards blindly. Since many contests require entry fees, blind submissions will just waste your money. As in the Publishers of Poetry section, each listing here contains one or more Roman numerals in its heading. These "codes" will not only help you narrow the list of contests and awards, but they can also help you evaluate your chances of winning (and recouping your expenses).

The **I** code, for instance, is given to contests that are very open to beginners. While these contests may require small fees, or membership in the sponsoring organization, they typically are not exploitive of poets, beginning or otherwise. Keep in mind, however, that if a contest charges a $5 entry fee and offers $75 in prizes, then the organizers only need 15 entries to cover the prizes. Even though fees may also go toward providing a small honorarium for the judge, 100 entries will surely net the organizers a tidy profit—at the expense of the participating poets. Be careful when deciding which of these contests are worth your money.

The **II** code follows the name of general literary contests, usually for poets with some experience. This code may also follow awards for recently published collections, such as The Poets' Prize and the Kingsley Tufts Poetry Award, or fellowships designed for poets of "demonstrated ability," such as the Guggenheims. And competitions like the Great Lakes Colleges Association New Writers Award (new to this edition), a first-book contest that accepts submissions from publishers only, are also listed under this code. If you're just beginning, start building a reputation by having your work accepted by periodicals, then try your hand at these competitions.

Of all the codes, however, perhaps the most useful is **IV**, which designates specialized contests and awards. That is, you—or your poetry—must meet certain criteria to be eligible. Some contests are regional, so only poets from a certain area may enter. For example, fellowships and grants offered by state and provincial arts councils are only open to residents of the particular state or province. Some of these programs are detailed here. For those not found, see the list of State and Provincial Grants following this section.

Other contests are limited to certain groups, such as women or students. For instance, the Emerging Lesbian Writers Award is a new listing that offers a $10,000 prize to lesbian writers who have published at least one piece of writing, but not more than one book. And the "Giorgio La Pira" International Literary Prize (also new to this edition) is open only to poems written in Italian.

A few contests are for translations only. Still others are limited to poets writing in certain forms or on certain subjects. If you write sonnets, for example, consider the Salmon Arm Sonnet Contest. One award limited to a certain subject is the Boardman Tasker Award, which only considers work that deals with the mountain environment. Competitions that primarily consider themselves specialized are often open to both beginning and established poets.

While most of the contests and awards in this section are open to entries, there are a few to which you cannot apply. These are coded **V**, indicating that the winners are chosen by nomination—often by an anonymous committee. See the listing for The Whiting Writers' Awards, for example. We include such awards because winning one is a very high honor and it is not only helpful to know these awards exist, but it is also important to know that you should not attempt to apply for them.

In addition to the listings in this section, there are contests and awards (particularly those sponsored by journals) mentioned in listings in other sections of this book. For those, you should refer to the list of Additional Contests and Awards at the end of this section and consult the listings noted there for details.

Once you've narrowed down the contests and awards you want to enter, treat the submission process just as you would if you were submitting to a magazine: Always send a SASE for more information. Many contests want you to submit work along with their specific entry form or application. Others offer guidelines that detail exactly how they want poetry submitted. Also, deadlines for entries are often subject to change and if your work arrives after the deadline date, it may automatically be disqualified. Finally, request a list of recent winning entries for any contest you are considering. This will give you a good idea of the kind of work the judges appreciate. However, this may not apply if the judges change each year.

OUR OWN EXPERIENCE

In the last edition of *Poet's Market*, we announced our very first poetry contest. The contest received more than 600 submissions from almost every state in the U.S. and from a few countries overseas. And not only was it a success as far as response, but we learned a great deal from the experience. In the article on page 6, we share with you what we learned so that you may benefit from our experience and, perhaps, see the submission process from another point of view.

On page 7 of this edition, you will also find the announcement for the *1998 Poet's Market* Poetry Contest. And to read the winning poems from the *1997 Poet's Market* Poetry Contest, see the endleaves at the front and back of this book. But whether you are entering our contest or one of the contests listed in this section, we wish you the best of luck!

AAA ANNUAL NATIONAL LITERARY CONTEST; ARIZONA LITERARY MAGAZINE (I), 3509 Shea Blvd., Suite 117-PM, Phoenix AZ 85028-3339, sponsoring organization Arizona Authors' Association, award director Iva Martin. 42 lines maximum, $5 entry fee, submit between January 1 and July 29. Prizes are $125, $75, $40 and 6 honorable mentions of $10 each. Include SASE with entry for contest results; no material will be returned. Winners are announced and prizes awarded in October. Winning entries are published in a special edition of *Arizona Literary Magazine*. Entries must be typed, double-spaced on 8½ × 11 paper. Send SASE for more information and entry rules.

MILTON ACORN POETRY AWARD; PRINCE EDWARD ISLAND LITERARY AWARDS (IV-Regional), The Prince Edward Island Council of the Arts, 115 Richmond St., 115 Richmond St., Charlottetown, Prince Edward Island C1A 1H7 Canada. Awards are given annually for poetry. Writers must have been resident of Prince Edward Island at least 6 of the 12 months before the contest. Submit November 28 through February 15. For the Milton Acorn Poetry Award, participants may submit as many entries as they wish, each of no more than 10 pgs. Entry fee: $6/entry. Prizes: A trip for 2 via Air Nova between any two points (excluding Boston), first prize; $200 and $100, second and third prizes.

THE AIR CANADA AWARD (IV-Regional), % Canadian Authors Association, Box 419, Campbellford, Ontario K0L 1L0 Canada, phone (705)653-0323, fax (705)653-0593, e-mail canauth@redden. on.ca. The Air Canada Award is an annual award of two tickets to any Air Canada destination, to a Canadian author, published or unpublished, under 30 who shows the most promise. Nominations are made before April 30 by Canadian Authors Association branches or other writers' organizations and the award is given at the CAA banquet in June.

AMERICAN-SCANDINAVIAN FOUNDATION TRANSLATION PRIZE; SCANDINA-VIAN REVIEW (IV-Translation), 725 Park Ave., New York NY 10021, for the best translation into English of a work (which may be poetry) of a Scandinavian author after 1800; $2,000, publication in the *Scandinavian Review*, and a bronze medallion. To enter, first request rules. Deadline: June 3.

ANDREAS-GRYPHIUS-PREIS; NIKOLAUS-LENAU-PREIS (II, IV-Foreign Language), Die Künstlergilde e.V., Hafenmarkt 2, D-73728, Esslingen a.N., Germany, phone 0711/3969 01-0. "The prize is given annually to German-speaking authors who are dealing with the particular problems of the German culture in eastern Europe or to the best published literary works (which may be poems) that promote understanding between Germans and eastern Europeans." Prizes awarded: 1 Grand Prize of DM 15,000; 2 prizes of DM 7,000. Submissions judged by an 8-member jury. They also sponsor the Nikolaus-Lenau-Preis for German-speaking poets. The prize is named in honor of Nikolaus Lenau, "a poet who facilitated understanding with the people of eastern Europe." The prize of DM 12,000 is awarded in 3 parts. Only 3 unpublished poems/entrant. Write for details.

ARIZONA STATE POETRY SOCIETY ANNUAL CONTEST (I, II, IV), 317 Hackney Ave., Globe AZ 85501, director Audrey Opitz. Contest for various poetry forms and subjects. Prizes range from $10-75; first, second and third place winners are published in the winter edition of *The Sandcutters*, the group's quarterly publication, and names are listed for honorable mention winners. Contest information available for SASE. Fees vary. Deadline: August 31. "ASPS sponsors a variety of monthly contests for members. Membership is available to anyone anywhere."

ARKANSAS POETRY DAY CONTEST; POETS' ROUNDTABLE OF ARKANSAS (I), over 25 categories, many open to all poets. Brochure available in June; deadline in September; awards given in October. For copy send SASE to Verna Lee Hinegardner, 605 Higdon, Apt. 109, Hot Springs AR 71913.

ARTIST TRUST; ARTIST TRUST GAP GRANTS; ARTIST TRUST FELLOWSHIPS (IV-Regional), 1402 Third Ave., Suite 404, Seattle WA 98101, phone (206)467-8734. Artist Trust is a nonprofit arts organization that provides grants to artists (including poets) who are residents of the state. It also publishes, three times a year, a journal of news about arts opportunities and cultural issues.

ARTS RECOGNITION AND TALENT SEARCH (ARTS) (II, IV-Students), National Foundation for Advancement in the Arts, 800 Brickell Ave., Suite 500, Miami FL 33131, phone (305)377-1140, president Dr. William H. Banchs. "ARTS is a national program designed to identify, recognize and encourage young people who demonstrate excellence in Dance, Music, Music/Jazz, Music/Voice, Theater, Visual Arts, Photography and Writing." Offers annual awards of $3,000 (Level 1), $1,500 (Level 2), $1,000 (Level 3), $500 (Level 4) and $100 (Level 5). Submit up to 6 poems in up to but not more than 10 pgs. Open to high school seniors and young people aged 17 or 18 by or on December 1 of the award year. Send SASE for entry form and guidelines. Entry fee: $25 (June 1 early application deadline), $35 (October 1 regular application deadline).

ARVON INTERNATIONAL POETRY COMPETITION (I, II), Kilnhurst, Kilnhurst Rd., Todmorden, Lancashire OL14 6AX England, phone 01706 816582, fax 01706 816359, jointly sponsored by Duncan Lawrie Limited and *The Observer*. Poems (which may be of any length and previously unpublished) must be in English. First prize is £5,000 ($8,425), and other cash prizes. The competition is biennial. Distinguished poets serve as judges. Though the contest (which raises funds by entry fees) may be better known internationally, the major function of the Arvon Foundation is to offer writing courses at three retreats: at Totleight Barton, Sheepwash, Beaworthy, Devon EX21 5NS, phone 01409 231338; at Lumb Bank, Heptonstall, Hebden Bridge, West Yorkshire HX7 6DF, phone (01422) 843714; and at Moniack Mhor, Teavarran, Kiltarlity, Beauly, Inverness-shire 1V4 7HT, phone (01463) 741675. These are residential programs at attractive country retreats, offered by established writers in subjects such as poetry, playwriting, short fiction, radio drama, and words and music. The tuition is £275 for, typically, 5 days, which includes tuition, food and accommodations, and there is scholarship available from the foundation for those who cannot otherwise afford to attend.

BARNARD NEW WOMEN POETS PRIZE; WOMEN POETS AT BARNARD; BARNARD NEW WOMEN POETS SERIES; BEACON PRESS (IV-Women), Barnard College, 3009 Broadway, New York NY 10027-6598, phone (212)854-3453. Women Poets at Barnard holds open competition and annual series. The winner receives an award of $1,000 and publication in the Barnard New Women Poets Series, Beacon Press. The competition is open to any woman poet with a book-length ms who has not yet published a book (exclusive of chapbooks). Deadline: October 1. Send SASE for guidelines.

BAVARIAN ACADEMY OF FINE ARTS LITERATURE PRIZE (V), Max Joseph-Platz 3, 80539 Munich, Germany. An award of DM 30,000 given annually to an author in the German language, to honor a distinguished literary career—**by nomination only**.

‡BAY AREA BOOK REVIEWERS ASSOCIATION AWARDS (IV-Regional), 11A Commercial Blvd., Novato CA 94949, phone (415)883-2353, fax (415)883-4280, contact Jon Sharp, offers annual awards which recognize "the best of Northern California (from Fresno north) fiction, poetry, nonfiction, and children's literature." Submissions must be previously published. Submit 3 copies of each book entered. Open to Northern California residents. Send SASE for guidelines. Deadline: December 1. They also sponsor the Fred Cody Award, an annual award for lifetime achievement given to a writer who also serves the community, and give, on an irregular basis, awards for outstanding work in translation and publishing.

GEORGE BENNETT FELLOWSHIP (II), Phillips Exeter Academy, 20 Main St., Exeter NH 03833-2460, provides a $5,000 fellowship plus room and board to a writer with a ms in progress. The Fellow's only official duties are to be in residence while the academy is in session and to be available to students interested in writing. The committee favors writers who have not yet published a book-length work with a major publisher. Send SASE for application materials. Telephone calls strongly discouraged. Deadline: December 1.

‡BEST OF OHIO WRITERS WRITING CONTEST (IV-Regional), Ohio Writer Magazine, P.O. Box 91801, Cleveland OH 44101, award director Linda Rome, offers annual contest for poetry, fiction, creative nonfiction, and children's fiction plus special categories for students grades 7-9 and 10-12. Prizes: $100 first prize, $50 second prize, $25 third prize, plus publication in a special edition of *Ohio Writer*. Submit up to 3 typed poems, no more than 2 pages each. Open to Ohio residents only. "Entries will be judged anonymously, so please do not put name or other identification on manuscript. Attach a 3 × 5 card with name, address, city, state, zip, and day and evening phone number. Manuscripts will not be returned." Entry fee: $5 for subscribers, $10 for nonsubscribers. (With $10 entry fee, you will receive subscription to *Ohio Writer*.) Deadline: June 30. Winners will be announced in the September/October issue of *Ohio Writer*. (See listing for *Ohio Writer* in Publications Useful to Poets.)

THE BOARDMAN TASKER AWARD (IV-Specialized: mountain literature), The Boardman Tasker Memorial Trust, 14 Pine Lodge, Dairyground Rd., Bramhall, Stockport, Cheshire SK7 2HS United Kingdom, secretary Dorothy Boardman, offers prize of £2,000 to "the author or authors of the best literary work, whether fiction, nonfiction, drama or poetry, the central theme of which is concerned with the mountain environment. Entries for consideration may have been written by authors of any nationality but the work must be published or distributed in the United Kingdom between November 1, 1996 and October 31, 1997. (If not published in the U.K., please indicate name of distributor.) The work must be written or have been translated into the English language." Submit ms in book format. "In a collection of essays or articles by a single author, the inclusion of some material previously published but now in book form for the first time will be acceptable." Submissions accepted from the publisher only. Four copies of entry must be submitted with application. Deadline: August 1, 1997. 1995 winner was *Geoffrey Winthrop Young* by Alan Hankinson, published by Hodder Headline.

BOLLINGEN PRIZE (V), Beinecke Rare Book and Manuscript Library, Yale University, P.O. Box 208240, New Haven CT 06520-8240, a biennial prize of $25,000 to an American poet for the best poetry collection published during the previous two years, or for a body of published poetry written over several years. **By nomination only.** "All books of poetry by American poets published during the two-year period are automatically considered." Judges change biennially. Prize awarded in January of odd-numbered years.

‡BP NICHOL CHAPBOOK AWARD (IV-Regional), 316 Dupont St., Toronto, Ontario M5R 1V9 Canada, $1,000 (Canadian) prize for the best poetry chapbook (10-48 pgs.) in English published in Canada in the preceding year. Submit 3 copies (not returnable). Entries close March 31.

BRITISH COMPARATIVE LITERATURE ASSOCIATION/BRITISH CENTRE FOR LIT-ERARY TRANSLATION COMPETITION (I, IV-Translations), (formerly B.C.L.A. Translation Competition), Dept. of English Literature, The University of Glasgow, Glasgow G12 8QQ United Kingdom, competition secretary Dr. Stuart Gillespie, offers annual awards of £350 1st prize and £150 2nd prize, plus other prizes for specific languages. Submissions must be unpublished translations of literary works or excerpts from any language into English. Submit 25 double-spaced typed pgs. Write to competition secretary for entry form and guidelines. Entry fee: £5/entry. Deadline: February 28, 1997. "Winning translations will be published in the annual *Comparative Criticism* (Cambridge University Press). Winners who wish to become Translators in Residence at the British Centre for Literary Translation, University of East Anglia, Norwich, will be given special consideration for one of the Centre's bursary awards."

BUCKNELL SEMINAR FOR YOUNGER POETS; STADLER SEMESTER FOR YOUNGER POETS (IV-Students), Bucknell University, Lewisburg PA 17837, phone (717)524-1853, director John Wheatcroft, includes the Stadler Semester for Younger Poets, the Seminar for Younger Poets and the Poet-in-Residence Series. The Stadler Semester is distinctive in allowing undergraduate poets almost four months of concentrated work centered in poetry. Guided by practicing poets, the apprentice will write and read poetry and will receive critical response. The two Fellows selected will work with Bucknell's writing faculty. The visiting Poet-in-Residence also will participate in the program. Fellows will earn a semester of academic credit by taking four units of study: a tutorial or individual project with a mentor poet, a poetry-writing workshop, a literature course, and an elective. Undergraduates from four-year colleges with at least one course in poetry writing are eligible to apply; most applicants will be second-semester juniors. Send a 10- to 12-page portfolio and a letter of presentation (a brief autobiography that expresses commitment to writing poetry, cites relevant courses and lists any publications. Also include a transcript, two recommendations (at least one from a poetry-writing instructor), and a letter from the academic dean granting permission for the student to attend Bucknell for a semester. Application deadline for the Stadler Semester is November 1. Students chosen for the fellowships will be notified by November 25. The Bucknell Seminar For Younger Poets is not a contest for poems but for 10 fellowships to the Bucknell Seminar, held for 4 weeks in June every year. Seniors and juniors from American colleges are eligible to compete for the 10 fellowships, which consist of tuition, room, board, and spaces for writing. Application deadline for each year's seminar is March 1. Students chosen for fellowships will be notified by April 8. Please write for details.

THE BUNTING FELLOWSHIP PROGRAM (IV-Women), Radcliffe College, 34 Concord Ave., Cambridge MA 02138, phone (617)495-8212, supports women of exceptional promise and demonstrated accomplishment who want to pursue independent study in the creative arts in a multidisciplinary setting. The stipend is $33,000 for a fellowship period, September 15 through August 15, and requires residence in the Boston area. Awards 6-10 fellowships. Applicants in creative arts should be at the equivalent stage in their careers as women who have received doctorates two years before applying. Deadline is October 15.

‡CALIFORNIA BOOK AWARDS OF THE COMMONWEALTH CLUB OF CALIFOR-NIA (IV-Regional), 595 Market St., San Francisco CA 94105, phone (415)597-6700, fax (415)597-6729, website http://www.sfgate.com/~common, award director Michael Brassington, annual awards "consisting of not more than two gold and eight silver medals" for books of "exceptional literary merit" in poetry, fiction and nonfiction (including work related to California and work for children), plus 2 "outstanding" categories. Submissions must be previously published. Submit at least 3 copies of each book entered with an official entry form. (Books may be submitted by author or publisher.) Open to books, published during the year prior to the contest, whose author "must have been a legal resident of California at the time the manuscript was submitted for publication." Send SASE for entry form and guidelines.

CALIFORNIA WRITERS' ROUNDTABLE POETRY CONTEST (I), under the auspices of the Los Angeles Chapter, Women's National Book Association, 11684 Ventura Blvd., Suite 807, Studio City CA 91614-2652, phone (818)789-9175, chairman Lou Carter Keay. Annual contest with $50, $25 and $10 cash prizes for unpublished poems on any subject, in various forms, not more than 42 lines in length. WNBA members may submit free; nonmembers pay $3/poem entry fee. Send SASE for guidelines. Deadline: September 30.

CANADIAN AUTHORS ASSOCIATION LITERARY AWARDS; CANADIAN AU-THORS ASSOCIATION (IV-Regional), Box 419, Campbellford, Ontario K0L 1L0 Canada, phone (705)653-0323, fax (705)653-0593, e-mail canauth@redden.on.ca. $5,000 and a silver medal in each of 4 categories (fiction, poetry, nonfiction, drama) to Canadian writers, for a published book in the year of publication (or, in the case of drama, first produced), deadline December 15. Nominations may be made by authors, publishers, agents or others. (Also see The Air Canada Award in this section.)

CAPRICORN POETRY AWARD (II); OPEN VOICE AWARDS (I, II); THE WRITER'S VOICE, Writer's Voice, 5 W. 63rd St., New York NY 10023, phone (212)875-4124. Capricorn Poetry Award, a cash prize of $1,000 and a reading at The Writer's Voice, limited to writers over 40. $15 entry fee. Deadline: December 31. Send SASE for application guidelines. Open Voice Awards, annual awards, $500 honorarium and a reading at The Writer's Voice, open to both published and unpublished poets who have not previously read at The Writer's Voice. $10 entry fee. Deadline: December 31. Send SASE for application form. "Write 'Genre' on the envelope." The Writer's Voice is a literary center sponsoring weekly readings, writing workshops, writing awards and other activities.

‡CHICANO/LATINO LITERARY CONTEST (II), Dept. of Spanish & Portuguese, University of California-Irvine, Irvine CA 92717, contest director Prof. Alejandro Morales, is an annual contest focusing on 1 of 4 genres each year; poetry (1997), drama (1998), novel (1999), short story (2000). Prizes: First, $1,000, publication and transportation to Irvine to receive the award; second, $500; and third, $250. Work may be in English or Spanish. Only one entry/author. Open to US citizens or permanent residents of the US. Send SASE for guidelines. Deadline: April 30. Most recent contest winner was Evangeline Blanco. Judge was Novelist José Agustín. Winners will be notified by letter by October 30. Prizes will be awarded during a ceremony in November.

CINTAS FELLOWSHIP PROGRAM (IV-Regional), Arts International, Institute of International Education, 809 United Nations Plaza, New York NY 10017, makes awards of $10,000 to young professional writers and artists of Cuban lineage living outside of Cuba. Call (212)984-5370, for applications and guidelines. Deadline for applications: March 1.

CLARK COLLEGE WRITERS CONTEST (I), % Arlene Paul, 4312 NE 40th St., Vancouver WA 98661-3535, jointly sponsored by Clark College, The Oregon State Poetry Association and Washington Poets' Association, awards prizes of $100, $150 and $200, for poems up to 25 lines, unpublished, not having won another contest. Send 2 copies, one not identified, one with name, address and phone number. Type name, address and phone number on a 3×5 card, include title and first line on card. Entry fee: $3/poem (make checks payable to Clark College Foundation). May purchase book of winners' poems for $4 plus $1 postage. Deadline: February 5. Winners announced at April Workshop. (For information about The Oregon State Poetry Association, see listing in Organizations Useful to Poets.)

‡COLORADO BOOK AWARDS (IV-Regional), Colorado Center for The Book, P.O. Box 360, Denver CO 80201, phone (303)273-5935, fax (303)273-5934, e-mail 103332.1376@compuserve.com, website http://www.aclin.org/~ccftb, award director Suzan Moore, offers annual award of $500 plus promotion for books published in November or December of the year prior to the award or published anytime during the year of the award. Submissions may be entered in other contests. Submit 6 copies of each book entered. Open to residents of Colorado. Send SASE for entry form and guidelines. Entry fee: $30. Deadline: December 31. Most recent award winner Luis Alberto Urrea. Judges were Tom Auer of the *Bloomsbury Review* and Katherine O'Neill previous editor of *Poesis* poetry magazine. Winner will be announced at a ceremony/dinner in April. "We are a nonprofit organization affiliated with the Library of Congress Center for The Book. We promote books and reading. We annually sponsor the Rocky Mountain Book Festival which attracts 40,000 people. It's free and includes 300 authors from throughout the country. We are moving into the home of Thomas Hornsby Ferril, Colorado's former poet laureate. This historic home will be used as a literary center and a tribute to Ferril's life and work."

INA COOLBRITH CIRCLE ANNUAL POETRY CONTEST (IV-Regional), 2712 Oak Rd., #54, Walnut Creek CA 94596, treasurer Audrey Allison, has prizes of $10-50 in each of several categories for California residents and out-of-state members only. Three poems per contestant, but no more than 1 poem in any one category. Poems submitted in 2 copies, include name, address, phone number and member status on 1 copy only. Enclose a 3×5 card with name, address, phone number, category, title, first line of poem and status as member or nonmember. Members of the Ina Coolbrith Circle pay no fee; others pay $5 for 3 poems (limit 3). Send SASE for details. Deadline is August.

ABBIE M. COPPS POETRY COMPETITION; GARFIELD LAKE REVIEW (I, II), Dept. of Humanities, Olivet College, Olivet MI 49076, phone (616)749-7683, contest chairperson Linda Jo

Scott. Annual contest awarding $150 prize and publication in the *Garfield Lake Review*. $2/poem entry fee for unpublished poem up to 100 lines. Submit unsigned, typed poem, entrance fee, and name, address and phone number in a sealed envelope with the first line of the poem on the outside. Judge to be announced. Deadline: February 15.

COUNCIL FOR WISCONSIN WRITERS, INC. (IV-Regional), Box 55322, Madison WI 53705. Offers annual awards of $500 or more for a book of poetry by a Wisconsin resident, published within the awards year (preceding the January 13 deadline). Entry form and entry fee ($10 for members of the Council, $25 for others) required.

CREATIVE ARTIST PROGRAM (IV-Regional), Cultural Arts Council of Houston/Harris County, 1964 West Gray, Suite 224, Houston TX 77019-4808, phone (713)527-9330. Offers annual awards of $5,000 to Houston visual artists, writers, choreographers and composers selected through an annual competition. The program also offers Artist Project grants. Deadline for entry is in the fall. Write for application forms and guidelines.

CREATIVE WRITING FELLOWSHIPS IN POETRY (II, IV-Regional), Arizona Commission on the Arts, 417 W. Roosevelt St., Phoenix AZ 85003, phone (602)255-5882, literature director Tonda Gorton, offers biennial prizes of $5,000-7,500. Poetry fellowships awarded in odd-numbered years. Submissions can be previously published or unpublished, and can be entered in other contests. Submit 10 pgs. maximum on any subject. Open to Arizona residents over 18 years old. Send SASE for entry form. Entry deadline is in September of the year prior to the award.

‡**CRUMB ELBOW PUBLISHING POETRY CONTESTS (I, IV-Themes)**, P.O. Box 294, Rhododendron OR 97049, phone (503)622-4798, award director Michael P. Jones, offers annual awards of publication and copies, "for both established poets and beginners to introduce their work to new audiences by having their work published in a collection of poetry." Crumb Elbow sponsors 7 contests all having different themes. They are the Scarecrow Poetry Harvest Contest (deadline August 1), Old Traditions & New Festivities: Winter Holiday Poetry Contest (deadline October 1), Natural Enchantment: Henry David Thoreau Poetry Contest (deadline February 1), Centuries of Journeys: History & Folk Traditions Poetry Contest (deadline April 1), Onward to the New Eden! Oregon Trail Poetry Contest (deadline January 1), Westward! Historic Trails Poetry Contest (deadline November 1), and Beyond the Shadows: Social Justice Poetry Contest (deadline June 1). Submissions may be entered in other contests. Submit at least 3 poems or verses. All submissions should be typed and accompanied by SASE. Send SASE for entry form and guidelines. Entry fees range from $2 for 3 poems to $15 for 22-30 poems. The award director says, "Have fun with your creativity. Explore with your words and don't be afraid of themes or to try something different."

DALY CITY POETRY AND SHORT STORY CONTEST (I), Serramonte Library, 40 Wembley Dr., Daly City CA 94015. Contest held annually, awarding prizes of $40, $25, $20, $15 and $10 in various categories and $5 for honorable mention. All winners also receive certificates. Entry fee: $1/poem or $2/story. Stories must be unpublished. Send SASE for rules; attn: Ruth Hoppin, coordinator. Contest opens September 1. Postmark deadline: January 15.

BILLEE MURRAY DENNY POETRY AWARD (II), % Janet Overton, Lincoln College, 300 Keokuk St., Lincoln IL 62656. Annual award with prizes of $1,000, $500 and $250. Open to poets who have not previously published a book of poetry with a commercial or university press (except for chapbooks with a circulation of less than 250). Enter up to 3 poems, 100 lines/poem or less at $10/poem. (Make checks payable to Poetry Contest—Lincoln College.) Poems may be on any subject, using any style, but may not contain "any vulgar, obscene, suggestive or offensive word or phrase." Winning poems are published in *The Denny Poems*, a biennial anthology, available for $5 from Lincoln College. Send SASE for entry form. Postmark deadline: May 31.

MILTON DORFMAN NATIONAL POETRY PRIZE (II), % Rome Art & Community Center, 308 W. Bloomfield St., Rome NY 13440. Annual award for unpublished poetry. Winners for 1995: Elton Glaser, first place; Deborah DeNicola, second place; and John McMoy, third place. Judge for 1995 was Margaret Lloyd. Prizes: $500, $200 and $100. Entry fee: $3/poem (American funds only; $10 returned check penalty); make checks payable to: Rome Art & Community Center. Include name, address and phone number on each entry. Poems are printed in Center's Newsletter. Contest opens July 1. Deadline: November 1. Winners are notified by December 1. Send SASE for results.

‡**EMERGING LESBIAN WRITERS AWARD (IV-Lesbian)**, Astraea National Lesbian Action Foundation, 116 E. 16th St., New York NY 10003, phone (212)529-8021, fax (212)982-3321, e-mail anlaf@aol.com, website http://www.imageinc.com/astraea/, contact Program Director, offers an annual award of $10,000 to "support the work of emerging lesbian writers, and to acknowledge the contribu-

tions of established lesbian writers to our movement and culture." Submissions must be previously published and may be entered in other contests. Submit 10-15 pgs. of collated poetry. "You may only submit in one category (fiction or poetry) per year." Open to US residents who have published "at least one piece of writing (in any genre) in a newspaper, magazine, journal or anthology; but not more than one book." Submit 3 copies of ms with completed cover sheet and 1-paragraph bio. Send SASE for entry form and guidelines. Entry fee: $5. Deadline: March 8. Most recent award winners include Pamela Crow and Adrian Oktenberg. Applications are judged by a panel of lesbian writers who remain anonymous until after the competition. Applicants are notified by mail after June 30.

FLORIDA INDIVIDUAL ARTIST FELLOWSHIPS (II, IV-Regional), Florida Division of Cultural Affairs, Dept. of State, The Capitol, Tallahassee FL 32399-0250, phone (904)487-2980, annually offers an undetermined number of fellowships in the amount of $5,000 each. "The Individual Artist Fellowship Program is designed to recognize practicing professional creative artists residing in Florida through monetary fellowship awards. The program provides support for artists of exceptional talent and demonstrated ability to improve their artistic skills and enhance their careers. Fellowships may be awarded in the following discipline categories: dance, folk arts, interdisciplinary, literature, media arts, music, theatre and visual arts and crafts." Submissions can be previously published or unpublished. Submit 3-5 representative poems, single or double-spaced. "Reproductions of published work may not be submitted in published format. Open to Florida residents of at least 18 years of age who are not enrolled in undergraduate or graduate programs. Seven copies of the work sample must be included with 7 copies of the application form. Write for entry form and guidelines. Deadline: January 25.

FOSTER CITY INTERNATIONAL WRITERS' CONTEST (II), F.C. Arts & Culture Committee, 650 Shell Blvd., Foster City CA 94404, phone (415)345-5731. Yearly competition for previously unpublished work. $10 entry fee, $250 prize with certificates of merit awarded to 2nd, 3rd and 4th runners-up. Send SASE for instructions. Deadline: November 1. Awards announced January 15.

FRIENDS OF DOG WATCH OPEN POETRY COMPETITION (I), 267 Hillbury Rd., Warlingham, Surrey CR6 9TL England, phone 01883-622121, contact Michaela Edridge. Annual competition for poems up to 40 lines. Cash prizes. Entry fees: £2/poem. Contest information available for SASE (or SAE and IRCs). Deadline: January 1.

GEORGIA STATE POETRY SOCIETY, INC.; BYRON HERBERT REECE AND EDWARD DAVIN VICKERS INTERNATIONAL AWARDS; THE REACH OF SONG ANNUAL ANTHOLOGY; GEORGIA STATE POETRY SOCIETY NEWSLETTER (I, IV-Anthologies, form), P.O. Box 120, Epworth GA 30541-0120. The society sponsors a number of contests open to all poets, described in its quarterly newsletter (membership $20/year). Sponsors an annual anthology, *The Reach of Song*. The Byron Herbert Reece and the Edward Davin Vickers International Awards have prizes of $250, $100, $50, $25, $15 and $10. Entry fee: $5 first poem, $1 each additional. Deadline: January 31, Reece Awards; November 20, Vickers Awards. Send SASE for guidelines. Sample newsletter: $2; *Reach of Song:* $10.

JOHN GLASSCO TRANSLATION PRIZE (IV-Translation, regional), Literary Translators' Association of Canada, 3492, avenue Laval, Montreal, Quebec H2X 3C8 Canada. $500 awarded annually for a translator's first book-length literary translation into French or English, published in Canada during the previous calendar year. The translator must be a Canadian citizen or landed immigrant. Eligible genres include fiction, creative nonfiction, poetry, published plays and children's books. Write for application form. Deadline: February 15.

‡GREAT LAKES COLLEGES ASSOCIATION NEW WRITERS AWARD (II), GLCA, The Philadelphia Center, North American Bldg., 121 S. Broad St., 7th Floor, Philadelphia PA 19107-4577, phone (215)735-7300, fax (215)735-7373, director Mark Andrew Clark, Ph.D., offers annual award to "the best first book of poetry and the best first book of fiction among those **submitted by publishers**. The winning authors tour several of the Great Lakes Colleges reading, lecturing, visiting classes, doing workshops, and publicizing their books. Each writer receives an honorarium of at least $300 from each college visited, as well as travel expenses, hotel accommodations, and hospitality. Usually, one winner (fiction) tours in the fall, and the other winner (poetry) tours in the spring, following the competition." Submissions must be previously published. Submit 4 copies of galleys or the printed book plus a statement stating author's agreement to commit to the college tour. Send SASE for guidelines. Deadline: February 28. Most recent award winners were *Human Nature* (poetry) by Alice Anderson and *Cannibal* (fiction) by Terese Svoboda (both published by New York University Press).

GREEN RIVERS WRITERS' CONTESTS (I, IV-Themes, forms), 1043 Thornfield Lane, Cincinnati OH 45224, contact Contest Chairman, offers 6 contests for poetry on various themes and in various forms. Entry fees range from $5-8 for nonmembers, prizes range from $5-150. Send SASE for rules. Deadline: October 31.

GROLIER POETRY PRIZE; ELLEN LA FORGE MEMORIAL POETRY FOUNDATION, INC. (II, IV-Themes), 6 Plympton St., Cambridge MA 02138, phone (617)547-4648, award director Louisa Solano. The Grolier Poetry Prize is open to all poets who have not published either a vanity, small press, trade or chapbook of poetry. Two poets receive an honorarium of $150 each. Up to 4 poems by each winner and 1-2 by each of 4 runners-up are chosen for publication in the *Grolier Poetry Prize Annual*. Opens January 15 of each year; deadline May 1. Submit up to 5 poems, not more than 10 double-spaced pages. Submit one ms in duplicate, without name of poet. On a separate sheet give name, address, phone number and titles of poems. Only 1 submission/contestant; mss are not returned. $6 entry fee includes copy of *Annual*, checks payable to the Ellen La Forge Memorial Poetry Foundation, Inc. Enclose self-addressed stamped postcard if acknowledgement of receipt is required. For update of rules, send SASE to Ellen La Forge Memorial Poetry Foundation before submitting mss. The Ellen La Forge Memorial Poetry Foundation sponsors intercollegiate poetry readings and a reading series, generally 10/semester, held on the grounds of Harvard University. These are generally poets who have new collections of poetry available for sale at the Grolier Poetry Book Shop, Inc., which donates money toward costs (such as rental of the auditorium). They pay poets honoraria from $100-400 and occasionally provide overnight accommodations (but not transportation). Such poets as Mark Strand, Philip Levine, Robin Becker, Donald Hall and Brigit Pegeen Kelly have given readings under their auspices. The small foundation depends upon private gifts and support for its activities.

GUGGENHEIM FELLOWSHIPS (II), John Simon Guggenheim Memorial Foundation, 90 Park Ave., New York NY 10016. Approximately 158 Guggenheims are awarded each year to persons who have already demonstrated exceptional capacity for productive scholarship or exceptional creative ability in the arts. The amounts of the grants vary. The average grant is about $28,000. Application deadline: October 1.

HACKNEY LITERARY AWARDS; BIRMINGHAM-SOUTHERN COLLEGE WRITER'S CONFERENCE (II), Birmingham-Southern College, Box 549003, Birmingham AL 35254. This competition, sponsored by the Cecil Hackney family since 1969, offers $4,000 in prizes for novels, poetry and short stories as part of the annual Birmingham-Southern Writer's Conference. Novels postmarked by September 30. Poems and short stories must be postmarked by December 31. Send SASE for Hackney guidelines. Winners are announced at the conference, which is held in the spring. (Also see Writing Today in Conferences and Workshops.)

THE HODDER FELLOWSHIP (II), The Council of the Humanities, 122 E. Pyne, Princeton University, Princeton NJ 08544, is awarded for the pursuit of independent work in the humanities. The recipient is usually a writer or scholar in the early stages of a career with one or two published books. Preference is given to applicants outside academia. "The Fellowship is designed specifically to identify and nurture extraordinary creative potential rather than to honor distinguished achievement." **Candidates for the Ph.D. are not eligible.** The Hodder Fellow spends an academic year in residence at Princeton working independently. Applicants must submit a résumé, sample of previous work (10 pgs. maximum, not returnable), a project proposal of 2 to 3 pgs., and SASE. The announcement of the Hodder Fellow is made in February by the President of Princeton University. Deadline: November 15.

HENRY HOYNS FELLOWSHIPS (II), Dept. of English, 219 Bryan Hall, University of Virginia, Charlottesville VA 22903, are fellowships in poetry and fiction of varying amounts for candidates for the M.F.A. in creative writing. Sample poems/prose required with application. Deadline: February 1.

IRISH AMERICAN CULTURAL INSTITUTE LITERARY AWARDS (IV-Ethnic, foreign language), 1 Lachawanna Place, Morristown NJ 07960, for Irish writers who write in Irish or English, **resident in Ireland,** with published work. A total of $10,000 in prizes awarded every year.

‡THE JAPAN FOUNDATION ARTIST FELLOWSHIP PROGRAM (IV-Specialized: US residents with Japanese affiliations), The Japan Foundation New York Office, 152 W. 57th St., 39th Floor, New York NY 10019, phone (212)489-0299, fax (212)489-0409, director general Mr. Natsuo Amemiya, offers annual fellowships of 2-6 months in Japan (during the Japanese fiscal year of April 1 through March 31) for "accredited professional writers, musicians, painters, sculptors, stage artists, movie directors, etc." Submissions may be entered in other contests. Open to citizens or permanent residents of the US. "Affiliation with a Japanese artist or institution is required. Three letters of reference, including one from the Japanese affiliate must accompany all applications." Send SASE for entry form and guidelines. Deadline: December 1.

JOHANN-HEINRICH-VOSS PRIZE FOR TRANSLATION (V), German Academy for Language and Literature, Alexandraweg 23, 64287 Darmstadt, Germany, is an annual award of DM 20,000 for outstanding lifetime achievement for translating into German, **by nomination only**. 1994: Werner von Koppenfels. 1995: Rosemarie Tietze.

‡**CHARLES JOHNSON AWARD FOR FICTION AND POETRY (IV-Ethnic, students)**, English Dept. 4503, Southern Illinois University at Carbondale, Carbondale IL 62901-4503, phone (618)453-5321, award director Ricardo Cortez Cruz, offers annual award "intended to support increased artistic and intellectual growth, plus encourage excellence and diversity in creative writing." Prizes: $500 and a signed copy of a Johnson book will be awarded in each genre. Submissions must be unpublished and may be entered in other contests. Submit 3-5 poems on no more than 6 typed pages. Entries will not be returned. Open to ethnic or minority students in the US or to US students whose work "explores issues of minority/marginalized culture." Send SASE for guidelines. Postmark deadline: January 28. Recent award winners were Linda K. Wright and Frank Lamont Phillips. The judges for upcoming contest will be bell hooks (fiction) and Gloria Anzaldúa (poetry). All winners and finalists will be notified by letter in April. Results will also be announced in the September issue of *AWP Chronicle*. "When submitting, students need to be sure to include full address, phone number, and name of college or university that they are attending."

THE CHESTER H. JONES FOUNDATION NATIONAL POETRY COMPETITION (II), P.O. Box 498, Chardon OH 44024, an annual competition for persons in the USA, Canadian and American citizens living abroad. Prizes: $1,000, $750, $500, $250, and $50 honorable mentions. Winning poems plus others called "commendations" are published in an anthology available for $3.50 from the foundation. Submissions must be unpublished. Submit no more than 10 entries, no more than 32 lines each. Send SASE for latest brochure. Entry fee $2 for the first poem, $1 each for others. Deadline: March 31. Distinguished poets serve as judges. 1996 judges were John Drury, Marie Ponsot and Diane Wakoski.

KENTUCKY ARTISTS FELLOWSHIPS (II, IV-Regional), Kentucky Arts Council, 31 Fountain Place, Frankfort KY 40601, award director Irwin Pickett, offers biennial fellowships of $5,000 to "encourage excellence and assist Kentucky artists in the professional development of their various art forms and careers." Next fellowships awarded in 1998. Fellowship recipients will be selected by a panel of out-of-state professional artists in a "blind jurying" process. Submit 15 pgs. of poetry maximum, 1 poem/page. Open to Kentucky residents who have lived in the state 1 year immediately prior to the fellowship application deadline. Send SASE for entry form (available in July). Deadline: September 15.

‡**"GIORGIO LA PIRA" INTERNATIONAL LITERARY PRIZE (IV-Foreign language)**, "G. Donati" Study Centre, Piazza S. Francesco, Pistoia 60-51100 Italy, phone (0573)367251, fax (0573)27140, contact Secretary, offers prizes of 1.500.000 lire (first prize), 1.000.000 lire (second prize) and 500.000 lire (third prize). Submit 2 copies each of 3 poems *in Italian*, not more than 40 lines each. Send SASE for guidelines. Entry fee: 25.00 lire. Winners must collect prizes in person.

LAMPMAN AWARD (IV-Regional); OTTAWA INDEPENDENT WRITERS, 265 Elderberry Terrace, Orleans, Ontario K1E 1Z2 Canada, phone (613)841-0572, is a $400 award for a published book of English-language poetry by writers in the National Capital region. Submit 3 copies of each title by February 28. Membership in Ottawa Independent Writers is $60/year, and offers their newsletter, programs and registration at reduced fees for workshops.

LATINO LITERATURE PRIZE (IV-Ethnic/Nationality), Latin American Writers Institute, Hostos Community College, 500 Grand Concourse, Bronx NY 10451, phone (718)518-4195, award director Isaac Goldemberg, offers annual prize of $1,000. Submissions must be previously published and can be entered in other contests. Only open to books written in English or Spanish by Latino authors living in the US. Send SASE for guidelines. Deadline: May 28. Recent winners include Oscar Hijuelos, Alma Luz Villanueva, Marjorie Agosín and Laura Riesco. The Institute also publishes *Brújula/Compass*, a bilingual journal devoted to Latino writing in the US.

THE STEPHEN LEACOCK MEDAL FOR HUMOUR (IV-Humor, regional), Stephen Leacock Associates, P.O. Box 854, Orillia, Ontario L3V 3P4 Canada, phone (705)325-6546, award chairman Mrs. Jean Bradley Dickson, for a book of humor in prose, verse, drama or any book form—by a Canadian citizen. Submit 10 copies of book, 8×10 b&w photo, bio and $25 entry fee. Prize: Silver Leacock Medal for Humour and Laurentian Bank of Canada cash award of $5,000. Deadline: December 31. The 1995 winner was *Fear of Frying and Other Fax of Life* by Josh Freed (Véhicule Press). The committee also publishes *The Newspacket* 3 times/year.

THE LEAGUE OF MINNESOTA POETS CONTEST (I, IV-Students), 1510 S. Seventh St., Brainerd MN 56401, contact Doris Stengel. Offers 20 different contests in a variety of categories and prizes of $5-75 for poems up to 55 lines, fees of $3 to enter all categories for members and $1/category for nonmembers. There is one category for students in grades 7 through 12 and one category for elementary students through grade 6. Deadline: July 31. Winners are not published. Write for details.

LETRAS DE ORO SPANISH LITERARY PRIZES (IV-Foreign language), Iberian Studies Institute, North-South Center, University of Miami, P.O. Box 248123, Coral Gables FL 33124, fax (305)284-4406. Awards include a general prize of $2,500 and publication of the book-length entry. For creative excellence in poetry written in the Spanish language. Write for guidelines. Deadline: October 12.

‡LONDON WRITERS COMPETITION (IV-Regional), Wandsworth Borough Council, Room 224, Town Hall, Wandsworth High St., London SW18 2PU United Kingdom, phone (0181)871-7380, fax (0181)871-7630, chairman Martyn Goft OBE, offers annual award of £1,000 each in poetry and short story plus publication. Submissions must be unpublished. Open to residents of Greater London (UK). Submit no more than 50 lines (poetry); 2,000-5,000 words (short story). Send SASE for entry form and guidelines. Entry fee: £2 (poetry), £3 (short story). Deadline is in July. Most recent contest winners were Betsy Tobin and Tamar Yoseloff. Copies of previous winning poems may be obtained by sending £2.50 to the address above. "Wandsworth Borough Council is a local government body in London. The Council Arts and Libraries division arranges an annual series of events which take place in the Borough."

MASSACHUSETTS STATE POETRY SOCIETY, INC.; NATIONAL POETRY DAY CONTEST; GERTRUDE DOLE MEMORIAL CONTEST (I), 64 Harrison Ave., Lynn MA 01905, president Jeanette C. Maes, both annual contests are open to all poets. The National Poetry Day Contest, deadline August 1, offers prizes of $25, $15 and $10 (or higher) for each of 25 or more categories; $3 fee for entire contest. The Gertrude Dole Memorial Contest, deadline March 1, offers prizes of $25, $15 and $10; $1 entry fee, one prize/poet. Send SASE for contest flyer.

MID-LIST PRESS FIRST SERIES AWARD FOR POETRY (I), Mid-List Press, 4324 12th Ave. S., Minneapolis MN 55407-3218, phone (612)822-3733, senior editor Lane Stiles. "The First Series Award for Poetry is an annual contest we sponsor for poets who have never published a book of poetry. The award includes publication and an advance against royalties." Individual poems within the book manuscript can be previously published and can be entered in other contests. Submit at least 65 single-spaced pages. "Other than length we have no restrictions, but poets are encouraged to read previous award winners we have published." Recent award winners include Neva Hacker, Jeff Worley, Neil Shepard, Douglas Gray, Stephen Behrendt, J.E. Sorrell and Mary Logue. Submissions are circulated to an editorial board. Send #10 SASE for guidelines. Entry fee: $10. Accepts submissions October 1 through February 1. "The First Series Award contest is highly competitive. We are looking for poets who have produced a significant body of work but have never published a book-length collection. (A chapbook is not considered a 'book' of poetry.)"

MILFORD FINE ARTS COUNCIL ANNUAL NATIONAL POETRY CONTEST (I, II), 40 Railroad Ave. S., Milford CT 06460, contact contest chairperson, awards 3 prizes of $50, $30 and $20. Submissions must be unpublished, have not received any other awards and not be submitted for publication. Poems must be typed, single-space on white standard paper with name and address on middle back of page. Each poem should be "10-30 lines plus title—rhymed or unrhymed—any style, any subject. Poetry will be judged on clarity, originality and universal appeal." Include SASE for contest results. Open to adults in the US. Send SASE for guidelines. "Observe rules, otherwise disqualified." Entry fee: $2 for the first entry, $1 for each additional. Open to entries September 15 through January 31.

MISSISSIPPI VALLEY POETRY CONTEST (I, II, IV), sponsored by North American Literary Escadrille, P.O. Box 3188, Rock Island IL 61204, director S. Katz, annually offers prizes of approximately $1,500 for unpublished poems in categories for students (elementary, junior and senior high), adults, Mississippi Valley, senior citizens, jazz, religious, humorous, rhyming, haiku, ethnic and history. Fee: $5 for up to 5 poems; 50 lines/poem limit. Fee for children: $3 for up to 5 poems. Professional readers read winning poems before a reception at an award evening in mid-May. Deadline: April 1.

MONTANA ARTS FOUNDATION POETRY CONTEST; MARY BRENNEN CLAPP MEMORIAL AWARD (IV-Regional), P.O. Box 1872, Bozeman MT 59771, annual contest with a September 15 deadline. Open to Montana poets only, for 3 unpublished poems up to 100 lines total. Mary Brennen Clapp Memorial Award of $50 and prizes of $40, $30 and $20. Must submit 3 poems and cover letter. Send SASE for guidelines.

JENNY MCKEAN MOORE FUND FOR WRITERS (II), Dept. of English, George Washington University, Washington DC 20052, provides for a visiting lecturer in creative writing about $40,000 for 2 semesters. Apply by November 15 with résumé and writing sample of 25 pgs. or less. Awarded to poets and fiction writers in alternating years.

‡NASHVILLE NEWSLETTER POETRY CONTEST (I), P.O. Box 60535, Nashville TN 37206-0535, editor/publisher Roger Dale Miller. Founded 1977. Reporting time 6-10 weeks. Published quarterly. Sample copy: $3. Awards prizes of $50, $25 and $10 plus publication in newsletter, and at least 50 Certificates of Merit. Any style or subject up to 40 lines. One unpublished poem to a page with name and address in upper left corner. Entry fee of $5 for up to 3 poems. Must be sent all at once. "All other nonwinning poems will be considered for possible publication in future issues." Recent contest winners include Marie E. Martinez, Jerry R. Jax and Mary Kline.

NATIONAL BOOK AWARD (II), National Book Foundation, 260 Fifth Ave., Room 904, New York NY 10001, phone (212)685-0261, award directors Neil Baldwin, Meg Kearney and Kevin LaFollette, offers annual grand prize of $10,000 plus 4 finalist awards of $1,000. Submissions must be previously published and **must be entered by the publisher**. Send SASE for entry form and guidelines. Entry fee: $100/title. Deadline: July 15.

NATIONAL ENDOWMENT FOR THE ARTS; FELLOWSHIPS FOR CREATIVE WRITERS; FELLOWSHIPS FOR TRANSLATORS (II), Attn: Literature Heritage & Preservation Division, Room 720, Nancy Hanks Center, 1100 Pennsylvania Ave. NW, Washington DC 20506, phone (202)682-5451. Fellowships for Creative Writers is a program of individual grants for American writers of poetry, fiction and creative nonfiction. Applications for prose and poetry are accepted in alternating years. Awards of $20,000 are made each year to published writers. Applications are reviewed and recommendations for funding are made by an advisory panel composed of experts from the literature field. In reviewing applications, advisory panelists consider solely the literary quality of the manuscripts submitted. To be eligible, a poet must have in publication a volume of at least 48 pages, or 20 or more poems or pages of poetry in five or more literary publications in the last 5 years. A limited number of $20,000 fellowship grants are awarded to published translators of creative literature for translation projects from other languages into English. Matching grants are also available to nonprofit organizations that have had programming for 4 years. Phone or write for guidelines and application for ms in March 1998. Anticipated deadlines: May 1998 for both the 1998 translation fellowships and the 1998 poetry fellowships.

NATIONAL POETRY SERIES ANNUAL OPEN COMPETITION (II), P.O. Box G, Hopewell NJ 08525, between January 1 and February 15 considers book-length mss (approximately 48-64 pgs.). Entry fee: $25. Manuscripts will not be returned. The 5 winners receive $1,000 each and are published by participating small press, university press and trade publishers. Send SASE for complete submissions procedures.

NATIONAL WRITERS ASSOCIATION ANNUAL POETRY CONTEST (I), 1450 S. Havana, Suite 424, Aurora CO 80012, award director Sandy Whelchel, an annual contest with prizes of $100, $50 and $25. Entry fee: $10/poem; additional fee charged if poem is longer than 40 lines. All subjects and forms are acceptable. Deadline: October 1.

NATIONAL WRITERS UNION ANNUAL NATIONAL POETRY COMPETITION (II), P.O. Box 2409, Aptos CA 95001, phone (408)457-7488, fax (408)427-2950, award director Don Marsh. See National Writers Union listing under Organizations Useful to Poets. The Santa Cruz/Monterey Local 7 chapter at this address sponsors an annual competition with entry fee: $3/poem; prizes of $200, $100 and $50 plus publication in newsletter, with prominent poets as judges. Send SASE for rules beginning in April. Deadline: September 30.

THE NATIONAL WRITTEN & ILLUSTRATED BY . . . AWARDS CONTEST FOR STUDENTS; LANDMARK EDITIONS (IV-Students), P.O. Box 270169, Kansas City MO 64127, award director David Melton, is an annual contest for unpublished work for a book written and illustrated by a student. Three books published, one from each of 3 age categories (6-9; 10-13; 14-19). Send #10 SAE with 2 first-class stamps for rules.

NEUSTADT INTERNATIONAL PRIZE FOR LITERATURE; WORLD LITERATURE TODAY (V), University of Oklahoma, 110 Monnet Hall, 630 Parrington Oval, Norman OK 73019-0375. Award of $40,000 given every other year in recognition of life achievement or to a writer whose work is still in progress; **nominations from an international jury only**.

NEW JERSEY STATE COUNCIL ON THE ARTS FELLOWSHIP PROGRAM (II, IV-Regional), CN 306, 20 W. State St., Trenton NJ 08625-0306, phone (609)292-6130, award director Steven R. Runk, offers fellowship grants that currently range between $5,000-12,000. Submissions can be previously published or unpublished and can be entered in other contests. Submit 5-8 pgs. maximum; any subject, any style. Open to New Jersey residents, except matriculated undergraduate and graduate students. Call or write for application and guidelines. Deadline is mid-December of each year.

‡NEWBURYPORT ART ASSOCIATION ANNUAL SPRING POETRY CONTEST (I), Charron Dr., Newburyport MA 01950, contest coordinator Rhina P. Espaillat, awards prizes of $100, First; $50, Second; and $25, Third; plus Honorable Mentions. Submit any number of unpublished poems; no restrictions as to length, style or theme. Open to anyone over 16 years old. Send 2 copies of each poem, typed on 8½×11 paper with SASE for notification of contest results. Send SASE for guidelines. Entry fee: $3/poem. Make checks payable to Newburyport Art Association. Postmark deadline: March 21. Most recent contest winners include Ellin Anderson, Ross R. Whitney and Len Krisak. Judge was X.J. Kennedy. Prizes are awarded at a ceremony in May.

OHIOANA BOOK AWARDS; OHIOANA KROUT MEMORIAL AWARD FOR POETRY; OHIOANA QUARTERLY; OHIOANA LIBRARY ASSOCIATION (IV-Regional), Ohioana Library Association, 65 S. Front St., Suite 1105, Columbus OH 43215. Ohioana Book Awards given yearly to outstanding books. Up to 6 awards may be given for books (including books of poetry) by authors born in Ohio or who have lived in Ohio for at least 5 years. The Ohioana Poetry Award of $1,000 (with the same residence requirements), made possible by a bequest of Helen Krout, is given yearly "to an individual whose body of work has made, and continues to make, a significant contribution to the poetry of Ohio, and through whose work as a writer, teacher, administrator, or in community service, interest in poetry has been developed." Nominations to be received by December 31. *Ohioana Quarterly* regularly reviews Ohio magazines and books by Ohio authors. It is available through membership in Ohioana Library Association ($20/year).

NATALIE ORNISH POETRY AWARD (IV-Regional); SOEURETTE DIEHL FRASER TRANSLATION AWARD (IV-Translations, regional); TEXAS INSTITUTE OF LETTERS, % James Hoggard, T.I.L., P.O. Box 9032, Wichita Falls TX 76308-9032. The Texas Institute of Letters gives annual awards for books by Texas authors in 8 categories, including the Natalie Ornish Poetry Award, a $1,000 award for best volume of poetry. Books must have been first published in the year in question, and entries may be made by authors or by their publishers. Deadline is January 4 of the following year. One copy of each entry must be mailed to each of three judges, with "information showing an author's Texas association . . . if it is not otherwise obvious." Poets must have lived in Texas for at least two consecutive years at some time or their work must reflect a notable concern with matters associated with the state. Soeurette Diehl Fraser Translation Award ($1,000) is given for best translation of a work into English. Same rules as those for Natalie Ornish poetry award. Write during the fall for complete instructions.

‡P.A.L.S. CLUB NEWSLETTER CONTESTS; POEM AND LETTER SOCIETY OF AMERICA (I), P.O. Box 60535, Nashville TN 37206-0535, founded 1988, offers 2-4 poetry contests per year, with $5 fee for nonmembers for up to 3 poems, prizes of at least $50, $25 and $10 and at least 50 Certificates of Merit. Membership is $20 a year. Members pay no entry fees for contests and receive the newsletter free. Recent contest winners include Jay Barton, Barbara States and Marthe Strom Rodrigue.

PACIFIC NORTHWEST WRITERS CONFERENCE ADULT LITERARY CONTEST (I), 2033 Sixth Ave., Suite 804, Seattle WA 98121-2546, phone (206)443-3807. For information, please request a contest brochure. Complete entry form must accompany entry.

PANHANDLE PROFESSIONAL WRITERS (I), P.O. Box 19303, Amarillo TX 79114, contact contest chairman, open to all poets, any subject or form, 50 lines maximum, limit of 2 poems/entry, awards of $25, $20 and $15, fee $7.50 for 2 poems. Send SASE for contest rules. Deadline: on or before June 15. Recent winners include Maisle Rubinstein, Ray Fernandez and Christina D. Smith.

PAUMANOK POETRY AWARD COMPETITION; THE VISITING WRITERS PROGRAM (II), SUNY Farmingdale, Farmingdale NY 11735, phone (516)420-2031, director Dr. Charles Fishman. The Paumanok Poetry Award Competition offers a prize of $1,000 plus an all-expense-paid feature reading in their 1997-98 series. They will also award two runner-up prizes of $500 plus expenses for a reading in the series. Submit cover letter, 1-paragraph literary bio, up to 5 poems (published or unpublished), and $12 entry fee postmarked by September 15. Check payable to SUNY Farmingdale Visiting Writers Program (VWP). Send SASE for results. Results will be mailed by December 20. Poets who have read in their series include Hayden Carruth, Allen Ginsberg, Linda Pastan, Marge Piercy, Joyce Carol Oates, Louis Simpson and David Ignatow. The series changes each year, so entries in the 1996 competition will be considered for the 1997-98 series, entries in 1997 for the 1998-99 series, and so on.

‡JUDITH SIEGEL PEARSON AWARD (I, IV-Women), Wayne State University/Family of Judith Siegel Pearson, 51 W. Warren, Detroit MI 48202, phone (313)577-2450, offers an annual award of $250 for "the best creative or scholarly work on a subject concerning women." The type of work accepted rotates each year: fiction, 1997; plays and nonfictional prose, 1998; poetry, 1999. Submissions must be unpublished. Submit 4-10 poems on 20 pgs. maximum. Open to "all interested writers and scholars." Send SASE for guidelines. Deadline: March 1. Winner announced in April.

‡PEN CENTER USA WEST LITERARY AWARD IN POETRY (IV-Regional), PEN Center USA West, 672 S. Lafayette Park Place, #41, Los Angeles CA 90057, phone (213)365-8500, fax (213)365-9616, award director Sherrill W. Britton, offers annual $500 cash award to a book of poetry published during the previous calendar year. Open to writers living west of the Mississippi. Submit 4 copies of the entry. Send SASE for entry form and guidelines. Deadline: December 31. The 1995 award winner was Jack Gilbert. Judges were Holly Prado, Maurya Simon and Gary Soto. Winner will be announced in a spring press release and then honored at a ceremony in Los Angeles.

PENNSYLVANIA POETRY SOCIETY ANNUAL CONTEST; PEGASUS CONTEST FOR STUDENTS, 801 Spruce St., West Reading PA 19611-1448, phone (610)374-5848, newsletter editor and recording secretary Ann Gasser. The deadline for the society's annual contest, which has 12 categories open to nonmembers and 4 to members only, is January 15. Grand prize category awards 3 prizes of $100, $50, $25 and three poems may be entered at $2 each for members and nonmembers alike. All other categories award three prizes of $25, $15 and $10 and permit one poem in each category. Twelve categories are open to all poets; nonmembers pay $1.50 per category 2-12. PPS members pay $2.50 total for entries in categories 2-16. For information about the annual contest send a SASE to Lillian Tweedy, contest chairman, 2488 New Franklin Rd., Chambersburg, PA 17201. For information about the Pegasus Contest for Students, write to Anne Pierre Spangler, contest chairman, 1685 Christine Dr., R.D. #2, Lebanon PA 17042. Deadline for the Pegasus contest is March 1. The Carlisle Chapter of PPS sponsors the "Kids 'N Critters" contest which has a deadline of October 31. For information send SASE to Jessie Ruhl Miller, 670 West Louther St., Carlisle PA 17013. The Pennsylvania Poetry Society publishes a quarterly newsletter and an annual *Prize Poems* soft cover book, containing prize-winning and honorable mention award poems. Prize poems in the Pegasus contest are published in a booklet for the schools which enter. PPS membership dues are $15/year. Make check payable to PPS, Inc. and mail to Richard R. Gasser, Treasurer, at the above address.

PENUMBRA POETRY COMPETITION (I, IV-Form), Tallahassee Writers' Association, P.O. Box 15995, Tallahassee FL 32317-5995, poetry chairperson Barbara Hogan, offers annual prizes of $50, $20 and $10 in each category, plus publication and one copy of a chapbook. Submission must be unpublished. No simultaneous submissions. Two categories: (1) poetry of up to 50 lines (shorter poetry is of equal value) and (2) 3-line haiku. "Poems on $8\frac{1}{2} \times 11$ paper; haiku on 3×5 cards. Please send two copies of each entry. On the back of one copy only, write author's name, full address, telephone number, and source of contest information." Send SASE for guidelines. Entry fee: $5/poem, $3/haiku. Deadline: June 30.

THE RICHARD PHILLIPS POETRY PRIZE (II), The Phillips Publishing Co., P.O. Box 121, Watts OK 74964, award director Richard Phillips, Jr. Annual award of $1,000 open to all poets. Submit 40-page ms, published or unpublished poems, any subject, any form. Include $10 reading fee/ms, payable to Richard Phillips Poetry Prize. Mss are not returned. Send SASE for guidelines. Postmark deadline: September 5. "Winner will be announced and check for $1,000 presented October 15." Publication is the following year. Most recent prize winner was Kathryn Presley. "There are no anthologies to buy, no strings attached. The best manuscript will win the prize."

‡THE POETRY CENTER BOOK AWARD (II), 1600 Holloway Ave., San Francisco CA 94132. Method for entering contest is to submit a published book and a $10 entry fee. "Please include cover letter noting author's name, book title(s), name of person or publisher issuing check and check number." Book must be published and copyrighted during the year of the contest and submitted by December 31. "Beginners may enter but in the past winners have published several previous books." Translations and anthologies are not accepted. Books should be by an individual living writer and must be entirely poetry. Prize (only one) is $500 and an invitation to read for the Poetry Center. No entry form is required. Recent winners include Jane Hirshfield and Barbara Guest. "The Poetry Center and American Poetry Archives at San Francisco State University celebrated its fortieth year in 1994. Its archives is the largest circulating tape collection of writers reading their own work in the United States."

POETRY OF HOPE AWARD (II, IV-Themes), P.O. Box 21077, Piedmont CA 94620, awarded annually, $200 first prize (adult division), $100 first prize (junior division) for a poem up to 20 lines expressing "the spirit of hope" using inspirational themes. Themes should speak to the "healing" of social problems (i.e., war/peace, spiritual self-transformation, human rights, the homeless, the earth/ecology, etc.), hope for the highest good for all of creation. Application needed. No fee. Send SASE. Deadline: December 30.

‡**THE POETRY SOCIETY OF VIRGINIA ANNUAL CONTESTS (I, II, IV-Forms)**, 42 Twin Oaks, Rustburg VA 24588, phone (804)821-1709, contest chairperson Lisa Stinnett, offers 18 contests in various categories including: the Bess Gresham Memorial (garden or gardeners); Brodie Herndon Memorial (the sea); Judah, Sarah, Grace and Tom Memorial (inter-ethnic amity); Cenie H. Moon Prize (women); Karma Deane Ogden Memorial (PSV members only); Edgar Allen Poe Memorial and the Alice Sherry Memorial. (All of the previous contests are open to any form, have limits of 32-48 lines, and some have specific subjects as noted.) The following group of contests require specific forms: the J. Franklin Dew Award (series of 3-4 haiku), Carleton Drewry Memorial (lyric or sonnet about mountains), Handy Andy Prize (limerick), Emma Gray Trigg Memorial (lyric, 64-line limit, PSV members only), Nancy Byrd Turner Memorial (sonnet). The last group of contests are open to elementary, middle school and high school students only: Elementary School Prize (grades 1-5, any form or subject, 24-line limit), Middle School Prize (grades 6-8, any form or subject, 24-line limit), Musings/Northern VA Poets Prize—Grades 6-8 (sonnet, Shakespearean or Petrarchan, any subject), Shenandoah University Prize (grades 9-12, any form or subject, 32-line limit). All poems are open to nonmembers except those noted above. Cash prizes range from $10-100. Contest information available for SASE. Entry fees: Adults, $2/poem; $1/high school entry; no fee for elementary school entries. Send **all student entries** to Claudia Gary Annis, 217 Nottoway St. SE, Leesburg VA 22075, phone (703)771-9342. Deadline for all contests is January 19.

POETS' CLUB OF CHICAGO INTERNATIONAL SHAKESPEAREAN/PETRARCHAN SONNET CONTEST (II, IV-Form), 130 Windsor Park Dr., C-323, Carol Stream IL 60188, chairman LaVone Holt, is open to anyone **except** members of Poets' Club of Chicago. Submit only 1 entry of either a Shakespearean or Petrarchan sonnet which must be original and unpublished and must not have won a cash award in any contest sponsored previously by the Club. Write for rules, include SASE, no earlier than March. No entry fee. Prizes of $50, $35 and $15 plus 2 honorable mentions. Postmark deadline: September 1. Winners will be notified by October 15. Send SASE with entry to receive winners' list. The Poets' Club of Chicago meets monthly to critique original poetry, read and man the Poetry Room in the Harold Washington Library, and read at open-mike coffeehouses. Members also conduct workshops at area high schools by invitation.

POETS' DINNER CONTEST (IV-Regional), 2214 Derby St., Berkeley CA 94705, phone (510)841-1217. Since 1926 there has been an annual awards banquet sponsored by the ad hoc Poets' Dinner Committee, usually at Spenger's Fish Grotto (a Berkeley Landmark). Three typed copies of original, unpublished poems in not more than 3 of the 8 categories are submitted anonymously without fee, and the winning poems (grand prize, 1st, 2nd, 3rd) are read at the banquet and honorable mentions awarded. **Contestant must be present to win.** Cash prizes awarded; honorable mention, books. The event is nonprofit. Send SASE for contest rules. Deadline: January 25.

POETS OF THE VINEYARD CONTEST (I), P.O. Box 12154, Santa Rosa CA 95406, an annual contest sponsored by the Sonoma County Chapter (PofV) of the California Federation of Chaparral Poets with entries in 7 categories. These include traditional forms, free verse, haiku/senryu and tanka and a themed category on grapes, vineyards, wine, viticulture. Send SASE for a copy of the current contest rules and deadline. Prizes in each category are $20, $15 and $10, with a grand prize chosen from category winners ($50). Entry fee: $2/poem. Prize winning poems will be published in the annual anthology, *Vintage*. Every winning poet will receive a complimentary copy of the anthology in which his/her poem appears.

THE POETS' PRIZE (II), The Poets' Prize Committee, % the Nicholas Roerich Museum, 319 W. 107th St., New York NY 10025, phone (212)864-7752, award directors Robert McDowell, Frederick Morgan and Louis Simpson. Annual cash award of $3,000 given for a book of verse by an American poet published in the previous year. The poet must be an American citizen. Poets making inquiries will receive an explanation of procedures. Books may be sent to the committee members. A list of the members and their addresses will be sent upon request with SASE.

POETS RENDEZVOUS CONTEST; INDIANA STATE FEDERATION OF POETRY CLUBS (I), % Dottie Mack, P.O. Box 643, Huntertown IN 46748. The Poets Rendezvous Contest offers $1,000 in prizes for poems in 25 categories, $5 fee covers all 25 categories in different forms and subjects, September 1 deadline. The Indiana State Federation of Poetry Clubs also has contests with January 15 and June 15 deadlines for poems no longer than 1 page, $1/poem fee, prizes of $25, $15 and $10 with 3 honorable mentions. Write for details.

PRESIDIO LA BAHIA AWARD; SUMMERFIELD G. ROBERTS AWARD (IV-Regional), Sons of the Republic of Texas, 1717 Eighth St., Bay City TX 77414, phone (409)245-6644, contact Melinda Williams. Both may be awarded for poetry. The Presidio La Bahia Award is an annual award or awards (depending upon the number and quality of entries) for writing that promotes research into and preservation of the Spanish Colonial influence on Texas culture. $2,000 is available, with a minimum first prize of $1,200. Entries must be in quadruplicate and will not be returned. Deadline: September 30. The Summerfield G. Roberts Award, available to US citizens, is an annual award of $2,500 for a book or manuscript depicting or representing the Republic of Texas (1836-46), written or published during the calendar year for which the award is given. Entries must be submitted in quintuplicate and will not be returned. Deadline: January 15.

PULITZER PRIZE IN LETTERS (II), % The Pulitzer Prize Board, 702 Journalism, Columbia University, New York NY 10027, phone (212)854-3841, offers 5 prizes of $3,000 each year, including 1 in poetry, for books published in the calendar year preceding the award. Submit 4 copies of published books (or galley proofs if book is being published after November), photo, bio, entry form and $20 entry fee. July 1 deadline for books published between January 1 and June 30; November 1 deadline for books published between July 1 and December 31.

‡QSPELL LITERARY AWARDS; QUEBEC SOCIETY FOR THE PROMOTION OF ENGLISH LANGUAGE LITERATURE (IV-Regional), 1200 Atwater Ave., Montreal, Quebec H3Z 1X4 Canada, phone/fax (514)933-0878, contact Award Director, offers annual awards of $2,000 each for poetry, fiction and nonfiction. Submissions must be previously published. Open to authors "who have lived in Quebec for 3 of the past 5 years." Submit a book published between May 15 of the preceding year and May 15 of the current year. "Books should have at least 48 pgs." Write for entry form. Entry fee: $10/title. Deadline: May 31. Most recent award winner was D.G. Jones (1995). Judges were Ray Filip, Nicole Brossard and Eric Ormsby. Winner will be announced in November. "QSPELL was formed in 1988 to honor and promote literature written in English by Quebec authors."

QUINCY WRITERS GUILD WRITING CONTEST (I), P.O. Box 433, Quincy IL 62306, offers annual award for original, unpublished poetry, fiction and nonfiction. Cash prizes based on dollar amount of entries. 1st, 2nd and 3rd place will be awarded in all categories. Send SASE for guidelines. Entry fee: $2/poem; $4/nonfiction or fiction piece. Entries accepted from January 1 through April 15. Recent contest winners include "Working with Lionel" by Ted. D. Barber (poetry), "Country Dreams" by Renie Burghardt (nonfiction), and "The Demon Ponies of Griffith Park" by Evelyn Villegas (fiction). The Quincy Writers Guild meets monthly and consists of Quincy-area writers working in various genres.

REDWOOD ACRES FAIR POETRY CONTEST (I), P.O. Box 6576, Eureka CA 95502, offers an annual contest with various categories for both juniors and seniors with entry fee of 50¢/poem for the junior contests and $1/poem for the senior contests. Deadline: June 3.

‡ROANOKE-CHOWAN POETRY AWARD (IV-Regional), North Carolina Literary and Historical Association, 109 E. Jones St., Raleigh NC 27501, phone (919)733-7442, contact Secretary, offers annual award for "an original volume of poetry published during the twelve months ending June 30 of the year for which the award is given." Open to "authors who have maintained legal or physical residence, or a combination of both, in North Carolina for the three years preceding the close of the contest period." Submit 3 copies of each entry. Most recent award winner was Robert Watson (1995). Winner will be announced during the annual meeting in November.

MARY ROBERTS RINEHART FOUNDATION AWARD (V), Mail Stop Number 3E4, The Mary Roberts Rinehart Award, English Dept., George Mason University, Fairfax VA 22030-4444. Two grants are made annually to writers who need financial assistance "to complete work definitely projected." The amount of the award depends upon income the fund generates; in the past the amount was approximately $900 in each category. Work by poets and fiction writers is accepted in odd numbered years, e.g., 1995, 1997. **A writer's work must be nominated by an established author or editor**; no written recommendations are necessary. Nominations must be accompanied by a sample of the nominee's work, up to 25 pgs. of poetry and 30 pgs. of fiction. Deadline: November 30.

ANNA DAVIDSON ROSENBERG AWARD (IV-Ethnic), Judah L. Magnes Museum, 2911 Russell St., Berkeley CA 94705, offers prizes of $100, $50 and $25, as well as honorable mentions, for up to 10 pgs. of 1-3 unpublished poems (in English) on the Jewish Experience. There is also a Youth Commendation for poets under 19, a Senior Award if 65 or over and a New/Emerging Poet Award. Do not send poems without entry form; write between April 1 and July 15 for form and guidelines (enclose SASE). Deadline: August 31. Recent winners have included Jane Jacobson, Alicia Ostriker, Myra Sklarew and Phillip Terman. The Magnes Museum is the third largest Jewish museum in the country and sponsors numerous programs in the arts and literature.

SALMON ARM SONNET CONTEST (IV-Form), Salmon Arm & Dist. Chamber of Commerce, Box 1270, Salmon Arm, British Columbia V1E 4P4 Canada. An annual contest for unpublished sonnets. Prizes: $100-500 and books. Entry fee: $6/poem. Limit 2 entries. New juvenile category for 18 and under, entry fee: $2/poem plus $6 to enter the main contest. Deadline: June 1. Copies of winning entries will be sent to all entrants.

SAN FRANCISCO FOUNDATION; JOSEPH HENRY JACKSON AWARD; JAMES D. PHELAN AWARD (IV-Regional), % Intersection for the Arts, 446 Valencia St., San Francisco CA 94103. The Jackson Award ($2,000) will be made to the author of an unpublished work-in-progress in the form of fiction (novel or short stories), nonfictional prose, or poetry. Applicants must be residents of northern California or Nevada for three consecutive years immediately prior to the deadline date of January 31, and must be between the ages of 20 and 35 as of the deadline. The Phelan Award ($2,000) will be made to the author of an unpublished work-in-progress in the form of fiction (novel or short stories), nonfictional prose, poetry or drama. Applicants must be California-born (although they may now reside outside of the state), and must be between the ages of 20 and 35 as of the January 31 deadline. Mss for both awards must be accompanied by an application form, which may be obtained by sending a SASE to the above address. Entries accepted November 15 through January 31.

SAN MATEO COUNTY FAIR FINE ARTS COMPETITION (I), P.O. Box 1027, San Mateo CA 94403-0627, phone (415)574-3247, for unpublished poetry. Adult and youth divisions. Write or call for entry form and additional information. Adult Division awards of $100, $50, and $25; fee $10 for each poem. Youth Division awards of $50, $25 and $15; no fee. Limit 2 entries per division. June 28 deadline for poems.

CARL SANDBURG AWARDS (IV-Regional), sponsored by Friends of the Chicago Public Library, 400 S. State St., 10S-7, Chicago IL 60605, phone (312)747-4907, are given annually to native-born Chicago authors or present Chicago-area writers for new books in 4 categories, including poetry. Each author receives $1,000. Publisher or authors should submit 2 copies of books published between June 1 of one year and May 31 of the next. Deadline: August 1.

‡SASKATCHEWAN WRITERS GUILD ANNUAL LITERARY AWARDS; CITY OF RE-GINA WRITING AWARD (IV-Regional), SWG Literary Awards Convenor, Box 3986, Regina, Saskatchewan S4P 3R9 Canada, phone (306)757-6310, offers 3 prizes of $1,000 for long ms (every fourth year for poetry) and 3 prizes of $150 and $75 honorable mentions for 1 poem up to 100 lines. Open to Saskatchewan writers only. $15 entry fee for long mss, $4 for single poems. Deadline mid-June. (Contact for more details.) CRWA of $3,300 awarded annually to a writer living in Regina as of January 1 of the previous year to work for 3 months on a specific project. Deadline: March 15.

SCOTTISH INTERNATIONAL OPEN POETRY COMPETITION; THE AYRSHIRE WRITERS' & ARTISTS' SOCIETY (I), 42 Tollerton Dr., Irvine, Ayrshire, Scotland. Open to all poets. Inaugurated in 1972 it is the longest running poetry competition in the U.K. Entries are free, restricted to two per person and should be accompanied by SASE (or SAE and IRCs). December deadline. Special award ceremony March. First prize, U.K. Section, MacDiarmid Trophy and $100. First prize, International Section, The International Trophy. Scots Section, The Clement Wilson Cup. Diplomas are awarded to runners up. Competition opens September each year. Most recent winner of the International Trophy was Geraldine Mills (Ireland). "The Society, a charitable organisation, is dedicated to the promotion of poetry and poets of every calibre."

SOCIETY OF MIDLAND AUTHORS AWARD (IV-Regional), P.O. Box 10419, Chicago IL 60610-0419, is for authors from Midland states: IL, IN, IA, KS, MI, MN, MO, NE, ND, SD, OH, WI. It is an annual cash award and a plaque given at a dinner. Books in each calendar year are eligible, not self-published. Deadline January 15 of award year. Send SASE for entry form; books must be submitted to each of 3 judges, not to above address. The Society of Midland Authors provides camaraderie and encouragement to writers practicing their art in the heartland. Membership is by invitation only and restricted to authors of books "demonstrating literary style and published by a recognized publisher." However, as a public service, their monthly meetings are open to anyone who wants to attend.

SOUTH DAKOTA STATE POETRY SOCIETY CONTESTS (I), Present Chairman of S.D. State Poetry Society Contests Myra Osterberg, P.O. Box 613, Salem SD 57058, phone (605)425-2886, 12 categories. Deadline: August 31.

SPARROWGRASS POETRY FORUM (I), Dept. PM, 203 Diamond St., Box 193, Sistersville WV 26175, phone (800)685-0848, offers 6 annual free contests, each of which has $1,000 in prizes, including a $500 grand prize. Entrants are solicited to buy an anthology, but you do not have to buy the anthology to win. Send 1 original poem, no longer than 20 lines. Name and address at the top of the page. Any style, any subject. Contest deadlines are the last day of every other month.

SPRINGFEST AND WINTERFEST POETRY CONTESTS; MILE HIGH POETRY SOCIETY (I), P.O. Box 21116, Denver CO 80221, phone (303)657-8461, award director Jane C. Schaul. Each spring and fall they offer a contest with $300 1st prize, $100 2nd prize, and two 3rd prizes of $50 each for maximum 36-line poems. Entry fee $3/poem. Deadlines: June 30 and December 31. Send SASE for details. The Springfest 1995 winners were Ramon Del Castillo, Romaine L. Miller, Barbara R. Dubois and Elizabeth Aiello.

‡STARVING ROMANTICS POETRY COMPETITION (I, II), Starving Romantics, 93 Charnwood Place, Thornhill, Ontario L3T 5H2 Canada, phone (905)731-8055, award director I.J. Schecter, offers annual awards for poetry that "hearkens to the style of Romantic poetry." First place: $125 plus recitation at literary venues; Second place: $50 plus recitation; Third place: $25 plus recitation; Fourth through Tenth: recitation plus free entry for the following year. Submissions must be unpublished and may be entered in other contests. Submit up to 5 poems maximum, typed on one side of page. Include separate cover sheet with name and address and SASE for notification. Send SASE for guidelines. Entry fee: $3/poem. Deadline: July 31. Winners notified by September 30. The director says, "Too much of today's poetry is superficial and lifeless. Starving Romantics was created with the hope of reclaiming poetic integrity on behalf of its Romantic masters—Wordsworth, Shelley, Byron, and others of the period. Send me something which evokes the formidable beauty of Romantic Poetry and you've got a strong chance."

WALLACE E. STEGNER FELLOWSHIPS (II), Creative Writing Program, Stanford University, Stanford CA 94305, phone (415)725-1208, administrator Gay Pierce, 5 in poetry, $15,000 plus tuition of $4,800, for promising writers who can benefit from 2 years instruction and criticism at the Writing Center. Previous publication not required, though it can strengthen one's application. Deadline: Postmarked by the first working day after January 1.

‡TENNESSEE LITERARY AWARDS (I), Tennessee Mountain Writers, P.O. Box 4895, Oak Ridge TN 37831-4895, phone (423)482-6567, contact award director, offers annual awards of $250 in each of 3 categories—fiction, poetry and essay. Second and third place winners in each category will receive $150 and $75, respectively. Submissions must be unpublished. Submit 3-5 poems/entry. "The group of poems in any single entry may, but need not, be related." Send SASE for guidelines. Entry fee: $10 (make checks payable to Tennessee Mountain Writers). Postmark deadline: September 30. "Winners in each category are chosen by an outside judge after initial screening by Board members." Winners announced the first week of January. Tennessee Mountain Writers also sponsor a conference. (See listing in Conferences and Workshops section.)

TOWSON STATE UNIVERSITY PRIZE FOR LITERATURE (II, IV-Regional), Towson State University, College of Liberal Arts, Towson MD 21204-7097, phone (410)830-2128, award director Dean of the College of Liberal Arts, offers annual prize of $1,000 "for a single book or book-length manuscript of fiction, poetry, drama or imaginative nonfiction by a young Maryland writer. The prize is granted on the basis of literary and aesthetic excellence as determined by a panel of distinguished judges appointed by the university. The first award, made in the fall of 1980, went to novelist Anne Tyler." The work must have been published within the three years prior to the year of nomination or must be scheduled for publication within the year in which nominated. Open to Maryland residents under 40 years of age. Submit 5 copies of work in bound form or in typewritten, double-spaced ms form. Send SASE for entry form and guidelines. Deadline: May 15.

TRILLIUM BOOK AWARD; PRIX TRILLIUM (IV-Regional), Ministry of Citizenship, Culture and Recreation, Cultural Partnerships Branch, 77 Bloor St. W, 3rd Floor, Toronto, Ontario M7A 2R9 Canada, is given annually for a book in English and a book in French by Ontario authors. Submissions of published books are by publishers. Winning authors in each category receive $12,000; publishers of the winning books also receive $2,500 each. Awards given in April. Deadline: December 31.

KINGSLEY TUFTS POETRY AWARD; KATE TUFTS DISCOVERY AWARD FOR POETRY (II), The Claremont Graduate School, 740 N. College Ave., Claremont CA 91711, phone (909)621-8974, award chairman Jack Miles. The Kingsley Tufts Poetry Award is a $50,000 prize awarded annually to a book published during the previous year. Unpublished book-length mss created during the previous year are also acceptable, if poet has publication credits. Subject and form are open. No translations. Submit 5 copies with entry form. Entry form must accompany submission. Deadline: September 15. Manuscripts scheduled for publication between September 15 and December 31 may be submitted in ms form or held for the next competition. The Kate Tufts Discovery Award for Poetry is an annual $5,000 prize awarded to a "first or very early work by a poet of genuine promise." Submission requirements and deadline are the same as Kingsley Tufts Poetry Award. (Work may be entered in only one award.) Both awards are presented at a ceremony in April. Entrants to the Kingsley Tufts Award must "agree to reproduction rights, be present at the award ceremony and spend a week in residence at the Claremont Graduate School." Send SASE for rules and entry forms.

UTAH ORIGINAL WRITING COMPETITION (II, IV-Regional), Utah Arts Council Literary Program, 617 E. South Temple, Salt Lake City UT 84102-1177, award director Guy Lebeda, offers annual awards in 7 categories: novel, nonfiction book, book-length collection of poetry, juvenile book, poetry, short story and personal essay. Prizes range from $200-1,000 and a $5,000 publication prize is awarded to one of the book-length first place winners from the previous year's competition. Open to Utah residents only. "Submit work in standard publishing ms style." Write for entry form. Deadline: mid-June.

THE VICTORIAN FELLOWSHIP OF AUSTRALIAN WRITERS; FAW AWARDS (IV-Regional), FAW (Vic) Inc., P.O. Box 528, Camberwell 3124, Australia, all awards for Australian authors. The FAW Anne Elder Poetry Award (prizes of $1,000 and $500) is for a first published book of poetry. The FAW Christopher Brennan Award is a bronze plaque to honor an Australian poet who has written work of sustained quality and distinction (entries not required; award by committee). The FAW John Shaw Neilson Poetry Award (prizes of $500 and $250) is for an unpublished poem of at least 14 lines. The FAW Fedora Anderson Young Writers' Poetry Award ($150 and $75) is for unpublished poems by Australian writers 15-20 years old. The FAW C.J. Dennis Young Writers' Poetry Award (prizes of $100 and $50) is for unpublished poems by Australian writers 10-14 years old.

THE W.D. WEATHERFORD AWARD (IV-Regional), Berea College, CPO 2336, Berea KY 40404, contact chairman, for the published work (including poetry) which "best illuminates the problems, personalities, and unique qualities of the Appalachian South." Work is nominated by its publisher, by a member of the award committee or by any reader. The award is for $500 and sometimes there are special awards of $200 each. Deadline: December 31 of the year work was published.

WEST HAVEN COUNCIL OF THE ARTS, P.O. Box 17594, West Haven CT 06516. An annual national poetry contest open April 15 to September 15. Entry fee: $2 for the first poem, $1 each additional to a maximum of $5. Prizes of $50, $25 and $15 will be awarded plus publication in the annual poetry anthology, *Sound and Waves of West Haven*. Send SASE for guidelines.

‡WESTERN HERITAGE AWARDS (IV-Specialized), National Cowboy Hall of Fame and Western Heritage Center, 1700 NE 63rd St., Oklahoma City OK 73111. Since 1960, this national museum has awarded excellence in western literature, music, television and film. Principle creators of winning entries in 15 categories receive the bronze "Wrangler," an original sculpture by artist John Free, during special awards ceremonies held at the museum each March. The 1995 award for poetry went to Jane Candia Coleman for her book *The Red Drum*, published by High Plains Press. Entry forms are mailed annually in September for works published between January 1 and November 30 of that year. Deadline for entries: November 30.

WESTERN STATES BOOK AWARDS; WESTERN STATES ARTS FEDERATION (IV-Regional), Dept. PM, 236 Montezuma Ave., Santa Fe NM 87501, presents annual book awards to outstanding authors and publishers. The awards include cash prizes of $5,000 for writers and their respective publishers. Mss must be written by an author living in Alaska, Arizona, California, Colorado, Idaho, Montana, Nevada, New Mexico, Oregon, Utah, Washington or Wyoming. Award given to books to be published in fall of the award year. Work must already have been accepted for publication by a publisher in one of these states. Work must be submitted by the publisher, submitted in ms form (not previously published in book form). Publisher must have published at least 3 books. Write for more information.

WFNB ANNUAL LITERARY CONTEST; THE ALFRED G. BAILEY AWARD; WRITERS' FEDERATION OF NEW BRUNSWICK (IV-Regional), P.O. Box 37, Station A, Fredericton, New Brunswick E3B 4Y2 Canada, offers prizes of $200, $100, $30, for unpublished poems of up to 100 lines (typed, double-spaced). Open to New Brunswick residents only. The Alfred G. Bailey Award is a $400 prize given annually for poetry mss of 48 pgs. or more. May include some individual poems that have been published. Entry fee: $10 for members, $15 for nonmembers. Send SASE for guidelines. Deadline: February 14.

WHITING WRITERS' AWARDS; MRS. GILES WHITING FOUNDATION (V), 1133 Avenue of the Americas, 22nd Floor, New York NY 10036-6710, director Gerald Freund. The Foundation makes awards of $30,000 each to up to 10 writers of fiction, nonfiction, poetry and plays chosen by a selection committee drawn from a list of recognized writers, literary scholars and editors. Recipients of the award are selected from nominations made by writers, educators and editors from communities across the country whose experience and vocations bring them in contact with individuals of unusual talent. The nominators and selectors are appointed by the foundation and serve anonymously. **Direct applications and informal nominations are not accepted by the foundation.**

‡**STAN AND TOM WICK POETRY PRIZE (I)**, Wick Poetry Program, Kent State University, P.O. Box 5190, Kent OH 44242-0001, phone (330)672-2672, e-mail wickpoet@kentvm.kent.edu, award director Maggie Anderson, offers annual award of $1,000 and publication by The Kent State University Press. Submissions must be unpublished and may be entered in other contests. Submit 48-68 pages of poetry. Open to poets writing in English who have not yet published a full-length collection. Entries must include cover sheet with poet's name, address, telephone number and title of ms. Send SASE for guidelines. Entry fee: $10. Deadline: May 1, 1997. Most recent contest winner was Lise Coffman (1995). Judge was Alicia Suskin Ostriker. Judge for 1996 contest was Yusef Komunyakaa.

OSCAR WILLIAMS & GENE DERWOOD AWARD (V), Community Funds, Inc., 2 Park Ave., New York NY 10016, is an award given annually to nominees of the selection committee "to help needy or worthy artists or poets." **Selection Committee for the award does not accept nominations.** Amount varies from year to year.

WISCONSIN ARTS BOARD FELLOWSHIPS (II, IV-Regional), Wisconsin Arts Board, 101 E. Wilson St., 1st Floor, Madison WI 53702, phone (608)266-0190, award director Kate LaRocque, offers fellowships to "recognize the significant contributions of professional artists." Open to Wisconsin residents who are *not* fulltime students. Write for entry form and guidelines. Deadline: September ("call for exact date").

WORLD ORDER OF NARRATIVE AND FORMALIST POETS (II, IV-Subscription, form), P.O. Box 580174, Station A, Flushing NY 11358-0174, contest chairman Dr. Alfred Dorn. This organization sponsors contests in at least 15 categories of traditional and contemporary poetic forms, including the sonnet, blank verse, ballade, villanelle, free verse and new forms created by Alfred Dorn. Prizes total at least $5,000 and range from $20 to $300. Only subscribers to *The Formalist* will be eligible for the competition, as explained in the complete guidelines available from the contest chairman. "We look for originality of thought, phrase and image, combined with masterful craftsmanship. Trite, trivial or technically inept work stands no chance." Postmark deadline for entries: April 24, 1997. Recent contest winners include Annie Finch, Rhina Espaillat, Melissa Cannon and Roy Scheele. (For more information on *The Formalist*, see their listing in the Publishers of Poetry section.)

WORLD'S WORST POETRY CONTEST (IV-Regional), Pismo Bob's True Value Hardware and Nursery, 930 Price St., Pismo Beach CA 93449, phone (805)773-NAIL, fax (805)773-6772, award director "Pismo Bob" Pringle. Contest for "bad (not necessarily conforming to normality)" poetry that mentions Pismo Beach. The contest is simple to enter. Just send a poem or poems to "Pismo Bob" Pringle, originator of the contest. The poems must include the word "Pismo," but aside from that there are no literary requirements. "In addition to the sheer pride of being the world's worst bard, the Chosen One will also win a free round trip to the wonderful shores of Pismo Beach, California." Deadline: September 30.

WRITERS AT WORK FELLOWSHIP COMPETITION (II), Writers at Work, P.O. Box 1146, Centerville UT 84103, phone (801)292-9285, offers annual awards of $1,500 and $500 plus publication in *Quarterly West* (first place only). Submissions must be unpublished and can be entered in other contests, "but must be withdrawn if they win another contest." Submit 6 poems, 10 pgs. maximum, subject and form open. Entry must include 2 copies of ms, 2 #10 SASEs and cover letter stating name, address, phone number, genre and title of ms. "No names on mss." Mss will not be returned. Open to any writer who has not published a book-length volume of original work. Entry fee: $12/entry (make check payable to Writers at Work). Postmark deadline: March 15.

WRITERS' GUILD OF ALBERTA BOOK AWARD (IV-Regional), Writer's Guild, 11759 Groat Rd., 3rd Floor, Edmonton, Alberta T5M 3K6 Canada, phone (403)422-8174, awarded in six categories, including poetry. Eligible books will have been published anywhere in the world between January 1 and December 31. Their authors will have been a resident in Alberta for at least 12 of the 18 months prior to December 31. Contact the WGA head office for registry forms. Unpublished manuscripts are not eligible. Except in the drama category, anthologies are not eligible. Five copies of each book to be considered must be mailed to the WGA office no later than December 31. Submissions postmarked after this date will not be accepted. Exceptions will be made for any books published between the 15th and 31st of December. These may be submitted by January 15. Three copies will go to the three judges in that category; one will remain in the WGA library; and one will be placed in a

WGA book display around the province. Works may be submitted by authors, publishers, or any interested parties.

WRITERS UNLIMITED (I), %Voncile Ros, 4709 New Hope Ave., Pascagoula MS 39581-3040, offers an annual literary competition, deadline September 1. There are up to 20 categories with cash prizes up to $50 and other prizes. Do not use the same poem for more than one category. $5 entry fee covers entries in all categories up to 20. Send SASE for contest rules.

WYOMING ARTS COUNCIL FELLOWSHIP COMPETITION (II, IV-Regional), 2320 Capitol Ave., Cheyenne WY 82002, phone (307)777-7742, award director Michael Shay, offers up to four annual awards of $2,000 each. Submissions can be entered in other contests. Submit 10 pgs. maximum. Open to poets residing in Wyoming for 2 years prior to award. "No name should appear on manuscript." Send SASE for entry form and guidelines. Deadline: July 1.

Additional Contests and Awards

The following listings also contain information about contests and awards. See the General Index for page numbers, then read the listings and send SASEs (or SAEs and IRCs) for specific details about their offerings. Note: Double daggers (‡) preceding titles indicate listings new to this edition.

Abiko Quarterly With James Joyce Studies
Academy of American Poets, The
Advocate
Aegina Press, Inc.
African Voices
Albatross
‡A.L.I. (The Avon Literary Intelligencer)
Alicejamesbooks
‡Amaranth
Amelia
America
American Poetry Review
American Tolkien Society
‡Amethyst Review, The
Analecta
‡Anamnesis Press
Anhinga Press
Anterior Poetry Monthly
Antietam Review
Appalachia
Appalachian Heritage
Appalachian Writers' Association Conference
Apropos
‡Arc: Canada's National Poetry Magazine
Arkansas Press, The University of
Arkansas Writers' Conference
‡artisan, a journal of craft
Associated Writing Programs
Atlanta Review
‡Authors
Bay Area Poets Coalition (BAPC)
Bellingham Review, The
Bell's Letters Poet
Beloit Poetry Journal, The
Black Bear Publications
Black Warrior Review, The
Block's Poetry Collection
Blue Penny Quarterly
Blue Unicorn, A Triquarterly of Poetry
Bohemian Chronicle
BOOG Literature
Borderlands: Texas Poetry Review

Bread Loaf Writers' Conference
‡Buffalo Bones
ByLine Magazine
Calapooya Collage
Canada Council, The
Canadian Writer's Journal
‡Candlelight Poetry Journal
Cape Rock, The
Caribbean Writer, The
Carolina Quarterly, The
Center Press
Chelsea
Chiron Review
Claremont Review, The
Cleveland State University Poetry Center
Climbing Art, The
‡Cló Iar-Chonnachta
Cochran's Corner
Comstock Review, The
Connecticut River Review
Copper Canyon Press
Country Woman
Cover Magazine
CQ (California State Poetry Quarterly)
Crab Creek Review
Craft of Writing
Crazyhorse
Cream City Review
Cricket
Crucible
Cumberland Poetry Review
Cutbank
‡Dancing Jester Press
‡Dead Metaphor Press
Deep South Writers Conference
Defined Providence
Devil's Millhopper Press, The
Dominion Review, The
Dream Shop, The
Eagle's Flight
Echoes Magazine
1812
Eighth Mountain Press, The
ELF: Eclectic Literary Forum
Elk River Review
Envoi

Epoch
Equinox Press
Excursus Literary Arts Journal
Explorations
Explorer Magazine
Expressions
Expressions Forum Review
Fauquier Poetry Journal
Federation of British Columbia Writers
Feelings: America's Beautiful Poetry Magazine
‡First Time
‡Floating Bridge Press
Flume Press
Folio: A Literary Journal
Footwork: The Paterson Literary Review
Formalist, The
Frogmore Papers
Frogpond: Quarterly Haiku Journal
Fudge Cake, The
‡Gaslight: Tales of the Unsane
Gentle Survivalist, The
Georgetown Review
Geppo Haiku Worksheet
‡Gerbil: A Queer Culture Zine
Glass Cherry Press, The
Golden Isis Magazine
Grain
Greensboro Review, The
Haiku Headlines: A Monthly Newsletter of Haiku and Senryu
Half Tones to Jubilee
Harp-Strings Poetry Journal
Heartlands Today, The
Heaven Bone Magazine
Helicon Nine Editions
Hellas: A Journal of Poetry and the Humanities
Hippopotamus Press
Home Planet News
‡Hopewell Review
Housewife-Writer's Forum
Hubbub
Hyacinth House Publications

GET YOUR WORK INTO THE RIGHT BUYERS' HANDS!

You work hard... and your hard work deserves to be seen by the right buyers. But with the constant changes in the industry, it's not always easy to know who those buyers are. That's why you'll want to keep up-to-date and on top with the most current edition of this indispensable market guide.

Keep ahead of the changes by ordering *1998 Poet's Market* today. You'll save the frustration of getting poems returned in the mail, stamped MOVED: ADDRESS UNKNOWN. And of NOT submitting your work to new listings because you don't know they exist. All you have to do to order the upcoming 1998 edition is complete the attached order card and return it with your payment or credit card information. Order now and you'll get the 1998 edition at the 1997 price—just $22.99— no matter how much the regular price may increase! *1998 Poet's Market* will be published and ready for shipment in September 1997.

Keep on top of the fast-changing industry and get a jump on selling your work with help from the *1998 Poet's Market*. Order today! You deserve it!

Turn over for more books to help you get your poems published

---

☐ **Yes!** I want the most current edition of *Poet's Market*. Please send me the 1998 edition at the 1997 price – $22.99.* (NOTE: *1998 Poet's Market* will be ready for shipment in September 1997.) #10516

I also want:

Book # _____ Price $_____

Book # _____ Price $_____

Book # _____ Price $_____

Book # _____ Price $_____

Subtotal $_____

*Add $3.50 postage and handling for one book; $1.00 for each additional book.

Postage and handling $_____

Payment must accompany order.
Ohioans add 6% sales tax.

Total $_____

☐ **FREE CATALOG.** Ask your bookstore about other fine Writer's Digest Books, or mail this card today for a complete catalog.

**VISA/MasterCard orders call
TOLL-FREE 1-800-289-0963**

☐ Payment enclosed $_____ (or)

Charge my: ☐ Visa ☐ MasterCard Exp._____

Account # _____

Signature_____

Name_____

Address _____

City_____ State _____ Zip _____

Phone Number _____
(will be used only if we must contact you regarding this order.)

**30-Day Money Back Guarantee
on every book you buy!**

Mail to:
Writer's Digest Books
1507 Dana Avenue
Cincinnati, OH 45207

6897

More Great Books to Help You Write and Sell Your Poetry!

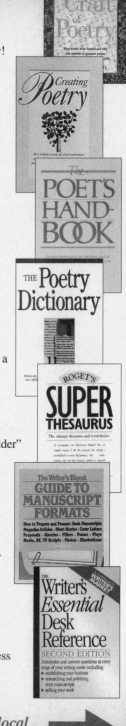

‡Icon
‡i.e. magazine, A Journal of
    Literature and the Arts
Imago: New Writing
Intercultural Writer's Review,
    The
International Black Writers
Iowa Press, University of
Iowa Woman
‡Jacaranda
Jackson's Arm
‡Joyful Noise: The Journal of
    Christian Poetry
Kalliope, a journal of women's art
Kinesis
‡Lacunae Magazine
League of Canadian Poets, The
Ledge Poetry and Fiction
    Magazine, The
Light and Life Magazine
Lines n' Rhymes
‡Listening Eye, The
Literal Latté
Literature and Belief
‡Litteratura Magazine
Loft, The
Long Island Quarterly
Lotus Poetry Series
Louisiana Literature
Lucidity
Madison Review, The
Malahat Review, The
‡Manitoba Writers' Guild Inc.
‡Many Mountains Moving
Maryland Poetry Review
Massachusetts Press, The
    University of
Maverick Press, The
Mid-American Review
Midwest Poetry Review
Midwest Writers' Conference
‡Minority Literary Expo
Mississippi Valley Writers
    Conference
Missouri Review
Mr. Cogito Press
Mockingbird
Modern Haiku
‡M.O.O.N. Magazine
‡Moose Bound Press
(m)öthêr TØñgué Press
‡MPF Muse Letter, The
Mudfish
My Legacy
Mystery Time
Nation, The
National Federation of State
    Poetry Societies, Inc.
Nebraska Review, The
Negative Capability
New England Poetry Club
New Era Magazine
‡New Frontiers of New Mexico
‡New Hampshire Writers &
    Publishers Project
New Horizons Poetry Club
New Letters
New Press Literary Quarterly,
    The
new renaissance, the
‡New Spirit Press
Nimrod: International Journal of

Contemporary Poetry and
    Fiction
‡Nite-Writer's International
    Literary Arts Journal
North Carolina Writers' Network
North, The
Northeastern University Press
Nostalgia: A Sentimental State of
    Mind
‡no roses review
Oak, The
‡Oatmeal and Poetry
Ohio State University Press/The
    Journal Award in Poetry
Onionhead
Oracle Poetry
Orbis: An International Quarterly
    of Poetry and Prose
Oregon State Poetry Association,
    The
Owl Creek Press
‡Oxford Poetry
Ozark Creative Writers
    Conference
‡Pacific Coast Journal
Painted Bride Quarterly
Palanquin/TDM
Panhandler, The
‡Paper Boat Magazine
Paris Review, The
Parnassus Literary Journal
Pasque Petals
Passager: A Journal of
    Remembrance and Discovery
‡Pavement Saw
Pearl
PEN American Center
‡Peregrine: The Journal of
    Amherst Writers & Artists
Perivale Press
Permafrost: A Literary Journal
Peterloo Poets
‡Piedmont Literary Review
Pig Iron
Pikeville Review
Pitt Poetry Series
Pittsburgh Quarterly, The
Plainsongs
Plowman, The
Plum Review, The
Poems & Plays
Poet Magazine
Poetic Page
Poetry
Poetry Committee of the Greater
    Washington Area, The
Poetry Harbor
Poetry Ireland Review
Poetry Miscellany, The
Poetry Northwest
‡Poetry Nottingham International
Poetry Society of America
‡Poet's Attic, The
Poets at Work
Poet's Fantasy
‡Poet's Guild, The
‡Poets Journey, A
Poet's Review
Poets' Roundtable
Potpourri
Prairie Schooner
Princeton University Press

Pudding House Publications
Purdue University Press
Quarterly Review of Literature
    Poetry Book Series
Radcliffe Quarterly
‡Rambunctious Press
Rio Grande Press
River City
‡River Oak Review
Riverstone, A Press for Poetry
Rockford Review, The
Rosebud
St. Davids Christian Writers
    Conference
Salmon Run Press
Santa Barbara Review
Santa Barbara Writers'
    Conference
Sarabande Books, Inc.
Scavenger's Newsletter
‡Seasons of the Muse
Sewanee Review, The
Sheila-na-gig
Shenandoah
Silhouette
Silver Apples Press
Silver Wings
Silverfish Review
Sinipee Writers Workshop
‡Skipping Stones: A
    Multicultural Children's
    Magazine
Slate & Style
Slipstream
Smith Publisher, Gibbs
Society of American Poets, The
Songwriters and Poets Critique
Sonora Review
Southern California Anthology,
    The
Southern Humanities Review
Southern Poetry Association
Southern Poetry Review
Southwest Florida Writers'
    Conference
Southwest Review
Sow's Ear Poetry Review, The
Spitball
Spoon River Poetry Review, The
Staple
State of Maine Writers'
    Conference
State Street Press
Still Waters Press
Story Line Press
Studio, A Journal of Christians
    Writing
Sub-Terrain
Sun Dog: The Southeast Review
Taproot Literary Review
Tears in the Fence
‡Tennessee Mountain Writers
    Conference
Tesseract Publications
Texas Tech University Press
Tickled by Thunder: The
    Magazine That Set Fiction
    Free
Time of Singing, A Magazine of
    Christian Poetry
Trenton State College Writers
    Conference

Unforgettable Fire, The
‡University of Arizona Poetry
  Center
Unterberg Poetry Center of the
  92nd Street Y, The
Vegetarian Journal
Verve
Virginia Quarterly Review, The
Voices Israel
W.I.M. Publications (Woman in
  the Moon)
Washington Writers' Publishing
  House
Waterways: Poetry in the
  Mainstream
West Wind Writers & Artists
  Project
Westerly
Western Humanities Review

Weyfarers
‡Whetstone (Canada)
Whetstone (IL)
Whiskey Island Magazine
White Eagle Coffee Store Press
White Pine Press
White Review: A Gay Men's
  Literary Quarterly, James
White River Writers' Workshop
Wildwood Journal
Willow Review
Willow Springs
Wind Publications
Wisconsin Press, University of
Wisconsin Regional Writers'
  Association
Woodley Memorial Press
Woodnotes
Worcester Review

‡Word Works, The
WORDS—The Arkansas Literary
  Society
World-wide Writers Service, Inc.
WoRM fEASt!
Wormwood Review Press
‡Write Way, The
Writers' Center Press
Writer's Digest
Writer's Exchange
Writer's Journal
‡Writers of Kern
Writing Today
‡Wyoming Writers, Inc.
Yale University Press
‡Yalobusha Review, The
Yankee Magazine
Zuzu's Petal Quarterly Online

State and Provincial Grants

Arts councils in the United States and Canada provide assistance to artists (including poets) in the form of fellowships or grants. These grants can be substantial and confer prestige upon recipients; however, **only state or province residents are eligible**. Because deadlines and available support vary annually, query first (with a SASE).

UNITED STATES ART AGENCIES

Alabama State Council on the Arts, *Becky Mullens, Performing Arts Program Manager, 1 Dexter Ave., Montgomery AL 36130-1800; (334)242-4076*

Alaska State Council on the Arts, *Shannon Planchon, Grants Officer, 411 W. Fourth Ave., Suite 1-E, Anchorage AK 99501; (907)269-6610*

Arizona Commission on the Arts, *Tonda Gorton, Public Information Officer, 417 W. Roosevelt, Phoenix AZ 85003; (602)255-5882*

Arkansas Arts Council, *Sally Williams, Artists Program Coordinator, 1500 Tower Bldg., 323 Center St., Little Rock AR 72201; (501)324-9150*

California Arts Council, *Carol Shiffman, Individual Fellowships, 1300 I St., Suite 930, Sacramento CA 95814; (916)322-6555*

Colorado Council on the Arts and Humanities, *Daniel Salazar, Individual Artists Program Director, 750 Pennsylvania St., Denver CO 80203-3699; (303)894-2619*

Connecticut Commission on the Arts, *Linda Dente, Grants Information, 1 Financial Plaza, Lobby, 755 Main St., Hartford CT 06103; (203)566-7076*

Delaware State Arts Council, *Barbara King, Coordinator, Individual Artist Fellowships, Carvel State Office Building, 820 N. French St., Wilmington DE 19801; (302)577-3540*

District of Columbia Commission on the Arts and Humanities, *Carlos Arrien, Program Coordinator, Stables Art Center, 5th Floor, 410 Eighth St. NW, Washington DC 20004; (202)724-5613*

Florida Arts Council, *Valerie Ohlsson, Arts Consultant, Division of Cultural Affairs, Florida Dept. of State, The Capitol, Tallahassee FL 32399-0250; (904)487-2980*

Georgia Council for the Arts, *Ann Davis, Program Manager, Community Arts Development, 530 Means St. NW, Suite 115, Atlanta GA 30318-5793; (404)651-7920*

Hawaii State Foundation on Culture & Arts, *Hinano Campton, Artist Grant Coordinator, 44 Merchant St., Honolulu HI 96813; (808)586-0300*

Idaho Commission on the Arts, *Diane Josephy Peavey, Literature Director, P.O. Box 83720, Boise ID 83720-0008; (208)334-2119*

Illinois Arts Council, *Richard Gage, Communication Arts Director, 100 W. Randolph, Suite 10-500, Chicago IL 60601; (312)814-6750*

Indiana Arts Commission, *Beth Bashara, Interim Artist Manager, 402 W. Washington St., Room W072, Indianapolis IN 46204-2741; (317)232-1268*

Iowa Arts Council, *Julie Bailey, Grants Coordinator, Capitol Complex, 600 E. Locust, Des Moines IA 50319-0290; (515)281-4451*

Kansas Arts Commission, *Tom Klocke, Program Coordinator, Jay Hawk Tower, 700 Jackson, Suite 1004, Topeka KS 66603; (913)296-3335*

Kentucky Arts Council, *Irwin Pickett, Program Branch Manager, 31 Fountain Place, Frankfort KY 40601-1942; (502)564-3757*

Louisiana State Arts Council, *James Border, Program Director, 1051 N. Third St., Room 420, Baton Rouge LA 70802; (504)342-8180*

Maine State Arts Commission, *Alden C. Wilson, Director, State House, Station 25, 55 Capitol St., Augusta ME 04333-0025; (207)287-2724*

Maryland State Arts Council, *Charles Camp, Grants Officer, 601 N. Howard St., Baltimore MD 21201; (410)333-8232*

Massachusetts Cultural Council, *Lisa Sasier, Public Information, 120 Boylston St., 2nd Floor, Boston MA 02116; (617)727-3668*

Arts Foundation of Michigan, *Kim Adams, Executive Director, 645 Griswold, Suite 2164, Detroit MI 48226; (313)964-2244*

Minnesota State Arts Board, *Karen Mueller, Program Associate, Park Square Court, 400 Sibley St., Suite 200, St. Paul MN 55101; (612)215-1600*

Mississippi Arts Commission, *Kathleen Stett, Program Administrator, 239 N. Lamar St., Suite 207, Jackson MS 39201; (601)359-6030*

Missouri Arts Council, *Michael Hunt, Program Administrator, Wainwright State Office Complex, 111 N. Seventh St., Suite 105, St. Louis MO 63101; (314)340-6845*

Montana Arts Council, *Fran Morrow, Director of Art Services/Programs, 316 N. Park Ave., Suite 252, Helena MT 59620; (406)444-6430*

Nebraska Arts Council, *Nancy Quinn, Grants Officer, 3838 Davenport, Omaha NE 68131-2329; (402)595-2122*

Nevada State Council on the Arts, *Susan Bofkoff, Executive Director, 602 N. Curry, Carson City NV 89710; (702)687-6680*

New Hampshire State Council on the Arts, *Audrey Sylvester, Artists Services Coordinator, Phoenix Hall, 40 N. Main St., Concord NH 03301; (603)271-2789*

New Jersey State Council on the Arts, *Steve Runk, Grants Coordinator, CN 306, 3rd Floor, Roebling Bldg., 20 W. State St., Trenton NJ 08625; (609)292-6130*

New Mexico Arts Division, *Eleanor Broh-Kahn, Administrative Secretary, 228 E. Palace Ave., Santa Fe NM 87501; (505)827-6490*

New York State Council on the Arts, *Jewelle Gomez, Director, Literature Program, 915 Broadway, New York NY 10010; (212)387-7020*

North Carolina Arts Council, *Deborah McGill, Literature Director, Department of Cultural Resources, 221 E. Lane St., Raleigh NC 27601-2807; (919)733-2111*

North Dakota Council on the Arts, *John Carroll, Assistant Directoor, 418 E. Broadway, Suite 70, Bismark ND 58501-4086; (701)328-3954*

Ohio Arts Council, *Bob Fox, Literature Coordinator, 727 E. Main St., Columbus OH 43205; (614)466-2613*

State Arts Council of Oklahoma, *Betty Price, Executive Director, P.O. Box 52001-2001, Oklahoma City OK 73152-2001; (405)521-2931*

Oregon Arts Commission, *Vincent Dunn, Assistant Director, 775 Summer St. NE, Salem OR 97310; (503)986-0082*

Pennsylvania Council on the Arts, *John Moore, Literature Program Director, Finance Bldg., Room 216, Harrisburg PA 17120; (717)787-6883*

Institute of Puerto Rican Culture, *P.O. Box 4184, San Juan PR 00905; (809)724-0700*

Rhode Island State Council on the Arts, *Randold Rasenbaum, Director, Individual Artist Program, 95 Cedar St., Suite 103, Providence RI 02903; (401)277-3880*

South Carolina Arts Commission, *Steve Lewis, Literary Arts Director, 1800 Gervais St., Columbia SC 29201; (803)734-8696*

South Dakota Arts Council, *Dennis Holub, Director, 800 Governors Dr., Pierre SD 57501; (605)773-3131*

Tennessee Arts Commission, *Alice Swanson, Director of Literary Arts, 404 James Robertson Pkwy., Suite 160, Nashville TN 37243-0780; (615)741-1701*

Texas Commission on the Arts, *Rita Starpattern, Program Director, Visual and Communication Arts, P.O. Box 13406, Austin TX 78711-3406; (512)463-5535*

Utah Arts Council, *Amanda Pahnke, Assistant Director, 617 E. South Temple, Salt Lake City UT 84102; (801)533-5895*

Vermont Council on the Arts, *Nicolette Clarke, Executive Director, 136 State St., Drawer 33, Montpelier VT 05633-6001; (802)828-3291*

Virgin Islands Council on the Arts, *Marie Daniel, Grants Officer, 41-42 Norre Gada, St. Thomas VI 00802; (809)774-5984*

Virginia Commission for the Arts, *Susan FitzPatrick, Program Coordinator, 223 Governor St., Richmond VA 23219; (804)225-3132*

Washington State Arts Commission, *Artist Fellowship, Karen Gose, Executive Director, 234 E. Eighth Ave., Olympia WA 98504-2675; (360)753-3860*

West Virginia Arts and Humanities Division, *Jill Ellis, Grants Coordinator, Cultural Center, 1900 Kanawha Blvd. E., Charleston WV 25305-0300; (304)558-0220*

Wisconsin Arts Board, *Kate LaRocque, Individual Artists Program Director, 101 E. Wilson St., 1st Floor, Madison WI 53702; (608)266-0190*

Wyoming Council on the Arts, *Michael Shay, Literary Arts Coordinator, 2320 Capitol Ave., Cheyenne WY 82002; (307)777-7742*

CANADIAN PROVINCES ART AGENCIES

Alberta Arts and Cultural Industries Branch, *Clive Padfield, Director, 10158 - 103 St., 3rd Floor, Edmonton, Alberta T5J 0X6; (403)427-6315*

British Columbia Arts Council, *Cultural Services Branch, Walter Quan, Coordinator of Individual Awards Program, 800 Johnson St., 5th Floor, Victoria, British Columbia V8V 1X4; (604)356-1728*

Manitoba Arts Council, *Pat Sanders, Writing/Publishing Officer, 525 - 93 Lombard Ave., Winnipeg, Manitoba R3B 3B1; (204)945-0422*

New Brunswick Department of Tourism, Recreation and Heritage, *Arts Branch, % Desmond Maillet, P.O. Box 6000, Fredericton, New Brunswick E3B 5H1; (506)453-2555*

Newfoundland Department of Municipal and Provincial Affairs, *Cultural Affairs, % Elizabeth Channing, P.O. Box 1854, St. John's, Newfoundland A1C 5P9; (709)729-3650*

Nova Scotia Department of Education, *Cultural Affairs, % Peggy Walt, P.O. Box 578, Halifax, Nova Scotia B3J 2S9; (902)424-4442*

The Canada Council, *General Information Officer, P.O. Box 1047, 350 Albert St., Ottawa, Ontario K1P 5V8; (613)566-4365*

Ontario Arts Council, *Lorraine Filyer, Literature Officer, 151 Bloor St. W., 6th Floor, Toronto, Ontario M5S 1T6; (416)961-1660*

Prince Edward Island Council of the Arts, *Judy McDonald, Executive Director, 115 Richmond, Charlottetown, Prince Edward Island C1A 1H7; (902)368-4410*

Saskatchewan Arts Board, *Gail Paul Armstrong, Literary & Multidisciplinary Arts Consultant, 3475 Albert St., Regina, Saskatchewan S4S 6X6; (306)787-4056*

Government of Yukon Arts Branch, *Laurel Parry, Arts Consultant, P.O. Box 2703, Whitehorse, Yukon Y1A 2C6; (403)667-5264*

Resources
Conferences and Workshops

Conferences and workshops are valuable resources for many poets, especially beginners. A conference or workshop serves as an opportunity to learn about specific aspects of the craft, connect with and gather feedback from other poets and writers, listen to submission tips from editors, and revel in a creative atmosphere that may stimulate one's muse.

In this section you'll find listings for 72 conferences and workshops—more than a dozen of which are new to this edition. Some, such as The Asheville Poetry Festival in Asheville, North Carolina, are specifically geared to poets. Most, however, are more general conferences with offerings for a variety of writers, including poets.

A "typical" conference may have a number of workshop sessions, keynote speakers and perhaps even a panel or two. Topics may include everything from writing fiction, poetry, and books for children to marketing one's work. Often a theme, which may change from year to year, will be the connecting factor.

Other conferences and workshops cover a number of topics but have an overriding focus. For example, you'll find two gatherings for Appalachian writers. There are also events geared to women writers and Christian writers. And the Writing Workshop in Lexington, Kentucky, is specifically designed to aid adults ages 55 or older.

Despite different themes or focuses, each listing in this section details the offerings available for poets. Each also includes information about other workshops, speakers and panels of interest. It is important to note, however, that conference and workshop directors were still in the organizing stages when contacted. Consequently, some listings include information from last year's events simply to provide an idea of what to expect this year. For more up-to-date details, including current costs, send a SASE to the director in question a few months before the date(s) listed.

BENEFITING FROM CONFERENCES

Without a doubt, attending conferences and workshops is beneficial. First, these events provide opportunities to learn more about the poetic craft. Some even feature individual sessions with workshop leaders, allowing you to specifically discuss your work with others. If these one-on-one sessions include critiques (generally for an additional fee), we've included this information.

Besides learning from workshop leaders, you can also benefit from conversations with other attendees. Writers on all levels often enjoy talking to and sharing insights with others. A conversation over lunch can reveal a new market for your work, or a casual chat while waiting for a session to begin can acquaint you with a new resource.

Also, if a conference or workshop includes time for open readings and you choose to participate, you may gain feedback from both workshop leaders and others. For some, however, just the relief from the loneliness of writing can make a conference or workshop worthwhile.

Another reason conferences and workshops are valuable is the opportunity they provide to meet editors and publishers who often have tips about marketing work. The availability of these folks, however, does not necessarily mean they will want to read your latest collection of poems (unless, of course, they are workshop leaders and you have individual meetings scheduled with them).

Although editors and publishers cannot give personal attention to everyone they meet, don't be afraid to approach them. If they weren't interested in speaking to writers, they wouldn't have agreed to attend the conference. However, if the editor or publisher's schedule is too full to allow discussion of your work, ask if you may follow up with a letter after the event. This will give you the benefit of his or her undivided attention and, perhaps, develop into a contact in the poetry field.

SELECTING A CONFERENCE OR WORKSHOP

When selecting a conference or workshop to attend, keep your goals in mind. If you want to learn how to improve your craft, for example, consider one of the events entirely devoted to poetry or locate a more general conference where one-on-one critique sessions are offered. If you're looking for more informal feedback, choose an event which includes open readings. If marketing your work seems like an ominous task, register for a conference that includes a session with editors. And if you also have an interest in other forms of writing, an event with a wide range of workshops is a good bet.

Of course, also take your resources into consideration. If both your time and funds are limited, search for a conference or workshop within your area. Many events are held during weekends and may be close enough for you to commute. On the other hand, if you want to combine your vacation with time spent meeting other writers and working on your craft, consider workshops such as those sponsored by The Writers' Center at Chautauqua. In either case, it is important to at least consider the conference location and be aware of activities to enjoy in the area.

Still other factors may influence your decision. Events that sponsor contests, for instance, may allow you to gain recognition and recoup some of your expenses. Similarly, some conferences and workshops have financial assistance or scholarships available. Finally, many are associated with colleges or universities and offer continuing education credits. You will find all of these options included here. Again, send a SASE for more details.

For other conferences and workshops, see *The Guide to Writers Conferences* (Shaw-Guides, Inc., P.O. Box 1295, New York NY 10023) or the May issue of *Writer's Digest* magazine (available on newsstands or directly from the publisher at 1507 Dana Ave., Cincinnati OH 45207).

AMERICAN CHRISTIAN WRITERS CONFERENCES, P.O. Box 110390, Nashville TN 37222, phone (800)21-WRITE, director Reg Forder. Annual 3-day events founded in 1981. Held throughout the year in cities including Houston, Dallas/Ft. Worth, Boston, Minneapolis, Chicago, St. Louis, Detroit, Orlando, Atlanta, Miami, Phoenix and Los Angeles. Usually located at a major hotel chain like Holiday Inn. Average attendance is 100. **Open to anyone. Conferences cover fiction, poetry, writing for children.** Cost is $199, participants are responsible for their own meals. Accommodations include special rates at host hotel. They also sponsor an annual Caribbean Christian Writers Conference Cruise each November. Send SASE for brochures and registration forms.

ANTIOCH WRITERS' WORKSHOP, P.O. Box 494, Yellow Springs OH 45387, phone (513)866-9060, director Judy DaPolito. Annual 7-day event founded in 1986. Usually held in July at Antioch College in the village of Yellow Springs. "The campus is quiet, shady, relaxed. The village is unusual for its size: a hotbed of artists, writers and creative people." Average attendance is 70. **Open to everyone. "We create an intense community of writers and cover fiction, poetry and writing for children plus playwriting, screenwriting, mystery and nonfiction. Also talks by editors, agents, and others in the industry."** Offerings specifically available for poets include an introductory class in writing poetry, an intensive seminar, night sessions for participants to share poetry, and critiquing. Speakers for the 1996 conference included Virginia Hamilton and Colette Inez. Cost for 1996 conference was $475; scholarships and some work-study fellowships are available (including the Judson Jerome Scholarship sponsored by *Writer's Digest* magazine). Both graduate and undergraduate credit is available for an additional fee. Campus dining room meal ticket is $110 (for 20 meals); must be purchased in advance. Transportation from airport is provided. Information on overnight accommodations is available and includes housing in campus dorms. Individual critiques available. Submit work for critique in advance with $60 fee for poetry; $60 fee for story, book or script. Send SASE for brochures and registration forms. Antioch Writers' Workshop is supported in part by Poets & Writers, Inc.

APPALACHIAN WRITERS' ASSOCIATION CONFERENCE, Dept. of English, WCU, Cullowhee NC 28723, phone (704)227-7264, program chair Steve Eberly. Annual 3-day event founded in 1980. 1997 dates: July 11-13. Location: Madison Dorm and Conference Center on the campus of Western Carolina University. Average attendance is 65. **Open to Appalachian writers, "including any interested writers in Kentucky, Tennessee, Georgia, South Carolina, North Carolina, Virginia, West Virginia and other kindred spirits." The conference is designed "to share readings, workshops, marketing tips and skills relating to poetry, fiction and essays; to celebrate the successes, common bonds and concerns of writers in the Appalachian region."** Special features include "Readings by the Creek," a picnic and open readings, at WCU picnic grounds. Cost for conference ranges from $120-160, including room (2 nights), meals and registration. Local accommodations on campus are arranged by AWA. A list of other accommodations is available on request. Poetry, fiction and essay contests are sponsored as part of the conference. Entry requirements: $15/year membership fee, $5/year for students. Judges are published regional writers. Send SASE for brochures and registration forms.

APPALACHIAN WRITERS WORKSHOP, P.O. Box 844, Hindman KY 41822, phone (606)785-5475, director Mike Mullins. Annual 5-day event founded 1977. Usually held at the end of July or beginning of August. Location: Campus of Hindman Settlement School in Knott County, KY. "The campus is hilly and access for housing is limited for physically impaired, but workshop facilities are accessible." Average attendance is 60-70. **Open to "anyone regardless of sex, age or race." Conference is designed to promote writers and writing of the Appalachian region. It covers fiction, poetry, writing for children, dramatic work and nonfiction.** Offerings specifically available for poets include daily sessions on poetry, individual critique sessions and readings. Staff for 1996 included Lee Smith, Hal Crowther, Jim Wayne Miller, James Still and Barbara Smith. Cost for workshop is approximately $350 for room, board and tuition. Information on overnight accommodations is available for registrants. Accommodations may include special rates at area hotels "once our facilities are filled." Submit mss for individual critiques in advance. Send SASE for brochures and registration forms. A few years ago they published *A Gathering At The Forks*, an anthology of the best work from past workshops. Write for information.

ARKANSAS WRITERS' CONFERENCE, 1115 Gillette Dr., Little Rock AR 72207, phone (501)225-0166, director Clovita Rice. Annual 2-day event founded 1944. Always held the first weekend of June at the Holiday Inn West in Little Rock. Average attendance is 200. **Open to all writers. The conference is designed to "appeal both to beginning and already active writers with a varied program on improving their writing skills and marketing their work."** Offerings specifically available for poets include poetry contests and sessions with poetry editors. In 1996, the guest speakers were Leonard Bishop, author of *Dare to Be a Great Writer* (Writer's Digest Books); Andrea Hollander Budy, nationally known award-winning poet; Victor Fleming; Grif Stockley; and Gina Wilkins. Other special features include an awards luncheon (door prizes such as *Writer's Market* and *Poet's Market*) and banquet, and the announcement of the person selected for Arkansas Writers' Hall of Fame. Cost for 1995 conference was $10 registration for 2 days, $5 for 1 day. Five dollar fee to cover entry to 36 contests. Limousine service from airport to Holiday Inn West is provided. Accommodations include special rates at host hotel. Individual critiques are available. Thirty-six contests (4 require attendance and 8 are limited to Arkansas residents) are sponsored as part of the conference. Each contest has a chairman who will judge or secure a judge. Send SASE for brochures and registration forms after February 1 each year. Clovita Rice, conference director, is editor of *Voices International* (see listing in the Publishers of Poetry section).

‡THE ASHEVILLE POETRY FESTIVAL, P.O. Box 9643, Asheville NC 28815, phone (800)476-8172, fax (704)298-5491, e-mail festival@poetryalive.com, website http://www.poetryalive.com, director Allan Wolf. Annual 3-day event founded 1994. Usually held the second weekend in July at the campus of the University of North Carolina-Asheville. Average attendance is 600. **Open to "everyone and anyone. Our focus is poetry. Our mission is to bring together poets of different voices, styles, and backgrounds to celebrate the diversity of poetry and the spoken word."** Workshops for the 1996 festival included "Using metaphor: Telling the Truth But Telling It Slant"; "Place as Window: Using Place to Generate New Poems"; "Turn So-So Language into Language that Soars"; "Publishing

Poetry for Children"; and "The Art of Performing Poetry." Speakers at the last festival included Sharon Doubiago, Lee Bennett Hopkins, Ntozake Shange, Marc Smith, Patricia Smith, Henry Taylor, James Tate and Anne Waldman. Other special features included continual open mics, a poetry slam with cash prize, and readings by featured poets. Cost for the 1996 festival was $50 (weekend pass). Individual workshop prices vary from $5-35. "Participants are responsible for their own travel and lodging." Information on overnight accommodations is available for registrants. Accommodations include special rates at area hotels. Individual critiques are also available. Submit up to 10 poems on 10 pgs. maximum with $40 reading fee by June 1. Write or call for brochures and registration forms.

‡**ASPEN WRITERS' CONFERENCE**, P.O. Drawer 7726, Aspen CO 81612, phone (970)925-3122, fax (970)920-5700, executive director Jeanne McGovern. Annual week-long event founded 1975. Usually held the second week of June. Location: The Aspen Institute, Aspen Meadows campus or other site in Aspen. Average attendance is 60. **Open to all writers. Conference includes intensive writing workshops in poetry, fiction and nonfiction**. In 1996, offerings specifically available for poets included two poetry workshops, craft lectures and readings by faculty and participants. Speakers at last conference were David Guteron (keynote); Marcia Southwick and Gerald Stern (poetry); Ron Carlson and Shelby Hearon (fiction); and Madeleine Blais (nonfiction). Cost for 1996 conference was $495, does not include meals or lodging. Transportation to and from on-site lodging and event is available. Information on overnight accommodations is available for registrants. In 1996, cost of on-site accommodations was $50/person/day double occupancy. "We accept poetry in advance that will be discussed during workshop." Send SASE for brochures and registration forms.

AUSTIN WRITERS' LEAGUE SPRING AND FALL WORKSHOPS, 1501 W. Fifth St., Suite E-2, Austin TX 78703, phone (512)499-8914, executive director Angela Smith. Biannual workshops founded 1982. "Each workshop series has 12-18 workshops. Workshops are usually 3- or 6-hour sessions." Usually held weekends in March, April, May and September, October, November. Location: St. Edward's University Moody Hall. Average attendance is 15 to 200 per workshop. **Open to all writers, beginners and advanced. Workshops cover fiction, poetry, writing for children, nonfiction, screenwriting, book promotion and marketing, working with agents and publishers, journal writing, special interest writing, creativity, grantwriting, copyright law and taxes for writers.** Offerings specifically available for poets include at least 2 workshops during each series. Poetry presenters have included Lorenzo Thomas, Laurel Ann Bogen, Bobby Byrd and Benjamin Saenz. Past speakers have included Sandra Scofield, Sue Grafton, Peter Mehlman, Gregg Levoy, Lee Merrill Byrd and several New York agents and editors. "Occasionally, presenters agree to do private consults with participants. Also, workshops sometimes incorporate hands-on practice and critique." Cost is $35-75. Members get discount. Cost includes continental breakfast and refreshments for breaks. Meals not included. Arrangements can be made in advance for airport transportation. Information on overnight accommodations is available for registrants. Accommodations include special rates at area hotels. Requirements for critiques are posted in workshop brochure. Send SASE for brochures and registration forms. The Austin Writers' League publishes *Poetography*, an anthology of poems selected by jury, and *The Austin Writer*, a monthly publication of prose and poetry selected from submissions each month. These poems are eligible for six $100 Word Is Art awards presented in December of each year. Poetry guidelines for other publications, awards and grants programs, and market listings are available through the League library.

AUTUMN AUTHORS' AFFAIR, 1507 Burnham Ave., Calumet City IL 60409, phone (708)862-9797, president Nancy McCann. Annual 3-day event founded 1983. The 1996 conference will be held October 11, 12 and 13 at the Hyatt Lisle in Lisle, IL. Average attendance is 200-275. **Open to anyone. Conference covers fiction, but Professor Charles Tinkham of Purdue University-Calumet, called "the poet of the people," usually gives a poetry workshop "covering the entire realm" of writing poetry. "We have between 40-75 published authors and qualified speakers at the conference each year."** Saturday-only and weekend packages, including most meals, are available. Information on overnight accommodations is also available. Send SASE for brochures and registration forms which include the cost of each package, special hotel rates and itinerary.

BENNINGTON SUMMER WRITING WORKSHOPS, Bennington College, Bennington VT 05201, phone (802)442-5401 ext. 160, fax (802)442-6164, assistant director Priscilla Hodgkins. Annual 2-4 week event founded 1977. Usually held in July. Located at Bennington College Campus. "A 550-acre site in the Green Mountains of southwestern Vermont." Average attendance is 80-90 students/session, 12/workshop. **"Open to everyone over 18 years of age. Conference is designed to provide small classes and tutorials with distinguished faculty in fiction, nonfiction and poetry. There is time to write and revise while in residence at Bennington College."** Offerings specifically available for poets include readings and workshops. "Student readings are held several times each week and offer all students valuable experience of reading before an audience." In 1996, guest speakers included Jonathan Holden, Ed Ochester, Lynn Emanuel, Bruce Weigl, Chase Twichell, Frank Bidart, Donald

Hall and Wyn Cooper. Cost for 1996 was $1,380 for 2-week tuition including room and board; $2,280 for 4-week tuition including room and board. "Participants may take room and board at the college or a list of local motels, inns, B&Bs is available." On-site accommodations include single rooms in college houses. Linens are supplied. "Students may take meal plan without staying on campus. Those who do stay on campus are automatically enrolled in meal plan. All prospective participants must submit a writing sample with their application. This is reviewed by an admissions panel. This or another writing sample (12 pages of poetry) is critiqued by faculty in workshop and in tutorial. Students also critique each other's work." Call or write for brochures and registration forms. Affiliated with Associated Writing Programs and Writers Conferences and Festivals.

BREAD LOAF WRITERS' CONFERENCE, Middlebury College, Middlebury VT 05753, phone (802)388-3711 ext. 5286, administrative coordinator Carol Knauss. Annual 12-day event founded 1926. Usually held in mid-August. Average attendance is 230. **Conference is designed to promote dialogue among writers and provide professional critiques for students. Conference usually covers fiction, nonfiction and poetry.** Cost for 1996 conference was $1,600, including tuition, room and board. Fellowships and scholarships for the conference are available. "Candidates for fellowships must have a book published. Candidates for scholarships must have published in major literary periodicals or newspapers. A letter of recommendation, application and supporting materials due by April 1. Awards are announced in June for the conference in August." Taxis to and from the airport or bus station are available. Individual critiques are also available. Send for brochures and application forms.

BROCKPORT WRITERS FORUM SUMMER WORKSHOPS, 350 New Campus Dr., SUNY-Brockport, Brockport NY 14420, phone (716)395-5713, fax (716)395-2391, director Dr. Stan Rubin. Annual 7-day event founded 1980. Usually held the second week in July. Average attendance is 60-75. **Open to all writers, "advanced beginners through published authors." Workshop usually covers fiction, poetry, creative nonfiction, journals/autobiography and fantasy/science fiction.** Panels for 1996 are on publishing, craft and on individual genre. Offerings specifically available for poets include poetry workshop with 2 nationally known leaders. Guest speakers at the last conference included Peter Stitt, editor of *The Gettysburg Review*, and Hilda Raz, editor of *Prairie Schooner*. Other special features include individual conferences (critiques) for all participants, access to the Brockport Writers Forum videotape library and readings by faculty and participants. "Up to 3 college credits—graduate or undergraduate—can be earned." Cost for conference is approximately $450, lodging is extra. "We provide lunches and some dinners." Scholarship available. Transportation to and from the event is provided as required. Private and semiprivate, air-conditioned accommodations available in on-site conference center. Send SASE for brochures and registration forms. "We publish occasional broadsides and pamphlets of participant and faculty work."

CAPE WRITING WORKSHOPS OF CAPE COD WRITERS' CENTER, c/o Cape Cod Writers' Center, P.O. Box 186, Barnstable MA 02630, phone (508)375-0516, director Joseph Ryan. Annual week-long event founded 1985. Usually held the second week of August at the Parish House, St. Mary's Church, Barnstable. Average attendance is 10/workshop. **Open to everyone. Workshops usually cover poetry, fiction, scriptwriting, travel, science fiction, magazine article writing and children's book writing and illustration.** Cost is $395; participants are responsible for meals although "plentiful snack spreads" are included. "Twenty hours of practically individual attention is given, including one personal critique." Private transportation recommended. Contact Bed & Breakfast Cape Cod for housing information. Send SASE for brochures and registration forms.

CHARLESTON WRITERS' CONFERENCE, Lightsey Conference Center, College of Charleston, Charleston SC 29424-0001, phone (803)953-5822, fax (803)953-1454, director Paul Allen. Annual 4-day event founded 1989. Usually held in March at the College of Charleston, founded 1770, in historic downtown Charleston, South Carolina, "a setting renowned for its beauty, history and intimacy." Average attendance is 150. **Open to everyone. Conference covers fiction, poetry and nonfiction.** Past offerings have included a panel discussion on issues in writing and workshops covering various genres. Speakers at last conference included Joyce Carol Oates, Andrew Hudgins, Martha Collins, Andrea Hollander Budy and Cecile Goding. Cost for 1996 conference was $140 ($75 for students); participants are responsible for their own meals. Information on overnight accommodations is available for registrants. Accommodations include special rates at hotels within walking distance of conference. Individual critiques are also available. Submit up to 5 poems on 8 pgs. maximum in advance with $50 fee. Send SASE for brochures and registration forms or call Judy Sawyer at phone number above.

CRAFT OF WRITING, University of Texas at Dallas, Center for Continuing Education, Box 830688, Mail Station CN1.1, Richardson TX 75081, phone (214)883-2204, fax (214)883-2995, director of continuing education Janet Harris. Annual 2-day event founded 1983. 1996 dates were September 20 & 21. Location: Omni Richardson Hotel. Average attendance is 175. **Open to all writers. Confer-**

ence covers the creative, technical and business aspects of writing. Offerings specifically available for poets include workshops and critique sessions. Speakers at the 1996 conference included Donald Maass, Donald Maass Literary Agency; Jim Donovan, Literary Agent; Deborah Adams, The Herman Literary Agency; and Susan Allison, Putnam Berkley Group. Other special features include 28 workshops covering all facets of a writer's world, discussion sessions conducted by editors and agents, and tips for marketing yourself and your writing. Cost for 1996 conference was $195, includes 1 lunch and 1 banquet. Accommodations include special rates at the Omni Richardson where conference is held. Group critiques are available. Bring 3- to 8-page ms with you and sign up at registration desk. Contest sponsored as part of conference. You must be registered for the conference by July 19 to enter contest. Manuscript must be sent with registration. Write for brochures and registration forms.

DEEP SOUTH WRITERS CONFERENCE, %English Dept., USL Box 44691, University of Southwestern Louisiana, Lafayette LA 70504, phone (318)482-5478, director Jerry McGuire. Annual 3-day event founded 1960. Usually held the third week in September at the University of Southwestern Louisiana in Lafayette, LA. Average attendance is 200. **Open to anyone. "The conference emphasis is on adult writing. Within workshops, we cover poetry, fiction and scriptwriting. We have also had children's literary workshops."** A speaker at the last conference was Tim O'Brien. Cost for 1996 conference was $50 registration for readings and craft lectures. Includes one catered reception. Special fee for workshops. Information on overnight accommodations is available for registrants. Accommodations include special rates at area hotels. Individual critiques are also available. "Supplement fee is required plus sample of work." Contest sponsored as part of conference. Submit $10 entry fee and up to 3 poems. Manuscripts are not returned. Send SASE for contest rules and registration forms. Query about other literary forms. Sponsors the Spring Literary Festival. They also publish an anthology of prize-winning work, *The Chapbook*.

‡**DESERT WRITERS WORKSHOP**, P.O. Box 68, Moab UT 84532, phone (800)860-5262 or (801)259-7750, fax (801)259-2335, contact director of programs. Annual 3-day event founded 1985. Usually held the second weekend in November at Pack Creek Ranch in the foothills of the LaSal Mountains. Attendance is a maximum of 30. There is a limit of 10 for each session of the workshop. **Open to all. Workshop covers 3 categories—fiction, nonfiction and poetry.** Cost for 1996 is $400, including meals, instruction and lodging. "All participants stay at Pack Creek." Individual critiques are also available. "Participants will be able to mail some samples to their instructor before the workshop for critique." Send SASE for brochures and registration forms.

‡**EASTERN KENTUCKY UNIVERSITY CREATIVE WRITING CONFERENCE**, Case Annex 467, Richmond KY 40475-3140, phone (606)622-5861, director Harry Brown. Annual 5-day event founded 1964. Usually held Monday through Friday of the third week in June. Location: Eastern Kentucky University. Average attendance is 15. **Open to poetry, fiction and drama writers. The conference is designed to "help writers interested in increasing their skills in writing poetry, fiction and drama; and to offer networking."** Offerings specifically available for poets include workshop discussions and individual conferences. Speakers at last conference were Dorothy Sutton, Normandi Ellis, George Ella Lyon and Reginald Gibbons. Cost for 1995 conference was $75 undergraduate and $109 graduate (in-state fees), $207 undergraduate and $302 graduate (out-of-state fees); participants are responsible for their own meals. "Conference attendees can eat at EKU grill or cafeteria or at nearby restaurants." In 1995, housing in on-site facilities cost $55/week single occupancy, $39/week double occupancy. Individual critiques are available. Submit ms in advance. Send SASE for brochures and registration forms.

‡**FEMINIST WOMEN'S WRITING WORKSHOPS, INC.**, P.O. Box 6583, Ithaca NY 14851, co-director Kit Wainer. Annual 8-day event founded 1974. Usually held in early July. Location: Hobart and William Smith Colleges, Geneva, New York. Average attendance is 45. **Open to "feminist women writers." Workshop usually covers fiction, poetry, journal writing, playwriting, personal essay, autobiography, journalism and performance.** Offerings specifically available for poets include daily workshops, critiques and readings. Cost for 1996 workshop was $535, including tuition, room, board and all events. "We try to help arrange car pools." Participants are housed in a campus residence. Individual critiques while at the conference are optional. "We require a work sample for first-time attendees prior to acceptance." Submit "writing sample (nonreturnable) of up to 10 pgs. Type of sample is your choice. Work in progress, autobiographical writing, nonfiction prose or experimental writing are as welcome as fiction, poetry or drama." Send SASE for brochures and registration forms.

FESTIVAL OF POETRY, Robert Frost Place, Franconia NH 03580, phone (603)823-5510, executive director Donald Sheehan. Annual week-long event founded in 1978. Usually held first week of August at Robert Frost's mountain farm (house and barn), made into a center for poetry and the arts. Average attendance is 50-55. **Open to poets only.** Faculty has included Luci Topahonzo, William W. Cook, Molly Peacock, Martin Espada, Dana Gioia and Ellen Bryant Voigt. Cost is $375-395 tuition, plus a

$25 reading fee. "Room and board available locally; information sent upon acceptance to program." Application should be accompanied by 3 sample pages of your work. Send SASE for brochures and registration forms.

FESTIVAL OF POETS AND POETRY AT ST. MARY'S; EBENEZER COOKE POETRY FESTIVAL, St. Mary's College of Maryland, St. Mary's City MD 20686, phone (301)862-0239. An annual event held during the last two weekends in May. Approximately 18 guest poets and artists participate in and lead workshops, seminars and readings. Concurrent with the festival, St. Mary's College offers a 2-week intensive poetry writing workshop and a 10-day writer's community retreat. **The poetry workshop engages the participants in structured poetry writing experiences. Intended for anyone with a serious interest in writing poetry**, it offers four college credits or may be taken as a non-credit course. **The retreat, designed for the serious writer, offers individual plans for writing alone or in conjunction with other participants.** Three 90-minute workshop sessions are organized for participants. There is also a 12-day fiction writing workshop offered during the festival. For applications or more information on these workshops or the festival, please write to Michael S. Glaser at the above address. The Ebenezer Cooke Poetry Festival is a biennial event in August of even numbered years, held in the name of the first Poet Laureate of Maryland. Poets from Maryland and the surrounding areas are invited to give 5-minute readings, enjoy a crab feast and otherwise celebrate together.

THE FLIGHT OF THE MIND, WOMEN'S WRITING WORKSHOPS, 622 SE 29th Ave., Portland OR 97214, phone (503)236-9862, director Judith Barrington. Annual events founded 1983. Usually held at the end of June, beginning of July. Two workshops in summer for 7 days each at "a rustic retreat center (Dominican owned) right on the wild McKenzie River in the foothills of the Oregon Cascades." Average attendance is 65 women/workshop in 5 different classes. **Open to women writers. Workshops cover fiction, poetry, essays, screenwriting, special-topic classes (e.g. "landscape and memory") with a feminist philosophy.** In 1996 workshop leaders included Ursula K. Le Guin, Naomi Shihab Nye and Charlotte Watson Sherman. Cost for workshop (including tuition, all meals and room) was $685 and up depending on accommodations chosen. Scholarships available. Transportation to and from the event is provided. Participants are selected on the basis of work submitted. Peer critique groups form at workshop. "Competition is discouraged." Send first-class stamp for brochures and registration forms.

FLORIDA SUNCOAST WRITERS' CONFERENCE, Dept. of English, University of South Florida, Tampa FL 33620, phone (813)974-1711, fax (813)974-2270, directors Steve Rubin and Edgar Hirshberg. Annual 3-day event founded 1970. 1997 dates: February 6-8. Location: University of South Florida, St. Petersburg campus. Average attendance is 350. **"Open to students, teachers, established and aspiring writers. Conference covers all areas—fiction, poetry, nonfiction, children's, mystery/ detective, romance, etc."** Offerings specifically available for poets included seminars, workshops, poetry readings and ms evaluation. Speakers at past conferences included Peter Meinke, Sharon Olds, Nikki Giovanni, Yevgeny Yevtushenko, Maxine Kumin, Michael Dennis Brown, Toi Derricotte, Marge Piercy and Carolyn Forché. Cost for 1996 conference was $115; $95 for students and teachers. Information on overnight accommodations is available for registrants. Accommodations include special rates at area hotels. Manuscript evaluation available at extra cost. Write for brochures and registration forms. They also publish *Sunscripts*, an anthology of writing from Florida Suncoast Writers' Conference. All participants eligible to submit.

FLORIDA SUNCOAST WRITERS' WEEKEND WORKSHOP, Dept. of English, University of South Florida, Tampa FL 33620, phone (813)974-1711, fax (813)974-2270, directors Steve Rubin and Ed Hirshberg. Annual 3½-day event founded 1995. Usually held in April at the University of South Florida, Tampa campus. Average attendance is 75-80. **"Open to all writers, beginning and advanced. Workshop covers poetry, fiction and nonfiction."** Offerings specifically available for poets include poetry workshop and readings. Speakers at past conferences included Tobias Wolff, Dannie Abse, Peter Meinke and Michael Dennis Browne. Other special features include intensive small-group seminars, guest speakers and a banquet. Cost for conference is $195, includes ms evaluation and banquet. Transportation to and from the event is provided. Information on overnight accommodations is available for registrants. Accommodations include special rates at area hotels. Manuscript evaluation available for each participant. Write for brochures and registration forms. They also publish *Sunscripts*, an anthology of writing from Suncoast programs participants.

‡FOOTHILL WRITERS' CONFERENCE, 12345 El Monte Rd., Los Altos Hills CA 94022, phone (415)949-7316 or 949-7436, conference co-directors Kim Silveira Wolterbeek and Jim Whearty. Annual 6-day event founded 1975. 1996 dates were June 27 through July 2. Location: Foothill College campus in Los Altos Hills. **Open to everyone. Conference includes panel discussions and manuscript workshops; poetry one-on-one sessions; and poetry and prose readings.** Panels for the 1996 conference included the List Poem, the state of the novel, nature and art, women's issues, and multicultural literature. Offerings specifically available for poets included an one-on-one manuscript workshop. Speakers at the last conference were Kim Addonizio, Alan Cheuse, Jim Houston, Jane Hirshfield and Roshi Rustomji-Kerns. Cost for 1996 conference was $75, included enrollment fees and admission to faculty afternoon and evening readings, intensive writing workshops, and lectures and panels by faculty (college credit available). Individual critiques available on a first come, first serve basis. "Sign up posted on the first day of conference." Send SASE for brochures and registration forms.

GREEN RIVER WRITERS CONFERENCE/RETREAT, Green River Writers, 403 S. Sixth St., Ironton OH 45638, secretary D.H. Spears, phone (614)533-1081, provides a weekend workshop, then 5-day retreat at the University of Louisville's Shelbyville campus [contact Mary E. O'dell at (502)245-4902]. Participants may take part in only the conference or the retreat or both. 1996 conference speakers were Max Garland (poetry), Dick Hague (essay) and Garry Baker (fiction). Submissions are accepted for editing workshops. Submit up to 2 poems or 8 pgs. maximum for short stories and essays. Retreat participants may schedule impromptu sessions with fellow participants and staff or work alone. Cost for 1996 conference/retreat was $75, $40 each for only conference or retreat. Rooms are available at the conference center for $20/night for private room, $16/night for shared room. Beginning writers are furnished with advisors. Details available for SASE.

HARVARD SUMMER WRITING PROGRAM, 51 Brattle St., Dept 733, Cambridge MA 02138, phone (617)495-4024, fax (617)495-9176, e-mail summer@hudce.harvard.edu, website http://www.harvard.edu/summer/. Annual 8-week event. 1997 dates: June 23 through August 15. Location: Harvard University. Average attendance is 300. **Open to all levels, from beginner to published author. Course offerings include creative, expository and professional writing.** Offerings specifically available for poets included beginning poetry, intermediate poetry and graduate level poetry courses. Other special features included small classes, undergraduate and graduate credit, individual conferences, access to the Writing Center at Harvard, visiting writers, a reading series and a literary magazine. Instructors are writers, editors, and faculty members from Harvard as well as other universities. Cost for 1996 conference was $1,410/course (2 courses is considered full-time), plus $2,360 for room and board (dormitory housing). Phone or write for brochures or request via e-mail. Their catalog is also available on the internet.

HAYSTACK WRITING PROGRAM, School of Extended Studies, Portland State University, P.O. Box 1491, Portland OR 97207, phone (800)547-8887 ext. 8500, fax (503)725-4840, contact Maggie Herrington. Annual summer program founded 1968. One-week courses over the six weeks of the program. 1996 dates: July 1 through August 9. "Classes are held in the local school of this small coastal community; some evening lectures and other activities." Average attendance is 10-15/class; 350 total. **Open to all writers. One-week workshops cover fiction, poetry, mystery, radio essay and nonfiction.** Cost for workshops is $110-360; participants pay for their own lodging and meals. Accommodation options range from camping to luxury hotels. Write for brochures and registration forms (no SASE necessary).

THE HEIGHTS WRITER'S CONFERENCE, Writer's World Press, P.O. Box 24684, Cleveland OH 44124, phone (216)481-1974, fax (216)481-2057, conference director Lavern Hall. Annual 1-day event founded 1991. Usually held the first Saturday in May. "The conference is held at the Marriott hotel in Beachwood, OH. Conference rooms are centrally located and handicapped accessible. Lunch is served in the ballroom." Average attendance is 100. **"Open to all writers who are interested in learning about the craft and business of writing and networking with professionals. We cover a variety of genres including poetry, fiction, science fiction, romance, mystery, travel, etc.** We don't have themes; however, each year two intensive hands-on workshops will vary. In 1996, the workshops were in poetry and screenwriting. These intensive workshops are limited to 25 students who must pre-register and are taken on a first come, first serve basis." Guest speaker for the last conference was Ralph Keyes, who spoke on "The Courage to Write." They say, "Our format is unique. We have four major sessions (two in the morning and two in the afternoon) with three concurrent one-hour seminars. In addition, we offer two 2½-hour intensive workshops, one in the morning, the other in the afternoon. The genre teaching workshops vary each year." Cost for 1996 conference was $70 preregistration; $85 late registration. "All activities are included: continental breakfast, seminars/workshops, lunch with guest speaker program, networking reception and author autographing at conclusion of day. In addition there are many free handouts and The Writer's Book Shop offers a selection of writing-related books. We provide accommodation information upon request for those arriving the day before." Critiques are handled through speakers directly. Send SASE for brochures, map and area hotels. Information on local poetry readings and poetry publishers soliciting work available.

HIGHLAND SUMMER WORKSHOP, P.O. Box 7014, Radford University, Radford VA 24142, phone (703)831-5366, director Grace Toney Edwards. Annual 2-week event founded 1978. Usually held the last 2 weeks in June. Location: Radford University campus. Average attendance is 20-25. **Open to everyone. "The conference, a lecture-seminar-workshop combination, is conducted by well-known guest writers and offers the opportunity to study and practice creative and expository writing within the context of regional culture." Topics covered vary from year to year. Poetry, fiction and essays (prose) are generally covered each year.** In 1996, the first week of the workshop was led by poet Bill Brown, author of *The Art of Dying, Holding on By Letting Go* and *What the Night Told Me*. The second week was led by Don Secreast, author of *Red Velvet and White Trash* and *When The Rat Becomes Light*. Cost for the conference ranged from $406-925 plus $15/day for meals. Individual meals may also be purchased. On-site housing costs range from $16-26/night. On-site accommodations are available at Norwood Hall. Accommodations are also available at local motels. Send SASE for brochures and registration forms.

HOFSTRA UNIVERSITY SUMMER WRITERS' CONFERENCE, 375 Hofstra University, U.C.C.E., Hempstead NY 11550-1009, phone (516)463-5997, fax (516)463-4833, e-mail dcelcs@hofst ra.edu, director Lewis Shena. Annual 10-day event founded 1972. Usually starts the Monday after July 4th. Location: Hofstra University. Average attendance is 50-60. **Open to all writers. Conference covers fiction, nonfiction, poetry, children's writing, stage/screenwriting and, on occasion, one other area (science fiction, mystery, etc.).** Guest speakers (other than the workshop leaders) "usually come from the world of publishing." There are also "readings galore and various special presentations." Cost for 1996 conference was $300/workshop. Additional fee of $450 for air-conditioned dorm room, one dinner and coffee/tea on a daily basis. For those seeking credit, other fees apply. Individual critiques are also available. "Each writer receives a half hour one-on-one with each workshop leader." They do not sponsor a contest, but "we submit exceptional work to various progams sponsored by Writers Conferences and Festivals." Write for brochures and registration forms (available as of April).

‡**INDIANA UNIVERSITY WRITERS' CONFERENCE**, Ballantine Hall 464, Indiana University, Bloomington IN 47405, phone (812)855-1877, director Maura Stanton. Annual week-long event founded 1940. Usually held the last week in June at the university student union. Average attendance is 100. **Open to all. Conference covers fiction and poetry.** Offerings specifically available for poets included workshops and classes. Speakers at last conference included Gerald Stern (poetry) and Frances Sherwood (fiction). Cost for 1996 conference was $180 for conference and classes, $280 for conference, classes and workshop; plus $25 application fee. Information on overnight accommodations is available for registrants. "Rooms available in the student union or in a dorm." Individual critiques are also available. Submit 10 pgs. of poetry in advance. "All manuscripts are considered for scholarships." Send SASE for brochures and registration forms.

IOWA SUMMER WRITING FESTIVAL, University of Iowa, 116 International Center, Iowa City IA 52242-1802, phone (319)335-2534, fax (319)335-2740, coordinators Amy Margolis and Peggy Houston. Annual event founded in 1987. Held each summer in June and July for six weeks, includes one-week and weekend workshops at the University of Iowa campus. Average attendance is 125/week. **Open to "all adults who have a desire to write." Conference offers courses in nearly all writing forms. In 1996, offerings available for poets included 18 poetry classes for all levels.** Speakers were George Barlow, Michael Carey, Rosemary Daniell, Timothy Liu, Ken McCullough and Jane Mead. Cost for 1996 conference was $150 for a weekend course and $350-375 for a week course. Participants are responsible for their own meals. Accommodations available at the Iowa House and the Holiday Inn. Housing in residence hall costs about $25/night. Participants in week-long workshops will have private conference/critique with workshop leader. Send for brochures and registration forms.

THE IWWG SUMMER CONFERENCE, The International Women's Writing Guild, P.O. Box 810, Gracie Station, New York NY 10028, phone (212)737-7536, executive director Hannelore Hahn. Annual week-long event founded 1978. Usually begins on the second Friday in August and runs through following Friday. Location: Skidmore College in Saratoga Springs, NY. Average attendance is 400. **Open to all women. Fifty-six workshops offered. "At least four poetry workshops offered for full week."** Cost is $600 for conference program and room and board. "Critiquing available throughout the week." Send SASE for brochures and registration forms. The International Women's Writing Guild's bimonthly newsletter publishes and features hundreds of outlets for poets. See listing in Organizations Useful to Poets.

LIGONIER VALLEY WRITERS CONFERENCE, Box 8, RR 4, Ligonier PA 15658, phone (412)238-5749, fax (412)238-5190, president Louis A. Steiner. Annual 3-day event founded 1986. Usually held in July. "This is a relaxing, educational, inspirational conference in a scenic, small town." Average attendance is 80. **Open to anyone interested in writing. Conference covers fiction, creative nonfiction, poetry and writing for children.** Poetry workshops each day. 1996 workshops conducted by Jim Daniels. Cost for conference is approximately $200, including some meals and picnic. Participants are responsible for their own dinner and lodging. Information on overnight accommodations is available for registrants. Individual critiques are also available. Must send samples in advance. Send SASE for brochures and registration forms. "We also publish *The Loyalhanna Review*, a literary journal, which is open to participants."

MARITIME WRITERS' WORKSHOP, UNB Dept. of Extension, Box 4400, Fredericton, New Brunswick E3B 5A3 Canada, phone (506)454-9153, fax (506)453-3572, coordinator Glenda Turner. Annual 1-week event founded 1976. Usually held the first week in July. Location: University of New Brunswick campus. Average attendance is 50. **Open to all writers. Workshop covers fiction, nonfiction, poetry and writing for children.** Offerings specifically available for poets included a daily workshop group for poets, limited to 10 participants, and individual conferences arranged with instructors. Speakers at last conference were Ann Copeland and Nino Ricci (fiction); Douglas Burnet Smith (poetry); Mark Abley (nonfiction); Janet Lunn (writing for children). Other special features included readings. Cost for 1996 conference was $300 plus $270 for room and board. Scholarships are available. "All participants must submit a manuscript which is then 'workshopped' during the week." Write for brochures and registration forms.

MIDLAND WRITERS CONFERENCE, Grace A. Dow Memorial Library, 1710 W. St. Andrews, Midland MI 48640, phone (517)835-7151, fax (517)835-9791, conference co-chairs Margaret Allen, Eileen Finzel and Katherine Redwine. Annual 1-day event founded 1979. Usually held the second weekend in June at the Grace A. Dow Memorial Library in Midland, MI. Average attendance is 100. **Open to any writer, published or unpublished. Conference includes sessions that vary in content.** In 1995, Nick Bozanic of Interlocken Fine Arts Academy conducted a 2-hour poetry workshop, and the keynote speaker was Dave Barry. "We always have a well-known keynoter. In the past we have had Judith Viorst, Kurt Vonnegut, Mary Higgins Clark, David McCullough, P.J. O'Rourke." Cost for 1996 conference was $45 until 2 weeks prior to the event ($55 after that). For students, senior citizens and handicapped participants, cost was $35 until 2 weeks prior to the event ($45 after that). Information on overnight accommodations is available for registrants. Send for brochures and registration forms.

MIDWEST WRITERS' CONFERENCE, 6000 Frank Ave. NW, Canton OH 44720-7599, phone (216)499-9600, fax (216)494-6121, assistant director of continuing studies Debbie Ruhe. Annual 2-day event founded 1968. 1996 dates: October 4-5. Location: Kent State University Stark Campus in Canton, Ohio. Average attendance is 350. **Open to aspiring writers in any category, but the writing contest is directed toward fiction, nonfiction, juvenile literature and poetry. "The conference provides an atmosphere in which aspiring writers can meet with and learn from experienced, established writers through lectures, workshops, competitive contests, personal interviews and informal group discussions."** Offerings specifically available for poets include a lecture session in the poetry area and a contest. Past panelists have included Joyce Carol Oates, Edward Albee, Kurt Vonnegut and John Updike. One special feature of the conference is an all day book fair which includes several Ohio small presses. Cost for 1996 conference is $65, including conference registration, workshops, keynote address, lunch and ms entry fee. Contest entry fee exclusively: $40 for two mss and $10 for each additional ms. Participants are responsible for other meals. Information on overnight accommodations is available for registrants. Special conference rates are available through the Sheraton Inn. Individual critiques are also available in the areas of poetry, fiction, nonfiction and juvenile literature. Submit one individual poem up to 200 lines. Contest sponsored as part of conference. "Work must be original, unpublished and not a winner in any contest at the time of entry." Judging is performed by local professionals in their appropriate categories. Send SASE for brochures and registration forms. Co-sponsor of the Midwest Writers' Conference is the Greater Canton Writers' Guild, 919 Clinton Ave. SW, Canton OH 44706-5196.

MISSISSIPPI VALLEY WRITERS CONFERENCE, 3403 - 45th St., Moline IL 61265, phone (309)762-8985, founder/director David R. Collins. Annual week-long event founded in 1973. Usually held the second week in June at the Liberal Arts College of Augustana College. Average attendance is 80. **Open to all writers, "beginning beginners to polished professionals." Conference provides a general professional writing focus on many genres of writing. Offers week-long workshop in poetry.** Evening programs as well as daily workshops are included. Cost for 1995 conference was $25 registration, $40 one workshop, $70 two workshops, $30 each additional workshop. Conferees may stay on campus or off. Board and room accommodations are available at Westerlin Hall on Augustana campus, 15 meals and 6 nights lodging approximately $200. Individual critiques are also available. Submit up to 10 poems. Awards presented by workshop leaders. Send SASE for brochures and registration forms.

MOUNT HERMON CHRISTIAN WRITERS CONFERENCE, P.O. Box 413, Mount Hermon CA 95041, phone (408)335-4466, fax (408)335-9218, director of specialized programs David R. Talbott. Annual 5-day event founded 1970. Always held Friday through Tuesday over Palm Sunday weekend. 1997 dates: March 21-25. Location: Full hotel-service-style conference center in the heart of the California redwoods. Average attendance is 150-200. **Open to "anyone interested in the Christian writing market." Conference is very broad-based. Always covers poetry, fiction, article writing, writing for children, plus an advanced track for published authors.** In 1995, offerings specifically available for poets included a 4-day, 8-hour track on "Writing the Published Poem," plus individual one-hour workshops on poetry. "We usually have 34 teaching faculty. Faculty is made up of publishing reps of leading Christian book and magazine publishers, plus selected freelancers." Other special features included an advance critique service (no extra fee); residential conference, with meals taken family-style with faculty; private appointments with faculty; and an autograph party. "High spiritual impact." Cost for 1996 conference was $650 deluxe; $545 standard; $465 economy; including 13 meals, snacks, on-site housing and $285 tuition fee. No-housing fee: $435. $15 airport, Greyhound or Amtrack shuttle from San Jose, CA. Send SASE for brochures and registration forms.

NAPA VALLEY WRITERS' CONFERENCE, Napa Valley College, 1088 College Ave., St. Helena CA 94574, phone (707)967-2900, managing director Anne Evans. Annual week-long event founded 1981. Usually held the last week in July or first week in August at Napa Valley College's new facility in the historic town of St. Helena, 30 minutes north of Napa in the heart of the valley's wine growing community. Average attendance is 36 in poetry and 36 in fiction. **"The conference has maintained its emphases on process and craft, featuring a faculty as renowned for the quality of their teaching as for their work. It has also remained small and personal, fostering an unusual rapport between faculty writers and conference participants. The poetry session provides the opportunity to work both on generating new poems and on revising previously written ones. Participants spend time with each of the staff poets in daily workshops that emphasize writing new poems—taking risks with new material and forms, pushing boundaries in the poetic process."** The 1996 poetry staff was Jane Hirshfield, Marie Howe, Robert Pinsky and David St. John. "Participants register for either the poetry or the fiction workshops, but panels and craft talks are open to all writers attending. Evenings feature readings by the faculty that are open to the public and hosted by Napa Valley wineries." Cost is $450, not including meals or housing. There are some limited partial scholarships, depending on donations. A list of valley accommodations is mailed to applicants on acceptance and includes at least one reduced-rate package. "Through the generosity of Napa residents, limited accommodations in local homes are available on a first-come, first-served basis." All applicants are asked to submit a qualifying ms with their registration (no more than 5 pgs. of poetry or 10-15 pgs. of fiction) as well as a brief description of their background as a writer. Application deadline: June 1. Send SASE for brochures and registration forms.

THE NAROPA INSTITUTE WRITING & POETICS SUMMER PROGRAM, 2130 Arapahoe Ave., Boulder CO 80302, phone (303)444-0202, director of writing & poetics Reed Bye, director emertis Anne Waldman, director of summer writing program Max Regan. Annual month-long summer program founded in 1974. Held from mid-June to mid-July, participants may attend from 1-4 weeks. "We are located on 3.7 acres in the center of Boulder, Colorado. The campus houses a performing arts center, meditation hall, classrooms, offices and library. Many of the summer lectures are held under a huge tent on our back lawn." Average attendance is 100-120. **Open to anyone; students attending for credit must obtain department's permission. "It is a convocation of students, scholars, fiction writers, poets and translators. In dialogue with renown practitioners of verbal arts, students confront the composition of poetry and prose."** The 1995 and 1996 summer programs included emphasis in these areas: "Dharma/Ecopoetics, International Writers, The Oral Tradition and Experimental/Wild Forms, performance poetry and gender issues." Offerings specifically available for poets include lectures, readings (both student and faculty), workshops and one-on-one interviews with guest faculty. Conference speakers have included Allen Ginsberg, Anselm Hollo, Bobbie Louise Hawkins, Jack Collom, Bernadette Mayer, Michael McClure, Ron Silliman, Michael Ondaatje, Nathaniel Mackey and Eagle Cruz. Cost for 1 week is $315 (non credit), $495 (BA credit), $690 (MFA credit). Lab fees are $10/week. Four scholarships are available for minority students. Participants are responsible for their own meals. "Student services can help find places to stay." Work to be critiqued does not need to be sent in advance. "During the weekly workshops and personal interviews, every writer will have a chance to be critiqued by professional poets/fiction writers." Write for brochures and registration forms. "We also sponsor student readings and have an informal summer magazine and a school sponsored magazine, *Bombay Gin*."

NEBRASKA WRITERS GUILD CONFERENCE, 515 N. 87th St., Omaha NE 68114, phone (402)391-2267, president Mark Manhart. Biannual 1-day event founded 1925. Usually held in April and October at various locations statewide. Average attendance is 50-75. **"Open to members and any writers. Conference covers all areas of writing, publishing and marketing."** Guest speaker at the last conference was poet Roy Scheele. Other special features included a book fair and book exchange. Cost for conference was $35/member, $40/nonmember. Information on overnight accommodations is available for registrants. Send SASE for brochures and registration forms.

‡**OAKLAND UNIVERSITY WRITERS' CONFERENCE**, Division of Continuing Education, 265 SFH, Oakland University, Rochester MI 48309-4401, phone (810)370-3120, fax (810)370-3137, e-mail jakobows@oakland.edu, director Nadine Jakobowski. Annual 1½-day event founded 1961. 1996 dates: October 18-19. 1997 dates: October 17-18. "The Oakland University Writers' Conference is conducted in the university student center, in meeting rooms and large dining/meeting areas, plus adjoining classroom buildings with lecture halls." Average attendance is 400-500. **Open to beginning through professional adult writers. "No restrictions as to geographic area." The conference is designed to "help writers develop their skills, to provide information (and contact) for getting published; to provide a current picture of publishing markets; to furnish a venue for networking. All genres of writing are covered."** The conference offers "critiques, both one-on-one and group, as well as auditing, on Friday. On Saturday, 36 concurrent sessions dealing with all aspects and a variety of genres of writing are offered in a total of four time slots. A well-known professional writer speaks at lunch. A panel of the major speakers answers questions in the concluding session." Cost for 1995 conference was $25-35 for Friday critiques; $60 for Saturday conference plus $8 for lunch. "Discounts are not offered." Information on overnight accommodations is available for registrants. Work must be submitted, in advance, for individual critiques. Brochures and registration forms available each September 1 prior to the October conference.

OZARK CREATIVE WRITERS CONFERENCE, 6817 Gingerbread Lane, Little Rock AR 72204, phone (501)565-8889, conference counselor Peggy Vining. Annual 3-day event. Held in October at the Inn of the Ozarks in Eureka Springs, Arkansas. 1996 dates: October 10-12. **Open to all writers.** Registration fee is $35 prior to September 1. Various writing contests sponsored as part of conference. Awards of $25, $15 and $10 ("some higher") for all types of writing. Send #10 SASE for brochure after April 1.

PORT TOWNSEND WRITERS' CONFERENCE, c/o Centrum, P.O. Box 1158, Port Townsend WA 98368, phone (360)385-3102, fax (360)385-2470, director Carol Jane Bangs. Annual 10-day event founded 1974. Usually held the second week in July at a 400-acre state park at the entrance to Puget Sound. Average attendance is 160. **Open to "all serious writers who pass our preliminary manuscript screening." Conference usually covers fiction (no genre fiction), poetry, creative nonfiction, and writing for children.** Offerings specifically available for poets include "three limited-enrollment workshops, private manuscript conference, open-mike readings, faculty readings and technique classes." Speakers at the last conference were Percival Everett, Ursula Hegi, Joyce Thompson, Bill McKibben, Sue Halpern, Carol Muske, Marvin Bell, Cornelius Eady, Kay Morgan, Anna Hines, Josip Novakovich and David Rigsbee. Cost for the 1996 conference was $425 tuition including workshop, ms conference, classes, readings, lectures; $300 tuition without workshop or ms conference; plus $330 optional for dormitory housing and 3 meals per day. Information on overnight accommodations is available for registrants. Individual critiques are also available, however "you must be enrolled in a manuscript workshop." Send SASE for brochures and registration forms.

‡**SAGE HILL WRITING FALL POETRY COLLOQUIUM**, P.O. Box 1731, Saskatoon, Saskatchewan S7K 3S1 Canada, phone/fax (306)652-7395, executive director Steven Ross Smith. Annual 21-day event founded 1995. Usually held the first three weeks in October at "the peaceful milieu of St. Peter's College, adjoining St. Peter's Abbey, in Muenster, 150 kilometers east of Saskatoon." **Open to poets, 19 years of age and older, who are working in English. The colloquium offers "an intensive three-week workshop/retreat designed to assist poets with manuscripts-in-progress. Each writer will have a significant publishing record and will wish to develop his/her craft and tune a manuscript. There will be ample time for writing, one-on-one critiques, and group meetings to discuss recent thinking in poetics. Eight writers will be selected. Writers in and outside Saskatchewan are eligible."** Cost for 1996 was $700, included tuition, accommodations and meals. "A university registration fee of $25 will be added if taking this course for credit." Transportation from Saskatoon can be arranged as needed. On-site accommodations included in cost. Send SASE for brochures and registration forms.

‡**SAGE HILL WRITING SUMMER EXPERIENCE**, P.O. Box 1731, Saskatoon, Saskatchewan S7K 3S1 Canada, phone/fax (306)652-7395, executive director Steven Ross Smith. Annual 7-day and 10-day events founded in 1990. Usually held the end of July through the beginning of August. The Summer Experience is located at St. Michael's Retreat, "a tranquil facility in the beautiful Qu'Appelle Valley just outside the town of Lumsden, 25 kilometers north of Regina." Average attendance is 54. **Open to writers, 19 years of age and older, who are working in English. No geographic restrictions. The retreat/workshops are designed to "offer a special working and learning opportunity to writers at different stages of development. Top quality instruction, a low instructor-writer ratio, and the rural Saskatchewan setting offers conditions ideal for the pursuit of excellence in the arts of fiction, poetry, playwriting, and writing young adult fiction."** Offerings specifically available for poets include a poetry workshop and poetry colloquium. In 1996, the faculty included

Rosemary Nixon, William Robertson, Janice Kulyk Keefer, Di Brandt and Patrick Lane. Cost for 1996 conference ranged from $425-495, included instruction, accommodations and meals. Limited local transportation to the conference is available. "Van transportation from Regina airport and a downtown hotel, to Lumsden will be arranged for out-of-province travellers." On-site accommodations offer individual rooms with a writing desk and washroom. Individual critiques offered as part of workshop and colloquium. Writing sample required with application. Application deadline: May 1. Send SASE for brochures and registration forms.

ST. DAVIDS CHRISTIAN WRITERS CONFERENCE, 87 Pines Rd. East, Hadley PA 16130, phone (717)394-6758, registrar Audrey Stallsmith. Annual 5-day event founded 1957. Usually held in June at the campus of Geneva College in Beaver Falls, PA. Average attendance is 100-120. **Open to "anyone interested in writing." Conference is designed to "train and develop skills of writers for Christian and secular markets."** Offerings include a series of advanced classes that require prior acceptance to attend. Cost for conference is $400-500, including classes, room and board. Price varies according to choice of study packages. Housing in on-site facilities costs $200-230. Individual critiques are also available. "Must have a body of work to submit." Contest sponsored as part of conference. "Must be a conference attendee. Faculty members judge contest." Send SASE for brochures and registration forms.

SANTA BARBARA WRITERS' CONFERENCE, P.O. Box 304, Carpinteria CA 93014, phone (805)684-2250, fax (805)684-7003, conference director Barnaby Conrad. Annual week-long event founded in 1973. Held the last Friday to Friday in June at the Miramar Hotel on the beach in Montecito. Average attendance is 350 people. **Open to everyone. Covers all genres of writing.** Workshops in poetry offered. Past speakers have included Ray Bradbury, Phillip Levine, Sol Stein, Dorothy Wall, Gore Vidal and William Styron. Cost for 1996 conference, including all workshops and lectures, 2 al fresco dinners and room (no board), was $1,015 single, $745 double occupancy, $350 day students. Individual critiques are also available. Submit 1 ms of no more than 3,000 words in advance with SASE. Competitions with awards sponsored as part of conference. Send SASE for brochures and registration forms.

‡SBPI WRITERS' CONFERENCE, P.O. Box 2197, Redmond WA 98073, phone (206)836-8634, fax (206)868-4022, e-mail MEQU95A@prodigy.com or SBPI@MSN.com, publisher Stephen Bruno. Annual 3- or 4-day event founded 1995. 1997 conference to be held in November. The conference will be held at various sites. The 1996 conference was held at Lake Washington Technical College, Kirkland WA. Average attendance is 200-300. **Open to established and emerging writers working in all genres. Conference covers fiction, poetry, writing for children, nonfiction, freelance writing, specialty writing, self-publishing, trade writing and photography.** Offerings specifically available for poets include awards and scholarships, readings, and many workshops on the craft of writing poetry and finding paying markets. Speakers at last conference included Molly Giles, winner of the Flannery O'Connor Award; Philip Deaver, director of the New Writers' Workshop in Orlando; Jon Franklin, twice winner of The Pulitzer Prize; Dorianne Laux, who won a Pushcart Prize for her poetry; and Mark Lewis, a two-time Emmy Award winner. Other special features were an interactive tradeshow that included step-by-step instructions on web page design, with authoring tools, hundreds of guide-lines, and information about writer's resources, colonies and retreats. Cost for 1996 conference was $225, included daily buffet lunch and snacks. Accommodations include special rates at area hotels plus discounted transportation to and from conference. "Some hotels offer free shuttle." Individual critiques are available for $45 reading fee. Submit a maximum of 8 poems, not to exceed 10 pgs., 30 days before conference. Contests sponsored as part of conference. Send SASE for brochures and registration forms. "We publish *Beyond Essence Magazine*, a literary, art, photography magazine that publishes poetry. We also publish poetry books."

SEWANEE WRITERS' CONFERENCE, 310 St. Luke's Hall, Sewanee TN 37383-1000, phone (615)598-1141, fax (615)598-1145, conference administrator Cheri B. Peters. Annual 12-day event founded 1990. Usually held the last 2 weeks in July at The University of the South ("dormitories for housing, Women's Center for public events, classrooms for workshops, student union building for dining, etc."). Attendance is about 105. **Open to poets, fiction writers and playwrights who submit their work for review in a competitive admissions process. "Genre, rather than thematic, work-shops are offered in each of the three areas."** In 1996, faculty members were fiction writers James Gordon Bennett, John Casey, Amy Hempel, Alice McDermott, Mary Morris, Tim O'Brien, Francine Prose and Robert Stone; poets Rachel Hadas, Anthony Hecht, Mark Jarman and Donald Justice; playwrights Dave DeChristopher and Romulus Linney. Other speakers included editors, agents and additional writers. Cost for 1996 conference was $1,200, including room and board. Each year scholar-ships and fellowships based on merit are available on a competitive basis. "We provide bus transporta-tion from the Nashville airport on the opening day of the conference and back to the airport on the closing day at no additional cost." Individual critiques are also available. "All writers admitted to the conference will have an individual session with a member of the faculty." A ms should be sent in advance after admission to the conference. Write for brochure and application forms. No SASE necessary.

SINIPEE WRITERS WORKSHOP, P.O. Box 902, Dubuque IA 52004-0902, phone (319)556-0366, director John Tigges. Annual 1-day event founded 1986. Usually held the 3rd or 4th Saturday in April on the campus of Loras College, Dubuque, Iowa. Average attendance is 50-100. **Open to anyone, "professional or neophyte," who is interested in writing. Conference covers fiction, poetry and nonfiction.** Cost for 1997 workshop is $60 pre-registration, $65 at the door. Scholarships covering half of the cost are traditionally available to senior citizens and to full-time students, both college and high school. Cost includes handouts, coffee and donut break, lunch, snacks in afternoon and book fair with authors in attendance available to autograph their books. Information on overnight accommodations is available for out-of-town registrants. Annual contest for nonfiction, fiction and poetry sponsored as part of workshop. There is a $5 reading fee for each entry (article/essay of 1,500 words, short story of 1,500 words or poetry of 40 lines). First prize in each category is $100 plus publication, second prize $50 and third prize $25. Entrants in the contest may also ask for a written critique by a professional writer. The cost for critique is $15/entry. Send SASE for brochures and registration forms.

SOCIETY OF THE MUSE OF THE SOUTHWEST (SOMOS), P.O. Box 3225, Taos NM 87571, phone/fax (505)758-0081, office manager Beth Enson. Founded 1983. "We offer workshops at different times during the year, at least one during the summer." Length of workshops vary. Held at various sites. Average attendance is 10-50. **Open to anyone. "We offer workshops in various genres—fiction, poetry, nature writing, etc."** In 1996 workshop speakers included Natalie Goldberg, Robin Becker, William Melvin Kelley and Judith Hill. Other special features include writing in nature/ nature walks and beautiful surroundings in a historic writer's region. Cost for workshops range from $50-175, excluding room and board. Information on overnight accommodations is available. Individual critiques are also available. Send SASE for brochures and registration forms. "We're affiliated with Blinking Yellow Books in Taos, which publishes local authors including poets."

SOUTHWEST FLORIDA WRITERS' CONFERENCE, P.O. Box 60210, Ft. Myers FL 33906-6210, phone (941)489-9226, fax (941)489-9051, director Joanne Hartke. Annual event founded 1980. Usually held the 4th Friday and Saturday in February on the campus of Edison Community College. Average attendance is 150-200. **Open to anyone interested in writing, including full-time high school and college students. "We cover many areas; in 1996 our offerings included poetry and writing for children. Sessions are usually varied to provide something for both beginning and published writers."** The 1996 poetry session was with Rochelle Holt. Cost for the 1996 Friday sessions was $30; the Saturday conference was $59, including a continental breakfast and lunch. Limited scholarships are usually available and full-time students can attend the conference for only $25. Information on overnight accommodations available for registrants. An annual contest (including poetry) is sponsored as part of the conference. Judges are published authors and writers in the Ft. Myers community. Send SASE for brochures and registration forms.

‡SQUAW VALLEY COMMUNITY OF WRITERS POETRY WORKSHOP, P.O. Box 2352, Olympic Valley CA 96146, phone (916)274-8551 or 583-5200, executive director Brett Hall Jones. Annual 7-day event founded 1969. 1997 dates: July 19-26. The workshop is held in The Squaw Valley Ski Corporation's Olympic House Lodge located in the Sierra Nevada near Lake Tahoe. "The workshop takes place in the off-season of the ski area. Participants can find time to enjoy the Squaw Valley landscape; hiking, swimming, river rafting and tennis are available." Average attendance is 52. **Open to high quality talented writers of diverse ethnic backgrounds and a wide range of ages. "The Poetry Program differs in concept from other workshops in poetry. Our project is to help our participants to break through old habits and write something daring and difficult. Workshops are intended to provide a supportive atmosphere in which no one will be embarrassed, and at the same time to challenge the participants to go beyond what they have done before. Admissions are based on quality of the submitted manuscripts."** Offerings include regular morning workshops, craft lectures and staff readings. "The participants gather in daily workshops to discuss the work they wrote in the previous 24 hours." Speakers at last conference were Yusef Komunyakaa, Brenda Hillman, Sharon Olds and Galway Kinnell. Cost was $555, included regular morning workshops, craft lectures, staff readings and dinners. Scholarships are available. "Requests for financial aid must accompany submission/application, and will be granted on the perceived quality of manuscript submitted and financial need of applicant." Transportation to workshop is available. "We will pick poets up at the Reno International Airport if arranged in advance. Also, we arrange housing for participants in local houses and condominiums on the valley. Participants can choose from a single room for $320/week or a double room for $220/week within these shared houses. We do offer inexpensive bunk bed accommodations on a first come first serve basis." Individual conferences are also available. "Only work-in-progress will be discussed." Send SASE for brochures and registration forms. "We also publish an annual newsletter."

STATE OF MAINE WRITERS' CONFERENCE, P.O. Box 7146, Ocean Park ME 04063, phone (207)934-9806 (summer), phone (413)596-6734, fax (413)782-1746 (winter), director Dick Burns. Annual August event founded 1941. Usually runs from Tuesday evening to Friday noon. 1997 dates: August 19-22. Average attendance is 50-75. **Open to any interested person. Conference is "very eclectic, covers writing to publishing."** Every year there is a poetry tournament including a poetry booklet, Poems to be Put on Trees Contest and Beach Inspiration Poetry. "In 1995, there was a Haiku Workshop. Something similar is expected to be continued annually." In 1996 cost was $75. Those 21 and under may attend at half price. Information on overnight accommodations is available for registrants. "Local accommodations are reasonable." There are many contests, 15-20/year. Separate contest announcement is available in advance to registrants. Send SASE for brochures and registration forms.

‡TENNESSEE MOUNTAIN WRITERS CONFERENCE, P.O. Box 4895, Oak Ridge TN 37831-4895, phone (423)482-6567, executive director Patricia Hope. Annual 3½-day event founded 1989. 1997 dates: April 16-19. Location: Garden Plaza Hotel in Oak Ridge. Average attendance is 150-200. **Open to "all aspiring writers, including students." Conference covers fiction, poetry, nonfiction and writing for children, plus special classes on romance, mystery, business, etc.** Speakers at last conference included David Bradley, Sandra Blanton, Alexa Selph, Katy Koontz, Dana Wildsmith and Michael Seidman. Other special features included a contest in conjunction with conference offering prizes to adults/students and a book fair featuring participants' books. Cost for 1996 conference was $165 for full participants, $120 for day-only participants, $35 for students. Information on overnight accommodations is available for registrants. Host hotel provides discount to participants. Cost for 1996 was $60/night. Individual critiques are also available. Submit up to 10 pgs. prior to conference. Send SASE for brochures and registration forms. Tennessee Mountain Writers also sponsor the Tennessee Literary Awards which is separate from the conference. (See listing in Contests and Awards section.)

TRENTON STATE COLLEGE WRITERS CONFERENCE, Trenton State College, Hillwood Lakes CN 4700, Trenton NJ 08650-4700, phone (609)771-3254, director Jean Hollander. Annual 1-day event founded 1981. Usually held the beginning of April at Trenton State College Campus. Average attendance is about 800. **Open to anyone. Conference covers all genres of writing. "We usually have a special presentation on breaking into print." 12-15 separate poetry and fiction workshops as well as readings are offered.** In 1996 the featured speaker was Alice Walker. Cost in 1995 was $40 for day session; additional cost for workshops and evening session. Discounts available for students. Information on overnight accommodations is available for registrants. Poets and fiction writers may submit ms to be critiqued in writing by workshop leaders. Poetry and short story contest sponsored as part of conference. 1st prize: $100; 2nd prize: $50. Judges are workshop leaders and a special panel from the English Dept. Write or call for brochures and registration forms.

‡TŶ NEWYDD WRITERS' CENTRE, Taliesin Trust, Llanystumdwy, Cricieth, Gwynedd LL52 0LW Wales, Great Britain, phone 01766 522811, fax 01766 523095, director Sally Baker, founded 1990. 4½-day course held throughout the year. Courses run Monday evening through Saturday morning at Tŷ Newydd, "a house of historical and architectural interest situated near the village of Llanystumdwy. It was the last home of Lloyd George, the former British prime minister. It stands in landscaped gardens and has fine views over Cardigan Bay towards the mountains of Meirionnydd." Average attendance is 16/course. **Open to anyone over 16 years of age. Courses are designed to "promote the writing and understanding of literature by providing creative writing courses at all levels for all ages.** Courses at Tŷ Newydd provide the opportunity of working intimately and informally with 2 professional writers." Courses specifically for poets, of all levels of experience and ability, are offered throughout the year. Cost for a 4½-day course is £255 (inclusive), some weekend courses available, cost is £100 (inclusive). Transportation to and from Centre is available if arranged at least a week in advance. Participants stay at Tŷ Newydd House in shared bedrooms; single bedrooms available on a limited basis and for an additional fee. "Vegetarians and people with special dietary needs are catered for but please let us know in advance. Course participants help themselves to breakfast and lunch and help to prepare one evening meal as part of a team. Participants should bring towels and their own writing materials. Some typewriters and word processors are available." Send SASE for brochures and registration froms.

UNIVERSITY OF WISCONSIN-MADISON'S SCHOOL OF THE ARTS AT RHINE-LANDER, 726 Lowell Hall, 610 Langdon St., Madison WI 53703-1195, administrative coordinator Kathy Berigan. Annual 5-day event founded 1964. Usually held the third or fourth week in July. Held at a local junior high school. Average attendance is 300. **Open to all levels and ages.** Offerings specifically available for poets include poetry workshops. Guest speaker at last workshop was Thomas

Bontly. Cost for 1996 workshop ranged from $130-265. Information on overnight accommodations is available for registrants. Write for brochures and registration forms.

WESLEYAN WRITERS CONFERENCE, Wesleyan University, Middletown CT 06457, phone (203)685-3604, fax (203)347-3996, director Anne Greene. Annual 5-day event founded 1956. Usually held the last week in June on the campus of Wesleyan University. The campus is located "in the hills overlooking the Connecticut River, a brief drive from the Connecticut shore. Wesleyan's outstanding library, poetry reading room, and other university facilities are open to participants." Average attendance is 100. **Open to both experienced and new writers. The participants are an international group. The conference covers the novel, short story, fiction techniques, fiction-and-film, poetry, literary journalism and memoir.**" Special sessions in 1996 included "How Poets Make a Living," "Beyond Daily Journalism," "Fiction and Film Writing," and "Publishing." Offerings specifically for poets included manuscript consultations and daily seminars with Pulitzer Prize-winner Henry Taylor, and panel discussions with Robert Phillips and Kate Rushin. Other faculty included Dorothy Allison, Amy Bloom, Robert Stone, Tom Drury, Lis Harris and James Lardner. Cost in 1996, including meals, was $635 (day rate); $740 (boarding rate). "Wesleyan has special scholarships for journalists who are interested in poetry and fiction techniques. Request brochure for application information." Information on overnight accommodations is available. "Conference participants may stay in university dormitories or off campus in local hotels." Individual critiques are also available. Registration for critiques must be made before the conference. Send SASE for brochures and registration forms.

WESTERN RESERVE WRITERS AND FREELANCE CONFERENCE, 34200 Ridge Rd., #110, Willoughby OH 44094, phone (216)943-3047 or (800)653-4261, e-mail fa837@cleveland.freenet.edu, coordinator Lea Leever Oldham. Annual 1-day event founded 1983. Usually held the second Saturday in September. Average attendance is 150. **Open to "writers, published and aspiring." Conference usually covers fiction, nonfiction, poetry, articles, books, sometimes photography and other freelance subjects, copyright, writing for children, etc.** "We always include a presentation specifically for poetry." Cost for conference is about $49, plus lunch. Participants can make arrangements one-on-one for possible time with guest speakers. Send SASE for brochures and registration forms.

WESTERN RESERVE WRITERS MINI CONFERENCE, 34200 Ridge Rd., #110, Willoughby OH 44094, phone (216)943-3047 or (800)653-4261, e-mail fa837@cleveland.freenet.edu, coordinator Lea Leever Oldham. Annual ½-day conference founded 1991. Usually held the last Saturday in March. Average attendance is 100. **Open to "published and aspiring writers." Conference usually covers fiction, nonfiction, poetry, writing for children, articles and romance writing.** "We always have a session with a published poet." Cost for conference is $29, including morning refreshments. Attendees can make their own arrangements with presenters for possible critiques. Send SASE for brochures and registration forms.

WHITE RIVER WRITERS' WORKSHOP, Lyon College, P.O. Box 2317, Batesville AR 72503-2317, phone (501)793-1766, fax (501)698-4622, director Andrea Hollander Budy. Annual 7-day event founded 1995. Usually held the third week of June at the "campus of Lyon College on the banks of the White River in the foothills of the Arkansas Ozarks. This workshop offers a beautiful setting, rich with opportunities to experience the natural and cultural attractions of this region." Limited to 50 participants. **Open to poets. "Workshop is designed as an intensive for poets in poetry, translation and presentation. Serious poets are invited to work on new poems and/or translations. All are also invited to work on oral presentation."** In 1996, speakers were C.D. Wright, Lawrence Raab, Lee Potts, Stephen Dunn, Philip Dacey and Andrea Hollander Budy. Special features included panels, craft lectures and readings. Also, all faculty and fellows available for one-on-one guidance. Cost for 1996 workshop was $425 plus $325 for room and board. "Five scholarships and five fellowships are awarded each summer. The scholarships (which cover tuition costs only) are available to poets who have not yet published a first full-length book but who have published individual poems in established and reputable literary journals. Fellowships (which cover tuition and room and board) are awarded to poets who have published at least one, but no more than two, full-length poetry collections. Applications for scholarships and fellowships are due by April 1." Transportation to and from the event is available. "A van or taxi will be available for a reasonable fee." All participants are expected to live on campus during the week-long event. Write for brochures and application forms. Applications are read and evaluated as they are received. Application deadline is May 15. Early application is suggested, as only up to fifty participants are accepted.

WILDACRES WRITERS WORKSHOP, 233 S. Elm St., Greensboro NC 27401, phone/fax (910)273-4044, director Judith Hill. Annual week-long event founded 1983. Usually held the second week in July at "a beautiful retreat facility in the Blue Ridge Mountains of North Carolina." Average attendance is 100. **Open to all "serious adult writers." Conference covers fiction, poetry, screen**

and play writing, and nonfiction. **"We have two poetry workshops with a limit of twelve to a class.** In total, we have eleven writers on staff who read and give programs. Plus we have an agent in residence." Cost is approximately $410, including a double room, all meals and ms critique. Van transportation to and from the Asheville Airport is provided. Send SASE for brochures and registration forms. Some years they also publish *The Wildacres Review*.

WISCONSIN REGIONAL WRITERS' ASSOCIATION, 912 Cass St., Portage WI 53901, phone (608)742-2410, president Elayne Clipper Hanson. Biannual conferences founded in 1948. Usually held first Saturday in May and last weekend in September at various hotel-conference centers around the state. Average attendance is 100-130. **Open to all writers, "aspiring, amateur or professional." All forms of writing/marketing rotated between conferences. "The purpose is to keep writers informed and prepared to express and market their writing in a proper format." Poetry covered once a year.** In 1996, spring speakers included Phyllis Kasper, psychotherapist, "Creativity & Sensuality into Your Writing"; John Brooks, "Writing Your Life Story"; and Scott Edelstein, literary agent. A book fair is held at both conferences where members can sell their published works. A banquet is held at the fall conference where writing contest winners receive awards. Writing contest winners receive awards at the spring conference as well. Spring conference is approximately $30-35, fall conference approximately $35-40. Spring conference includes coffee and sweet rolls, lunch and hors d'oeuvres at book fair. Fall conference also includes dinner and entertainment. Information about overnight accommodations is available for registrants. "Our organization 'blocks' rooms at a reduced rate." Sponsors 3 writing contests/year. Membership and small fee are required. Send SASE for brochures and registration forms. "We are affiliated with the Wisconsin Fellowship of Poets and the Council of Wisconsin Writers. We also publish a newsletter four times a year for members."

THE WRITERS' CENTER AT CHAUTAUQUA, Box 408, Chautauqua NY 14722, phone (716)357-2445 (June-August) or (717)872-8337, director Mary Jean Irion. Annual event founded 1988. Usually held 9 weeks in summer from late June to late August. Participants may attend for one week or more. "We are an independent, cooperative association of writers located on the grounds of Chautauqua Institution." Average attendance is 30 for readings and speeches, 12 for workshops. **Readings and speeches are open to anyone; workshops are open to writers (or auditors). The purpose is "to make creative writing one of the serious arts in progress at Chautauqua; to provide a vacation opportunity for skilled artists and their guests (one each); and to help learning writers improve their skills and vision."** Workshops are available all 9 weeks. Poetry Works meets 2 hours each day offering 1 hour of class for every hour of workshop. In 1996, leaders included Michael Waters, Stephen Sandy, Carol Frost and Margaret Gibson. Prose Works offers 2 hours a day in fiction and nonfiction, writing for children and Young Writers' Workshops. Poets are welcome to explore other fields. Other special features include 2 speeches a week and 1 reading, usually done by the Writers-In-Residence. Cost is $70/week. Participants are responsible for gate fees, housing and meals and "may bring family; sports, concerts, activities for all ages. A week's gate ticket to Chautauqua is $165/adult (less if ordered early); housing cost varies widely, but is not cheap; meals vary widely depending on accommodations—from fine restaurants to cooking in a shared kitchen." Access is best by car or plane to Jamestown, NY, where a limousine service is available for the 14 miles to Chautauqua ($18). Phone number for Accommodations Directory Service is available for registrants. Individual critiques are also usually available. Information published in spring mailing. Send SASE for brochures and registration forms.

WRITERS' FORUM, Community Education Dept., Pasadena City College, 1570 E. Colorado, Pasadena CA 91106-2003, phone (818)445-0704, contact Meredith Brucker. Annual 1-day event founded 1954. Usually held all day Saturday in early-March at Pasadena City College. Average attendance is 200. **Open to all. Conference covers a wide variety of topics and always includes one poet.** Speakers have included poet Ron Koertge, *ONTHEBUS* editor Jack Grapes, Philomene Long speaking on "Poetry for Non-poets," and Myra Cohn Livingston describing "Poem Making" for children. Cost for the 1996 conference was $85, including lunch. Write for brochures and registration forms. No SASE necessary.

WRITING TODAY, BSC A-3, Birmingham AL 35254, phone (205)226-4921, fax (205)226-4931, director of special events Martha Andrews. Annual 2-day event founded 1978. 1996 dates were April 12-13. Location: Birmingham-Southern College campus. Average attendance is 400-500. **Open to "everyone interested in writing—beginners, professionals and students. Conference topics vary year to year depending on who is part of the faculty."** In 1996, Shelby Foote was the major speaker and Grand Master Award recipient. Other speakers at the last conference were Albert Murray, Terrence Rafferty and James Tate. Cost for 1996 conference was $85 before deadline ($90 after deadline), including lunches and reception. Cost for a single day's events was $45, including luncheon. Either day's luncheon was only $20. $10 cancellation fee. Information on overnight accommodations is available for registrants. Accommodations include special rates at area hotels. Individual critiques are also available. In addition, the Hackney Literary Awards competition is sponsored as part of the conference. The competition, open to writers nationwide, offers $2,000 in prizes for poetry and short stories and a $2,000 award for the novel category. Send SASE for conference information and see the listing for the Hackney Literary Awards in Contests and Awards.

WRITING WORKSHOP, % Donovan Scholars Program, University of Kentucky, Ligon House, 658 S. Limestone St., Lexington KY 40506-0442, phone (606)257-2657, fax (606)323-4940. Annual event founded 1966. Usually held in June, the workshop runs from Sunday afternoon to Friday afternoon. Location: Lexington area. Average attendance is 35-50 (maximum). **Open to "adults aged 55 or older who share an interest in writing and wish to learn more about how to express their thoughts in the written form. We offer classes in fiction, nonfiction, children's literature/juvenile novel and poetry."** Offerings specifically available for poets include "classes instructed by established writers in the field of poetry, whether local or elsewhere." Cost is $325/person, includes classes, meals and double occupancy room. Writers may register as full-student status, which requires a ms to be submitted for critique, or as auditor status, which does not require a ms. Send SASE for brochures and registration forms. *Second Spring*, their yearly publication, contains the written work of past workshop participants.

YELLOW BAY WRITERS' WORKSHOP, Center for Continuing Education & Summer Programs, The University of Montana, Missoula MT 59812, phone (406)243-6486, fax (406)243-2047, program manager Lee Hynson. Annual week-long event founded 1988. Usually held mid-August at the University of Montana's biological research station located on beautiful Flathead Lake. The facility includes informal educational facilities and rustic cabin and dorm living. Average attendance is 60. **Open to all writers. Conference offers two workshops in fiction, one in nonfiction and one in poetry.** In 1996, workshop faculty included William McKibben, David Long, Deirdre McNamer and Pattiann Rogers. Elizabeth Grossman, a literary agent with Sterling Lord Literistic in New York, will be joined by Emilie Buchwald, publisher/editor of Milkweed Editions, and Sue Halpern, editor of *Doubletake*, for a forum on their areas of expertise. Cost for 1996 workshop was $435, commuter fee; $735, tuition and single-occupancy lodging/meals; $705, tuition and double-occupancy lodging/meals. Round-trip shuttle from Missoula to Yellow Bay (85 miles) is available for $40 and a specific airfare package is offered. Applicants must send a writing sample. Full and partial scholarships are available. Deadline for scholarship applications is June 10. Send SASE for brochures and registration forms.

Writing Colonies

Writing colonies are places for writers (including poets) to find solitude and spend concentrated time focusing on their work. While a residency at a writing colony may offer participation in seminars, critiques or readings, the atmosphere of a colony or retreat is much more relaxed than that of a conference or workshop. Also, a writer's stay at a colony is typically anywhere from one to twelve weeks (sometimes longer), while time spent at a conference may only run from one to fourteen days.

Like conferences and workshops, however, writing colonies and retreats span a wide range. Yaddo, perhaps the most well-known colony, limits its residencies to writers "who have already achieved some recognition in their field and have new work under way," whereas Walker Woods offers residencies to writers completing their first books. Hedgebrook is limited as well. It only offers residencies to women writers. The N.A.L.L. Art Association (new to this edition), on the other hand, limits its residencies to writers who are members of the association. And, in addition to listings for colonies across the United States, this section contains listings for residencies in Canada, the Dominican Republic, France, Ireland, the Italian Alps and Spain.

Despite different focuses and locations, all writing colonies and retreats have one thing in common: They are places where you may work undisturbed, usually in very nature-oriented and secluded settings. A colony serves as a place for rejuvenation, a place where you may find new ideas for poems, rework old ones, or put the finishing touches to a collection. For an in-depth look at a writing colony, see the interview with Elizabeth Guheen, executive director of the Ucross Foundation Residency Program, on page 520.

SELECTING A WRITING COLONY

When selecting a colony or retreat, the primary consideration for many writers is cost, and you'll discover that arrangements vary greatly. The Millay Colony for the Arts, Inc., for instance, has no fee. Other colonies provide residencies as well as stipends for personal expenses. Some suggest donations of a certain amount. Still others offer residencies for tidy sums but have financial assistance available.

When investigating the various options, consider meal and housing arrangements and your family obligations. Some colonies provide meals for residents, while others require residents to pay for meals. Some colonies house writers in one main building; others provide separate cottages. (In both cases, you are given private work space, although you must usually bring along your own reference materials and typewriter or personal computer.) A few writing colonies have provisions for spouses and families. Others prohibit families altogether.

Overall, residencies at writing colonies and retreats are competitive. Since only a handful of spots are available at each place, you often must apply months in advance for the time period you desire. A number of locations are open year-round, and you may find that planning to go during the "off-season" lessens your competition. Other colonies, however, are only available during certain months. In any case, be prepared to include a sample of your best work with your application. Also, know what project you'll work on while in residence and have alternative projects in mind in case the first one doesn't work out once you're there.

Each listing in this section details fee requirements, meal and housing arrangements, and space and time availability, as well as the retreat or colony's surroundings, facilities and special activities. Of course, before making a final decision, send a SASE to the colonies or retreats that interest you to receive their most up-to-date details. Costs, application requirements and deadlines are particularly subject to change.

For other listings of writing colonies, see *The Guide to Writers Conferences* (available from ShawGuides, Inc., P.O. Box 1295, New York NY 10023), which not only provides information about conferences, workshops and seminars but also residencies, retreats and organizations. Another resource is *Havens for Creatives*, available from ACTS Institute, Inc. (P.O. Box 30854, Palm Beach Gardens FL 33420-0854).

THE EDWARD F. ALBEE FOUNDATION, INC.; THE WILLIAM FLANAGAN MEMO-RIAL CREATIVE PERSONS CENTER ("THE BARN"), 14 Harrison St., New York NY 10013, phone (212)226-2020, for information and application forms. The Albee Foundation maintains the center (better known as "The Barn") in Montauk, on Long Island, offering 1-month residencies for writers, painters, sculptors and composers, open June 1 through October 1, accommodating 6 persons at a time. Applications accepted at the above address by regular mail only January 1 through April 1. Fellowship announcements by May 15. "Located approximately 2 miles from the center of Montauk and the Atlantic Ocean, 'The Barn' rests in a secluded knoll that offers privacy and a peaceful atmosphere. The foundation expects all those accepted for residence to work seriously and to conduct themselves in such a manner as to aid fellow residents in their endeavors. The environment is simple and communal. Residents are expected to do their share in maintaining the condition of 'The Barn' as well as its peaceful environment."

‡**ALTOS DE CHAVÓN**, % Parsons School of Design, 2 W. 13th St., Room 707, New York NY 10011, New York coordinator Carmen Lovente, arts/education director Stephen D. Kaplan. Offers 3½-month residencies to artists working in various fields: painting, sculpture, dance, music, crafts, writing, etc. "The village of Altos de Chavón is located on the southeast coast of the Dominican Republic, an 1½-hour drive from the bustling capital city of Santo Domingo." Accommodates 15 international artists during the year in "comfortable" apartments with small balconies and kitchenettes; basic furniture and some housewares provided. Individual studio space available near apartments. "Many artists agree to teach an occasional workshop in their area of expertise." Cost for residencies is $300/month and a $100 nonrefundable registration fee; participants are responsible for airfare, meals and daily living expenses. To be considered, submit a letter of interest, sample of work and résumé. Artist couples may apply. "A panel meets in New York in July to select the participants for the following year." Write for more information.

ATLANTIC CENTER FOR THE ARTS, 1414 Art Center Ave., New Smyrna Beach FL 32168, phone (904)427-6975, program director Nicholas Conroy, program assistant Jim Frost. The center was founded in 1979 by sculptor and painter Doris Leeper, who secured a seed grant from The Rockefeller Foundation. That same year the center was chartered by the state of Florida and building began on a 10-acre site. The facility now covers 67 acres. The center was officially opened in 1982. Since 1982, 65 Master Artists-in-Residence sessions have been held. At each of the 3-week sessions, internationally known artists from different disciplines conduct interdisciplinary workshops and lectures and critique works in progress. They also give readings and recitals, exhibit their work and develop projects with their "associates"—mid-career artists who come from all over the US to work with them. The center is run by an advisory council which chooses Master Artists for residencies, helps set policies and guides the center in its growth. The process of becoming an associate is different for each Master Artist. Recent poets in residence at the center include Rachel Hadas (January 1995), Sonia Sanchez (May 1995) and Ntozake Shange (May 1996). Poet and Pulitzer Prize-winner Carolyn Kizer is scheduled to be at the center in January 1997 and Poet David Lehman in May 1997.

‡**BYRDCLIFFE ARTIST COLONY**, The Woodstock Guild, 34 Tinker St., Woodstock NY 12498, phone (914)679-2079, fax (914)679-4529, executive director Caroline Harris, founded 1901. Offers 1-month residencies from June through September to visual artists, crafts people, writers, musicians and theater artists at an historic 600-acre colony in the Catskill Mountains, 1½ miles from the Woodstock village center and 90 miles north of New York City. Accommodates 10 residents in Villetta Inn, "a spacious turn-of-the-century mountain lodge," in single and double rooms with shared bathrooms and kitchen; separate individual studio space also available. Activities include hiking, concerts, theater, art exhibitions and literary events. Cost ranges from $400-500, including meals. Reduction offered to residents staying more than 1 session. Limited scholarships available. Send SASE for application forms and guidelines. Work sample, project description, résumé, reviews, contact information for 2 references

and $10 fee, must accompany application. Application deadline: April 1.

‡CENTRE INTERNATIONAL DE POÉSIE MARSEILLE (CIPM), Centre de la Vieille Charité, 2 rue de la Charité, 13002 Marseille France, phone (91 91 26 45), fax (91 90 99 51), contact Eric Giraud or Olivier Devers. Offers 3-month residencies to 4 poets a year (2 French, 2 foreigners). The 4 residents chosen are paid and have a book published by CIPM. Residents are housed in a second or third floor studio near the Centre. Accommodates 2 residents at one time in single rooms with private baths and kitchens; desks and reference materials available. Computers and typewriters available at the CIPM library, a 3-minute walk from the studio. Activities include lectures, readings, and "meeting with people in the library once during the residency." There is no cost to the individuals chosen, instead they are given 8,000 French francs each month of the residency. To be considered, the poet must have published at least one book and submit a written plan of work to be done. Write for further details.

CENTRUM, Residency Program, P.O. Box 1158, Port Townsend WA 98368, offers 1-month residencies, September through May, for writers, composers, choreographers and printmakers. Centrum provides individual cottages, a stipend of $75/week and solitude. Families welcome. Located in Fort Worden State Park on the Strait of Juan de Fuca. Also sponsors the Port Townsend Writers' Conference (See Conferences and Workshops) and other seminars. Contact Carol Jane Bangs, Literature Program Manager, for more information on these programs.

CHATEAU DE LESVAULT, 58370 Onlay, France, phone 33-03-86-84-32-91, fax 33-03-86-84-35-78, director Bibbi Lee. This French country residence is located in the national park "Le Morvan" of western Burgundy, halfway between Nevers and Autun and is surrounded by green hills and forests. The chateau accommodates 5 residents at a time in 5 large rooms with private baths, fully furnished and equipped for working. The facilities of the chateau are at the disposal of residents, including the salon, library and grounds. Requests for residencies from October through April should be made at least 3 months in advance. The cost is 4,500 FF per month for room, board and utilities.

THE CLEARING, Box 65, Ellison Bay WI 54210, phone (414)854-4088, resident managers Donald and Louise Buchholz, "is first a school, then a place of self-discovery." Founded in 1935, The Clearing celebrated its 60th anniversary in 1995. It is made up of cabins and lodges in a rustic setting overlooking Green Bay, it offers a variety of courses, including courses in writing and poetry, May through October. Fees include tuition, room (dormitory or twin-bedded room) and board.

DOBIE-PAISANO PROJECT, Attn: Audrey N. Slate, Main Building 101, The University of Texas, Austin TX 78712. Offers two annual fellowships of $7,200 and 6-month residency at Frank Dobie's ranch, Paisano, for native Texans, those who have resided in the state at least 2 years, or writers with published works about Texas. Write for application and guidelines. Application deadline: January 24, 1997.

DORLAND MOUNTAIN ARTS COLONY, P.O. Box 6, Temecula CA 92593, established 1979. A 300-acre nature preserve which offers 1-month residences for writers, visual artists and composers in a rustic environment with no elecricity, propane appliances (refrigerator, water heater, cooking stove, some lights) and oil lamps. Residents provide their own meals. A donation of $300/month is requested. Send SASE for application form and guidelines. Deadlines are the first of September and March.

DORSET COLONY HOUSE RESIDENCIES; AMERICAN THEATRE WORKS, INC., P.O. Box 519, Dorset VT 05251, managing director Mr. Gene Sirotof. Residencies available to writers fall and spring for periods of 1 week to 2 months for intensive work. Requested fee of $95/week, but ability to pay is essential in awarding residencies.

FINE ARTS WORK CENTER IN PROVINCETOWN, 24 Pearl St., Provincetown MA 02657, provides monthly stipends of $375 and studio/living quarters for 7 uninterrupted months for 21 young artists and writers (fiction writers, playwrights and poets) who have completed their formal training and are capable of working independently. The center arranges readings and slide presentations and visits from other distinguished writers and artists. Sessions run from October 1 through May 1. Applications, accompanied by a $35 processing fee, must be received by February 1. To receive an application and program brochure, send a SASE to Writing Fellowship. Unlike the winter residency, the Summer Program offers open-enrollment workshops with "an outstanding faculty in the visual arts and writing." The 10-week program consists of 40 one-week workshops in poetry, fiction, nonfiction, painting, sculpture, installation, printmaking and photography. Write for catalog of course descriptions and registration materials.

‡FUNDACIÓN VALPARAÍSO, Apt. 836, 04638 Mojácar Playa, Almería Spain, phone/fax (34)50-47 23 80, manager Bibi Petersen, founded 1992. Offers 1-month residencies (except in March, August

and between Christmas and New Year) to writers, painters, sculptors, musicians, etc., from all countries at a converted olive oil mill in Andalucia, Spain. Accommodates 8 residents at one time in single rooms with private baths and shared kitchen facilities; one computer and a small library also available. Residents *do not* pay for accommodations and meals. However, "traveling costs and insurance are not paid." To be considered, submit publication with application for the Board to evaluate. Write for application form. Application deadline: May/June and December.

GELL WRITERS CENTER OF THE FINGER LAKES, %Writers & Books, 740 University Ave., Rochester NY 14607, phone (716)473-2590, fax (716)729-0982, director Joseph Flaherty. Offers 1-week to 1-month residencies on a year-round basis for writers and readers who "seek a quiet and restorative time away from their usual routine. The center is located at the southern end of Canandaigua Lake, in the center of New York State's famous Finger Lakes region. Rich in natural diversity, the area contains one of the world's great grape-growing regions, as well as many fine cultural and recreational attractions such as hiking trails. Visitors stay in The Gell House, a completely furnished hillside home surrounded by a beautifully landscaped yard and 23 acres of woodlands." Accommodates 2 writers at a time in single rooms with private baths and shared kitchen facilities; private desks and an extensive library available. Activities include workshops, lectures and readings at a nearby literary center. Cost is $25/day for members of Writers & Books; $35/day for nonmembers. Memberships are available. Participants are responsible for own meals. Send SASE for application forms, guidelines and membership information for Writers & Books. A 5- to 10-page work sample must accompany application.

‡GUEST HOUSE AT NEW LIGHT STUDIOS, 1890 Turtle Town Hall Rd., Beloit WI 53511, phone (608)362-8055 or 365-7907, fax (608)362-1417, e-mail blakeley@als.lib.wi.us, partner Sharon Blakeley, founded 1992. Offers 3-day to 1-month residencies throughout the year to writers/artists working in any field at New Light Studios, located between Chicago and Madison in the Wisconsin countryside. "The guest house is simple, self-contained and quiet. Two of the three artist-partners reside in nearby farmhouses." Accommodates up to 4 residents at one time in a 2-bedroom house with bath and fully equipped kitchen. "Since we emphasize privacy, we accept dual residencies for artists previously unknown to each other only by special arrangement with those concerned." Desks and a small library of reference books available. Residents may bring their own computers and typewriters, or arrangements can be made locally for borrowing needed equipment. "We host poetry readings on a regular basis. Residents are invited to read their own work. Participation is encouraged but not mandatory. Residents may attend cultural events at nearby Beloit College. We can provide transportation." Residencies are free "to deserving artists who desire solitude for their work." Residents are responsible for their own meals. "Special arrangements can be made for meals to be furnished for a fee." Hourly bus service from Chicago's O'Hare Airport to Beloit available. "We provide transportation from the bus to New Light." Send SASE for application materials and more details. "We want to provide quiet inspiration and encouragement for artists, especially poets. We encourage artists at all stages of their careers to apply. (The partners in New Light Studios are artists themselves. We have received encouragement from others, and want to return the favor.)" Application deadline is 30-60 days prior to desired date of residency.

THE TYRONE GUTHRIE CENTRE, Annaghmakerrig, Newbliss, Co. Monaghan, Ireland, phone (353)47-54003, fax (353)47-54380, resident director Bernard Loughlin. Offers residencies, normally 3 weeks to 3 months, for artists, including poets. "Each resident has a private apartment within the house . . . and all the centrally heated comfort an Irish Big House can afford. It is set on a wooded estate of 400 acres and overlooks a large lake. The house is surrounded by gardens and a working dairy farm. Couples or small groups of artists may stay for up to a year in Maggie's Farm, a cottage on the estate, and have use of studios at the Big House. Five newly built, self-contained farmyard cottages are also available for individuals and couples for longer stays. To qualify for residence it is necessary to show evidence of a significant level of achievement in the relevant field. Once accepted, Irish artists are asked to contribute what they can afford toward the cost of their stay. Overseas artists are expected to pay the whole cost of a residency."

HAMBIDGE CENTER FOR CREATIVE ARTS AND SCIENCES, P.O. Box 339, Rabun Gap GA 30568, phone (706)746-5718. The Center is located on 600 acres of unspoiled wooded slopes, mountain meadows and streams, near Dillard, Georgia. It is listed on the National Register of Historic Places. Resident Fellowships of 2 weeks to 2 months are awarded to individuals engaged in all artistic disciplines for the purpose of solitude and the pursuit of creative excellence. Those accepted are given a private cottage equipped with a kitchen, living and studio/work space. Center is open from March through December. For more information and application forms send SASE. Deadline for initial scheduling review is January 31, however, applications are accepted year round.

HAWK, I'M YOUR SISTER; WOMEN'S WILDERNESS CANOE TRIPS; WRITING RETREATS, Beverly Antaeus, P.O. Box 9109, Santa Fe NM 87504-9109. This organization offers

CLOSE-UP

Residencies provide more than wide open spaces

"A residency is an award of time and great care," says Elizabeth Guheen, executive director of the Ucross Foundation Residency Program in Clearmont, Wyoming. "We are going to take great care of you while you're here, and allow you to do your work. It is not just a space." Located at the confluence of three crystal creeks in the shadow of the Bighorn Mountains and the heart of high plains country, space, however, is something for which the foundation is not at a loss.

Elizabeth Guheen

© Val Burgess

Established in 1983, the Ucross Foundation Residency Program is hosted year-round in the restored facilities of the historic Pratt & Ferris Cattle Company. On the 22,000-acre sprawl, residents create, eat and sleep in one of a handful of renovated, red-planked out-buildings collectively (and affectionately) known as "Big Red."

Each year more than 60 artists and writers—poets, painters, composers, sculptors, photographers and playwrights—come to Ucross's wide open spaces to focus on specific projects, to refocus on what they want to do next. They come to start something, to finish something, to do something over again. They come to consider, to reconsider. This is true of not only Ucross, but of any artists' retreat.

"Residencies hold time open," says Guheen, a visual artist herself and a former fine arts instructor. "When you come for your residency, it's here waiting for you—the time you asked for. It's about being able to focus not just for a few hours. It's about being able to focus five days, ten days, thirty days in a row. That's pretty unusual in whatever you're doing in life—to concentrate on one thing and do nothing but that—and to have that activity validated by everyone and everything that's going on around you. You are given the sense that you are doing the right thing. You are doing what you are supposed to be doing. No guilt."

Dozens of residency programs exist across the United States and abroad. Programs vary, but most provide a few basic things: individual workspace, living accommodations and, perhaps most important, uninterrupted time—often free of charge. At Ucross, there is no charge for the residency. All candidates, however, must send a $20 processing fee with their application, and if accepted, are asked to submit a $50 deposit which is refunded after the residency's completion.

Residents must also make arrangements for their own transportation to Ucross, but cars are not welcome on-site. Instead, residents are offered weekly trips into town. The goal, after all, is to avoid as many distractions as possible.

CLOSE-UP, *Guheen*

Only eight individuals are in residence at Ucross at any given time, and their terms can last anywhere from two weeks to two months. They come from all stages of professional careers, from unpublished initiates, attempting to complete a first novel or book of poetry, to established (and award-winning) authors and artists. Each candidate requests the specific dates and duration of the residence in his or her application.

For the director, coordinating requests can sometimes be a logistical nightmare. "My only frustration is not being able to provide the exact times residents request," says Guheen. "We get as close as we can, and I've never had any complaints once they get here. Even if it's not for as long as they asked. Once they are in residence that is all forgotten."

But getting accepted into a residency is no easy task. "Some applicants believe the application is just a process," says Guheen. "But it is one of competition and peer review." Along with an application, a candidate for the residency program is required to submit a work sample, a project description, and three recommendations from qualified individuals, largely instructors or other professionals who are familiar with the candidate's work. Almost 1,000 candidates apply to Ucross each year, but only 60 or so are selected.

The most significant criterion for evaluating applicants is the quality of the work sample. A selection committee comprised of professionals from the arts and humanities—university professors, museum curators and working artists and writers, some of whom are former Ucross residents—carefully reviews each submission.

Secondary to quality work is a complete application. "This is important," says Guheen, "because it indicates intention and seriousness on the part of the applicant. The application process gives us the information we need to evaluate or determine whether we have something to offer this person."

Another major consideration in granting a residency is the project proposal. Project proposals are chances for applicants to communicate to reviewers who they are, what they want, and how residencies would make differences in their work. "The project proposal is also very important. By that, I don't mean it has to be long or excruciatingly detailed. It simply has to provide us with insight as to why an applicant wants to come to Ucross," Guheen says.

Of course, a proposal and work sample must somehow correlate. "If you are proposing to come to Ucross to write poetry, your work sample should be poetry," she says. For instance, very rarely does an applicant submit poetry, then decide that he or she would like to do a lengthy, narrative nonfiction memoir. However, it does happen.

In Ucross's 15-year history, more than 600 artists have been involved with the program. Of that number, about half have been writers and poets, including the Pulitzer Prize-winning E. Annie Proulx, author of *The Shipping News*, and award-winning poets Gregory Donovan and Fred Marchant. "We don't have any sort of 'quota,'" says Guheen. "We don't accept so many writers, so many painters, so many poets. Once the work has been accepted, we just make the space that is appropriate."

Each resident's day begins basically the same: a quick breakfast and a short

CLOSE-UP, *continued*

hike across the ranch—about one-half mile—to a studio located in a separate building. From there, however, everyone sets his or her own personal work schedule—whether it's working on a project in-studio or just sitting creekside with a notepad and jotting down thoughts under a crisp, blue sky. At noon, lunch is delivered in a sack. And in the evening, residents may enjoy a communal dinner prepared by a professional chef, with all special dietary instructions carefully heeded.

This "cared for" aspect is a little hard to describe, says Guheen. "We do cater to the residents; we take care of a lot of the day-to-day things—like meals and shopping. We try to make their work process as easy as possible, so they can accomplish what they came here to do."

It is not unusual, she says, for an artist who had been working in "fits and starts," trying to complete something, to finally finish it during his or her residency at Ucross. That's not to say the program is in any way quantitatively oriented. It isn't about completing so many poems, finishing so many pages, painting so many pictures. "We don't want there to be any sense that a resident is to be counting what is actually produced," says Guheen. "Some people come here because they are actually coming down from completing a big project, and they need to regroup to consider what they are going to do next. This can be a good place to accomplish that as well. Sometimes it takes as much time to start something as it does to finish it."

In general, a residency doesn't always conclude at the end of any visitor's stay. Often residents use the experience to rearrange their lives back home. It can help them focus on what it is that they can do differently to get similar results in their permanent surroundings. "Sometimes it's just a simple thing like saying 'I'm going to have the place I write be different from the place I live,' " says Guheen. "I've had many people tell me long after their residencies were up that the experience continues to shape their work well into the future."

—*Patrick Souhan*

"[Residencies are] about being able to focus five days, ten days, thirty days in a row. That's pretty unusual in whatever you're doing in life—to concentrate on one thing and do nothing but that . . . "

—*Elizabeth Guheen*

wilderness retreats for women, many of them with writing themes, including A Writing Retreat with Sharon Olds in Montana and A Writing Retreat with Deena Metzger in New Mexico. The canoe trips are held all over North America plus Russia and Peru, and typically last 8 days-2 weeks with fees of $1,000-2,500. Write for annual listing of specific trips, a few offered for women and men.

HAWTHORNDEN CASTLE INTERNATIONAL RETREAT FOR WRITERS, Hawthornden Castle, Lasswade, Midlothian EH18 1EG Scotland, phone (0131)440-2180, contact administrator, founded 1982. Offers 8 four-week sessions from February through July and September through December for dramatists, novelists, poets or other creative writers who have published one piece of work. Located in a "remotely situated castle amid wild romantic scenery, a 30-minute bus ride to Edinburgh." Accommodates 5 writers at a time in study bedrooms with communal breakfasts and evening meals; desks, typewriters for hire, and limited reference materials available. Board and lodging are free. Write for application forms and guidelines. Application deadline is the end of September for upcoming year.

HEDGEBROOK, 2197 E. Millman Rd., Langley WA 98260, phone (360)321-4786, founded 1988. Offers 1-week to 3-month individual residencies from early January through May and mid-June through early December for "women writers of all ages and from all cultural backgrounds. The Hedgebrook community, on 30 acres of farmland and woods located on Whidbey Island in Washington State, seeks to balance human needs with those of the earth while providing a nurturing environment in which creativity can thrive." Accommodates 6 writers at a time. "Each writer has her own cottage with writing space, living room, sleeping loft, small kitchen, bathroom, electricity and a woodstove. Writers gather for dinner in the farmhouse every evening and may read in the living room/library afterwards. A bathhouse serves all six cottages." Public libraries with excellent interlibrary loan located within 2-6 miles. Computers available for rent. Activities include occasional cultural celebrations and field trips. Free room and board. Limited, need-based travel scholarships are available. Send SASE for application forms and guidelines. When sending application, include writing sample. Application deadlines: April 1 for residencies from mid-June to mid-December; September 30 for mid-January through May.

KALANI HONUA OCEANSIDE ECO-RESORT, RR2, Box 4500, Pahoa HI 96778-9724, phone (808)965-7828 or (800)800-6886, fax (808)965-9613 (call first), director Richard Koob, founded 1980. Offers 2-week to 2-month residencies on a year-round basis for visual, literary, folk and performing artists. "Kalani Honua is situated near Kalapana on the big island of Hawaii on 113 acres of secluded forest and dramatic coastline, 45 minutes from the city of Hilo and one hour from Hawaii Volcanoes National Park. Visitors stay in 4 two-story wooden lodges and 8 private cottage units that provide comfortable accommodations." Accommodates 100 (generally about 5 artists-in-residence) at a time in private rooms with full meal service plus optional kitchen facilities and shared or private baths; private desks and access to computers, typewriters and reference material available. Activities include a variety of dance, drawing, fitness and mind/body classes; also available are an olympic pool, sauna, volleyball, tennis, basketball and fitness room. Cost ranges from $45/night (multiple occupancy) to $85/night (private cottage); plus $25/day for meals. Stipends are most available in the periods of May through July and September through December. Stipends provide for 50% of lodging costs; balance is responsibility of the artist (stipends may *not* be applied toward dorm lodging or camping, or reduction in food or transportation costs). Send SASE for application forms and guidelines. When sending application, include $10 fee.

THE MACDOWELL COLONY, 100 High St., Peterborough NH 03458, phone (603)924-3886, founded 1907, "to provide creative artists with uninterrupted time and seclusion to work and enjoy the experience of living in a community of gifted artists." Residents receive room, board and exclusive use of a studio. Average residency is 6 weeks. Ability to pay for residency is not a factor. Application deadlines: January 15 for summer (May through August); April 15 for fall/winter (September through December); September 15 for winter/spring (January through April). Please write or call for application and guidelines.

THE MILLAY COLONY FOR THE ARTS, INC., East Hill Rd., P.O. Box 3, Austerlitz NY 12017-0003, e-mail application@millaycolony.org, founded in 1973, assistant director Gail Giles. Provides work space, meals and sleeping accommodations at no cost for a period of 1 month. Send SASE for brochure and application forms and apply with samples of your work before February 1 for June through September; before May 1 for October through January; before September 1 for February through May. Applications also can be accessed via e-mail.

MONTALVO CENTER FOR THE ARTS; MONTALVO BIENNIAL POETRY COMPETITION (IV-Regional), Box 158, Saratoga CA 95071, phone (408)741-3421, presents theatre, musical events and other artistic activities. They have an Artist Residency program, director Judy Moran, which has 5 apartments available for artists (including poets) for maximum 3-month periods. (No children or pets.) Limited financial assistance available. Deadlines: March 1 (fall and winter) and September 1 (spring and summer) of every year. They offer a biennial poetry competition in odd-numbered years (1997, 1999, etc.). Open to residents of Oregon, Nevada, Washington and California, with a prominent judge, with a first prize of $1,000 (and artist residency), other prizes of $500, $300 and 8 honorable mentions. Submit 3 poems in duplicate with $5 entry fee. Deadline: October 2. Send SASE for rules.

MY RETREAT, P.O. Box 1077, South Fallsburg NY 12779, phone (914)436-7455, owner Cora T. Schwartz, founded 1993. Offers "a room of one's own" for a weekend, week or month on a year-round basis for writers, poets and "artists of life." Located in the foothills of the Catskill Mountains, My Retreat is approximately 90 miles northwest of New York City. An unpretentious, peaceful setting consisting of a main house and cottages. The modest 1950-style cottages (open May through October) have seven furnished bedrooms, three kitchens and four bathrooms. Accommodates 5-12 guests depending on season. Cottages also have private accommodations with own kitchen/porch/bathroom and single or double bedrooms. The main house, with five bedrooms, is available year-round. There are screened and open porches, and a library of mostly vintage books for lending or for sale. Activities include ongoing workshops and informal readings. Nearby activities include a park with a lake for row boating and a pool, horseback riding, downhill skiing, art galleries, gift shop, classes at an ashram and a local museum. Cost per person starts at $85 for the weekend and $185 for one week, including continental-style breakfast. There is a two night minimum. Residents are responsible for the remainder of their meals. Special rates available on longer stays of 1 week or more. Send SASE for information.

‡N.A.L.L. ART ASSOCIATION, 232, Blvd. de Lattre, Vence 06140 France, phone (33)93 58 1326, fax (33)93 58 0900, founded 1993. Once an artist becomes a member of N.A.L.L. (annual donation of 500 French francs required), houses are available on a monthly basis throughout the year. Open to all artists. The N.A.L.L. (Nature, Art and Life League) is located between Vence and Saint-Paul, fifteen minutes from the Mediterranean Sea and Nice-Cote d'Azur Airport, and "consists of independent houses or cabins, complete with equipped kitchens and baths and each is quietly situated on a wooded hillside connected by rustic terraced trails." Accommodates up to 4 residents at one time. Large studios are available, but "each artist must have his own supplies." Activities include exhibitions, lectures and workshops. Cost ranges from 1,500-10,000 francs. To be considered, send work sample, an outline of education and accomplishments, and brief description of future projects. Write for further details.

‡NAUTILUS FOUNDATION, P.O. Box 368, Lloyd FL 32337, phone (904)997-1778, fax (904)997-0440, president Francois Bucher, founded 1987. Offers 3-week residencies from February through October to published poets and writers at the Foundation's grounds in Lloyd, "an unspoiled 400-acre wooded area blessed with wildlife, brooks and ponds." Accommodates 2 residents at one time in single rooms with private baths and kitchen facilities; a large library with reference materials available. No cost, however, residents are required to pay utilities. Some meals provided. Participants responsible for transportation to and from retreat. To be considered, send résumé. Send SASE for more details.

THE NEW YORK MILLS ARTS RETREAT, 24 N. Main Ave., Box 246, New York Mills MN 56567, phone (218)385-3339, fax (218)385-3366, coordinator Kent Scheer. Offers 1- to 4-week residencies on a year-round basis for emerging artists and writers of demonstrated quality and commitment. "The retreat is a 15-acre retired farmstead located three miles outside the small town of New York Mills. Loft space is provided in the upstairs of the old dairy barn while the original farm home serves as shared living quarters." Accommodates one writer/artist at a time in a single room with shared bath and kitchen. Work space and supplies are simple and minimal. A private loft is available for concentrated work. "All residencies in our program are supported by the Jerome Foundation. In this way we can provide stipends for 5 to 7 visiting artists annually. Beyond this, we will do all the necessary coordination for any artists interested in funding themselves for a personal retreat within our community. Artists and writers selected for our program receive up to $1,500 as a stipend. The criteria are artistic excellence as demonstrated by work samples, commitment to the arts as demonstrated by the résumé and a creative proposal for interaction with the community of New York Mills." Send SASE for application forms and guidelines. When sending application, include a résumé, artist's statement and a retreat proposal. Application deadlines: June 1 and January 1.

THE NORTHWOOD UNIVERSITY ALDEN B. DOW CREATIVITY CENTER, 3225 Cook Rd., Midland MI 48640-2398, phone (517)837-4478, fax (517)837-4468, founded 1979. Offers fellowships for 2-month summer residencies at the Northwood University Campus. Travel, room and board plus $750 stipend for personal expenses and/or project materials. No families/pets. Applicants can be undergraduates, graduates, or those without any academic or institutional affiliation, including citizens of other countries (if they can communicate in written and spoken English). Projects may be in any field, but must be new and innovative. Write for application. Annual deadline is December 31 for the following summer.

It's where **Faulkner** and **Cheever**
submitted their early work.

It's where **Salinger, Saroyan,
McCullers** and **Mailer**
were first published.

And now it's where **today's most
exciting new writers**
come to show you their talent.

To Subscribe, mail this form in the attached envelope. You'll get 4 quarterly issues at the introductory rate of just $19.96, a savings of 28% off the newsstand price.

NAME

ADDRESS

CITY

STATE ZIP

☐ Payment enclosed ☐ Bill me

Charge my ☐ Visa ☐ MC

Exp. _____

Signature _____

Outside U.S. add $7 (includes GST in Canada) and remit in U.S. funds. Allow 4-6 weeks for first issue delivery. Annual newsstand rate $27.80.

TTPM6-STY

STORY

‡**PENDLE HILL**, 338 Plush Mill Rd., Wallingford PA 19086-6099, phone (800)742-3150 or (610)566-4507, fax (610)566-3679, e-mail chuckfager@aol.com, website http://www.quaker.org/pen dle-hill, outreach associate Bobbi Kelly, founded 1930. Sojourns from 1 day to 1 month offered year round. Three 10-week residential study courses offered from October through June. Open to "all who seek a peaceful, spirit-centered setting." Pendle Hill's facilities include 16 buildings which house informal classrooms and meeting rooms, a library, bookstore, crafts studio and housing for students and staff. The buildings are "set on 23 acres of beautiful woods and gardens." Accommodates 60 residents at one time in single rooms with shared baths; communal dining. Twenty-four-hour library and typewriters available. "Classes in the resident program are open to sojourners. Weekend conferences also available. Guests may organize interest groups for writing support or readings." Cost for resident study is $3,875/term, $11,300/year, including room and board. Nightly rates available for sojourns. Limousine ride from airport available for $17. "Some financial aid available for Resident Program. Requires some work in exchange." Write for application forms and guidelines. "No application necessary to sojourn."

PUDDING HOUSE PUBLICATIONS, 60 N. Main St., Johnstown OH 43031. See listing in Publishers of Poetry section.

RAGDALE FOUNDATION, 1260 N. Green Bay Rd., Lake Forest IL 60045, founded 1976, provides a peaceful place and uninterrupted time for 12 writers, composers and artists. Meals, linen and laundry facilities are provided. Each resident is assigned private work space and sleeping accommodations. Couples are accepted if each qualifies independently. Residents may come for 2 weeks to 2 months. The fee is $105/week. Some full and partial fee waivers available. The foundation also sponsors poetry readings, concerts, workshops and seminars in writing. Ragdale is open year-round except for the month of May and 2 weeks at Christmas. Send SAE for application. Apply by January 15 for residencies in June through December and June 1 for January through May. Application fee: $20.

SPLIT ROCK ARTS PROGRAM, University of Minnesota, 306 Wesbrook Hall, 77 Pleasant St. SE, Minneapolis MN 55455, phone (612)624-6800, fax (612)625-2568, e-mail srap@mail.cee.uwn.e du. The program is a summer series of week-long workshops in the visual and literary arts and in the nature and applications of creativity, on the Duluth campus of UM "in the green hills overlooking Lake Superior." The 1996 faculty included Charles Baxter, Carol Bly, Michael Dennis Browne, Sharon Doubiago, Heid Erdrich, Janet Holmes, Jane Howard, Mary LaChapelle, Phillip Lopate, Naomi Shihab Nye, Alberto Rios, Martha Roth, Jane Resh Thomas, Catherine Watson, Will Weaver and Susan Welch. Tuition is $374-404 with an additional charge for graduate credit. Housing ranges from $168-246, depending on type of accommodation. Most students choose single or double rooms in 2-bedroom apartments on campus. Other housing options also available. Meals are in UMD's cafeteria, cooked by participants in their apartments, or in Duluth restaurants. Write or call for complete catalog in March.

UCROSS FOUNDATION RESIDENCY PROGRAM, 2836 US Hwy. 14-16, Clearmont WY 82835, phone (307)737-2291, executive director Elizabeth Guheen. There are 8 concurrent positions open in various disciplines, including poetry, each extending from 2 weeks to 2 months. No charge for room, board or studio space, and they do not expect services or products from guests. However, there is a $20 application fee required, plus $50 refundable deposit if accepted. Send SASE for information and application guidelines. Residents are selected from a rotating panel of professionals in the arts and humanities. Semiannual application postmark deadlines are March 1 (fall session) and October 1 (spring session).

VERMONT STUDIO CENTER; VISUAL ARTISTS AND WRITERS RESIDENCIES, P.O. Box 613NW, Johnson VT 05656, phone (802)635-2727, founded 1984. Offers 2-week Writing Studio Sessions led by prominent writers/teachers focusing on the craft of writing. Independent Writers' Retreats for 2, 4 or more weeks are also available year-round for those wishing more solitude. Room, working studio and meals are included in all programs. Generous work-exchange Fellowships are available. Write or call for more information and application.

VIRGINIA CENTER FOR THE CREATIVE ARTS, Mt. San Angelo, Sweet Briar VA 24595, director William Smart. Provides residencies for 12 writers (and 9 visual artists and 3 composers) for 2 weeks to 2 months at the 450-acre Mt. San Angelo estate. All accommodations provided. The normal fee is $30/day. Financial assistance is available.

WALKER WOODS, 1397 La Vista Rd. NE, Atlanta GA 30324, phone/fax (404)634-3309, founder Dalian Moore, founded 1993. Offers 2-week to 8-month residencies to "writers completing their first book (novels, short story collections, nonfiction, poetry, etc.)" and also to foreign authors writing or translating a first book in the English language." Located on 1½ acres in North Atlanta, Walker Woods, the home of the late Reuters foreign correspondent Richard Leigh Walker, "features a waterfall into a pond stocked with colorful coy fish, two bridges crossing a stone-lined stream (a tributary of the Chattahoochee River), hot tub, inspiration garden, and a three-story tree house currently in design. Writers may share a room or have one of their own, and meals are taken communally—with residents cooking for each other." Accommodates 8 writers at a time in three private suites (two with bathrooms), shared and convertible rooms. Kitchen and library are also shared. A computer system with laser printer is available on a reservation basis, but "each writer selected for residence will have a work station with WordPerfect software at their disposal." A fax machine and other office features are also available. Activities at Walker Woods include a public introduction of writers in residence. "A party is held in each writer's honor, with a full public relations campaign that introduces them nationally. Writers have the opportunity to share new work and offer shared critique, and many nights patrons and community arts leaders join in for dinner and readings. Writers in residence are also listed with speakers bureaus in the immediate area and included in radio, television and public appearances made by Dalian Moore. They are also included in cultural programs with the symphony, ballet, museums and other institutions. Last year, Walker Woods became a gathering place for writers and V.I.P.s from 50 different countries at 12 major monthly events." Cost ranges from $300-600/month depending on accommodation and needs. "Everyone in residence takes up small projects on the property (be it planting a tree or flower bed) or assisting with general upkeep of the property—we live as a family. Pet friendly, but please make arrangements ahead of time." Partial scholarships are available on a competitive basis. Send SASE for application forms and guidelines. Application deadlines for partial scholarships are quarterly, and there is a onetime $20 application fee.

THE HELENE WURLITZER FOUNDATION OF NEW MEXICO, Box 545, Taos NM 87571. Offers residencies to creative, *not* interpretive, artists in all media, for varying periods of time, usually 3 months, from April 1 through September 30, annually. Rent free and utilities free. Residents are responsible for their food. No families. No deadlines on application. However, all residencies are assigned into 1998.

YADDO, Box 395, Saratoga Springs NY 12866-0395, phone (518)584-0746, founded 1900, offers residencies to writers, visual artists, composers, choreographers, film/video artists and performance artists who have already achieved some recognition in their field and have new work under way. During the summer 35 guests can be accommodated at a time, 14 during the winter, approximately 200/year. The hours 9-4 are a quiet period reserved for work. Send SASE for applications to: Admissions, Yaddo, address above. Application deadlines are January 15 and August 1. A $20 application fee is required.

Organizations Useful to Poets

The organizations listed in this section offer encouragement and support to poets and other writers through a wide variety of services. They may sponsor contests and awards, hold regular workshops or open readings, or release publications with details about new opportunities and area events. Many of these groups provide a combination of these services to both members and nonmembers.

The PEN American Center, for instance, holds public events, sponsors literary awards, and offers grants and loans to writers in need. Poets seeking financial assistance should also refer to the listing for the Authors League Fund or contact the arts council in their state or province (see State and Provincial Grants on pages 495-497).

Many organizations provide opportunities to meet and discuss work with others. Those with access to computers and modems can connect with poets around the world through computer online services like the CompuServe Information Service. The National Federation of State Poetry Societies, Inc. and the Canadian Poetry Association are both national organizations with smaller affiliated groups which may meet in your state or province. And for those seeking gatherings more local or regional in focus, there are organizations such as the New Hampshire Writers & Publishers Project, Ozark Poets and Writers Collective, and Writers of Kern (all of which are new to this edition).

In addition to local and regional associations, there are also organizations which focus on helping certain groups of writers. For instance, the Writers Information Network (also new to this edition) provides encouragement, advice and networking for Christian writers. Also, the International Women's Writing Guild supports women writers through various national and regional events and services.

For organizations close to home, check for information at the library or contact the English department at a nearby college. Your local branch of the YMCA is also a good source for information on writing groups and programs. In fact, The National Writer's Voice Project sponsors both open-mike readings and readings by nationally known writers in approximately 15 YMCAs throughout the country. For more information, contact your local YMCA or the New York-based offices of the National Writer's Voice Project at (212)875-4123.

If you are unable to find a local writer's group, however, start one by placing an ad in your community newspaper or posting a notice on the library bulletin board. There are sure to be others in your area who would welcome the support, and the library might even have space for your group to meet on a regular basis.

To locate some of the larger organizations (or representative samples of smaller groups) read through the listings that follow. Then send a SASE to those groups that interest you to receive more details about their services and membership fees. Also refer to the list of Additional Organizations Useful to Poets at the end of this section.

THE ACADEMY OF AMERICAN POETS; FELLOWSHIP OF THE ACADEMY OF AMERICAN POETS; WALT WHITMAN AWARD; THE JAMES LAUGHLIN AWARD; HAROLD MORTON LANDON TRANSLATION AWARD; THE LENORE MARSHALL POETRY PRIZE; THE ERIC MATHIEU KING FUND; THE RAIZISS/DEPALCHI TRANS-LATION AWARD; THE TANNING PRIZE, 584 Broadway, Suite 1208, New York NY 10012-3250, phone (212)274-0343, founded 1934, executive director William Wadsworth. Robert Penn Warren wrote in *Introduction to Fifty Years of American Poetry*, an anthology published in 1984 containing one poem from each of the 126 Chancellors, Fellows and Award Winners of the Academy: "What does the Academy do? According to its certificate of incorporation, its purpose is 'To encourage, stimulate and foster the production of American poetry. . . .' The responsibility for its activities lies with the Board of Directors and the Board of 12 Chancellors, which has included, over the years, such figures as Louise Bogan, W.H. Auden, Witter Bynner, Randall Jarrell, Robert Lowell, Robinson Jeffers, Marianne Moore, James Merrill, Robert Fitzgerald, F.O. Matthiessen and Archibald MacLeish—certainly not members of the same poetic church." They award fellowships, currently of $20,000 each, to distinguished American poets (no applications taken)—61 to date—and other annual awards. The Walt Whitman Award pays $5,000 plus publication of a poet's first book by a major publisher. Mss of 50-100 pgs. must be submitted between September 15 and November 15 with a $20 entry fee. Entry form required. Send SASE. The James Laughlin Award, for a poet's second book, is also a prize of $5,000. Submissions must be made by a publisher, in ms form, prior to publication. The Academy distributes 3,000 copies to its members. Poets entering either contest must be American citizens. The Harold Morton Landon Translation Award is for translation of a book-length poem, a collection of poems or a verse-drama translated into English from any language. One award of $1,000 each year to a US citizen. Only publishers may submit the book. Write for guidelines. The Lenore Marshall Poetry Prize is a $10,000 award for the most outstanding book of poems published in the US in the preceding year. The contest is open to books by living American poets published in a standard edition (40 pgs. or more in length with 500 or more copies). Self-published books are not eligible. Publishers may enter as many books as they wish. Deadline: June 1. Write for guidelines. The Eric Mathieu King Fund assists noncommercial publishers of poetry. Send SASE for guidelines. The Raiziss/dePalchi Translation Award is for outstanding translations of modern Italian poetry into English. A $5,000 book prize and a $20,000 fellowship are given in alternate years. No applications accepted for the book prize. Submissions for the fellowship are accepted in odd-numbered years from September 1 through November 1. The Tanning Prize, of $100,000, is given annually for proven mastery in the art of poetry. No applications are accepted. *American Poet* is an informative periodical sent to those who contribute $25 or more/year or who are members. Membership: $45/year. The Academy inaugurated the first Annual National Poetry Month in April 1996. It also sponsors a national series of poetry readings and panel discussions, and offers for sale select audiotapes from its archive of poetry readings.

ADIRONDACK LAKES CENTER FOR THE ARTS, P.O. Box 205, Rte. 28, Blue Mountain Lake NY 12812, phone (518)352-7715, fax (518)352-7333, director Robert C. Lilly. An independent, private, nonprofit educational organization founded in 1967 to promote "visual and performing arts through programs and services, to serve established professional and aspiring artists and the region through educational programs and activities of general interest." Open to everyone. Currently has 1,300 members. Levels of membership available are individual, family and business. Offerings available for poets include workshops for adults and children, reading performances, discussions and lectures. Offers a "comfortable, cozy performance space—coffeehouse setting with tables, candles, etc." Computers available for members and artists. Publishes a triannual newsletter/schedule that contains news, articles, photos and a schedule of events. "All members are automatically sent the schedule and others may request a copy." Sponsors a few readings each year. "These are usually given by the instructor of our writing workshops. There is no set fee for membership, a gift of any size makes you a member." Members meet each July. Send SASE for additional information.

ASSOCIATED WRITING PROGRAMS; AWP CHRONICLE; THE AWP AWARD SERIES, Tallwood House, MS 1E3, George Mason University, Fairfax VA 22030, founded 1967. Offers a variety of services to the writing community, including information, job placement assistance, publishing opportunities, literary arts advocacy and forums. Annual individual membership is $50; placement service extra. For $20 you can subscribe to the *AWP Chronicle* (published 6 times/year), containing information about grants and awards, publishing opportunities, fellowships, and writing programs. They have a directory, *The Official Guide to Writing Programs*, of over 250 college and university writing programs for $23.95 (includes shipping). The AWP Award Series selects a volume of poetry (48 pg. minimum) each year ($10 entry fee for members; $15 for nonmembers) with an award of $2,000 and publication. Deadline: February 28. Send SASE for submission guidelines. Query after November. Their placement service helps writers find jobs in teaching, editing and other related fields.

THE AUTHORS GUILD, INC., 330 W. 42nd St., New York NY 10036, phone (212)563-5904, executive director Paul Aiken, "is an association of professional writers which focuses its efforts on the legal and business concerns of published authors in the areas of publishing contract terms, copyright, taxation and freedom of expression. We do not work in the area of marketing mss to publishers nor do we sponsor or participate in awards or prize selections." Send SASE for information on membership.

AUTHORS LEAGUE FUND, 330 W. 42nd St., New York NY 10036. Makes interest-free loans to published authors and professional playwrights in need of temporary help because of illness or an emergency. No grants.

‡**THE BEATLICKS**, 1016 Kipling Dr., Nashville TN 37217, phone (615)366-9012, e-mail kameleon 2@aol.com, editors Joe Speer and Pamela Hirst. Founded in 1988 to "promote literature and create a place where writers can share their work." International organization open to "anyone interested in literature." Currently has 200 members. "There is no official distinction between members, but there is a core group that does the work, writes reviews, organizes readings, etc." Offerings available for poets include publication of work (They have published poets from Australia, Egypt, India and Holland.), reviews of books and venues, readings for local and touring poets and a poetry hotline. "We have also hosted an open mic reading in Nashville since 1988. We have read in bars, bookstores, churches, libraries, festivals, TV and radio. We produce an hour show every Friday on public access TV. Poets submit audio and video tapes from all over. We interview poets about their work and where they are from." Publishes two newsletters: *Speer Presents* (monthly) and *Beatlicks Poetry Newsletter* (bimonthly). Subscription: $10/year. Members meet twice a month. Send SASE for additional information. "We promote all the arts."

BERGEN POETS, 180-G1 Summit Ave., Summit NJ 07901, phone (908)277-6245, fax (908)277-2171, president Ms. Roberta L. Greening, founded in 1969 to "bring together poets and friends of poetry in our area, help the individual in writing and appreciation of poetry, and add to the cultural life of the community." Open to anyone in the community interested in poetry. "Our base is in Bergen County, New Jersey. However, our members extend from New York to Florida." Currently has 50 members. Offerings available to poets include workshops on craft and readings at area facilities. "Our meetings are held at various public libraries and local bookstores." Publishes a quarterly newsletter at an annual cost of $5 to new members. Sponsors open-mike readings following featured members' readings. Membership dues are $5 to receive newsletter and meeting announcements. Members meet a minimum of 4 times/year. Send SASE for additional information. "Bergen Poets is one of the oldest poetry organizations in the state of New Jersey."

BEYOND BAROQUE LITERARY/ARTS CENTER, 681 Venice Blvd., Venice CA 90291, phone (310)822-3006, director Chase L. Frank. A nonprofit arts center established in 1968 that has been funded by the NEA, state and city arts councils and corporate donations. Members get a calendar of events, discounts on regularly scheduled programs, discounts in the bookstore, and invitations to yearly events only open to members. Beyond Baroque contains a bookstore open 5 days a week, including Friday evenings to coincide with regular weekly readings and performances. About 130 writers are invited to read each year; there are also open readings and poetry and fiction workshops.

BLACK CULTURAL CENTRE FOR NOVA SCOTIA, 1149 Main St., Dartmouth, Nova Scotia B2Z 1A8 Canada, phone (902)434-6223, or (800)465-0767, fax (902)434-2306. Founded in 1977 "to create among members of the black communities an awareness of their past, their heritage and their identity; to provide programs and activities for the general public to explore, learn about, understand and appreciate black history, black achievements and black experiences in the broad context of Canadian life. The centre houses a museum, reference library, small auditorium and workshops."

BURNABY WRITERS' SOCIETY, 6584 Deer Lake Ave., Burnaby, British Columbia V5G 2J3 Canada, contact person Eileen Kernaghan. Corresponding membership in the society, including a newsletter subscription, is open to anyone, anywhere. Yearly dues are $25. Sample newsletter in return for SASE with Canadian stamp. The society holds monthly meetings at The Burnaby Arts Centre (located at 6450 Deer Lake Ave.), with a business meeting at 7:30 followed by a writing workshop or speaker. Members of the society stage regular public readings of their own work.

THE WITTER BYNNER FOUNDATION FOR POETRY, INC., P.O. Box 10169, Santa Fe NM 87504, phone (505)988-3251, fax (505)986-8222. The foundation awards grants exclusively to nonprofit organizations for the support of poetry-related projects in the area of: 1) support of individual poets through existing nonprofit institutions; 2) developing the poetry audience; 3) poetry translation and the process of poetry translation; and 4) uses of poetry. The foundation "may consider the support of other creative and innovative projects in poetry." Grant applications are accepted annually from January 1 through February 1; requests for application forms should be submitted to Steven Schwartz, executive director, at the address above.

THE CANADA COUNCIL; GOVERNOR GENERAL'S LITERARY AWARDS; INTERNATIONAL LITERARY PRIZES, P.O. Box 1047, 350 Albert St., Ottawa, Ontario K1P 5V8 Canada, phone (613)566-4376. Established by Parliament in 1957, the Canada Council "provides a wide range of grants and services to professional Canadian artists and art organizations in dance, media arts, music, theatre, writing, publishing and the visual arts." The Governor General's Literary Awards, valued at $10,000 (Canadian) each, are given annually for the best English-language and best French-language work in each of seven categories, including poetry. Books must be first-edition trade books written, translated or illustrated by Canadian citizens or permanent residents of Canada and published in Canada or abroad during the previous year (October 1 through September 30). Collections of poetry must be at least 48 pgs. long and at least half the book must contain work not published previously in book form. In the case of translation, the original work must also be a Canadian-authored title. Books must be submitted by publishers with a Publisher's Submission Form, which is available from the Writing and Publishing Section. All entries must be received at the Canada Council by August 31. The Canada Council administers two International Literary Prizes (Canada-French Community of Belgium, Canada-Switzerland) of $2,500-3,500 (Canadian) and the Canada-Japan Book Award worth $10,000 (Canadian). Winners are selected by juries. Except for the Canada-Japan Book Award, applications are not accepted.

CANADIAN CONFERENCE OF THE ARTS (CCA), 189 Laurier Ave. E., Ottawa, Ontario K1N 6P1 Canada, phone (613)238-3561, fax (613)238-4849, is a national, nongovernmental, not-for-profit arts service organization dedicated to the growth and vitality of the arts and cultural industries in Canada. The CCA represents all Canadian artists, cultural workers and arts supporters, and works with all levels of government, the corporate sector and voluntary organizations to enhance appreciation for the role of culture in Canadian life. Each year, the CCA presents awards for contribution to the arts. Regular meetings held across the country ensure that members' views on urgent and ongoing issues are heard and considered in organizing advocacy efforts and forming Board policies. Members stay informed and up-to-date through *Blizzart*, a newsletter, which is published 5 times a year, and receive discounts on conference fees and on all other publications. Membership is $30 (plus GST) for Canadian individual members, $35 for US members and $45 for international members.

CANADIAN POETRY ASSOCIATION; POEMATA, 340 Station B, London, Ontario N6A 4W1 Canada, e-mail resource.center@onlinesys.com, national coordinator Wayne Ray. A broad based umbrella organization that aims to promote the reading, writing, publishing, purchasing and preservation of poetry in Canada through the individual and combined efforts of its members; to promote and encourage all forms and styles of poetry; to promote communication among poets, publishers and the general public; to promote the establishment and maintenance of poetry libraries and archives in educational institutions across Canada; and to develop an international connection for Canadian poets through *Poemata,* its bimonthly magazine, and events organized by independent, locally-run chapters. Through its 6 autonomous local chapters, CPA organizes poetry readings, literary and social events. Membership is open to anyone with an interest in poetry, including other literary organizations, for $25/year. *Poemata* publishes articles, book reviews and essays related to writing. Sample newsletter: $3.

CANADIAN SOCIETY OF CHILDREN'S AUTHORS, ILLUSTRATORS & PERFORM-ERS, 35 Spadina Rd., Toronto, Ontario M5R 2S9 Canada, phone (416)515-1559, fax (416)515-7022, is a "society of professionals in the field of children's culture. Puts people into contact with publishers, offers advice to beginners, and generally provides a visible profile for members; 365 professional members and over 1,000 associates who are termed 'friends.' An annual conference in Toronto the last week of October provides workshops to people interested in writing, illustrating, and performing for children." Membership is $60 for professional members (and a free copy of the Membership Directory); $25 for associates/year. Both include a subscription to the quarterly *CANSCAIP News*.

‡COMPUSERVE INFORMATION SERVICE, 5000 Arlington Centre Blvd., P.O. Box 20212, Columbus OH 43220, phone (800)848-8199 from outside Ohio or (614)457-8600 from within Ohio or outside the US, fax (614)538-1780. An international online information service available via modem from any computer. On CIS are many forums on specialized topics of interests, including Litforum. This is basically a bulletin board where various members post and respond to public messages (though you may communicate with them privately, too, either through the CompuServe Mail system or by leaving private messages in Litforum). A CompuServe membership is $9.95/month for 5 hours of online time; each additional hour is $2.95. The CompuServe Information Manager software is free and available in a Windows, Mac or OS/2 platform. There are many services available through CIS (in addition to electronic mail), but most of the action is in the forums. In Litforum sometimes the talk is quite funny, often bawdy, and far-ranging, though there is a lot of practical, professional communication, too, and many people make contact via Litforum with agents, editors, other writers, researchers, and so on, that prove quite useful. You join Litforum (anyone can join; a number of the regulars are not even writers—just people interested in literature, writing, publication, chitchat), read the messages posted in some or all of the 17 sections (on such things as poetry and lyrics, fiction, nonfiction, speculative fiction, and so on), respond to any that you wish to, or just lurk. Each section has a library where you can post material you have written or download material by others, and comment if you wish. There is also a workshop for which you can request admission (and you're in automatically) where each writer has a turn to have material criticized by the other workshop members.

COUNCIL OF LITERARY MAGAZINES AND PRESSES, 154 Christopher St., Suite 3-C, New York NY 10014-2839. Compiles an annual directory useful to writers: The *Directory of Literary*

Magazines, which has detailed descriptions of over 600 literary magazines, including type of work published, payment to contributors and submission requirements. The directory is $15 postage paid and may be ordered by sending a check to CLMP.

COWBOY POETRY GATHERING; WESTERN FOLKLIFE ROUNDUP; WESTERN FOLKLIFE CENTER, 501 Railroad St., Elko NV 89801. Both of these gatherings are sponsored by Western Folklife Center, Box 888, Elko NV 89803, phone (702)738-7508, fax (702)738-2900, e-mail wfc@sierra.net. There is an annual 6-day January gathering of cowboy poets in Elko. The Western Folklife Roundup is held annually the last weekend in August. The Western Folklife Center publishes and distributes books and tapes of cowboy poetry and songs as well as other cowboy memorabilia. The well-established tradition of cowboy poetry is enjoying a renaissance, and thousands of cowboy poets participate in these activities. For further information and details, contact the Center, or visit their website http://www.westfolk.org.

FEDERATION OF BRITISH COLUMBIA WRITERS, M.P.O. Box 2206, Vancouver, British Columbia V6B 3W2 Canada, manager Corey Van't Haaff. The federation "is a nonprofit organization of professional and emerging writers of all genres." They publish a newsletter of markets, awards and literary news/events; act as "a network centre for various other provincial writer's organizations; host, promote and organize workshops, readings, literary competitions and social activities; distribute directories which are distributed to schools, businesses, and organizations which may request the services of writers; and represent writers' interests to other professionally related organizations."

INTERNATIONAL WOMEN'S WRITING GUILD, P.O. Box 810, Gracie Station, New York NY 10028, phone (212)737-7536, website Hanelore@http://www.iwwg.com, founded 1976, "a network for the personal and professional empowerment of women through writing." The Guild publishes a bimonthly 32-page newsletter which includes members' needs, achievements, contests, and publishing information. A manuscript referral service introduces members to literary agents. Other activities and benefits are 13 annual national and regional events, including a summer conference at Skidmore College (see listing under Conferences and Workshops); "regional clusters" (independent regional groups); job referrals; round robin manuscript exchanges; sponsorship of the "Artist of Life" award; and group health insurance. Membership in the nonprofit Guild costs $35/year in the US and $45/year foreign.

JUST BUFFALO LITERARY CENTER, 2495 Main St., Suite 436, Buffalo NY 14214, phone (716)832-5400, fax (716)832-5710, founded 1975 by executive director Debora Ott. It offers readings, workshops, master classes, an annual competition for Western New York writers, Spoken Arts Radio broadcasts on National Public Radio affiliate WBFO, and Writers-in-Education programs for school-age populations. Just Buffalo acts as a clearinghouse for literary events in the Greater Buffalo area and offers diverse services to writers and to the WNY region. "Although we are not accepting submissions for publication at this time, we will review works for possible readings."

THE LEAGUE OF CANADIAN POETS; POETS IN THE CLASSROOM; WHO'S WHO IN THE LEAGUE OF CANADIAN POETS; POETRY MARKETS FOR CANADIANS; NATIONAL POETRY CONTEST; GERALD LAMPERT AWARD; PAT LOWTHER AWARD, 54 Wolseley, 3rd Floor, Toronto, Ontario M5T 1A5 Canada, phone (416)504-1657, founded 1966, contact Edita Petrauskaite. The league's aims are the advancement of poetry in Canada and promotion of the interests of professional, Canadian poets. Information on full and associate membership can be obtained by sending a SASE for the brochure, League of Canadian Poets: Services and Membership. The league publishes a biannual *Museletter* (30 pgs., magazine-sized) plus six newsletters; *Poets in the Classroom*, on teaching poetry to children; a directory called *Who's Who in The League of Canadian Poets* that contains 1 page of information, including a picture, bio, publications and "what critics say" about each of the members; and *Poetry Markets for Canadians* which covers contracts, markets, agents and more. The league's members go on reading tours, and the league encourages them to speak on any facet of Canadian literature at schools and universities, libraries or organizations. The league has arranged "thousands of readings in every part of Canada"; they are now arranging exchange visits featuring the leading poets of such countries as Great Britain, Germany and the US. The league sponsors a National Poetry Contest with prizes of $1,000, $750 and $500; the best 50 poems published in a book. Deadline: January 31. Entry fee: $6/poem. Poems should be unpublished, under 75 lines and typed. Names and addresses should *not* appear on poems but on a separate covering sheet. Please send SASE for complete rules, info on judges, etc. Open to Canadian citizens or landed immigrants only. The Gerald Lampert Award of $1,000 is for a first book of poetry written by a Canadian, published professionally. The Pat Lowther Award of $1,000 is for a book of poetry written by a Canadian woman and published professionally. Write for entry forms.

THE LOFT; LOFT-MCKNIGHT AWARDS; THE NATIONAL PRIZE IN POETRY AND FICTION, Pratt Community Center, 66 Malcolm Ave. SE, Minneapolis MN 55414, phone (612)379-8999, founded 1974, executive director Linda Myers. The Loft was started by a group of poets looking for a place to give readings and conduct workshops and has evolved into "the most comprehensive literary center in the country," offering opportunities for writers in all genres and at all levels of development, managed by a 21-member board of directors and staff of 12. Membership: 2,400. In addition to membership dues, financial support came from tuition for creative writing classes, fees from benefit performances, and contributions from individuals, corporations and foundations. The Loft offers over 100 courses each year in addition to 40 workshops and panels. Its reading series presents established and emerging writers throughout Minnesota and the Mentor Series and Creative Nonfiction Program feature nationally known writers. The Loft publishes *A View from the Loft*, a monthly magazine on craft. The Loft-McKnight Awards are offered annually to Minnesota writers: 8 awards of $7,500 each, 3 in poetry, 5 in creative prose; 2 Awards of Distinction, $10,500 each. The Mentor Series, Creative Nonfiction Program, and Inroads Programs provide opportunities for area writers to study intensively with local and national writers. The National Prize in Poetry and Fiction awards $1,000 annually to a poet and fiction writer; winning works are published in the *Michigan Quarterly Review* (see listing in the Publishers of Poetry section).

MAINE WRITERS & PUBLISHERS ALLIANCE; MAINE IN PRINT; MAINE WRITERS CENTER, 12 Pleasant St., Brunswick ME 04011-2201, phone (207)729-6333, founded 1975, outreach coordinator Cate DiMarzio. This organization is "a nonprofit organization dedicated to promoting all aspects of writing, publishing, and the book arts. Our membership currently includes over 1,500 writers, publishers, librarians, teachers, booksellers and readers from across Maine and the nation. For an individual contribution of $30 per year members receive a range of benefits including *Maine in Print*, a monthly compilation of calendar events, updated markets, book reviews, grant information, interviews with Maine authors and publishers, articles about writing and more. The alliance distributes selected books about Maine and by Maine authors and publishers, and it maintains a bookstore, reference library, performance space and word processing station at the Maine Writers Center in Brunswick. MWPA regularly invites writers to conduct Saturday workshops." Reviews books of poetry only by Maine-based presses and poets. "We also have extensive ongoing workshops in fiction and poetry and offer an annual fall writing retreat."

‡MANITOBA WRITERS' GUILD INC., 206-100 Arthur St., Winnipeg, Manitoba R3B 1H3 Canada, phone (204)942-6134, fax (204)942-5754. Founded in 1981 to "promote and advance the art of writing, in all its forms, throughout the province of Manitoba." Regional organization open to "any individual with an interest in the art of writing." Currently has 430-500 members. Levels of membership are Regular and Student/Senior/Fixed income. Programs and services include: the Manitoba Workshop Series, intensive one-day sessions conducted by professional writers; Open Workshops, monthly evening sessions held in the fall and winter; an Annual Literary Conference, which is held 3 days in the fall and includes panel discussions, readings, performances and special events; the Mentor Program, a limited number of promising writers selected to work one-on-one with experienced mentors; the Manitoba Literary Awards which include the McNally Robinson Book of the Year Award and the John Hirsch Award for Most Promising Manitoba Writer, all awards are to "recognize and celebrate excellence in Manitoba writing and publishing"; the Café Reading Series, a weekly series showcasing emerging and established local writers; the Writers' Resource Centre, containing information about writing, publishing, markets, as well as Canadian periodicals and books by Manitoba authors; and a studio offering writers comfortable, private work space. Published 7 times/year, their newsletter, *Word-Wrap*, includes feature articles, regular columns, information on current markets and competitions, and profiles of Manitoba writers. They also publish *The Writers' Handbook*, the Guild's "comprehensive resource manual on the business of writing." Membership fees are $40 Regular, $20 Student/Senior/Fixed Income. Send SASE for additional information.

NATIONAL FEDERATION OF STATE POETRY SOCIETIES, INC. Membership Chairperson: Barbara Stevens, 909 E. 34th St., Sioux Falls SD 57105; Contest Chairperson: Claire Van Breeman Downes, 1206 13th Ave. S.E., St. Cloud MN 56304. "NFSPS is a nonprofit organization exclusively educational and literary. Its purpose is to recognize the importance of poetry with respect to national cultural heritage. It is dedicated solely to the furtherance of poetry on the national level and serves to unite poets in the bonds of fellowship and understanding." Any poetry group located in a state not already affiliated but interested in affiliating with NFSPS may contact the membership chairperson. Canadian groups may also apply. "In a state where no valid group exists, help may also be obtained by individuals interested in organizing a poetry group for affiliation." Most reputable state poetry societies are members of the National Federation and advertise their various poetry contests through the quarterly bulletin, *Strophes*, available for SASE and $1, editor Kay Kinnaman, Route 3, Box 348, Alexandria IN 46001. Beware of organizations calling themselves state poetry societies (however named) that are not members of NFSPS, as such labels are sometimes used by vanity schemes trying to sound respectable. Others, such as the Oregon State Poetry Association, are quite reputable, but they don't belong to NFSPS. NFSPS holds an annual meeting in a different city each year with a large awards banquet, addressed by an honorary chairperson. They sponsor 50 national contests in various categories each year, including the NFSPS Prize of $1,500 for first place; $500, second; $250, third; with entry fees ($3 for the entire contest for members, $5 for NFSPS Award; $1/poem for nonmembers and $5 for NFSPS Award, up to 4 poems/entry). All poems winning over $10 are published in an anthology. Rules for all contests are given in a brochure available from Kay Kinnaman at *Strophes* or Claire Van Breeman Downes at the address above; you can also write for the address of your state poetry society. Scholarship information is available from Pj Doyle, 4242 Stevens Ave., Minneapolis MN 55409.

THE NATIONAL POETRY FOUNDATION; SAGETRIEB; PAIDEUMA, University of Maine, 5752 Neville Hall, Room 302, Orono ME 04469-5752, publications coordinator Marie McCosh. "The NPF is a nonprofit organization concerned with publishing scholarship on the work of 20th century poets, particularly Ezra Pound and those in the Imagist/Objectivist tradition. We publish *Paideuma*, a journal devoted to Ezra Pound scholarship, and *Sagetrieb*, a journal devoted to poets in the imagist/objectivist tradition, as well as books on and of poetry. NPF occasionally conducts a summer conference." Sample copies: $8.95 for *Paideuma* or *Sagetrieb*.

NATIONAL WRITERS UNION, 113 University Place, 6th Floor, New York NY 10003, phone (212)254-0279, e-mail nwu@nwu.org, website http://www.nwu.org/nwu. Offers members such services as a grievance committee, contract guidelines, health insurance, press credentials, car rental discounts, and caucuses and trade groups for exchange of information about special markets. Members receive *The American Writer*, the organization's newsletter. Membership is $80 for those earning less than $5,000/year; $132 for those earning $5,000-25,000; and $180 for those earning more than $25,000.

NEW ENGLAND POETRY CLUB, 2 Farrar St., Cambridge MA 02138, president Diana Der-Hovanessian, founded in 1915 by Amy Lowell, Robert Frost and Conrad Aiken to "bring the best poets to the area and foster fellowship among writers." National organization open to beginning poets, professional poets and teachers of poetry. Currently has 500 members. Offerings available for poets include a newsletter with poetry information, free admission to readings and contests and free participation in workshops. Nationally known writers regularly give readings that are open to the public. Sponsors open-mike readings for members only. Membership dues are $20. Readings and workshops are held monthly. Of the 12 contests they sponsor, 9 are open to nonmembers for an entry fee of $3/poem. Entries must be original, unpublished poems in English. Send SASE for details or membership information to Victor Howes, 137 West Newton St., Boston MA 02118.

‡NEW HAMPSHIRE WRITERS & PUBLISHERS PROJECT, P.O. Box 2693, Concord NH 03302-2693, phone (603)226-6649, fax (603)226-0035, executive director Patricia Scholz-Cohen. Founded in 1988 "to foster the literary arts community in New Hampshire, to serve as a resource for and about New Hampshire writers, to support the development of individual writers, and to encourage an audience for literature in New Hampshire." State-wide organization open to anyone. Currently has 750 members. Offerings specifically available for poets include workshops, seminars and information about poetry readings and slams held throughout northern New England. Sponsors a day-long workshop and 4- to 6-week intensive courses. Also sponsors a biennial award. Publishes *Ex Libris*, a bimonthly newsletter for members only. Members and nationally known writers give readings that are open to the public. Also sponsors open-mike readings. Membership dues are $35/year; $20/year for Seniors and students. Members meet annually. Send SASE for additional information.

THE NORTH CAROLINA POETRY SOCIETY; BROCKMAN/CAMPBELL BOOK AWARD CONTEST, 518 West Main St., Mt. Olive NC 28365, president Cecil Cahoon. Founded in 1932 to "foster the writing of poetry; to bring together in meetings of mutual interest and fellowship the poets of North Carolina; to encourage the study, writing, and publication of poetry; and to develop a public taste for the reading and appreciation of poetry." Regional organization open to "all interested persons." Levels of membership available are Regular ($20/year) and Student ($5/year). NCPS conducts 3 general meetings and numerous statewide workshops each year, sponsors annual poetry contests with categories for adults and children (open to anyone, with small fee for nonmembers; December/January deadline; cash prizes), publishes the contest-winning poems in the annual book *Award Winning Poems*; publishes a newsletter and supports other poetry activities. They also sponsor the annual Brockman/Campbell Book Award Contest for a book of poetry (over 20 pgs.) by a North Carolina poet (native-born or current resident for 3 years). $100 cash prize and a Revere-style bowl is awarded. $5 entry fee for nonmembers. Deadline: May 1. For details, send SASE to Sharon A. Sharp, P.O. Box 3345, Boone NC 28607. For membership information, send SASE to address at beginning of listing.

NORTH CAROLINA WRITERS' NETWORK; THE NETWORK NEWS, P.O. Box 954, Carrboro NC 27510, established 1985. Supports the work of writers, writers' organizations, independent bookstores, little magazines and small presses, and literary programming statewide. $35 membership dues annually brings members *The Network News*, a 28-page bimonthly newsletter containing organizational news, national market information and other literary material of interest to writers, and access to the Resource Center, other writers, workshops, conferences, readings and competitions, and a critiquing service. 1,600 members nationwide. They also publish the *North Carolina's Literary Resource Guide*, an annual including information about retreats, fellowships, markets, writers groups, conferences, agents and literary organizations. Available to members for $5 postpaid and to nonmembers for $6.50 postpaid. Annual fall conference features nationally-known writers, publishers and editors. It is held in a different North Carolina location each year in November. Also sponsors competitions in short fiction, one-act plays and nonfiction essays for North Carolinians and members.

THE OREGON STATE POETRY ASSOCIATION, % Linda Smith, 471 NW Hemlock, Corvallis OR 97330, phone (503)753-3335; newsletter editor Elizabeth Bolton, P.O. Box 219006, Portland OR 97225. Founded for "the promotion and creation of poetry," the association has over 200 members, $18 dues, publishes a quarterly *OSPA Newsletter*, and sponsors contests twice yearly, October and April, with total cash prizes of $300 each (no entry fee to members, $3/poem for nonmembers; out of state entries welcome). Themes and categories vary. For details write to OSPA, P.O. Box 219006, Portland OR 97225 after August 1 and February 15 each year. The association sponsors workshops, readings and seminars around the state.

‡**OZARK POETS AND WRITERS COLLECTIVE**, P.O. Box 3717, Fayetteville AR 72702, phone (501)443-7575, e-mail bjmoossy@aol.com, co-chairpersons Lisa Martinovic and Brenda J. Moossy. Founded reading series in 1993, incorporated in 1995, "to support and promote community involvement in Ozark literary arts; to encourage an appreciation of local writers by providing access to their work through readings, publications, workshops and other events; to ensure that the experience of writing and reading remain a vital part of life in the Ozarks. Regional organization open to any interested poets and writers. "Most participants come from the Ozarks, which encompasses parts of Arkansas, Missouri and Oklahoma." Offerings available for poets include monthly slams with cash prizes and biweekly informal poetry workshops. "OPWC also runs a weekly column in the *Northwest Arkansas Times* with space to showcase local and not so local poets, provide information about upcoming readers and events, and invite comment about the feast of poetry and all its flavors." Nationally and locally known writers give readings that are open to the public. The readings are held on the last Wednesday of each month and are immediately followed by an open mic session. Board members meet the second Wednesday of every month; interested poets and writers may attend the meetings. Send SASE for additional information.

PEN AMERICAN CENTER; PEN WRITERS FUND; PEN TRANSLATION PRIZE; GRANTS AND AWARDS, 568 Broadway, New York NY 10012, phone (212)334-1660, "is the largest of more than 100 centers which comprise International PEN, founded in London in 1921 by John Galsworthy to foster understanding among men and women of letters in all countries. Members of PEN work for freedom of expression wherever it has been endangered, and International PEN is the only worldwide organization of writers and the chief voice of the literary community." Its total membership on all continents is approximately 10,000. The 2,700 members of the American Center include poets, playwrights, essayists, editors, novelists (for the original letters in the acronym PEN), as well as translators and those editors and agents who have made a substantial contribution to the literary community. Membership in American PEN includes reciprocal privileges in foreign centers for those traveling abroad. Branch offices are located in Cambridge, Chicago, Portland/Seattle, Baton Rouge and San Francisco. Among PEN's various activities are public events and symposia, literary awards, assistance to writers in prison and to American writers in need (grants and loans up to $1,000 from PEN Writers Fund). Medical insurance for writers is available to members. The quarterly *PEN Newsletter* is sent to all members and is available to nonmembers by subscription. The PEN Translation Prize is sponsored by the Book-of-the-Month Club, 1 prize each year of $3,000 for works published in the current calendar year. They publish *Grants and Awards* biennially, containing guidelines, deadlines, eligibility requirements and other information about hundreds of grants, awards and competitions for poets and other writers: $10 postpaid. Send SASE for booklet describing their activities and listing their publications, some of them available free.

PITTSBURGH POETRY EXCHANGE, P.O. Box 4279, Pittsburgh PA 15203, phone (412)481-POEM. Founded in 1974 as a community-based organization for local poets, it functions as a service organization and information exchange, conducting ongoing workshops, readings, forums and other special events. No dues or fees. "Any monetary contributions are voluntary, often from outside sources. We've managed not to let our reach exceed our grasp." Their reading programs are primarily committed to local and area poets, with honorariums of $25-75. They sponsor a minimum of three major events each year in addition to a monthly workshop. Some of these have been reading programs in conjunction with community arts festivals, such as the October South Side Poetry Smorgasbord—a series of readings throughout the evening at different shops (galleries, bookstores). Poets from out of town may contact the exchange for assistance in setting up readings at bookstores to help sell their books. Contact Michael Wurster at the above address or phone number.

THE POETRY COMMITTEE OF THE GREATER WASHINGTON AREA, % The Folger Shakespeare Library, 201 E. Capitol St. SE, Washington DC 20003, phone (202)544-7077, executive director Saskia Hamilton. An independent, nonprofit group, the membership (by invitation) consists of about 60 people who represent major and minor poetry organizations in the metropolitan area. Annual sponsors of Celebration of Washington Poetry, a reading and book sale highlighting area poets and presses, the Columbia Book Award for best book of poetry by Washington area poet within the past calendar year and the Columbia Merit Award for service to area poetry.

THE POETRY PROJECT AT ST. MARK'S CHURCH-IN-THE-BOWERY, 131 E. 10th St., New York NY 10003, phone (212)674-0910, was established in 1966 by the US Dept. of H.E.W. in an effort to help wayward youths in the East Village. It is now funded by a variety of government and private sources. Artistic Director: Ed Friedman. Program Coordinator: JoAnn Wasserman. From October through May the project offers workshops, talks, staged readings, performance poetry, lectures, an annual 4-day symposium, literary magazines and a series of featured writers who bring their books to sell at the readings. If the reading is a publication party, the publisher handles the sales.

POETRY RESOURCE CENTER OF MICHIGAN, %English Dept., Wayne State University, 51 W. Warren, Detroit MI 48202, phone (810)754-9645, president Cindi St. Germain, "is a nonprofit organization which exists through the generosity of poets, writers, teachers, publishers, printers, librarians and others dedicated to the reading and enjoyment of poetry in Michigan." The *PRC Newsletter*, which includes a calendar of events, is available by mail monthly for an annual membership donation of $25 or more ($15 for students and seniors), and is distributed free of charge at locations throughout the state. To obtain copies for distribution at poetry functions, contact the president or any member of the PRC Board of Directors.

POETRY SOCIETY OF AMERICA; POETRY SOCIETY OF AMERICA AWARDS, 15 Gramercy Park, New York NY 10003, phone (212)254-9628, is a nonprofit cultural organization in support of poetry and poets, member and nonmember, young and established, which sponsors readings, lectures and workshops both in New York City and around the country. Their Peer Group Workshop is open to all members and meets on a weekly basis. They publish a newsletter of their activities and sponsor a wide range of contests. The following are open to members only: Alice Fay Di Castagnola Award ($1,000); *Writer Magazine*/Emily Dickinson Award ($100); Cecil Hemley Memorial Award ($300); Lucille Medwick Memorial Award ($500); Lyric Poetry Award ($500). Nonmembers may enter as many of the following contests as they wish, no more than 1 entry for each, for a $5 fee: Louise Louis/ Emily S. Bourne Student Poetry Award, $100 for students in grades 9-12; George Bogin Memorial Award, $500 for a selection of 4 to 5 poems which take a stand against oppression; Robert H. Winner Memorial Award, $2,500 for a poem written by a poet over 40, still unpublished or with one book. (All have a deadline of December 22; awards are made at a ceremony and banquet in late spring.) The Society also has 2 book contests open to works submitted by publishers only. They must obtain an entry form, and there is a $10 fee for each book entered. Book awards are: Norma Farber Award, $1,000 for a first book; William Carlos Williams Award, $1,000 for a book of poetry published by a small, nonprofit or university press, by a permanent resident of the US—translations not eligible. The Shelley Memorial Award of $2,000-6,000 is by nomination only. For necessary rules and guidelines for their various contests send #10 SASE between October 1 and December 22. Rules and awards are subject to change. Membership: $40.

POETS & WRITERS, INC. See listing under Publications Useful to Poets.

POETS HOUSE: THE REED FOUNDATION LIBRARY; THE POETRY PUBLICATION SHOWCASE; DIRECTORY OF AMERICAN POETRY BOOKS; POETRY IN THE BRANCHES; NYC POETRY TEACHER OF THE YEAR, 72 Spring St., New York NY 10012, phone (212)431-7920, founded 1985, executive director Lee Ellen Briccetti. Poets House is a 30,000-volume (noncirculating) poetry library of books, tapes and literary journals, with reading and writing space available. This comfortably furnished literary center is open to the public year-round. Over 30 annual public events include 1) poetic programs of cross-cultural and interdisciplinary exchange, 2) readings in which distinguished poets discuss and share the work of other poets, 3) workshops and seminars on various topics led by visiting poets, 4) an annual $1,000 award for the designated NYC Poetry Teacher of the Year, and 5) an inhouse conference for high school teachers of poetry. In addition, Poets House has begun a 3-year pilot collaboration with The New York Public Library, Poetry in the Branches, aimed at bringing poetry into NYC neighborhoods—through collection-building, public programs, seminars for librarians, and poetry workshops for young adults—in three branch libraries around the City. Finally, each fall Poets House hosts the Poetry Publication Showcase—a comprehensive exhibit of the year's new poetry releases from commercial, university, independent, and micro presses across the country. Related Showcase events include receptions, panel discussions, and a contributor's poetry reading, which is open to the public and of special interest to poets, publishers, booksellers, distributers and reviewers. (Note: Poets House is not a publisher.) Following each Showcase, copies of new titles are added to the library collection and an updated edition of the *Directory of American Poetry Books*—edited by Poets House and available by mail for $23—is compiled. "Poets House depends, in part, on tax-deductible contributions of its over 550 nationwide members." Membership levels begin at $40/year, and along with other graduated benefits each new or renewing member receives a free copy of the most current directory.

POETS THEATRE, RD 2, Box 155, Cohocton NY 14826, director Beatrice Obrien, founded 1981. Sponsors readings and performances with limited funding from Poets & Writers. For a mostly conservative, rural audience. A featured poet, followed by open reading, monthly.

POETS-IN-THE-SCHOOLS. Most states have PITS programs that send published poets into classrooms to teach students poetry writing. If you have published poetry widely and have a proven commitment to children, contact your state arts council, Arts-in-Education Dept., or other writing programs in your area to see whether you qualify. Three of the biggest programs are Teachers & Writers Collaborative, Inc., 5 Union Square W., Seventh Floor, New York NY 10003, phone (212)691-6590; California Poets-in-the-Schools, 870 Market St., Suite 1148, San Francisco CA 94102, phone (415)399-1565; and Writers & Artists-in-the-Schools, COMPAS, 304 Landmark Center, 75 W. Fifth St., St. Paul MN 55102, phone (612)292-3249, which includes both writers and artists in their program.

SCOTTISH POETRY LIBRARY; SCHOOL OF POETS; CRITICAL SERVICE, Tweeddale Court, 14 High St., Edinburgh EH1 1TE Scotland, phone (031)557-2876, director Tessa Ransford, librarian Penny Duce. It is a reference information source and free lending library, also lending by post and has a travelling van service lending at schools, prisons and community centres. The library has a computerized catalogue allowing subject-based searches and indexes of poetry and poetry magazines. The collection comprises over 15,000 items of Scottish and international poetry. The School of Poets is open to anyone; "at meetings members divide into small groups in which each participant reads a poem which is then analyzed and discussed." Meetings normally take place at 7:30 p.m. on the first Tuesday of each month at the library. They also offer a Critical Service in which groups of up to 6 poems, not exceeding 200 lines in all, are given critical comment by members of the School: £15 for each critique (with SAE).

SONGWRITERS AND POETS CRITIQUE, 11599 Coontz Rd., Orient OH 43146, phone (614)877-1727, founded in 1985 by Ellis Cordle. A nonprofit association whose purpose is to serve songwriters, poets and musicians in their area. The president of the organization says, "We have over 200 members from over 16 states at several levels of ability from novice to advanced, and try to help and support each other with the craft and the business of poetry and songs. We have published writers and recorded artists. We share information about how to pitch, send and package a demo and who to send it to. We also have a songwriting contest for member writers." Annual dues are $25.

SOUTHERN POETRY ASSOCIATION; THE POET'S VOICE, P.O. Box 524, Pass Christian MS 39571, founded 1986, poetry editor Mildred Klyce. SPA offers networking, publishing, free critique service for members through Round Robin Groups and assistance in publishing chapbooks. $12 annual membership fee includes *The Poet's Voice* quarterly newsletter. The association sponsors a number of contests, including Voices of the South, Yarn Spinner, Poetry in Motion, Special People; some are for members only; some, such as the Voices of the South Contest, are open to all. Prizes total $200 with $3 entry fee/poem (28-line limit). June 1 deadline. High scoring poems are published in an anthology (which the poet is not required to purchase). Send #10 SAE with 64¢ postage for details. *The Poet's Voice* contains poetry book reviews, articles on great poets of the past, current activities, input from SPA members and contest winning poems.

THE THURBER HOUSE; JAMES THURBER WRITER-IN-RESIDENCE, 77 Jefferson Ave., Columbus OH 43215, phone (614)464-1032, officially opened in 1984. It is "one of the most diversely active of all restored writer's homes." The Thurber House has a staff of 8, over 50 volunteers and 22 board members. Its budget comes from state, local and national arts councils; foundations; corporate, business and individual sponsors; and sales. Listed on the National Register of Historic Places, The Thurber House is a literary center, bookstore and museum of Thurber materials. Programs include writing classes, author readings, Thurber celebrations, events for children and an art gallery. The Thurber House sponsors a writer-in-residence program that brings 2 journalists, a playwright, a poet or a fiction writer to spend a season living and writing in The Thurber House while teaching a course at The Ohio State University. Each writer will receive a stipend and housing in the third-floor apartment of Thurber's boyhood home. "Please send a letter of interest and a curriculum vita to Michael J. Rosen, literary director."

‡UNIVERSITY OF ARIZONA POETRY CENTER, 1216 N. Cherry Ave., Tucson AZ 85719, director Alison Deming. Founded in 1960 "to maintain and cherish the spirit of poetry." Open to the public. The Center is located in two historic adobe houses near the main campus and contains a nationally acclaimed poetry collection that includes over 27,000 items. Programs and services include: a library with a noncirculating poetry collection and space for small classes, poetry-related meetings and activities; facilities, research support, and referral information about poetry and poets for local and national communities; the Free Public Reading Series, a series of 12 to 18 readings each year featuring poets, fiction writers, and writers of literary nonfiction; a guest house for residencies of visiting writers and for use by other University departments and community literary activities; a one-month summer residency at the Center's guest house offered each year to an emerging writer selected by jury; and poetry awards, readings, and special events for undergraduate and graduate students. Publishes a biannual newsletter. Send SASE for additional information. "We do not have members, though one can become a 'Friend' through a contribution to our Friends of the Poetry Center account."

THE UNTERBERG POETRY CENTER OF THE 92ND STREET Y; "DISCOVERY"/THE NATION POETRY CONTEST, 1395 Lexington Ave., New York NY 10128, phone (212)415-5760. Offers annual series of readings by major literary figures (weekly readings October through May), writing workshops, master classes in fiction and poetry, and lectures and literary seminars. Also co-sponsors the "Discovery"/*The Nation* Poetry Contest. Deadline early February. Send SASE for information. "No phone queries, please."

WELFARE STATE INTERNATIONAL, The Ellers, Ulverston, Cumbria LA12 0AA England, phone 01229-581127, fax 01229 581232, founded 1968, artistic director John Fox, is a "celebratory arts company of national and international status creating functional poetry both visual and verbal, for ceremonial occasions. Commissions range from small-scale domestic celebrations to city-scale spectaculars." They publish poster poems in limited editions, dramatic songs and interludes for performance works, and poetic masques.

WALT WHITMAN CULTURAL ARTS CENTER, Second and Cooper St., Camden NJ 08102, executive director René L. Huggins, program coordinator J. Daniel Johnson, phone (609)964-8300. A writers' center, founded 1975, it offers a variety of programs such as Notable Poets and Writers Series, Walt Whitman Poetry Series, school programs, adult and children's theater, musical presentations and Fine Art Exhibitions. Their regular season runs September through June. During the summer months they provide a children's theater series entitled "10 Fridays of Fun."

WOODLAND PATTERN, P.O. Box 92081, 720 E. Locust St., Milwaukee WI 53212, phone (414)263-5001. Executive director Anne Kingsbury calls it "a semi-glamorous literary and arts center." Kingsbury regards the center as a neighborhood organization; it includes a bookstore that concentrates on contemporary literature, much of it small press, much of it poetry, and also on multicultural children's literature. It also incorporates a multipurpose gallery/performance/reading space, where exhibitions, readings, a lecture series, musical programs and a reading and study group are held. The *Woodland Pattern Newsletter*, mailed free to 2,800 people, contains an annotated calendar and pieces about visiting writers.

WORDS—THE ARKANSAS LITERARY SOCIETY, P.O. Box 174, Little Rock AR 72203, phone (501)661-9389, e-mail 71044.3371@compuserve.com, president H.K. Stewart, founded in 1984 to "help support literature and literary activities in the state of Arkansas. WORDS is a statewide group of people who love the language and encourage its use and celebration by Arkansans. Some of us are writers; some of us are readers. All hope, together, to accomplish good things for our state." Currently has over 200 members. Offerings available for poets include an annual contest and workshops, periodic readings and a quarterly newsletter. The annual literary contest awards a $250 prize in three categories: poetry, fiction and nonfiction. Deadline: early June. They also support the Porter Fund Award, an annual state award for literary excellence. The quarterly newsletter, *Words from WORDS*, includes information on contests, readings, events, submission information, reviews, workshops, in-state conferences and other items of interest for members. It is not generally distributed to nonmembers. WORDS helps support different literary readings—some by members and some by nationally known writers. Some of the readings offer open-mike time. Membership dues are $20/year for an individual or family, $10/year for students and senior citizens. Board meetings are held quarterly and are open to anyone. Send SASE for additional information. "WORDS always welcomes suggestions, ideas, and volunteers to help support and nurture the literary community in Arkansas."

WORLD-WIDE WRITERS SERVICE, INC.; WRITERS INK; WRITERS INK PRESS; WRITERS UNLIMITED AGENCY, INC., P.O. Box 698, Centereach NY 11720-0698, phone

(516)821-2945, founded in 1976, Writers Ink Press founded 1978, director Dr. David B. Axelrod. "World-wide Writers Service is a literary and speakers' booking agency. With its not-for-profit affiliate, Writers Unlimited Agency, Inc., it presents literary workshops and performances, conferences and other literary services, and publishes through Writers Ink Press, chapbooks and small flat-spined books as well as arts editions. **We publish only by our specific invitation at this time.**" *Writers Ink* is "a sometimely newsletter of events on Long Island, now including programs of our conferences. We welcome news of other presses and poets' activities. Review books of poetry. We fund raise for nonprofit projects and are associates of Westhampton Writers Festival and Jeanne Voege Poetry Awards. Arts Editions are profit productions employing hand-made papers, bindings, etc. We have editorial services available at small fees ($50 minimum), but only after inquiry and if appropriate. We are currently concentrating on works in translation, particularly Chinese."

THE WRITER'S CENTER; WRITER'S CAROUSEL; POET LORE, 4508 Walsh St., Bethesda MD 20815, phone (301)654-8664, website http://www.writer.org, founder and artistic director Allan Lefcowitz, executive director Jane Fox. This is an outstanding resource for writers not only in Washington DC but in the wider area ranging from southern Pennsylvania to North Carolina and West Virginia. The Center offers 200 multi-meeting workshops each year in writing, word processing, and graphic arts. It is open 7 days a week, 10 hours a day. Some 2,300 members support the center with $30 annual donations, which allows for 5 paid staff members. There is a book gallery at which publications of small presses are displayed and sold. The center's publication, *Writer's Carousel*, is a 24-page magazine that comes out 6 times a year. They also sponsor 80 annual performance events, which include presentations in poetry, fiction and theater. The Center is publisher of *Poet Lore*—100 years old in 1989 (see listing in the Publishers of Poetry section). This year the Center also has a computer on-line service with news and information about the Washington metropolitan literary community. The number to connect with the service via modem is (301)656-1638.

‡**WRITERS INFORMATION NETWORK**, The Professional Association for Christian Writers, P.O. Box 11337, Bainbridge Island WA 98110, phone (206)842-9103, fax (206)842-0536, director Elaine Wright Colvin. Founded in 1983 "to provide a much needed link between writers and editors/publishers of the religious publishing industry, to further professional development in writing and marketing skills of Christian writers, and to provide a meeting ground of encouragement and fellowship for persons engaged in writing and speaking." International organization open to anyone. Currently has 1,000 members. Offerings available for poets include market news, networking, editorial referrals, critiquing and marketing/publishing assistance. Sponsors conferences and workshops around the country. Publishes a 20- to 24-page bimonthly newsletter containing industry news and trends, writing advice, announcements and book reviews. Membership dues are $25. Members meet quarterly. Send SASE for additional information.

‡**WRITERS OF KERN**, P.O. Box 6694, Bakersfield CA 93386-6694, phone (805)871-5834, president Barbara Gabel, founded 1993. Writers of Kern is the Bakersfield Branch of the California Writers' Club and is open to "published writers and any person interested in writing." Currently has 100 members. Levels of membership available are professional, writers with published work; writers working toward publication; and students. Membership benefits include "meetings on the third Saturday of every month, except in September which is our conference month, with speakers who are authors, agents, etc., on topics pertaining to writing; several critique groups including fiction genres, nonfiction and poetry; a monthly newsletter with marketing tips; access to club library; and discount to annual conference." The conference is held on the third Saturday in September. They also sponsor an annual writing contest held May through June. Winners are announced at the conference. Membership dues are $35/year. Send SASE for additional information.

THE WRITERS ROOM, 10 Astor Place, 6th Floor, New York NY 10003, phone (212)254-6995, fax (212)533-6059, provides a "home away from home" for any writer who needs a place to work. It is open 24 hours a day, 7 days a week, offering desk space, storage and comraderie at the rate of $165/quarter. It is supported by the New York State Council on the Arts, the New York City Department of Cultural Affairs and other private sources. The Writers Room also offers monthly readings and semimonthly workshops for its residents. Call for application.

‡**WYOMING WRITERS, INC.**, P.O. Box 987, Thermopolis WY 82443-0987. Founded in 1974 to "encourage writers." Regional organization open to "writers, poets, and those interested in the writing profession." Wyoming Writers sponsors an annual workshop each June and an annual writing competition. Also publishes the *Wyo-Writer*, a newsletter published 10 times a year that provides information on writing, marketing, contests and organizations. Membership dues are $25/year. Send SASE for additional information.

Additional Organizations Useful to Poets

The following listings also contain information about organizations useful to poets. See the General Index for page numbers. Note: Double daggers (‡) preceding titles indicate listings new to this edition.

Air Canada Award, The
Arkansas Poetry Day Contest
Bay Area Poets Coalition (BAPC)
California Writers' Roundtable
    Poetry Contest
Canadian Author
Canadian Authors Association
    Literary Awards
Capricorn Poetry Award
‡Colorado Book Awards
Comstock Review, The
Connecticut River Review
Coolbrith Circle Annual Poetry
    Contest, Ina
Council for Wisconsin Writers,
    Inc.
CQ (California State Poetry
    Quarterly)
Dream Shop, The
Emerald Coast Review
Equinox Press
Frogpond: Quarterly Haiku
    Journal
Georgia State Poetry Society, Inc.
Grolier Poetry Prize

Intro
Jewish Women's Literary Annual
Lampman Award
Lines Review
Maryland Poetry Review
Midwest Villages & Voices
Midwest Writers' Conference
‡MPF Muse Letter, The
New Horizons Poetry Club
‡Newburyport Art Association
    Annual Spring Poetry Contest
Northwoods Press
Onionhead
Oracle Poetry
Outrider Press
‡P.A.L.S. Club Newsletter
    Contests
Pasque Petals
Pennsylvania Poetry Society
    Annual Contest
‡Peregrine: The Journal of
    Amherst Writers & Artists
Philomel
‡Piedmont Literary Review
Poem

Poetry
Poetry Harbor
Poetry Ireland Review
‡Poetry Nottingham International
Poets' Roundtable
Pudding House Publications
Rockford Review, The
Science Fiction Poetry
    Association
‡Small Press Genre Association
Society of American Poets, The
Washington Review
Washington Writers' Publishing
    House
Weyfarers
WFNB Annual Literary Contest
Wisconsin Regional Writers'
    Association
Woodnotes
Worcester Review
‡Word Works, The
Xanadu
Young Voices Magazine

Publications Useful to Poets

The publications in this section are designed to help poets with all aspects of writing and publishing poetry. While few are actual markets, many detail new publishing opportunities in addition to providing information on craft, advice on marketing, or interviews with poets and writers.

Poets & Writers Magazine, in fact, is one of the most useful resources for both poets and fiction writers. In addition to informative articles and interviews, it includes calls for submissions and contests and awards. *Writer's Digest*, on the other hand, covers the entire field of writing and features market listings as well as a monthly poetry column by Michael J. Bugeja, author of *The Art and Craft of Poetry* (Writer's Digest Books).

Other publications, such as *Dusty Dog Reviews*, *Small Press Review* (see Dustbooks) and *Literary Magazine Review*, include reviews of poetry books and chapbooks or reviews of small press magazines. These reviews provide further insight into the different markets.

For poets seeking resources more regional in focus, six of the new listings in this section are publications that include, among other items, markets, news and events for specific areas of the U.S. and Canada. For example, *First Draft* publishes information of interest to Alabama writers, *Next . . . Magazine* provides information on happenings in Southern California, and *Word: The Literary Calendar* focuses on literary events in Ontario, Canada. In addition to these publications, we have also added *Slam*, a magazine that contains information on poetry slams held in various locations around the world.

Finally, for those interested in various publishing opportunities, this section also includes information about other market directories as well as materials on self-publishing. And, in addition to the listings that follow, you will find other useful publications, such as *Canadian Author* and *New Writer's Magazine*, noted in Additional Publications Useful to Poets at the end of this section.

To determine which of these publications may be most useful to you, read sample issues. Many of these books and periodicals may be found in your local library or located on newsstands or in bookstores. If you are unable to locate a certain magazine, order a copy directly from the publisher. For books, send a SASE with a request for the publisher's current catalog or order information.

R.R. BOWKER; LITERARY MARKET PLACE; BOOKS IN PRINT, 121 Chanlon Rd., New Providence NJ 07974, phone (908)464-6800. *LMP* is the major trade directory of publishers and people involved in publishing books. It is available in most libraries, or individual copies may be purchased (published in September each year; standing order price: $170.96). *BIP* is another standard reference available in most libraries and bookstores. Bowker publishes a wide range of reference books pertaining to publishing. Write for their catalog.

CANADIAN POETRY, English Dept., University of Western Ontario, London, Ontario N6A 3K7 Canada, phone (519)661-3403, founded 1977, editor Prof. D.M.R. Bentley. A biannual journal of critical articles, reviews and historical documents (such as interviews). It is a professionally printed, scholarly edited, flat-spined, 100-page journal which pays contributors in copies. Subscription: $15. **Sample: $7.50. Note that they publish no poetry except as quotations in articles.**

DUSTBOOKS; INTERNATIONAL DIRECTORY OF LITTLE MAGAZINES AND SMALL PRESSES; DIRECTORY OF POETRY PUBLISHERS; SMALL PRESS REVIEW; SMALL MAGAZINE REVIEW, P.O. Box 100, Paradise CA 95967. Dustbooks publishes a number of books useful to writers. Send SASE for catalog. Among their regular publications, *International Directory* is an annual directory of small presses and literary magazines, over 6,000 entries, a third being magazines, half being book publishers, and the rest being both. There is very detailed information about what these presses and magazines report to be their policies in regard to payment, copyright, format and publishing schedules. *Directory of Poetry Publishers* has similar information for over 2,000 publishers of poetry. *Small Press Review* is a monthly magazine, newsprint, carrying current updating of listings in *ID*, small press needs, news, announcements and reviews—a valuable way to stay abreast of the literary marketplace. *Small Magazine Review*, which began publication in June, 1993, is included within *Small Press Review* and covers small press magazines in a similar fashion.

DUSTY DOG REVIEWS, 1904-A Gladden, Gallup NM 87301, phone (505)863-2398, founded 1990, editor/publisher John Pierce. *Dusty Dog Reviews* is a review magazine appearing 3 times/year, reviewing small press poetry books and chapbooks, 75-100/issue average length 200 words. Subscription: $7.50. Sample: $3. Open to unsolicited reviews. Poets should send books for review consideration to Dave Castleman, 512 Tamalpais Dr., Mill Valley CA 94941. "All editors and publishers whose poetry books/chapbooks get reviewed will receive one copy of the issue in which the review appears." The editor advises, "Become very familiar with *Poet's Market* and what is said at the beginning of the book. The small press magazines are often one-person staff and work very hard for you, the poet. Be patient with them, and support the magazines you like. If poets don't subscribe to the magazines that publish them, it is very hard for the magazines to continue publishing."

‡**FIRST DRAFT: THE JOURNAL OF THE ALABAMA WRITERS' FORUM**, The Alabama Writers' Forum, Center for the Arts & Humanities, Pebble Hill, Auburn University, Auburn AL 36849-5637, phone (334)844-4947, fax (334)844-4949, e-mail cahawf@mail.auburn.edu, website http://www.auburn.edu/~cahawf, editor Jeanie Thompson, founded 1992, appears 3 times a year, publishing news, features, book reviews, and interviews relating to Alabama writers. "We do not publish original poetry or fiction." It is 28 pgs., 8½×11, professionally printed on coated paper and saddle-stitched with b&w photos inside and on the cover. Lists markets for poetry, contests/awards and workshops. Sponsored by the Alabama Writers' Forum, "the official literary arts advocacy organization for the state of Alabama." Reviews books of poetry by "Alabama poets or from Alabama presses." Subscription: $25/year. Sample postpaid: $3.

LAUGHING BEAR NEWSLETTER; LAUGHING BEAR PRESS, P.O. Box 36159, Denver CO 80236, phone (303)744-3624, founded 1976, editor Tom Person. *LBN* is a monthly publication of small press information for writers and publishers containing articles, news and reviews. Cost: $12/year. Send SASE for sample copy. *LBN* is interested in short (200- to 300-word) articles on self-publishing and small press. Pays copies.

THE LETTER EXCHANGE, published by The Readers' League, P.O. Box 6218, Albany CA 94706-0218, editor/publisher Stephen Sikora. Published 3 times each year, *The Letter Exchange* is a digest-sized magazine, 36 pgs., that publishes 4 types of listings: regular (which are rather like personal classifieds); ghost letters, which contain lines like "Send news of the Entwives!"; amateur magazines, which publicizes readers' own publishing ventures; and sketch ads, in which readers who would rather draw than write can communicate in their chosen mode. All ads are coded, and readers respond through the code numbers. Subscription to *The Letter Exchange* is $22/year, and sample copies are $9 postpaid for current issue. Poets who are so inclined often exchange poems and criticism with each other through this medium.

LITERARY MAGAZINE REVIEW, Dept. of English Language and Literature, The University of Northern Iowa, Cedar Falls IA 50614-0502, founded 1981, editor Grant Tracey. A quarterly magazine (digest-sized, saddle-stitched, about 48-64 pgs.) that publishes critiques, 2-5 pgs. long, of various literary magazines, plus shorter "reviews" (about ½ page) of new journals during a particular year. Single copies: $5; subscriptions: $12.50/year.

‡**MINNESOTA LITERATURE**, One Nord Circle, St. Paul MN 55127, phone (612)483-3904, editor Mary Bround Smith, founded 1975. *ML* appears 10 times a year (September through June), providing news and announcements for Minnesota writers. Regularly features "Minnesota literary events such as readings, lectures, workshops, conferences and classes; news of publications written by Minnesotans or published in Minnesota; and opportunities for writers, such as grants, awards and want-ads." It is 8½×11, 8 pgs. (two 11×17 sheets folded), unbound. Subscription: $10 for 10 issues.

‡**NEXT . . . MAGAZINE**, Orange Ocean Press, P.O. Box 13019, Long Beach CA 90803, phone/fax (310)930-0587, e-mail nextmag@aol.com, editor G. Murray Thomas, founded 1994, is a monthly publication providing a calendar of southern California poetry events, news and reviews. It is 16-24 pgs., newsprint, with photos and cartoons, accepts ads. Reviews books, chapbooks, tapes, CDs, videos

and performances of poetry in 100-500 words. Poets may send books for review consideration to Attn: Reviews. Single copy: free; subscription: $18/year. "*Next . . . Magazine* covers the rapidly growing performance poetry scene in southern California with a monthly calendar, news, reviews, commentary and lots of humor. We are an essential resource for poets in southern California."

OHIO WRITER, P.O. Box 91801, Cleveland OH 44101, editor Linda Rome, is a bimonthly newsletter for Ohio writers or those connected with Ohio. It is 16 pgs., professionally printed in colored ink on off-white stock, containing news and reviews of Ohio writing events, publications and regional opportunities to publish. Subscription: $12/year, $18 for institutions. It also sponsors an annual contest for Ohio writers. See the Best of Ohio Writers Writing Contest listing in the Contests and Awards section.

OPEN HORIZONS, P.O. Box 205, Fairfield IA 52556-0205, phone (515)472-6130, fax (515)472-1560; e-mail John Kremer@bookmarket.com, publisher John Kremer, publishes how-to books about book publishing and self-publishing, such as *1001 Ways to Market Your Books*, *Directory of Book Printers*, and *Book Publishing Resource Guide* (also available on IBM PC or Macintosh disk as a database). Send SASE for catalog.

OXFORD UNIVERSITY PRESS, 198 Madison Ave., New York NY 10016, phone (212)726-6000, founded 1478, literature editor T. Susan Chang (NY), is a large university press publishing academic, trade and college books in a wide variety of fields. **Not accepting poetry mss.** "Our list includes editions of English and American poets for classroom use, thematically-oriented anthologies and critical studies of poets and their work for general readers. Unfortunately, we do not publish new poetry by contemporary writers."

PARA PUBLISHING, Box 8206-880, Santa Barbara CA 93118-8206, phone (805)968-7277, orders (800)727-2782, fax (805)968-1379. Author/publisher Dan Poynter publishes how-to books on book publishing and self-publishing. *Is There a Book Inside You?* shows you how to get your book out. *The Self-Publishing Manual, How to Write, Print and Sell Your Own Book* is all about book promotion. *Publishing Short-Run Books* shows you how to typeset and lay out your own book. Poynter also publishes *Publishing Contracts on Disk, Book Fairs* and 19 Special Reports on various aspects of book production, promotion, marketing and distribution. *Free* book publishing information kit. Newly available through Para Publishing is a 24-hour fax service called Fax-On-Demand. This service enables you to obtain free documents on book writing and publishing; and lists of workshops and presentations offered by Dan Poynter. Call (805)968-8947 from your fax machine handset, then follow the voice prompts to hear a list of documents and to order. The fax machine will retrieve the documents and print them instantly. This is a good way to sample Para Publishing's offerings.

PERSONAL POEMS, %Jean Hesse, Villa B-7, 16591 Perdido Key Dr., Pensacola FL 32507, phone (904)492-7909. Jean Hesse started a business in 1980 writing poems for individuals for a fee (for greetings, special occasions, etc.). Others started similar businesses, after she began instructing them in the process, especially through a cassette tape training program and other training materials. Send SASE for free brochure or $25 plus $4.50 p&h (make checks payable to F. Jean Hesse) for training manual, *How to Make Your Poems Pay*.

POETRY BOOK SOCIETY, Book House, 45 East Hill, London SW18 2QZ England. A book club with an annual subscription rate of £37, which covers 4 books of new poetry, the *PBS Bulletin*, and a premium offer (for new members). The selectors also recommend other books of special merit, which are obtainable at a discount of 25%. The Poetry Book Society is subsidized by the Arts Council of England. Please write (Attn: Betty Redpath) for details or phone 0181-877-1615 (24-hour fax/answer service).

‡**POETRY CALENDAR**, 611 Broadway #905, New York NY 10012, phone (212)260-7097, fax (212)475-7110, editor Molly McQuade, founded 1975. "*Poetry Calendar* is a monthly publication (not published in July and August) that lists literary events in metropolitan New York. Eleven-thousand copies are distributed each month providing a comprehensive schedule of poetry and fiction readings, performances, lectures, exhibits, workshops and related activities. The *Calendar* also includes reviews, essays, and interviews." It is 24-32 pgs., 8½ × 11, newsprint, saddle-stitched. Subscription: $20. Sample available for free.

THE POETRY CONNECTION, 13455 SW 16 Court #F-405-PM, Pembroke Pines FL 33027, phone (954)431-3016, editor/publisher Sylvia Shichman. *The Poetry Connection*, a monthly newsletter, provides information in flyer format. Poets, writers and songwriters receive information on how to sell their poetry/books, poetry and musical publications and contests, and obtain assistance in getting poetry published. *TPC* has information on writing for greeting card companies, poetry and songwriting publications, and greeting card directories. Sample issue: $5 plus $2 postage. Send SASE for more information.

‡**POETRY FLASH**, 1450 Fourth St. #4, Berkeley CA 94710, phone (510)525-5476, fax (510)525-6752, editor Joyce Jenkins, founded 1972, appears 10 times a year including double issues. "*Poetry Flash*, a Poetry Review & Literary Calendar for the West, publishes reviews, interviews, essays and information for writers. Poems, as well as announcements about submitting to other publications, appear in each issue." *PF* focuses on poetry, but its literary calendar also includes events celebrating all forms of creative writing in areas across the nation. It is about 40 pgs., printed on newsprint. Lists markets for poetry, contests/awards and workshops. *Poetry Flash* also sponsors a weekly poetry reading series at Cody's Books in Berkeley and sponsors the Bay Area Book Reviewers Association. (Also see listing in Contests and Awards.) Reviews books and chapbooks of poetry. Poets may send books for review consideration. Subscription $16/year. Sample postpaid: $2. "We publish one to three poems per issue—sometimes more in a special feature." Even though *Poetry Flash* publishes a limited amount of poetry, work published here has also been selected for inclusion in *The Best American Poetry 1996*.

POETS & WRITERS, INC.; A DIRECTORY OF AMERICAN POETS AND FICTION WRITERS; LITERARY AGENTS; LITERARY BOOKSTORES; POETS & WRITERS MAGAZINE, 72 Spring St., New York NY 10012, phone (212)226-3586 or (800)666-2268 (California only), website http://www.pw.org, is a major support organization. Its many helpful publications include *Poets & Writers Magazine*, which appears 6 times a year ($18 or $3.95 for a single copy), 88 pgs., magazine-sized, offset, has been called *The Wall Street Journal* of our profession, and it is there that one most readily finds out about resources, current needs of magazines and presses, contests, awards, jobs and retreats for writers, and discussions of business, legal and other issues affecting writers. P&W also publishes a number of valuable directories such as its biennial *A Directory of American Poets and Fiction Writers* ($24.95 paperback), which editors, publishers, agents and sponsors of readings and workshops use to locate over 7,000 active writers in the country. (You may qualify for a listing if you have a number of publications.) They also publish *Literary Agents* (available for $10); *Literary Bookstores* (available for $12); a series of eight chapbooks, "Into Print: Guides to the Writing Life," that includes *Out of the Slush Pile and Into Print*; *Contracts and Royalties: Negotiating Your Own*; *On Cloud Nine: Writers' Colonies, Retreats, Ranches, Residencies, and Sanctuaries*; and *Helping Writers Help Themselves: A National Guide to Writers' Resources*; and a list of literary resources for writers in all 8 regions of the country. The chapbooks and resource lists are available from P&W for $12.95.

POETS' AUDIO CENTER; THE WATERSHED FOUNDATION, P.O. Box 50145, Washington DC 20091. This is an international clearinghouse for ordering any poetry recording available, from both commercial and noncommercial producers. Catalog available free ("an introduction to our collection"); they stock over 500 titles. **Foundation not accepting applications at this time.**

‡**PO'FLY**, P.O. Box 1026, Ashland KY 41105, e-mail poflye@aol.com, website http://members.aol.com/POFlye, publisher Michael Elton Crye, is a quarterly publication "founded as a crossroads, a place between trenches, a meeting place where all voices are heard. A gathering of information and inspiration for working artists, *PO'Fly* acts as both a resource and a showcase." Regular features include articles/commentary on poetry; book reviews; market, event and contest listings; local resources; and information on poetry readings. They also publish poetry and fiction. "Do not submit poetry via e-mail." Pays copies. It is 20 pgs., 8½×11 (five 11×17 sheets folded in half), unbound. Subscription: $6-10 for 4 issues. Sample postpaid: $2-3.

BERN PORTER INTERNATIONAL, 22 Salmond Rd., Belfast ME 04915, founded 1911. A monthly journal that both reviews books of poetry and publishes poetry. Also provides sleeping bag space for poets and writers May 1 through November 1 for the cost or freewill contribution. No smoking. No drugs. No telephone.

PUSHCART PRESS, P.O. Box 380, Wainscott NY 11975. Publishes a number of books useful to writers, including the Pushcart Prize Series—annual anthologies representing the best small press publications, according to the judges; The Editors' Book Award Series, "to encourage the writing of distinguished books of uncertain financial value"; *The Original Publish-It-Yourself Handbook*; and the Literary Companion Series. Send SASE for catalog.

‡**SLAM**, 24 Arlington St., Medford MA 02155, (617)488-3636, e-mail bosslam@aol.com, editor Michael R. Brown, founded 1992, is a quarterly publication containing international news and events on poetry slams. "*Slam* is the official publication of the poetry slam." It is 4 pgs., 8½×11, offset. Subscription: $6/year, add $4 for first-class mail. Sample copy available for free.

THE WASHINGTON INTERNATIONAL ARTS LETTER, P.O. Box 12010, Des Moines IA 50312-9401, phone (319)358-6777, fax (319)358-6786. Appears 4 times/year, 6- to 8-page newsletter on grants and other forms of assistance for the arts and humanities—mostly lists various programs of support to artists, including many for poets. Reviews books of poetry. Subscription: $124 full rate; $55 for individuals; $82 for institutions. Send all orders and requests for information to the address above.

‡**WHERE POETS SPEAK**, 1516 South 16th Ave., Birmingham AL 35205, phone (205)933-6012, editor Gene Crutcher, founded 1991, is a monthly publication providing "listings of other publications that consider poetry for publication, listings of coffeehouses, bookstores or other places that schedule poetry readings, especially 'Open Mike' nights. Also publish reviews of other publications I receive from time to time, and fill up blank space with poems I have found recently that I like." Devoted entirely to poetry. *WPS* is 4 pgs., 5×7 (8½×11 sheet folded). "Occasionally 6 pages and once or twice I have had an 8-page issue." Reviews books and chapbooks of poetry. Poets may send books for review consideration. Subscription: $10/year. Sample copy available for "a poem or a buck or nothing. I don't do this to make money but to encourage youngsters to write. I am *not* a poet, but I am a pretty good oral interpreter. I will often start reading something at a reading if I sense that the people there are too timid to begin. Once the ice is broken, they often reveal some fine works."

‡**WORD: THE LITERARY CALENDAR**, 378 Delaware Ave., Toronto, Ontario M6H 2T8 Canada, phone (416)536-4308, fax (416)588-4198, publisher Mike O'Connor, founded 1995, a monthly publication providing an "all inclusive calendar of literary events, book launches, readings, slams and workshops in Ontario (also lists contests and calls for submissions)." It is 8 pgs., 8½×11, offset printed, unbound, with ads. Subscription: $10/year. Make checks payable to Insomniac Press. "All listings are free. An excellent resource for poets in Ontario."

‡**WORDWRIGHTS CANADA**, P.O. Box 456 Station O, Toronto, Ontario M4A 2P1 Canada, director Susan Ioannou, publishes "books on poetics in layman's, not academic terms, such as *Writing Reader-friendly Poems: Over 50 Rules of Thumb for Clearer Communication* and *The Canadian Writers' Contest Calendar*." They consider manuscripts of such books for publication, paying $50 advance, 10% royalties and 5% of press run. They also conduct "Manuscript Reading and Editing Services, as well as The Poetry Tutorial correspondence course for writers." Request order form to buy samples.

WRITER'S DIGEST BOOKS; WRITER'S DIGEST, 1507 Dana Ave., Cincinnati OH 45207, phone (800)289-0963 or (513)531-2690. Writer's Digest Books publishes a remarkable array of books useful to all types of writers. In addition to *Poet's Market*, books for poets include *The Poet's Handbook* by Judson Jerome, *Creating Poetry* by John Drury and *The Art and Craft of Poetry* by Michael J. Bugeja. Call or write for a complete catalog. *Writer's Digest* is a monthly magazine about writing with frequent articles and market news about poetry, in addition to a monthly poetry column. See the listing in the Publishers of Poetry section.

Additional Publications Useful to Poets

The following listings also contain information about publications useful to poets. See the General Index for page numbers. Note: Double daggers (‡) preceding titles indicate listings new to this edition.

Northwoods Press
Oak, The
Oregon State Poetry Association
‡Papyrus
Parnassus: Poetry in Review
PEN American Center
Pequod: A Journal of
  Contemporary Literature and
  Literary Criticism
‡Piedmont Literary Review
Poetry Ireland Review
Poetry Resource Center of
  Michigan
Poetry Society of America
Poets House: The Reed
  Foundation Library

Poets' Roundtable
Prosetry: Newsletter For, By and
  About Writers
Rio Grande Press
Scavenger's Newsletter
‡Small Press Genre Association
Smith, The
Southern Poetry Association
‡Squaw Valley Community of
  Writers Poetry Workshop
Third Alternative, The
‡University of Arizona Poetry
  Center
Verse
Wildacres Writers Workshop
Wisconsin Regional Writers'

Association
World-wide Writers Service, Inc.
‡Write Way, The
Writer, The
Writer's Center, The
Writer's Exchange
Writers Forum (England)
‡Writers Information Network
Writer's Journal
Writer's Lifeline
‡Writers of Kern
Writer's World
‡Wyoming Writers, Inc.
Xanadu

U.S. and Canadian Postal Codes

United States

AL	Alabama
AK	Alaska
AZ	Arizona
AR	Arkansas
CA	California
CO	Colorado
CT	Connecticut
DE	Delaware
DC	District of Columbia
FL	Florida
GA	Georgia
GU	Guam
HI	Hawaii
ID	Idaho
IL	Illinois
IN	Indiana
IA	Iowa
KS	Kansas
KY	Kentucky
LA	Louisiana
ME	Maine
MD	Maryland
MA	Massachusetts
MI	Michigan
MN	Minnesota
MS	Mississippi
MO	Missouri
MT	Montana
NE	Nebraska
NV	Nevada
NH	New Hampshire
NJ	New Jersey
NM	New Mexico
NY	New York
NC	North Carolina
ND	North Dakota
OH	Ohio
OK	Oklahoma
OR	Oregon
PA	Pennsylvania
PR	Puerto Rico
RI	Rhode Island
SC	South Carolina
SD	South Dakota
TN	Tennessee
TX	Texas
UT	Utah
VT	Vermont
VI	Virgin Islands
VA	Virginia
WA	Washington
WV	West Virginia
WI	Wisconsin
WY	Wyoming

Canada

AB	Alberta
BC	British Columbia
LB	Labrador
MB	Manitoba
NB	New Brunswick
NF	Newfoundland
NT	Northwest Territories
NS	Nova Scotia
ON	Ontario
PEI	Prince Edward Island
PQ	Quebec
SK	Saskatchewan
YT	Yukon

Glossary

A3, A4, A5. Metric equivalents of 11¾×16½, 8¼×11¾ and 5⅞×8¼ respectively.

Bio. A short biographical paragraph often requested with a submission; it is commonly called a "bio." In your bio, publishers may ask you to note your most recent and noteworthy publication credits.

Chapbook. A small book of approximately 20-25 pages of poetry. Such a book is less expensive to produce than a full-length book collection, though it is seldom noted by reviewers.

Cover letter. Letter accompanying a submission; it usually lists titles of poems and gives a brief account of publishing credits and biographical information. (See sample on page 13.)

Digest-sized. Approximately 5½×8½, the size of a folded sheet of conventional typing paper.

Flat-spined. What many publishers call "perfect-bound," glued with a flat edge (usually permitting readable type on the spine).

Galleys. Typeset copies of your poem(s). You should proofread and correct any mistakes and return galleys to editors within 48 hours of receipt.

IRC. International Reply Coupon, postage for return of submissions from another country. One IRC is sufficient for one ounce by *surface mail*. If you want an airmail return, you need one IRC for each half-ounce. Do not send checks or cash for postage to other countries: The exchange rates are so high it is not worth the inconvenience it causes editors. (Exception: Many Canadian editors do not object to U.S. dollars; use IRCs the first time and inquire.)

Magazine-sized. Approximately 8½×11, the size of conventional typing paper unfolded.

ms, mss. Manuscript, manuscripts.

Multi-book review. Also known as an omnibus or essay review. A review of several books by the same author or by several authors, such as a review of four or five political poetry books.

Multiple submission. Submission of more than one poem at a time; most poetry publishers *prefer* multiple submissions and specify how many poems should be in a packet. Some say a multiple submission means the poet has sent another manuscript to the same publication before receiving word on the first submission. This type of multiple submission is generally discouraged.

p. Abbreviation for pence.

pg., pgs. Page, pages.

Perfect-bound. See Flat-spined.

Query letter. Letter written to a publisher to elicit interest in a manuscript or to determine if submissions are acceptable.

Rights. First North American serial rights means the publisher is acquiring the right to publish your poem first in a U.S. or Canadian periodical. All rights means the publisher is buying the poem outright. Selling all rights usually requires that you obtain permission to reprint your work, even in a book-length collection.

Saddle-stapled. What many publishers call "saddle-stitched," folded and stapled along the fold.

SAE. Self-addressed envelope.

SASE. Self-addressed, stamped envelope. *Every* publisher requires, with any submission, query or request for information, a self-addressed, stamped envelope. This requirement is so basic it is repeated in bold type at the bottom of a number of pages throughout this book. The return envelope (usually folded for inclusion) should be large enough to hold the material submitted or requested, and the postage provided—stamps if the submission is within your own country, IRCs if it is to another country—should be sufficient for its return.

Simultaneous submission. Submission of the same manuscript to more than one publisher at a time. Most magazine editors *refuse to accept* simultaneous submissions. Some book and chapbook publishers do not object to simultaneous submissions. In all cases, notify them that the manuscript is being simultaneously submitted if that is what you are doing.

Slush pile. The stack of unsolicited manuscripts received by an editor or publisher.

Status. The current situation concerning a particular manuscript: 1) The manuscript was never received. 2) We received the manuscript but cannot locate it. 3) We received and rejected said manuscript. 4) We are still considering it. 5) We are in the process of accepting your manuscript.

Subsidy press. See Vanity press.

Tabloid-sized. 11×15 or larger, the size of an ordinary newspaper folded and turned sideways.

Vanity press. A slang term for a publisher that requires the writer to pay publishing costs, especially one that flatters an author to generate business. These presses often use the term "subsidy" to describe themselves. Some presses, however, derive subsidies from other sources, such as government grants, and do not require author payment. These are not considered vanity presses.

Visual poetry. A combination of text and graphics usually only reproduced photographically.

Indexes

Chapbook Publishers

A chapbook is a slim volume of a poet's work, usually 20-25 pages (although page requirements vary greatly). Given the high cost of printing, a publisher is more apt to accept a chapbook than an entire book from an unproven poet.

Some chapbooks are published as inserts in magazines. (The winner of The Tennessee Chapbook Prize, for instance, is published as an insert in *Poems & Plays*.) Others are separate volumes. Whenever possible, request submission guidelines and samples to determine the quality of the product.

You'll find many presses, particularly those that sponsor chapbook contests, charge reading fees. Avoid any over $10. (Some folks go as high as $15 for book-length manuscripts, but chapbooks are easier to process.)

If your chapbook is published, by the way, you may still participate in "first-book" competitions. For more information about both chapbook and book publishing, read Charting Your Path to Poetry Publication, beginning on page 10.

Following are publishers who consider chapbook manuscripts. See the General Index for the page numbers of their market listings. Note: Double daggers (‡) preceding titles indicate listings new to this edition.

Insects Are People Two
Intercultural Writer's Review, The
International Black Writers
Inverted-A, Inc.
Jackson Harbor Press
Jackson's Arm
Lake Shore Publishing
Ledge Poetry and Fiction Magazine, The
Lilliput Review
Limited Editions Press
‡Lockhart Press, The
Lone Willow Press
Lucidity
Luna Bisonte Prods
Mad River Press
‡Malevolence
‡Manifold
Maverick Press, The
Mayapple Press
‡Melting Trees Review
‡Merrimack Books
Mid-American Review
(m)öthêr TØñgué Press
Negative Capability
‡Nerve Cowboy
New Earth Publications
New Hope International
New Orleans Poetry Journal Press
‡New Spirit Press
Oasis Books
Ohio Review, The
Olympia Review
ONTHEBUS
‡open unison stop
Outrider Press
Owl Creek Press
‡Pacific Coast Journal
Palanquin/TDM
Panhandler, The
‡Paper Boat Magazine

Paradox
Parting Gifts
‡Pavement Saw
Pearl
‡Pennywhistle Press
‡Peregrine: The Journal of Amherst Writers & Artists
Perivale Press
Permafrost: A Literary Journal
Permeable Press
Petronium Press
Phase and Cycle
‡Pine Press
Pirate Writings
Plowman, The
Poems & Plays
Poetic Space: Poetry & Fiction
‡Poetical Histories
Poetry Harbor
Poetry in Motion
Poetry Miscellany, The
Poets at Work
Poets' Roundtable
Potato Eyes
Prairie Journal, The
Press Here
Pudding House Publications
PYX Press
‡RACS/Rent-A-Chicken Speaks
Rag Mag
Red Candle Press, The
Red Dancefloor Press
Red Herring Poets
Riverstone, A Press for Poetry
Runaway Spoon Press, The
St. Andrew Press
Scavenger's Newsletter
Score Magazine
Serpent & Eagle Press
Shamal Books
Sheila-na-gig
Ship of Fools

Silver Apples Press
Silverfish Review
Slipstream
Southern Poetry Association
Sow's Ear Poetry Review, The
Stand Magazine
State Street Press
Still Waters Press
Sub-Terrain
Tak Tak Tak
"Teak" Roundup
texture
Third Half Literary Magazine, The
Tightrope
Time of Singing, A Magazine of Christian Poetry
Touchstone Literary Journal
Tower Poetry Society
Trout Creek Press
‡Underwhich Editions
Urbanite, The
Voyant, The
W.I.M. Publications (Woman in the Moon)
Waterways: Poetry in the Mainstream
West of Boston
White Eagle Coffee Store Press
Whole Notes
Wind Publications
Windless Orchard, The
‡Wineberry Press
‡Wooden Head Review
World-wide Writers Service, Inc.
WoRM fEASt!
Wormwood Review Press
Writers Forum (England)
xib
‡Xiquan Publishing House

Geographical Index

Use this index to locate small presses and magazines in your region. Much of the poetry published today reflects regional interests. In addition, publishers often favor poets (and work) from their own areas. Also, keep your neighboring areas in mind for other publishing opportunities.

Here you will find the names of U.S. publishers arranged alphabetically within their state or territory. Following them are lists of publishers in Canada, the United Kingdom, and other countries. See the General Index for the page numbers of their corresponding listings. Note: Double daggers (‡) preceding titles indicate listings new to this edition.

Alabama
Alabama Literary Review
Aura Literary/Arts Review
Birmingham Poetry Review
Black Warrior Review, The
Catamount Press
Dreams and Nightmares
Elk River Review
Laureate Letter, The
Livingston Press
‡Melting Trees Review
‡Minority Literary Expo
National Forum: The Phi Kappa
    Phi Journal
Negative Capability
Poem
Southern Humanities Review
Sticks

Alaska
Alaska Quarterly Review
Explorations
Intertext
‡Moose Bound Press
Permafrost: A Literary Journal
Salmon Run Press

Arizona
Bilingual Review Press
Coyote Chronicles: Notes from
    the Southwest
Forever Alive
Hayden's Ferry Review
Newsletter Inago
Sonora Review
South Ash Press
‡Xiquan Publishing House

Arkansas
Arkansas Press, The University of
Bloodreams: A Magazine of
    Vampires & Werewolves
Crazyhorse
Graffiti Off the Asylum Walls

Hyacinth House Publications
Kansas Quarterly/Arkansas Re-
    view
Lucidity
Nebo: A Literary Journal
Slant: A Journal of Poetry
Voices International

California
Acorn, The
Advocacy Press
Amelia
‡American Indian Studies Center
Anthology of Magazine Verse &
    Yearbook of American Poetry
Apostolic Crusade, The
Arshile
Arundel Press
Athena Incognito Magazine
Bakunin
Bay Area Poets Coalition (BAPC)
Berkeley Poetry Review
‡Big Head Press
Bishop Publishing Co.
‡Black Cross
Black Scholar, The
Black Sheets
Blowfish Catalog, The
Blue Unicorn, A Triquarterly of
    Poetry
Bottomfish
‡Cannedphlegm
Cat Fancy
Caveat Lector
Center Press
‡Cherry Street Grill
Christian Poet
City Lights Books
Clutch
College & Career Publishing
CQ (California State Poetry Quar-
    terly)
Crazyquilt Quarterly

Creative With Words Publications
    (C.W.W.)
Daniel and Company, Publisher,
    John
Dragon's Teeth Press
Epicenter
‡Faultline
‡Five Lines Down
Flume Press
‡Found Street Press
Free Lunch
Fudge Cake, The
Geppo Haiku Worksheet
GLB Publishers
Greenhouse Review Press
Haight Ashbury Literary Journal
Haiku Headlines: A Monthly
    Newsletter of Haiku and Sen-
    ryu
Harcourt Brace & Company
Hard Row to Hoe
Idiot, The
Indefinite Space
India Currents
Intercultural Writer's Review,
    The
International Olympic Lifter
    (IOL)
‡Jacaranda
Jewish Spectator
Juggler's World
‡Junction Press
Konocti Books
Kuumba
Lamp-Post, The
Left Curve
Liberty Hill Poetry Review
Libra Publishers, Inc.
Lynx, A Journal for Linking Poets
Lynx Eye
Mind in Motion: A Magazine of
    Poetry and Short Prose
Mind Matters Review
‡Minotaur Press

Mockingbird
‡Modern Words
Moving Parts Press
Mythic Circle, The
nerve
New Earth Publications
New Horizons Poetry Club
New Methods: The Journal of Animal Health Technology
Nocturnal Lyric, Journal of the Bizarre
NV Magazine
Olive Press Publications, The
ONTHEBUS
Ortalda & Associates
Oxygen
‡Pacific Coast Journal
Panjandrum Books
Papier-Mache Press
Pearl
‡Perceptions
Perivale Press
Permeable Press
‡Poet Papers
‡Poetry Connexion, The
‡Poet's Guild, The
Poets On:
Press Here
Prisoners of the Night
Prosetry: Newsletter For, By and About Writers
Pygmy Forest Press
PYX Press
Radiance: The Magazine for Large Women
‡Rattle
Red Dancefloor Press
‡Reed
‡Route One
San Fernando Poetry Journal
Santa Barbara Review
Santa Monica Review
Scream Press
‡Seasons of the Muse
Sequoia
Sheila-na-gig
Silver Wings
‡Sinister Wisdom
‡Small Press Genre Association
Southern California Anthology, The
‡Spillway
Steelhead Special, The
Stone Soup, The Magazine by Young Writers and Artists
‡Sublime Odyssey
Summer Stream Press
‡360 Degrees
Threepenny Review, The
tight
Tucumcari Literary Review
Turkey Press
Urbanus Magazine
Verve
Virgin Meat

Vol. No. Magazine
W.I.M. Publications (Woman in the Moon)
‡Western Tales
‡Wind-Mill, The
Wishing Well, The
Woodnotes
Wormwood Review Press
Writing For Our Lives
xib

Colorado

Arjuna Library Press
Blue Mountain Arts, Inc.
‡Buffalo Bones
Climbing Art, The
Cloud Ridge Press
Coffeehouse
Colorado Review
Communities: Journal of Cooperative Living
‡Dead Metaphor Press
Denver Quarterly
Dry Creek Review, The
Hen's Teeth
High Plains Literary Review
‡Many Mountains Moving
Phase and Cycle
Pueblo Poetry Project
Three Continents Press Inc.
Virtue: The Christian Magazine for Women
Writers' Forum

Connecticut

‡Amaranth
‡Brass City
Broken Streets
Chicory Blue Press
Connecticut Poetry Review, The
Connecticut River Review
‡Papyrus
Potes & Poets Press, Inc.
‡Rolling Penny Review
Singular Speech Press
Small Pond Magazine of Literature
‡Twilight Ending
Wesleyan University Press
Yale University Press

District of Columbia

Aerial
American Scholar, The
Conscience
Folio: A Literary Journal
G.W. Review
Middle East Report
New Republic, The
Sojourners
Washington Review
Washington Writers' Publishing House

‡Wineberry Press
‡Word Works, The

Florida

Albatross
Anhinga Press
Apalachee Quarterly
Bohemian Chronicle
‡Candlelight Poetry Journal
Cathartic, The
Cats Magazine
Central Florida Contemporary Poetry Series, University of
‡Chaff
Churchman's Human Quest, The
Ediciones Universal
Emerald Coast Review
Florida Review, The
‡Grey Matter
Gulf Stream Magazine
Half Tones to Jubilee
Harp-Strings Poetry Journal
‡Home Times
‡Implosion: A Journal of the Bizarre and Eccentric
International Quarterly
Kalliope, a journal of women's art
National Enquirer
New CollAge Magazine
New Writer's Magazine
Nuthouse
Onionhead
Panhandler, The
‡POETRY Digest
Poetry of the People
Runaway Spoon Press, The
Science Fiction Poetry Association
‡Silver Web: A Magazine of the Surreal, The
‡Siren, The
Sun Dog: The Southeast Review
Tampa Review
Thoughts for All Seasons: The Magazine of Epigrams
‡Write Way, The
Yesterday's Magazette

Georgia

Atlanta Review
baby sue
Chants
Chattahoochee Review, The
Classical Outlook, The
Dickey Newsletter, James
feh!
Georgia Journal
Georgia Press, University of
Georgia Review, The
‡Habersham Review
Ice Cold Watermelon
‡Linwood Publishers
Midwest Poetry Review
Old Red Kimono, The
Parnassus Literary Journal

Expressions Forum Review
Feminist Studies
Gut Punch Press
Jewish Vegetarians Newsletter
Johns Hopkins University Press, The
Maryland Poetry Review
‡Maryland Review
Nightsun
Oracle Poetry
Passager: A Journal of Remembrance and Discovery
Pegasus Review, The
Plastic Tower, The
Poet Lore
Samsara
Scop Publications, Inc.
Shattered Wig Review
‡Situation
Social Anarchism
Vegetarian Journal
WoRM fEASt!

Massachusetts

Aboriginal SF
Adastra Press
AGNI
Amherst Review, The
Appalachia
Ark, The
Arts End Books
Atlantic, The
‡Aurorean: A Poetic Quarterly, The
‡Backspace
Bay Windows
Boston Phoenix: Phoenix Literary Section (PLS), The
Boston Review
‡Brave New Tick, (the)
Button Magazine
Christian Science Monitor, The
Christopher Publishing House, The
College English
Dead of Night Publications
‡Djinni
Eidos Magazine: Sexual Freedom & Erotic Entertainment for Women, Men & Couples
Faber and Faber, Inc.
Figures, The
‡Freezer Burn Magazine
Godine, Publisher, David R.
Harvard Advocate, The
Houghton Mifflin Co.
Little River Press
Loom Press
Mad River Press
Massachusetts Press, The University of
Massachusetts Review, The
Muddy River Poetry Review
Muse Portfolio
new renaissance, the

Next Phase
96 Inc
Northeast Arts Magazine
Northeastern University Press
Old Crow Review
Osiris, An International Poetry Journal/Une Revue Internationale
Paramour Magazine
Partisan Review
‡Pearl, The
‡Peregrine: The Journal of Amherst Writers & Artists
Ploughshares
‡Point Judith Light
Poultry, A Magazine of Voice
Provincetown Arts
Radcliffe Quarterly
‡Rugging Room, The
Tightrope
West of Boston
Worcester Review
Writer, The
Zephyr Press
Zoland Books Inc.

Michigan

‡Above the Bridge Magazine
American Tolkien Society
‡Angelflesh Press
Bennett & Kitchel
Centennial Review, The
Clubhouse
Expedition Press
Gazelle Publications
Hartland Poetry Quarterly, The
Howling Dog
Japanophile
Lotus Poetry Series
MacGuffin, The
Mayapple Press
Michigan Quarterly Review
‡Mobius
Nada Press
Passages North
Pen and Ink Magazine
Poetic Page
Rarach Press
Red Cedar Review
Riverrun
Struggle: A Magazine of Proletarian Revolutionary Literature
Sulfur Magazine
‡Third Coast
Touch
‡Verbal Expression
Wayne State University Press
Witness

Minnesota

Ally Press Center
Ascent
Coffee House Press
‡Conduit
Evergreen Chronicles, The

Expressions
‡Gaslight: Tales of the Unsane
Graywolf Press
Guild Press
Hurricane Alice
Loonfeather
Lutheran Journal, The
M.I.P. Company
Mankato Poetry Review
Meadowbrook Press
Midwest Villages & Voices
Milkweed Editions
New Rivers Press
‡Oatmeal and Poetry
Place in the Woods, The
Poetry Harbor
Poetry in Motion
Poetry Motel
Rag Mag
‡Sidewalks
Sing Heavenly Muse!
Sisters Today
Slate, The
‡Spout Magazine
Studio One
White Review: A Gay Men's Literary Quarterly, James
Writer's Journal

Mississippi

Bell's Letters Poet
Cross Roads: A Journal of Southern Culture
Georgetown Review
Mississippi Review
‡Yalobusha Review, The

Missouri

Afro-Hispanic Review
Anterior Poetry Monthly
‡BkMk Press
Cape Rock, The
Chariton Review Press, The
Communications Publishing Group
Gospel Publishing House
‡Green Hills Literary Lantern
Helicon Nine Editions
Laurel Review
Missouri Review
‡MPF Muse Letter, The
Nazarene International Headquarters
New Letters
Offerings
‡Pleiades
River Styx Magazine
Sharing the Victory
Timberline Press
Unity Magazine
Webster Review

Montana

‡Chinook Press
Corona

New Directions Publishing Corporation
New Press Literary Quarterly, The
‡New Spirit Press
New York Quarterly
New Yorker, The
Nomad's Choir
Northern Centinel, The
Norton & Company, Inc., W.W.
Outerbridge
Oxford University Press
Pantheon Books Inc.
Parabola: The Magazine of Myth and Tradition
Paradox
Paris Review, The
Parnassus: Poetry in Review
‡Pavement Saw
PeopleNet DisAbility DateNet
Pequod: A Journal of Contemporary Literature and Literary Criticism
Persea Books
Philomel Books
Pipe Smoker's Ephemeris, The
Pirate Writings
Pivot
Poetry New York: A Journal of Poetry and Translation
Quarterly, The
†Queen of All Hearts
Queen's Mystery Magazine, Ellery
‡RACS/Rent-A-Chicken Speaks
Response
Review: Latin American Literature and Arts
Rocket Press
Round Table: A Journal of Poetry and Fiction, The
Sachem Press
St. Martin's Press
Segue Foundation
Seneca Review
Serpent & Eagle Press
Shamal Books
Shofar
Slate & Style
Slipstream
Smith, The
‡Space and Time
Spirit That Moves Us, The
Spring: The Journal of the E.E. Cummings Society
State Street Press
Stevens Journal, The Wallace
Street Press
13th Moon
Turnstile
Ultramarine Publishing Co., Inc.
Unforgettable Fire, The
Unmuzzled Ox
Viking Penguin
Villager, The

Water Mark Press
Waterways: Poetry in the Mainstream
White Pine Press
Women's Studies Quarterly
‡Writes of Passage
Xanadu

North Carolina
Black Mountain Review
Carolina Quarterly, The
Carolina Wren Press
Cold Mountain Review
Crucible
Deathrealm
French Broad Press
Greensboro Review, The
International Poetry Review
Minnesota Review, The
‡New Native Press
Parting Gifts
Pembroke Magazine
Report To Hell
Sanskrit
Southern Poetry Review
Sun, The
Tar River Poetry
‡Wake Forest University Press

North Dakota
North Dakota Quarterly

Ohio
Anathema Review
Antioch Review, The
Artful Dodge
Ashland Poetry Press, The
Bits Press
‡Black River Review
Cincinnati Poetry Review
Cleveland State University Poetry Center
Confluence
Dream Shop, The
Field
Generator
Grasslands Review
Heartlands Today, The
Hiram Poetry Review
Hopscotch: The Magazine For Girls
‡Icon
Implosion Press
Inkslinger
Journal, The
Kaleidoscope: International Magazine of Literature, Fine Arts, and Disability
Kenyon Review, The
‡Listening Eye, The
Luna Bisonte Prods
Luna Negra
‡Malevolence
Mark: A Literary Journal
Mid-American Review

‡New Thought Journal
Nexus
Ohio Review, The
Ohio State University Press/The Journal Award in Poetry
‡"Over The Back Fence" Magazine
Oxford Magazine
Pig Iron
Pudding House Publications
Riverwind
St. Anthony Messenger
Ship of Fools
Silhouette
Solo Flyer
Spitball
Straight
Vincent Brothers Review, The
Whiskey Island Magazine
‡Wooden Head Review
Writer's Digest

Oklahoma
ByLine Magazine
Cimarron Review
Eagle's Flight
manna
Midland Review
Nimrod: International Journal of Contemporary Poetry and Fiction
Ogalala Review, The
Surprise Me
texture
Westview: A Journal of Western Oklahoma

Oregon
Beacon
‡Bear Essential, The
Calapooya Collage
Calyx, A Journal of Art & Literature by Women
Eighth Mountain Press, The
Fireweed: Poetry of Western Oregon
Furry Chiclets: A Lawpoets Creation
Hubbub
Literary Fragments
Midwifery Today
Mr. Cogito Press
Northwest Literary Forum
Northwest Review
‡open unison stop
Oregon East
Plazm Magazine
Poetic Space: Poetry & Fiction
Pointed Circle, The
Portland Review
Prescott Street Press
Sandpiper Press
Silverfish Review
‡Skipping Stones: A Multicultural Children's Magazine

Brunswick Publishing Corporation
Callaloo
Chronicle of the Horse, The
Chrysalis Reader, The
Conservative Review
Dominion Review, The
Fauquier Poetry Journal
5th Gear
Hollins Critic, The
Intro
‡Lingo: a language art journal
Lintel
Lyric, The
‡Masonia Roundup
Orchises Press
Phoebe
‡Piedmont Literary Review
Pocahontas Press, Inc.
Ranger Rick Magazine
Reflect
St. Andrew Press
Shenandoah
Sow's Ear Poetry Review, The
Verse
Virginia Quarterly Review, The
William and Mary Review, The
Writer's World

Washington
Ag-Pilot International Magazine
Arnazella
Bellingham Review, The
Bellowing Ark Press
‡Brooding Heron Press
Cleaning Business Magazine
Copper Canyon Press
Crab Creek Review
Fine Madness
‡Floating Bridge Press
Frontiers: A Journal of Women
    Studies
‡George & Mertie's Place:
    Rooms With A View
Improvijazzation Nation
‡L'Epervier Press
‡Lockhart Press, The
‡Murderous Intent
‡Muse of Fire
Olympia Review
Open Hand Publishing Inc.
Owl Creek Press
‡Paper Boat Magazine
Poetry Northwest
Poets. Painters. Composers.
Score Magazine
Seattle Review
Slightly West
Spindrift
Willow Springs
Young Voices Magazine

West Virginia
Aegina Press, Inc.
‡Bohemian Bridge

Wisconsin
Abraxas Magazine
Acorn Whistle
Blank Gun Silencer
Block's Poetry Collection
Caxton Ltd., Wm
Country Woman
Cream City Review
Fox Cry
Glass Cherry Press, The
Jackson Harbor Press
Juniper Press
Madison Review, The
Magazine of Speculative Poetry,
    The
Modern Haiku
‡M.O.O.N. Magazine
Poet's Fantasy
Rosebud
Seems
Student Leadership Journal
Touchstone
‡256 Shades of Grey
Wisconsin Academy Review
Wisconsin Press, University of
Wisconsin Review

Wyoming
High Plains Press
Housewife-Writer's Forum
Owen Wister Review

Canada
Afterthoughts
Amber
‡Amethyst Review, The
Anjou
Antigonish Review, The
‡Arc: Canada's National Poetry
    Magazine
Ariel, A Review of International
    English Literature
Arsenal Pulp Press
Atlantis: A Women's Studies
    Journal
‡Authors
Beach Holme Publishers
Beneath the Surface
Borealis Press
Canadian Author
Canadian Dimension: The Maga-
    zine for People Who Want to
    Change the World
Canadian Literature
Canadian Writer's Journal
Capers Aweigh Magazine
Capilano Review, The
‡Carleton Arts Review
‡Carousel Magazine
Chickadee Magazine
Church-Wellesley Review, The
Claremont Review, The
Compenions
Cosmic Trend

Coteau Books
Dalhousie Review, The
Dance Connection
Dandelion
Descant
Ekstasis Editions
Ellipse
Event
Fiddlehead, The
Filling Station
Fireweed: A Feminist Quarterly
‡Firm Noncommittal: An Interna-
    tional Journal of Whimsy
Goose Lane Editions
Grain
Green's Magazine
Guernica Editions Inc.
‡Harbour Publishing
‡Hecate's Loom Magazine
‡House of Anansi Press
Indigo Magazine: The Spanish-
    Canadian Presence in the Arts
‡Madame Bull's Tavern
Malahat Review, The
(m)öthêr TØñgué Press
Musicworks
New Quarterly, The
On Spec: The Canadian Magazine
    of Speculative Writing
Our Family
Plowman, The
Poetry WLU
Prairie Fire
Prairie Journal, The
Prairie Publishing Company, The
Presbyterian Record, The
Press Gang Publishers
Prism International
Queen's Quarterly: A Canadian
    Review
Ronsdale Press
Room of One's Own
Sister Vision Press
Sub-Terrain
"Teak" Roundup
Tessera
‡Textshop
Thalia: Studies in Literary Humor
Thistledown Press Ltd.
Tickled by Thunder: The Maga-
    zine That Set Fiction Free
Tower Poetry Society
Townships Sun
Tyro Publishing
‡Underwhich Editions
Unmuzzled Ox
Vehicule Press
Voyant, The
Wascana Review
West Coast Line
Western Producer Publications
‡Whetstone
White Wall Review
Windsor Review